The Macmillan
Guide to Britain's Nature Reserves

The Macmillan
Guide to Britain's
Nature Reserves

Foreword by
HRH The Prince of Wales

Accounts of the reserves researched and written by
Jeremy Hywel-Davies and Valerie Thom

*Supplement to the Papermac edition
researched and written by*
Linda Bennett

*Publication of this book has been made possible by
Gulf Oil Corporation in association with the
Royal Society for Nature Conservation*

MACMILLAN

First published 1984 by Macmillan London Limited

First published in paperback 1986 by
PAPERMAC
a division of Macmillan Publishers Limited
4 Little Essex Street London WC2R 3LF
and Basingstoke

Associated companies in Auckland, Delhi, Dublin, Gaborone,
Hamburg, Harare, Hong Kong, Johannesburg, Kuala Lumpur, Lagos,
Manzini, Melbourne, Mexico City, Nairobi, New York, Singapore
and Tokyo

Hywel-Davies, Jeremy
    The Macmillan guide to Britain's nature reserves.
    1. Natural areas—Great Britain—Guide-books
    2. Great Britain—Description and travel—1971-
    —Guide-books
    I. Title II. Thom, Valerie III. Bennett, Linda
    508.41   QH77.G7

ISBN 0–333–42102–7

Filmset in Apollo by Filmtype Services Limited,
Scarborough, North Yorkshire
Originated by Adroit Photo Litho Limited, Birmingham

Printed in Hong Kong

Picture research: Juliet Brightmore
Design: Robert Updegraff
Maps: Hilary Evans

Frontispiece: Lake District National Park – Hausgill waterfalls in the
Honister Pass.

Contents

Foreword

With all the pressures on our countryside the conservation of wildlife has become a matter of national concern. While it is true that much of our landscape as it now stands was created by man in the first place, the increase in population coupled with the need to grow more food, to build more houses and factories and to provide space for leisure have in the last half century done immeasurable damage to our natural resources. Some of this damage was unavoidable, but some has been caused by our own greed and our lack of concern for future generations.

For many years the conservation organisations have been working to identify and protect the more important wildlife habitats by the creation of nature reserves. It is a measure of their success that 550,000 acres of importance to wildlife survival have now been secured in nearly 2000 reserves. In fact the forty-six nature conservation trusts between them protect nearly 1400 of these sites.

Important as this achievement is, there is a danger of assuming that the objects of conservation can be fulfilled simply by creating reserves. We certainly need the reserves, in many cases just to ensure the survival of some endangered species; but we also need a much broader approach as well to make certain that those who own and occupy and use land regard conservation as part of their responsibility. Conservation cannot be relegated to reserves alone and requires a conscious and continual effort from all those who care for the land.

In the Duchy of Cornwall we have a number of important reserves and plan to have more in the future. At the same time in conjunction with the conservation organisations and our tenants we are reviewing ways in which we can improve our whole approach to both conserving and encouraging wildlife throughout the estate. There is no reason why many of those species of wildlife which survive in reserves should not in time re-establish themselves in other places, given that people are encouraged to care that they should do so.

This Guide is a mammoth work and I hope that it will do much to help people to explore the rich heritage of our islands. It has taken four years of dedicated work to prepare for publication and includes details of some 2000 sites. For the expert it will provide an invaluable reference work. For others it will provide an essential introduction to the richness and wealth of our wildlife. As Patron of the Royal Society for Nature Conservation I welcome its publication.

Charles.

List of Contributors

Editorial Advisers

Robert E. Boote CVO *Vice-President of the Royal Society for Nature Conservation, and Council Member of a number of voluntary bodies.*
Bernard Gilchrist MBE *Chief Executive of the Scottish Wildlife Trust.*
Dr Franklyn Perring *General Secretary of the Royal Society for Nature Conservation, writer and broadcaster.*

Research Officers

Jeremy Hywel-Davies *Writer on wildlife and the countryside. Author of the English and Welsh entries in the Guide.*
Valerie Thom *Writer and consultant on countryside interpretation. Author of the Scottish entries in the Guide.*
Linda Bennett *Editor of* Natural World, *the magazine of the Royal Society for Nature Conservation. Author of the Supplement to the Papermac edition.*

Authors of the Introductions

Dr I.P. Bainbridge *Conservation Liaison Officer of the Northumberland Wildlife Trust.*
M.E. Ball *Deputy Regional Officer, Nature Conservancy Council (North-West Scotland Region).*
G.H. Ballantyne *Former Vice-Chairman of the Fife and Kinross Branch of the Scottish Wildlife Trust.*
John A.G. Barnes *Former Vice-Chairman of the Cumbria Trust for Nature Conservation.*
Rennie Bere CMG *Past President of the Cornwall Trust for Nature Conservation and former Director and Chief Warden of the Uganda National Parks.*
Dr R.D. Bowden *Member of several Cheshire Conservation Trust committees.*
Dr H.J.M. Bowen *Member of the Botanical Society of the British Isles and the British Lichenological Society, and author of* Flora of Berkshire.
W.R. Brackenridge *Countryside Ranger for Stirling District Council, and Honorary Secretary of the Central Region Branch of the Scottish Wildlife Trust.*
Michael E. Braithwaite *Honorary Secretary of the Tweed Valley Branch of the Scottish Wildlife Trust.*
Elaine R. Bullard MBE *Member of the Botanical Society of the British Isles and of a number of Scottish wildlife organisations.*
Peter Cunningham *Member of several Scottish wildlife organisations.*
Andrew Currie *Assistant Regional Officer, Nature Conservancy Council (Skye and Lochalsh District).*
Dr J.G. Dony MBE *Honorary Fellow of the Linnean Society and Honorary Keeper of Botany at Luton Museum and Art Gallery.*

Phil Drabble *Writer and broadcaster.*
Tom Dunn MBE *Writer, broadcaster and naturalist.*
D.M. Eagar *Council Member of the British Ecological Society and the North Wales Naturalists' Trust.*
Dr Trevor Elkington *Chairman of the Derbyshire Naturalists' Trust and Senior Lecturer in Botany at the University of Sheffield.*
Ted Ellis *Author and broadcaster.*
Ian Evans *Assistant Director (Natural Sciences), Leicestershire Museums Service, and Council Member of the Leicestershire and Rutland Trust for Nature Conservation.*
P. Evans *Conservation Officer of the Kent Trust for Nature Conservation.*
F. Fincher *Author, naturalist and active member of many local and national wildlife organisations, including the Worcestershire Nature Conservation Trust.*
Richard Fitter *Author, broadcaster, Chairman of the Fauna and Flora Preservation Society, Past President of BBONT, and Committee or Council Member of several national and international wildlife organisations.*
Julie Gaman *Administrative Officer of the Durham County Conservation Trust.*
Larch S. Garrad *Assistant Keeper of the Manx Museum and National Trust.*
Dr Mary E. Gillham *Author, and Past Chairman of the Glamorgan Naturalists' Trust.*
Dr Henry Heal *Member of the former Northern Ireland Nature Reserves Committee, founder member of the Ulster Trust for Nature Conservation and Fellow of the Royal Entomological Society.*
Dr Peter G. Hopkins *Honorary Secretary of the Dumfries and Galloway Branch of the Scottish Wildlife Trust, and Chairman of the Wigtownshire Branch of the Scottish Ornithologists' Club.*
P.N. Humphreys *President of the Gwent Ornithological Society, Vice-President of the Gwent Trust for Nature Conservation, and Honorary Veterinary Surgeon to the Wildfowl Trust.*
T. Illsley *Horticultural journalist, Fellow of the Linnean Society, Council and Education Committee Member of the Essex Naturalists' Trust.*
Dr Ralph Kirkwood *Reader in Biology at the University of Strathclyde.*
Peter Lawson *Member of several national and local wildlife organisations, including the Suffolk Trust for Nature Conservation.*
Ian Mercer *Chairman of the Devon Trust for Nature Conservation and Chief Officer, Dartmoor National Park.*

Dr Pat Morris *Writer, Lecturer in Zoology at Royal Holloway College, University of London, Vice-president of the London Wildlife Trust and Patron of the Avon Wildlife Trust.*
Dr J.M. Newton *Secretary of the Scientific and Conservation Committee and Assistant Conservation Officer of the Lancashire Trust for Nature Conservation*
W.H. Palmer *Deputy President of the Cambridgeshire and Isle of Ely Naturalists' Trust and Fellow of the Linnean Society.*
Susan Parker *Former Lecturer in Geography, University of Durham.*
Morley Penistan *Chartered Forester and Chairman of the Gloucestershire Trust for Nature Conservation.*
Dr I.D. Pennie *Former President of the Scottish Ornithologists' Club.*
Brian Playle *Assistant Director of Arts (Museums), Nottingham City Council.*
Will Prestwood *Former Conservation Officer of the Shropshire Trust for Nature Conservation, and Joint Editor of the* Ecological Flora of Shropshire.
John Price *Vice-Chairman of the Wiltshire Trust for Nature Conservation.*
Michael Romeril *Conservation Officer of Jersey.*
John Sankey *Former Warden of Juniper Hill Field Studies Centre, Box Hill.*
David Saunders *Conservation Administration Officer of the West Wales Naturalists' Trust.*
Dr A.A. Savage *Lecturer in Environmental Sciences.*
Michael M. Scott *Writer and broadcaster.*
David Shirley *Conservation Officer for the Education Dept of Hertfordshire County Council.*
Dr F.M. Slater *Curator of the University of Wales Institute of Science and Technology Field Centre, and Vice-Chairman of the Herefordshire and Radnorshire Nature Trust.*
A.E. Smith OBE *Chairman of the Lincolnshire and South Humberside Trust for Nature Conservation and former General Secretary of the Royal Society for Nature Conservation.*
Dr C.E.D. Smith *Chairman of the Somerset Trust for Nature Conservation.*
Dr Rosalind A.H. Smith *Assistant Regional Officer, Nature Conservancy Council (Perth and Kinross District).*
Bob Smyth *Journalist, with a particular interest in the environment, and Chairman of the London Wildlife Trust.*
Dr Fay R. Stranack *Chairman of the Conservation Committee and Council Member of the Hampshire and Isle of Wight Naturalists' Trust, and a Fellow of the Zoological Society of London.*
David Streeter *Author, broadcaster, Reader in Ecology at the University of Sussex, and Deputy President of the Sussex Trust for Nature Conservation.*
Dr A. Tasker *Lecturer in Ecology, environmental consultant, and Chairman of the Warwickshire Nature Conservation Trust.*
W.G. Teagle *Life Fellow of the RSPB and a Scientific Fellow of the Zoological Society of London.*
Dr Michael J. Thompson *Council Member of the Yorkshire Naturalists' Trust and of the Mammal Society, and Fellow of the Linnean Society.*
Peter Thomson *Former Tutor at Bristol Polytechnic, and member of the Herefordshire and Radnorshire Nature Trust.*
Bobby Tulloch *RSPB representative in Shetland.*
Ron Wilson *Head of Everdon Field Centre, Daventry.*
Peter Wormell BEM *Assistant Regional Officer, Nature Conservancy Council (North Argyll, Cowall and Bute District).*
Dr Mark Young *Lecturer in Zoology at the University of Aberdeen, and Chairman of the Aberdeen and Kincardine Branch of the Scottish Wildlife Trust.*

Acknowledgements

Jeremy Hywel-Davies would like to acknowledge the help of the officers of all the county conservation trusts; the Nature Conservancy Council – in particular Malcolm Rush for his invaluable assistance; the Forestry Commission; the Royal Society for the Protection of Birds – especially for the very helpful liaison work of Anthony Chapman; the Royal Society for Nature Conservation; the National Trust; the County and District Councils; and the many and varied bodies involved in conservation today. He would also like to thank those who have helped in the research and compilation, particularly Caroline Carless, Annabel Seddon, Sarah Tester, and Dr Terry Stevens (for access to his PhD thesis on nature trails in Wales); Angela Dyer, who began it, and Esther Jagger, who took over the daunting task, for their editing toil; also all those people throughout the country whose friendship and hospitality enabled him to survive for weeks at a time in the confines of a camper van.

Valerie M. Thom is grateful to the staff of the Forestry Commission, the National Trust for Scotland, the Nature Conservancy Council and the Royal Society for the Protection of Birds, and to both members and staff of the Scottish Wildlife Trust, who assisted her by providing information, or by commenting constructively on her draft entries, for the sites under their care. Her special thanks go to those who made time to accompany her in the field: Mrs Elspeth Hamilton, Colin McLean and Dr Ian Pennie of the SWT, Ray Hawley of the RSPB, Derrick Warner of the NTS and Robbie Brydson and David Duncan of the NCC.

The Royal Society for Nature Conservation acknowledges with gratitude the generosity of Gulf Oil Corporation in waiving their royalties on this book in favour of the Society.

How to Use the Guide

Entries are arranged alphabetically under counties or regions of England, Wales and Scotland. The precise order is shown in the Contents list.

Each county or regional section contains a map showing sites open to the general public, with details of size, population, physical features, climate and major land use. An introduction highlights the main points of interest and characteristics of each county or region.

Factual information is given at the beginning of each entry, in this form:

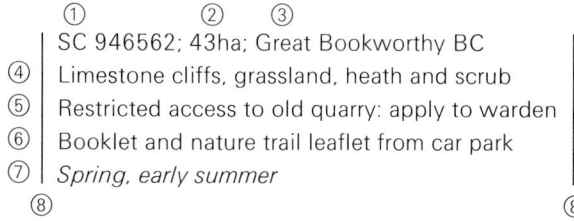

Key

① Ordnance Survey map reference (every OS map contains clear instructions on how to read it) or, in the case of very large sites, reference to the map. For sites marked *Permit only* apply to the managing body (see addresses on p.666) unless otherwise stated.

② Area in hectares, or length in kilometres, as appropriate. (One hectare is approx. 2½ acres; one kilometre is approx. five-eighths of a mile.)

③ Manager/owner of site (for key to abbreviations, see p.664).

④ Brief description of site.

⑤ Details of any restrictions.

⑥ Availability of leaflets or other information.

⑦ Best season(s) for visiting site.

⑧ Indicates sites that have ceased to exist since publication of the first edition of the *Guide*.

Sites with access limited to members of trusts or other bodies, or to holders of special permits, are not shown on the map or given OS references.

Cross references to other sites mentioned in the text are shown in CAPITALS on their first mention in any entry.

A list of addresses of nature conservation trusts, wildlife organisations and other managing bodies of sites is on p.727.

An index of species is on p.742, and an index of sites is on p.767.

New sites, and changes in the status of existing ones, are listed in the Supplement on p.658.

A glossary of naturalists' terms is on p.738.

Introduction

This Guide brings together for the first time sites of wildlife interest in Britain to which the public may have some form of access. The majority of sites are designated Nature Reserves but we have included, especially in parts of the country where there are few formal Nature Reserves, a number of sites such as country parks, walks and trails and other areas where wildlife may be enjoyed.

To achieve this our research officers have visited many of the two thousand sites described and have consulted the owners or managers of them all. This four-year quest has been supported by the Royal Society for Nature Conservation and by many other organisations and individuals; it was made possible by the generosity of Gulf Oil Corporation.

Our basis for inclusion of a site is that members of the public should have access either by common law rights, or by membership of a club or trust which gives access by right of membership or by special permit. (All sites in the latter category are marked *Permit only* in the text.) Exceptions have been made on two criteria: where we believe that an endangered or rare species would be threatened by publication of any information about the site where it is found, or where the owner of a site at present allowing access to a limited section of the public would be unwilling to continue such arrangements if an account were published here. We have taken the best advice available on these delicate issues, but in the last resort have made our own judgement.

Our aim has been to be comprehensive, but inevitably at the first attempt there will be omissions and errors and we would be grateful for information on these from our readers. The information published here was the latest available at the time of going to press. In succeeding editions we intend to cover also Northern Ireland, the Channel Islands and the more distant offshore islands. It has not been possible to include individually all the sites owned or managed by the Forestry Commission, the Woodland Trust, the Ministry of Defence and the various water authorities, and readers should apply for information to the appropriate addresses (see p.666).

We have taken great pains to ensure the accuracy of the Guide at the time of going to press. Every entry has been shown to a representative of the owner or managing body, and the text has been read by two other advisers in addition to our own staff.

In Scotland we have used the modern regions, though dividing Highland and Strathclyde into two to make them less unwieldy. In Wales we have used the modern counties. In England we have had to take a more pragmatic approach, using a combination of old and modern counties in our section titles, and basing our structure in general on the areas covered by the nature conservation trusts, many of which still retain titles relating to the pre-1974 administrative counties. The geographical area of each section is coloured green on the map.

Each section is introduced by a well-known naturalist living in the area and possessing an extensive knowledge of its characteristics. The longer entries in each section have been selected for their perspective on the magnificent diversity of habitats in Britain, and because they are large enough to sustain much public use; many of them offer interpretative facilities. The increasing emphasis on and support for wildlife in cities is reflected in this Guide. London in particular has been given a separate section to allow for adequate treatment, which in later editions we may extend to other major cities.

Readers will no doubt wish to support the work of the trusts and other organisations involved in the management of many of the sites included here. The addresses of the relevant bodies are on p.666.

At a time when public interest in our natural heritage has never been stronger, but when paradoxically threats to its future seem to be gathering force, we hope that this Guide will encourage both the sensitive use and enjoyment of Britain's wildlife.

England

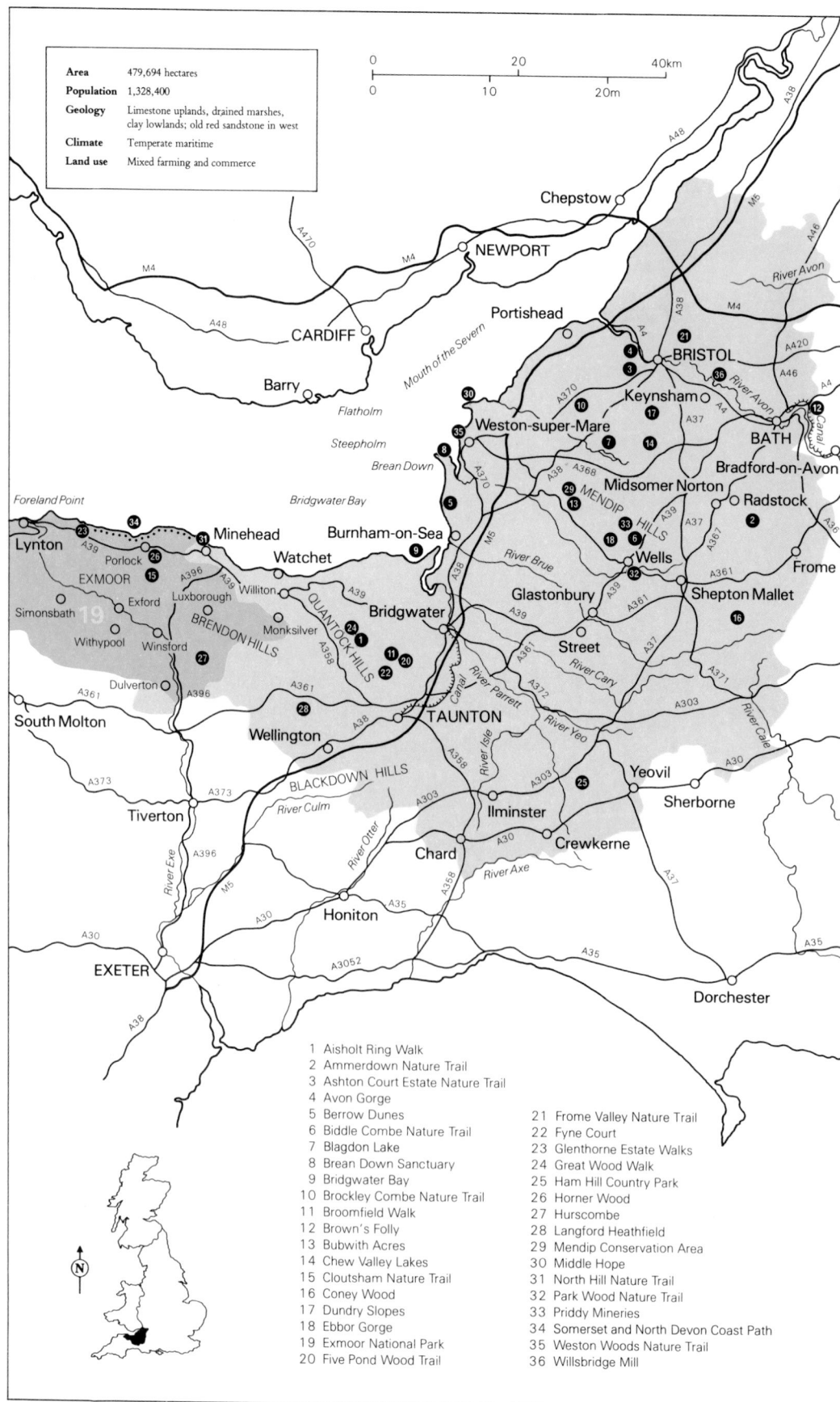

Area	479,694 hectares
Population	1,328,400
Geology	Limestone uplands, drained marshes, clay lowlands; old red sandstone in west
Climate	Temperate maritime
Land use	Mixed farming and commerce

1 Aisholt Ring Walk
2 Ammerdown Nature Trail
3 Ashton Court Estate Nature Trail
4 Avon Gorge
5 Berrow Dunes
6 Biddle Combe Nature Trail
7 Blagdon Lake
8 Brean Down Sanctuary
9 Bridgwater Bay
10 Brockley Combe Nature Trail
11 Broomfield Walk
12 Brown's Folly
13 Bubwith Acres
14 Chew Valley Lakes
15 Cloutsham Nature Trail
16 Coney Wood
17 Dundry Slopes
18 Ebbor Gorge
19 Exmoor National Park
20 Five Pond Wood Trail
21 Frome Valley Nature Trail
22 Fyne Court
23 Glenthorne Estate Walks
24 Great Wood Walk
25 Ham Hill Country Park
26 Horner Wood
27 Hurscombe
28 Langford Heathfield
29 Mendip Conservation Area
30 Middle Hope
31 North Hill Nature Trail
32 Park Wood Nature Trail
33 Priddy Mineries
34 Somerset and North Devon Coast Path
35 Weston Woods Nature Trail
36 Willsbridge Mill

Avon and Somerset

For their size the two counties of Avon and Somerset form what is probably the most geologically complicated piece of land in the world. To the naturalist and country-lover it is a region of considerable contrast in both its landscape and wildlife. Its mellow golden towns and villages, its lush countryside and coast, provide delight for every visitor.

The landscapes range from the Mendip Hills, carboniferous limestone deposits rising in places to over 300m; to the Somerset Levels, once an extensive marsh; to Taunton Deane, a vale of rich agricultural land; and the two gentle ridges of the Quantock and Brendon Hills. The area also encompasses part of wild, windswept Exmoor, rising to 300m on Dunkery Hill, and has a remarkably unspoilt coastline of over 110km.

A rough quadrilateral drawn between Weston-super-Mare, Glastonbury, Taunton and Bridgwater contains the unique Somerset Levels, a former marsh which has been partially drained over the centuries. The area is below sea level as far as 9km inland, which can lead to severe flooding where the rivers meet the sea at Burnham. An enormous number of rare plants and insects are supported here on some 8000km of ditch and rhyne, which in addition enjoy a large resident breeding bird population. The Levels are also resting places for numerous birds of passage from northern Europe, en route to or from places as far away as southern Africa. The coast between Burnham and Minehead attracts migrating waders and duck.

The Levels are of European importance in terms of ecological vitality, but, if their extremely valuable wildlife is to be saved, at least one-eighth of the area must be placed under some sort of control to prevent its destruction. Wildlife in this rich dairying country is threatened by modern farming methods and by the extraction of peat. Today tremendous efforts are being made by the various wildlife conservation bodies and by local authorities to lead Avon and Somerset through these problems, but if something is not done, particularly in the Levels, the next 50 years could see major deterioration in the region's wildlife.

The beautiful natural wealth of the Mendip Hills can be viewed from public trails on nature reserves at EBBOR GORGE, Black Rock and Long Wood (MENDIP CONSERVATION AREA). The rich limestone woodlands here contain a wide range of spring flowers, including herb-Paris, and butterflies such as brimstone, orange tip, fritillaries and speckled wood. Breeding birds include blackcap, willow warbler and chiffchaff, and there is a good chance of seeing roe deer. Woodland management at Long Wood has set out to encourage wildlife and in May and early June there are few woods with which to compare it for beauty and tranquillity. In nearby Velvet Bottom special plants from Roman and later lead spoil heaps, such as alpine penny-cress and spring sandwort, can be found.

Leigh Woods and the AVON GORGE near Bristol, and BROWN'S FOLLY near Bath, are also areas of limestone grassland with mixed woodland and scrub. Plants such as wild thyme, common rock-rose and carline thistle can be found on the fine downland turf, together with many insects, including marbled white and green hairstreak butterflies, and the greater horseshoe bat which roosts in the old mines.

15

At the western end of the Mendip Hills is BREAN DOWN, a bird sanctuary famous as a stopping-off place for thousands of birds on migration, and the site of the rare white rock-rose which flowers profusely between April and July. Also on the migration route is the reserve at BRIDGWATER BAY, where at all times of year waders can be viewed on the mudflats from hides erected by the Nature Conservancy Council. The reserve's most remarkable feature is the hundreds of shelduck which moult there in July.

An idea of the wildlife of the Brendon Hills in west Somerset can be obtained at HURSCOMBE reserve at the northern end of the new Wimbleball Lake. The wildfowl of the lake, buzzard and raven above, and whinchat in the gorse make it a birdwatcher's paradise. The frogs, butterflies and marsh plants of the rich, wet grassland ensure that there is something to capture the attention of every nature-lover.

FYNE COURT, in the Quantock Hills, is the headquarters of the Somerset Trust for Nature Conservation. Much modified by man, the estate nevertheless contains much of interest – from stately old beech trees to three artificial ponds and lakes. The snowdrop and foxglove seasons are two favourite visiting periods, and the interpretative centre helps visitors gain an understanding of the animal and plant life of the area.

Apart from its magnificent display of wildlife, Avon and Somerset is a region of great scenic beauty offering dramatic views. From Wills Neck, the highest point of the Quantocks, it is possible to see no fewer than three National Parks: EXMOOR to the west, DARTMOOR (Devon) to the south west, and the BRECON BEACONS (Powys) in Wales to the north.

C.E.D. SMITH

Aisholt Ring Walk

ST 182338; *c.*9km; STNC
Circular trail in the Quantocks
Booklet from STNC
All year

The walk includes Wills Neck, which is the highest point in the Quantocks and affords some spectacular views over Somerset and into Devon and Wales.

Aller Wood

Permit only; 2ha; STNC reserve
Mixed woodland
Spring, summer

The small reserve, set within a much larger area of ancient woodland, includes an attractive range of ground plants below a canopy of oak, ash and small-leaved lime.

Ammerdown Nature Trail

ST 715534; *c.*2km; STNC
Woodland trail
Leaflet from STNC or site dispenser
Spring, early summer

The chiefly coniferous plantations through which the trail runs include some native trees. Roe deer are present.

Asham Wood

Permit only; 33.4ha; STNC reserve
Rich woodland
No access off public right of way
Spring, early summer

The wood contains a very good range of tree species with a particularly rich ground flora, including meadow saffron, which is encouraged by active coppicing.

Ashton Court Estate Nature Trail

ST 554726; 2.5–3.7km; Bristol Naturalists' Soc.
Walk laid out on old estate
Booklet from site, BNS or Bristol City Council
Spring, early summer

A great variety of wildlife interest is demonstrated by the trail which crosses both lime-rich and acid soils, showing a variety of typical species from green hellebore and common rock-rose to silver birch and bracken. The woodland is of mixed exotic and native species giving, with the shrubs and grassland, a wide range of habitat enjoyed by fallow deer, by kestrel, wood warbler and goldcrest, and by comma, painted lady, silver-washed fritillary and holly blue butterflies.

Avon Gorge

ST 553731; 105ha; NCC reserve
Wooded limestone gorge
Leaflet from NCC
Spring, early summer

The reserve lies on the western side of the Avon Gorge, clothed with woodland and scrub, quarried out into slabby scallops and topped with the ancient Leigh Woods. The general feel of the woodland is of high oak forest with ash and beech over a thin shrub layer of dogwood, hawthorn, hazel, spindle and yew. There are dark areas of impenetrable yew and holly as well as old coppiced small-leaved lime. The Avon Gorge is important for the endemic Bristol whitebeam and Bristol rock-cress, and species of biogeographical importance such as honewort, hutchinsia and spiked speedwell.

Nightingale Valley, a gorge within a gorge, runs down from the plateau to the river below, showing yet another face of the reserve. Here huge old oaks stand over slopes of bramble and thickets of young ash trees. Steeper slopes of unstable scree spread

below rocky faces, cascaded with ivy, and form stony gardens of pink herb-Robert, yellow cory-dalis and dense shining plumes of hart's-tongue. Because of the narrow steepness of the valley, trees on the lower slopes must reach upwards to the light and some old ashes here are enormous.

Where the saplings grow, with bramble, on the less steep slopes, the scree is stable enough for a shallow soil to form and so for typical woodland plants to find a footing. The ground cover in the plateau woods above is chiefly bramble, with bracken, honeysuckle and species such as wood sage and bluebell. On the slopes, more rich in lime, dog's mercury and enchanter's-nightshade grow with traveller's-joy and wild madder. Less usual plants include columbine, green hellebore, ivy broomrape, toothwort and bird's-nest orchid.

Other slopes, rocky and scrub-covered rather than wooded, have a mixture of lime-loving shrubs such as privet, wayfaring-tree, dogwood, common and less common whitebeam species, with a rich variety of herbs: small scabious, common rock-rose, salad burnet and many more, including the unusual spring cinquefoil and autumn squill.

The reserve contains a good range of woodland bird species, mammals and insects.

Avonmouth

Permit only; 10ha; AWT reserve
Bird-rich lagoons
All year

Lying in the Severn Estuary flight line, the reserve attracts a wide range of waterbirds with maximum interest at migration times.

Backside Wood

Permit only; 4.8ha; STNC reserve
Mixed woodland
Spring, early summer

Grassland and a pond add to the range of wildlife interest of the wood which includes oak, ash and wych elm and is a refuge for badger and buzzard.

Berrow Dunes: open sea, strand, sand dunes and level marsh.

Berrow Dunes

ST 293540; 135.6ha; Sedgemoor DC reserve
Dunes and foreshore
Booklet from STNC
Late spring, early summer

The dunes, slacks and pools support a good insect and plant life, including lesser bulrush, marsh helleborine and heath spotted-orchid; the foreshore and mudflats are best for winter bird life.

Biddle Combe Nature Trail

ST 569488; 4km; Wells Nat. Hist. and Arch. Soc.
Valley trail through grass and woodland
Leaflet from Wells Museum
Spring, summer

The often damp trail passes through a good range of habitats with opportunities to see grassland, woodland and streamside plants and animals, with the accent on lime-loving species.

Blackmoor

Permit only; 10ha; Bristol University reserve
Educational reserve
Spring, summer

A typical range of lime-loving plants grows around the pools and slopes of the old lead workings.

Blagdon Lake

ST 516596; 178ha; Bristol Waterworks Co.
Large reservoir
Permits required for hides and access to banks
All year

Described under CHEW VALLEY LAKES.

17

Brean Down: looking inland to Weston-super-Mare. A rocky island linked to the flat farmland behind.

Brean Down Sanctuary

ST 296586; 64ha; NT reserve
Limestone headland
Booklet from NT
All year

A great whale-backed ridge of limestone jutting out into the mudflats of the Severn Estuary, Brean Down was one of the earliest bird sanctuaries established by the RSPB. It forms an important landmark for migrating birds and insects.

The limestone ridge slopes down towards the north with a steeper, rougher face turned to the south. The plants vary according to the depth of soil and the exposure, which is so wild at times that only a few elder and hawthorn shrubs can survive. Privet and bramble form a low scrub which, together with bracken on the deeper soils and occasional heather, provides shelter for the smaller migrants. Rock samphire may be found on the seaward edges of the down, while grassy areas contain not only coastal plants such as thrift and buck's-horn plantain but also typical lime-loving herbs such as salad burnet, wild thyme and horse-shoe vetch. The undoubted treasures of the area, though, grow in the shallowest, most rocky turf: dwarf sedge, Somerset hair-grass and white rock-rose all have very restricted distributions and are therefore of great interest to plant geographers.

The cliffs and rocky jumbles provide nest sites for birds such as jackdaw, kestrel and rock pipit while the scrubland and grassland are used by stonechat, meadow pipit and skylark. Mallard and shelduck breed in the area and are joined in spring and autumn by many migrant species. Then the mudflats below the down and the saltmarsh behind it teem with birds. Redshank and oystercatcher, snipe and curlew, godwit, knot, lapwing and golden plover gather here for food or shelter. Geese may fly in from the Arctic to feed or a visiting peregrine may maraud the tired migrants.

One of the special pleasures of the down is its position, an outlier of the Mendip Hills and a pointer to the island of STEEPHOLM; it stands above the huge spread of Berrow mudflats and the wider spread of the Somerset Levels behind.

Bridgwater Bay

ST 278464; 2400ha; NCC reserve
Estuary, saltflats and lagoons
Access limited to rights of way and public hides
Leaflet from NCC, Taunton
Winter and migration times

A rising tide, flooding the huge shallow bay, pushes vast numbers of wildfowl and waders into the shelter of the Parrett Estuary, where they may be watched from hides, or on to the scrapes by the hides. A feature of the reserve is that it is a moulting ground for shelduck, and at any time of year these strikingly beautiful birds may be seen feeding on the mudflats or flighting strongly across the estuary. Another important gathering is that of whimbrel in spring; up to 1000 pause here before moving northwards to breed; with perhaps around 200 curlew also present this provides an ideal opportunity to study the differences between the two birds.

Many thousand duck congregate in winter, with up to 2500 each of shelduck, mallard and wigeon together with smaller numbers of pintail, shoveler and teal. At migration times large flocks of dunlin, black-tailed godwit, lapwing, oystercatcher and redshank spread out across the mudflats or stand roosting in packed ranks when the tide drives them off their feeding grounds. Small numbers of bar-tailed godwit, knot, grey plover and turnstone are also usually present.

Although the islands and the higher sandbanks provide a high-tide roost, the birds are never still for long. The smaller birds are always busy, gaining their neat quickness at the expense of a constant hunger, but larger birds may stand for a while and then seem seized by a communal restlessness. Whole flocks will move together, walk fast into the wind and suddenly lift, simultaneously to swing in a wide circle, glide back all wings still together and then all beating, to drop exactly on to the bank where they stood a few moments before. This magic unison is a fascinating aspect of many wader species but one of the most spectacular sights might be to see the whole assembly of resting birds leap into the air and break into swirling flocks: a peregrine falcon, black-masked like a highwayman, may be overhead.

The area is also one of note for the botanist with a variation of habitat from grassland to open mud and sand, including a spread of marsh and a shingle bank. Yellow horned-poppy occurs beside the path to the hides while other shingle species include henbane and knotted clover. Sea clover grows on the sea wall of the Parrett with honewort in the grassland beside it.

Brockley Combe Nature Trail

ST 483663; 3.2km; AWT
Woodland trail
Leaflet from AWT
Spring, early summer

The trail runs through a wooded limestone valley with a good range of native trees and of typical woodland birds.

Broomfield Walk

ST 222322; *c.*8km; STNC
Country walk
Booklet from STNC
Spring, early summer, autumn

The walk passes through a range of agricultural land, woodland and coniferous forest with some spectacular viewpoints overlooking Somerset or over the River Severn into Wales.

Brown's Folly

ST 798664; 12.8ha; AWT reserve
Limestone downland, woodland and scrub
No entry to old mine shafts
Leaflet from AWT
Spring, early summer

A great shoulder of rock from which the famous Bath stone was quarried, Brown's Folly stands high above the valley of the River Avon, terraced by the benches of the old mine workings whose scars are covered now with a rich mix of woodland, scrub and grassland.

The reserve contains a wide variety of habitat, from high semi-natural downlands to the woods below, with rocky grottos, woodland glades and areas of dense or open scrub. The key to the general pattern is the underlying limestone, encouraging a colourful and varied range of plants and animals.

The downland benches, open to the sun, sheltered by the slopes behind them and the scrub around, are opulent with limestone flowers and filled with the quick movement of insects. Wild thyme, common rock-rose, common bird's-foot-trefoil, harebell and lady's bedstraw attract the butterflies common blue and marbled white, the caterpillar of the common blue feeding on clovers, trefoils and vetches and that of the marbled white on grasses. Green hairstreak butterflies may also be seen, which argues the presence of gorse or broom on which their larvae feed.

The benches overlook mixed woodland and, sitting on a cushion of herb-rich grassland, one can look out into the canopy of ash, beech, birch and oak with darker conifers behind. The woods are very varied and range from mature woodland to newly planted trees or to dark thickets of tangling thorns. The woodland shows typical limestone shrub species, dogwood, privet and spindle, wayfaring-tree and whitebeam, with traveller's-joy lacing the edges or climbing into the canopy, while the scrub and grassland areas are also rich in species including both cowslip and the spectacular woolly thistle.

The reserve makes up about one-third of a site of special scientific interest scheduled for its geological importance. Two strata of oolitic limestone are exposed, the Bath oolite and the Combe Down oolite, in beds some 3–4m thick, previously mined for building stone. The mines are extensive and house an important colony of greater horseshoe bat.

Bridgwater Bay: the Parrett Estuary.

Bubwith Acres

ST 470537; 5.2ha; STNC reserve
Limestone heath, downland and scrub
Permit only off right of way
Spring, summer

Outcrops of rock carry sprays of maidenhair spleenwort, wall-rue and the rather uncommon rustyback, while the limestone heath is characterised by a mixture of acid and lime-loving plants such as salad burnet, heather and dwarf thistle. The scrub encourages a variety of birds including linnet, stonechat and whitethroat.

Burtle Moor

Permit only; 14.8ha; STNC reserve
Grazing marsh
Spring, early summer

Characteristic birds of the Somerset Levels, curlew, redshank and snipe, breed among a mix of marsh plants such as marsh-marigold, marsh pennywort, ragged-Robin and meadow thistle.

Catcott

Permit only; 14ha; STNC reserve
Fen meadow and heathy wetland
Spring, summer

The track which divides the reserve is a narrow straight drove, defined by low alders, by drains filled with bulrush, yellow iris and reed sweet-grass, sometimes almost a tunnel beneath the trees, sometimes an open peaty lane where the summer air is filled with the continual whizz and zigzag of dragonflies.

After the last ice age, an acid raised bog developed in this area, overlying the rich fen peat beneath, but very little of the bog survived the drainage and peat digging which have turned the Somerset Levels to farmland. South of the drove, however, surrounded by a belt of wet woodland, a number of acid species still survive.

Broad stands of bog myrtle surround a mix of bog and fen plants, a luxuriant aromatic jungle sheltered by trees and shrubs. The acid-loving plants include cross-leaved heath and purple moor-grass, together with common cottongrass, tormentil and creeping willow, with marsh pennywort and devil's-bit scabious grading into a fenlike mix of bittersweet and meadowsweet, of hemp-agrimony, yellow loosestrife and yellow iris, purple-loosestrife, ragged-Robin, skullcap and milk parsley. The wet woodland, or carr, is mainly of birch, alder and grey willow but is varied with alder buckthorn and guelder-rose or, where drier, ash and hawthorn. The ground cover contains a variety of species including two uncommon ferns, the tall royal fern and the attractive small marsh fern.

One of the very few areas unspoiled by peat extraction or modern farming, the meadows at Catcott contain a wonderful mixture of plants associated with traditional management. The grazed meadows contain marsh bedstraw, marsh-marigold, jointed rush, common spike-rush and creeping-Jenny while the hay meadows have deep spreads of taller plants, wild angelica, common meadow-rue, meadowsweet and meadow thistle, with yellow loosestrife, water dock, marsh cinquefoil and southern marsh-orchid.

The rich dampness of the reserve encourages a great range of insects, including several butterfly species, together with a range of woodland birds with particularly good numbers of willow tit. The meadowlands offer breeding sites for curlew, redshank and snipe.

Cheddar Cliffs

Permit only; 80ha; NT reserve
Limestone cliffs
Spring, summer

The cliffs carry a variety of plants according to soil depth, light and dampness. Several unusual species occur including lesser meadow-rue, green-winged orchid and Cheddar pink.

Cheddar Wood

Permit only; 39.2ha; STNC reserve
Small-leaved lime woodland
Spring, early summer

Purple gromwell is a speciality among a fine range of lime-loving plants in an ancient coppice woodland which contains ash, hazel, small-leaved lime, field maple, oak and wild service-tree.

Redshank breed on the meadows of Catcott.

Chew Valley Lake: a fine site for waterbirds.

Chew Valley Lakes

ST 570615; 656ha; Bristol Waterworks Co.
Large reservoirs
Permits required for hides and access off picnic areas
Booklet from BWC
All year

Chew Valley Lake, some 489ha in size, and BLAG-DON LAKE form together a large area of water which attracts a wide variety of birds. Blagdon is smaller, deeper and more enclosed, with clearer water and a wider variety of water animals associated with an abundance of submerged water plants. Chew Valley Lake itself is much larger and shallower, which makes it more attractive to waterfowl.

The natural banks and the island on Chew Valley Lake make it a fine site for nesting waterbirds such as gadwall, mallard, pochard, ruddy duck, shelduck, shoveler and tufted duck. Outside the breeding season duck tend to move between the two reservoirs. To lessen the impact of recreation a sanctuary area, the Chew Valley Lake reserve, has been established in the most southerly bay.

Although the winter wildfowl are perhaps the most impressive facet of these waters, the interest extends all year long – the range of resident species is constantly reinforced or deserted by travellers or is joined by birds which have come here to breed.

At any time of year the lakes and their surrounds may hold varying numbers of gadwall, great crested grebe, ruddy duck, curlew, kingfisher, little owl, kestrel and all three native woodpeckers. In spring wintering duck, geese, swans, waders and other birds move north to breed and the lakes become staging posts for passage birds or breeding sites for southern-wintering species. Swallow, sand and house martin, sedge and reed warbler and yellow wagtail fly in to breed while common sandpiper, bar-tailed and black-tailed godwit, sanderling, ruff and little stint pass through. Occasionally predators such as osprey and marsh harrier may be seen, while the resident sparrowhawks look forward to the influx of smaller birds, some of which may remain to breed, birds

such as whinchat, whitethroat and lesser whitethroat, garden warbler and grasshopper warbler.

By autumn the migrant breeders will begin to leave and a return passage will sweep back southwards through the reservoirs. Marsh harrier and osprey may be reinforced by peregrine and hobby. Arctic, black, common, little and sandwich tern may pause to hunt across the waters while greenshank, redshank, spotted redshank, green and wood sandpiper, knot and grey plover feed on the muddy edges.

In winter many goosander, goldeneye and wigeon may be seen, with increased numbers of mallard, pochard, tufted duck and teal, with Bewick's and occasional whooper swan and a wide variety of predators, waders, sheltering seaduck and finch flocks.

The Chew Valley Lakes are important examples of eutrophic reservoirs, different in that one, Blagdon, does not suffer from dense algal blooms. Chew Valley Lake is the site of a ringing station.

Cleeve Heronry

Permit only; 3.2ha; AWT reserve
Woodland
Spring, early summer

The reserve has been established to protect one of the most important heronries in the south west, a site which may hold over 40 breeding pairs.

Cloutsham Nature Trail

SS 903438; 5km; ENPC–NT
Moorland and woodland trail
Booklet from ENP Information Centre, Minehead
Summer, spring

Covering a small part of the Holnicote Estate on the edge of HORNER WOOD, the trail winds through moor and valley land, crossing the attractive East Water stream. It provides a range from damp oak woodland to open gorse moor with a rich animal life, which includes red deer and raven, brown trout and buzzard, not far from the bracken and heather top of Dunkery Beacon.

Coney Wood

ST 692389; 1.2ha; WdT reserve
Mixed woodland
Spring, early summer

This small attractive woodland stands beside a tributary of the River Alham and holds a resident population of badger.

Dolebury Warren

ST 450590; 6.4ha; AWT–NT reserve
Acid heath, limestone grassland and scrub
Spring, early summer

Heather, bell heather, western gorse and bilberry characterise the acid area below slopes of limestone grassland with typical species such as common rock-rose.

Dommett Wood

Permit only; 13.8ha; STNC reserve
Beech woodland
Spring, early summer

The woodland, standing on a steep scarp slope, is varied with heathland clearings and is noted for bluebells. Badger and roe deer are among the larger animals.

Dundon Beacon

Permit only; 28ha; STNC reserve
Limestone downland, scrub and woodland
Leaflet from STNC
Spring, early summer

The ancient oak–ash woodland contains some splendid field maple, a tall contrast with the spread of scrub where nightingales may be heard, while the butterfly-rich grassland has lime-loving plants such as autumn lady's-tresses, bee orchid and musk mallow.

Dundry Slopes

ST 582669; 3.6ha; AWT reserve
Wet meadow and scrub
Spring, early summer

With areas of scrub developing towards woodland, there is a surprising range of habitat for such a small area which includes an attractive variety of wetland plants and insects.

Durleigh Reservoir Sanctuary

Permit only; 31ha; WWA reserve
Birdwatchers' reservoir
Key available from reservoir ranger on request
All year

A hide overlooks the reservoir so that watchers may observe the extensive reedbeds and willow swamp where migrant warblers breed. Many species of duck together with Bewick's swan may visit the sanctuary in winter.

Ebbor Gorge

See map; 46ha; NCC reserve
Wooded limestone gorge
Permit only off pathways
Leaflets from site or NCC
Spring, early summer

To see the gorge at Ebbor you must park, walk down through the green woodland and follow the climbing path through the rocks which form the walls of the chasm.

Despite the fact that the gorge has long been dry, it was cut by the action of water, presumably by the meltwater which followed the thaw of each ice age, and at one time the headwaters of the River Axe flowed through here. Now the Axe emerges at Wookey Hole, having cut itself a new channel underground. In massive limestones water dissolves out channels and flows through these, dissolving away the rock to form long cave systems and often flowing suddenly out of a fissure.

The gorge is cut back into the Mendip plateau, where the tops of the cliffs level off and a small area of limestone heath occurs, although much of this higher land is invaded by ash woods, and near the

edge of the scarp thinner soils show a remnant of limestone grassland. Gorse, heather and foxglove, heath bedstraw and common bent are found where rain has washed the lime out of deeper soils, but where the soils are shallow and exposure has inhibited scrub a splendid variety of lime-loving plants may occur. Here, high above the rich green carpet of the lower woods, are salad burnet and fairy flax, marjoram, common milkwort, common rock-rose, carline thistle, large thyme, wild thyme, horseshoe vetch, false brome and quaking-grass together with pale St John's-wort and common bird's-foot-trefoil, betony, mouse-ear hawkweed and eyebright.

Below, in the damp shade of the gorge, are gardens of ferns, brittle bladder-fern, uncommon in the south, the rare Tunbridge filmy-fern, hart's-tongue, maidenhair fern, maidenhair spleenwort, polypody, rustyback and wall-rue. Other plants enjoy the shelter: wood melick, shining crane's-bill and wall lettuce grow here, together with hairy rock-cress and herb-Robert which also grow well on the screes.

Although the main rock of the Mendips is limestone, folding in response to earth movements, later deposition, erosion and faulting have led to a mix of different rocks occurring at the surface. No river runs through the gorge and water is often underground in limestone, but a stream will be seen in the Primrose Valley below the ravine, and this occurs because coal measures form the bedrock. Although lime-loving plants such as hart's-tongue and hard shield-fern occur on the coal measures soils, so too do more general species such as male-fern, lady-fern and broad buckler-fern, while even the acid-loving hard fern can find a suitable habitat and marsh or moorland plants – small and plicate sweet-grass for instance – may be found near the source of the stream.

Small damp meadows provide a site for ragged-Robin, marsh-marigold, meadowsweet, greater bird's-foot-trefoil and lesser spearwort, together with fine stands of common twayblade in patches of scrub and an autumn display of meadow saffron. Other areas of the valley floor and the lower woodland slopes carry scattered oak and ash standards over a shrub layer of coppiced hazel. Coppiced hazel was used as long ago as the late Bronze Age

Ebbor Gorge: white rock contrasts with green shade.

The spectacular water-cut ravine of Cheddar Gorge in the Mendip Conservation Area.

when it was laid as a trackway across the bogs of parts of the Somerset Levels. Fuel too was much in demand at the time when the Romans mined and processed lead from the mineral veins within the Mendips, so that the techniques of coppicing and wood management will have been practised for many centuries.

The chief importance of the Ebbor woodlands lies in the spread of ash and oak over a typical limestone shrub layer throughout much of the reserve. The age pattern seems to indicate a widespread planting, or a general regrowth, around the mid-nineteenth century, followed by a heavy thinning around the time of World War I. This has led to a high-forest woodland where large standards are scattered among a younger generation of trees to give a mix of ash and oak with smaller ash, wych elm, field maple and common whitebeam. Hornbeam occurs occasionally, thought to be native here at its western limit, and beech has long been established, shown by the use of beech stakes in the Bronze Age hazel-pole roadways. Small-leaved lime may be locally common in some places while the varying understorey in-

cludes a scatter of hazel and hawthorn but also the characteristic limestone species dogwood, privet, spindle and wayfaring-tree with guelder-rose and holly, tangles of honeysuckle and spreads of traveller's-joy.

Spring brings a carpet of bluebells to floor the woodland, varied with wood anemone, lesser celandine and primrose, and later drifts of dog's mercury, enchanter's-nightshade and bramble, woodland grasses, ferns and clumps of great woodrush. Splashes of colour are added by yellow archangel, bugle, goldilocks buttercup, early dog-violet and wood-sorrel with less common plants such as broad-leaved helleborine, greater butterfly-orchid, nettle-leaved bellflower and purple gromwell.

With its wide range of habitat, the reserve is obviously attractive to animals. The mammals include resident fox and badger, together with a typical range of small mammals such as wood mouse, voles and shrews. Among the birds are the characteristic western species grey wagtail and buzzard, together with woodcock which is uncommon in western England. Typical woodland birds include green and great spotted woodpecker, treecreeper and nuthatch, with tawny owl, kestrel and sparrowhawk; among the birds of scrubland and clearings are grasshopper warbler, whitethroat and goldfinch, cuckoo and meadow pipit.

Butterflies enjoy the range of woodland, scrub and grassland and over 30 species have been recorded. Woodland species include purple hairstreak, white-letter hairstreak, white admiral and the two fritillaries, silver-washed and high brown. The dark green fritillary is more a butterfly of the open country, a fast-flying species which might be seen with marbled white, brown argus, common, chalkhill or silver-studded blue around the plateau edge above the gorge. Just as we saw that the plateau might have acid plants on the deeper leached soils and lime-loving plants in the shallow turf so do we see the butterflies which utilise them. Even within one family, butterfly species have evolved to cope with the different food plants available: brown argus and chalkhill blue feed on lime-loving common rock-rose and horseshoe vetch respectively, while silver-studded blue feeds on acid gorse, broom, heather or even bilberry; common blue, the most widespread of this family, bases its success on trefoils, vetches and clovers and so can survive almost anywhere.

Ebbor Gorge is both a magnificent limestone ravine and a splendid limestone woodland reserve, full of beauty and richness. With its caves, its cliffs, its deep green woodlands, it forms an important feature of the Mendips.

Edford Wood

Permit only; 15.6ha; STNC reserve
Mixed woodland
Spring, early summer

The reserve protects a block of ancient woodland straddling a river, where ash and alder, birch and oak stand above a typical rich ground cover while the river adds its own wildlife interest.

Exmoor National Park

See map; 68,635ha; ENPC
Uplands, valleys, woods and coast
Booklets and leaflets from ENPC
Spring, summer

High on the north coast of Devon and Somerset, facing Dartmoor across a broad sweep of lowland fields, looking north across the huge estuary of the River Severn to Wales, Exmoor stands as a land of heather and bracken, of peat bogs, mires and steep valleys draining south to the lowlands or, fast and sudden, cutting the hog-backed coastal hills to the sea. The valleys are dressed with splendid woods, rich in wildlife, while the uplands are the domain of the Exmoor pony and the woods and valleys home to red deer.

The Exmoor, alone of British ponies, seems to have missed the improvements of modern breeding techniques and to represent a type of British hill pony which in many ways parallels the primitive Przewalski's horse. The red deer winter in the valley woodlands and roar at the autumn rut. Apart from the breeding season, hinds and stags remain separate, and at any time of year these beautiful animals are a magnificent sight on the hills.

The range of habitat is a splendid mix of moorland and valley types with the extra interest of the coast which adds rocky cliffs, small bays and the special attraction of saltmarsh. The heathland is usually dominated by heather in association with plants such as bilberry, bracken, bristle bent and gorse. Near the coast bell heather and western gorse may be dominant. The wetter and more peaty moorland carries abundant purple moorgrass in association with deergrass, common and hare's-tail cottongrass and heath spotted-orchid. *Sphagnum* mosses are common in the patches of bog, where cross-leaved heath, round-leaved sundew, bog asphodel and pale and large-flowered butterwort may also be found.

Lankcombe waterslide: an upland Exmoor stream cuts through oak coppiced woodland.

Pinkworthy pond: the stillness of dawn at an Exmoor pool.

Raven, buzzard, merlin perhaps, curlew and ring ouzel, wheatear, whinchat and stonechat are among the birds of the moorland, while dipper and grey wagtail may be seen on the streams. Where the streams cut down into the steep winding valleys, woodlands such as HORNER WOOD add a wide range of typical bird life and the coastal sites hold guillemot and razorbill, with ringed plover and dunlin where beaches or saltmarshes break the line of the cliffs.

Some of the fascination of the natural history of Exmoor may be seen in the presence of both northern and oak eggar moths. The northern eggar is a heather-feeding upland race which here may be a glacial relict species while the oak eggar is a lowland race feeding on plants such as bramble and hawthorn. Both races remain as separate populations by having evolved different lifestyles.

The whole area is a wonderful pattern of farmland and open country, of valley, woodland and coast with the ancient hunting forest, the moorland Forest of Exmoor, at its heart. The National Park Committee publish several guides, such as that for the CLOUTSHAM NATURE TRAIL, to explain the interest of the park.

Five Pond Wood Trail

ST 224275; 1.5km; NT–STNC
Woodland nature trail
Leaflet from STNC
Spring, early summer

The trail runs through a streamside woodland rich in bluebell, marsh-marigold and other spring flowers.

Frome Valley Nature Trail

ST 622765; 4.5km; Bristol Naturalists' Soc.
Riverside trail
Booklet from site or Bristol City Council
Spring, summer

The fast-flowing river contains attractive water-plants such as arrowhead and river water-crowfoot, while the trail includes several areas of other interest where plants such as ivy broomrape and yellow archangel occur. Over 70 bird species have been recorded here including heron, kingfisher and grey wagtail, with redstart, spotted flycatcher, sparrowhawk and kestrel.

Fyne Court

ST 223321; *c.*9ha; NT–STNC reserve
STNC headquarters, old estate woodlands and ponds
Leaflets from information centre
Spring, early summer

An arboretum, lake, ponds, beech woodland and old quarry area provide a wide range of habitat with a good variety of plants and animals. The buildings house the offices of STNC, a shop, lecture hall and an interpretative centre for the Quantocks.

Glenthorne Estate Walks

SS 794486; 1.6–3.2km; ENPC
Wooded coastline trails
Leaflet from ENPC
Spring, early summer

A nature trail, including the pinetum and the beach, together with two shorter walks, demonstrate some of the wildlife interest of this nineteenth-century estate with its views across the River Severn to South Wales.

Goblin Combe

Permit only; 9ha; AWT reserve
Steep valley woodland and limestone grassland
Spring, early summer

The approach to the reserve is along a woodland footpath deep in the bed of the combe, which hints at the brilliance of the limestone site ahead. Tall ash trees, beech, sycamore and yew stand above hazel and box; the ground cover has the richness expected of limestone with deep beds of dog's mercury and enchanter's-nightshade fringed with wood melick. The shrub layer includes privet and field maple, while rubbly screes fanning downwards from unseen cliffs above may show stinking hellebore. Where the crags do show between the trees they are hung with ivy and decorated with the lifting crowns of hart's-tongue.

Within the reserve an area of dense old coppice woodland, under some large old oak trees, gives way to more scree and then to craggy downland. The screes are bare of plants, or colonised by bramble, wild madder and wild rose, with privet and sapling yew beginning to stabilise them. Wood sage and marjoram show as the scree consolidates into grassland and the smaller herbs appear.

These downland slopes are shallow-turfed but support an amazing variety of small, colourful plants which include quaking-grass, common rock-rose, yellow-wort, common centaury, wild thyme, common bird's-foot-trefoil and dwarf thistle, while taller than these are small scabious and ploughman's-spikenard. Along with many other butterflies common blue, small copper and marbled white may be seen on the sunlit slopes.

Above the slopes the grassland levels out, a most spectacular viewpoint from which the combe is overlooked, a vista of mixed woodland, dark yew contrasting with ash, beech and oak, against the sloping uniform dark background of the conifer plantations to the west. Here, above the broken slopes with thickets of hawthorn, whitebeam, yew, ash, spindle and wayfaring-tree, the more acid-loving birch and oak take over and bell heather shows in the grassland, adding a heathland touch to this beautiful limestone reserve.

Small copper butterfly on marjoram.

Great Breach and New Hill Woods

ST 505325; 79.4ha; STNC reserve
Mixed woodland, and limestone grassland
Spring, summer

The mainly oak–ash woodland, lying on heavy clay above slopes of limestone grassland, includes both small-leaved lime and hornbeam, with alder in the wettest places, above a wide range of smaller plants. Over 500 species of fungi occur and the blend of wood and grassland has attracted 52 species of butterfly. Nightingale and woodcock are among the breeding birds.

Great Wood Walk

ST 165360; 8km; STNC
Circular walk chiefly in FC woodlands
Booklet from STNC
Spring, early summer

This Quantock walk through coniferous woods and parkland offers the possibility of seeing red deer.

Ham Hill Country Park

ST 478167; 62ha; Yeovil DC
Disused quarries and spoil heaps
Booklet from Yeovil DC
Spring, summer

Limestone quarrying has left spoil heaps and hollows, together with old quarry faces of rock, which combine to give a variety of wildlife interest from plants such as common rock-rose, autumn lady's-tresses, musk thistle and ploughman's-spikenard to birds such as kestrel and yellow-hammer or butterflies such as small copper, marbled white and dingy skipper.

Horner Wood

SS 897454; 405ha; NT
Mixed woodland
Permit only off pathways
Spring, early summer

In early spring a cold wind blows across the higher slopes of Exmoor but the valley woodlands, like Horner Wood, are sheltered from the biting breeze; if you walk through the woods you will see how the trees grow tall in the sheltered valleys or low and stunted where they near the crest of the combe.

Most of the wood is several thousand years old, indicated by the presence of ivy-leaved bellflower, bilberry, goldenrod, scaly male-fern, Cornish moneywort, slender St John's-wort, lesser skullcap, wood spurge and bitter vetch. These plants are part of a suite of woodland species which do not colonise easily in the west; the presence of one or two is not conclusive, but that of most of the species is very strong evidence for ancient woodland. The wood, of course, has not remained unchanged but has been strongly modified by centuries of management and it is a mosaic of different

types. Horner is now mainly high-forest, grown on from the old coppice stools, but the patterns of previous management give it a varied appearance.

Hazel and holly or birch and rowan make up most of the understorey while the ground cover is often a dense spread of bramble; but an interesting change may be seen as the woods climb higher and bracken and bilberry show in the higher oakwoods which merge into heather, bell heather and gorse as they meet the open moor.

The streams attract typical birds such as dipper and grey wagtail while the variation of the site is answered by woodland species which include the western trio of wood warbler, redstart and pied flycatcher with many other commoner birds. The most dramatic of the mammals is undoubtedly the red deer and Horner Wood is one of their three main winter strongholds.

The wood holds a very fine lichen flora, with over 10 species recorded including many that are rare. The aerial epiphyte *Usnea articulata*, now confined to south western England, is present and the species occurring are representative of the characteristic types of ancient woodland in north western Europe.

Hurscombe (Wimbleball Lake)

SS 974317; 18.6ha; STNC reserve
Reservoir-side old farmland
Access only on public rights of way
Leaflet from STNC or site dispenser
Spring, early summer

Farmland, reverting to scrub and marsh, an old larch plantation and hedges, provide a good variety of habitat, while the reserve already attracts several species of wintering duck.

Langford Heathfield: bramble, bracken, oak and birch − a good example of dry acid woodland.

Langford Heathfield

ST 100236; 91.5ha; STNC reserve
Lowland heath, ancient woodland
Permit only off pathways
Spring, summer

A fine variety of habitat, oak woodland, birch and willow scrub, dry and wet acid heathland, attracts birds and butterflies to the reserve. The wildlife interest, the richness of warblers, of wetland sedges and other plants, will be illustrated by a nature trail as soon as this is established.

Limebreach Wood

Permit only; 6ha; AWT reserve
Old coppiced woodland
Spring, early summer

A block of important ancient woodland containing old coppiced small-leaved lime, the reserve is to be re-coppiced to restore its richness.

Littleton Brickpits

Permit only; 6ha; AWT reserve
Extensive reedbed
Can be overlooked from sea wall at ST 590912
Spring, autumn

The reserve is a good site for migrant birds and typical reedbed species such as reed bunting, reed and sedge warbler.

Littleton Wood

Permit only; 0.5ha; AWT–NT reserve
Woodland
Spring

The reserve was established to protect a colony of the very local yellow star-of-Bethlehem.

Mascall's Wood

Permit only; 4.8ha; STNC reserve
Ancient woodland and grassland
Spring, early summer

A fine variety of trees such as ash, hazel, holly, small-leaved lime, field maple, oak and yew above a rich ground cover contrasts with the sunlit limestone grassland which adds to the range of butterflies and other animals.

Mendip Nature Conservation Area

ST 482545; 586ha; STNC reserves
Cheddar limestone reserves represented by Black Rock, Long Wood, Velvet Bottom and others
Leaflets from STNC
Spring, early summer

Black Rock, Long Wood and Velvet Bottom reserves lie around the winding drove in a beautiful and fascinating complex of woodland, scrub, grassland and craggy rocks: a complex which includes broad-leaved woods and conifers, with grassland rich in limestone flowers, with the changes brought by quarrying and mining. Effectively the area is Y-shaped with Long Wood lying along one arm and Velvet Bottom occupying the other, with Black Rock Reserve beside the drove which forms the stem.

Long Wood contains a good variety of tree species but ash is probably the most successful, with an understorey of hazel and hawthorn and the lime-loving group of dogwood, privet, spindle, wayfaring-tree and field maple. The limestone influence is underlined by rich-woodland plants such as dog's mercury and enchanter's-nightshade with the unusual herb-Paris, while recent coppicing encourages a brilliant show of flowers in spring. Steep, rocky slopes are thickly ferned, a wonderful green spread of hart's-tongue, male-fern and lady-fern, polypody, broad buckler-fern, maidenhair spleenwort and hard shield-fern, while the valley bottom is damp enough for meadowsweet and willow species along the stream bed. During the summer the stream disappears into a swallow hole, emerging again below the Cheddar Gorge.

The shoulder of the drove outside the wood is rich in downland plants where scrub with bracken and foxglove opens out. Primrose and eyebright, lady's bedstraw, common rock-rose and common centaury, wild thyme and common bird's-foot-trefoil, slender St John's-wort and quaking-grass, carline thistle, dwarf thistle, harebell, violet and small scabious all occur.

Velvet Bottom: where lead was once worked.

Velvet Bottom is a narrow grassy valley, hummocked and pitted at first by old lead workings, then dropping in levels, below, where lead was filtered out. The valley sides are rich in limestone plants but the bottoms are still so highly contaminated that intensive grazing is dangerous and the grassland is deep and coarse. The twisting valley is sheltered and rich in butterflies.

Black Rock reserve, a slope above the drove, is chiefly steep grazed grassland, with a block of planted conifers and areas of native woods, a rich reserve with over 200 tree and flower species recorded. The limestone flowers again appear, and the open scrub is good for butterflies and songbirds.

The complex's special interests probably lie in the geological features shown in the quarries, in archaeological features such as Rhino Cave in Long Wood, where hyena and woolly rhinoceros teeth have been found, and in the ecological significance of the lead-contaminated Velvet Bottom which was worked from pre-Roman times until the 1880s.

Middle Hope

ST 330660; 8ha; NT–AWT reserve
Limestone grassland, scrub and saltings
Access by foot only from Sand Bay car park
All year

The limestone flowers are attractive in spring and early summer, with bird interest in Sand Bay and the Severn Estuary all year round but particularly at migration times.

Midger

Permit only; c.9ha; GTNC reserve
Limestone woodland
Permit may be extended to cover 32ha of neighbouring estate
Leaflet from GTNC or AWT
Spring, early summer

The mixed woodland contains a good range of tree and shrub species and a rich ground cover including the lime-loving specialities green hellebore, columbine and herb-Paris. Woodland bird interest is increased by the presence of streamside species.

Peony grows wild on Steepholm.

Mill Water

Permit only; 0.8ha; Tony Parsons, Barnfield,
Tower Hill Rd, Crewkerne, Somerset
Small wetland
Spring, summer

A pond, the old millstream, a fine area of reed-swamp and a spread of scrub make up a most attractive small reserve with a good range of insects and birds, protected and recorded by the enthusiasm of its owner.

North Hill Nature Trail

SS 968474; 5km; ENPC
Foreshore-to-moorland circular walk
Booklet from ENPC
Spring, summer

The trail climbs from the harbour up the land-slipped cliffs through planted woodlands and tang-les of bramble, ivy, honeysuckle and madder, to the moorland where gorse and western gorse flower high above the Bristol Channel and bilberry and heather blow in the fresh upland breeze.

Park Wood Nature Trail

ST 551458; c.3km; Wells Nat. Hist. and Arch. Soc.
Circular walk from Wells centre through woodland
Booklet from Wells Museum
Spring, early summer

The trail passes the moat of the Bishop's Palace and crosses, through meadowland, to a good damp woodland nearby.

Priddy Mineries

ST 547515; 49.2ha; STNC reserve
Wetland and limestone grassland
Permit only off rights of way
Spring, summer

An area of former mineral workings, the reserve includes limestone grassland while large pools

provide a wide range of interest such as breeding great crested newt and a variety of dragonflies and water beetles.

Priors Park Wood

Permit only; 8ha; STNC reserve
Limestone valley woodland
Spring, early summer

Ash woodland fills the valley, on one side dry with mature oak and blackthorn scrub, on the other wet with alder, willow and spreads of pendulous sedge. The ground cover is varied and includes unusual species such as herb-Paris.

Rodney Stoke

Permit only; 35ha; NCC reserve
Limestone woodland and some grassland
Leaflet from NCC
Spring, early summer

Chiefly ash woodland, the reserve also supports a wide range of other species and a good ground flora including nettle-leaved bellflower, meadow saffron and purple gromwell. The woodland, scrub and grassland encourage some 30 butterfly species.

Screech Owl

Permit only; 25ha; SCC reserve
Disused brickpit
All year

The wetland reserve, part of a group of old brick-pits, is centred on a pond rich in invertebrate species together with a fine stand of common reed. The reedbed provides a winter roost for large num-bers of starling and is a site at which uncommon birds such as little gull and spotted crake have been recorded; duck such as shoveler may often be seen on the marshy ground near the river.

Shapwick Heath

Permit only; 221ha; NCC reserve
Remnant of Somerset Levels fenland
Spring, summer

Marsh and fen on rich peatlands, most of which have now been destroyed by drainage or cutting, the reserve contains a rich variety of plants such as marsh fern and an outstanding range of insects.

Somerset and North Devon Coast Path

SS 793487–971467; 25km; CC
Part of long-distance coastal footpath
Booklet from CC or HMSO bookshops
Spring, summer

From County Gate to Minehead the path, part of the South West Peninsula Coast Path, undulates from sea level to the high curves of the hills above the Bristol Channel. Hedgerow, scrub, copse and woodland, grassland, farmland and heather moors provide a wealth of wildlife interest.

South Hill

Permit only; 2.8ha; STNC reserve
Limestone grassland and scrub
Spring, summer

The old quarry, where rock was worked for lime-stone flags, has been colonised by a fine variety of lime-loving plants and scrub, and attracts both breeding birds and butterflies.

Steepholm

Permit only; 20ha; Kenneth Allsop Memorial Trust reserve
Steep-cliffed limestone island
Access by boat from Weston-super-Mare
Leaflets from KAMT
Day trips Saturdays April–October

This fascinating island reserve supports an interesting range of plants, including wild leek and peony. Animals include slow-worm, which may grow half a metre long, breeding cormorant, lesser and great black-backed gull, and an important colony of herring gull. Peregrine falcon have now returned to the island. There is a small colony of muntjac, and a large number of hedgehogs.

Street Heath

Permit only; 7.6ha; STNC–SCC reserve
Lowland heath
Spring, summer

Old peat diggings, wet heath and birch woodland combine to provide a wide range of habitat in which many attractive insects and birds may be found. The plant life includes species such as bog asphodel, common butterwort, lesser butterfly-orchid and heath spotted-orchid.

Tealham Moor

Permit only; 45ha; STNC reserve
Grazing marsh in ten blocks
Spring, summer

A splendid example of the Somerset Levels marshlands, the reserve holds a fine range of typical plants and of wetland breeding birds such as snipe, redshank and yellow wagtail. An artificial scrape increases the interest for waterbirds and in winter attracts a variety of wildfowl and waders.

Thurlbear Wood

Permit only; 10.4ha; STNC reserve
Rich mixed woodland, limestone scrub and grassland
Spring, early summer

The woods lie on a shoulder of the limestone, part-ly on the level top and partly on the slope, a mix of sunny clearings, wide rides, pathways, blocks of old and newly coppiced woodland, filled throughout with lime-loving and rich-woodland shrubs and flowers, with the sound of songbirds or the mew of a circling buzzard hunting nearby.

The upper woodland is chiefly old coppiced hazel with field maple and hawthorn below oak standards, although some fine old ash trees have been left as standards, as well as at least one huge wild cherry tree. Wild rose and bramble grow in the shrub and ground cover and the richness of the

The Somerset Levels: flooding provides a refuge for waterbirds and ensures a wealth of wetland plants in summer.

Thurlbear Wood: field maple above coppiced hazel typifies this limestone woodland.

wood is underlined by spindle and much privet. Wide areas are carpeted with ivy from which spring clumps of stinking iris together with wood spurge, dog's mercury, and small violets. Beneath the trees, left to grow on as standards, the woodland floor is a bright mosaic of plants: together with the plants already mentioned are species such as bugle, enchanter's-nightshade, ground ivy, honeysuckle and primrose, wild strawberry, wood avens and woodruff with a variety of grasses and sedges and growths of holly, ash and guelder-rose.

Below the slope the limestone influence becomes even more marked and, indeed, it was once quarried and worked: an old lime kiln still stands, now capped with trees and shrubs. Here dogwood and wayfaring-tree are added to the understorey and traveller's-joy to the woodland edges. The reserve includes a block of grassland clumped and hedged with open scrub, a wonderful site for butterflies and songbirds. Characteristic of this almost downland scrub, shrubs are clumped in groups of several species – dogwood, privet, field maple, hawthorn, hazel and wild rose in a single spray. The grassland itself, though rather coarse, still contains a range of downland species, with lady's bedstraw, salad burnet and quaking-grass beneath

small scabious and greater knapweed, and is also hummocked with rounded ants' nests which provide a foothold for the smaller plants.

Vigo Wood

Permit only; 14ha; STNC reserve
Mixed woodland
Spring, early summer

The oak–ash woodland contains some unusual pollarded trees and stands above a rich ground cover. Areas of bracken and scrub attract a good range of breeding birds and the reserve is notable as a wintering ground for woodcock.

Westcombe

Permit only; 4.8ha; STNC reserve
Mixed woodland
Spring, summer

In the past otter have been recorded on the river which borders the reserve, but despite their decline Westcombe still holds the fascination of a typical mixed woodland.

Westhay Moor

Permit only; 12.8ha; STNC reserve
Remnant of raised bog
Spring, summer

Only two small areas of the Somerset peat moors have been saved from peat extraction and Westhay Moor demonstrates, with a mix of species such as *Sphagnum* mosses, cottongrasses, deergrass, heather and cross-leaved heath, much of the beauty that has been lost.

Weston Moor

Permit only; 4ha; AWT reserve
Rich wetland reedbed
No access March–August
Autumn, or overlook in spring, summer

The reserve may not be entered between March and August because it is now the last remaining reedbed in the Gordano Valley and is managed to retain its breeding populations of reed, sedge and grasshopper warbler. Because of agricultural drainage, the wetland has been drying out, severely threatening the reedbeds, but the AWT has now erected a windpump which will lift water into the reserve and encourage a stronger growth of the vital common reed.

Weston Moor is flushed with drainwater from the limestone ridges which enclose the valley, and in the past this led to the development on some 5m of peat of a rich fen-type vegetation. Drying out of the peat has meant that many of the beautiful and important plants have been suppressed by the invasion of bramble, hemp agrimony and rosebay and great willowherb, but it is hoped that a reversal of this trend will reward the installation of the pump. Even in its generally drier state the reserve is still an exciting rich wetland with the reedbeds full of yellow iris and purple-loosestrife, greater bird's-foot-trefoil and meadowsweet. Tussocks of purple moor-grass replace some areas of reed and these are bright with tormentil, marsh thistle, devil's-bit scabious, marsh pennywort and water mint. In damper areas the uncommon marsh fern flourishes while drier areas are taken over by bracken.

A number of shrubs have grown up, spreading from the strip of woodland on the east edge of the reserve. These include birch and hawthorn, willow, guelder-rose, alder and a particularly good growth of alder buckthorn, important as a foodplant of the brimstone butterfly. The woodland belt itself is chiefly alder, with sycamore, hawthorn, willow and ash, and stands above a ground cover of ivy with ferns such as broad buckler-fern and lady-fern.

Some 50 flowering plants have been recorded, with a good range of insects and mammals.

Weston Woods Nature Trail

ST 327627; 1–3km; Woodspring DC
Mixed woodland
Leaflet from WDC
Spring, early summer

The woodland is largely a planted area of sycamore with oak, ash, sweet chestnut and poplar trees above a rather limited ground cover which includes toothwort. Birds include woodland species such as warblers, goldcrest and kestrel, while sunlit clearings are enjoyed by butterflies such as brimstone, comma and peacock.

Sedgemoor: King's Sedgemoor Drain in summer, with grazing marsh and yellow water-lilies.

West Sedgemoor

Permit only; 200ha; RSPB reserve
Wet grazing marsh
All year

Probably the most important spring passage site for whimbrel in all Britain and one of the richest for breeding waders in south west England, the reserve consists of low-lying meadows intersected by ditches where curlew, black-tailed godwit, lapwing, redshank and snipe breed. In winter the shallow pools attract golden plover, mallard, teal and occasional Bewick's swan, together with huge numbers of lapwing.

Wetmoor

Permit only; 20ha; GTNC reserve
Damp ancient woodland
Booklet and leaflet from GTNC
Spring, early summer

The fine coppiced woodland has rich butterfly, moth and insect life, a good variety of spring flowers and abundant nightingales.

Willsbridge Mill

ST 665707; 8ha; AWT reserve
Wildlife and countryside centre
Leaflet at site
All year

The steep-sided valley of the Siston Brook contains a disused quarry and a deep old railway cutting which show the geological interest of the area, while woodland, scrub, meadowland and ponds display a good range of wildlife.

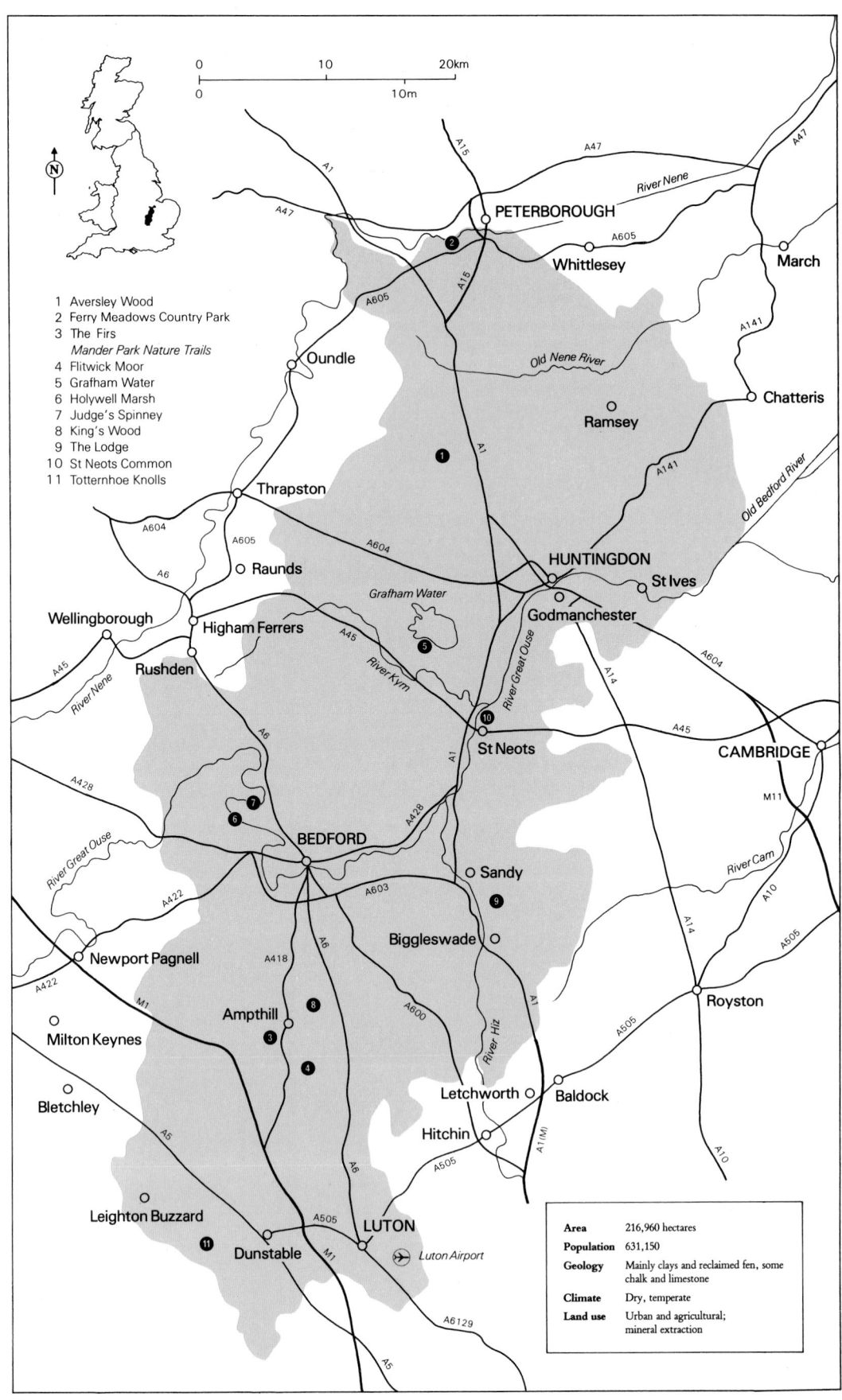

0   10   20km

0   10m

N

1   Aversley Wood
2   Ferry Meadows Country Park
3   The Firs
    Mander Park Nature Trails
4   Flitwick Moor
5   Grafham Water
6   Holywell Marsh
7   Judge's Spinney
8   King's Wood
9   The Lodge
10   St Neots Common
11   Totternhoe Knolls

PETERBOROUGH

Whittlesey

March

River Nene

A47

A47

A15

A1

A605

Old Nene River

Oundle

Ramsey

Chatteris

A141

Thrapston

HUNTINGDON

St Ives

A604

A604

Raunds

Grafham Water

Godmanchester

A605

A6

Wellingborough

Higham Ferrers

A45

River Kym

River Great Ouse

A14

A604

Rushden

River Nene

St Neots

CAMBRIDGE

A428

A6

A1

A45

M11

River Cam

Judge's Spinney

Holywell Marsh

BEDFORD

Sandy

River Ouse

A10

A422

Newport Pagnell

A603

A505

Milton Keynes

A418

A6

King's Wood

Biggleswade

A600

Royston

M1

Ampthill

The Firs

Flitwick Moor

River Hiz

A505

A14

Bletchley

Letchworth

Baldock

A1(M)

A10

Leighton Buzzard

A505

Hitchin

A5

Totternhoe Knolls

Dunstable

LUTON

A505

M1

Luton Airport

A6129

A5

Area	216,960 hectares
Population	631,150
Geology	Mainly clays and reclaimed fen, some chalk and limestone
Climate	Dry, temperate
Land use	Urban and agricultural; mineral extraction

Bedfordshire
and Huntingdonshire

To the passing visitor, Bedfordshire and the former county of Huntingdonshire would appear to offer little of interest to the naturalist. Both areas are low-lying and Bedfordshire has been greatly affected by twentieth-century urbanisation, although Old Huntingdonshire, which was ceded to Cambridgeshire in 1974, remains largely rural. The county naturalists' trust which covers this area was formed in 1960, before local government reorganisation, and retains its former name and responsibilities.

Much of the landscape is influenced by the River Ouse, which enters Bedfordshire at Turvey to take a winding course before leaving Old Huntingdonshire at Earith, where the river is only about 5m above sea level and just entering fen country. When the fens were drained in the seventeenth century, some relics remained on the margins; two of these are now reserves, and the especially rich WOODWALTON FEN, with its dykes, damp droves, woodland, meadows and heath, is one of the oldest reserves in Britain.

Following the ice ages the Ouse, much larger then than now, changed its course from time to time, depositing spreads of gravel which have been much exploited in recent years to leave behind flooded pits. These, initially rich in bird life, are soon colonised by plants which, with management, can also be of interest. A more permanent ornithological interest is maintained at the only large reservoir, GRAFHAM WATER, part of which is a reserve managed by the county trust. Before the increases in the gravel workings and recent improvements to the river, water meadows were a feature of the riverside, but unfortunately few of these remain today.

Higher ground, capped by glacial debris, rises on both sides of the river. Much of this is still wooded, but there was probably more woodland in the time of Neolithic man. Remnants of this presumably primeval deciduous woodland have a rich vegetation and associated animal life, those to the north of the river differing in some respects from those to the south. In many of the southern woodlands in Old Huntingdonshire, oxlips replace the more familiar primrose. One of each of these types of woodland is conserved.

The Oxford clay is exposed south of Bedford and has been much exploited by London Brick PLC, leaving a series of flooded pits which, unlike the gravel workings, are slow to colonise with plant growth. They are comparatively recent and, given time, may develop more than their present mainly ornithological interest. As a result of these mineral workings there is now more open water in the two counties than at any time since the aftermath of the ice ages.

Geologically, Old Huntingdonshire is comparatively simple, with clay soils dominating all but the riverside lowlands. These provided many rich pastures in the past, most of which are now improved and retain little of their former vegetation. One relic, undoubtedly the richest in this part of Britain, is now, happily, a trust reserve.

By contrast, the geology of mid-Bedfordshire is complex, largely because of a layer of lower greensand which crosses the county. Apart from small adjacent blocks of greensand in neighbouring Buckinghamshire and Cambridgeshire, there are no other exposures of this rock in Britain north of the Thames. Most of its sandy soils made poor agricultural land, and areas left as heathland provided an impoverished pasture. There were some excellent woods, mainly on shallow deposits of clay overlying the greensand, and it is not surprising that many of these are now conifer plantations, with some of the older woods completely replanted with conifers. Some remnants of the heathland are now protected, one as a local nature reserve and another in an RSPB reserve at Sandy. The animals and plant life of these greensand woods are very different from those on the glacial debris, but only one area enjoys full protection.

In an area so complex in its soils there are a number of marshes, many of them small, where clay underlies the sand and other pervious strata. FLITWICK MOOR, Bedfordshire's largest wetland and fortunately mainly a trust reserve, is, however, more like a fen, having been formed by reedbeds accumulating in a waterlogged valley.

The southern part of Bedfordshire is scenically the most attractive, with a long stretch of chalk downland, too steep in many places to have been ploughed, and rising to 243m on the summit of Dunstable Downs. The downland was grazed by sheep for many centuries until about 50 years ago. Since then there has been some deterioration caused by scrub invasion, but most of it remains, with its colourful and attractive vegetation and associated animals, especially insects. It is, however, by no means uniform. One hill, presumed to be virgin pasture, has been claimed to have more rare flowers to a square metre than any other site in the British Isles; another is a medieval castle site with a downland developed in not more than seven centuries, and it, too, has its own plant rarities. Most of the downland is now owned or leased by agencies concerned with its protection. Much is open to the public, and it is already showing signs of wear and tear.

For the naturalist who relishes a wide horizon and is not intimidated by urban sprawl, there is much to be found in this region.

J. G. DONY

Arlesey Old Moat

Permit only; 2.4ha; B and HWT reserve
Derelict moat, stream and developing woodland
Spring, early summer

The moat has been colonised by bulrush, greater pond-sedge and reed sweet-grass with water fig-wort and comfrey at the margins. Ash woodland is developing in drier parts of the reserve, alder carr in wetter places. Breeding birds include reed bunting, sedge warbler and redpoll.

Aversley Wood

TL 160817; 60ha; WdT
Ancient woodland
Spring, early summer

This large, partly ancient, woodland contains ash, hazel, field maple, oak, and wild service-tree above a superb spring display of bluebell. Dense thickets of blackthorn provide a habitat for black hairstreak butterfly.

Bankside

Permit only; 2ha; B and HWT reserve
Meadow grassland with pond
Spring, early summer

The hayed grassland varies from dry to damp and contains rich-meadow species such as salad burnet, cowslip and pignut, wild angelica and meadow crane's-bill. The ponds contain both bulrush and lesser bulrush together with many other wetland plants and are surrounded by willow scrub, attractive to warblers. Introduced fritillary, marsh sow-thistle and the alien purple toothwort are well established.

Southern aeshna is a common dragonfly of the ponds and pools of the south.

Begwary Brook Marsh

Permit only; 4ha; B and HWT reserve
Lake, marsh and riverside
Spring, summer

An excellent place for bird life, including passage migrants following the river. A fine range of wetland plants occurs from the willow scrub, water mint and orange balsam of the lake to the tall spread of meadowsweet, great willowherb, reed sweet-grass and other species of the marsh.

Cople Pits

Permit only; 1.9ha; B and HWT reserve
Disused gravelpits
Spring, summer

Eleven small pits are variously overgrown with scrub or managed as areas of open water to provide

Felmersham Gravel Pits: white water-lily fringes the pool in summer.

a wide range of habitat suitable for breeding amphibians and dragonflies or offering sheltered sites for breeding birds. A good range of warblers nests here, together with mallard, moorhen and birds such as goldfinch and redpoll.

Felmersham Gravel Pits

Permit only; 21 ha; B and HWT reserve
Disused gravel workings
Spring, summer

Shallow spreads of water, marsh, grassland, hedges and developing woodland form a very varied reserve which attracts a good range of both breeding and passage birds and provides an excellent site for damselflies and dragonflies.

Ferry Meadows Country Park

TL 145975; 200ha; Peterborough Dev. Corpn
River meadows, lakes formed by gravel extraction, and woodland
Leaflets from PDC and site
All year

Throughout lowland Britain, the glacial rivers have spread deposits of gravels along their valleys and these, increasingly, are being exploited by man. When gravel-digging is finished, the pits are often raw slopes and banks of sandy waste, lapped by the empty waters of a new lake, but are then colonised by plants which attract a host of bright insects and other small animals to the new range of habitat. Birds tend to follow old river courses in their seasonal migrations and often use the new lakes before the gravel extraction has finished. Careful planning and management can create excellent conditions for wildlife.

Nene Park is a regional park being created along 10km of the River Nene, from the centre of Peterborough to the A1. Ferry Meadows, its centrepiece, includes three large connecting lakes formed by the excavation of sand and gravel, to a predetermined level, between 1972 and 1977. The combination of water, grassland and woodland at Ferry Meadows provides habitats for a wide range of wildlife.

Colt's-foot and willowherb grow in abundance on the lake edges, together with planted soft rush, bulrush and branched bur-reed, which shelter amphibians and attract dragonflies. Natural colonisation of the lakes has also taken place. Varying methods of grassland management ensure the development of different plant associations. Some fields are mown only after the plants have flowered and set seed, encouraging their survival and providing food and shelter for insects and birds. Certain areas have been sown with wild flower seed. New trees are restricted to species such as alder, willow, dogwood, blackthorn, hazel, lime and ash.

The woodland harbours hedgehog, mole, wood mouse, weasel and grey squirrel, while along the river banks water vole, bank vole and brown rat thrive. Brown hare, rabbit, stoat and fox can be seen in the meadows.

Nearly 180 bird species have been recorded, remarkable for an inland site so near a town. Some 110 species rest and feed on passage, and about the same number breed. Since the park was opened in 1978 a 4 ha shallow lake (wader scrape) with islands has been created as a sanctuary. Many waders including dunlin, common sandpiper and ruff may be seen at the water's edge, while terns and gulls feed over the lakes and swift and swallow swoop and glide above. Mallard and Canada and greylag goose breed here, while winter brings flocks of pochard, tufted duck and teal, and sometimes wigeon, goosander and other scarcer species.

Birds which breed in the meadows and sanctuary include lapwing, snipe, reed bunting and yellow wagtail, with species that favour the willow plantations and beds of common reed such as turtle dove, reed warbler and sedge warbler. The open areas of gravel attract shingle-nesting birds and may, in part, account for the colonisation of Britain by little ringed plover since the 1950s. Ringed plover, little ringed plover and common tern breed on certain gravel islands carefully maintained free of the vegetation that would otherwise choke their nest sites. Redshank, snipe and water rail rely on plant growth to camouflage their nests and young from predators, and inhabit the overgrown islands, wet meadows and other areas of rank vegetation.

The Firs

TL 028376; 12.4ha; BCC reserve
Heather–bracken heath
Booklet from B and HWT or BCC
Spring, summer

The best remaining area of heathland on the greensand in Bedfordshire, The Firs includes some fine sweeps of heather heath, with bracken, birch, gorse, broom and acid grasses, together with a wetland where purple moor-grass grows with gipsywort, giant horsetail, skullcap and marsh violet. The typical heathland linnet and yellowhammer are present while the woodland provides a habitat for kestrel and great spotted and lesser spotted woodpecker.

Flitwick Moor

TL 046354; 28ha; B and HWT reserve
Wetland and wet woodland
Permit only off rights of way
Booklet from B and HWT
Spring, summer

During the Dark Ages, when Roman rule had decayed, the River Flit was no longer contained by drainage systems and spread across the area of the moor to form a great fen of common reed which grew, collapsed and grew in yearly cycles until it had built a bed of peat across the clays beneath. Chalybeate springs, rich in iron, bubbled through the clay and impregnated the peat. A fall in water level enabled much of the moor to return to grazing

Flitwick Moor: meadow and woodland.

land, a rich fen-marsh for fattening stock or leying, where small amounts of peat were dug and where gorse was cut from the drier parts for fuel. Later the peat was dug commercially and used, for its iron-richness, in purifying gas; this, and a further drying out, advanced the change to woodland.

Flitwick Moor is now a damp birch woodland varied with areas of open water, or with jungles of wetland plants and thickets of scrub. Common reed still shows in swampy areas, with bulrush invading the open pools together with water fig-wort and water-plantain, rushes, sedges and colonising alder, birch and willow.

Drier, but still damp, areas may have a tremendous growth of plants such as butterbur, comfrey and meadowsweet, sedges, reed sweet-grass and yellow iris and this whole rich mix is hedged around and sheltered within vigorous thickets of alder, crab apple, hawthorn and willow, while old pollard crack willows stand on the streamside. The rather uncommon small teasel occurs together with marsh-marigold and hop.

Alder occurs in many of the wetter places but most of the present woodland is birch. Where the peat is driest and well lit, birch and oak stand above a carpet of wavy hair-grass which thins as the wood becomes deeper and wetter. Here the ground cover is thick with mosses, with sprays of fern, or tussocked with sedges; some areas are dry enough for bracken and honeysuckle, some wet and acid enough for common cottongrass and *Sphagnum* moss.

Ninety bird species have been recorded in this attractive mosaic of woodland and wetland which contains breeding populations of water rail and grasshopper warbler.

With plentiful water, some 200 plant species and over 100 each of mosses and fungi, the insect variation is predictably wide and includes some 140 species of plant-feeding sawflies.

Gallows Hill Field

Permit only; 0.4ha; B and HWT reserve
Small plantation
Spring, early summer

Seedling oak trees have been planted, the first step in an attempt to restore an area of woodland to reverse the trend towards the destruction of the Old Huntingdonshire woods.

Gamsey Wood

Permit only; 4ha; B and HWT reserve
Ancient woodland
Spring, early summer

Most of the standard oaks have been felled but elm and coppiced ash provide a canopy, with hazel, Midland hawthorn, hawthorn and wild service-tree, over a ground layer which includes yellow archangel, pendulous sedge, enchanter's-nightshade and primrose. Large quantities of dead wood attract both insects and insect-eating birds.

Grafham Water

TL 143672; 148 ha; B and HWT reserve
Mainly farmland, woodland and open water
Access to sanctuary area by permit only
Leaflets and booklets from B and HWT
All year

The reserve is designed to provide a zone of undisturbed shoreline with creeks where waterfowl can retreat from the disturbance of sailing boats and fishermen. In the main it is modern farmland, poor in species, but it provides nesting sites for lapwing, skylark and yellow wagtail and supports a few interesting plant species – cowslip, great burnet, woolly thistle and sulphur clover still occur. The woodland is mostly recent but contains breeding grasshopper and willow warbler, chiffchaff and lesser whitethroat, while nettle-leaved bellflower, spurge laurel and musk mallow may be found. Common blue, small copper and orange-tip are among the 20 butterfly species recorded.

The reservoir is huge, some 628ha when full, and often birds may be so far away that a telescope is needed, but a number of viewpoints offer opportunities to observe inshore birds and include the B and HNT hide which may be visited from the MANDER PARK NATURE TRAILS.

In winter there are good numbers of mallard, teal, wigeon, tufted duck, coot, pochard, goldeneye and shoveler, with great crested grebe, dunlin and several thousand lapwing. This is a noted site for goldeneye, a non-breeding winter visitor. Easterly gales may bring in more typically coastal species, such as scaup and smew, while throughout the winter the reservoir forms an important roost for gulls.

Breeding species include great crested and little grebe, shoveler, shelduck, redshank, both ringed and little ringed plover, occasional garganey and gadwall, and possibly teal and water rail.

On passage arctic, black and common tern, little gull, black-tailed and bar-tailed godwit, greenshank, knot and ruff may be seen with common, curlew, green and wood sandpiper.

The possible conflict between conservation and leisure pursuits is resulting in a considerable amount of research into bird distribution related to disturbance. The case for a sanctuary at Grafham is clearly stated in the number of birds which frequent the reserve in the fishing season and underlined by the numbers which leave it when perhaps 1000 naturalists tramp the nature trail on open days.

Holme Fen

Permit only; 263.6ha; NCC reserve
Birch woodland
Leaflet from NCC
Spring, early summer

Old fenland, drained, turned into farmland and then disused, the reserve is now the finest lowland birch wood in the country. Alder, elder, oak and willow are mixed with the birch but much of it is pure birch woodland with a wide age structure. Recent peat extraction has left flooded pits which will be increased by current workings and which add to the interest of the site, while relict species from the former fen such as heather, cross-leaved heath, bog myrtle, *Sphagnum* mosses and the rare fen wood-rush still occur. The wood is particularly rich in fungi.

Holme Fen: birches in spring.

Holywell Marsh

SP 991536; 0.2ha; B and HWT–Stevington PC
reserve
Tiny wetland
Spring, summer

A spring line, where water drains from the limestone, is populated by a rich variety of wetland plants including a fine stand of white poplar and a tremendous show of butterbur.

Judge's Spinney

TL 018542; 1.4ha; B and HWT–BCC reserve
Beech woodland
Spring, early summer

A beech hanger on clay, the wood contains spurgelaurel. Birds include both green and great spotted woodpecker.

King's Wood

TL 037393; 29ha; BCC reserve
Mixed woodland and meadow
Spring, early summer

The old-meadow grassland and ancient woodland, on lime-rich clay or more acid greensand, contain a range of plants from meadow grasses to high-forest ash, oak and elm. The ground cover includes yellow archangel, goldilocks buttercup and small teasel, with a shrub layer of hawthorn, hazel and dogwood providing shelter for a good variety of woodland birds.

Lady's Wood

Permit only; 6.8ha; B and HWT reserve
Mixed woodland
Spring, early summer

Field maple, with coppiced ash, forms the major woodland tree since the ash and oak standards were felled around 1950. A dense understorey of bramble, blackthorn and hawthorn, elder, privet and wild rose proves suitable for songbirds such as nightingale.

The Lodge

TL 188478; 41.6ha; RSPB reserve
Heathland and woodland around RSPB
headquarters
Not open on Sundays except to RSPB or
B and HWT members
Leaflets from site
Spring, early summer

Hen harrier, hoopoe or golden oriole do not occur every day at The Lodge but they have been seen either on or over the reserve. Generally the range of birds is that characteristic of woodland and heath and the variety has been increased by the construction of an artificial lake where green sandpiper occasionally visit and where martins and swallows hawk for insects. A public hide has been erected here and a second not far away overlooks the tiny Jack's Pond, set in woodland.

The Lodge: winter woods, bracken and heathland.

The reserve lies on a shoulder of sandstone, giving acid soils which grow bracken, heather and fine small grasses, with heath bedstraw and occasional broom. Birch or oak woodland or small plantations contrast with the spread of heathland and cover the slopes where small valleys have been cut down into the greensand.

Where the trees thin and the heather shows, tree pipit, linnet and yellowhammer may be seen, while open heath with scrub and scattered trees is the favourite habitat of nightjar, which has nested in some years. Around 130 species have been identified on or over the reserve and some 50 species usually breed.

Among the mammals are large numbers of grey squirrel, a variety of small mammals including yellow-necked mouse, and a population of muntjac deer. Reptiles and amphibians are represented by common lizard and by toad and smooth newt.

Butterflies include painted lady, comma and holly blue, and there is a splendid variety of other insects including beetles and dragonflies. Among almost 300 species of moth are the unusual pine hawk, cream-spot tiger and rosy footman.

Mander Park Nature Trails

TL 143672; 1.2 and 2.4km; B and HWT
Waterside nature walks
Hide open September–March, Sundays only
Booklet from B and HWT
All year

Part of GRAFHAM WATER. Gadwall, mallard, shelduck, shoveler and tufted duck breed nearby and may be seen from the hide together with seasonal migrants such as greenshank, spotted red-shank or little stint.

Marston Thrift

Permit only; 5.2ha; B and HWT reserve
Mixed woodland
Spring, early summer

Oak, coppiced ash and hazel stand on a damp slope of boulder clay with a ground cover which includes southern wood-rush at its only known locality within the county.

Monks Wood

Permit only; 156.8ha; NCC reserve
Mixed woodland
Leaflet from NCC
Spring, early summer

Monks Wood is not only a superb example of an-cient oak–ash woodland on lime-rich clays but is also one of the best researched woods in the country. Most of the wood was clear-felled in the early part of this century, and some of the area drained and tilled for farming, but all except the cleared fields has returned to woodland cover and the reserve is now managed to foster a wealth of wildlife interest.

Marston Thrift: coppice with standards.

Before World War I Monks Wood used to be regularly coppiced. Tall oak standards stood above cropped stools of ash, field maple and hazel with other species such as small-leaved elm and horn-beam. Now the coppicing has been reinstated and a fine mosaic of different-age stands adds to the variation encouraged by blocks of high-forest woodland contrasting with areas left unmanaged. Add to these the fields with their scrub develop-ment, the wide rides and the several woodland ponds and it is easy to see why Monks Wood is so rich in varied species. Wild service-tree is plenti-ful, spreading by growing from suckers; the under-storey contains both hawthorn and Midland haw-thorn together with their hybrids, in addition to colourful shrubs such as dogwood, privet, spindle and occasional guelder-rose, with buckthorn, willow, wayfaring-tree and dense thickets of blackthorn.

On higher ground, where the Oxford clay is capped by chalky boulder clay, traveller's-joy tangles its way upwards towards the sun, while the ground cover throughout the wood varies accord-ing to the amount of shade. Cowslip occurs in suit-able open sites and primrose is widespread; one of the features of the springtime woodland is the cowslip–primrose hybrid, sometimes called the false oxlip, which grows where the parent plants meet. Surprisingly the oxlip does not occur here, although it is present in Cambridgeshire woods not far away. Woodland edges and hedgerows contain an attractive speciality, crested cow-wheat, a summer plant found in sites which seem to represent the boundaries of ancient woodlands.

Monks Wood: autumn sunlight slants across a ride to the woodland edge.

Many other fascinating plants may be found, such as yellow archangel, lesser centaury, herb-Paris, spurge-laurel and wood spurge, small teasel, star-of-Bethlehem, musk mallow and a range of orchids which includes common twayblade, bird's-nest and early-purple orchid, common spotted-orchid and greater butterfly-orchid, with occasional species such as the delicate violet helleborine.

The broad rides are a most important facet of the reserve: the margins are managed to represent woodland edge, a well-mown central track grading into taller herbs, into scrub, and into high woodland. This provides space and variation which attracts a fine range of insects. The really distinctive species of the reserve is black hairstreak, first identified here in 1828, for which Monks Wood became the classic site. All three British hairstreaks may be present in the wood, which also holds a good range of moths, including at least two uncommon species, concolorous and light orange underwing. The reserve contains a typical community of woodland birds, with wetland species attracted by the numerous pools, and is a notable site for nightingale.

An outstanding variety of beetles has been recorded at Monks Wood; for the 156.8ha of the reserve, over 1000 species are recognised, including *Osphya bipunctata* for which it is the principal site.

Old Warden Tunnel

Permit only; 2ha; B and HWT reserve
Lime-rich scrub and grassland
Spring, summer

A cutting and the tunnel baulk of a disused railway, the reserve contains grassland filled with lime-loving cowslip, oxeye daisy, hairy violet and spiny restharrow, with spreads of scrub and rough grass attractive to many small mammals and birds.

Pingle Wood Cutting

Permit only; 1.2ha; B and HWT reserve
Lime-rich grassland, scrub and woodland edge
Spring, summer

Gorse, hawthorn and Midland hawthorn are among the scrub species which, with plants such as kidney vetch, bee orchid and common spotted-orchid, attract a good range of insects, birds and other animals.

Ramsey Heights Clay Pits

Permit only; 3.4ha; B and HWT reserve
Flooded clay workings
Interpretative centre open for school parties only
Nature trail leaflets from B and HWT
Spring, summer

The ponds have been invaded by common reed, varied with both bulrush and lesser bulrush, fringed with yellow iris and several species of willow, which provide nesting sites for sedge warbler, reed bunting and a variety of tits. Both three-spined and nine-spined stickleback may be found in the open water areas.

Raveley Wood

Permit only; 5.7ha; B and HWT reserve
Mixed woodland
Spring, early summer

Probably an ancient woodland, most of the standard ash and oak trees have been felled but a variety of species such as Midland hawthorn, dogwood, spindle and privet occurs, with small-leaved elm, over a ground cover which includes goldilocks buttercup, wood millet, early-purple orchid and common twayblade. The wood contains a sizeable rookery and is a breeding site for birds such as blackcap, willow tit and spotted flycatcher.

Redshanks Spinney

Permit only; 0.8ha; B and HWT reserve
Mixed woodland
Spring, early summer

The tiny woodland has developed on peat in an area of intensive agriculture. The ground cover is virtually limited to common nettle and violets but there is considerable variation in tree and shrub species reinforced by recent plantings.

St Neots Common

TL 183613 and 201613; 41.8ha; various bodies
Grassland and marsh
Spring, summer

Much of the area is used for recreation but the wetter, less popular parts contain marsh arrowgrass, meadow saxifrage and both early and southern marsh-orchid, together with good breeding populations of frog and common toad.

Sharnbrook Summit

Permit only; 8.4ha; B and HWT reserve
Lime-rich scrub and grassland
Spring, summer

Excavated material from the railway cutting encourages a splendid range of plants including zigzag clover, wild liquorice and hairy violet, with a scrub of bramble, hawthorn and wild rose, attracting small birds such as whinchat and insects such as green hairstreak, dark green fritillary and five-spot burnet moth.

Shepherds Close

Permit only; 1.2ha; B and HWT reserve
Plantation reverting to natural woodland
Spring, early summer

A good variety of shrubs, together with ash and oak saplings, are set to grow on into woodland when the planted poplars are harvested. Grassland species, such as cowslip, adder's-tongue and the uncommon grass vetchling occur, while some 15 species of breeding birds have been recorded.

Green-winged orchid is a neutral grassland species.

Totternhoe Knolls

SP 986216; 13.6ha; B and HWT–BCC reserve
Chalk grassland, scrub and woodland
Leaflet from B and HWT or BCC
Spring, summer

The Knolls, crowned by the site of a Norman castle, have been much changed by the hand of man. Originally they formed a wooded outlier of the Chiltern Hills, then the trees were cleared and sheep grazed the chalky slopes; the chalk itself was found to contain a layer of harder rock, Totternhoe Stone, which was quarried for building; sheep lost favour, trees were planted on the slopes and scrub invaded the grassland; the softer chalk was quarried for cement.

The beech trees, planted on the slope above the village, still stand but the tangle of scrub on the top of the hill has been cleared to provide open grassland, while the hills and holes below the old castle site are grazed to maintain their richness of chalkland plants.

From the car park the reserve is approached by a rising ancient track from which the great curves of recent quarrying are seen. The open grassland is deep, comprising mainly coarse grasses, but fringed with hawthorn and wild rose, an ideal site for warblers or tree pipit.

The hills and holes, the Knolls proper, are artefacts of quarrying, shallow turfed and ablaze with chalkland plants. Here are lady's bedstraw, common bird's-foot-trefoil and salad burnet, cowslip, eyebright, basil thyme and wild thyme, yellow rattle and yellow-wort, wild mignonette and quaking-grass. This is also a refuge for less common plants and several orchid species occur together with adder's-tongue, clustered bellflower, autumn gentian and both horseshoe and kidney vetch.

The scrub is full of lime-loving ash, privet and spindle, festooned with traveller's-joy and white bryony. Hawthorn, sycamore, bramble and wild rose add to the tangle of thick cover which encourages nesting birds and grades into the woodland. The woodland proper is deeply shaded by

tall beech trees. The understorey and ground cover are sparse, with spreads of ivy, characteristic of secondary woodland, together with violets and sanicle.

The short chalk grassland is the major interest and here may be seen most of the many moths and butterflies, which include the typical chalk downland moths, small purple-barred and dark pyrausta, with little and chalkhill blue butterflies. Some 40 species of bee and wasp are recorded and include three species of *Osmia*, a family of shell-nesting mason bees.

Upwood Meadows

Permit only; 6ha; B and HWT–NCC reserve
Old-meadow grassland
Spring, summer

A rare and beautiful remnant of the ancient unimproved meadows of the area, the reserve is rich in grassland plants, with heath-grass growing unexpectedly among quaking-grass and red fescue, with betony, cowslip, dropwort, dyer's greenweed and devil's-bit scabious, together with species rare or local in East Anglia such as sulphur clover, saw-wort and a magnificent show of greenwinged orchid.

Waresley Wood

Permit only; 28.7ha; B and HWT reserve
Ancient woodland
Spring, early summer

An ancient mixed woodland over coppiced hazel, the reserve, which includes part of the adjacent Gransden Wood, has a rich ground cover including oxlip, primrose and their hybrid, with hairy woodrush, adder's-tongue, greater butterfly-orchid, bird's-nest, early-purple and fly orchid. Badger and fallow deer visit the wood which has a typical range of woodland birds and insects.

Wistow Wood

Permit only; 8.4ha; B and HWT reserve
Mixed woodland
Spring, early summer

Most of the standard trees have been removed and the wood is mainly old coppiced ash with many small field maples above a ground cover which includes the only sizable colony of ramsons in the county.

Woodwalton Fen

Permit only; 208ha; NCC reserve
Fenland remnant
Leaflet from NCC
Spring, summer

Wetlands are always under threat: drainage will change them into farmland, rubbish dumping will build a base on which houses and factories can be built. In Hereward the Wake's time the wetlands stretched into Norfolk, Suffolk and Lincolnshire, a continuous spread of bog and fen, wet *Sphagnum* mosses and reedbeds, alder woodland and vast meres. Woodwalton Fen and WICKEN FEN (Cambridgeshire), two of Britain's most important areas of fenland, total less than 500ha; if we have saved that area of fenland, we have lost approximately 800 times more.

Even what we have saved is suffering from drainage; the fields around Woodwalton are lower than the reserve and much of the fen has progressed to woodland where once it was open wetland. What remains, however, is a marvellous complex of fen and open water, of woodland and wet heath.

Barton Hills: a fine example of chalkland, typical of the landscape of the southern part of Bedfordshire.

Woodwalton Fen: the wetland richness of the entrance to the reserve.

The reserve is dissected by water-filled dykes and by damp droves which pass from blocks of woodland, willow, birch and alder, to broad spreads of mixed fen, to damp meadows and patches of wet heath.

The heathland area is characterised by purple moor-grass, heather and cross-leaved heath which contrast with the spread of the mixed-fen blocks where common reed, yellow loosestrife, common meadow-rue and milk parsley grow, together with purple and wood small-reed, and with the rare fen violet and fen wood-rush. The open waters may be fringed with marsh sow-thistle or decorated with bladderwort, flowering-rush or water-violet, while both these and the mixed-fen areas are sites for water dock.

The insects include the hornet clearwing moth, a splendid example of mimicry, together with the more uncommon marsh carpet and concolorus, and ruddy sympetrum and large red damselfly.

One of the main specialities of Woodwalton is the colony of large copper butterflies (*Lycaena dispar batavus*). The original fenland race, *Lycaena dispar dispar*, became extinct last century and in 1927 the present colony was introduced from Holland. It is carefully maintained and predation minimised by removing as many larvae as possible to protected food plants of water dock. The adults are then released when they hatch in July.

Wymington Meadow

Permit only; 2ha; B and HWT reserve
Old-meadow grassland
Spring, summer

The lime-rich meadow is a mosaic of tall coarse grasses and closely grazed turf which contains cowslip, dropwort, green-winged orchid, yellow rattle and woolly thistle, together with a scrub of hawthorn and wild rose.

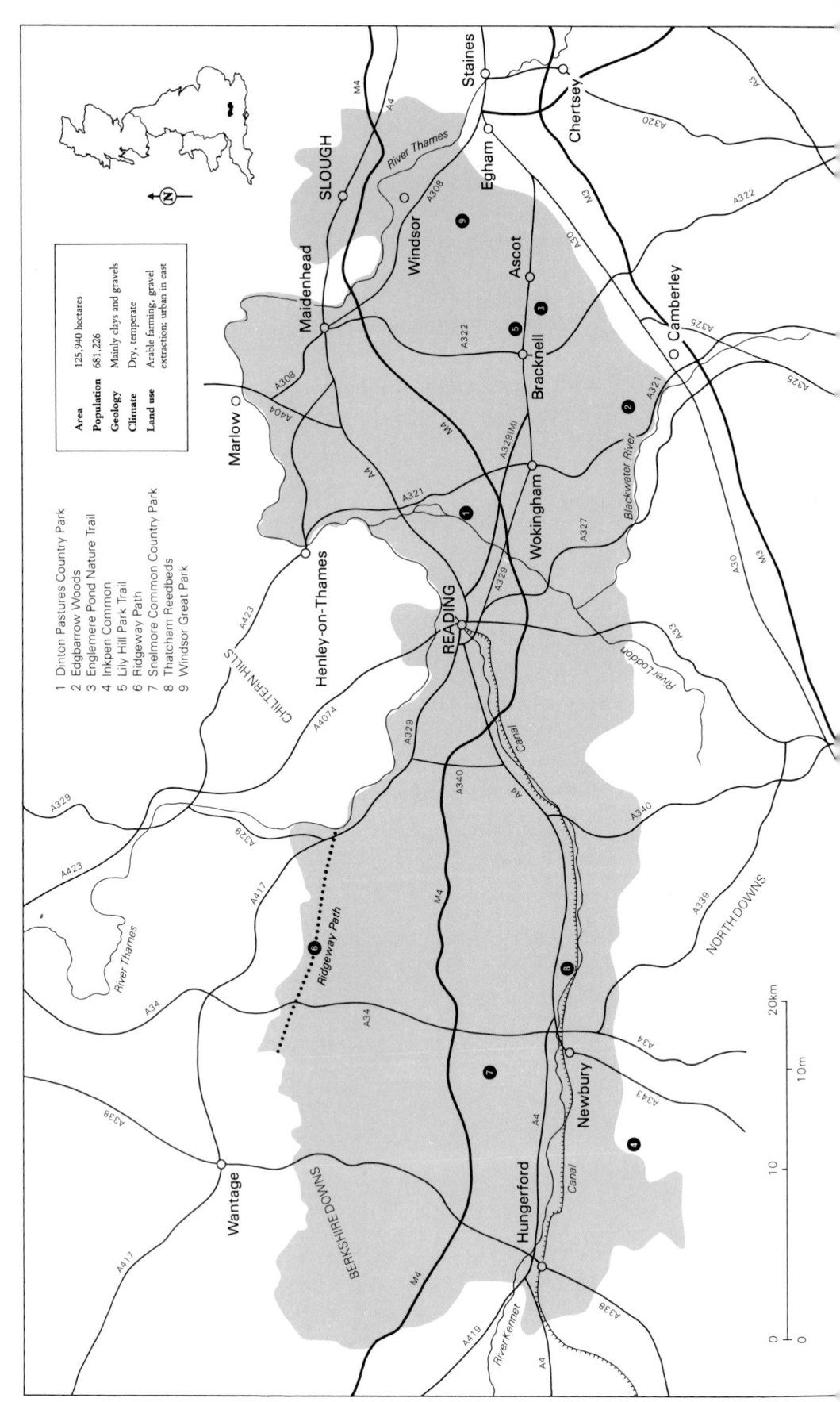

Area 125,940 hectares
Population 681,226
Geology Mainly clays and gravels
Climate Dry, temperate
Land use Arable farming, gravel extraction; urban in east

1 Dinton Pastures Country Park
2 Edgbarrow Woods
3 Englemere Pond Nature Trail
4 Inkpen Common
5 Lily Hill Park Trail
6 Ridgeway Path
7 Snelmore Common Country Park
8 Thatcham Reedbeds
9 Windsor Great Park

Berkshire

The Royal County of Berkshire extends over the region once called the Royal Forest of Windsor, which stretched from Windsor to Hungerford, and includes the lower reaches of two Thames tributary streams, the Kennet and the Loddon; the Loddon has given its name to two rare and beautiful plants, a lily and a pondweed. In the north west and extreme south west, chalk, which underlies so much of the county, gives rise to rolling waterless downland similar to the whalebacked South Downs. In the east the dominant soils, supporting a rather monotonous plant life, have formed on heavy, ill-drained London clay. In parts of the south and south east there are large infertile tracts of plateau gravels and sandy Eocene beds that support heath vegetation, which reverts to birch and oak woodland if not regularly burnt. Exposed rock is extremely rare in the county though sandstone boulders, called sarsens, occur very locally near Lambourn and support interesting lichens.

Historical records show that by AD 1600 only a tenth of the county was still wooded, and the proportion of woodland has changed very little in the last four centuries. The natural forest was probably oak, with alder in the wetter valleys and some beech around Streatley and Bisham. Beech does not appear to have extended along the Berkshire Downs. From the evidence of certain plants, lichens and bark beetles, fragments of ancient forest have been located at Windsor, Ashridge Wood, Clay Hill, Snelsmore, Hamstead Park, Riva Copse (which has the rare snail *Ena montana*) and other sites. One old-woodland plant, the wild service-tree, is widespread east of Reading. Elms have long been a feature of the hedgerows, but only sucker shoots have survived the recent outbreak of disease. This has had a disastrous effect on associated species, such as bark lichens and the large tortoiseshell and white-letter hairstreak butterflies.

Heathland has declined in area following its use for building, gravel extraction and conifer plantation. The abandoned gravelpits, however, can provide nesting sites for sand martin or little ringed plover and, near Ascot, an old brickpit has developed into a *Sphagnum* bog. Dwarf gorse does not occur further west than Berkshire, nor does the bent *Agrostis curtisii* occur much further east, but both grow at INKPEN COMMON.

The relative proportions of grassland and arable have fluctuated dramatically since the early eighteenth century. Today, there is more than twice as much arable as grassland, but 50 years ago the reverse was true. It is now hard to find old permanent meadows and pastures, though most of them have traces of ridge and furrow. All types of grassland can still be seen in the county, however, from the acid ridges of WINDSOR GREAT PARK, with their flora of dwarf ephemeral plants, mosses, ferns and lichens, to the orchid-rich chalk turf of the Berkshire Downs, Inkpen Downs or Winter Hill near Maidenhead. On the chalk, there are at least two good colonies of pasqueflower, and a few sites for rarities like the stone curlew, and the Adonis blue and silver-spotted skipper butterflies. Rich alluvial meadows are found by the Thames between Streatley and Reading and near Cookham, by the upper Loddon where there is a fine fritillary field, and especially along the Kennet. The Kennet is the favoured habitat of the tiny snail *Vertigo moulinsiana*. At least one reedbed along the Kennet has had bearded tits nesting on occasion.

The clear streams of the Pang and Kennet, with their sheets of common water-crowfoot in summer, contrast with the muddy Thames where all submerged vegetation is shredded by powerboats. The Thames still has one rare mollusc, *Gyraulis acronicus*, found nowhere else in Britain, but the river's aquatic plants are now confined to backwaters. Another freshwater mollusc, the tiny *Pisidium tenuilineatum*, has only been found on the Loddon. A large gravelpit at Sandhurst is remarkable for its wealth of aquatic plants, which include six-stamened waterwort and needle spike-rush, which forms a fringing turf kept short by grazing Canada geese. By the lower Loddon many huge gravelpits are now being dug, and it is to be hoped that an equally rich aquatic flora will spread there.

The weedy vegetation of Berkshire is extensive, but the widespread use of weedkillers has made good fields hard to find. Areas close to towns affected by planning blight are often weed refuges. On the chalk wild candytuft, pheasant's-eye, the small fumitories and broad-fruited cornsalad are extremely local, but may be survivors of three millennia of arable farming. On acid soils mousetail, lesser snapdragon and lamb's succory are sporadic. A few corncockle plants are kept going each year by a co-operative farmer. Among the rather large number of alien plants established in Berkshire are yellow figwort, the dock-like beet *Beta trigyna*, and spring crocus which colours a whole field at Inkpen each year.

H.J.M. BOWEN

Dinton Pastures Country Park

SU 785718; 111ha; Wokingham DC
Flooded gravelpits
Leaflets from WDC or site
Spring, early summer

Even so close to the motorway the lakes draw a good variety of birds, while the plant life of meadow, lakeside and water is attractively varied and includes the delicate summer snowflake, a plant locally called the Loddon lily. A nature trail guide illustrates much of the interest of the park and demonstrates the wildlife importance of these gravel pits which now form chains along so many of our major river valleys.

Edgbarrow Woods

SU 837632; 31.2ha; Bracknell DC reserve
Lowland heath
Leaflet from BDC
Spring, summer

The higher ground is wooded with planted or self-sown Scots pine, birch and rowan, but the dry

Bee orchid at Hurley Chalk Pit.

heaths carry a good range of characteristic species such as heather, bell heather, gorse and dwarf gorse, while the wetter areas are distinguished by cross-leaved heath, purple moor-grass and bog asphodel. Among the butterflies recorded regularly are grayling and silver-studded blue, and both fox and emperor moths may be found on the dry heath.

Englemere Pond Nature Trail

SU 902684; 1.2km; Bracknell DC
Lake and heathland
Leaflet from BDC
Spring, summer

Waterbirds, reedbed birds and insect takers such as swallow and sand martin may be seen at the lake, which has considerable stands of common reed and grades through fringes of *Sphagnum* mosses, common cottongrass and the attractive marsh St John's-wort to spreads of heath and invading woodland, rich in many forms of typical wildlife.

Hurley Chalk Pit

SU813820; 1.4ha; BBONT reserve
Disused chalkpit
Spring, summer

Open chalk, scree, scrub grassland and a narrow beech woodland all contribute to the variety of this tiny reserve, rich in plant species such as bee, fragrant and pyramidal orchid and the strange-looking earth-star fungus.

Inkpen Common

SU 382641; 10.4ha; BBONT reserve
Heathland with small bog
Spring, early summer

Although the limestone and chalk areas of Britain are quite outstanding in the variety and beauty of their plant life, one of the compensations of the more acid areas is the richness and subtlety of their colours; though gorse may sometimes look as brash and vivid as yellow-wort or cowslip, in a heathland setting, moderated by the colours of heather, bell heather and paler cross-leaved heath, it seems to glow like captured sunshine. Inkpen Common shows both the subtle colours of the heathlands and also the gemlike smaller plants adapted to such areas.

Gorse and birch form a scrub which shelters the common, providing, with hawthorn, a choice of nesting sites suitable for linnet and nightingale and, perhaps, ground-nesting nightjar. Much of the common is kept open, mown from time to time to keep the scrub from taking over, the effect being that of areas of coarse grass, with regrowing heather being separated by gorse hedges. The grassland contains typical acid heathland plants such as sheep's sorrel, heath bedstraw and tormentil with heath milkwort and lousewort.

The common has suffered badly from fire damage in the past, allowing in invaders such as rosebay willowherb, but heather is regrowing now, a contrast in its tender greenness with the unburned uncut areas where gorse and birch scrub stand above the coarse and leggy old heather plants. Broom complements the gorse, while bell heather shows brighter and larger flowers than the heather, with pale clusters of cross-leaved heath where the ground is damper. The damper ground supports common spotted-orchid and, by the stream, a belt of wet woodland, full of willow, is bright with marsh-marigold, lesser spearwort and ragged-Robin.

On the drier areas bracken may alternate with the grassland, and seedling oak trees have become established with rowan but, as with most heathland areas, the most attractive plants are in the

Summer snowflake, also known as Loddon lily after the river of that name.

wetter parts. Among the other small bog plants at Inkpen are the typical bog asphodel and bogbean, the latter far more attractive than its name.

A speciality of the reserve is the presence, in the grassy paths, of pale dog-violet which is not known to occur at any other site in Berkshire.

Typical rolling chalkland of the Berkshire Downs, rich in orchids.

Lily Hill Park Trail

SU 887694; 34.8ha; Bracknell DC
Ornamental parkland
Tree trail leaflet from BDC
Spring, early summer

A wide variety of exotic tree and shrub species forms most of the park woodland, but sufficient native trees have invaded to improve the resident wildlife and the range of birds includes greenfinch, nuthatch, treecreeper and long-tailed tit.

Moor Copse

SU635742; 22.4ha; BBONT reserve
Damp woodland and riverside
Spring, early summer

Three areas of woodland make up the major part of this reserve, which is bisected by a river. The woods are surprisingly different from each other, providing a range of type over a small area, while the river adds further interest.

Little grebe, water rail and moorhen breed along the river, together with mallard and tufted duck, and the sheltered banks provide ideal sites for water vole and water shrew. One of the specialities of the reserve is the richness of its Lepidoptera, with upwards of 300 species recorded.

Ridgeway Path

SU 464848–595807; 15km; CC
Part of ancient chalkland way
Leaflet from CC and booklet from HMSO bookshops
Spring, summer

Based on an age-old route along the top of the hills, the Ridgeway Path gives a superb picture of chalk downland north of the Thames, with its wide high skies and rich pattern of colourful chalkland flowers.

Snelsmore Common Country Park

SU 463711; 58.4ha; Newbury DC
Lowland heath
Leaflet from NDC
Spring, summer

Woodland, heathland and valley bog are the main aspects of the common, encouraging a good range of bird life which includes nightjar, grasshopper warbler and woodcock, with occasional visits from sparrowhawk and hobby, while the plants include bog asphodel and bogbean.

Thatcham Reedbeds

SU 501673; 12.8ha; Newbury DC reserve
Reedbeds, marsh and wet woodland
Permit only off rights of way
All year

The reserve is part of a more extensive area which makes up one of the largest and most important reedbeds in southern England. Its continuity as a wetland area and the deep beds of common reed make Thatcham Reedbeds a very important staging post for migrant birds, a reservoir of winter food and shelter and a remnant of a once more widespread habitat.

The reserve is mainly reedbed, marsh and wet woodland, where the marsh is a mix of grasses, sedges and tall herbs and the wet woodland consists chiefly of alder and willow species standing over a damp ground cover of pendulous sedge and great horsetail.

The importance of the reedbeds can be seen in the presence of several uncommon moths, the larvae of which all live on or in common reed alone— moths such as brown-veined, obscure, silky, southern and twin spot wainscot. The marshes are also very important for other moths and an expert might need only to look at a list of Thatcham's moths to describe some of the marsh plants there: the blackneck moth predicts tufted vetch, the butterbur moth tells of spreads of the butterbur plant, the dentated pug of yellow loosestrife, the scarce burnished brass of hemp-agrimony and the scarlet tiger of comfrey. All are rare moths, and all are present here because of the large populations of their food plants. Other typical plants include wild angelica, yellow iris, common meadow-rue, great willowherb, common twayblade and species of marsh-orchid.

Of course, such large undisturbed areas of tall plants also provide a vital site for birds. In spring and autumn, Thatcham may be flocked with migrants, including warblers, swallows and martins. In summer, too, warblers abound and the reedbeds, marshes and scrub hold large breeding numbers of reed and sedge warbler, together with grasshopper warbler, nightingale, water rail, little grebe and tufted duck.

In winter, some 50 bird species have been recorded, including up to 1000 wrens, with flocks of goldcrest, treecreeper and tit species, with gatherings of finches, with siskin and redpoll, redwing and fieldfare, and pochard, teal, wigeon, snipe and jack snipe.

The reedbeds have attracted uncommon species such as great reed warbler, Baillon's crake and spotted crake, while the area is the only known Berkshire site for the stonefly *Leuctra geniculata* and the beetles *Leistus rufescens* and *Phyllobius viridicollis*.

Windsor Great Park

SU 953735; 6000ha; Crown Estate Commissioners
Ancient hunting forest
Booklet from NCC
Spring, early summer

An oak tree near Forest Gate is reputed to be some 800 years old; the acorn from which it grew would have fallen only just over a century after William the Conqueror invaded England; certainly many generations passed while it grew from a twiggy sapling into the gnarled ancient which stands there

now. Many of the other old oak trees, hollow, riven, seemingly stunted, are thought to be some 500 years old. This continuity of woodland life, shared only with a very few old forests, preserves at Windsor a wonderful community of plants and animals, rivalled in variety and interest only by the NEW FOREST (Hampshire and the Isle of Wight).

A tree left to itself will become huge and over-mature, and will weaken and die. If it is periodically cropped, fresh shoots grow up with renewed vigour and the old stem may become virtually immortal; this explains the great age of the pollards, cropped at a high level to prevent grazing animals such as the deer of the Royal Hunting Forest or the commoners' beasts from feeding off the regrowing shoots; it also explains the great open parklike areas where grazing prevented new trees from establishing themselves. The large mature oaks in the park were planted from Elizabethan times onwards to supply timber for the ships of the navy; many of these still survive and may be contrasted with the pollards.

Roughly half of the present area of the Great Park and Forest is wooded, a mixture of ancient pollards with park trees, high-forest woodland, coppice, mixed woodland and coniferous trees. Old beech woodland supplements the importance of the oak and the NCC have declared an 18ha block of the finest surviving original oak–beech woods as a forest nature reserve. Oak is the food plant for

Windsor Great Park: an ancient oak towers over the open scrub of the royal hunting forest.

over 280 species of insects and beech too has its complement of important species.

The area has long been famous for its bird life with breeding species including sparrowhawk and little owl, a number of warblers, all three British woodpeckers and other insect-takers such as nuthatch, treecreeper and redstart. On the heathland fringe to the south hobby, nightjar, woodlark and stonechat breed, while Virginia Water, renowned for its wildfowl, is one of the foremost sites for mandarin duck, now a British breeding species, together with gadwall, pochard, shoveler, shelduck, tufted duck, teal and wigeon. Over 30 butterfly species are recorded including silver-studded and holly blue, painted lady, white admiral and five species of skipper. Red and fallow deer are present but rarely seen and there are populations of roe and muntjac. Some 400ha of the Great Park have now been set aside as a deer park; 19 red hinds were brought from Balmoral in 1979 and the herd has now multiplied to over 300.

The greatest interest to naturalists probably lies in the fungi and insects associated with the ancient trees. The fungi include rare species of *Boletus* while over 2000 beetle species have been identified here, together with a number of rare Diptera, including *Chrysopilus lactus* and *Rainieria calceata* at their only known British locality.

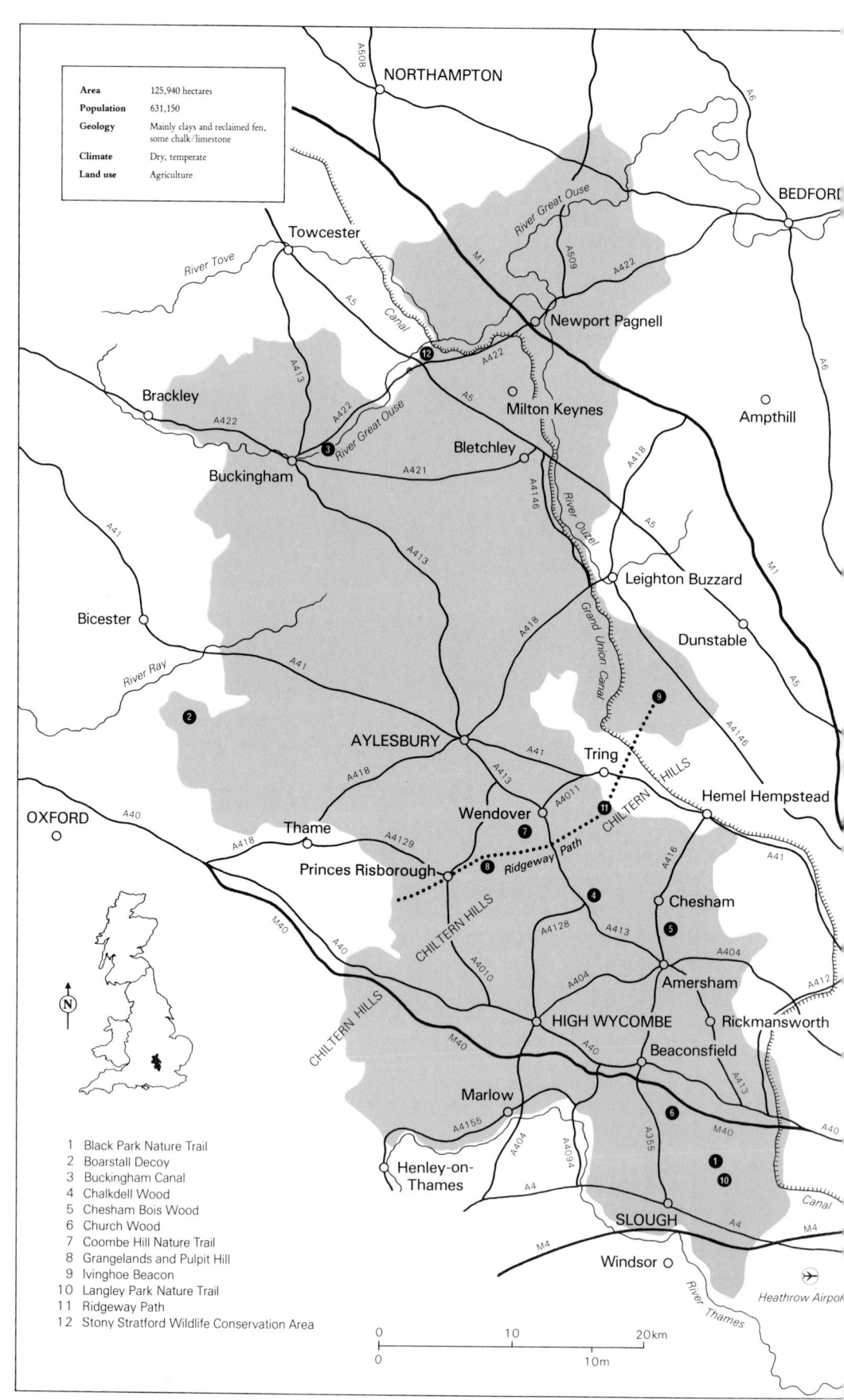

Area	125,940 hectares
Population	631,150
Geology	Mainly clays and reclaimed fen, some chalk/limestone
Climate	Dry, temperate
Land use	Agriculture

NORTHAMPTON

BEDFORD

A508

River Tove

Towcester

River Tove

A5

Canal

M1

River Great Ouse

A509

A422

A6

Newport Pagnell

Brackley

A413

A422

River Great Ouse

A5

A422

Milton Keynes

Ampthill

A422

A5

Buckingham

3

A421

Bletchley

A4146

River Ouzel

A418

A5

A41

Bicester

River Ray

A41

A418

A418

Grand Union Canal

Leighton Buzzard

M1

Dunstable

A4146

A5

2

9

AYLESBURY

A41

A4011

Tring

CHILTERN HILLS

OXFORD

A40

A418

A418

A413

Wendover

7

11

Hemel Hempstead

A41

Thame

A4129

Ridgeway Path

8

Princes Risborough

CHILTERN HILLS

A4128

A413

4

A416

Chesham

5

A40

M40

A4010

A404

Amersham

A404

A412

CHILTERN HILLS

M40

A404

HIGH WYCOMBE

A40

Rickmansworth

Beaconsfield

A413

6

Marlow

A4155

A404

A4094

A355

M40

A40

Henley-on-Thames

A4

1

10

SLOUGH

A4

M4

Windsor

M4

River Thames

Heathrow Airport

N

1 Black Park Nature Trail
2 Boarstall Decoy
3 Buckingham Canal
4 Chalkdell Wood
5 Chesham Bois Wood
6 Church Wood
7 Coombe Hill Nature Trail
8 Grangelands and Pulpit Hill
9 Ivinghoe Beacon
10 Langley Park Nature Trail
11 Ridgeway Path
12 Stony Stratford Wildlife Conservation Area

0	10	20km
0	10m	

Buckinghamshire

Like Caesar's Gaul, Buckinghamshire is divided into three parts: a northern region that is part of the Midlands; the Vale of Aylesbury in the middle, considered by many to be the most English part of the English countryside; and the core of the Chilterns in the south, sandwiched between Oxfordshire and Hertfordshire and sloping down to the opulent towns and villages of the Thames Valley.

Northern Buckinghamshire lies largely on oolitic limestone, although it is not marked by the characteristic stone walls of the Cotswolds to the south west or Northamptonshire to the north east. It is very agricultural limestone countryside, from which any rolling lime-rich downland has long since been eliminated by the plough and the government grant. But it is also still very wooded, with some fine fragments of the extensive oak forest that once covered most of the Midlands – SALCEY FOREST, which is half in Northamptonshire, as is Whittlewood Forest, and Whaddon Chase. The eastern side of this region is now being slowly engulfed in the new town of Milton Keynes, leaving an isolated fragment of rural Buckinghamshire north of the Ouse around the eighteenth-century poet William Cowper's magical little town of Olney, perhaps the only place in the county with an echo of the flavour of an eighteenth- or nineteenth-century market town.

Despite the rapid growth of the town of Aylesbury, the Vale is still very rural and you can still find gated roads and splendid minor roads that take you through the green countryside, deserted since the Enclosures, straight to the old county town of Buckingham. Here is as good a place to search for deserted villages as anywhere in the Midlands. Again the Vale is very agricultural, with only scattered woodlands to vary the hedged landscape of green and brown fields. But it is still a hedged landscape, and the farmers and landowners deserve praise for resisting the temptation to rip out hedges as others have done elsewhere in England. At the eastern end of the Vale, on the borders of Bedfordshire, is one of the few areas north of the Thames where the greensand becomes an important landscape feature. The mini-escarpments and fragments of heathland still surviving around the Brickhills are similar to those of Wealden Sussex.

To many people Buckinghamshire means the Chilterns, and it was the Chilterns that gave the county its nickname, 'Beechy Bucks', which nowadays has faint echoes of John Betjeman's Metroland and the early motoring era, when venturesome London motorists discovered the wealth of woodland on their doorstep. The Chilterns form an astonishingly rural area so near to London, with more single-track roads than you will find elsewhere until you reach the Pennines or the Welsh Marches. There are still plenty of trees, most of them beeches, and more rare orchids than anywhere else in England west of the Medway.

Although the Chilterns are chalk hills, there is very little typical chalk grassland, for the tops of the hills are covered with a thick layer of clay with flints. Going south towards the Thames, the chalk is covered with various tertiary sands and gravels, culminating in Burnham Beeches with its ancient pollard trees including a few oaks. What little chalk downland there is lies mainly between IVINGHOE BEACON and the Chequers estate to the south. This stretch still has such treasures as pasqueflower and musk orchid, not to mention one of the three boxwoods in England that may be native.

The Thames itself is very respectable and sedate in Buckinghamshire, but there are still towpath walks around Great and Little Marlow, and the towering cliff of Cliveden bows the river out into what is now Berkshire on both banks. Even this tamed part of the Thames can still offer a fine stand of the Thames's special flower, summer snowflake, sometimes called the Loddon lily.

If the two-thirds of the county that lie north of the Chiltern escarpment have little semi-natural habitat left, except for a few oakwoods and a handful of marshy meadows, the Chilterns fully make up for the deficiency. Their beechwoods and chalk grasslands, many of them belonging to or managed by the National Trust and BBONT, put them high among the parts of southern England that every naturalist ought to know.

R.S.R. FITTER

Amersham Main Substation Nature Trail

Permit only; 2km; CEGB
Circular trail in substation grounds
Leaflet from CEGB or BBONT
Restricted site for use by Bucks Education Authority and BBONT
Spring, early summer

This varied trail runs through woodland and grassland rich in plant and animal life. Numerous bird species include blackcap, coal and marsh tit, goldcrest, kestrel and nuthatch.

Bernwood Forest

Permit only; 409ha; NCC–FC reserve
Invertebrate reserve
Spring, autumn

This large tract of mixed woodland includes a ride system.

Black Park Nature Trail

TQ 005833; 0.8km; BCC
Nature walk in country park
Booklet from site or BCC
Spring, early summer

The trail, laid out in part of the County Council's green belt estate, contrasts broad-leaved woodland with coniferous plantations and the plants and animals of the acid gravels with those of the lake.

Boarstall Decoy

SP 623151; 7.2ha; BBONT–NT reserve
Duck decoy in mixed woodland
Limited opening Good Friday–August Bank Holiday. No access at other times
Spring, summer

The practical working of a traditional decoy is demonstrated here, where the curious duck are worked down a narrowing netted channel by the antics of a trained decoying dog; at the psychological moment, the catcher appears behind the ducks and frightens them further in, to the keepnet where they may be handled, ringed and released.

Buckingham Canal

SP 728357; 0.5km; BBONT reserve
Disused canal
Spring, summer

Open water and marshy areas make this reserve a good one for wetland plants and insects.

Buttler's Hangings

SU818962; 4ha; BBONT reserve
Chalk grassland
Spring, summer

Rich downland with plants such as wild candytuft and blue fleabane; 26 species of butterfly have been recorded.

Calvert Jubilee

SP684252; 35.2ha; BBONT reserve
Flooded claypit
Dangerous without a guide
All year

The pit is a deep islanded pool partly surrounded by sheltering trees and scrub. Some of the land around has been cleared, providing an open plateau which is being recolonised by vegetation, while the undisturbed margins are rich in scrub and meadow species with good numbers of common spotted-orchid. The islands should become breeding sites for mallard and tufted duck, both of which have bred in the past, and will increase the year-round interest of the site. The development of scrub and woodland will add a further range of habitat to attract breeding birds.

Boarstall Decoy: duck are trapped here by methods dating back for centuries.

The depth of the pool provides a more suitable site for divers than for dabblers, and probably explains the only infrequent visits of heron and kingfisher, but numbers generally should increase as the protected nature of the reserve is recognised. Even now well over 100 species have been recorded including great grey shrike and osprey.

Regular breeding species include great crested grebe, moorhen and coot on the pool, with the trees and scrubland providing nest sites for green woodpecker, magpie and bullfinch, and warblers such as blackcap and garden, sedge and willow warbler. Grasshopper warbler and nightingale are probable breeders.

Despite the lack of ideal shallows, the reserve may still draw visits from the passage waders — greenshank, redshank and common sandpiper, with rarer occurrences of other species. Black and common tern have also been recorded.

Tufted duck have two peaks, one in late summer when birds gather in the safety of the reserve to go through their moult, another when winter numbers build. Winter brings in the largest numbers of waterbirds. Regular wintering species include mallard, pochard and wigeon with smaller numbers of teal and with occasional gadwall, pintail, scaup and shoveler, goldeneye and goosander. The pool may be visited by Slavonian or black-necked grebe, and when the duck flight out to feed in the evening, it forms an important winter roost for gulls.

Chalkdell Wood

SP 900012; 1 ha; WdT
Small beech woodland
Spring, early summer

The woodland surrounds an old chalk quarry. Mainly beech, it includes lime and Scots pine above a typically varied Chiltern shrub layer. A rookery adds to the interest.

Chesham Bois Wood

SP 960003; 16 ha; WdT
Beech woodland
Spring, early summer

The wood is rich in species such as bluebell, together with coralroot, adapted to the shade.

Church Wood

SU 973873; 14 ha; RSPB reserve
Mixed woodland, and scrub grassland
Spring, early summer

Woodland and grassy scrub, together with a recently built pond, provide a wide range of suitable sites for birds in the reserve and this has resulted in some 80 recorded species, over half of which breed. The wood, on a slope of flinty clay above a chalky bedrock, is very varied, chiefly of birch but with areas of oak, beech, and ash and mixed throughout with other species including tall exotic conifers. Much of the ground cover is dense bramble, providing ideal nest sites for many small birds, but clearings and more open areas allow a good variety of woodland plants to flourish. The grassland area, the paddock, has been invaded by willow and aspen, tangled with bramble, or has an open scrub of hawthorn, again providing convenient nest sites and singing posts.

Some 200 plant species have been identified, which show both the rather acid nature of the clays, with birch—oak—bramble as a natural cover, and the effect of chalk in adding more interesting species such as hornbeam, yew and box. Butcher's-broom is found in clumps within the wood, as are green hellebore and Solomon's-seal. Primrose, bugle, wood spurge and violets grow in the open rides, while damper clearings show ragged-Robin and common spotted-orchid. The pool adds a further range of plants such as sedges, rushes and yellow iris.

A good variety of butterflies includes white admiral, purple and white-letter hairstreak and the beautiful holly blue; mammals include muntjac deer, fox and weasel, together with grey squirrel.

The major management at Church Wood is for the birds which share the habitats. Blackcap and garden warbler nest in the less dense woodland and tall bramble; magpie and jay prefer the taller trees; pheasant, and woodcock nest upon the ground; hole-nesting birds find, or make, holes in the standing trees or use the nest boxes provided. The pool encourages water-loving species; mallard and moorhen will breed there, heron visit, pied and sometimes grey wagtail work the edges, and snipe probe the marshy ground. The wood sees the spring and autumn passage of many other species, with wintering flocks of fieldfare and redwing, siskin and redpoll.

Coombe Hill Nature Trail

SP 853063; 2 km; NT
Chiltern Hills walk
Leaflet from NT
Spring, summer

Part of the interest of the trail is its clear demonstration of the difference between the chalk slopes and the clay-with-flints hilltop where acid plants such as broom, gorse and heather contrast with the chalk-loving species such as juniper, yew and whitebeam below. The trail affords superb views across the clay vale and to the Cotswolds and the Berkshire Downs.

Dancers End

SP900095; 31 ha; BBONT reserve
Wood, scrub and grassland
Spring, summer

A very rich variety of plant species, with abundant Chiltern gentian, and of associated insects, may be seen in the interesting contrast between acid clay with flints above and chalk richness below.

Gomm Valley

SU898922; 4ha; BBONT reserve
Chalk grassland, scrub and woodland
Spring, summer

Generally rather overgrown with scrub, the reserve is notable for its butterflies with over 30 species recorded.

Grangelands and Pulpit Hill

SP827049; 20ha; BBONT reserve
Chalk downland, scrub and beech woodland
Spring, summer

This complex of three areas is rich in plant species such as bird's-nest orchid and narrow-leaved helleborine, with a good variety of butterflies and birds.

Ivinghoe Beacon

SP 961168; 400ha; NT
Chalk grassland and scrub
Spring, summer

The Beacon, and the Ivinghoe Hills just to the south, lie close to the Hertfordshire border and look out across the Vale of Aylesbury, a great plain below the sheltering slopes of the Chilterns. The slopes are rich in plant life, butterflies and birds and the views are so spectacular that they draw large crowds of visitors.

The slopes of the Beacon are grassed or trodden into chalky pathways while the hills have an open scrub of hawthorn, with species such as wayfaring-tree and whitebeam, over deep or thinner grassland depending on the steepness of the slope. Competition from the coarser grasses tends to smother the small chalk plants where the

Gomm Valley: an area of woodland adds to the wide variety of the reserve, famous for its chalkland butterflies.

soil is deeper, so the richest areas are those steep slopes where the soil is shallowest. Salad burnet and common rock-rose are widespread and there are good numbers of cowslip, even under the denser areas of scrub, but the banks of the old cart-tracks and the steepest slopes of the hills hold the richest collection of plants and attract the widest range of chalkland butterflies.

Kidney vetch and horseshoe vetch, both important food plants for blue butterfly species, grow with common bird's-foot trefoil, milkwort and wild thyme. Bladder campion, wild mignonette, yellow rattle and quaking-grass also occur, together with common-spotted orchid, fragrant orchid and, here and there, adder's-tongue.

Deep coarse grasses, gorse and mixed scrub on the hilltops show where the chalk is topped by clay with flints and mark the upper level of the chalkland richness. In the natural course of events the whole area would return to woodland, only small areas remaining as herb-rich grasslands with chalkland flowers, areas too steep for scrub to gain a foothold. Grazing and scrub clearance are the usual methods for keeping grassland open, often at the expense of excluding public access.

The public are so often accused of damage through trampling and flower picking that the points of greatest interest here are not only that some trampling acts as a grass control, in the absence of grazing, and allows the smaller plants to gain a foothold, but also that some of the finest shows of fragrant orchid stand beside and in a much-used pathway – with not a sign of damage.

Langley Park Nature Trail

TQ 016824; 1.6km; BCC
Parkland and woodland including gardens
Booklet from BCC
Spring, early summer

A number of ancient oak trees with many exotics and coniferous plantations add interest to the trail which is laid out in part of the County Council's green belt estate.

Ridgeway Path

SP 770013–961168; 30km; CC
Part of ancient chalkland way
Leaflet from CC and booklet from HMSO bookshops
Spring, summer

The final, eastern section of this fascinating long-distance way passes briefly through a limb of Hertfordshire before ending at the steep chalk knoll of IVINGHOE BEACON. As well as the beauties of its plants, butterflies and birds, the path gives spectacular views across the plain of the Vale of Aylesbury.

Salcey Forest

Permit only; 13.2ha; BBONT–Northants TNC
reserve
Remnant of ancient oak forest
Spring, early summer

Described under Northamptonshire.

Stony Stratford Wildlife Conservation Area

SP 785412; 22.3ha; BBONT reserve
Disused gravel workings
Permit only to main reserve area
All year

Opened in 1980, this reserve was set up with considerable help from the Milton Keynes Development Corporation. Gravel was extracted from the site for the building of the new A5 road and the area was restored and designed first and foremost for breeding redshank and other waders. Considerable work has been carried out, including the erection of a hide and nesting boxes, and the transfer of water plants from the nearby Grand Union Canal. Shingle and mud islands have been established in the now water-filled pits, along with the scrub islands which provide cover for nesting. Sand martin and kingfisher banks have also been constructed. A good selection of waders and wildfowl now make use of the reserve, including ringed plover, curlew and redshank.

Chiltern downland: the slopes around Ivinghoe show the curving beauty of the chalklands.

Cambridgeshire

At first sight Cambridgeshire seems a flat and, in places, almost treeless landscape with a complete hemisphere of sky filled, at times, with quite spectacular cloud formations. Some people may prefer hills and mountains but there is much of interest here and even the fens have a charm of their own – and a unique plant and animal life – for those who get to know them.

Geologically and historically, Cambridgeshire has three distinct regions which may be called the fen, the field and the forest. Most of the fen is in the northern half of the county, the old Isle of Ely, and the soil is almost entirely silt or peat. In former times much of it was under shallow water or at least liable to winter flooding. The field lies across the southern part of Cambridgeshire on a subsoil of solid chalk; probably it has always been more or less open grassland. Overlying this chalk to the south east, where Cambridgeshire marches with Essex and Suffolk, and to the west, towards Bedfordshire, is a thick deposit of heavy boulder clay which once supported dense forest. Most of the county has now been drained or cleared for cultivation but in each of the three regions there remain a few large, and many small, relics of the former vegetation and their characteristic insects and birds.

In Neolithic times, some 5000 years ago, the area that is now fenland was a gently undulating plain covered with dense woodland; through it flowed streams and rivers carrying water northwards to the sea from the higher ground in the south and east. The rising sea level gradually slowed these rivers at their outflow, so that the silt they carried was dropped to form the silt fen in the north of the county. South of these silt deposits there was a gradual rise in the level of fresh water, drowning

the trees of the woodland and creating ideal conditions for reeds and other aquatic plants. As the vegetation died it accumulated and partially decayed in the fresh water to form peat which thickened, as the water level rose, to become several metres thick in places. This rise must have been fairly rapid because the growing peat covered and then preserved the now dead and fallen trees; even today trees are occasionally found in the peat as 'bog oaks', and they are sometimes far larger than any living oaks in Britain.

Large-scale reclamation of the fens did not start until the seventeenth century, although small parts, such as by Ramsey Abbey in the Middle Ages, were drained and cultivated earlier. Two long canals, the Old Bedford River and the New Bedford River, were cut across the fenland to carry the waters of the River Ouse straight to the estuary and to the sea beyond King's Lynn. As it was drained, the peat shrank very rapidly at first, and then continued to waste away under cultivation, so that the level of the farmland was lowered in relation to the rivers. Pumping was soon necessary to keep the land drained; wind pumps were used at first, replaced later by steam and now diesel and electric pumps. Considerable areas of fenland are now well below high-tide level; the fields are surrounded by dykes (ditches) which carry water into main drains leading to the pumps where it is lifted into the rivers, often several metres higher than the land. These dykes and drains are bordered by water plants such as reed and also support many aquatic insects including water beetles and mayfly larvae. The washes between the two Bedford rivers are fairly wet all the year and usually flooded in winter, when they attract large flocks of migratory birds. The world-famous nature reserve of WICKEN

FEN is open to the public all the year; it is an extensive area of undrained fen where rare fenland plants and insects may be found, such as marsh-orchids and great fen-sedge.

The chalk region of south Cambridgeshire was probably never thickly wooded; it was mostly open grassland grazed by wild cattle and deer in prehistoric times and more recently by flocks of sheep. The Icknield Way, that ancient route from Salisbury Plain to Breckland, comes into Cambridgeshire at Royston and runs along the chalk escarpment through Newmarket and beyond. Crossing it are several earthworks, notably FLEAM DYKE and the DEVIL'S DYKE, constructed in early Saxon times to protect East Anglia, then the most cultured part of England, from the barbarians further west. These banks and ditches, of imposing proportions, ran from the impassable fen across the open grassland to the impenetrable forest. In time they became overgrown with the rich and varied vegetation of the chalk grassland through which they passed. Early last century most of this grassland was enclosed and cultivated, destroying this vegetation together with the butterflies and other insects which it supported. Today, apart from some very interesting roadside verges, these ancient earthworks are the best places in Cambridgeshire to see pasqueflower, bee and fragrant orchid, common rock-rose, clustered bellflower, and many other treasures of chalk grassland.

Until early Saxon times areas of south east and south west Cambridgeshire were almost continuous mixed oak forest, with some marshy places where drainage was poor. Most of this was cleared and cultivated during the next 400 to 500 years, but every parish retained one or two woods to provide for its needs; there is nearly as much woodland in south Cambridgeshire now as there was at the time of the Norman Conquest. Fortunately several of these ancient woods have been preserved as nature reserves; HAYLEY WOOD is the best known and most fully documented. Like many others, this wood is directly derived from the primeval 'wildwood', that is, it has never been cleared and replanted. It has, however, been much modified by coppicing with standards. This practice has continued since the thirteenth century, perhaps even two or three centuries earlier. Woodland vegetation is in three distinct layers: trees, shrubs, and herbaceous plants. In Hayley Wood the principal trees are oak and ash; the main shrub is hazel, though others are present; and the ground flora includes oxlip, bluebell, wood anemone, and many other herbaceous species.

As a conservation measure to encourage the ground flora, coppicing has been revived in Hayley Wood since the early 1960s. Just under half a hectare alongside the main ride is cut every winter by volunteer labour, so visitors are able to see there each stage of the subsequent regrowth. Coppicing involves cutting the shrubs and often the ash, too, to near ground level every ten years or so. The hazel then sends up many straight stems which were once used for hurdle making and other rural crafts.

W.H. PALMER

Bassenhally Pit

Permit only; 8.8ha; Cambient reserve
Woodland, scrub, grassland and wetland
Spring, early summer

The reserve is noted for its invertebrate life and for a very rich plant life, including lesser water-plantain.

Beechwood

TL 486548; 4.8ha; Cambient reserve
Beech woodland
Spring, early summer

Pure beechwoods are uncommon on the Cambridgeshire chalk and the beechwood shade eliminates virtually everything beneath it. A few plants survive where the canopy becomes thinner, and the beautiful white helleborine occurs on the woodland floor.

Buff Wood

TL 283509; 15.6ha; University Botanic Garden reserve
Mixed woodland
Permit only, except to north western section
Spring, early summer

Coppicing has been reinstated in this rich boulder clay wood which is centred on a nucleus of ancient woodland. It contains a mix of oak, ash, elm, aspen and hazel, with a considerable block of hornbeam above a ground cover noted for oxlip, primrose and their hybrids. A fine colony of green hellebore may be seen with commoner spring flowers such as wood anemone, bluebell and lesser celandine, and some beautiful displays of orchids.

Cherry Hinton–Lime Kiln Close

TL 484556; 3ha; Cambridge City Council
Recolonised chalk workings
Spring, summer

These chalkpits have been famous among naturalists for over 300 years. The public open space demonstrates a complete range of habitat from chalk grassland through scrub to woodland.

Chippenham Fen

Permit only; 105ha; NCC reserve
Breckland valley fen
Can be overlooked from public footpath at
TL 653690
Spring, summer

This superb area of very varied habitat includes old peat diggings, unimproved wet meadows, and old planted woodlands grading through scrub to fen. The reserve contains spreads of great fen-sedge and black bog-rush, saw-wort and meadow thistle,

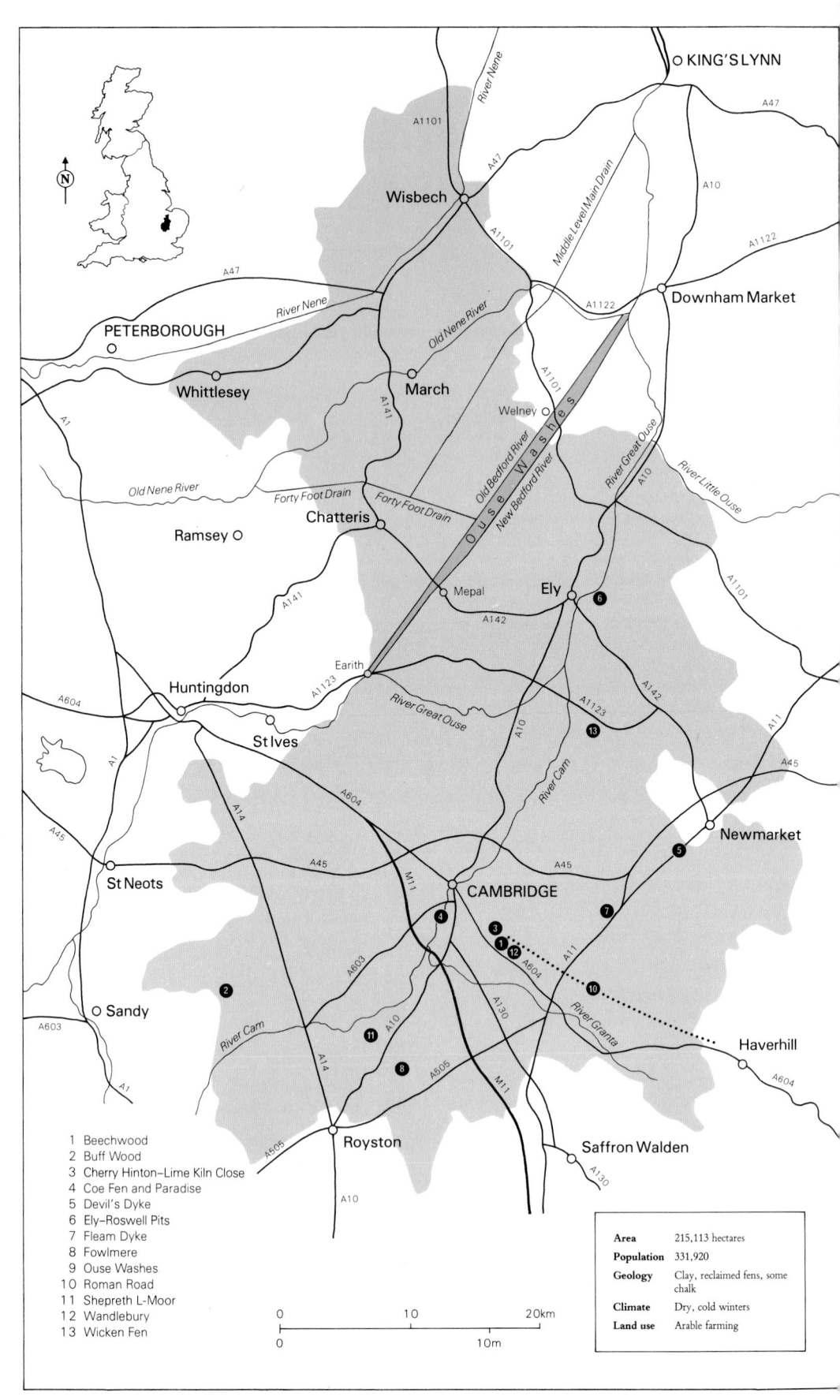

KING'S LYNN

River Nene

A1101

A47

A47

A10

A1122

Wisbech

A1101

Middle Level Main Drain

A1122

Downham Market

A47

River Nene

PETERBOROUGH

Old Nene River

A1101

March

Welney

Whittlesey

A141

River Great Ouse

A10

River Little Ouse

Old Nene River

Forty Foot Drain

Forty Foot Drain

Old Bedford River

New Bedford River

O u s e W a s h e s

Chatteris

Ramsey

Mepal

Ely   **6**

A142

A1101

Earith

A1123

River Great Ouse

A1123

A142

Huntingdon

A10

13

St Ives

A604

A11

A141

A14

River Cam

A45

A45

Newmarket

A45

5

St Neots

A45

A603

CAMBRIDGE

7

M11

4

A603

A10

3

1

12

A11

2

A604

A130

10

Sandy

River Cam

River Granta

Haverhill

A603

11

A604

A505

M11

8

A1

A14

Royston

Saffron Walden

A505

A130

A10

1 Beechwood
2 Buff Wood
3 Cherry Hinton–Lime Kiln Close
4 Coe Fen and Paradise
5 Devil's Dyke
6 Ely–Roswell Pits
7 Fleam Dyke
8 Fowlmere
9 Ouse Washes
10 Roman Road
11 Shepreth L-Moor
12 Wandlebury
13 Wicken Fen

0   10   20km

0   10m

Area	215,113 hectares
Population	331,920
Geology	Clay, reclaimed fens, some chalk
Climate	Dry, cold winters
Land use	Arable farming

locally uncommon species such as bogbean, common butterwort, columbine and grass-of-Parnassus, and displays of marsh helleborine, fragrant orchid and southern marsh-orchid. Birds include water rail and grasshopper warbler.

Cinques Common

Permit only; 2.4ha; Cambient reserve
Acid heathland
Spring, early summer

The reserve protects part of an acid heath, unique in the county, where plants such as mat-grass, heather, heath bedstraw and heath-grass grow.

Coe Fen and Paradise

TL 448575; 9.2ha; Cambridge City Council reserve
Grazing land and marshy island
Nature trail leaflets from Cambient
Spring, summer

The grazing land of Coe Fen is coloured with buttercups and fringed with streamside plants and willows, while Paradise is clumped with alder, buckthorn and willow above marsh plants such as reed canary-grass, comfrey, marsh-marigold, purple-loosestrife and reed sweet-grass. The river and plants attract insects as food for birds.

Devil's Dyke

TL 570660–654585; 34ha; Cambient–CCC reserve
Linear chalk earthwork
Spring, summer

From Reach to Stetchworth, the Devil's Dyke runs arrow-straight across the land, an ancient earthwork over 11km long. The dyke is surprisingly varied, here an embankment thick with scrub, there an open slope of downland, a splendid mosaic of chalkland plants which delight in the dry shallow soils. Here are the characteristic plants of southern lime-rich soils: salad burnet and quaking-grass, horseshoe vetch, common rock-rose, squinancywort, clustered bellflower and dropwort. Tor-grass, typical of chalk and limestone, is quite uncommon in Cambridgeshire but, particularly where the spread of scrub has been held at bay, it is not uncommon here.

Scrub can cause great problems on ungrazed grassland but regular clearance of open scrub maintains a habitat for the special plants while denser spreads of blackthorn and hawthorn provide a suitable habitat for birds.

Among the plants for which the dyke is famous is the spring-flowering pasqueflower, together with rare spring-sedge, purple milk-vetch, bloody crane's-bill and a number of uncommon mosses. But, although these uncommon plants must be protected, the real importance of the dyke is its place as a guardian of chalkland, not a special site for plants of great rarity but a natural garden of mixed downland flowers which reminds us of what we have lost to the plough.

Dog House Grove

Permit only; 0.8ha; Cambient reserve
Woodland and ponds
Spring, early summer

Seven small fish ponds add to the interest of this tiny woodland where ash and elm stand above an understorey of hawthorn and encourage a good range of woodland birds.

Ely–Roswell Pits

TL 547805; 32ha; AWA reserve
Flooded clay workings, meadowland, scrub and woodland
Nature trail leaflet from Cambient
All year

The digging of clay to maintain river banks has resulted in a series of waters, the Roswell Pits, close to the course of the River Great Ouse. Besides the plants which respond to the varied range of habitat, such as common reed and bulrush, common meadow-rue, purple-loosestrife and bee orchid, a good range of birds is attracted. Breeding species include great crested grebe, shoveler, reed and sedge warbler and typical scrub and woodland birds such as redpoll and blackcap. Wintering wildfowl may include pochard, tufted duck and less common visitors such as goldeneye and Slavonian grebe. Migration times might show greenshank, black-tailed godwit and ruff with, occasionally, black, common and little tern on passage.

Fleam Dyke

TL 548542; 18ha; various owners
Linear earthwork
No access off rights of way
Spring, summer

Rather similar to DEVIL'S DYKE, although perhaps not quite so rich in uncommon plants, Fleam Dyke attracts a good range of birds to its scrub-covered slopes and is notable as the only East Anglian site for juniper.

In spring the Devil's Dyke is bright with pasqueflower.

Fordham Woods

Permit only; 8.9ha; Cambient reserve
Wet woodland
Spring, early summer

The woods form a continuous block, bordered by
a river, and contain tall stands of ash and alder,
with poplar, willow and sycamore, above a dense
damp undergrowth. Bird life is rich and varied and
includes kingfisher and nightingale.

Fowlmere

TL 407462; 26ha; RSPB reserve
Derelict water-cress beds
Spring, summer

Winter is fascinating for the number of birds
which come to shelter in the tall reedbeds and thick
plant cover of the reserve, but the spread of colour
through spring and summer, the profusion of
plants such as water forget-me-not, purple-
loosestrife and great willowherb, offset by the
summer songbirds, blackcap, whitethroat and perhaps nightingale, make this a very special time of
year. In autumn waders such as redshank, green
sandpiper and snipe may be seen with duck such
as mallard and teal. Hen harrier occasionally winter. The principal nesting species is reed warbler,
with up to 100 pairs. Sedge and grasshopper warbler, reed bunting and water rail also occur.

*Reed warbler is a characteristic bird of English
reedmarshes.*

Fulbourn Educational Reserve

Permit only; 26.8ha; Cambient reserve
Woodland and grassland
Spring, summer

Wide diversity in a relatively small area makes
Fulbourn Fen an ideal site for education. Wych elm,
alder, oak and ash, characteristic fenwood trees,
together with a number of introduced species,
stand above woodland plants such as bugle, primrose and sanicle. The grassland varies from damp-
loving plants, purple moor-grass, reed canary-
grass and common meadow-rue, to plants of drier
lime-rich meadows such as cowslip, hairy violet
and quaking-grass. Some 60 bird species have been
recorded, and a network of streams or drainage
dykes adds further variety.

Gamlingay Meadow

Permit only; 1ha; Cambient reserve
Small damp heathland
Spring, early summer

Like CINQUES COMMON, the meadow is a remnant of
an acid heath, unique in Cambridgeshire, and is of
great interest for its acid flora.

Hayley Wood

Permit only; 48.8ha; Cambient reserve
Mixed woodland
Spring, early summer

The woodland is set on chalky boulder clay, a
poor-draining rich clay which here carries the
classic East Anglian pattern of coppiced ash, field
maple and hazel under standards of oak confined
by an ancient earth bank. Other tree species include aspen and spreads of elm while both
hawthorn and Midland hawthorn occur in the
shrub layer which, with the pattern of rides and
clearings together with blocks of recent coppice,
adds much to the variation of the wood. Further
variation is provided by the inclusion of a triangle
of secondary woodland, a recolonised area of ridge-
and-furrow farmland which was cut off from the
neighbouring field when the railway line was laid;
a length of the line itself, now disused, is also incorporated, together with the ancient hedge of Old
Hayley Lane.

This gives a fine spread of habitat which holds
around 280 flowering plants, around 80 mosses and
liverworts and 370 fungi. Apart from the oxlip
population, one of the largest in Britain, Hayley
Wood holds other old-woodland plants such as
dog's mercury, herb-Paris and wood millet, with
plants of ancient wood margins such as saw-wort
and crested cow-wheat.

For liverworts and mosses Hayley Wood rivals
WICKEN FEN and includes not only several species
rare in Cambridgeshire but also *Nowellia curvifolia*,
unknown in much of the south.

The most obvious mammals, at least in terms of
their footprints, are fallow deer, probably derived

from the parkland herd at Waresley. A good range of woodland birds includes both great spotted and lesser spotted woodpecker, treecreeper, long-tailed, marsh and willow tit, linnet, redpoll and several warbler species, with winter visits from species such as redwing and from fieldfare and flocks of tits and finches.

Knapwell Wood

Permit only; 4.4ha; Cambient reserve
Mixed woodland
Spring, early summer

A tiny fragment of ancient woodland, the reserve contains a fine variety of tree species, mainly oak, ash, small-leaved elm and field maple, above an understorey of hazel, blackthorn, dogwood, elder, guelder-rose, hawthorn, Midland hawthorn and spindle. For such a small wood the show of spring flowers is remarkable and includes oxlip, wood anemone, bluebell, early-purple orchid and primrose.

Madingley Brickpits

Permit only; 0.8ha; Cambient reserve
Flooded claypits
Spring, summer

A specialist reserve, the group of pits contains an interesting range of simple waterplants and algae, protozoa and aquatic invertebrates; it is mainly used for educational and research purposes.

Norwood Road

Permit only; 2.6ha; Cambient reserve
Scrub, marsh and pond
Spring, summer

Hawthorn scrub, reedmarsh and a pond make up a small urban reserve which is not only extremely rich in bird life but also contains alder buckthorn, uncommon in the county, and good numbers of adder's-tongue. Wetland birds such as reed and sedge warbler, mallard, coot and moorhen breed, while the dense hawthorns provide ideal nest sites for many woodland species.

Ouse Washes

See map; 2500ha; Cambient–RSPB–WT reserve
Winter-flooded fen meadows
Leaflets from Cambient, RSPB or WT
Winter

The wild and desolate fenlands of East Anglia remained unchanged for many centuries. Attempts to drain them were not successful until the early seventeenth century when a Dutchman, Cornelius Vermuyden, was commissioned by the Earl of Bedford and a group of landowners to turn the wetlands into spreads of farmland. Vermuyden dug first one and then a second parallel cut running from Earith almost to Downham Market, designed to straighten the meanders of the River Great Ouse and take the main flow of winter floodwater so that the meadows in between, and not the surrounding rich fen soils, were flooded.

Wood anemones, with occasional oxlips, spread across the floor of Hayley Wood.

The embanked Old and New Bedford Rivers, which form the bounds of the washes, run roughly parallel for about 22km, separated by fen meadows up to 1km wide. The meadows slope slightly upwards from river to river, so that when the washes are flooded the water varies in depth across the meadows. This variation contributes much to the value of the washes, since anything less than bank-to-bank flooding provides a range from wet meadow grassland through shallows to waters around 1m deeper, an ideal situation for dabbling duck and waders.

The meadows themselves are rich in plants, wide spreads of rushes and sedges, reed canary-grass and reed sweet-grass, thistles and docks, and plants such as common meadow-rue and creeping-Jenny. Water-dropwort species are plentiful, with the uncommon small and tasteless water-pepper, the rare mousetail and, over 30km from the coast, plants such as sea aster, sea club-rush and wild celery, evidence of early flooding from the sea. The ditches and river banks are colourful with comfrey, nodding bur-marigold, meadowsweet and purple-loosestrife, and fringed with flowering-rush. Small copper and common blue are among the meadow-land butterflies while the rare large tortoiseshell may be seen where osier beds grow by the rivers. Moths include large numbers of cinnabar, feeding on the plants of marsh ragwort, with wetland species such as fen and obscure wainscot and cream-bordered green pea while, above the rivers, dragonflies hawk in the sun.

With the flowering-rush are many other attractive water plants such as fringed and yellow water-lily, frogbit and sweet-flag, while 16 species and hybrids of pondweed and all four native duckweed species have been recognised. The ditches are rich in animal life and hold particularly good numbers of water snails together with beetles, mayfly larvae and ten-spined stickleback. The rivers are famous for their fish, for near-record rudd and large pike, for bream, perch, roach, tench, eel and zander, the last an introduction from Eastern Europe which feeds on smaller fish. Mammals of the rivers and dykes include water vole and mink with occasional coypu, while the meadows provide a habitat for the prey species – bank and short-tailed vole, common and pigmy shrew and both harvest mouse and wood mouse – hunted by stoat, weasel and fox.

The birds are what most people come to the washes to see and the managing bodies have provided excellent hides. The Wildfowl Trust reserve at WELNEY (Norfolk) is reached from the east of the washes, with the car park and visitor centre at TL 539933, so that the light is best for viewing in the mornings; conversely the RSPB–Cambient holdings are reached from the west, with the car park and visitor centre at TL 478871, south of Manea, where viewing is best in the afternoon.

Although the vast numbers of birds present in winter flood times make this the most popular time to visit, the washes hold important breeding colonies and are fascinating at any time. Among the most notable breeding birds are black-tailed godwit and ruff, both rare breeders outside this small area. Other breeding birds include mallard, shoveler, gadwall, pochard, shelduck, teal, tufted duck, and occasionally a few pairs of garganey and pintail, smaller birds such as reed and sedge warb-ler, reed bunting and yellow wagtail, meadow pipit and skylark, a pair or two of short-eared owls to harass the meadows' small mammals, and lapwing and redshank with large numbers of snipe. Some 60 species have been recorded as breeding here and, with the success of the ruff and black-tailed godwit, an exciting occurrence in recent years has been the several attempts by black tern to recolonise the site.

The sheer numbers of winter wildfowl are amazing. Up to 40,000 wigeon have been recorded, with several thousand mallard, pintail, pochard and teal, and lesser numbers of gadwall, shoveler, shelduck and tufted duck. Over 3000 Bewick's swan have been counted, with gatherings of mute and whooper swan, while small numbers of smew and goldeneye might be seen with the diving duck, and birds such as lapwing, golden plover, redshank, ruff and snipe join the wigeon on the water's edge and the grassland. Above the water line short-eared owl and kestrel take the small mammals which move to the banks to escape from the rising flood: the narrowness of the long flooded washes means that birds are easily seen.

The washes demand conservation for so many reasons. For their historical interest alone they merit it; for their plants they are nationally important; for their breeding birds they are equally irreplaceable. As an inland winter wildfowl site, the washes are quite without peer, with a seventh of the British population of wigeon and a fifth of the north west European population of Bewick's swan.

The Ouse Washes in summer: grazing marshes where black-tailed godwit and ruff may breed.

Overhall Grove

Permit only; 17ha; Cambient reserve
Mixed woodland
Can be overlooked from public footpath at
TL 337633
Spring

In summer the woodland floor is deep in coarse herbs and rough meadow-grass but the wood is famous for its spring displays of oxlip and bluebell, splendid beneath the budding spread of small-leaved elm, ash, elder, hawthorn, field maple and oak. A typical range of woodland birds adds to the interest. The reserve also contains an outstanding variety of historic earthworks.

Papworth Wood

Permit only; 7.2ha; Cambient reserve
Mixed woodland
Spring

Similar to OVERHALL GROVE for its relatively recent invasion by small-leaved elm and dense ground cover of summer plants, Papworth Wood has a long recorded history but does not contain ancient woodland species such as oxlip and dog's mercury and seems, therefore, to have been wholly cleared and then recolonised. In spring, however, the wood shows a splendid array of wood anemone, bluebell and primrose.

Adder's-tongue, a small, unusual grassland fern.

Roman Road

TL 494547–560498; 8km; CCC
Ancient trackway
Spring, summer

The road was already old when some sections were improved in Roman times and, as with the DEVIL'S DYKE, its verges have become a refuge for many important species which have been ploughed out of existence in the adjoining, once rich, fields; among the uncommon plants here are purple milk-vetch and perennial flax.

Shepreth L-Moor

TL 386476; 7.2ha; Cambient reserve
Rough-grazed marshy pasture
Permit only off rights of way
Spring, summer

Grading from rough grassland to reedmarsh, the reserve holds the increasingly uncommon parsley water-dropwort and a range of wetland sedges. The bird life contrasts with that of the fields around and includes species such as grasshopper warbler and kingfisher.

Soham Meadows

Permit only; 32ha; Cambient reserve
Damp and wet meadows
Spring, early summer

One of the most important areas of grazing meadows in the county, the pastures contain old-meadow species such as pepper saxifrage and adder's-tongue, evidence of ridge-and-furrow ploughing, and a splendid range of plants which include autumn gentian, bee orchid and meadow saxifrage. Small ponds, hedges and areas of scrub add to the variation of the meadows and attract small birds to a site already well populated with species such as redshank and snipe.

Sutton Wash

Permit only; 3.5ha; Beds and Hunts NT reserve
Old fen flood meadow
Spring, summer

Part of the OUSE WASHES, the reserve lies at the drier end of the meadowland and, although invaded by common nettle and tufted hair-grass, contains characteristic plants such as reed canary-grass, reed sweet-grass and meadowsweet, and provides a nesting site for lapwing and yellow wagtail.

Thriplow Meadows

Permit only; 4.4ha; Cambient reserve
Damp meadows
Spring, early summer

Outstanding for their colonies of marsh-orchids, the meadows also contain drier areas of chalkland turf which fall, increasing in wetness, to the margin of a small stream. Mallard may be seen, with nesting lapwing, redshank and snipe.

Wandlebury

TL 493533; 44ha; Cambridge Preservation Soc.
Country park with Iron Age fort
Booklet from site
Spring, early summer

Built on the chalk of the Gog Magog Hills, the ancient fort and its surrounds have been planted with a wide variety of tree and shrub species, though small areas of chalk turf still survive. The variation of the site encourages a good range of breeding birds and in winter Wandlebury shelters and feeds a further variety of species.

Wicken Fen

TL 563705; 272ha; NT reserve
Relict fenland
Booklet from site or NT
Spring, summer

The general impression at Wicken is of a huge spread of wet, rich scrub divided by damp mown trackways and deep stands of tall herbs, pooled here and there and cut by waterways, but, viewed at close range the plant life reveals its variety and thus its earlier history. The scrub, a rich habitat for warblers and other small birds, is a stage in the natural change to woodland and its presence is due to the fact that mowing of the reeds and sedges had died out by the end of the nineteenth century. In these rich wetlands open water tends to give way to reedbed, reedbed to sedgebed, sedgebed to spreads of alder buckthorn and then to a mixed scrub, as now, of buckthorn, alder buckthorn and guelder-rose which would probably end as oak—ash woodland.

To maintain the widest range of variation of fenland types, the progression is stopped at different stages by controlling scrub and by varying mowing regimes. A windmill, once used to drain the farmlands, is now employed to pump water into the fen and much time and effort are spent in maintaining the water levels to protect the fenland species.

The value of this work is obvious. The droves, beautiful with southern marsh-orchid, yellow rattle and meadow thistle, the stands of mixed fen showing meadowsweet, common meadow-rue, yellow loosestrife, hemp-agrimony, wild angelica, milk-parsley, common reed and great fen-sedge, the spreads of scrub which shelter marsh fern, the whole rich spectrum of fenland plants is a natural wilderness, a reservoir of wildlife in the level farmland landscape.

Open waters, the lodes, ditches and pools support bulrush and lesser bulrush, greater bladderwort, fine-leaved water-dropwort, greater spearwort and lesser water-plantain. The reserve attracts a variety of birds from songbirds to snipe and shoveler, from wigeon to woodcock, from roosts of starling to long-eared owl, hen harrier and great grey shrike. Most of the reserve may be overlooked from the Tower Hide which gives views across both the Sedge Fen and the mere in Adventurer's Fen.

This, one of the oldest and the most famous reserves in Britain, is a site for much scientific research into the ecology of fenland. It protects a wealth of semi-natural habitat which was once a widespread facet of the fens of eastern Britain.

Wicken Fen: common reed and willow scrub fringe a pool starred with white water-lily.

Cheshire

The Dee, that ancient natural barrier between Wales and England, still forms the Cheshire boundary and the traveller who crosses the bridge between the villages of Holt and Farndon can view a microcosm of the county, with the small red sandstone cliff, the black and white half-timbered houses echoed by the black and white Friesian cattle grazing on the lush green pasture, and, especially, the river itself. The picture is, of course, one of modern Cheshire modified by man and agriculture; but the scene is the key to the origins of the environment and to the original habitats which survive amid intensive dairy farming.

Two thousand years ago Cheshire consisted of woodlands, wetlands and water. For centuries little changed, until the industrial revolution gained momentum and south Lancashire began to make urban demands on the countryside. The woodlands provided materials for houses and boat building, and the wood was also used for charcoal burning and in tanning. After the clearance of the forest and draining, the wetlands provided excellent pasture for dairy cattle. The meres and mosses, too difficult to drain, remained essentially unaltered, as did much of the Dee Estuary.

Although the true Cheshire coastline is short, the large inlets of the Dee and Mersey Estuaries are tidal far inland, helping to create a mild climate. Cheshire is protected by the Pennines to the east and also by the Welsh Mountains. Rainfall is moderate. The land undulates gently and the water drains only slowly into the major rivers – the Dee, Gowy and Weaver.

Geologically, the county is composed of three main types of rock. In west Cheshire are the triassic red sandstones which outcrop on the Wirral peninsula but principally form the mid-Cheshire ridge, where they are often displayed in colourful road and railway cuttings. The ridge rises to over 220m as it runs north–south from Frodsham to Duckington. Along the top is the Sandstone Trail. In the east of the county, towards the Peak, are the gritstones of the Pennines, rising to nearly 600m. Between the two, on the salt-bearing marls, are the meres and wetlands.

All the lowland areas are covered by layers of sand, silt and boulder clay, and over the last 12,000 years a series of lakes has developed. Low-lying hollows filled with water and gave rise to that well-known local feature, the mere. Meres were also formed by natural subsidence when the ground water partly dissolved the underlying marls. The solution formed from chemicals in clay and marls is alkaline and rich in nutrients. Eighteenth- and nineteenth-century farmers used this fact to advantage and dug marlpits. The marl was used for marl spreading, an early form of 'liming', and the water-filled pits which resulted are still used as ponds from which cattle drink. Today many of these ponds, like the meres, support a rich flora.

In the Weaver Valley particularly there are brine springs and, although industrial extraction over the years has lowered the 'salt table', in some places a saltmarsh flora can still be found many kilometres from the sea. The uncontrolled extraction of brine by previous generations has resulted in the formation around Northwich, Middlewich and Sandbach of water-filled hollows known as flashes, some of which contain salt water, too. Modern salt extraction leaves no lasting mark on the surface.

The fate of a mere is to disappear. A rich vegetation develops around the edges and slowly extends to the centre. Ultimately a moss is formed and eventually even woodland may develop where there was once open water. Mosses can be eerie and dangerous

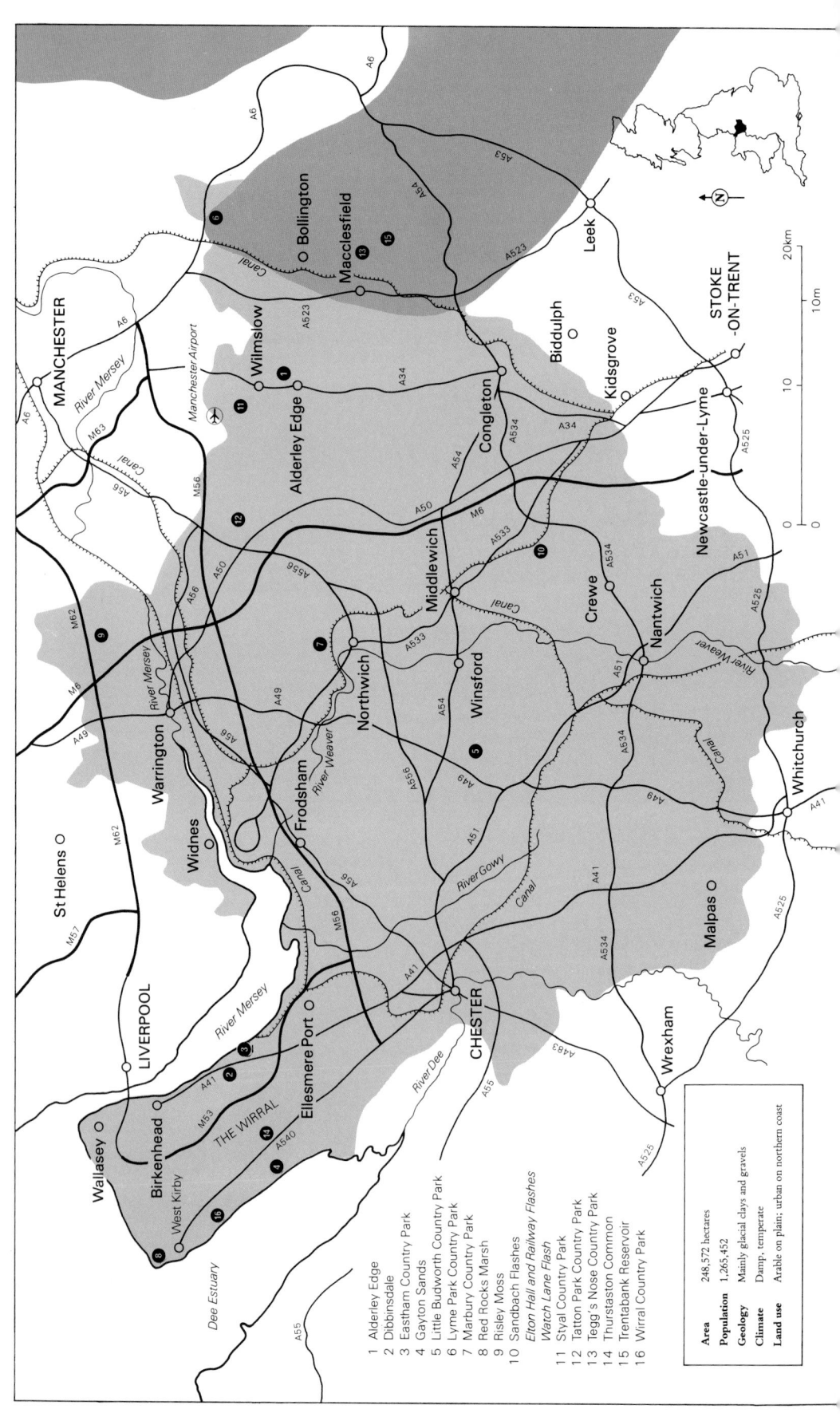

1 Alderley Edge
2 Dibbinsdale
3 Eastham Country Park
4 Gayton Sands
5 Little Budworth Country Park
6 Lyme Park Country Park
7 Marbury Country Park
8 Red Rocks Marsh
9 Risley Moss
10 Sandbach Flashes
    Elton Hall and Railway Flashes
    Watch Lane Flash
11 Styal Country Park
12 Tatton Park Country Park
13 Tegg's Nose Country Park
14 Thurstaston Common
15 Trentabank Reservoir
16 Wirral Country Park

Area	248,572 hectares
Population	1,265,452
Geology	Mainly glacial clays and gravels
Climate	Damp, temperate
Land use	Arable on plain; urban on northern coast

places. Often the skeletons of trees can be seen, which have grown on a floating blanket and eventually sunk under their own weight and drowned. The rate of transition from mere to moss varies from place to place and results in an interesting range of plant and animal life. In the meres there are water-lilies and reedbeds; on the mosses bog-rosemary and the insect-eating sundew. Great crested grebe and duck decorate the open water, while reed and sedge warbler hide in the reedbeds. The shallow inland flashes support large numbers of waders. Many of these sites are close to roads and public footpaths, for instance BLACK LAKE in Delamere Forest, and the SANDBACH FLASHES.

Woodland once covered the remainder of the county. Pedunculate oak grew on the heavier clay soils, with sessile oak on the sand and gritstones. Intermediate forms are now frequent. These woodlands remain only on slopes which are too steep for agriculture along the Pennine margin, where the best sessile oaks remain, and along the incised river valleys. These so-called clough woods have a particularly rich plant life. They are often inaccessible and several have been acquired as nature reserves.

The higher parts of the mid-Cheshire ridge supported heathland or a lighter oak–birch woodland, some of which remains relatively untouched. The Sandstone Trail follows the ridge and some fine old woodland, also with sessile oak, can be found here.

Another legacy of the early development of the chemical industry is some exciting artificial habitats. Limestone in Cheshire has long since been quarried away, but the lime beds formed from the dumping of industrial lime waste, similar in part to dune slack and in part to waste ground, support a range of lime-loving plants which would not otherwise be found here. The orchids are a particular delight: in some places acres of fragrant orchids grow like bluebells, complete with the occasional white form. On other lime beds hybrid orchids can be found, of which the parents can only be guessed.

No portrait of Cheshire is complete without a mention of the Dee and Mersey Estuaries. These shallow tidal flats are of international importance as breeding grounds for numerous bird species and as the feeding ground of migrants. Ducks and waders, geese and, at low tide, smaller birds can be seen in abundance, and in spring and autumn a lucky ornithologist may spot some rare foreign bird which has followed the wrong migration route.

Here in north Cheshire industry is never far away, but throughout the rest of the county the majority of the land is used for agriculture. This rural industry has left many of the meres and wetlands relatively unscathed. These habitats, together with the lime beds and the estuaries, make Cheshire internationally important for naturalists and a most valuable natural amenity for everyone.

R.D. BOWDEN
A.A. SAVAGE

Alderley Edge

SJ 860776; 88.4ha; NT
Sandstone escarpment
Spring, early summer

The well-wooded sandstone heights tower some 100m above the surrounding countryside and provide an outlook across the Cheshire plain to the Pennines beyond.

Black Lake

Permit only; 0.4ha; CCT reserve
Floating bog
Spring, summer

An area of open water supports a *Sphagnum* raft which shows an attractive variety of bog plants, such as common cottongrass, cranberry and cross-leaved heath.

Danes Moss

Permit only; 13.4ha; CCT reserve
Woodland and wetland
Spring, summer

The woodland, of Corsican pine fringed by purple moor-grass with areas of oak and bracken, stands on a raised bog modified by drainage and peat-cutting. About a third of the reserve, lower and now flooded, is being recolonised by *Sphagnum* and, on its borders, by other typical bog plants, including bilberry, common and hare's-tail cottongrass, cross-leaved heath and heather. This attracts winter wildfowl, and breeding birds which include unusually large numbers of willow warbler. Much of the reserve can be seen from the footpath on the northern edge.

Typical of Cheshire's damp lime wastes are marsh orchids.

Dibbinsdale

SJ 345827; 47ha; Wirral BC reserve
Mixed deciduous woodland
Leaflet from WBC Dept of Leisure Services or site
Spring, summer

A range of habitats includes meadows, reedbeds, parkland and grassland, while the woods lining the valley sides, predominantly ash and wych elm, may be a relict of ancient woodland dating back to the last ice age. Breeding birds include tawny owl, kingfisher, great spotted woodpecker, nuthatch, treecreeper, willow tit and grasshopper warbler, and the reserve is very rich in invertebrates.

Eastham Country Park

SJ 364818; 30.4ha; Wirral BC
Mixed woodland and foreshore
Nature trail leaflet from site or WBC Dept of Leisure Services
Spring, early summer

The woodland stands over a rich ground cover which includes a fine show of bluebell and Solomon's-seal. Typical birds may be seen in the park while seabirds abound on the estuary that runs beside it.

Elton Hall and Railway Flashes

No access; 30ha; CCT reserve
Subsidence ponds
Elton Hall Flashes may be overlooked from the minor road at SJ 725595
All year

Part of the SANDBACH FLASHES reserves.

Oystercatchers fly in to join the ranks of waders on Little Eye.

Gayton Sands

SJ 273790; 2000ha; RSPB reserve
Saltmarsh and mudflats
Autumn, winter

High tides force thousands of waders off the wide mudflats to roost on the saltmarsh, and in winter they are complemented by an important concentration of water rail. In addition wildfowl, particularly pintail and shelduck, and smaller birds such as finches, brambling, water pipit and their predators, hen harrier, merlin, short-eared owl and peregrine may be seen.

Hilbre Island

Permit only; 6ha; Wirral BC reserve
Small estuary islands
Permit and leaflet from WBC Dept of Leisure Services
Autumn, winter

In summer the three islands, Little Eye, Little Hilbre and Hilbre itself, low, flat platforms set in the estuary of the River Dee, are filled with the colour of plants such as thrift and common bird's-foot-trefoil. Stunted clumps of heather and bell heather, dwarf stands of bracken sheltering bluebells, coastal plants such as Danish scurvygrass, buck's-horn plantain and sea sandwort make a bright display with lady's bedstraw, harebell and clear yellow hawkweeds. Gulls and terns fly above the estuary, while oystercatcher hunt round the rocky platforms, and smaller birds may occur: wheatear on the islands, perhaps, dunlin or turnstone on the shoreline, and redshank probing the muds. On a low-tide summer day the sands are busier with walkers than with birds, but in autumn the birds begin to gather and the sky can be literally darkened by vast flocks of knot and

dunlin which whirl like smoke above the water to roost on the tiny islands. Purple sandpiper regularly gather with bar-tailed and black-tailed godwit, sanderling, greenshank, spotted redshank and curlew sandpiper, little stint and whimbrel. Arctic, common, little and Sandwich tern gather in the estuary before emigrating; gull records include glaucous, Iceland, little, Mediterranean and Sabine's gull, and other seabirds include the pirates: arctic, great, pomarine and long-tailed skua. On the deeper waters beyond the rocks red-throated and great northern diver, eider, scaup and long-tailed duck may be seen.

The bird observatory on Hilbre contributes important information on longevity and movements. For example, the first purple sandpiper ringed here was reported five years later shot in Greenland.

Little Budworth Country Park

SJ 590655; 33ha; CCC
Sandy heathland
Leaflet from CCC or site
Spring, early summer

Little Budworth Common lies on a spread of glacial sands where heather, gorse and bracken heath alternate with invading birch woodland and are varied by bogs where cranberry and common cottongrass grow on the *Sphagnum* mosses. The park is noted for its range of insect and fungus species, and typical birds include tree pipit and redpoll.

Lyme Park Country Park

SJ 966842; 528ha; NT–Stockport MBC
Old parkland
Spring, early summer

The great spread of parkland with its splendid trees is also famous for its red deer.

Marbury Country Park

SJ 651763; 76ha; CCC
Woodland and grassland
Leaflet from information centre
Spring, early summer

The country park, run by Cheshire County Council and housing the headquarters of the Cheshire Conservation Trust, offers attractive woodland walks. Of special interest is the hide overlooking Budworth Mere and MARBURY REED BED.

Marbury Reed Bed

Permit only; 6ha; CCT reserve
Reedbed and woodland
Spring, summer

The bird hide in MARBURY COUNTRY PARK conveniently overlooks the reserve, which shows a progression from open water through reedbed to wet and dry woodland. Plants include flowering-rush and marsh cinquefoil while great crested and little grebe, coot and moorhen nest.

Mount Farm Ponds

Permit only; 0.2ha; CCT reserve
Series of small ponds
Spring, early summer

With one exception the five ponds are interconnected but each differs in some way from the other four. Plant life includes marsh cinquefoil, greater pond-sedge and ragged-Robin, with devil's-bit scabious in the surrounding grassland.

Plumley Lime Bed

Permit only; 23ha; CCT reserve
Herb-rich grassland, scrub and lagoon
Spring, summer

Plants on the lime bed include common centaury, yellow-wort, fragrant orchid, common spotted-orchid, northern, southern and several hybrid marsh-orchids, while the lagoon, fringed with reed-bed, woodland and scrub, attracts waders, waterfowl and many species of warblers.

Red Rocks Marsh

SJ 204884; 4ha; CCT reserve
Reedmarsh, grassland and dunes
Permit only off pathways
Spring, early summer

At the north west corner of the Wirral peninsula, sand from the mouth of the River Dee has been heaped up into two low dune ridges which hold a fresh-to-brackish marshland. The slack, or dip, between the ridges is mainly filled with reedmarsh fringed with damp, lime-rich grassland. The comparatively small area shows an excellent variation of species and forms a long, narrow ribbon beside the estuary. Whereas in larger reserves one might have to walk for considerable distances to appreciate the complete range, here a few paces can span each habitat.

The fore dune, facing across to the Welsh coast, is stabilised by lyme-grass and marram and carries a characteristic range of open-sand plants such as sand sedge and sea sandwort, sea-milkwort, sea rocket and the prickly but beautiful sea-holly. Behind these, they become less specialised, merging into a rich, damp grassland.

This grassland separates the ridge from the reed-marsh and is continued around the northern rim of the long, damp slack where common spotted-orchid and marsh-orchid species hybridise to give a wonderful variation of colour. Common bird's-foot-trefoil, quaking-grass and spreads of kidney vetch show in the drier grassland with wild asparagus and parsley-piert on open areas, soft pink restharrow and white-flowered Danish scurvygrass in the damper places, and meadow crane's-bill above the taller grasses. The wet marsh is filled with common reed, fringed by club-rush, with gipsywort, yellow iris, water mint, meadow-sweet and sedges, and varied by clumps of alder and grey willow in which passage migrants shelter.

Natterjack toad, now rare, is easily distinguished by its yellow dorsal stripe.

The DEE ESTUARY, described under Clwyd, is noted for its bird life, with nearby HILBRE ISLAND a most important high-tide roost. Dunlin and knot are a typical winter feature here, together with wildfowl such as shelduck and pintail. Other animals include common toad and frog, but pride of place among the amphibians of the reserve must go to the natterjack toad, in its only breeding colony on the peninsula.

Risley Moss

SJ 663921; 81ha; Warrington New Town Dev. Corpn reserve
Woodland and remnant raised peat bog
Permit required from head ranger to visit peat bog area
Leaflets and nature trail guide from interpretative centre
Spring, early summer

Excellent interpretative displays and leaflets explain the origins and history of Risley Moss, which developed in a hollow of the glacial clays of the Mersey Valley. The driest part of the moss contains a waymarked nature trail which winds past pools, through clearings and dense birch woodland. It starts and finishes at the interpretative centre which stands on a wooded mound of clay, much richer in woodland plants and animals than the surrounding peat. Both areas are havens for wildlife and provide nesting sites for some 34 species of birds, including six species of warbler, spotted flycatcher, and tawny owl. Fox, stoat and weasel are frequently seen and kestrel, sparrowhawk, little owl and barn owl regularly visit. Buzzard, hen harrier, merlin and short-eared owl have been recorded in autumn and winter. Dragonflies have increased considerably and 11 species have been recorded to date.

A raised water-table controlled by sluices is encouraging a return to mossland conditions in the open peatlands. Bracken and birch are being removed, and the purple moor-grass is gradually withdrawing as the peat becomes waterlogged, while *Sphagnum* mosses and cottongrass species are beginning to spread. Open pools have been excavated to improve conditions for wildfowl and waders, and a further 14 bird species breed on the peatland. Teal, mallard and waders such as snipe, curlew and woodcock breed here; migration times bring whimbrel, redshank, golden plover and green sandpiper. Many other visiting birds may be seen at different times of the year and, although the mossland may be entered only by permit holders, a tall observation tower overlooks the wetland area and provides a vantage point for birdwatchers.

Rostherne Mere

Permit only; 150ha; NCC reserve
Large lowland lake
No access is allowed but permit holders may use the observatory
Leaflet from NCC; permit from Manchester Ornithological Soc.
Late summer, autumn, winter

The A.W. Boyd Observatory overlooks the mere and provides an excellent vantage point. It may also be observed from Rostherne churchyard and from several different places along the surrounding lanes.

The lake, the largest and deepest of the Cheshire meres, was probably formed by a combination of kettle-hole development (see SHEMMY AND SOUTH MOSSES) and of subsidence due to the washing out of buried salt-beds, as in the case of the SANDBACH FLASHES. It lies in a great bowl of farmland and woodland, much of it fringed with common reed and lesser bulrush. The lake itself, some 48.7ha in size, is unusually deep, reaching in places 30m. It is generally unsuitable as a feeding site for dabbling ducks and waders but, as a result of the increase in disturbance to most of the other Cheshire meres, it has become spectacularly successful as a daytime roost.

The numbers of duck build up in late summer and autumn to reach a winter peak which may total upwards of 5000 birds. At night they fly out to feed in the surrounding areas, and then their place on the roosts is taken by incoming swarms of gulls. This winter night-time gull roost may total up to 20,000 birds which, with the day population of duck, exerts a real pressure on the balance of the lake; the lower levels are reported to have become virtually sterile as a result of the input of guano.

Mallard and teal make up the greatest numbers of duck, with smaller groups of pintail, pochard, shoveler, tufted duck and wigeon, and species such as goldeneye, ruddy duck and goosander. Other wetland birds such as water rail and several species of wader may winter here or visit at migration times. The surrounding area of woodland and farmland provides nest sites for other birds and feeding sites for migrants. Over 180 species have been identified on the reserve and there is no time of year when Rostherne mere is totally without interest.

Sandbach Flashes

SJ 725595 and 727607; 51ha; CCT reserves
Subsidence ponds and wetlands
All year

The Sandbach Flashes comprise ELTON HALL AND
RAILWAY FLASHES and WATCH LANE FLASH, a chain
of ponds and wetlands caused by subsidence. Some
200 million years ago a change to desert conditions
dried up great salty lakes which stood across the
Cheshire–Shropshire area and left a thick deposit
of salt-rich sediment. Brine, formed where the salt
beds met the lower limit of ground water, has long
been used as a source of commercial salt; the flashes
were formed by subsidence as the land above
collapsed after the salt had been removed.

None of the reserves is open to visitors but all
may be overlooked from rights of way. The range
of habitat is wide: from open water, through lime
beds and mud to sedge- and reedbeds, woodlands
and wet meadows; from drowned dead trees to
reedswamps and spreads of alder and wet willow
carr. The high salinity of these pools encourages
unusual plants such as sea aster and lesser sea-
spurrey.

The breeding birds include mute swan, little
grebe, mallard, tufted duck, lapwing, redshank
and reed bunting, with little ringed plover, common sandpiper, and grasshopper, reed and sedge
warbler. In winter wildfowl such as pochard,
shoveler and pintail fly in while spring and
autumn passages bring waders such as ruff and
green sandpiper. Occasionally less common species
appear and there are records of avocet, spoonbill
and semi-palmated sandpiper.

Delamere Forest, an FC area of hardwoods.

Shemmy and South Mosses

Permit only; 6ha; CCT reserve
Two connected basin mires
Spring, summer, autumn

The dark lines of the conifer plantations which
hide and shelter the reserve fall away to reveal first
a shoulder of heather and bell heather and then a
birch and bracken slope which falls to the rich
russet, green and soft purple of the moss. This
change from an invariant, often gloomy, area into
one of subtle colours is one of the chief pleasures
of a basin mire or valley bog, since they so often
form small pockets of richness in wide areas of acid
monotony.

Basin mires are a feature of the great plain of
Cheshire and Staffordshire, formed over holes in
the sands and clays washed down by glacial action.
Some of the holes are thought to have been formed
when the sands or clays settled around a huge mass
of ice which later melted to form a 'kettle hole'.
Vegetation eventually grows clear across the
water's surface forming a layer of peat which carries a distinctive range of plants.

These mires may be dangerous. Perhaps as little
as one metre of floating peat may lie above many
metres' depth of water; the surface of the moss will
flex and dip with a person's weight. Not only are
they dangerous but the peat itself is highly vulnerable to trampling, and the beauties of the moss are
easily destroyed.

The chief impression given by Shemmy and
South Mosses is of a level or gently hummocked
Sphagnum lawn. Areas of open peat are often
densely covered with round-leaved sundew, while
the *Sphagnum* hummocks may support cross-
leaved heath, heather, bog rosemary, cranberry

and crowberry. The site attracts birds, with a good range of insects in the damp mire and adjacent dry heathland, including almost 150 species of spider.

Styal Country Park

SJ 835830; 25.5ha; NT
Wooded valley
Leaflet from CCC
Spring, early summer

The park, set in the Bollin Valley, is rich in both river and woodland wildlife.

Tatton Park Country Park

SJ 745816; 400ha; NT–CCC
Parkland and meres
Leaflets from CCC or information centre at site
Spring, summer

Melchett Mere attracts a good variety of wetland birds and the walk which encircles it provides an opportunity for studying them closely. The parkland surrounds provide a habitat for scrub and woodland species and a variety of trees may be seen by following the Foresters' Walk.

Tegg's Nose Country Park

SJ 950733; 54ha; CCC
Pennine outlier
Spring, early summer

A shoulder of Pennine gritstone with truly panoramic views gives a spread of bracken, gorse and bilberry which attracts typical moorland birds.

Thornton Wood

Permit only; 6.2ha; CCT reserve
Mixed valley woodland
Spring, early summer

A good range of trees including alder, hazel, holly and grey willow varies the mixed oak woodland. Water-plantain and reed canary-grass grow in the valley with bramble, bracken, foxglove and bluebell on the drier, more acid slopes. Dingy shell and small yellow wave moths occur.

Thurstaston Common

SJ 244853; 75.2ha; NT
Acid heathland
Late summer

Good exposures of the upper mottled sandstone may be seen and the site contains heather, bracken and scrub.

Trentabank Reservoir

SJ 964712; 20ha; CCT–NWWA reserve
Wooded reservoir
No access to reservoir
Spring, summer

A number of waterfowl may be observed in winter but the main importance lies in the heronry which may be seen from the road.

Warburton's Wood: ramsons and bluebells cover the floor in spring.

Warburton's Wood

Permit only; 3ha; CCT reserve
Valley woodland and grassland
Spring, early summer

The clough is cut through glacial sands and keuper marl to the hard sandstone below, giving both acid and lime-rich soil conditions with a particularly good range of plants.

The lower, river, end of the valley is lined with ash, small-leaved lime and oak over an understorey of wild cherry, elder, hawthorn, hazel and holly. The steep slopes to the stream are thick with hart's-tongue and other ferns and with ramsons, ground-ivy and enchanter's-nightshade, while the shallower upper slopes have a great variety of woodland species. In spring the wood shows a wonderful display of bluebell, wood anemone and wood-sorrel, red campion, primrose, early and common dog-violet, early-purple orchid and yellow archangel.

More acid areas of oak above hazel, hawthorn and rowan stand over bramble and bluebell, and richer flushes contain woodruff and opposite-leaved golden-saxifrage. Honeysuckle and wild rose, greater bellflower and guelder-rose occur, and the presence of wild service-tree together with small-leaved lime suggests that the woodland is ancient.

The banks around the wood are either damp, jungled with great horsetail, hogweeds, buttercups, vetches and banks of bramble, or dry, full of butterflies and the flowers of lime-rich grassland: betony and common bird's-foot-trefoil, common milkwort and quaking-grass, cowslip and its hybrid with the woodland primrose. More uncommon species such as dyer's greenweed and lady's-mantle may be found, and the reserve also contains smooth sedge and pale sedge.

Wirral Country Park looks over the sands of the Dee Estuary to Wales.

Watch Lane Flash

No access; 14.5ha; CCT reserve
Subsidence pond
The reserve may be overlooked from the car park at
SJ 727607 and from the lanes around
All year

One of the SANDBACH FLASHES reserves.

Wirral Country Park

SJ 237834; 43ha; Wirral BC
Disused railway line and surrounds
Leaflets from site or WBC
All year

Embanked above or cut through the varied rocks
of the Wirral, the country park gives superb opportunities to observe the wildlife of the area.

Wybunbury Moss

Permit only; 12ha; NCC reserve
Floating bog
Spring, early summer

The reserve demonstrates a range from mixed
woodland, through marsh and reedswamp, to
hummocked floating bog. The reedswamp, where
richer waters occur, contains bulrush, common
reed, great fen-sedge and occasional marsh fern
while damp fields are rich in species such as
ragged-Robin and devil's-bit scabious. The pine–
birch woodland grades into mixed deciduous
woods, adding to the wide diversity of habitats
which attracts a good range of birds and an
interesting variety of insects.

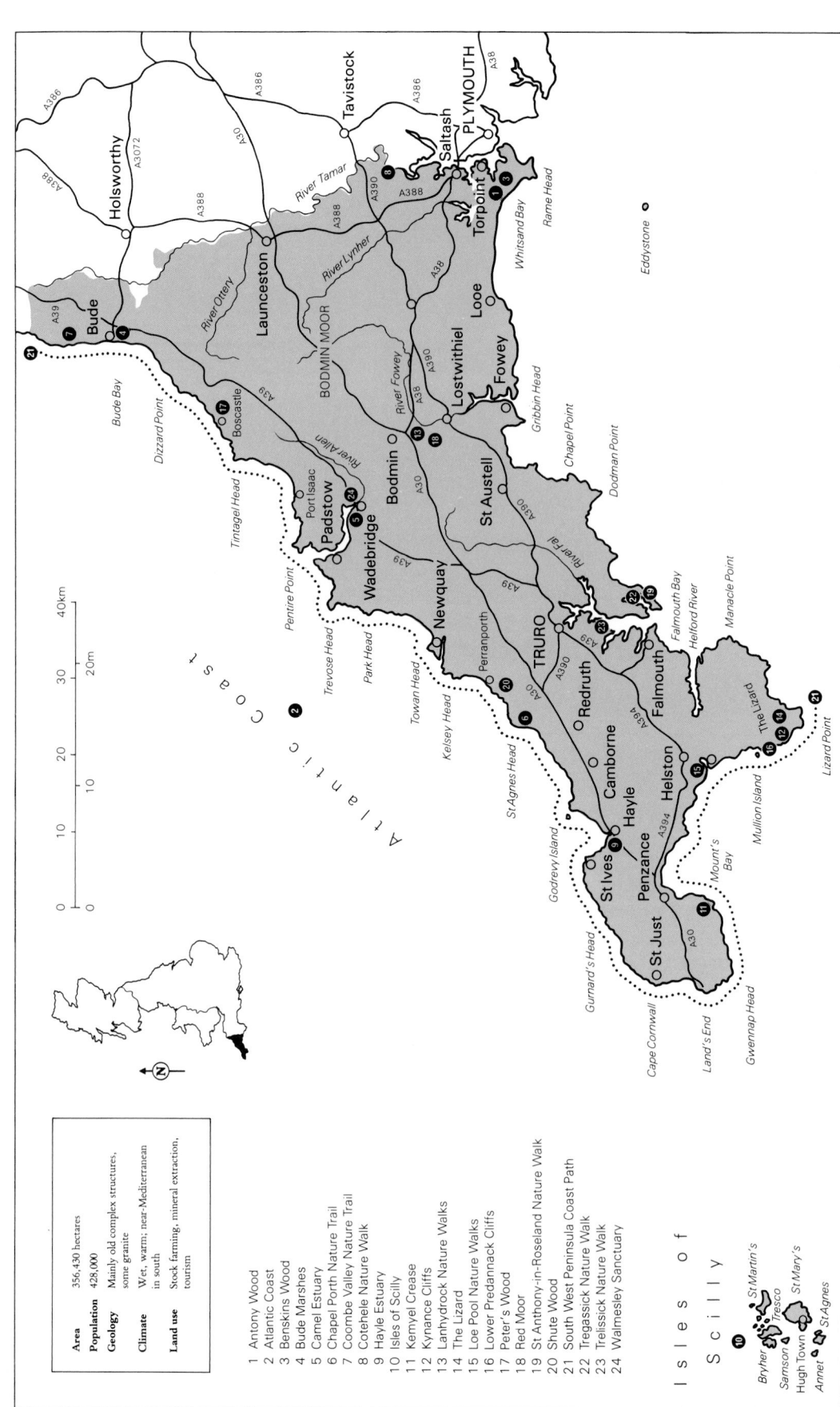

Area	356,430 hectares
Population	428,000
Geology	Mainly old complex structures, some granite
Climate	Wet, warm; near-Mediterranean in south
Land use	Stock farming, mineral extraction, tourism

1 Antony Wood
2 Atlantic Coast
3 Benskins Wood
4 Bude Marshes
5 Camel Estuary
6 Chapel Porth Nature Trail
7 Coombe Valley Nature Trail
8 Cotehele Nature Walk
9 Hayle Estuary
10 Isles of Scilly
11 Kemyel Crease
12 Kynance Cliffs
13 Lanhydrock Nature Walks
14 The Lizard
15 Loe Pool Nature Walks
16 Lower Predannack Cliffs
17 Peter's Wood
18 Red Moor
19 St Anthony-in-Roseland Nature Walk
20 Shute Wood
21 South West Peninsula Coast Path
22 Tregassick Nature Walk
23 Trelissick Nature Walk
24 Walmesley Sanctuary

Cornwall
and the Isles of Scilly

Cornwall is the most southerly county in Britain and the most westerly in England. Almost an island, cut off from the rest of the country by the River Tamar, it is over 120km long with no part of it more than 24km from the sea. This shape and situation mean that Cornwall has a relatively warm and wet climate, with tearing salt-laden winds constantly sweeping across a landscape full of strong contrasts: bare cliff faces scorched by the wind, then followed suddenly by great swathes of brightly coloured flowers; stark, desolate moors with pockets of wetland alive with their own glorious plant life; ancient oakwoods in the valleys; deep-cut lanes; and the ever-changing shoreline.

The soils themselves are mostly derived from Devonian and carboniferous sedimentary rocks known as the Cornish killas, and from the granite spine which runs through the length of Cornwall, though exposed only on the higher moors: Bodmin Moor, Hensbarrow, Carnmenellis and West Penwith, where the granite actually meets the sea. China clay and the lodes of tin and copper are derivatives of the granite; their excavation and exploitation have created a strange 'lunar' landscape which presents formidable conservation problems.

The highest hills are on Bodmin Moor (Brown Willy, 420m, and Rough Tor, 400m), an area of open moorland, tors, clitter slopes, bogs and streams. There is less heather than there used to be because of grazing pressure and improvement schemes, but orchids, insect-eating sundews, bogbean and other wetland plants may be found, as well as rare mosses and lichens. Mysterious, isolated Dozmary Pool, an upland tarn steeped in Cornish legend, nestles among the hills and attracts

wintering wildfowl and wading birds, as do certain recently constructed reservoirs, notably Crowdy which already looks convincingly natural and is a favourite haunt of ornithologists.

The granite of the moors reappears from the ocean as the ISLES OF SCILLY, a group of 145 rocks and islands, only five of which are inhabited. The Scillies are famed for their breeding colonies of seabirds and for rare migrants, grey seals and the Scilly shrew which, unlike most of its kind, favours stony beaches. The island of Annet is a nature reserve, and the whole group is carefully protected.

The moorland and plateau surfaces of THE LIZARD, the heel of Cornwall, are not part of the granite but consist of alkaline soils derived from Pre-Cambrian serpentinite rocks and boulder-strewn gabbro. They support a unique plant life including Cornish heath and a number of lime-loving plants which are rare in Cornwall. This important area is now well protected by the LOWER PREDANNACK reserves.

The Lizard is only a small though by no means insignificant part of Cornwall's greatest glory, the 650km long coast which reaches its climax in the bare rocks and towering cliffs of north Cornwall, High Cliff (223m) being the highest point. The line of harsh, wild north-coast cliffs is broken only at a few places: the CAMEL ESTUARY, rich in bird life; the HAYLE ESTUARY, a favourite refuge for migrating and wintering waders; and the dune areas of Penhale Sands and Phillack Towans where the lime-rich sand supports fascinating plant communities. At Dizzard a strange stunted oak forest stretches down exposed landslip slopes almost to sea level. Below Beeny, Pentire Head and Godrevy

77

seals breed, and gorse, thrift, spring squill, scurvygrass, kidney vetch, common bird's-foot-trefoil, rock samphire and wild carrot abound. There are countless nesting places for seabirds – auks, fulmar, kittiwake and other gulls – and one or two peregrine eyries. Stonechat, jackdaw, wheatear and pipits enliven the cliff tops. The coast itself is bare, but sheltered valleys inland are often wooded, two of the best examples being at Marsland on the Devon border (described under WELCOMBE AND MARSLAND VALLEYS) and the Valency Valley at Boscastle, both of which contain reserves. And wherever the sea meets the land, there is the constantly varying scene of moving tides exposing and then covering again mussel beds, banks of seaweeds, and rock pools.

The south coast is different in character. Here the scenery is gentler, and the cliffs are lower and less abrupt. Most Cornish rivers flow towards the south and open out into estuaries bounded by woods and edged by saltmarsh where waders and wildfowl feed. All the river valleys are interesting to naturalists, and there are reserves proper in both the TAMAR and FAL-RUAN ESTUARIES.

Inland, deciduous woods are mostly dominated by oak and ash with hazel, hawthorn, holly and willows in the valley bottoms; a varied ground flora is seasonally ablaze with bluebells. Sadly many such ancient woods have been replanted with conifers.

Here visitors will find quarries rich with ferns; stone-wall Cornish hedges and sunken lanes bright with foxglove, honeysuckle, stonecrops and primrose. There are marshes, bogs, inland waters and scrubby hillsides. Mammals – notably badger, fox and even a few red deer – birds of the woods, countryside and coast, and countless invertebrates amount to an exceptional diversity of wildlife.

The pressures upon this rich natural heritage, particularly those of uncontrolled tourism, are severe; nature reserves protect only a very small part of it. But the National Trust is extremely active in Cornwall. Many of the best stretches of coast, some fine woods such as those of LANHYDROCK, and the upper slopes of Rough Tor are safely in the ownership of the National Trust, and introduce a wide public to Cornwall's landscapes and wildlife.

RENNIE BERE

Antony Wood

SX 401547; 0.1 ha; WdT
Mixed woodland
Spring, early summer

A small area of land has been planted up with saplings to provide a broad-leaved woodland when the trees grow to maturity.

Atlantic Coast

See map; 260km; various bodies
Mainly rocky coastline
Spring, summer

Most of the south west of England is made from a huge downfold of land where twisted and buckled rocks have been bent into a U-shaped fold running from west to east. The fold is as wide as the whole peninsula and meets the sea end-on on this western coast, where the gales eat into the softer rocks more deeply than into the hard ones. The Devon–Cornwall border lies near to the centre of the fold so that each county reflects the sequence of rocks, but Cornwall is barricaded by other types as well, those which cooled from a molten flow thrusting up from the magma, such as the rocks which drove steam and scalding water through the layers above and which altered and realtered the layers around them to set the seams of tin and lead which drew the Cornish miners. These, granite and gabbro, dolerite and basalt, for instance, and the very ancient serpentine and schist of the Lizard, contribute much to the magic of the coast.

The SOUTH WEST PENINSULA COAST PATH picks its way from headland to headland, overlooking sandy coves which winter gales may strip to bare bones of rock and spring storms bury in sand

again. It climbs to cliffs where the land slopes gently and then falls, suddenly, sheer, to the sea. It crosses long sweeps of heathland or tilted grasslands spread with flowers. The plateau shows how ancient seas have levelled the land, while the modern sea lies, at times a level lake, at other times a roaring force which seems to shake the land.

The surrounding sea is the reason for the mild climate of the peninsula, a climate closer to the Mediterranean than to many other parts of Britain. It encourages plants which cannot grow in colder

Herring gulls nest on the Cornish cliffs.

The Atlantic Coast: wind and weather have carved out spectacular bays.

conditions but, at the same time, imposes other pressures. Salt winds blow across the cliffs and prune the coastal plain as rigorously as any formal gardener; plants must cope not only with the salt, not only with the winter violence which threatens to uproot them, but also with the drying effect of the sea breeze and the general lack of water near the cliffs. Stream-cut valleys break the line of the sea cliffs, some of them drowned river courses made into tidal estuaries by the relative change in sea level; sands and muds have filled the valley bottoms and the tidal reaches often run far inland. By contrast, some of the valleys hang above sea level, and streams meander between their steep sides to tumble in waterfalls on to the beach below. Here the sea cuts back the cliffs more quickly than the stream can deepen the valley; freshwater plants line the hanging valleys while the estuaries are fringed with saltmarsh plants. Near Godrevy, the Red River spills across a sandy beach and stains the sea with red; mining, far upstream, has filled the river with mineral pollution.

Pollution is fortunately far from evident along most of the cliffs and this is a coast of clear coves where grey seal haul out on low-tide rocks and breed on sheltered beaches or swim perfectly camouflaged in the rocky waters of the bays. Above the water, the seabirds wheel and fulmar, kittiwake, lesser black-backed, great black-backed and herring gull nest on the cliffs. Arrowing out from their rocky ledges or bobbing on the waves are breeding guillemot and razorbill, and occasionally puffin may be seen. Other fish-catchers, cormorant and shag, are also resident, and gannet may hunt the waters just offshore, perhaps coming from breeding colonies somewhere on the Channel Islands or Grassholm.

However beautiful the birds may be, however magnificent the seascape of rugged cliffs above sweeping thunderous waves, the colour and variety of the plant life is everywhere a rich and emphatic feature of the coast. Cliffs, the highest lifting to over 200m, may be topped with a dwarf-shrub heathland, varied with sloping sunlit grassland. The wealth of colour of the commoner coastal plants such as thrift and common bird's-foot-trefoil forms a backcloth for rare and uncommon species: hairy greenweed, shore dock, slender bird's-foot-trefoil, and the parasitic carrot broomrape which grows on the roots of wild carrot. The heathland is bright with western gorse and the subtle colours of heather and bell heather, with burnet rose and tangles of honeysuckle and wild madder. In April and May the bristle bent grassland is a blue sheen of spring squill which gives way later to the colours of sheep's-bit and betony, buck's-horn and sea plantain, and the delicate, strange-looking flower sprays of Portland spurge. An interesting and attractive flowering plant is the *coccinea* variety of kidney vetch, dusky red instead of yellow.

The dramatic red of bloody crane's-bill may show in the richer grassland together with other lime-loving plants such as salad burnet and fairy flax. Both heath and pale dog-violet appear in spring with a sub-species of early gentian, *cornubiensis*, known only from this coast. Other specialities of the western Cornish coast, where golden samphire, rock sea-spurrey and sea spleenwort grow on the cliffs, are the soft-leaved sedge, a plant of lime-rich pasture, heath pearlwort and maidenhair fern. All these treasures occur on the coast from the border down to Land's End, but the ancient rocks of the Lizard carry an even more wonderful magic. On the largest outcrop of serpentine in Britain, a unique association of Lusitanian plants grows in the warm, damp climate.

Serpentine is a basically very rich rock which gives rise to a thin heathland soil supporting an incredible assortment of rarities. The cliffs themselves are not as high as some of the younger rocks but form magnificent craggy headlands with jagged islands and picturesque, sea-shattered coves; this is a place of beauty and a botanist's paradise. Dwarf and pigmy rush, pillwort, three-lobed crowfoot, chaffweed and yellow centaury are some of the plants of note, together with spring and autumn squill, land quillwort and spotted cat's-ear. Fringed rupturewort and several unusual clovers are found nowhere else in mainland Britain. Cornish heath, abundant on the Lizard, its only native site, occurs with several colour variations, while a feature of the coastlands is the number of species which grow as prostrate or dwarf varieties. Many plants, particularly those in very exposed positions, tend to remain stunted but seeds which are set in more suitable sites will give rise to plants of normal size. The Lizard varieties, though, are separate races and breed true to their dwarf or prostrate forms. Dwarf populations of betony, oxeye daisy, common knapweed, devil's-bit scabious and saw-wort may be found, together with prostrate forms of wild asparagus, broom, dyer's greenweed, privet and juniper.

Sandymouth, north Cornwall, in winter sunshine at low tide.

Besides the slopes of coastal grassland and heath, drainage from inland gives rise to small mires where marsh plants grow. Common reed occurs with great fen-sedge above plants such as purple moor-grass, sea rush, black bog-rush and royal fern, while smaller plants include pale butterwort. The shallower soils carry populations of chives and green-winged orchid while slopes of gorse and wind-pruned blackthorn shelter spreads of bluebells.

Inland are further splendid stretches of heath, rich mires and pools, varying with the underlying soil and filled with a fascinating range of plant life. The Lizard is too exposed to carry woodlands, and for fine woods we must return to the more north westerly coast. Here, on more friable rock given to landslips, wind-pruned oak woods may be found, mixed with birch and rowan over shrubs of hawthorn, hazel and holly, gorse, wild privet and spindle. Blackthorn scrub gives additional shelter while the varied soils encourage a ground cover of rich-wood plants such as sanicle and ramsons, contrasting with bilberry, common cow-wheat and heather. Valley woodlands are similarly varied and provide a habitat for birds to contrast with that of the cliffs. Butterflies, too, delight in the grassland and heath, scrub and woodland, and include grayling, brown and green hairstreak, high brown, dark green, pearl-bordered, small pearl-bordered, marsh and silver-washed fritillary, dingy and grizzled skipper and marbled white.

The estuaries draw seasonal numbers of wildfowl and waders, although the south coast of Cornwall is better supplied with suitable sites, and

Bell heather, thrift and a mosaic of lichens.

lying as it does at the Atlantic limit of England, Land's End may see some notable migrant birds.

This whole magnificent coast, from the Lizard round to the northern border with Devon, contains an exceptional range of habitats. To watch a year on any small stretch of its length must be the dream of every naturalist; to know the full magic of every change of season, the ebb and flow of life from cliff top to sea bed, the power of the storm and the still of evening, would be a dream which would fill many lifetimes; to snatch only a brief time here is to know that you must return.

Benskins Wood

SX 409539; 1.1ha; WdT
Mixed woodland
Spring, early summer

With views across Plymouth Sound and the Tamar, the site consists of both standing woodland and open areas replanted with young trees.

Bude Marshes

SS 207062; 3.2ha; North Cornwall DC reserve
Coastal marshland
All year

The hide offers views of winter snipe and autumn migrants. The marshland includes yellow iris and common reed, shelters breeding reed and sedge warbler, and is visited by heron and kestrel.

Camel Estuary

SW 980735; c.800ha; various bodies
Long tidal mudflats and saltmarsh
All year

A disused railway line has been established as a waterside walk from which the waders and wild-fowl of the estuary may be seen. A small flock of white-fronted geese winter in the estuary.

Cecil Stevens Memorial Hide

Permit only; RSPB
Hide overlooking the Fal–Ruan Estuary
All year

Described under FAL-RUAN ESTUARY.

Chapel Porth Nature Trail

SX 697495; 3.2km; CCC
Atlantic coast nature trail
Booklet from CCC
Spring, summer

A splendid range of features includes a stream-cut valley, typical coastal heathland and magnificent rocky cliffs. Stonechat, rock pipit, raven and buzzard may be seen, together with fulmar, kittiwake, guillemot and gannet.

Coombe Valley Nature Trail

SS 203116; up to 2.5km; CTNC
Wooded valley trail, much planted with conifers
Booklet from CTNC
Spring, early summer

The trail includes areas of broad-leaved trees and may reveal such interesting plants and animals as winter heliotrope and autumn crocus, dipper and kingfisher, and silver-washed fritillary.

Cotehele Nature Walk

SX 423681; 2.4km; NT
Riverside woodland
Spring, early summer

A circular trail has been laid out in the woodlands of Cotehele, a large estate on the western bank of the Tamar, which includes river and marshland as well as woods.

Drift Reservoir

SW435291; 36ha; CTNC reserve
Reservoir and margins
All year

The reservoir is noted for rare and vagrant birds, due to its position as the most south westerly body of fresh water in mainland Britain, and provides a site for many migrant wintering and breeding species. The margins are variously woodland, wet woodland, scrub and herb-rich meadows, with a good range of plants including both heath spotted-orchid and southern marsh-orchid.

Fal-Ruan Estuary

SW 875405–SW886412; 100ha; CTNC reserve
Inland estuary
All year

Probably the most beautiful of the inland estuaries of Cornwall, the Fal-Ruan is a winding fingered spread of pale mudflats ringed by gently sloping hills, sheltered, quiet and inaccessible. The land around is privately owned, without rights of way, and the only access is to CTNC members or to key-holders of the CECIL STEVENS MEMORIAL HIDE.

The mudflats are unusually rich in suitable food for waders, particularly in ragworms. This is due to the high levels of mica-rich kaolin clays which have been washed down from china clay works higher up the river and which encourage a plentiful supply of tiny bacterial food.

When high tides cover the mudflats the estuary becomes a shallow saltwater lake, lapping the low cliffs below the woodland and washing across the narrow fringe of saltmarsh. This is a habitat of considerable local interest containing not only typical saltmarsh plants, but also three species uncommon in Cornwall: celery-leaved buttercup, lesser sea-spurrey and common saltmarsh-grass. One area of the estuary is of special fascination for its complete succession from mudflats to saltmarsh to alder–willow and to birch–oak woodland, a most uncommon occurrence in Britain, where most tidal areas have been altered by reclamation for grazing or for building.

A host of gulls may rest on the mudflats here, including such uncommon species as Mediterranean gull, and this is a site for winter birds. Mallard, shelduck, teal, wigeon and occasional shoveler may be seen with waders such as black-tailed godwit, dunlin, oystercatcher and lapwing, curlew, grey and golden plover, greenshank, ruff and spotted redshank and, perhaps, green, wood and curlew sandpiper. Uncommon birds recorded include osprey, spoonbill, glaucous gull and whiskered tern.

Hawke's Wood

SW 987709; 3.6ha; CTNC reserve
Mixed woodland
Spring, early summer

A small, plant-rich quarry adds to the variety of the wood which includes oak with ash, holly, sycamore, hazel and guelder-rose, with alder and birch along a stream. The upper slopes are more acidic with oak, originally coppiced, over hazel, hawthorn, holly and gorse. Many other species occur throughout the reserve which contains a typical range of woodland birds.

Hayle Estuary

SW 553373; c.100ha; various bodies
Sandflats, mudflats and saltmarsh
All year

Lying beside the busy A30, the Hayle Estuary has none of the quiet beauty of the FAL-RUAN yet still attracts good numbers of birds and, above all, is easily accessible. The estuary is formed by two arms of tidal waters lying south and east of the town and may be overlooked from various points on the roads which run beside them.

The southern arm is probably the more important: some 70ha of sandy flats are spread in a wide bowl, nowhere more than 500m wide, between the

A30 and the single-track railway line on its western side. The sands become more muddy where the river drains into the basin, and here saltmarsh adds further variation. Below the head of the estuary a non-tidal embanked pool, the Carnsew Basin, forms a permanent deep-water area suitable both as a roost and as a fishing ground for divers. An additional range of habitat, and one which may be welcomed by smaller migrants, is provided by an area of scrub and woodland which lies beside the railway at the river end of the estuary.

The eastern arm is even more easily studied since a trackway runs along its northern bank. It is a much smaller narrow strip of muddier flats which passes into a small reedmarsh by the river inflow. Low water provides a good feeding area for waders and, like RADIPOLE in Dorset, the fact that the area lies entirely within the edge of the town seems to make no difference to the birds. Summer numbers of birds will obviously be smallest but there may be much of interest to see here at any time. Winter wildfowl include wigeon, teal and shelduck, with occasional goldeneye, goosander and red-breasted merganser or less common species such as Slavonian grebe. Waders, in winter or on spring and autumn passage, include numbers of dunlin, lapwing and golden plover, together with birds such as curlew, bar-tailed godwit, knot, oystercatcher, grey and ringed plover, redshank, sanderling and turnstone.

The Hayman

SW 750498; 1.8ha; CTNC reserve
Wet steep wooded valley
Spring, early summer

The woodland is oak above a rather thin acid ground cover and sweet chestnut over a richer array of bluebell, enchanter's-nightshade and sanicle, with a show of ferns on the wet ground near the stream. Most of the commoner woodland mammals and birds are present with the extra interest of a rookery.

Knot are typical of estuaries such as Hayle.

Isles of Scilly

See map; 1600ha; Duchy of Cornwall–NCC
Small group of islands
Booklets and guide from local newsagents and
bookshops
Spring, summer

*Wingletang Down, St Agnes: wind-pruned
heathlands littered with rocks top many of the
islands.*

If you visit the low archipelago on a summer's day when the bright light is dashed upwards from fine white granite sands and waves driven by the long ocean breezes break in a diamond glitter on the beaches, it is hard to believe that the peace of the Scillies could ever be disturbed. Stay here when 30m waves drive in and try to drown the islands, when the spray-laden gales howl across the rocky islets, at their highest point only 20m above the crests of the waves, when the sand and shingle beaches move by the power of wind and water — then you will see how jealous the sea is of Britain's most westerly outcrop.

The Scillies group consists of five inhabited islands, with around 40 more which are large enough for land plants, and more than three times as many high-tide rocks too small or too exposed for vegetation. From several of the islands, old field walls run out into the central sea, showing how it was only won by the tides when a single granite island was drowned, long after the ice ages, and only a low-lying ring of hills was left above the water. At the time of the ice the island was possibly still joined on to Cornwall but a rise in the sea of perhaps 100m isolated the granite knoll when the glacial ice-cap melted. The island, at that time, seems to have been wooded, dressed with oak and hazel across the central lower plateau, with the hills probably used as grazing lands. As the water-level rose further, the central fields were slowly flooded and eventually the pattern of rocks and islands became established.

Even the splendid ATLANTIC COAST of Cornwall is affected partly by the influence of mainland Britain: rivers discharge fresh water into the sea, and coastal towns contribute wind-borne pollution. The Scillies, however, have only one stream that is worthy of mention and are largely watered by rainfall and blown by unpolluted winds. The air thus has a startling clarity, and the sunlight attains a brilliance never seen on the mainland. The offshore waters, unmuddied by river flows, are so clear that even the moon can light the sandy shallows.

The sea life, encouraged by these tidal waters, is as rich and attractive as the shores themselves. Where sand has been washed across the shallows, such beautiful sea snails as the common necklace shell and netted dog whelk may be found, together with strange-looking worm-like creatures such as *Glossobalanus* where the sand becomes slightly muddy. *Chaetopterus*, a weird three-part tube-dwelling worm, lives in the wet sand, and the wide variety of beach types contains a rich assortment of sea-anemones. Snakelocks, dahlia and beadlet anemone spread their tentacles, together with the beautiful coral-like organ-pipes of *Corynactis viridis* and the rare small Devonshire cup coral. The common sea-urchin favours rocky shores and is strongly spined for protection, while the heart-urchin and rarer purple heart-urchin live buried under the sands and tend to be hairy rather than spined. An outstandingly beautiful member of this family, and one which is elsewhere only found in deeper waters, is the feather star, an elegant starfish with five pairs of feather-like arms.

The tides which rise and fall across the beaches stir the trailing thong-weed, the flat wrack, bladder wrack and serrated wrack which zone the rocky shores, the knotted wrack which grows in sheltered waters, and the low encrusting weeds which grow where the wind and waves are roughest. They lap low rocky cliffs or wind-blown dunes where land plants begin to show, and where the battle is no longer how to survive at low water but how to survive in the face of salt splash and spray.

The sands and dunes have a characteristic plant life: sea-rocket, sea sandwort and prickly salt-wort below spreads of marram and sand sedge, of yellow horned-poppy, sea bindweed and spiny sea-holly, sea spurge and Portland spurge, or a low cover of buck's-horn plantain and sea stork's-bill. The rocky cliffs carry plants such as sea beet, common scurvy-grass, rock sea-spurrey and thrift, with shore dock, rock samphire, navelwort, tree-mallow and the alien Hottentot-fig. Above are cliff tops decorated with spring squill and sea pearlwort, giving way to sweeps of wind-pruned heathland, occasional thickets of gorse and western gorse, or stands of bracken where the soils are deep enough.

Bracken performs an important function on the Scillies, sheltering woodland plants whose woodland cover has long since been removed. It forms a canopy where plants such as bramble, foxglove, balm-leaved figwort and wood spurge in turn shelter bluebell, lesser celandine, ground-ivy and common bird's-foot-trefoil. Marsh vegetation occurs occasionally by the freshwater pools, with plants such as bulrush and common reed, with yellow iris, ragged-Robin and royal fern, but in general plants must be acid-tolerant, due to the granite beneath, and are often fleshy or very tough-skinned to avoid drying out in the wind. Danish scurvy-grass and sea spleenwort, found on inland heaths, show how the salt blows across the islands.

A large number of alien species have been planted or have colonised the islands, but several native plants are of particular note. The dwarf pansy of the acid dunes is found only here on the Scillies and on the Channel Islands; the low cliffs have the best British populations of shore dock, small tree-mallow and orange bird's-foot. The heathlands, of heather and bell heather, are subjected to a wind-pruning so severe that they tend to resemble a sea where waves of plants, grey and dead on the windward side, break green in the lee of their own lower foliage. The relative freedom from frost, coupled with high humidity, makes the Scillies a wonderful early-growing site provided that plants can be sheltered from the high winds and the spray. The complex of tiny fields and shelter belts is a picturesque feature of the islands.

Characteristic animals include a subspecies of meadow brown butterfly, and an island race of common blue which is only known from Tean. Grey seal breed in small numbers and are plentiful in summer, but the mammal speciality is the tiny Scillies shrew, an attractive insectivore widespread on the heathlands and which frequently hunts among the rocks on the shore.

Marram, on the edge of Tresco, overlooks the inter-tidal flats.

Annet Head, above a spread of thrift.

The islands are also important for bird life. The best time is probably May and June, when cushions of thrift and stands of rank weeds shelter varied colonies of seabirds. Annet, an important breeding island, is closed to visitors from mid-April to August to afford some privacy to birds such as storm petrel, Manx shearwater and puffin, together with raucous colonies of gulls. Puffin numbers unfortunately have fallen, part of a recognised national decline, but they may still be seen arrowing low across the waves or floating buoyantly on the water. Manx shearwater and storm petrel too are burrow or crevice nesters which only visit to breed, wintering in distant seas, but neither is commonly seen on the Scillies, being nocturnal at their breeding sites. Guillemot and razorbill nest here; whereas razorbill is the less common in mainland colonies, here it considerably outnumbers guillemot.

Other breeding birds include both common and roseate tern, fulmar, kittiwake, cormorant and shag, with waders such as ringed plover and oystercatcher, and a varied range of land birds, from duck such as gadwall, shoveler and teal to goldcrest, linnet, rock pipit and stonechat. The ducks may often be observed around the fresh-water pools, which also attract some interesting passage waders. Birds such as little stint and purple sandpiper may be seen at migration times, while the position of the islands encourages landfalls of many uncommon European and Transatlantic species. Pectoral sandpiper and Baltimore oriole from America have been recorded, together with alpine swift and golden oriole; other visitors include Lapland and ortolan bunting, Pallas's and yellow-browed warbler, tawny pipit and red-breasted flycatcher, and a host of commoner migrants.

Although the island complex is scattered over a large spread of water, the land area is surprisingly small and the wealth of wildlife is outstanding in its variety. July and August are quiet from the birdwatchers' point of view but the life of the tides is still full of interest; spring is spectacular for plants while autumn brings the largest numbers of migrants; winter itself may be full of gales but never a time of savage cold; the whole year is filled with a rhythm of fascination.

Kyemel Crease

SW 460244; 2ha; CTNC reserve
Mainly coniferous coastal woodland
Permit only off right of way
Spring, early summer

The woodland has developed from shelter belts planted on a 2ha, steep, sloping sea cliff where 121 tiny fields were once cultivated. It is now so darkly shaded that ground cover is virtually confined to Italian lords-and-ladies and ferns such as hart's-tongue and male-fern.

Kynance Cliffs

SW 688132; 26ha; CTNC reserve
Coastal cliffs, grassland and heath
Spring, summer

The cliffs are formed from serpentine which supports a wonderful variety of typical LIZARD plants and provides attractive nesting sites for birds.

Lanhydrock Nature Walks

SX 099635; various lengths; NT
Mixed woodland
Information boards at site
Spring, early summer

The Lanhydrock woodlands, straddling the River Fowey, are as important for their wealth of wildlife as for the beauty of their walks.

The Lizard

SW 701140; 400ha; reserves managed by various bodies
Complex of coast and heath
Spring, summer

The incredibly complicated geology of the Lizard has given rise to rock formations which carry a very special range of plants. It provides a superb scenery of heathland, and of coastal cliffs (described under LOWER PREDANNACK CLIFFS).

Most of the West Lizard is formed of serpentine, a rock which occurs nowhere else in Britain except on Anglesey and in Scotland; it is particularly rich in magnesium, and, with the warm south westerly climate, provides a special range of habitats.

The Downs support a unique variety of plants in dry to wet heathlands with stretches of mixed gorse and heather, damp tall heath, and contrasting dry short heathland away from the serpentine.

Main Dale, on the Lizard: short heath strewn with boulders formed from gabbro.

Cornish heath, found only in Cornwall, is one of the main plants of the mixed heath, together with a variety of unusual species including dwarf rush, pigmy rush, Dorset heath and chives. Spring squill makes a wonderful April show with both pale and common dog-violet and their hybrids. The damper situations contain tall heath where sprays of black bog-rush are mixed with purple moor-grass and Cornish heath while, even on the serpentine, some areas are acid enough for bog asphodel and small spreads of peat where species such as round-leaved sundew grow.

The short heath grows on the more granitic soil derived from gabbro, another rock formed from molten materials. Cornish heath does not grow on these more acidic soils; here the cover is generally of bristle bent with spreads of heather, bell heather, cross-leaved heath, purple moor-grass and western gorse. Areas of peat are rich in *Sphagnum* mosses and many plants in common with the tall heath, but plants such as pale butterwort, common butterwort – uncommon in the county – tawny sedge and lesser butterfly-orchid may also occur.

Other plants of interest include the grass-like fern pillwort, yellow centaury, three-lobed crowfoot and the very rare heath *Erica williamsii*, a cross between Cornish heath and cross-leaved heath.

Loe Pool Nature Walks

SW 639259; various lengths; NT
Shingle bank, freshwater lake and surrounding woodland
Information boards at site
All year

An extensive system of footpaths demonstrates shingle, lake and woodland plants in an area renowned for its birds.

Lower Predannack Cliffs

SW 660163; 16ha; CTNC reserve
Cliffs and coastal heathland
Spring, summer

Smaller examples of the heaths described under THE LIZARD occur on Lower Predannack Cliffs, together with an excellent spread of the coastal heathland so characteristic of the Lizard peninsula. The geology is a complex mix of rocks giving soils which support a magnificent range of plants set on steep slopes above the cliffs themselves.

The shallower slopes are closely covered with gorse and heather, in early spring decorated with lesser celandine and small violets; the grassy steeper slopes are filled with a wide range of small plants: spring squill, kidney vetch, wild thyme, sea campion and common scurvy-grass. The rocks are encrusted with lichens and plants such as navelwort. Wet places by the streams may have a marsh vegetation of yellow iris, meadowsweet and purple moor-grass with hart's-tongue on the damp rocks and bluebell and primrose on the banks, while damp areas may be deep in black bog-rush, Cornish heath and cross-leaved heath.

The coast provides a wide range of contrasts, from sheltered stream-cut valleys to very exposed cliff slopes. Stunting is a characteristic of the area, and along the Lizard coast may be found distinct populations of dwarf varieties of betony, oxeye daisy, common knapweed, saw-wort and devil's-bit scabious. An alternative to remaining small in order to avoid exposure is to lie down to get out of the wind, and this reaction is another characteristic. Prostrate varieties of wild asparagus, broom, dyer's greenweed, privet and juniper occur on the Lizard cliffs.

The area is known not only for these specialities but also for its rare or uncommon species such as twin-flowered, upright and long-headed clover, another clover, *Trifolium occidentale*, fringed rupturewort, spring sandwort, thyme broomrape and hairy greenweed.

Lower Predannack Cliffs, of course, do not hold all these plants but, as a representative of the Lizard coast, the reserve is both beautiful and fascinating in the variety of its wildlife.

Pelyn Woods are a mixed woodland typical of old estates.

Lower Predannack Downs

SW 690145; 60ha; CTNC reserve
Typical Lizard heathland
Spring, early summer

The drier heathland carries characteristic plants such as Cornish heath, while the wetter slopes provide a habitat for species such as black bog-rush.

Lower Tamar Lake

Permit only; 20.4ha; SWWA
Bird sanctuary
All year

A hide overlooks the lake where over 170 bird species have been recorded. Winter wildfowl include gadwall and goldeneye, and the marsh has become an important breeding site.

Pelyne

SX 179598; 3.7ha; CTNC reserve
Wooded valley
Spring, early summer

Oak, beech, birch, wild cherry, holly and rowan form the major part of the reserve which includes a stream, a pond, a wet meadow and the remains of a small disused lead mine.

Pelyn Woods

SX 092586; 40.4ha; CTNC reserve
Old estate woodland
Spring, early summer

Beech, sweet chestnut and sycamore, rhododendron and laurel have been planted but oak and ash over hazel, holly, hawthorn and rowan are native. An attractive torrential stream adds wetland interest to a typical range of woodland plants and animals.

Pendarves Wood

SW 641377; 24ha; CTNC reserve
Old estate woodland and educational reserve
Spring, early summer

A nature trail runs through oak, ash, beech and sycamore woodland with dense spreads of laurel and rhododendron where an ornamental lake attracts winter wildfowl and is a breeding site for dragonflies and damselflies.

Peter's Wood

SX 113910; 10ha; CTNC reserve
Steep valley woodland
Spring, early summer

The steep narrow valleys which cut through the sea cliffs of Cornwall to drain into the Atlantic form an unusually sheltered environment in the wind-swept coastal belt. At their mouths they provide the tiny harbours once so important here, while further inland they often hold slopes of woodland too steep to farm.

Peter's Wood has been much modified by planted trees, such as beech and sycamore, yet evidence seems to indicate that some, at least, is ancient woodland. Apart from the alien species, oak is the main tree cover, with birch, ash and wild cherry above an often sparse shrub layer including holly, hazel, rowan and guelder-rose. The wood is rather acid, with wide spreads of great wood-rush and hard fern, but damp flushes and the deeper soils of the valley floor, where hazel, hawthorn, alder and willow grow, contain nutrients enough for plants such as ramsons and opposite-leaved golden-saxifrage. Spring brings a typical show of woodland plants such as wood anemone, bluebell, primrose and wood-sorrel to contrast with hart's-tongue and lady-fern. Bilberry and common cow-wheat underline the acid nature of the wood but the richer valley floor adds marshland plants such as meadowsweet and hemlock water-dropwort. Among the interesting ferns of the reserve are the unusual royal fern and Tunbridge filmy-fern.

The river which once cut the valley is a feature of the reserve, a route by which animals such as mink might enter the area, a hunting ground for birds such as dipper and a breeding ground for insects which might feed the resident Leisler's, Daubenton's and long-eared bats. The rather sparse bird life is typical of these woodlands, with blackcap, whitethroat, willow warbler and chiffchaff, goldcrest, wren and buzzard.

Porthcothan Valley

SW 870713; 7.2ha; CTNC reserve
Sheltered valley
Spring, early summer

The valley contains a range of habitats which include streamside meadowland, woodland and an old quarry. Badger breed on the reserve and birds include nesting sparrowhawk and buzzard.

Red Moor

SX 070615; 24ha; CTNC reserve
Wetland heath, scrub and woodland
Spring, summer

While man's activities have generally been so destructive in the modification of wild areas to fit the pattern of industry or farming, in a very few cases a wilderness has been created of benefit to wildlife. Red Moor is just such a case: working alluvial tin has left a marvellous complex of pools and wetlands, of hills and holes which are now a jungle, thick with wet woodland, scrub, reed-marsh, heath and bog. This is a reserve where a great range of habitats may be studied in a relatively small area, and where plants and animals can survive undisturbed deep in farmland.

One of the attractive features of the reserve is the mosaic nature of the site: an old bank, dry and thick with polypody, hard fern and gorse, may overlook a silted pool, wooded with willow like a rich dark mangrove swamp; a few metres away a screen of trees shelters the waters of the main pool, where it fills from a wide spread of bulrush reed-swamp, or where low coppiced oakwoods stand with every upper branch bunched with grey-green lichen. Clearings may be filled with tall gorse and leggy stands of heather, or with damp spreads of purple moor-grass and *Sphagnum* or dry heath invaded by birch.

Around 100 species of birds have been recorded here. Nightjar have bred on the heathland, an ideal site for typical birds such as stonechat, linnet and yellowhammer, while the wetlands attract waterbirds and may be fished by birds such as heron. As one would expect from such a varied site, there is an excellent range of insects and spiders, and the wetlands of Red Moor encourage a variety of specialised animals including 11 recorded species of dragonfly.

St Anthony-in-Roseland Nature Walk

SW 868329; 6.4km; NT
Coastal trail
Information board at site
Spring, summer

Circling part of the famous Roseland peninsula, the trail includes woodland and farmland, set beside a creek of the Percuil River or above the rocky cliffs of the open coast.

Shute Wood

SW 742522; 0.2ha; WdT
Mixed woodland
Spring, early summer

The tiny copse, important for wildlife in an area where woods are sparse, has been doubled in size by the planting of a block of young oak saplings.

South West Peninsula Coast Path

SS 212174–SX 455534; 427km; CC
Part of coastal footpath
Spring, summer

Running around the spectacular coastline of Cornwall, the path passes through a superb range of coastal habitats from Plymouth, in the south, to the Marsland Valley, part of WELCOMBE AND MARSLAND VALLEYS reserve, in the north.

Ancient parkland at Trelissick, overlooking the Fal Estuary. Old parklands are often rich in fungi, lichens and uncommon insects.

Tamar Estuary

SX 430610;400ha; CTNC reserve
Saltmarsh and mudflats
All year

The wide mudflats of the Tamar, fringed with saltmarsh, provide a suitable habitat for birds such as shelduck, curlew, oystercatcher and redshank, together with a small but regular wintering population of avocet outside the reserve area.

Tregassick Nature Walk

SW 857340; 3.2km; NT
Riverside trail
Spring, summer

From Percuil the walk follows the banks of the attractive tidal river and ends at Tregassick Farm, not far north of the ST ANTHONY-IN-ROSELAND NATURE WALK.

Trelissick Nature Walk

SW 837396; 3.2km; NT
Woodland and parkland walk
Spring, summer

The circular trail includes the high-forest woodland on the slopes above the River Fal where cormorant and heron may be seen.

Tremelling

SW 550340; 2.8ha; CTNC reserve
Mixed woodland
Spring, early summer

The small damp reserve contains willow, sycamore, holly, ash, blackthorn, hawthorn and hazel above a good show of woodland flowers and ferns.

Ventongimps Moor

SW 781513; 8ha; CTNC reserve
Wet and dry heath with pools
Spring, summer

The moor is slightly tilted, with streamlets draining through to the wet wooded brook at the boundary, but is varied by low, level plateaus which carry spreads of dry heath. These dry heaths contain common and western gorse, heather and bell heather and are filled with magnificent stands of Dorset heath. Below them, the wet heaths are a deep pattern of purple moor-grass, Dorset heath and black bog-rush, dissected by the streamlets where clumps of rushes, yellow iris and plants such as royal fern grow. Along the edges of the streams are groves of aromatic bog myrtle, while the wet willow woodland is floored with yellow iris, meadowsweet and water mint. This lower woodland is fringed with oak, birch and hazel while above the moor is a belt of coppiced woodland with a dense ground cover of bramble giving way to gorse as it grades into the heath.

Further variety is added by a number of pools varying from shallow, probably summer-dry, pits, through deeper pools rich in water plants, to a very deep, crystal-clear pond. Some of the pools provide breeding sites for frogs and for the 13 recorded species of dragonfly. Snipe and other woodland birds breed on the moor itself while the woodlands attract a typical range of nesting and visiting species.

Ventongimps Moor: the deep, clear pond in early summer.

Merely to list a few of the plants and animals of the reserve, however, is to do far less than justice to a quite exceptional heathland. Pale butterwort and yellow centaury are among the uncommon species here but the whole mosaic of colour, of richly scented plants and bright insects, in a valley bottom surrounded by formal farmland, combines to form a special wilderness. No one who visits Ventongimps can fail to stand against any further loss of our irreplaceable southern heaths.

Walmesley Sanctuary

No access; 17ha; Cornwall Bird-Watching and Preservation Soc.
Wet grassland and foreshore
The sanctuary may be overlooked from SW 987744
Autumn, winter

White-fronted geese are fewer now than in former years, but duck include pintail and wigeon, and autumn brings waders such as wood and green sandpiper, greenshank and ruff.

Welcombe and Marsland Valleys

Described under Devon.

Woodland

Permit only; 3.6ha; CTNC reserve
Woodland, scrub and heath
Spring, early summer

Old coppiced oak with hazel, gorse scrub and herb-rich grassy heath contain plants such as common cow-wheat, bladderseed, bastard balm, heath spotted-orchid and lesser butterfly-orchid. The reserve is particularly rich in butterflies, including the attractive marsh fritillary.

Cumbria

Cumbria can claim as rich a diversity of scenery and habitat as any English county. The still unspoilt beauty of the LAKE DISTRICT NATIONAL PARK, which lies at its heart, draws thousands of visitors from all over the world. So small that it could all be enclosed by a circle with a 32km radius, it contains an astonishing variety of mountain, crag, scree, moorland, valleys and ravines, becks, waterfalls, rivers, tarns and lakes, old oakwoods and new conifer forests, slopes of heather and bracken, and a wealth of ever-changing colour.

But the Lake District occupies only a part of the county of Cumbria. To the north of the National Park it includes the extensive farmlands of the Solway Plain, to the east a stretch of limestone upland, the wide Eden Valley and the high Pennines beyond, while the limestone hills and woods of south Cumbria have a gentler charm and interest of their own. The county is bounded on the west by a long and varied coastline between the great estuaries of the Solway Firth and Morecambe Bay, including fine sand dune systems and saltmarshes as well as the high sandstone cliffs of ST BEES HEAD.

The mountainous area of the Lake District is made up of three broad bands of different types of rock running roughly north east to south west. In the north are Skiddaw slates, a rather soft rock which forms the smoothly rounded shapes of Skiddaw and the fells west of Derwentwater. Adjoining them to the south are the harder Borrowdale volcanics which produce the rugged crags of most of the central Lake District. South of Ambleside and Coniston lie Silurian slates and mudstones with lower hills and gentler slopes. Almost encircling the Lake District proper is a broad band of carboniferous limestone, with striking exposures of creviced bare rock known as limestone pavements. Subsequently, the whole of Cumbria has been carved by great glaciers during the ice ages. Ice scoured out the deep U-shaped valleys, made the great rocky corries and basins of tarns in the fells, dammed streams with moraines, creating swamps

and lakes, and deposited in valleys and plains the rocks, gravel and till that underlie the present Cumbrian lowlands.

The much maligned climate of Cumbria is actually as varied as its geology. The heavy rainfall of the central fells and valley heads (some 3100mm a year at Seathwaite in Borrowdale) drops rapidly away from the mountains (under 1000mm on the Solway Plain and southern coast). Temperature shows similar local variations. Air frost is recorded on about 160 days every year on the high fells, but on only 30 days at Grange-over-Sands. Snow often lies in high gullies into June, but is rarer by the southern estuaries than almost anywhere else in England.

Severe climatic conditions combined with steep slopes and shallow soils make agriculture and even forestry impossible on the higher hills. Low temperatures and high winds inhibit the growth of vegetation, and trees are scarce and stunted on exposed slopes over 300m above sea level. Selective grazing by mountain sheep has impoverished plant life and prevented the regeneration of trees, so that fellsides that were once wooded even above 300m are now reduced to mat-grass and bracken. On the plains and in the wider valleys the mixed farms include some arable land, but Cumbria has not suffered the widespread destruction of hedges like some eastern and southern counties.

The great conifer forests planted by the Forestry Commission and private landowners have affected Cumbria's scenery and wildlife. Dense sitka spruce, the usual choice for quick growth on wet acid soils, allows no ground flora and only limited insect and bird life, but the deciduous woodlands of south Cumbria, which once supplied several rural industries, still support a rich and varied wildlife. Modern industry, apart from tourism, seriously affects the Cumbrian countryside only around Carlisle, Barrow and the west Cumberland coalfield.

The animal and plant life of Cumbria is rich and varied. There are small gems of arctic–alpine flora

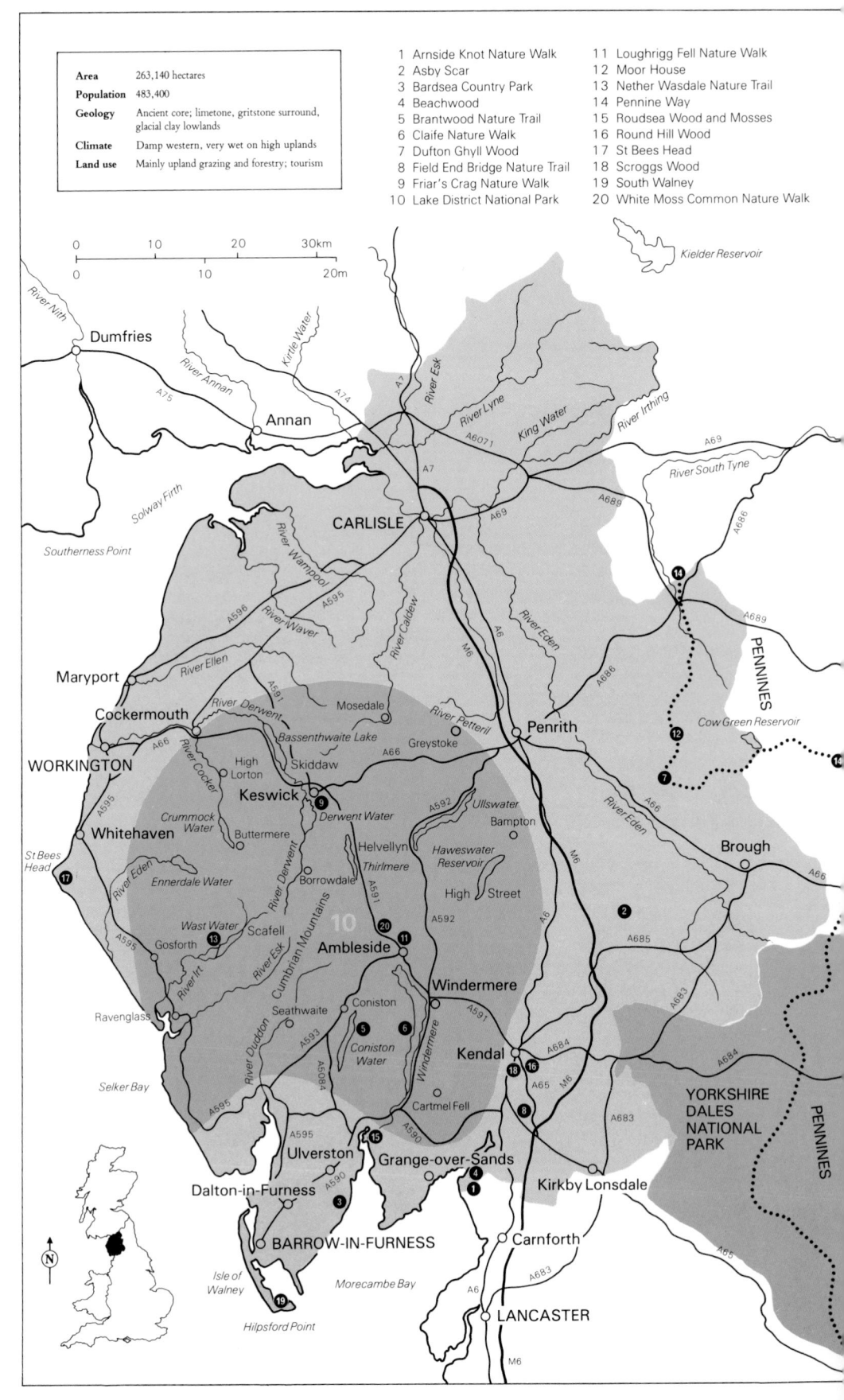

Area	263,140 hectares
Population	483,400
Geology	Ancient core; limetone, gritstone surround, glacial clay lowlands
Climate	Damp western, very wet on high uplands
Land use	Mainly upland grazing and forestry; tourism

1 Arnside Knot Nature Walk
2 Asby Scar
3 Bardsea Country Park
4 Beachwood
5 Brantwood Nature Trail
6 Claife Nature Walk
7 Dufton Ghyll Wood
8 Field End Bridge Nature Trail
9 Friar's Crag Nature Walk
10 Lake District National Park
11 Loughrigg Fell Nature Walk
12 Moor House
13 Nether Wasdale Nature Trail
14 Pennine Way
15 Roudsea Wood and Mosses
16 Round Hill Wood
17 St Bees Head
18 Scroggs Wood
19 South Walney
20 White Moss Common Nature Walk

0   10   20   30km
0   10   20m

Kielder Reservoir

River Nith
Dumfries
River Annan
River Annan
Kirtle Water
Annan
A75
A74
A7
River Esk
River Lyne
King Water
A6071
River Irthing
A69
River South Tyne
A69
CARLISLE
A7
A69
A686
A689
PENNINES
Solway Firth
Southerness Point
River Wampool
River Waver
River Caldew
M6
A6
River Eden
A686
Cow Green Reservoir
14
Maryport
River Ellen
A596
A591
Mosedale
River Petteril
Greystoke
Penrith
River Eden
A66
12
7
14
Cockermouth
River Derwent
Bassenthwaite Lake
A66
WORKINGTON
A66
High Lorton
Skiddaw
Keswick
9
Derwent Water
Ullswater
Bampton
A592
River Eden
Brough
A66
Whitehaven
A595
Crummock Water
Buttermere
Helvellyn
Thirlmere
Haweswater Reservoir
A66
St Bees Head
17
River Eden
Ennerdale Water
River Derwent
Borrowdale
A591
High Street
Wast Water
Scafell
10
20
A592
2
A685
Gosforth
13
River Esk
Cumbrian Mountains
Ambleside
11
A591
Windermere
Ravenglass
River Irt
Seathwaite
A593
Coniston
5
6
Windermere
A591
A684
Kendal
18
16
A683
Selker Bay
River Duddon
A5084
Coniston Water
Cartmel Fell
A65
M6
YORKSHIRE DALES NATIONAL PARK
A595
A590
15
8
A683
PENNINES
Ulverston
Grange-over-Sands
4
1
Kirkby Lonsdale
Dalton-in-Furness
A590
3
Carnforth
A6
A683
N
BARROW-IN-FURNESS
A85
Isle of Walney
19
Morecambe Bay
Hilpsford Point
LANCASTER
M6

on a few high crags and flushes; certain insects, like the small mountain ringlet, occur in England only on the mountain slopes; and, for centuries, Cumbrian crags have provided a breeding refuge for raven, peregrine and buzzard. Wild red deer and a few pine marten still survive. The lakes, tarns and streams of Lakeland have been intensively studied for many years by scientists from the Freshwater Biological Association headquarters on Windermere, and glacial relicts such as char and whitefish have been found in some Cumbrian waters.

The wildlife of the central Lake District receives some protection through land ownership by the National Trust and the Lake District Special Planning Board; both bodies offer public access to large areas of countryside. The policy of the Cumbria Trust for Nature €onservation is to safeguard the survival of specialised habitats or rare species, especially where these are threatened by damaging development or excessive visitor pressure. Fens, bogs, limestone pavements, saltmarshes and sand dunes have been bought or leased for this purpose. A mosaic of sanctuaries has been established throughout the county for the preservation of the local fauna and flora. Large colonies of breeding seabirds, rare species of butterflies and moths and many scarce and interesting plants are already being given invaluable protection, and further acquisitions are constantly under review. Although permits are required to visit many of the county's nature reserves, free access can be gained to many sites so that careful visitors may still enjoy the wealth of Cumbrian wildlife, particularly in the National Park itself where unusual plants such as touch-me-not balsam grow in acid woods, or yellow loosestrife fringes the lakes which radiate outwards like the spokes of a wheel. Many wildfowl, such as mallard or even red-breasted merganser, breed around the lakes and, in spring, magnificent whooper swan may be seen.

JOHN A.G. BARNES

Arnside Knot Nature Walk

SD 451773; 1–5km; Arnside PC–NT
Limestone trail
Leaflet from Arnside PC Clerk, local shops or NT information centre
Spring, summer

The circular trail has a rich flora and fauna including typical woodland birds, red squirrel, moths and butterflies.

Asby Scar

NY 648103; 160ha; NCC reserve
Upland grassland and limestone pavement
Spring, early summer

A rim of limestone forms a broken curve around the Lake District and lines the Vale of Eden. It supports a very specialised range of plant life and is fashioned by erosion into a unique scenery.

Limestone dissolves, effervescing in acid solutions, and since rainwater is a weak acid the hard rock is slowly dissolved away. A limestone pavement forms where clints, or horizontal slabs of rain-washed rock, are separated by twisting grikes, the fissures, which may be several metres deep. Where soils are developed over and around the pavement, a rich variety of plants may grow. HERVEY shows limestone grassland bright with common rock-rose and wild thyme, scrubbed with juniper, a sheep-grazed upland full of colour, while LANCELOT CLARK STORTH, ungrazed, has developed into woodland, splendidly varied and gladed with flowers such as dropwort. Asby Scar, by contrast, shows the hard, grey world of open rock.

The limestone here appears as wide pavements set in grassland or as long, low cliffs, or scars, in the side of the hill. Where the pavement is shallow, the grikes themselves may be open and grassed, often filled with acid plants such as bilberry, heather and tormentil because water has leached the calcium carbonate downwards to give an acid soil. As the pavements deepen, the grikes become deep, dark, humid places which protect the special plants of the pavement from the sheep.

Each damp, cool pit is a small garden of ferns and plants such as wall lettuce, mountain melick and lesser meadow-rue, hart's-tongue, green spleenwort and brittle bladder-fern. Rigid buckler-fern and limestone fern, both extremely uncommon in this country, occur here.

The clints and grikes of a limestone pavement may be treacherous underfoot; where the water washes out the grikes, it also tends to undercut the clints and quite large slabs of pavement may tilt unexpectedly.

Asby Scar: water dissolves the rock to form a spectacular limestone pavement.

Bardsea Country Park

SD 300742; 32ha; CCC
Coastal woodland
Spring, early summer

An area of oak–beech woodland lies above some 2.4km of shoreline, consisting mainly of shingle and mudflats.

Barkbooth Lot

Permit only; 12ha; CTNC reserve
Rough grassland and scrub
Spring, early summer

Acid-loving scrub species occur here together with a small spread of heather to vary the grassland surrounding a small tarn or pool. Over 60 bird species have been recorded on the reserve.

Beachwood

SD 452786; 0.5ha; CTNC reserve
Meadowland and woodland
Spring, early summer

The tiny limestone reserve contains a woodland which includes ash, spindle and whitebeam, together with an area of grassland rich in spring and summer flowers. An amazing diversity of plants includes 12 fern species, with both adder's-tongue and rustyback, lime-loving plants such as columbine, green hellebore, herb-Paris and Solomon's-seal with a number of transplanted species including stinking hellebore, angular Solomon's-seal, lily-of-the-valley, spurge-laurel and the alien white butterbur.

Blelham Bog

Permit only; 2ha; NT–NCC reserve
Small tarn-side bog
Spring, summer

The reserve protects a *Sphagnum* bog developing from wet willow woodland beside a tarn important for research into the enrichment of acid pools.

Bowness Gravel Pits

Permit only; 7.2ha; CTNC reserve
Disused gravel workings
All year

Set on the fringes of the Solway Firth saltmarshes, the flooded pits and areas of scrub attract a variety of birds, adding to the interest of the plant life which includes aquatic species and a variety of orchids.

Brantwood Nature Trail

SD 313958; 4km; Brantwood Estate, Coniston Water
Lakeland nature trail
Spring, early summer

The trail winds through the 100ha estate of Brantwood and includes splendid views across the fells.

Claife Nature Walk

SD 388954; 2.4km; NT
Mixed woodland trail
Leaflet from NT information centres
Spring, early summer

Beside Lake Windermere, the circular walk passes through broad-leaved woodland with a typical bird life which includes the attractive pied flycatcher. The walk includes areas of planted conifers together with a lakeside stretch where waterbirds may be seen.

Clawthorpe Fell

Permit only; 14ha; NCC reserve
Two sections of limestone pavement
Spring, summer

The pavements provide a splendid contrast between the lowland GAIT BARROWS (Lancashire) and the upland mass of ASBY SCAR. They carry a dramatic range of plants such as bloody crane's-bill, lily-of-the-valley and dark-red helleborine, and a fine variety of ferns including polypody and rigid buckler-fern.

Dorothy Farrer's Spring Wood

Permit only; 1.4ha; CTNC reserve
Mixed woodland
Spring, early summer

The wood is a rich mix of species and includes ash, birch, bird cherry, hazel, oak and rowan over a ground cover of bluebell, bramble, dog's mercury and early-purple orchid.

Dorothy Farrer's Spring Wood: the tumbling small stream at the woodland edge.

Curlew, whose call is perhaps the most evocative sound of the mosses.

Drumburgh Moss

Permit only; 90ha; CTNC reserve
Raised bog
Spring, summer

A fine remnant of the Solway mires, Drumburgh is rich in plants such as cross-leaved heath, heather, both common and hare's-tail cottongrass and several species of *Sphagnum*. Bog asphodel, cranberry and bog-rosemary are frequent while resident birds include curlew, snipe and red grouse.

Dubbs Moss

Permit only; 7.2ha; CTNC reserve
Fen and woodland
Spring and early summer

The reserve consists of alternating damp and raised dry ground with a fen vegetation in the wetter areas and hawthorn scrub or woodland on the drier ones. The scrub contains early-purple orchid, common twayblade and common spotted-orchid, while the woodland holds abundant mosses and ferns.

Dufton Ghyll Wood

NY 687250; 10ha; WdT
Mixed valley woodland
Spring, early summer

Just off the PENNINE WAY, the wood lies in a narrow valley, a mix of beech, oak and birch with spectacular views across the Pennines or out to the distant Lakeland fells.

Field End Bridge Nature Trail

SD 526850; 1km; CTNC
Canal-side nature trail
Leaflet from CTNC
Spring, summer

The canal is rich in small water animals, in fish such as pike, perch, roach and eel, and in plants such as horsetails, sedges, water mint, hemlock water-dropwort and water-plantain. Birds of field, hedgerow and wetland may be seen.

Friars Crag Nature Walk

NY 264227; 2.4km; NT
Lake-edge and woodland walk
Leaflet from NT information centres
Spring, early summer

Overlooking Derwent Water with its scatter of wooded islands, the trail circles along the shore and through mixed woodland to give a picture of typical Lakeland with its woodland birds and waterbirds.

Glasson Moss

Permit only; 58ha; NCC reserve
Remnant of acid raised bog
Spring, summer

The bog has a hollow–hummock structure, rich in *Sphagnum* mosses and in species such as common and hare's-tail cottongrass, cross-leaved heath, cranberry, heather and crowberry. Fringed by bog myrtle, the site has unusual mosses as well as an abundance of white beak-sedge and bog-rosemary.

Grubbins Wood

Permit only; 7.2ha; CTNC reserve
Old coppiced limestone woodland
Spring, early summer

The woodland contains yew, oak, beech, ash and small-leaved lime above spindle, buckthorn, wayfaring-tree and whitebeam. Green and stinking hellebore, baneberry, columbine and Solomon's-seal are part of an outstanding flora.

Hay Bridge

Permit only; 88ha; Hay Bridge Nature Reserve
Soc. reserve
Rusland Valley deer sanctuary
Leaflets and permit from Warden, Low Hay Bridge,
Bouth-by-Ulverston, Cumbria LA12 8JG
Spring, summer

The habitat ranges from upland fell through woodland, lime-rich flushes, fen, raised bog and pasture, to river bank and open tarns and gives a splendid variety of scenery. The plant life ranges from bracken and wavy hair-grass through oak and birch, primrose, cowslip, grass-of-Parnassus and orchid species, yellow iris and devil's-bit scabious, bog-rosemary and royal fern, field wood-rush and sweet vernal-grass, to monkeyflower and marsh woundwort. The reserve is a breeding site for mallard and little grebe, and over 100 species of birds have been recorded. Mammals include red and roe deer, badger and red squirrel. Two nature trails have been laid out, and there is a deer museum.

Hervey

Permit only; 100ha; CTNC reserve
Limestone outcrops, grassland and woodland
Spring, summer

Hervey reserve stands between ASBY SCAR and LANCELOT CLARK STORTH in the progression of limestone scenery from open rock to woodland.

The low cliffs, or scars, are still bare and barren but, over much of the rock, a thin soil has been laid by glaciation.

The reserve is sited on a long low scarp which dips towards the east, giving a line of cliffs and steep scree slopes on the western side which is thickly dressed with woodland. This high-forest woodland passes up into open stands of birch and to a scrub of species such as juniper, ash and yew. Much of the top, however, is grassed, mainly with blue moor-grass, although some areas are acid enough for heather, heath bedstraw, tormentil, mat-grass and common bent. An unexpected pool lies between two of the scars where bogbean and common butterwort may be found but generally the hilltop is open, dry upland, with shelves of limestone grassland where common rock-rose, wild thyme and harebell grow.

The pavements are thin and brittle and there are many areas of level scree where loose, flat limestone slabs litter the grassland. Here, summer shows vivid yellow spreads of biting stonecrop and low, creeping herb-Robert. Here, too, may be the characteristic pavement plants such as lesser meadow-rue, limestone polypody and rigid buckler-fern, green spleenwort and commoner species such as maidenhair spleenwort and wall-rue.

Where red grouse clucked and grumbled around Asby Scar, the woodland and scrub at Hervey invite a greater range of birds. Buzzard and woodcock breed in the neighbourhood and skylark, meadow pipit and tree pipit on the hilltop; the reserve is a vantage point from which black grouse, nightjar, raven and the majestic golden eagle have been seen.

High Stand Observation Tower

Permit only; FC
Raised hide
Permit from Head Forester, Spadeadean Forest, FC,
High Stand Office, Armathwaite, Carlisle, Cumbria
CA4 9SY
Spring, early summer

The hide overlooks a pond and clearing in the Spadeadean Forest where, at dawn and dusk, roe deer, fox, badger and a variety of wildfowl may be seen.

Ivy Crag Wood

Permit only; 1.6ha; CTNC reserve
Mixed woodland
Spring, early summer

Oak with ash, wild cherry and species such as beech, sweet chestnut, Douglas fir and rhododendron stand over dry slopes of bracken or a damper, lower springtime spread of snowdrop and wild daffodil. Characteristic woodland birds include buzzard; among the mammals are roe deer.

Hervey: juniper, stunted by the continual wind, grows on the limestone plateau.

Lake District National Park

See map; 224,300ha; LDSPB
Uplands and lakes
Leaflets from National Park Centre, Brockhole,
Windermere
Spring, early summer

The Lake District National Park reflects most people's image of Cumbria, where rugged crags are mirrored in deep, still meres, but the park includes a far wider range of scenery than this. The largest national park in the whole country, but still only 32km across, the designated area rises from tidal shores to the peak of England's highest mountain, from sea level to almost 1000m.

The park meets the sea above MORECAMBE BAY (Lancashire), one of the two most important sites for winter waders in Britain, or laps the dunes and shingles at the edge of the Irish Sea. A fine example of duneland is conserved at RAVENGLASS.

Once, all but the coastal dunes, marshes, mountain tops and bogs of Cumbria were thick with a varied woodland. The rocks of the park are mainly acid, where sessile oakwoods grow best, but here and there more lime-rich rocks occur where the main dome of the Lakeland hills is ringed by an outcrop of limestone. Many of the natural woodlands have gone now, replaced on the upland slopes with conifers, but some remain. On limestone the main tree is probably ash, with a delicate open canopy which encourages a rich ground cover. Here yew may stand, with whitebeam above spreads of lily-of-the-valley or, perhaps, dark-red helleborine. The woodland edges may be tangled

Wastwater, deepest of the lakes, lies ringed by steep fells close to Scafell Pike.

with climbers, traveller's-joy and white bryony, and give way to farmland below, to limestone grassland, scrub and broken pavements above, where columbine, bloody crane's-bill, common and hoary rock-rose, the tiny mountain everlasting and plants such as fragrant orchid and lesser butterfly-orchid grow with wild rose and juniper.

Juniper is a distinctive shrub of many of the uplands, growing on both the lime-rich and acid slopes of the Cumbrian hills. High on the crags it may be severely dwarfed, a subspecies adapted to exposure, but in the oak–birch woodlands which grow on the acid soils juniper shrubs may become several metres tall. Hawthorn, hazel, holly and rowan grow in the understorey, forming a most attractive woodland which ranges from small, exposure-pruned oaks at the upper limits of the woods to a belt of alder and willow where woodland cover runs down to the lakes. These acid woods may contain, in their less acid parts, such unusual species as alpine enchanter's-nightshade and wood fescue or touch-me-not balsam, food plant of netted carpet moth.

Woodland birds include the more common species, with tree pipit, woodcock and the western trio of pied flycatcher, wood warbler and redstart. Coniferous woodlands attract a range of species, depending much on the thickness and height of plantations, and also hold numbers of two of the noted mammals of the park, red squirrel and our largest native species, red deer. Pine marten, too, may occur in coniferous woodland, although these uncommon animals will often hunt above the tree line. Badger and fox are generally woodland species, though foxes often breed in the upland rock falls.

From a bird's-eye view the lakes lie like the spokes of a giant wheel. They were scoured out during the ice ages by glaciers which deepened the valley bottoms and dammed the water behind great banks, or moraines. Most of the lakes are extremely deep, with the bed of the deepest, Wastwater, almost 18m below sea level.

The lakes may be fringed with tall herbs, such as yellow loosestrife and stands of common reed, while small plants such as white water-lily and quillwort with spreads of shoreweed grow in the shallow lake margins. In some of the fish which come to breed in the shallows further effects of glaciation can be seen; thawing ice trapped glacial relicts in the lakes and, as in SNOWDONIA (Gwynedd), char and whitefish are found in some Cumbrian waters. Another glacial relict, *Mysis relicta*, is a small freshwater shrimp found in Ennerdale. It is rarely seen, unless it is trapped, because it feeds by night and spends its days deep in the lower waters.

Mallard, teal, tufted duck and, recently, red-breasted merganser are among the birds which breed around the lakes, while grey wagtail and common sandpiper may be seen at the waterside. In winter, the lakes provide shelter for large roosts of gulls but probably the most dramatic visitors are the beautiful wild whooper swan. Occasionally

Bewick's swan may be seen on the winter lakes, or a low shape in the water might be a black-necked or Slavonian grebe, a black-throated, red-throated or great northern diver; diving birds, however, are most likely to be represented by goosander or goldeneye, pochard or tufted duck.

The core of the Lakeland fells is a great uplifted dome of slates rent by volcanic lavas and baked by the heat of cooling granite, covered by later slates and limestones, raised up and eroded by time and weather, shattered and sculpted by ice. The basic shape of the modern fells seems to have been cut when the raised dome shed radiating rivers. These cut down faster than the overall erosion so that

Langdale Pikes, towering above the dale, are characteristic of the heart of the National Park.

their pattern was superimposed upon the core rocks. In repeated glaciations the valleys were scoured by ice, plucking the rocks from the steep sides, carving into the plateaus to form the peaks and knife-edge ridges we know, while frost split and shivered the standing rock to fall in long slopes of scree. Each different rock was eroded differently, and much of the wonderful variety of the fells lies in the rich confusion of those rocks.

On the mountain tops exposure may be severe – these are bitter sites on which to survive, where snow may fall from mid-September to May or even into early June, where winds are as dangerous to plants from their drying effects as from sheer destructive force or biting cold. Yet, even among the high crags, plants grow; dwarf willow may mature, carrying catkins a mere 2mm long on a shrub which is only 2.5cm tall. On ledges and screes, in gullies and corries, a trickle of water may encourage flowers wherever the site is safe from sheep. Alpine lady's-mantle, alpine saw-wort, purple, yellow, mossy and starry saxifrage, roseroot and mountain sorrel grow with coastal plants, designed to cope with exposure, such as thrift, sea campion and sea plantain. In well-sheltered sites shade-tolerant plants may grow, such as water avens, wood anemone, wood crane's-bill, wood-sorrel, great woodrush and a variety of ferns, with globeflower or mountain avens, moss campion, alpine catchfly, alpine scurvygrass, shrubby cinquefoil and lesser meadow-rue, holly and parsley fern, brittle bladder-fern or oblong woodsia. Like the specialities of the lakes below, many of these plants are glacial relicts.

Bearberry, bilberry, cranberry, cloudberry and cowberry occur on the moors and bogs, where wet spreads of *Sphagnum* mosses may be decorated with all three British sundews, common butterwort, bog-rosemary and, here and there, the tiny rare bog orchid.

To match the wealth of plant life is a fine variety of insects. The distinctive emperor moth may often be seen on the heather moors while the northern influence which characterises much of the wildlife may be recognised in another heather feeder, the northern eggar. Another distinctive northern species is the mountain ringlet butterfly, a small high-upland species which uses mat-grass as a food plant and which only flies when the sun shines.

These, and other insects, spiders and small invertebrates make up much of the diet of birds such as wheatear and ring ouzel, while carrion on the sheep walks encourages raven, buzzard, and golden eagle. Peregrine, too, hunt across the moorlands, watchful for red grouse or smaller prey, and merlin might hawk after meadow pipit and skylark.

Thousands of people use the park for recreational pastimes; for those who look, the Lake District National Park in its range from mountain top to seashore has a wealth of wildlife and beauty perhaps unparalleled in the country.

Lancelot Clark Storth: a fine wooded pavement.

Lancelot Clark Storth

Permit only; 56.2ha; CTNC reserve
Limestone pavement, woodland and scrub
Spring, summer

Where HERVEY consists of flat scree and fragmentary pavement, and ASBY SCAR has wide pavements pocketed with basins, the pavements of Lancelot Clark Storth are generally of massive clints with long fissured grikes more reminiscent of parts of GAIT BARROWS (Lancashire). Within the woodland, which may be dense and impenetrable, are six separate pavements stepping up the slopes with an altitude range of some 100–250m. The pavements form wooded clearings within the woodland or, at the higher levels, may lie among bracken and heather where glacial soils around the rock have been leached of nutrients by filtering rain.

In the grassland on and around the limestone pavements are typical colourful plants such as lady's bedstraw, oxeye daisy, common milkwort and wild thyme, with biting stonecrop, common valerian, common spotted-orchid and dropwort. Trees and shrubs grow in the grikes and sometimes tangle across the clints in a superb mix of species such as ash, blackthorn, bramble and birch, bird cherry, elm, hawthorn, hazel and holly, ivy, juniper, oak, wild rose, rowan, whitebeam and yew. The wooded pavements, as a group, have been evaluated as among the richest in the British Isles.

The whole range of variation is superb; common cow-wheat and bilberry may signal the change to more acid soils yet lie within a few metres of species in the pavements such as wall lettuce, ploughman's-spikenard and splendid sprays of hard shield-fern; the sun may slant through the leaves of lime-loving trees to fall on acid plants such as heather and bracken; the massive clints may lie grey, bare and open to the sky or, beneath the trees, be moist and green with mosses.

Birds as different as wren and woodcock, goldcrest and curlew are recorded here, together with warblers, treecreeper and long-tailed tit.

Loughrigg Fell Nature Walk

NY 375047; 4km; NT
Fell and farmland trail
Leaflet from NT information centres
Spring, early summer

From Ambleside the trail crosses the river and climbs the slopes of Loughrigg Fell before swinging back to the start. Upland, farmland, woodland and riverside wildlife may be seen at various points on the circular walk.

Low Park Bothy Observation Hides

Permit only; FC
Bird and deer hides
Permit from Head Forester, Millfield Lodge, Hutton Roof, Penrith
All year

The hides overlook a series of small ponds at which waterfowl, red deer and a variety of other animals may be seen.

Meathop Moss

Permit only; 48ha; CTNC reserve
Raised bog
Spring, summer

The bog still retains the characteristic plants: bog asphodel, white beak-sedge, cranberry, bog-rosemary, heather and cross-leaved heath. Insects include emperor, northern eggar, Manchester treble-bar and purple-bordered gold moths.

Moor House

NY 730325; 4000ha; NCC reserve
Blanket bog and sheep walk
Permit required off public paths
Leaflets from NCC
Early summer

On a clear summer's day the reserve may show well the huge areas of blanket peat mire and the long valleyed slopes of grassland to the west. But this is not typical. It rains or snows for about two-thirds of the year.

This is a western flank of the Pennines where peat fills the drift-covered dip slope of a limestone scarp which faces across the Vale of Eden. The glacial drift is impervious to water and has held up drainage to form the peats, 2–8m deep, across it. The drier areas are spreads of hare's-tail cotton-grass and heather, varied with cloudberry, crowberry and bilberry, which change, on the high plateau of Knock Fell, for instance, to areas where common cotton-grass and heath rush replace the heather or, where the peat lies wetter, to mires of common cotton-grass and deergrass with *Sphagnum* mosses, heather, cross-leaved heath and plants such as round-leaved sundew and bog asphodel.

The scarp slopes on the Eden Valley side are typical sheep walks with steep grasslands cut by tumbling becks where limestone outcrops enrich the shallow turf or deeper soils carry more acid grasses. This is the highest area of carboniferous limestone in the country, rising to 750m and capped on the fells by thick layers of sandstone. Exposures of the rock are rich in plants such as spring sandwort and mossy saxifrage while old lead workings, in which the reserve abounds, add alpine penny-cress and alpine scurvygrass, together with autumn gentian and mountain pansy. High-level springs and streamlets may be sites for mountain plants such as alpine foxtail, pale forget-me-not and starry saxifrage, while lime-rich mires contain a fine variety of sedges together with marsh saxifrage, hairy stonecrop, three-flowered rush and grass-of-Parnassus.

Ring ouzel, meadow pipit, wheatear and dipper nest. Red grouse are present in some numbers, and breeding waders include curlew, lapwing, golden plover, snipe and common sandpiper. Among the insects recorded here are two montane moths, northern dart and red carpet.

The River Brathay near Ambleside.

Nether Wasdale Nature Trail

NY 147048; 5.5km; CTNC
Lakeland trail
Leaflet from CTNC
Spring, early summer

Beside Wastwater, where mallard, red-breasted merganser and common sandpiper may be seen, the trail includes woodland, marsh and bog with dramatic views to the fells where buzzard, peregrine and raven ride the wind.

North Fen

Permit only; 1.6ha; NCC reserve
Small wetland
Spring, summer

The reserve shows an interesting range from open water through reedswamp and sedgebeds to a wet scrubland. Common reed and bulrush, tufted-sedge, greater tussock-sedge, bottle sedge and bladder-sedge grade into a varied wetland which includes purple moor-grass and bog myrtle.

Park Wood

Permit only; 15ha; NCC reserve
Limestone woodland
Spring, early summer

The ash woodland is well lit and contains dense areas of hazel, varied with field maple, and an attractive ground cover including herb-Paris and common twayblade. The shrubby nature of the wood is particularly good for bird life.

Pennine Way

NY 698489–815286; 50km; CC
Part of long-distance way
Leaflet from CC or booklet from HMSO shops
Spring, summer

The trail runs from the county boundary near Alston and winds among the upland moors to swing east and cross into County Durham just south of the vast Cow Green Reservoir. A superb example of high peat moorland is crossed in the course of the trail, including the huge high tract of MOOR HOUSE.

Ravenglass

Permit only; 383ha; CCC reserve
Duneland peninsula
Spring, summer

Towards the tip of the peninsula a deep spread of nettles, docks and ragworts caps an area of dunes overlooking the estuary, the beach and the inner dune slacks. The gullery, a dense cover of plants encouraged by guano, is sited like some ancient fort where guards can watch for enemies approaching. This was once one of the largest colonies of black-headed gull in Europe and the site of important research. The reserve is closed to visitors for the last two weeks of May, the peak hatching time.

Ravenglass also contains a superb range of dune features, together with shingle, saltmarsh and inter-tidal mud. The large central slack areas are surrounded by vegetated and open dunes, with the long beach of the Irish Sea to the west and the wonderful backdrop of the Lakeland fells to the east.

Cross Fell: jumbles of rock where the Pennine Way crosses the moorland.

The plant life is as rich and varied as the scenery and includes the uncommon Isle of Man cabbage on the shingle with characteristic saltmarsh plants such as glasswort, common sea-lavender and sea-purslane, towards its northern limit in Britain, in the saltmarsh. The duneland plants include both Portland spurge and sea spurge with sea bindweed and more unexpected species such as bloody crane's-bill, field gentian and carline thistle.

Besides the breeding black-headed gulls are colonies of other seabirds, including arctic, common, little and Sandwich tern, together with waders such as oystercatcher and ringed plover and wildfowl such as red-breasted merganser and shelduck. Wheatear and skylark nest in the grasslands while snipe and lapwing may be seen on the grazing marshes above the reserve. Other animals include a good population of adder and all six native amphibians, the freshwater pools holding breeding colonies of frog, common and natterjack toad, with great crested, palmate and smooth newt.

Roudsea Wood and Mosses

SD 335825 and 351802; 69ha; NCC reserve
Mixed woodland
Permit only off rights of way
Leaflet from NCC
Spring, early summer

Surrounded by peatland and saltmarsh, two ridges of slate and limestone are divided by a narrow alluvial valley to give a fascinating spectrum from acid woodland on the older slates, through the damp valley to lime-rich woodland and then to acid woodland again on the edge of the Holker Mosses.

The ridge of slate is a wood where oak and birch, rowan and holly stand above a rather thin understorey of hazel. The floor is generally dry, carpeted with wavy hair-grass and acid plants such as foxglove and hard fern, or with spreads of bracken where the trees are widely spaced; where the soil is wet alder shows above tussocks of purple moorgrass.

The limestone woodland is darker. Ash and oak are the main trees with birch, small-leaved lime and other lime species, with crab apple, wild cherry, a scatter of sycamore and occasional dark spreads of yew. The understorey is chiefly of hazel, with hawthorn and holly, thickets of blackthorn and shrubs such as buckthorn, guelder-rose and spindle. The ground cover contains a wealth of plants such as giant bellflower, columbine, herb-Paris and lily-of-the-valley, bird's-nest orchid and toothwort. More open areas contain species such as tor-grass, ploughman's-spikenard and pyramidal orchid.

To the west, dividing the limestone from the slates, is the narrow valley which lies between the ridges and contains a small tarn, where waterplantain and lesser water-plantain grow. It is floored with a damp mire rich in sedges such as greater and lesser tussock-sedge, brown sedge, bladder-sedge, cyperus sedge and large yellow-sedge at its only known station in Britain.

Animals include badger, roe deer and red squirrel, with occasional red deer and otter, and a variety of breeding birds such as redstart, sparrowhawk, tawny owl, woodcock, curlew, mallard and shelduck.

Round Hill Wood

SD 526909; 0.3ha; WdT
Small stand of mature trees
Spring, early summer

A small area of woodland on the edge of Kendal, the trees provide an important refuge for wildlife and harbour a well-established rookery.

Rusland Moss

Permit only; 25ha; NCC reserve
Wet and dry heath
Spring, summer

The moss has been partially cut and drained and invaded by Scots pine and scrub, but still contains typical areas of heather and cross-leaved heath with plants such as round-leaved sundew, bog myrtle, common and hare's-tail cottongrass, with royal fern in the willow carr and a fringe of fenlike marsh, rich in such species as hemp-agrimony, yellow iris, marsh lousewort, common valerian and dyer's greenweed.

Hare's-tail cottongrass, typical of the mosses.

St Bees Head

NX 959118; 5km; RSPB reserve
Spectacular sandstone cliffs
The cliffs are sheer and very dangerous; do not leave the footpath
Spring, summer

The cliff path climbs and winds above Cumbria's westernmost point, where a changing pattern of plants reflects the soils; common bird's-foot-trefoil, thrift, harebell and sheep's-bit, wild thyme and restharrow give way to sweeps of heather, bell heather and gorse with smaller plants such as tormentil and heath bedstraw while, here and there, bloody crane's-bill, kidney vetch, early-purple orchid, meadow saxifrage, orpine and rock samphire add their colours to the scene.

Above and beyond this spread of colour, birds sail on the wind – herring gull, kittiwake, fulmar: several thousand pairs of these seabirds nest on the ridged sandstone cliffs which also serve as breeding sites for auks, for guillemot and black guillemot, for razorbill and puffin. This is the only English colony of black guillemot but, unfortunately, neither it nor the puffin is plentiful – though their small numbers are balanced by several thousand pairs of guillemot, together with over 600 razorbill.

Other birds of the cliffs and the coastal strip include rock pipit, jackdaw, kestrel and occasionally raven, with corn bunting and linnet, stonechat, whitethroat and willow warbler, while sparrowhawk from the nearby woodlands, peregrine and merlin may hunt along the reserve. Waders such as curlew, oystercatcher and whimbrel may be seen moving along the line of the coast. Offshore birds such as terns, gannet and Manx and sooty shearwater may be seen, while arctic and great skua occur occasionally and, on the sea, there may be non-breeding common scoter and red-throated diver.

Scroggs Wood

SD 509908; 1.2ha; WdT
Riverside woodland
Spring, early summer

Sited on a broad meander of the River Kent, the mixed woodland provides an important wildlife oasis on the fringes of urban Kendal.

Siddick Pond

Permit only; 20.2ha; Allerdale DC reserve
Lake and reedbeds
All year

Lying close to the coast, the reed-fringed pool has a range of typical birds, such as mallard, little grebe and reed bunting, and is notable for passage birds and storm-blown vagrants.

Smardale Gill

Permit only; 12ha; CTNC reserve
Limestone woodland and disused railway line
Spring, early summer

Some 50 species of birds including goldcrest and redstart breed in the woodlands of ash and birch with aspen, hazel, oak, small-leaved lime and spindle, with occasional conifers. More open areas contain less common species such as bird's-eye primrose, fragrant orchid, melancholy thistle and common wintergreen.

South Walney

SD 215620; 92ha; CTNC reserves
Rough meadowland, sand dunes, saltmarsh and mudflats
Closed Monday except Bank Holidays
Booklets and nature trail leaflets from CTNC
All year

Built from glacial deposits, Walney Island is set at the mouth of MORECAMBE BAY (Lancashire), poised between the tides and the Furness peninsula. Above the deposits, sands have been blown to form a dune system in which lesser black-backed and herring gull have established one of the largest colonies in Europe. The dunes are part of an area which includes wet and dry meadowland, fresh-water marsh, open pools, shingle and saltmarsh, low-tide muds and high-tide spreads of water: an enormous range of habitat reflected by the plant life and encouraging an excellent range of birds.

Glasswort, sea aster, sea-lavender, lax-flowered sea-lavender and sea-purslane grow on the mudflats. Sands or shingles hold such coastal species as sea beet, sea bindweed and sea campion, sea-holly, sea-milkwort, sea rocket and sea spurge, with Portland spurge, yellow horned-poppy and thrift. Further inland a total contrast is provided by acid, marshy grassland where heather and cross-leaved heath are seen, grading into drier heath bed-straw, sheep's sorrel and tormentil, gorse and spreads of bracken. Ground disturbed by gravel working contains some fascinating plants: viper's-bugloss, ploughman's-spikenard and henbane.

Besides the thriving colony of lesser black-backed and herring gull are smaller numbers of greater black-backed gull. Other breeding species include land birds such as lapwing, meadow pipit and skylark, together with mallard, shelduck and moorhen, oystercatcher, ringed plover and the most southerly breeding colony of eider on Britain's west coast. Wintering flocks include thousands of oystercatcher with large numbers of mallard, teal and wigeon and other waders such as curlew, grey plover, redshank and turnstone.

Spruce Knott Observation Tower

Permit only; FC
Wildlife hide
Permit from Chief Forester, Grizedale, Hawkshead, Ambleside
Spring, early summer

Overlooking Wood Moss Tarn, a haven for wild-fowl and a grazing and watering site for red and roe deer, the hide may be booked for morning or evening sessions.

White Moss Common Nature Walk

NY 348065; 1.2km; NT
Woodland, fell and farmland walk
Leaflet from NT information centre
Spring, early summer

Lake, stream, woodland, open fell and pasture land combine to provide a picture of Cumbrian Lakeland, rich in scenery and bird life.

St Bees Head: weathered red sandstone cliffs provide nest sites for many seabirds.

Derbyshire

Derbyshire's natural landscapes range from the wild open moorlands of the north to the flat lowlands of the Trent Valley in the south. Framed within the county is the southernmost extension of the Pennines, the Peak District, making it the meeting place of many southern and northern plants and animals and thus giving a unique flavour to the area's wildlife. The natural contrasts between the north and south of the county are accentuated by long-established man-made differences in land use, exploitation of mineral resources and density of population.

South of the Trent the land is used mostly for agriculture, and retains little of the forest which originally covered it. The Trent Valley itself is exploited for its sand and gravel deposits. Worked-out pits, if they have not been filled with ash from one of the power stations which line the river banks, fill with water and provide valuable refuges for wildfowl migrating along the valley and for a range of breeding wetland birds. HILTON GRAVEL PITS forms a link in a chain of such sites. Reservoirs, when not over-used for recreation, are also important nesting and resting sites for wildfowl, as at Staunton Harold where part of the adjoining SPRING WOOD has been set aside as a reserve.

Eastern Derbyshire, formerly covered by forest, lies largely on coal measures rocks, which give rather heavy, acid soils. Today agriculture, industry and coal mining all coexist, and as a result the area is densely populated. Little natural vegetation has survived except for small pockets unsuitable for agriculture: OAKERTHORPE reserve forms one of these sites, where spring lines along a stream have created a marsh with fringing woodland. The extreme north-east is intensively cultivated, but small areas with semi-natural vegetation exist in disused quarries. Probably the only remnants of natural vegetation are in gorges developed in the limestone, the best known being Cresswell Crags, famous for the prehistoric remains found in its caves.

Travelling westwards the land rises and agriculture becomes less intensive with more permanent pastures. Woodlands are increasingly common, particularly in stream valleys: OGSTON WOODLANDS is typical of them. Once probably supporting mainly oak, it now contains a mixture of oak, ash, elm, sycamore and other trees and has a well-developed herb layer, dominated in spring by carpets of bluebell.

Most of north and west Derbyshire forms part of THE PEAK NATIONAL PARK. There are two distinct regions in the park: the Dark Peak, made by a horseshoe of millstone grit rocks, predominantly forming high moorlands, which encircle the White Peak, a carboniferous limestone massif dissected by the Derbyshire Dales.

The lower slopes and valleys of the millstone grit were originally covered with woodlands, mainly sessile oak, but the majority of these have been replaced by permanent pasture in the valleys and sheep-grazed heather moorland above. A few woodlands still remain, one of the best being LADYBOWER WOOD, and have a distinctive upland character, in sharp contrast to the oakwoods of the lowlands. Above about 300m the moors stretch virtually unbroken, a pattern of drab greens and browns, of heather and crowberry, with great spreads of cottongrass in the wetter areas; the moorland turns briefly purple in August when the heather blooms. Birds provide the greatest natural history interest of these uplands, particularly birds of prey which still maintain a foothold despite pesticide poisoning and increased disturbance from visitors. A large area of the wildest region, the KINDER–BLEAKLOW UPLANDS, forms a fascinating moorland reserve.

The richest wildlife area in Derbyshire is undoubtedly the White Peak, the limestone heart of the National Park. Much of the area is permanent pasture and hay meadow, but often supporting a much greater range of common wild plants than in the lowlands. Incised into this limestone plateau are the Dales, steep-sided valleys, all originally cut by streams but now largely dry, except for those containing the main rivers of the Peak – the Wye, Lathkill and Dove. The Dales have been less affected by man than other parts of the Peak, but past lead mining, limestone quarrying, wood cutting for fuel and extensive sheep grazing have modified them all to some extent. Today the original wooded sides are a mosaic of grass, scrub and woodland, interspersed with rocky crags and spoil heaps left by mining. Each of these habitats has its own uncommon plants. The grasslands may contain bloody crane's-bill, Jacob's-ladder, globeflower or mossy saxifrage. Scrub, often of hazel, has its own associated flora including columbine and lily-of-the-valley, while woodland, although usually dominated by ash and elm, often includes whitebeam, yew and bird cherry. On the old lead mine spoils tips grow characteristic spring sandwort and alpine penny-cress.

Among the best of the Derbyshire sites for its wildlife interest is Lathkill Dale (DERBYSHIRE DALES); its river is fed by deep-seated springs, but the upper reaches completely disappear at intervals. There are several extensive reserves along the River Wye, the largest being MILLER'S DALE, where the daleside includes grassland, scrub and woodland, each with its own characteristic plants and animals.

TREVOR ELKINGTON

Black Rocks

Permit only; 0.5ha; DNT reserve
Scrub and grassland
Spring, early summer

Old mine spoil heaps encourage lead-tolerant species such as spring sandwort and moonwort. Dark green fritillary butterfly and small elephant hawkmoth, Mother Shipton and gold spangle moth are among the invertebrate species that have been recorded at this site.

Blake Moor

Permit only; 6ha; DNT reserve
Disused railway line
Can be overlooked from right of way at SK 153628
Spring, early summer

A feature of the reserve is its wealth of ferns which include black and green spleenwort, brittle bladder-fern, hart's-tongue, lemon-scented and limestone fern, hard shield-fern and limestone polypody.

Broadhurst Edge Wood

Permit only; 6ha; DNT reserve
Mixed woodland
Spring, early summer

Oak, with birch, rowan, Scots pine, beech and sycamore stands above moorland heather, bilberry, cowberry and crowberry. There is an interesting selection of the commoner woodland birds.

Brockholes Wood

Permit only; 9ha; DNT reserve
Mixed woodland
Spring, early summer

Oak, birch and rowan over wavy hair-grass, purple moor-grass, bilberry and heather form a woodland which is reminiscent of the ancient forest cover.

Broomfield

Permit only; 1.5km; Derbyshire College of Agriculture reserve
Disused railway line
Permit from the Principal, Derbyshire College of Agriculture, Broomfield, Morley, Derbyshire
Spring, summer

An amazing degree of variation in so small an area makes this a most interesting reserve where there is not only a range from the plants of disturbed ground on areas of ballast, through grassland, scrub and marsh, to woodland, but also a variety of soils. The range from acid to lime-rich soils encourages some 280 plant species including locally uncommon heath-grass and bitter vetch, downy oat-grass and cowslip, fairy flax and wild carrot.

Buxton Country Park

SK 050727; 40ha; Buxton and District Civic Assn
Broad-leaved woodland
Leaflets and nature trail guides from interpretative centre
Spring, early summer

The park centres around the show cave of Poole's Cavern but also includes a sizeable spread of mixed woodland. Ash, beech, elm and sycamore stand above a rich ground cover and are varied with occasional clearings and meadow lands where plants such as mountain everlasting and mountain pansy may be found.

Cheedale

Permit only; 24ha; DNT reserve
Ash woodland and limestone grassland
Spring, summer

Birch, bird cherry, elm, rowan and whitebeam grow in the fine ash woodland with blackthorn, buckthorn, dogwood and guelder-rose. There is a rich ground cover and the wide range of habitat encourages a considerable variety of birds.

Cromford Canal

SK 333544–350520; 3km; DNT reserve
Derelict canal
Spring, summer

From the Cromford Canal, raised above the River Derwent, there are splendid views over the valley, and the sheltered quiet of this unrestored waterway, with no pleasure boats to stir the mud, makes it a place of peace and beauty.

Rich colour is laid clear through the canal, from emergent plants at the water's edge to waterweed growing across the bottom. Three-spined stickleback or roach may be seen in the shallows, or perhaps there might be the crocodile shape of a young pike, basking in a pool of sunlight.

The plant life is richly varied along the length of the canal with dense stands of reed sweet-grass foresting the whole width, with a fringe of lesser pond-sedge and spreads of water horsetail or with broad-leaved pondweed showing the slow flow of water. Branched and unbranched bur-reed, bulrush, square-stalked St John's-wort, water forget-me-not, water mint and yellow iris lift at the water's edge or form small rich marshes, mixed with reed sweet-grass, in the shallower parts of the canal while the towpath is dressed with meadowsweet, hemp-agrimony, great willowherb, thistles, buttercups and vetches.

Arrowhead, flowering-rush and water-plantain are among the most beautiful water plants, flowering after the vivid spring blaze of marsh-marigold, while clumps of meadow crane's-bill add further colour to the towpath. The shrubs and hedgerow trees, the leaning alders and the shaded woods of the farmland complete a very attractive scene.

In summer the reserve is alive with movement — the movement of water-snails, of water-insects, of fish, of waterbirds and, above the canal, of songbirds, butterflies, hoverflies and dragonflies. In winter finches and other small birds come to feed on the plant seeds, with redpoll and siskin foraging in the alders and birch.

The Matlock Field Club have made a preliminary survey of the reserve and have published an exemplary booklet describing it. Permission must be obtained from the Derbyshire Naturalists' Trust before removing any plant or animal material for educational or scientific purposes.

Derbyshire Dales

SK 203662 (Lathkill Dale) and SK 141725
(Monk's Dale); 234ha; NCC reserve
Limestone valleys, streams, woodlands, cliffs,
screes and grasslands
Permit only off rights of way
Leaflets from NCC
Spring, summer

This composite reserve consists of five of the best and most representative dales on the carboniferous limestone of the Peak District. Between them they safeguard and demonstrate examples of the whole range of species and habitats associated with that formation. Two of the five — Lathkill Dale and Monk's Dale — are described here.

To look at the river in Lathkill Dale in summer it is hard to imagine that, when the last ice age released its water, this gentle stream was a roaring torrent which carved the shape of the valley. After the land had warmed and the waters subsided, woodland would have spread back across the hills and valleys until cleared by man for farming and fuel. Despite this, Lathkill Dale still contains much woodland.

Some of that woodland has been modified; beech, Scots pine and sycamore were planted and the sycamore has grown on as secondary woodland, but much of the lower valley is filled with ash woods, mixed with species such as rowan, buckthorn, the uncommon rock whitebeam, wych elm, guelder-rose, hawthorn, hazel, field maple and privet. The ground cover contains plants such as water avens, nettle-leaved bellflower, lily-of-the-valley, yellow star-of-Bethlehem and mezereon as well as much dog's mercury. Green hellebore and bird's-nest orchid occur in the dale, though outside the reserve.

The grasslands are full of characteristic species such as common bird's-foot-trefoil, marjoram, quaking-grass and common rock-rose, with dropwort and wild thyme.

The south-facing slopes are extremely rich, with up to 54 species of plant recorded in a square metre, a contrast with the plateau edge above, where plants such as wavy hair-grass, sheep's fescue, bilberry and heather grow.

Field garlic and spring cinquefoil occur on the valley slopes while old mine spoil heaps, tainted with lead, show the characteristic spring sandwort, together with plants such as common spotted-

Lathkill Dale: a classic White Peak valley.

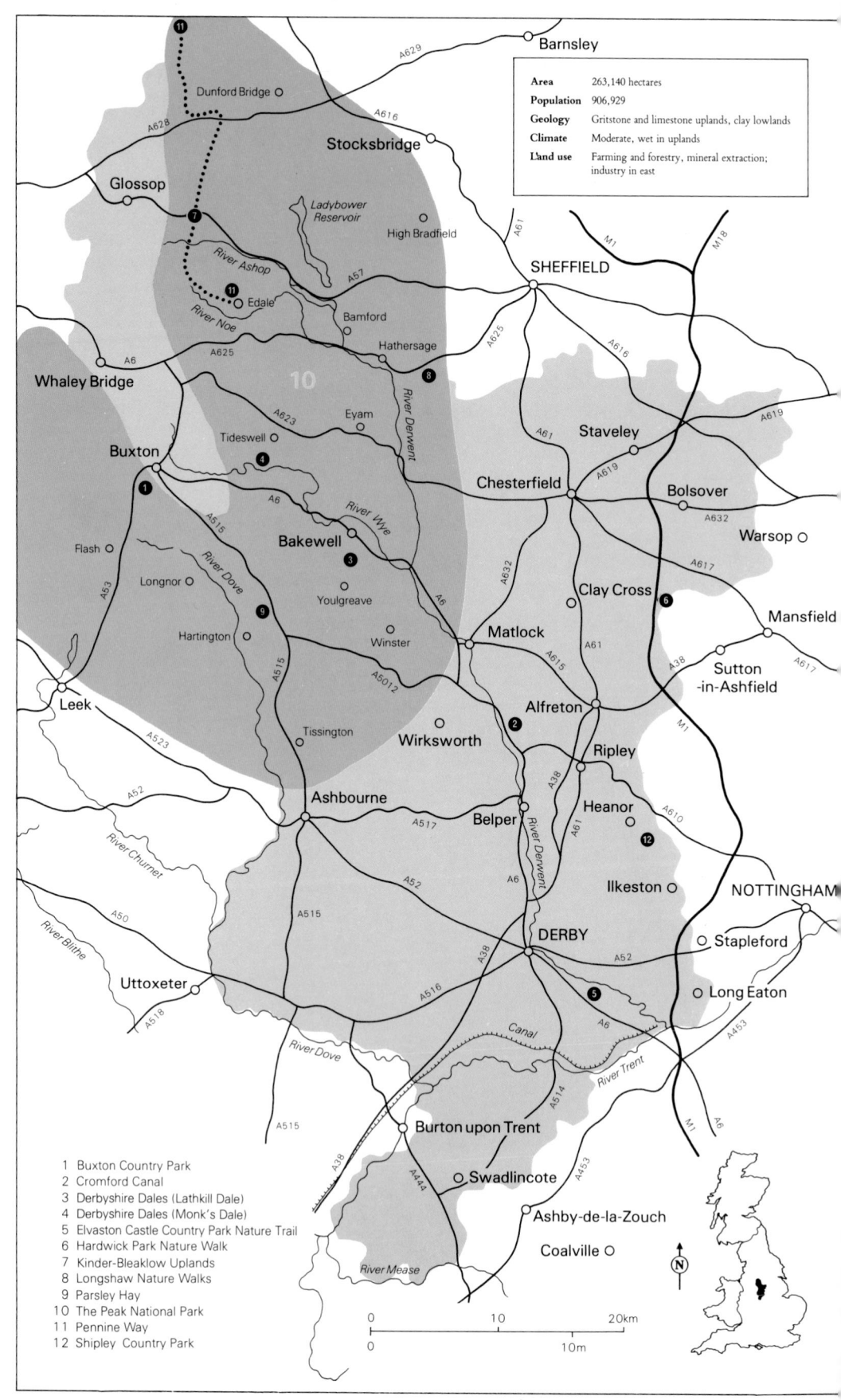

Barnsley

Area	263,140 hectares
Population	906,929
Geology	Gritstone and limestone uplands, clay lowlands
Climate	Moderate, wet in uplands
Land use	Farming and forestry, mineral extraction; industry in east

Dunford Bridge

Stocksbridge

Glossop

Ladybower
Reservoir

High Bradfield

River Ashop

SHEFFIELD

Edale

River Noe

Bamford

Hathersage

Whaley Bridge

10

Staveley

Eyam

River Derwent

Buxton

Tideswell

Chesterfield

Bolsover

Warsop

Bakewell

Flash

Longnor

Youlgreave

River Dove

Clay Cross

Mansfield

River Wye

Winster

Matlock

Sutton
-in-Ashfield

Hartington

Leek

Tissington

Wirksworth

Alfreton

Ripley

Ashbourne

Belper

River Derwent

Heanor

Ilkeston

NOTTINGHAM

River Churnet

Uttoxeter

DERBY

Stapleford

River Blithe

Long Eaton

River Dove

Burton upon Trent

Canal

River Trent

Swadlincote

Ashby-de-la-Zouch

Coalville

River Mease

1 Buxton Country Park
2 Cromford Canal
3 Derbyshire Dales (Lathkill Dale)
4 Derbyshire Dales (Monk's Dale)
5 Elvaston Castle Country Park Nature Trail
6 Hardwick Park Nature Walk
7 Kinder-Bleaklow Uplands
8 Longshaw Nature Walks
9 Parsley Hay
10 The Peak National Park
11 Pennine Way
12 Shipley Country Park

0   10   20km

0   10m

N

orchid. Rock outcrops, too, have their special plants such as thale cress, fine-leaved sandwort, rue-leaved and mossy saxifrage and common whitlowgrass, while down in the valley bottom are stands of Jacob's-ladder.

Monk's Dale has been less changed than Lathkill Dale and contains a superb range of woodland, scrub, grassland, scree and rocks, with spring-fed flushes and an area of marsh. The plants include such varied species as herb-Paris and narrow-leaved cottongrass, globeflower, bloody crane's-bill and grass-of-Parnassus.

Monk's Dale in the Derbyshire Dales: scrub invades the long slopes of limestone grassland in this beautiful dale, relatively untouched by the hand of man.

clearings are light enough for bluebell, primrose, ramsons and violets. The stream and lake attract mallard and tufted duck, grey wagtail and king-fisher, while woodland species include blackcap, garden and willow warbler, nuthatch and lesser spotted woodpecker.

Drakelow Wildfowl Reserve

Permit only; 8.8ha; CEGB reserve
Islanded lagoons, scrub and farmland
Booklet from CEGB
All year

The reserve lies in a loop of the River Trent which increases the open-water area and helps to attract wetland birds to the site. A field centre and an educational nature trail have also been established here.

Elvaston Castle Country Park Nature Trail

SK 413332; 1.5km; DCC
Woodland and wetland trail
Leaflets from park centre or DCC
Spring, early summer

Oak, birch, ash and beech stand above an under-storey, thick with rhododendron, but woodland

Fenny Bentley Cutting

Permit only; 3ha; DNT reserve
Disused cutting
Can be overlooked from right of way at SK 170505
Spring, early summer

The reserve contains plants characteristic of damp rich meadowland: wild basil, cowslip, primrose, yellow rattle, common spotted-orchid, common twayblade, wild angelica, water avens, ragged-Robin and meadowsweet.

Hardwick Park Nature Walk

SK 453640; 2.5km; NT
Parkland trail
Leaflet from site
Spring, early summer

The trail circles through ponded parkland with a wetland area where reed and willow warbler breed in a sanctuary rich in plants such as bulrush, mare's-tail and common spike-rush.

Hilton Gravel Pits

Permit only; 29ha; DNT reserve
Worked-out gravelpits
All year

At Hilton the old river gravels of the Trent were dug to form a series of pools which now give a splendid range of habitats from open water to woodland. Generally the area seems rich and damp, with swamp and marshy clearings beside an islanded tree-lined lake, but raised banks between the wetlands are dry enough for small woodlands of oak, hawthorn and birch or have been planted with pine. Willow is the main tree of the wet woodlands, a wide mix of species dominated by crack willow, of which there are some very large examples. Dense cover, thick with common nettle, bramble and rosebay willowherb, grades to a low willow swamp edged with plants such as gipsywort and cyperus sedge.

The glades, once sedimentation lagoons, are damp and colourful, shrubbed with low birch and willow saplings, thick with rushes, sedges, horsetails and plants such as the tall marsh thistle with a fine show of southern marsh-orchid, common spotted-orchid and their hybrids. Like the glades, small pools are sheltered among the trees, mirroring stands of bulrush, water horsetail and water-plantain.

The main body of water is a breeding site for diving birds such as little and great crested grebe and is big enough to draw winter waterfowl. Bewick's swan, black-necked and Slavonian grebe have been recorded; bearded tit and merlin have been seen on the reserve; and some 120 bird species have been recognised.

Great crested and smooth newt, frog and common toad breed in the smaller pools, together with a good variety of dragonflies, while butterflies include common blue, brimstone, small copper and painted lady, and eyed hawkmoth, pale oak eggar, small bloodvein and scallop shell moths have been recorded.

Hopton Tunnel Cutting

Permit only; 2ha; DNT reserve
Disused railway cutting
Spring, early summer

The steep limestone cuttings support plants such as wild basil, thale cress, lady's-mantle and burnet saxifrage. A good variety of insects includes common blue, small copper and painted lady butterflies with moths such as six-spot burnet and pimpinel pug.

Kinder–Bleaklow Uplands

SK 090929; 4500ha; PPJPB
High acid uplands
Summer

The road from Glossop winds south eastwards across the moors to Sheffield; running east–west between Holden Clough and Lady Clough it crosses the watershed between the streams which run back to Glossop or on to the Ladybower Reservoir; here the PENNINE WAY crosses from Bleaklow to Kinder Scout; to north and south lie great areas of peat bog. This is the Dark Peak: a huge upland mass of millstone grit, carved by valleys, bordered by edges where the hard rock stands in crags above the land below. The tops are plateaus, wide spreads of blanket mire, deep peat eroding to leave a complex of gullies and hummocks. The gullies wind and twist, cut down to the bare rock and walled by slopes of peat higher than a man.

To gain an idea of the uplands one might follow the Snake Path up the Ashop Clough, to join the Pennine Way and climb to Kinder Scout, follow the Edge toward Fairbrook Naze and look out over a quite magnificent prospect of rock, valley and moorland. The grazed slopes are mainly grassland, dissected by streams draining the peatlands above. The peat tops are thick with a springy carpet of bilberry, crowberry, cowberry, a damp moorland spread of hare's-tail and common cottongrass. Bracken shows on some of the drier slopes and contrasts with the purple of heather. Cloudberry, the only real mountain plant here, is near its southern limit in Britain and can occur in abundance.

The uplands are a site for birds such as curlew, dunlin, red grouse, merlin, ring ouzel and golden plover. Apart from the curlew these are all moorland and mountain birds, and their distribution in Britain is limited to areas of upland moor.

Kinder Downfall plunges from the edge of Kinder Scout.

The Dark Peak is of great importance as one of the best examples of blanket mire in the country but, sadly, is an area where peat hags are eroding: active peat formation no longer occurs and the huge bogs are in a state of degeneration.

Ladybower Wood

Permit only; 16ha; DNT reserve
Woodland, scree and crags
Spring, early summer

A remnant of old upland forest, the woodland is oak with birch and rowan over acid grasses and bluebell, lesser celandine and wood-sorrel. More open areas, the massive block screes and the crags, contain heather, bilberry, cowberry and crowberry.

Longcliffe Cutting

Permit only; 1ha; DNT reserve
Disused cutting
Can be overlooked from right of way at SK 235557
Spring, early summer

The reserve is dominated by broken limestone crags thick with woodland. A more open slope carries a population of hutchinsia.

Longshaw Nature Walks

SK 267800; various lengths; NT
Parkland, woodland and moorland
Leaflet from site or PPJPB information centres
Spring, summer

A fine range of gritstone habitats – open moorland and wooded river valley as well as the pond and meadowland, the plantations and grazing land of the park – provide a rich show of plants and birds.

Miller's Dale

Permit only; 64ha; DNT reserves
Limestone quarries and old lead mine spoil heaps, grassland, woodland and scrub
Spring, summer

Ash and wych elm in the woods stand above a scrub of hazel and guelder-rose, while the open hillsides support a typical limestone flora including common rock-rose, wild thyme, marjoram and common bird's-foot-trefoil, plants which attract butterflies such as common blue. The old quarries, too, have been colonised by these plants, along with oxeye daisy and wild rose.

Oakerthorpe

Permit only; 3ha; DNT reserve
Pond and marsh
Spring, summer

Derbyshire is noted for its uplands and its dales but, where the grits and limestones dip, some areas still keep their cover of coal measures. Oakerthorpe lies in just such a dip, less rich than the limestone, but richer than the grits. The woods which hedge the wetland are of field maple, hawthorn, birch and crab apple, above bluebell, wood-sorrel and yellow archangel. The wetland, though, is the most important feature of the reserve.

The artificial pond makes a strong contrast with the acid bogs and streams of the gritstones and is fringed by marshes of bulrush, soft and jointed rush and great willowherb. The damp grassland is rich in marshland species, such as wild angelica and meadowsweet, giving way to field scabious and oxeye daisy on the higher drier parts.

Although small, the reserve contains a good range of habitats, from tall trees through birch scrub, through dry and damp grassland to marsh and to water, crystal clear, which encourages an interesting variety of animals. Grass snakes frequent the marshy fringes, hunting for smaller creatures such as the breeding amphibians: frog, common toad and common newt. Some 75 species of birds have been recorded including woodland birds such as tawny owl, great spotted and lesser spotted woodpecker, woodland and scrub birds such as the warblers, blackcap, chiffchaff, whitethroat and lesser whitethroat, and wetland birds such as kingfisher, water rail, and sedge warbler. Butterflies include common blue, small copper and large skipper while among the moths is the uncommon latticed heath. The pool and marsh also attract such insects as brown hawker dragonfly and azure and large red damselflies.

Ogston Woodlands

Permit only; 32ha; DNT reserve
Mixed woodlands
Spring, early summer

The reserve constitutes one of the largest blocks of broad-leaved woodland in lowland Derbyshire – a stretch of valley woods with great variation. One area probably represents primary woodland here, an area with a continual woodland cover dating back to its recolonisation after the last ice age. Most of Ogston, however, has been changed and a variety of alien species has been planted. Trees such as beech and sycamore were introduced, shrubs such as rhododendron were probably planted for pheasant cover, and stands of conifers such as larch were established for their rapid growth. The effect is to give a wide variety of habitat in a very variable uneven-aged mixed wood. The primary woodland is oak with rowan and holly, on an area of very shallow soil over millstone grit, but most of the rest is a mix of oak, ash, beech, silver birch, wych elm and rowan, with alder along the valley bottom and with sycamore dominating some parts of the wood. The understorey varies from areas of impenetrable rhododendron to a more open and varied shrub layer which includes hazel and guelder-rose. The ground cover is equally varied, ranging from head-high bracken to springtime spreads of wood anemone, bluebell and wood-sorrel. Climbing corydalis, creeping-Jenny and moschatel are among the small plants, with species such as wood horsetail, wood speedwell and wood stitchwort, while the rocky narrow gorges cut by the stream are rich in ferns and mosses.

Snow on the fringes of the Peak National Park: Stannage Edge by the Hallam Moors.

A hide has been built, near some splendid huge old beech trees, which overlooks a small damp clearing. Some 70 species of birds have been recorded, together with a typical range of woodland mammals. The birds include spotted flycatcher, nuthatch and treecreeper, green and great spotted woodpecker, small birds such as tits and larger predators such as sparrowhawk and tawny owl.

Overdale

Permit only; 17ha; DNT reserve
Upland pasture
Spring, early summer

Spreads of bracken rise above plants such as foxglove and wood-sorrel, slopes of acid heath contain heather and crowberry, streams and small wetlands hold plants such as marsh violet, and a 3m waterfall encourages liverworts.

Parsley Hay

SK 147628; 3ha; DNT reserve
Limestone cutting
Spring, summer

On a small area of heath, heather and heath bedstraw contrast with such plants as cowslip and common rock-rose. A good variety of birds and insects may be seen.

The Peak National Park

See map; 140,378ha; PPJPB
Spectacular uplands and valleys
Leaflets from PPJPB
Spring, summer

The Peak National Park was the first in Britain and still characterises the basic concepts: most of the land remains in private hands but, by special agreements, the public can walk over many of the open moorlands; with the founding of the park in 1951, work to achieve 'the right to roam' was begun. In the south lie the farmlands and dales of the White Peak, in the north the horseshoe curve of moorland which dominates much of the park. This is the high land of peat bogs, of long cliffs of millstone grit, a desolate land where climbs are rewarded by views over huge stretches of open moor and deep-cut valleys.

The Dark Peak is a plateau, twice as high as the southern limestone, reaching over 600m on Kinder Scout. It curves away at its outer edges, sloping down to the plains of Cheshire and Staffordshire or the lowland spread of south Yorkshire while the inner edge, the curve which has been eroded to reveal the soft Edale shales and the limestone of the White Peak, stands as a broken line of gritstone cliffs. The slopes are generally grassland or heather moor, the plateau top a wide desert of peat.

To many people, a blanket bog conjures a picture of sweeps of heather patterned with cross-leaved heath, *Sphagnum* mosses and plumes of common cottongrass. The peat of the Dark Peak is dark indeed, for the plants which build up typical blanket bogs are long since dead, probably killed by pollution from the cities; *Sphagnum* moss remains may be found on the plateau but, in the main, the peatland itself is dying. Without a cover of plants, the peat is desiccated by wind – the rains which drench the plateau wash it away. Just as the gritstone plateau is dissected by stream-cut valleys so, in a miniature form, is the overlying peat. The exciting bleakness of the high Dark Peak lies in the deeply eroded hags of peat, the pattern of gullies cut down to the glittering gravels of millstone grit which frets the hummocks of peak like a twisting maze. The land is not wholly bare of vegetation: the islands of peat may be dressed with hare's-tail cottongrass, plants such as bilberry, cowberry, crowberry and occasional cloudberry may be found, heather and cross-leaved heath occur, while mat-grass and rushes are colonising the gullies.

Below the plateau, heather and bilberry grow thick on the upper slopes, giving way to spreads of grassland, mat-grass and purple moor-grass, and are varied with other moorland plants such as cross-leaved heath and bell heather. On the East Moor, the eastern arm of the gritstone horseshoe lying above the Derwent reservoirs, a hybrid of bilberry and cowberry occurs which has its main site on CANNOCK CHASE (Staffordshire); it is known from only a very few places, all in Midland Britain. The West Moor, too, holds an interesting range of plants, particularly those of wetter situations; fine wet mires can still be found with bog plants such as bog asphodel and cranberry, bogbean, marsh cinquefoil, heath spotted-orchid and northern marsh-orchid, together with their hybrids.

The Northern Moor, the KINDER—BLEAKLOW massif, is perhaps the least rich in plant life. It is higher and covered with dissected peat hags, but has strong populations of cloudberry and crowberry, together with almost pure spreads of bilberry. These high bleak moors are the most southerly site for good breeding numbers of many typical northern birds such as red grouse, curlew and dunlin.

On the White Peak the frowning rocks give way to a land where white stone walls are laid in patterns across the curves of a plateau of pale hard limestone, where spectacular dales have been cut down through the rock and where brilliant limestone flowers contrast with the sombre moors of the Dark Peak. The White Peak is less open to the public. The fields of the plateau are worked, for grazing and for fodder, but several of the dales are conserved and public footpaths run through them.

Ash seems to be the natural woodland cover, varied with shrubs such as hawthorn and hazel above a rich ground cover. Where woodland has been cleared hawthorn and hazel tend to invade unless grazing keeps the grassland open. Grassland, though, is now more widespread than scrub

and woodland cover and the sloping dale sides are patterns of green shallow pasture, filled with flowers, banded with scars of white stone. Each dale is subtly different from the next, whether through aspect, soil type or history, and the whole limestone complex of cliffs, screes, grasslands, scrub and woodlands, together with the rivers and marshy banks, contains a remarkable range of uncommon and beautiful species.

Rock exposures and screes, where pockets of soil encourage plants, might carry ferns such as rustyback, green spleenwort, brittle bladder-fern and limestone fern, with plants such as Nottingham catchfly and spring cinquefoil. Thale cress, hairy rock-cress and narrow-leaved bitter-cress might be found, with fine-leaved and slender sandwort, while old lead mine spoil heaps are coloured with spring sandwort and mountain pansy. Open or scrub-scattered grassland might contain dwarf thistle and tor-grass near to their northern limit, spreads of common rock-rose and kidney vetch and a wonderful range of lime-loving plants such as bloody crane's-bill and lesser meadow-rue, carline and musk thistle, marjoram, small scabious and dropwort. Damper soils may carry taller plants.

Where the grassland gives way to scrub woodland and ash woods, gorse, hazel and hawthorn, blackthorn, dogwood and yew might stand above plants such as sanicle, while the woodland proper is thick with dog's mercury. Ash is the main woodland type but here, too, are aspen, blackthorn and buckthorn, bird cherry, dogwood, elder and wych elm, guelder-rose, hawthorn, hazel, small-leaved lime and field maple, privet and spindle and several species of whitebeam. The woods may

Edale Moor: snow lies long on a typical Dark Peak peat hag.

contain both giant and nettle-leaved bellflower, with unusual plants such as yellow star-of-Bethlehem. Woodland may also cling to the steep river cliffs where yew and whitebeam stand above long curtains of mountain currant.

The park contains many other facets of wildlife interest but the marriage of Dark and White Peak scenery is one of the most fascinating aspects of central Britain. Sightseer, walker, naturalist or geologist – no one can fail to fall under the spell of the Peak.

Pennine Way

SE 078047–SK 124857; 30km; CC
Part of long-distance way
Spring, summer

Completing the crossing of the KINDER–BLEAKLOW peat bogs before dropping down to the trail's end at Edale, the way passes through the splendid moorland of the millstone grit before it gives way to the limestone of the Dales.

Risley Glebe

Permit only; 0.6ha; DNT reserve
Small damp meadowland
Can be overlooked from right of way at SK 461359
Spring, early summer

Surrounded by hedges and scrubbed with clumps of hawthorn, blackthorn, bramble, dogwood and elder, the damp pasture, drained by a small stream, contains an interesting variety of plants such as wild angelica, fleabane, cowslip, yellow rattle and adder's-tongue.

Selby

Permit only; 40ha; DNT reserve
Woodland, scrub and grassland
Spring, summer

Part of MILLER'S DALE.

Shipley Country Park

SK 426458; 400ha; DCC
Parkland, woodland and water
Leaflets from ranger post or DCC
All year

The most important conservation areas are centred at Mapperley Reservoir, where a hide is available and a nature trail has been established. Mallard, pochard, tufted duck and, occasionally, goldeneye and shoveler visit in winter while woodland birds include nuthatch and great spotted woodpecker.

Spring Wood

Permit only; 20ha; DNT reserve
Mixed woodland
All year

The main block of Spring Wood is a private commercially managed woodland standing above the bank which slopes down to Staunton Harold Reservoir. This bank has been colonised to the water's edge and now forms the reserve, a long narrow belt of woodland with some derelict pasture which has been planted with trees and shrubs in order to screen the approach to a hide overlooking part of the reservoir.

The reserve contains some fine areas of tall high-forest trees, of standard trees and of pure or almost pure stands of birch. The standards are chiefly oak with ash and alder above a rather thin understorey of hazel. Where the bank is dry, birch woodland grows over deep bracken and bramble under which carpets of bluebell and greater stitchwort show in spring; where streams drain down to the reservoir, the ash and alder stand above a richer ground cover of plants such as opposite-leaved golden-saxifrage, dog's mercury and enchanter's-nightshade, yellow pimpernel, wood-sorrel, sedges and ferns such as lady-fern and male-fern. Further variety is added by a stand of Scots pine, by an unexpected area of box beneath ash and oak trees and by spreads of dense rhododendron growing on the drier ground.

The big trees encourage birds such as lesser spotted woodpecker, nuthatch, treecreeper and tawny owl. The more shrubby areas attract summer warblers such as blackcap, whitethroat and garden warbler, or more uncommon visitors, for instance sedge and grasshopper warbler. Red-poll are usually present, reinforced in winter by flocks of goldfinch and siskin. Good numbers of great crested grebe and mute swan may be seen on the reservoir, gathered for their autumn moult. In winter, the waters form a sizeable gull roost and attract wildfowl such as pochard, shoveler, tufted duck, wigeon and occasional goldeneye.

The mammals include resident fallow deer, and the insects wetland species such as brown hawker dragonfly and woodland species such as hornet.

Tissington Station Cutting

Permit only; 2.4ha; DNT reserve
Limestone woodland, scrub and grassland
Can be overlooked from right of way at SK 182525
Spring, summer

Over 120 flowering plants have been recorded in a mix of ash woodland over plants such as giant bellflower, hawthorn and wild rose and grassland filled with cowslip and meadow crane's-bill. There are also marshy areas containing water avens and meadowsweet.

Watford Lodge

Permit only; 0.5ha; DNT reserve
Small pond
Spring, summer

The pond, fringed with bulrush, water-plantain, marsh-marigold and cuckooflower, has breeding newts, common toad and frog. The area is suitable for wetland birds and winter migrants.

Devon

From Atlantic-torn Hartland Point to the soft chalk of Beer in the south east, and from sea-level Dartmouth to the 666m summit of Dartmoor, Devon offers immense variety to the observer. Straddling the south west peninsula of England, with no higher ground to the west, it is bathed by the warm, moist air from over the Gulf Stream. Mildness is the climatic keynote, and softness the land's characteristic. Only on the most exposed western cliffs, and within Dartmoor's tor-ringed high plateau, do animals, plants and people have to struggle. In deep, narrow valleys sheltered even from the westerly wind, ferns and mosses give the oakwoods a sub-tropical luxuriance. Between the valleys massive Devon hedge banks shelter primroses, bluebells, marjoram and orchids. Copses support buzzard, raven and heron. Badgers trundle, and foxes dash, across lanes sunk below the fields by a thousand years of farming traffic.

Geologically Devon divides about the River Exe. West of it the bulk of the land is formed of slates and thin sandstones. They are old hard rocks, standing on end, interleaved in the south with the odd limestone, lava and volcanic ash. They lap around the great boss of the Dartmoor granite, which rises to high plateaus carrying peat up to 4m thick in places. The landscape thus formed is crossed from Dartmoor to the sea by a set of radiating rivers. The Taw flows north westwards to Barnstaple, the rest to the southern coast. The Teign and the Dart are largest; Avon, Erme, Yealm, Plym and Tavy have shorter runs to the sea. Tamar and Exe rise in Cornwall and Somerset respectively, both close to the north coast, but flow south either side of Dartmoor to the English Channel. East of the Exe, softer, younger rocks prevail. They run in procession from Exeter eastwards as new red sandstone with pebble beds, marls, greensand and chalk. This landscape is a succession of vales and flat-topped ridges capped by flint gravel, drained by the Otter, Axe, Sid and Yarty, smaller lowland streams meandering through water meadows with willows and alder.

Within this general pattern there are unique 'islands'. The lignites and clays of the Bovey Basin form a black-and-white sandwich well exposed in pits both new and abandoned. The china clay deposits of south west Dartmoor form a near-sterile landscape of their own, and the schists from Bolt Tail to Start Point are a southerly bastion protecting 96km of eastern coast from the Atlantic.

Devon is the only county in England with two separate coastlines. The north coast is entirely within the 'hard rock' landscape and all exposed to the Atlantic. Only the low entrance of the Taw–Torridge Estuary, with the great flat of BRAUNTON BURROWS across its entrance, relieves the continuous cliffline. LUNDY ISLAND is more exposed still, but houses the only puffins in the county. In contrast the southern and south eastern coast changes from hard to softer rock around the north end of Torquay, though the coastal character pivots about Start Point. To the west Atlantic attack means that rocky shores are narrow and exposed – only in the estuaries of Tamar, Plym, Yealm, Erme, Avon and Kingsbridge are sheltered shores found, and mud to support waders masks much of the bedrock within them. East of Start, beaches proliferate. The shingle of Start Bay supports its own flora, as do the remnant sand dunes at the mouth of the Exe. The Dart is the last narrow, steep-sided, oakwooded estuary. The Teign and the Exe are in wide shallow vales, with more mudbanks and sandbanks and hence bigger flocks of birds. The Otter and the Axe are now very small, much silted and saltmarshy. East of the Exe the cliffs are soft, crumbly and unstable. Landslips are common and the biggest – from Axmouth to Lyme Regis – forms a 14km-long reserve. The whole spectrum of seaboard habitat is within these

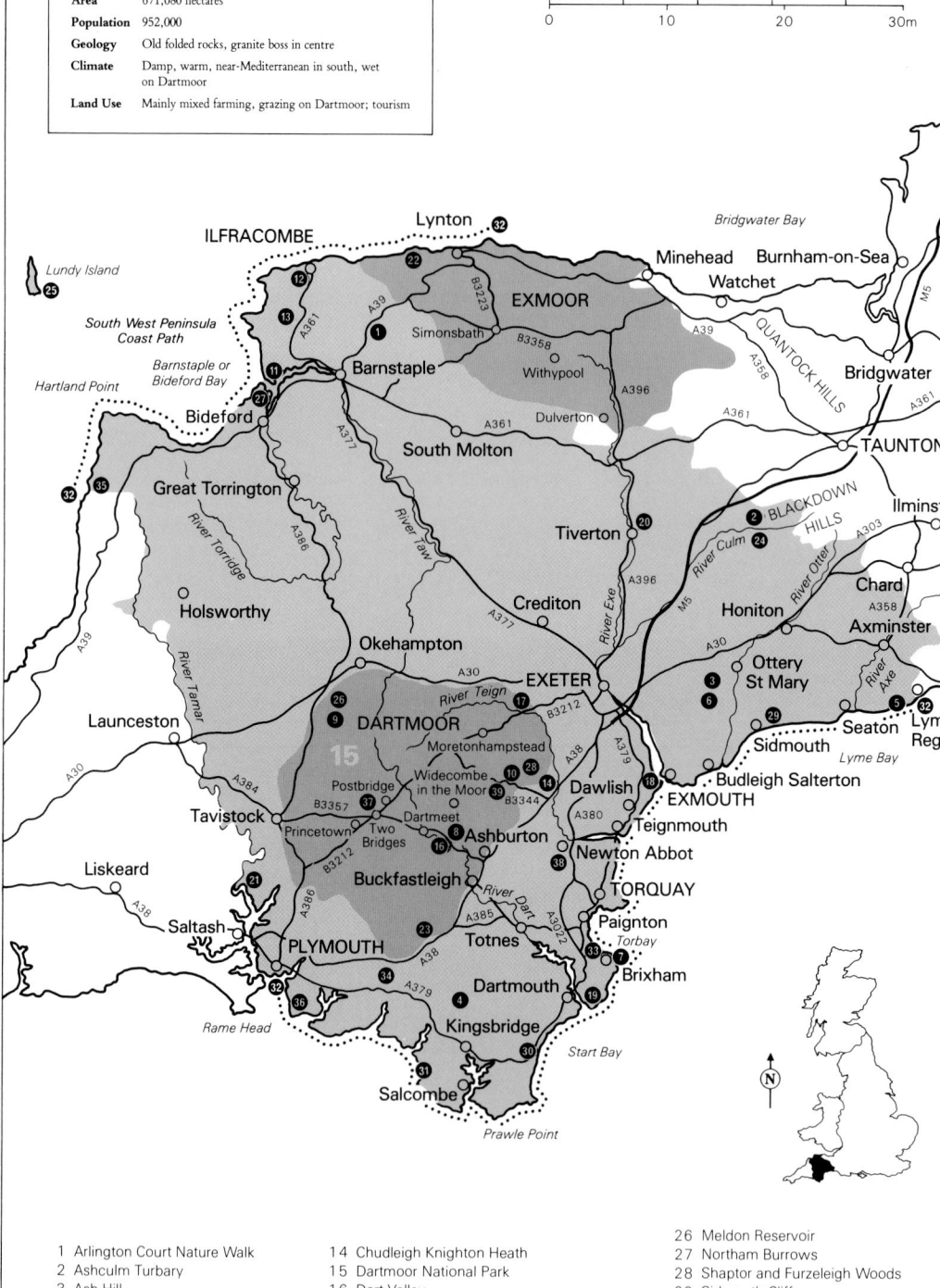

Area	671,080 hectares
Population	952,000
Geology	Old folded rocks, granite boss in centre
Climate	Damp, warm, near-Mediterranean in south, wet on Dartmoor
Land Use	Mainly mixed farming, grazing on Dartmoor; tourism

1 Arlington Court Nature Walk
2 Ashculm Turbary
3 Ash Hill
4 Avon Valley Woods
5 Axmouth–Lyme Undercliffs
6 Aylesbeare Common
7 Berry Head Country Park
8 Blackadon
9 Black Tor Copse
10 Bovey Valley Woodlands
11 Braunton Burrows
12 Cairn Top
13 Chapel Woods
14 Chudleigh Knighton Heath
15 Dartmoor National Park
16 Dart Valley
17 Dunsford and Meadowhaydown Woods
18 Exe Estuary
    Dawlish Warren
19 Froward Point
20 Grand Western Canal
21 Hangingcliff Wood
22 Heddon Valley Nature Walk
23 Lady's Wood
24 Lickham Common
25 Lundy Island
26 Meldon Reservoir
27 Northam Burrows
28 Shaptor and Furzeleigh Woods
29 Sidmouth Cliffs
30 Slapton Ley
31 South Huish Marsh
32 South West Peninsula Coast Path
33 Sugarloaf Hill and Saltern Cove
34 Tod Moor
35 Welcombe and Marsland Valleys
36 Wembury Point
37 Wistmans Wood
38 Wolborough
39 Yarner Wood

240km of coast. Kittiwake and rainbow limpet breed here, while gannet and basking shark are seen from the beach.

Warm but damp, the Devon year has a high number of rain days. Fog and mist are common at the sea's edge and on Dartmoor and Exmoor. The other side of that same coin is that snow is rare, and lies only briefly even on the moors. Frost days are few and far between on the southern coast, and grass stops growing only for a very short time. Even a warm wind off the Atlantic blows strongly across plateau tops, and shelter is still sought by living things well inland.

All this adds up to a superior grass-growing landscape and for 3000 years Devonians have been graziers. South Devon and Red Devon cattle; South Devon, Devon Closewool, Dartmoor Greyface and Exmoor sheep; Dartmoor and Exmoor ponies are testimony to that. From Anglo-Saxon times the stock-rearing and dairying enterprise has been integrated into a mixed farming system for the self-sufficiency necessitated by remoteness from large towns. A pattern of small fields and woods separated by large earth and stone banks, all enmeshed in a dense network of deep narrow lanes, is the physical expression of that economy. Farmsteads and villages, with orchards, ponds and mills, seem to grow out of the hillsides and valley heads. This man-made landscape continues to support a rich plant and animal life, with gentle transitions to the seashore one way, and up on to stone-walled moors and blanket bogs the other.

IAN MERCER

Arlington Court Nature Walk

SS 611405; 2.4km; NT
Lakeside and river walk
Spring, early summer

The circular trail includes the lake, a wildfowl sanctuary overlooked by a heronry, and the riverside woodlands where raven and buzzard breed.

Ashculm Turbary

ST 147158; 6.4ha; DTNC reserve
Wet heath
Spring, summer

A range of habitats from acid bog to birch scrub and wet alder–willow contains purple moor-grass, cross-leaved heath and round-leaved and oblong-leaved sundew. Some 40 bird species have been recorded here, along with a wide variety of other animals.

Ash Hill

SY 065927; 0.7ha; DTNC reserve
Small woodland
Spring, early summer

This tiny reserve consists of a triangular stand of beech varied by occasional pine trees.

Avon Valley Woods

SX 736509; 40ha; WdT
Mixed woodland
Spring, early summer

For roughly 3km the steep woodlands follow the valley of the Avon as old oak coppice with sweet chestnut, birch and alder at the riverside. The woods are rich in shrubs with splendid spring flowers and a good range of animal life including woodland and riverside birds.

The chalk and sandstone Axmouth–Lyme Undercliffs, above Charton Bay.

Axmouth–Lyme Undercliffs

SY 268896–329916; 320ha; NCC reserve
Wooded cliffs and slopes
Permit only off right of way
Dangerous site with unstable cliffs
Leaflet from NCC
Spring, early summer

One winter's night in 1839, a huge chalk floe of cliff slid towards the sea, pushing in front of it the tumbled debris of many minor falls and opening up behind it a chasm into which an only slightly smaller section of cliff collapsed. Six broad hectares of chalk and sandstone had moved, unseen, in a single night to form an island of land in the loosely tumbled slopes below the fields. This and many smaller slips of rock make up the Undercliffs, altered every year by newer falls.

In places there are planted trees, conifers, everlasting and turkey oak, beech and ash, but much of the woodland has developed naturally, particularly the dense tangle which now fills the chasm behind Goat Island. The natural cover on

these lime-rich rocks, where purple gromwell grows, is ash and field maple over blackthorn, dogwood, hazel and spindle, thickly tangled with traveller's-joy. On the seaward slopes a wind-pruned scrub is contoured by exposure: dogwood, field maple, privet, spindle and wayfaring-tree with blackthorn and hawthorn, bramble, ivy, honeysuckle, traveller's-joy and wild madder. Shaded places are thick with hart's-tongue, male-fern, broad buckler-fern and soft shield-fern, while paths are edged with yellow archangel, dog's mercury, enchanter's-nightshade, herb-Robert, wood spurge and pendulous sedge. Water still drains down through the slopes to cause new falls, providing sites for common bird's-foot-trefoil, biting stonecrop, carline thistle and common rock-rose, with marshy sumps where a wet sandy porridge is filled with rushes, sedges and plants such as water mint, purple-loosestrife, great horsetail, bog pimpernel and the rare fen orchid.

The area is rich in animal life – adder and common lizard bask on the open slopes, badger and roe deer enjoy the secrecy of the thickets; sunlit glades and banks of flowers are alive with insect life: this is a key site for the wood white butterfly. The scrub provides food and shelter for many migrant birds; breeding species include herring gull, nightingale and long-tailed tit, goldcrest, stonechat and rock pipit, while buzzard, kestrel and sparrowhawk hunt across the reserve.

Aylesbeare Common

SY 057898; 180ha; RSPB reserve
Lowland heath
No access off footpaths
Extreme danger of fire; no smoking
Spring, early summer

While avocet, marsh harrier and peregrine may be spreading once more as British breeding species and recent colonisers such as collared dove are extending their breeding range, the Dartford warbler seems doomed as a native species. Most British warblers are summer visitors but the Dartford is not a migrant species. Essentially it is a bird of the western Mediterranean where winters are mild enough; it has either never evolved, or has lost, the urge to move in autumn. These birds were once widespread in the south of England, but savage winters have cut their numbers down while forestry and farming have drastically reduced the lowland heaths. A national crash followed the winter of 1962–3, reducing the population to less than 100 pairs and wiping out the colony at Aylesbeare. By 1978 they had recolonised, only to vanish again that winter. Obviously Aylesbeare is close enough for juveniles from the Dorset strongholds, such as ARNE, to reach the heathland here but, if our climate grows colder, the Dartford warbler may become extinct in the British Isles.

Better-adapted species, though, still inhabit the heathland where curlew nest beside the valley bogs and nightjar breed in the dry heath. Linnet,

stonechat and yellowhammer sing from the gorse, while the woodland fringe provides a habitat for tree pipit and green woodpecker, and buzzard and raven wheel above the reserve.

The heath is considered the finest of the Budleigh Salterton pebble heaths, a spread of heather, bell heather and western gorse which curves into shallow valleys and drains into small bogs. The change from dry to wet heath is marked by a change to cross-leaved heath and to a show of sedges, cottongrass and plants such as royal fern and bog asphodel, lifting between tussocks of purple moor-grass. The wettest places are rich in *Sphagnum* with white beak-sedge, round-leaved sundew, bog pimpernel and plants of western and south-western bogs – pale butterwort, oblong-leaved sundew and many-stalked spike-rush. Mineral-rich water seepages are marked by less acid-loving plants such as black bog-rush, devil's-bit scabious, marsh thistle, carnation and tawny sedge, while the green and russet *Sphagnum* mosses give way to brown moss species.

The reserve attracts a wide range of insects, with a variety of dragonfly species, with heathland moths such as emperor and fox, and an exceptional 32 species of butterflies recorded, including silver-studded blue and grayling, purple hairstreak and silver-washed fritillary.

Berry Head Country Park

SX 943564; 43ha; Torbay BC reserve
Limestone cliffs, grassland, heath and scrub
Restricted access to old quarry: apply to TBC
Booklet and nature trail leaflet from TBC or car park at site
Mid-May–mid-July

The country park, to the south of urban Torbay, consists of a headland capped with scrub and bracken–gorse–heather heathland, which is the largest exposure of Devonian limestone in Britain. Its magnificent range of plants and birds is so

White rock-rose is an uncommon plant of hard limestone crags.

The Bovey Valley Woodlands form a corridor running into the heathland of the moor.

important that the park is also scheduled as a nature reserve.

Below the heath a shallow turf curves to the sheer cliffs, filled with a colourful blend of lime-loving and coastal plants such as white and rock stonecrop, sea campion and thrift. Some of the special plants are uncommon and may represent a range of species which survived the ice ages here. White rock-rose, honewort, goldilocks aster, small hare's-ear and small restharrow grow together nowhere else in the country: small hare's-ear occurs in Sussex on chalk, the rest on western limestones. These plants seem unable to spread from their present small colonies and their strange distribution is a puzzle which may never be fully solved.

For the birdwatcher this is also a special site: Berry Head holds one of the very few south coast colonies of auks. Around 150 pairs of guillemot nest on the cliffs, together with small numbers of razorbill and other seabirds such as fulmar and kittiwake. Other cliff-breeders include jackdaw and rock dove × feral pigeon, while crevices in the sea cliffs and the quarry hold important gatherings of several bat species.

The heathland holds resident birds such as linnet and stonechat and affords a breeding or resting site for many small migrants, including black redstart, while buzzard and kestrel may often be seen hunting over the headland. The park also provides an ideal place for sea-watching: cormorant and gannet are frequent and passage birds may use the reserve as a staging post or be seen flying offshore.

Blackadon

SX 712732; 36.4ha; DTNC reserve
Wooded valley slope and moorland
Spring, early summer

Oak woodland over bilberry rises from the River Webburn to an area of coppiced birch below slopes of grass–heather moorland invaded by bracken. Mosses, ferns and lichens are prolific.

Black Tor Copse

SX 567890; 28.9ha; Duchy of Cornwall–NCC reserve
Dwarf high-Dartmoor woodland
Spring, early summer

Set in a valley near Dartmoor's highest point, the dwarf oaks and the tumbled rocks are thick with lichens, mosses and ferns, a shelter for birds such as ring ouzel.

Bovey Valley Woodlands

SX 789801; 71.2ha; NCC reserve
Old coppiced woodland
Permit only off rights of way
Spring, early summer

Oak and hazel, with a variety of other tree species, fill the valley of the River Bovey with an abundance of lichens and riverside boulders thick with mosses, liverworts and ferns. The reserve varies from woodland to valley bog and has a typical bird life which includes pied flycatcher, redstart and wood warbler with dipper and grey wagtail.

119

A colony of yellow iris at Braunton Burrows.

Bradley Pond

Permit only; 4ha; DTNC reserve
Disused claypit
Spring, summer

Birch, grey willow and oak woodland is developing around an old ball clay working, colonised by a fringe of wetland plants and supporting a wide range of aquatic invertebrates.

Braunton Burrows

SS 464326; 604ha; NCC reserve
Coastal dune system
No access to military zones when red flags are flying
Leaflet from NCC
Spring, summer

At low water the beach seems to reach as far as the horizon while the sand bars and ridges of the estuary form a foraging ground for shelduck and oystercatcher. The strand line tells of the life of the sands; empty shells of shore crab and masked crab mix with Baltic tellin, mussel and common whelk, with the egg cases of dogfish, the rounded tests of heart urchins, and the seaweed-like fronds of hornwrack.

Where the edge of the dunes meets the sea are special plants which can live in this sand-blown environment, including sea-holly, sea bindweed and the uncommon and beautiful sea stock. Marram, typical of most dune systems, binds the sand of the dunes and helps to build the ramparts which shelter the rich plant life behind them.

Braunton is an outstanding dune system where a wide range of conditions from the open sand of the beach to thick scrub may be seen in a full progression. The first small slacks are open spreads of lichens and mosses, rabbit-bitten turf and scatters of low plants such as biting stonecrop and common stork's-bill. Larger slacks further inland begin to show shrubby cushions of privet, patches of restharrow and plants such as Portland and sea spurge, viper's-bugloss, wild thyme and sprays of stinking iris.

Larger, wetter slacks, varied with shingle and pools of standing water, are a wonderful pattern of scrub and colourful plants – mounds of privet and dense tangles of bramble, clusters of willows and rushy herb-rich areas, wet places where marsh-orchids stand above tangles of creeping willow, fringed with clumps of sharp rush, contrasting with short-turfed sandy pockets of plants such as hound's-tongue. The reserve is also of great importance for its spreads of water germander and round-headed club-rush.

Further inland stunted hawthorn appears, with stands of bracken where the lime has been washed out of the topsoil. Damper areas are still amazingly rich, with the scrub becoming more varied and forming a mix of hawthorn, blackthorn, privet, willow and buckthorn, with birch in the drier sites, with yellow rattle and kidney vetch, common twayblade, hemp-agrimony, red campion and ragged-Robin and, everywhere, the flower spikes of the orchids.

The animal life of the dunes corresponds to their variation. The lime-richness encourages snails, the wealth of plant life draws insects, and many mammals and birds breed and hunt here.

Brownsham

SS 287257; 30ha; DTNC reserve
Heathy grassland and woodland
Summer

The wet heathy grassland on the reserve is very rich in meadow plants. Scrub covers large areas and there is some mixed deciduous woodland. A 'tree library' contains examples of all native tree and shrub species.

Cairn Top

SS 515463; 7.6ha; DTNC reserve
Hillside with mixed woodland
Spring, early summer

A small area of open hill top, surrounded by gorse and blackthorn, contrasts with steep slopes where mixed deciduous trees and conifers stand above a varied ground cover.

Chapel Wood

SS 483415; 6ha; RSPB reserve
Mixed woodland
Spring, early summer

The woodland of oak, ash, birch, hazel, willow and alien species contains birds such as buzzard and raven which are limited to the west in southern Britain.

Chudleigh Knighton Heath

SX 838776; 74ha; DTNC reserve
Lowland heath
Spring, early summer

Small ponds, containing such interesting plants as common bladderwort, occur in a wide spread of wet and dry heathland, scrub and woodland where nightingales breed and attractive small plants such as pale dog-violet may be found. This is the last extensive area of lowland heathland remaining in the Bovey Basin.

Dartmoor National Park

See map; 94,500ha; DNPA
Moorland with granite tors and fringing valleys
Leaflets from DNPA and information caravans
No access to MOD ranges when in use
Spring, early summer

Dartmoor, the Cornish granites of Bodmin, St Austell, Carnmenellis and Land's End, the Scillies and the underwater outcrop of Haig Fras are all great masses which stand up from one huge buried reef of granite and represent bosses of rock which have been uncovered by erosion. When the Dartmoor granite was forced into the folded carboniferous crust many metres of layered rocks stood above the tors; time has now stripped these softer rocks away and the bare grey granite stands against wind and rain. Even this hard rock cannot hold for ever and one of the characteristic sights of the Moor is the clitters, the screes of huge boulders which frost has shattered from the tors.

The spreads of heather are varied with bright small plants such as tormentil, heath bedstraw and heath milkwort, together with bilberry and bell heather, with cross-leaved heath and purple moorgrass in damper situations. Bristle bent is one of the typical grasses, a fine-leaved, tufty grass which only grows in the south west and South Wales, often found with mat-grass and other grasses on the open moors which surround the central bogs.

Lydford Gorge: many of Devon's rivers flow off the moor and cut through the valley woods.

The bogs vary from the eroded peats on some of the open hills to the dangerous quaking spread of Fox Tor Mires, from tiny wet hollows filled with vivid bog mosses to trembling bogs around the upland streams. Heather and cross-leaved heath grow on the blanket bogs, with common and hare's-tail cottongrass and occasional crowberry, while the valley mires have a richer vegetation where round-leaved sundew grows on the *Sphagnum* mosses with plants such as bog asphodel, pale butterwort, marsh St John's-wort and ivy-leaved bellflower, bogbean and bog pimpernel.

While the open moors are heavily grazed by ponies, cattle and sheep the clitters are almost as hard to graze as the bogs and often support a luxuriant growth of plants. The crevices protect the plants from grazing and give shelter from the wind: this may be why some clitters carry the only native woods of the moor. BLACK TOR COPSE, Piles Copse and WISTMAN'S WOOD are strange small thickets of twisted oaks which cling close to the slopes of the moorland, dramatically gnarled and stunted. The lack of air pollution encourages splendid growths of lichens and mosses, so that these woods have long been famous for the species which clothe the trees.

At lower altitudes, the moorland edge is dissected by valleys where the granite meets the softer rocks around it. The rivers have cut deep gorges where oak woodland spreads on the steep sides and alders line the river bank. The valleys wind through the in-country, where the heat of the cooling granite often altered the older rocks to provide minerals sought by miners, and these valleys form a vital aspect of the wildlife interest of the park.

Although winter floods may sweep through them, scouring the narrow alluvial flats and the islands, the valleys are sheltered from storms and spring brings wild daffodil, primrose, wood anemone, bluebell and ramsons to flower under the trees.

The rivers which drain the moor are all torrential, for heavy rain on the uplands will gather to pour down the narrow valleys. Salmon come to breed in the shallow gravels, waiting for the spate to bring them enough depth of water to run. All the life of the river must be adapted to cope with flood, from the freshwater limpets to the mayfly nymphs, from the fish to the caddisfly larvae. The rivers, fishing sites for heron and kingfisher, are worked by dipper and grey wagtail, and provide hunting grounds and passage routes for otter and feral mink.

Cumberstone Tor: rock-strewn grasslands and tors are typical of the granite, bog and heath landscape of the Dartmoor National Park.

The valley woods beside the rivers are attractive sites for bird life. Truly moorland birds such as dunlin, red grouse and golden plover may occur in small numbers, and the high moor also provides nest sites for skylark and meadow pipit, ring ouzel, wren and wheatear, for stonechat and whinchat in rough moorland or snipe and common sandpiper in the bogs, but the valley woodlands are far more rich in birds. Buzzard and raven are frequent across the moor and often fly out from the surrounding woodlands but, while the raven is mainly a bird of the open sheep walks, the buzzard is an opportunist, just as much at home in farmland.

In the valleys, several of them nature reserves, all three British woodpeckers may be present, together with nuthatch and treecreeper and the western trio of pied flycatcher, redstart and wood warbler. Woodcock are uncommon in the south west peninsula but may be found in some of the woodlands where they nest, often in a sparse cover of bracken or tangle of bramble. The woods are frequently noisy with the raucous calls of jays, although magpies prefer more open situations, and provide nest sites for predators such as buzzard, kestrel, sparrowhawk and tawny owl. In winter they may shelter flocks of smaller birds: long-tailed and coal tits, finches, and gatherings of fieldfares and redwings which feed on the scrubland berries.

Several Dartmoor valleys have been flooded to form reservoirs and, while there is a loss of moorland habitat, there is some gain in wetland wildlife, in breeding and wintering wildfowl and in visitors such as osprey.

The open moors offer little shelter and are often too wet for small mammals and, while the moorland foxes may find sanctuary in the clitters, the valley slopes provide far more suitable homes. In valleys, too, fallow deer and badger make regular, well-worn pathways, and a good range of woodland mammals live in the shelter there.

Buzzard, characteristic of the National Park, nest in the valley woodlands and can be seen soaring above Dartmoor.

Of course, the moorland should be seen in all its moods, and these can change with startling rapidity, but the sheer size of the National Park and the wide diversity within it ensure that, even when the uplands are thick with mist or enveloped in drowning rain, there is always somewhere to excite the naturalist.

Dart Valley

SX 672733–704704; 364ha; DNPA–DTNC reserve
Valley woodland and heath
Spring, early summer

In one of the most attractive of the Dartmoor valleys, the reserve is a stretch of wooded riverside and steep-sloped open heath. The Dartmoor rivers spread to all points of the compass from the rain-fed peat bogs deep in the heart of the Moor, cutting through the granite and the hills of slates and shales which lie around it. In parts of the reserve the heathland changes from gorse and acid grasses to a richer mix of species, and great clitters give way to finer slaty screes as the narrow valley leaves the granite and small valley plains become more frequent.

The narrow steepness of the gorge has preserved the valley from agricultural improvement. The lower slopes are wooded, an oak woodland with hazel, birch, holly and beech, which grades through birch and bracken scrub to the open heathland above. The woods are very varied, a mosaic of coppiced areas with stands of almost pure birch, with alder at the water's edge, with taller trees in the deeper soils below and small, slow-growing copses on the arid steep scree slopes. Similarly, the ground cover may be rich in mosses

A feeder stream at Burrator: moss-covered rocks in low oak woodlands watered by rushing streams typify the change from open moorland.

and ferns on a tumble of boulders or be a more typical woodland spread of grasses and shade-loving plants.

The rapid flow of the torrential river is rich enough in oxygen for fish such as salmon and brown trout to breed, and for the insect larvae on which the dipper feeds. From dipper and grey wagtail to buzzard and raven high above, the valley is rich in bird life. Woodcock, green woodpecker and marsh tit, redstart, whinchat and ring ouzel, meadow pipit and skylark are among the breeding species, while winter may bring flocks of goldcrest, coal tit and long-tailed tit. Otter and mink may occur and the woods and scrub provide a suitable habitat for fox and badger. The reserve provides an invaluable natural corridor into the centre of the Moor.

Dawlish Warren

SX 981787; 70ha; DTNC–Teignbridge DC reserve
Sand dunes, scrub and marsh
No access to golf course
All year

Part of the EXE ESTUARY, providing an important staging post for many immigrant birds.

Dendles Wood

Permit only; 29ha; NCC reserve
Oak–beech woodland
Spring, early summer

Beech trees, up to 300 years old, stand above a ground cover of little more than mosses but, where the trees become more mixed, holly, hazel and rowan, for instance, grow with bluebell, bracken, bramble, wood-sorrel and woodland grasses. Birds include buzzard, pied flycatcher, redstart, grey wagtail and wood warbler, with silver-washed fritillary and green hairstreak among the insects.

Dunsford and Meadhaydown Woods

SX 805883; 56ha; DTNC–NT reserve
Mixed valley woodland
Booklet from DTNC
Spring, early summer

The slopes are covered with an open woodland of old coppiced oak while blackthorn, hazel and spindle or level plains of grass and bracken spread across the valley floor. The reserve is noted for its wild daffodils and has a good range of woodland birds, including the locally uncommon lesser spotted woodpecker. There are large colonies of wood ant and some 23 butterfly species including pearl-bordered and silver-washed fritillaries.

Exe Estuary

SX 980785; 12sq.km; various owners
Large area of open water, mudflats, saltmarsh and sandy spit
No access to golf course at Dawlish Warren
All year

The great estuary, one of eleven in the county, forms the most important wetland in the whole south west peninsula. Sand, pushed into a long narrow spit by the eastward thrust of the long-shore drift, almost closes the estuary mouth at DAWLISH WARREN, while wide sandflats spread from 'The Point at Exmouth, holding the river against the western shore. The estuary may be overlooked from footpaths along the shoreline, north from Powderham at SX 973845 and south from Lympstone at SX 992836, and from a hide.

The habitats include mudflats thick with the seaweed *Enteromorpha*, and with dwarf and narrow-leaved eelgrass; saltmarsh building around spreads of cord-grass with species such as glasswort; the dunes and scrub of Dawlish Warren, where the rare sand crocus grows; and areas of common reed together with grazing marshes at the northern head of the estuary.

Enormous numbers of wigeon winter here with flocks of dark-bellied Brent geese. Large flocks of mallard, shelduck and teal, with lesser numbers of eider, goldeneye, pintail and red-breasted merganser, are usually present along with mute swan and Canada goose, common scoter, pochard, scaup, shoveler and tufted duck. Dunlin and oystercatcher together will probably outnumber all the other waders but there are still good numbers of curlew, bar-tailed and black-tailed godwit, lapwing and redshank, with smaller numbers of golden, grey and ringed plover, turnstone, knot and sanderling. Avocet, greenshank, spotted redshank, ruff, curlew sandpiper, purple sandpiper and whimbrel may occur, while stormy weather may bring in many unexpected birds.

Dark-bellied Brent geese on the Exe Estuary.

Froward Point

SX 904496; 22.8ha; DTNC–NT reserve
Coastal woods and cliffs
Spring, early summer

Coniferous and mixed woodland, scrub and cliffs provide nesting sites for birds, while the cliff-top grassland contrasts with the wooded areas and provides a stand for sea-watching near the mouth of the River Dart.

Grand Western Canal

SS 963124–ST 074195; 17.6km; DCC
Linear park based on old canal
Leaflets from DCC
Spring, summer

Devon has very few slow waters but the old Tiverton Canal provides an example of a lowland waterway rich in plant and animal life.

Hangingcliff Wood

SX 425655; 3ha; DTNC reserve
Mixed woodland
Spring, early summer

The mainly broad-leaved wood contains typical woodland birds and is set on steep cliffs overlooking the TAMAR ESTUARY (Cornwall).

Heddon Valley Nature Walk

SS 655483; 3.2km; NT
Coastal valley walk
Spring, summer

The circular walk follows the valley through fine oak woodlands and damp rich meadows to the sea at Heddon Mouth.

Higher Kiln Quarry

Permit only; 1.2ha; DTNC reserve
Disused quarry
Cave system and study centre–museum let to William Pengelly Cave Studies Trust
Access to caves and museum: Mr D. Curry, Plymouth Museum (tel. Plymouth 668000, ext. 4376)
Spring, early summer

The main interest of this reserve is an extensive Devonian limestone cave system containing colonies of bats at certain times of year. Fossil remains of straight-tusked elephants, narrow-nosed rhinoceros, hippopotamus and bison can be seen where they fell through an opening into the caves about 10,000 years ago.

Isley Marsh

Permit only; 56.7ha; DBWPS reserve
Small marshland
All year

The reserve, set on the edge of the Taw Estuary, is important for spring and autumn passage birds and winter waders and wildfowl.

Lady's Wood

SX 687591; 3.2ha; DTNC reserve
Coppiced woodland
Spring, early summer

Active coppicing maintains oak and ash standards over ash and hazel, with some grey willow, while part is left uncoppiced. There is a good show of springtime flowers and the wood is a noted site for dormouse.

Lickham Common

ST 126122; 4ha; DTNC reserve
Heath and carr
Spring, early summer

Open areas are dominated by purple moor-grass, with bracken in drier parts and bog myrtle in wetter places; alder and alder buckthorn occur in the wet woodland, with old coppiced birch and willow, while standard oak trees prefer the drier sites. Roe deer and fox are present.

Lundy Island

SS 143437; 450ha; Landmark Trust–NT reserve
Granite island
Passage bookings from the Administrator, Lundy via Ilfracombe, Devon
Booklet from site or LT
Spring, summer

The granite of Lundy is later than that of Dartmoor, perhaps as young as 50 million years old, and forms a sea-washed island about 5km long and less than 1km wide. The western cliffs are generally high and steep while the eastern side is sloped to lower cliffs and hung with valleys; all around, deep rocky coves echo the sound of the sea. Not only is Lundy a nature reserve above sea level, it has also been designated a marine nature reserve. The rocky foreshores and tidal zones are rich in seashore life and, some 17km from the mainland, provide a site where oceanic species may occur.

Above, the slopes and cliff ledges are filled with cushions of thrift and of sea-coast plants which give way to the heather, bracken and acid grasses of the peat. Here and there, pools provide water for grazing stock and a habitat for wetland plants, reinforced by small patches of bog.

The island is of special interest to botanists and coleopterists as the site for Lundy cabbage, which grows nowhere else in the world, and for two species of beetle which live on it.

Some 40 species of breeding birds nest around the island, taking advantage of the habitat range which includes, with the cliffs and moorland, woodlands of sycamore, rhododendron scrub, derelict quarries and tumbledown buildings, stone walls, grassland and gardens. The island's emblem, the puffin, is sadly diminished but still occurs with guillemot and razorbill while other seabirds include fulmar, kittiwake and shag with lesser black-backed and great black-backed gulls and herring gull. A few Manx shearwater still breed on the island and raven nest on the rocky crags of the

The magnificent Lundy coastline stands above clear waters where grey seals are frequently observed.

Kittiwake and guillemot breed on the hard granite cliffs of Lundy.

cliffs, with wheatear and rock pipit flitting among cliff-top boulders and with small songbirds in the woods and the pockets of scrub. Over 400 different birds have been recorded on Lundy and there is always the chance of sighting some rare or unusual species.

Meldon Reservoir

Permit only; 5.6ha; DTNC reserve
Sanctuary area in moorland reservoir
May be overlooked from slopes around e.g.
SX 563915
All year

In winter the reservoir may contain waterfowl, such as goldeneye and goosander, while early summer shows breeding stonechat, whinchat and wheatear. The banks contain both wet and dry heath with bog asphodel and heath spotted-orchid. The contrast between the ungrazed area of the reserve and the moor beyond is impressive.

New Bridge

Permit only; 2.2ha; DTNC reserve
Mixed woodland
Spring, early summer

The woodland, mainly oak, is bounded in part by the River Teign, in part by a large tip of clay waste; it contains a range of habitats including those suitable for colonising species and for water plants.

Northam Burrows

SS 444298; 263ha; DCC reserve
Coastal sand dunes and saltmarsh
Booklet from DCC
All year

The fascinations of the seashore, of rock pool and sandy beach, of saltmarsh, sand dune and estuary are all here, set in the mouth of the Taw and the Torridge. Plants such as glasswort, sea spurge and sea-holly colonise the mud and sand, common stork's-bill and wild thyme attract butterflies such as common blue and brown Argus, and skylark, wheatear, ringed plover and shelduck, curlew and oystercatcher may be seen.

Old Sludge Beds

Permit only; 5.2ha; DTNC reserve
Reedswamp and open water
All year

Common reed, bulrush, hemlock and willows provide a habitat attractive to birds, particularly small migrants.

Shaptor and Furzeleigh Woods

SX 819797; 78ha; WdT
Mixed woodland
Spring, early summer

Considerably varied, containing both dwarfed oaks and areas of coppice with planted beech and invading birch, the woods contain an excellent range of characteristic plants and animals including a good variety of birds.

Sidmouth Cliffs

SY 130872 and 146875; 7.5ha; DTNC reserve
Cliff slopes
Booklet from DTNC
Spring, summer

Two blocks of undercliff, separated by private land, form the reserve, parts of which have been colonised by bramble, blackthorn, ash and sycamore scrub which is rich in birds and insects.

Slapton Ley

SX 826431; 190ha; FSC reserve
Freshwater lagoon, reedbeds, mixed woodlands and shingle
Permit only to woodlands and Higher Ley, from South Hams Countryside Unit, Slapton Ley Field Centre, Slapton
Leaflets from South Hams Countryside Unit
All year

The beach, the misnamed Slapton Sands, is the most south westerly shingle in Britain, apart from a few small fragments, and carries a fine variety of plants. Ray's knotgrass, shore dock, sea radish and yellow horned-poppy grow on the long stretch of shingle while, beyond the road, the back slope of the ridge is thick with a cover of bramble and gorse and a mixed low tangle of scrub. Behind the ridge

The South West Peninsula Coast Path includes dramatic scenery such as this near Hartland.

is the Ley, 100ha in area and up to 3m deep: a rich lake, full of plant and animal life. The Higher Ley is an almost continuous reedbed, a fen, invaded by willow, with quiet pools where mink and otter survive – a sanctuary for some of the shyer birds.

Over 230 birds have been recorded here: the curve of the bay is such that the Ley offers shelter from south western winds. Spring and autumn offer passages of migrants while winter brings its regular seasonal flocks and storms at sea or bitter cold inland will bring birds here for shelter.

Shingle-breeding birds are gone, the visitor pressures are probably too high, and the same stress may deflect the breeding wildfowl, but great crested grebe, mallard and water rail, Cetti's and occasional grasshopper warbler, stonechat, grey wagtail and goldcrest all breed on the reserve. Nesting nearby, cormorant, fulmar and great black-backed gull declare the closeness of the sea and, in winter, gulls gather here in huge flocks – perhaps 10,000 birds roosting on the shingle beach and the Ley.

South Huish Marsh

No access; 1.5ha; DBWPS reserve
Wet pasture
May be overlooked from SX 677414
Autumn, winter

Migration times and winter are probably best here, when waders and wildfowl may be seen in the marshy grassland.

South Milton Ley

Permit only; 16.2ha; DBWPS reserve
Coastal reedbed
All year

A hide may be used by permit holders but the main importance of the reserve is as a ringing station. Reed and sedge warbler, occasional grasshopper and Cetti's warbler are among the breeding species while autumn brings a large roost of yellow wagtail and, in recent years, gatherings of bearded tit.

South West Peninsula Coast Path

North Devon: SS 213174–793487; South Devon: SX 493531–SY 332916; 256km; CC
Part of long-distance way
Leaflet from CC or booklet from HMSO bookshops
Spring, summer

Both the North and South Devon coastlines form part of the long-distance path which includes a wide spectrum of coastal scenery and habitat.

Sugarloaf Hill and Saltern Cove

SX 895583; 51.5ha; Torbay BC reserve
Small cove and coastal grassland
Spring, summer

Part of the reserve includes the active railway line and is out of bounds to visitors. The open-access grasslands and shallow cliffs are rich in flowers and typical scrub plants and the rocky shore is important for the wildlife of its tidal zones.

Tod Moor

SX 624540; 6.8ha; DTNC reserve
Wet heath
Spring, summer

Wet, heathy grassland supports marsh plants such as bogbean and marsh-marigold. Oak–hazel coppice, hedgerows and gorse scrub add variety and encourage a good population of birds.

Welcombe and Marsland Valleys

SX 214174; 208ha; RSNC reserve
Coastal valley woodlands, scrub and grassland
Permit only off rights of way
Spring, summer

Including land in both the valleys and straddling the border between Devon and Cornwall, the reserve contains a magnificent range of habitat, from the weirdly folded rocks at Welcombe Mouth, through streamside valley woodland, to once-farmed fields high up in the valleys which are tending to revert to forest.

Much of the reserve is tall high-forest woodland, damp and sheltered in the deep valleys, with alder and willow along the marshy stream sides and with oak and mixed woodland in the valley bottoms and

Small pearl-bordered fritillary can be seen in Welcombe and Marsland Valleys.

Badgers frequently inhabit the woodlands of south western England.

clothing the drier slopes. The oakwoods stand over hazel and holly above a ground cover of bramble varied with bluebell, hard fern and male-fern, honeysuckle and creeping soft-grass. Spindle and privet mark areas of richer ground where dog's mercury, primrose, sanicle and hart's-tongue grow on the woodland floor, and higher slopes may be acid enough for bilberry, common cow-wheat, heather and tormentil.

Mixed woodland of ash and sycamore tends to contain oak in the drier sites but, in damper situations, contains much alder over plants such as wild daffodil and yellow pimpernel or marsh plants including common valerian, marsh-marigold and meadowsweet. Beech in places reduces ground cover to a spread of ferns, while other areas are wet enough for alder–willow carr. A full range from grassland to woodland may be seen: the old fields are invaded by bracken and bramble, then by a scrub of gorse and thorn trees, then by a secondary woodland which stands over hawthorn and blackthorn. These old fields seen from the opposite slope, make a wonderful pattern on the hillside.

Other major habitats are the gorse heath, which holds acid plants such as lousewort, heath milkwort and trailing St John's-wort, and the short-tufted coastal grassland. The coastal turf is rabbit-grazed, trodden by visitors and exposed to bitter winds and salt spray, yet it carries a vivid range of such plants as spring squill, sea campion, thrift, restharrow, wild carrot and kidney vetch with a host of other small herbs.

There is a rich diversity of animals, with a good range of cliff-breeding, grassland, scrub and woodland birds. Mammals include badger and, among the insects, the reserve is particularly rich in butterflies with five species of fritillary.

129

Wembury Marine Conservation Area

SX 507484; 6km; WMCA Advisory Group reserve
Rocky foreshore and adjacent shallow water zone
Spring, summer

Comprising a length of rocky coast from Gara Point to Fort Bovisand at the mouth of Plymouth Sound, the reserve was set up in 1981 by voluntary agreement between landowners and users of the area, including the DTNC. The intertidal reefs at Wembury are regularly visited by educational parties, while the rocky sublittoral areas are of great interest to divers. Wembury Point (SX 502482) is important for waders and migratory birds.

Wistlandpound Reservoir

Permit only; 2ha; DBWPS–SWWA reserve
Wooded reservoir
Permit from SWWA
All year

The DBWPS manage a section of the reservoir where two hides overlook the coniferous woodland and a bay with a small artificial island. Birds include winter wildfowl and woodland species such as buzzard and sparrowhawk.

Wistman's Wood, probably the best-known wood on Dartmoor, is formed of stunted ancient oaks growing among large boulders.

Wistman's Wood

SX 612772; 24ha; Duchy of Cornwall–NCC reserve
Dwarfed moorland oakwood
Leaflet from NCC
Spring, early summer

The stunted oak woodland grows on a boulder-strewn slope, thick with mosses and lichens in conditions of harsh exposure, exceptionally high rainfall and frequent mists.

Wolborough

SX 866703; 5.2ha; DTNC reserve
Small fen area
Spring, summer

The reserve is mainly wet birch and willow carr over *Sphagnum* moss, but also includes areas of fen and reed, which are uncommon in the county.

Yarner Wood

SX 785788; 150ha; NCC reserve
Oak–birch woodland
Permit only off marked trails
Leaflets from site or NCC
Spring, early summer

A mainly oak woodland, with birch colonising disused farmland, and with areas of moorland and planted conifers, the reserve contains wood warbler and pied flycatcher with holly blue and white admiral butterflies.

Dorset

Enter Dorset from almost any direction and you feel that here is a county that has survived into the late twentieth century relatively unscathed by modern development, with most of its wild, rugged coast unspoiled and unpopulated, and its hinterland little changed from the countryside of Hardy's novels. Only at Dorset's eastern limits is this illusion completely shattered. Here Bournemouth, Christchurch and Poole form an extensive built-up area. It has obliterated a vast expanse of heath and subjugated most of its shoreline, but protection has been given to the wild beauty of Christchurch Harbour and HENGISTBURY HEAD, where the imposing eminence of Warren Hill broods over the bird-haunted levels of STANPIT MARSH.

West Dorset is quite another world. Its soft countryside melts imperceptibly into that of Devon, with deep lanes and sleepy villages, the rich pastures of the Marshwood Vale, and the oddly isolated hills capped with upper greensand. Different again are the chalk uplands which make a broad sweep over central Dorset and stretch a slender arm across the so-called ISLE OF PURBECK, which forms its south eastern corner. Chalk downland is Dorset's main scenic feature, but little now remains of its characteristic grassland. Some remnants which have escaped the modern plough are now enshrined in reserves like FONTMELL DOWN, but survival of the chalk plant life and its invertebrates often depends on the steepness of the hill slope and the legal protection afforded to the county's rich legacy of archaeological sites. It is indeed fortunate for present-day naturalists that these hills were cleared, grazed, settled, cultivated and defended in prehistoric times. The Neolithic and Bronze Age barrows which break the skyline, the Iron Age ramparts which crown the summits of the higher hills, the linear earthworks, circles, trackways and field systems now offer sanctuary, in an age of intensive farming, to such threatened species as chalkhill blue and marsh fritillary, fragrant orchid, clustered bellflower and knapweed broomrape.

In the south east of the county chalk hills enclose the tertiary sands and clays of the Poole Basin, once covered with heathland and bog that developed after Bronze Age man had stripped the woodland and scrub. For centuries the heaths survived virtually unchanged, providing fuel for humans and fodder for their livestock. Grazing, browsing and heather-burning ensured their treelessness and created a great wilderness of melancholy beauty, the fictional Egdon Heath of Thomas Hardy and Gustav Holst. Now the heathland mantle lies in shreds. The disintegration process began slowly but by 1900 much had already been ploughed into oblivion or sealed beneath the streets of Bournemouth, and now the expansion of Poole is taking its toll. Other areas have been ripped apart for their sand and clay, probed for oil, used by the military, smothered in domestic rubbish, swamped by conifers or converted into grassland. It is unfortunate that these southern heaths are the principal habitat of rare species such as Dartford warbler, sand lizard, smooth snake, marsh gentian and Dorset heath. Other species, especially among the invertebrates, are equally vulnerable but much less publicised. Their fate depends on the retention of a few large heathland reserves, which must be scientifically managed to prevent their reversion to woodland.

Recent conifer plantations account for much of the woodland on the tertiary deposits, and self-sown birches and pines are well established on those parts of the heath which have escaped fire. Oakwood with hazel is characteristic of the vales – the hazel is no longer coppiced to a great extent – with ash and beech on the lime-rich soils. Quite small deciduous woods can sometimes retain such

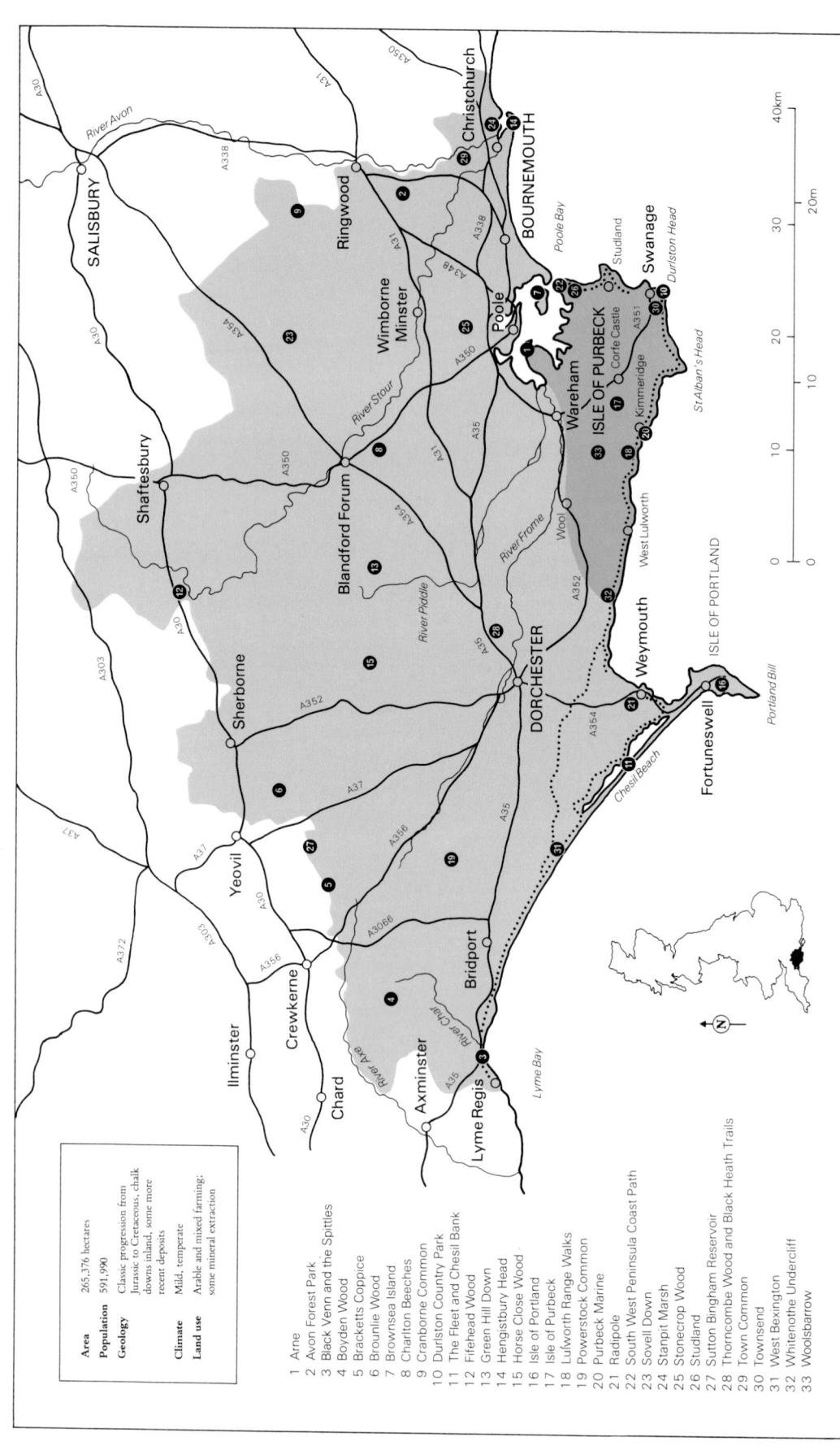

Area   265,376 hectares
Population   591,990
Geology   Classic progression from
              Jurassic to Cretaceous, chalk
              downs inland, some more
              recent deposits
Climate   Mild, temperate
Land use   Arable and mixed farming;
              some mineral extraction

1 Arne
2 Avon Forest Park
3 Black Venn and the Spitlles
4 Boyden Wood
5 Bracketts Coppice
6 Brounlie Wood
7 Brownsea Island
8 Charlton Beeches
9 Cranborne Common
10 Durlston Country Park
11 The Fleet and Chesil Bank
12 Fifehead Wood
13 Green Hill Down
14 Hengistbury Head
15 Horse Close Wood
16 Isle of Portland
17 Isle of Purbeck
18 Lulworth Range Walks
19 Powerstock Common
20 Purbeck Marine
21 Radipole
22 South West Peninsula Coast Path
23 Sovell Down
24 Stanpit Marsh
25 Stonecrop Wood
26 Studland
27 Sutton Bingham Reservoir
28 Thorncombe Wood and Black Heath Trails
29 Town Common
30 Townsend
31 West Bexington
32 Whitenothe Undercliff
33 Woolsbarrow

treasures as lungwort, heath lobelia, greater butterfly-orchid, broad-leaved helleborine, white admiral and silver-washed fritillary, and the much-maligned conifer plantations are not without interest. The forests of Purbeck and Wareham are the daytime retreat of sika deer, and the BROWNSEA pinewoods accommodate a heronry and a population of red squirrel.

Dorset has four main rivers: the Avon (shared with Hampshire) and the Stour drain into Christchurch Harbour, while the Piddle and Frome are received into vast Poole Harbour, which, with its saltings, mudflats, creeks and islands is Dorset's most impressive wetland. It is the haunt of migrating waders and summering terns, and the winter quarters of several thousand wildfowl, some of which move to the freshwater lake of STUDLAND's Little Sea.

One of Britain's long-distance footpaths begins on the Studland side of the narrow harbour entrance. Legions of students have descended upon Lulworth to examine its Cove and to look at the sea-carved arches of Stair Hole and Durdle Door and the places which gave their names to Kimmeridge clay and Purbeck marble, studied the development of Studland's acid dunes, followed the ghost of Mary Anning across the fossil-bearing lias of Lyme Regis, and stood upon the quarried heights of Portland to gaze upon the great westward sweep of Chesil Bank and the shingle-shielded waters of THE FLEET.

The ISLE OF PORTLAND holds itself aloof from the rest of Dorset, its back to Weymouth and its lowered head pointed at the unseen coast of France, somewhere beyond the tide race and the plunging gannets. First impressions may be unfavourable – it is bleak, grey and practically treeless – but Portland has character, and even without its bird observatory, rare plants, raised beach and ancient fields it would still exert a strange fascination on the visitor.

Further east, beyond Lulworth, lie the shores of Purbeck; the restless cliffs of Kimmeridge clay, the spray-lashed headlands of Portland stone, and the tilted, faulted Purbeck Beds, which dip beneath the waves at Peveril Point. Along this coast fulmar glide past jostling guillemot, the weary Channel-crossing migrants find rest in scrub-filled gullies, and downland butterflies and orchids still decorate the cliff-top fields of limestone grassland.

Dorset provides an embarrassment of riches for the naturalist, in its towns as well as in its countryside. Where else, save at Weymouth's reedy wilderness of RADIPOLE, can the sounds of water rail and bearded tit mingle with those of motor traffic and diesel trains?

W.G. TEAGLE

Arne

SY 984885; 525ha; RSPB reserve
Rich heathland and estuary margin
Permit only to main body of reserve
Leaflet from RSPB
All year

The mudflats, saltmarsh and reedbeds, the birch, oak and coniferous woodlands and the small old fields and roadside verges add to the variation of the reserve, but the main importance of Arne is the splendid heathland. Heather, bell heather and dwarf gorse are spread across the thin acid peats, with cross-leaved heath where the soil is damper and with fine stands of Dorset heath. Wetter sites are also rich in bog species, such as *Sphagnum* mosses, white beak-sedge and all three British sundews and, with open pools formed from old bomb craters, provide an important habitat for some of the special insects of the reserve, such as small red damselfly, downy emerald, scarce ischnura, scarce and southern aeshna.

A special feature of the Dorset heathlands is their colonies of reptiles and, here at Arne, all six British species may be found.

Considerable spreads of gorse grow in the coombs and around the heathlands, providing suitable nest sites for another Arne speciality, the tiny Dartford warbler, a rare non-migratory bird always threatened because, at the limit of its range, it cannot survive hard winters. Over 170 species of birds have been noted here, with impressive winter flocks of the larger waders, with a good range of wildfowl in winter and a fine variety of passage birds, including several hundred black-tailed godwit on spring migration. Breeding birds include species of heathland, woodland and marsh, such as stonechat, nightjar, sparrowhawk and redshank, while the reedbeds provide a nesting site which has attracted bearded tit.

Although a permit is required to visit the main body of the heathland, the Shipstal Point area is open at all times; a nature trail is laid out during the summer months and the Point provides a bird-watching site from which summer terns and winter wildfowl may be seen.

One of Arne's special plants is Dorset heath.

Dartford warbler, a bird of the Dorset heathlands.

Avon Forest Park

SU 128023; 600ha; DCC
Heathland and plantations
Spring, summer

A relict area of the Dorset heathlands, the park includes a spread of grassland and heath within coniferous woodlands. Dartford warbler occur on the heath which is also a site for smooth snake and sand lizard.

Black Ven and the Spittles

SY 353931; 64.4ha; DNT reserve
Undercliff, landslip, grassland and circular walk
This site is dangerous
Spring, early summer

Continual slipping opens a wide range of habitat from scrub woodland, on stable areas, to open sloping faces and puddingy mires where slips are frequent. Unimproved meadows form the western section of the reserve and contain a rich grassland flora. Cowslips flower on steeper banks, while the wet flushes support orchids and other wetland plants and harbour snipe in winter. Insects include great green bush cricket, while among the mammals are roe deer, fox and badger.

Boyden Wood

ST 404026; 0.8ha; WdT
Young broad-leaved woodland
Spring, early summer

An area of farmland, now returned to woodland by planting with deciduous trees, will form a haven for many types of wildlife as it develops towards maturity.

Bracketts Coppice

ST 517072; 21.6ha; DNT reserve
Woodland and scrub grassland
Permit only off right of way
Spring, early summer

Bracketts Coppice is a rather wet woodland, divided by a stream and by blocks of grassland. The wood is mainly of oak standards over a mixture of ash, birch, holly and old hazel coppice with shrub species such as wild rose, guelder-rose and privet. Generally the ground cover is fairly thin but there is a great deal of variation; areas of woodland grasses alternate with splays of fern, with woodland flowers such as bugle, primrose and violet or with spreads of enchanter's-nightshade or carpets of ivy. One of the most spectacular aspects of the reserve is a show of pendulous sedge, in some places covering the entire woodland floor.

Bramble, hawthorn and honeysuckle grow among the other shrubs and, in places, the ground is thick with young blackthorn seedlings, while an area of denser woodland is filled with ash saplings beneath the coppiced hazel. The natural climax on these lime-rich clays of fuller's earth is probably oak–ash woodland, but above the stream it is acid enough for bracken. The stream itself is edged with ferns and rich-wood plants such as dog's mercury and wood spurge.

The grasslands are also damp, with tussocks of purple moor-grass, rushes, sedges, and plants such as devil's-bit scabious, fleabane, tormentil, sawwort and common spotted-orchid. Scrub, spreading from the woodland, varies these clearings with birch, blackthorn, dogwood, gorse, hazel, hawthorn and wild rose. The damp-meadow plants, scrub and woodland edge make these grassland areas most attractive to a good range of butterflies and birds and they probably harbour the deer whose tracks may be seen in the wood.

Brounlie Wood

ST 601118; 1.5ha; WdT
New woodland and wetland
Spring, early summer

A mixture of tree species has been planted in a small area which includes three ponds.

Brownsea Island

SZ 032877; 100ha; DNT–NT reserve
Estuary island
Regular guided visits; no dogs
Boat service from Poole Quay or Sandbanks Ferry
Leaflet from DNT
April–September

The reserve occupies slightly less than half of the island and, even if you cannot coincide with the regular guided walk, the open-access part of the island is well worth a visit and a public hide affords views across the lagoon.

The lagoon is one of the first features you notice on reaching the island; backed by reedbeds and scattered with islands, it provides an opportunity to see some of the waterbirds. In late summer, 100 or more cormorants rest on the sea wall or spread their wings on islets while herons, which nest in the pines on the North Ridge in the second largest heronry in Britain, regularly visit the lagoon.

The island is basically two ridges, built of tertiary gravels divided by a clay-lined valley which opens on to the lagoon. The lagoon, the valley, the North Ridge and an area of foreshore make up the reserve, which contains red squirrel, sika deer and the heronry. The North Ridge is wooded with pine trees, varied with several exotic species, which stand over an often dense scrub of rhododendron. The ridge slopes down to the central valley, where two lakes provide freshwater pools for waterfowl, and falls in a steep short scarp to the reedmarsh and the lagoon. A further range of habitat is added by a wet woodland of willow and alder between the lakes and the reedmarsh and by spreads of grassland, heath and mixed woodland in the southern half of the island.

Common and Sandwich tern breed on the islands in the lagoon, little grebe, mallard, teal and tufted duck may nest by the lakes, and the reedbed and marsh provide sites for birds such as reed and sedge warbler, reed bunting and, probably, water rail. Other breeding species include great and lesser black-backed, black-headed and herring gull and shelduck.

Charlton Beeches

ST 897041; 1.2ha; WdT
Narrow roadside woodland
Spring, early summer

The small stand of large trees provides a refuge for woodland wildlife in an area comprising mainly arable farmland.

Cranborne Common

ST 103112; 42.8ha; DNT reserve
Typical Dorset heathland
Permit only off right of way
All year

The habitats range from dry heath, with gorse and heather, through wet heath and bog, with bog asphodel and good populations of dragonflies and crickets. The reserve is notable for reptiles and breeding birds, including nightjar and Dartford warbler.

Durlston Country Park

SZ 032773; 104.4ha; DCC
Coastal limestone grassland, scrub, old quarry workings and part of long-distance way
Leaflets from information centre or DCC Planning Dept; interpretive displays; warden service; guided walks in summer
Spring, summer

Although not strictly a nature reserve, Durlston Country Park is managed as a wildlife sanctuary. Many visitors are attracted by the superb seascapes and the view across to the Isle of Wight, but there is also a variety of limestone features from open rock to deep grassland and scrub.

The land, generally, slopes steeply towards the sea, where sheer Jurassic limestone cliffs stand exposed to the force of the wind. The cliff-top walk, part of the SOUTH WEST PENINSULA COAST PATH, provides dramatic views of seabirds and their nesting colonies. The importance of shelter is shown by the scrub on these slopes: the lower stands of blackthorn are spectacularly pruned while higher up, although still showing signs of wind sculpting, the scrub is more variable with hawthorn, gorse and bramble and, above and behind the crest of the headland, a belt of taller scrub is thick with traveller's-joy.

Brownsea Island, one of the last English strongholds of red squirrel.

A great variety of lime-loving plants may be seen on the grassland slopes where deeper soils carry gorse, bramble and wild rose over coarse grasses, clovers and thistles, and shallow soils are filled with bright small herbs. This gives a patterned hillside, a mosaic of taller grassland and low herb gardens full of common bird's-foot-trefoil, kidney and horseshoe vetch, lady's bedstraw and salad burnet, restharrow, yellow-wort and common centaury, carline thistle, dwarf thistle and quaking-grass.

Above the grassland is a broken plateau, an area of the hills and holes of old quarry workings and of slabby limestone walling. The steep thin sunny slopes are ideal sites for such plants as pyramidal orchid while deeper, sheltered soils show taller plants such as greater knapweed, wild parsnip and woolly thistle, or bracken where rain has washed the lime from the soil.

The scrub provides shelter and feeding for migrant birds while the plants attract a great range of butterflies including Adonis, chalkhill and small blue, marbled white, dark green fritillary and Lulworth skipper.

Fifehead Wood

ST 778218; 20ha; WdT
Oak–ash woodland
Spring, early summer

Dry and wet woodland with oak and ash standards over old hazel coppice; part of the wood was once wet enough to support an osier bed.

The Fleet and Chesil Bank

SY 568840–668754; 800ha; Strangways Estate
Large tidal lagoon and shingle beach
No access to part of Chesil Bank in nesting season, and no access at any time to sanctuary
All year

The huge storm beach is one of the five largest shingle ridges in Europe and the lagoon behind it is sheltered and shallow, a sanctuary and feeding ground for waterbirds. This lagoon, the Fleet, is open to the sea in Portland Harbour and lies behind the eastern half of the shingle bank which extends for over 25km from the ISLE OF PORTLAND.

The western part of the Fleet is a sanctuary and contains the famous Abbotsbury Swannery where mute swan have bred for centuries; winter numbers of these birds may approach 1000. They feed on the richest beds of brackish-water plants remaining in Britain, for the lagoon holds good amounts of eelgrass, with both narrow-leaved and dwarf eelgrass and beaked tasselweed. Wigeon, too, are attracted here and several thousand may be present in winter, together with very large numbers of coot, Brent goose, gadwall, goldeneye, pintail and pochard. Shelduck, shoveler, teal and tufted duck also winter on the Fleet, with red-breasted merganser here and in Portland Harbour.

Small numbers of waders may feed on the muddy shingle edges or on the clay beaches of the

The Chesil Bank protects the Fleet from the sea.

Fleet, including species such as dunlin, bar-tailed godwit, lapwing, oystercatcher, ringed and grey plover and redshank. The shingle is an important breeding site for common and little tern and is wardened in summer to protect them from disturbance; no access is permitted at this time.

Westwards, beyond the Fleet, the shingle lies against the land, backed by arable slopes, small lagoons, and an interesting area of reedbed at WEST BEXINGTON where reed-nesting birds and migrants may be seen. The shingle has developed a good range of typical plants such as sea-kale and yellow horned-poppy. Within its length the Chesil Bank contains populations of rough clover, shrubby sea-blite and sea pea, and is also the only known British site for *Mogoplistes squamiger*, a species of wingless cricket.

Fontmell Down

Permit only; 57.2ha; DNT–NT reserve
Chalk downland, scrub and woodland
Spring, summer

Time has carved the edge of the Dorset Downs into smoothly rounded shoulders of chalk which curve into steep dry coombs and which stand high above the clays of the vales. Fontmell Down overlooks the Vale of the Stour and the other great chalk banks which thrust out into the plain.

The reserve itself is a dry valley patterned with scrub, with woodland along one side. The slopes are steep, full of chalkland flowers and butterflies and scattered clumps and thickets of lime-loving scrub. Blackthorn, hawthorn, bramble, gorse and wild rose, dogwood, wayfaring-tree, whitebeam, privet, holly and yew are tangled with traveller's-joy and honeysuckle. The woodland proper is chiefly of planted conifers, which the DNT intend to replace with native hardwoods, but it also contains beech, ash and whitebeam, with birch and with spectacular spreads of traveller's-joy, in places covering entire trees.

The grassland plants are exceptionally rich and grow in great profusion on the thin chalk soils or on the mounded ant hills which cover the slopes. Quaking-grass, harebell, carline and dwarf thistle, lady's bedstraw and common bird's-foot-trefoil, with restharrow, small scabious, wild thyme and salad burnet are among the typical plants. Other less common species include early gentian, clustered bellflower, bastard-toadflax and autumn lady's-tresses while, to the south of the reserve, is an additional small plot which is managed for an interesting population of greater knapweed parasitised by knapweed broomrape.

Green Hill Down

ST 792037; 12ha; DNT reserve
Chalk downland, clay-with-flints capping
Permit only off bridleway; no dogs
Spring, summer

Scrub and scattered oak, ash and beech add variety to an area of grassland which, with a small pond, contains a wide range of habitat and includes a strong population of marbled white butterfly.

Hartland Moor

Permit only; 258ha; NCC–NT reserve
Fine example of Dorset heath
Leaflet from NCC
Spring, early summer

One of the best remaining examples of southern lowland heath, the reserve contains dry and wet heathland grading into saltmarsh. Animals include a number of rare insects and all six native reptiles.

Hengistbury Head

SZ 175907; 100ha; Bournemouth BC reserve
Low coastal promontory
Leaflet from BBC
Spring, autumn

A circular trail demonstrates the promontory which includes heathland, woodland, grassland, ponds, dunes, saltmarsh and seashore, important as a staging post for spring and autumn migrants.

Hod Hill

Permit only; 2.6ha; NT reserve
Chalk downland
Spring, summer

The two small blocks of fine unimproved grassland contain chalkland plants and butterflies.

The chalkland of Fontmell Down overlooking the Vale of the Stour.

Dorset

Holton Heath

Permit only; 80ha; NCC reserve
Heathland and woodland
Spring, summer

A belt of saltmarsh and reedbed adds a further range of habitat to a varied area of dry heathland with stands of birch and Scots pine. The heathland is rich in animal species such as spiders, wasps and butterflies, including both grayling and silver-studded blue. Smooth snake and sand lizard are present and breeding birds include stonechat and, possibly, Dartford warbler.

Horse Close Wood

ST 715045; 16.4ha; WdT
Mixed woodland
Spring, early summer

Under oak standards the wood is a mix of alder, ash, oak and hazel coppice and contains one of the very few Dorset populations of meadow saffron. There is a typical range of woodland birds and a large and active badger sett.

Isle of Portland

SY 682738; *c.*1050ha; various bodies
Massive limestone outcrop
All year

Connected with the mainland by the pebble ridge of the Chesil Bank, the island provides a site for formal wildlife studies in the presence of a ringing station and bird observatory. Cliffs and quarries demonstrate the geology and fossils of the limestone, supporting an exciting range of plant and insect life, while the island is a staging post for migrant birds and a superb site for sea-watching.

Isle of Purbeck

See map; *c.*22,000ha; various bodies
Chalk and limestone hills set between heathland and sea
Spring, summer

Purbeck's seaward defences are the cliffs, where layered and buckled rocks provide ideal nesting sites for birds and shallow ledges on which plants can grow above the reach of the sea. The sea continually carves and whittles the rocks away, forming complex and spectacular bays, such as Lulworth Cove. Until the sea cut through the long ridge to the east, the Isle of Purbeck was joined to the Isle of Wight: the chalk which forms the Old Harry rocks is continued as the Needles. From WHITENOTHE to Worbarrow Bay the chalk is exposed on the cliffs and then gives way to a varied range of rocks, including the oil-rich shales of Kimmeridge, which continues round Durlston Head and meets the chalk again beyond Swanage. This is the only site in Britain where chalk and Jurassic limestone lie side by side; with exposures of Wealden sands, of gault and Kimmeridge clays, it draws geologists from all over the world to visit the Purbeck coast.

The cliffs and coves, the wave-cut platforms and fissured slabs of rock are also rich in wildlife and a long section of the coastline, including the cliffs, the beach and the seabed for a kilometre offshore, has been scheduled as the PURBECK MARINE RESERVE to protect its plants and animals.

The cliffs themselves may be sheer towers of hard rock or steep crumbling faces, ranging from dazzling chalk to dark shales; green slopes and

Holton Heath's dry heathland runs to the saltmarsh edge of Poole Harbour.

Wet heathland is typical of one of the aspects of Hartland Moor.

jungled spreads of scrub show where landslips have broken the rock face, while the pale limestone may be marked by caves, old quarry workings cut in the face of the cliffs. These caves are important sites for bats and hold colonies of greater horse-shoe, Bechstein's and grey long-eared bat, while the cliffs provide nesting sites for birds such as fulmar and kittiwake, shag and cormorant, guillemot, razorbill and perhaps a few pairs of puf-fin. The cliff tops are rich in plants, with notable species such as wild cabbage, Italian lords-and-ladies and early spider-orchid growing among a host of colourful flowers. A fine variety of insects includes Adonis, chalkhill, little and common blue with marbled white and dark green fritillary but-terflies, together with wart-biter cricket and long-winged cone-head. The jumbles of the landslips provide cover for breeding buzzard and larger mammals such as fallow deer and badger.

Inland, where soft rocks separate the limestone from the chalk, a spread of agricultural land gives a scenery of fields and hedges, of farmsteads and small villages protected by the chalk ridge to the north. This shallow vale is watered by small streams which drain the hills and flow either to the sea at Swanage or northwards into Poole Harbour, cutting the chalk where Corfe Castle stands, dominating the gap. Beyond the chalk, stretching up to the River Frome and Poole Harbour, are the outlands of Purbeck, the lowland heaths and bogs.

The chalk forms a ridge which runs from east to west, rising to around 200m and generally over 100m. Except where the slopes are steep, farming

has modified the grassland and most of the chalk-land flowers have been lost but, on these steeper slopes, some characteristic downland remains. Some of the scarps are wooded and oak and hazel coppice contrasts with the wide plantations on the plain below.

The heaths have formed on coarse sands, laid down in tertiary times, where clays prevent free drainage and assist the development of the mires. These wet and dry heaths include STUDLAND, HARTLAND MOOR and ARNE and form a striking contrast with the higher land of Purbeck; where the hills are rich in lime-loving plants, the heath-lands are far more acid; where all but the steepest upland slopes are farmed, the heaths form an open wilderness. These heaths once stretched from here almost to Dorchester, Thomas Hardy's inspiration for the daunting Egdon Heath, but they have been ploughed, planted with conifers and buried under houses and industry. Now only a broken scatter of heathland remains, a last small refuge for plants and animals unique in the British Isles.

Adder and grass-snake, slow-worm and common lizard slither or scuttle among stands of Dorset heath and here, but nowhere else in Britain, they share their hunting grounds with smooth snake and sand lizard. The sand lizard may occur as far north as AINSDALE DUNES in Lancashire, but the smooth snake only occurs in southern England and the Dorset heaths are the stronghold of both these species. For the Dartford warbler, also, Dorset is a key area, and other typical heathland birds include linnet, stone-chat and yellowhammer with nightjar and hobby.

To these special animals of the heaths might be added insects such as feathered footman moth, dragonflies from the pools and mires such as scarce coenagrion, scarce blue darter, scarce aeshna and small red damselfly, and other interesting species such as heath and large marsh grasshoppers. The wetter areas, too, contain a splendid range of plants which includes brown beak-sedge, intermediate bladderwort, marsh clubmoss, royal fern, great sundew, marsh gentian and the delicate small bog orchid. The heathlands provide a wide diversity of interest, are visually wild and beautiful and, coloured with Dorset heath, filled with the scent of bog myrtle, are an irreplaceable part of our national heritage.

The Isle was made when the Alps were built, raised by the huge pressures which lifted the spire of the Matterhorn, though the forces which reached southern England were no more than the ripples of that great upheaval. The layers of rock laid down before this time were thrown into folds, buckled and faulted, attacked by erosion as they lifted above the sea and then cut back to form the present coastline. The youngest rock, the tertiary sands and clays which form the heaths, laps at the foot of the ridge of chalk which was forced into a high-pitched fold. Within the fold were earlier Wealden Beds, sands, clays and shales laid down when a huge river drained from the west, carrying material from as far as Dartmoor, while under the Wealden Beds were limestones folded across the Kimmeridge clay.

The alternation of hard and soft rocks makes for sudden coves and curving bays, for sloping cliffs and sheer rock faces, for a range of variation which equals the magic of the heaths – a day spent on Purbeck can be unforgettable.

Stair Hole and Lulworth Cove demonstrate the astonishing geology of the Isle of Purbeck.

Lulworth Range Walks

SY 882804; various lengths; MOD
Coastal downland
The range is still used: visitors must keep to marked footpaths
For open days see local press or tel. Bindon Abbey 462721, ext. 859
Leaflets from exhibition centre, DCC or DNT
Spring, summer, on open days only

Several walks have been laid out in an area rich in lime-loving plants and animals. Over 2000ha of downland with around 10.5km of coast make up the range.

Morden Bog

Permit only; 149ha; NCC reserve
Dry heath, bog and old decoy ponds
Spring, early summer

An exceptionally rich heathland holds a very varied insect population. The surrounding FC woodland encourages a good variety of bird life and supports a large deer population.

Powerstock Common

SY 540963; 13.4ha; DNT reserve
Oak woodland, scrub, grassland and disused railway
Permit only off bridleway and tracks
Spring, early summer

The reserve is made up of several areas within the FC plantations which cover much of the common. Where the bridleway passes through one of the oakwoods, the ground is damp and heavy, a slope of clay with an understorey of hazel, varied with stands of dense blackthorn or with shrubs such as spindle, privet and dogwood. Ash standards occur with the oaks and the less dense areas are floored with rich-wood species such as primrose, violet and dog's mercury. Bracken grows in well-lit drier parts, with bramble and red currant, and gives way in damper shade to broad buckler-fern or male-fern; the wettest clays are marked by clumps of pendulous sedge and occasional grey willow.

The open grassland field is also damp, a spread of purple moor-grass, filled with wetland plants and ringed with trees. Cross-leaved heath and heather, devil's-bit scabious, tormentil, fleabane and betony contrast with rushes, sedges and horsetails, and a small pond at the edge of the meadow has a variety of water plants including lesser spearwort and bogbean.

The forest tracks provide another very varied habitat, fringed with drainage ditches and marshy places thick with meadowsweet and yellow iris, with rushes and pendulous sedge, edged with stands of common spotted-orchid, with vetches, clovers, knapweeds and carpets of creeping cinquefoil. Heather and gorse spread beside the tracks beneath young plantations of conifers which form an open scrub, highly suitable for hunting birds such as sparrowhawk. Taller plantations, with their dark forest floors, have little undergrowth, but the many animal tracks which cross the rides indicate that they probably shelter some of the larger mammals here. Another habitat is provided by the bracken-covered slopes which run up to the crest of the old common. The bracken is dense and laced with bramble, some of it planted with conifers, but a variety of saplings have become established and show how the native woodland would easily spread, if it were given the opportunity to do so.

The disused railway line adds a cutting (to which there is no access), suitable for lime-loving species, and the area as a whole is rich in insects and supports a wide range of birds and other animals, including fallow, sika and roe deer.

Purbeck Marine Reserve

SY 909788; *c.*650ha; DNT reserve
Cliff top to as far as 1km offshore
Leaflets from information centre or DNT
Spring, summer

Although marine nature reserves have been established at LUNDY ISLAND (Devon) and SKOMER ISLAND (Dyfed), Purbeck is the first reserve of its kind to be set up on the mainland. Several organisations and landowners have entered into a voluntary agreement to conserve the wildlife interest of a length of the Purbeck coast. The reserve is wardened and has an excellent interpretative centre at Kimmeridge Bay, a deep curve dominated by the great shaly cliffs which fall to the Kimmeridge Ledges.

Over the 7km of the reserve the cliffs, up to 165m, are very variable in their geology and are often highly unstable, providing an enormous range of coastal situations.

The difference in height between high and low tides is relatively small, less than 2m, but the shallow slope of the beaches means that a wide area is exposed at low water, ideal for seashore studies. The seashore at low tide can show much of the change from land to water life. The pools at various stages down the beach will hold the plants and animals which are typical of that zone. Barnacles shut their doors and limpets clamp close to the rocks, keeping in the moisture they need to survive

Kimmeridge Bay: the sea-cut ledges form an important feature of the marine reserve.

St Aldhelm's Head on the South West Peninsula Coast Path.

until the next tide; animals which move easily make their way to crevices which still stay damp or slide into jungles of seaweed to keep themselves moist. Drying out is the chief danger to these animals and plants – those of the upper beach may have to survive for hours out of water, those at the lower end may only have to cope for minutes.

Channelled wrack marks the top zone, followed by bladder wrack, with knotted wrack in sheltered areas, and then serrated wrack. Below this, and in the deeper pools, sea-lettuce and kelp mark the margin of the tides. Throughout the zones the animals move or live cemented to the rocks or seaweeds, a wonderful variety of colour, shape and size.

The reserve is mid-way between the western and eastern basins of the Channel and contains several species at or near the limits of their normal distribution. These include cushion starfish, wart-let anemone, and a range of algae and of molluscs including Pandora shell.

Radipole

SY 676796; 78ha; RSPB reserve
Reedbeds and open water
All year

A most important staging post for migrating birds: many species have been recorded here. The reed-beds provide nesting sites for birds such as bearded tit and warblers, while the lake varies enough in depth to attract dabblers and diving ducks.

South West Peninsula Coast Path

SY 344928–SZ 042860; 116km; CC
Very varied section of long-distance way
Leaflet from CC or DCC, or booklet from HMSO bookshops
Spring, summer

The pathway begins at Lyme Regis and ends at Poole Harbour. On its way it passes through or by a variety of areas of wildlife interest from BLACK VEN AND THE SPITTLES in the west to STUDLAND in the east.

Sovell Down

ST 992108; 1.6ha; DNT reserve
Chalk grassland and scrub
Permit only off rights of way
Spring, summer

The reserve is rich in chalkland plants, with over 135 species recorded. It contains a good range of butterflies while the scrub provides feeding and nesting sites for small birds.

Stanpit Marsh

SZ 169920; 49.7ha; Christchurch BC reserve
Estuary marshland
No access off rights of way
Information caravan
All year

The reserve ranges from grazing marsh to fresh-water marsh and saltmarsh, and from estuary waters to ditches and pools. Waders, together with birds such as shelduck and heron, are attracted to the site.

Stonecrop Wood

SY 988955; 0.8ha; WdT
Mixed woodland
Spring, early summer

Mainly a birch woodland, Stonecrop Wood is situated on the urban outskirts of Broadstone and provides a valuable retreat and shelter for wildlife in that area.

Studland

SZ 034836; 631ha; NCC–NT reserve
Dry and wet heathland, lagoon and woodland
There is severe danger of fire: do not drop matches or cigarettes
Leaflets from NCC
Spring, early summer

Some of the specialities of the reserve are hidden within the heathland which makes up most of the area, but two nature trails have been set up to show the general wildlife interest. An observation hut, open on Sundays or by appointment, overlooks the Little Sea, a freshwater lagoon which in winter may hold up to 2000 duck.

The Sand Dune Nature Trail includes a stretch of foreshore, outside the reserve, which demonstrates a good variety of shells together with birds such as oystercatcher, ringed plover, common and Sandwich tern and perhaps, in winter, red-breasted merganser, common scoter and eider. The trail proper begins in the dunes which are stabilised by sand couch, lyme-grass and marram, decorated with sheep's-bit, common centaury and sea bindweed. Behind the first ridge a damp gully, a slack, has developed and in the damper areas characteristic plants are found. Cross-leaved heath and round-leaved sundew, bog myrtle, purple moor-grass and common cottongrass occur while similar sites hold royal fern, great sundew and marsh gentian. Grey willow, birch and gorse form clumps of scrub, and occasional pools, old bomb craters, may contain greater bladderwort. The drier levels and intervening ridges are thick with heather, here and there laced with lesser dodder, a parasite which grows on heather and gorse.

The Woodland Trail, open from April to September, leads through birch, grey willow and aspen, gladed with bluebell and bramble, with blackthorn, hawthorn and elder scrub. Part of the trail overlooks the Little Sea, a site for the rare spring quillwort. The woodland contains typical bird life and roe deer may be frequent. The reserve is home to all six British reptiles and is rich in insects, with a fine range of dragonflies.

Studland Heath: wet and dry heathland, forming the major part of the reserve, stretches towards the sea.

Sutton Bingham Reservoir

ST 543095; 1.6ha; WWA
Reservoir and marshy fringes
All year

Only a small part of the reservoir lies in Dorset, with the rest in Somerset, but throughout the year a good variety of water birds may be seen on and around it.

Tadnoll Meadows

Permit only; 44ha; DNT reserve
Heathland, damp meadowland and bog
Spring, summer

Heathland, of heather, bell heather and cross-leaved heath, and species-rich meadowland with plants such as water avens, great burnet and common spotted-orchid, grade into a spread of purple moor-grass and *Sphagnum*, with abundant stands of bog myrtle. The reserve is noted for smooth snake and for good numbers of roe deer and resident badger.

Thorncombe Wood and Black Heath Trails

SY 726922; 3.5km; DCC
Woodland and heathland trails
Leaflet from DCC
Spring, early summer

The trail passes through mixed woodland and scrub-covered heath with the added interest of two old ponds. A good variety of birds may be seen together with characteristic butterflies.

Townsend

SZ 025783; 12.8ha; DNT reserve
Limestone grassland and scrub
Leaflet from DNT or DCC
Spring, summer

The area has been extensively quarried, giving scrub-filled hollows, good for small birds such as nightingale, to contrast with herb-rich stony banks. Plants such as kidney vetch, horseshoe vetch and sainfoin attract a good range of butterflies including Lulworth skipper and little blue.

West Bexington

SY 525870; 16ha; DNT reserve
Shingle beach and reedbed
No access to reedbed
Spring, early summer, autumn

Sea-kale, sea campion and yellow horned-poppy grow on the section of the Chesil Bank included within the reserve, while the wetland behind is filled with common reed, important for nesting and migrant birds. The reserve forms an integral part of THE FLEET complex.

Whitenothe Undercliff

SY 765813; 46ha; NT–DNT
Scrub, clay and chalk grasslands, wetland and crags
Some sections may be dangerous, particularly after rain
Spring, early summer

This is a superbly varied area, backed by cliffs up to 140m high, which overlooks the great sweep of Weymouth Bay and the humpbacked ISLE OF PORTLAND. The landslips have formed a series of slopes, terraces and gullies, a complex of wet and dry situations filled with a wide range of plants. There is a contrast not only between the wet and dry areas but also in exposure: because of the hummocked and tilted slopes, some places lie completely open to the strong sea winds while elsewhere

Whitenothe, like the Axmouth–Lyme Regis landslip, shows how the cliffs have slumped downwards, providing a rich range of habitat.

hidden pockets are sheltered by banks and scrub, warm and windless on all but the stormiest days.

The thickets of scrub on the more stable slopes and filling the drier gullies are very varied – perhaps a tangle of blackthorn, hawthorn, wayfaring-tree, privet, elder, bramble and wild rose. Ivy, honeysuckle, traveller's-joy and wild madder climb around the edges of the paths or up the shrubs, and this riot of vegetation is mirrored in the damper areas where groves of great horsetail, hart's-tongue and stinking iris grow. Some of the gullies are wet enough for common reed and fleabane, rushes and stands of great willowherb, and damp washes from the soft collapsing cliffs are colonised by colt's-foot and plants such as yellow-wort, restharrow and viper's-bugloss. Less disturbed or stable areas are grassed and filled with lime-loving plants, including a number of orchids.

The animal life, too, is rich, and the population of small mammals may be hunted by kestrel or buzzard. Small birds nest in the thickets, which also provide shelter for migrants, and the grasslands are nesting sites for meadow pipit and skylark. The scrub also gives cover to other animals – roe deer lie up in the daytime – while warm banks are sunning sites for adder. Among the insects, a good range of species includes Lulworth skipper and great green bush-cricket.

Woolsbarrow

SY 892925; 7.6ha; DNT reserve
Dry heathland and Iron Age hill fort
No access away from tracks
Summer

A fine heathland area, an oasis among FC plantations, the reserve contains classic heathland species. It is a focal point for birds such as nightjar, as well as reptiles and insects, including wood tiger beetle.

Durham, Cleveland, and Tyne and Wear

From the high windswept moorlands of the Pennines in the west to the beaches and cliffs in the east, Durham, Cleveland and Tyne and Wear show a remarkable variety in their landscape and have much more to offer than the traditional pit-village image often portrayed by the media. Although the region bears the scars of past and present extractive and manufacturing industries, it also contains extensive areas of great natural beauty and biological interest. The Durham County Conservation Trust exists to safeguard the wildlife and natural environment of the area covered by those parts of Durham and Tyne and Wear that lie between the rivers Tyne and Tees, while the Cleveland Nature Conservation Trust manages the rest of the region.

The Wear and Tees, which are fast-flowing torrents in their upper reaches, have enlarged their valleys through time to form the Pennine Dales, and in its middle course the Wear has cut down a steeply incised meander, on the 'peninsula' of which stands the splendid Norman cathedral of Durham city. Between Sunderland and Teesmouth the magnesian limestone plateau has been dissected by smaller streams, producing the coastal denes which are a unique feature of the landscape.

Wide contrasts in land use can also be observed across the region. Mineral extraction, once of great importance in the Pennine area, is now much reduced, leaving scars which are in the process of healing. The population is gradually moving east and the land is reverting to hill farming and grouse moor. In the east heavy industry still exists, especially opencast and deep mining of coal and quarrying of the magnesian limestone, and yet here too

can be found some of the richest botanical sites.

Geologically there are three main zones: the Permian magnesian limestone block running the length of the coastline and broadening inland from north to south, the central low-lying area of carboniferous shales, coals and sandstones, and the western dales where the underlying carboniferous limestone has a mantle of glacial deposits capped with peat. While the eastern plateau is also covered by varying depths of glacial clays in its central parts, the magnesian limestone outcrops along the coastal cliffs and is also at the surface in places along the west of the escarpment.

The eastern part of the county was probably the first to be cleared of its primary post-glacial forests and is now mostly used for farming in between the pockets of industry. In places where the soils are too thin and the slopes too steep for farm machinery there are patches of herb-rich magnesian limestone grassland. Where the coast has been incised, forming deep ravines known as denes, in some cases with almost vertical sides, woodland has often survived for hundreds of years. CASTLE EDEN DENE, the most famous of these, is the largest and possibly also the most natural; it is particularly significant for its plants and insects. Along the northernmost stretch of the coast the Permian rocks have formed massive cliffs, and at Marsden Bay there is an impressive offshore sea stack, MARSDEN CLIFFS, the most important breeding colony of seabirds to be found between the FARNE ISLANDS (Northumberland) and BEMPTON CLIFFS (YORKSHIRE).

The central lowlands of the valley of the River Wear and its tributaries used to be the site of the

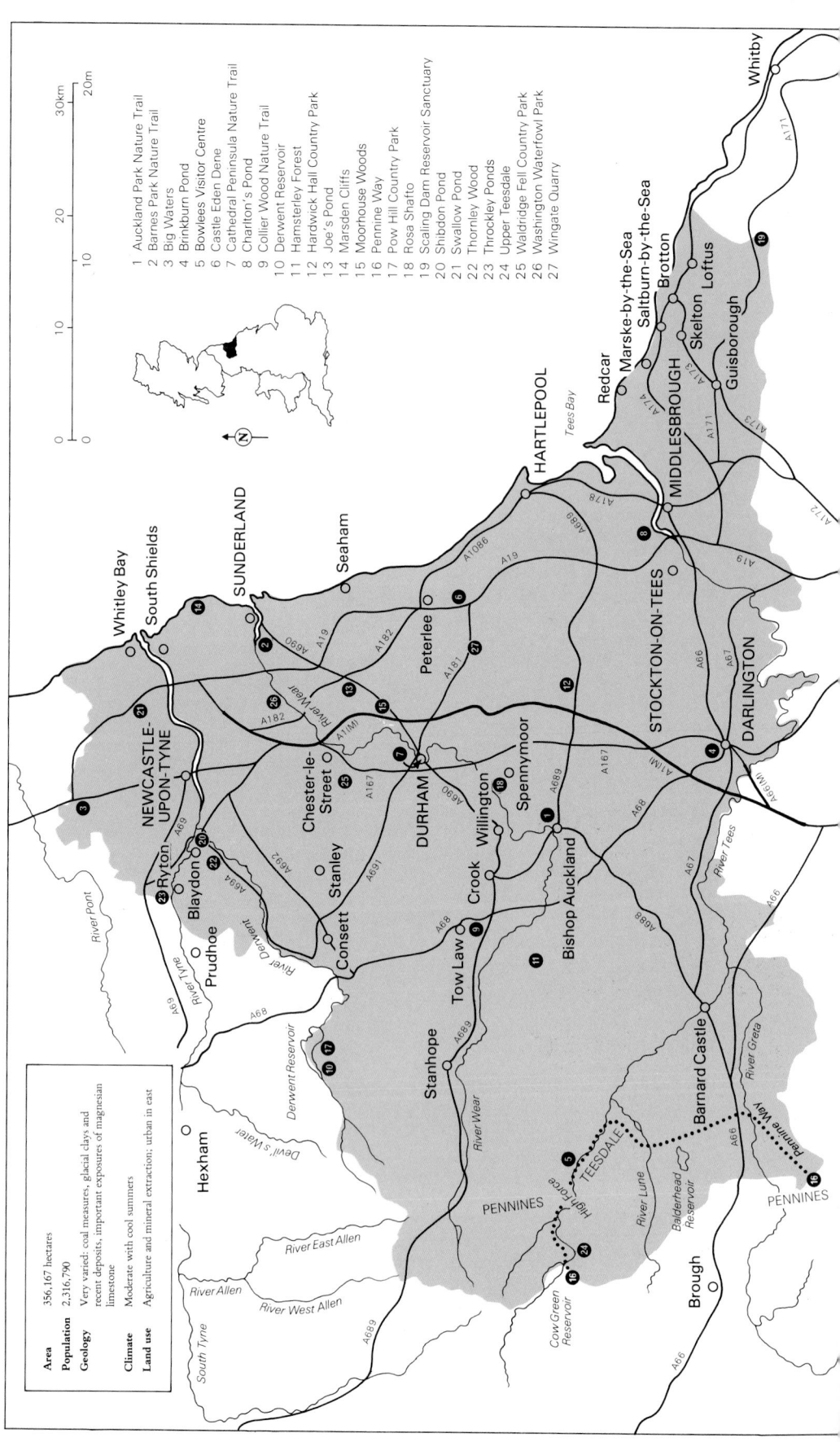

Area	356,167 hectares
Population	2,316,790
Geology	Very varied: coal measures, glacial clays and recent deposits, important exposures of magnesian limestone
Climate	Moderate with cool summers
Land use	Agriculture and mineral extraction; urban in east

1 Auckland Park Nature Trail
2 Barnes Park Nature Trail
3 Big Waters
4 Brinkburn Pond
5 Bowlees Visitor Centre
6 Castle Eden Dene
7 Cathedral Peninsula Nature Trail
8 Charlton's Pond
9 Collier Wood Nature Trail
10 Derwent Reservoir
11 Hamsterley Forest
12 Hardwick Hall Country Park
13 Joe's Pond
14 Marsden Cliffs
15 Moorhouse Woods
16 Pennine Way
17 Pow Hill Country Park
18 Rosa Shafto
19 Scaling Dam Reservoir Sanctuary
20 Shibdon Pond
21 Swallow Pond
22 Thornley Wood
23 Throckley Ponds
24 Upper Teesdale
25 Waldridge Fell Country Park
26 Washington Waterfowl Park
27 Wingate Quarry

great Durham coalfield. Of the hundreds of mines seen here a few years ago, less than a handful remain. During the last 20 years the towering heaps of shale have disappeared in a massive reclamation programme carried out by the County Council. Most of the projects have resulted in the return of the land to agriculture, but in some cases, as at Roddymoor near Crook, reclamation has taken the form of an experimental tree-planting programme.

In the western dales the wider valley bottoms are now mainly mixed farmland, but on the slopes and ridges sheep and grouse moor occupy much of the open spaces. There are also quite extensive stretches of plantation, of which the largest is HAMSTERLEY FOREST, with good numbers of roe deer, adder, slow-worm and other reptiles as well as an interesting variety of insects.

The upper dales, which converge on the Cross Fell group of hills, are as perfect an example of wilderness as anything in Britain south of the Scottish border. UPPER TEESDALE is internationally famous for its unique assemblage of arctic–alpine plants and invertebrates. To help the tourist understand Teesdale an information centre has been established at BOWLEES which is visited by thousands of visitors every year. High Force, the highest waterfall in England, and Cauldron Snout are two of the scenic attractions where the great basaltic Whin Sill can be seen to its best advantage. Close by, the Cow Green Reservoir broods darkly

between the high hills. Although the scenery in Upper Weardale is less spectacular, it is of a similar beauty, and the road to Cumbria climbs up to over 666m at Killhope summit.

Upper Derwentdale has its beauty spots too, and not far from industrial Consett is Coombe Bridges, where the river forms a deep gorge in the limestone strata. The Hisehope Burn joins the Derwent here after flowing across grouse moorland well known both for its junipers (the local people refer to it as Juniper Valley) and for its moorland insects. The Derwent Valley also supports large stretches of relatively undisturbed deciduous woodland where dominant oak provides an important habitat for birds and mammals. At the DERWENT RESERVOIR in the far north west an extensive nature reserve has been established. The reservoir is a favourite spot for birdwatching: large populations of wildfowl occur in winter and many other species are seen at migration times.

The region's wide variations in altitude and topography, together with the influence of man, are reflected in its diversity of vegetation and wildlife habitats. Durham, Cleveland, and Tyne and Wear contain much to excite the visitor with an interest in wildlife and the natural environment.

TOM DUNN
JULIE GAMAN
SUSAN PARKER

Auckland Park Nature Trail

NZ 215803; 2km; Wear Valley DC
Trail in parkland around tributary of River Wear
Leaflet from DCCT
Spring, summer

Parkland trees and exotics, hawthorn scrub and native trees provide a rich habitat for birds; a stream adds further interest to the trail.

Barnes Park Nature Trail

NZ 383557; 1km; Sunderland BC
Trail in parkland along stream
Leaflet from DCCT
Spring, summer

Ash, yew, holly and privet with exotic and native shrubs and flowers attract insects, such as orange-tip butterfly, and many birds.

Big Waters

NZ 227734; 15ha; NWT reserve
Large mining subsidence pond and grassland
Permit only to fenced western area
All year

The large pond is thickly fringed with reed canary-grass and bulrush, the wet grassland rich in old-meadow plants such as great burnet. Breeding birds include coot, great crested grebe and tufted duck, with winter teal and shoveler.

Bishop Middleham Quarry

Permit only; 9.1ha; DCCT reserve
Limestone quarry, grassland and woodland
Spring, summer

Autumn gentian, fairy flax, moonwort, blue moor-grass, common rock-rose, northern marsh-orchid, pyramidal and fragrant orchid are among flowers which draw a good range of butterflies including browns, skippers and common blue.

Bishop Middleham Quarry: limestone cliffs above the species-rich grassland.

Blackhall

Permit only; 32ha; DCCT reserve
Coastal limestone grassland with foreshore
Spring, summer

The grassed sea cliff, clay-topped and often marshy and prone to landslip, was built beneath an ancient sea, a reef of magnesian limestone. Its special plants include blue moor-grass, bird's-eye primrose, bloody crane's-bill and large wintergreen. The beautiful grass-of-Parnassus grows in damp places with common butterwort, in a very different habitat from its more usual mires. Common rock-rose, restharrow and common bird's-foot-trefoil, with wild thyme and characteristic limestone and sea-coast plants, grow all around the damper gullies where yellow iris shows the wettest places and a fine display of orchids may be seen.

There is a wide variety of habitat for insects. Blackhall attracts common blue, one of our best known but still very beautiful butterflies, as well as a colony of Castle Eden Argus. One reason for the common blue's wide spread is that the caterpillars feed on a relatively wide selection of plants, particularly clovers, trefoils and vetches. The Castle Eden Argus is more specific, feeding only on common rock-rose, and this particular form of Argus butterfly is found only in the north east coastal strip. The uncommon cistus forester moth, a relative of the burnets, also occurs on the reserve.

The limestone rocks conceal the rare sea spleenwort, while the foreshore has an interesting range of plants and animals despite colliery pollution. Included among the seashore animals are at least four sea anemones – beadlet, plumose, and two species of *Sagartia*. Waders and seabirds visit the coastal shingles and lagoons, and migration times may bring sightings of birds as varied as arctic skua and snow bunting.

Bowlees Visitor Centre

NY 907283; trail 1.4km; DCCT
Interpretative centre and trail
Leaflets from centre or DCCT
Spring, summer, autumn

The centre, established to explain the natural history and land uses of Teesdale, also displays some of its special plants, rescued from a now-flooded valley. The trail mounts through ash woodland, upland turf and hawthorn scrub to the fern-rich dampness of a spectacular waterfall where streamside birds include dipper and yellow wagtail.

Brinkburn Pond

NZ 282161; 0.4ha; DCCT reserve
Small pond
Spring, summer

The pond is fringed with marsh-marigold, yellow iris and willows and provides a breeding site for frog, common toad, smooth newt and birds such as mallard and moorhen.

Castle Eden Dene

NZ 410387; 200ha; NCC reserve
Deep wooded ravine
Leaflets from PDC
Spring, summer

The Dene is a long narrow valley which cuts through the high coastal plateau to the sea, a valley in which the river twists and turns, gathering tributaries, until it spills out against the shingle bank thrown up by the North Sea tides. The woods are very varied, sometimes clinging to steep slopes, sometimes curving gently to the stream, and they are pierced by a network of paths which run the length of the Dene. Clearings and streamside glades are filled with flowers while the spectacular limestone cliffs are cascades of ivy.

Castle Eden Dene is probably the least spoilt of the valleys which cut through the plateau of magnesian limestone. The rock was laid down in Permian times, some 200 million years ago, under circumstances rather similar to the Great Barrier Reef today. By the ice ages the land had been lifted above the sea and, at some point in the long period of advancing and melting ice, a torrent of water drained through the Dene to carve its way to the sea. Eventually the raw valley was buried under a glacial silt of rubble and ground-up rock. The head of the Dene is cut into this clay, fairly steep-sloped with the stream meandering through the valley bottom. Below this the clay slopes are less steep but the river finds a major fault in the soft magnesian limestone and runs through a narrow deep ravine. Lower again the valley opens, cut in the clay and the limestone, while further down the river plain is a wide spread of clay in which the stream curves between long valley slopes; limestone does not show again until the sea cliffs are reached.

Ash and yew would probably be the most widespread trees had nature been left to manage the Dene unaided, but oak has been encouraged because of the value of its timber. In the early nineteenth century the *Castle Eden* was launched, a ship built from Eden timber, and trees such as beech and sycamore have also been introduced. Blocks of conifers have been planted, together with horsechestnut, hornbeam and sweet chestnut; rhododendron, too, has been introduced to spread in a densely shading understorey, but a fine variety of native shrubs and trees still survives. Alder grows along the valley bottom where bird cherry occurs, wild cherry is scattered, mainly around the woodland edges, while other species include rowan, blackthorn, hawthorn, hazel, holly and elder.

The smaller plants are as varied as the trees, a superb range of species from acid-lovers such as heather, heath milkwort and tormentil to the lime-loving plants which are found in the turf of the sea cliffs. Spring in the woods brings a show of wood anemone, bluebell, primrose, ramsons and delicate violets set in a sea of dog's mercury. A hybrid between the primrose and cowslip occurs, which closely resembles the oxlip, confined to East

A splendid mix of woodland fills the valley of Castle Eden Dene.

Anglian woods. Another hybrid, found later in the year, is the cross between water avens and wood avens – a very variable cross which can produce an attractive suite of colours ranged between the two.

Several wild geraniums may be found throughout the reserve, including herb-Robert, meadow, wood and bloody crane's-bill. Bloody crane's-bill is not a common plant and, although it occurs fairly widely north of the Humber–Severn line and sparsely south of it, it is a rather local species. Many other uncommon plants occur within the Dene. The wide shelf of magnesian limestone provides a northern site for several species more typical of the chalk. Giant bellflower is a plant of open northern woodlands but here also are fly and bird's-nest orchid, more characteristic of downland woods. Columbine, too, is more common on the chalk, while the Dene supports plants of widespread but rather local occurrence, such as herb-Paris, lily-of-the-valley and round-leaved wintergreen.

Wetter places show marsh-marigold, marsh arrowgrass and spreads of opposite-leaved golden-saxifrage while dame's-violet lines the riverside; sanicle, woodruff, enchanter's-nightshade and sprays of ferns, such as male-fern, hart's-tongue and hard fern, grow in the woods while the sea-cliff grassland is rich in common bird's-foot-trefoil, wild thyme, carline and musk thistle, marjoram, cowslip and blue moor-grass, the sea shingle with plants such as restharrow, sea plantain and sea rocket.

Blomer's rivulet, barred carpet and the tiny *Acrolepiopsis betulella* moths were all first captured at the Dene, which is also famous for the Castle Eden Argus butterfly. A great variety of insects lives in the valley and provides food for a typical range of common woodland birds. Although there have been records of nuthatch breeding in Northumberland and some evidence that a few may breed as far north as Tayside in Scotland, here at Castle Eden Dene they are at their normal limit. Other birds include bullfinch and linnet, goldcrest and great spotted woodpecker. In summer migrant warblers arrive, such as blackcap or even grasshopper warbler, while winter may bring visits from brambling, siskin, waxwing, and perhaps even great grey shrike. Cold weather may drive dipper down from the upland streams when redshank and dunlin feed in the shelter of Denemouth and migrants such as snow bunting move down the coast. Other waders may visit from time to time including snipe, common and curlew sandpiper, greenshank and little stint, while migration times bring sightings of numerous terns. Buzzard may occasionally hunt the area, competing with the local predators – kestrel, sparrowhawk and tawny owl.

The resident mammals range in size from roe deer to pigmy shrew. There is a good population of badger, with numbers of native red squirrel.

Quiet is one of the features of the Dene, cut so deep below the surrounding land, and no one who visits it and enjoys its beauty can fail to hope that it remains undisturbed. The woods, of course, will change with time: great trees will fall and saplings

149

The larch plantation at Castle Eden Dene.

take their place; the Castle Eden Burn will continue to work at the clays and the limestone, finding the points of weakness and subtly changing the shape of the valley; all the natural change of erosion will come, in time, to the Dene. As long as it is conserved, however, for peaceful walks and for wildlife, it will safeguard not only the special plants and animals but also the very idea of natural things to set against our steel and concrete values.

Cathedral Peninsula Nature Trail

NZ 272422; 0.8km; DCCT–DCC
Urban trail along River Wear
Leaflet from DCCT
Spring, summer, autumn

Following a meander of the River Wear around Durham Cathedral, the trail shows a variety of alien and native trees with common woodland and waterside plants and birds.

Charlton's Pond

NZ 467232; 9ha; Stockton-on-Tees BC reserve
Flooded clay workings
No access to sanctuary in eastern part of reserve
All year

Good stands of common reed and bulrush, together with dense hawthorn scrub, attract winter numbers of starling and migrants such as waxwing; breeding birds include common sandpiper and common tern.

Collier Wood Nature Trail

NZ 129364; 0.4km; DCCT–DCC
Woodland trail
Leaflet from DCCT or DCC
Spring, summer

The trail is laid out in a mixed woodland with good spring flowers including bluebell, cowslip and primrose. The variety of animal life, particularly birds and insects, is nicely demonstrated in seasonal leaflets devised by the DCCT.

Cowpen Marsh

Permit only; 75ha; CNCT reserve
Grazing marsh and inter-tidal saltmarsh
Hide
Spring, summer

Shelduck, waders, yellow wagtail and meadow pipit breed on the marshland bordering Greatham Creek on the Tees Estuary. Passage and wintering birds include mallard, teal, curlew, bar-tailed godwit, grey plover and redshank. The public hide, overlooking Seal Sands, can be reached from the car park. The saltmarsh plants are of particular interest.

Derwent Reservoir

No access; 93ha; Sunderland and South Shields Water Co.
Western end of large reservoir
May be overlooked from lanes at NY 985519, 991524, 995528 and from Pow Hill Country Park
All year

In winter mallard, wigeon, teal and tufted duck, goldeneye, goosander and pochard spread across the reservoir, but disturbance confines most birds to the sanctuary area throughout the rest of the year. Autumn attracts passage waders and in spring and summer the sanctuary holds breeding waders and wildfowl. The B6306 overlooks the main section of the reservoir and public access is permitted on the private road across the dam.

Gravel Hole Quarry

Permit only; 1.5ha; CNCT reserve
Lime-loving scrub and grassland
Spring, summer

Small scabious, quaking-grass and orchids are among the plants which attract butterflies such as small heath and dingy skipper. The scrub contains a typical range of bird life.

Hamsterley Forest

NZ 093312; 4372ha; FC
Large area of FC woodland with pockets of native trees
Leaflets from information centre
Spring, summer

Despite the great sweeps of conifers casting their dense shade, many parts of Hamsterley Forest are sunlit, rich in wildlife and colourful wild flowers, drained by the Bedburn Beck and its fast-running tributary streams. The Pennington Beechwood, at about 300m, is one of the highest beech-woods in the country but many of the native trees are in scattered belts and streamside woodlands – a mix of alder, ash and silver birch with grey and crack willow. Drier slopes have oak, beech and rowan with sycamore and a considerable diversity of undergrowth.

This undergrowth forms a complicated pattern which reflects the type of soil, the wetness and the shade. Under the conifers, where the sun strikes through, damp clearings glisten with liverworts and opposite-leaved golden-saxifrage. The wider clearings and woodland edge show foxglove, lady's-mantle and bush vetch, while richer land, beside the beck, has bluebell, ramsons and wood-sorrel. A good variety of plants occurs where level gravelled places, ringed with small steep rocky cliffs, show that the river once ran wider. They provide a habitat for meadow crane's-bill, raspberry and banks of common dog-violet below the dripping mossy rocks which are clumped with heather and bilberry. Drier banks on more open gravel soils are thick with bracken, gorse and broom and small plants such as heath bedstraw.

Old meadows, too, lie in the river valley within the forest, where cowslip and primrose give way to yellow rattle and meadowsweet. Where limestone outcrops give a richer soil, common bird's-foot-trefoil grows with vetches, clovers and a number of orchid species.

The large size of the forest encourages roe deer, red squirrel, badger and fox with woodland birds such as crossbill, goldcrest and siskin, pied flycatcher, redstart and wood warbler, and with dipper, grey wagtail and mallard by the beck.

Hardwick Hall Country Park

NZ 347292; 16ha; DCC
Old parkland
Leaflet from DCC
Spring, summer

A nature trail, set on a raised boardwalk, winds across the silted bed of a lake, an area of rich fen and wet woodland which provides a habitat for typical birds.

Hawthorn Dene

Permit only; 66ha; DCCT reserve
Rich coastal valley woodland
Spring, summer, autumn

The deep ravine was formed in the same way as CASTLE EDEN DENE and in many ways is similar to that site: its native woodland would be ash with hazel and holly in the understorey, giving a well-lit forest, but imported trees have added to this pattern and give still greater variation. Beech, elm, wych elm, sycamore, horse-chestnut, larch and walnut, crab apple and spindle vary the valley woods.

This is a colourful site in spring alight with snowdrop, wood anemone, woodruff and ramsons, while wet places are bright with marsh-marigold and grasslands with primrose and cowslip. Later, wood crane's-bill, wood and water avens and giant bellflower show among the trees, with common twayblade and beautiful Jacob's-ladder. The

Hamsterley Forest: the steep wooded slopes drain down to the Bedburn Beck.

grassland areas show bloody crane's-bill, harebell, common centaury and marjoram, with dyer's greenweed, common rock-rose and yellow rattle; while orchids include early-purple orchid, common spotted-orchid, northern marsh-orchid and, in the coastal grassland, fragrant orchid.

The valley has an active badger sett with good numbers of fox, stoat and weasel, and with roe deer resident. There are excellent breeding populations of tits and treecreeper, with warblers in summer and waxwing as a notable winter visitor.

Joe's Pond

NZ 329488; 4.4ha; DCCT reserve
Scrub-encircled pond
Leaflet from DCCT
Spring, summer

This deep freshwater pond, sheltered by a thick belt of blackthorn, hawthorn and willows, contains two small islands. A good range of water plants is fringed with bulrush, giant horsetail and northern marsh-orchid, while breeding birds include little grebe, mallard and tufted duck.

Marsden Cliffs

NZ 397650; c.1km; South Tyneside MBC reserve
Limestone sea cliffs
Spring, summer

The splendid magnesian limestone cliffs carry typical species such as cowslip, common rock-rose and thrift and hold the most important colonies of seabirds between the FARNE ISLANDS (Northumberland) and BEMPTON CLIFFS (Yorkshire). Breeding birds include kittiwake, fulmar, cormorant and herring gull with a few pairs of lesser black-backed gull, while winter brings migrant species such as snow bunting.

Moorhouse Wood

NZ 310460; 8ha; DCCT–NT reserve
Small mixed woodland
Leaflet from DCCT
Spring, summer

Much of the wood is regrowing from old stumps, giving a coppiced effect, but there are still a number of mature trees, including some fine hornbeams. Field rose occurs, around the northern limit of its range, and the clearings are deeply carpeted with white drifts of woodruff in early summer. There is a good range of typical woodland birds and the butterflies include meadow brown and small copper.

Pennine Way

NZ 815286–897067; 45km; CC
Long-distance way
Leaflet from CC or booklet from HMSO bookshops
Spring, summer

This part of the Pennine Way passes through a fine range of valley and upland moors including a section of the River Tees with the spectacular High Force waterfall.

Pow Hill Country Park

NZ 010513; 18ha; DCC
Moorland above reservoir
Leaflet from DCC
All year

Consisting of a small area of moorland above the Derwent Reservoir, the park contains a bird hide from which the waterbirds of the sanctuary may be observed.

Kittiwake, one of the seabird species which breed on Marsden Cliffs.

Great spotted woodpecker searching for grubs.

Raisby Quarry

Permit only; 12ha; DCCT reserve
Quarry and limestone grassland
Spring, summer

Scrub woodland covers much of the reserve but open areas contain lime-loving plants such as pale St John's-wort, fragrant orchid and dark-red helleborine together with wayfaring-tree and burnet rose.

Rosa Shafto

NZ 245350; 30.8ha; DCCT reserve
Mixed woodland
Leaflet from DCCT
Spring, summer

The woodland is shaped roughly like a straggling letter H with an extended cross-piece, giving, in effect, a great deal of 'edge' to the woods which, with their fine variety of tree species, makes this a most interesting reserve. There is a range from beech high forest to grassland and scrub with hawthorn and guelder-rose, with oak, ash, birch and rowan, willow and alder, sycamore and grey poplar together with a variety of conifers.

With this wide diversity of trees, the reserve has a very varied geography. In some parts the woodland floor slopes steeply down to narrow streams, in others shallow banks, thick with bramble or dense with bracken, grade into marshy areas full of meadowsweet and meadow buttercup. In another part the woodland floor is level, dark under tall trees but with a ground cover typical of rich mixed woodland. As well as the streams which drain the woods, a small pool adds to the habitat range and attracts common frog and newts.

The broad-leaved woodlands are filled with primrose, wood anemone and bluebell; rich woodland areas have sanicle and woodruff, honeysuckle and thick bramble tangles, with ivy spreading where the shade is too deep for wood-sorrel or dog's mercury to grow. Herb-Robert, wood crane's-bill and wood avens grow by the paths and in clearings, while water avens shows in damper ground, together with common spotted-orchid and common wintergreen.

The wide range of trees and woodland types gives rise to good bird populations: 94 species have been recognised here, including birds which are locally uncommon such as great spotted woodpecker. A large population of warblers breeds in the reserve and includes chiffchaff, whitethroat, garden and willow warbler.

Scaling Dam Reservoir Sanctuary

No access; 23ha; NWA reserve
Part of large reservoir
May be viewed from hide at NZ 744125
All year

Breeding and wintering wildfowl may be observed from the bird hide while the surrounding heather moors may give sightings of short-eared owl and hen harrier in winter.

Shibdon Pond

NZ 195628; 13.6ha; DCCT–Gateshead MBC reserve
Subsidence pond and wetland
Visitors must keep to authorised paths
All year

Mown grassland slopes down to the edge of Shibdon Pond and gives way to a jungled tangle of marsh plants, a most welcome contrast as far as wildlife is concerned. Reedbeds and clumped trees fringe much of the pond, with stands of reed sweet-grass and great willowherb, while the wetland grades into an area of acid heathland with heather and *Sphagnum* mosses. There are spreads of hawthorn scrub, adding to the habitat range, and colourful populations of common spotted-orchid.

The great variety of birds which visit this essentially urban reserve come because of the richness of the site – the suitability of nesting places and the availability of plant or animal food. This richness is demonstrated, too, by good populations of other animals. Eels and several coarse fish species live in the pond and there are good numbers of frog, common toad, smooth and palmate newt here and in the marsh. Water voles are plentiful, feeding on water plants, while typical mammals emphasise the richness of the insect life: at dusk both pipistrelle and noctule bat fly out over the pond and marshland, twisting and diving to take gnats and larger insects.

The water rail is one of the most interesting residents at Shibdon, breeding here in early summer but seldom seen except when winter ice may drive it out from the frozen marsh to feed.

Among the other breeding birds are summer visitors including yellow wagtail, lesser white-throat, grasshopper and sedge warbler. Wildfowl include goldeneye, tufted duck, pochard, teal and shelduck; among many other birds which visit the reserve, the most spectacular are probably heron and kingfisher.

Swallow Pond

NZ 301693; 14ha; NWT reserve
Subsidence pond
Visitors must keep to right of way
Spring, autumn, winter

Bulrush and branched bur-reed are among the plants colonising the pond, where breeding birds include coot, little grebe and mallard; migration times bring passage waders and winter birds such as whooper swan.

Thornley Wood

NZ 185612; 33ha; Gateshead MBC reserve
Mixed woodland
Spring, early summer

The mixed oak and coniferous woodland in a steep-sided valley contains damp areas with attractive plants such as southern marsh-orchid. A good range of animals includes typical woodland birds with mammals such as badger, fox and fallow deer.

Cronkley Fell, Upper Teesdale: the mosaic of fields below the moorland.

Throckley Pond

Permit only; 7.2ha; NWT–Tyne and Wear CC reserve
Lowland pond and colliery spoil heaps
Visitors must keep to footpaths
Spring, summer

The pond has a developing wetland vegetation while the spoil heaps support a range from colonisers to thick birch and pine woodland. Birds include breeding mallard, redstart, whitethroat and great spotted woodpecker; snipe, fieldfare, red-wing and brambling may visit in winter.

Trimdon Grange Quarry

Permit only; 4.8ha; DCCT reserve
Limestone quarry with scrub and woodland
Spring, summer

Plants include autumn gentian, early-purple orchid, cowslip, carline thistle and zigzag clover. Burnet moth, common blue and orange-tip but-terflies are among the insects associated with the site, while the scrub and woodland hold large numbers of breeding birds including abundant yellow-hammer and willow warbler.

Upper Teesdale

NY 840280; 3500ha; NCC reserve
Dale and upland moor
Visitors must keep to footpaths
Booklet from NCC
Spring, summer

The richness of Upper Teesdale has been well known for generations and the reserve was established to defend the vulnerability of much of the area, a unique mosaic of habitats of international importance. The DCCT has set up an interpretative station at the BOWLEES VISITOR CENTRE.

Waldridge Fell Country Park

NZ 254494; 130ha; DCC
Heathland, bog and woodland
Spring, summer

Semi-natural woodland adds extra interest to a spread of insect-rich heathland and bog, containing plants such as heather, bell heather, bilberry and crowberry, with cross-leaved heath, common and hare's-tail cottongrass, bogbean and a variety of sedges.

Washington Waterfowl Park

NZ 330565; 41.2ha; WT
Ponds, river, reedbeds and woodland
Leaflet from visitor centre
All year

The site includes a wild area with feeding stations and hides which overlook woodland, ponds and reedbeds where ducks, waders and many other birds may be seen. There are fine views of the collection area, which includes many 'at risk' wildfowl, from the visitor centre. The wild area is accessible also to handicapped visitors.

Whitburn Bird Observatory

Permit only; DCCT reserve
Small observation station
Cliff-top path out of bounds when rifle range in use
All year

The observatory was established for watching and recording the coastal movements of seabirds and passage migrants. In winter the cliff top is a favourite area for snow bunting and shore lark, with occasional Lapland bunting, while waders may be seen moving south to feed on the tidal banks below Whitburn.

Wingate Quarry

NZ 373376; 22.5ha; DCC reserve
Old limestone workings
Spring, summer

The magnesian limestone grassland flora unique to County Durham and Tyne and Wear may be seen here – spoil heaps, steep slopes and rocky crags are covered with a rich pattern of plants. A few areas of hawthorn scrub and the ivy-hung ledges of some of the steeper cliffs provide nest sites for birds while the ponds contain a good range of animals such as horse leech and smooth and great crested newt. The plants include quaking-grass, greater knapweed and species such as common twayblade, common spotted-orchid and fragrant orchid.

Washington Waterfowl Park: lapwing and gulls at a scrape in the wild area.

Witton-le-Wear

Permit only; 33.6ha; DCCT reserve
Lakes, wetland, grassland, scrub, woodland and
gravel island
All year

Greylag goose, largest of the grey geese, are a winter visitor at Witton-le-Wear.

From the flat roof of the laboratory building you can look out across the reserve, across the wide spread of the islanded Marston Lake, across grassland and young plantations to the line of trees which marks the River Wear. A narrow woodland of mature alders faces a gravel island in the Wear while a smaller alder copse shelters the West Lake. This is a widely varied reserve with a wealth of different habitats from the rushing river to the calm of the lakes, from the rich sludge lagoons of a sewage farm to the dry grassland under the young plantations, from the low damp meadowland to the tall alders. The habitat range is reflected in the plants and animals found here.

Bulrush and water-plantain grow around the lake edges with marsh-marigold in wet places by the stream, with butterbur on the river bank and cuckooflower in the damper grasslands, where common spotted-orchid and northern marsh-orchid occur with a range of hybrids. In drier parts of these old gravel workings viper's-bugloss, gorse and broom, wild mignonette and meadow crane's-bill grow with burnet rose and guelder-rose.

Four hides in different parts of the reserve overlook the lakes, the river and the sewage farm. Around the scrub and woodland, tree pipit, linnet and goldfinch may be seen, together with several warblers including whitethroat and garden, sedge and willow warbler. The sludge lagoons attract waders such as green sandpiper, greenshank and snipe, while the gravel island in the river may hold little ringed plover, oystercatcher, common sandpiper and pied wagtail, with dipper, heron and kingfisher. Many waterbirds visit the lakes including little grebe, mallard, teal and tufted duck, with winter goldeneye, pochard, wigeon, shoveler and greylag goose.

Essex

In some ways a county of extremes, ranging from the highly rural to the heavily industrialised, most of Essex comprises agricultural land. It contains a wide variety of wildlife habitats, but perhaps the county's greatest attraction to the naturalist is the wide, flat and desolate shores of the North Sea, with their wealth of birds and other coastal life.

The shape and appearance of Essex are the result of considerable geological action. Imagine the county as a basin of chalk with its rim appearing at Saffron Walden and re-emerging at Grays Thurrock. Into this basin has been deposited a layer of London clay, varying in depth and covering the chalk over much of southern Essex. Glacial action has then deposited a further layer of fertile boulder clay over much of the London clay in the north west, creating contours up to 120m, and stretching as far as from Chelmsford to Colchester.

South of Chelmsford, much of Essex is industrial and densely populated, owing to the development of new towns such as Harlow and Basildon, combined with the major road systems serving London and the Dartford Tunnel, which links Essex and Kent under the Thames. The two airports at Stansted and Southend increase the activity in an already busy area. Small farms and smallholdings are found in southern Essex, concentrating on mixed livestock and arable cropping and reflecting the varied soil types.

In former times the county was heavily wooded inland, and the numerous rivers resulted in extensive saltings and poorly drained areas. From the twelfth century onwards drainage of the coastal area and clearing of woodlands was begun for settlement and agriculture, and the county shows evidence of extensive settlement from the fourteenth century, resulting in the loss of certain types of habitat. The only remnants left today of these extensive woodlands are EPPING and HATFIELD FORESTS, together with a scattering of smaller woods.

Epping Forest, on the edge of London, with its conservation centre at High Beach as a focal point for detailed exploration, is particularly rewarding for naturalists in autumn, when fungi and the spectacular leaf colour of beech, hornbeam and oak, the main species here, can be admired. Hanningfield Reservoir offers exciting opportunities to birdwatchers, as does the Thames Estuary: the reserves at LEIGH and nearby Two Tree Island are excellent for wildfowl, waders and Brent geese.

The northern half of Essex presents a different picture: more sparsely populated, the area is farmed intensively, producing wheat, barley, sugar beet and seed crops, with little livestock. Market towns such as Braintree, Halstead, Great Dunmow and Saffron Walden serve the area, and the surrounding countryside is rich in ancient villages and hamlets. Medieval timber-framed houses, barns and farmhouses, together with the extensive use of thatch and plaster, make it attractive to the general visitor, but naturalists may be disappointed since nature reserves are few. Several areas of woodland have, however, been retained: HALES WOOD, for instance, near Saffron Walden, harbours oxlip, various orchids and herb-Paris. Two other similar woods in the vicinity, WEST WOOD and SHADWELL WOOD, are owned by the Essex Naturalists' Trust, the largest county trust in England.

The county's seaboard, cut by a number of rivers, has a character of its own. In the north the Stour, flowing through Constable country, separates Essex from Suffolk. The Colne is navigable as far as Colchester and passes the Trust's major reserve at FINGRINGHOE WICK on its southern edge, while at its mouth lies COLNE ESTUARY with its outstanding plant, animal and bird life. The BLACKWATER ESTUARY encompasses Mersea Island and Bradwell atomic power station. The rivers Crouch and Roach dissect the DENGIE peninsula, while the southernmost river, the Thames, is the county boundary.

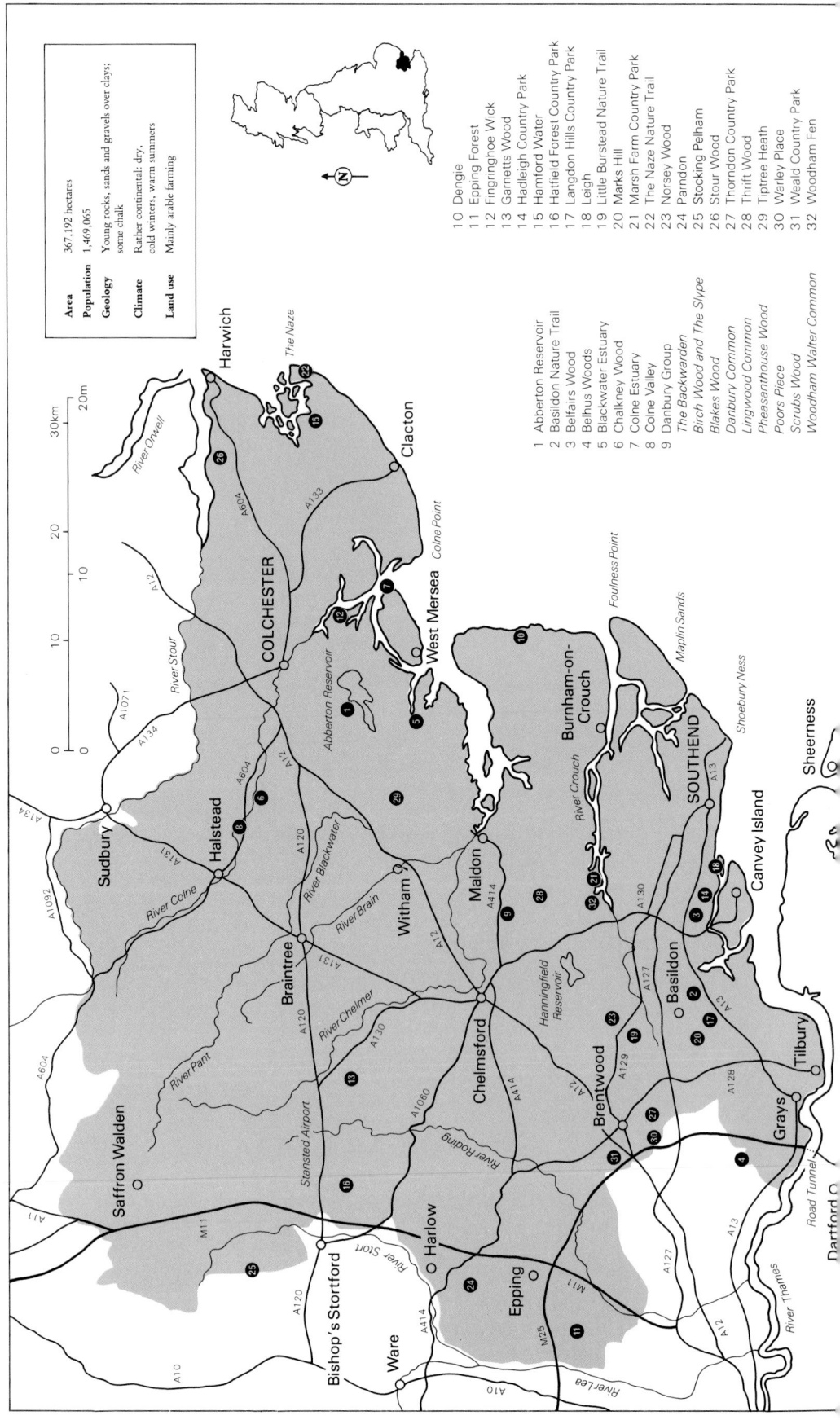

Area	367,192 hectares
Population	1,469,065
Geology	Young rocks, sands and gravels over clays; some chalk
Climate	Rather continental: dry, cold winters, warm summers
Land use	Mainly arable farming

1 Abberton Reservoir
2 Basildon Nature Trail
3 Belfairs Wood
4 Belhus Woods
5 Blackwater Estuary
6 Chalkney Wood
7 Colne Estuary
8 Colne Valley
9 Danbury Group
  The Backwarden
  Birch Wood and The Slype
  Blakes Wood
  Danbury Common
  Lingwood Common
  Pheasanthouse Wood
  Poors Piece
  Scrubs Wood
  Woodham Walter Common

10 Dengie
11 Epping Forest
12 Fingringhoe Wick
13 Garnetts Wood
14 Hadleigh Country Park
15 Hamford Water
16 Hatfield Forest Country Park
17 Langdon Hills Country Park
18 Leigh
19 Little Burstead Nature Trail
20 Marks Hill
21 Marsh Farm Country Park
22 The Naze Nature Trail
23 Norsey Wood
24 Parndon
25 Stocking Pelham
26 Stour Wood
27 Thorndon Country Park
28 Thrift Wood
29 Tiptree Heath
30 Warley Place
31 Weald Country Park
32 Woodham Fen

Much of eastern Essex is low-lying, with few trees, and is protected by a sea wall with saltings on the sea side. On the other side is land which when drained makes highly productive farmland. Four ideal centres for exploring these habitats are Goldhanger, Tollesbury, Bradwell-on-Sea and Burnham-on-Crouch. North of Colchester the land is flat and open, with fertile soil. Near the seaside resorts of Walton, Frinton, and Clacton nature reserves reveal the wide variety of species found on coastal sand and shingle, backed by saltings which are very rich in marine flora and fauna and show the constant erosive force of the sea.

In short, Essex offers the visitor far more variety than a cursory glance at the map will reveal. Its woodland and coastal heritages still support a vast array of wildlife resources.

T.ILLSLEY

Abberton Reservoir

TM 962185; 470ha; Essex Water Co.
Large reservoir
Permit only except to public birdwatching site
Leaflet from EWC
Winter

With its wide, shallow estuaries, its long salt-marshes and mudflats, Essex attracts an incredible quantity of wetland birds and Abberton, not far inland, is the most important reservoir in Britain for wintering duck. Its flocks of thousands of mallard, pochard and tufted duck, of hundreds of goldeneye and shoveler, are among the highest in the country, while huge numbers of wigeon and teal and smaller numbers of gadwall contribute to its international importance. If all eight duck were present in maximum numbers, they would make an astounding total of over 25,000; add to this over 5000 coot and many other waterbirds, with thousands of waders such as lapwing, golden plover and snipe on the pastures around the water, and some idea can be gained of Abberton's value to winter wildlife.

The reservoir lies in three sections. The largest part, some 400ha, is ringed by a steeply sloping concrete apron, although parts are shallow enough for an island and shoreline spreads of mud to show in times of drought and to attract good numbers of feeding waders. The other sections have natural banks, well grown with rushes, reeds and scrub, and provide a wider range of habitat where some duck breed and where reed and sedge warbler and reed bunting nest. The roads on the causeways between the areas provide excellent observation points and the birdwatching site has a large hide. This, some 30m long, also overlooks artificial islands on which common tern have bred while a second, smaller hide overlooks an area of flood meadow south of the reservoir.

Other winter species include mute and Bewick's swan with occasional whooper swan, smew, goosander, shelduck and great crested grebe while there is always a chance of rarer birds, such as black-necked, red-necked and Slavonian grebe and red-throated diver. Passing through on migration are uncommon waders such as spotted redshank, little stint and curlew sandpiper. Bearded tit and water rail are regular autumn visitors and osprey are often recorded on spring and autumn passage. Other birds of prey, such as hen and marsh harrier and short-eared owl, may visit and hunt the surrounding pastures, while sudden panic among the duck may mean a peregrine scything overhead. Although waterfowl numbers and movements are fewest in summer, the reservoir forms an important moulting site and perhaps 200 mute swan may be accompanied by several thousand pochard and tufted duck.

Not only is Abberton of great importance as a sanctuary for wildfowl, it is also a site where much research is conducted to monitor mortality rates and migration patterns of north west European populations. Over 70,000 duck have been ringed here, and recoveries of the ringed birds have been reported from places as far afield as Iceland, the Azores, Senegal and Siberia.

Aubrey Buxton

Permit only; 10ha; ENT reserve
Parkland, woods and small lakes
Spring, early summer

A most attractively varied area rich in woodland birds and waterfowl.

The Backwarden

TL 782039; 12ha; ENT reserve
Woodland, heath and wetland
Nature trail guide from ENT
Spring, early summer

Part of the DANBURY GROUP.

Little grebe, sometimes known as dabchick.

Old Hall Marshes: old grazing marsh, saltmarsh and tidal marshes in the Blackwater Estuary.

Basildon Nature Trail

TQ 715876; 6km; Basildon Dev. Corpn
Countryside nature trail
Leaflet from BDC
Spring, early summer

The trail has been laid out in an area of woodland, scrub and grassland, divided by hedges and stream; much of this is in old plot-land – tiny fields, pastures and derelict gardens which provide a fine range of habitats for plants and animals.

Belfairs Wood

TQ 787874; 36ha; Southend-on-Sea BC reserve
Mixed woodland
Spring, early summer

Heath fritillary is one of the uncommon butterflies which may be seen in the rich oak, birch and hornbeam woodland.

Belhus Woods

TQ 565825; 37.2ha; ECC reserve
Woodland and wetland
Spring, early summer

Gravel and claypits with stands of common reed provide wetland interest in an area of old woodland where oak, ash and wild cherry grow above an understorey of hazel. Wood anemone and bluebell make a colourful display in spring, while the variation of coppiced woodland, together with the reedbeds, attracts a good range of warblers and woodland birds.

Birch Wood

TL 789068; part of a 54ha block; ENT reserve
Mixed woodland
Spring, early summer

Part of the DANBURY GROUP.

Blackwater Estuary

TL 940070; 654ha; RSPB–NCC reserve
Grazing marshes, saltmarsh and mudflats
Permit only off rights of way
All year

Long walks on the banked sea wall afford views over the ditches and marshes of the grazing meadows and the tidal saltmarsh and mudflats. Spring birds include mallard, shelduck, shoveler, curlew, redshank and grey plover, and there are high winter numbers of dark-bellied Brent goose.

Blakes Wood

TL 775064; 33.4ha; ENT reserve
Mixed woodland
Spring, early summer

Part of the DANBURY GROUP.

Bonner's Saltings

Permit only; 24.8ha; ENT reserve
Tidal saltmarsh
This area is dangerous as visitors could be caught on a rising tide
All year

Summer saltmarsh plants such as sea aster and sea-lavender add to the year-round interest of waders and wildfowl.

Butler's Grove

Permit only; 0.2ha; Basildon Nat. Hist. Soc. reserve
Woodland and scrub
Spring, early summer

The reserve includes a pond, and embraces plants of the remaining woodland – primrose and early-purple orchid – with meadow species such as cowslip. Although small, the site has obvious value in an area of widespread urban development.

Chalkney Wood

TL 873273; 25.2ha; ECC reserve
Coppiced woodland
Spring, early summer

A splendid area of old small-leaved lime, it is being returned to its coppiced tradition and this regular opening up of the leaf canopy encourages a wealth of woodland flowers, insects and birds. Bluebells provide a brilliant springtime carpet and the bushy half-grown coppice forms ideal territory for a nightingale population.

Chigborough Lakes

Permit only; 18.4ha; ENT reserve
Flooded gravelpits
All year

Wet willow woodland, marsh, scrub and rough grassland shelter stretches of open water which include two sizeable lakes. An interesting range of plants includes blue fleabane, golden dock and common spotted-orchid, while the wetland habitats encourage nesting birds such as tufted duck, little grebe and sedge warbler. In winter, duck include gadwall, shoveler and teal.

Colne Estuary

TM 075155; 608ha; NCC–ENT reserve
Saltmarsh, shingle and mudflats
Colne Point permit only
All year

It is difficult to think of any season when the estuary, with its range of open water, mudflats, sand, shingle, saltmarsh and grazing marshes, is not full of fascination. The variety of habitat is reflected clearly in the changing plant life. Throughout the reserve, which includes both sides of the Colne mouth, a superb range of sand and shingle plants grows, two of the most dramatic being yellow horned-poppy and sea-holly. Sea bindweed sprawls its pink and white striped bells over clumps and hedges of shrubby sea-blite, glossy-leaved sea beet and grey-green sprays of aromatic sea wormwood. Sea sandwort and prickly saltwort show where the sand grades into shingle, while sea heath grows on sandy patches on the shingle banks, with marram and, unexpectedly, rock sea-lavender on some areas of drier, sandy gravel.

The saltmarshes are beautiful in summer with lawns of common sea-lavender, a haze of delicate violet above the rich green leaves. Here too are sea aster and thrift, with glasswort, an odd-looking, fleshy-jointed plant which grows on the muddy edges of the marsh or in the salt pans where gullies have been cut off. Sea-purslane edges the pans and gullies, trapping the sediments and building up the marsh, together with annual sea-blite and sea arrowgrass. On higher parts golden samphire stands among common saltmarsh-grass, which forms a grazing sward for winter wildfowl.

The mudflats and marshes attract large flocks of dark-bellied Brent goose, a speciality of the east coast shallows which flies in from Arctic Russia and Siberia to find unfrozen winter feeding grounds. Mute swan may be here in numbers and the duck include goldeneye and mallard, pintail, shelduck, teal and wigeon. Thousands of waders, such as curlew, dunlin, bar-tailed godwit, knot, golden, grey and ringed plover, redshank and turnstone, probe in the soft mud, feed on the strandline or rest on the pastures. Grebe and diver species may be seen fishing the deeper waters away from the shore.

In spring and autumn the reserve is enriched by many passage migrants, including greenshank and whimbrel, and in summer breeding birds may be seen. There is an important colony of little tern and the shingle banks provide ideal sites for oyster-catcher and ringed plover. Redshank nest on the raised saltmarshes but higher tides, or the general lowering of eastern Britain, have led to the marshes flooding more frequently than of old and breeding is frequently unsuccessful.

The reserve is particularly rich in insects and other invertebrates and provides a superb illustration of the importance of the Essex coast.

Colne Valley

TL 862296 2.1ha; ENT reserve
Disused railway line
Spring, early summer

Developing scrub on the old railway banks is being colonised by woodland species such as dog's mercury and provides an ideal nesting site for songbirds such as whitethroat.

Colne Estuary: low water discloses the intricate pattern of inter-tidal muds.

Copperas Wood

Permit only; 13.6 ha; ENT reserve
Mixed woodland
Spring, early summer

Small-leaved lime is found in the woodland, which is mainly oak with coppiced sweet chestnut, together with woodland flowers such as climbing corydalis, common cow-wheat and woodruff. The reserve is rich in butterflies and moths and contains a good variety of bird life.

Danbury Common

TL 782044; 63ha; NT reserve
Woodland and heathland
Spring, early summer

Part of the DANBURY GROUP.

Danbury Group

For map references see individual sites; 185ha;
ENT–NT reserves
Mixed woodland and heathland
Leaflets from ENT
Spring, early summer

A long but highly rewarding circular walk takes in all nine sites in this group of woodlands. Even the names possess a magic of their own: THE BACK-WARDEN, LINGWOOD COMMON and BLAKES WOOD, BIRCH WOOD and WOODHAM WALTER COMMON, PHEASANTHOUSE WOOD, POORS PIECE, SCRUBS WOOD and DANBURY COMMON. They lie around the village as a rich and complex range of wildlife havens between the urban centre and the surrounding farmland. The Danbury Ridge, between the Chelmer and the Crouch, is formed from gravels heaped on London clay and capped with boulder clay, an ancient sandwich which provides an enormous range of habitats.

From The Backwarden, with its pools in the clay beneath and heathland on the slopes, one can cross through Lingwood Common to the lime-rich clays of Blakes Wood, a journey which takes in a range from reed sweet-grass, heather, *Sphagnum*, bluebell and wood anemone to yellow archangel, wood spurge and moschatel. Every area within the group possesses its special attraction. The Backwarden climbs from richer clays through areas of heath. Lingwood Common – it is thought the name implies lime trees rather than ling or heather – passes upwards into clays richer in species than the lower slopes; the limes are gone, but the wood has old coppiced oak and hornbeam with areas of birch and scrub, and sweet chestnut in a spectacular coppiced block. Blakes Wood is a rich-wood site which has an excellent structure, standard oak over coppiced hazel, hornbeam and sweet chestnut with early-purple orchid and spectacular bluebells in spring. Birch Wood is carpeted in wood anemone and offers an early summer blaze of broom in the clearings, while Woodham Walter Common boasts valley bogs with acid-loving plants, an extraordin-ary area of stunted coppiced oak and lime-rich areas containing species such as sanicle, greater butterfly-orchid, and superb lily-of-the-valley. Pheasanthouse Wood, with some splendid oak and holly, has an attractive area of *Sphagnum* bog and, with Poors Piece, also contains lily-of-the-valley. The latter reserve was once a source of wood for the poor of the parish; some pollard oak argues that earlier it might have been common land. Scrubs Wood is more varied and includes a small pond with yellow iris, greater spearwort and water-plantain. Danbury Common slopes back down beside The Backwarden, a more open heathland with some areas of coppiced wood, generally more rich in scrubland species with banks of vivid gorse and broom and with typical grassland flowers such as tormentil.

The group makes a wonderfully diverse wildlife refuge with breeding birds such as blackcap, garden warbler and lesser whitethroat, hawfinch, redpoll, all three species of native woodpecker and occasional nightingale and wood warbler. Butterflies include comma, purple hairstreak and speckled wood, and there is a wide variety of moths.

Dengie

TR 030090–020960; 3025ha; NCC–ENT reserve
Mudflats, saltmarsh and shingle
No access off right of way
All year

A very open coastline attracts good winter numbers of grey plover, knot and sanderling.

Elms Spinney

Permit only; 0.6ha; ENT reserve
Marsh and thicket
Spring, early summer

Wetland plants include cuckooflower, ragged-Robin and pendulous sedge with common meadow-rue, rare in Essex.

Purple hairstreak: these beautiful butterflies may be seen flying high round oaks in summer.

Epping Forest

TQ 412981; 2430ha; Corpn of the City of London
Ancient wood pasture, grassland and wetland
Spring, early summer

A visitor to St Paul's Cathedral stands less than 20km from the heart of the ancient forest of Epping, parts of which have probably been wooded since Neolithic times. When the arctic conditions of the last ice age withdrew and the huge ice melt-water rivers subsided, woodland, probably dominated by small-leaved lime, spread across this part of England. Small-leaved lime is now uncommon in Britain, although some fine coppiced woodlands such as COLLIN PARK WOOD (Gloucestershire) still survive.

As time passed this wildwood altered; clearance for farming stripped the trees from the better soils, leaving spreads of woodland where deer and cattle grazed. Small-leaved lime with its sweet and slender saplings would have been preferentially grazed, so that when the old trees died they were replaced by beech, hornbeam and oak which took over the forest. On areas of poorer soil heaths developed, providing better grazing and forming a mosaic of woodlands and plains.

By the early twelfth century fallow deer were widespread, and Henry I declared the whole county the Royal Forest of Essex, where bylaws protected the deer. Even then the woodlands were probably little different from now but, had it not been declared a Royal Forest, Epping might have been further eroded by agriculture or been en-

High Beach, Epping Forest: autumn leaves begin to fall from the beech trees.

closed for coppicing. If it had been left to itself the woodland would have continued to change as old trees died and fluctuating grazing pressures prevented or allowed new trees to grow; indeed, with enough grazing animals the whole woodland might have been lost to heath, but the traditional system of pollarding established an equilibrium. When a young tree is topped, perhaps 3m from the ground, it puts out a crown of shoots which grow out of reach of grazing animals. This not only provides a regular crop of wood but also reduces the need for sapling growth, since the tree never matures but survives virtually indefinitely provided that the process of pollarding continues.

Even while Christopher Wren was raising his great cathedral, a visitor to Epping Forest might have stepped back into medieval England. From the twelfth until the nineteenth century, the forest stood as a great spread of wood pasture where the only changes were seasonal and cyclical, where deer and cattle grazed the plains and browsed beneath recent pollards. Provided the pollards were regularly cut they would continue to grow their crowns of poles, and provided they were harvested in rotation there was always a supply of wood, of fresh-grown grazing beneath them and of shade – a perfectly balanced system which benefited man and beast.

The varied pattern of plains and wood pasture can still be observed but, sadly, this is in decline.

The pollards have been uncut for a hundred years and their huge crowns cast a deep shade over much of the once rich woodland. Grazing, too, has declined and the plains have been overcome with thickets of birch or tangles of blackthorn and hawthorn. Where oak, often grown on for timber, was scattered throughout the beech of the higher sands and gravels and the hornbeam of the more loamy slopes, the trees have often been overtopped and killed by the shade of the pollards, although oak still dominates the heavier clays with a dense understorey of holly.

The great beech pollards themselves are threatened by their size and liable to crash down in storms or, with their huge canopies of leaves, lose so much water that they readily succumb to drought. Their shade has destroyed the undergrowth so that plants such as primrose and butcher's-broom are increasingly rare. Shade on the plains, together with lack of grazing, is also the cause of the loss or rarity of heather and of heathland birds and insects such as nightjar and emperor moth.

The forest, however, still remains the largest spread of old woodland, unimproved grassland and wetland in this part of England; an area of trees ranging from saplings in the clearings to pollards perhaps four centuries old; an area, varied in its geology from free-draining gravels and sands to clays, which provides a range of habitat from dry woodland to marshland, bogs and pools.

One of the important features of ancient wood pasture is the continuity of old standing timber which supports a number of beetles adapted to this specific habitat. Where wild service-tree, butcher's-broom and pendulous sedge suggest that some of Epping's woods have stood for many thousands of years, another wood containing these species may have been clear-felled and allowed to grow again. The presence of these beetles, how-

Overgrown pollards in Epping Forest.

ever, indicates that ancient trees have had an unbroken succession at Epping, that at no time was all of the woodland cleared, that this is genuinely an ancient forest.

Almost 1400 species of beetle associated not only with woodland, but also with the remnants of the heathy plains and the ponds, bogs and marshes, may be found. Epping Forest can stand comparison with any other British forest of similar size and is surpassed for variety only by WINDSOR FOREST (Berkshire) and the NEW FOREST (Hampshire), both very much larger than Epping.

The forest has probably always been of relatively restricted importance for moths and butterflies, a site where vagrants might occur but which lacked the range of shrubs and varied herbs attractive to many species. The edges of the woods hold the widest variation, and here and around the clearings common and holly blue, small, large, dingy and Essex skipper, comma and small copper may be found, together with purple hairstreak near oak, while moths might include red-belted clearwing, gold tail, common footman, leopard lobster and the migrant humming-bird hawkmoth.

Slow-worm and common lizard, adder and grass snake survive in the forest although the dark, bare ground and leaf mould under the overgrown pollards do not provide a suitable habitat and they are limited to clearings and plains. Both snakes are excellent swimmers and, while the two lizards prefer the drier sites, are often recorded from the wetland areas which also form the breeding grounds of the forest's amphibians. Common toad, migrating to the deeper pools where it lays long strings of eggs, is certainly more numerous than the frog, partly perhaps because frog spawn is laid in shallow pools where it tends to float in collectable masses easily reached by children. Crested, smooth and palmate newt are found in these pools, with the crested, like the common toad, seeming to prefer the deeper, darker waters.

The bird life is mainly restricted to the common woodland birds, with summer visitors such as blackcap, whitethroat and willow warbler nesting in the scrub, and with tree-loving species such as nuthatch, treecreeper and all three British woodpeckers. Redpoll is now a regular breeding species while redstart and hawfinch are the special forest birds, the redstart on account of its preference for old woodland and the hawfinch as a specialist in hornbeam. Several species, such as buzzard and peregrine, have either withdrawn from the area or, like the sparrowhawk, were hounded before the days of conservation by keepers, whose pole traps also took birds such as red-backed shrike and wryneck. Nightjar, wryneck, red-backed shrike and woodlark have all disappeared but the causes may be associated as much with national changes as with changes in habitat or disturbance.

One radical and distressing change is the loss of the forest's large mammals. The small mammals all seem to be surviving but badger and fallow deer are effectively gone. Both may occur in the wood but breeding seems unlikely, although the small muntjac deer is probably breeding. It is sad that the forest, established for its fallow and red deer herds, should no longer hold them, due in part to the altering habitat and loss of suitable cover, in part to human disturbance and to sudden death on the roads.

The forest, though, is still a magical place and a memorial to a very ancient tradition, a place of fascination for its wildlife and history. Such a mighty spread of woodland, so close to the city, is a national heirloom beyond price.

Slow-worm, a legless lizard and not a snake, is bronze-coloured, harmless and sun-loving.

Fingringhoe Wick

TM 041195; 50ha; ENT reserve
Old gravel workings, saltmarsh and mudflats
Restricted visiting for non-members
Leaflets from ENT
All year

The headquarters of the ENT, Fingringhoe Wick, has an interpretative centre which includes an observation tower, and a number of hides overlooking the river, the saltmarsh and scrape and the lake. Two nature trails demonstrate the variety of the site. The gravel workings have left hummocks, banks and level clearings, hollows, ponds and gullies; these may be filled, or scrub-lined, or grassed and rich in bright small flowers, or lie as wetlands thick with reeds, or sheltered open waters.

The spread of Geedon Marsh, overlooked from the scrape hide and the nature trail, shows the characteristic plants of the east coast marshes. Glasswort and sea aster catch the tidal muds and slowly raise the level of the marsh to suit plants such as thrift and sea-purslane, sea plantain and common sea-lavender. In winter dark-bellied Brent goose, dunlin and curlew flock here in thousands, grazing the common saltmarsh-grass or probing the mud for food. The tidal river also draws geese to feed on its brackish-water plants, while the flats and scrape attract greenshank, redshank, spotted redshank, ringed plover, lapwing and snipe.

The freshwater pools are very varied. Some, filled with common reed, form breeding sites for reed and sedge warbler and resting places for migrant bearded tit; the large lake attracts winter mallard, pochard, shoveler, teal and tufted duck, and breeding coot, little grebe, moorhen and mute swan; some pools hold bulrush and water-plantain or are willow-ringed and filled with birdsong.

Songbirds are a feature of the reserve with its wealth of scrub and trees – willow and bramble tangles mingle with thickets of gorse and broom, while mixed coniferous woodland contrasts with hedges, and copses of hawthorn with wide, winding paths and open, heath-like glades. Chiffchaff, garden and grasshopper warbler, blackcap and nightingale, whitethroat, lesser whitethroat and willow warbler are recorded, with autumn flocks of passage migrants and winter fieldfare and redwing.

The heathland areas, sheltered by scrub and open to the sun, are ideal sites for butterflies such as wall brown, small heath and skipper species, all of which feed on grasses as caterpillars, as well as peacock and small tortoiseshell, which need common nettle, and purple hairstreak, whose larval plant is oak. The Essex skipper, not uncommon here, is widespread on the continent; in Britain it is limited to the south.

Much of the reserve's interest is the result of its mixed geology. Glacial gravels on the London clay are capped with boulder clay and brickearth, giving a variation of acid and calcareous influence. The very varied aspects of the site provide a mosaic of shelter and exposure.

Garnetts Wood

TL 635815; 24.8ha; ECC reserve
Coppiced woodland
Spring, early summer

Like its sister woodland, CHALKNEY WOOD, it is a
fine spread of ancient small-leaved lime, actively
coppiced to recreate the varied structure of such
woodlands. It provides a range from forest glade to
densely shaded thickets and attracts a fine variety
of wildlife.

Great Holland Pits

Permit only; 17.6ha; ENT reserve
Old gravel workings
Spring, early summer

A great diversity of habitat – ponds, rough grassland, woodland, wetland and a stream – contains
plants ranging from bulrush through moschatel
and mousetail to carline thistle and blue fleabane;
birds include nightingale and waterfowl.

Hadleigh Country Park

TQ 795868; 136ha; ECC
Grassland and reclaimed marshland
All year

The park overlooks Canvey Island and the huge
Thames Estuary: its main natural history interest is
coastal bird life, in particular the wintering east
coast Brent geese.

Hainault Forest Country Park

TQ 476926; 387ha; GLC
Old woodland, scrub and grassland
All year

Remnant of an old Royal Forest, the site is
described under Greater London.

Orange-tip butterfly on cuckooflower.

Hales Wood

Permit only; 8ha; NCC reserve
Oak and ash woodland
Spring, early summer

An old coppice-with-standards woodland, the
reserve has a good range of rich-wood plants and
is renowned for its show of oxlip.

Hall Wood

Permit only; 2.4ha; ENT reserve
Small mixed woodland
Spring, early summer

The wood is chiefly oak, with some ash and elm,
and contains a flourishing rookery.

Hamford Water

TM 235260; 688ha; NCC reserve
Mudflats
No access off rights of way
All year

Summer birds include ringed plover and little tern,
while the mudflats in winter hold many thousands
of waders and wildfowl, including curlew, grey
plover, pintail and dark-bellied Brent goose.

Hatfield Forest Country Park

TL 546199; 420ha; NT
Parkland and woodland
Nature trail leaflet from NT or at site
Spring, early summer

Hatfield Forest was once part of the Forest of Essex,
where kings hunted deer, but was later enclosed
and coppiced. Oaks were left to grow as standards,
to provide timber for ships, while hornbeam, ash
and hazel were cropped for fuel and for fencing
materials. Open parkland was left between the coppices, and here, although within the woods many
of the standards have been felled, some fine old
trees still stand above the open grassland, their
huge, straight trunks and spreading, perfect
crowns contrasting with the shrubby coppices.
  A nature trail which starts beside the ornamental
lake passes HATFIELD FOREST MARSH, an ENT
reserve, and demonstrates some characteristics of
the woods and parkland. The lake attracts Canada
goose, pochard and tufted duck in winter to swell
the numbers of resident moorhen, coot and mallard.
A lucky summer visitor might see a female mallard
flap 'broken-winged' across the park ahead – look
the other way and a brood of piping ducklings may
skitter to the water or into the pathside cover.
  The coppiced woodland by the lake shows the
beautiful fluted columns of hornbeam above
woodland flowers such as primrose, lesser celandine and sanicle with an understorey, typical of
rich woodlands, containing hazel, hawthorn,
spindle and field maple. The woodland opens on to
hawthorn and wild rose, a grassy scrub which

Nightingales nest in thick cover, and are heard most clearly after dusk and before dawn.

overlooks the marsh and may reveal birds such as reed bunting and snipe, the vivid flags of yellow iris or the strangely beautiful marsh cinquefoil.

The denser coppiced woodland has little ground cover except a thick floor of dog's mercury, but the rides are full of blue bugle and germander speedwell, while the woodland edge is bright with lesser celandine, ground ivy, wild strawberry and wild rose. Orange-tip butterflies and whites dance in the sunlit clearings, and where the woodlands open into a hummocked open space meadow brown and common blue may be seen.

This area of mounds and ditches, Portingbury Hills, is sheltered and warm. Anthills are gardens of small flowers and there is a wonderful show of cowslip, hairy and perforate St John's-wort, valerian, teasel, common gromwell and common spotted-orchid.

The woods and clearings may have changed much since the Normans hunted here but they still hold such special plants as herb-Paris and violet helleborine, and nightingales still sing in the evening stillness.

Hatfield Forest Marsh

Permit only; 3.6ha; ENT reserve
Small lime-rich marsh
Spring, summer

Willow and hawthorn scrub surround a jungle of bulrush, common reed and great willowherb, a rich variety of rushes, sedges and horsetails, with plants such as water mint, cuckooflower and marsh cinquefoil. The fauna includes a good range of birds and insects.

Hitchcock's Meadows

Permit only; 3.8ha; ENT reserve
Lime-rich grassland, scrub and marsh
Spring, early summer

The grassland slopes are rich in species such as heath dog-violet, meadow saxifrage, green-winged orchid and autumn lady's-tresses; insects include glow-worm, and an interesting variety of bird species is attracted to the scrub and hedges.

Langdon Hills Country Park

TQ 696862 and 681867; 121.6ha; ECC
Woodland and rough grassland
Spring, early summer

An area of old farmland and woodland, the country park lies in two blocks, One Tree Hill and Westley Heights, which encompass some fine woodland with a mix of species incuding ash, hornbeam, field maple, oak and wild service-tree, together with heath-like open areas and ancient meadowland.

Leigh

TQ 835850; 257ha; NCC–ENT reserve
Reclaimed marsh, saltmarsh and mudflats
No access off marked footpaths
Leaflet from NCC
Winter

The saltmarsh, one of the richest in the Thames Estuary, includes at least five species of glasswort, both common and the less usual lax-flowered sea-lavender, golden samphire, thrift, sea arrowgrass and sea wormwood. The marshes are much divided

Leigh: one of the richest saltmarshes in the Thames Estuary.

by muddy runnels which drain down to wide areas of mud with prolific spreads of common and narrow-leaved eelgrass and the soft green alga *Enteromorpha*. Despite looking like seaweeds the eelgrasses are flowering plants, an important source of winter food for wildfowl.

Above the marsh the reclaimed land, a jungle of scrub and rough grassland, provides welcome food and shelter for migrant birds. Much of the reclamation was done by tipping and the result is a bewildering mix of normal colonisers, such as bramble, wild rose, willow, hawthorn and gorse over yarrow, teasel and coarse grasses, together with species such as apple and laburnum, over hyacinth, purple iris and yellow tulip. Coastal species such as alexanders flourish here with the dramatic alien milk thistle. Drainage dykes contain a rich assembly of water plants, including soft and rigid hornwort, horned pondweed and beaked tasselweed, and are fringed with saltmarsh rush and hairy buttercup. This vigorous plant cover is ideal for small mammals: short-tailed vole and water vole are hunted by resident predators such as fox and weasel, by kestrel, which regularly visit the island, and by short-eared owls in winter.

Winter is the time for geese. Some 10,000 to 20,000 dark-bellied Brent geese fly in from the far north east to feed on the east coast shallows while the western coasts receive an influx of light-bellied Brent geese. In autumn and winter many of the dark-bellied Brent geese may be seen at Leigh or flying between here and their main centre on the Foulness–Maplin sands. Brent, smallest of our winter geese, could only be confused with barnacle or Canada goose, but both these have white on their faces while Brent have a white half-collar halfway down their necks.

Rising tides bring the waders in from the flats to roost. The mudflats are extremely rich in bristle worms, small shrimp-like creatures and shellfish such as laver spire shell and common cockle. As the waters cover the mud the waders move to the salt-marsh and flock head-to-wind until they fall again. Then curlew, dunlin and redshank stand grouped with others such as knot and bar-tailed godwit, and with mallard, shelduck and other wildfowl.

Among the insects of the reserve are a number of uncommon moths including Essex skipper and the only Essex population of marbled white.

Lingwood Common

TL 783057; 22ha; NT reserve
Woodland, scrub and heathland
Spring, early summer

Part of the DANBURY GROUP.

Little Burstead

TQ 674931; 5.5km; Basildon DC
Countryside trail
Leaflet from BDC
Spring, early summer

The trail is an attractively varied route through heathland vivid with gorse and broom, along old hedgerows with gnarled pollard oaks, past the Wilderness where a lake marks the source of the River Crouch, alongside a pond on Little Burstead Common where yellow water-lily and arrowhead grow beneath tall bulrushes, and past farmland where lapwing wheel and dive.

Loshes Meadow

Permit only; 6.8ha; ENT reserve
Woodland and meadow
Spring, early summer

Six species of speedwell have been identified on the reserve, which slopes from gravels to London clay, while other plants include moschatel and yellow archangel. Among the breeding birds are blackcap, reed bunting and willow tit.

Maldon Wick

Permit only; 6.4ha; ENT reserve
Disused railway line
Spring, early summer

The reserve comprises 1.2km of old embanked line, rich in flowering plants, on which some 25 species of butterflies have so far been recorded.

Marks Hill

TQ 684874; 17ha; Basildon Nat. Hist. Soc. reserve
Woodland and rough grassland
Leaflet and nature trail guide from Basildon DC or BNHS
Spring, early summer

The reserve is mainly woodland which has grown up since the original tree cover was cleared for development, but areas of ancient woodland remain, where wild service-tree grows with oak, hornbeam and field maple, and the woods are being returned to coppice management. The ground cover includes wood anemone, bluebell and yellow archangel, and the varied plant life of the grassland, woods and pond encourages a good range of insects and birds.

Marsh Farm Country Park

TQ 814961; 96ha; ECC
Riverside farmland and saltmarsh
Winter

Although the spread of marshy fields and dykes is fascinating at any time of year, in winter it attracts a good variety of birds including the east coast speciality, Brent goose.

The Naze Nature Trail

TM 265235; 2km; ENT–Tendring DC
Coastal trail
Leaflet from ENT
All year

The trail passes the JOHN WESTON reserve and in places gives good views over the sheltered mudflats of HAMFORD WATER. The cliffs here show a classic exposure of red crag, a highly fossiliferous rock, and the promontory as a whole is important for migrant birds.

Ringed plover breed mainly on coastal sites, on sand and shingle beaches.

John Weston

TM 266245; 8ha; ENT reserve
Grassland and scrub
Spring, summer

The reserve protects some of the typical plants and animals of the Naze, which is noted for strawberry clover, slender thistle and pepper-saxifrage, holds breeding ringed plover and oystercatcher and provides a landfall for migrant birds.

Newland Grove

Permit only; 3.2ha; ENT reserve
Woodland and grassland
Spring, early summer

A length of river bank adds interest to this small area of woodland and meadow.

Norsey Wood

TQ 692957; 67ha; Basildon DC reserve
Coppiced woodland
Leaflets from BDC
Spring, early summer

The reserve has probably been wooded for thousands of years, although the coppiced sweet chestnut is a recent introduction, and the mixed woodland, coppiced now to continue an ancient tradition, is rich in locally uncommon species such as Midland hawthorn, butcher's-broom and lily-of-the-valley. Ponds within the wood contain mare's-tail and water-violet, while adder's-tongue occurs among the grasslands. The trees, including oak and hornbeam with alder, ash, hazel and willow, are a haunt for woodcock in winter as well as a breeding site for nuthatch, tree pipit and redpoll.

Northey Island

Permit only; 132ha; NT reserve
Estuary island
All year

The island, reached by a low-tide causeway, includes saltmarshes supporting characteristic plants such as sea-purslane, while sea beet and shrubby sea-blite grow on the rocky sea wall, and the saltings are rich in wetland bird life – curlew, redshank, and winter flocks of Brent geese. A hide overlooks the BLACKWATER ESTUARY.

Parndon

TQ 444073; 23.6ha; Harlow DC reserve
Ancient woodland
Spring, early summer

This splendid woodland lies partly on lime-rich boulder clay and partly on London clay, a chain of springs providing wetlands where the two clays meet. The richer woodland, characterised by dog's mercury, changes to hornbeam woodland on the lower London clay, and, like all the old woods of Essex, offers a fine variety of insects and woodland birds.

Pheasanthouse Wood

TL 787065; part of a 54ha block; ENT reserve
Mixed woodland
Spring, early summer

Part of the DANBURY GROUP.

Poors Piece

TL 788068; part of a 54ha block; ENT reserve
Mixed woodland
Spring, early summer

Part of the DANBURY GROUP.

Rat Island

Permit only; 14ha; ENT reserve
Small saltmarsh island
No access in breeding season
All year

The reserve is a low-lying island, site of a small colony of common tern and a large nesting community of black-headed gull.

Ray Island

Permit only; 19ha; ENT reserve
Saltmarsh and island
All year

The saltmarsh backs on to a shingle foreshore above which the island is grassed and scrub-covered. The scrub shelters and feeds migrant bird species, while waders such as oystercatcher and ringed plover, and wildfowl such as shelduck, may be seen on the saltings, shingle and open mud.

Blackcap and young at their nest.

Roman River Valley

Permit only; 11.5ha; ENT reserve
Wetland and woodland
Spring, early summer

The wood consists of oak standards with coppiced hornbeam, while the marsh contains a good range of wetland plants. Among the insects found here are large emerald and rosy footman moths, while breeding birds include blackcap, willow tit, garden warbler and whitethroat.

St Peter's Marsh

Permit only; 0.05ha; ENT reserve
Tiny wetland
Spring, early summer

One of the smallest reserves in the country, it is planted with poplar and bounded by old elm trees. Frogs breed prolifically and the site is visited by a surprising range of birds, including warbler species and snipe.

Sawbridgeworth Marsh

Permit only; 12ha; ENT–H and MTNC reserve
Marsh and wet pasture
Spring, summer

A superb wetland area, the reserve is described under Hertfordshire.

Scrubs Wood

TL 787058; part of a 54ha block; ENT reserve
Mixed woodland
Spring, early summer

Part of the DANBURY GROUP.

Shadwell Wood

Permit only; 6.4ha; ENT reserve
Coppiced woodland
Spring, early summer

This small, damp wood is a botanist's treasure trove in which over 20 species of tree and shrub stand above a remarkable ground cover. The sloping, chalky boulder clay provides a soil wet enough to fill the rides with meadowsweet and rich enough for a great variety of lime-loving plants. Continued coppicing creates a range of habitat which, left to itself, only a much larger wood could equal, since it provides the equivalents of clearings, scrub and thickets with tall trees.

Oak, ash and elm have been left to grow as standards, maiden trees allowed to form full-crowned big timber trees, around which the other trees and shrubs are periodically cut. The stems are trimmed comfortably close to the ground, and from the stump or stool new shoots spring to form first bushy clumps, then scrub-like areas, and finally thickets of lifting poles. The poles are harvested to provide firewood or fencing materials and the cycle is repeated. After putting up a full growth of trunk and bough a tree eventually loses its vigour and dies; the standards then have to be replaced and younger trees grown on, but the coppice stools seem to have an indefinite life, with their vigour renewed at every cutting time.

Not only are new shoots put up when the stools are cut, but the light let in renews the woodland floor: plants may lie dormant under thick growth, but when the light floods in again they respond immediately. The regular pattern of cutting, with a different area coppiced every year, ensures circumstances suited to particular plants. This, and the richness of the soil, accounts for the wonderful variety of the wood. Spectacular shows of bluebell, wood anemone, cowslip, and primrose occur in the newly coppiced blocks, with one of the specialities of the wood, oxlip. Where cowslip and primrose grow together, their hybrid – false oxlip – may often appear, but here true oxlip flourishes, which only occurs on these south eastern clays. Spring brings to this small woodland the blue of bugle, the white of ramsons and wood sorrel, the yellow of lesser celandine and goldilocks buttercup, the delicate colours of early and common dog-violet, of hairy violet and the fragrant sweet violet.

Holly and yew have cast their shade throughout the winter but now other trees and shrubs come into leaf. Blackthorn, hawthorn and Midland hawthorn, field maple, hornbeam and hazel, dogwood, privet, spindle, wayfaring-tree and guelder-rose all help to make the wood so fascinating, as do some of the smaller plants: hard, spiky butcher's-broom, uncommon slender vervain, tiny, delicate round-leaved fluellen, and showy alien Oregon-grape. After the early-purple orchid, the paths are often so crowded with common spotted-orchid and common twayblade that visitors must tread with care; bee and pyramidal orchid and greater

Oxlip is a speciality of south eastern woods on clay soils, such as Shadwell Wood.

butterfly-orchid may also be found. Among other plants of interest are spurge-laurel, herb-Paris and star-of-Bethlehem, all of fairly local distribution.

Shotgate Thickets

Permit only; 2ha; ENT reserve
Woodland and pond
Spring, early summer

A small oakwood, a dense blackthorn and hawthorn thicket and a large pond provide a range of habitat which also contains buckthorn, golden dock and dyer's greenweed, attracting over 50 bird species, while butterflies include speckled wood, comma and orange-tip.

Skippers Island

Permit only; 93.2ha; ENT reserve
Pasture, scrub and saltmarsh
All year

Unusual plants include adder's-tongue, dyer's greenweed and lax-flowered sea-lavender which, with a good range of breeding birds, make this an unusually rich reserve. Insects include short-winged conehead and Roesel's bush cricket, together with ringlet butterfly and starwort shark and scarce footman moth. Among the birds are breeding kestrel, oystercatcher and shelduck, with migrant and wintering waders and wildfowl.

171

Stocking Pelham

TL 457286; 28ha; CEGB reserve
Grassland, spinneys, ponds and mature hedges
Restricted site for use by Essex and Herts
Education Authorities, ENT, and H and MTNC
Nature trail guide from CEGB, ENT or
H and MTNC
Spring, early summer

Plant life here includes developing chalk grassland and flora. An ancient hedgerow is a feature. There are over 60 bird species, among them blackcap, greenfinch, treecreeper, willow warbler and woodpeckers.

Stour Wood

TM 195311; 53.6ha; WdT
Ancient woodland
Spring, early summer

Although most of the woodland is now sweet chestnut coppice, wild service-tree indicates probable continual tree cover since the last ice age; 14 mammal species and 40 of breeding birds are recorded.

Stow Maries Halt

Permit only; 2.4ha; ENT reserve
Disused railway line and meadow
Spring, summer

The reserve protects the unusual cypress spurge, together with a colony each of glow-worm and speckled wood butterfly.

Thorndon Country Park

TQ 604915 and 635899; 144.4ha; ECC
Old parkland, lakes and woods
Spring, early summer

The park is in two sections, once part of an old deer enclosure where ancient oaks and hornbeams still stand above grassy clearings. Younger woodlands and lakes now add to the variety of the site, and the unimproved parkland is rich in insects and bird life; even the alien conifers add to the variation, while the streams and marshes are full of interest.

Thrift Wood

TL 790107; 19.2ha; ENT reserve
Mixed woodland
Permit only off rights of way
Spring, early summer

The wood is chiefly oak, with birch and ash over hornbeam coppice. Common cow-wheat occurs in the ground cover and extra interest is added by a fair-sized pool.

Tiptree Heath

TL 884149; 24ha; Tiptree PC
Heathland
Spring, early summer

The block of heathland, unusual in Essex, offers a good show of the typical plants of this kind of habitat such as gorse, heather and tormentil, with heath milkwort and cross-leaved heath in the damper parts.

Turner's Spring

Permit only; 2.6ha; ENT reserve
Small wood and meadow
Spring, early summer

The reserve consists of an area of mixed woodland and wet meadow only a short distance from AUBREY BUXTON.

Warley Place

TQ 583908; 5.4ha; ENT reserve
Old ornamental garden and parkland
Nature trail leaflet from ENT
Spring, early summer

An amazing range of native and exotic plants makes this a most attractive reserve, and it has become a haven for many birds and butterflies. Unusual species include spring crocus.

Weald Country Park

TQ 574940; 173.5ha; ECC
Ancient deer park and ornamental lakes
Spring, summer

The park contains extremely ancient oaks and hornbeams and is still a haunt of fallow deer. The lakes attract typical bird life, while younger plantations add to the habitat range.

Weeleyhall Wood

Permit only; 31.2ha; ENT reserve
Mature oak woodland
Spring, early summer

The unmistakable song of a nightingale from a shrubby part of the wood might be heard across the surrounding fields, making an attractive accompaniment to the approach along an open, tree-lined cartway. Within the wood the trees are tall, except in the recent Corsican and Scots pine blocks which, filled with seedling birch and rosebay willowherb, make a strong contrast with the older trees. Much of the reserve is high-forest oak: open, almost park-like trees over an amazing show of bluebell in spring – not the spread of bluebell which hurries to flower before the leaf canopy closes overhead, but a knee-deep wash of shimmering blue-purple in well-lit glades between the trees. The dark oaks rise from a living sea which fills the woodland floor and breaks, at the edges of the rides, in the white of greater stitchwort. Smaller spring flowers, particularly along the paths and rides, include wood anemone and wood-sorrel, bugle, primrose and species of violet. Red campion may make a patriotic pattern with greater stitchwort and bluebell.

Bracken and bramble grow in the open oak woodland where forest trees include scattered mature larch and an occasional fine, full-grown Scots pine. The conifers may not be native but do provide an extra range of habitat and winter food for several small bird species. The importance of the oak, though, is supreme – almost 300 insect species depend on it as a food plant and many more are associated with it less directly. One of our oldest and most long-lived species, the oak has given animals many thousands of years in which to evolve to use it to the full. Leaf-eaters, bud-eaters, bark-eaters, borers – the oak is home and larder to a greater variety of species than any other native tree. Indeed, only where oak has stood for centuries, allowed to age like some of the WINDSOR GREAT PARK (Berkshire) or NEW FOREST (Hampshire) trees, can some species survive: certain beetles, for instance, live only in such old oaks.

Another planted tree here is sweet chestnut, but more unusual, in the wetter parts, are fine stands of old coppiced alder which have grown into slender, tall clumps with attractive, rounded leaves. Willows also occur in the damp areas, with plants such as yellow pimpernel and moschatel. Beech, occasional holly, crab apple and hawthorn add to the diversity of trees, while the range of high forest, coppice and young plantation is varied with clearings, containing opportunist plants such as common mullein. Small ponds form an attractive addition to the habitat range of the reserve. This variation encourages a range of woodland birds such as blackcap, chiffchaff, green woodpecker and jay, and of butterflies, moths and other insects. Among plants of regional interest are yellow arch-angel and butcher's-broom.

Westhouse Wood

Permit only; 3ha; ENT reserve
Mixed woodland
Spring, early summer

This remnant of an ancient coppiced woodland contains not only a good range of tree species, some of them lifting from fine old coppice stools, but also a number of ponds. Spring flowers include abundant bluebell, and active coppicing is intended to encourage variation.

West Wood

Permit only; 23.2ha; ENT reserve
Mixed woodland
Spring, early summer

The pathways lead through a great variety of woodland, through high-forest trees and coppiced areas, through swampy clearings and by thick plantations, the whole a mix of types rich in both plant and animal life. Where WEELEYHALL WOOD shows splendid tall oak woodland and SHADWELL WOOD rich coppice on chalky clays, West Wood shows a great diversity of species, partly on clay and partly on gravel, part dry, part damp.

Much of the central area is planted up with Norway spruce, a fast-growing softwood tree, but most trees elsewhere are mixed native broad-leaved species. Elm and ash, particularly, stand over hawthorn, hazel, spindle and plentiful field maple. Elder and willow also grow in the understorey and there are dense drifts of blackthorn scrub.

The woodland floor is as varied as the shrubs and trees: dense areas of bramble alternate with gardens of smaller plants, open spreads of swampy sedges, and grassy, flower-filled rides. Spring brings oxlip and bluebell, green dog's mercury and other rich-wood species such as sanicle and the unmistakable garlic-smelling ramsons. Lesser celandine, with speedwell and forget-me-not species, bugle and ground ivy add yellow and blue to the springtime colour, while the rides are thick with early-purple orchid. By early summer St John's-wort species are out and the delicate-patterned lilac spires of common spotted-orchid stand in the rides in their hundreds.

Pools, in the clearer areas, offer water-crowfoot species, brilliant yellow marsh-marigold, and a breeding site for newts and numerous water insects; the pools are edged with rushes, sedges and clustered water mint, attracting butterflies.

The breeding birds include blackcap, chiffchaff and garden warbler in the deciduous trees, with goldcrest and redpoll in the conifers, and with great and lesser spotted woodpecker and tawny owl. The owls hunt within the clearings mice and voles, which may also be taken by weasel, stoat or fox. Deer slots are often found in the open rides. These rides and the grassy damp of the clearings prove suitable for ringlet butterfly, while other species include small and large skipper, green-veined white and brimstone; the presence of the last-named species argues a growth of buckthorn on the chalky clay, or alder buckthorn on the more acid gravels.

Witton Wood Spinney

Permit only; 0.04ha; ENT reserve
Tiny urban reserve
Spring, early summer

Probably once a garden, the reserve offers an urban retreat for songbirds and insects, particularly butterflies.

Woodham Fen

TQ 798975; 8ha; ENT reserve
Saltmarsh, grassland and scrub
Spring, summer

Stands of rush encourage a good population of reed bunting, while yellow wagtail usually breed. The insects include six-spot burnet moth and Essex skipper butterfly. There is a good ground flora.

Woodham Walter Common

TL 790065; part of a 54ha block; ENT reserve
Mixed woodland
Spring, early summer

Part of the DANBURY GROUP.

173

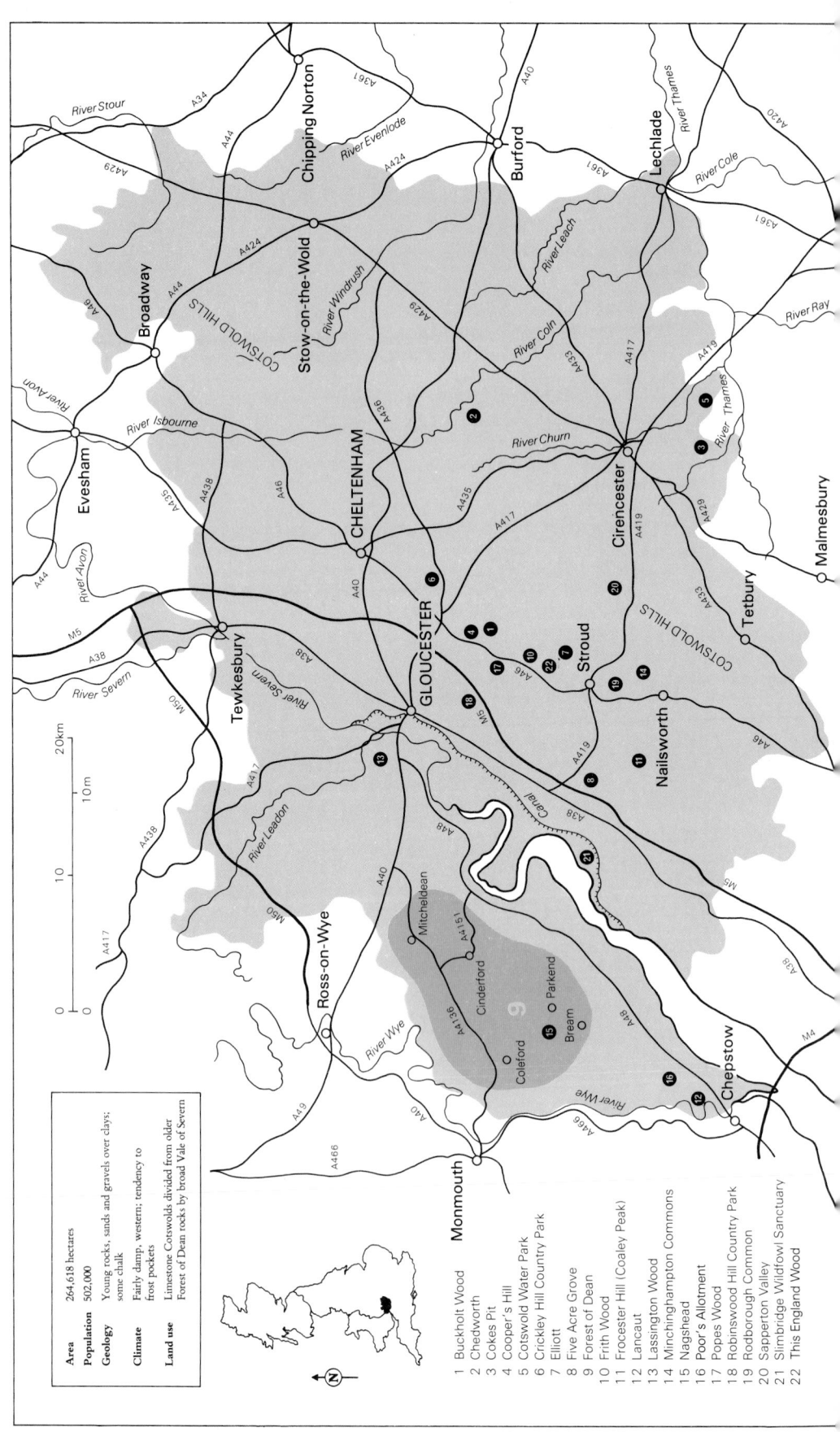

Area	264,618 hectares
Population	502,000
Geology	Young rocks, sands and gravels over clays; some chalk
Climate	Fairly damp, western; tendency to frost pockets
Land use	Limestone Cotswolds divided from older Forest of Dean rocks by broad Vale of Severn

1 Buckholt Wood
2 Chedworth
3 Cokes Pit
4 Cooper's Hill
5 Cotswold Water Park
6 Crickley Hill Country Park
7 Elliott
8 Five Acre Grove
9 Forest of Dean
10 Frith Wood
11 Frocester Hill (Coaley Peak)
12 Lancaut
13 Lassington Wood
14 Minchinhampton Commons
15 Nagshead
16 Poor's Allotment
17 Popes Wood
18 Robinswood Hill Country Park
19 Rodborough Common
20 Sapperton Valley
21 Slimbridge Wildfowl Sanctuary
22 This England Wood

Gloucestershire

Though lacking wild coast and mountain, this is a county of great richness and diversity. Eastward, from the limestone cliffs of the Wye gorge, the land bears a forest shading traces of the working of coal, iron and sandstone. Beyond, a rich red rolling landscape of orchards, farms and copses borders the wide plain of the lower Severn. The heavy pastures of the Gloucester and Berkeley Vales were once golden with cowslips. Above the vale runs the long rampart of the Cotswolds, hung with beechwoods where the rock is harder, and humpy fields where sand and clay have slumped. The beech reaches back into the Stroudwater Valley, but is succeeded by ash to the north and south.

The Cotswolds, whose golden stone has been used for centuries to build fair towns and pretty villages, slope gently eastward again, in arable farms and coverts, down to the long, well-watered valleys leading to the young Thames. Salt water laps the Severn saltings and mudflats, the winter base for wildfowl and waders. Only in the far north west of the county is there a small corner of true hill land, the southern tip of the Malverns, where a bone of granite and schist shows through the gentler contours of less old rocks.

There is no wild heath, no acid wilderness: the hand of man shows everywhere in the landscape. Management has rarely been unsympathetic, and up to the 1940s the rich countryside had evolved from medieval sheepwalks and eighteenth-century remodelling of agriculture and of the whole landscape, producing a web of fields and copse, hedged and walled, between the remaining great woods. These woods of oak and ash, in the FOREST OF DEAN, in Over Severn, in the vales and on the clayey upper levels of the Cotswolds, were still managed very much on traditional lines, though plantation of oak, fir and larch was succeeding the smallwood producing coppices. Where the limestone surfaced beechwoods thrived, some stored up from coppice, others planted in the last two centuries on the great estates. Some commons still remained among all this good husbandry of field and wood: on the high Cotswolds at Cleeve at 350m, on lower ground in the Stroudwater Hills, in the vales beside the Severn and the Stratford Avon, on the Malverns and within the Royal Forest of Dean, where only a limited area was enclosed.

As farming practice has intensified with the introduction of fertilisers and herbicides, traditional land management has been superseded, and semi-natural wood and grassland and its associated wildlife have disappeared. Much of what remains has been surveyed and noted for conservation by establishing reserves and by consultation with and advice to owners and managers. The list shows great diversity: among woodlands there are ancient beech, oak associated with small-leaved lime, elm, field maple, crab apple, wild cherry, whitebeam and wild service-tree beyond the Severn and beside the Wye; a plainer oakwood with birch and rowan in the Forest of Dean; one of ash, field maple, elm and whitebeam on the Wold; with willow and alder in the wet vale. A few meadows remain rich in flowers, bearing cowslips and orchids in the vale, wild daffodils in the west and an astonishing variety of spring and summer flowers in the Wold.

The gorge of the Wye contains nationally important woodland sites, some contained in reserves which conserve the native limes and whitebeams. At LANCAUT there is an unusual transition from salting to oakwood; within the Forest of Dean oaks two herds of fallow deer wander; pied flycatcher nest in the remaining oakwoods now being conserved; and there are wet places kept for their insects. Many trails are laid out to show people these wilder areas. Wild daffodil are reasonably safe in the pure sessile oakwoods of Over Severn, complementing the drifts of bluebells, and are succeeded in clearings by campion and foxglove. The great lime coppice of COLLIN PARK WOOD is still managed on traditional lines. In these sandstone woods wild cherry flowers plentifully on the margins. On the level fields and saltings beside the Severn, the wildfowl gather and find special shelter and exotic cousins under the protection of the Wildfowl Trust at SLIMBRIDGE; from here Bewick's swan and other wildfowl flight out to flooded fields and wet pastures. In summer warblers sing in the osiers of former claypits by the river.

In the Cotswolds the hanging beechwoods shelter a special flora: some continental orchids reach their northern limit here and are watched over carefully. The interspersed commons carry many orchids of varying rarity and occasional juniper, and locally pasqueflower and meadow clary. Elsewhere much of the ancient grassland has gone, but some samples are managed well in the old way, to the benefit of many butterflies as well as an abundance of flowers. In one place an ancient boxwood still survives.

Nightingale visit the dense thorns of the vale and upland on the edge of their northern range, and hobby hawk for flying quarry over the tall woods. There are curlew in the river meadows; dipper and kingfisher work many streams; but sadly the barn owl, symbol of the Gloucestershire Trust for Nature Conservation, is now rare. In the flooded gravelpits of the upper Thames and on Severnside many waterfowl share water space with sailors and fishermen, and some pits reserved for wildlife are densely populated by human visitors at winter weekends.

Most streams are clear and hold trout; salmon are still caught in the wicker putchers made from wands cut in lowland woods; and there is still a rich harvest of elvers in season. Seals can be seen in the Severn mouth. Gloucestershire hopes to claim the otter as a resident again, though it regrets its mink, descended from fur-farm escapes and now a pest. Roe deer are spreading up from Wiltshire to share the woods with fallow deer, a few muntjac deer and many foxes. Some of the plentiful badgers have unhappily caught tuberculosis and reinfect cattle.

Like many more in the Midlands, the elms have survived only as swarms of hedgerow suckers. Gloucestershire still has a good mixture of woods, fields, hedges, streams, pools and some marsh, the home of many plants and animals, and some 50 reserves conserve examples of most of them.

MORLEY PENISTAN

Ashleworth Ham

No access; 40.9ha; GTNC reserve
Flood meadows and woodland
Can be viewed from hides adjacent to public road
All year

The chief interest must be the wildfowl in winter, when thousands of duck may be observed from the hides, but there is also a varied population of breeding birds and a good range of wetland plants such as meadowsweet, great burnet and golden dock.

Badgeworth

Permit only; 394sq m; GTNC reserve
Tiny wetland and pond
June

The reserve is established to protect a rare buttercup, adder's-tongue spearwort.

Baunhill Quarry

Permit only; 0.02ha; GTNC reserve
Geological site
All year

This seabed exposure of the middle Jurassic period contains fossil oysters with marine worm and mollusc workings.

Barn owl at its nest hole: unfortunately it is now a steadily decreasing species.

Betty Daws Wood

Permit only; 8.8ha; GTNC reserve
Fragment of ancient woodland
Spring, early summer

The mainly oak woodland, including small-leaved lime and wild service-tree, has a good show of spring flowers with abundant wild daffodil.

The Severn Vale, looking across the lowlands and into Wales.

Bourton Wood Nature Trail

Permit only; 5km; Batsford Estate
Commercially managed and ancient woodland
Access generally restricted to GTNC members and
school parties
Trail guide and permit form from Batsford Estate
Office, Moreton-in-Marsh
May–September

The woodland has a good range of flowers and is
rich in birds and mammals.

Buckholt Wood

SO 894131; 100ha; NCC–GTNC reserve
Beech high forest
Spring, summer

One of the COTSWOLD COMMONS AND BEECHWOODS.

Chedworth

SP 051138; 1.5km; GTNC reserve
Disused railway line
Car park for members only
Spring, early summer

The reserve runs either through cuttings, rich in
lime-loving plants such as large thyme, basil
thyme and blue fleabane, or raised on an embankment with good views over the surrounding woodlands. The cuttings show important exposures of
middle Jurassic inferior oolitic limestone.

Cokes Pit

SU 026953; 3.2ha; GTNC–GCC reserve
Flooded gravelpit in Cotswold Water Park
Access restricted
All year

The islanded lake is easily viewed from the roads
around it and often contains a good range of wildfowl including less usual species such as red-
crested pochard.

Collin Park Wood

Permit only; 14ha; GTNC reserve
Coppiced small-leaved lime woodland
Spring, early summer

A superb damp woodland of coppiced small-leaved
lime and oak stands over a dense, rather acid
ground cover with much bramble and bracken but
also species such as bluebell, primrose and yellow
archangel.

Cooper's Hill

SO 886142; 54.8ha; GCC reserve
Woodland, scrub and limestone grassland
Leaflet from GCC or GTNC
Spring, early summer

Spectacular views across Gloucestershire and over
the Severn Vale into Wales give extra interest to a
reserve which demonstrates some of the characteristic Cotswold woodland plants, together with
scrub and grassland.

Cotswold Commons and Beechwoods

SO 894131 (Buckholt Wood); 270ha; NCC reserves
Beech high forest
Spring, summer

These reserves consist of several more or less contiguous woodlands which, collectively, form a
superb example of beechwoods on the Cotswold
limestone. One of these, Buckholt Wood, is
described here.

Tall beech trees stand throughout the wood over
younger beech with a scatter of other species such
as common whitebeam, oak and wych elm or ash,
alder and willow where the soils are deep and
damp. The wood is often steeply tilted, sloping
down in flinted folds, a cover to the hillside which
probably dates from the last ice age. Although

animals are not grazed there now, the woods are unenclosed and rights of common apply.

Below the high-forest beech the understorey contains a variety of shrub or sapling species such as ash, hawthorn, hazel, holly, wayfaring-tree, wild cherry and yew, with a considerable invasion of young sycamore. This shrub layer stands over a ground cover of bramble and wild rose with carpets of gleaming ivy and such rich-wood plants as dog's mercury and enchanter's-nightshade, sanicle, primrose and violet, woodruff and wood spurge. Climbing tangles of traveller's-joy and dark clumps of the strange green hellebore underline the lime-rich nature of the soil, and where a ride is edged by a grassy bank this is confirmed by a limestone grassland with salad burnet, small scabious and the tall ploughman's-spikenard.

Although at least part of the wood was once coppiced, present management involves removal of timber trees, achieved by thinning rather than clear-felling, and the former coppice areas have virtually disappeared. The heavy thinning opens out the woodland but leaves the essential beech cover and does not destroy the character of the wood. Bramble tends to spring up and fill the open clearings but this is later replaced by sapling trees and a good woodland structure. In places the soil becomes less lime-rich and stands of bracken and bluebell appear with honeysuckle, replacing traveller's-joy, while deeper, damper soils are shown by sprays of pendulous sedge.

These Cotswold beechwoods are important not only as fine examples of the natural woods which once covered all these hills, and as havens for woodland wildlife, but also for the unusual plants which still survive because they have been undisturbed for thousands of years.

Among these important Cotswold beechwood species are common wintergreen, generally a northern species but found here on the limestone and also in some East Anglian fens, narrow-lipped and green-flowered helleborine, and both bird's-nest orchid and yellow bird's-nest, two saprophytes that are characteristic of old beech woodland.

Cotswold Water Park

SU 026597; 5666ha; GCC–Wilts CC
Flooded gravel workings
Leaflets from GCC or WCC
All year

Not many kilometres from Cricklade the River Thames is a young stream risen from the plain below the Cotswold Hills. The plain is an older river bed and the Thames at its mightiest is a rivulet compared with the flow of water which once ran here. This spread of level land was made by a huge flow of water which seeded the earlier surface with the gravels that are now a more valuable harvest than crops or cows. Vast shallow diggings remove the gravels to leave lakes of lime-rich

Cotswold Water Park: flooded gravelpits have become rich waters full of wildlife.

water which, when all the extraction ends, will total around 1600ha.

Although there are obvious dangers in encouraging the destruction of one form of habitat to replace it with another, this enormous new wetland must make some slight recompense for loss of others. The eventual spread of waters will form the largest body of marl lakes in the country, which will encourage a richness of plant and invertebrate life to feed great numbers of fish and birds.

Where birds are known to migrate by sight along river courses and valleys, they will also drop down to a spread of water; no one visiting the area, already widely flooded, could fail to see how wetland birds must be attracted here. Many of the large flooded pits will be used for recreation which will keep wildlife away, but some, as with the GTNC reserves of COKES PIT, EDWARD RICHARDSON and WHELFORD POOLS, will provide oases of peace among the disturbance. Already over 120 species have been recorded although many of them depend upon a habitat which may be affected by further gravel working. In such an important area continual efforts will be made to establish nature reserves and, as the water area grows, the importance of the Water Park must grow. Already Bewick's swan, garganey, water rail, grasshopper warbler, little ringed plover, spotted redshank, terns, gulls and a host of smaller birds have been recorded. Osprey on passage have inspected the waters and, as the scars of digging fade beneath spreads of vegetation, the lakes should acquire increasing attraction for other predators. Apart from the interest of the growing list of uncommon species such as marsh warbler and white-winged black tern, the Water Park is of great importance for the study of the plant colonisation of these waters and of the developing animal life within them.

Crickley Hill Country Park

SO 936163; 60ha; GCC
Woodland, scrub and limestone grassland
Leaflets from information centre or GCC
Spring, summer

The drive up to the country park passes through grazed meadows shaded by parkland oak trees, and there is a spectacular view from this shoulder of Cotswold limestone. Trampled pathways crossing old limestone workings indicate heavy use but this adds to the variety of the site since it keeps open areas which can be colonised by tiny plants.

A nature trail demonstrates a good range of characteristic Cotswold plants. The first impression of the scrubland area leading to the woodland is that of a great mix of species, one of the features of lime-rich scrub. Ash, elder, blackthorn, hawthorn, hazel, holly and wayfaring-tree are tangled together with wild rose and traveller's-joy; beech and field maple stand above banks of bramble; grassy path edges are decorated with small herbs such as salad burnet or tall betony.

Water rail adjusting its clutch of eggs.

The woodland itself is typically beech with some very large old trees and a number of ancient oaks. Old coppiced hazel and holly form the understorey with a ground cover which varies with the amount of shade; under a dense canopy the woodland floor is virtually bare, except for a brief show of bluebells before the leaves are cut out the light; where light can get in, bramble tends to take over but elsewhere typical rich-wood plants such as dog's mercury, violets and sanicle may be found. An area of recent coppicing is thick with rosebay willowherb, a blaze of colour compared to the rather sombre show in the shaded wood. Tall ash trees also grow in the woodland; like beech they can grow on very shallow soils: an old stone quarry here shows just how little soil there is covering the rubble above the solid rock.

Beyond the wood is scrub and grassland, again the mixed scrub species, clumped in and around glades of herb-rich grass. Harebell, eyebright, wild thyme and small scabious fill the clearings, together with more uncommon species such as clustered bellflower and autumn gentian.

The grassland in the more busy areas is heavily trampled but is still rich in species such as yellowwort and ploughman's-spikenard, or viper's-bugloss, carline and dwarf thistle and common rockrose. Where the grassland is deeper many of the smaller species disappear but harebell and salad burnet persist and taller plants such as greater knapweed show with musk mallow and woolly thistle.

Daneway Banks

Permit only; 17ha; GTNC reserve
Limestone scrub and grassland
Spring, early summer

A superb range of lime-loving flowers such as columbine, clustered bellflower and meadow saffron are complemented by a good range of insects and scrubland birds.

Edward Richardson

Permit only; 10ha; GTNC reserve
Scrub and flooded gravelpits
Spring, early summer

The ponds are too small to attract regular visits from the most unusual bird species but kingfishers, for instance, are frequently seen here and the variety of plant and insect life is extremely good.

Elliott

SO 877067; 9.6ha; GTNC reserve
Limestone grassland
Spring, summer

This small area of grazed common land is rich in lime-loving species, such as kidney vetch , autumn gentian and several orchids and in associated insects. A good variety of butterfly species is recorded.

Fairplay Ponds

Permit only; 1.6ha; GTNC reserve
Ponds and wet heathland
Spring, early summer

A mixture of acid and lime-rich areas add interest to a wetland showing purple moor-grass with western gorse, and a good display of lemon-scented fern.

Five Acre Grove

SO 791042; 5ha; GTNC reserve
Mixed woodland
Spring, early summer

Some 34 woodland bird species breed in the oak and ash woodland which stands over a good mix of species including wild service-tree, spindle and field maple.

Forest of Dean

See map; 10,935ha; FC
Mixed woodland
Leaflets from FC
Spring, early summer

The Dean is set between two rivers, the Wye and the Severn, on a tract of hilly ground which is built from very varied rocks. It lies between South Wales and the main body of England, forming an island wilderness where wildlife is conserved in a wide variety of habitats. Although conservation is an implicit concern of FC management, the importance of the Dean is underlined by the fact that it contains several nature reserves, managed jointly by the FC and such bodies as the NCC, RSPB and GTNC.

Much of the Dean has been wooded for thousands of years but has suffered sweeping changes since man began to modify his environment so widely. Nature, of course, has forced its own changes with woodland, returning after the

Longhorn beetle on bramble in the Forest of Dean.

last ice age, gradually developing from near-Arctic conditions to a blend of birch and Scots pine, similar to present Scottish forests, and then to a rich mixed woodland of which only echoes remain.

The forest spreads across a tract of land which has been warped by great earth movements and weathered by time to show a central core of coal-seamed sandstones, clays and limestones surrounded by old red sandstone and by older Silurian rocks. This mix of tilted rocks provides hills, plateaus and valleys of a widely varying nature, reflected in the forest trees. Sessile oak, the oak of the western woodlands, with wych elm, small-leaved lime, hazel, holly and rowan would have been mixed with trees such as ash, wild cherry, field maple, whitebeam and yew on richer sites, with alder and species of willow in wetter places.

The forest, now, can tell a history of man in Britain. The open lands between the spreads of woodland in the Dean began with the forest-clearer, Neolithic man, and were enlarged and confirmed by farmers since, by Romans and Saxons, by Englishmen who resented the Norman deer and by men who also worked in the woods to find timber for their wars. Areas of coppice are reminders of the medieval management when wood was needed for charcoal and bark for tanning, and large quantities of poles were used for baskets, hurdles and building materials. Massive clearances fed wood to the two world wars and, even now, quarries and mines are worked to extract stone and coal from the forest.

Despite all the felling, clearing and planting, mining, quarrying, drainage and general alterations to the Dean, the forest still holds a splendid mix of ancient plantations and new. The woods form a mosaic of conifers and hardwoods, a pattern largely imposed by the variation of the soils, while rotational planting, thinning and cropping ensure the very wide habitat range.

The broad-leaved woodland is mainly pedunculate oak with beech, sweet chestnut, rowan, holly and sessile oak, standing above a ground cover of bracken, bramble or grasses. The predominantly high-forest structure possesses little understorey, since sheep-grazing severely inhibits new growth – the woods are often composed of equal-aged tall trees. Other types of woodland contribute variety, with alder in the wetter sites and with ash, beech, large-leaved lime and wych elm. Birch will invade wherever it can while the variation is further increased by areas of young plantation, grassland, heathland, bogs, pools, streams and rivers.

Unmanaged areas on the limestone outcrops have the richest plant life, perhaps where abandoned quarries leave slopes too steep to be worth replanting. Beech and wych elm are mixed with ash, birch, sweet chestnut, oak, rowan and sycamore above a shrub layer of holly and yew with dogwood, elder, guelder-rose, hawthorn, hazel, field maple, willow and wild rose. The ground cover may be equally rich and may contain such uncommon species as autumn crocus, herb-Paris and bird's-nest orchid.

Together with the variation provided by the managed woodlands there is a range of heath and bog habitats where plants such as purple moor-grass, bilberry, heather, bell-heather, cross-leaved heath, bog asphodel and bog pimpernel may be found.

Sheep are not the only grazing animals in the Dean – there are also two herds of fallow deer, one based on High Meadows Woods, the other around Speech House. Small mammals such as shrews, voles and mice are quarry for stoat, weasel and fox, and several species of bat may be recorded. Very occasionally otter or polecat may occur.

The bird life varies according to the habitat. New plantations may encourage shrub and heath-land species such as tree pipit, whinchat, linnet and nightjar; the range in taller woodland includes goldcrest, redstart, warblers and all three native woodpeckers. Among the more interesting birds of the Dean are pied flycatcher and raven, around their eastern limit in southern Britain, and breeding populations of hawfinch and crossbill. Water adds an important range of habitat to the forest – dipper, kingfisher and visiting heron may be seen. The ponds and marshy areas draw winter migrants such as snipe, jack snipe, teal and whooper swan.

Water, too, provides a habitat for a range of dragonflies and damselflies while the grasslands, heath and woodlands are rich in other insects. Over 30 species of butterfly have been recorded including both grassland and woodland species. Brown argus, grayling, holly blue and white admiral have been recorded together with dark green, high brown, pearl-bordered, small pearl-bordered and silver-washed fritillary.

Among the specialities of the Dean are spectacular colonies of the exotic Martagon lily and a number of outstanding ancient woodland lichens, in particular those growing on the oaks

The mixed woodlands of the Forest of Dean.

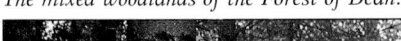

around Speech House. Declared, in 1938, as England's first National Forest Park, the Dean remains a wonderfully varied wildlife sanctuary – a place of fascination at any season.

Foxes Bridge Bog

Permit only; 5.3ha; GTNC reserve
Ancient marshland
Spring, early summer

Sphagnum mosses and plants such as marsh St John's-wort and marsh violet, a possible food plant for small pearl-bordered fritillary, characterise this area of bog.

Frith Wood

SO 877086; 22ha; GTNC reserve
High-forest beech woodland
No access off cleared tracks
Spring, early summer

Frith Wood is an even-aged woodland. Slender, straight, very tall beech trees stand above the woodland floor, so tall that the canopy resembles a vaulted cathedral roof. The reserve lies on both sides of a narrow limestone ridge and this enables light to enter horizontally, to encourage a dense understorey of saplings and shrubs. An area of high-forest oak and ash lies near the plateau top of the ridge, standing over bare rubbly slopes with spreads of bramble and dog's mercury.

Thinning in the northern wing has opened some of the woodland, although many tall beech trees still stand, and this area is notable for old quarries filled with ash, whitebeam and yew, with steep ivy-covered slopes and spreads of rich green hart's-tongue, topped with lesser periwinkle. The southern wing is far more densely dressed, fringed at its lower edge with birch and oak saplings mixing with the lime-loving ash, yew, whitebeam and field maple. Strong young saplings of beech, hawthorn, hazel, holly and elder also occur, together with traveller's-joy and wild rose.

The ground cover is similarly varied with more acid areas showing stands of bracken and rides lined with rosebay willowherb and raspberry, with pendulous sedge and great willowherb in wetter places. The woodland grasses include wood melick, a lime-loving decorative grass which often grows on sunny banks or pathways, while the more open shrubby understorey may stand over carpets of woodruff or enchanter's-nightshade. Wood spurge and spurge-laurel may both be found with sanicle. Orchid species include broad-leaved helleborine.

The understorey offers both ideal nest sites for many woodland birds and also cover for small animals, the limestone providing a source of shell-building material for a good variety of snails while the woodland edge and clearings caused by tree-felling make attractive areas for butterflies.

The felling programme will lead to one of the most fascinating aspects of the woodland. As the fully mature beech trees are felled young saplings will replace them with a more mixed-age commun-

Marbled white butterfly, typical of grasslands such as Frocester Hill.

ity, varied with other species. Provided sycamore growth is controlled, this should lead to the development of an interesting woodland and provide a progression rewarding to monitor.

Frocester Hill (Coaley Peak)

SO 794009; 5.6ha; GTNC reserve
Limestone grassland and scrub
Leaflet from GTNC or GCC
Spring, summer

Superb views across the River Severn to Wales add to the interest of the ungrazed grassland, scrub and wooded quarry. A good range of species is found including both nettle-leaved and clustered bell-flower, with insects such as marbled white and holly blue butterflies and scarlet tiger and ghost moths.

Hobbs Quarry

Permit only; 1ha; GTNC reserve
Geological reserve
All year

The chief importance of the quarry is an exposure of slump strata of Wenlock series limestone, although there is also an interesting small area of woodland with a ground cover which includes primrose and spurge-laurel.

Lancaut

ST 539967; 24ha; GTNC reserve
Woodland and quarry above the tidal River Wye
Permit only off public rights of way
Spring, early summer

From the road above, the path slopes steeply down through woodland to a tiny derelict chapel from which it descends again to the bank of the River Wye. The river bends downstream in a spectacular curve of vertical rock and the northern side of the gorge is thickly clothed with woodland.

The waters are deep and muddy with an enormous tidal range, either exposing steep banks of glutinous mud or lapping the narrow saltmarsh zone below the woodland. The edge of the mud is thick with English scurvygrass, a fleshy plant with sprays of small white flowers, and sea aster, lifting its small flower clusters above all but the highest tides. Above this narrow lower zone is the saltmarsh proper with spear-leaved orache and buck's-horn plantain, common sea-blite, sea plantain, sea-milkwort and sea-spurrey.

The river terrace is grassed and often quarried below the wooded slopes; in the stony banks a profusion of lime-loving plants take advantage of the open sunny position. Common rock-rose and yellow-wort vie with varieties of St John's-wort in the brightness of their colour, contrasting with the subtler shades of the tiny hairy violet or the rare lesser calamint. On the open limestone ledges ox-eye daisy, red valerian and naturalised wallflower give the effect of window boxes.

In the cooler, deeper soils of the woodland a variety of species grow together. Small-leaved lime and wild service-tree, with varieties of whitebeam, grow with yew, field maple, oak and ash above luxuriant stands of woodland ferns. Bright spring flowers such as bluebell, primrose and violet make an attractive show before the leaf canopy closes over, a strategy also employed by wood spurge and spurge-laurel, while the climbing wild madder ensures its sunlight by growing on the woodland fringes and pathway edges.

The woodland contains a typical range of mammals and birds, while the cliffs provide nesting sites for a variety of species. On the river below are cormorant, heron and shelduck, though the muddiness of the water conceals elvers and salmon.

Lassington Wood

SO 803203; 6ha; Tewkesbury BC–GTNC reserve
Mixed woodland
Spring, early summer

Lime-rich clays encourage a good variety of woodland species, with much ash over spurge-laurel and goldilocks buttercup. Nightingale nest, together with a good range of woodland birds.

Laymoor Quag

Permit only; 3.5ha; GTNC reserve
Wet heathland
Spring, early summer

The reserve contains a rich variety of heather, purple moor-grass and *Sphagnum* mosses and is notable for petty whin, uncommon in the county.

Littleton Wood

Permit only; 0.7ha; AWT reserve
Mixed woodland
Spring, early summer

The small woodland is most notable as a stronghold for yellow star-of-Bethlehem.

Lower Lodge Wood

Permit only; 4.45ha; GTNC reserve
Mixed woodland
Spring, early summer

Since Dutch elm disease killed off the majority of the elms, the woods mainly consist of oak and ash over a hazel understorey. The ground cover includes spurge-laurel, and bird's-nest orchid and earth star fungus can be found in those places where beech trees grow.

Merring Meend

Permit only; 1.6ha; GTNC reserve
Pools and wetland
Spring, early summer

Probably the last of the natural pools remaining in the FOREST OF DEAN, Merring Meend is the only site still to contain that beautiful pink-flowered wetland species, bogbean. Nodding bur-marigold also occurs on the reserve and there is a good range of wetland insects to complement the plants.

Minchinhampton Commons

SO 858013; 232ha; NT
Limestone grassland
Spring, summer

A superb sweep of limestone grassland, the commons contain a characteristic variety of lime-loving plants such as clustered bellflower and several orchid species.

Mythe Railway

Permit only; 2.8ha; GTNC reserve
Disused railway line
Spring, early summer

Wetland plants such as common comfrey, together with lime-loving species such as wild liquorice and spindle, add to the interest of this small reserve which also contains a good variety of butterflies and birds.

Nagshead

SO 606080; 153ha; RSPB reserve
Mixed woodland
Leaflet from RSPB
Spring, early summer

Part of the great FOREST OF DEAN, the reserve consists of a varied range of woodland types including recent Forestry Commission plantations with both enclosed and open woodland. The classic birds of mature western woodland, pied flycatcher, redstart and wood warbler, are present with dipper and grey wagtail by the stream, while the conifers attract birds such as goldcrest and sparrowhawk to the taller stands of trees. The largest mammals to be found here at Nagshead are fallow deer, which graze the rides or the clearings under the open woods in the dawn or dusk. During the daytime, while the deer are quietly lying up, these places may be bright with butterflies such as white admiral and speckled wood.

Over Ponds

Permit only; 4ha; GTNC reserve
Ponds and marshland
Spring, early summer

The ponds contain interesting plants such as nodding bur-marigold, narrow-leaved water-plantain and frogbit, while flowering-rush occurs in the marsh. Water rail have been recorded.

Pit House Pond and Bog

Permit only; 0.2ha; GTNC reserve
Acid wetland
Spring, early summer

The tiny wetland, contrasting with the forest around it, contains western gorse with delicate bog plants such as cross-leaved heath, marsh violet and bog asphodel.

Plump Hill Dolomite Quarry

SO 661172; 1ha; GTNC reserve
Disused quarry
Spring, summer

The quarry face is unstable and should be avoided, although the reserve may be visited for its interesting range of plants, among which are white horehound and autumn lady's-tresses.

Poor's Allotment

ST 559995; 28.3ha; Poor's Allotment Trustees reserve
Heathland and limestone grassland
Spring, summer

Acid soils over sandstone faulted against limestone give a most unusual mix of heathland with western gorse, all three common heathers and bilberry, and limestone grassland with species such as carline thistle, common rock-rose and wild thyme. A small pond adds further interest to the reserve.

Popes Wood

SO 875128; 26ha; GTNC–NCC reserve
Beech woodland
Visitors must keep to paths and tracks
Spring, early summer

The fine high-forest beech woodland with a rich lime-loving ground cover is part of an NNR established to protect its wealth of interest. Characteristic plants include green hellebore, spurge-laurel and several orchid species.

Robinswood Hill Country Park

SO 835157; 97ha; Gloucester City Council
Cotswold outcrop
Spring, summer

A taste of the wildlife of the Cotswolds on the southern edge of Gloucester, Robinswood Hill is topped by downland above more acid older rocks. A nature trail leads to the summit viewpoint, demonstrating the variation as the marlstones and sands give way to limestone and plants such as greater knapweed and small scabious appear.

Rodborough Common

SO 852035; 96.8ha; NT
Limestone grassland
Spring, summer

A level plateau, falling steeply along the edge, Rodborough Common bears a great variety of attractive limestone flowers characteristic of the Cotswold downlands. The plateau has generally deeper soils than the steep, soft limestone slopes and is a mosaic of short and deeper grassland according to the grazing and the depth of soil. Even in the areas of coarser grasses, yellow rattle and common spotted-orchid, kidney vetch and greater knapweed are found. Where the grasses are shorter, small scabious, harebell, common bird's-foot-trefoil and common rock-rose, cowslip and eyebright, common milkwort and lady's bedstraw, wild thyme and autumn gentian, salad burnet, quaking-grass and the lime-loving hoary plantain hint at the variety these limestone grasslands can carry. Much of the interest of the area lies in determining why some plants are on the slopes but not the plateau – why some prefer shallow turf while others shun it.

A shallow quarry-like depression at the top of the slope demonstrates the plants which can survive on the almost scree-like soft limestone. Yellow-wort and carline thistle grow on the very

thin soils, with herb-Robert on the rocks themselves; scrublike bramble, wild rose and hawthorn throw up a protective screen which may have helped ash saplings avoid grazing animals. The ubiquitous wood sage has established a foothold here although, like the scrub, it does not generally appear upon the slopes. More characteristic lime-loving plants include the delicate pink common restharrow with bee and pyramidal orchid.

The pyramidal orchid also appears in coarser grassland lower down, together with common spotted-orchid and yellow rattle, so it cannot prefer thin soils. For yellow-wort and carline thistle, though, it seems to be true: wherever the slope is only thinly grassed, the two appear together. The slopes are faintly terraced, either by soil creep or grazing animals or both, and the small banks so formed are crowded with bright small flowers such as horseshoe vetch and marjoram, oxeye daisy and clustered bellflower, in addition to the species found in the short grass of the plateau. To complement the common restharrow above, spiny restharrow occurs on the slopes, while tiny saplings of birch and oak appear, pointers to the natural progression of grassland, through scrub, to woodland. Woodland does occur below the common and in some places scrub is beginning to spread up into the sloping grassland.

Of special interest here are two species of local distribution, pasqueflower and wild liquorice, together with a good range of orchids including a particularly good show of early-purple, green-winged, fragrant and pyramidal.

The rich variety of limestone plants attracts an appropriate range of insects, including blues and marbled white among the butterflies with six-spot burnet among the moths.

Sandhurst

Permit only; 7.5ha; GTNC reserve
Flooded brickpits
Spring, summer

Two areas of old brickpit workings, one of them converted to an osier bed, form an interesting wetland reserve with a good variety of plants and animals. The clays of the Severn Vale were dug for brick-making and here, when the brickpits became uneconomical in the early part of the century, willows were planted and managed to provide slender wands for basket-making and spars for thatching. The osier willow is allowed to grow until it has established itself, and then the crown

The Cotswold beechwoods, such as Popes Wood, are a special feature of Gloucestershire.

is cut out so that growth is concentrated into producing finger-thick flexible straight shoots which are harvested to stimulate a further crop.

The most important osier beds were planted in the northern section, a complex of pools and banks where the willows are still maintained to preserve nesting sites. Hemlock water-dropwort and fine-leaved water-dropwort fringe the pools while the alder and willow woodland shading them contains damp-loving species such as guelder-rose, remote and swamp meadow-grass, bladder-sedge, cyperus sedge and wood club-rush. Great bellflower raises its tall blue-purple flowered stem and orange balsam shows a jewel-like delicacy compared with the large-flowered Indian balsam which lines many river banks. The pools themselves contain whorled water-milfoil together with the beautiful rose-pink flowering-rush, white-flowered frogbit and the speciality of the reserve, greater bladderwort, which had disappeared from the area before the reserve was established. Clearance the following summer let light into the pools and in most years there is a brilliant show of yellow blooms.

The southern area is more unkempt. A scrub of willow, hawthorn and blackthorn, backed by a colourful jungle of nettle, meadowsweet and meadow crane's-bill, bright yellow tansy and common toadflax, common comfrey and great willow-herb which, with a variety of vetches, shelters a sizeable open pool. The pool contains stands of arrow-head, water-plantain and flowering-rush, with rigid hornwort hidden beneath the quiet waters.

Mallard, shoveler and teal have been recorded together with heron, kingfisher and water rail and with sedge and reed warbler in the osiers or surrounding scrub. Siskin and redpoll may feed in the alder stands of the northern pool when winter brings them down from colder latitudes. Insects are numerous and, with a good range of dragonflies and damselflies, include the spectacular musk beetle and a rare water beetle, *Agabus undulatus*.

Sapperton Valley

SO 939034; 3.7ha; GTNC reserve
Disused canal
Spring, summer

Parts of the canal are thick with marsh-marigold, yellow water-lily and plants such as purple-loose-strife, while the towpath shows woodland influence, with yellow archangel and wood melick. Typical woodland and some wetland birds may be seen.

Silk Wood

Permit only; 8.5ha; GTNC reserve
Remnant of ancient woodland
Spring, early summer

Oak over coppiced hazel is the main pattern throughout, but other species include field maple and wild cherry, with a rich ground cover including herb-Paris and meadow saffron. White admiral and silver-washed fritillary are among the butterflies and there is a good range of woodland birds.

Slimbridge Wildfowl Sanctuary

SO 723048; 800ha; WT
Mudflats, saltmarsh, grazing meadows and lagoons
Leaflets from reception centre
Winter

The headquarters of the Wildfowl Trust houses the world's largest wildfowl collection, but beyond this is the Severn Estuary and natural salt grassland, together with the great open levels of reclaimed saltmarsh, the New Grounds, where winter weather brings thousands of wild birds to rest and feed. A series of carefully designed hides along the south and west overlook these meadows where up to 20,000 wildfowl may be seen.

White-fronted geese are one of the Slimbridge specialities, flying in here from Europe every winter to form the largest flock in the country. Bewick's swan is another, with up to 600 present in the winter. They, too, fly in from Europe, from the high cold north west, to gather in the lagoons to wait for feeding time. The swans can then be seen at close quarters and, since the beak marking is different in every bird, they can be individually recognised. One swan was seen in the winter of 1982–3 making his twentieth consecutive visit.

Whooper swan are occasionally seen, while mingling with the huge flocks of white-fronted geese are numbers of feral greylag and Canada geese, with regular barnacle, bean, Brent, pink-footed and lesser white-fronted geese. The rare lesser white-fronted goose is seen at Slimbridge nearly every winter: this is the only site in the country where birdwatchers may hope to see it.

Thousands of wigeon and mallard, perhaps a thousand pochard and teal, hundreds of tufted duck, pintail, gadwall and shelduck, with smaller numbers of shoveler, may be present. Several hundred coot winter, while the cold, short days are busy with the movement of wader flocks, of large gatherings of curlew and huge congregations of dunlin and lapwing.

In times of passage, the lagoons may be visited by small but regular numbers of migrant waders. Bar-tailed and black-tailed godwit, ruff, ringed, little ringed, grey and golden plover, green and wood sandpiper, curlew sandpiper and whimbrel are regular visitors while merlin may prey on the smaller passage migrants. Spring also brings swallow and house martin and, while they feed on insects above the lagoons and meadows, a hobby can sometimes be seen harrying them.

Uncommon birds may also occur but the sanctuary is not merely concerned with adding to its bird list: important research, through recording and ringing, is conducted on bird numbers and migrations.

Snows Farm

Permit only; 21.3ha; GTNC reserve
Limestone grassland and woodland
Spring, summer

Bee and fly orchid and greater butterfly-orchid are among the great variety of attractive plants here which draw many species of butterfly. A brook

Wild geese on the Dumbles, part of the vast expanse of mudflats, marsh and meadow land that forms the Slimbridge Wildfowl Sanctuary.

increases the habitat range and adds to the interest of the reserve.

Stenders Quarry

Permit only; 2.8ha; GTNC reserve
Disused quarry
Spring, early summer

The quarry is not only geologically important, with exposures of carboniferous limestone shales, lower dolomite and the junction with the old red sandstone, but also carries limestone woodland and grassland with cowslip, primrose and autumn gentian.

Stuart Fawkes

Permit only; 8.3ha; GTNC reserve
Limestone grassland
June, July

Cowslip and common restharrow are among approximately 70 plants recorded here, but the reserve was established to protect a fine colony of the very local meadow clary.

This England Wood

SO 875083; 2ha; WdT
New plantation
Spring, early summer

A small field has been planted up with some 1400 young broad-leaved trees and will, in time, grow on to maturity colonised by woodland plants and animals.

Westbury Brook Mine Pond

Permit only; 0.2ha; GTNC reserve
Small pond
Spring, summer

The pond, hidden within a plantation, is lined with rushes and bulrush, contains bog pondweed and supports both common and palmate newt.

Whelford Pools

Permit only; 20ha; GTNC reserve
Flooded gravelpits
All year

Two large pits with sheltering high hedges and well-vegetated margins provide ideal breeding and wintering sites for waterbirds. There is a hide.

Wigpool

Permit only; 1.6ha; GTNC reserve
Small wetland
Spring, early summer

The pool has lost much interest through drying out but still contains *Sphagnum* mosses and is fringed with tufted hair-grass and purple moor-grass.

Witcombe Reservoirs

No access; 28ha; STWA
Reservoir and surrounds
Can be viewed from public right of way
at SO 904149
Winter

The open water areas contain wintering wildfowl and the muddy edges occasional waders. Black tern visit at migration times, and great crested grebe breed.

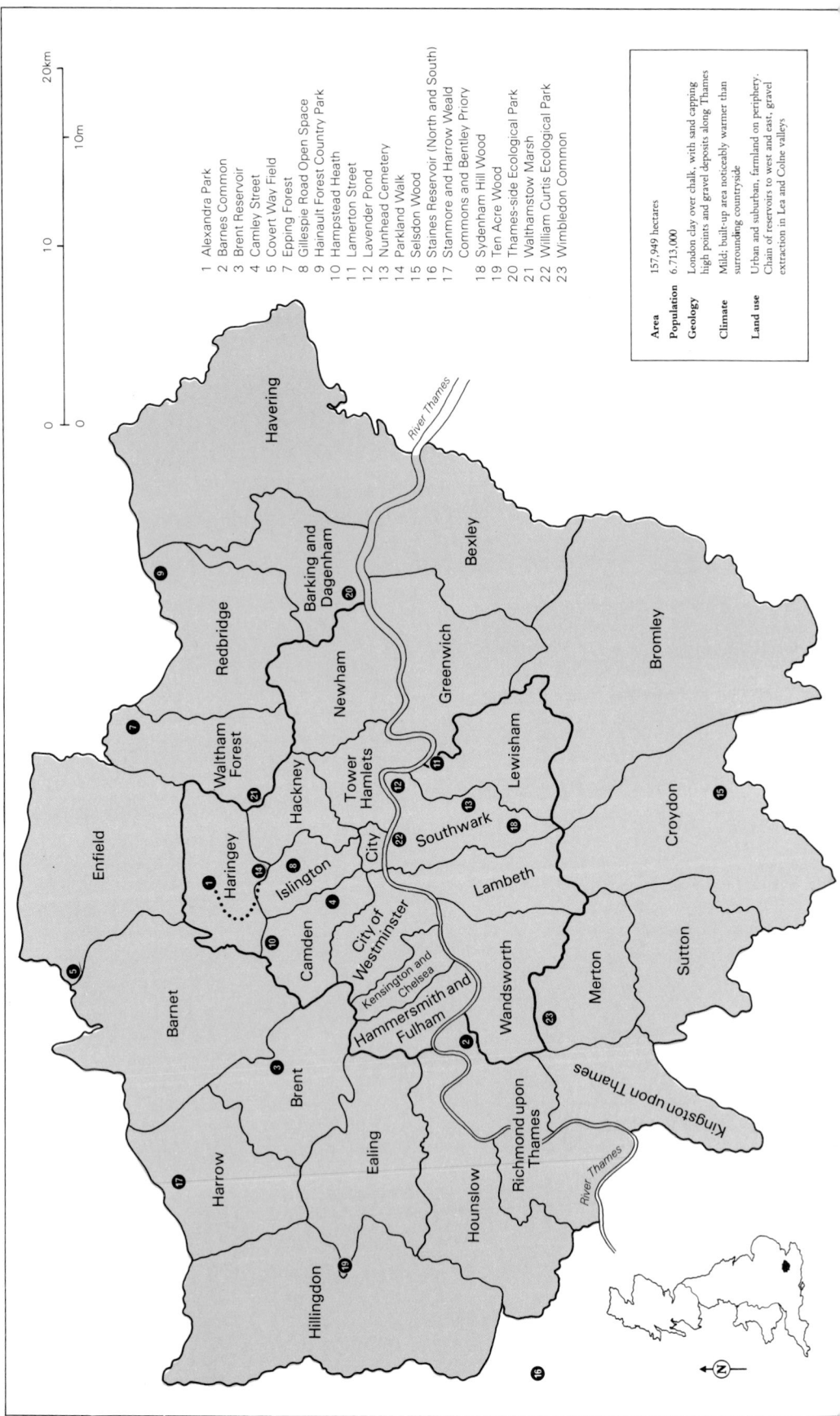

1	Alexandra Park
2	Barnes Common
3	Brent Reservoir
4	Camley Street
5	Covert Way Field
7	Epping Forest
8	Gillespie Road Open Space
9	Hainault Forest Country Park
10	Hampstead Heath
11	Lamerton Street
12	Lavender Pond
13	Nunhead Cemetery
14	Parkland Walk
15	Selsdon Wood
16	Staines Reservoir (North and South)
17	Stanmore and Harrow Weald Commons and Bentley Priory
18	Sydenham Hill Wood
19	Ten Acre Wood
20	Thames-side Ecological Park
21	Walthamstow Marsh
22	William Curtis Ecological Park
23	Wimbledon Common

Area	157,949 hectares
Population	6,713,000
Geology	London clay over chalk, with sand capping high points and gravel deposits along Thames
Climate	Mild; built-up area noticeably warmer than surrounding countryside
Land use	Urban and suburban, farmland on periphery. Chain of reservoirs to west and east, gravel extraction in Lea and Colne valleys

Greater London

Despite the mass of buildings in the central areas, the suburban sprawl of the 1920s and 1930s, and the motorways and high-rise estates of the last two decades, London's 6½ million inhabitants co-exist with a surprising variety of wildlife in the city's 1550 sq. km. Birds in vast numbers visit its reservoirs and gravelpits. Fish are returning to the lower Thames as it reverts to the purity of centuries ago. Habitually rural animals such as foxes flourish within the sound of Big Ben. And an incredible diversity of plant species is found within the Greater London area.

Londoners can ramble in expansive heathland such as WIMBLEDON COMMON or wander through bluebell woodland on HAMPSTEAD HEATH. They can crouch in hides overlooking open water, they can study the bankside life of Thames-feeding streams such as the Rivers Crane and Brent on the north bank, or the Wandle and Pool to the south, and in wellington boots they can squelch through WALTHAMSTOW MARSH by the side of the River Lea.

As well as surviving riches, the metropolis offers an ersatz but wide range of habitats which Richard Mabey memorably christened 'the unofficial countryside'. Unkempt nineteenth-century cemeteries such as the one at NUNHEAD have become fortuitous havens for wildlife. Scattered vacant sites, such as the old Brompton Hospital in Chelsea, now ST LUKE'S NATURE GARDEN, offer unexpected pockets of open space some undisturbed since the last war. Exhausted gravel diggings as at RUXLEY GRAVEL PITS are enthusiastically adopted by bird life discovering advantages over life in the official countryside – a warmer microclimate, regular food supplies and fewer pesticides. Most dramatic of all are the chalk cliffs of SPRINGWELL QUARRY, carved into the side of the Colne Valley, where kestrel find nest sites on ledges high above the disused quarry floor.

Perhaps most curious are those reserves founded on artifice – London's attempt to compensate for the open spaces still being lost each year to factory estates such as that threatening the Chiswick Triangle, to motorways like the one aiming at Oxleas Wood on Shooter's Hill and one of London's innermost farms, or to mineral extraction as at Fray's Farm Meadows. Best known of these modern equivalents of the old physick gardens is the WILLIAM CURTIS ECOLOGICAL PARK on the Thames opposite the Tower of London. On a former lorry park which may eventually be redeveloped are young woodland, a pond dug by volunteers, and a rubble-based grassland which is tramped over by thousands of teacher-led schoolchildren every year.

Inevitably it is the fringes of the region, where London approaches surrounding Kent, Surrey, Buckinghamshire, Hertfordshire and Essex, which are more generously provided with farmland. Yet even here formal reserves support the greatest variety of wildlife. In former Middlesex OLD PARK WOOD offers springtime flowers and birdsong rare in less protected circumstances. Further north the cattle grazing at Bentley Priory make an essential contribution to the equilibrium of this part of the STANMORE AND HARROW WEALD C/ of the Thames at the mouth of th London's last saltmarsh, endar yacht marina, but at the sou/ GLC territory Charles Darwir is safe under official protec/

At Barking, on the as power station, the THAME and orchids bloom alrea(

patch of disused railway embankment in Lewisham harbours the delightful BROOKMILL ROAD reserve, created by voluntary effort with the local council's blessing. In the middle of a giant post-war estate at Camberwell a former prefab site is now a regular visiting place for children from the adjacent school cataloguing the bird, plant and insect life – BENHILL ROAD NATURE GARDEN being an excellent example of the now common partnership between schools, tenants' associations, local wildlife groups and borough councils.

An extra ingredient in what London has to offer the wildlife explorer are the aids to understanding provided at appropriate places. William Curtis is open every day and has ever-patient wardens in attendance. LAVENDER POND has its own attendant and a nature centre in prospect. An energetic group at ALEXANDRA PARK have created a PARKLAND WALK, with an information centre near Finsbury Park. The most ambitious scheme, and the one nearest to the West End and City, is that at CAMLEY STREET where, courtesy of the GLC, the Inner London Education Authority and the London Borough of Camden, an interpretative centre is to be established on the banks of the Regent's Canal.

The nearer a site is to central London, the more important is the protection offered by formal reserve status. Designation as Sites of Special Scientific Interest deters interference from most quarters, but most effective of all are the activities of ordinary people, many of them discovering an interest in wildlife for the first time, who rush to the defence of local sites which for one reason or another face extinction. The increasing and welcome willingness of London's 32 boroughs to recognise the desirability of creating official nature reserves, often in response to campaigns organised by local people, offers ever-expanding prospects for the safeguarding and enhancement of natural environments.

A recent survey of conservation groups identified their members' interest in the countryside as being primarily aesthetic, scientific or 'corporeal' – the last referring to those people who enjoy a healthy day in the fresh air. London has more than enough to satisfy all three inclinations.

BOB SMYTH

Alexandra Park

Wood Green, N22; 4ha; Haringey Wildlife Group–
Alexandra Palace Dev. Team reserve
Woodland, scrub, grassland and pond
Information centre
All year

A spread of adjoining habitats occupies this part of Alexandra Park at the edge of the old racecourse and next to the New River reservoirs. Woodland is accompanied by dense scrub. The former racecourse is managed as meadow grassland, and a new pond sustains plant and insect species as well as wildfowl.

Barn Elms Reservoirs

Permit only; 34ha; TWA
Open water with shallow margins
All year

A favourite spot for birdwatchers for many years: its regulars include great crested grebe, grey heron, gadwall and Canada goose. Among migrants are common sandpiper, sand martin and yellow wagtail with occasional wheatear and whinchat. Large numbers of gulls and wildfowl visit in winter, while summer visitors include swift and meadow pipit.

Barnes Common

Rocks Lane, Barnes, SW13; 71ha
Grassland and scrub
y–July

...mon supports a workaday stock of plants, ...insects and birds, with burnet rose a

Benhill Road Nature Garden

Camberwell, SE5; 0.5ha; local management association reserve
Grass and trees
May–July

Over 40 wild plant species have already established themselves on this former prefab site. Small tortoiseshell butterfly and garden tiger moth are among the insect life already flourishing, while increased variety will result from tree planting and a new pond.

Burnet rose, probably the most attractive of the several rose species growing on Barnes Common.

Brent Reservoir

Welsh Harp, West Hendon, NW9; 47.2ha; BWB
Open water
January–February, April, August–September

A reservoir since 1835, its sloping banks and silted areas at the entry of the River Brent and Silk Stream exhibit the succession from open water to willow carr with beds of common reed and bulrush. Gadwall, a fairly uncommon duck, appreciate the shallow water as a wintering site.

Brookmill Road

Permit only; 0.25ha; Lewisham Wildlife Group (LWT) reserve
Coppice and chalk grassland on former railway line ballast
May–July

Woodland has established itself on an old railway line, the chalk ballast supporting chalkland plants and associated insect species.

Camley Street

St Pancras, NW1; 1ha; LWT reserve
Scrub, grassland and canalside marsh
May–July

On a former canalside coal depot an ecological park is being established, safeguarding the existing goat willow scrub and grassland – common blue butterflies are in evidence here – with skullcap and reed sweet-grass intruding from along the canal.

Covert Way Field

Hadley Wood, Enfield; 6.5ha; Enfield Nat. Hist. Soc. reserve
Scrub, tall grassland and coppice
April–July

Tree cover of ash, oak, hawthorn and various willows supplementing the Hadley Common woodland accompanies tall grassland, an area of which is mown in order to produce a herb-rich pasture.

Darlands Lake

TQ 244934; 5.1ha; H and MNT reserve
Lake and marsh
April–June, September

A former duck refuge; around the lake are marshy areas, mature alder woodland and damp grassland. Breeding birds include a variety of warblers, mandarin duck and goldcrest.

Downe Bank

Permit only; 7ha; KTNC reserve
Chalk grassland, beech and oak woodland with hazel coppice
All year

Predominantly hazel coppice and chalk grassland: the former has a rich ground flora, including toothwort and spurge-laurel, chronicled by Charles Darwin who lived for 40 years in nearby Down House.

Camley Street: rosebay willowherb, often known colloquially as 'fireweed' because of the rapidity with which it colonised bomb sites during World War II.

Epping Forest

Chingford Plain, Rangers Road, Chingford, E4; 2430ha; Corpn of the City of London
Ancient wood pasture, grassland and wetland
Spring, early summer

Situated inside the Greater London boundary at the southern tip of the Forest, Pole Hill is one of the outstanding parts of the area, the rest of which is described in greater detail under Essex. The hill provides a vantage point offering extensive views over the Lea Valley and its rich grassland includes plants such as dyer's greenweed.

Gillespie Road Open Space

Highbury, N5; 1ha; LB Islington reserve
Grassland, scrub, whips and pond
May–July

A fine specimen of progressive landscape architecture, this nature park on old railway sidings abounds in naturalised lupins rooted in the clinker. Whitethroat find the planting of alder, birch and field maple attractive, and a new pond is lavishly planted with species such as water-plantain, water-soldier and yellow iris.

Buddleia, an introduced species, has nectar-rich flowers that attract butterflies such as peacock.

Hainault Forest Country Park

Fox Burrows, Romford Road, Chigwell Row; 387ha; GLC
Old woodland, scrub and grassland
All year

While most of the area provides active recreational facilities such as golf, fishing and horse riding, parts of this former royal hunting forest, bought by the London County Council in 1903, are common land and secondary woodland.

Hampstead Heath

NW1 and NW3; 324ha; GLC
Woodland, sandpit and meadow
All year

One of the earliest conservation battles saved the Heath from development, and areas of special interest around Ken Wood include traditional woodland complete with bluebells, a valley bog and its mosses, a wild flower meadow, and the South Meadow grassland and scrub which are visited in season by migrants such as yellowhammer.

Harefield Place

Harefield Place Golf Course; 3.9ha; Hillingdon Nat. Hist. Soc. reserve
Woodland, pond and wet meadow
Key available from warden
May–July

Originally established as a bird sanctuary based on its woodland; a pond and marsh now increase its interest, and animals include white-letter hairstreak butterfly and an unexpectedly wide range of small mammals.

Kempton Park West Reservoir

Permit only; 8.5ha; TWA
Open water
All year

Though less attractive to duck than some of the other reservoirs in the Greater London area, Kempton Park West can usually offer tufted duck, pochard and great crested grebe with terns among other migrant species.

Lamerton Street

Deptford, SE8; 1ha; local management association–LWT reserve
Shrubs and butterfly garden with pond
June–August

Small skipper, small tortoiseshell, peacock and a dozen other species of butterfly flourish on the buddleia bushes and brambles that dominate the cobbled walkway which leads up to Deptford High Street.

Lavender Pond

Rotherhithe Street, SE16; 1ha; Ecological Parks Trust reserve
Pond and reedbed
July–September

Lavender Pond is a prime example of a wholly artificial nature reserve; its Thames-water pond supports shoals of fish, four species of dragonfly and various water birds. Other communities represented here are alder carr, together with plants typical of flood meadows and species commonly found on waste ground.

Litten

Oldfield Lane, Greenford; 1.6ha; LB Ealing reserve
Thicket, grassland and pond
May–July

This small educational reserve packs an interesting variety of habitats into a small space: two ponds, a grove of oak and elm, thickets and grassland are the basis for a range of plant and animal inhabitants.

Nunhead Cemetery

Linden Grove, Peckham, SE15; 11ha; LB Southwark reserve
Wood and grassland
May–July

Though the nature reserve area is dominated by sycamore, 100-plus plants have already been recorded which include dog's mercury, meadow crane's-bill and meadow vetchling. Foxes and up to seven butterfly species, including speckled wood, red admiral and meadow brown, may be seen.

Old Park Wood

TQ 049913; 7.7ha; H and MNT reserve
Woodland
April–June

Ancient oak woodland with hazel understorey: its rich ground flora includes coralroot as well as thin-spiked wood-sedge. This wood is one of the best places in London for spring flowers.

Parkland Walk

Alexandra Palace, N22, to Cranley Gardens, N10 (0.7km) and Holmesdale Road, N6, to Finsbury Park, N4 (2.8km); LB Haringey
Woodland, scrub, grassland and ecological corridor
All year

Disused as a railway line for more than 20 years, the site is now managed on an ecological basis, and is colonised by woodland, scrub and coarse grassland. One section runs from Alexandra Park to Highgate Woods, the second section from Highgate tube station to Finsbury Park, passing the information centre at Stapleton Road, N4.

Perivale Wood

Permit only; 11ha; Selborne Soc. reserve
Ancient woodland
April–October

The wood has special claim to fame as one of the oldest nature reserves in Britain, for it has been owned and managed since 1904 by the Selborne Society; their name is a tribute to Gilbert White, whose *Natural History of Selborne* still inspires new generations of naturalists. Sandwiched between the railway and the Paddington arm of the Grand Union Canal, the mainly oak woodland is interspersed with patches of hazel coppice, ash and wild service-tree.

A profusion of bluebells in spring is accompanied by large numbers of breeding blackcap and other birds. Other woodland flowers including red campion make a vivid display, while grasses such as wood millet are an indication of the wood's age. Coppicing of the hazel is being reinstated; the hazel wands are used for hedging around the fields next to the wood.

The grassland on the south and east sides encompasses a marshy pond and associated plants such as cuckooflower. The reserve, sometimes known as the Brent Valley Bird Sanctuary, is one of London's only two statutorily recognised Local Nature Reserves; the other is RUISLIP, further up the Brent Valley.

To be visited as part of any trip to Perivale is nearby Horsenden Hill, whose unimproved hay meadow includes dyer's greenweed and ragged-Robin. Its hedgerows, survivors of ancient woodland, are fringed with herbs such as dog's mercury. The hilltop offers a panorama across west London, south to Richmond, north to Harrow, and westwards as far as the Thames terraces at Windsor.

Hornbeam, beech, oak and hazel form a canopy over Old Park Wood's fine bluebell display.

Queen Mary Reservoir

Permit only; 283ha; TWA
Open water
All year

Part of the reservoir is a protected area for birds, with black-necked grebe a regular, and shoveler and goosander among fairly frequent visitors.

Ruislip

Permit only; 4.5ha; Ruislip and District Nat. Hist. Soc. reserve
Open water and marsh
All year

This segment of former reservoir, built to feed the Grand Union Canal and its Paddington arm, offers open water and surrounding marshland of unusual richness containing a range of plants, insects and molluscs. Drier parts consist of heathland vegetation and developing scrub. As added interest excavated chalk debris supports characteristic chalk grassland. Breeding willow tit and kingfisher are among the birds to be seen here.

The reserve, one of London's two Local Nature Reserves, is surrounded not only by the complex of Ruislip Woods but also by other ancient vestiges. A pre-Roman greenway runs through Mad Bess Woods and a medieval trackway crosses Poor's Fields between Ruislip and North Woods. One of the largest oak-and-coppiced-hornbeam areas left, it presents a contrast to the pollards of Epping Forest. Whereas Epping was open for grazing, Ruislip Woods were enclosed and pannage laws restricted the area to pigs rooting for acorns.

Whitethroat, an attractive warbler that breeds both at Ruislip and at Selsdon Wood.

The glaciers of the last ice age reached the limit of their southward progress around here, and in a ditch dug across Poor's Fields plants of the tundra are revealed after thousands of years of quiescence.

In winter the woodland is a haven for woodcock, and water rail lurk in the densest part of the swamp. Summer sees breeding woodpeckers, hawfinch, wood warbler and tree pipit, and sometimes a nightingale in Poor's Fields.

Ruxley Gravel Pits

Permit only; 20ha; KTNC reserve
Open water and marsh
All year

The contrasting textures of these flooded gravelpits, which act as side reservoirs for the River Cray, are an exciting spectacle for visitors looking from the Sidcup side towards the wooded banks on the Kent side of the valley. The ponds are frequented by migrant wildfowl such as gadwall and tufted duck, and by grey wagtail; they also support many freshwater invertebrates. Surviving marshland vegetation from before the days of water authority drainage schemes is of special interest. But above all it is the atmosphere of this oasis on the edge of the built-up area of south east London which makes Ruxley a source of such immense pleasure to the visitor.

St Luke's Nature Garden

Permit only; 5ha; Kensington and Chelsea Wildlife Group (LWT) reserve
Grass and scrub
May–July

On the basement of the old Brompton Hospital bladder-senna (appropriate name!) spreads among the buddleia, attracting butterflies and large numbers of burnet moth. A kestrel inhabits the gothic tower of St Luke's church opposite.

Selsdon Wood

Court Wood Lane, Selsdon, Croydon; 81ha; NT–LB Croydon reserve
Woodland and bird sanctuary
May–July

The woodland ranges from 200-year-old oaks to recent plantings of beech, larch and spruce, with rotational coppicing in parts, and ground flora including early-purple orchid. Breeding birds include long-tailed tit, blackcap, treecreeper, whitethroat and spotted flycatcher. Grassland pasture occupies a quarter of the reserve.

Springwell Quarry

Permit only; 0.5ha; LWT reserve (under negotiation)
Chalkpit
May–July: wildlife; all year: viewpoint

A former quarry carved into the chalk of the eastern bank of the River Colne, once the course of the

Thames itself, Springwell offers a spectacular view across the valley from its tall cliffs. Kestrel nest on the most inaccessible ledges, while wayfaring-tree and yellow-wort lodge on undisturbed crevices.

On the quarry floor chalkland plants include salad burnet, meadow crane's-bill and fumitory. Soapwort is presumably a relic of former sheep-rearing, being used to wash lanolin out of wool.

On the other side of the canal water pipit are among the rare visitors attracted by the water-cress beds fed by Colne water. Stockers Lake, one of the most important of the old gravel diggings, is favoured by goldeneye, shoveler, pochard and tufted duck in winter. Maple Cross sewage farm, visitable by permit, requires no permit from wintering snipe and waders, including redshank.

Redpoll and siskin abound among the alders which flank the Colne. Along its banks and that of its sister, the Frays River, green sandpiper and kingfisher are among the jewels of London's richest wildlife area.

Staines Reservoirs, North and South

Hanworth; 172ha; TWA
Open water
All year

A winter count here recorded 5000 pochard – one of the largest concentrations in the British Isles – and 4000 tufted duck – only 500 less than the highest national count at LOCH LEVEN (Tayside). Other regulars are teal, wigeon and common sandpiper.

Thousands of wildfowl, such as these tufted duck at Staines, make for London's reservoirs in winter.

Stanmore and Harrow Weald Commons and Bentley Priory

Common Road, Harrow Weald; 133ha;
H and MNT (reserve only)
Heathland, scrub and some woodland
Permit only to reserve
All year

This common land comprises bracken, gorse and broom with developing birch scrub and woodland on Harrow Weald, and beech and oak on Stanmore Common. Cattle still graze on the Bentley Priory grassland next to the formal reserve, consisting of a lake fringed by bulrush.

Sydenham Hill Wood

Sydenham Hill, SE26; 11ha; LWT reserve
Woodland
All year

A majestic survivor of the ancient forest that formerly covered southern London, the woodland includes areas once known by individual names such as Fernbank and Lapsewood. Originally oak forest, the wood is now a patchwork of oak, hazel and hornbeam coppice together with holly and impressively large beeches. Rhododendron and bamboo have invaded from the Victorian garden which protected it from development.

The surroundings of Ten Acre Wood in London's Green Belt, an essential buffer between town and country.

The rich bird life in the wood includes great spotted woodpecker, thought to breed here, together with marsh tit, long-tailed tit, treecreeper, nuthatch, chiffchaff, willow warbler, blackcap and spotted flycatcher, and with winter woodcock. Woodland flowers include wood anemone, Solomon's-seal, southern wood-rush and ramsons; wood melick is among the unusual grasses.

One of the reserve's curious features is the track of the railway built to take visitors to the Crystal Palace. A long tunnel, barred against intruders, may provide a good harbourage for bats. Alongside the railway embankment path an undrained marsh where grey wagtail once bred has been excavated to form a pond.

Other parts of the wood are being restored to the working wood that existed before Victorian encroachments. The hazel is being coppiced once again, and the sycamore that is being eradicated is being put to use as rotting timber in other less mature reserves. Where it can be spared without detriment to the wood, soil is being taken to other wildlife sites so that the mixture of seeds within it may in time produce infant versions of Sydenham Hill Wood.

Tarleton's Lake

Permit only; 2.8ha; H and MNT reserve
Lake, marsh, sandpit and wood
June–July

Birds abound here, and while orchids are a special feature other rare species include flowering-rush and moschatel.

Ten Acre Wood

Charville Lane, Hayes; 4.5ha; LWT reserve
Oak woodland and meadow
All year

A fine stand of oak standard woodland with hazel coppice and Midland hawthorn on the edge of Yeading Brook includes herb-Robert in its ground flora.

Thameside

River Road, Creekmouth, Barking; 13.2ha;
Thameside Assn. reserve
Grassland, lagoon and dykes
All year

On the unpromising foundation of wasteland on the site of the old Barking power station, the reserve already has an unexpected variety of plants such as the hybrid between common spotted-orchid and southern marsh-orchid growing on a soil which is mostly pulverised fuel ash. The area is drained by dykes but marsh and pools remain. Skylark and meadow pipit feature among the grassland birds and in winter short-eared and barn owl quarter the flats, alert for unsuspecting mice and voles.

An active management scheme is developing a spectrum of habitats while at the same time making them accessible to visitors and students. In the often grim terrain left in the wake of obsolete industries in this part of eastern London, an urban farm will be an added attraction.

196

Nearby, Barking Bay survives as a short but rewarding stretch of estuary mud and sand where pochard and other diving duck congregate with shelduck. Their refuge is, however, threatened by possible development of the area as a marina.

Upper Wood

Farquhar Road, Crystal Palace, SE19; 3ha;
Ecological Parks Trust reserve
Woodland
All year

Mature trees including oak, lime and horse-chestnut are among the 20-plus species forming a woodland which, after years of neglect, is being managed to increase plant and animal diversity and provide a range of wildlife interest for visitors.

Walthamstow Marsh

Spring Hill, Clapton, E5; 35.2ha; Lea Valley
Authority reserve
Flood meadow
All year

The marsh is to join WALTHAMSTOW RESERVOIRS as a Site of Special Scientific Interest – it forms the last ancient grassland in the Lea Valley. The plant life includes fen-type communities of sedges, meadowsweet and reedbeds, and over 350 plant species have been recorded. Sedge warbler are present in summer, snipe and teal in winter.

Walthamstow Reservoirs

Permit only; 133ha; TWA
Open water
All year

In addition to its famous heronry this group of reservoirs is an important breeding site for mute swan, Canada goose, pochard, mallard and tufted duck. Other nesting birds include kingfisher, pied and yellow wagtail and skylark. Thirty species of wader have been recorded among migrants, including greenshank and redshank in spring and autumn, plus snipe, dunlin and green sandpiper. Several warbler species, finches and great spotted woodpecker may also be seen.

Walton Reservoirs

Permit only; 90ha; TWA
Open water
All year

The nine reservoirs offer concentrations of diving duck and other wildfowl plus sightings of the rarer grebes and many rare ducks.

William Curtis Ecological Park

16 Vine Lane, Tooley Street, SE1; 2ha;
Ecological Parks Trust reserve
Grass and pond
All year

A pioneering example of the ecologically sympathetic layout of urban wasteland, the park now has a range of trees including alders and six different willow species; a pond which attracts mallard and nesting coot; and undergrowth covering former house basements which provides shelter for frog, toad and slow-worm. Three hundred plant species have been recorded and 30 species of birds, including heron, black redstart and goldcrest. William Curtis stands on part of the South Bank development area, and is a classic instance of what can be achieved on a short-term basis.

Wimbledon Common

Parkside, Wimbledon, SW19; 341ha
Heath and bogs
All year

Higher, gravelly areas are, not surprisingly, grassland with gorse and birch scrub, while the lower clay slopes feature oak woodland with hornbeam and birch – redstart are among the large breeding bird population. A couple of valley bogs harbour bogbean, round-leaved sundew, bog asphodel and bog mosses. Animals include badger, grass snake, common lizard, and a large insect population including many butterflies.

Barking power station's disused chimneys stand over remnant saltmarsh at Thameside.

Hampshire and the Isle of Wight

The stark white pinnacles of the Needles present a marked contrast with the flat mudlands and marshes of the mainland coast, epitomising the dramatic variety of landscape and wildlife to be found in the two counties. Additionally the Isle of Wight contains eroding cliffs and the only piece of rocky shore in the area, as well as sandy beaches and estuaries.

Although the central chalk ridge dominates the Isle of Wight scenery, as do the South Downs in Hampshire, the presence of other geological formations gives rise to a range of soil types supporting varied plant and animal communities. The poorer soils in the west of Hampshire bear the unique NEW FOREST, a mosaic of ancient oak and beech woodland intermixed with lowland heath and valley bog, modified by human influence over many centuries and currently under considerable recreational pressure. In the other area of poor soil, in north east Hampshire, it is heathland species that predominate.

The richer soils derived from chalk strata support the WEALDEN EDGE hanging woodlands near Petersfield, with their abundant specialised flora and fauna. More woodland, less diverse but still interesting, grows on the Hampshire Basin tertiary strata. These woods are remnants of one of Hampshire's Royal Forests, the Forest of Bere, and indeed the county contains about 10 per cent of all the ancient woodlands of England and Wales. Viewed from the high points of Hampshire the well-wooded appearance of the landscape is remarkable, especially since large tracts of countryside, including some parts of the chalk downs, are farmed intensively. The shortage of plant and animal life on farmland makes another contrast with the exceptional richness of the remaining semi-natural chalk grassland. Some of this valuable habitat type is conserved in a number of reserves, large and small, in both Hampshire and the Isle of Wight. Orchids, butterflies and a wide range of animals and plants, together with the yew and whitebeam woods on the slopes, provide a further aspect of wildlife diversity.

Rising in the chalk hills and flowing into the Solent are several large rivers and many smaller streams. Most are noted for their trout fisheries, implying a wealth of small aquatic animals, and the unpolluted state of most of Hampshire's rivers is a direct result of their importance to anglers. Otter still occur on some of Hampshire's rivers, and havens are being established.

The equable climate of central southern England enables a number of species to survive at the northern end of their range: four plants and two insects occur nowhere else in England. Similarly the position of Hampshire and the Isle of Wight places them where the eastern continental and western Oceanic–Lusitanian floras overlap. The North Sea and Atlantic waters mix in a zone surrounding the island and washing the shores of the mainland; the considerable variety of marine fauna and flora, which includes a number of introduced species, is probably connected with this.

The population increase in Hampshire, resulting from London overspill in the north and urban expansion in the south, forms yet another sharp distinction from the sparsely settled agricultural regions of the county. The Isle of Wight, on the other hand, experiences seasonal population differences, with a massive influx of holidaymakers in the summer and relative peace and quiet in the winter. Residents are not slow to appreciate the natural environment and its wildlife, carrying on the tradition of study started by Hampshire's two best-known naturalists, Gilbert White of Selborne fame and W.H. Hudson.

In addition to their local and national importance for wildlife conservation, several sites are of international significance. Notable among them are the New Forest and the three linked harbours of Portsmouth, LANGSTONE and Chichester – the last actually in West Sussex – where wintering wildfowl and waders occur in considerable numbers.

These rich and varied wildlife resources are safeguarded by reserves, owned and managed by a range of agencies: parts of the coastline are under the protection of the Nature Conservancy Council, Hampshire Country Council, the Forestry Commission, the Royal Society for the Protection of Birds and the National Trust, as well as the Hampshire and Isle of Wight Naturalists' Trust. Similarly the woodlands and chalk grassland are protected by one or more of these organisations. But general public awareness of the value of wildlife is perhaps the best safeguard of all, ensuring the retention of these habitats.

FAY R. STRANACK

Ashford Chace

SU 729266; 86.4ha; HCC reserve
Beech–yew–ash hanger
Spring, early summer

Part of the WEALDEN EDGE HANGERS.

Basingstoke Canal

SU 719514–784513; 12km; HCC reserve
Reopened canal
Spring, summer

The canal and towpath pass through woodland and fields, adding their wildlife interest to yellow water-lily and purple-loosestrife, little grebe and moorhen, dragonflies and damselflies.

Basingstoke Canal Flashes

Permit only; 1.4ha; H and IOWNT reserve
Shallow pools adjoining the canal
Spring, summer

When the canal was dredged these wetlands were conserved as sanctuaries for such uncommon plants as frogbit, flowering-rush, narrow-leaved water-plantain, water-soldier and water-violet. The insects are particularly varied and interesting.

Blackdam

Permit only; 4ha; H and IOWNT reserve
Streamside, marshland and scrub
Booklet from H and IOWNT
Spring, summer

All stages from open water through marsh to dry land are represented and contain a fine range of plant and animal wildlife. Adder's-tongue, water avens, bluebell and cowslip are among the attractive plants while birds include corn bunting and water rail among 50 species recorded.

Brook Nature Trail

SZ 391839; 3.2km; IOW Nat. Hist. and Arch. Soc.
Countryside trail
Leaflet from IOW Tourist Board
Spring, summer

The circular walk includes land on both lower greensand and chalk, showing the contrast of the brilliant small downland plants such as clustered bellflower, lady's bedstraw and common centaury with the more robust and common flowers of the farmland.

Broughton Down

Permit only; 14.4ha; H and IOWNT reserve
Chalk grassland, scrub and woodland
Spring, summer

A fine chalk grassland, which includes the unusual field fleawort, grades through scrub into beech–oak–yew woodland. Insects include chalkhill blue and dark green fritillary butterflies with moths such as ruby tiger and large yellow underwing.

Broxhead Common

SU 806374; 44ha; HCC reserve
Dry heathland
Spring, summer

Situated on rising ground, this small remnant of dry heathland enjoys fine views over the well-wooded landscape of east Hampshire. Mature and regenerating heather occupies the higher ground while common and dwarf gorse, birch and pine have extensively colonised the lower slopes, providing nest sites for tree pipit, whitethroat and redpoll.

Calshot Marshes

SU 480010; 48ha; HCC reserve
Saltmarsh and mudflats
Spring, autumn, winter

A wide area of cord-grass saltmarsh and tidal mudflats which may be overlooked from the Calshot end of the LEPE AND CALSHOT COUNTRY PARK, it is good for migrants and winter birds.

Carisbrooke Walk Nature Trail

SZ 484876; 6.4–8 km; IOW Nat. Hist. and Arch. Soc.
Countryside walk
Leaflet from IOW Tourist Board
Spring, early summer

A wood where badgers breed, a shady deep-sunk lane and a sunlit stream are characteristic island features of the circular walk, which in early summer is loud with songbirds.

199

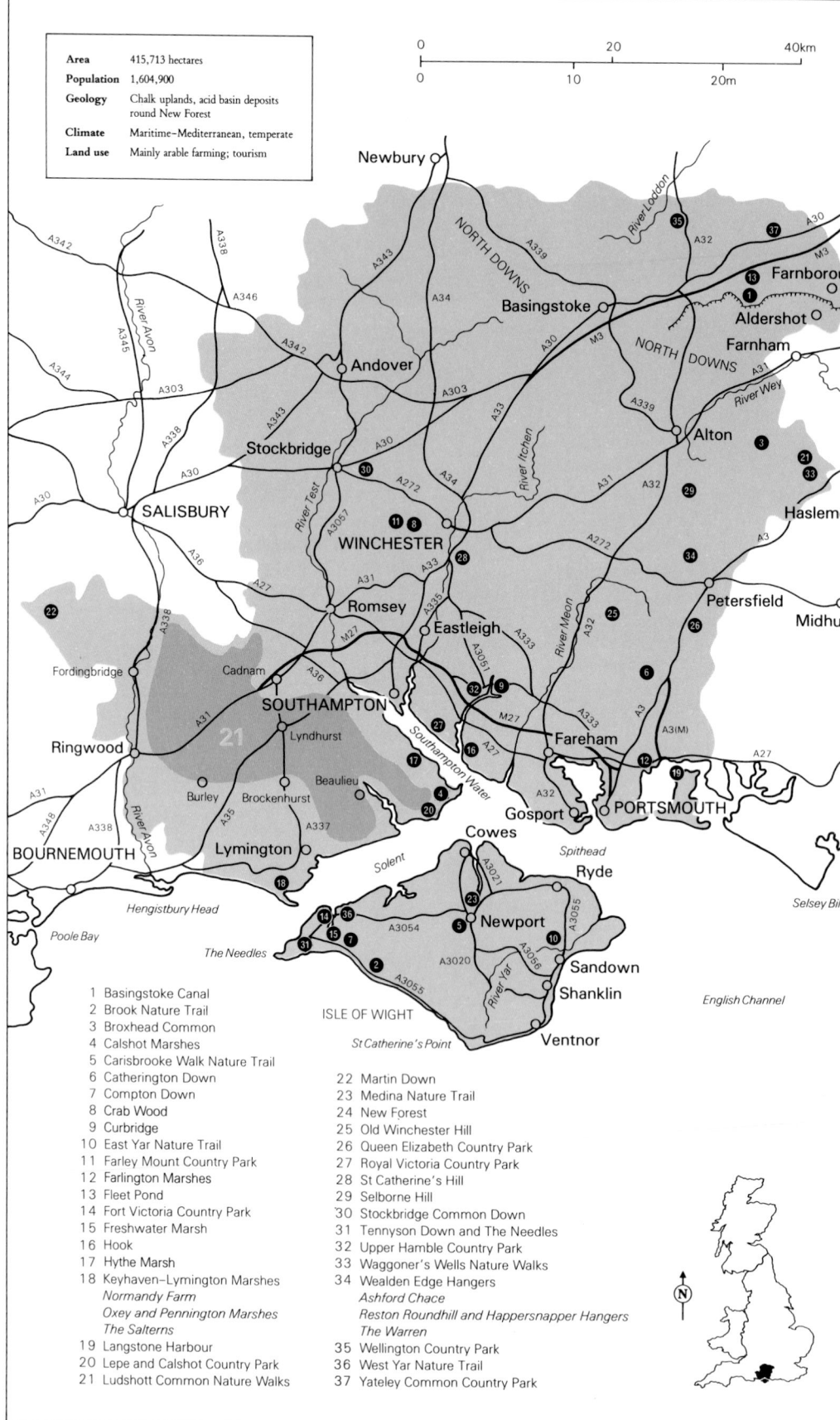

Area	415,713 hectares
Population	1,604,900
Geology	Chalk uplands, acid basin deposits round New Forest
Climate	Maritime–Mediterranean, temperate
Land use	Mainly arable farming; tourism

0 20 40km

0 10 20m

Newbury

NORTH DOWNS

Basingstoke

NORTH DOWNS

Farnborough

Aldershot

Farnham

Andover

Alton

Stockbridge

Winchester

Romsey

Eastleigh

Haslemere

Petersfield

Midhurst

SALISBURY

Cadnam

Fordingbridge

SOUTHAMPTON

Lyndhurst

Fareham

PORTSMOUTH

Ringwood

Burley   Brockenhurst   Beaulieu

Gosport

Cowes

Ryde

BOURNEMOUTH

Lymington

Solent

Spithead

Selsey Bill

Hengistbury Head

Newport

Sandown

Poole Bay

The Needles

Shanklin

ISLE OF WIGHT

English Channel

St Catherine's Point

Ventnor

1 Basingstoke Canal
2 Brook Nature Trail
3 Broxhead Common
4 Calshot Marshes
5 Carisbrooke Walk Nature Trail
6 Catherington Down
7 Compton Down
8 Crab Wood
9 Curbridge
10 East Yar Nature Trail
11 Farley Mount Country Park
12 Farlington Marshes
13 Fleet Pond
14 Fort Victoria Country Park
15 Freshwater Marsh
16 Hook
17 Hythe Marsh
18 Keyhaven–Lymington Marshes
   Normandy Farm
   Oxey and Pennington Marshes
   The Salterns
19 Langstone Harbour
20 Lepe and Calshot Country Park
21 Ludshott Common Nature Walks

22 Martin Down
23 Medina Nature Trail
24 New Forest
25 Old Winchester Hill
26 Queen Elizabeth Country Park
27 Royal Victoria Country Park
28 St Catherine's Hill
29 Selborne Hill
30 Stockbridge Common Down
31 Tennyson Down and The Needles
32 Upper Hamble Country Park
33 Waggoner's Wells Nature Walks
34 Wealden Edge Hangers
   Ashford Chace
   Reston Roundhill and Happersnapper Hangers
   The Warren
35 Wellington Country Park
36 West Yar Nature Trail
37 Yateley Common Country Park

N

Catherington Down

SU 689141; 12ha; HCC–H and IOWNT
Chalk grassland
Spring, summer

The unploughed banks of the ancient field system bear chalkland flowers such as clustered bell-flower, round-headed rampion and dropwort. Several orchid species include autumn lady's-tresses. A good range of butterflies may be present.

The Chase

Permit only; 47.6ha; H and IOWNT reserve
Conifer woodland and lake with alder wetland
All year

The reserve is most interesting for its bird life which includes all three native woodpeckers, a good range of warblers, kingfisher near the lake, and wintering siskin and redpoll in the alder carr.

Compton Down

SZ 368854; 40ha; NT
Chalk grassland
Spring, summer

Inland, chalk downland often stands above a level plain marked with the patterns of towns and villages, but Compton Down looks out across the sea. It forms part of the most southerly flank of chalk in the country, crowned with a turf of herbs and grasses. The soil is sometimes deep enough for gorse and coarse grasses to grow, sometimes a shallow broken cover over open, herb-rich rubbles.

The deeper soils are filled with plants such as cowslip, flowering before the grass grows tall, salad burnet, small scabious and pyramidal orchid, later plants which can lift above the shade, or common rock-rose, leaning on the stronger stems to raise its yellow flowers to the light. Ragwort and gorse grow with occasional hawthorn and taller lime-loving species such as wild parsnip.

The thinner soils are filled with small, more delicate bright flowers such as wild thyme, harebell, quaking-grass and yellow-wort. The soft pink of restharrow complements the blue selfheal, the tiny eyebright, clusters of horseshoe and kidney vetch, lady's bedstraw and squinancywort. Clustered bellflower and bee orchid contrast with the prickly carline and dwarf thistle. While the summer show of chalkland flowers is wonderful, in spring the down is decorated with a spread of early gentian and early-purple and green-winged orchid to add to the vivid colour of the cowslips.

The southerly position of the down makes it an ideal site for migrant butterflies. Clouded yellow and Berger's clouded yellow are both attracted by the wealth of vetches, while other butterflies include Adonis, chalkhill and little blue with dark green fritillary. The blue butterflies, too, are attracted to leguminous plants such as vetches and trefoils, both Adonis and chalkhill blue particularly associated with horseshoe vetch. The dark green

fritillary feeds as a caterpillar on violets like most of the British fritillaries, but an exception to this rule, and one which in Britain is limited to the Isle of Wight, may stray on to the down: the Glanville fritillary generally feeds on plantains and breeds on the undercliff nearby. Marbled white may also occur on these southern slopes although the breeding colony prefers a more northerly aspect.

The juxtaposition of the down and the sea implies a maritime influence which adds to and varies the characteristics of the chalk, reflected in the variety of the insects which includes such uncommon species as the rare weevil *Apion millum*.

Coulters Dean

Permit only; 5.2ha; H and IOWNT reserve
Chalk grassland and scrub
Spring, summer

A rich variety of chalkland plants includes clustered bellflower and round-headed rampion with orchids such as bee and fragrant. The butterflies include Duke of Burgundy and dingy skipper.

Crab Wood

SU 436298; 36ha; HCC–H and IOWNT reserve
Old oak woodland
Spring, early summer

Many of the higher chalk areas are covered by clay with flints, where deeper soils have developed than on the bare chalk. These soils once carried dense oak forest, of which Crab Wood is a remnant. Most of the larger oaks have been felled but some remain, together with a number of fine old beech trees, overtopping the hazel understorey. The diversity of plants reflects the varying depth of soil, the nutrient status and water-holding capacity. Ash, field maple, spindle, wayfaring-tree, yew and privet interlaced with traveller's-joy grow where the soil is rich. Holly, hawthorn and willows with aspen, birch and honeysuckle reflect the damper state of the soils with lower nutrient content.

Where glades have been opened up in the course of management, primrose, violets and the local specialities Solomon's-seal and lily-of-the-valley

Glanville fritillary occurs only on the Isle of Wight.

flower in spring. Where the light is less dog's mercury and enchanter's-nightshade grow, while under the dense shade of the beeches bluebell flourishes with scattered bird's-nest orchid and early-purple orchid. On richer soils woodruff, sanicle, pignut and wood spurge appear, and in damper hollows pendulous sedge, perforate St John's-wort and common spotted-orchid are found. Wood melick and nettle-leaved bellflower border the paths.

The wide range of birds also reflects the differing habitats. Open areas suit nightjar, scrub attracts nightingale, and all three woodpecker species are found as well as the more common woodland birds. Roe and fallow deer have been seen; dormouse, hedgehog and the usual woodland small mammals are also present.

Moths include some rarities; among the butterflies are white admiral, a melanistic form of silver-washed fritillary and Duke of Burgundy.

Curbridge

SU 528118; 5.6ha; H and IOWNT reserve
Mixed woodland and wetland
Spring, early summer

A good variety of spring flowers is matched by the riverbank plants, with freshwater species grading into saltmarsh where the unusual marsh-mallow may be found. There is a wide range of bird and insect species.

East Yar Nature Trail

SZ 576857; 4.8km; IOW Nat. Hist. and Arch. Soc.
Riverside walk
Leaflet from IOW Tourist Board
Spring, summer

A delightful walk along the eastern River Yar is bright with the flowers of comfrey, water forget-me-not and yellow iris. Damp meadows may show the flower spikes of common spotted-orchid while reedbeds give cover to reed and sedge warbler, little grebe and moorhen.

Farley Mount Country Park

SU 409293–433293; 106.5ha; HCC
Chalk downland and woods
Spring, summer

The chalk downland is spangled with characteristic plants, including the uncommon bastard-toadflax and beautiful pyramidal orchid, while the woods include CRAB WOOD.

Farlington Marshes

SU 679045; 120ha; H and IOWNT reserve
Damp grassland and scrub, freshwater marsh, pools and ditches
Spring, autumn, winter

An integral part of LANGSTONE HARBOUR, the reserve contains an interesting variety of plants and is an important roost and feeding ground for dark-bellied Brent goose, wigeon and teal, with waders such as black-tailed godwit and smaller birds such as bearded tit.

Fleet Pond

SU 816553; 56ha; Hart DC reserve
Open water, heath and woodland
Spring, early summer

Heathland, with mixed broad-leaved and coniferous woodland, covers roughly half of the reserve while the pond itself forms a fairly large body of water. Great crested grebe and Canada goose are among the breeding species and the reserve has been visited by such rarities as great reed warbler from Europe and transatlantic blue-winged teal.

Fort Victoria Country Park

SZ 339898; 20ha; IWCC
Wooded coastal landslips
Nature trail leaflet from IWCC
Spring, early summer

Below the limestone of the clifftops are beds of sands and clays which periodically collapse when water drains down from above. This has led to a tumbled overgrown wilderness, full of wildlife, which is explored by the nature trail laid out within the woods. The area is rich in tangles of lime-loving traveller's-joy.

Freshwater Marsh

SZ 347862; 16ha; South Wight BC reserve
Rich marsh and river course
Nature trail leaflet from SWBC
Spring, summer

A nature trail overlooks the main body of the marsh, an attractive spread of common reed and marsh plants such as bulrush, flowering-rush, yellow iris and yellow loosestrife, purple-loosestrife, meadowsweet and water-plantain. Alder and birch woodland fringes the western River Yar, which rises in the marsh, and, with the reedbeds, encourages a variety of birds including reed, sedge and willow warbler, reed bunting and nightingale. Butterflies are well represented, with a chance of migrants such as clouded yellow and Berger's clouded yellow, and several characteristic wainscot moths breed in the marshy reedbeds.

Holmesley Gravel Pits

Permit only; 3.2ha; H and IOWNT reserve
Scrub and flooded diggings
Spring, summer

Common duck such as mallard overwinter here but the muddy foreshore is attractive to waders and has drawn breeding redshank while the shingle banked islands are a suitable site for nesting little ringed plover. Willow scrub around the pits provides sites for many songbirds and encourages a good range of insects on which they feed.

Cord-grass spreads across the muds in a typical Hampshire saltmarsh.

Hook

SU 490060; 200ha; HCC reserve
Estuary shore
Winter

The reserve includes a wide range of habitat from the mudflats and saltmarsh of the tidal shore, through brackish meadows and freshwater marsh, to woodland. A great variety of birds may be seen throughout the year, from winter wildfowl and waders such as curlew and dunlin, to summer sedge warbler, stonechat and yellowhammer.

Hythe Marsh

SU 433073; 8.8ha; H and IOWNT reserve
Cord-grass saltmarsh
Summer

This area of specialist interest supports a wide range of genetically varied populations of cord-grass.

Keyhaven–Lymington Marshes

SZ 300908–333945; 277.6ha; HCC–H and IOWNT
Estuary coastal strip
No access off rights of way
All year

Hurst Spit is a long shingle ridge which forms the western limit of the area and shelters a wide spread of mudflats. The mudflats stretch on, outside the sea wall, to the Lymington River some 5km north eastwards and are backed by grazing marshes and coastal scrub. There is a splendid variety from open mud through saltmarsh to shingle or grazing marsh with brackish ditches and lagoons, with scrub and woodland, providing great interest for birdwatchers and botanists.

From Hurst Castle, a long trudge along the pebbles of the Spit, or north eastwards along the sea wall footpath from Keyhaven, the mudflats stretch in a gullied, puddled, inhospitable-looking spread. The channels turn and twist, cut deep into the muds, so that a flock of waders flying low may disappear, seeming to fly right down into the mud, but reappear springing out of the ground as clean as they flew into it.

A narrow saltmarsh has developed along the edge of the shingle where glasswort, sea aster, sea plantain and annual sea-blite begin to stabilise the muds and grade into the typical plants of the pebble spit. Here and in the grass of the castle area is a wealth of fascinating plants including sea campion, sea-kale, sea-lavender, sea-purslane and sea wormwood, with yellow horned-poppy, golden samphire, thrift, hare's-foot clover, kidney vetch and wild thyme. The sea wall, too, is faced with many of these species and is backed by grazed grasslands and marshy, heathlike scrubs of gorse and birch. Pools behind the sea wall provide an extra habitat and some have developed stands of common reed. A number of unusual plant species occur, including a subspecies of little-Robert, *Geranium purpureum forsteri*, which has a very limited distribution on stabilised shingle.

In winter Brent geese feed on the areas of eelgrass and *Enteromorpha* seaweeds while the muds are rich in small molluscs and other sea animals on which waders and wildfowl feed. Spring passage may bring red-throated diver, common scoter, arctic and great skua, little gull and black tern, while autumn brings numbers of waders such as black- and bar-tailed godwit, greenshank and grey plover, spotted redshank, ruff, common and curlew sandpiper, little stint and whimbrel.

In winter up to 500 Brent geese may be present with similar numbers of shelduck and teal and smaller flocks of duck such as goldeneye, long-tailed duck, mallard, pochard and wigeon. Huge flocks of dunlin may be here and large numbers of lapwing. A few Slavonian grebe and goosander are recorded and there is a November gathering of red-breasted merganser. There have been occasional sightings of surf scoter and whiskered tern.

Langstone Harbour

SU 697058; 554ha; RSPB reserve
Inter-tidal marshes and mudflats
Spring, autumn, winter

No access is possible to the reserve itself but the area is easily overlooked from the coast footpath along the north shore. In winter over 6000 dark-bellied Brent geese may be present, with spring and autumn passages of waders such as black-tailed godwit and grey plover.

Lepe and Calshot Country Park

SZ 456986 and SU 480012; 49.5ha; HCC
Cliff top and foreshore
Winter

The park itself, in two separate sections, is mainly used as a picnic spot from which to view the Isle of Wight and the Solent. In winter, however, low tide may provide good feeding grounds for waders such as turnstone and oystercatcher.

Long Aldermoor

Permit only; 2.4ha; H and IOWNT reserve
Wet woodland and grassland
Spring, early summer

The small but interesting reserve, with a range from heathland to marsh, contains species such as bog asphodel and heath spotted-orchid.

Lower Test Marshes

SU 364150; 110ha; H and IOWNT reserve
Reedbeds, water meadows, grassland and saltmarsh
Permit only beyond footpaths
All year

Over 450 plant and 170 bird species have been recorded on this very varied reserve. The water meadows include marsh-marigold, water avens and green-winged orchid while the birds range from wintering wildfowl and waders to breeding reed warbler and snipe.

Ludshott Common Nature Walks

SU 850360; various lengths; Ludshott Common Committee–NT
Heathland walks
Leaflet from Grayshott post office and newsagents
Spring, summer

An interesting range of heathland plants and bird life may be seen on the common, which adjoins the woodland surrounding WAGGONERS WELLS.

Martin Down

SU 058192; 249ha; NCC reserve
Chalk downland, chalk heath and scrub
Leaflet from NCC
Spring, summer

A very wide range of habitat, from a superb mix of chalkland scrub, with ash, buckthorn, dogwood, hawthorn, privet, spindle and wayfaring-tree, through spreads of dense gorse, of chalk heath with heather and gorse, to tall or short-grazed grassland, the reserve is rich in plant life and animal species. Among the downland plants are local species including chalk milkwort, early gentian, field fleawort and dwarf sedge, with a variety of orchids including bee, fly, frog and burnt; among the insects is an outstanding range of butterflies, with Adonis, chalkhill and small blue, silver-spotted skipper and Duke of Burgundy. The bird life varies from songbirds such as nightingale in summer to winter predators such as short-eared owl and hen harrier.

Medina Nature Trail

SZ 501895; 3.2–4.8km; IOW Nat. Hist. and Arch. Soc.
Riverside trail
Leaflet from IOW Tourist Board
Spring, summer

The trail runs from Newport Quay beside the tidal waters of the River Medina which show good examples of saltmarsh, with typical plants such as Townsend's cord-grass, sea-purslane and sea beet, and in late summer may be visited by cormorant, dunlin, bar-tailed godwit and ringed plover.

Micheldever Spoil Heaps

Permit only; 7.6ha; H and IOWNT reserve
Old chalk rubble, scrub and woodland
Spring, summer

The beech woodland contains such characteristics species as bird's-nest orchid, while the spoil heaps contain a good range of chalkland plants and include less usual species, for instance cut-leaved germander.

Duke of Burgundy, a mainly southern butterfly, lays its eggs on cowslip and primrose.

New Forest

See map; 37,560ha; FC and others
Woodland, heath and wetland
Leaflets from FC
All year

Bramshaw Wood in the New Forest: high-forest woodland where fallow, roe and red deer may be seen.

Walking among the huge old trees or across the heather heathland of the forest, you might tread the unmarked paths where primitive man once hunted. Where you see a high-forest woodland of beech and oak or spreads of acid grasses patterned with heather and dwarf gorse, he moved in a fearful twilight, in an ancient wildwood of oak, hazel, elm and small-leaved lime. He, and the men who followed him, have changed the wildwood to the present forest and have driven off or exterminated much of its ancient wildlife but, even so, to walk here is to walk in the largest spread of old lowland woodland in north west Europe, in one of the richest reservoirs of wildlife in Britain today.

Just under half of the forest is covered by varied woodland which forms a mosaic among and around wide spreads of grass and heather heathland or bowls of marsh and bog. The main woodland trees are beech and oak, trees around 200 to 300 years old which stand as high-forest woodland fringed with a younger mix of oak with beech, birch and other species such as ash, sweet chestnut, sycamore, hawthorn and Scots pine. The understorey is mainly holly, which stands above a very thin ground cover often limited by grazing pressure to nothing but grey-green cushions of the moss *Leucobryum glaucum*. On deeper soils there may be thick tangles of bramble and bracken or, where the woods are growing on richer clays, a more general spread of common woodland plants.

Although uncommon plants occur, such as narrow-leaved lungwort, coral-necklace and beech fern, together with a superb range of western species of lichens at their eastern limit, the woods are perhaps most outstanding for their richness of animal life. A small number of red, a few hundred roe and perhaps around 600 fallow deer remain as a memorial to the original purpose of the forest. The fallow has always been the chief member of these, at least partly because it tends to wander less. Sika deer, having spread from Beaulieu, now add to the numbers of forest deer but modern grazing will never sustain the earliest seventeenth-century count of almost 400 red deer and over 7500 fallow.

The deer are seldom seen or heard but in early summer the birds will be hard to miss. The forest woodlands contain both large and small timber, riven and rotting pollards, young trees and shrubs in a pattern of copses and clearings; suitable habitat is therefore available for outstanding numbers of woodland birds. Hawfinch, redstart, wood warbler and lesser spotted woodpecker are all rather locally spread in southern England – all may be present here, together with green and great spotted woodpecker, treecreeper and nuthatch. There are good numbers of predators and the forest has for a long time been a breeding site for buzzard and honey buzzard, hobby, kestrel, sparrowhawk and tawny owl.

The woods are also outstanding for their insects – for the presence of Britain's only cicada, the New Forest cicada, for a wide variety of moths and butterflies, and for a range of beetles probably unique in the British Isles; more species of beetle have been identified here than in any similar area in Britain.

The heathlands vary between wide acid grasslands filled with bristle bent, a characteristically south western fine-leaved grass, and spreads of heather with dwarf gorse or with cross-leaved heath in damper sites. A contrast with the summer cool of the woodlands, they are warm wide levels or shallow slopes, sheltered by occasional breaks of gorse and scattered with Scots pine, oak or hawthorn scrub. Purple moor-grass is spread throughout the heathlands, replacing bristle bent where the land is wettest, while deeper soils are marked by stands of bracken. Although the sandy heathlands support uncommon plants such as wild gladiolus and yellow centaury, the greatest variation appears in wet heathland, or where the heathlands grade into bog and marsh.

These valley mires are as richly varied as the other main habitats with lawns of *Sphagnum* mosses below the wet heath and with richer areas of fenlike marsh. These richer areas usually lie where slow streams run through the centre of a bog, where alder and willow grow above clumps of greater tussock sedge, a linear wet woodland fringed with common reed, or where black bog-rush, marsh St John's-wort and uncommon species such as broad-leaved and slender cottongrass show the course of the water. Touch-me-not balsam, our only native balsam, occurs in these alder carrs, together with a local speciality, Hampshire-purslane, a small creeping shallow-water plant, which grows only here and on Jersey. These stream-fed or spring-fed central areas vary according to the richness of the water supply and may show as a stand of common reed, tall above *Sphagnum* and sharp-flowered rush, or as a swamp of bog myrtle and purple moor-grass.

All three British sundews occur while, scattered among heather and cross-leaved heath, scented bog myrtle, tussocks of purple moor-grass and slender white beak-sedge and deergrass, are plants such as lesser skullcap, bog asphodel and meadow thistle, with more uncommon species including bog-sedge and slender sedge, brown beak-sedge and bog orchid, rare in the south of England.

The animal life of the open plains and the wetlands of the forest is no less varied and is equally specialised. The valley bogs and pools are rich in insects, from the biting midges and mosquitoes of late summer, to the dragonflies and damselflies, which include two species better known in Mediterranean areas, *Ceriagrion tenellum* and *Ischnura pumilio*. The relatively undisturbed deeper parts of the forest hold several species which survive at the northern limits of their range. The Dartford warbler is an example, a non-migratory warbler which lives and breeds on heathlands; in good years the population builds, but one bad winter can almost wipe it out.

New Forest ponies in a typical heathland setting, a contrast to the shelter of the woods.

The New Forest heaths are a hunting ground for the elegant hobby.

Redshank, curlew and snipe are better adapted birds which breed in these open parts of the forest, together with heathland species such as stonechat, linnet and yellowhammer and less common birds such as nightjar. In winter the berry-bearing shrubs may be feeding posts for fieldfare and redwing, while the heathlands may be hunted by predators – hen harrier, merlin, peregrine and occasional red-footed falcon.

While man has largely changed his role from the Neolithic hunter who walked the wildwood, throughout the history of the area he has had a profound effect on the ancient woodland. The forest today, with its mighty trees and its atmosphere of immemorial glades, is almost entirely made by man. The hunting forest of the Domesday Book was already a complex of woodland and heath, and was largely protected as such, but by the fifteenth century the accent began to change. Timber became more important than deer. During the seventeenth century in some places 90 per cent of the major trees were removed to provide materials for the navy's ships. The younger trees seem to derive from the burst of regeneration which followed the Removal Act, the huge cull of 6000 fallow deer after 1851, with a second burst to correspond with World War II. In terms of modern production the forest supplied, in the 10 years of the two world wars, almost 750,000 tons of timber.

As long as adequate spreads of broad-leaved woodland survive among the heaths and valley mires, the New Forest will remain as one of the finest sites for wildlife in the country, a reminder of the woods and wild heathlands we have lost elsewhere.

Newtown

Permit only, 338ha; IWCC reserve
Mudflats and saltmarsh
Permit from site or IWCC; reserve can be overlooked from public right of way
Winter

The old harbour contains an interesting range of plants, including Townsend's cord-grass, sea-heath and golden samphire, and provides a nest site for black-headed gull and a wintering area for wildfowl such as Brent goose, teal and wigeon, and for waders such as curlew, redshank and black-tailed godwit.

Noar Hill

Permit only; 12ha; H and IOWNT reserve
Old chalkpits and scrub
Spring, summer

Yellow-wort, autumn gentian and kidney vetch are typical of the chalkland flowers which grow here and attract a good variety of insects. The butterflies include both marbled white and Duke of Burgundy.

Normandy Farm

SZ 330940; 36ha; HCC reserve
Coastal grazing marshes
All year

Part of KEYHAVEN–LYMINGTON MARSHES.

North Solent

Permit only; 640ha; NCC reserve
Saltmarsh and grazing marsh
All year

Breeding colonies of terns, together with the largest colony of black-headed gulls in Britain, provide summer interest in an estuary reserve which contains an exceptional variety of fresh-water and saltmarsh plants while supporting large numbers of passage and wintering waders and wildfowl. Part of the reserve may be overlooked from the public footpath from Beaulieu to Bucklers Hard.

Old Burghclere Lime Quarry

Permit only; 6ha; H and IOWNT reserve
Disused chalk quarry
Spring, summer

Colonising chalkland plants include kidney vetch and fly orchid and attract such butterflies as little blue. Slow-worm is usually present.

Old Winchester Hill: a superb example of chalk downland varied with scrub and woods.

Old Winchester Hill

SU 647210; 60ha; NCC reserve
Chalk downland, scrub and woodland
Visitors must keep to marked pathways: danger from
unexploded missiles
Leaflets from car park or information centre
Spring, summer

The highest point of the reserve, within the ramparts of the Iron Age hill fort, overlooks the valley of the Meon with views across to the NEW FOREST and to the Isle of Wight. Below this point the downland falls in slopes and folds of scrub and woodland, a rich mosaic of chalkland habitat.

The woodland is in blocks separated by grassland and generally fringed by hawthorn scrub. Yew is the classic Hampshire downland tree and, left to itself, the whole reserve might develop into yew forest. This is prevented by careful management which also sustains some areas of broadleaved woods, beech and ash over coppiced hazel, to give the greatest degree of variation. The hawthorn scrub is rich in other shrubby species, filled with buckthorn, dogwood, privet, spindle, wayfaring-tree, whitebeam and tangling traveller's-joy. A large area of juniper scrub is important for insects. The range of grassland, scrub and woodland here is a classic demonstration of the transition from one stage to the next.

Near the car park a layer of clay above the chalk is deep enough for tormentil and gorse but, lower down and on the ramparts of the fort, the soils are thin and highly alkaline and superbly dressed with lime-loving species. Here are yellow-wort and clustered bellflower, fine spreads of horseshoe and kidney vetch, late-summer-flowering autumn gentian and, on the ramparts, a speciality of the reserve, one of the largest populations in the country of round-headed rampion. More common downland plants include hawkbit species, lady's bedstraw and crosswort, eyebright and salad burnet, yellow rattle, oxeye daisy, cowslip and wild mignonette. In the sheltered slopes between the woods are dark mullein and musk mallow while the reserve boasts some 14 orchid species. There are unusually large colonies of fragrant and frog orchid and greater butterfly-orchid.

Woodland birds include all three native woodpeckers while the wood edge and scrub attract a good range of warblers and other small birds. Kestrel and sparrowhawk are frequently seen. Harvest and yellow-necked mouse have been recorded and larger mammals include roe deer and badger. Butterfly species include chalkhill blue, dark green fritillary and Duke of Burgundy.

Oxenbourne Down

Permit only; 83.6ha; H and IOWNT reserve
Chalk grassland, scrub and yew woodland
Spring, summer

The main woods contain mixed-age yew trees, with other lime-loving species such as whitebeam and juniper, allied with areas of chalk grassland and contrasting with oak woodland and small areas of chalk heath. Breeding birds include blackcap, lesser whitethroat and nightingale.

Oxey and Pennington Marshes

SZ 330940; 71.6ha; HCC reserve
Coastal grazing marshes
All year

Part of KEYHAVEN–LYMINGTON MARSHES.

Queen Elizabeth Country Park

SU 717186; 560ha; HCC–FC
Mixed woodland, downland and scrub.
Leaflets from HCC or park centre
Spring, summer

A good variety of habitat may be observed from the trails within the park which interpret the nature of the woods and downland.

Reston Roundhill and Happersnapper Hangers

SU 749271; 17.6ha; HCC reserve
Beech–ash hanging woodland
Spring, early summer

Part of WEALDEN EDGE HANGERS.

Royal Victoria Country Park

SU 457080; 58ha; HCC
Woodland, parkland and coastal shores
All year

Inland, there is a contrast between open beech woodland and marshy areas where common reed and wet alder and willow scrub give shelter to birds such as reed bunting, blackcap, willow warbler and nightingale. A further range of habitat is added by parkland trees and by the saltmarsh, shingle, muds and gravels of the shoreline, where birds such as curlew, oystercatcher and redshank may be seen. A nature trail demonstrates the wildlife interest.

Royden Woods

Permit only; 340ha; H and IOWNT reserve
Mixed deciduous woodland, heathland, grassland and river banks
Spring, early summer

This large and very varied reserve has a magnificent mix of tree and shrub species with a great variety of smaller plants. Specialities include royal fern and narrow-leaved lungwort, with buzzard and sparrowhawk among the birds.

St Catherine's Hill

SU 841275; 30ha; H and IOWNT reserve
Chalk grassland and scrub
Spring, summer

A steep grassy knoll just outside Winchester, the reserve contains a wide variety of chalkland flowers and shrubs, including privet, dogwood, kidney vetch and common rock-rose. Beautiful downland butterflies such as chalkhill blue may be seen, with Adonis blue in occasional good summers.

Gilbert White once walked on Selborne Hill, a varied Hampshire woodland.

The Salterns

SZ 330940; 14ha; HCC reserve
Coastal grassland and marsh
All year

Part of KEYHAVEN–LYMINGTON MARSHES.

Selborne Hill

SU 735337; 97.4ha; NT
Mixed woodland and beech hanger
Spring, early summer

No natural history of Hampshire could leave out the territory of Gilbert White. Selborne Hill, composed of Selborne Common and Selborne Hanger, is a fine example of woodland on the clay-capped Hampshire chalk. The common occupies the more level land, a plateau which falls abruptly to the village where beechwoods hang upon the slope.

The plateau varies from open scrubland around wide grassy clearings to high-forest woodland and areas of coppice. Old pollard beech trees argue the common status, when pigs and cattle roamed and the stems were cut above their browsing height to provide both poles for firewood and fencing and herbage for winter stock feed. Coppicing must have started later, when animals no longer grazed, and new young shoots could grow uneaten from the lower hazel stools. The clay supports such acid-loving species as tormentil, gorse and birch with sweeps of bracken around the grassy clearings, grading into elder, hawthorn and hazel scrub.

The woods themselves, chiefly beech or oak standards over a rich variety of species including ash and blackthorn, holly, buckthorn, dogwood

and spindle, stand above a ground cover which varies both with the density of the shade and with the depth of the clay over chalk. Under pure beech cover there is very little that can survive, but ride edges and clearings show white drifts of greater stitchwort, bright red campion, wood-sorrel, dog's mercury and enchanter's-nightshade, yellow arch-angel, ferns and foxglove, wild rose and honey-suckle. The clay thins higher up and traveller's-joy replaces honeysuckle, with wood spurge, sanicle and woodruff beneath the trees.

The hanger is a steep one, of tall straight beech trees with an understorey of ash, young beech, yew, holly, hazel, hawthorn, dogwood, wayfaring-tree and spindle. The ground cover is mainly woodruff and ivy, dog's mercury and sanicle but, where the light strikes through, wood melick lines the path-ways while wood spurge, spurge-laurel, violets and nettle-leaved bellflower, with Solomon's-seal, wall lettuce and ferns such as hart's-tongue, hard shield-fern and male-fern, occur.

Where CRAB WOOD demonstrates a woodland on clays and WEALDEN EDGE HANGERS are excellent steep chalk woodlands, the variation of Selborne Hill is what makes it so rewarding and fascinating.

Shutts Copse

Permit only; 4.4ha; H and IOWNT reserve
Old hazel coppice
Spring, early summer

A rich woodland plant life, including such species as Solomon's-seal and greater butterfly-orchid, is encouraged by continuing the coppice manage-ment of the wood.

Stag Copse

Permit only; 2.4ha; H and IOWNT reserve
Mixed woodland
Spring, early summer

Woodland is not now widespread on the Isle of Wight. The reserve has a good range of tree species over hazel and holly with a ground cover which includes bluebell and butcher's-broom. A good variety of common mammal and bird species in-habits the wood.

Stockbridge Common Down

SU 377347; 89ha; NT
Ungrazed downland and scrub
Spring, summer

A long sweep of ungrazed grassland with tilted mixed rich scrub and a thick shrub cover on the highest land, the down gives a picture of the an-cient Salisbury Plain edge before ploughing turned the turf to endless cereals. In the days of great sheep flocks the downland would have been shorter, the small chalk herbs more widespread, but even now the coarser grasses can only colonise the deeper soils so pathways or pockets of shallow soil still contain a good variety of species.

Meadow pipit, along with skylark a classic bird of open country.

The upper scrub on the clay cap of the chalk contains hawthorn, gorse and blackthorn, an ex-cellent shelter for birds, while the scrub on the sloping chalk is a mix of species such as dog-wood, privet, spindle and juniper, wild rose and hawthorn with an occasional young oak. Giant hogweed and wild parsnip stand above the grasses here, together with other plants sufficiently robust to reach for light. Agrimony, ragwort and common toadflax show varied shades of yellow to contrast with the blue small scabious. Dark purple heads of greater knapweed stand beside tall spikes of knap-weed broomrape, a curious parasite which lives upon their roots and lifts its flower spikes perhaps some 60cm high. Lady's bedstraw puts up a vivid fizz of yellow flowers but cannot compare in delicacy with the exquisite pale dropwort, which grows here in great profusion.

The spread of grassland, although so much of it is deep and coarse, is filled with these elegant flowers, with the tall columns of wild mignonette, with yellow rattle and occasional dark mullein. Marjoram and betony may be found with the beautiful nodding musk thistle while path edges and shallow turfs have squinancywort and wild thyme, common rock-rose, kidney vetch and com-mon bird's-foot-trefoil.

The varied slopes and scrubland areas prove attractive for butterflies, including marbled white and species of blue, for mammals such as short-tailed vole, for hunting kestrel and owl species and for a variety of other birds such as skylark and meadow pipit in the grassland or linnet and yellowhammer in the scrub.

Swanpond Copse

Permit only; 4.4ha; H and IOWNT reserve
Small coppice-with-standards woodland
Spring, early summer

Goldilocks buttercup and narrow-leaved lungwort are among the interesting plants in this mainly damp woodland. There is a good range of tree and shrub species with an attractive variety of woodland birds.

Tennyson Down and the Needles

SU 324855; 77.6ha; NT reserve
Coastal chalk downland and scrub
Spring, summer

Tennyson Down differs from COMPTON DOWN to the east in not curving steeply towards the sea but rather dropping sheer into it. On the northern side the land falls steeply to Alum Bay but the sea has carved the south side into shining cliffs of chalk. At the western end the cliffs are weathered into the stacks of the Needles.

The sheltered northern side of the down has a fine development of mixed scrub species which suddenly stops when it reaches the height of the grassland plateau above. The chalkland plants on top are stunted by the sea winds – pigmy clustered bellflowers which open in the very short turf, short-stemmed harebells and the well-adapted dwarf thistle.

Lower, and less exposed, is a fine mixture of species, carline and musk thistle, lady's bedstraw and salad burnet, milkwort, eyebright, wild thyme and squinancywort, yellow-wort, quaking-grass and hoary plantain. In the Needles reserve, overlooking the stacks themselves, masses of kidney vetch, thrift, wild mignonette and pyramidal orchid sway in the breezes together with an unexpected plant for a chalk sea headland, yellow horned-poppy.

Areas of chalk heath, with heather, bell heather and tormentil or wind-pruned blocks of gorse, occur on the down and gorse again may be found in the dense mixed scrub. This scrub is a steep rich mixture of privet, hawthorn, ash, spindle and small-leaved cotoneaster, tied and tangled with traveller's-joy and honeysuckle. Path edges are thick with wild madder and fringed with stinking iris and ivy.

The scrub is of great interest as one of the very few areas where gorse and blackthorn grow together with privet, a highly lime-loving species. The site is also notable for large colonies of early-purple orchid and for bastard-toadflax and heath-grass in the maritime chalk grassland.

The downland is some 147m above sea level and rather exposed for much bird life, but skylarks may still be seen, together with a variety of gulls, and cormorant and shag. The guillemot, razorbill and puffin colonies are now depleted but there is scope for seawatching at passage times.

The Needles, teeth of chalk: part of a ridge which once ran westwards to the coast of Dorset.

Titchfield Haven

A tree-lined hammer pond at Waggoners Wells.

Permit only; 86.26ha; HCC reserve
Lagoons, marshes and grazing meadows by
River Meon
The lower part of the reserve may be overlooked from
SU 533024
Permit and leaflets by prior arrangement from the
Naturalist Ranger, Haven Cottage, Cliff Road, Hill
Head, Fareham (tel. Stubbington 2145)
Chiefly winter but interesting all year

The reedbeds and marshes, grazing meadows and
lagoons of Titchfield Haven form an oasis of quiet
between the urban spread of Southampton and the
Gosport–Portsmouth complex to the east. The
major part of the reserve remains a sanctuary area,
grazing marsh and reedbeds along the winding
River Meon. These marshes, where winter wigeon
feed, are overlooked from the Meadow hide, are
often hunted by kestrel or barn owl and are the
most northerly stretch of the reserve to which the
public have access.

The Suffern hide overlooks the Meon, with
sweet-grass marshes on the nearer side and common reed filling the further bank. Here are duck
and gulls, heron, coot and moorhen, with an
occasional wader on the muddy, tidal shores. The
Meon shore and Pumfrett hides overlook lagoons,
islanded scrapes with flats and shallows for the
dabblers and waders, with deeper waters for the
diving ducks.

Over the last few years the reserve has become
an important wintering site for curlew, godwit,
bittern, shoveler, mallard, teal and wigeon. Breeding birds include reed and sedge warbler, little
grebe and water rail, together with an increasing
colony of bearded tit, while spring migrants include a great variety of small birds, for instance
warblers, together with such waders as curlew and
greenshank, and seabirds such as black, common
and little tern. Autumn brings the return of several
of these species with others including spotted redshank, common and green sandpiper, hobby and
short-eared owl. The closeness of the reserve to the

Solent also affords the chance to see great crested
and Slavonian grebe, divers, and Brent geese in
winter.

Insects include holly blue butterfly, the unusual
wainscot moths, *Nonagria algae* and *Leucania ob-
soleta*, and a range of dragonflies and damselflies.

Upper Hamble Country Park

SU 490114; 163ha; HCC
Riverside woodland
Spring, early summer

An area of mature oak stands above the River
Hamble, with small-leaved lime and wild service-
tree, uncommon in the county. The rich ground
cover includes good spreads of bluebell and
primrose, with more unusual plants such as
butcher's-broom and hard shield-fern. The insects
include white admiral while a typical range of
woodland birds is present.

Upper Titchfield Haven

Permit only; 16.8ha; H and IOWNT reserve
Freshwater marsh, meadow and scrub
Spring, autumn, winter

Contrasting with the LOWER TEST MARSHES, Upper
Titchfield is not tidal but still contains an interesting range of plants and attracts a good variety of
bird life.

Waggoners Wells Nature Walks

SU 863354; 2km; Ludshott Common Committee–
NT
Lakeside, woodland and heath walks
Leaflet from Grayshott post office and newsagents
Spring, summer

Two trails show the natural history interest of
a chain of small lakes, originally hammer ponds,
set among woodland on the edge of LUDSHOTT
COMMON.

The Warren

SU 728288; 24.8ha; HCC–H and IOWNT reserve
Beech–yew–ash hanging woodland
Spring, early summer

Part of WEALDEN EDGE HANGERS.

Wealden Edge Hangers

SU 729266, 749271 and 728288; 129.2ha; HCC
reserves
Steep woodlands on chalk slopes
No access off rights of way
Spring, early summer

These are spectacular steep woodlands, chiefly of beech, ash and yew, which cling to the sides of the weathered mass of chalk that overlooks the farmland of the Weald. The chalk which covered the dome of the Weald has been worn away to leave a fluted, steep escarpment. Woodland once covered the plateau above and spread across the plain beneath, but only the slopes were steep enough to avoid the plough and now the scarp stands, dark with trees, between the open fields and spreading villages, a haven for chalkland wildlife.

Yew, if left alone, would probably replace all other trees and clothe the slopes with a strange dark forest, cool and silent even on the hottest day. Groves of yew spread down the scarps, showing as a deep green mass among the paler deciduous trees.

Beech forms almost as dense a canopy as yew and only early spring bluebell or adapted plants such as bird's-nest orchid or white helleborine survive beneath its shadow. Ash is far more open and lets in light for privet and field maple, dogwood and whitebeam, spindle, hawthorn and blocks of coppiced hazel.

Mixed woodland thus gives the widest range of species and in these areas the ground cover is full of plants such as wood spurge and ramsons,

Deadly nightshade's sombre flowers give way to highly poisonous black berries.

dog's mercury and enchanter's-nightshade, climbing traveller's-joy and carpets of ivy. The slopes lean at all angles, steep, sunny, shaded, shallow, and so afford a great deal of variety. Sunny open banks are thick with hart's-tongue or show chalk-loving species such as tutsan, deadly nightshade and nettle-leaved bellflower.

Bracken, above, marks the clay cap of the plateau, while birds sing in the treetops or in the deep clear air, but the slopes of chalk have a special thrill of their own. A tall woodland of beech may open on to a clear-felled hillside aflame with yellow mullein and rosebay willowherb. The heat of the clearing is suddenly lost in the green gloom of a yew copse or found again on a flowery bank where yellow-wort and common rock-rose, common bird's-foot-trefoil and wild thyme defy the dark of the woods and where musk mallow stands among tangles of wild rose.

Wellington Country Park

SU 724626; 244ha; Wellington Enterprises
Lake, woodland and meadowland
Leaflets from Wellington Office, Stratfield Saye,
Reading, RG7 2BT
Spring, early summer

Five nature trails show the variation of beech, oak and coniferous plantations, open parkland and the lake. Roe and fallow deer occur in the woodlands, where open rides provide sites for such butterflies as comma, white admiral, purple emperor and speckled wood, and the lake attracts great crested grebe, feral Canada goose and goosander. There are also many species of fungi.

West Yar Nature Trail

SZ 354897; 8km; IOW Nat. Hist. and Arch. Soc.
Riverside trail
Leaflet from IOW Tourist Board
Spring, summer

The trail follows the West Yar River to FRESHWATER MARSH, passing from the tidal area to fresh water above the sluice valve, and includes much of interest. Among the plants are the rather uncommon marsh-mallow, and the saltmarsh species sea arrow-grass and sea-purslane. A fine range of birds includes curlew, dunlin, redshank and ringed plover.

The Wildgrounds

Permit only; 30.4ha; Gosport BC reserve
Woodland and pond
Spring, early summer

Birch and pollarded oak form a bird-rich woodland above a rather acid ground cover of bracken and bramble, while hazel and sweet chestnut are grown for coppicing and young oak saplings have also been planted to revitalise the woods. All three native woodpeckers, bullfinch, linnet and goldfinch occur. The pond encourages nesting mallard and adds to the insect life of the reserve.

Winnall Moors

Permit only; 43ha; H and IOWNT reserve
Freshwater marsh and water meadows
Spring, early summer

The moors represent the remnants of now redundant water meadows, lying between the city of Winchester and the River Itchen. The site is dissected by many drains and dykes with raised drier strips between. Plants of freshwater marsh are abundant both in species and numbers: marsh-marigold, southern marsh-orchid, meadowsweet, yellow loosestrife, purple-loosestrife, water avens and yellow iris occur together with common reed, rush and sedge species. The alien monkeyflower also grows here, mixed with great willowherb. The damp grassland carries a wide range of grass species accompanied by angelica, ragged-Robin, hemp-agrimony, comfrey, gipsywort, valerian, greater bird's-foot-trefoil and common spotted-orchid. Some tree species have been planted in the past, including the hybrid black Italian poplar, in addition to the existing native willows, alder, ash, hawthorn and guelder-rose.

The reserve supports a wide range of birds at all seasons: winter visitors include wildfowl and waders, migrants pass through in spring and autumn, while many species stay to breed in spring and summer. Little grebe, moorhen, duck and mute swan nest beside the river; on the open grassland some waders breed and, in the reed beds, sedge warbler and reed bunting rear their young.

Grazing is an essential part of the management of the reserve, while leasing of the fly fishing rights also brings in income for management. During the fishing season visitors are asked to keep away from the river bank which has had to be fenced to provide mutual protection for the cattle and the bank.

Such rich wetlands are now very scarce due to advanced drainage techniques, so the conservation of these sites is particularly urgent. The very diverse fauna and flora, not yet exhaustively catalogued, demonstrate the great ecological value of these relics of a now obsolete farming method.

Yateley Common Country Park

SU 822597, 838594; 197ha; HCC
Heathland and pools
Nature trail leaflet from site or HCC
Spring, early summer, autumn

The heathland of south Hampshire is echoed north of the great chalk mass by the part of the county which lies within the heathy London Basin. A fine show of acid heather land may be found at Yateley Common where a nature trail demonstrates the interest of the site.

The 2km trail begins at Wyndham's Pool, an artificial lake popular for fishing and picnics. Away from the valley the scrub opens out as heathland; the gravelled sandy ground is thick with heather and bell heather by thickets and belts of birch and Scots pine. Gorse and broom form a colourful lower scrub and provide a sheltered area for many small heathland birds. Both downy and silver birch are found together with gorse and dwarf gorse.

Where the ground becomes damper cross-leaved heath replaces bell heather, although in some parts all three species may be found. Tussocks of purple moor-grass mark the damper ground while a small area near the pool edge is acid enough for *Sphagnum* mosses to grow, together with typical bog plants such as common cottongrass and round-leaved sundew. The pools in general, though, are richer than the heath above and support a marshy vegetation rather than that of a bog. Horsetail species and bulrush grow around the margins with marsh St John's-wort and marsh pennywort, water-plantain, yellow iris and floating white and yellow water-lily. A willow swamp stands at the head of the pool, varied with alder buckthorn, but once away from the wetland area the common returns again to open heathland or to a woodland of birch and grey willow with occasional rowan.

The narrow leaves of the gorses, broom and heathers are evolved to reduce their surface area and so save water loss by evaporation. Water is obviously at a premium on sands and gravels which drain so fast and this causes a further problem for the plants: there tends to be much dry material and a constant threat of sweeping fires.

Low regrowing heather, the patches of acid grassland, the open rides between woodlands and the scrubland belts make fine hunting grounds for predators – kestrels may often be seen hovering over the clearings. Jay and magpie scavenge the common and typical heathland birds such as linnet and stonechat with goldfinch, dunnock and many small woodland and garden birds may be found. Butterflies include peacock, red admiral and painted lady with common and silver-studded blue, small heath, brimstone and comma. The pool encourages a good variety of dragonflies and damselflies.

Chalk streams drain into the Itchen through the marsh and water meadows of Winnall Moors.

Hereford and Worcester

The MALVERN HILLS with their splendid views form a spectacular divide between the two former counties of Herefordshire and Worcestershire, now known collectively as Hereford and Worcester. Wildlife interests are served by the Worcestershire Nature Conservation Trust, and by the Herefordshire and Radnorshire Naturalists' Trust.

With the River Wye, wooded hills, areas of high-quality agricultural land, flood meadows grazed by the characteristic white-faced cattle, many villages linked by narrow lanes, and relatively little industrial development, Herefordshire itself has been described as one of the most uniformly beautiful counties in Britain. It is almost completely surrounded by hills rising to 300m or higher. The Malverns lie to the east, the Black Mountains to the west, and the FOREST OF DEAN (Gloucestershire) to the south, while the north west Herefordshire uplands form a link with the south Shropshire hills to the north. The central area is divided by lower hills into three lowland basins dominated by the city of Hereford in the centre, and the towns of Leominster to the north and Ross-on-Wye to the south.

The underlying rocks of the whole county are Palaeozoic or older, and characteristic of highland Britain. The Malverns, rising to about 425m, are made of Pre-Cambrian schists, gneisses and igneous rocks while, at their south western extremity, around Hollybush Hill, is Herefordshire's only area of Cambrian and Ordovician rocks. The western foothills of the Malverns, the north west Herefordshire uplands between Ludlow and Presteigne and the Woolhope Hills, are all Silurian scarplands formed largely from limestones. These areas are often wooded and do not possess such a rich flora as other limestones in the country, but are still interesting. Reserves found on them include COTHER WOOD near the Malverns, and NUPEND, COMMON HILL AND MONUMENT and LEA AND PAGET'S WOOD in the Woolhope Hills.

Most of the rest of the county is underlain by old red sandstone. Marls, producing heavy, rich soils, underlie the Leominster and Hereford lowlands and sands, giving rise to light but fertile soils, as around Ross-on-Wye. Hills such as Dinmore, Aconbury and the uplands around the Golden Valley break the lowlands and contain rubbly limestone bands which add diversity to their plant and animal life. In the south west the Black Mountains provide habitats for ring ouzel and red grouse.

At Symond's Yat the Wye enters the spectacular gorge by which it leaves the county. Rising sharply above it is the Great Doward, the only carboniferous limestone in Herefordshire, and the area with the richest flora. Some of it is now protected in the LEEPING STOCKS, WOODSIDE and WHITE ROCKS reserves, all part of the DOWARD GROUP.

During the ice ages, glaciers left behind morainic deposits, kettle-hole lakes, gravel spreads in the lowlands, diverted rivers and old lake floors. These features are most in evidence in the Lugg and Arrow valleys and the Wye Valley west of Hereford.

Many fine half-timbered buildings bear witness to the former importance of native woodlands, of which many fragments still remain, often on slopes too steep for ploughing or clearance. These woods frequently contain oak as well as ancient coppiced small-leaved lime, large-leaved lime and wild service-tree, while spurge-laurel, herb-Paris and stinking iris are among the ground flora on richer soils. Fallow deer are widespread, many woods boast a badger colony, and dormice may occupy nest boxes intended for pied flycatchers. Woodland paths and rides provide edge habitats for a wealth of butterflies and moths, including silver-washed fritillary and, much more rarely, white admiral. Few of the woods have escaped clearance or coppicing at some time, and coppicing is being reintroduced in some of them. Species-rich

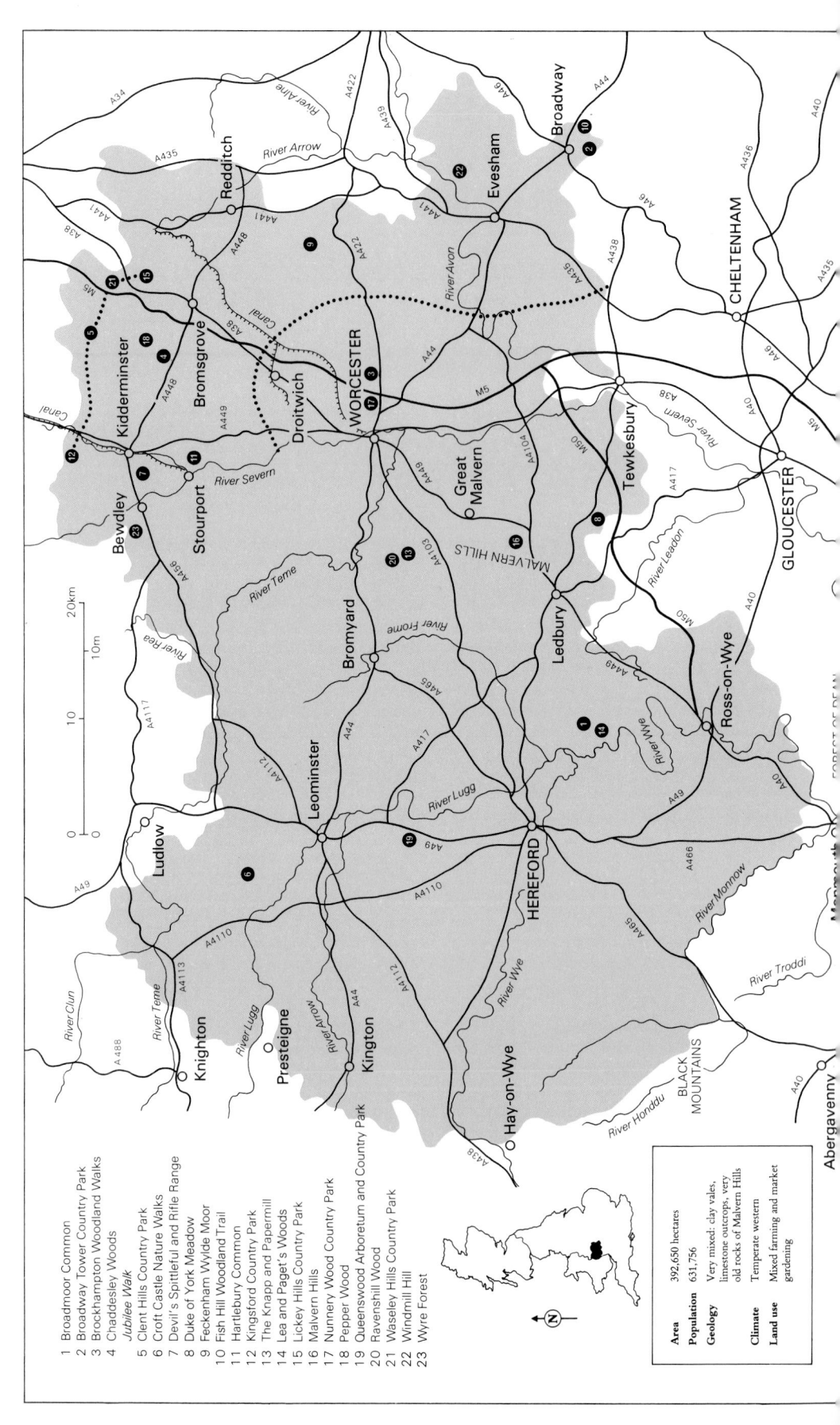

1 Broadmoor Common
2 Broadway Tower Country Park
3 Brockhampton Woodland Walks
  Jubilee Walk
4 Chaddesley Woods
5 Clent Hills Country Park
6 Croft Castle Nature Walks
7 Devil's Spittleful and Rifle Range
8 Duke of York Meadow
9 Feckenham Wylde Moor
10 Fish Hill Woodland Trail
11 Hartlebury Common
12 Kingsford Country Park
13 The Knapp and Papermill
14 Lea and Paget's Woods
15 Lickey Hills Country Park
16 Malvern Hills
17 Nunnery Wood Country Park
18 Pepper Wood
19 Queenswood Arboretum and Country Park
20 Ravenshill Wood
21 Waseley Hills Country Park
22 Windmill Hill
23 Wyre Forest

Area	392,650 hectares
Population	631,756
Geology	Very mixed: clay vales, limestone outcrops, very old rocks of Malvern Hills
Climate	Temperate western
Land use	Mixed farming and market gardening

'natural' grasslands, with hairstreaks and marbled whites, as well as orchids, cowslips, meadow saffron and adder's-tongue, are now very rare.

The old county of Worcestershire, mainly agricultural, is small and landlocked, but its geographical position brings it within the range of many species of limited distribution. Birds such as nightingale, pied flycatcher, dipper, nuthatch, grey wagtail, ruddy duck, little ringed plover, buzzard and hobby nest, and plants include traveller's-joy, giant bellflower, tutsan, wood crane's-bill, wild liquorice, narrow-leaved everlasting-pea, navelwort, mistletoe, wood spurge, wayfaring-tree, woolly thistle, stone parsley and stinking iris.

The pattern of soils ranges from light sands that suffer from wind blow to very heavy clays which are mainly basic and cover a substantial area in the south east and centre. Acid soils are confined mainly to the Lickey Hills in the north east, an area around Kidderminster, and the Malvern Hills and Castlemorton Common in the south west; but cultivation and enclosure have so altered these soils that heather grows only in a restricted area.

Wetlands have probably suffered most, with the drainage of Longdon Marsh, Feckenham Moors, Moseley Bog, bogs on the Lickey Hills and HARTLEBURY COMMON. The Great Bog of WYRE FOREST still remains but its size hardly justifies the name. Of these areas only Hartlebury Common retains any really acid bog. The best such area lies between Kidderminster and Stourport, at WILDEN MARSH, and attempts are being made to keep as much as possible. Worcestershire still houses many of the country's marsh warblers.

Probably all the lakes in the county are artificial – either created in the landscape around country houses, or caused by subsidence following brine extraction. The construction of some of these latter pools has impeded drainage and produced marshy areas to compensate for drainage elsewhere. The Droitwich area has long been known for salt-loving plants associated with its 'salt springs' and normally found near coasts.

Though there is plenty of agricultural grassland, good limestone grassland is now very restricted, and unimproved meadows have also greatly diminished in number, but a few good examples remain. EADES MEADOW is considered one of the best examples of its kind in the country.

Worcestershire still retains much woodland, largely through sharing Wyre Forest with Shropshire. Wyre Forest is the only area in which the true service-tree *Sorbus domestica* has ever been found, but it seems fairly certain that the original tree was planted and it never gained a serious hold. These native woods contain small-leaved lime, wild service-tree and yew, with a scattering of large-leaved lime that suggests that some, at least, might be genuinely native. The River Teme is still in good condition, as are other smaller streams that provide haunts for aquatic plants and animals.

F. FINCHER
PETER THOMSON

Aileshurst Coppice

Permit only; 1.4ha; WNCT reserve
Small mixed woodland
Spring, early summer

The reserve was established to protect some fine colonies of yellow star-of-Bethlehem.

Badgers Hill

Permit only; 2.2ha; WNCT reserve
Scrub woodland
Spring, early summer

Mainly hawthorn but with tree species such as ash, oak and turkey oak, the reserve is on lime-rich clays and includes a small area of grassland with adder's-tongue and greater butterfly-orchid. Nightingale may breed in the scrub.

Blind Lane Coppice

Permit only; 1.8ha; WNCT reserve
Old sunken lane and meadow
Spring, early summer

The meadow has been planted up with trees and, with seedlings from the old lane, serves as a tree nursery. Eventually, when these young trees have matured, the area will form a wood.

Yellow star-of-Bethlehem, a dramatic spring flower, is uncommon but fairly widespread.

Boynes Coppice and Meadow

Permit only; 1.2ha; WNCT reserve
Old-meadow grassland
Spring, early summer

Ancient ridge-and-furrow meadowland, Boynes Coppice and Meadow is rich in species such as dyer's greenweed, pepper-saxifrage, adder's-tongue and green-winged orchid. Small plantations of larch with standard oak trees flank the reserve.

Briar Hill Coppice

Permit only; 1.6ha; WNCT reserve
Steep woodland
Spring, early summer

Large poplar trees stand with a mixture of other species over a ground cover which includes giant bellflower and small teasel, both rather local species.

Broadmoor Common

SO 601363; 13.6ha; H and WCC
Heathland and scrub
Spring, early summer

Heathland, among the rich vales and limestone outcrops of Hereford and Worcester, is unusual; the common, scrubbed with scattered trees and gorse, is rich in insects and birds such as linnet and yellowhammer, and noted for its colonies of spiny restharrow.

Broadway Tower Country Park

SP 114360; 14ha; Mr Hans Will
Cotswold scarp parkland
Guidebook from shop
Spring, early summer

Two trails lead through the mixed broad-leaved woodland which crowns the summit, giving spectacular views across the lowlands into Wales. The woods contain badger and fox together with a typical range of woodland birds.

Brockhampton Woodland Walks

SO 893543; 1.6km, 2.4km; NT
Mixed woodland and lakeside walks
Leaflet from post office
Spring, early summer

Mixed broad-leaved and coniferous woodland and stands of mature oak encourage birds, including buzzard, raven, pied flycatcher and woodcock, while the small lake adds mallard and little grebe.

Brotheridge Green

Permit only; 2ha; WNCT reserve
Disused railway line
Spring, early summer

A variety of slope and soil type encourages a wide range of plants including privet, blackthorn, bramble and several vetches, attracting over 30 species

Brotheridge Green: a former railway line now reclaimed by nature.

of butterfly. These include marbled white, white-letter hairstreak and both dingy and grizzled skipper. Badger setts are present and there is a good variety of breeding birds.

Chaddesley Woods

SO 914736; 100ha; NCC reserve
Oak woodland and conifer plantations
Permit only off rights of way
Leaflet from NCC
Spring, early summer

Oak with birch, rowan and areas of hazel coppice forms the main tree cover, while small-leaved lime, wild service-tree and Midland hawthorn indicate that it is probably ancient woodland. The ground cover varies with the change in soils and includes bracken, bilberry and bluebell with yellow arch-angel and herb-Paris. The plantations are managed so as to demonstrate that conservation need not necessarily be the enemy of the practice of commercial forestry. The JUBILEE WALK has been established in Chaddesley Woods.

Clent Hills Country Park

SO 927798; 148ha; H and WCC
Rough grassland and woodland
Leaflet from H and WCC
All year

Bracken and foxglove, gorse scrub and mixed woodland provide a range of habitat suitable for linnet, tree pipit, redstart, kestrel and sparrow-hawk; mammals include fox and fallow deer.

Common Hill and Monument

Permit only; 2ha; H and RNT reserve
Limestone scrub and grassland
Spring, summer

Typical limestone plants include spring cinquefoil, adder's-tongue, pale St John's-wort and green-winged orchid. The reserve is rich in insects, in particular marbled white butterfly. Many species of moth, including two of burnet moth, are present, as well as glow-worm.

Cother Wood

Permit only; 1.6ha; H and RNT reserve
Limestone grassland and scrub
Spring, summer

Dyer's greenweed, yellow-wort, bee orchid and greater butterfly-orchid characterise this attractive small area, pitted by old quarry workings.

Court Wood

Permit only; 2.4ha; H and RNT reserve
Mixed woodland
Spring, early summer

Oak woodland invaded by ash, birch, wych elm, yew and sycamore, the reserve also contains small plantations of beech and conifers. Despite its small size 21 species of breeding birds occur, including both pied and spotted flycatcher.

Croft Castle Nature Walks

SO 463655; various lengths; NT
Parkland walks
Leaflets from site
Spring, early summer

Splendid avenues and mixed woodland hold buzzard, goldcrest and pied flycatcher while, from the peak of the limestone escarpment, views are said to stretch over 14 counties.

Devil's Spittleful and Rifle Range

SO 815752; 60ha; WNCT reserve
Heathland and birch woodland
Spring, early summer

One of the best examples of heathland in the county, the reserve shows good spreads of heather with gorse and bracken, blocks of birch woodland and a small oakwood. Grassland reveals harebell and wild pansy. A good range of insects includes the waved black moth.

Doward Group

Permit only; 16.5ha; H and RNT reserves
Limestone woodland, grassland and scrub
Spring, early summer

High above the valley of the River Wye the three reserves protect an area of characteristic wood- and meadowland. The presence of wild service-tree suggests that one of the woodland areas may be ancient, but generally, as boundary banks, old walls and tumbled stone-walled sheepfolds show, the woods are mostly secondary, returning to colonise cleared areas. The reserves are close enough to circle through all three, though any one would repay a lengthy study, but taken together they display a splendid range of open grassland, scrub and woodland.

WOODSIDE contains high-forest oak and beech over an understorey which includes ash, dogwood, field maple, whitebeam and yew with blackthorn, hawthorn, hazel and holly, together with wild service-tree. It is varied with stands of almost pure beech where ground cover is extremely thin and with more recently coppiced areas showing a well-developed understorey and a good variety of woodland plants. LEEPING STOCKS has fine beech trees marking the old field boundaries with coppiced oak and hazel and a great range of tangled scrub woodland. WHITE ROCKS has the same wide range of species including spindle and wayfaring-tree with sweet chestnut and sycamore. Throughout all the woods and scrubland areas the ground cover varies with the degree of shade or with changes in the soil so that acid-loving species such as bracken, birch and common cow-wheat may stand close to sanicle and marjoram, wood spurge and wood melick. Good populations of spurge-laurel are present together with ropes and drapes of traveller's-joy.

The more open areas range from stands of birch, bracken and rosebay willowherb to scrub-fringed gladed grasslands and have their finest show in a small paddock hidden against the woods. Beneath the cover of taller plants the paths are filled with plants such as ploughman's-spikenard and meadow saffron. The Woodside meadow is rich in lime-loving species and also contains a small area of heather, together with cowslip, common rock-rose and wild thyme, yellow-wort, harebell, marjoram, eyebright and greater knapweed, small scabious, quaking-grass and restharrow. Common bird's-foot-trefoil, vetches, violets and grasses provide attractive larval food for butterflies.

Throughout the area a fine variety of plants includes columbine, deadly nightshade and blue fleabane with bee, fly and green-winged orchid and broad-leaved and white helleborine.

Butterflies include common and holly blue, pearl-bordered and silver-washed fritillary, marbled white and, occasionally, white admiral. The birds are typical of scrub and woodland and may include nightingale.

Doward Quarry

Permit only; 1.3ha; H and RNT reserve
Disused quarry
Spring, summer

The quarry has recently been worked out and stands as bare limestone walls; the special fascination of this reserve will be to watch the gradual recolonisation of the site.

Drake Street Meadow

Permit only; 0.3ha; WNCT reserve
Rich grassland
Spring, early summer

The tiny meadow, crossed by a stream, contains a great variety of plants including unexpected species such as bluebell and woodland violets, with old-meadow flowers such as cowslip and green-winged orchid.

Duke of York Meadow

SO 782354; 2.3ha; WNCT reserve
Old-meadow grassland
Restricted opening: see board at site
Spring, early summer

An area of lowland unimproved grassland, the meadow is beautiful in spring with a show of wild daffodil, uncommon in the county, and with attractive pasture species such as cowslip and green-winged orchid.

Eades Meadow and Fosters Green Meadows

Permit only; 12.2ha; WNCT reserve
Old-meadow grassland
Access only on open days
Summer

In May the reserve is a perfect wild flower garden with large old parklike oak trees standing in a wonderful spread of natural colour. The slightly tilted meadow has damper areas with cuckooflower, ragged-Robin and marsh-marigold while the drier grassland is filled with spectacular displays of cowslip and green-winged orchid. Adder's-tongue is also present and sheltered spots and old hedgerows contain bluebell, bugle, primrose, goldilocks buttercup, wood anemone and violets.

Woodland flowers are present because the area was once part of the Royal Forest of Feckenham, a hunting forest which commoners' rights would probably have maintained as woodland pasture until the farm became established. The hedges are certainly many centuries old. At one time the meadow was subdivided, the oak trees mark the lines of other hedges, and the western parts show evidence of ridge-and-furrow ploughing. No ploughing has occurred in living memory, though, and this is why the grassland is so rich.

In July the meadow is cut for hay and by September the short sward is scattered with meadow saffron, the speciality of the reserve. The burning summer of 1976 did much to damage the large population of this strange and beautiful flower but there is still an attractive autumn show. Meadow saffron survives in a number of woodlands in this part of the country, but, with the exception of Eades Meadow, its finest grassland populations have long been destroyed by ploughing. Meadow saffron lifts its leaves in spring to build its corm throughout the summer and flower in the autumn.

Grazing animals might strip the leaves, depriving the corm of its food source, and so the plant has evolved a poisonous leaf. To ensure that his stock is not poisoned, man, the farmer, normally ploughs the meadows. In fact the leaf becomes quite edible when cut and dried at haytime and a haying regime safeguards the plant at Eades Meadow.

Eywood Pool

Permit only; 7.2ha; H and RNT reserve
Freshwater lake and woodland
All year

This attractive tree-fringed pool has drawn over 100 species of bird including great crested grebe, pochard, shoveler, redstart and pied flycatcher. The reserve lies within the private land of a large estate and the hide overlooks both water and woodland, arable fields and oaks over grassland.

Feckenham Wylde Moor

SP 012603; 11.2ha; WNCT reserve
Wetland and open water
All year

An area of undrained peat marsh, the reserve contains wide spreads of rushes and sedgebeds, including sea club-rush, uncommon in inland sites. An artificial lake will attract more wetland birds to add to the numbers of duck and passage waders which already visit and, it is hoped, encourage others to breed. Among the breeding species already present are snipe. A hide is open to the public at all times.

Meadow saffron, an autumn-flowering species, is a speciality at Eades Meadow.

Hartlebury Common: lowland heath is uncommon in Hereford and Worcester.

Fish Hill Woodland Trail

SP 120369; 0.5km; H and WCC
Cotswold scarp trail
Spring, early summer

The short trail is set in some 5ha of the steep Cotswold Edge near BROADWAY TOWER COUNTRY PARK. The characteristic lime-loving plants are set off by magnificent views of the distant Welsh hills.

Fred Dale

Permit only; 22.8ha, WNCT–West Midland Bird Club reserve
Woodland and brookside meadows
Spring, early summer

A mixed oak woodland, coppiced and gladed in places, sweeps of bracken, heather and bilberry, and streamside meadows rich in lady's-mantle and cowslip, attract fallow deer, a good range of butterflies and kingfisher, dipper, pied flycatcher, wood warbler, grey wagtail, redstart and nuthatch. The reserve is part of WYRE FOREST.

Grovely Dingle

Permit only; 8.4ha; WNCT–NT reserve
Steep valley woodland
Spring, early summer

The series of narrow, thickly wooded ravines contain oak, wych elm, wild service-tree, moschatel, wood speedwell and woodruff. It is the only site in the county for the uncommon wood barley.

Harris' Woodlands

Permit only; 581.2ha; L.G. Harris & Co. Ltd
13 commercial woodlands
Permit from WNCT or L. G. Harris
Spring, early summer

These varied woodlands, mostly sycamore, ash, alder and birch managed for commercial purposes, encourage a good range of woodland birds and insects. Six further woodlands are held by L. G. Harris and Co. Ltd in Warwickshire.

Hartlebury Common

SO 820705; 91ha; H and WCC reserve
Lowland heath
Leaflets from H and WCC
Spring, early summer

Broom, gorse and heather heathland, scrub woodland, bogs and pools make this one of the most important sandy acid areas in the locality. Marsh cinquefoil and bogbean show in the wetlands while harebell, shepherd's cress and buck's-horn plaintain may be found on the heath. Among the birds stonechat and whinchat occur and over 100 moth and butterfly species have been recorded.

Holywell Dingle

Permit only; 3.6ha; H and RNT reserve
Steep wooded ravine
Spring, early summer

A great variety of tree species stand over bluebell, moschatel and lesser periwinkle. Raven, kestrel, buzzard, pied flycatcher and nuthatch may be seen. Fox and badger may be present.

The Knapp and Papermill: old pollards line the Leigh Brook.

Hunthouse Wood

Permit only; 24.4ha; WNCT reserve
Mixed valleyside woodland
Spring, early summer

The path twists among mixed tree species standing above an understorey of coppiced hazel, thick with bracken, bramble and rosebay willowherb, while clearings allow a show of bugle, yellow pimpernel, violets and wood-sorrel. Lower down, a bridge crosses a damp flushed area widely spread with dog's mercury and enchanter's-nightshade, over-looked by tall dead elms. The stream has alder, ash and oak above the hazel with broad buckler-fern, tumbles of thickly mossed logs and marsh plants such as giant horsetail and the uncommon alternate-leaved golden-saxifrage and small teasel.

Gigantic wild cherry trees are a feature of the wood, together with large-leaved lime, forming a contrast to slender birch or willow and to the delicate plants of the woodland floor. The variation increases along the winding pathway: wet and dry gullies, steep and shallow banks, tall dead standing trees and fallen giants thick with fungi and filled with burrowing insects. Damper places have square-stemmed St John's-wort and carpets of bugle; richer soils support dogwood, yew and field maple over wood spurge and selfheal; more acid areas show foxglove, honeysuckle and wood sage; the whole is a wonderful complex mix with interest for all.

The key to this variation is in the ground beneath. The stream has cut down through an outcrop of coal measures, an alternation of lime-stone, sandstone and coal which may be seen in the cliffs along the valley and which, with the varying degree of wetness, gives the mixture of lime-rich and more acid soils.

A variety of animals enjoy the refuge of the reserve. Badgers breed, with an abundance of woodland birds, including several warbler species, reinforced by dipper and grey wagtail at the stream-side, and tawny owl, sparrowhawk and buzzard.

Ipsley Alders

SP 076676; 17.8ha; WNCT reserve
Fen marsh
Booklet from WNCT
Spring, summer

This fen marsh is supplied with water from a spring emerging under the layer of peat on the marsh. This type of habitat is rare in the area and supports plants such as the marsh stitchwort, marsh wound-wort and a number of rushes, especially the blunt-flowered rush. It is attractive to reed bunting and snipe, and many dragonflies inhabit the pools.

Jubilee Walk

SO 914736; 1.5km; NCC
Waymarked trail
Leaflet from dispensers or NCC
Spring, early summer, autumn

The walk passes through CHADDESLEY WOODS. A stream-fed pool adds wetland interest.

Kingsford Country Park

SO 823820; 87ha; H and WCC
Coniferous woodland and heathland
Leaflet from H and WCC
Spring, early summer

The country park adjoins 162ha of National Trust and Staffordshire CC birch heathland at KINVER EDGE (Staffordshire). The wildlife of the heather-bracken heathland and of the birch or coniferous woodland is demonstrated by a waymarked nature trail. The bird life varies from goldcrest to green and great spotted woodpecker while open areas are suitable for adder and common lizard.

The Knapp and Papermill

SO 748522; 24ha; WNCT reserve
Valley woodland, pasture and brook
All visitors should sign record book
Nature trail booklet from site or WNCT
Spring, early summer

The reserve enjoys a wide range of habitat within a relatively small area. The steeper slopes are clothed with woodland which, containing both small-leaved lime and wild service-tree, seems likely to have shaded the valley for many thousands of years. Shallower slopes are grassed, in some places returning to woodland, while the val-ley bottom is marshy, containing some interesting wetland plants. The Leigh Brook adds the special fascination of running water.

The brook is lined with coppiced alder and ash and pollarded crack willow, standing above small teasel and Indian balsam. Butterbur and common comfrey spread across the banks while water-crowfoot trails in the fast-flowing water. An earlier watercourse has become a marsh with sedges, rushes, marsh-marigold and great horsetail.

The lower land is rich in plants such as early-purple orchid and common spotted-orchid. The drier bank shows cowslip and primrose, growing together with their hybrid form. Longer slopes of grassland further upstream, an area of unimproved meadowland, are rich in common bird's-foot-trefoil, yellow rattle, devil's-bit scabious and musk mallow, contrasting with more acid patches of bracken and broom.

In a small coppice near the brook tangles of traveller's-joy loop over spindle, dogwood and remnants of coppiced wych elm with, where bramble is not too thick, a good variety of plants such as wood melick, woodruff, wood spurge and nettle-leaved bellflower. The woodland proper is varied with standard oak over coppiced hazel and some superb areas of coppiced small-leaved lime where goldenrod blazes in late summer and sprays of polypody decorate the trees. The woods hold good shows of hart's-tongue and soft shield-fern on damp and shaded slopes and here, in the shade of the main woodland, violet helleborine grows.

The variety of the reserve attracts a range of typical birds while moths include the local silver cloud and waved black, with butterflies such as silver-washed fritillary, holly blue and dingy skipper. Some 20 mammal species have been recorded and include a resident population of badger.

Knowles Coppice

Permit only; 7.7ha; WNCT reserve
Mixed woodland and brookside meadows
Spring, early summer

The woodland is typical of much of WYRE FOREST, consisting in the main of oak with birch, larch and occasional holly. The meadows are rich in cowslip and devil's-bit scabious while the brook attracts dipper, kingfisher and grey wagtail.

Lickey Hills: a magnificent vista from the woodland slopes of the country park.

Lea and Paget's Woods

SO 597342 and 598344; 9ha; H and RNT reserve
Mixed limestone wood
Spring, early summer

The two separate areas of woodland contain ash, birch and field maple, with a hazel understorey; Paget's Wood also has mature oak and plentiful wild cherry. The ground cover includes wild daffodil and various orchids, while Paget's Wood also supports wild liquorice. Bird life is abundant, with all three native woodpeckers, warblers and other typical woodland species.

Leeping Stocks

Permit only; 7.7ha; H and RNT reserve
Limestone woodland and scrub
Spring, early summer

Part of the DOWARD GROUP.

Lickey Hills Country Park

SO 986758; 213ha; City of Birmingham BC
Steep hilly parkland
Spring, early summer

The park gives splendid views from its steep grassed and wooded slopes and contains a children's nature trail.

Long Meadow

Permit only; 5.2ha; WNCT reserve
Unimproved hay meadow
Spring

Spring, before the meadow is closed for mowing, shows a fine variety of ancient-pasture species such as cowslip, green-winged orchid and adder's-tongue.

Malvern Hills

SO 768454; 600ha; Malvern Hills Conservators
Narrow ridge of ancient hills
Spring, summer, autumn

Lifting spectacularly from the farmland around, the Malvern Hills are a narrow switchbacked ridge formed from some of the oldest rocks in the country. They are wooded on their lower slopes, blanketed with bracken and scrub, but the ancient hilltops are open to the skies.

Where the rock was quarried to make our roads, plants are beginning to return. The slopes and cliffs are scattered with gorse and broom, with garden escapes such as buddleia, with wood sage and navelwort. Bare rock is thick with stonecrops, such as orpine, while ledges and quarry floors develop a scrub of bramble and wild rose, ash, elder, hawthorn, sycamore and willow. Mosses, lichens and ferns are plentiful, with an abundance of polypody. Small birds breed in the scrub; jackdaw and feral dove nest on the cliffs; kestrels hang in the up-draughts above. The slopes are full of butterflies such as the beautiful small copper or wall brown.

Above the quarries the land lifts steeply upwards, scrub-covered with bracken and bramble, with rosebay willowherb, gorse and broom and an invading woodland of hawthorn, rowan, birch and sycamore. Higher still is open grassland, with harebell and tormentil, heather, sheep's sorrel and bilberry. The complex nature of the rocks gives richer grasslands where lady's bedstraw, common bird's-foot-trefoil and wild thyme grow.

The Malvern Hills, composed of some of the most ancient rocks in Britain, rise from the plain.

Passing downwards again, the scrub grades into woodland. The mosaic of clumped gorse, hawthorn and heather, standing in a grassland filled with hawkbits, crosswort, broom and wild rose, gives way to oak, ash, birch, hazel and occasional yew, to fine old oak trees over open mossy grasses or richer blocks of coppiced hazel with plants such as violets, wood spurge and wood-sorrel, shrubs such as dogwood and field maple, holly and wild cherry.

Much of the attraction of the site is its variety. For over 15km the hilltops rise and fall and the hillsides change in steepness; the valleys themselves may be grassed or filled with scrub or woodland. Public pressure is high in certain places but quiet areas, rich in wildlife, are plentiful. The woods are rich in typical bird life and, above, the circling of a buzzard may enrich the summer sky.

Marsh Warbler Sites

Permit only; 9ha; WNCT reserves
Nine separate areas of marshland
Summer

Beds of nettle, great willowherb and meadowsweet, often flanked by pollarded willows, hawthorn and blackthorn, provide nest sites for marshland birds such as reed, sedge and marsh warbler and reed bunting. Up to one third of Britain's marsh warbler population breeds on these reserves.

Melrose Farm Meadows

Permit only; 2ha; WNCT reserve
Old-meadow grassland
Spring, autumn

Thick hedges surrounding the meadows add additional variety to the reserve, noted for its grassland species such as cowslip, saw-wort, green-winged orchid and meadow saffron.

Moccas Park

Permit only; 140ha; NCC reserve
Ancient deer park
Spring, early summer

The higher slopes are wooded while the lower areas are occupied by sweeps of grassland under fine old parkland oak and sweet chestnut. Mosses and lichens are particularly notable and the beetles include three species known only from this site in Britain.

Mowley Wood Track

Permit only; 1.3ha; H and RNT reserve
Disused railway line
Spring, early summer

Isolated from roads and houses, the scrub development on the railway banks is well suited to woodland birds.

Newbourne Wood

Permit only; 4.4ha; WNCT reserve
Coniferous and mixed woodland
Spring, early summer

The commercial plantation, now being converted to broad-leaved woodland, has great promise as an educational reserve with a range from dry to damp ground and the presence of three small pools.

Nunnery Wood Country Park

SO 877543; 25ha; H and WCC
Mixed woodland
Leaflets from H and WCC
Spring, early summer, autumn

Continuous woodland has certainly been present for some 900 years and oak, ash, aspen, hawthorn and hazel, managed as coppice with standards, allows good plant variation including common cow-wheat, hairy woodrush and violet helleborine. Woodland birds include all three native woodpeckers with nightingale and woodcock.

Nupend Wood

Permit only; 4.8ha; H and RNT reserve
Superb yew woodland and limestone scrubland area
Spring, summer

Mixed deciduous trees, with wild service-tree, stand above bluebell, stinking iris and stinking hellebore. Elsewhere yew prevents undergrowth. Sparrowhawk and tawny owl are resident, with summer warblers including occasional grasshopper warbler. Butterflies are plentiful and the reserve is well known for its fungi.

Penny Hill Bank

Permit only; 0.8ha; WNCT reserve
Limestone grassland
Spring, summer

Columbine, autumn gentian and ploughman's-spikenard characterise the herb-rich grassland which, sheltered by scrub and belts of woodland, attracts such butterflies as green hairstreak, dingy skipper and wood white.

Pepper Wood

SO 938745; 53.6ha; WdT
Mixed woodland
Spring, early summer

Once managed as coppice with standards, the wood is now overgrown, but a return to regular management is underway and should encourage a richer diversity of wildlife.

Queenswood Arboretum and Country Park

SO 517515; 68ha; H and WCC
Woodland and arboretum
Leaflet from H and WCC, and catalogue at site; visitor centre
Spring, early summer, autumn

The arboretum contains an important collection of trees on the plateau above a good mixed native woodland dominated by oak. The varied soils of the slopes support devil's-bit scabious, primrose and common spotted-orchid. The bird life is equally varied, including sparrowhawk and woodcock.

Marsh warbler, a Worcestershire speciality.

Randan Wood

Permit only; 4.8ha; WNCT reserve
Mixed woodland
Spring, early summer

The reserve contains a wide variety of trees such as small-leaved lime, wild service-tree, and alder buckthorn, of plants such as ivy broomrape and tutsan, of mammals such as badger and yellow-necked mouse, and many bird species. Over 300 fungi have been the subject of special study.

Ravenshill Wood

SO 739539; 20ha; WNCT–Miss M.E. Barling reserve
Mixed coniferous and broad-leaved woodland
Nature trail guides at discovery centre, and book about site from WNCT
Open March–October inclusive

The limestone areas support spindle, herb-Paris and broad-leaved helleborine beneath the woodland cover, filled with the birdsong of warblers or the roding flight of woodcock. A pool encourages wetland birds while badger and fox are plentiful. Insects include wood white butterfly.

Rhydspence

Permit only; 0.2ha; H and RNT reserve
Tiny woodland
Spring, early summer

A small area of woodland, close to the River Wye, contains a variety of typical plants and birds.

Pied flycatcher, a bird of upland valley woods and tree-lined watersides.

Romers Wood and Motlins Hole

Permit only; 18ha; H and RNT reserve
Mixed woodland
Spring, early summer

The two woodlands are separated by a large field and contain a mix of trees, chiefly oak and ash, over an understorey which includes hazel, holly and guelder-rose, with spring-fed streams thick with great horsetail. Over 30 breeding bird species have been recorded from the woods.

Upton Warren

Permit only; 24ha; WNCT reserve
Pools rich in bird life
All year

The pools, formed by subsidence due to underground salt extraction, range from open shallow ponds to lakes surrounded by bulrush swamp, great willowherb, sedges, rushes, yellow iris and water-plantain; some are surrounded by open fields, others by belts of alder and willow. The larger pools are deep enough for diving duck while the margins and the smaller ponds are ideal for dabblers and waders. Birds form the main attraction and some 150 species are recorded in an average year. Uncommon birds may occur at any time and there is a great variety of breeding species, spring and autumn migrants and wintering birds. The saltmarsh areas are some of the most extensive and important in inland Britain. They contain reflexed saltmarsh-grass, spear-leaved orache and sea-spurrey.

Spring may bring visits from black and common tern, travelling from Africa to breed in continental Europe, or from arctic tern, nearing the end of its stupendous 16,000km journey from the Antarctic seas to nest on sea coasts from Britain up into the Arctic. The waders, similarly, pass through on passage and include bar-tailed and black-tailed godwit, curlew and whimbrel, common and wood sandpiper, dunlin, greenshank and ruff. The summer residents include swallow and house martin, warblers, spotted flycatcher and cuckoo. Great crested grebe, mallard, tufted and ruddy duck, Canada goose and mute swan are resident, together with moorhen, coot and kingfisher. The hedges and woodlands hold a range of other birds, such as finches, tits and crow family species, together with green woodpecker, treecreeper and little owl.

As the breeding season ends, passage birds pass through again and the summer visitors move back to their winter quarters, sometimes preyed upon by hunters such as hobby. The winter birds arrive, driven down by the cold, and until the spring returns they shelter and feed here. Wigeon, pintail and goldeneye join the resident duck species while snipe and jack snipe probe the margins of the pools and water rail skulk in the marshes. Redwing and fieldfare gorge themselves on the hedgerow berries, and goldcrest and siskin feed busily among the trees.

Wilden Marsh: scrub is invading the old grazing marshland.

Waseley Hills Country Park

SO 979768; 54ha; H and WCC
Rough grassland, scrub and woodland
Leaflets from H and WCC; visitor centre
Spring, early summer

Sedgbourne Coppice, within the park, is managed as a conservation zone. Two ponds and a marsh increase the interest of the wood which provides a magnificent carpet of bluebell in spring. Gorse and broom encourage scrubland birds such as yellowhammer and linnet, while the Coppice area attracts a typical range of birds that favour woodland habitats.

Wern Wood

Permit only; 0.8ha; H and RNT reserve
Steep mixed woodland
Spring, early summer

Ash and oak, with wych elm, holly and grey willow, and a block of poplar over an understorey of elder, form the tree cover of the reserve while the woodland floor is distinguished by both giant and spreading bellflower. Summer warblers fill the wood with birdsong.

Wessington Pasture

Permit only; 10.8ha; H and RNT reserve
Grassland returning to woodland
Spring, early summer

Spindle and oak are among the trees present, and there is a good show of wild daffodil beneath them in spring. All three British woodpeckers are present, with breeding warbler species. In autumn an interesting and colourful range of fungi can be observed.

White Rocks

Permit only; 5.2ha; H and RNT reserve
Limestone woodland, scrub and grassland
Spring, summer

Part of the DOWARD GROUP.

Wilden Marsh

Permit only; 32.6ha; WNCT reserve
River valley marshes
Spring, summer

Marsh arrow-grass, marsh cinquefoil and southern marsh-orchid are only three of the attractive wetland plants. Willow and alder scrub provides shelter for migrant and resident birds while spectacular old pollard willows form a special habitat. The site forms part of the county's most important area of marshland.

Windmill Hill

SP 072477; 6ha; WNCT reserve
Limestone scrub and grassland
Spring, summer

The limestone grassland contains greater knapweed, wild liquorice and both common and spiny restharrow, and supports a good variety of butterflies. Small birds nest in the scrub and there is evidence of badger and fox.

Woodside

Permit only; 3.6ha; H and RNT reserve
Woodland and limestone grassland
Spring, early summer

Part of the DOWARD GROUP.

Wyre Forest

SO 759766; 300ha; NCC reserve
Mixed woodland
Permit only off rides and paths
Leaflet from NCC
Spring, early summer

The Wyre Forest reserve protects a part of one of the best remaining native woodlands in the country, a superbly varied area which lies beside the River Severn and is centred around a fast-flowing stream, the Dowles Brook. This stream is one of the richest in the area and the whole reserve forms one of the most important wildlife environments in the Midlands.

Wyre Forest was the first site where *Enoicyla pusilla*, our only land-living caddis larva, was discovered. It is known now from a very few other localities but Wyre is still an important site for the species. This is also the only caddis species with a female which cannot fly. The larvae shelter in elegant tapered cases, made of a mosaic of grains of sand. The cases are lined with a tube of silk, to which the larvae attach themselves, living in damp woodland mosses, feeding on dead leaves, eating them into filigreed skeletons; in late autumn they hatch out to mate, lay and die.

Oak is the key to the major part of the woodland, a fine spread of developing high forest which has grown up from coppiced stools. A small part of the forest is still coppiced oak, the wood used to make rustic furniture while the stripped bark is used in leather tanning, but coppicing here dates back to the Middle Ages and much of Wyre was harvested for charcoal and bark. More than half of the present woodland is converted to alien trees but the remnant forest still shows a great variation: the old coppiced oak on the plateaus, rich mixed woods in the valleys, woodland meadows and glades filled with a richly varied wildlife.

One of the special features of the forest is that it draws together so many forms and facets of British woodland. The plateau oakwoods have much in common with the coppices of Wales, the valley woods are similar to the Wye Valley's southern Welsh borders, mixed woods on clay have echoes of woodlands in East Anglia, and several plants and animals meet here on the very edge of their ranges.

The oak woodland may form stands of oak and birch, above an acid ground cover of bilberry, bracken, heather, wood sage, common cow-wheat and lily-of-the-valley. Lily-of-the-valley is generally found in hilly limestone woods but occasionally it may be found in sandy oakwoods, as in the DANBURY GROUP (Essex).

Oak and birch may stand above an area of growing oak coppice or give way to oak standards above a thin understorey of birch, of occasional holly or yew, over a spread of bracken and bramble.

Wyre Forest: high-forest oak in the Fred Dale reserve.

Even-aged oak, a closed canopy growing towards high forest, may have a variety of plants beneath it, bracken, bilberry, heather and wood sage.

The forest lies on coal measures, a very mixed range of rocks which includes sandstones, conglomerates, marls and bands of *Spirorbis* limestone. The richer rocks may give rise to less acid soils which were recognised in earlier times and have been cleared for grazing: bright small woodland meadows with a rich spread of plants such as betony, common bird's-foot-trefoil, lady's bedstraw, harebell, yellow rattle and wild thyme, with the more unusual green-winged orchid, adder's-tongue and meadow saffron.

Dowles Brook brings another change of scene, with shrubs such as blackthorn, hawthorn, hazel, guelder-rose and rowan, with ash and alder above a show of wild rose, hard fern, broad buckler-fern, wood melick, wood spurge and wood-sorrel. Alder, dogwood, small-leaved lime, wild service-tree and willow grow in the valley, where damp flushes are marked by clumps of pendulous sedge, hemp-agrimony and meadowsweet.

Britain boasts two native oaks, the sessile and the pedunculate, and typical tracts of both kinds occur here in the forest. Mountain melick and wood crane's-bill also occur here around the southernmost limit of their range. Uncommon and beautiful plants such as columbine and narrow-leaved helleborine glow in the shade of the woods, together with bloody crane's-bill and intermediate wintergreen.

The richness and variety of the habitats of the forest and their associated plant life encourage a range of insects of every shape and size, from tiny creatures which live in the leaf litter, to the southern aeshna, one of our largest dragonflies. Alder buckthorn, common nettle, woodland violets, bilberry, oak, cuckooflower and various grasses are food plants for some of the forest's butterflies: for brimstone, comma, high brown and silver-washed fritillary, for green and purple hairstreaks, orange-tip and speckled wood. An extraordinary range and abundance of moths is recorded, with national rarities such as alder kitten. Add to these a range of flies, wasps, bees, beetles and ants, and the forest can be seen as a teeming city where every niche, from the woodland floor to the topmost leaves of the oaks, is a natural home for some species of insect. Similarly, a whole range of snails and slugs, worms, flatworms, spiders and harvestmen, centipedes, millipedes, woodlice and other small animals forms part of the pattern of life here.

Dowles Brook holds trout, salmon, chub, eel and lamprey, freshwater shrimp and crayfish, and a host of insects and insect larvae and other invertebrates. Attracted by this wooded stream, dipper, kingfisher and grey wagtail may often be seen, while the aerial hunter, here in the woods, is the beautiful pied flycatcher, which matches the dancing insect flight with wonderful skill and deftness.

Dowles Brook, full of fish and insect life at the heart of Wyre Forest, attracts dipper and kingfisher.

Once more the varied nature of the forest ensures a wide range of suitable sites for birds. The wood warbler is found only where a closed leaf canopy ensures a sparse ground cover, whereas dense bushes are favoured by occasional grasshopper warbler. Where holes are available they may be taken by redstart, nuthatch or tits, while hole makers, great spotted, lesser spotted and green woodpecker all breed. Other birds include woodcock, kestrel, sparrowhawk and tawny owl, with, from time to time, long-eared owl in the conifers which adjoin much of the reserve.

The commoner woodland mammals, mice, voles and shrews, hedgehog and mole, stoat, weasel, badger and fox, may be found in the forest, together with fallow deer and several species of bat. The deer were hunted here over centuries and, particularly during Plantagenet and Tudor times, Wyre was one of the favourite Royal Forests. The ancient forest laws have helped to preserve at Wyre a tract of land which is now one of the finest woodland reserves in lowland Britain. Few sites can equal its variation of woodland types nor the wealth of plant and animal life it holds.

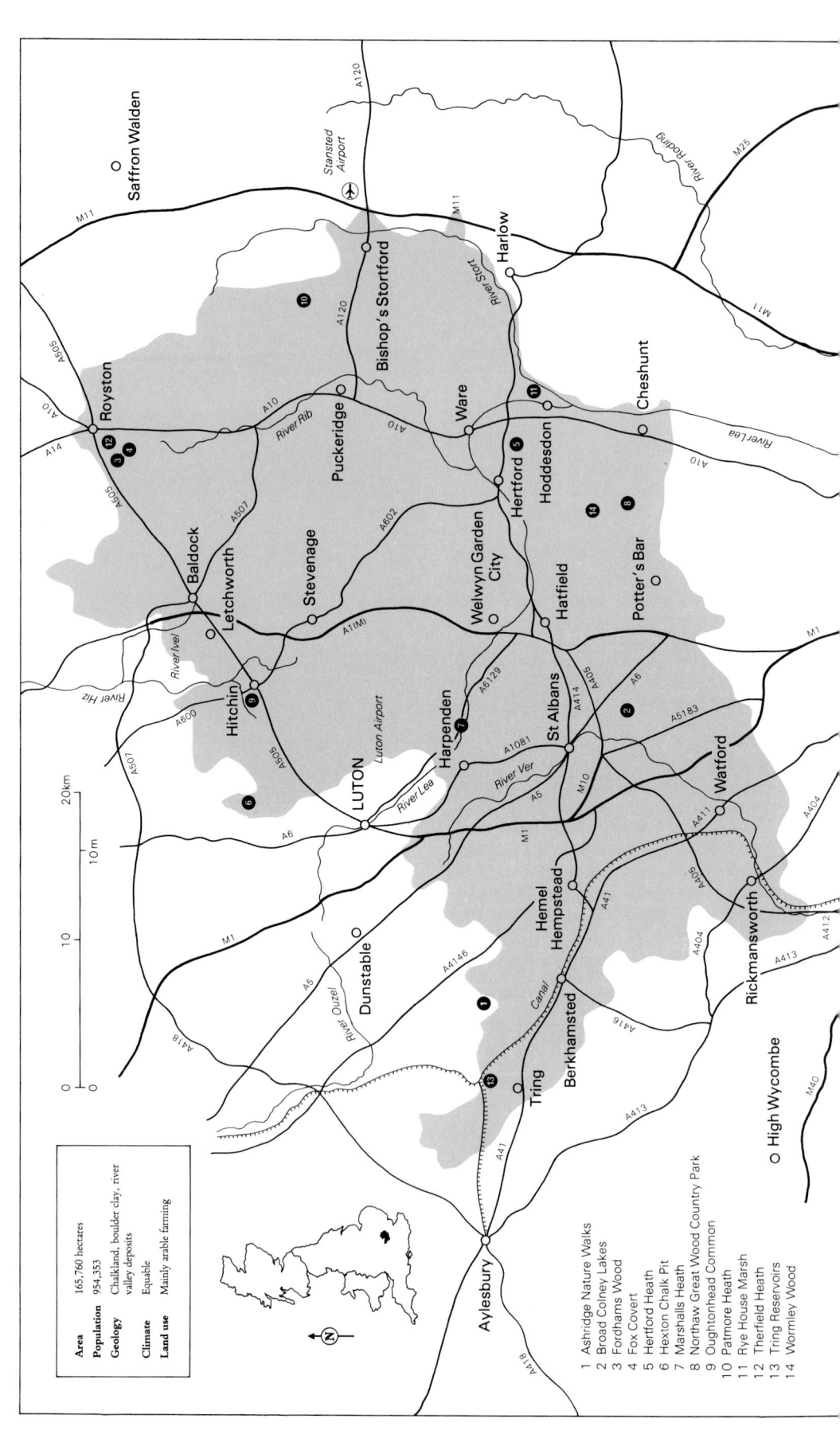

Area 165,760 hectares
Population 954,353
Geology Chalkland, boulder clay, river valley deposits
Climate Equable
Land use Mainly arable farming

1 Ashridge Nature Walks
2 Broad Colney Lakes
3 Fordhams Wood
4 Fox Covert
5 Hertford Heath
6 Hexton Chalk Pit
7 Marshalls Heath
8 Northaw Great Wood Country Park
9 Oughtonhead Common
10 Patmore Heath
11 Rye House Marsh
12 Therfield Heath
13 Tring Reservoirs
14 Wormley Wood

Hertfordshire

'Talk of PLEASURE GROUNDS, indeed! What that man ever invented under the name of pleasure grounds, can equal these fields in Hertfordshire!' wrote William Cobbett in *Rural Rides*. Though Cobbett was writing in 1822, he would still today find much to delight him in Hertfordshire's agricultural scenery. He might bitterly regret the loss of so much woodland and so many hedgerow trees, but he would find no shortage of pleasure grounds.

From the clayey fringes of London Hertfordshire extends 50km northwards to the tail of the Chilterns at Royston, and on the way a meandering modern traveller would pass through some of Britain's finest deciduous woodland. He could follow chalk streams flanked by ancient meadows and discover small marshes. Here and there patches of acid heathland, scattered with gorse or other scrub, might impede the journey, but finally he would emerge on open downland.

Although tranquil places for wildlife abound, it would be foolish to ignore the significance of Hertfordshire's other face. Rigorous exploitation of the land for farming, forestry and minerals has both impoverished and enriched the natural history as much as have the rocks, soil and climate. Within undulating vistas of wood and field new towns such as Stevenage and Hemel Hempstead help support a population which has quadrupled since the turn of the century. More people make more demands on the countryside for building and recreation. Yet despite all the pressures, and its proximity to London, Hertfordshire retains a distinctly rural character.

Much of the county is founded on chalk. The Chilterns sweep along its western edge from Chorleywood to Berkhamsted and Tring; they also line the northern rim from the Hexton hills to Royston. On the steeper slopes these areas of mixed farming have stretches of downland still unploughed and agriculturally unimproved. Most of this grassland, first cleared in Neolithic times, is now mingled with scrub through loss of grazing, but the largest piece of remaining open downland is THERFIELD HEATH, a site of national importance. The traditional woodland of the thinner soils is beech, long associated with the furniture industry, but in many places, notably at ASHRIDGE, it is mixed with oak and other hardwoods.

Elsewhere the solid chalk is strewn with a variety of superficial deposits. Most of the north and east, from Stevenage to Buntingford and Bishops Stortford, is covered with chalky boulder clay, a till providing deep loam well suited to arable production. The landscape rolls gently, the fields are large and the woodlands of oak, ash and hazel are major wildlife sanctuaries.

In the centre and south the soils are generally more acidic; around St Albans and Harpenden this is caused by the covering of clay with flints and, further south, by the Reading beds and London clay. In this region are isolated patches of acid heathland, such as Nomansland Common and Bricket Wood, the remnants of large common grazings which were strung across the county on the poorer soils before enclosure. Some of these vital heathland refuges, such as HERTFORD HEATH and PATMORE HEATH, are now protected as H and MTNC nature reserves.

The typical woodlands of the heavier soils are oak and hornbeam. For centuries many thousands of acres were managed as hornbeam coppice, providing wood for local use and domestic fuel for the towns; usually the coppices were interspersed with oak standards to provide mature timber. This woodland management gave an incomparable diversity of plants, insects and birds. However commercial coppicing of hornbeam and of hazel, its counterpart on the more calcareous soils, has now all but ceased. Other rich woodlands developed from wood pasture, many of which after the nineteenth-century enclosures were planted or allowed to regenerate naturally. Today they form valuable parts of the major woodlands at NORTHAW, Broxbourne and WORMLEY, existing alongside acres of old coppice. Some attempts have been made by the H and MTNC and by local authorities to reintroduce coppicing for conservation purposes; the best examples are at Northaw, Bencroft Wood and the Trust reserve near Stevenage. Nevertheless, most coppice remains derelict and much more has been cleared; some has gone to agriculture, but most has been replanted with conifers.

Virtually all Hertfordshire's rivers flow south to the Thames. Many, like the Chess, Mimram and Rib, are delightful chalk streams containing trout and crayfish. Riverside water-cress beds are frequent, but most of the valley sides have been drained for agriculture so that only a few marshes remain; the best are STANBOROUGH REED MARSH, SAWBRIDGEWORTH MARSH and RYE HOUSE MARSH. There is a similar scarcity of riverside meadows, but examples can still be found at Hertford and in the valleys of the Mimram, Stort and Chess.

The two largest rivers, the Lee and the Colne, leave Hertfordshire in the south east and south west respectively. Both valleys contain large deposits of river terrace gravels, heavily exploited in the past 50 years; the resulting chain of water-filled pits has great potential for wildlife, and some may eventually achieve the richness of the TRING RESERVOIRS which now have reserve status.

Parkland estates have always been a major feature of the Hertfordshire countryside. Through centuries of woodland planting, landscaping and management, Hatfield, Knebworth and Tring have made considerable contributions to its natural history. Improvements in transport and the rise in population have now brought a demand for more parks of a different nature. Large parts of the Lee and Colne valleys form regional parks providing public recreational facilities; all these areas make some provision for the conservation of wildlife and its study.

Hertfordshire's commons, public open spaces, even village greens and ponds are today also under increasing pressure from public recreation. Some of them, like Harpenden and Chipperfield commons, are locally important wildlife habitats. Fortunately, many of these too are now being managed in ways which blend conservation interests with those of recreation. Thus the parks, or pleasure grounds, complement in a valuable way the series of county nature reserves.

DAVID SHIRLEY

Alpine Meadow

Permit only; 1ha; H and MTNC reserve
Chalk grassland
Spring, summer

The small meadow set between scrub woodland and a larch plantation has a rich diversity of plants including several uncommon in the county. Spring brings a show of primrose while later-flowering plants include wild carrot, marjoram, common spotted-orchid and common twayblade.

Ashridge Nature Walks

SP 971131; 1.2 and 2.4km; Herts Nat. Hist. Soc. and Field Club–NT
Common land and woodland
Leaflet from local newsagents or NT
Spring, summer

Above the Vale of Aylesbury, the walks pass through mixed woodland of oak, ash, beech, birch and sycamore, a sanctuary for fallow and muntjac deer, while birds include redpoll and woodcock.

Ashwell Quarry Springs

Permit only; 0.3ha; H and MTNC reserve
A minor source of the River Cam
Spring, summer

Two small springs rise from the chalk and contain a number of uncommon animals adapted to very pure cold waters. Among them are the flatworms *Crenobia alpina* and *Polycelia felina*.

Balls Wood

TL 345105; 55.4ha; H and MTNC reserve
Mixed woodland and FC plantation
Spring, early summer

The mainly broad-leaved woodland contains damp rides, ditches and ponds. The ground cover ranges from bramble to dog's mercury and enchanter's-nightshade while the rides may be filled with bugle, meadowsweet, ragged-Robin, pendulous sedge and common spotted-orchid. Also present here are

Part of the mixed woodland traversed by Ashridge Nature Walks.

goldilocks buttercup, slender St John's-wort, wood spurge and wood small-reed, white admiral butterfly, a fine range of bird life and fallow and muntjac deer.

Barkway Pit

TL 381366; 0.3ha; H and MTNC reserve
Geological site
All year

The main interest is a unique exposure of chalk, showing crushing by movement of Pleistocene ice, and in places thrusting over the boulder clay.

Blagrove Common

Permit only; 4.3ha; H and MTNC reserve
Rich damp meadow
Spring, early summer

Blagrove Common is recognised as one of the richest grasslands on the Hertfordshire chalky boulder clay, a moist mix of clays and chalk rubble spread by ice age meltwaters. Grazing has kept the meadow clear of scrub and ensured a wonderful range of plants. Spectacular avenues of early and southern marsh-orchid and common spotted-orchid line the damper areas which carry water from the springs above. The beauty of old pasture, unimproved by drainage or fertilizer, makes this a very special site indeed.

Brown, carnation, common, distant and remote sedge may be found with false fox-sedge, few-flowered spike-rush and bristle club-rush; ragged-Robin and cuckooflower, marsh-marigold, lesser spearwort and meadowsweet, devil's-bit scabious and lady's-mantle add to the rich variation. The meadow is a mosaic of wet and damp areas, a fragment of farmland to echo the centuries before man turned to modern farming methods.

Chemical fertilisers both encourage the grasses, so that they shade out smaller plants, and discourage plants adapted to the original circumstances. 'Weeds' may also be actively removed by herbicides and areas too wet for meadow grasses can be drained. When man improves his grasslands the insect life also suffers. In the absence of pesticides large skipper, found at Blagrove, might survive since its caterpillars feed on grasses, but species such as small copper would lose their food plants, the 'weeds': docks and sorrels.

Among the pasture and farmland birds recorded here are snipe, reed bunting, cuckoo and turtle dove.

Broad Colney Lakes

TL 175033; 11ha; H and MTNC reserve
River and flooded gravelpits
All year

Developing ash woodland, together with alder and willow around the pools, provides shelter and nest sites for small birds, while coot, moorhen, mallard, tufted duck and great crested grebe may be seen among the bulrush reedswamp, on the open pools or the river.

Cassiobury Park, set beside the River Gade.

Cassiobury Park

Permit only; 5.2ha; H and MTNC reserve
Wetland and wet woodland
Spring, summer

Lying beside the River Gade, the reserve, part of a larger park of the same name, contains many lagoons and watercourses, the remains of old water-cress beds. A splendid diversity of marsh-land vegetation is complemented by a rich animal life including many species of birds, insects and fish, over 30 species of river mollusc and a characteristic chalk-stream animal, the crayfish. Alder–willow woodland increases the variation.

Chorleywood Dell

Permit only; 2.5ha; H and MTNC reserve
Grassland and scrub
Spring, summer

The grassland, almost surrounded by scrub and trees, grows on chalk variously overlain by clay and gravel. The rich variety of plants includes cowslip, fairy flax, field scabious, pyramidal orchid, false oat-grass and quaking-grass.

Fordhams Wood

TL 337398; 10.9ha; H and MTNC reserve
Beech woodland
Spring, early summer

Woodland and scrubland birds alike are attracted to the reserve where beech is varied with ash, elm and sycamore or with a colourful scrub of lilac, birch and privet. The wood adjoins FOX COVERT.

Fox Covert

TL 337398; 1.5ha; H and MTNC reserve
Beech woodland
Spring, early summer

Mature beech trees stand over an essentially bare sweep of fallen leaves through which lift the elegant flower spikes of white helleborine.

Hertford Heath

TL 350106 and 354111; 25ha; H and MTNC reserve
Wet and dry heath, scrub and moorland
Spring, early summer

The heath has developed on pebble gravels above London clay with a woodland of oak, beech and hornbeam over holly, blackthorn, hawthorn and hazel, with birch and rowan over bracken. Heather, heath bedstraw, tormentil and sheep's sorrel characterise the open heathland areas where purple moor-grass spreads to marshy areas and pools with stands of bulrush. The attractive lousewort and petty whin occur.

Hexton Chalk Pit

TL 107299; 0.02ha; H and MTNC reserve
Tiny disused chalkpit
Spring, summer

The downland turf is filled with colourful plants including some five orchid species with yellow-wort and the introduced purple toadflax.

Oak and hornbeam woodland typifies sites such as Hopkyns Wood.

Hopkyns Wood

Permit only; 0.6ha; H and MTNC reserve
Old coppiced woodland
Spring, early summer

Part of a larger woodland, the reserve is oak, over hornbeam, with a spring ground cover of primrose and ramsons. Dormouse and roe deer have been recorded in the wood which contains a long-established badger sett.

Hunsdon Meads

Permit only; 27.5ha; H and MTNC–ENT reserve
Old-meadow grassland
Spring, early summer

An attractive area of marshy meadowland, Hunsdon Meads shows the special beauty of unimproved grassland when the brilliant yellow of marsh-marigold, in the wetter parts, is followed by a show of cowslip, green-winged orchid, adder's-tongue and yellow rattle.

Kings Langley Lake

Permit only; 5.2ha; H and MTNC reserve
Species-rich lowland lake
All year

Willow, alder and birch stand around the waters of the lake which hold several species of water-lily, together with breeding birds such as mallard, tufted duck and little grebe or winter pochard, teal and wigeon. Grey wagtail, kingfisher and snipe may be seen; some 60 birds and over 100 plants have been recorded.

Kingfisher: no other British bird can claim such vivid beauty.

Lemsford Springs

Permit only; 3.7ha; H and MTNC reserve
Derelict water-cress beds
Spring, summer

The hide overlooks a spread of small lagoons, butterbur marsh and wet willow woodland where breeding mallard and moorhen pick among water forget-me-not and monkeyflower. The lime-rich springs encourage an exceptional range of molluscs and the varied plant life, which includes the unusual star-of-Bethlehem, attracts a good variety of insects: the butterbur moth is known nowhere else in the county.

Marshalls Heath

TL 161149; 3.6ha; H and MTNC reserve
Acid heath
Spring, early summer

Before the heaths were ploughed for farmland, spreads of acid-loving plants were common in the county; now such areas are rare. Marshalls Heath contains not only the typical plant life of such heathlands but also a fine variety of insects.

Northaw Great Wood Country Park

TL 283038; 100ha; Welwyn and Hatfield DC
Mixed woodland
Spring, early summer

Although mainly clear-felled in the 1930s, the woodland is probably ancient. Beech tends to shade out the birch on the shallow gravels but

there is still a rich mix of oak and hornbeam, managed by coppicing and pollarding, which results in a fine range of habitat for birds. The wood is a noted site for nightingale.

Oughton Head

Permit only; 5.8ha; H and MTNC reserve
Alder–willow woodland
Spring, early summer

Mature alder–willow woodland is uncommon in Hertfordshire and offers additional interest in the complex described under OUGHTON HEAD COMMON.

Oughton Head Common

TL 172307; 16ha; HCC
Wetland and river
No access off rights of way
Spring, summer

The northern bank of Oughton Head is protected as OUGHTON HEAD reserve but a public footpath follows the southern side and runs between the river and the common. The whole forms a composite site which centres on the river.

The River Oughton seeps quietly out of the chalk, gently washing the muddy bottom of the channel in chalk-clean runnels which combine gradually to build a rivulet. Surprisingly quickly the young stream is a river, a smooth flow of crystal water which meanders between tall leaning trees beside the wetland of Oughton Head Common.

The river offers pure well-oxygenated water over chalk shingle where it flows fast and shallow, a habitat for stoneflies; where it slows enough for sediments to form, water plants can take root, to provide both food and shelter for many other animals. As it deepens, fish such as three-spined and ten-spined stickleback or bullhead can survive, to be prey for kingfisher, while further down rudd or brown and rainbow trout might be taken by heron or mink. The river bank is almost marsh-like in the upper reaches, grading upwards into a woodland of alder and willow. Trees and scrub line the banks downstream and stand above a spread of plants, suitable cover for water shrew and water vole.

The marsh is a varied area of willow scrub and pooled wetland, filled with greater pond-sedge and greater tussock-sedge, yellow iris and purple-loosestrife, hemp-agrimony and meadowsweet. This is a place for dragonflies and damselflies, for reed and sedge warbler, water rail and moorhen, and for predators such as sparrowhawk. The woodland contains a fine variety of trees and shrubs above a ground cover which includes such species as woodruff, and its birds are reinforced by winter groups of redpoll and siskin feeding in the alders. Muntjac deer may shelter in the scrub and woodland, where the variation of willow species is of considerable interest: six species – white, goat, grey, crack, bay and purple willow – have all been recorded.

Patmore Heath

TL 443257; 9.3ha; H and MTNC reserve
Acid grassland and scrub
Spring, early summer

A number of pools provide wetland interest in an area of grass heath which contains several plants uncommon in Hertfordshire, such as heath-grass, heath rush and marsh speedwell.

Pryors Wood

Permit only; 10.7ha; H and MTNC reserve
Mixed woodland
Spring, early summer

Summer warblers sing in an area of self-sown woodland where oak, birch and wild cherry attract typical species such as green, great spotted and lesser spotted woodpecker together with scrub or woodland-edge birds such as tree pipit.

Purwell Ninesprings

TL 206293; 7ha; H and MTNC reserve
Wetland and wet woodland
All year

Alder woodland, wet meadows, stands of reed sweet-grass and common reed provide an attractive habitat for reed bunting, reed and sedge warbler in summer, redpoll and siskin in winter and a variety of birds during the spring and autumn migration times.

Reed Chalk Pit

Permit only; 0.3ha; H and MTNC reserve
Geological site
All year

The deep pit shows not only the transition from middle to upper chalk but also evidence of disturbance by glaciation. The fossil record is unusually well demonstrated, including one brachiopod for which this is the type-locality.

Ridlins Mire

Permit only; 1ha; H and MTNC reserve
Small lime-rich marsh
Spring, early summer

Great horsetail and brown sedge spread across the marsh and are the main components of the lime-rich peats. Spring shows a spread of marsh-marigold and marsh valerian.

Royston Pit

Permit only; 0.6ha; H and MTNC reserve
Disused chalkpit
Spring, summer

Ash woodland is colonising the old chalkpit, which shows evidence of geological faulting. The ground cover includes plants such as butcher's-broom and yellow archangel.

Rye House Marsh

TL 386100; 7ha; RSPB reserve
Wetland
Leaflets from site or RSPB
All year

From the public hide the rich green of the reed sweet-grass marsh may appear busy with the small movements of birds while the high hedge of alder and willow is filled with the sound of warblers, a contrast with the harsh scream of a common tern overhead. The reedswamp is patterned with yellow iris, marsh thistle, comfrey, bulrush and stinging nettle, a deep fenlike vegetation, damp and sheltered to encourage the wealth of insects on which many of the birds rely for food. Although the reserve is set beside the busy River Lee, the noise of its surroundings seems to fade in the undisturbed sanctuary of the marsh.

The Lee is a migration route and the many pools and lagoons in the area draw down migrants to rest and feed while on passage. In spring and autumn many of these may be seen on the marsh: birds such as little ringed plover, redshank, common sandpiper, green sandpiper and yellow wagtail. Reed and sedge warbler breed, together with reed bunting, greenfinch and goldfinch, linnet and redpoll, with common tern nesting on rafts in one of the lagoons nearby. Winter brings large roosts of corn bunting, meadow pipit, yellowhammer and yet more reed buntings. The marsh is also a wintering site for kingfisher, water rail, snipe and jack snipe, for teal and, sometimes, water pipit, bittern and bearded tit.

The larger part of the reserve, to which access is by permit only, includes areas of more mixed marshland vegetation, with stands of common reed fringed by willow trees and scrub, varied with small lagoons and ditches. Hides overlook the large lagoons beside the reserve, the site of the tern rafts and a winter roost for black-headed gull, mallard, shoveler and tufted duck, or for passage birds such as garganey, pintail and great crested grebe.

Large numbers of swift, swallow, house martin and sand martin pass through on passage; in winter the marsh shelters blue tit and long-tailed tit, wren and starling, fieldfare and redwing. The whole reserve is a richly varied area which provides a vital sanctuary in a heavily used semi-urban setting.

Sawbridgeworth Marsh

Permit only; 12ha; H and MTNC–ENT reserve
Marsh and wet pasture
Spring, summer

Sawbridgeworth is a superb marshland in an open sunlit valley. It is a patchwork of reedbeds and sedgebeds, of drier and wetter areas filled with a wide range of plants. This is undoubtedly the finest marsh in the region.

A scatter of trees and shrubs breaks the open spread of the marsh where alder, elder, hawthorn,

Stanborough Reed Marsh: a small wetland with a good range of breeding birds.

Sawbridgeworth possesses one speciality unknown anywhere else in the country outside east Norfolk, a rare wetland snail usually found on the floating leaves of water plants: the slender amber snail.

Stanborough Reed Marsh

Permit only; 3ha; H and MTNC reserve
Reedmarsh and wet woodland
Spring, early summer

An excellent range of wetland plants includes common meadow-rue and needle spike-rush, while the reedmarsh and wet woodland attracts a wide variety of birds, including reed and sedge warbler with wintering bearded tit, known to have bred at least once.

Therfield Heath

TL 348406; 169ha; HCC
Chalk downland
Spring, summer

Outside the close-cut grassland of the golf course, a wide variety of downland plants gives colour to the steep chalk slopes and attracts the colourful butterflies of the Heath. The land slopes smoothly northwards, curved into deep hollows; beyond FOX COVERT, a narrow shoulder provides a south-facing bank.

In spring the Heath is lit with cowslip but a far more striking plant must take pride of place: this is one of the few remaining national sites for pasqueflower, a deep-violet crocus-like flower with a silky outside and vivid yellow stamens. In summer the slopes are bright with common milkwort, clustered bellflower, wild mignonette and common rock-rose; salad burnet and wild thyme grow with horseshoe vetch, purple milk-vetch and dropwort. Wild candytuft, a southern rather local species, may be found among the grasses, together with bastard-toadflax and the rare spotted cat's-ear, while lesser meadow-rue, field fleawort and bee and fragrant orchid occur on the Heath.

The birds include the expected downland species, skylark and meadow pipit, with corn bunting and, where scrub and woodland fringe the reserve, with wood and grasshopper warbler. Kestrel hunt across the slopes and in winter short-eared owl has been recorded, together with golden plover and brambling. Brown hare and rabbit graze the downland and common lizard may be seen, but the main animal interest must be the butterflies.

Brown Argus, common, chalkhill and holly blue, and dingy, Essex, large and small skipper are among the butterflies of Therfield, a fascinating range linked to the plant life. The skippers generally rely upon the grasses, the Argus on common rock-rose, chalkhill blue on horseshoe vetch, holly blue in a complex brood-pattern on ivy and holly, while the common blue uses a range of clovers, trefoils and vetches.

guelder-rose, birch and several willow species provide singing posts for warblers and mark the curving line of the river or old boundaries within the marsh itself. Stretching between them, stands of common reed give way to banks of reed sweet-grass, to sedgebeds or to tall ranks of great willowherb. The drier sedge beds are mown or grazed and are filled with yellow rattle and meadowsweet, while damper parts are bright with yellow iris, ragged-Robin, hemp-agrimony, common valerian, water mint, comfrey and the tall spears of bulrush. In spring marsh-marigold catches the eye while summer shows southern marsh-orchid, purple-loosestrife and water forget-me-not, fen bedstraw and common marsh-bedstraw, to contrast with whorl-grass, lesser pond-sedge and carnation, common and brown sedge. Other plants of note include marsh valerian and marsh arrowgrass with blunt-flowered rush, rare outside eastern England.

The marsh is particularly rich in insects, such as dragonflies and damselflies, butterflies including common and holly blue, orange-tip and small copper, and the midges and mosquitoes which attract insectivorous birds. Breeding birds include reed bunting, reed and grasshopper warbler, grey wagtail and snipe. Winter brings flocks of small birds to feed on the seed heads, fieldfare and redwing to the shrubs, redpoll and siskin to the alder and birch and birds such as water rail and jack snipe to the deep shelter of the marsh itself.

Tring Reservoirs

SP 919141; 19ha; NCC reserve
Banks and woodland around four reservoirs
No access off footpaths
Nature trail leaflets and hide permits from NCC
All year

The nineteenth-century navvies who dug the reservoirs at Tring, who changed the marshy lime-rich meadows to a group of man-made lakes, can hardly have realised that they were building a nature reserve – the spread of water is now so rich in wildlife that it was scheduled in 1955. Open water is rare in the porous chalklands and these stream-fed reservoirs form an important wetland site. The reservoirs are marl lakes, waters which only form on chalk or limestone, particularly rich in nutrients and supporting an abundance of water plants, fish and insects to provide a plentiful food supply for waterbirds while the fringing vegetation gives nesting cover.

Among the submerged plants are spreads of rigid hornwort, spiked water-milfoil and Canadian waterweed which provide habitats for many different animals. Dragonfly and damselfly larvae hunt here; water beetles, such as lesser water boatman, scud about – out of 33 British species over one-third are recorded here; water snails graze the algae and may be prey themselves to some of the leeches; 13 British leeches are recognised, 7 of which have been noted here at Tring.

Tring Reservoirs: a man-made habitat of great wildlife importance.

On the muddy margins which show when the water draws down, only adapted plants survive, including the uncommon species orange foxtail, round-fruited rush and mudwort. Above these is a varied fringe of plants, from deep beds of common reed, reed sweet-grass and bulrush to marsh-like spreads of gipsywort, meadowsweet, water mint, yellow iris and skullcap or orange balsam. Trees and scrub form a shelter behind the fringe of vegetation which in early summer may show both early and southern marsh-orchid.

The reservoirs were built to feed water to the Grand Union Canal, the waterway linking Birmingham with London. Near Tring, the canal runs over a high point so that traffic moving through the locks draws water away from the summit; the reservoirs make up this loss. The canal carries large numbers of pleasure-boats which have a profound effect upon the waters of the reserve. In spring the reservoirs are full, with little call on the water; by summer the canal is busy and levels fall; autumn sees maximum drawdown, before the winter rains refill the reservoirs and the cycle begins again.

The importance of this is that it matches the pattern of bird life: by the time the nestling waterbirds leave the shelter of the margins the shallows offer a rich supply of food, by the time the autumn waders arrive the mudflats are exposed, and by the time the winter wildfowl fly in for food and shelter the maximum spread of water is available for their roost. Mutually beneficial to canal user and naturalist, this ebb and flow, together with the lack of large waters nearby, must have much to do with the rich and varied bird life of the reserve.

In spring the resident birds begin their courtship, although the fascinating display of the great crested grebe may be seen here as early as midwinter. Little grebe will call and coot and moorhen will be busy building nests. At Tring there are insufficient nest sites in the woodland for heron and the heronry has been sited at water level in the reedbeds. Mute swan, feral Canada goose, mallard, pochard, shoveler and tufted duck all begin to prepare for nesting, joined by the summer visitors who have made this their breeding ground. Birds such as reed and sedge warbler and spotted flycatcher come from Africa to nest, joining the resident corn bunting, reed bunting and pied wagtail, while a host of other travellers pass through to their breeding grounds. Moorland birds such as wheatear and grassland pipits, wetland birds such as grey and yellow wagtail, passage waders and wildfowl may visit the area in spring. Little ringed plover chose this for its first ever nest site in Britain; occasionally the water is low enough to expose suitable shingle again but generally the birds move on, together with ringed plover, turnstone, sanderling and bar-tailed and black-tailed godwit. Scaup and shelduck may well pass through and, perhaps, osprey and merlin.

Summer is the quietest time, when the resident birds are feeding their young, when the sky may be filled with house martins, swallows and swifts hawking for insects. At dusk the hunt is taken over by pipistrelle and noctule bats or by the more uncommon Brandt's bat, which was trapped at Wilstone in 1975, the first record for Hertfordshire. As the summer draws into autumn the passage birds return. Migratory birds often choose one route by which to fly to their breeding grounds and another to return. Arctic, common and black tern are regular spring migrants but autumn rarely brings as many southwards. Conversely, ruff are rare in spring but regularly pause in autumn when knot, wood sandpiper and little stint may be seen. Autumn brings large numbers of migrant swallows, martins and swifts, sometimes hounded by the fast-flying hobby. Redshank, greenshank, green and common sandpiper may fly in to the spreads of mud laid bare by the falling waters, but soon the days begin to chill and the first birds of winter arrive.

Large flocks of wintering duck may gather, made up of both resident species and new arrivals. Mallard, pochard, shoveler, teal, tufted duck and wigeon with goldeneye and pintail ride the waves of the winter wind and Bewick's swan flies in from northern Russia. Thousands of gulls, black-headed, herring and common, forage the winter countryside and return to roost. Lapwing, snipe and jack snipe probe the shallow water's edge or crouch against the wind in the marshy meadows while the reedbeds may shelter pied and grey wagtail, bearded tit and bittern.

The trees and scrub also attract birds; siskin and redpoll may often be seen in the alders, woodcock and brambling may be present. Redwing and fieldfare cluster on the fields and hedgerows, great grey shrike may be recorded, stonechat and twite may be uncommon visitors and, rarely, cirl or snow bunting may be seen.

One of the special features of Tring Reservoirs is that the nature reserve accommodates interests as diverse as fishing, birdwatching and strolling, as well as controlling the water, yet offers the wildlife a place of sanctuary. Public hides have been sited overlooking Tringford and Wilstone Reservoirs and the paths allow good views of the other waters here. The nature trail involves a walk of some 3km. Tring Reservoirs may be a man-made habitat but it is one of exceptional wildlife value.

Wormley Wood

TL 317062; 136ha; WdT
Mixed woodland
Access may also be gained from car park at
TL 327062
Spring, early summer

The wood is a superb spread of mainly sessile oak standards over hornbeam coppice. Other trees include ash, birch and pedunculate oak, with wild service-tree and areas of high-forest oak and hornbeam. The ground flora varies from acid wood anemone, bluebell and honeysuckle to a richer mix including yellow archangel and woodruff. Most is ancient, primary woodland, but blocks of birchwood, blackthorn and hawthorn scrub mark the sites of fields.

Great crested grebe, one of the most spectacular of British-breeding waterbirds.

Kent

Known as the Garden of England because of the extensive orchards which thrive on the favourable southerly climate and rich soils, the county is famous for beautiful countryside, from the rolling hills of the North Downs and the white cliffs of Dover to the broad, flat, reed-fringed pasture of north Kent. The characteristic wildlife habitats of Kent, notably the old deciduous woodland of the Weald, the chalk grasslands of the North Downs, and the marshlands of north Kent and Romney Marsh, relate to the geology of the county, which changes to the north east following the contours of the High Weald sands, the Low Weald clays, the greensands, the chalk and finally, on the eastern edge of the county, the tertiary beds of gravel and sands, laid down over the soft white upper chalk. It is this change of bedrock that accounts for much of the diversity of land use, habitat and wildlife found in Kent.

The county is still extensively wooded. Stands of the ancient oakwood remain, but commercial chestnut coppice and plantation forest account for most of Kent's woodlands. However, many areas of semi-natural woodland are still found, from the steep-sided, spring-fed valleys or ghylls of the High Weald, clothed with oak and ash, crab apple and wild cherry, bluebell and bracken, to the beech hangers on the summits and slopes of the Downs.

The main agricultural activities are fruit growing, arable farming, dairy cattle and sheep. Hedgerows still fragment the agricultural landscape. On the flat clay vale of the Low Weald sheep and cattle feed in the wet meadows edged by broad and blooming hedges of blackthorn and hawthorn, wild service-tree, elm, ash and hazel, while in the fruit-growing belts along the Medway Estuary and in central Kent tall shelter hedges of alder and poplar stand upright between orchards of bowed apple and cherry. Where the pasture has escaped the ravages of herbicides and chemical fertilisers, such as on the steep scarp faces of the Downs, and in pockets on the clay vale, traces of the agricultural past can be found. Remnants of downland rich in yellow vetches, sweet-scented herbs and orchids are reminders of intensive sheep farming, and the network of narrow roads linking the small Kentish towns and villages reflects former agricultural wealth. Old hay meadows, not used for silage or turned over to barley but still cut annually and fertilised lightly with manure, support many plants. Grass species such as barley and oat-grass, oxeye daisy, buttercup, ragged-Robin and cowslip, and more often than not the heady-scented pepper-saxifrage and the curious adder's-tongue, are all vulnerable to drainage and the plough and remain only in these meadows.

The coastline is as varied as the rest of Kent. The sharp chalk cliffs of Dover and Deal are constantly eroding but support a diversity of plants, some, such as the early spider-orchid, seeking lime-rich pastures, others, for instance rock samphire, the constantly changing cliff faces, and still others, such as sea-kale, the shingle beaches. The Stour Estuary around SANDWICH is a mosaic of pasture, saltmarsh and sand dunes, but the adjacent cliffs of Thanet indicate the presence of chalk, reflected in the flora. The coast at Romney Marsh in the south is remarkable for its history of reclamation as well as its special flora and fauna. Both marsh-mallow and marsh frog are common, and the Marsh's ornithological importance relies on the intricate field and dyke system which still remains in some areas. The marshes and estuaries provide wintering grounds for birds such as bar-tailed godwit, hen harrier and Brent goose, and breeding sites for shelduck, redshank and garganey; few other areas are so rich in both numbers and species.

Kent's natural history relates closely to its proximity to continental Europe. The southerly winds carry over unusual insects: painted lady and red admiral butterflies often arrive in this way, and many of the recordings of unusual moths made in central Kent can be attributed to this migration. Bird migrants travelling across continental Europe seek the nearest land mass and so direct themselves towards Sandwich and DUNGENESS. Bird observatories have been established at both places to monitor their movements, and both areas are now protected by official status and the establishment of nature reserves.

Plants, though less mobile, still reflect the continental influence. The abundant roadside weed hoary cress is sometimes known as Thanet weed because it first became established there after being brought over in straw from Europe. Other species are on the most northerly limit of their range, and subject to the wild fluctuations in population size caused by small climatic changes which are characteristic of species at the edge of their distribution. Orchids are the most striking example. At least five species are more abundant in Kent than anywhere else in Britain. At least twice as many more are commonly found here. Orchids of woodland and pasture occur, but the best representatives are those of the chalk downland. Common spotted-orchid, man, pyramidal, fragrant, bee and fly orchid are all frequently found on the Downs.

Kent also provides the only remnants of habitat suitable for many other plant and animal species. FOLKESTONE WARREN and ORLESTONE FOREST support unique assemblages of plants and insects; BLEAN WOODS contain one of the last British breeding colonies of heath fritillary, and sub-angled wave and lesser bell moths are restricted to Orlestone Forest. Other species in decline in Britain still remain common here; wild service-tree is found frequently in hedgerow, woodland and coppice; dormouse and harvest mouse are still often recorded in Kent; and nightingale, although found throughout southern Britain, is most abundant in east Kent.

Kent is under severe pressure from urban development and population expansion, from intensification of agriculture, and from the expansion of communications with Europe, especially the development of motorways. All these influences threaten wildlife, but conservation bodies throughout the county continue to protect its variety and uniqueness.

P. EVANS

Bedgebury Pinetum

TQ 715338; 40ha; FC
National pinetum established by FC and Royal Botanic Gardens, Kew
Booklet at site or from FC
All year

Over 200 tree species with a further 200 varieties of conifers are ranged within an area which includes two streams and a lake.

Blean Woods

TR 118611; 66.5ha; NCC reserve
Coppiced woodland
Permit only off paths and rights of way
Leaflet from NCC
Spring, early summer

Oak standards over coppiced ash, beech, sweet chestnut and hornbeam spread across the London clay with small areas of acid heath where gravels overlie it. A good range of woodland wildlife is present and the area is important as a beach-head from which continental species may spread into Britain.

Bough Beech Reservoir

TQ 495494; 18ha; KTNC reserve
North lake and part of reservoir
Booklet from information centre
All year

The information centre illustrates the importance of the reserve both as a breeding and wintering site for birds and as a staging post for migrants. Garganey, common scoter and osprey are occasionally recorded on passage, together with a good range of waders.

Brenchley Wood

TQ 648418; 2.8ha; KTNC reserve
High Weald woodland
Spring, early summer

In contrast to the clay and chalk of much of Kent, the High Weald is acid sandstone, reflected here by the intrusion of birch into the oak–beech woodland and by boggy areas with *Sphagnum* mosses.

Bough Beech Reservoir provides a site for waterbirds among farmland and woods.

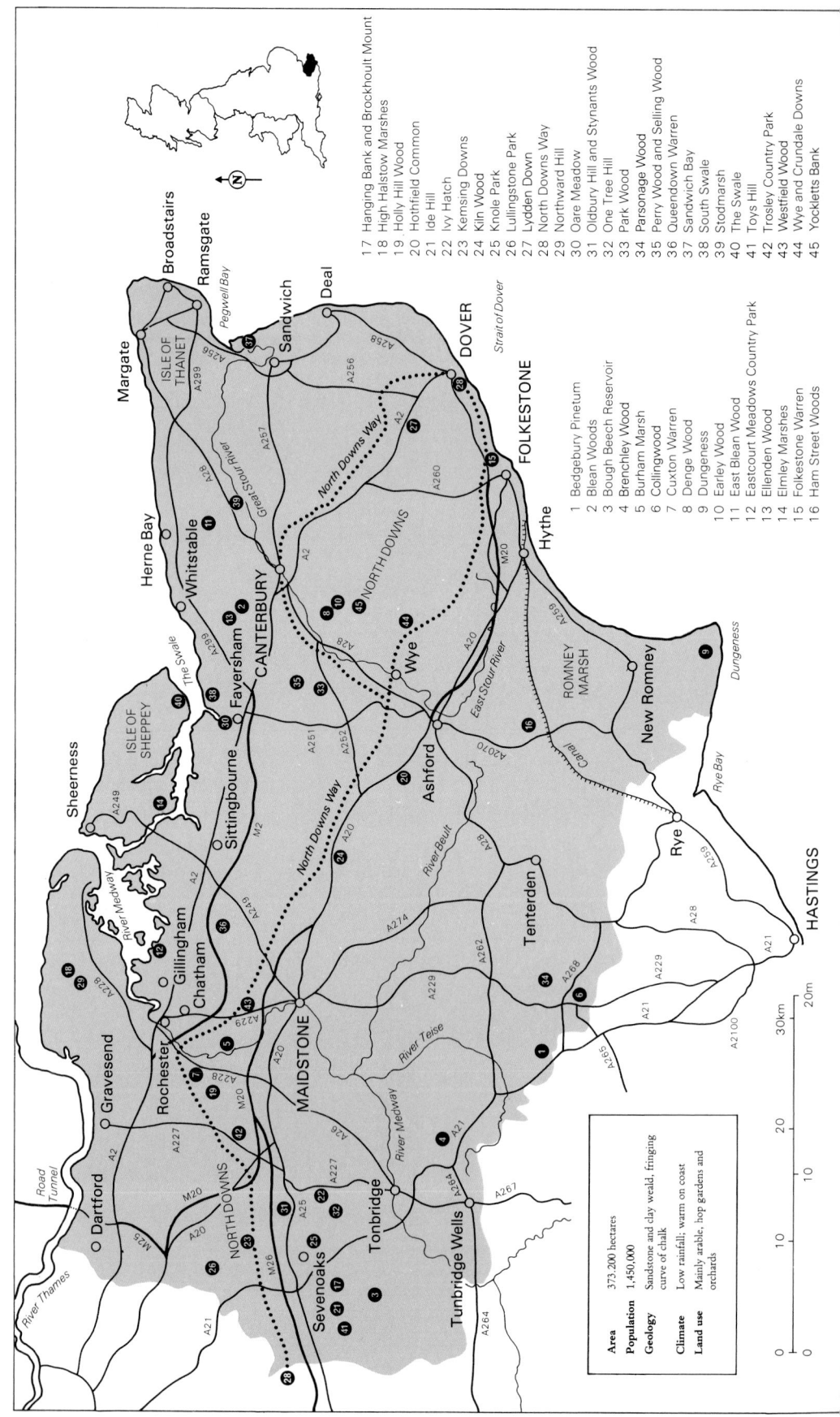

17 Hanging Bank and Brockhoult Mount
18 High Halstow Marshes
19 Holly Hill Wood
20 Hothfield Common
21 Ide Hill
22 Ivy Hatch
23 Kemsing Downs
24 Kiln Wood
25 Knole Park
26 Lullingstone Park
27 Lydden Down
28 North Downs Way
29 Northward Hill
30 Oare Meadow
31 Oldbury Hill and Stynants Wood
32 One Tree Hill
33 Park Wood
34 Parsonage Wood
35 Perry Wood and Selling Wood
36 Queendown Warren
37 Sandwich Bay
38 South Swale
39 Stodmarsh
40 The Swale
41 Toys Hill
42 Trosley Country Park
43 Westfield Wood
44 Wye and Crundale Downs
45 Yockletts Bank

1 Bedgebury Pinetum
2 Blean Woods
3 Bough Beech Reservoir
4 Brenchley Wood
5 Burham Marsh
6 Collingwood
7 Cuxton Warren
8 Denge Wood
9 Dungeness
10 Earley Wood
11 East Blean Wood
12 Eastcourt Meadows Country Park
13 Ellenden Wood
14 Elmley Marshes
15 Folkestone Warren
16 Ham Street Woods

Area	373,200 hectares
Population	1,450,000
Geology	Sandstone and clay weald, fringing curve of chalk
Climate	Low rainfall; warm on coast
Land use	Mainly arable, hop gardens and orchards

Burham Down

Permit only; 85.2ha; KTNC reserve
Woodland, scrub and chalk grassland
Spring, summer

The reserve contains the characteristic plants, wild thyme, trefoils and vetches, which attract a good range of butterflies. The scrub and woodland provide nest sites for small birds while the cliffs of disused chalkpits are breeding sites for kestrel.

Burham Marsh

TQ 714624; 40ha; KTNC reserve
River bank, marsh and reedbeds
No access off public footpath
All year

The vegetation is interesting, particularly for the rare marsh sow-thistle, but the reedbeds and river probably provide the greatest general interest, for wetland birds and resting migrants.

Burnt Oak Wood

Permit only; 28ha; KTNC reserve
Damp oak woodland
Spring, early summer

The wood is chiefly oak standards over hazel and hornbeam coppice on heavy clay. There is little ground cover, due to the dense canopy, but pathway edges and open glades are attractive to woodland butterflies such as white admiral.

Chiddingstone

Permit only; 6.8ha; KTNC reserve
Woodland, marsh and pools
Spring, early summer

A series of old brickpits provides a range from open water through bulrush reedswamp to dry ground and woodland, containing wild service-tree and oak with an area of conifers. Wood sandpiper has been recorded on passage while breeding species include kestrel and tawny owl.

Collingwood

TQ 761292; 2.4ha; KTNC reserve
Woodland and lake
Spring, early summer

The wood contains a variety of planted exotics, together with native trees, and the lake is bright with water-lilies, fringed by bulrush. Spotted flycatcher and several tit species breed and the lake may be visited by kingfisher.

Denge Wood

TR 108525; 25.6ha; WdT
Coppiced woodland, scrub and grassland
Spring, early summer

The woodland, composed of hornbeam and sweet chestnut coppice, includes an area of chalk scrub and grassland together with old earth banks topped with hornbeam pollards. Active coppicing encourages a rich variety of wildlife.

Denton Bank

Permit only; 3.6ha; KTNC reserve
Steep chalk grassland
Spring, early summer

A show of cowslip and early-purple orchid in the spring is followed by characteristic chalkland species.

Dungeness

TR 063196; 480ha; RSPB reserve
Extraordinary shingle expanse with scrub and lagoons
Leaflet from information centre or RSPB
All year

Dungeness, often described as the largest shingle ridge in Britain, perhaps in Europe, is a desert plain of shingle, a great expanse of rounded stones combed into lines and curves by a giant hand. It looks inhospitable and yet it is a special, magical place, the best in Britain for sea-kale, fine-leaved sheep's-fescue and dwarf broom, a site for the uncommon Nottingham catchfly and stinking hawksbeard. It is a place for scrub and stony grassland, for sweeps of open shingle, for natural and man-made pools, for huge skies and sea breezes, above all for migrant insects and for birds. Spring and autumn bring the passage migrants: black tern, wryneck, bluethroat and hosts of other birds. In autumn the numbers are higher, and the reserve is noted for whitethroat, lesser whitethroat and firecrest.

Dungeness: an oasis of shingle wilderness visited by many spring and autumn migrants.

Some 40 to 45 species usually breed on the reserve, although some 60 in all have been recorded, with the shingle and shingle islands in the lagoons providing sites for black-headed, common and herring gull, for common and little tern. Hides have been built overlooking some of the pools and a trail laid out from which the range of habitat can be observed. Gorse, blackthorn, elder and bramble scrub provides nest sites for many birds, including magpie and carrion crow in the absence of taller trees, while the wetland areas contain breeding shelduck and little grebe, occasionally shoveler and water rail. Throughout the summer the croaking of marsh frogs can be heard. Eight of these European animals were brought to Romney Marsh in 1935; since then they have spread up waterways to colonise Dungeness. Newts also live in the pools and grass snake and common lizard may often be seen.

In winter the lagoons hold sheltering flocks of wildfowl including mallard, pintail, pochard, teal, tufted duck and wigeon with occasional gadwall, goosander and smew. Hen harrier, merlin and short-eared owl may hunt the area for smaller birds such as shore lark and snow bunting.

Migrant butterflies such as painted lady, clouded yellow and the rarer pale clouded yellow add seasonal interest to the resident species, which include Essex skipper, while moths include brown-tail. Among rarer moths are toadflax brocade, pigmy footman and Sussex emerald.

Earley Wood

TR 120505; 15.2ha; WdT
Coppiced woodland
Spring, early summer

Coppiced hazel, hornbeam and sweet chestnut encourage a wide range of plants to follow spring bluebell. An avenue of fine old beech runs through the wood which harbours a large badger sett.

East Blean Wood

TR 182647; 11.6ha; KTNC reserve
Old coppiced woodland
No access off rights of way
Spring, early summer

Oak and ash standards, over a variety of coppice species including hornbeam and field maple, stand above a ground cover rich in spring with wood anemone, bluebell, lesser celandine and lesser periwinkle. Typical woodland birds are present.

Eastcourt Meadows Country Park

TQ 805684; 24ha; Gillingham BC
Estuary-side grassland, scrub and trees
All year

The country park lies on the southern edge of the Medway Estuary and provides a site from which the various marshes, islands and creeks may be overlooked.

Ellenden Wood

TR 103622; 68ha; KTNC reserve
Coppiced woodland
No access off rights of way
Spring, early summer

Oak and hornbeam are the main tree species with occasional wild service-tree, although many of the finest examples of the latter have been felled. Breeding birds in the woodland include all three native woodpeckers and there is an interesting range of insects.

Elmley Marshes

TQ 926704; 1360ha; RSPB reserve
Grazing marsh, lagoons, saltmarsh and mudflats
All year

Gadwall, mallard, pochard, shelduck, shoveler and tufted duck are among the breeding species of Elmley, together with lapwing, ringed plover, oystercatcher and redshank. All are present in some numbers throughout the year but another important nesting species, yellow wagtail, flies south to winter in West Africa. In summer the breeding birds provide the greatest interest here, with perhaps an occasional marauding marsh harrier, and it is then that the plant life of the reserve is at its best.

The wide grasslands, generally dry now, are scattered with daisies, buttercups, clovers and thistles, whose autumn heads will provide food for later small migrant birds. The shallow margins of the ditches and lagoons are fringed with sea club-rush while deeper areas have stands of common reed and lesser bulrush, waving above water-crowfoot species. The saltmarsh areas are filled with sea aster, sea lavender and thrift contrasting with the grey-green sea-purslane, with the fleshy spikes of glasswort and, in one site, the yellow heads of golden samphire.

As the colours fade in autumn the migrant birds begin to arrive, moving away to warmer places or driven down from the colder north. Curlew, redshank and greenshank, golden plover and lapwing, black-tailed godwit, spotted redshank, ruff and snipe, common, green and wood sandpiper – there is a continual movement into and out of the reserve. Smaller birds such as linnet, greenfinch and reed bunting move in flocks across the area, at peril from hunting short-eared owl, hen and marsh harrier or other predators.

By midwinter the resident species have been increased in numbers and others flock in to rest and feed, either on the flooded marshes or the mudflats of the Swale. White-fronted and Brent geese winter with red-breasted merganser and pintail, with dunlin, knot, turnstone and grey plover; bitter weather may bring in a host of other birds to add to the variety. In spring the flow of migrants reverses direction, the wintering birds disperse and the annual round of breeding and rearing young begins again.

Folkestone Warren

TR 242373; 140ha; Shepway DC reserve
Chalk cliffs, chalk grassland and scrub
Spring, summer

One of the best southern sites for migrant butterflies and moths, the Warren also contains areas of chalk grassland, landslips and open cliffs, with plants including sea-heath, rock sea-lavender and privet.

Ham Fen

Permit only; 6ha; KTNC reserve
Relict fenland
Spring, summer

A fine show of marsh fern, with areas of sedge, distinguishes the marsh while birch and alder, ash and grey willow woodland attracts many species of birds. Little grebe, mallard, teal and occasional kingfisher may be seen at the central stream.

Ham Street Woods

TR 004337; 97ha; NCC reserve
Coppice-with-standards woodland
No access off paths and rights of way
Leaflet from NCC Regional Office, Church Street, Wye
Spring, early summer

The woods are chiefly oak over hornbeam, hazel and sweet chestnut, though many other species may be found, over a fine spring display of woodland plants. Birds include hawfinch, nightingale and nuthatch while the varied nature of the woods makes the reserve a site for many moths and butterflies.

Water-crowfoot flowering in a drainage ditch at Elmley Marshes.

Hanging Bank and Brockhoult Mount

TQ 497518; 38.8ha; NT
Mixed woodland
Spring, early summer

The mixed woodland, clothing the crest of a hill, is attractive both for its wildlife interest and for its splendid views across BOUGH BEECH RESERVOIR and the Weald.

Hawkenbury Bog

Permit only; 0.4ha; KTNC reserve
Small acid wetland
Spring, summer

A spring-fed mire filled with soft rush and purple moor-grass, the reserve contains *Sphagnum* mosses with plants such as round-leaved sundew, unusual in Kent.

High Halstow Marshes

TQ 799763; 52ha; NCC reserve
Saltings and mudflats
No access off right of way
Winter

The spread of reclaimed saltings and saltmarsh is a breeding site for gadwall, garganey, mallard, pochard, pintail, shelduck, shoveler and teal; winter wildfowl may include white-fronted geese with waders including curlew, grey and golden plover, dunlin, knot and redshank. Heron from adjoining NORTHWARD HILL may frequently be seen feeding or flying across the marshes.

Holly Hill Wood

TQ 667627; 12.8ha; Tonbridge and Malling BC
Mixed woodland
Spring, summer

The woodland, at one of the highest points in Kent, has extensive views across the Downs to the Medway Valley.

Hothfield Common

TQ 969459; 56ha; KTNC–Ashford BC reserve
Heathland and bog system
Nature trail leaflet from KTNC
Spring, early summer

Heathland and bog are uncommon in Kent but the reserve is an excellent example of these habitats, safeguarded by careful management.

Acid sands are spread across a layer of impermeable rock to give a pattern of raised ground separated by narrow bogs. The higher ground is wooded, with ancient beech, oak, planted Scots pine and sweet chestnut, while much of the drier lower areas are covered with bracken and birch. Areas of the original cover, heather grading into purple moor-grass, can still be seen but, without control, the birch and bracken will spread.

The drier areas slope down into the bogs where cross-leaved heath joins the heather and purple moor-grass fringes the wetter parts. Here is the typical bog development, a spread of *Sphagnum* mosses decorated with tiny plants such as heath milkwort, yellow tormentil and bog asphodel. Common cottongrass in the wettest places and hare's-tail cottongrass in drier parts show white-plumed heads while all around are heath spotted-orchid and bog pimpernel. Here also is round-leaved sundew, quite rare in Kent. The bogs are highly vulnerable to trampling and must on no account be walked upon, but an excellent cause-way has been built across the largest and from it all these species may be seen.

Below the mires is a more marshy area with clumps of tussock-sedge, spreads of marsh pennywort, stands of rushes, marsh bedstraw and greater bird's-foot-trefoil, water mint, yellow iris, ragged-Robin and devil's-bit scabious. The marsh grades into an area of willow and alder swamp.

The range of habitat encourages a variety of birds, with 35 species recorded as breeding. The high-forest woodland of the ridge tops is suitable for nuthatch, treecreeper and green woodpecker while the open scrub and wetland areas attract reed bunting, tree pipit, yellowhammer and a variety of warblers. Common lizard, grass-snake and adder occur and the insects include dragonflies and damselflies, together with several sand wasps and the day-flying orange underwing moth.

Hunstead Wood

Permit only; 4.8ha; KTNC reserve
Dry and wet woodland
Spring, early summer

Steep sloping beech woodland falls to a stream and pond, thick with alder and birch, sharp-flowered rush and *Sphagnum* mosses. Solomon's-seal is one of the attractive plants of the dry woodland while birds include breeding nightingale and occasional woodcock.

Rare wart-biter cricket occurs on Lydden Down.

Ide Hill

TQ 487517; 12.8ha; NT
Mixed woodland
Spring, early summer

A stand of mature trees, a mix of oak, sweet chestnut and conifers, the woodland lies on a ridge of greensand overlooking the Weald.

Ivy Hatch

TQ 588548; 0.8ha; KTNC reserve
Wet woodland
Spring, early summer

Grey willow and alder grow in the main wet part of the wood while drier areas have hazel, ash and oak. American skunk-cabbage has spread within the reserve, most of which was formerly a nut orchard.

Kemsing Downs

TQ 550594; 14.4ha; KTNC reserve
Woodland and chalk grassland
Spring, summer

Chalkland scrub and a disused chalkpit add to the variety of the reserve which includes lime-loving oak, birch, ash and yew woodland, containing characteristic species such as spurge-laurel, and a fine area of chalk downland. Butterflies include brown Argus, chalkhill blue, Essex, dingy and grizzled skipper.

Kiln Wood

TQ 888515; 6ha; KTNC reserve
Coppiced and old-coppice woodland
Spring, early summer

Kiln Wood lies on gault clay, a rather level very wet wood, actively coppiced to encourage a fine array of woodland plants. The recently cut area provides a scrublike habitat with bushy clumps of foliage lifting from the coppice stools. Among the new growth are spreads of damp-loving and woodland plants: bugle, rushes and sedges, including pendulous sedge, stands of rosebay and great willowherb and clusters of square-stalked St John's-wort. Willow, ash and hazel are the main coppice species here and the presence of antiquated farm machinery, together with meadow plants such as cuckooflower, suggest a secondary wood grown up on once-cleared farmland.

The older part of the wood, less recently coppiced, is mainly oak, ash and hornbeam with occasional field maple and birch over an under-storey of hawthorn, hazel and elder. The drier parts have a splendid show of springtime bluebell with wood anemone and primrose. A characteristic plant of the damper clays is yellow archangel. Wild rose tangles and climbs around clearings and path edges, where openings in the canopy let in the light, and guelder-rose adds its colour to the woods. Early-purple orchid, common twayblade and common spotted-orchid are present, with herb-Paris.

The old Pilgrims' Way followed the curve of the North Downs above the Weald.

Buckler-fern species grow thick in the valley where a small stream runs, together with the delicate lady-fern, while further wetland interest is added by a small pond which lies across the boundary of the reserve. The pond is fringed with marshlike vegetation such as gipsy-wort but its chief interest is a fine colony of water-violet.

Birds include species of woodland and scrub: nuthatch and treecreeper, warblers and nightingale. Kingfisher may visit the sheltered pool.

Knole Park

TQ 532543; 400ha; NT
Extensive deer park
Access on foot only
Spring, summer

The old parkland still holds deer, and the park trees and woodland attract a range of birds and insects.

Lullingstone Park

TQ 515636; 120ha; Sevenoaks DC
Parkland and woodland
Spring, early summer

Areas of woodland and stretches of parkland afford a good range of wildlife habitat.

Lydden Down

TR 278453; 21.2ha; KTNC reserve
Superb chalk grassland
Spring, summer

Too steep for ploughing, the long slopes of downland have probably stood unchanged since man first cleared them to graze his flocks of sheep. This is fine chalk grassland, the pride of Kent, where typical lime-loving plants such as yellow-wort and salad burnet grow with the less common chalk milkwort and dropwort. Common rock-rose grows here with wild thyme, cowslip, dyer's greenweed, common bird's-foot-trefoil and horseshoe vetch. Wild mignonette is found in the deeper grassland while the shorter swards are flecked with tiny eyebrights, common centaury and small violets.

One of the specialities of Kentish downland is its magnificence of orchids. Fragrant orchid and autumn lady's-tresses both occur, standing among the commoner plants with the strange elegance of their kind.

Gorse scrub with occasional hawthorn and dogwood tops the downland and, with a narrow belt of hawthorn on the deeper soils below, provides shelter and nest sites for birds. The grassland flowers are attractive to butterflies including marbled white and common and chalkhill blue. Among the other insects are two of particular note: the reserve contains populations not only of great green bush cricket but also of wart-biter cricket.

North Downs Way

TQ 428557–TR 319412; 123km or 139km; CC
Long-distance way
Leaflet from CC or booklet from HMSO bookshops
Spring, summer

Based on the old Pilgrims' Way from Winchester to Canterbury, the way follows the line of the Kentish Downs and winds through Rochester and Canterbury to Dover. An alternative route from Boughton Lees takes the walker south to Folkestone and along the sea coast of the white cliffs to Dover.

Northward Hill

TQ 784761; 54ha; RSPB reserve
Oak woodland and scrub
Spring, early summer

The reserve is chiefly important for its heronry, the largest in Britain and possibly western Europe, but also contains breeding nightingale, hawfinch and long-eared owl. A high-level observation platform affords an opportunity to overlook the treetops and the fields below which stretch to the estuary of the Thames.

Oare Meadow

TR 007627; 2.8ha; KTNC reserve
Small grazing meadow
Spring, early summer

A small tidal stream adds to the interest of the rather acid grassland while wet flushes, fed by springs, provide a habitat for freshwater plants such as brooklime. Trees and scrub attract a variety of birds.

Oldbury Hill and Styants Wood

TQ 578559; 60.7ha; NT
Mixed woodland
Spring, early summer

An Iron Age hill fort adds archaeological interest to this large area of varied woodland.

One Tree Hill

TQ 560532; 13.6ha; NT
Mixed woodland
Spring, early summer

Broad-leaved woodland crowns the spine of a hill with wide views across the farmland, hedges and woods of the Kentish Weald.

Orlestone Forest

Permit only; 11.2ha; KTNC reserve
Oak–hornbeam woodland
Spring, early summer

An area of old coppiced woodland now being allowed to grow on to high forest, the reserve, like many of the east Kent woodlands, is a notable site for butterflies which may include white admiral and purple emperor and moths such as the unusual lesser belle and Clifden nonpareil.

Park Gate Down

Permit only; 8ha; KTNC reserve
Woodland, scrub and unimproved chalk grassland
Spring, summer

The scrub and woodland areas shelter songbirds such as nightingale while the grassland is rich in typical chalkland species, for instance cowslip and early-purple orchid, together with bee, lady and pyramidal orchid.

Park Wood

TR 045525; 22ha; WdT
Coppiced woodland
Spring, early summer

A fine remnant of the old Challock Forest, the wood is chiefly hazel, hornbeam and chestnut coppice with a rich variety of other shrubs and plants. Active coppicing increases the interest of the wood.

Parsonage Wood

TQ 797329; 9.2ha; KTNC reserve
High Weald woodland
Spring, early summer

Clay overlies the High Weald sands, supporting an oak–beech woodland with rich-wood species such as ash and field maple. Small pools add a wetland interest and a stream-cut ghyll, rich in liverworts, mosses and ferns, cuts down to the sandstone beneath.

Perry Wood and Selling Wood

TR 045556; 60ha; Swale BC reserve
Mixed woodland
Spring, summer

In this attractive area of woodland, with a good range of rich-wood plants, active sweet chestnut coppicing is practised.

Queendown Warren

TQ 827629; 7.2ha; KTNC reserve
Chalk, grassland, scrub and woodland
Leaflet from site or KTNC
Spring, summer

The records of Queendown Warren stretch back to the time of Henry III when it was, in fact, a commercially managed rabbit warren – a source of meat and fur.

Around the grasslands dense spreads of hawthorn, beech and elder are laced together with traveller's-joy; tall beech trees stand in a mixed scrub of broom, birch and hawthorn, hornbeam, oak and sweet chestnut; ash, dogwood, hawthorn and hazel, hornbeam, oak and wayfaring-tree are clustered in the deeper soils at the foot of the slopes. The grassland slopes themselves are banked and terraced with impressive beeches standing like parkland trees among the rich array of smaller plants. Cowslip and violet are followed by the typical range of downland plants, common rock-rose and wild thyme, marjoram and common milkwort, common bird's-foot-trefoil, horseshoe vetch and a splendid range of orchids. Bee and fly orchid and early spider-orchid are all well represented together with burnt, green-winged and man orchid. Scrub and woodland add extra habitats and both white and broad-leaved helleborine occur.

The woodland is very varied with blocks of high-forest beech and oak contrasting with areas where oak, ash, birch and wild cherry have been left as standards above an understorey of coppiced sweet chestnut. Bluebell, honeysuckle and yellow archangel are encouraged by active coppicing.

This wide range of habitat provides suitable food and shelter for a great variety of animals. Grasshopper populations are good and there are breeding colonies of both common and chalkhill blue butterfly. Despite myxomatosis, there are large numbers of rabbits, hunted by fox, stoat and weasel. Adders enjoy the warmth and shelter of the slopes and there is a good range of typical scrub and woodland birds such as breeding warblers, tit species and woodpeckers.

Sandwich Bay

TR 356593; 400ha; KTNC–RSPB–NT reserve
Grassland, beach and foreshore, dunes and saltmarsh
Toll levied on access road
All year

Shingle and dunes contain plants such as sea bindweed, sea-holly and sea sandwort, old slacks may have a show of southern marsh-orchid and pyramidal orchid. A spectacular plant is the giant sharp rush while among the most fascinating are the parasitic bedstraw and carrot broomrape. The reserve lies on a bird migration route and has long been famous among ornithologists.

Sevenoaks Wildfowl Reserve

Permit only; 54ha; Jeffery Harrison Memorial Trust
Flooded gravelpits
Permit and leaflet from warden
All year

Flooded gravel workings have been developed as a wetland reserve, where floating rafts provide nest sites for waterbirds and the shores have been designed to give the best conditions for breeding species.

Smallman's Wood

Permit only; 12ha; KTNC reserve
Old coppiced woodland
Spring, summer

A remnant of the old ORLESTONE FOREST, the reserve is no longer actively coppiced but contains some fine oak standards over a spring show of bluebell. Woodpeckers and treecreeper are plentiful while there is an excellent variety of moths and butterflies including white admiral.

South Swale

TR 035648; 21ha; KTNC reserve
Beach and foreshore
Permit only off rights of way particularly during breeding season
Winter

An attractive range of plants such as yellow horned-poppy and sea-lavender adds interest in summer, but the reserve is chiefly notable for its winter wildfowl and waders, for perhaps 500 Brent geese, and for migrants such as shore lark and snow bunting.

Stockbury Hill Wood

Permit only; 2.8ha; KTNC reserve
Rich chalk woodland
Spring, early summer

Bird's-nest, fly and lady orchid add their special beauty to this small area of yew, hornbeam, oak and beech woodland, which contains colonies of chalkhill and holly blue butterflies and is a breeding site for hawfinch and nightingale.

Knot may flock in their thousands above the Kentish saltmarshes in winter.

Stodmarsh

TR 222607; 160ha; NCC
Open water and dykes, reedbeds and grazing
meadows
No access off Lampen Wall and riverbank footpaths
Leaflet from NCC
All year

The Stodmarsh is a superb wetland area through
which a flood protection bank, the Lampen Wall,
winds to join the riverbank flood wall and from
which the whole wide marsh is overlooked. The
wetlands of the Stour Valley were all but
eradicated by drainage but subsidence due to underground coal workings has lowered much of this
area and recreated the marshes which are so attractive to many birds.

The edges of the lagoons and the wide reedbeds
are filled with common reed and bulrush. The open
dykes contain bogbean, greater bladderwort and
greater spearwort, water forget-me-not, flowering-
rush, marsh cinquefoil and frogbit. Marsh stitchwort and common meadow-rue grow on the banks,
with hawthorn, willow and alder scrub along the
waterways.

The list of birds breeding on the reserve is long
and varied, with lapwing, redshank and snipe on
the meadows, reed bunting, reed and sedge warbler in the reedbeds, coot, moorhen and great crested grebe by the lagoons. Cetti's warbler has
colonised the scrub, with grasshopper warbler in
the drier marshland, while the reedswamp proper
gives cover for rare breeding species – bittern,
bearded tit and Savi's warbler. Nesting duck

*Stodmarsh: mining subsidence has brought back
rich wetlands to the Stour Valley.*

include gadwall and garganey, mallard, pochard,
teal, shelduck and shoveler.

In winter dabbling duck such as mallard and teal,
with smaller numbers of shoveler and wigeon,
frequent the flooded meadows while the lagoons
are dotted with diving birds such as tufted duck
and pochard. Occasionally winter will bring flights
of wild swans or geese from the north and birds
may be driven in from the sea by storms. Passage
birds such as arctic, black and common tern pass
through in spring and autumn together with ruff
and black-tailed godwit; migrant swallow, swift or
martin may be pursued by hobby; seasonal visitors
such as hen and marsh harrier or osprey may hunt
the marshes.

The Swale

TR 032662; 220ha; NCC reserve
Grazing marshes, saltmarshes, lagoons and mudflats
Permit only off right of way
Leaflet from NCC
Winter

Like SOUTH SWALE, the reserve has impressive winter numbers of waders, wildfowl and smaller
migrant birds. The grazing marshes provide breeding sites for many species while the shell beach
holds birds such as ringed plover. The large lagoon
contains one of Britain's largest populations of sea
club-rush.

Toys Hill

TQ 469517; 152ha; NT
Mixed woodland
Spring, summer

Beech, oak, sweet chestnut and coniferous woodland stand on the brow of a greensand ridge; the
wood is attractive both for its wildlife and for its
splendid views across the Weald.

Trosley Country Park

TQ 634613; 64ha; Kent CC
Chalk woodland, scrub and grassland
Nature trail leaflet from information centre
Spring, summer

High-forest beech, hornbeam, oak and ash woodland, with whitebeam, wild cherry and coppiced
hazel, caps the steep escarpment which shows good
examples of chalkland scrub and grassland.

Westerham Wood

Permit only; 43.2ha; KTNC reserve
Coppiced woodland
Spring, early summer

Possibly the best remaining Kentish coppice-with-
standards wood on lime-rich gault clays, the
reserve is chiefly oak over coppiced ash, hazel and
hornbeam with a ground cover of species such as
herb-Paris and green hellebore. There is a typical
range of woodland bird life and a good variety of
butterflies and moths.

Westfield Wood

TQ 754607; 5ha; KTNC reserve
Steep yew woodland with areas of mixed wood
Spring, early summer

The medieval Pilgrims' Way from Winchester to Canterbury followed the line of the North Downs chalk to keep above the heavy clay and the forests of the Weald. The great chalk scarp still stands, a long stretch of wooded slopes from which the pilgrims must have seen the slow work of the axes in the shrinking Wealden forests and the spreading change to farmland.

Westfield Wood, on the flanks of the Medway Gap, is a good example of these steep chalk woodlands. Yew has colonised the main part of the slopes, a deep green shade varied only by the white bones of the ground beneath and the gnarled red-brown of the lifting trunks. Nothing grows beneath the yews, for too little light can penetrate, but there is a special quality of ancient, almost sepulchral, peace within the wood. Where the canopy opens the woodland floor is filled with plants: carpets of dog's mercury are patterned with sanicle and common twayblade, ivy or stinking iris. The fringes of the yew-wood get most light and here young saplings and shrubs of ash, privet, sycamore and wayfaring-tree are tangled with traveller's-joy above yellow archangel and stinking hellebore. Burnet rose, guelder-rose, spindle, whitebeam and beech also occur here.

Above the yew-wood the soils deepen to allow a spread of ash and beech, oak, wild cherry and field maple with an area of coppiced hazel. The ground cover is varied with tangles of bracken, bramble and rosebay willowherb, with the woodland plants wood anemone and bluebell,

The Devil's Kneading Trough is a fine example of a dry valley at Wye and Crundale Downs.

wood-sorrel, yellow pimpernel and with the less common species butcher's-broom and green hellebore.

This variety of woodland is typical on chalk where a cap of clay with flints encourages more acid plants such as bracken and bluebell with, lower down, a spread of lime-loving ash and beech, grading into dense yew woodland. Yew is probably the climax here and, left to itself, would eventually spread and shade out everything else. The present structure, though, is rich and varied and provides a range of habitat for many woodland animals.

Most of the old badger setts have been taken over by rabbits but a small population of badger still uses the wood. The yew woodland is not attractive to many birds, although goldcrest may be present and the red fruits may draw thrushes in the autumn. The mixed woodland above is rich in typical birds, as are the fields and hedgerows around.

Wye

TR 077455; 100ha; NCC reserve
Chalk downland, scrub and woodland
No access off rights of way
Leaflets and nature trail guide from information centre or NCC
Spring, summer

From the Broad Downs, the slopes of the reserve plummet to the level plain below, spread with fields, hedges, copses and farms, villages and small towns. A shepherd, tending the great sheep flocks which used to graze these North Downs slopes, would notice many changes. The sheep themselves have virtually disappeared and the long slopes of close-cropped grass have been reclaimed by coarser grasses, by spreads of scrub and by woodland. This is a wholly natural change, and he might be interested to see the great variety which it has brought to the Downs.

He would recognise in the few sheep-browsed areas the herb-rich short grass he knew so well; he would see other slopes where coarser grasses shade out the tiny plants but which have a typical different plant and animal life of their own. He would see where woodland has grown up bringing shade to the open chalkland, and where thickets and gladed spreads of scrub have invaded the grassy slopes. He would notice that, where the skylark's song was the music of earlier years, a richer counterpoint of birds can be heard: if he stood until the long shadows drew across the plain and the songbirds began to fall silent, where dusk was a silent time on the open downland, broken perhaps by the deep grumble of a ewe or the distant bark of a fox, the shepherd might today be enchanted by the song of a nightingale.

The story of these long slopes and coombs of chalk began more than 60 million years ago when the chalk was laid down at the bottom of the sea. At a time when most of Britain was buried deep beneath the waves, over 350m of chalky sediments were laid down on the older deposits to form a fine white rock. When the land was uplifted, weathering agents such as heat and cold, wind and water were able to work on the new surface, and over much of the country the chalk was worn away. The Weald was domed higher than much of this southern land and once the chalk was removed the weathering agents could reach the softer clays beneath. In the same way the clay was stripped from the sandstones of the core of the Weald and was then eroded away between these sandstones and the chalk.

The general effects of weathering would probably have produced a fairly regular slope to the chalk but one of the features of the scarp today, well shown at Wye, is the series of spectacular coombs and deep gullies which run towards the plain. These were almost certainly caused by the ice ages which did so much to form our modern landscape. Although the ice cap never reached this far south, the Downs were still subjected to arctic conditions. When snow and ice on the tops of the Downs began to thaw, the water would have run off on the surface, cutting the coombs in the chalk. At the same time, frozen moisture held in the surface would cause frost shattering and flake away the rock. Magnificent fluted slopes were carved on the edge of the Downs in this way and the Devil's Kneading Trough at Wye is a fine example.

The chalk poses problems for plant life, particularly in coping with its dryness, and the first plants to grow here, before a soil develops, must be highly adapted for these conditions. Sheep's fescue, one of the typical grasses of the short turf of chalk

grassland, keeps its stomata hidden from the drying effect of the wind by rolling the edges of its leaves. Other plants, such as hoary plantain and dwarf thistle, grow low rosettes of leaves, keeping their stomata safe from the wind close against the ground, lying low to avoid grazing, and preventing other plants from growing too close to them; around one-third of all chalk-sward plants conform to this low rosette pattern. Some plants form mats, which carry the same advantages – wild thyme and common bird's-foot-trefoil, for example – while others have fleshy water-storing leaves, like biting stonecrop, or slow down the drying airstream by being hairy, like lesser hawkbit. Whatever their specially chosen shape, these plants form a fascinating herb-rich turf.

Unless it is continually grazed, this short chalk sward will be colonised by taller plants, such as torgrass, which shade the small herbs out. Much of the colour is lost, although some special plants prefer this habitat, but the coarser grasses are less liable to grazing and in their shade and cover shrubs can begin to find a foothold. Eventually an open scrub of elder, blackthorn, hawthorn, dogwood, spindle, wild privet and wayfaring-tree will spread, an area where many attractive plants can survive in the glades and a splendid site for blackcap, willow warbler and whitethroat, as well as nightingale.

In the shelter of the scrub, forest trees begin to seed and the down grows on towards woodland. Beech or yew will eventually form a densely shaded wood where only specially adapted plants can survive but ash, until taken over by one of these two, lets in more light and may form an airy woodland rich in plants.

One of the special features of the reserve is the richness of its orchid populations. In the short dry turf of the Kentish Downs, and generally only in

Fly orchid, one of many species in the fine orchid colonies at Wye and Crundale Downs and at Yockletts Bank.

the Wye and Folkestone districts, late spider-orchid is a very special plant: on the reserve it is possibly at its most north westerly site. Early spider-orchid also grows here but flowers before its cousin and is rather more widespread: it prefers to grow fairly near to the sea and is found as far west as Dorset. Bee and burnt orchid, musk and man orchid are also short-turf plants, although man orchid may sometimes be found growing in open scrub on steep slopes.

The deeper grasses, scrub and woodland are sites for shade-tolerant plants, for commoner species such as fragrant and pyramidal orchid, although these are often found in the shorter swards, and a habitat for the more uncommon fly orchid. In the scrub and woodland clearings lady orchid grows: almost wholly restricted to Kent, it is among our most beautiful plants. For its orchids alone the reserve is a site of exceptional interest and beauty.

Yockletts Bank

TR 125477; 24.8ha; KTNC reserve
Particularly fine chalk woodland
Spring, summer

Where WESTFIELD WOOD is chiefly dense yew cover, Yockletts Bank shows a wonderful range of rich chalk woodland species. This is a classic Kentish site, one of the best chalk woodlands in the county. It is comprised of slopes of chalk capped with deposits of clay and, although yew is present, it has never achieved the density of Westfield and active coppicing of the other species has increased the range of habitat.

Yockletts Bank: chalk woodland at its best, with a wide range of scrub and woodland plants.

The clay grows springtime drifts of bluebell, ramsons, wood anemone, common figwort and lords-and-ladies. Oak trees stand over coppiced sycamore and sweet chestnut with thickets of blackthorn.

The lower woodland, on the chalk, is chiefly of ash, beech and hornbeam above an understorey of coppiced hazel. Dogwood, field maple, yew and wild rose, with hawthorn, elder and wayfaring-tree, contribute to the variety of shrubs and spread above a typical range of varied rich-wood plants. Primrose and wood spurge, violets and woodruff make an attractive show in spring, together with ramsons, sanicle, dog's mercury, enchanter's-nightshade and yellow archangel.

The open banks and pathway edges retain their grassland species: cowslip and common milkwort, common rock-rose, wild thyme and salad burnet. Chalkland grasses and sedges grow, surrounded by sapling spindle, wayfaring-tree and dogwood. Yockletts Bank has splendid colonies of common twayblade and common spotted-orchid, of early-purple, fly and pyramidal orchid. Greater butterfly-orchid may also be found but the chief excitement is the population of lady orchid, probably one of the finest in the county. Lady orchid is one of our most beautiful orchids and is virtually limited to Kent, where it is found mainly in woods and shady places growing on the chalk.

Green and great spotted woodpecker nest in the larger trees while the areas of scrub and coppice provide sites for nightingale and warblers. There is a flourishing badger population.

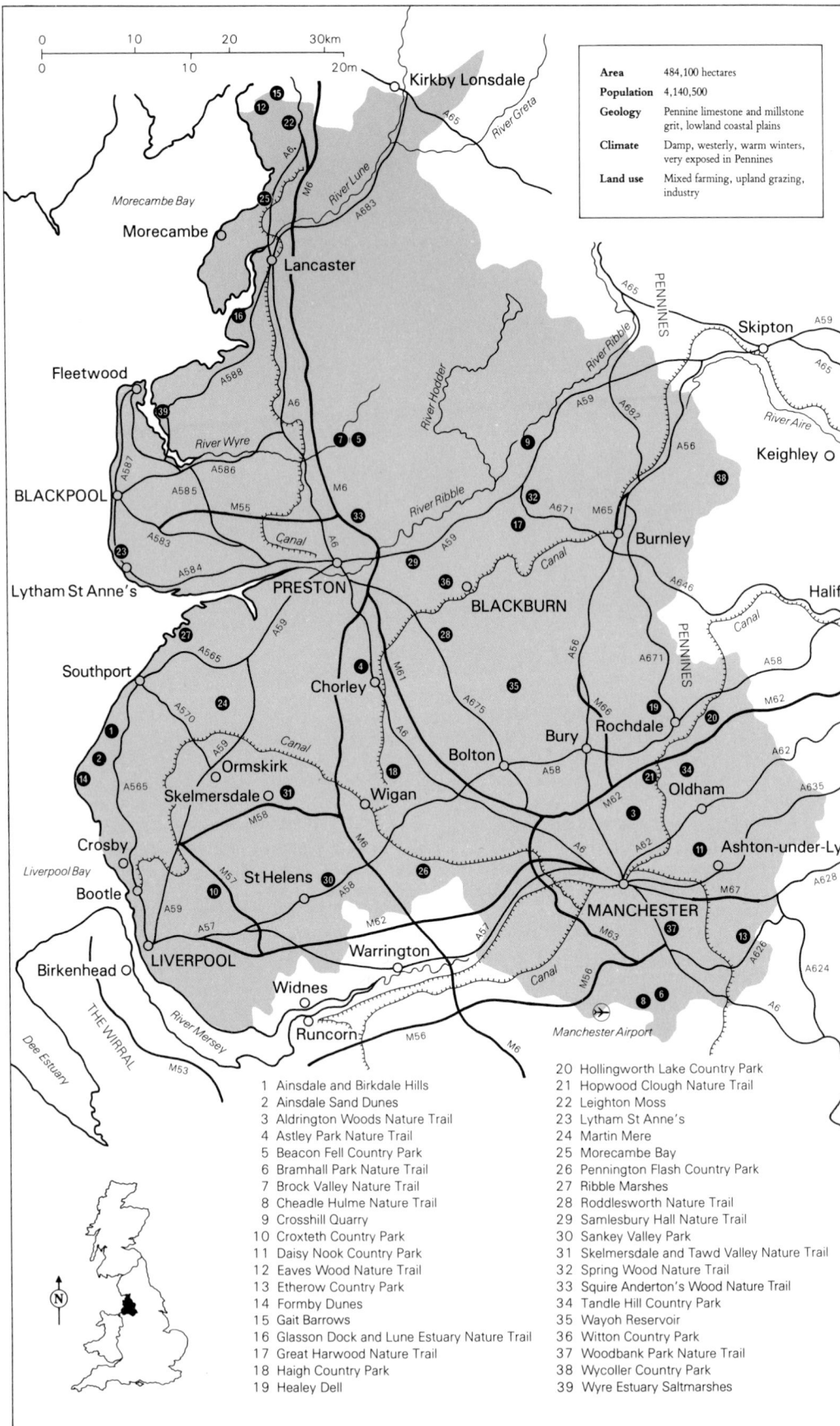

Area	484,100 hectares
Population	4,140,500
Geology	Pennine limestone and millstone grit, lowland coastal plains
Climate	Damp, westerly, warm winters, very exposed in Pennines
Land use	Mixed farming, upland grazing, industry

1 Ainsdale and Birkdale Hills
2 Ainsdale Sand Dunes
3 Aldrington Woods Nature Trail
4 Astley Park Nature Trail
5 Beacon Fell Country Park
6 Bramhall Park Nature Trail
7 Brock Valley Nature Trail
8 Cheadle Hulme Nature Trail
9 Crosshill Quarry
10 Croxteth Country Park
11 Daisy Nook Country Park
12 Eaves Wood Nature Trail
13 Etherow Country Park
14 Formby Dunes
15 Gait Barrows
16 Glasson Dock and Lune Estuary Nature Trail
17 Great Harwood Nature Trail
18 Haigh Country Park
19 Healey Dell

20 Hollingworth Lake Country Park
21 Hopwood Clough Nature Trail
22 Leighton Moss
23 Lytham St Anne's
24 Martin Mere
25 Morecambe Bay
26 Pennington Flash Country Park
27 Ribble Marshes
28 Roddlesworth Nature Trail
29 Samlesbury Hall Nature Trail
30 Sankey Valley Park
31 Skelmersdale and Tawd Valley Nature Trail
32 Spring Wood Nature Trail
33 Squire Anderton's Wood Nature Trail
34 Tandle Hill Country Park
35 Wayoh Reservoir
36 Witton Country Park
37 Woodbank Park Nature Trail
38 Wycoller Country Park
39 Wyre Estuary Saltmarshes

Lancashire and Greater Manchester

The grim, huddled mill towns and coal tips of industrial south Lancashire – now mostly within Merseyside and Greater Manchester – are transformed northwards into the beautiful valleys of the Ribble and Lune and finally the delightful woods, crags and pastures of Silverdale. The mudflats, saltmarshes and sand dunes of the coast pass eastwards into the arable plain and rise to the extensive upland moors of the Pennines. Thus Lancashire, on a small scale, offers most of the variation in scenery for which England is renowned.

On this western side of the Pennine chain the climate is generally moist and mild, with a lack of extremes. In the winter the coastal resorts are as warm as any in Britain outside the extreme south west. Heavy and prolonged snowfall is extremely rare, but the region's notorious reputation for rain has some justification – annual rainfall rises sharply from 760mm on the coast to over 1500mm on the fells.

Limestone provides the basis for the beautiful wooded, rocky landscape of the Silverdale area with its very rich plant and animal life. Typical limestone upland scenery with potholes, caverns and gills is found on Leck Fell, in the extreme north east, at 627m the highest point in the county. Further south the uplands are mostly formed of acid sandstones and grits of the millstone grit series, separated in the extreme south by the deep valleys of the coal measures. On the coastal plain the Triassic rocks are largely covered by a thick layer of glacial drift, and more recently peat, which provides the fertile soils of the Fylde and west Lancashire.

The most important wildlife habitats lie along the coastline. In spite of heavy pressures from Merseyside and the Fylde for recreation and development, the coastal dunes are still of great importance for wildlife, and are represented in both national nature reserves such as AINSDALE SAND DUNES and local ones such as LYTHAM ST ANNES.

The vast mudflats and saltmarshes of MORECAMBE BAY and the estuaries of the RIBBLE, WYRE and Lune are of international importance as winter feeding grounds and roosts for huge numbers of waders and wildfowl. It is very pleasing that the Nature Conservancy Council was able to purchase Banks Marsh on the Ribble to prevent its reclamation for agriculture, the fate of so much saltmarsh all round the country. To see thousands of pink-footed geese feeding on the marshes or flying, or dense clouds of dunlin or knot wheeling through the air, is an experience few birdwatchers will ever forget.

The formerly extensive lowland mosses were largely drained for agriculture in past centuries, and only tiny fragments remain. LEIGHTON MOSS is the happy result of reversion to the 'wild' after drainage and agricultural use. Now its extensive reedbeds, carefully managed for maximum benefit to wildlife, form an important northern outpost of fenland habitats.

In the north of the county the shallow limestone soils have proved much less amenable to agricultural improvement than other lowland areas. The main damage by man has been through the quarrying of limestone, initially for local buildings and burning in lime kilns, and now for a variety of construction purposes. GAIT BARROWS is a fine example of limestone pavement, with its associated unique flora.

Here on the limestone are to be found the most extensive areas of semi-natural woodland as well as pastures with a wealth of colourful plants. Both habitats are included in the National Trust property, EAVES WOOD. Outside the Silverdale area deciduous woodland is largely confined to valley sides, too steep to be used for agriculture. The Lune and Ribble valleys possess some particularly fine examples, such as REDSCAR AND TUNBROOK WOODS. Further south HEALEY DELL is an excellent ravine woodland which has survived close to a built-up area.

In the east of the county the extensive heather moors of Leck Fell and the Forest of Bowland are managed primarily for grouse, and have very limited public access. The result is some of the least disturbed open moorland in England, where huge colonies of gulls and some rare upland birds are able to breed. Further south the West Pennine Moors provide an important recreation area for Greater Manchester. Of the many reservoirs now accessible to the public, WAYOH and Rivington are of particular importance for their wildlife. Efforts are being made to protect the most sensitive and interesting upland areas from excessive public pressure.

Heavily industrialised south Lancashire provides some unusual wildlife habitats in the form of industrial tips, marshes, flashes and disused mill lodges. Impressive displays of marsh-orchids, far removed from natural habitats, and some unusual birds, show that man's activities are not always detrimental to wildlife. MERE SANDS WOOD and HASKAYNE CUTTING are two examples of valuable nature reserves on man-made habitats, and show that conservation of wildlife is an activity that is carried on throughout the diversity of landscape and environment that Lancashire represents.

J.M. NEWTON

Ainsdale and Birkdale Hills

SD 298127; 191.6ha; Sefton BC reserve
Rich coastal dune system
Spring, summer

A superb range from open to fixed dunes dressed with flowers, Ainsdale and Birkdale Hills protects a range of important plants including the beautiful grass-of-Parnassus and the very local dune helleborine.

Ainsdale Sand Dunes

SD 290105; 492.5ha; NCC reserve
Huge area of sand dunes, slacks and woodland
Permit only off marked paths
Nature trail leaflets from field office or NCC
Spring, early summer

This superb duneland reserve has public trails through the woodland and foredune-slack areas where lime-rich sands encourage sea spurge and sea-holly, sea-buckthorn, early marsh-orchid, marsh helleborine, kidney vetch, yellow-wort and autumn gentian. Specialities include grass-of-Parnassus and round-leaved wintergreen, with the rare dune helleborine and pendulous helleborine, while a great variety of insects and birds frequents the dunes and pinewoods which also contain a population of red squirrel.

Alkrington Woods Nature Trail

SD 864053; 3.2km; Rochdale MBC
Woodland trail
Leaflet from RMBC
Spring, early summer

The trail is laid out in an area of beech woodland varied with oak and birch. The soil is sandy and badly drained, giving dry spreads of bracken contrasted with shallow pools and boggy patches, with the additional interest of the river bank. A good range of woodland birds frequents the area.

Arbour Quarry

Permit only; 8.4ha; Bridgewater Estates Ltd reserve
Mainly geological site
Permit from LTNC
All year

The reserve offers fine exposures of reefknoll limestone containing brachiopods, corals, crinoids, lamellibranchs and trilobites, of great interest to geologists. The damp floor of the quarry supports a rich marshland vegetation.

The foredunes at Ainsdale Sand Dunes: sand, heaped around marram, shelters the rich slacks.

The Trough of Bowland, a spectacular pass through the Lancashire moors.

Astley Park Nature Trail

SD 574183; 2.4ha; Chorley BC
Woodland trail
Leaflet from CBC
Spring, early summer

A lake, attracting mallard and pied wagtail and fringed with water-plantain, contrasts with rather dense woodland where oak, beech, alder, sweet chestnut and sycamore stand above hawthorn, holly and bracken. A typical range of birds includes great spotted woodpecker and kestrel and the area is noted for its fungi.

Beacon Fell Country Park

SD 565427; 74ha; LCC
Upland conifer woods and moorland
Booklet from information centre at SD 578423 or LCC
Spring, early summer

Some small bogs have developed on the acid millstone grit which caps the fell but the general cover is coniferous woodland. From the summit, some 266m, there are superb views across the surrounding farmland and moorland.

Birch Moss Covert

Permit only; 6ha; CCT reserve
Birch woodland
Spring, early summer

Birch–bracken woodland, in which oak and Scots pine have been planted, has developed on an area of dried-out raised bog. Large numbers of small mammals attract fox, stoat and weasel together with sparrowhawk and kestrel.

Bramhall Park Nature Trail

SJ 890863; 2km; Stockport MBC
Parkland and lakes
Leaflet from SMBC
Spring, early summer

The park contains open grassland and mixed woodland including alder, beech, birch and sweet chestnut with conifers and, with the extra attraction of two lakes, is rich in birds such as pied wagtail, nuthatch and kestrel.

Brock Valley Nature Trail

SD 548431; 2.4km; M.J. Fitzherbert-Brockholes– R. Walmsley-Cottam
Riverside nature trail
Leaflet from LTNC
Spring, early summer

The trail follows a torrential stream which has cut down through glacial sands and gravels to the boulder clay beneath. Indian balsam and butterbur grow on the banks where dipper, pied and grey wagtail and common sandpiper may be seen. The rather uncommon marsh stitchwort may be found.

Brookheys Covert

Permit only; 1.8ha; CCT reserve
Woodland and wetland
Summer

Oak, with crab apple, holly, hazel and several willow species, stands above a varied ground cover, except where dense rhododendrons shade out all smaller plants. The flooded marlpits contain greater spearwort and water-violet and attract heron and kingfisher, while the woodland draws characteristic birds such as blackcap and spotted flycatcher.

Cheadle Hulme Nature Trail

SJ 875855; 3.6km; Stockport MBC
Pasture and hedgerow trail
Leaflet from SMBC
Spring, early summer

Open grassland and species-rich old hedges, alder, elder, hawthorn, hazel, holly, oak, rowan and willow, laced with hop, honeysuckle and wild rose, provide a habitat for birds such as chiffchaff and willow warbler.

Compstall

Permit only; 15.4ha; CTC reserve
Woodland and wetland
Spring, summer

Steeply wooded slopes fall to a marshy flood plain where reedbeds and stands of sweet-flag lift above the herb-rich swamp. Open-water areas invite waterfowl and winter duck may include goldeneye, mallard, pochard, shoveler, teal and wigeon. The mix of woodland and wetland encourages a generally good bird life, with warblers singing from the lower slopes and dipper or grey wagtail working the river.

Cotterill Clough

Permit only; 5.6ha; CCT reserve
Wooded valley
Spring, early summer

The range from plateau woodland and valley slopes to wet woodland floor includes oak, ash and coppiced alder above a range of ground cover from acid bramble and bracken, through rich-wood yellow archangel and dog's mercury to a dense, damp spread of plants such as marsh-marigold and pendulous sedge. A good variety of mosses, liverworts, ferns and fungi parallels an interesting animal life.

Crosshill Quarry

SD 746436; 6ha; Ribble Valley BC reserve
Disused quarries and woodland
Spring, summer

The areas of limestone grassland are varied with a scrub of ash and hawthorn and contain a variety of lime-loving plants such as small scabious and lady's bedstraw. Bee orchid and common spotted-orchid occur.

Croxteth Country Park

SJ 399943; 208ha; Merseyside MBC
Parkland and farmland
Leaflet from MMBC
Spring, early summer

Over 100 species of bird have been recorded in this area of varying habitat where ponds and pastureland contrast with broad-leaved and coniferous woodland.

Daisy Nook Country Park

SD 921004; 34.5ha; Oldham MBC–Greater Manchester Council
Canal and valley land
Spring, early summer

The undeveloped river valleys of the great industrial areas are of vital importance to wildlife as corridors by which plants and animals can spread. Much of the country park is managed to this end and the open waters of the canal, rich in wetland life, add a further range of interest.

Dark Lane Tip

Permit only; 4ha; CCT reserve
Scrub woodland
Spring, summer

An old tip, colonised by elder and hawthorn above coarse grassland, has been planted with a variety of native trees and attracts a wide variety of birds and butterflies. The reserve is a good example of a wildlife habitat created on the urban fringe.

Dean Wood

Permit only; 10ha; LTNC–NWWA reserve
Wooded valley
Spring, early summer

The steep-sided narrow valley is filled with a typical mixed woodland damp and shady enough to encourage a luxuriant growth of ferns.

East Wood

Permit only; 5ha; RSPB reserve
Woodland and pools
Spring, early summer

The woodland is rich in tree species which, with shrubs such as holly and rhododendron, attract a good variety of birds including breeding warblers such as blackcap. The pools add wetland interest.

Woodcock, a ground-nesting woodland wader, is endowed with excellent camouflage.

The strange bleak beauty of limestone pavement at the heart of Gait Barrows.

Eaves Wood

SD 467762; 3.2km; NT
Woodland nature trail
Leaflet from NT or LTNC
Spring, early summer

The hillside, with areas of limestone pavement, carries a mixed woodland of oak, ash, small-leaved lime, beech and yew over an understorey which includes buckthorn, privet and spindle. Among the woodland birds, marsh tit, great spotted woodpecker and woodcock occur, while mammals include red squirrel.

Etherow Country Park

SJ 965909; 65ha; Stockport MBC
Wooded valley slopes and marshes, reservoir and pools
Spring, summer

The River Etherow winds among steep slopes, often well-wooded, and through spreads of marsh and fishponds. The quieter sections of the canal and river, the undisturbed spreads of marsh and of mixed woodland, provide a sanctuary for wildlife. COMPSTALL is part of this park.

Formby Dunes

SD 275083; 188.8ha; NT reserve
Foreshore, dunes and woodland
Formby Point nature trail guide available from NT, LTNC or Merseyside MBC
Spring, summer

As at AINSDALE SAND DUNES to the north, Formby has a full range from open beach, through dunes and slacks, to wooded dunes behind. The area includes commercial asparagus fields and a special reserve established to protect a population of continental red squirrel, introduced many years ago.

Gait Barrows

SD 480772; 70ha; NCC reserve
Limestone pavement, woodland, meadows and wetland
Permit only off public right of way
Leaflet from NCC
Spring, early summer

Hidden in the heart of a mixed woodland is a fluted, riven, potholed, gently sloping pavement of limestone, a rock garden filled with shrubs and colourful flowers. The rock has bright green ferns springing from every crevice, biting stonecrop spreading in cushions, juniper and yew showing dark above bloody crane's-bill.

Hart's-tongue and hard shield-fern are plentiful, with the more unusual rustyback and rare rigid buckler-fern, making a contrast with tutsan, hemp-agrimony, saw-wort, northern bedstraw and angular Solomon's-seal. Lily-of-the-valley and dropwort show beneath the scrub, which grades into taller woodland where glacial soils lap the edges of the limestone. The scrub is varied with yew, hazel, ash and oak, juniper, holly, wild privet, dogwood, buckthorn, small-leaved lime and spindle, clumped or single shrubs lifting from the larger crevices. As rich a mix of smaller plants grows among the scrub: deadly nightshade, mountain melick, fingered sedge and stone bramble, pale St John's-wort and dark-red helleborine.

Where the edges of the pavement are more broken and dissected the shrub thickens into woodland and then into an area of high-forest, generally coppiced hazel under oak, ash and sycamore. Hornbeam and beech are also present and there are thickets of silver birch. Pathways and glades provide openings in the woodland which has a variable ground cover, often thick with bramble and bluebell, primrose, sanicle and common dog-violet. The reserve includes an area of grazed rich meadowland which grades through marsh and fen to the pool of Little Hawes Water, completing an exceptional range of limestone habitat.

Not only is the site perhaps the most important single example of carboniferous limestone clint and grike pavement in the country, but it is also interesting as the most northerly scrub community to include together spindle, wild privet, buckthorn, dogwood and small-leaved lime, all of which are near their northern limit.

Bird's-eye primrose, a speciality of damp northern meadows in early summer.

Glasson Dock and Lune Estuary Nature Trail

SD 457562; 3.2km; BWB–LCC–W. and J. Pye Ltd
Estuarine and canal nature trail
Leaflet from LTNC
All year

Saltmarsh plants, sea aster, English scurvygrass and thrift, lime-loving plants on the disused railway line and freshwater plants, flowering-rush and yellow iris, by the canal complement the range of birds from mallard and yellow wagtail to common and arctic tern, shelduck and redshank. Passage migrants may be seen on the estuary while winter may bring wigeon and red-breasted merganser.

Great Harwood Nature Trail

SD 745339; 6.4ha; Great Harwood Civic Soc.
Woodland and pasture trail
Leaflets from local library and GHCS members
Spring, early summer

The varied walk includes a stretch of the River Calder with a deeply wooded ravine, rich in species such as alder, beech, bird cherry, dogwood and hazel, with the added interest of an ancient clapper bridge crossing a tributary stream.

Haigh Country Park

SD 596087; 150ha; Wigan MBC
Plateau and valley slopes
Spring, early summer

A nature trail has been laid out on the lower, wooded, valley slopes above the River Douglas, a valley which is also noted for its geology.

Haskayne Cutting

Permit only; 2.8km; LTNC–NWWA reserve
Disused railway line
Nature trail leaflet, acting as permit, from LTNC
Spring, early summer

The nature trail illustrates many interesting features which include wetland, grassland and scrub, an associated range of insects and birds, an exposition of the geology and a chance to see marsh-orchids and their hybrids.

Hawes Water

Permit only; 2.4ha; LTNC reserve
Woodland, cliff, grassland and wetland
Spring, summer

A limestone cliff scattered with yew overlooks an area of grassland and marsh beside the lake. Among the many unusual plants are black bog-rush and bird's-eye primrose.

Healey Dell

SD 883159; 70ha; Rochdale BC reserve
Narrow moorland-edge valley
Nature trail booklet from warden's hut or RBC
Spring, early summer

The River Spodden, draining Rooley Moor, Brown Wardle Hill and the western slopes of Inchfield Moor, rushes south to join the River Roach through the narrow wooded clough of Healey Dell. It was water, of course, which cut the winding valley: waterfalls and sculpted grottoes, such as the Fairy Chapel, result from changes in the hardness of the rock and contribute much to the fascination of the site.

The valley opens to the south and thus is warmer and more sheltered than the land around, a circumstance which encourages a rich variety of ferns, mosses and liverworts. Woodlands hang above the water, adding to the shade and the humidity, providing suitable conditions for lady-fern and lemon-scented fern, while the hard rocks are acid enough for hard fern. The woods themselves are varied, the western bank being covered with ancient oak–birch woodland, while the eastern side has been modified with planted trees, most of them sycamores.

The ground cover under the older woods is typical of acid moor-edge sites with heather and bilberry, wavy hair-grass and tormentil. Open areas are thick with bracken while the trees tend to be widely spread and small. Below the woodland a disused railway line crosses the river by a viaduct on which grows the locally uncommon hart's-tongue. The ballast for the line was limestone gravel which has allowed an unexpected range of lime-loving plants to colonise the valley.

The wetter areas, where nutrients are easiest to absorb, tend to be the richest parts of any site. Healey Dell is no exception and the damper parts have horsetails and cuckooflower, marsh-marigold, marsh violet, ragged-Robin, water forget-me-not and water mint, water avens and a host of others. An interesting range of hybrids of both southern and northern marsh-orchid with common spotted-orchid may be seen.

Birds of woodland, scrubland, open fields and water occur, together with passage migrants and seasonal visitors. Birds such as blackcap, garden warbler and woodcock, tawny owl and kestrel, snipe, redpoll and twite, pied and grey wagtail, siskin and waxwing, all may be seen in season, either breeding or feeding in the valley. Butterfly records are sparse but moths are plentiful, including flame shoulder, burnished brass and beautiful golden Y, or hedge and rosy rustic, true lover's knot, brown-spot binion and bright-line brown-eye, spinach, and ear and snout.

Hollingworth Lake Country Park

SD 939153; 84ha; Rochdale MBC
Large reservoir
Winter

The lakeside trail provides excellent views across the water at any time of year but winter is likely to be best for waterbirds, when disturbance is at its lowest. A closed sanctuary holds a variety of breeding birds in summer.

Leighton Moss: an important site for otter, bittern and bearded tit.

Hopwood Clough Nature Trail

SJ 878079; 3.3km; Rochdale MBC
Wooded valley
Leaflet from RMBC
Spring, early summer

An attractive series of small woodlands, oak and birch over fine acid grasses and bracken, over bluebells in spring with marsh-marigold in the wetter parts, lies along the narrow valley where a small lake adds wetland interest.

Leighton Moss

SD 478752; 130ha; RSPB reserve
Pools, reedbed, marsh and scrub
Permit only off right of way or to other than public hide
Leaflet and permits from reception centre
All year

Leighton Moss has 80ha of deep rich reedbeds, set around spreads of open water, grading into marsh and scrub and filled with a wealth of wildlife. Because the reeds want to colonise the water, the marsh to grow into the reedbeds and the woodland to capture the marsh, a very high level of management is required to maintain the balance, but this effort is not unrewarded: the reserve is a wonderful reservoir of wildlife, not of birds alone but of both plants and animals.

The waters are shallow meres only 15–60cm deep, filled with an underwater jungle of plants, such as rigid hornwort and amphibious bistort, fringed with mare's-tail, water dock, yellow iris, bulrush and common reed. The marsh above the reedbed is a brilliant mix of species, of sedges and rushes, of tall plants such as meadowsweet, common meadow-rue, purple-loosestrife, common valerian and great willowherb, with marsh-marigold, water mint and the unusual small marsh dandelion in the wetter places and with smaller marsh and wet-meadow plants – ragged-Robin, yellow rattle, marsh valerian, southern marsh-orchid and common spotted-orchid – forming a lower tier of colour to balance the scatter of shrubs. In early summer the orchids are beautiful, not only for their colourful flower spikes but also for the wide range of hybrid plants which occur. The shrubs too are richly varied with alder, birch, buckthorn and alder buckthorn, guelder-rose and spindle, contrasting with the taller oak and ash of the woodland proper. Gorse and bracken provide a further contrast on a small area of heath while coppiced willow, managed for its rich insect life, adds yet another bird-rich habitat. At the opposite end of the reedbeds, the freshwater marsh changes to saltmarsh and an interesting range of plants includes marsh arrowgrass, reed canary-grass, salt-marsh rush, grey club-rush and sharp rush.

With a range from open water right through to woodland the reserve could hardly fail to be rich in insects. Bright summer days may see brown aeshna, our largest dragonfly, with common sympetrum and four-spotted libellula, together with damselflies such as common blue and common ischnura, with large red and common coenagrion.

Reed bunting: the male, seen here at the nest, is easily told by his black head and white collar.

Butterflies are drawn by the richness of the marsh: peacock and small tortoiseshell come to lay their eggs on common nettle, orange-tip on cuckooflower, small copper on docks and sorrels. Around the woodland edge, holly blue, pearl-bordered, small pearl-bordered and high brown fritillary fly.

Over 300 moths have been recorded including poplar, eyed, large elephant and small elephant hawkmoth, together with reedbed moths such as fen and bulrush wainscot which feed on common reed and bulrush respectively. Other species of interest include scarce prominent, sprawler, old lady and an uncommon coastal species, feathered ranunculus.

Frog and common toad breed in the waters of the reserve and fish include three-spined and ten-spined stickleback, rudd, perch, pike and eel. Leighton Moss has long been known as an important site for otter. Eels are among the favourite food of otters and the shallows afford good opportunities for seeing them hunting their prey. Other mammals include stoat and weasel, with both red and roe deer and occasional visiting fallow. The woods hold red squirrel and provide a roost for some of the bats recorded on the reserve: five species have been identified, the commonest being pipistrelle and noctule.

The Moss is superbly sited just above the huge estuary of MORECAMBE BAY which, with the Wash, forms one of the two most important wader sites in Britain. The reserve can therefore provide a bad-weather refuge as well as a site for many breeding birds. Over 200 species have been recorded and over 70 breed. This is the only regular site for breeding bittern in northern England, estimated in one year to be 20 per cent of the national numbers, and holds a thriving colony of bearded tit. Besides these, the reserve boasts breeding garganey, a duck unique among British waterfowl in being a summer migrant. Other breeding waterfowl include large numbers of mallard, with pochard, shoveler, teal and tufted duck. A rare British breeder, the spotted crake, has nested here in the marsh, while the reedbed provides a regular site for the equally secretive water rail. Redshank, snipe, lapwing and woodcock represent the waders, although oystercatcher have nested on the islands of the meres and curlew breed nearby. The reedbeds, marsh and woodland provide a fine range of nest sites for smaller birds and in early summer the Moss is filled with the sound and movement of grasshopper, reed and sedge warbler, reed bunting, spotted flycatcher and yellow wagtail.

Spring and autumn bring splendid passages of migrants, waders such as whimbrel, bar-tailed godwit, spotted redshank and ruff, birds such as little gull, black and common tern, perhaps a hunting goshawk, hobby, merlin or harrier and always the possibility of visitors such as little bittern, little egret, night heron or purple heron.

With winter flocks of finches and small birds feeding on the rich store of seeds in the reeds, the

Breeding in high northern latitudes, whooper swan come to winter on British waters.

scrub and the marshland, with dramatic numbers of teal, with other duck including goldeneye, pintail and wigeon, with occasional long-tailed duck and scaup, and with a great variety of winter species to complement the birds that are present at other seasons, Leighton Moss is a wonderful site the whole year round.

Lewis Garden

SD 625304; 1ha; Samlesbury Hall Trustees–CPRE–BTCV
Former Japanese water garden
Leaflet from CPRE
Spring, early summer

Mature oak and ash, with other trees and shrubs, stand above a varied ground cover. A stream, ponds and marsh add wetland interest and support a range of birds typical of these habitats. Practical conservation work is carried out.

Lytham St Annes

SD 309307; 16ha; Lytham BC reserve
Sand dunes and slacks
Booklet from information hut or LTNC
Spring, summer

For several kilometres great rolling dunes of sand have been heaped up by the wind off the sea to form a dominant feature of the coastline here. The dunes are separated from housing development by the main road; while holidaymakers cross to play and picnic on the sands a smaller semi-natural area lies to the east of the road, ignored by most of the visitors: this is the Lytham St Annes reserve.

The first impression is of a gently rolling sweep of green, pale and spiky where marram grows or deeper, smoother green where finer grasses spread, the whole small area starred with vivid splashes of colour. The sands are full of small shell particles, making them rich in lime. At MERE SANDS WOOD they are hard and shiny, with an acid-loving plant life, but here the sands are soft and covered with

lime-loving yellow rattle and kidney vetch, wild pansy, carline thistle, biting stonecrop and yellow-wort. Probably the most dramatic-looking plant present here is common evening-primrose but some more fascinating species flourish in the moist dune slacks.

A small pool is close enough to the underlying peat for acid-loving plants such as marsh pennywort and common cottongrass, but the richer areas support round-leaved wintergreen, marsh helleborine, early marsh-orchid and creeping willow.

A wealth of insect life enjoys the warm flowered slopes, the protection of tangling dewberry or the shelter of blocks of scrub. White satin, cinnabar and burnet moths, all day-flying species, are common while the butterflies include grayling, common blue, green-veined white and small copper. Five species of bumble bee frequent the reserve and the two-spot, seven-spot and twenty-two-spot ladybird may be seen. Reptiles are represented by common lizard and the birds include skylark, meadow pipit, linnet and stonechat with occasional kestrel.

Martin Mere

SD 428145; 36ha; WT reserve
Marshlands and lagoons
Leaflets from reception centre
All year

As with most of the Wildfowl Trust sanctuaries, considerable importance is placed on the collection of penned or pinioned waterfowl, but the 8ha man-made mere and the 105ha marshland area attract a spectacular range of wild birds. In winter, the meadows provide a roost and feeding ground for many thousands of waterfowl. Over 10,000 pink-footed geese migrate annually from Greenland and Iceland to the reserve. Whooper swan fly here from Iceland and Bewick's swan cross the Baltic from Russia. Martin Mere is now an important wintering ground for both species.

Among the wintering duck some, like mallard, are present all year but are reinforced by visitors from continental Europe; some, scaup for instance, are solely winter visitors. Shoveler breed in Britain but the summer birds fly south to be replaced by northern cousins: gadwall, goldeneye, pintail, pochard, shelduck, teal, tufted duck and wigeon, birds from Iceland, from western, northern and eastern Europe gather here for shelter and for food. The reserve is well known for its very large numbers of wintering teal, and for pintail in autumn.

Other birds fly through on passage or stay to breed. Curlew, dunlin, bar-tailed and black-tailed godwit, greenshank, lapwing, golden and grey plover, ringed plover and little ringed plover visit or breed in the sanctuary, with oystercatcher, sanderling and common, curlew, green, purple, marsh and wood sandpiper, redshank and spotted redshank, whimbrel, snipe, woodcock and many others. Martin Mere has the largest wintering population of ruff on any site in the United Kingdom.

Gulls and terns include little gull and glaucous gull, with arctic, black, white-winged black, common and little tern. Kingfisher may hunt the waters of the mere. Hen harrier are quite common, and Montagu's and marsh harrier are occasional visitors. Hobby, merlin and peregrine also occur. Short-eared owl hunt the meadows and both great grey and red-backed shrike have been recorded.

Mere Sands Wood

Permit only; 40ha; LTNC reserve
Flooded sand workings
Spring, summer

Mixed woodland, coniferous or oak over ash and rowan with alder, willow and rhododendron scrub, surrounds an area of islanded lagoons. The woodlands contain red squirrel and provide a habitat for warblers, while the water attracts mallard, shelduck and tufted duck.

Morecambe Bay

SD 468666; 2485ha; RSPB reserve
Sandflats and saltmarsh
Access to the sands free at all times, but beware
of quicksands and tides
Information from Leighton Moss reception centre
All year

The huge estuary between Cumbria and Lancashire is a wide flat tidal plain, fascinating at any time of year. In winter it is probably the finest site in Britain for enormous numbers of waders. The sands are the dominant feature once the tide has ebbed, sands which look like a wet bare barren waste but which contain incredible riches of seafood for the birds. A classic animal of muddy sandflats, the Baltic tellin, is a small shellfish about 2cm long, and may occur at Morecambe in densities of over 5000 per square metre. The tiny laver spire shell, and an extraordinary-looking small shrimp-family animal called *Corophium volutator*, are also here in enormous numbers.

Around the sandflats are areas of saltmarsh, rich in sea-milkwort, thrift and sea club-rush with more uncommon plants such as lesser centaury and strawberry clover. These are high-tide roosts for the waders and wildfowl and breeding sites for meadow pipit, skylark, lapwing, redshank and oystercatcher. Behind the marshes are banks thick with hawthorn scrub or low cliffs of limestone with bloody crane's-bill, yew, whitebeam, wild rose and juniper.

Passage migrants as varied as osprey and Bewick's swan, little gull, little stint and little tern may be seen in season, together with an occasional merlin or peregrine.

Roughly a quarter of the country's winter populations of bar-tailed godwit, knot, oystercatcher and turnstone come here to feed and shelter, with important numbers of curlew, dunlin and redshank – around a quarter of a million waders may be present. The Wash may have greater numbers of winter wildfowl but Morecambe often holds hundreds of grey-lag geese, mallard and pintail, with more than 1000 each of wigeon and shelduck, with pink-footed geese, red-breasted merganser, goldeneye, pochard, shoveler, scaup and teal. A great variety of other species may occur – the complete list of those recorded here contains over 160 birds.

The rising tide brings winter waders to roost on tidal sandflats as at Morecambe Bay.

Pennington Flash Country Park

SD 646985; 263ha; Greater Manchester Council–
Wigan MBC
Large lake and surrounds
Winter

Over 150ha of open water attracts many sailing
enthusiasts and fishermen but in winter the undisturbed flash may draw an interesting variety of
waterbirds. A nature trail and a small reserve increase the wildlife interest.

Redscar and Tunbrook Woods

Permit only; 30ha; LTNC reserve
Mixed valley woodlands
Spring, early summer

The fine mixed woodland includes oak, ash, beech,
wild cherry, elm and sycamore above a varied
ground cover, with yellow archangel and field
maple approaching the northern limit of their
spread. The diversity of woodland type is reflected
in an interesting range of insects and a variety of
birds.

Ribble Marshes

SD 374208; 3226ha; NCC reserve
Saltmarsh and mudflats
Permit only to Hesketh Out-Marsh and
study-sanctuary zone; the saltmarsh is dangerous
Leaflet from NCC
All year

The sea wall overlooks the flats and marshes of the
River Ribble and the grazing marshes behind, an
important breeding site for lapwing, oystercatcher,
redshank and shelduck. Winter populations include the largest gatherings of pink-footed geese in
north west England, with many duck and waders.
The best place for birdwatching is the coastal road
overlooking Crossens Marsh.

Roddlesworth Nature Trail

SD 665215; 2km; NWWA
Woodland and streamside nature trail
Spring, early summer

The nature trail passes through a range of habitat
which includes lemon-scented fern, lady-fern and

265

adder's-tongue, marsh cinquefoil and marsh-marigold, acid plants such as heather and tormentil. The bird life is equally varied with redstart, wood warbler and woodcock, curlew and kingfisher.

Sankey Valley Park

SJ 535966; 8km; St Helens MBC
Restored canal and towpath
Spring, summer

The long narrow park is based on a greenway along the canal where common spotted-orchid shows beneath planted alder and willow. The birds include heron and kingfisher among common woodland and scrub species.

Skelmersdale and Tawd Valley Nature Trail

SD 487061; 1.2km; Skelmersdale Dev. Corpn
Mainly educational trail
Leaflet from LTNC
Spring, early summer

The trail explores the wildlife interest of the valley which forms a natural corridor from the farmland to the very heart of the town of Skelmersdale.

Common spotted-orchid is a widespread and beautiful flower of early summer.

Spring Wood Nature Trail

SD 740364; 1.5km; LCC
Mixed woodland
Leaflet from LTNC
Spring, early summer

The woodland is mainly mature with a high closed canopy, extremely rich in birds and one of the few sites locally where wood warbler may be seen.

Squire Anderton's Wood Nature Trail

SD 560337; 0.8km; Central Lancashire Dev. Corpn
Woodland trail
Leaflet from LTNC
Spring, early summer

The mixed woodland has the added interest of a stream and the ground cover includes wood anemone, lords-and-ladies, ramsons and woodruff. Birds include goldcrest and treecreeper with several tit and warbler species.

Tandle Hill Country Park

SD 907087; 44ha; Oldham MBC
Grassland and woodland
Spring, early summer

A nature trail demonstrates the interest of the grassy hillside crowned with beech and conifers.

Upper Coldwell Reservoir

Permit only; 5ha; LTNC–NWWA reserve
Upland reservoir
Spring, summer

The rather bleak upland reservoir is fringed by marshland, containing common butterwort and grass-of-Parnassus and providing a breeding site for great crested grebe and tufted duck.

Wayoh Reservoir

SD 732170; 50ha; LTNC–NWWA reserve
Open water, marsh, grassland, scrub and woodland
Permit only off rights of way
All year

The reserve is rich in animals and plants, with the marsh and woodland containing marsh-marigold, marsh valerian and alpine scurvygrass, five species of horsetail, seven of ferns and shrub species such as bird cherry. Winter wildfowl include mallard, pochard and tufted duck while warblers breed in the woodland and great crested grebe may be seen on the reservoir.

Witton Country Park

SD 665276; 89.6ha; LCC
Old estate parkland
Nature trail booklet from Blackburn Museum
Spring, early summer

Ornamental parkland and natural woodland provide a good range of habitat illustrated by the nature trail.

Woodbank Park Nature Trail

SJ 914904; 1.6km; Stockport MBC
Riverside parkland and woodland
Leaflet from SMBC
Spring, early summer

Filling a wide meander of the River Goyt, close to the heart of Stockport, the park contains a fine variety of trees and smaller plants and attracts birds such as chiffchaff, willow warbler and yellow wagtail.

Wycoller Country Park

SD 926395; 140.8ha; LCC
Moorland-edge country park
Nature trail leaflet from site or LCC
Spring, early summer

This attractive river valley area lies in the old Forest of Trawden.

Wyre Estuary Saltmarshes

SD 346486; 104ha; LTNC reserve
Ungrazed estuarine marshes
Spring, summer

As the tides rise and fall in the estuary of the Wyre, the shallows are washed with a spread of river-borne silts; where plants such as common cord-grass form a filter, the silts begin to make a tidal marsh. Gradually, around the spiky stems, the muds build upwards until a new area of low-tide land is formed. More plants move in and form a better silt trap until eventually a saltmarsh forms, flat as a lawn, which stands above most high tides

Wayoh Reservoir: scrub and woodland surround the marsh grassland.

but which still must survive the wash of the sea when the moon lifts the spring tides up to the low sea wall.

These lawns of saltmarsh look level but are fissured by creeks and are ponded with small salt pans. The creeks drain the marshes and build levees on their banks. These raised banks are formed as silt is deposited, assisted by the fringe of sea-purslane, when the creeks are full. When the spring tides come the creeks are overtopped and the whole marsh may be flooded in minutes.

When the floods subside the marshes return to their normal green spread but a tiny extra layer of silt has been laid and slowly they continue to rise. The salt pans have been refreshed and the plants and animals which live in them, even more than those of the marsh in general, must adapt to an amazing range of salinity from almost pure seawater in spring, through brackish water diluted by rain, to a dried-out brine in summer.

In summer the sea wall, edged with common bird's-foot-trefoil, clovers and vetches, with sea campion, harebell and restharrow, surrounds a mosaic of sea-lavender, sea aster and thrift, contrasting with common scurvygrass, sea plantain, glasswort and the varying shades of green of the grasses.

The marshes show excellent examples of vegetational zonation and are of interest for the presence of common, lax-flowered and rock sea-lavender growing together in one site.

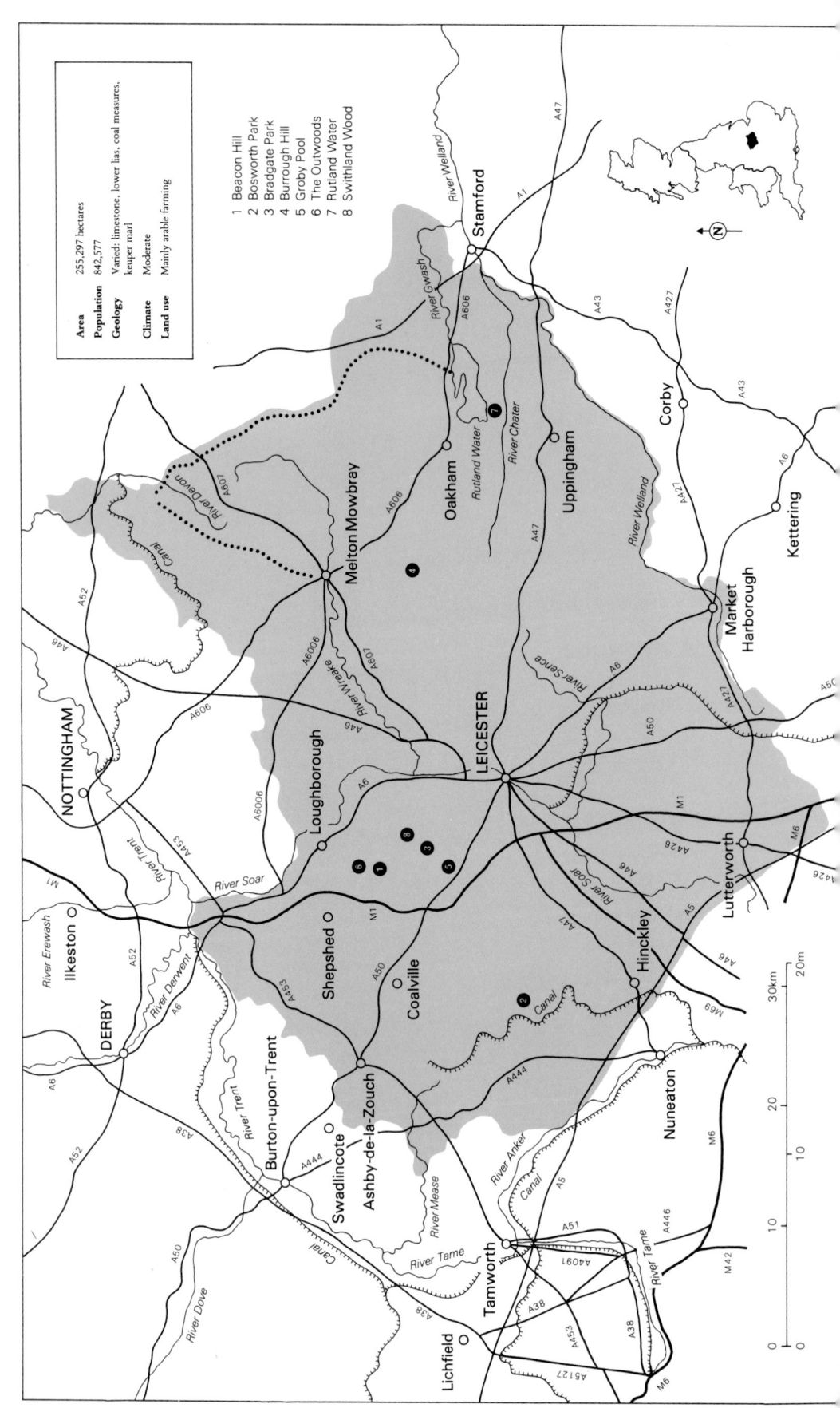

Area	255,297 hectares
Population	842,577
Geology	Varied: limestone, lower lias, coal measures, keuper marl
Climate	Moderate
Land use	Mainly arable farming

1 Beacon Hill
2 Bosworth Park
3 Bradgate Park
4 Burrough Hill
5 Groby Pool
6 The Outwoods
7 Rutland Water
8 Swithland Wood

N

River Welland
Stamford
A1
River Gwash
A606
A47
A43
A427
Corby
A43
A6
Kettering
Oakham
Rutland Water
River Chater
Uppingham
A47
River Welland
A427
Market Harborough
A50
A6
A421
A5C
Melton Mowbray
A606
River Wreake
A607
A606
A46
River Eye
River Devon
Canal
A607
A52
A46
NOTTINGHAM
A606
A6006
Loughborough
A6
LEICESTER
River Soar
River Sence
A6
River Soar
A46
A426
Lutterworth
M1
A5
A426
Shepshed
M1
A50
Coalville
Canal
Hinckley
A47
A5
M69
Ilkeston
A52
River Erewash
River Trent
M1
A453
DERBY
River Derwent
A6
A52
Burton-upon-Trent
River Dove
A50
A38
A444
A444
A444
Swadlincote
Ashby-de-la-Zouch
A453
River Mease
Nuneaton
M6
A444
River Anker
Canal
A5
Tamworth
River Tame
A51
A446
A4091
A38
A53
Lichfield
A38
A51127
M6
M42
River Tame
M42

0   10   20   30km
0   10   20m

Leicestershire and Rutland

Though Leicestershire, including the old county of Rutland in the east, is not nationally renowned for its wildlife, the discerning visitor who is prepared to explore its footpaths and byways can find much of beauty and interest. One part, Charnwood Forest, is unique: a buried mountain chain of hard Pre-Cambrian rocks, yielding relatively inhospitable soils, it largely held its own against the forces of agricultural improvement until the early nineteenth century, when it was finally enclosed. The moorland which survived this process harbours plants such as bilberry and heather, cottongrass and cross-leaved heath. Athough its rocky outcrops are no longer the haunt of raven and kite, whinchat and meadow pipit still nest in their vicinity; it is also the stronghold of adder, common lizard and slow-worm. Substantial parts of the Forest are now public open space, but complementing these are two large nature reserves: one, on the flanks of the ULVERSCROFT Valley, spans a whole cross-section of characteristic habitats, from a rocky ridge studded with bilberry down through heath grassland and ancient woodland to species-rich grassland and marsh in the valley bottom.

On the eastern flank of Charnwood Forest lies the valley of the Soar, running north through Leicester and Loughborough to join the Trent. Although much 'improved', its upper reaches still adjoin some small valley marshes where plants such as meadow-rue and marsh-orchid grow. Extensive areas of the valley north of Leicester are marred – or not, according to your point of view – by gravelpits. As these are worked out and abandoned they flood, and the reedswamp and willow scrub now developing in and around them provide excellent feeding and nesting sites for a variety of waterfowl and other birds.

The rolling hills of east Leicestershire and western Rutland were for many centuries sheep pasture. They are capped in places by a warm brown ironstone, out of which many of the older houses in the villages are built. The edge of this ironstone is often marked by a steep scarp, at the foot of which are small spring-fed flushes, where great horsetail, marsh-marigold and tussock-sedge jostle for space with fleabane and spotted-orchid. The last-named plant is also a feature of some of the old quarries where iron ore was dug, and one, with a stretch of the disused mineral line which served it, is now a nature reserve.

The ironstone scarp is drained by streams: some find their way into tributaries of the Soar, but others flow south and east into the Welland. The heavy and intractable clay soils of these latter valleys are one reason for the survival there of a number of ancient woodlands, some of which have happily so far escaped the drastic effects of reafforestation. Their overgrown ash, field maple and hazel coppice shelters a rich ground flora including herb-Paris, greater butterfly-orchid and violet helleborine. Nightingale nests in dense thickets of blackthorn, and redstart in the hollow ash trees in nearby hedgerows.

One valley, that of the EYE BROOK, was for many years a mecca for local birdwatchers, the attraction being a reservoir built there in 1940. Since the mid-1970s, however, many have transferred their allegiance to the huge new reservoir a little to the north east, RUTLAND WATER. With a surface area of 1250ha this is the largest man-made lake in southern Britain; there is a 140ha nature reserve at the western end, and to date over 200 species of bird have been recorded there. Careful management and its geographical position make this reservoir a magnet for waterfowl in particular.

Rutland, once England's smallest county and still rightly jealous of its individuality, has another attraction for the naturalist – its eastern limestone plateau. Two centuries ago its limestone heaths rivalled the wolds of Lincolnshire; nowadays they are sadly curtailed and the colourful lime-loving plants eke out a somewhat precarious existence on roadside verges and in churchyards and, in greater quantity, in abandoned quarry workings. Sulphur clover, pyramidal orchid, clustered bellflower and autumn gentian may still be found, among many others.

Moorland, marsh, woodland and limestone grassland are some of the highlights of Leicestershire's natural history, but are not all that the area has to offer. Though scattered and often remote from roads, there still survive, for example, unimproved hay meadows on lime-rich clays, where in May green-winged orchids flower in hundreds among cowslips. Later in the year dropwort, burnet and betony provide very different colours, and the season closes with devil's-bit scabious and hoary ragwort.

Fields of this kind are of course the exception in a landscape which, like most of the rest of lowland England, is either arable or ley. However the hedgerows which divide the fields retain their interest whatever the crop, and those of Leicestershire are no exception. In a journey from the acid soils of the north west, through the Soar Valley and east on to the limestone, 30 or more different kinds of hedgerow trees and shrubs may be seen, some found everywhere but others highly selective in their soil preferences. Holly and oak are a feature of the western hedges, buckthorn with trailing hops those of the central valley, and wayfaring-tree and spindle those of eastern Rutland.

The lowland landscape does not stand still and Leicestershire is no exception. Its hard rock quarries supply aggregate to most of south east England, and coalmining on a huge scale threatens areas that are traditionally agricultural. However there are still large areas of countryside where people can observe nature's astonishing ability to accommodate disturbance and management by man that extends back over several millennia. Despite the loss of some rarities, this remains a fascinating study for anyone with a mind to enquire and eyes to see.

IAN EVANS

Ambion Wood and Shenton Cutting

Permit only; 20ha; L and RTNC reserve
Woodland and disused railway line
Spring, early summer

Close to Bosworth Field, where red kites must have gathered like vultures after the battle, the old Nuneaton to Ashby de la Zouch railway line runs right past the edge of Ambion Wood.

The cutting is hedged with oak and ash, a clue to the rich boulder clay of the site, while the slopes have been invaded with a scrub of hawthorn, wild rose and bramble forming tilted glades of rough grassland filled with tor-grass, cowslip and yellow rattle, with common spotted-orchid, common twayblade and hairy violet. The ballast bed of the old line is rich in small plants and common centaury, fairy flax, imperforate St John's-wort and fern-grass may be found. It forms an avenue in which butterflies, common blue and small heath perhaps, fly in the sun around rosebay and great willowherb or rest on vetches or common bird's-foot-trefoil. Other insects are plentiful and moths include chimneysweeper, which argues the presence of its food plant, pignut.

Shade is a keynote of Ambion Wood, where oaks stand above deep thickets of hawthorn, and blackthorn, although clearings let light in to the damp woodland floor and the structure throughout is considerably varied. Away from the tangles of thorns, this fine old wood is a mix of oak with ash and wych elm over an understorey of Midland hawthorn, with old coppiced hazel, field maple, guelder-rose and willow above a varied ground cover.

The clearings are often marshy, with great willowherb, thistles, rushes, bramble and bittersweet, but where the ground is drier, under the trees, the woodland plants include goldilocks buttercup, wood-sorrel, broad-leaved helleborine and early-purple orchid, with narrow buckler-fern and lady-fern.

A dark pool inside the wood, with the bordering Ashby de la Zouch Canal, adds a range of wetland interest, increasing the variety of insects. The woodland birds range from woodpeckers, in the tall timber trees, to warblers in the thickets and scrub. On a sunlit summer day the clearings are filled with birdsong.

Beacon Hill

SK 510145; 67ha; LCC
Upland and woodland
Leaflet from LCC
Spring, early summer

Beacon Hill is one of the highest points in the county and contains a great variety of plant and animal life in an area which includes grassland, bracken, woods and moorland.

Bloody Oaks Quarry

Permit only; 1.2ha; L and RTNC reserve
Small disused limestone quarry
Spring, summer

The rabbit-grazed old quarry is a shallow working, bordered by farmland and woodland, with an attractive scrub cover and rich areas of lime-loving plants such as marjoram, yellow-wort and common rock-rose.

Bosworth Park

SK 413033; 34.8ha; LCC
Traditional parkland with lake
Leaflet from LCC
Spring, early summer

The lake, stream and small ponds add a wetland interest to the grassland and fine old parkland trees of this remnant of a seventeenth-century deer park.

Bradgate Park

SK 523116; 320ha; Bradgate Park Trust
Heathland and woodland
Leaflets from information centre
Spring, early summer

The large area of grassland, heath and bracken, with small woodlands and rocky outcrops, adjoins SWITHLAND WOODS, overlooks Cropston Reservoir, and has a deer sanctuary.

Broombriggs

Permit only; 7.6ha; L and RTNC reserve
Large field and spinneys
Spring, early summer

Although this area of grassland is still actively farmed, new planting of oak, birch and rowan next to the spinneys should greatly enhance its wildlife value.

Brown's Hill Quarry

Permit only; 5ha; L and RTNC reserve
Disused quarry
Geology: all year; plants: early summer

The geological importance lies in an excellent exposure of middle lias marlstone with the basal beds of the overlying upper lias. The chief botanical interest is a spectacular show of common spotted-orchid together with numbers of bee orchid.

Burrough Hill

SK 766115; 34ha; LCC
Hill grassland and woodland
Booklet from LCC
Spring, early summer

The grassed hill fort affords splendid views across east Leicestershire and over the spread of Burrough Hill covert below with its typical woodland bird life and butterflies.

Charley

Permit only; 224ha; L and RTNC reserve
Moorland and heath
Spring, early summer

One of the few remaining areas of heather moorland and grassland heath in the county, the reserve contains a fine show of plants such as heather, cross-leaved heath, purple moor-grass, bilberry, crowberry, lesser skullcap and the strange-looking small fern, moonwort.

Cribb's Meadow

Permit only; 4ha; L and RTNC reserve
Unimproved meadowland
Spring, early summer

A railway line, long closed, has a thick cover of scrub on its banks, enhancing the value of the site to wildlife and increasing the sheltered nature of the meadows. The two fields lie on either side of this line, aligned east–west between hedges and the embankment, open to the warmth of the mid-day sun and sheltered from chilly winds. The essential nature of the rich old grasslands is unaltered and the county's heritage of beautiful old-meadow flowers is protected here.

In spring cowslip makes a brilliant show together with green-winged orchid. Buttercups add their brilliance and, later in the year, common bird's-foot-trefoil spreads across the meadows. The scrub species, wild rose and hawthorn, which had moved out into the meadow, have now been removed, and there is still a rich variety of smaller plants. Lady's bedstraw and yellow rattle occur with great burnet, an indicator of unploughed grassland. An even more important indicator of an old-meadow site is the presence together of green-winged orchid, adder's-tongue, pepper-saxifrage and common spotted-orchid.

The embankment and ballast of the disused railway line are full of varied plants and, with the hedges, contain ash, blackthorn, crab apple, dogwood, hawthorn, oak and willow. Bramble and wild rose tangle the sunlit fringes of the scrub while acid-loving gorse contrasts with kidney vetch and oxeye daisy. Herb-Robert and perforate St John's-wort spread across the levelled ballast, with banks of rosebay willowherb and ragwort.

This variety of plant life attracts beautiful small butterflies such as the common blue and small copper and the scrub encourages warblers and yellowhammer.

Moonwort, an uncommon fern of dry grassland.

Croft

Permit only; 6ha; L and RTNC reserve
River and river meadows
Spring, summer

The River Soar winds through water meadows before squeezing between two shoulders of hill at Croft. Rocky exposures are crowned with gorse and hawthorn while the richer meadows contain alder and willow along the stream with bulrush, water forget-me-not and arrowhead.

Dimminsdale

Permit only; 6.8ha; L and RTNC reserve
Old limestone workings
Spring, early summer

Much of the reserve is now covered with scrub and woodland but there are still small areas of limestone grassland and an interesting change to acid conditions where millstone grit overlies the richer limestone. Flooded quarries add wetland interest and the range of plants includes bulrush, water-lily and giant bellflower, heath bedstraw, harebell and tormentil. A good variety of bird life includes mallard on the pools and woodcock in the woodland.

Eye Brook Reservoir

Permit only; 160ha; AWA reserve
Large reservoir
Winter

Although permits are required to enter the reservoir area itself, it is easily overlooked from a minor road at SP 850960. Once the premier birdwatchers' reserve of the county, its importance has now been usurped by RUTLAND WATER but good numbers of winter wildfowl still feed and shelter here. Species include mallard and wigeon with pochard, teal, goldeneye and goosander.

Grand Union Canal

Permit only; 32km; L and RTNC reserve
Length of working canal
Spring, summer

The canal has an attractive range of waterside plants such as arrowhead, flowering-rush and greater tussock-sedge, together with a great variety of fish, dragonflies and beetles, with the special interest of a colony of Daubenton's bat in one of the tunnels.

Grantham Canal

Permit only; 13km; LTNC reserve
Rich canal site
Spring, summer

An outstanding variety of water plants includes both branched and unbranched bur-reed, with common reed, flowering-rush and lesser water-parsnip.

Great Bowden Pit

Permit only; 1.6ha; L and RTNC reserve
Small marsh
Spring, summer

An old pit has developed a fine small marsh which contains not only typical species such as bulrush but also plants more characteristic of acid bogs such as *Sphagnum* mosses and common cottongrass. Snipe may fly in to feed in winter.

Great Fenny Wood

Permit only; 4ha; L and RTNC reserve
Mixed woodland
Spring, early summer

Lying in a very wet area of waterlogged gravels, the wood is a mix of crack willow, oak and ash which has been growing and regenerating naturally, unmanaged for around a century. A rich variety of insects encourages a good range of birds, including spotted flycatcher, willow warbler and treecreeper. Tawny owl and kestrel breed.

Great Merrible Wood

Permit only; 12ha; L and RTNC reserve
Rich woodland
Spring, early summer

In summer Great Merrible stands like a tilted green island in a rolling sea of golden cornfields. A superb wood, it echoes the sound of tractors at sowing time, harvest and ploughing, but stays still, cool and disturbed only by the wind for the rest of the year.

It is a damp wood on heavy lime-rich clays where some very fine ash and oak trees dominate a spread of coppiced hazel. A good variety of other species includes buckthorn, dogwood, field maple, guelder-rose and spindle with hawthorn and Midland hawthorn.

Beneath this mix of shrubs and trees the ground cover varies with the shade and wetness. Rides are thick with meadowsweet and great horsetail; well-lit clearings are tangled with bramble; bluebell, dog's mercury and enchanter's-nightshade spread beneath the trees. Scattered throughout the drier slopes nettle-leaved bellflower grows in good numbers, with herb-Paris and violet and broad-leaved helleborine.

There is a good variety of woodland birds and the wood is a notable pigeon roost. Mammals include wood mouse, fox and stoat.

Groby Pool

SK 524081; 13.6ha; Hinckley and Bosworth BC
reserve
Freshwater lake
All year

The pool is privately owned but may be overlooked from the road. A fine reedswamp attracts a wide variety of small birds while duck may be seen on the open water and kingfisher may visit.

Herbert's Meadow

Permit only; 2ha; L and RTNC reserve
Unimproved grassland
Spring, summer

Heathy grassland and scrub give way to marshy ground where a fine range of plants includes bog pimpernel, marsh violet and flea sedge. Green-winged and heath spotted-orchid occur, with fragrant orchid at one of the only two Leicestershire sites.

Holwell Mineral Line

Permit only; 0.8km; L and RTNC reserve
Disused railway line
Spring, early summer

Meadow crane's-bill, cowslip and common spotted-orchid grow on the drier parts while wetter areas are rich in great horsetail, meadow-sweet and spreads of various sedges. There is a similar variation of shrubs from dogwood, wild privet and guelder-rose to osier and grey willow.

Canals were once busy trade routes, but now provide corridors of great wildlife importance.

King Lud's Entrenchments

Permit only; 2.4ha; L and RTNC reserve
Limestone grassland and scrub
Spring, summer

A rich limestone plant life, well attended by butterflies and other insects, includes autumn gentian, basil thyme and purple milk-vetch.

Knaptoft Pond

Permit only; 0.2ha; L and RTNC reserve
Small field pond
Spring, summer

The small pond, shaded by willows, contains ivy-leaved duckweed and water-plantain and, fringed by redshank, hard rush and soft rush, provides an attractive site for snipe and mallard. Notable are greater spearwort and flowering-rush.

273

Launde Big Wood

Permit only; 40ha; FC–L and RTNC reserve
Remnant of old Leighfield Forest
Spring, early summer

Most of the large timber has been removed from the wood but a varied range of soils has encouraged a wide variety of ground cover. Early-purple orchid, yellow archangel and giant bellflower occur in the richer areas while more uncommon plant species include herb-Paris, toothwort, broad-leaved helleborine and greater butterfly-orchid.

The Miles Piece

Permit only; 0.4ha; L and RTNC reserve
Grassy bank and marsh
Spring, summer

Despite its small size the reserve contains over 70 species of flowering plant including the rather uncommon marsh arrowgrass with marsh-marigold and ragged-Robin.

Narborough Bog

Permit only; 8.4ha; L and RTNC reserve
Marsh, reedbed and wet woodland
Spring, summer

For all its small size Narborough, on the banks of the River Soar, contains a wide range of wetland habitats. In the past, attempts have been made to drain the woodland and an unusual short-pitched ridge-and-furrow surface has resulted, but the trees have moved back in and returned the wood to a wonderful willow swamp where the warm damp encourages a rich variety of plants. Ash, elder, oak, field maple and guelder-rose, hawthorn, rowan and sycamore grow among the willows while a great tangle of bramble, wild rose, red currant, common reed and meadowsweet is varied with rosebay willowherb and common twayblade where the ground is not so wet. In these drier parts ash replaces willow while sycamore grows tall along the river.

Beside the wood, between it and the railway line which separates the northern from the southern part of the reserve, is a reedbed, a tall dense stand of common reed filled with meadowsweet and yellow iris, varied with an open scrub of willow and guelder-rose. The river borders both wood and reedbed, fringed with plants such as nodding bur-marigold, celery-leaved buttercup, skullcap and water-plantain, with yellow iris and arrowhead. South of the embankment is the marshland area where alder, oak and willow show the lines of old ditches and stand above a superb mix of wetland and damp-meadow plants. Wild angelica and great burnet show above a spread of buttercups, of cuckooflower and yellow rattle, with ragged-Robin, meadowsweet and common meadow-rue, with rushes, sedges such as lesser pond-sedge, tufted-sedge and slender tufted-sedge, brown, carnation and common sedge, with marsh-

marigold, marsh arrowgrass and marsh bedstraw, marsh thistle and marsh valerian. In June the site is dotted with southern marsh-orchid.

The reserve is rich in bird life – in woodland birds such as spotted flycatcher, blackcap, chiffchaff, whitethroat, willow warbler and woodcock and in wetland species such as yellow wagtail and snipe.

North Quarry

Permit only; 4ha; L and RTNC reserve
Geological site
All year

Near BROWN'S HILL QUARRY, North Quarry shows a particularly fine exposure of the 'paper shales' of the upper lias basal beds, together with the beds immediately above them.

The Outwoods

SK 515159; 40ha; Charnwood BC
Mixed woodland
Spring, early summer

Mainly oak and coniferous woodland caps a long ridge of high ground overlooking the fields and hedges of the Soar Valley.

Pickworth Great Wood

Permit only; 120ha; L and RTNC reserve
Mixed woodland
Spring, early summer

Originally an ash–field maple woodland, the reserve contains a rich ground cover with many interesting species such as toothwort, herb-Paris, bird's-nest orchid and greater butterfly-orchid.

Rutland Water

SK 897049; 140ha; L and RTNC–AWA reserve
Reservoir shores and lagoons
Permit only to Egleton section
Leaflets from L and RTNC and interpretative centre
All year

With a shoreline over 38km long, Rutland Water is the second largest man-made lake in England. It stands at the heart of a minor lakeland formed by the spread of Midlands reservoirs and, lying close to the migration routes along the Welland and Nene rivers, has become of national importance for many waterfowl.

The reserve is a vindication of careful planning and excellent management, a site designed specifically for wildlife. Shallow lagoons have been created by building banks which may be over-topped when the water is high but which hold their levels when the reservoir draws down. The levels can be individually controlled so that suitable deeps for diving duck can be maintained at the same time as shallow water for waders and dabbling duck. Because the reservoir is used for recreation the area is zoned to give maximum sanctuary to the reserve itself.

Vast, man-made Rutland Water, on bird migration routes, is of supreme importance for waterfowl.

The reserve falls into three parts. The northern section, Burley Fishponds, consists of an area of reedbed, a nesting site for warblers and other reed-marsh birds, which is scheduled as a research site and has no public access. The middle section, reached from Egleton, is open to permit holders or to members of the L and RTNC. The southern section is open to anyone. Both the Egleton and the southern, Lyndon, areas have excellent observation hides while the Egleton section includes the chain of three lagoons.

The fields around the foreshore are grazed and managed to include paddocks of rich old-meadow grassland and damp areas full of orchids as well as more general spreads of reseeded land. Almost 40,000 trees and shrubs have been planted to grow on into new woodland, scrub and shelter belts, almost invariably of species which might occur here naturally.

The number of bird species recorded at Rutland Water now stands at over 210 and includes more than a dozen species of breeding waterfowl. Ruddy duck and Canada goose may derive from collection escapes but both breed here, together with greylag goose, a feral breeder on lowland waters. Great crested and little grebe, mute swan, gadwall, mallard, pochard, shelduck, shoveler and tufted duck, coot and moorhen all breed.

The spring and autumn wader passage is out-standing for an inland water and several of the waders remain to breed; oystercatcher, for example, have nested on the artificial islands – some overgrown, some shingle-covered to provide a range of sites. Little ringed plover are shingle-nesting birds, and one of the strangest records of breeding success comes not from the nature reserve

but from the reservoir's main car park where, in 1978, one pair nested and raised three of their young right in the centre, despite the fact that perhaps 3000 cars had used the site. Ringed plover also use the shingled islands while redshank generally prefer those covered with vegetation. Snipe, woodcock and lapwing are probable breeders and their characteristic territorial displays may be seen in spring and early summer.

Other ground-nesting birds which breed in the grasslands around the reserve include partridge, red-legged partridge and pheasant, meadow pipit and skylark, together with yellow wagtail, a summer visitor from across the Sahara Desert. The hedges and woodlands which shelter the pastures are rich in breeding birds including wood pigeon and turtle dove, rook and jackdaw. The migrant blackcap, chiffchaff, whitethroat and lesser whitethroat, with garden, reed, sedge and willow warbler, sing in the spring sunshine, marking this area of scrub or reedbed as their breeding territory for the coming summer. Spotted flycatcher may be seen with greenfinch, goldfinch, linnet, bullfinch, redpoll and yellowhammer.

Autumn brings a passage of migrant species – warblers and other summer birds leave, the rush of swallows, swifts and martins moves southwards and waders rest briefly on the lagoons before flying on. Curlew sandpiper, common, green and wood sandpiper pass through with dunlin, ruff, greenshank, spotted redshank and little stint. Occasional bar-tailed and black-tailed godwit, turnstone and sanderling occur, although their major passage is in the spring. Whimbrel may join curlew which are here in greater numbers now, as are snipe and ringed plover.

Golden plover, jack snipe and woodcock numbers build as they come to Rutland Water to winter and as the days grow shorter groups of waterfowl arrive, the birds for which the reservoir has become such a vital site. Regular numbers of coot, little and great crested grebe, gadwall, goldeneye, goosander, mallard, pochard, teal, tufted duck, wigeon and mute swan amount to over 9000 birds, with great northern diver and cormorant, pintail, red-crested pochard and scaup, red-breasted merganser, and sometimes Bewick's and whooper swan.

Now that migrant terns have moved on south, the seabirds are represented by huge passage roosts of thousands of lesser black-backed gull and by winter roosts of great black-backed, common, black-headed and herring gull. The reservoir annually adds to its list of unexpected birds which come here from all points of the compass. Other seabirds include gannet, Manx shearwater, great and arctic skua, red-necked phalarope and Sabine's, Iceland and Mediterranean gull. Red-throated pipit, pomarine skua, collared pratincole, alpine swift, white stork, pectoral sandpiper and long-billed dowitcher have also been recorded.

Although the reserve requires time for its new vegetation to mature and develop, Rutland Water is not only a wonderful place for birds but is also a splendid example of what can be achieved by considered management and a spirit of cooperation. For this, as well as for its waterfowl numbers, the reserve must be rated as one of at least national importance.

Red-legged partridge, a breeding bird of the farmland around Rutland Water.

Swithland Woods

SK 538129; 58.4ha; Bradgate Park Trust
Mixed woodland
Spring, early summer

In the middle of a remnant of the ancient Charnwood Forest is a deep quarry, steep-sided, dressed with acid-loving plants and drowned in still blue-green water. The slates which were quarried here are Pre-Cambrian – even though they are the youngest of the Charnian rocks they are over 550 million years old. A similar smaller quarry occurs in the northern part of the woods, but most of the rest of the area is covered with younger deposits, varying soils which contribute much to the variety.

The major part is high-forest oak, tall and sturdy on the deeper soils, smaller and gnarled on the thin ground above the slates. These shallow acid soils support fine grasses with areas of bracken, wood sage and foxglove and stands of birch. The wettest of the soils, a marshy area to the south, is an alder–ash wood over an understorey of young ash, elder, blackthorn and hazel, with bramble and red currant, with rosebay willowherb, common valerian and common nettle, red campion, yellow pimpernel and bugle. Old coppiced alder and ash occur again where a stream has cut down through the woodland and stand over broad buckler-fern and pendulous sedge.

Most of the wood is ancient – the oaks were probably once coppiced but left for at least a century to grow towards high-forest. With the oaks, small-leaved lime is widespread while the ground cover is a mix of woodland grasses, bramble, great wood-rush, wood-sorrel and bluebell, with yellow pimpernel, hairy wood-rush and common cow-wheat: plants characteristic of ancient Midland woods. Hazel is the chief species of the understorey, often tangled with honeysuckle, while sandier soils show spreads of bracken and bramble.

An area of scrub has oak, blackthorn, hawthorn, birch and hazel over deep grasses from which great burnet and meadowsweet lift. Smaller grassland plants may be seen in a grazed paddock, an ancient unimproved meadow, which lies within the wood: common spotted-orchid shows in early summer and a number of rather uncommon plants, such as betony, saw-wort and adder's-tongue, survive here.

The wide variety of habitat encourages an equivalent diversity of animal life with interesting populations of butterflies, moths and birds.

Ulverscroft

Permit only; 52ha; L and RTNC reserves
Woodland, heathland, meadow and marsh
Spring, early summer

A long slope of the ancient Charnwood Forest is protected by a group of reserves which display an enormous range of habitat. Much of the area is a spread of heathland and scrub; a lot of the woodland is planted – conifers with sycamore and sweet chestnut – but part of the fascination is the change in character from acid higher ground to richer land below.

Charnwood Forest from Bradgate Park, looking across the River Soar to the Wolds.

From the top of the ridge it is possible to pass from woodland to heath, from scrub to wood, from open meadow to marshland. The first small woodland is oak with beech over a thin ground layer which opens on a great sheet of bracken. Oak and rowan, birch and holly grow among the bracken while pathway edges and more open areas show foxglove, bluebell, rosebay willowherb with gorse, bilberry, sheep's sorrel, tormentil and wavy hair-grass. Lower down a semi-mature oak–rowan wood over bracken, honeysuckle and bluebell shows how the upper part will change, unless its open nature is maintained, although this wood is modified with planted sweet chestnut and Scots pine and the shapes of earlier fields are marked by old hedgerow beech trees.

An area of scrub heathland is thick with birch, oak, rowan, hawthorn and holly, with gorse and western gorse, wild rose and rosebay willowherb. Open grassy glades are scattered with common bird's-foot-trefoil and tormentil, fringed with heather and flooded with the song of yellowhammer and linnet. Below the scrub is an ancient woodland replanted with larch, spruce and sweet chestnut with beech and sycamore, which has a ground cover of bluebell and foxglove. Beyond this are the marshes and the meadows.

The marshes have a rich show of meadowsweet and marsh-marigold, of willow and alder over horsetails and rushes, greater bird's-foot-trefoil, betony and water mint. Common spotted-orchid stands among sprays of sedge while a small pool contains bulrush. The meadows have a superb mix of grassland and wetland plants: a willow swamp grades into pasture full of ragged-Robin and buttercups, yellow rattle and vetches, drier humps where tormentil and heath bedstraw show acid influence, and damper places where greater bird's-foot-trefoil and common spotted-orchid grow.

The Wailes

Permit only; 2ha; L and RTNC reserve
Oxbow lake and marsh
Spring, summer

The oxbow lake, artificially created when the river was straightened, has largely silted up but still includes two deep pools, fringed with water-pepper and lesser water-parsnip. The marsh is thick with rushes and sedges and contains marsh arrowgrass, creeping-Jenny and marsh valerian. Reed bunting and snipe probably breed.

Wymondham Rough

Permit only; 12ha; L and RTNC reserve
Unimproved grassland and wood
Spring, early summer

The grassland is different from that at CRIBB'S MEADOW but still contains a great variety of species including the beautiful dropwort, while the woodland and the small marsh area add further interest. Harvest mouse may be found in the hedgerows.

Lincolnshire and South Humberside

Under great skies and swept by fresh sea winds, the low hill ranges of Lincolnshire command spacious views over sea and estuaries, over the fenland plain and far into the eastern Midlands. This wide-ranging scenery is matched by a diversity of wildlife, including many rare plants, insects, amphibians and birds, which give national distinction to some of the county's reserves.

The historic county of Lincolnshire is largely rural and agricultural. Apart from the industrialised belt along the Humber in what is now South Humberside, there are few towns and a small population. The county's landscape and wildlife have been greatly influenced by changing patterns of agriculture over the centuries – initially by forest clearance and grazing, later by enclosures and ploughing, and more recently by intensive agriculture and some afforestation.

These land uses took place on a mosaic of rocks and soils. The harder rocks gave rise to two distinctive and roughly parallel blocks of upland country. In the west, limestone forms a narrow ridge broadening in the south into a gently sloping plateau and giving an almost continuous escarpment towards the Vale of Trent. In the east, the chalk Wolds stretch from the Humber towards the Wash, forming a rolling plateau with small valleys.

The lowland parts of the area consist mainly of clays, but the soils and the scenery were remoulded in the ice ages. The marshland plain between the Wolds and the sea is built of boulder clays which also underlie the later silts and peats of the fenland and the Isle of Axholme. Sands and gravels spread widely over the claylands in the north west and along the edge of the fenland basin, which held a great lake in the last ice age.

On these rocks and soils many different kinds of natural vegetation developed, influenced by a climate which is, by British standards, extreme. The vegetation includes widespread deciduous woodland, open downland on the chalk and limestone hills, heaths over the sand-covered areas and saltmarshes along the coast.

The forest was gradually cleared for cultivation, although some older deciduous woods have survived in the Kesteven (Kest comes from Celtic *coed*, a wood) plateau and valleys, in the central clay vale, and on the boulder clays of the Wolds. The nature reserves reveal the distinctive character of these woods; BARDNEY FOREST, for example, is notable for the abundance, both in standard and coppice form, of the native small-leaved lime.

The open downlands were created by forest clearance and subsequent grazing but they had been largely destroyed by 1820 through ploughing and enclosure. Today, the colourful flowers of this rich habitat are confined to fragments of ancient turf, to old quarries and wide roadside verges.

The acid heaths were difficult to cultivate, but afforestation with conifers after 1920 and intensive agriculture after 1939 destroyed most of them. Only remnants now survive.

The old fenland, with its wealth of bird and insect life, was almost totally destroyed in the eighteenth and early nineteenth centuries. Apart from areas in the Isle of Axholme preserved for peat digging (the turbaries), not a vestige of fen has survived, although claypits, like those along the Humber bank, and later gravelpits in other areas, have provided some compensation for the loss of older wetlands.

Permanent grassland has disappeared rapidly in recent years. Even a field of cowslips is now an unusual sight, and once-common meadow flowers, such as green-winged orchid, have become rarities. The reserves of the L and SHTNC are now the last refuges of the rich and varied plant and animal communities of these old grasslands.

Lincolnshire's long coastline provides some striking contrasts. Between Mablethorpe and Skegness the bulge of the coast is subject to constant erosion, and the narrow, sandy beaches are backed by sea walls to prevent another flood disaster like that of the great North Sea surge in 1953. But north of Mablethorpe and south of Skegness the coast is more sheltered, and sand dunes and saltmarshes are formed here. The dunes at SALTFLEETBY–THEDDLETHORPE are several centuries old; those at GIBRALTAR POINT are of more recent origin and still developing. The great inlet of the Wash is fringed with saltmarshes, which are some of the most extensive in Britain.

Many of the saltmarshes have been extensively reclaimed for cultivation: nearly half the area of the Wash, for example, has been recovered since Saxon times, and reclamation has accelerated since the 1950s. Pressures of a different kind have affected other parts of the coast. Tiny coastal villages have been transformed into seaside resorts, and thousands of caravans and chalets now crowd along the sandy coastline. Fortunately, the finest sand dune areas in the north east and those further south at Gibraltar Point have been protected as nature reserves. Several of these are of national importance, while the vast migratory and wintering populations of waders and wildfowl in the Wash make it an estuary of vital European significance for wildlife.

A. E. SMITH

Axholme Line

SK 773997; 14ha; L and SHTNC reserve
Lime-rich disused railway line
Visitors must keep to central right of way
Spring, summer

A scrub of hawthorn, ash, aspen, elder, oak, dog rose and field maple shelters a spectacular show of green-winged orchid. Eighteen butterfly species have been recorded and the reserve is particularly rich in birdlife.

Baptist Cemetery

Permit only; 0.3ha; L and SHTNC reserve
Disused cemetery
Spring, summer

Mature trees above areas of scrub provide urban sanctuary for a variety of wildlife.

Barrow Blow Wells

Permit only; 2.8ha; L and SHTNC reserve
Small wetland
Spring, summer

A marsh, much of it common reed, surrounds three pools massed with pale green starwort. The reedbed is attractive to small birds including both reed and sedge warbler, as is a small woodland which grades into wet grassland, thick with sedges. There is a good variety of birds.

Bardney Forest

Permit only; 395ha; FC
Mixed woodland
Spring, early summer

Fragments of the old Bardney Forest, a once great spread of ash and small-leaved lime, are conserved by the FC for their ecological and historic importance. Generally managed as coppice with standards, they contain a rich and varied ground cover and are attractive to insects and birds.

Baston Fen

Permit only; 36.5ha; L and SHTNC reserve
Flood meadows and open water
All year

Over 230 plants have been identified here, including water-violet, lesser water-plantain, greater bladderwort and a rich community of marsh-orchids. More than 130 birds have been recorded, among them breeding snipe and redshank, tufted duck and shoveler, with wintering flocks of several hundred mallard, teal and wigeon.

Birds Wood

Permit only; 6.2ha; L and SHTNC reserve
Woodland, scrub and flooded sand workings
Spring, summer

Half of the reserve consists of flooded sandpits, with oak, birch and grey willow scrub on the spoil and with small ponds thick with common reed and bulrush. Seventy bird species have been recorded, with newts, frog and common lizard and 12 species of butterfly. The remaining area has yet to be worked for sand.

Blacktoft Sands

SE 843232; 184ha; RSPB reserve
Salt reedmarsh and lagoon
Leaflet from RSPB
All year

Until the lagoon was dredged, Blacktoft Sands was a reedbed, the largest single block of common reed in the country – virtually impenetrable and, where the tides wash most often, up to 3m tall. On higher ground within the reeds there are small rough grasslands of tangled couch where short-eared owl nest, and there is an area of saltmarsh where sea club-rush and sea aster grow. A low stone wall deflects the river, stabilising the reedmarsh, and beyond are mudflats and tide-washed shingle.

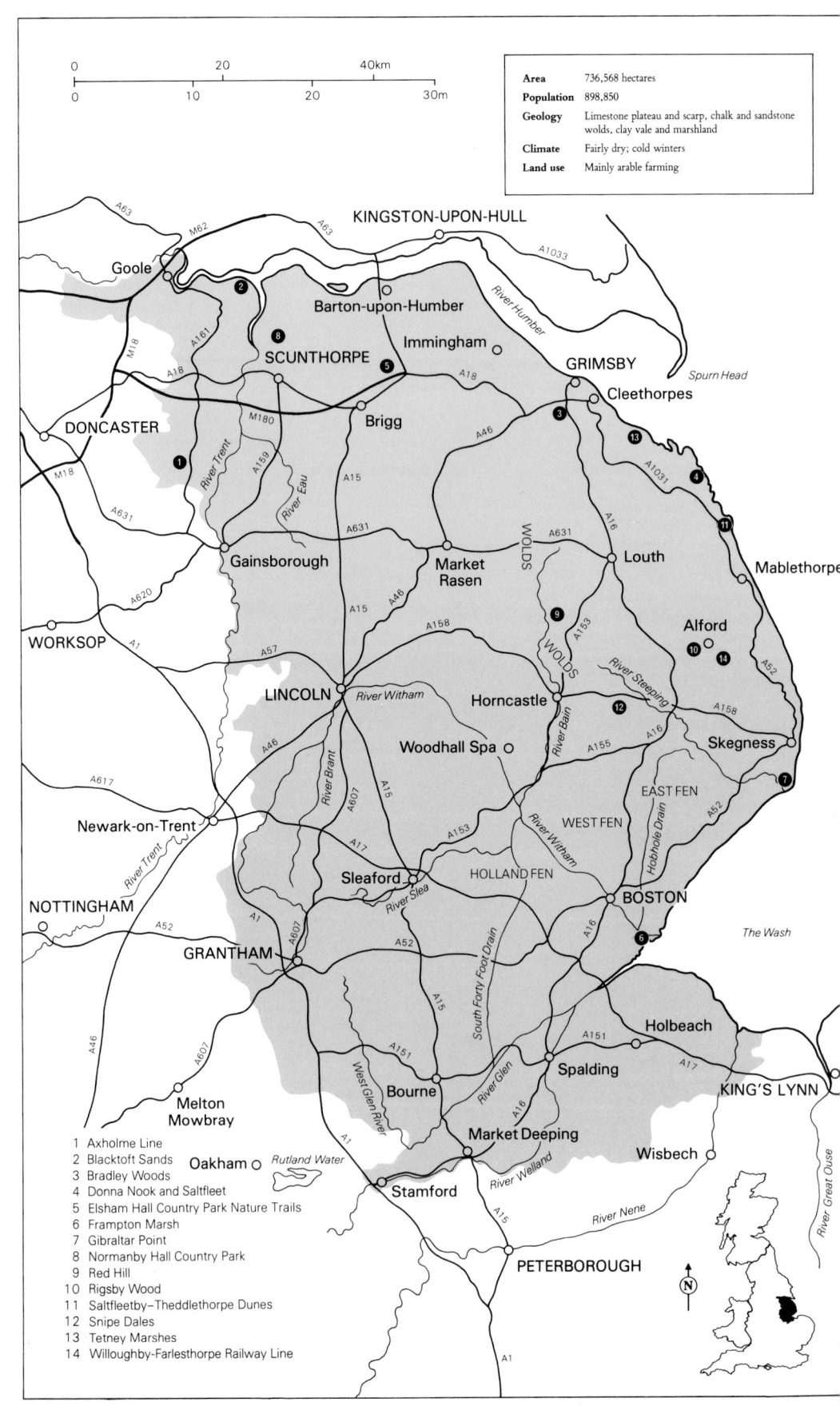

Area	736,568 hectares	
Population	898,850	
Geology	Limestone plateau and scarp, chalk and sandstone wolds, clay vale and marshland	
Climate	Fairly dry; cold winters	
Land use	Mainly arable farming	

KINGSTON-UPON-HULL

Goole

Barton-upon-Humber

SCUNTHORPE

Immingham

GRIMSBY

Cleethorpes

Spurn Head

DONCASTER

Brigg

WORKSOP

Gainsborough

Market Rasen

WOLDS

Louth

Mablethorpe

WOLDS

Alford

LINCOLN

River Witham

Horncastle

Woodhall Spa

River Bain

Skegness

Newark-on-Trent

EAST FEN

WEST FEN

River Witham

Hobhole Drain

NOTTINGHAM

Sleaford

River Slea

HOLLAND FEN

BOSTON

The Wash

GRANTHAM

South Forty Foot Drain

Holbeach

Melton Mowbray

Oakham

Rutland Water

Bourne

River Glen

Spalding

KING'S LYNN

Market Deeping

Wisbech

Stamford

River Welland

River Nene

PETERBOROUGH

River Great Ouse

1 Axholme Line
2 Blacktoft Sands
3 Bradley Woods
4 Donna Nook and Saltfleet
5 Elsham Hall Country Park Nature Trails
6 Frampton Marsh
7 Gibraltar Point
8 Normanby Hall Country Park
9 Red Hill
10 Rigsby Wood
11 Saltfleetby–Theddlethorpe Dunes
12 Snipe Dales
13 Tetney Marshes
14 Willoughby-Farlesthorpe Railway Line

Because the habitat varies little the range of breeding birds is not particularly wide, but there are important nesting communities. Bearded tit breed only in large reedbeds and Blacktoft is now an important stronghold with some 10 per cent of the national breeding numbers. Reed bunting, reed and grasshopper warbler and water rail also breed while redshank nest in the saltmarsh area and the reserve protects nesting mallard, teal and shelduck, and occasional marsh harrier.

Two public hides overlook the reserve – the lagoon may draw good numbers of autumn birds, with around 1000 teal and many kinds of wader. Dunlin in large numbers, redshank, lapwing and bar-tailed godwit, smaller numbers of little stint, ruff and little ringed plover gather here with, in winter, over 1000 pink-footed geese.

Boston Road Brickpit

Permit only; 1.8ha; L and SHTNC reserve
Wetland, grassland and old orchard
Spring, summer

Yellow water-lily, yellow iris and marsh-marigold shelter nesting coot, reed and sedge warbler and reed bunting.

Bradley Woods

TA 245058; 25ha; Grimsby BC
Mixed woodland
Spring, early summer

Oak, ash and elm with some coniferous woodland have an understorey including wild cherry and dogwood with beech, birch and blackthorn. Open wet areas are rich in bugle and common spotted-orchid, providing suitable glades for butterflies; other animals include badger and a variety of woodland birds.

Brumby Common

Permit only; 4ha; Scunthorpe BC reserve
Educational reserve
Permits from Normanby Hall Country Park or Scunthorpe Museum
Spring, early summer

Burton Gravel Pits, now flooded, provide an important wetland refuge near Lincoln.

A nature trail has been established to demonstrate the ecology of this area of heathland and lagoons.

Burton Gravel Pits

Permit only; 36.8ha; L and SHTNC reserve
Flooded gravelpits and woodland
All year

Sheltered by belts of woodland, the four lakes on which the reserve is based lie calm and peaceful, only some 5km from Lincoln. For wildfowl and waterbirds this is one of the most important sites in the county. The lakes vary in size, ranging from wide, islanded and relatively open waters to sheltered, shallow, marshy places, rich in plants such as bulrush and yellow iris, with the less common species galingale, mare's-tail and greater spearwort.

Generally the water is deep, suited to diving ducks, pochard and tufted duck, to great crested grebe and resident Canada goose, all of which breed here. Other birds include mute swan and mallard, marsh and reedbed birds at the water's edge, and the occasional kingfisher, while winter brings good numbers of varied waterbirds. The woodland areas are small but varied, with a range from brambled scrub to tall trees, both broad-leaved and coniferous, extensive enough to hold true woodland birds such as great spotted and green woodpecker.

The most interesting mammals here are probably the bats, which include noctule and Daubenton's bat. The noctule is fairly common in England and Wales but Daubenton's bat is less frequent and is generally only found hunting over water, flying in very low, wide circles to take and eat small insects. Both these bats are gregarious and may form colonies several hundred strong.

Burton Gravel Pits also attracts vagrant migrating birds, including red-crested pochard, an eastern European bird which occasionally overshoots its normal limits and has even, rarely, nested in this country. Red-necked grebe has occurred, a winter visitor also from eastern Europe, and black tern may be seen on passage.

Candlesby Hill Quarry

Permit only; 1.2ha; L and SHTNC reserve
Old chalkpit
Spring, summer

Wild thyme, wild pansy and other small plants attract butterflies and bees; the range from scrub to tall hawthorn and ash woodland holds breeding spotted flycatcher, finches and warblers.

Covenham Reservoir

Permit only; 80ha; L and SHTNC
Large open reservoir
Autumn, winter

The reservoir is a daytime roost for surface-feeding duck but is mainly important for diving ducks. Pochard and tufted duck, goldeneye, scaup, long-tailed duck and smew may occur with red-throated diver and several species of grebe.

Crowle Waste

Permit only; 116.8ha; L and SHTNC reserve
Partially flooded peat workings with bog and heath
Visitors must keep to paths and smoking is forbidden
Spring, summer

Crowle Waste is a wonderfully peaceful place, tawny with bracken, sheltered by dense belts of downy birch. It is a remnant of a vast domed bog stretching from the Trent to the Aire rivers around the head of the Humber Estuary. It is now much changed: the 3m deep peat of the old bog has been dug and the water level lowered by drainage. This has left a complex pattern of drowned diggings, separated by dry banks, and of canals connecting the diggings, providing a range from open water to dry scrub woodland.

The dry banks which carry the footpaths are thick with bracken and downy birch, which invaded as the water dropped, but spreads of heather occur in some of the drier areas, while the wet hollows may be plumed with hare's-tail cottongrass.

The wetter habitats carry a wide range of plants. In places willow swamp replaces the dry birch woodland and alternates with stands of common reed or *Sphagnum* bog, broken by pools and lanes of water twisting among the trees. This is a site for round-leaved sundew and common butterwort, bog rosemary, fen violet and marsh pea.

Adder and grass snake occur and over 30 bird species breed. The insects include large heath whose caterpillar feeds on cottongrass and is here around the south eastern limit of its range.

Dole Wood

Permit only; 2.7ha; L and SHTNC reserve
Mixed oak woodland
Spring, summer

A remnant of the old Kesteven Forest, the wood is mainly oak over coppiced hazel, and includes small-leaved lime, wild service-tree, hawthorn and Midland hawthorn. Yellow archangel, uncommon in these parts, grows on the woodland floor.

Donna Nook and Saltfleet

TF 421998 and 444958; 900ha; L and SHTNC reserve
Dune system, mudflats, saltings and sandflats
Do not enter bombing area when red flags are flying
All year

The reserve has a rich and varied plant life and over 250 bird species have been recorded, including rarities. Breeding birds include red-legged partridge, whitethroat, little grebe, ringed plover, and little tern; winter may bring shore lark, twite and Lapland bunting, knot, dunlin, short-eared owl and hen harrier. Grey and common seal may be seen.

Elsham Hall Country Park Nature Trails

TA 029120; 1–4km; Elsham Hall Country Park
Three varied trails
Spring, early summer

The trails are laid out around artificial lakes, plantations, mixed woodlands and downland in the attractive Lincolnshire Wolds.

Epworth Turbary

Permit only; 34ha; L and SHTNC reserve
Old peat workings with fen and wet heath habitats
The bog areas are particularly dangerous
Spring, summer

Sphagnum bog with common cottongrass and bog rosemary contrasts with richer fen where great fen-sedge, sneezewort, yellow loosestrife, purple-loosestrife and common meadow-rue occur. Much of the reserve is scrubbed with birch, creeping willow, alder buckthorn, oak and rowan, a habitat for birds such as green and great spotted woodpecker and woodcock.

Ewerby Pond

Permit only; 0.9ha; L and SHTNC reserve
Reed-fringed pond
Spring, summer

Common reed, bulrush, lesser bulrush, purple-loosestrife and great willowherb shelter breeding birds including reed and sedge warbler, mallard and tufted duck, little grebe and Canada goose.

Fir Hill Quarry

Permit only; 0.5ha; L and SHTNC reserve
Old chalkpit
Spring, summer

This small quarry supports many of the wild flowers of the chalk Wolds. Quaking grass, wild basil, marjoram, salad burnet, yellow-wort and pyramidal orchid grow here together with autumn gentian and wild thyme, among other species.

Frampton Marsh

TF 364384; 271ha; L and SHTNC reserve
Large area of saltmarsh and mudflat
Check tides before walking on the marsh: creeks fill
up rapidly
All year

It is a long walk from where one can park a car to
the Haven Bank, overlooking the reserve, but for
the naturalist it is well worth while. From the foot
of the bank the marsh stretches as far as the eye can
see, merges into the wide mudflats and flat waves
of the Wash, an endless level of green and grey,
incredibly only a fragment of the Wash marshes.

Frampton Marsh is part of the only unreclaimed
area of high saltmarsh in the south west Wash. The
marsh has developed from the mudflats by a
seaward growth of glasswort, common saltmarsh-
grass and common cord-grass which trap the unstable silts and build them slowly upwards. As the
mud builds up, other plants become established and
eventually the marsh is lifted so that only high spring
tides cover it. Creeks, lined with sea-purslane and
sea-blite, drain the land behind and carry the ebb and
flow of normal tides between rich swards filled
with sea aster and common sea-lavender.

A wealth of insects, molluscs and other small
animals live in the vegetation and thick muds,
providing food for vast populations of birds. The
reserve protects the largest black-headed gull colony in Britain, with considerable numbers of common tern and redshank, reed bunting, meadow
pipit and skylark. In winter the saltmarsh draws
large flocks of finches and buntings, birds such as
linnet and twite which feed on the seeds of the
saltmarsh plants, together with wildfowl such as
wigeon, mallard, teal, shelduck and Brent goose.

The Wash is the most important breeding area in
Britain for common seal and has international
status as a site for winter waders. The mudflats
provide a feeding ground for huge gatherings of
knot and dunlin, with other waders such as curlew,
whimbrel, greenshank and bar-tailed godwit.

Friskney Decoy Wood

Permit only; 5.8ha; L and SHTNC reserve
Woodland with old decoy pond
Spring, summer

The decoy pond stands in a mixed woodland,
largely bracken-covered but including climbing
corydalis, uncommon in east England. Over 40
species of birds breed and many autumn migrants
pause on the reserve; an added attraction is a
flourishing badger colony.

Furze Hill

Permit only; 4.7ha; L and SHTNC reserve
Valley grassland and stream
Spring, summer

A narrow valley meadow with brookside alder and
willow trees includes both opposite-leaved and the
more uncommon alternate-leaved golden saxifrage.
The drier hill grassland has strong growths of gorse
and plants such as dove's-foot crane's-bill,
parsley-piert and bird's-foot. Birds include linnet,
treecreeper and willow tit, and the sandy hillside
contains a badger sett.

Gibraltar Point

TF 556581; 428ha; L and SHTNC reserve
Coastal dunes and marshes
Leaflets from visitor centre
All year

To those who are used to a land where rocky cliffs
stand above the swell of the sea, to a clear-cut
definition of land and water, the edge of the Wash
must seem a place with no real boundaries, a place
where land and sea and sky flow one into the other
with their meeting place always just beyond reach
and never quite defined.

The Lincolnshire coast is a dynamic coast built
from sand and mud where dune systems form new
sea walls and saltmarshes lift from the mudflats.
Gibraltar Point has two main dune systems: one
raised in the eighteenth century, when it stood at
the edge of the sea, the other almost half a
kilometre eastwards, formed a century later and
holding the land it has won from the force of the
tides. This land between has been built up by a
saltmarsh, open towards the Wash where a new
marsh is forming and headed to the north by a
freshwater marsh, an area, like the sand dunes, rich
in animal and plant life and a wonderful
demonstration of the magic of these coasts.

The dunes are held in a delicate balance, for only
a thin skin of plants protects the sand from the
wind. A violent storm, combined with a high
spring tide, can still cut the dune ridge away and
any damage to the cover of plants can lead to a
blow-out, where the wind will scoop out a valley
of sand. Since human feet easily break the thin
plant cover, board-walks have been laid at Gibraltar Point. Eventually more seaward dunes may
form, while a shallow soil begins to cover the older
slopes; a deeper plant cover spreads, scrub and
trees begin to grow and the landward dunes
become stable, free of the threat of the sea.

At Gibraltar Point the whole progression from
open windblown sand can be clearly seen. The
sand and shingle ridges of the beach grade up to a
strand line where pioneer plants are able to survive. Sea rocket, sand couch and prickly saltwort
can tolerate the flood of the higher tides and help
to trap the blown sand. The strong roots of sand
couch help to bind the mounds of sand but, when
the young dune has been raised above the tides,
marram comes into its own. Marram, also a grass,
is the main builder of dunes, a plant which has a
phenomenal ability to grow upwards through
windblown sand, while lacing together the layers
below with a network of long white roots.

Although these plants help to hold the dune
together, it is still mobile, with sand blowing from

The complex of sea, sand and sea-buckthorn covered dunes at Gibraltar Point.

and over the face, dropping in the shelter behind and moving the ridge slowly inland. When another seaward dune shelters this one, the marram, without fresh windblown sand to stimulate it, tends to die out. Mosses, lichens and fine grasses spread and a host of plants such as ragwort, hound's-tongue and common bird's-foot-trefoil add brightness to the slopes. The most sheltered landward side of the ridge is filled with a dense jungle of spiny sea-buckthorn, varied with elder, hawthorn, wild privet and wild rose.

The earlier western dunes are the oldest part of the reserve, banks of sand thick with sea-buckthorn, elder and hawthorn. The sands of Gibraltar Point have been milled not only from hard pebbles but also from softer chalks and from fragments of sea shells, so the dunes are lime-rich with carpets of colourful flowers between the dense thickets of scrub. Cowslip, lady's bedstraw and an occasional pyramidal orchid may show in these glades while the thickets are floored with springbeauty in spring and early summer.

Between the two main dune systems and in the strip saltings between the newer dunes, the other main habitat has developed: the saltmarsh. Plants such as Townsend's cord-grass and glasswort colonise tidal muds by trapping material around their stems and leaves, forming low mounds. The cord-grass forms strong clumps which grow up through the muddy hummocks until they form low-water islands.

When the mounds have built up higher to form a shallow marsh dissected by winding creeks,

annual sea-blite and sea aster appear, plants which can survive a regular dip in sea water. More varied plants tend to trap more sediments and these newcomers help to raise the saltmarsh further until thrift and sea-lavender can become established.

The creeks are fringed by sea-purslane, a plant which is well adapted to trapping silt and which helps to raise the level of the banks. Every time the tides fill the creeks they spill silt through the fringe of plants and when the water falls the silt is trapped, building a low lip to the twisting channels. Between the creeks is spread a wonderful summer show of thrift and sea-lavender above a fine turf of grasses pricked with sea plantain and sea arrow-grass. Three kinds of sea-lavender grow here, common, lax-flowered and rock sea-lavender, while the old marsh contains stands of shrubby sea-blite, a shingle plant at probably its most northerly site in Europe.

Above the saltmarsh, the Bulldog Bank protects a freshwater marsh from tidal invasion, a ponded area of wet meadowland rich in sedges and rushes, meadowsweet, yellow iris and great willowherb. A mere, overlooked by a public hide, adds to the wetland interest and increases the great range of habitat.

Gibraltar Point is rich in animal life, in a wide spectrum from sand eel, piddock, lugworm and ragworm to rabbit and common seal, from the myriad spiders and insects to the countless birds which visit here to breed or feed or shelter. Some of the animals have to be able to cope with shifting sands, with clinging muds and with changes in salinity as the tides ebb and flow. Only a small range of very highly adapted species can cope, but they are present in enormous numbers. Marine worms, shellfish and tiny crustaceans such as *Corophium volutator* provide a vast supply of food for waders and wildfowl, while the salt-marshes are grazing grounds for other wildfowl and rich sources of plant seeds for smaller birds in winter.

The reserve protects an important breeding colony of little tern, which nest together with ringed plover on the sand and shingle of the Spit. To keep the birds from disturbance the Spit is closed in the breeding season.

The dunes provide nest sites for shelduck and short-eared owl, the scrub for birds such as whitethroat, sedge warbler and yellowhammer, while the marshes are filled with the vivid song of skylark and meadow pipit or the staccato notes of reed bunting.

In autumn the summer birds move south and the passage migrants and winter birds may be seen. The shelter of the thickets attracts birds such as pied and spotted flycatcher, goldfinch and redstart, while the flats and marshes are busy with feeding waders. By winter the Wash, one of the two most important wader sites in the British Isles, supports thousands of birds including curlew, dunlin, knot and oystercatcher, with bar-tailed godwit, grey and ringed plover, sanderling and redshank, wildfowl such as wigeon, mallard, teal and goldeneye, pink-footed and dark-bellied Brent geese; all these may occur around the reserve, together with fieldfare and redwing, snow bunting, waxwing and twite.

An excellent visitor centre, a nature trail and a field centre based on this fascinating and beautiful coastal reserve provide interpretation and the opportunity to learn more about both the reserve itself and the range of habitat which it embraces.

Haxey Turbary

Permit only; 9.8ha; L and SHTNC reserve
Wooded old peat workings
Spring, summer

The reserve is still rich in heathland wildlife and still holds characteristic bog mosses in the deeper cuttings, while the dense birch woodland provides a sheltered habitat for small mammals, adder and grass snake. Breeding birds include grasshopper warbler and nightingale.

Heath's Meadow

Permit only; 2.1ha; L and SHTNC reserve
Small grassland hayfields
Spring, early summer

The traditional July hay cutting followed by autumn grazing encourages a very good range of old-meadow plants such as cowslip, dyer's green-weed, green-winged orchid, common spotted-orchid, adder's-tongue, great burnet, devil's-bit scabious and saw-wort.

Hoplands Wood

Permit only; 14ha; L and SHTNC reserve
Mixed oak–ash woodland
Spring, summer

A reminder of the once great Middle Marsh forests of east Lincolnshire, oak and ash grow with birch, wych elm and alder above a rich understorey including hazel, dogwood and guelder-rose. Primrose and bluebell, wood and water avens, herb-Paris and a good variety of orchids may be seen. Breeding birds include great spotted woodpecker and woodcock.

Keal Carr

Permit only; 9.3ha; L and SHTNC reserve
Alder carr
Spring

In this, one of the finest examples of the alder carr woodlands of the south east Wolds, small tributary streams have cut valleys through the Spilsby sandstone down to the underlying Kimmeridge clay. At the junction of the porous rock and the impervious clay a spring line is formed, giving rise to flushes rich in wild flowers. In spring the gold of marsh-marigold and yellow saxifrage is striking. Other species include great horsetail, willowherbs, moschatel, bluebell, meadowsweet and yellow iris.

Killingholme Haven Pits

No access; 36ha; L and SHTNC reserve
Flooded claypits, grassland and scrub
Can be overlooked from public road
Spring, autumn

The four pits, with varying depths of water and bankside cover, provide a range of habitat exploited not only by breeding birds, such as little grebe and a number of warblers, but also by an exceptional range of migrant waders.

Sea buckthorn, a berry-bearing east coast shrub.

Kirkby Moor

Permit only; 56ha; L and SHTNC reserve
Heathland, woods and lake with hide
Spring, summer

The reserve is entered across a wide heathland, uncommon in the rich Lincolnshire countryside, edged with a large conifer plantation. The heathland makes up the greater part of Kirkby Moor and is a sweep of heather and bracken with occasional open areas of wavy hair-grass where heath bedstraw and heath speedwell show. Scattered rowan and hawthorn shrubs provide shelter for small birds and grade into scrub woodland as the heath drops towards the wetter, more fully wooded section of the reserve. Here there is a mosaic of dry woodland and marshy areas with a large pool, sheltered by trees and a fine stand of common reed.

While blue fleabane is one of the more interesting plants of the heathland, the marshland has a range of varied plants, with bog pimpernel, common cottongrass, common twayblade, skullcap, marsh violet and marsh-orchids in a rich mix of sedges and rushes. The woodland trees show good variety with birch-scrub clearings, thick with gorse and heather, surrounded by oak and hawthorn, grey willow, birch and rowan, with alder buckthorn, not a common shrub in Lincolnshire.

The pool is still and private, with rabbits feeding beneath the sheltering trees as tufted duck loaf near the middle. Coot and little grebe nest in the reedbeds and other breeding birds include mallard and great crested grebe. Green and great spotted woodpecker, woodcock and kestrel breed in the woods, with birds such as lesser redpoll on the heath. Siskin visit, and heron and kingfisher may be seen by the pool and streamsides.

Adder, slow-worm and grass snake occur on the reserve and badger are resident. The insect life is predictably rich with such a wealth of wetland, wood and heathland habitat; dragonflies abound; butterflies include brimstone and dark-green fritillary; the many moths include heath rustic,

Grass snake is distinguished by its yellow collar.

angle-striped sallow and broad-bordered bee hawkmoth. The pool contains a good variety of fish and water wildlife.

Langholme Wood

Permit only; 10.3ha; L and SHTNC reserve
Birch–oak woodland
Spring, summer

The woodland, developed on abandoned farmland and sandy heath, has an understorey of elder, hawthorn, bramble, broom and gorse, with clearings of heather and wavy hair-grass. Birds include warblers, such as blackcap, with redpoll, spotted flycatcher, goldcrest and tawny owl among 52 species recorded.

Linwood Warren

Permit only; 26.4ha; L and SHTNC reserve
Wet and dry heath, grassland and woodland
Spring, summer

In one of the rare Lincolnshire heathlands wet heath is characterised by marsh violet, sneezewort, heath spotted-orchid, round-leaved sundew and all three common heathers. With dry tracts of wavy hair-grass and woodlands, with bracken and lily-of-the-valley, the reserve contains over 200 moth and 21 butterfly species. Adder and slow-worm occur, red squirrel may be seen, and over 30 species of breeding birds include long-eared owl, nightjar and woodcock.

Little Scrubbs Meadow

Permit only; 2ha; L and SHTNC reserve
Old grassland
Spring, summer

Green-winged orchid, dyer's greenweed and great burnet grow with sneezewort and marsh valerian. Woods and scrub around the meadow hold nightingale, grasshopper warbler and woodcock.

Lowgate Pit

Permit only; 0.3ha; L and SHTNC reserve
Small pond
Spring, summer

The pond, fringed by trees and beds of common reed, holds a good fish population and provides nest sites for moorhen and reed and sedge warbler.

Mill Hill Quarry

Permit only; 1.6ha; L and SHTNC reserve
Disused chalkpit and spinney
Spring, summer

Chalk cliff, scree or herb-rich grassland with marjoram and bee orchid is flanked by scrub and taller woodland – ash, elm, beech and sycamore – providing a suitable habitat for warblers, finches, tawny owl, pied wagtail and spotted flycatcher.

Moor Closes

Permit only; 6.4ha; L and SHTNC reserve
Old grassland
Spring, summer

Four small grazed fields hold a mix of wet and dry meadow plants. The drier areas contain meadow saxifrage, dropwort and a rare subspecies of thrift, while the wetland species include marsh valerian, ragged-Robin, devil's-bit scabious, adder's-tongue, marsh-orchids, spotted-orchids and a wide variety of grasses, sedges and rushes.

Moor Farm

Permit only; 48ha; L and SHTNC reserve
Heath, pasture, bog and woodland
Spring, summer

A species list for Moor Farm would include some 200 plants, 73 birds, 21 butterflies and 180 moths – which implies a very good diversity of habitat. It derives from old agricultural land, with a range from acid bog through marsh, damp heath and pasture, scrub and woodland to an unusual sandy heath of a type more characteristic of the Norfolk–Suffolk Brecklands than of Lincolnshire.

This part of the reserve is grazed to keep an open herb-rich turf and, fringed with scrub, gorse and broom, is attractive to small birds. The sandy dry heath plants include common cudweed, bird's-foot and common centaury. Grading towards the marsh the soil is still quite dry and sandy, again with typical sand and gravel species and occasional plants more usual in lime-rich situations: basil thyme grows among early and silver hair-grass, with plants such as trailing St John's-wort.

Below these dry pastures the reserve becomes wet – marshy meadows thick with rushes and sedges, with wetland plants including lesser spearwort, purple-loosestrife and ragged-Robin. A small example of an acid mire contains *Sphagnum*, common cottongrass and cross-leaved heath, with tussocks of purple moor-grass, while damp heath shows typical plants such as heath spotted-orchid, lousewort and devil's-bit scabious. Woodland has invaded these damper parts, birch giving way to oak in the classic progression. Blocks of woodland are divided by belts of alder and oak, showing the lines of the old field boundaries, with a stand of more mature woodland around the old farmhouse.

Heathland, woodland and wetland birds are all represented and include linnet, spotted flycatcher, green woodpecker and woodcock, with nesting lapwing, redshank and snipe; winter-visiting duck include mallard and teal.

Normanby Hall Country Park

SE 887169; 1.2–3.2km; Scunthorpe BC
Old estate parkland
Spring, early summer

Four trails have been established here, with several ponds, a deer park and sanctuary.

Bearded tit breed only in sizeable reedbeds.

Rauceby Warren

Permit only; 8.3ha; L and SHTNC reserve
Old sand and gravelpits
Spring, summer

Most of the reserve consists of old workings, flooded in winter, with a lagoon which may hold water all year. Small areas of heathland turf remain with scrub, gorse and a Scots pine plantation. Breeding birds include partridge, mallard, sedge warbler and whitethroat. Smooth rupturewort, a tiny rare sand plant, occurs at one of its very few sites outside East Anglia.

Red Hill

TF 264807; 3.8ha; L and SHTNC–LCC reserve
Chalk grassland and quarry
L and SHTNC members only to hill grassland
Summer

The reserve is in two small blocks, half of it an old quarry in grassland, the other half a steep hill pasture with scrub and much coarse tor-grass.

The level grassland is probably a remnant of the old Lincolnshire Wold downland: here, and in the hummocked bowl of the quarry, there is a rich variety of lime-loving plants. In June clusters of kidney vetch vie in brilliance with yellow-wort and both bee and pyramidal orchid may be found. Throughout the summer this grassland is rich in flowers and later plants include basil thyme and autumn gentian.

The hill beyond the red chalk cliff shows well the natural change that these rich grasslands suffer if ungrazed; they underline the interplay between the grazing species and the grazed and illustrate a knotty conservation problem. The rich chalk grassland which we try to save is merely a stage in the progression through rough grassland and scrub

The spring colour of bluebells in Rigsby Wood.

to woods; to preserve it, it must be managed – not left to nature but grazed or mown to keep it at that stage.

Along with kidney vetch, various other vetches and clovers grow in the downland turf and, with the grasses, attract a range of butterflies, among them common blue and meadow brown, and moths, including abundant six-spot burnet. There is a breeding population of meadow pipit, uncommon this far inland in the county, and the rough grass of the hillside shelters common lizard.

The geological interest here is quite considerable. This is an exposure of red chalk, repeated at Hunstanton in north Norfolk, particularly rich in belemnites and brachiopods, and, lying below the lower chalk, paralleled by the gault in western counties.

Rigsby Wood

TF 420761; 15ha; L and SHTNC reserve
Ash–oak woodland
Spring, summer

Although some parts have been replanted, much of the wood is ash and oak over an understorey of ash and hazel. Early-purple orchid and woodruff, wood anemone, with ragged-Robin in the wetter places, show the richness of the site. A good range of woodland birds breed; woodcock and redpoll are frequent in winter.

Rosper Road Pools

No access; 10ha; L and SHTNC reserve
Flood reservoir and wet grassland
Can be overlooked from public road
Autumn, winter

Regular autumn waders include greenshank, spotted redshank, green, wood and curlew sandpiper and little stint, while up to 70 ruff may visit in winter and some remain to display in spring, together with black-tailed godwit.

Rush Furlong

Permit only; 0.5ha; L and SHTNC reserve
Old grassland
Spring, summer

A fragment of the old strip-farming system contains a wonderful show of green-winged orchid supported by over 60 species of flowering plant, including rough hawk's-beard, oxeye daisy, yellow rattle and adder's-tongue.

Saltfleetby–Theddlethorpe Dunes

TF 465924, 467917, 478901, 483893 and 489882; 478ha; NCC–L and SHTNC reserve
Dune system, freshwater marsh, sand and mudflats
Do not enter the RAF ranges when in use
Leaflet from NCC
All year

The long sandy Lincolnshire shores show wonderful examples of the ecology of this coast and the reserve is a fine illustration. From the sea, sand and shingle banks grade into wide sands and mudflats, backed by a saltmarsh with a dune system and freshwater marsh behind.

The sands shift and swirl in the tides but at the saltmarsh edge are trapped by plants such as annual sea-blite and glasswort. Thrift, sea plantain and sea-lavender, with sea-purslane along the winding creeks, colonise the saltmarsh proper while the landward side may also contain brackish-water species such as sea rush. Here the dunes lift, laced with sea couch, lyme-grass and marram. These old dunes are stable, richly overgrown with sand sedge, dewberry, viper's-bugloss, common centaury and common bird's-foot-trefoil. The sand is rich in shell-gravels – lime-loving carline thistle, fairy flax, bee and pyramidal orchid and the duneland form of lesser meadow-rue may be found. Large areas of dense sea-buckthorn scrub may be contrasted with a more open scrub of mixed, less spiny species.

Behind the dunes the freshwater marsh contains some elements of the seaward side – sea rush occurs in the more brackish parts – but wetter areas are thick with common reed and marsh plants such as water dock, skullcap and marsh pea. Both early and southern marsh-orchid grow in the fringes while other interesting plants include bog pimpernel, lesser water-plantain and autumn gentian. The wetland contains frog, smooth newt and common toad, with natterjack toad at its only site in Lincolnshire.

A wide variety of insects occur in the reserve with several unusual marsh and saltmarsh moths, with dragonflies and damselflies and many butterflies, including dark green fritillary and green hairstreak. Birds take great advantage of the diversity of habitat with meadow pipit, oystercatcher and redshank nesting at the top of the saltmarsh, skylark and shelduck in the dunes and dunnock, linnet, whitethroat and yellowhammer in the scrub. The marsh holds breeding snipe and mallard, with sedge warbler and reed bunting, and provides a winter roost for visiting hen harrier. Winter brings a host of visitors, with large flocks of fieldfare, redwing and starling feeding on the orange berries of sea buckthorn and with many waders on the flats, mainly dunlin with curlew, redshank and ringed plover.

Scotton Common

Permit only; 14.5ha; L and SHTNC reserve
Dry and wet heath
Spring, summer

Heather, bell heather, wavy hair-grass and developing birch, oak and pine woodland contrast with purple moor-grass, deergrass, cross-leaved heath and less common wet heath species such as marsh gentian, heath spotted-orchid and royal fern. Breeding birds include tree pipit and nightjar and the reserve is a haven for common lizard and adder.

Sea Bank Clay Pits

No access; total 17.2ha; L and SHTNC reserve
Flooded pits
Can be overlooked from public road
Winter

Eighteen species of duck are recorded, with Bewick's and whooper swan, red-throated diver, red-necked and Slavonian grebe, bittern and bearded tit. Breeding birds include great crested and little grebe.

The Shrubberies

Permit only; 3.2ha; L and SHTNC reserve
Old parkland
Spring, summer

Fine old oak and elm trees stand over grazed pasture, giving an old parkland habitat of a kind now very rare in the Lincolnshire Fens. Added interest is provided by a pond and marshy area. Twelve butterfly and some 40 bird species have been recorded.

Snipe Dales

RF 320863; 48ha; LCC–L and SHTNC reserve
Valley grassland
Visitors must keep to waymarked route
Spring, summer

The approach to the reserve is through a narrow area of woodland and marsh which opens on the long grassland valley, falling away to the dark shadows of a forestry plantation; here and there a gnarled hawthorn stands on the slopes, with gorse and great willowherb, breaking the curve of the grasslands.

New plantations of oak and ash, alder and willow are being established to restore the woods which once stood here, and eventually the reserve will hold a greater variation, but even now it shows a spread of plants and animals adapted to exploit the present range. The drier upper slopes are clothed with grasses but below the spring line and along the stream marsh-marigold, meadowsweet and ragged-Robin, water mint, water-cress and

Marsh-orchids in the damp slack grassland behind the dunes at Saltfleetby.

water avens grow. Both opposite-leaved and alternate-leaved golden-saxifrage occur in these damper parts, together with meadow saxifrage, while shaded streamside places show a good variety of ferns.

The lower part of the reserve is sheltered, warm and banked with gorse, a totally different habitat from that of the open slopes, though primrose and bluebell in the grassland show where woods once stood above the streams. Here in this lower part common spotted-orchid may be found and here too are many of the 11 butterfly species.

Linnet and yellowhammer nest in the gorse scrub area, with meadow pipit and reed bunting by the stream. The reserve holds six species of breeding warbler, including grasshopper warbler and whitethroat, and there is a sand martin colony in a bank of exposed sandstone. Visiting birds include heron, snipe and woodcock and the area is hunted by kestrel, short-eared owl and barn owl.

Sotby Meadows

Permit only; 6.1ha; L and SHTNC reserve
Old meadows
Spring, summer

Lime-rich old-meadow grassland contains a wonderful range of plants including dropwort, common twayblade and both green-winged and pyramidal orchid, together with the grassland ferns moonwort and adder's-tongue. Seventeen breeding birds are recorded from the hedgerows.

Surfleet Lows

Permit only; 3.4ha; L and SHTNC reserve
Flood meadows, pools and reedbed
The reserve is dangerous without a guide
All year

Parts of the reserve are highly saline and have an unusual range of species such as sea-milkwort and distant sedge, with hairy buttercup and golden dock. Reed warbler breed here, and winter birds include snipe, redshank, mallard, teal and wigeon.

Swaby Valley

Permit only; 3.6ha; L and SHTNC reserve
Lime-rich valley grassland and marsh
Spring, summer

The marsh has early and southern marsh-orchid together with local species such as marsh arrowgrass; the slopes contain salad burnet, small scabious and wild thyme with bee and pyramidal orchid. Sixteen butterfly species are recorded.

Tetney Blow Wells

Permit only; 13ha; L and SHTNC reserve
Open water, some grassland and woodland
Spring, summer

Reed-fringed pools supply a disused water-cress farm, now thickly grown with common reed, great willowherb and bulrush. Marsh-marigold, with cowslip in the grassland, is followed by buttercups and ragged-Robin. Breeding birds include mute swan, sedge warbler and spotted flycatcher.

Tetney Marshes

TA 360037; 1300ha; RSPB reserve
Saltmarsh, dunes and sandflats
Visiting by arrangement only
April–August

Outstanding as a site for breeding little tern, the reserve holds the largest east coast colony between Norfolk and the Scottish coast. Ringed plover and redshank also breed; autumn visitors include grey plover and curlew sandpiper while winter brings bar-tailed godwit and Brent goose.

Little tern, one of Britain's rarest and most elegant seabirds.

The Spilsby sandstone valleys of Snipe Dales, in the south east corner of the Lincolnshire Wolds.

Tortoiseshell Wood

Permit only; 11ha; L and SHTNC reserve
Oak–ash woodland
Spring, summer

Some fine standards of oak and ash grow above hazel, field maple and wild service-tree, with plants of lime-rich clays including herb-Paris, yellow archangel, early-purple orchid and greater butterfly-orchid. Fallow deer are frequently seen and breeding birds include nightingale and nuthatch, rare in Lincolnshire.

Westhorpe Pit

Permit only; 0.4ha; L and SHTNC reserve
Small pond and marsh
Spring, summer

Alder and grey willow fringe the pool, with a reed-bed which holds breeding reed warbler and reed bunting. The marsh contains a range of wetland plants including reed sweet-grass, great willowherb, field horsetail and yellow iris.

Willoughby-Farlesthorpe Railway Line

TF 467720–475736; 5ha; L and SHTNC reserve
Disused railway line
All year

A 2km length of former railway line has been developed as a delightful walk and a small nature reserve. Along the path grassy banks and the bed of the old track provide a habitat for a wealth of chalk and meadow plants including common rest-harrow, adder's-tongue, greater burnet and quaking-grass. The fringing scrub of hawthorn, bramble and wild rose attracts tits, whitethroat, turtle dove, linnet and redpoll, all of which nest, and large winter flocks of finches, fieldfare and redwing.

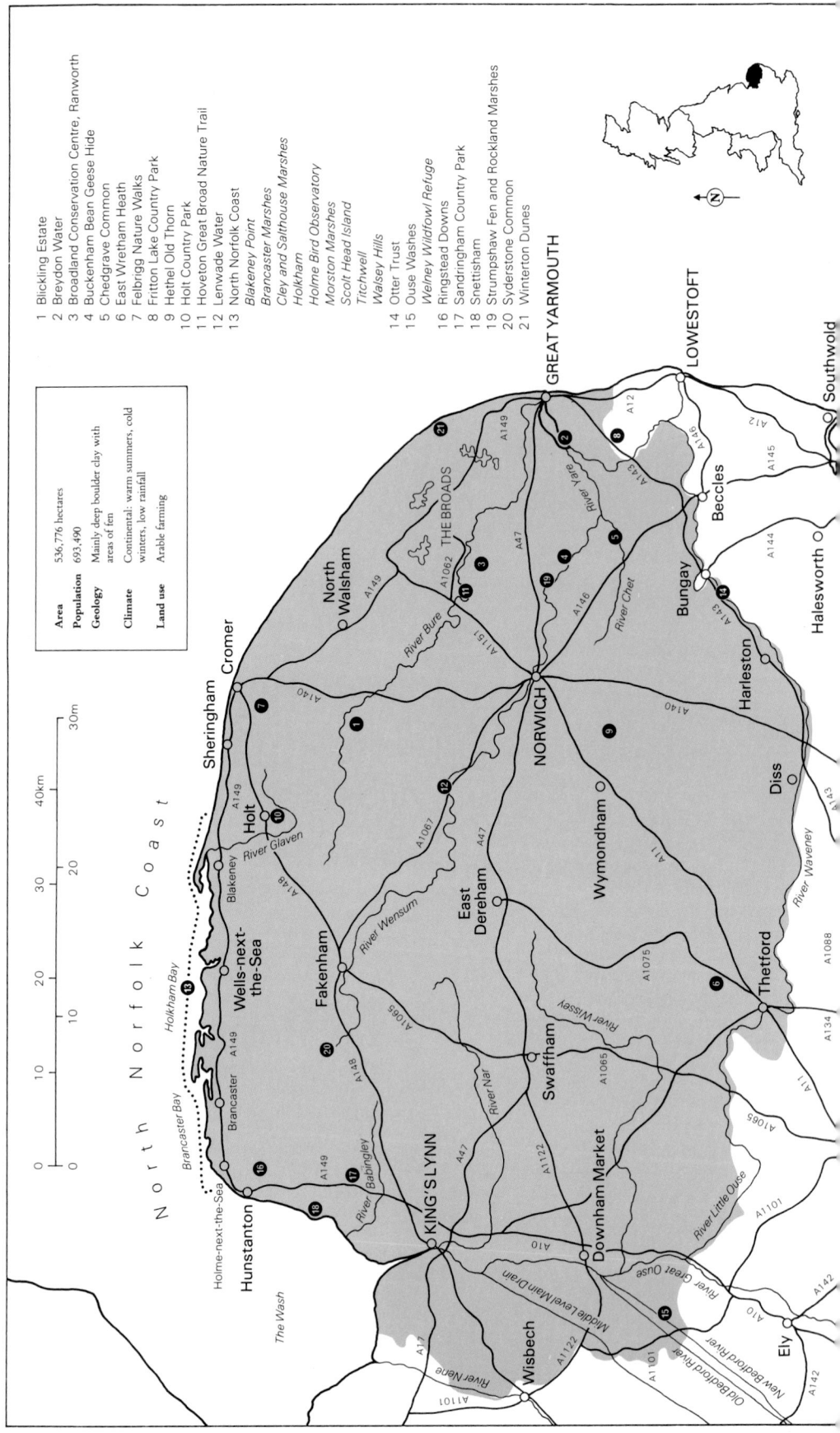

1 Blickling Estate
2 Breydon Water
3 Broadland Conservation Centre, Ranworth
4 Buckenham Bean Geese Hide
5 Chedgrave Common
6 East Wretham Heath
7 Felbrigg Nature Walks
8 Fritton Lake Country Park
9 Hethel Old Thorn
10 Holt Country Park
11 Hoveton Great Broad Nature Trail
12 Lenwade Water
13 North Norfolk Coast
    Blakeney Point
    Brancaster Marshes
    Cley and Salthouse Marshes
    Holkham
    Holme Bird Observatory
    Morston Marshes
    Scolt Head Island
    Titchwell
    Walsey Hills
14 Otter Trust
15 Ouse Washes
    Welney Wildfowl Refuge
16 Ringstead Downs
17 Sandringham Country Park
18 Snettisham
19 Strumpshaw Fen and Rockland Marshes
20 Syderstone Common
21 Winterton Dunes

Area	536,776 hectares
Population	693,490
Geology	Mainly deep boulder clay with areas of fen
Climate	Continental: warm summers, cold winters, low rainfall
Land use	Arable farming

Norfolk

Norfolk is bounded on the north and east by the vast open shores of its 130km long coastline, curving from the Wash round to Great Yarmouth, and in the west and south by rivers flanking the fens and broads. Its countryside is essentially flat lowland, but still contains considerable variety in its scenery and wildlife: the coast, the flood plains of rivers in the east, and especially the unique sandy Breckland in the west, ensure a fascinating and internationally important array of marine, shore, heath, woodland, marsh and fenland wildlife.

Naturalists have been aware of the richness of Norfolk's wildlife heritage since Sir Thomas Browne's research awakened interest in the seventeenth century. Outstanding botanists who later found inspiration in the county's plant life have included Sir James Smith, John Lindley and the Hookers. Naturalists' societies have flourished here since 1747. Local ornithologists participated eagerly in the earliest efforts to legislate for bird protection, and the wider interests of habitat conservation were served when the first of Britain's county naturalists' trusts was established here in 1926. Since then, with ever-growing popular support, thousands of hectares of dunes and saltings, heaths, fens, broads and woods have been safeguarded, supplemented by parallel efforts on the part of the National Trust, the RSPB and the NCC. The county now boasts a rich mosaic of protected habitats.

Among the delights of the coast one thinks first of the Wash, a huge bay which takes the outflow of the fenland rivers and is subject to great tides. Its sandbanks and mussel beds are ideal for common seal and its shores are a gathering ground for immense flocks of migratory waders. Jutting boldly to form a seaward bastion on its eastern flank, the multicoloured chalk and sandstone cliffs of Hunstanton support wild wallflower and are the haunt of fulmar.

For many kilometres to the east stretches the marshland coast, whose sand spits and shingle banks welcome large colonies of terns in the nesting season and are crowded with waders at all times. The fine dunes, notably at SCOLT HEAD ISLAND and BLAKENEY POINT, are a preserve of plants such as sea-holly and sea bindweed. Behind them lie extensive salt flats and tidal creeks where, in July, vast sheets of sea-lavender attract bees and butterflies. At several points, from HOLME to CLEY, hides exist for observing a wealth of birds. Breeding species include avocet, bearded tit and bittern, while there is no lack of interesting visitors at all seasons, but especially during the spring and autumn migrations.

At the western end of the coast the chalk surface, at beach level, is strewn with large flints which provide the chief habitat of inter-tidal marine life. Elsewhere unstable, crumbling cliffs and wave-washed sandy shores are unsuitable for permanent colonisation, even by seaweeds. East of Cromer the cliffs reach a considerable height, with landslips here and there, diminishing south eastwards from Mundesley and disappearing beyond Happisburgh to be succeeded by dunes bordering marshland and the broads.

The dune slacks and sub-maritime fens in the Horsey–WINTERTON region are specially interesting for their plants and are now the chief breeding ground for natterjack toad in the east of Britain. Hybrid marram is an abundant and conspicuous feature of the dunes.

The broads, famous among sailing enthusiasts, are a series of shallow pools occupying the sites of medieval peat workings in the flood plains of rivers converging on a common outlet at Great Yarmouth. With their surrounding reedswamps, fens, carrs and areas of reclaimed grazing marshes intersected by dykes, they form a paradise for wetland wildlife. Notable inhabitants include bittern, marsh harrier and bearded tit, the Norfolk dragonfly *Aeshna mixta*, swallowtail butterfly, several rare moths, marsh sow-thistle and water-soldier, while the Fens are known for their rich assortment of micro-fungi. Pollution of broadland waters as a result of ever-increasing recreational use has caused much concern in recent years, but remedial action is now in progress.

True heathland is relatively scarce in Norfolk: what there is is concentrated chiefly between Norwich and the Cromer–Holt ridge and on the greensand flanking the Wash. Its moister hollows hold various rare lowland mosses and, very locally, marsh gentian.

Oak–ash woodland with coppiced hazel and a rich ground flora is represented by a few large and ancient examples and fragments elsewhere, while the lighter, less calcareous soils support oak–birch communities less rich in species. Modern conifer plantations, mostly in the west, provide refuges for crossbill, woodpecker and titmouse, besides increasing numbers of red, roe and muntjac deer.

Red squirrel survive here and there, but greys have now usurped most of their territory.

Norfolk's great glory to the naturalist is the Brecklands, extensive grass heaths which until early this century formed a great tract of open country, with sheep walks and rabbit warrens, haunted by wheatear, stone curlew and, once, great bustard. Though forestry and agriculture have made great inroads into the area, its low rainfall and continental climate make it a unique wildlife habitat, and those parts which have escaped destruction are still a haven for special wild flowers, insects and spiders; this steppe-type flora and fauna is represented better here than anywhere else in Britain. The Breckland meres, supplied erratically by water rising from the underlying chalk, are another remarkable and delightful feature of this very special area in what is, to the naturalist, a very special part of Britain.

TED ELLIS

Alderfen Broad

Permit only; 29ha; NNT reserve
Small valley broad
Can be overlooked from TG 353196
Spring, summer

Rigid hornwort, white and yellow water-lily are the main plants in the broad itself which holds mallard, tufted duck and gadwall. Reedbed, fen and wet alder woodland provide cover for small birds.

Barton Broad

Permit only; 148ha; NNT reserve
Group of broads and edge vegetation
Right of navigation across broad
Spring, summer

Three broads, Irstead, Turkey and Barton itself, make up the reserve which includes, wet alder woodland, reed-beds, sedgebeds and stands of bulrush and lesser bulrush. Milk-parsley feeds swallowtail caterpillars and both bearded tit and great crested grebe breed. There is a small heronry.

Blakeney Point

TG 001464; 440ha; NT reserve
Shingle spit, saltmarsh and dunes
Booklets available from site or NT
All year

Part of the NORTH NORFOLK COAST.

Blickling Estate

TG 175287; 1907ha; NT
Parkland, woodland, farmland and lake
Spring, summer

The woods contain a range of typical breeding birds such as hawfinch and redstart while tufted duck and great crested grebe may frequently be seen on the lake. The estate is typical of many of the large East Anglian parklands.

Brancaster Marshes

TF 772450; 850ha; NT reserve
Beach, dunes and saltmarsh
All year

Part of the NORTH NORFOLK COAST.

Breydon Water

TG 475051; 453ha; Norfolk CC reserve
Huge inland estuary
All year

A great variety of waders and wildfowl visits the mudflats and grazing marshes of the reserve which may be overlooked from public footpaths. Avocet, spoonbill and black tern are regular visitors to the area while bean, Brent, pink-footed and white-fronted geese may be observed here.

Broadland Conservation Centre

TN 356149; 0.5km (trail); NNT
Wetland trail to broadland exhibition
Leaflets available at site
April–October except Mondays

Cars must be parked at TM 359146. The trail, constructed out of level duckboarding, passes through a range of broadland habitats, from wet woodland through increasingly wet fen to the floating conservation centre which overlooks Ranworth Broad. The trail illustrates typical plants, such as milk-parsley, food plant of the larvae of the swallowtail butterfly, and the exhibition demonstrates the problems and attractions of the extraordinary and fascinating wildlife environment of the broads.

Buckenham Bean Geese Hide

TG 342067; RSPB
Hide overlooking grazing marsh, river and reedbed
Winter

The hide is open daily from November to March but the best time for the geese is between December and February when around 200 bean geese, the only regular flock in Britain, may be seen together with a wide range of other wintering wildfowl.

Bure Marshes

Permit only; 412ha; NCC reserve
Wet woodland, fen and broads
Nature trail leaflet from NCC
Spring, early summer

The large area, ranging from open water through reedbeds and sedgebeds to alder woodland, contains a great range of classic fenland species. There is public access, by boat only, to the HOVETON GREAT BROAD NATURE TRAIL.

Chedgrave Common

TM 372993; 5ha; NNT reserve
Small grass heathland
Spring, early summer

The rough grassland, with bramble, gorse and frequent flowerspikes of southern marsh-orchid, may be seen from the public footpath along the river. Breeding birds include linnet and kingfisher.

Bure Marshes: drainage ditches divide the reedbeds from the woodland.

Cley and Salthouse Marshes

TF 054451; 266ha; NNT reserve
Freshwater, saltwater and grazing marshes, reedbeds and pools
Information from observation centre
April–October

Part of the NORTH NORFOLK COAST.

East Winch Common

Permit only; 32ha; NNT reserve
Heathland, bog and woodland
Spring, summer

Birch–oak woodland surrounds this relict area of acid heath where heather spreads around small bogs containing species such as bogbean and round-leaved sundew. Adders are abundant, as are birds such as nightingale, blackcap, linnet and yellowhammer.

East Wretham Heath

TL 914886; 147ha; NNT reserve
Breckland heath, meres and mixed woodland
Visitors must report to the warden at 10 a.m. or 2 p.m.; closed Tuesdays
Nature trail leaflets from warden or NNT
Spring, early summer

When the ice ages levelled the surface of Norfolk by spreading a layer of glacial debris across it, higher areas of the underlying chalk were thinly covered with sands and gravels to form the Breckland heaths. These, even up to the seventeenth

century, were wide treeless deserts, bone-dry and heather-covered, with low dune systems built up by driving sandstorms, but with here and there a spread of clay to hold water above the chalk and to form oases. Later, trees were planted to hold back the sands and gradually the heaths were tamed and turned to farming or to forestry but some areas still exist which retain the flavour of the Brecklands.

East Wretham Heath has been modified by its use as a wartime airfield yet it contains two of the finest Breckland meres, and good examples of acid grassland and heath combined with lime-loving species where the sands are thin over the chalk. The grassland is chiefly of wavy hair-grass with heather and plants such as harebell and heath bed-straw, with an open scrub of broom and hawthorn or giving way to a woodland of birch over bracken and Yorkshire-fog. Two planted woodlands are most interesting – an area of hornbeam, attractive to birds such as hawfinch and winter siskin, to butterflies such as ringlet and speckled wood, and a stand of splendid old Scots pine, planted about the time of the Battle of Waterloo. The pine plantation, an early attempt to consolidate the sands and form a shelter belt, now provides an ideal site for birds such as crossbill.

Where the sand is very shallow over the chalk, plants such as wild thyme, wild mignonette and dyer's greenweed show with species such as viper's-bugloss, bladder campion, hound's-tongue and the beautiful musk mallow. Reed canary-grass marks the fringes of the meres, with golden dock and knotted pearlwort, and with aquatic plants such as shining and fennel pondweed and amphibious bistort. The meres attract waterfowl and waders, gadwall, pochard, shoveler, teal and wigeon, goldeneye and little grebe, woodcock, spotted redshank, common, green and wood sand-piper. One mere may be empty while another is full and the species living in them may have to cope with temporary desiccation. The leech *Dina lineata*, which only occurs in temporary waters of southern Britain, is found here.

The great diversity of habitat attracts a wide range of birds from wren and willow warbler, skylark and swallow to nightingale, redstart and grasshopper warbler, to whinchat, wheatear and nightjar, to marauding hen harrier, hobby and merlin or tawny and long-eared owl. Adder, grass snake and common lizard may be seen while mammals include stoat, weasel and a resident population of roe deer.

Felbrigg Great Wood: fine old East Anglian estate beechwoods.

Felbrigg Nature Walks

TG 204403; 1.6 and 2.4km; NT
Woodland and lakeside walks
Leaflets from Felbrigg Hall
Woodland walk and Hall open afternoons
April–mid-October; closed Monday and Friday
except Bank Holidays
Spring, summer

The walks are set in old parkland and include an area of ancient beech woodland and an ornamental lake which, together with the stands of mixed woodland, attract an interesting and varied range of birds.

Fritton Lake Country Park

TG 472004; 68ha; Somerleyton Estate
Large lake and surrounding woodlands
Leaflets from information centre
April–September

The main feature of the park is the 3km long lake formed by peat cutting, as were the broads. Used in the past as a site for duck decoys, the lake is visited by a good range of waterbirds, while the woodland, too, is rich in birds.

Hardley Flood

Permit only; 36ha; NNT reserve
Open water and reedbeds, open mud and wet woodland
All year

The reserve may be overlooked from the footpath which passes CHEDGRAVE COMMON, but a permit allows access to two hides from which breeding species such as gadwall, pochard, shoveler and tufted duck or winter visitors such as teal and shelduck may be observed. Waders are frequent and the area may be hunted by hen and marsh harrier.

Hethel Old Thorn

TG 172004; 0.05ha; NNT reserve
Single tree
All year

A unique reserve consisting of a single hawthorn tree, reputed to have been planted in the reign of King John. It is considered to be the oldest member of its species in England.

Hickling Broad

Permit only; 549ha; NNT reserve
Large broad with reedbeds and sedgebeds, marshland, pools and woodland
Permits and leaflets from warden's office at TG 427222, except Tuesday; or enquire from NNT
Spring, summer

This magnificent broadland reserve protects one of the oldest and largest areas of open water in southern Britain, together with a rich variety of fringing reedbeds and sedgebeds, of grazing

The drainage ditches at Hickling Broad are filled with a rich mix of water plants.

marshes and drainage ditches, of shallow pools and woodlands. In early Iron Age or Roman times the sea level rose, or the land sank, and a layer of clay was deposited on the river peatlands. The sea then withdrew, allowing more peat to form and later, digging down until the clay contaminated their workings, peat diggers formed the broads, wide shallow waters floored with clay which then became filled and fringed with wetland wildlife.

Frogbit and holly-leaved naiad are among the water plants while the edges of the waterways are filled with common reed and lesser bulrush, with water-violet, marsh sow-thistle, milk-parsley and marshland species such as purple-loosestrife, cowbane, a poisonous relative of hogweed, hemp-agrimony, water dock and the delicate marsh fern. Great fen-sedge, black bog-rush and purple moor-grass form spreads in some of the damper areas while the old hay meadows have plants such as purple small-reed and the beautiful marsh pea. The grazing marshes are thick with stands of common spotted-orchid and southern marsh-orchid in early summer and with the slender lifting heads and pale-backed leaves of meadow thistle, while two characteristic ferns of the reserve, which grow in the drier alder and grey willow areas, are narrow and crested buckler-fern. Two more plants, sea-milkwort and marsh-mallow, are of particular interest because they normally grow in coastal sites and demonstrate the brackish nature of the water at Hickling Broad; salt seeps through from the sea 3–4km away.

The wonderfully rich and varied plant life is paralleled by the richness of the birds. This is a renowned area for bittern and bearded tit; marsh harrier breed in some years and it has been a nesting site for Montagu's harrier. The wetland fringes have populations of gadwall, pochard, shelduck, shoveler, tufted duck and great crested grebe with small numbers of garganey. The grazing meadows are breeding places for lapwing, redshank, snipe and yellow wagtail with a great variety of smaller birds in the reedbeds and sedgebeds and the woodlands, which also contain a number of heronries. Common tern fly in in spring to nest here, when numbers of passage migrants, including black tern and osprey, may be seen. In winter coot, teal, wigeon, pintail, goldeneye, scaup, Bewick's, mute and whooper swan may join the resident birds, while predators such as great grey shrike and hen harrier hunt across the marshes.

There is an important colony of swallowtail butterflies, a great range of common reed and bulrush specialists, such as Fenn's, flame, rufous and bulrush wainscot moths, and migrant species such as great brocade.

Hockham Fen

Permit only; 8ha; NNT reserve
Small fen
Visitors must be accompanied by honorary warden and the site is extremely dangerous
Spring, summer

Bogbean, cranberry, marsh cinquefoil, milk-parsley, water-violet and the rare narrow small-reed characterise this small rich fen which is full of birds such as willow tit, redpoll, great and lesser spotted woodpecker. Speckled wood and white admiral butterflies may be seen and the reserve provides shelter for roe deer and a wallowing site for red deer. The wet peat is particularly deep and treacherous.

Holkham

TF 892447; 3953ha; NCC reserve
Dunes, saltmarsh, sandflats, mudflats and farmland
Booklet from NCC
All year

Part of the NORTH NORFOLK COAST.

Holme Bird Observatory

TF 714449; 2.4ha; NOA
Reception centre set in pine belt
Leaflets from site
All year

Part of the NORTH NORFOLK COAST.

Holme Dunes

Permit only; 160ha; NNT reserve
Foreshore, dunes, saltmarsh, grazing marsh and open water
Permit from NNT warden or Holme Bird Observatory
All year

Part of the NORTH NORFOLK COAST.

Holme Marsh Bird Reserve

Permit only; 36ha; NOA reserve
Grazing marsh and pools
Permit from NNT warden or Holme Bird Observatory
All year

Part of the NORTH NORFOLK COAST.

Holt Country Park

TG 082375; 38.4ha; North Norfolk DC
Woodland
Spring, summer

Coniferous woodland, surrounding a small pond, and a bog within an area of heathland provide a good variation of habitat used by roe deer, fox and red squirrel. Adder, slow-worm and newt occur with frog and common toad; birds include tawny owl and woodcock.

Hoveton Great Broad Nature Trail

TG 322157; 0.8km; NCC
Nature trail illustrating broadland wildlife
Accessible only by boat
Leaflet from site or NCC
Weekdays only, May–mid-September

Part of the BURE MARSHES, the trail is laid out on duckboarding through a range of fen and wet woodland, with an observation hide overlooking Hoveton Great Broad itself. The trail is designed to explain to broads users the origins and wildlife of the area and may be visited by hiring a day boat from Wroxham.

Hoveton Great Broad is peaceful, a wide area of water fringed with fen and backed by alder carr, a wet woodland growing on the peat. The water is dotted with tufted duck and great crested grebe. Mallard float at the water's edge or scramble under the overhanging trees and the still grey shapes of heron stand poised in the shallows. Above, the visitor can follow the sweeping flight of swallow and house martin and the wonderful elegance of the common tern, for which a nesting raft is moored in front of the hide.

To reach the hide the pathway passes through alder and grey willow carr, floored with spreads of marsh fern, woody nightshade, yellow iris, sedges and mosses; honeysuckle and hop climb among shrub species such as alder buckthorn while more open areas show clumps of greater tussock-sedge and aromatic bog myrtle. Wild raspberry, red and black currant may be found and there is an example of the splendid royal fern while an interesting area of more solid peat has oak, ash, birch and hawthorn over guelder-rose and wild rose. The fen area at the waterside is rich in plants such as common reed, lesser bulrush, hemp-agrimony and meadowsweet with milk-parsley, locally common but nationally rare, which is the food plant for caterpillars of the swallowtail butterfly. Swallowtails may be seen here but are more plentiful at HICKLING BROAD.

The solid peat island, where the wider range of tree species grew, contains one of the keys to the making of the broads. They were, in fact, made by men digging for fuel, beginning over a century before the Normans invaded Britain. From then and until late in the fourteenth century, the sea level was relatively lower than it is now, and it was possible to dig huge pits some 3m deep before water seepage from the rivers made digging deeper uneconomic. Banks of uncut peat were often left between strip diggings and were topped by gravel tracks along which the peat was transported, gravels which have been found in cores taken from several of these banks. The banks would also have helped in preventing flooding from one strip to the next as the peat was worked out to the maximum depth and the digging then abandoned. The island at Hoveton Great Broad, like these banks, is clearly a remnant of the natural structure of broadland unaffected by the workings. After the rising sea level made further digging impractical, the river bank was cut to allow boats in for fishing, shooting or for working the developing fen for reeds and sedges. Now that the fens of Cambridgeshire, Huntingdonshire and Lincolnshire have been largely drained, the broads are the last stronghold of their wealth of wonderful plants and animals.

Holkham comprises a vast range of habitats.

Lenwade Water

TG 110184; 15ha; NNT reserve
Flooded gravel workings
Spring, summer

The pools are surrounded with scrub woodland and fringed with wetland plants such as bulrush, while small marshy areas contain bogbean, purple-loosestrife and ragged-Robin; climbing corydalis and lesser teasel are among the more unusual plants. Birds include common tern, great crested grebe and a variety of duck with sand martin, marsh tit and several warblers. Dragonflies, moths and butterflies are plentiful.

Martham Broad

No access; 60ha; NNT reserve
Wet alder woodland, reedbeds and sedgebeds, open water
Can be overlooked from footpaths around
TG 467201; right of navigation along Somerton dyke
All year

The plants include greater bladderwort and holly-leaved naiad, and the rich bird life includes species such as bearded tit and common tern, winter gadwall, mallard, pochard, shoveler, teal, tufted duck and wigeon, hunting marsh and hen harrier or passage migrants such as black tern.

Morston Marshes

TG 007443; 222.4ha; NT reserve
Grazing marsh, saltmarsh and tidal creeks
All year

Part of the NORTH NORFOLK COAST.

Common sea-lavender spreads across a north Norfolk saltmarsh.

North Norfolk Coast

See map; 40km; NCC–NNT–NOA–NT–RSPB reserves
Shingle, dunes and saltmarsh
Leaflets and booklets from managing bodies
All year

Almost all of the north Norfolk coast from Holme-next-the-Sea to Salthouse is protected by nature reserves which form a mosaic of sites of international importance. Sandbanks and shingle ridges provide shelter for saltmarsh to grow, and the marshes form one of the largest spreads in Britain. Wind-blown sand builds dunes on the shingle ridges; plants invade and stabilise the dunes, providing cover for breeding birds and a landfall for migrants. The wetlands contain pooled stands of reedmarsh unusually rich in bird life. Not only is there a classic show of the change from tideline to farmland but, because the aims of each reserve tend to differ, the habitat range increases.

The western end of SCOLT HEAD ISLAND and the fist of BLAKENEY POINT provide a wonderful example of shingle and sand interplay. Scolt Head Island may only be reached by boat, Blakeney by boat or by a long trudge along shingle, but both are quite superb in their strange and lonely beauty. Both lie beyond wide spreads of marsh, of low-tide muds, edged by lawns of sea-lavender, and both of them thrill to the harsh cries of the terns. The shingle ridges form the base on which hills of sand are built in the classic progression from sand couch and marram to herb-rich older dunes while, here and there, the wind has scooped out spectacular large blowouts which are cut back to the shingle below in a strange moonscape of sandy hills and lows.

The crests and the seaward sides of the shingle are too exposed, too mobile, for plants to survive but below the crests are vigorous stands of shrubby sea-blite, a plant of Mediterranean areas, together with sea-heath and matted sea-lavender around the northern edge of its range. All three plants seem well suited to these sandy or muddy shingles and grow with thrift and rock sea-lavender, yellow horned-poppy and sea campion and, where a soil has developed over the shingle, with a great variety of other plants.

Sea sandwort occurs on shingle and on sand and is often one of the first plants of the dunes, together with prickly saltwort and sea rocket, lyme-grass and sea-holly. Stable dunes may be patterned with lichens and mosses, with common stork's-bill and biting stonecrop.

Beyond the hedge of shrubby sea-blite, the sea-lavender lawns are spread. Here, too, the plants form a broad mosaic, with common scurvygrass, thrift, greater and lesser sea-spurrey, sea arrow-grass, sea plantain, sea-purslane, common and lax-flowered sea-lavender, and with stands of sea rush and common saltmarsh-grass. Some plants cope with long immersion more readily than others, so glasswort, sea aster and annual sea-blite form the lower marsh, while sea wormwood grows on the drier higher fringes. The marshes spread from Blakeney to Wells, from west of HOLKHAM to HOLME, a wonderful richness of creek-cut wilderness where redshank and curlew call.

At Holkham the land is generally fronted by sands, thrown up in long dune ridges on either side of the Holkham Gap, which are stabilised for much of their length by plantations of Corsican pine. The system of dunes and slacks contains typical plants such as lady's bedstraw, common centaury, ploughman's-spikenard and carline thistle, with creeping willow, marsh helleborine, early and southern marsh-orchid and, in drier sites, with bee orchid and Jersey cudweed. The huge reserve also covers the marshes from Wells across to Stiffkey, with the farmland and grazing marshes of Holkham north of the A149.

Holme, TITCHWELL and CLEY hold not only the features of shingle, sand and saltmarsh but also a range of brackish-water lagoons, freshwater marshes and reedbeds which provide an invaluable breeding site for many species of bird. Scolt Head and Blakeney are famous for their important terneries but these reserves also attract birds not seen since the fens were drained.

Cley and Titchwell, in particular, are managed mainly for their birds. Saltmarsh, brackish-water marsh and freshwater lagoons are maintained by embankments and series of sluices so that conditions can be controlled to support a wide range of bird life. The scrapes attract waders and dabbling duck while damp meadows provide a site for winter geese and for grazing duck. Reedbeds are managed for optimum growth, for cover, for nest sites and for insect life to feed the smaller birds. Whereas sand-dune development on one reserve might be encouraged deliberately, on another reserve it might be discouraged to preserve a site for shingle-nesting birds – the result is an increase in variation which, clearly, is of benefit to wildlife.

For birds, this is one of the outstanding coasts around the British Isles and it is a splendid site for migrants and a magnet for uncommon vagrants. Firecrest, hoopoe, osprey, great grey shrike, barred warbler and wryneck are regular visitors and such uncommon wanderers as red-spotted bluethroat, yellow-breasted bunting, collared flycatcher and nutcracker, scarlet rosefinch and red-rumped swallow, Bonelli's, fan-tailed, arctic and subalpine warbler form only part of a quite outstanding bird list.

Breeding birds of the shingle and dunes include common, little, Sandwich and a few pairs of arctic tern, together with ringed plover, oystercatcher and shelduck, while redshank and black-headed gull may nest both here and on the upper parts of the marshes. The dune woodlands at Holkham provide a site for common tree-nesting birds, as well as for conifer-loving species such as goldcrest and, occasionally, crossbill. The wide range of wetland habitat encouraged at Cley and Titchwell attracts reed bunting and reed warbler, water rail, mallard and moorhen, together with specialities such as wigeon, around the southern limit of their range, bearded tit, bittern, marsh harrier and avocet.

The passage birds are marvellously varied, from the first spring arrivals of wheatear, chiffchaff and sand martin, through exciting visitors such as little bittern, golden oriole and black-winged stilt, to the autumn migrants, the falls of hundreds of continental birds and, perhaps, to further rare vagrants such as Radde's bush warbler. Thousands of swallows, martins and swifts roost in the reedbeds on autumn passage while the spreads of sea-buckthorn and sea-blite feed and shelter a host of others. A great variety of waders, and of seabirds such as gannet and Manx shearwater, pass through on autumn migration when pomarine, long-tailed, great and arctic skua might harass the gulls and terns while, inland, marsh or Montagu's harrier hawk above the wetlands.

In winter hen harrier and short-eared owl hunt while purple sandpiper joins the waders which remain to winter here. Seaduck such as common and velvet scoter, long-tailed duck and eider may be seen offshore and the mudflats are feeding grounds for large flocks of Brent and small numbers of pink-footed and white-fronted geese. Gadwall, goldeneye, pintail, shoveler, teal and wigeon are among the winter wildfowl while smaller birds include brambling, greenfinch, goldfinch and siskin with Lapland and snow bunting, shorelark and twite.

Otter Trust

TM 315884; 12ha; Otter Trust reserve
Otter and waterfowl collection, river bank, pools and marshes
Nature trail leaflet from exhibition hall
Spring, summer

Wild birds are attracted to the waterfowl collection and may be watched from an observation hide at the lake while the nature trail looks briefly at stream and river habitats. The otter collection includes European and Asian short-clawed varieties.

Ouse Washes

TL 547946; 2500ha; Cambient–RSPB–WT reserve
Winter-flooded fen meadows
Leaflets from Cambient, RSPB or WT
Winter

Described under Cambridgeshire.

Otter are now uncommon in the wild.

Redgrave and Lopham Fens

Permit only; 134ha; STNC reserves
Rich fen, river and pools
Spring, summer

These reserves, mainly in Suffolk, are described there.

Ringstead Downs

TF 706400; 10.5ha; NNT reserve
Chalk downland
Spring, summer

A public track runs through this attractive dry valley in which the two sections of the reserve lie, filled with lime-loving plants such as common rock-rose, squinancywort and wild thyme. Scrub areas provide nest sites for birds such as white-throat and there is a good range of butterflies.

Roydon Common

Permit only; 57ha; NNT reserve
Dry heath, wet heath and fen
Can be overlooked from public right of way at
TF 680229
Spring, summer

Heather is widespread on the dry heath which grades into an area of cross-leaved heath, purple moor-grass and common cottongrass with deer-grass and *Sphagnum* mosses. Adder and common lizard are plentiful while the insects include a variety of dragonflies and two unusual wasps.

Bittern in typical alarm posture.

Sandringham Country Park

TF 689287; 240ha; Sandringham Estate
Parkland, woodland and heathland
Spring, early summer

The mixed coniferous and broad-leaved woodland attracts a good range of birds, including resident crossbill in the conifers, while the heathland affords a nesting site for birds such as nightjar and shelduck. Waymarked trails have been established to show the variation of the park.

Scarning Fen

No access; 4ha; NNT reserve
Small valley fen
Can be overlooked from public right of way at
TM 983120
Spring, summer

The moss and liverwort communities are most important here but there is a fine range of flowering plants including such species as meadowsweet and ragged-Robin, grass-of-Parnassus, common butterwort and great sundew. A good range of insects includes characteristic fen moths such as five-spot burnet and blackneck.

Scolt Head Island

TF 805465; 738ha; NCC–NT–NNT reserve
Shingle, dune and saltmarsh island
Access by prior arrangment with local boatmen at
TF 794445
May–mid-August

Part of the NORTH NORFOLK COAST.

Snettisham

TF 648335; 1300ha; RSPB reserve
Flooded shingle pits, tidal sand and mudflats
Leaflet from RSPB
All year

Snettisham lies within the great tidal estuary of the Wash: most the reserve consists of some 1250ha of inter-tidal muds and sandflats which may be over-looked from the sea wall or from the hide.

Above this splendid feeding ground, the reserve includes a further 43ha of young saltmarsh and shingle backed by flooded pits which are also over-looked by public hides and are attractive as high-tide and winter roosts. The saltmarsh has a typical range from the colonisers, glasswort and common cord-grass, through sea aster, sea-purslane and common saltmarsh-grass to plants such as sea arrowgrass and rock sea-lavender. The shingle above contains sea beet and shrubby sea-blite, sea-kale and species such as yellow horned-poppy, hound's-tongue, springbeauty and viper's-bugloss.

Although the greatest numbers of birds will be seen in winter, there is no season when the pits and mudflats lack interest. Even when the wintering birds have gone and the spring migration has passed, waders such as oystercatcher, ringed plover and redshank remain to breed, common tern nest on the islands of the pits and may be seen fishing them for sticklebacks or flying out to search for sand eels in the estuary where immature eider summer in relative shelter.

In autumn many of the summer birds move south and the autumn passage and build-up of wintering birds begin. At the height of winter a marvellous variety of wildfowl and waders may be present, from dunlin and sanderling to geese and wild swans. Thousands of knot, oystercatcher, redshank and bar-tailed godwit gather with curlew, grey plover and turnstone, with shelduck, Brent and pink-footed geese, with large numbers of mallard and with wigeon, teal and pintail. The pits form a night-time roost for Bewick's and whooper swan and draw good numbers of coot and little grebe, gadwall, mallard, pochard and tufted duck together with great crested grebe, red-breasted merganser, scaup, shoveler, teal and wigeon and occasionally smew and long-tailed duck.

Apart from its magnificent bird list, the reserve is of great importance as a sanctuary within the Wash which is of international importance for its winter wader populations and for its numbers of Brent and pink-footed geese and shelduck.

Sparham Pools

Permit only; 12ha; NNT reserve
Flooded gravelpits
Public footpath and car park at TG 073179
All year

Common evening-primrose and hound's-tongue grow on the gravel while birch, willow and gorse form a scrub under mature trees. Gadwall, mallard

Swallowtail butterfly, a speciality of Norfolk.

and tufted duck may be seen with Canada, Egyptian and greylag feral geese, while kingfisher and sand martin nest in the gravel cliffs. Insects include brimstone and orange-tip butterflies.

Strumpshaw Fen

TG 342067; 247ha; RSPB reserve
Fen, woodland and grazing marsh
Leaflets from site or RSPB
Closed Tuesdays and Fridays
All year

Where the HOVETON GREAT BROAD NATURE TRAIL is laid out in the Middle Bure broadland, where HICK-LING BROAD lies in the headwaters of the Thurne, Strumpshaw and Rockland straddle the lower, strongly tidal, reaches of the Yare and have an appropriately different basis to their fenland. The particular and interesting species are the same, with tall yellow marsh sow-thistle, white milk-parsley, marsh fern, bog myrtle, frogbit and water-soldier, marsh pea and tussock-sedges, marsh helleborine and southern marsh-orchid but, where the northern fens are filled with common reed and bulrushes, these tidal broads are overgrown with floating, spreading mats of tall reed sweet-grass. Common reed invades when the mats have formed but the swirling brackish tides have had a clear effect on the building of the fen.

As at HICKLING BROAD, the bird life is superb; the wide range of habitat – broad reedbeds, reed-swamp tussocked with sedges, willow and alder woodlands, open water, drainage ditches and graz-ing marsh backed by drier woods of birch, ash and oak – encourages a tremendous range of wetland and woodland birds. The woodlands hold all three native woodpeckers, are visited in winter by flocks of siskin and have a breeding population of wood-cock, an adapted wader whose closely related cousin, snipe, nests in the grazing meadows with

303

Strumpshaw Fen: flood meadows, fen and woods.

lapwing and redshank, skylark and yellow wagtail. The reedswamp and wetlands, the river and the small remaining area of open broad, are home and nesting ground for mallard, teal and pochard, for coot and moorhen, great crested and little grebe. Heron, common tern and kingfisher take their prey from the open waters and, in winter, wigeon fly in to rest and shelter.

Marsh harrier has returned to breed here, although bittern and Montagu's harrier have yet to make a return. Sedge, reed and grasshopper warbler come to nest in summer and recently Cetti's warbler has joined them. Bearded tit still breeds and so does the rarely seen shy water rail. Hen and Montagu's harrier visit and osprey fly over on passage.

On passage, too, waders such as common and green sandpiper and greenshank visit the reserve and, although they do not breed, bittern may pass through as well as rarities such as purple heron.

Swallowtail butterfly also occurs here.

Surlingham Broad

Permit only; 122ha; NNT reserve
Wet wood, fen and open water
Spring, summer

The wetland area may contain a great variety of wildfowl and waders, such as gadwall, shoveler, teal, green sandpiper, redshank and snipe, while the rare musk beetle is among the many insects present encouraged by the rich fen vegetation.

Thompson Common

Permit only; 125.6ha; NNT reserve
Wetland and woodland
Car park and trail at TL 934966
Spring, summer

The reserve combines the common and an area of Thompson Water which gives a fascinating complex of open water, pools, streams, wet meadows and mixed broad-leaved woodland. The wetland plants include bogbean and water-violet, the meadows provide grazing for roe deer, and a rich bird life includes snipe and bittern. Dragonflies and water beetles abound on the glacial pools or pingos.

Thursford Wood

Permit only; 10ha; NNT reserve
Mixed woodland and ponds
Spring, early summer

Oak standards over coppiced hazel with ash, beech, birch, field maple and alder grow with introduced conifers over a fine spring carpet of bluebell, wood anemone and wood-sorrel. Woodcock and tawny and long-eared owl have been recorded, with mallard, snipe and teal at the ponds.

Titchwell

TF 750436; 206ha; RSPB reserve
Foreshore, dunes, salt and freshwater marshes and reedbeds
Leaflets from reserve centre, open in summer
All year

Part of the NORTH NORFOLK COAST.

Upton Fen

Permit only; 50ha; NNT reserve
Fen and woodland surrounding the broad
Access very limited
Spring, summer

This superb fenland area completes the range of broadland types. HICKLING represents the higher waters of the river system, HOVETON GREAT BROAD the middle section and STRUMPSHAW the lower reaches. Upton is a broad, formed in a valley spur, no longer connected to the open river and so particularly undisturbed and unpolluted. For this reason access is strictly limited and only a few permits are available each year. The land-locked water stands surrounded by trees, jewelled with white water-lily and holding in its clear waters aquatic plants such as stoneworts, whorled water-milfoil and greater bladderwort.

Although we can point to the broads as protectors of fenland, it is only when we look at sites such as Upton Fen that we recognise the riches which we have lost and are still losing, through ignorance and through disturbance.

Walsey Hills

TG 062441; 0.3ha; NOA reserve
Thicket-covered hill
Information centre with warden, and hide
Spring, autumn

Part of the NORTH NORFOLK COAST, the hill is a superb vantage point for observing migrant birds, some of which land in the gorse bushes. Adder, slow-worm and several species of butterfly can be seen on the reserve.

Wayland Wood

Permit only; 34ha; NNT reserve
Damp clay woodland
Spring, early summer

The damp rich clays of Norfolk must have held a great variety of woodland before the Danes and Angles began to clear them. Some woods, however, were preserved for building timber and firewood, for charcoal to fire the blacksmith's forge, or for fencing and thatching materials, spars to clench the patterns on roof ridges or hurdles to hold the sheep at lambing or shearing time. Wayland Wood is managed on the coppice-with-standards principle where oak was left to grow on to maturity, to produce building timbers or the bones of wooden ships, while the lesser trees were cut low to provide crops of poles for more general purposes, harvested in rotation to permit a continuous supply. A few ash and birch trees stand with the oaks above a coppice layer of hazel and bird cherry varied with other species such as dogwood, willow and clumps of dark green holly.

The woodland floor is very damp, rides are filled with summer meadowsweet and, earlier in the year, spreads of bluebell, primrose and early-purple orchid show beneath the delicate drooping white flower clusters of bird cherry. Among the glories of a coppiced woodland are the glades in which the flowers that lie dormant under the earlier thick growth spring suddenly to life. Then, as the block of new coppice bushes over and shuts out the sunlight, the flowers will be depressed but will show again in a new coppiced block as soon as it is opened. Yellow star-of-Bethlehem grows here in good numbers at its only Norfolk site.

Burgh Common: rich fen vegetation and woods ring the quiet water.

Not only does coppicing encourage the wood-land flowers, it also increases the habitat range for birds. Where a high-forest wood has only rides and pathways to provide the 'edge' variety so impor-tant to many birds, and generally has only a rather thin understorey, a coppiced wood is gladed where the most recent cut has been taken, is equivalent to a bushy scrub where the standards rise through half-grown poles, and has a dense understorey where the coppice approaches harvesting stage.

At Wayland Wood woodcock and the exotic golden pheasant breed on the woodland floor, and there is a great diversity of warblers and small songbirds nesting in the coppice shrubs. Birds such as nuthatch and great and lesser spotted wood-pecker use the larger trees for nest-hole sites and feeding grounds.

Weeting Heath

Permit only; 138ha; NNT–NCC reserve
Typical Breckland heath
Spring, summer

The characteristic Breckland plants such as early forget-me-not and rue-leaved saxifrage, together with a number of rarer species, attract a wonderful range of butterflies including Essex skipper and holly blue, while the heath is noted for its range of breeding birds. Observation hides, for which a per-mit is needed (obtainable on site), are available from April to August.

Welney Wildfowl Refuge

TL 547946; 362.8ha; WT reserve
Large area of drains, lagoons and flood meadows
Leaflets from site or WT
All year

Part of the OUSE WASHES which, mainly in Cam-bridgeshire, are described there.

Winterton Dunes

TG 498197; 105ha; NCC reserve
Acid dune system
Leaflet from NCC
Spring, summer

Behind the dune ridge, which backs a sweep of sand and shingle, the ground is thrown into lower ridges and damp slacks, filled with a purple haze of heathers and overlooking a roughland of grazing marsh and scrub.

Marram, a strong tall spiky grass which can trap fresh sand and grow up through it, covers most of the dune ridge while the lower heath is a mix of acid species. The sands, which dry out at low tide and are blown up on to the dunes, are, unlike most East Anglian systems, almost without shell frag-ments and hence unusually acid. This encourages heather and bell heather in the drier parts which give way to cross-leaved heath in the damp slacks. Pools, some of which dry out in summer, are fringed with heather and cross-leaved heath or – the

Bewick's, mute and whooper swan feed at Welney Wildfowl Refuge.

deepest ones – are ringed and shaded by low stands of willow. Spreads of fern are a feature of the reserve, where broad and narrow buckler-fern and the rare crested buckler-fern grow together and royal fern lifts its dramatic fronds. There is also an outstanding growth of the very local grey hair-grass as well as the finest show in Britain of the hybrid *Ammocalamagrostis baltica*.

The scrub, between the reserve and the wood-land or grazing marsh, stands above spreads of heather and forms a welcome resting site for passage migrants such as brambling, redpoll, siskin, fieldfare and redwing. In winter you might be lucky enough to see a hen harrier hunting low over the marsh or the broad pale wings of a rough-legged buzzard circling overhead. Among the breeding birds is a good population of warblers, with chiffchaff and whitethroat, garden, reed, sedge and willow warbler likely to be present. The most important bird, though, is the least common of our terns. Little tern fly up from the tropics to breed on sandy shingles, and are extremely susceptible to disturbance.

Adders are plentiful on the reserve and the rarest of our amphibians, natterjack toad, occurs here, and croaks loudly from the pools. Natterjack is slightly smaller than common toad and is easily recognised by the yellow stripe down its back. It is very restricted in its range and occurs more frequently in coastal situations than inland.

The acid dunes at Winterton, breeding site for natterjack toad.

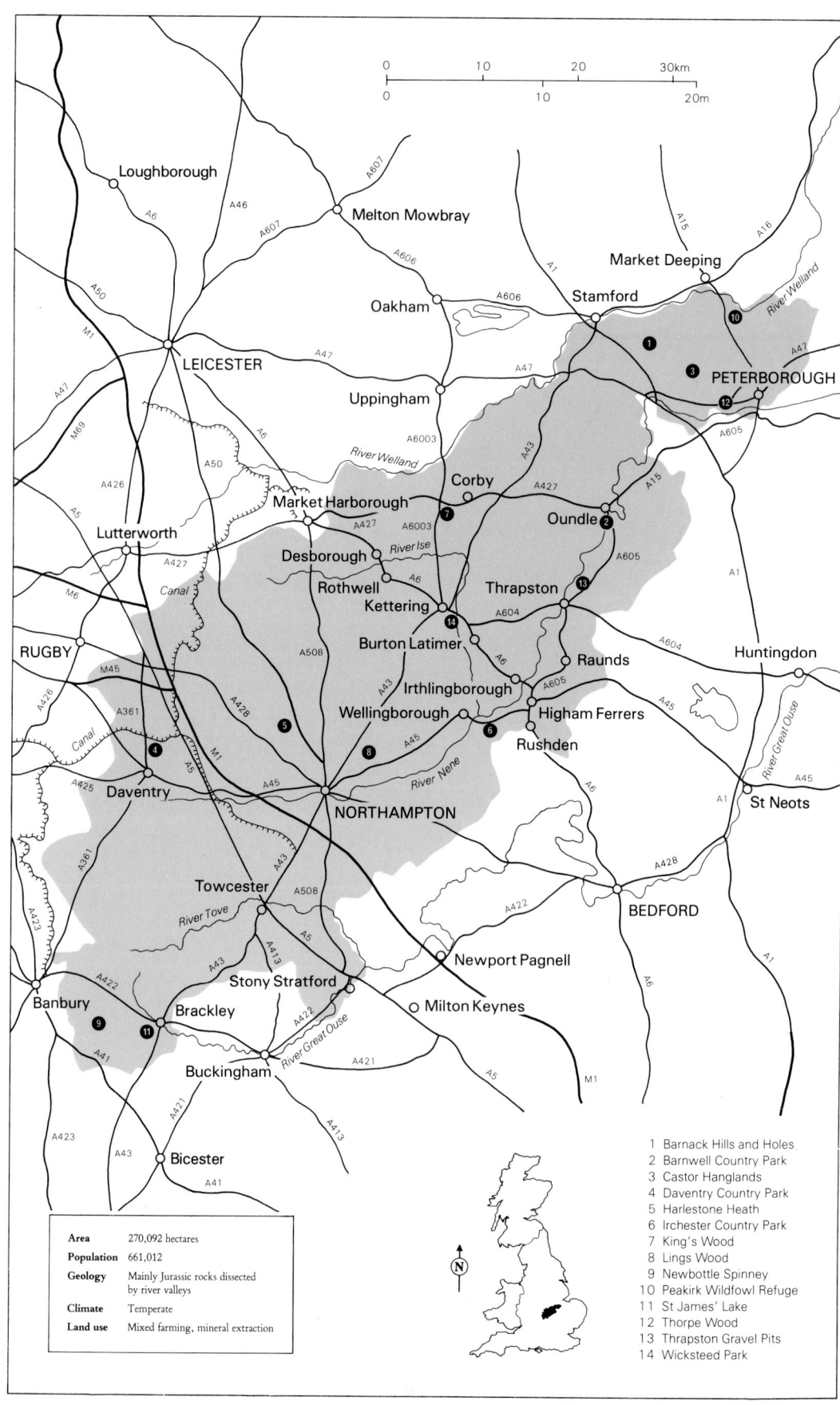

Loughborough

Melton Mowbray

Oakham

Market Deeping

Stamford

1 Barnack Hills and Holes

LEICESTER

PETERBOROUGH

3

10

12

Uppingham

Corby

7

Oundle **2**

A47

River Welland

Market Harborough

Lutterworth

Desborough

River Ise

Rothwell

Thrapston **13**

Kettering

14

RUGBY

Burton Latimer

Raunds

Irthlingborough

Wellingborough

Higham Ferrers **6**

Huntingdon

5

8

Rushden

4

Daventry

NORTHAMPTON

St Neots

River Nene

Towcester

BEDFORD

River Tove

Newport Pagnell

Banbury

9 **11**

Brackley

Stony Stratford

Milton Keynes

Buckingham

River Great Ouse

Bicester

Area	270,092 hectares
Population	661,012
Geology	Mainly Jurassic rocks dissected by river valleys
Climate	Temperate
Land use	Mixed farming, mineral extraction

N

1 Barnack Hills and Holes
2 Barnwell Country Park
3 Castor Hanglands
4 Daventry Country Park
5 Harlestone Heath
6 Irchester Country Park
7 King's Wood
8 Lings Wood
9 Newbottle Spinney
10 Peakirk Wildfowl Refuge
11 St James' Lake
12 Thorpe Wood
13 Thrapston Gravel Pits
14 Wicksteed Park

Northamptonshire and the Soke of Peterborough

One of the predominantly agricultural Midland shires, Northamptonshire has a relatively mild climate, no spectacular hills or jagged outcrops, and of course no coastline. Nevertheless the county contains a wide range of wildlife habitats from marsh to ancient forest remnants, acid heathland, lime-rich grassland, reservoirs, old gravelpits and other worked-out industrial sites.

The flat plain of the Nene Valley occupies much of the centre and north east of the county. Over the centuries the River Nene has cut a wide valley on its slow journey to the sea; its waters pass through Northamptonshire sands and great oolite limestone, and on either side low hills flank the valley.

There are distinct differences between this landscape and that of the Northamptonshire uplands, where weathering of the underlying clays has given rise to undulating countryside with gently rounded features. A somewhat hillier landscape lies between Daventry and the Oxfordshire border, the area often referred to as the Wolds. Seemingly undramatic, these relatively minor upland areas form one of the most important watersheds in central Britain. Here rise the Avon, Nene, Welland and Ouse, the last three making their way in a leisurely fashion eastwards to the Wash.

In past centuries changing patterns of agriculture shaped the face of the landscape, a process which is still going on, generally to the disadvantage of wildlife habitats. In more recent times, since the Industrial Revolution, mining of iron ore for the once flourishing but now defunct Corby steel works has placed additional burdens on wildlife and left innumerable scars in the north of the country. Yet industrial development such as iron ore and coal mining and gravel extraction have not always had adverse effects on wildlife, and over the past 30 years interesting and important plant and animal communities have evolved in some of these sites.

With the arrival of the boot and shoe industry for which the county has long been famous large numbers of oaks were felled in this hitherto well-wooded region, for the bark provided a valuable source of tannin. Yet in spite of this and earlier felling since Neolithic times to make way for human settlement and agriculture, some areas have retained their wooded character. Under the Normans almost half the county was covered by Royal Forests, remnants of which still survive at Rockingham, Salcey and Whittlebury, and the fact that so much woodland has been preserved is due in no small measure to later aristocratic landowners and their passion for hunting. What remains is only a fraction of the original woodland, but even so the casual observer today might be forgiven for thinking that the county is still well wooded, an illusion that is created by the numerous copses and spinneys.

A variety of nature reserves hold something of interest for most naturalists, whatever their speciality. Among woodland reserves SHORT WOOD, dominated by oak and ash and in springtime famous for its show of bluebells, is part of the ancient Rockingham Forest and one of the few Northamptonshire sites which support wood speedwell, rare in the county. The reserve in SALCEY FOREST provides nesting sites for several warblers, nightingale, treecreeper and woodcock. THORPE WOOD is an area of primary woodland, effectively unchanged since the ice ages. NEWBOTTLE SPINNEY supports such species as spotted-orchid, twayblade and wall lettuce. Rich in both plant and insect life, BEDFORD PURLIEUS, another vestige of Rockingham Forest, has probably been wooded since the ice ages. Small-leaved lime here is a relic from the days when the climate was milder; less common woodland species include wild liquorice and nettle-leaved bellflower. GLAPTHORN COW PASTURE supports the most vigorous colony of black hairstreak butterfly in Northamptonshire. KING'S WOOD, an area of ancient forest near industrial Corby, exhibits a variety of woodland types and is rich in moths, butterflies, birds and plants.

Though the county is dominated by farming, old grassland is becoming a thing of the past. In areas traditionally famed for livestock rearing new techniques are being adopted, and plants once common in such habitats are fast disappearing. In the north, excavations in past centuries from the stone quarries at BARNACK HILLS AND HOLES have given rise to grassland on limestone which supports a wide variety of lime-loving plants and associated butter-

flies. For more than two centuries now the area has been famous for the silky, deep violet pasqueflower, and recent grazing has been of considerable benefit to both pasqueflower and orchids.

The county in general is particularly rich in plants, and more than 1000 species have been recorded, some of them protected in reserves which are strongholds for species that were once common but are now rare.

Northamptonshire is well known for its bird life, and 170 species have been recorded regularly. PITSFORD RESERVOIR and STANFORD RESERVOIR are both important sites, especially for breeding and wintering waterfowl.

Though the landscape is soft and gentle and lacks spectacular contrasts, there is much of interest in Northamptonshire for both the experienced naturalist and the visitor who makes an effort to discover the county's unpretentious but undeniable wildlife riches.

RON WILSON

Barnack Hills and Holes

TF 075046; 22ha; NCC–NTNC reserve
Limestone grassland
Leaflet from NCC
Spring, summer

The medieval craftsmen who built the great cathedrals and abbeys of Peterborough, Ely, Bury St Edmunds and other south east towns used stone from here; from here the stone for several Cambridge colleges was cut and in the cutting limestone rubble was dug and heaped, delved out and banked, to form the hills and holes. By the sixteenth century the finest stone was gone and the pits and rubble piles were left for plants to colonise. Gradually, a shallow turf developed and stock was grazed among the limestone flowers until World War I, when grazing stopped and scrub and coarser grasses began to choke the site.

The reserve is now an open, hummocked, herb-rich turf, grazed to control the coarser upright and false brome, with a scrubland area of steep-banked Turkey oak, hawthorn and other trees. The scrub contrasts with the grassland and shows how its fragile ecology depends upon grazing.

In the wonderful variety of limestone flowers, pride of place must go to the pasqueflower, a plant with a very restricted range on lime-rich slopes in southern Britain. The reserve also has a good show of cowslip in spring, followed by a fine variety of summer plants. Typical lime-loving plants such as quaking-grass, small scabious, dropwort and common rock-rose grow together with more uncommon species. Horseshoe vetch contrasts with purple milk-vetch and squinancywort, with the tiny northern mountain everlasting and the tall spires of knapweed broomrape. The orchids, too – bee orchid, fragrant and pyramidal orchid and the extraordinary man orchid – provide a show of wonderfully delicate plants.

Fifty bird species are recorded on the reserve, with woodland birds in the scrub and species such as skylark in the grasses while the grassland flowers attract a wide range of insects.

Barnwell Country Park

TL 037874; 15ha; Northamptonshire CC
Flooded gravelpits and grassland
Leaflets from site
Spring, summer

Old gravel workings in a meander of the River Nene have become flooded to give a complex of tree-fringed open lagoons, scrub woodland and level grassland. The pools are lined with common reed, bulrush and common club-rush, with purple-loosestrife in summer. Some 126 bird species have been recorded here including breeding great crested grebe, reed bunting and yellow wagtail. Winter wildfowl include tufted duck and pochard, migrant common, arctic and black tern occur, and unusual birds include water rail and red-crested pochard.

Bedford Purlieus

Permit only; 22.8ha; NTNC reserve
Mixed woodland
Spring, summer

This small reserve lies within a much larger area, managed by the Forestry Commission, which is part of the once-great Royal Forest of Rockingham. It has been altered by coppicing and some replanting but still holds areas of primary woodland, the ancient heritage of continuity over many thousands of years. The soils are varied, encouraging a mosaic of lime-loving and more acid plants which may be unique in Britain, and this superb range of plants makes the site justly famous for its butterflies.

The richer areas have stands of ash, hazel, wych elm and field maple with birch, poplar and oak–hazel woodland in the acid parts. Small-leaved lime and English elm may be found and there is a considerable invasion by sycamore. The ground cover is equally varied, with rich-wood plants such as ramsons and woodruff, and more acid-loving species such as common cow-wheat, great wood-rush and hard fern. There is also a great diversity of much less common species. Lily-of-the-valley, columbine, herb-Paris, greater butterfly-orchid and fly orchid may be found while rides and clearings may contain deadly nightshade, wild liquorice and tall nettle-leaved bellflower. Other unusual plants include mountain melick and caper spurge.

The butterflies comprise species which rely on trees, on scrub, on shrubs, on herbs and on grasses for their larval food – species such as white-letter hairstreak and brown hairstreak, white admiral and pearl-bordered, high brown, dark green and silver-washed fritillary. The wide range of habitat also attracts a good variety of woodland birds.

Castor Hanglands

TF 118023; 45ha; NCC reserve
Woodland, scrub, grassland and wetland
No access to woodland off right of way
Leaflet from NCC
Spring, early summer

A fragment of the ancient Forest of Narborough, the woodland was enclosed and managed as coppice with standards, then later virtually clear felled. The grassland – common land – was kept open by grazing and then fell derelict; scrub began to invade as a step in the reversion to full tree cover.

Evidence such as the presence of wild service-tree shows that the woods are probably ancient, and a few oak standards remain above coppiced oak, ash, field maple and hazel, with occasional stands of birch and with species such as crab apple, aspen, dogwood, wych elm and willow, both hawthorn and Midland hawthorn, blackthorn, red currant, bramble and honeysuckle. The ground cover is chiefly that of rich woodland, with spreads of dog's mercury and bluebell, wood anemone, primrose and wood spurge and with damper areas showing plants such as ramsons, wood-sorrel and herb-Paris. A good range of woodland birds is present and the reserve protects a strong population of fallow deer.

The grasslands vary from areas of shallow lime-rich turf to more acid gorse and grass heath, but the most obvious feature is the spread of scrub which forms thickets and mazes of dense, colourful shrubs. This is a superb habitat for birds such as warblers, with its varied mix of crab apple, alder buckthorn, blackthorn, hawthorn, guelder-rose and bramble with wild rose and lime-loving shrubs such as buckthorn, privet, spindle and wayfaring-tree. Songbirds such as garden and willow warbler, whitethroat, lesser whitethroat and blackcap may be heard together with grasshopper warbler and nightingale.

A spring-fed pool and a number of ponds provide an extra interest with bulrush and yellow iris, early marsh-orchid and common spotted-orchid and a fine range of hybrids between the two. The pools attract dragonflies and damselflies, support breeding common toad and all three British newts; they may be visited by birds such as heron, mallard, teal and tufted duck.

The reserve is notable for its butterflies, particularly black hairstreak.

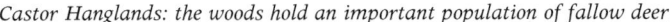

Castor Hanglands: the woods hold an important population of fallow deer.

The reservoir forms the focus around which Daventry Country Park is sited.

Collyweston Quarry

Permit only; 9ha; NTNC reserve
Limestone grassland, scree and scrub
Spring, summer

An area of worked-out oolitic limestone, the quarry was formerly mined for Collyweston tiles, which are a feature of the roofs of houses and barns round about. Humps and hollows produce a range of micro-habitats for lime-loving plants including an extensive population of dyer's greenweed.

Daventry Country Park

SP 575642; 70.8ha; Daventry DC
Reservoir and wetland
Leaflets from site or DDC
All year

A nature trail has been established to demonstrate the ecology of the area, which includes a designated nature reserve and which is rich in plant and animal life. A good range of birds includes breeding great crested grebe with passage waders including occasional curlew sandpiper, ruff and little stint. Winter wildfowl occur in reasonably good numbers.

Delf Spinney

Permit only; 4ha; NTNC reserve
Woodland and grassland
Spring, summer

The narrow strip of woodland between railway line and stream holds mixed ash, oak and willow with an understorey including hazel, buckthorn, dogwood and field maple. Bluebell, common dog-violet and dog's mercury characterise the ground cover, with a good show of broad-leaved helleborine in late summer. Some areas of wet grassland occur at the woodland edge with dry grassland sloping down from the railway line. Woodland birds include willow warbler, long-tailed tit, treecreeper and green woodpecker.

Denford Churchyard

Permit only; 0.02ha; NTNC reserve
Small riverbank scrubland
Spring, summer

Although very small, there is a range from over-grown river bank to alder–grey willow scrubland. Water figwort, purple-loosestrife, water forget-me-not and great willowherb grow in a confusion of common nettle, which is food for small tortoiseshell and peacock caterpillars and a nest site for mallard and moorhen. The scrub provides a habitat for birds such as whitethroat while the river attracts kingfishers.

Glapthorn Cow Pasture

Permit only; 28ha; NTNC reserve
Scrub and woodland
Spring, summer

The reserve is an old meadow which has reverted to scrub and woodland. Some fine old oak trees probably shaded the milking cows before the woods moved in and now stand high above a variety of younger trees and an impenetrable jungle of blackthorn. Generally, the wood is rather damp, with meadowsweet, hemlock and teasel among the grassy clearings; drier clearings may contain other non-woodland species such as musk mallow.

The wood attracts a range of breeding birds, with nightingale and warblers, in particular, taking advantage of the prickly safety of the black-thorn. Grassland butterflies such as large skipper, meadow brown and ringlet lay their eggs in the open rides and clearings. The *raison d'être* of the reserve, however, resides in the black hairstreak butterfly.

The black hairstreak is one of the largest and most beautiful of the hairstreaks and is the most local in its distribution: it is found only in certain Midland counties, in Northamptonshire, Cambridgeshire, Buckinghamshire and Oxfordshire. It is hard to know why this should be; many species are restricted by their food plants, but the black hairstreak uses blackthorn and this is a very widespread plant. Presumably the butterfly is a relict of a warmer British climate and only a few strong colonies have survived.

It was first recognised in the 1820s — a dark-coloured insect with underwings that are flushed with orange, while the hindwing carries a black-spotted orange band close to the edge; a scribble of white across both underwings is bordered with black. The female has an orange flush on the upper forewing while both sexes have an orange bar on the upper hindwing. They fly towards the end of June or the beginning of July and lay their eggs among the blackthorn scrub, on which the young caterpillars feed when they have hatched. When the caterpillar pupates, to make its final change to adulthood, it is obviously at great risk; it cannot move, yet its resting place, the blackthorn scrub, is attractive to small birds. The insect escapes, for-tunately for one so rare, by a beautiful example of camouflage — its pupa closely resembles a bird dropping.

Black hairstreak, one of our rarest butterflies.

Irchester Country Park

SP 912658; 81ha; Northamptonshire CC
Plantation, scrub and grassland on old ironstone workings
Leaflets from site
Spring, summer

Most of the country park consists of an alternation of dry slopes and wet dales, typical of disused open-cast workings, and much of this has been planted with conifers. Where tree cover is not too dense, good stands of common reed develop in the damp places and, because the ironstone lies below limestone, some interesting limestone plants such as blue fleabane and woolly thistle grow on the drier slopes. Ash widens the range of habitat available to the birds.

King's Wood

SP 864874; 45ha; NTNC–Corby DC reserve
Oak–ash woodland
Spring, summer

Part of the old Rockingham Forest, King's Wood is the best remaining wood for lichens. A mixed oak–ash woodland with an understorey of hazel, it is also outstanding for a number of very old oak trees which stand above a rich-wood ground cover including bluebell, wood-sorrel and sanicle. Orchids include common twayblade, early-purple orchid and common spotted-orchid. A wide variety of moths has been recorded and there is a good range of woodland birds.

Lings Wood

SP 802638; 22.4ha; NTNC reserve
Mixed woodland
Nature trail guide from NTNC headquarters, Lings House
Spring, summer

In the sixteenth century, Lings Wood was an area of heather and gorse, a heathland wooded with birches and an open common land. Silver birch and gorse still occur but much of the reserve is now given over to coniferous plantation with mixed broad-leaved trees which give a wide range of habitat. It does not show the old heathland ecology however and is strongly affected by the alien species present.

Sycamore is abundant in part of the reserve, which also contains sweet chestnut, horse-chestnut and Turkey oak and, while rhododen-dron makes a spectacular show in May and June, its thick shrub cover shades out anything beneath it. There is, however, a good variety of native trees including beech, crab apple, hazel and holly, oak, rowan and silver birch.

The importance of native trees to a woodland habitat is shown by the numbers of their insect associates; where oak has almost 300 British insects associated with it, sycamore has fewer than 30.

Ground cover within the reserve includes the woodland grass false brome, with beautiful small spring flowers such as sweet violet and lesser celandine. Dog's mercury also flowers in spring in richer parts of the wood, tending to grow in wide green drifts, each plant a low, many-leaved stem lifting to catch the light as the woodland trees leaf over. Dry, more open, areas may be filled with bracken, a tall fern that only strong plants such as foxglove can overtop. Foxglove and bracken are typical plants of drier acid areas and the lack of lime where rain has washed the top layers of the sands may be contrasted with damper places where a richer variety of plants may be found. Two wetland areas provide a further range of habitat with plants such as soft and toad rush, reed sweet-grass, water forget-me-not and branched bur-reed.

Insect life in the reserve is very varied – over 15 butterfly species are known – while the birds include treecreeper, all three British woodpeckers, redpoll, pied wagtail, tits and finches.

Newbottle Spinney

SP 517364; 16ha; NTNC reserve
Mixed woodland
Spring, summer

This is a most valuable reserve in a part of the county where very few woods remain. Mixed woodland occupies the central part, once quarried and now an area of 'hills and holes', with fine beech trees in the north and sweet chestnut and lime in the south. Primrose is followed by common twayblade and common spotted-orchid, with spindle in autumn. Birds include tawny and little owl, warblers, tits and all three woodpeckers.

Peakirk Wildfowl Refuge

TF 168069; 6.8ha; WT
Wildfowl collection and ancient duck decoy
Permit only to duck decoy
Leaflets from reception centre or WT
Spring, summer

The collection, set on the site of an old osier bed, attracts migrant waterfowl including shoveler, pochard, tufted duck and teal, and small passerines in winter. Nearby is an old decoy pond, the first written record of which appeared in 1670, with the unusual feature of eight arms. It is still used for ringing. Visited by winter wildfowl and passage waders, it is fringed with woodland where mallard and moorhen breed and dragonflies may be seen. An observation hide overlooks the main body of the pool.

Pitsford Reservoir

Permit only; 172ha; AWA–NTNC reserve
Part of reservoir and surrounds may be overlooked
from SP 783701
All year

Woods of young oak trees, conifers or mixed woodlands shelter the marshy edges where sweetgrasses, common fleabane and water mint grow with marsh and golden dock, trifid bur-marigold and pale persicaria; willow scrub, grading into beds of rushes and reed canary-grass, adds a further spread of cover for wetland birds.

Pintail may visit Pitsford Reservoir in winter.

Over 200 bird species have been recorded for the reservoir. Spring and autumn are the main times for movement. In spring the winter wildfowl leave and passage birds, such as waders and terns, fly through on their way to more northerly nesting sites; summer breeding birds arrive from the south. In autumn, the stream reverses and the summer breeders leave, the passage birds migrate back through and the winter birds return.

Winter brings good numbers of dabbling duck, such as mallard, teal and wigeon, together with smaller groups of pintail and shoveler. Diving duck, pochard, tufted duck, goldeneye and goosander share the deeper waters with great crested grebe. Less common divers occur from time to time and Pitsford's records include black-necked, red-necked and Slavonian grebe, eider, long-tailed duck and little auk. Small parties of Bewick's swan often occur with occasional visits from whooper swan and, although geese are uncommon here, records include pink-footed, white-fronted, barnacle and Brent geese. A sizeable winter gull roost, mainly of commoner species, has attracted unusual birds such as glaucous and Iceland gull, together with great and arctic skua.

A wonderful range of predators is recorded including hen harrier, marsh and Montagu's harrier, hobby, merlin and peregrine, osprey, buzzard, rough-legged buzzard, kestrel, sparrowhawk and great grey shrike. They often occur at migration times, as flocks of smaller birds pass through, when the muddy edges of the reserve are feeding sites for waders and when marsh terns – black and white-winged black tern – have been recorded.

Although some notable rarities have been recorded, such as long-billed dowitcher and yellowlegs, the chief importance of the reserve lies in the size of the area protected from disturbance.

Ramsden Corner Plantation

Permit only; 3.2ha; NTNC reserve
Rough grassland and scrub
Spring, summer

Sandy soil, wet in places, gives an open heathland with scattered trees over grassland and thickets of gorse and broom, suitable habitats for birds such as linnet and yellowhammer. Opposite-leaved golden-saxifrage, uncommon in the county, grows in the wetter places beside a stream which runs through the site.

Ravensthorpe Reservoir

No access; 45.6ha; AWA
Birdwatchers' reservoir
May be overlooked from SP 675712
All year

Mature, mainly deciduous, woodland surrounds the water which, in the reserve, is fringed by willow scrub and reedbeds. Around 170 bird species have been recorded, from breeding great crested grebe to wintering Bewick's and whooper swan, goldeneye and smew, while the woodland encourages a good range of smaller birds. Visiting birds include black-necked, red-necked and Slavonian grebe, with great grey shrike and great reed warbler.

St James' Lake

SP 582365; 8.8ha; South Northamptonshire DC
Reservoir and meadowland
All year

The major attraction of this small reserve lies in its bird life. It was built to hold storm-water from the town and floods in winter, increasing the open water area. Among the species recorded are little and black tern, shoveler and scaup, grey, pied and yellow wagtail and a great variety of water and waterside birds. Trees and shrubs on the reserve attract a range of other birds.

Salcey Forest

Permit only; 8.8ha; NTNC–BBONT–FC reserve
Oak woodland
Spring, summer

A tract of woodland on these lime-rich clays once formed the old Salcey Forest – this reserve protects one of the few small remnants. Oaks still stand, with an understorey of hazel, over a rich ground cover characteristically adapted to woodland life. Primrose and bluebell make a spectacular spring show, with wood-sorrel, goldilocks buttercup and both early and common dog-violet. Other typical rich-wood plants are dog's mercury and enchanter's-nightshade while early-purple orchid and common spotted-orchid occur, together with other species including the tall, white, scented greater butterfly-orchid.

The rides hold a rich variety of plants, particularly in the damper areas. Hawthorn and Midland hawthorn, blackthorn and wild cherry fill out the woodland edges, often tangled with honeysuckle or field rose, while damper parts have goat willow over a colourful mix of cuckooflower, ragged-Robin and meadowsweet; bush vetch and meadow vetchling are among the species which attract a range of butterflies to these rides. The woods were once a favourite site for white admiral, black hairstreak and purple emperor, and for the wood white, which still occurs.

Mammals include fallow and muntjac deer with grey squirrel, rabbit and fox and small mammals such as common shrew and wood mouse. The birds are varied and include blackcap, chiffchaff, garden and grasshopper warbler, willow warbler and whitethroat, which all breed in the area, as do redstart and spotted flycatcher. The nightingale has long been known as one of the specialities of Salcey.

Short Wood

Permit only; 24.8ha; NTNC reserve
Oak–ash woodland
Spring, summer

Short Wood has been described as the finest bluebell wood in Northamptonshire. It is a remnant of the ancient Royal Forest of Rockingham, and includes elements of the original woods as well as other areas which at one time have been cleared for agriculture and have then been allowed to revert to woodland.

Short Wood: a remnant of the ancient Forest of Rockingham.

Stanford Reservoir: the fringe of vegetation helps to attract a good range of birds.

This combination of primary and secondary woodland has been modified by past management to give a good variety of habitat. Part of the wood is ash high-forest, part coppiced ash, hazel and field maple with oak and ash standards, and part is most unusual high-stooled coppiced elm. The elms, springing straight and tall from chest-high stumps, give a rather open, uniform wood; the mixed coppice with standards provides a pattern of sturdy trees, understorey and a varied ground layer; the ash high-forest is full of tall trees and sunlit clearings. Wild service-tree may be found within the wood.

Hairy wood-rush, primrose, sweet violet and wood speedwell, a rarity in Northamptonshire, grow on the woodland floor. The spread and mix of these small plants are fairly even through the wood, indicating that the soil is uniform damp clay but, here and there, a group of different species indicates a change. Clumps of silver birch with stands of bracken show where the soil is lighter and more acid, while a richer area is marked by lime-loving species such as traveller's-joy and spindle. Orchids include early-purple orchid and common spotted-orchid together with more uncommon species such as greater butterfly-orchid, bird's-nest orchid and broad-leaved and violet helleborine.

There is a good range of woodland birds and the reserve shelters fallow deer and other mammals.

Stanford Reservoir

Permit only; 66ha; STWA–NTNC
Small reservoir
Permit from STWA; members only admitted to the 16ha NTNC reserve
Autumn, winter, spring

Some 135 bird species have been recorded on the reservoir including most of the migrant waders and common warblers together with large numbers of wildfowl and gulls. Regular winter visitors include mallard, pochard, shoveler, tufted duck, teal and wigeon with occasional pintail and goldeneye when bad weather drives them inland. Goosander are relatively common, with winter flocks of up to 30 birds, and terns and some of the less common gulls may be seen.

Thorpe Wood

TL 160986; 9.7ha; NTNC reserve
Oak–ash woodland
Spring, summer

Oak and ash trees stand over a coppice layer of hazel and field maple with a good rich-wood ground cover including bluebell, ramsons, nettle-leaved bellflower and wood melick. The butterflies are varied and a wide range of woodland birds breed here.

Thrapston Gravel Pits and Titchmarsh Heronry

TF 007796; 15ha; NTNC reserve
Flooded gravelpits, river, scrubland and woods
Permit only to heronry; visitors must keep to
rights of way
All year

Thrapston Gravel Pits is a large complex of open water, wetland, rough grassland and woodland, on the east side of which lies the NTNC reserve. The area has the added interest of an adjacent disused railway line.

The flooded pits, deep and suitable for divers, provide an ideal site for coot and great crested grebe, for winter gatherings of diving duck and roosts of gulls. The shallows around the edges of the pits and the islands attract dabblers such as mallard, shoveler, teal and feral Canada geese. Sandbanks around the area are tunnelled by sand martin, and open gravel shores provide nest sites for little ringed plover. Rough meadowland between the pits provides an ideal breeding site for redshank, yellow wagtail and corn bunting.

Where the gravels have been colonised by plantains, teasels and thistles, flocks of finches and migrant whinchat and stonechat may be seen in spring. The disused railway line, thick with blackthorn and hawthorn, attracts finches in autumn along with the migratory winter thrushes, fieldfare and redwing.

The railway line connects the main body of the gravelpits with the woodland block which holds the heronry at the northern end of the reserve. Titchmarsh Heronry has been designated as a reserve to protect the population of heron there.

About 40 nests form the breeding colony from which the adult birds fly out to feed on pools, rivers and streams for many miles around. Other species nesting in the wood include the warblers, blackcap and lesser whitethroat, with other woodland birds such as treecreeper and spotted flycatcher. Since the reserve lies in the migration flyway of the Nene Valley a wide range of unusual migrants may occur, and records from the area include bittern, red-necked and Slavonian grebe, marsh harrier, and roseate and white-winged black tern.

Walton Grounds

Permit only; 0.07ha; NNT reserve
Small area of grassland
Spring

The reserve was designated solely to protect a colony of green hellebore, a plant which generally grows in chalk woodlands.

Wicksteed Park

SP 880773; 59.5ha; Wicksteed Village Trust
Lake and pools
Nature trail leaflet from site
All year

Willow and alder stand by the open water areas while a shallow-water lagoon is fringed with marsh-marigold. Sedge warbler, pied and yellow wagtail, mallard, tufted duck, mute swan and Canada goose occur in summer, with pochard arriving in winter. Early in the year the lake is emptied for repairs and the muddy bottom attracts teal, with waders such as snipe, redshank and green sandpiper, and the alders are alive with redpoll and siskin.

Herons with young: in Britain herons usually build in trees, nesting communally like rooks.

Northumberland

From the line of the Cheviots marching along the Scottish border to the northern edge of the Pennine chain, from the moors and bogs of the Irthing Valley to the estuaries and islands of the county's north coast, Northumberland presents one of the widest ranges of habitats in any English county. Elements of the plant and animal life of upland and lowland Britain are found side by side, and internationally important examples of several habitats are protected within the county's nature reserves.

Away from the densely populated industrial conurbation around Tyneside, Northumberland is a quiet, rural county, with few towns and villages: old market towns such as Hexham and Morpeth nestle in the river valleys. The agriculture of the coastal plain and Tyne Valley gives way to the uplands in the west, long managed as sheep walk and grouse moor, but now increasingly coming under the green blanket of commercial forestry.

Northumberland's geology has moulded the county's land use concentrically around the massive granites of the Cheviot dome, which intrudes into the andesite lava flows of the long extinct Cheviot volcanoes. The sedimentary rocks of the carboniferous era sweep in a great eastern semi-circle around the flows. Nearest to Cheviot, only the oldest deposited cementstones remain; all that followed has been removed by erosion. The hard rock of the fell sandstone ridge stands out as a great scarp line, and the shales of the Scremerston coal group underlie the lower moors of the west. Several more smaller sandstone scarps outcrop in the limestone series, interspersed with shales, limestones and coals. In the south east these are overlain by the coal measure strata, into which the pits of the Geordie miners have been sunk for hundreds of years. Perhaps the most famous feature of the county's geology and landscape is the Great Whin Sill, forming a vast escarpment across the county, from Greenhead on the Cumbrian border east and north to the FARNE ISLANDS and Bamburgh Castle. Much of the western part forms a natural north-facing rampart on which stands Hadrian's Wall.

To the outsider, Northumberland is perhaps best known for its coast. The internationally famous Farne Islands offer probably the best opportunities in Britain for the general public to see large colonies of auks, cormorant, kittiwake and terns at very close quarters, with the added attraction of grey seal; the lesser known and inaccessible Coquet Island is an important reserve for terns, eider and puffin. To the north of these lie LINDISFARNE and Budle Bay, an internationally important complex of mudflats, saltmarshes and sand dunes. The mudflats and marshes are favoured by most of Spitsbergen's Brent geese and many other wildfowl and waders; bar-tailed godwit in particular feed on the enormous lugworm populations of the mudbanks. The Lindisfarne dunes form the keystone of one of the longest sand dune systems in Britain, running almost the length of the county; interspersed with hard rock outcrops, they still hold rich plant communities typical of sand dunes, with many rare and unusual species.

Like most of Britain lowland Northumberland has been changed markedly over the last few decades by new farming practices. Much ancient meadow has been lost, though sites still remain at the urban fringes or where the land is too rocky for cultivation. The Whin Sill outcrops and adjacent limestones often retain such grassland and support unusual plant species unique to the north east. Ancient woodlands too are few, restricted to the steep incised cleughs where deforestation was not practical or profitable. The reserves in the Coquet Valley conserve important alder, oak, ash and mixed deciduous and juniper woodland, and the valley woods of the Tyne, Allen and Derwent are also important. These areas, though, represent only a very small proportion of the 15 per cent of Northumberland which is afforested: the majority is commercial conifer plantation.

Northumberland's rivers are mostly clean, fast-flowing burns, spawning grounds for salmon and trout, breeding sites for many river birds, and home for the fast declining otter. The Tweed and Till in the north, the Coquet in the centre and the Tynes and Allens in the south are all important wildlife strongholds. The South Tyne and the Allens have the added interest of a unique flora which is tolerant of the high levels of lead and zinc found in the silts washed downstream from the now disused ore fields of the north Pennines.

Climbing north from the South Tyne, the 'Roman Wall country', with its distinctive series of scarpments, is one of the most varied areas of the county. In a short space of time the visitor passes through farmland and woodland, over the sandtone ridges with their heather cladding, and up to the great north-facing wall of the Whin Sill, with its unusual flora and nearby limestone outcrops. Nestling between the escarpments lie a series of loughs: Crag, GRINDON, Greenlee and Broomlee, important for winter wildfowl, invertebrates and aquatic plants, and virtually the only natural open water in the county. These are supplemented now by Tyneside's colliery subsidence ponds, the county estate lakes and the modern upland reservoirs. The newest and largest of these is Kielder Water, which fills 10 km of the North Tyne Valley, forms part of the BORDER FOREST PARK, and whose

potential for wildlife is yet to be realised.

Northumbrians divide the uplands into 'black land and white'. The black is the dark heather moorland of the acidic fell sandstones and shales, found on HARBOTTLE CRAGS and the imposing Simonside Hills; the white land comprises the grass-covered, rounded hills of the basic Cheviot lava flows, where the bigger Cheviot sheep have long been grazed. Cheviot itself is covered in blanket bog, and the range is dotted with granite tors reminiscent of West Country moors. The vestiges of an alpine flora may be found here, though it is sparsely spread. The north Pennine fells are different again: enclosed land rises to over 400m, nearly 170m higher than north of the Roman Wall, and the tilted plateau of the Alston block forms typical Pennine scenery, with limestones outcropping in the river valleys and burnsides, and blanket bog covering the tops. These, with the Cheviot moorlands, still form important strongholds for many of Britain's upland birds.

North of the Roman Wall lies the bleak moorland of Wark Forest, the eastern part reafforested with conifers. Here can be found prairie landscapes of purple moor-grass, and an internationally important series of bogs known collectively as the Irthinghead Mires. The wet climate and acid soils provide conditions which give rise to blanket, raised and valley bogs, intact for thousands of years, with rare plants in lawns of *Sphagnum*, breeding golden plover and the northern large heath butterfly. Isolated, many now surrounded by conifers, but protected as nature reserves, these are Northumberland's unknown jewels.

I.P. BAINBRIDGE

Arnold

NU 255197; 1.2ha; NWT reserve
Woodland and scrub
Visitors must keep to right of way
Spring, summer, autumn

An information centre explains the interest of the reserve, one of the few areas of semi-natural woodland and scrub near this stretch of coast. Sycamore, ash, elm and Scots pine stand above elder, hawthorn, blackthorn, honeysuckle, bramble and gorse. Bluebell and primrose are followed by foxglove, harebell, water avens and northern marsh-orchid. Blackcap, chiffchaff, sedge and willow warbler breed; lesser redpoll moult and migrants include bluethroat, red-breasted flycatcher, barred and icterine warbler and wryneck.

Gunnerton Nick

NY 9175; 5.6ha; NWT reserve
Quarries and grassland
Spring, summer

Two quarries, one in the Whin Sill, the other in Carboniferous limestone, are of exceptional ecological interest and both have grassland areas. The whinstone grassland has crested hair-grass,

hare's-foot clover, wild onion, dyer's greenweed and petty whin together with parsley fern. The limestone face is rich in common rock-rose, fairy flax, restharrow and small scabious, with meadow saxifrage and cut-leaved, long-stalked and wood crane's-bill on steep broken ground; the grassland is filled with cowslip and other colourful species. There are also stands of ash and scrub of blackthorn, hawthorn and hazel.

Barrow Burn Wood

NY 9106; 2.7ha; Northumberland CC–NWT reserve
Woodland
Spring, summer

Birch, oak, ash and hazel stand over ramsons, dog's mercury and primroses, while birds include dipper, redstart and pied flycatcher.

Bavington Carr

NY 9977; 13ha; NWT reserve
Wetland and marshy scrub
Spring, summer

An old lake, silted up, is rich in marsh-marigold, marsh cinquefoil, marsh ragwort and water mint

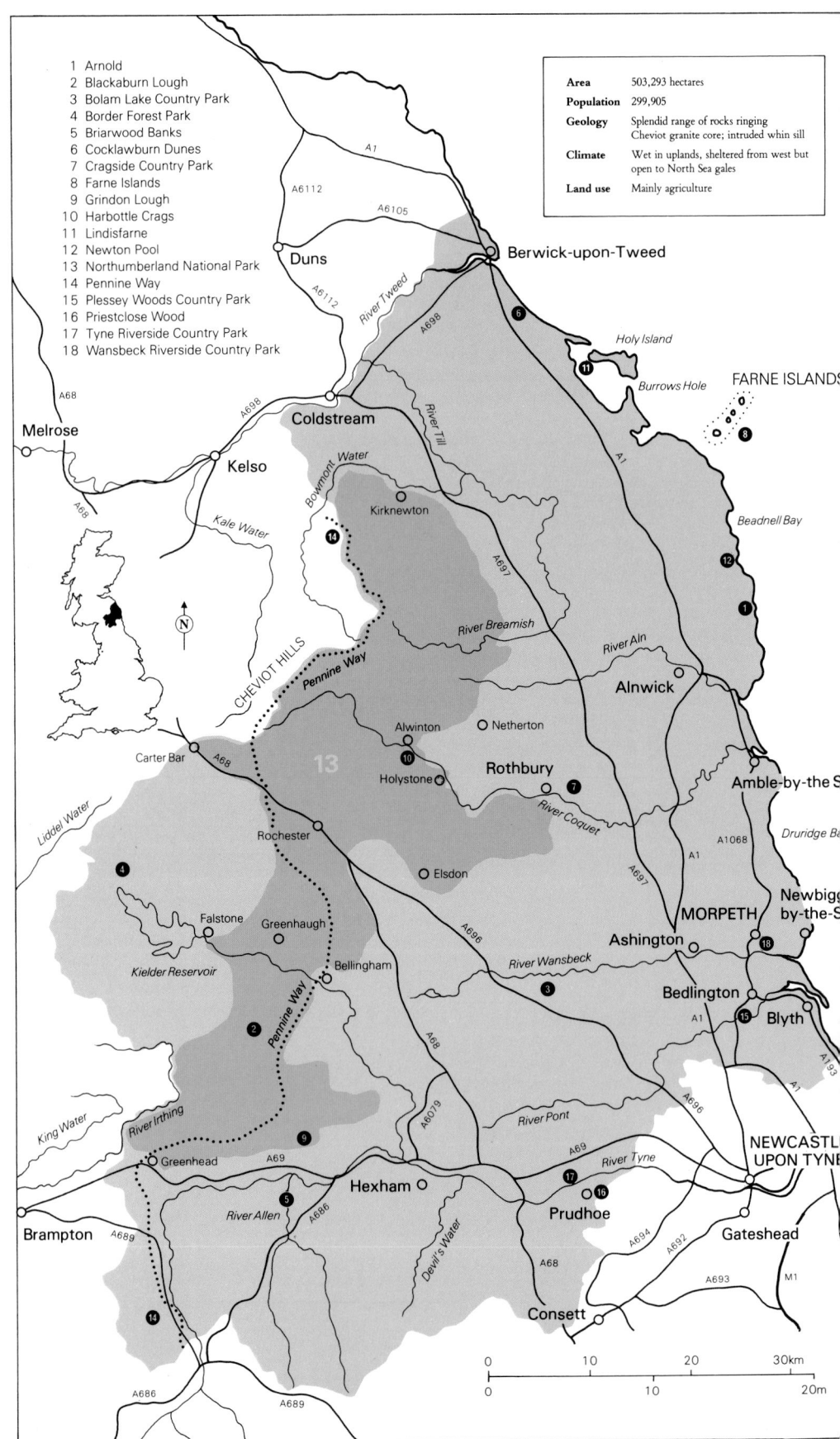

1 Arnold
2 Blackaburn Lough
3 Bolam Lake Country Park
4 Border Forest Park
5 Briarwood Banks
6 Cocklawburn Dunes
7 Cragside Country Park
8 Farne Islands
9 Grindon Lough
10 Harbottle Crags
11 Lindisfarne
12 Newton Pool
13 Northumberland National Park
14 Pennine Way
15 Plessey Woods Country Park
16 Priestclose Wood
17 Tyne Riverside Country Park
18 Wansbeck Riverside Country Park

Area	503,293 hectares
Population	299,905
Geology	Splendid range of rocks ringing Cheviot granite core; intruded whin sill
Climate	Wet in uplands, sheltered from west but open to North Sea gales
Land use	Mainly agriculture

Melrose
A68
Kelso
Duns
Coldstream
Berwick-upon-Tweed
A6112
A6105
A6112
A698
A698
River Tweed
River Till
Bowmont Water
Kale Water
Kirknewton
CHEVIOT HILLS
Pennine Way
River Breamish
River Aln
Alwinton
Netherton
Alnwick
13
Holystone
Rothbury
Amble-by-the-S
Carter Bar
A68
Rochester
Elsdon
River Coquet
A1068
Druridge Ba
A697
Liddel Water
Falstone
Greenhaugh
Bellingham
MORPETH
Newbigg
by-the-S
Kielder Reservoir
Pennine Way
River Wansbeck
Ashington
Bedlington
Blyth
A1
A696
A1
A193
King Water
River Irthing
A68
A6079
River Pont
NEWCASTL
UPON TYN
Greenhead
A69
A69
River Tyne
Hexham
Prudhoe
Gateshead
Brampton
A689
River Allen
A686
Devil's Water
A68
A694
A692
A693
M1
Consett
A686
A689

Holy Island
Burrows Hole
FARNE ISLANDS
Beadnell Bay

N

0   10   20   30km
0   10   20m

among reed canary-grass. Grey and crack willow grade into alder, birch and Scots pine, with mature alder over wet grassland. Redpoll, redstart, sedge and willow warbler breed while siskin, snipe and duck occur in winter. Roe deer are common.

Blackaburn Lough

NY 763796; 2ha; Borders Nat. Hist. Soc. reserve
Woodland lake
Car park at NY 804807, 4.8km from reserve
Spring, early summer

The lough grades into an acid swamp at one end and is completely surrounded by conifers. Black-headed gull, moorhen, mallard and tufted duck breed.

Black Pasture Quarry

NY 9369; 5ha; NWT reserve
Large sandstone quarry
Spring, summer

Huge old spoil heaps, thick with oak, ash and sycamore over typical woodland plants, contrast with richer areas where lime-loving plants include quaking-grass and fairy flax. More acid open spoil heaps show a sandstone vegetation with a scattered scrub of rowan, birch, Scots pine, hawthorn, blackthorn and gorse. Butterflies include red admiral, large skipper and small copper while among the birds are warblers, finches, woodcock, sparrowhawk and kestrel. The quarry exposes large sandstone beds in the great limestone series, including ripple bedding and fossiliferous horizons.

Bolam Lake Country Park

NZ 084820; 37ha; Northumberland CC
Wooded lake
Nature trail information from visitor centre
Spring, summer

A wildlife sanctuary – part of the lake – where waterbirds breed adds to the interest of an area of reedmarsh, lake and woodland.

Border Forest Park

NY 633935; 45,325ha; FC
Moorland and conifer forests
Leaflets from FC and site
Spring, summer

The forest park ranges from open moorland to the long, drowned valley of Kielder Water, probably the largest man-made lake in western Europe. The moors provide grazing for feral goat and breeding sites for black and red grouse, merlin and short-eared owl while the forests, now a mosaic of different-aged blocks, contain badger, roe deer, fox and red squirrel as well as birds such as siskin, crossbill, kestrel and sparrowhawk. The huge reservoir, with a wildlife sanctuary at its upper end, will attract breeding duck and large numbers of winter wildfowl while the whole forest park is rich in insects and other small animals.

Border Mires

Permit only; various sizes; FC reserves
Upland bogs
Spring, summer

Nine *Sphagnum* bogs, several of which are nationally important, have typical heather, hare's-tail cottongrass and crowberry in drier parts with cross-leaved heath, cranberry and bog-rosemary in the wet mires. Cloudberry and great sundew are only two of many unusual species.

Cocklawburn Dunes

NU 032482; 6ha; NWT reserve
Dunes and grassland
Spring, summer

The coastal dunes contain typical buck's-horn plantain, thrift and sea sandwort while the limestone outcrops and spoil heaps are filled with plants such as cowslip, bloody crane's-bill, autumn gentian, purple milk-vetch and kidney vetch. In winter, turnstone and purple sandpiper may be present with flocks of eider offshore.

Coom Rigg Moss

Permit only; 35ha; NCC reserve
Heather-clad blanket bog
Leaflet from NCC
Spring, summer

Coom Rigg Moss is one of the remnant areas of the original border mires, a great tract of rich blanket mire now largely destroyed by forestry plantations and the construction of a rocket-testing site. Large areas of the moss are covered with heather and hare's-tail cottongrass but there is a good variety of *Sphagnum* mosses together with characteristic bog plants such as round-leaved sundew, bog asphodel, bog-rosemary and cranberry.

Ford Moss

NT 9737; 71ha; NWT reserve
Lowland peat bog
Spring, summer

An extensive lowland bog, the moss is, in part, floating and much of it is heather-covered, with hare's-tail cottongrass and cross-leaved heath. There are areas of *Sphagnum* mosses with round-leaved sundew and its northern associate, cranberry. Bog myrtle occurs and the moss is fringed on its southern side by invading birch and pines.

Cragside Country Park

NU 072015; 280ha; NT
Parkland
Nature trail information from visitor centre
Spring, summer

Originally moorland, the park has been planted with trees and shrubs which, with the lakes, provide an attractive refuge for wildlife.

Crindledykes

NY 7867; 1ha; NWT reserve
Disused quarry
Spring, summer

Lime-loving autumn gentian, cowslip and fairy flax grow in the grassland while the quarry is of geological importance for good fold and fault features including a monocline section in the great limestone.

East Cramlington Pond

NZ 2975; 2.8ha; NWT reserve
Small pond and grassland
Spring, summer

The pond is shallow and fringed with yellow iris, water-plantain, branched bur-reed and great willowherb, with common spike-rush and with broad-leaved pondweed and common duckweed where the water deepens slightly. Early-purple orchid occurs in the grassland, and there is a good range of small water animals in the pond which also attracts occasional moorhen, duck and snipe.

Elf Hills

NZ 0186 11.6ha; NWT reserve
Mainly coniferous woodland
Spring, summer

The mainly coniferous plantations also include oak, beech and ash while the rides and clearings have now been colonised by birch, grey willow, hawthorn and rowan. The woods contain an old quarry and a small bog, adding to the habitat range, while a high seat has been built as an observation point. There is a good variety of woodland birds and roe deer, fox and red squirrel may be seen.

Farne Islands

NU 230370; 32ha; NT
Chain of offshore islands
Visits by boat, from Seahouses at NU 222323, may be dependent on weather
Strong headgear should be worn in early summer
Leaflets from NT shop in Seahouses
Late spring, summer, early winter

One stormy night in 1838 the captain of the *Forfarshire*, a paddle steamer bound from Hull to Dundee, mistook the light on the Longstone for that of the Inner Farne. He was aiming for the channel between the Farnes and the mainland, but instead he laid his ship fair and square into the rocky heart of the Outer Farnes and died, with 50 of his passengers and crew. William Darling and his 23-year-old daughter rowed twice across the roaring, tumbling waves to save the 11 who survived the night; Grace Darling became a national heroine.

To those few survivors the Farnes must have seemed a terrifying, savage world of tragedy and death. But they can show another face, a dapple of sunlit water round a fascinating range of rocks.

The islands are the last attempt of the Great Whin Sill, a shelf of stone which runs through the North of England, to show above the sea; further inland and northwards it appears at LINDISFARNE. The group consists of 28 small islands, the largest being Inner Farne (6.6ha), but the picture is confused in that many disappear at high tides while some, at low tide, become peaks connected by reefs of weed-covered rock, effectively one island.

North and South Wamses, Brownsman and Staple Island are the breeding grounds for a large population of grey seal, the most important east-coast colony south of the Orkneys. Where common seal delight in muddy sandbanks on which to haul themselves out of the sea, grey seal look for slabs of rock and shingle and thrive on the rocky coasts, breeding in isolated shingle coves or sea-racked islands. The seal shows in shallow sandy waters as a spotted, clear grey shape and disappears, wonderfully camouflaged, as soon as it crosses weedy rocks or shingle. These large animals are ungainly out of the water, but in it they slide effortlessly, sweeping their large hind flippers from side to side, balancing and levelling with their front ones.

The coat tends to be dappled: bulls are darker, spotted or patched with lighter grey, and cows are dark on the back, lighter underneath and marked with often conspicuous dark spots. They eat shellfish, crabs and lobsters but the basis of their diet is fish such as conger eel, herring, lumpsucker, pollack, ray, salmon, skate, whiting and wrasse,

The craggy rocks of the Farne Islands provide nesting sites for vast colonies of seabirds.

which is why seals have so often been destroyed by fishing interests. Another reason for their being hunted is for fur. The calves are born in early winter and for around two weeks are fed by the cows, lying dozing on the breeding ground like overfed large puppies. The baby coat is a beautiful deep-pile white which, around the time of weaning, is moulted for a mottled grey.

In the breeding season the nursery islands are in noisy turmoil. The bulls, hissing and snarling, establish their mating territories, fought for and guarded at the expense of food; they starve themselves throughout the mating season and do not feed for two months at a time. The cows feed their single calves, defending a territory around each one, snarling and hooting to keep intruders off; they also starve, until the calves are weaned, then mate and begin to feed again. Later the seals moult and then feed intensively until the next breeding season.

The calves grow, put on their second coats, play in the rock pools, move down to the sea and learn to feed on their adult diet. The Farnes community is relatively stable; unlike some breeding grounds where numbers fall dramatically, the seals here tend to stay around the islands, although once the breeding season is over they disperse to haul-outs and feeding grounds throughout the group. Until the following early winter the seals bask on low-water shelves and banks or bob upright in the water, curious to inspect a passing boat.

For birds the Farnes are best in early summer, but many stay all year and some pass through on migration. Peregrine falcon sometimes haunt the islands to take travelling linnet, skylark, fieldfare, redwing, snow bunting or a little auk blown down from the high Arctic pack-ice. The rocks are often white with gulls – common, great black-backed and herring gull – which clean the carcases of dead seal calves and scavenge on the drift line. Cormorant and shag stand or bob and dive in the icy waters where large numbers of eider float. Mallard, teal and long-tailed duck may visit the pond on the Brownsman. A great variety of birds is always present, from island wren to turnstone or purple sandpiper, and offshore occasional great northern diver.

Spring brings a change to the islands. The rocks always show shining seaweeds below high water mark, with rich yellow lichens above, but the loosening of winter's grip is marked by a show of green wherever winter's plants can survive. The migrants move back, some going north to breed and others, from the south or from the open seas, coming in to nest. By May thousands of seabirds squabble for nest sites or fly out to find food in the waters around. The islands are alive with every sort of bird activity from the eider dozing on her nest to the lesser black-backed gull sidling towards an unguarded clutch of eggs, from the buoyant flight of a tern to the guillemot's frenetic arrowing.

The distribution of the colonies is related to their needs; puffin nest in burrows so generally breed on

Grey seal, a speciality of the Farnes.

Brownsman, Inner Farne, Staple and the Wideopens where there is sufficient depth of soil. The Wideopens are a stronghold of lesser black-backed and herring gull, with further colonies on the Harcars and the Wamses; razorbill also nest on the Wideopens. Cormorant and fulmar, the one a large bird with an aggressive beak, the other a petrel capable of spitting nauseous liquid at an enemy, both breed on the Wamses and are, presumably, able to hold predators at bay. Most other species are concentrated on Brownsman, Inner Farne and Staple Island, avoiding the large colonies of gulls. Shag avoid the Megstone and North Wamses where cormorant breed and nest on the three main islands with eider, fulmar, kittiwake and puffin. Ringed plover and oystercatcher usually nest here, while razorbill breed on the Inner Farne and Staple Island, guillemot on Staple and Brownsman, and terns on Inner Farne and Brownsman. The arctic tern will also breed on Staple Island. Terns are fierce defenders of their nests, which is why protective headgear is essential for they can draw blood from a bare scalp.

The Longstone, Staple and Inner Farne are the only islands open to public landing, although the others may be overlooked from boats, and nature trails are laid out on the latter two which may be visited on a boat trip from Seahouses. The best time to visit is probably around low tide when the seals haul out. On a high-tide trip the sea may be full of bobbing curious heads but little more will be visible. There is, of course, a wealth of other wildlife interest on the Farnes, but for its breeding seabirds and its seals the reserve is one of international importance.

Flodden Quarry

NT 9135; 0.4ha; NWT reserve
Small quarry
Spring, summer

This small reserve protects unusual geological exposures in the Cheviot lava flows, but also contains an interesting range of habitats. The upper level of the quarry is grazed while the lower one has a scrub cover of elder, hawthorn, gorse and broom with elm and ash. The quarry faces carry such species as bluebell, harebell, dove's-foot crane's-bill and common stork's-bill with polypody and a good range of mosses, liverworts and lichens.

Goose's Nest Bluebell Bank

No access; 0.4ha; NWT reserve
Spectacular show of bluebells
May be overlooked from NY 980852
May

The reserve was established to protect one of the finest sweeps of bluebell in Northumberland.

Grasslees Burn Wood

NY 9597; 5.6ha; Northumberland CC–NWT reserve
Woodland
Spring, summer

Set on alluvial clay on a west-facing hillside, this reserve contains one of the largest alder woods in the county, with a wet moss-dominated floor. There are also stands of oak and birch, and lime-rich flushes with common butterwort and red rattle. Birds include pied flycatcher, wood warbler and redstart, and roe deer are common.

Flodden Quarry: a fine geological site.

Grindon Lough

No access; 88ha; NWT reserve
Shallow natural lake
May be overlooked from NY 806675
Winter

The lough is a noted site for shoveler, teal and wigeon, for whooper swan and for bean, greylag and pink-footed geese. Tufted duck and goldeneye are regular winter visitors.

Harbottle Crags

NT 927048; 156ha; NWT reserve
Upland heather moor, wetland and crags
No access away from nature trail
Booklet from NWT or site information centre
Spring, summer

Harbottle Crags includes great sweeps of heather and wet spreads of *Sphagnum* mosses, broken by low riven cliffs of hard abrasive fell sandstone. These hills were once well wooded with oak and birch and the gullies in the cliffs still shelter plants of high-level woodland such as climbing corydalis and chickweed wintergreen, but a programme of regular burning maintains the typical heather cover of a managed upland grouse moor.

Damp flushes are marked by purple moor-grass and bog myrtle while the wet mires are thick with common and hare's-tail cottongrass and vivid spreads of *Sphagnum* around pools where plants such as bog asphodel, cranberry, deergrass, round-leaved sundew and heath spotted-orchid grow.

The crags are spectacular low scarps of rock curving above the heather slopes and the bogs. Tall, leggy heather grows in the gullies and on the ledges, together with a varied range of plants, such as bilberry, cowberry and crowberry, broad buckler-fern, hard fern and bell heather, while the rocks themselves are rich in lichens and other specialised plants including the uncommon liverwort *Lepidozia pinnata*, and the fascinating luminous moss *Schistostega pennata*.

Below the crags, at the westernmost point of the reserve, is Harbottle Lough, a natural lake, acid and highly exposed. A fringe of soft rush and clumps of pale and bottle sedge provide some cover at the water's edge but generally the exposure is too severe for most wetland plants. The lough, however, provides a site where dragonflies and damselflies breed and draws an interesting range of waterfowl. Mallard, teal, tufted duck and heron are regular visitors and, in winter, the lake may attract whooper swan, greylag goose, goosander and goldeneye.

The birds of the moorland and cliffs include red and black grouse, ring ouzel, meadow pipit, wheatear and whinchat, curlew, lapwing, redshank and snipe, with predators such as short-eared owl, kestrel and occasionally merlin. Adders are common on the reserve and common lizard may be seen while insects include small heath butterfly with northern eggar, emperor and fox moths.

Holystone

NT 9402; 44ha; NWT–FC reserve
Dry and damp woodland, moorland and wetland
Spring, summer

Two reserves, about 1km apart, make up this composite site which provides a splendid example of upland and moor-edge valley woodland. The upland oakwood, with a ground cover of bracken and wood-sorrel or mosses such as the cushion-forming *Leucobryum glaucum*, has probably been coppiced in the past and contains the uncommon chickweed wintergreen. By contrast, the valley woods are far more varied – a mix of wych elm, oak and birch with aspen on the valley floor and with alder, ash and willow along the burn sides. An understorey of hazel, hawthorn and willow stands above wood anemone, red campion, dog's mercury and primrose and includes probably the finest show of juniper in the county. Scattered throughout the wood and ranging from young shrubs to bushes 10m tall, the juniper attracts specialised insects such as juniper pug moth.

More acid areas have a woodland of birch and oak, with planted conifers – which are to be removed – and with spreads of bracken and wavy hair-grass or *Sphagnum* mosses in the wet. Where wet flushes drain down from the moorland, common reed forms a dense stand, but the woodland edge is mainly marked by a fringe of crowberry and bilberry. The flushes themselves are fringed with bog myrtle and contain a fascinating range of plants including marsh lousewort, marsh violet, common butterwort, lesser twayblade and broad-leaved cottongrass.

The sloping heather moorland holds petty whin and provides a breeding site for curlew, red grouse and whinchat while the two areas of woodland attract such birds as pied flycatcher, redstart, wood warbler and woodcock, with dipper and grey wagtail by the burn and with visiting crossbill which breeds in the woodlands nearby.

Kielder Wildlife Observation Hide

Permit only; FC
Hide in the valley of the Kielder Burn
Spring, summer

The hide is sited on the edge of a mature spruce plantation looking across the burn to mixed woodland and forest with a small grazing area for roe deer. Fox and badger may be seen, together with a range of birds from dipper at the streamside to crossbill and siskin in the treetops.

Harbottle Crags cap a great spread of heather.

Lindisfarne

NU 096432; 3278ha; NCC reserve
Dunes, saltmarsh and mudflats
Causeway impassable at high tide
Leaflet from information caravan or NCC
All year

The low humped shape of Lindisfarne lifts up from a sea of shining mudflats or stands islanded at full tide. Shingle has been thrown up against a knoll of land and then banked up with wind-blown sands to make a natural breakwater which shelters vast flocks of winter birds. Eelgrass and fronds of *Enteromorpha*, a tubular green seaweed, spread across the mudflats, food for many of the winter wildfowl, with cordgrass and glasswort forming the basis from which the saltmarsh builds to a spread of common scurvygrass, sea aster and thrift. The dunes, above the saltmarsh, are stabilised with marram and contain a number of interesting plants including species such as viper's-bugloss and hound's-tongue. The sands are lime-rich, encouraging a wide variety of plants in the sheltered damp low slacks between the dunes: bog pimpernel and creeping willow with the beautiful grass-of-Parnassus and a wonderful show of orchids such as early and northern marsh-orchid, common spotted-orchid and marsh helleborine. Areas of heath grassland, rock exposures and low cliffs add to the range of habitat which contains floral elements of north and south. There are southern species such as rough clover and sand cat's-tail with northern coralroot orchid, curved sedge and saltmarsh flat-sedge.

Rabbits are plentiful on the island and form a useful study group because they are unlikely to be reinforced by mainland animals though foxes will cross to hunt. Grey seals haul out on offshore sandbanks but, although the other animals are full of interest, there is no doubt that the most dramatic impact on the island is that made by the great flocks of winter wildfowl, many thousands strong, and the vast, whirling clouds of waders.

Lindisfarne is the only regular wintering site in Britain for pale-bellied Brent goose, which flies down here from Spitsbergen, close to the edge of the polar ice, when winter gales and falling temperatures bring the pack-ice down to cover its Svalbard feeding grounds. This is also the country's most important coastal site for wigeon, averaging over 10,000 individuals and peaking at 25,000. Eider, mallard and shelduck are here in good numbers, with important flocks of greylag goose and whooper swan, red-breasted merganser, long-tailed duck, common scoter and teal. Thousands of dunlin, knot and bar-tailed godwit feed on the mudflats with lapwing, ringed, grey and golden plover and a wide variety of other waders which may include spotted redshank and purple sandpiper. Rarities may occur at any time, and passage migrants have included pine grosbeak, Richard's pipit, yellow-browed warbler and red-breasted flycatcher.

Little Harle

NZ 0183; 7ha; NWT reserve
Unimproved flood meadows
All year

The wet pasture holds yellow iris, marsh-marigold and ragged-Robin, with dipper and grey wagtail on the river meanders and wildfowl at flood times.

Little Mill

NU 2217; 10.8ha; NWT reserve
Disused quarry
Spring, summer

Ponds, scrub, grassland and a superb exposure of acre limestone support bulrush, water-plantain, fairy flax and wild carrot. Birds of scrub and wetland are resident and smooth newt and frog breed.

Lindisfarne rises from the low-tide mudflats where thousands of waders and wildfowl feed in winter.

Long Nanny Wood

NU 1928; 2ha; NWT reserve
Wet woodland and stream
Spring, early summer

Marsh-marigold, opposite-leaved golden-saxifrage and sweet violet are among the flowers of spring while bird interest includes a large rookery.

Lowick Quarry

Permit only; 4ha; NWT reserve
Limestone quarry
Spring, summer

The grassy quarry floor contains lime-loving plants such as fairy flax, wild mignonette and field scabious, but the reserve is probably most important for its geological exposures of folded great limestone.

Newton Pool

NU 243243; 9ha; NT
Freshwater lagoon
Autumn, winter

Containing an important colony of black-headed gull, the reserve probably holds a greater variety of birds in autumn, when passage ruff and red-shank may be seen, or in winter, when short-eared owl may hunt the marshy edges while goldeneye and pochard are on the pool. A hide overlooks the reserve.

327

Northumberland National Park

See map; 113,110ha; Northumberland CC
Northern uplands and farmland
Booklets from Northumberland CC or information
centres
Spring, summer

Set in the most northerly part of England, the national park protects a land which was made by
volcanoes and shaped by ice. Millions of years ago,
lava was forced from below as the mountains of
Scotland were raised; when the volcanoes died and
the lavas cooled, a second great surge of molten
rock thrust upwards but failed to reach the surface
and cooled underground as a huge boss of granite.
Over millions of years, the land was sometimes
submerged, sometimes raised, and was covered
with new layers of rock until the forces which
lifted the Pennines brought a violent change to the
scene. The younger rocks were driven and buckled
against the mass of granite and lava which now
forms the Cheviot Hills and the basis for our present
scenery was laid. At the same time a smaller underground thrust of molten rock was intruded underground and formed the special feature which is
known as the Great Whin Sill. The folded rocks
were slowly eroded to reveal the lavas and granite,
and the smoothing and scouring of the ice ages
continued the work of time.

The Cheviot is the core of the area and the
country changes around it in a pattern of con-
centric rings, with the soft rocks forming lowland
farming areas between harder ridges where crags

face inwards with long dip slopes behind. The
Cheviots provide an area of upland heath and grass
moor which is almost completely encircled by
farmland on soft shales and sandstones; beyond are
the hard fell sandstones which form the Simonside
Hills and moors such as HARBOTTLE CRAGS, while a
generally softer, more often farmed area lies, in
turn, beyond these. Throughout this outer ring,
however, occasional masses of sandstone give
spreads of heather moorland while the hard rocks
of the Whin Sill form the striking natural barrier on
which the Romans based part of Hadrian's Wall.

This widely varied area has a huge range of
habitat from the wholly agricultural lands of the
farms, through valley woodlands and rapid
streams, natural lakes caused by glaciation and
basin mires flushed by lime-rich waters, to the acid
bogs and peat moors of the uplands and the high
crags.

Much of the woodland is planted coniferous
forest, like the vast area of Kielder Forest in the
BORDER FOREST PARK which adjoins the western
edge of the national park, but some of the valleys
are wooded with native trees and contain an
interesting range of plants and animals. The
natural cover, except on the clay, is probably of
sessile oakwoods above bracken in light, dry
situations, or wavy hair-grass with plants such as
heath bedstraw and tormentil. There are
similarities between these woods and the oak-

*Looking southwards over Westnewton into the
Northumberland National Park.*

woods of North Wales and Cumbria – in the bird life too, for the trio of wood warbler, redstart and pied flycatcher often occurs in these woodlands – but the climate is drier and more eastern and the characteristic Atlantic mosses and liverworts are less common. Here, too, is a speciality which does not occur in the west, chickweed wintergreen, a plant of northern Scotland generally found on high moors or in pinewoods. Birch woodland may also be found, invading the moorland slopes, where it grows over heather, heath mosses and *Sphagnum*, which may hold lesser twayblade. Here, again, is a link with the western woods, for the rare lesser twayblade is also a mainly Scottish species but grows in Cumbria and Snowdonia; Northumberland is its only site in England east of the Pennines.

The torrential upland streams attract typical birds such as dipper and grey wagtail while winter brings many northern birds, wild swans and geese as well as flocks of duck, to the shallow Northumbrian loughs. These small lakes formed when ice sheets locally overdeepened their beds and they often lie beneath crags which must have channelled the flow of the ice. Where lime-rich water drains into the loughs, a marsh flora may develop and gradual silting of the pool will lead to a rich vegetation. Some, such as GRINDON LOUGH, are still open pools attracting waterbirds; others may have become basin mires where wet willow woodland stands among common reed, greater tussock-sedge and tall herbs such as meadowsweet and skullcap, where rushes and sedges make a rich pattern with marsh cinquefoil, marsh-marigold, mare's-tail, water mint and ragged-Robin.

In wet valley woods, alder may grow in glades hedged with bog myrtle where such plants as broad-leaved cottongrass, grass-of-Parnassus and marsh violet form a striking contrast with the bogs of the higher uplands. These blanket bogs form where the peats lie damp on the fell sandstones and the granite and, on the plateau of Cheviot itself, form communities of such plants as heather and hare's-tail cottongrass, cloudberry, bilberry and crowberry. Some of the moors contain very fine *Sphagnum* mires, mosaics of cranberry and cross-leaved heath with bog-rosemary and great sundew.

The fell sandstones, often managed as grouse moors, carry fine spreads of heather, with plants such as bilberry and occasional lesser twayblade, and may have great sheets of bracken on the lower valley slopes, while the granite supports dwarf cornel at one of its very few English sites, and the lavas around the granite core carry sweeping curves of mat-grass.

Rocky outcrops often hold interesting species, either because the plant requires a hard substrate or because only on difficult crags can it escape the grazing sheep. The Whin Sill has species such as parsley fern and dwarf male-fern, chives and maiden pink, and its soils have a fascinating flora of their own, a mix of acid and lime-loving plants. The fell sandstone crags may contain bearberry while, where lime-rich rocks occur in the Cheviot

The Bizzle, Cheviot, is situated at the heart of Northumberland's uplands.

Hills, a superb range of plants such as globeflower, roseroot, alpine saw-wort, mossy saxifrage and green spleenwort may be found and, where springs and rills wash the rocks, alpine and chickweed willowherb, hairy stonecrop and starry saxifrage may occur.

A wide range of animal life inhabits the park: from roe deer and feral goats to voles and shrews; from woodland birds such as redstart and pied flycatcher to moorland curlew, dunlin, golden plover, merlin and short-eared owl; from moths and butterflies of the lowland farms to those of heather and bilberry – a wealth of varied wildlife in the valleys, hills and moors.

Most of the national park is private land but rights of way allow access to many of its treasures and, although it may not be among the larger parks, it is certainly rich in beauty and fascination.

The dramatic face of the Great Whin Sill which carries the Pennine Way along Hadrian's Wall.

Pennine Way

NT 853269–NY 698479; 150km; CC
Long-distance way
Leaflet from CC and booklet from HMSO bookshops
Spring, summer

The way includes some of the wilder areas of the county, follows parts of Hadrian's Wall and the Scottish border, and provides superb views of the uplands of the NORTHUMBERLAND NATIONAL PARK.

Plessey Woods Country Park

NZ 238800; 41ha; Northumberland CC
Wooded river valley
Nature trail information from visitor centre
Spring, early summer

Set on the banks of the River Blyth, the park contains red squirrel and roe deer while typical birds include dipper, kestrel and tawny owl.

Priestclose Wood

NZ 107628; 15.2ha; NWT reserve
Broad-leaved woodland and scrub
Visitors must keep to the paths
Spring, summer

Oak and birch woodland, with sycamore, ash, yew, holly and willow, stands above a ground cover of woodland plants such as bluebell, wood anemone and dog's mercury. The reserve includes a small pond and marshland area. This variation, with a mature beech-oak woodland nearby, encourages a varied bird life which includes jay, great spotted woodpecker, treecreeper, wood warbler and woodcock.

Redpath and Fallowlees

NZ 0092; 1200ha; NWT reserve
Large block of conifer plantations
Spring, summer

Harwood Forest has been planted with Norway and sitka spruce and Scots and lodgepole pine over an area which includes, in the reserve, a small lough and a number of streams. Strips of marshland and semi-natural woodland, particularly of alder, fringe the streams while a number of unplanted grazing blocks have been left. Roe deer are abundant and there is a varied bird life which includes black grouse.

Beltingham and Williamston

NY 7864 and NY 6852; 5ha; NWT reserves
Woodland and scrub on river shingle
Spring, summer

Where the South Tyne deposits alluvium on its flood plain in times of spate, an unexpected range of plants appears; the bank looks almost like a sea-coast grassland, thick with tossing heads of thrift. The reserves contain communities of plants which seem quite out of place: common associates of thrift grow here, wild thyme and kidney vetch, together with plants expected from the moors, spring sandwort, alpine penny-cress and mountain pansy. The common denominator here is heavy metal; just as the sea-coast plants are adapted to cope with very high levels of exposure and of salt, so the moorland plants are adapted to similar factors and are often found around the spoil heaps of the mines. Both groups grow here on shingle contaminated by lead and zinc washed down from mining works upstream.

The River Tyne Gravels represent an important part of the ecology of Northumberland. The scrub and woodland hold a range of plants which, with the grassland, gives an exceptionally wide range of habitat for such a small area. The scrub and woodland trees include alder and grey alder, with silver birch, Scots pine, bird cherry and several willow species and with gorse and broom growing on the shingle. The flowering plants include a variety of characteristic northern species such as wood crane's-bill, sweet cicely, melancholy thistle and northern marsh-orchid, together with more widespread plants such as common spotted-orchid and great burnet.

In addition to the heavy-metal plants, the riverside has wet-loving species, including marsh-bedstraw and marsh-marigold, with wood club-rush and a number of alien plants, dame's-violet, Indian balsam, monkeyflower and blood-drop-emlets. Salmon and brown trout may be seen in the river, mammals include roe deer, fox and rabbit, and there is a good range of birds breeding in the area. Waterbirds and waders include goosander, oystercatcher, redshank and common sandpiper with waterside birds such as dipper and grey and pied wagtail. Sand martin breed along the river and may be seen taking insects over the water while woodland birds include blackcap, garden, grasshopper, sedge and willow warbler, goldfinch, redpoll and woodcock. Brambling, snipe and tawny owl may be seen at times.

Rothley Lake

NZ 0490; 21.2ha; NWT reserve
Part of a large artificial lake and woodland
Spring, summer

The lake is rich in wetland species while the planted woodlands contain exotic trees and a variety of invading native trees and shrubs. This variation encourages woodland birds and waterbirds. The limestone ballast on the old railway line has imported a lime-rich influence with plants such as fairy flax.

Sidwood Wildlife Observation Hide

Permit only; FC
Wildlife hide
Spring, autumn

The hide overlooks a varied woodland scene in which birds and mammals, such as roe deer and fox, are the main interest.

Silver Nut Well

NY 8991; 0.05ha; NWT reserve
Spring-fed pool
All year

Chalybeate, a form of iron carbonate carried in the upwelling springwater, reacts with sulphur-containing plant products in the deep mud of the pool to produce iron sulphide, which is precipitated on hazelnuts in the mud, giving them a silver-coloured coating which tarnishes in air. From the viewing platform churning silver-grey mud may be seen beneath the water surface and, occasionally, silver nuts appear and then sink back into the mud.

Slacks Plantation

NZ 1266; 1.6ha; NWT reserve
Quarry, woodland and scrub
Spring, summer

Mixed woodland and scrub has developed on the site of an old plantation and is chiefly of oak, birch, sycamore and gorse. There is a range of woodland plants with luxuriant bracken, which supports the white-flowering climbing corydalis, while the quarry has good moss and liverwort cover on its wet walls.

Holywell Pond

NZ 3175; 14.1ha; NWT reserve
Pond and old pasture
All year

Although winter and migrant birds, such as whooper swan, goldeneye, greylag goose and green sandpiper, are the special interest of the reserve, in spring and early summer the old pasture is rich in flowering plants while breeding birds at this time of year include little grebe, tufted duck and sedge warbler.

Tony's Patch

NY 8265; 1.6ha; NWT reserve
Mixed woodland
Spring, summer

A small but rich mixed woodland, a fragment of a larger old wood, Tony's Patch is mainly oak with elm, ash, birch, bird cherry, hawthorn, hazel and rowan. Honeysuckle tangles the trees above a varied ground cover including bluebell and early-purple orchid, woodruff, sanicle and ramsons. The northern wood crane's-bill occurs here together with toothwort and herb-Paris.

Tyne Riverside Country Park

NZ 086634; 80ha; Northumberland CC
Linear park beside River Tyne
Spring, summer, autumn

The river is tidal at this point and attracts water-birds and seabirds to add to the numbers of commoner species found in the mixed woodlands.

Wansbeck Riverside Country Park

NZ 257866; 58ha; Wansbeck DC
Tidal section of Wansbeck Valley
Nature trail information from WDC
Spring, autumn, winter

A wide diversity of birds visits the sheltered waters and woodlands of the park.

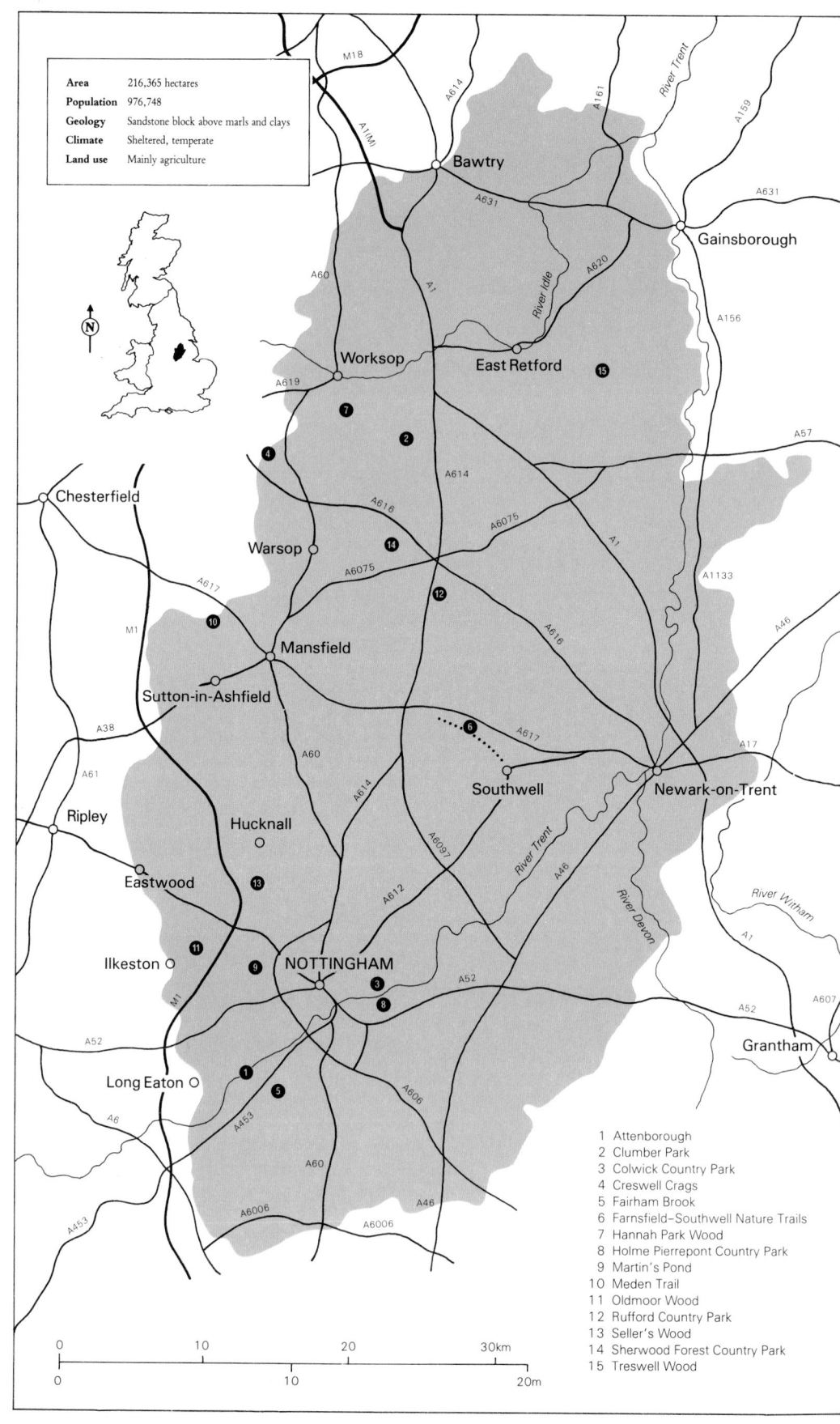

Area	216,365 hectares
Population	976,748
Geology	Sandstone block above marls and clays
Climate	Sheltered, temperate
Land use	Mainly agriculture

N

M18

A614

A161

River Trent

A159

A1(M)

Bawtry

A631

Gainsborough

A60

A1

River Idle

A620

A631

Worksop

A619

East Retford

⑮

A156

⑦

②

④

A614

A57

Chesterfield

A616

A6075

A1

Warsop

⑭

A1133

A6075

A617

⑫

A46

M1

⑩

A616

Mansfield

Sutton-in-Ashfield

⑥

A617

A17

A38

A614

Southwell

Newark-on-Trent

A61

Hucknall

A6097

River Trent

Ripley

River Witham

Eastwood

⑬

A6097

A46

River Devon

A1

⑪

A612

Ilkeston

⑨

NOTTINGHAM

③

A52

Grantham

⑧

A52

A607

A52

A52

A6

Long Eaton

①

⑤

A453

A606

A453

A60

A6006

A46

A453

A6006

A6006

20m

0   10   20   30km

0   10   20m

1 Attenborough
2 Clumber Park
3 Colwick Country Park
4 Creswell Crags
5 Fairham Brook
6 Farnsfield–Southwell Nature Trails
7 Hannah Park Wood
8 Holme Pierrepont Country Park
9 Martin's Pond
10 Meden Trail
11 Oldmoor Wood
12 Rufford Country Park
13 Seller's Wood
14 Sherwood Forest Country Park
15 Treswell Wood

Nottinghamshire

More famous for its historical and literary associations with Robin Hood and D.H. Lawrence, Nottinghamshire may not at first appear to warrant the attention of naturalists, but closer scrutiny reveals a landscape with a rewarding diversity of wildlife. Like many other Midland shires it enjoys a mixed economy based on agriculture and industry. Important extractive industries such as coal, gypsum, sand and gravel make a significant contribution to Britain's need for raw materials, while broad-based farming on the rolling clays flanking the Trent contrasts with the Forestry Commission's presence on the sandy central area of SHERWOOD FOREST.

In spite of man's considerable influence the pattern of landscape and land use still clearly reflects the county's geology, and a traveller journeying from west to east encounters a succession of rocks outcropping in roughly north–south bands which dip gently to the east. Exposed on the western fringe are the coal measure rocks of the Erewash Valley which have been exploited for coal down the centuries. This densely populated area is bordered to the east by a narrow, low ridge of magnesian limestone supporting interesting lime-loving plants, which disappears eastwards under a broad undulating tract of bunter sandstones. Stretching northward from Nottingham to south Yorkshire, this area of sandstones with its dry, pebbly soils was the nucleus for the historic royal hunting forest of Sherwood.

Sherwood still provides a home for red and fallow deer, and the significance of the degenerate oak and birch woodland as an important habitat for a rich variety of insects and spiders has been highlighted by a recent survey. However, relentless felling over the centuries has left little of the former open woodland, and modern farming practice enables even these poor soils to be economically cultivated; no less than 73 per cent of the county is now agricultural. Fortunately, under the Enclosure Acts substantial areas of Sherwood were enclosed to form the great estates of CLUMBER, Thoresby and Welbeck which are known today as the Dukeries. On such estates some magnificent areas of mature parkland are the legacy of wise landscaping and planting in the eighteenth century. It is likely that Sherwood was never more than sparsely peopled, but the last hundred years have seen an expansion of settlements such as Mansfield, Clipstone and Blidworth into thriving mining communities. If dry, sandy Sherwood belies the black wealth in its depths, a visitor would hardly guess, either, that beneath the dry soils the bunter sandstone provides an important source of water for industrial and domestic use.

Eastwards from Sherwood a low escarpment, again running north–south, heralds the keuper beds. Essentially red clays with sandstones at the base, these form pleasant, rolling country through which the majestic Trent has carved its course, virtually bisecting the county. The keuper clays on either flank present good agricultural land, giving soils rarely too heavy to work, yet retentive of moisture – an asset which has endeared them to rose growers. Feeding into the Trent from the west are streams flowing in winding, wooded valleys known locally as 'dumbles'.

Beyond the Trent to the south east the limestones at the base of the lias are indicated by a low ridge which can be recognised from Somerset to Lincolnshire. This ridge marks the northern boundary of the Vale of Belvoir, where intractable lias clays floor flat-lying pastures which are still important for grazing cattle whose milk is used in the production of Stilton cheese. From the Nottingham conurbation in the south west the Trent flows first through a series of wooded bluffs and then into a much broader floodplain downstream from Newark, where its tidal course is contained by levées.

Further north the Trent is joined by the River Idle, and together their washlands coalesce to form rich meadows – the Carrlands – subject to periodic flooding. Although major flood control work in this area has destroyed large refuges for wildfowl and waders, several small areas of washlands are fortunately being retained as nature reserves.

In a county where little natural woodland remains TRESWELL WOOD, FOX COVERT PLANTATION, SELLER'S WOOD and DYSCARR WOOD are important reserves where deciduous woods have developed on very different soils. The country-wide trend to 'improve' grassland and plough up pasture land has greatly affected the flowers, insects and birds favouring this habitat. The Trentside and other meadows, once alive with autumn and spring crocus, are almost a memory, while meadow-rue, water-dropwort, the burnets, saxifrages and other grassland flowers are now rare. To remedy this, meadows at EAKRING and WEST BURTON have been acquired and will be managed in the traditional manner.

The Trent, marked by five dominating power stations, assumes a regional importance for anglers and to the ornithologist it is a flightline for passage migrants, wildfowl, waders and passerines which are attracted to the fringing lagoons of old gravel workings. Adjacent to the Trent at ATTENBOROUGH, for example, 100ha of flooded gravelpits provide a nature reserve of great value for aquatic plants and wetland birds. The involvement at Attenborough between the Nottinghamshire Trust for Nature Conservation and the owners is an example of the spirit of co-operation which is necessary between landowners and conservationists if the best interests of wildlife are to be served.

BRIAN PLAYLE

Attenborough

SK 521343; 100ha; Butterley Aggregates Ltd– NTNC reserve
Flooded gravel workings
Permit only off pathways
Leaflets and key for bird hide from information caravan, if open, NTNC or works office
All year

The lakes are wholly artificial – gravel diggings from the old flood course of the Trent. After the glaciers melted, the rivers ran wide across the lower lands and spread huge fans and terraces of gravel; in many parts of the country the gravel is excavated, washed and sorted, and the pits which result provide an important new wildlife habitat.

Any new spread of water will attract a good number of birds. Before efficient drainage schemes controlled the winter rivers, thousands of hectares of farmland used to be flooded from autumn to spring; in autumn the flooded meadows would be rich in plant seeds and drowned delicacies which provided fine feeding for waterfowl. When the meadowland first flooded at RUTLAND WATER (Leicestershire) record numbers of wildfowl came to feed on the flush of food. Similarly, waders would find rich pickings in the shallows while predators learned that floods would both drive small mammals out into the open and encourage gatherings of feeding birds, an ideal hunting ground for short-eared owl and peregrine.

The chains of flooded gravelpits which lie along so many of our river plains, although they are not the seed-rich floods which the birds might have found in the past, are rich in water plants and animal life and are capable of feeding important numbers of waterfowl. Where the pits are protected as sanctuaries the birds will often remain and Attenborough is a fine example of the success of this idea.

When most of the winter duck and waders move off to breed, the first spring passage birds and summer visitors arrive; among the earliest arrivals of summer are sand martin and chiffchaff.

The grey twigs of winter turn to green and colour returns to the marshes and meadowland. Curled, fennel, horned and lesser pondweed, spiked and whorled water-milfoil and common water-starwort grow in the lakes while marshy fringes and ditches show arrowhead, flowering-rush and water-plantain, branched and unbranched bur-reed, bulrush, lesser bulrush and stands of common reed. The brilliant spring display of marsh-marigold is followed by fen and marsh flowers such as trifid bur-marigold, hemp-agrimony, yellow iris, mare's-tail, water mint and meadowsweet, by purple-loosestrife, square-stalked St John's-wort, ragged-Robin, common valerian and tubular water-dropwort. Wetland grasses, rushes and sedges add to the richness of plant life and include two unusual species, round-fruited rush and brown sedge.

Small patches of old-meadow grassland contain yellow rattle, great burnet and meadow saxifrage, while stands of meadow crane's-bill are a feature of the reserve. Rich neutral grasslands may support bents, salad burnet, common centaury, dropwort, eyebright, musk thistle and kidney vetch. The fragments of woodland and scrub contain spring plants, such as bluebell and goldilocks buttercup, and much interest lies in the rapid spread of willow carr. Over a dozen species, varieties and hybrids have been identified, including osier and almond, crack, goat, grey, purple and white willow. Alder is also frequent in the wetter woodland, important in winter as a food supply for small birds. The reclaimed land and spoil humps are grassed and clumped with scrub and show a good variety of colonising plants. Colt's-foot, feverfew, tansy,

Common tern breed at Attenborough.

mugwort and wormwood may be found and, in some places, southern marsh-orchid, common spotted-orchid and common twayblade.

Dragonflies such as common coenagrion, common ischnura and brown aeshna may be seen in the wetlands and over the pools while colourful summer flowers may attract red admiral, painted lady, peacock and other butterflies. One of the most interesting insects here is *Dytiscus circumcinctus*, a close relative of the great diving beetle, which is also present at Attenborough. These are among the largest British beetles and are rather similar but, whereas the great diving beetle is common in many marshy pools, *Dytiscus circumcinctus* is, generally, a beetle of the fens.

The reedmarsh, woodland and scrub provide nesting sites for several species of birds, including grasshopper, reed and sedge warbler, great spotted woodpecker and kestrel, while common tern breed on the islands. Duck include mallard and tufted duck, with high seasonal numbers of pochard and shoveler and occasional shelduck. In some years the reserve may hold a pair of garganey, attractive small duck which are unique in Britain in having the centre of their range at much lower latitudes than other duck: while most species fly north from Britain to breed, the garganey actually flies north to Britain and is only seen here during the summer.

The reserve is threatened by heavy pressure from the urban concentrations nearby, and by silting effects from continued gravel workings, but the islands provide a retreat where shyer animals can breed and the chain of lakes of differing ages provides a fascinating range of habitat. As mentioned above, gravelpits such as these have become an important feature of our landscape, have to a certain extent replaced the wetlands we have

lost, and have much to contribute in providing sites for wildlife. Sensitive management can change a flooded desert to a place of life and beauty. Attenborough shows such a splendid change, but at the same time it must be remembered that the now rich pits may have destroyed a previous richness, in this case ancient flood meadows with osier beds and willow holts recorded in Domesday Book. No promise of a future wetland reserve can compensate for such loss, and the siting of new pits throughout the country must be carefully monitored.

Bentinck Banks

Permit only; 5.7ha; NTNC reserve
Disused railway line
Spring, summer

The lime-rich soil encourages a good range of attractive flowers, attended by colourful butterflies, as at CLARBOROUGH.

Clarborough

SK 755825; 5ha; NTNC reserve
Lime-rich scrub and grassland
Spring, summer

Diesel trains now rush through the tunnel above which the reserve is sited but, where the first steam travellers saw raw embankments and spoil piled beside and over the line, modern passengers may catch a fleeting glimpse of lime-loving flowers and scrub.

The long narrow site provides a fine example of the way in which land will change to woodland if left to itself. Where the turf is short, typical plants of open downland occur, plants such as common bird's-foot-trefoil, cowslip, common centaury, common milkwort, bee orchid, hoary plantain and yellow-wort; where coarser taller grasses shade out the small plants, species which can lift above them survive – oxeye daisy, spiny restharrow, hairy St John's-wort, pyramidal orchid and common spotted-orchid. These areas of grassland occur as small clearings in the scrub, perhaps places where the soil is too shallow for easy woodland growth.

The spreads of taller grasses, though, show signs of the scrub invasion with thorny tangles of wild rose in the clearings, which are edged with shrubby wild privet, dogwood and hawthorn grading back into well-established scrub woodland. This taller scrub is a mix of hawthorn with ash, buckthorn, dogwood, elder, field maple, privet and sycamore and stands above a developing rich-wood ground cover of sanicle, woodruff and sheets of ivy varied with enchanter's-nightshade and plants such as wood anemone and woodland violets.

This is a very attractive small reserve where the tiny grasslands are glades of colour among the well-varied scrub, where banks and hollows provide a range of sheltered or more exposed sites. Typical scrub and woodland birds enjoy the sanctuary here while the herb-rich turf and flowering shrubs attract colourful butterflies.

The lake and woodland at Clumber Park attract a good variety of birds.

Clumber Park

SK 645773; 1273.5ha; NT
Parkland, heath and woodland
Nature trail information from visitor centre
Spring, summer

The bird interest is probably greatest when winter wildfowl come on to the lake, but the fine range of habitat in this old Sherwood Forest estate encourages a variety of breeding species and a rich diversity of plants.

Colwick Country Park

SK 600391; 105ha; Nottingham City Council
Parkland and lakes
Winter

Although a nature reserve provides some sanctuary for wildlife, birds are probably best seen on the lakes in winter when water sports have ceased.

Creswell Crags

SK 538744; 6.4ha; Nottinghamshire CC–
Derbyshire CC
Limestone gorge and lake
Leaflets from visitor centre
Spring, summer

Although the visitor centre lies in Derbyshire, the lake and most of the site is in Nottinghamshire. It contains spectacular crags festooned with ivy above a man-made lake where plants such as comfrey and monkeyflower grow and spotted flycatcher, pied wagtail and other birds feed on the plentiful insects.

Dyscarr Wood

Permit only; 13ha; NTNC reserve
Woodland, scrub and marsh
Spring, summer

One of the few remaining magnesian limestone woods in the county, the reserve contains an attractive diversity of lime-loving woodland plants together with the bonus of a stretch of species-rich marshland.

Eakring Meadows

Permit only; 10ha; NTNC reserve
Damp meadowland
Spring, summer

Old-meadow grassland beside a winding stream, the reserve contains great burnet, meadowsweet and ragged-Robin together with deep spreads of sedges and a good variety of meadow plants such as pepper-saxifrage, while an ancient hedge contains over 14 woody species including buckthorn and guelder-rose.

Fairham Brook

SK 562338; 10.1ha; NTNC reserve
Rough grassland and scrub
Spring, summer

Lying beside a slow shallow stream, the reserve is a spread of coarse grasses, clovers, vetches, thistles, rushes and sedges, varied with meadow crane's-bill, common meadow-rue, meadowsweet and willow scrub, attracting a good diversity of insects and small birds. Roach, chub and eel may be seen in the brook which is lined with hedgerow trees and occasional clumps of yellow iris or stands of common reed.

Farnsfield–Southwell Nature Trails

SK 675566–643573; 8.8ha; Nottinghamshire CC
Disused railway line
Spring, summer

A range from wet to dry, from acid to lime-rich habitats holds a good variety of plants and, with areas of scrub and mature trees, attracts breeding woodland birds.

Fox Covert Plantation

Permit only; 15ha; NTNC reserve
Mixed woodland
Spring, early summer

The sloping woodland of oak, birch, rowan, sweet chestnut and sycamore has a rather thin under-storey above a ground cover of acid grasses decorated with foxglove and heath bedstraw. A scrub-fringed ride, with banks of bramble, rosebay willowherb and gorse, increases the variation of the reserve which attracts a good range of birds including woodcock.

Hannah Park Wood

SK 590773; 5.6ha; WdT
Mixed woodland
Spring, early summer

A remnant of the northern edge of Sherwood Forest, the wood is mainly high-forest oak and beech but also contains an interesting area of yew.

Holme Pierrepont Country Park

SK 606386; 121.5ha; Nottinghamshire CC
Landscaped gravelpits
Winter

A nature reserve and hide have been established here at the National Water Sports Centre but con-siderable disturbance ensures that the best show of birds is that of winter waterfowl.

Kimberley Cutting

Permit only; 2ha; NTNC reserve
Disused railway cutting
Spring, summer

Wet flushes in the limestone cutting, which is primarily a geological site, increase the range of plants which include lime-loving flowers, scrub and woodland attractive to insects and birds.

Lady Lee Quarry

Permit only; 2.4ha; NTNC reserve
Disused quarry
Spring, summer

The old limestone working has been flooded and now forms an interesting pool within the quarry.

Martin's Pond

SK 526402; 4ha; Nottingham City Council–NTNC reserve
Pond, marsh and willow scrub
All year

Although parts of the bank may be lined with fishermen, much of the pool is edged by reed-swamp, in places dry enough for scrub to grow, which provides a sanctuary for birds such as reed and sedge warbler and lesser whitethroat. Over 150 plants have been recorded from the reserve and the reedswamp is rich in species such as marsh-marigold, ragged-Robin and yellow iris, together with bulrush, lesser bulrush and their hybrids.

The pond is ringed by a path from which the whole reserve may be seen – here the open water starred with white water-lily, there a stand of tall willow trees and scrub, rosebay willowherb on the drier banks, great willowherb in the marsh with golden dock, gipsywort, marsh arrowgrass and meadowsweet. A walkway has been built so that visitors can stand amid the spears of bulrush and look down into the marsh or watch the warblers in the willow scrub from an attractive vantage point.

Some 24 birds are known to have bred here, including great crested and little grebe, while the full list is over 70 species – a remarkable total for a site 1.5km within the city boundary. Water rail may be present in winter and the uncommon spotted crake has been recorded; woodcock too may visit when the marsh provides easier feeding in hard weather and other waders, redshank and greenshank, may occur at migration times.

Water animals include frog, common toad, two of our three newt species, water vole and oc-casional water shrew while, among other mam-mals, fox is a regular visitor.

Although Martin's Pond is not as rich as ATTEN-BOROUGH, nor as large, it is still a valuable wildlife site and, saved from conversion to a car park, is a splendid example of urban conservation.

Water vole, an attractive small mammal which may be seen in wetlands such as Martin's Pond.

Meden Trail

SK 506643–526646; 3.5km; NTNC
Disused railway line and riverside
Leaflet from NTNC or Mansfield DC
Spring, summer

Much of the trail is set in an area of magnesian limestone exposures, grassland and woodland containing fine ash standards with plants such as guelder-rose, ramsons, sanicle, wood melick and nettle-leaved bellflower.

Oldmoor Wood

SK 497428; 15.2ha; WdT
Mixed woodland
Spring, early summer

On the urban fringe of Nottingham, this mix of mainly high-forest beech, oak, sycamore, larch and pine forms an important wildlife refuge.

Rufford Country Park

SK 642648; 73.5ha; Nottinghamshire CC
Parkland and lake
Spring, summer

A wildlife sanctuary has been created in this Dukeries parkland which contains woodland and shrubs planted on the acid soils of Sherwood Forest.

Seller's Wood

SK 523455; 14.2ha; Nottingham City Council–
NTNC reserve
Mixed woodland
Spring, early summer

A particularly interesting wood on the edge of an area of recent housing development, Seller's Wood shows a good variation from acid to lime-rich woodland. Carpets of ivy indicate that at least some of the wood is secondary, ground which has been cleared and has now reverted to woodland, and the previous management of coppicing probably also involved some planting of sycamore.

The upper area of open heath gives way, through a zone of invading birch saplings, to a fine dry woodland of birch over bracken with rosebay willowherb, foxglove and gorse on the ride-edges and clearings, with scattered oak and rowan among the birches. Gradually the trees close in, shade reduces the bracken and the mix of species becomes more varied, with sycamore, hawthorn and hazel appearing above a ground cover shrubby with honeysuckle, bramble and sprays of ferns. An area of coppiced sycamore with ash, elm, hawthorn and hazel marks richer ground dampened by a stream, where the ground cover is a more open spread of bluebell, dog's mercury, woodland violets and grasses and where moles bring up mounds of rich dark soil to contrast with the sandy heathland above. Lower still the wood is a tall stand of trees where ash, dogwood, privet and spindle grow above wood melick and giant bellflower, all lovers of lime-rich soils, together with carpets of bluebell, where blackthorn and hawthorn form dense thickets of scrub and where willows and poplars mark the site of a dried-up small swampy basin.

The wood shows a great diversity in a relatively small area – sometimes dense tangles of overgrown coppice, sometimes open stands of pure birch, here an area of oak over hazel, there a sycamore copse. From its heathland edge to its taller woodland, a wide range of habitat is open to typical scrub and woodland birds, to butterflies, moths and many other animals.

Sherwood Forest Country Park

SK 627677; 202.5ha; Nottinghamshire CC
Fragment of ancient Sherwood Forest
Leaflets from visitor centre
Spring, summer

Huge old oaks separated by stands of birch grow above bracken and acid grasses; both pedunculate and sessile oak are present in a range from saplings to some of the largest in Britain and the area is home to a particularly important and wide variety of beetles.

Wilwell Farm Cutting: disused railway lines often make valuable nature reserves.

Staunton Quarry

Permit only; 3.2ha; NTNC reserve
Disused quarry
Spring, summer

The drowned limestone quarry provides an interesting wetland reserve, with the bonus of an area of mixed woodland.

Treswell Wood

Permit only; 48ha; NTNC reserve
Ancient coppice woodland
Leaflet from NTNC
April–September

The first reserve acquired by the NTNC, Treswell Wood is considered to be unique in the Midlands as a representation of consistently coppiced ancient woodland set on rich keuper marl. The wood was recorded in Domesday Book and, although modified by man, has probably never been wholly cleared since the days of the ancient wildwood; indeed, one of the insects here, speckled bush cricket, is rare in this part of the country since woodland or scrub is needed for its survival and, being flightless, it can hardly recolonise an area totally cleared of suitable woodland.

Ash and pedunculate oak are the main timber trees of the woodland, the standards left to grow above the coppice layer beneath, although most of the oaks were felled when heavy extractions occurred at the time of World War I and again in 1938 and 1958. Other trees, sometimes coppiced, sometimes allowed to grow on, are crab apple, aspen, wych elm, field maple, rowan and silver birch, with goat and grey willow and a shrub layer of hazel, hawthorn and Midland hawthorn, blackthorn, dogwood, elder, guelder-rose and occasional holly, while wild service-tree, like speckled bush cricket, underlines the woodland's antiquity. Wild service-tree, an indicator of old woodland, is here approaching its northerly limit.

Coppicing declined after the nineteenth century, with a probable reduction in the ground flora

Treswell Wood: set on deep clays, it forms a fine example of ancient coppiced woodland.

of the wood, but the NTNC have restarted management and should improve the variation within the reserve. Nevertheless a fine show of spring flowers includes wood anemone, bluebell, primrose and wood-sorrel while the damp rides are rich in such plants as wild angelica, selfheal and meadowsweet. An artificial pool is planted with common water-crowfoot, yellow iris and marsh-marigold, where damselflies and water-beetles breed and where woodland birds can often be observed as they come to drink.

A fine range of insects and birds may be seen in this excellent woodland, which can only improve as sympathetic management restores the old coppicing practices.

West Burton Meadow

Permit only; 0.8ha; NTNC reserve
Unimproved grassland
Spring, summer

Like EAKRING MEADOWS, the reserve contains a fine variety of old meadow plants.

Wilford Brick Pit

Permit only; 1.6ha; NTNC reserve
Disused brick workings
Spring, summer

Development of a marsh in the floor of the brickpit offers a rich community of wetland plants while the face of the working provides an important geological exposure.

Wilwell Farm Cutting

Permit only; 8ha; NTNC reserve
Disused railway line
Spring, summer

An exceptionally fine range of lime-loving plants grows on the slopes of the cutting which encourages colourful butterflies.

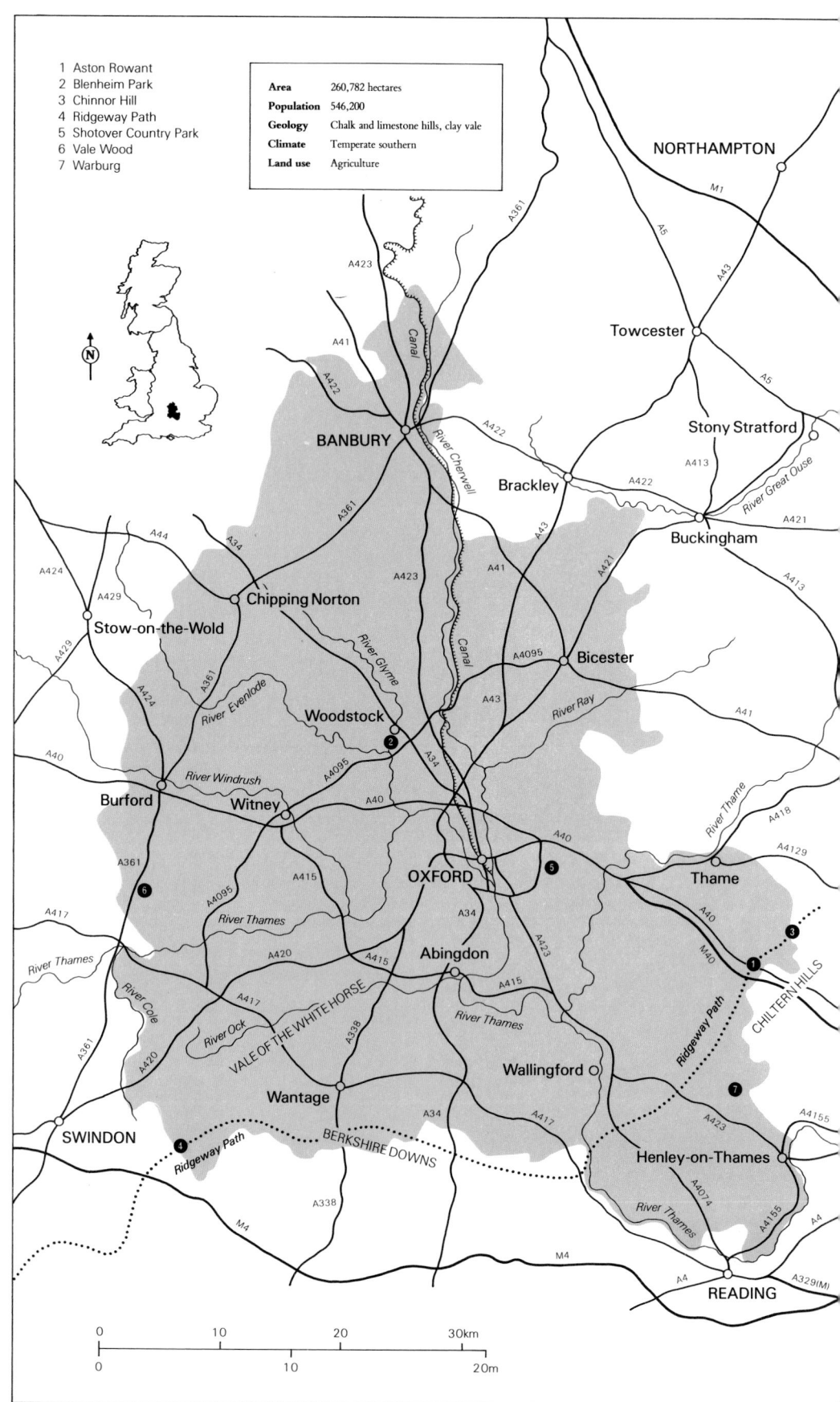

1 Aston Rowant
2 Blenheim Park
3 Chinnor Hill
4 Ridgeway Path
5 Shotover Country Park
6 Vale Wood
7 Warburg

Area	260,782 hectares
Population	546,200
Geology	Chalk and limestone hills, clay vale
Climate	Temperate southern
Land use	Agriculture

N

NORTHAMPTON

M1

A361

A423

Canal

A41

Towcester

A5

A5

A422

A422

Stony Stratford

River Great Ouse

A413

BANBURY

River Cherwell

Brackley

A422

A421

Buckingham

A361

A43

A41

A421

A413

A44

A34

A423

A41

A421

A424

A429

Chipping Norton

A423

Canal

A4095

Bicester

A41

Stow-on-the-Wold

River Glyme

River Ray

A429

A361

River Evenlode

Woodstock

A43

A424

Burford

River Windrush

Witney

A4095

A40

A34

River Thame

A418

A40

A40

A4129

OXFORD

⑤

Thame

A417

⑥

A4095

A415

A34

⑦

A4155

River Thames

A420

A415

Abingdon

A415

River Thames

A423

①

③

CHILTERN HILLS

River Thames

River Cole

A417

River Ock

VALE OF THE WHITE HORSE

A338

Wallingford ○

Ridgeway Path

A361

A420

Wantage

A34

A417

⑦

SWINDON

④

Ridgeway Path

BERKSHIRE DOWNS

Henley-on-Thames

A423

A4155

A4

A338

M4

A4074

River Thames

A4155

M4

A4

READING

A329(M)

| 0 | 10 | 20 | 30km |
| 0 | | 10 | 20m |

Oxfordshire

One of Britain's most inland counties, Oxfordshire comprises a large slice of the scarplands that lie between the Cotswolds in the west and the London clay of the lower Thames basin in the east. To travel to London from Banbury, in the extreme north of the county, involves a journey across rocks that represent millions of years of geological history, and explain the basis of Oxfordshire's present-day wildlife.

First come the lower Jurassic or lias rocks, then the middle lias that yields iron ore, still mined in parts of north Oxfordshire. These are succeeded by oolitic rocks which produce the lovely honey-coloured stone that has made Cotswold villages and Oxford colleges world-famous. A sandwich of upper Jurassic rocks follows, consisting of coral-lian limestone set between the Kimmeridge and the Oxford clay – the latter is quarried for a brick-works at Calvert, just across the Buckinghamshire border. The layered effect of the scarplands continues with the next sandwich, the gault clay enclosed between the lower and upper greensands. The upper greensand makes a distinct small escarpment between Postcombe and Watlington, rising to 144m at Adwell Cop.

Next come the great cretaceous system of rocks and the steep Chiltern escarpment, whose summits lie on average 100m above the Icknield Way at its foot. The beech-clad chalk hills of the Chilterns are quite distinct from those of the Berkshire Downs, now administratively in Oxfordshire. Whereas the Berkshire Downs recall the 'blunt, bow-headed, whale-backed' South Downs, the Chilterns, whose summits are covered with a thick deposit of clay with flints, are almost all wooded, except where farmland has replaced the trees. From the crest of the Chilterns the landscape slopes downhill all the way, and the chalk is progressively deeper down and covered with thicker layers of clays, sands and gravels.

The point of this geological odyssey across Oxfordshire is to show that most of the county consists of calcareous rocks. The first acid soils are not encountered until the clay with flints and scattered tertiary deposits on the top of the Chilterns. The plant and animal life of the county is almost entirely lime-loving, which makes common heather, for instance, one of the rarest plants in Oxfordshire, found only in a few spots – such as a small area of ASTON ROWANT – where rain has leached all the lime out of the topsoil. The naturalist will find bee, pyramidal and fragrant orchid, typical species of chalkland, and butterflies such as chalkhill blue and marbled white, whose larvae feed on chalk-loving plants, but such plants as sundews and *Sphagnum* mosses or such butterflies as grayling or silver studded blue will not be encountered.

While Oxfordshire is still rich in wildlife, as in most counties this richness is entirely the result of the ability of plants and animals to adapt to conditions created by man through the centuries. Excluding the large towns such as Oxford and Banbury and their associated industry, the county consists either of completely artificial habitats, for instance arable fields or grass leys (though traditional grassland management, still carried on at COLESHILL MEADOW and FOXHOLES, preserves old-meadow plant and butterfly species), or at best of semi-natural habitats. Among the latter are chalk grassland – a fine example of which can be found at Aston Rowant; beech and oak woodland; scattered fens – for instance the famous one at COTHILL, west of Abingdon; and the River Thames and its tributaries. Old sand- and claypits, such as those at DRY SANDFORD PIT and HENRY STEPHEN, and former railway lines such as HOOK NORTON RAILWAY CUTTING, become useful wildlife refuges when no longer needed for their original purpose.

Modern Oxfordshire is now more than ever the county of the Isis or Upper Thames. To the lower reaches of the Windrush, Evenlode, Cherwell, Ray and Thame on the north bank have been added the Ock on the south bank, together with its whole drainage basin, the Vale of the White Horse.

No part of the county can by any stretch of the imagination be called wilderness, but there are still places, such as the Isis Valley around Chimney and parts of the RIDGEWAY PATH on the Berkshire Downs, where, despite the intensive agriculture all around, with stuttering tractors and barbed wire fences, it is possible to feel remote from the everyday world. Naturalists in Oxfordshire can still find plenty to occupy them in its range of landscape and wildlife habitats, including a number of reserves owned or managed by BBONT, the Trust responsible for the three adjacent counties of Berkshire, Buckinghamshire and Oxfordshire; however naturalists are more and more likely to find themselves sharing the countryside with other users. The Ridgeway Path, for instance, has brought many newcomers to the county to enjoy the traffic-free walk along England's oldest road, that starts on the north coast of Norfolk and finishes far away on the Channel coast of Devon, and the County Council has pioneered the waymarking of circular walks from Banbury, Wantage and Witney.

RICHARD FITTER

Aston Rowant

SP 741967; 124ha; NCC reserve
Chalk grassland, scrub and woodland
No access off nature trail or rights of way
Leaflets from site or NCC
Spring, summer

While PEWSEY DOWN (Wiltshire) is a celebration of short-grazed open downland, Aston Rowant is a fine example of more varied Chiltern scarpland. The reserve is set on steep slopes of chalk, with tremendous views across the Vale of Aylesbury, and shows a wide range of chalkland habitat from open grassland through scrub to tall beech woodland. The forces which folded the chalk over Pewsey Vale seem to have had no striking effects in the Chilterns, so the high scarp of Aston Rowant must result from the general erosion of chalk from the lands which lie to the north.

A small area of chalk heath occurs where heather and other acid plants such as heath bedstraw are mixed with more lime-loving species, but most of the grassland and scrub lies on the long slopes where chalk is too close to the surface for acid plants to survive. The grassland is tightly grazed, containing typical downland plants – sheep's-fescue, glaucous sedge, salad burnet, common rock-rose and wild thyme with eyebright, common milkwort, quaking-grass and horseshoe vetch – or a slightly deeper, dense, colourful turf with common bird's-foot-trefoil, clovers and vetches, lady's bedstraw, common centaury, oxeye daisy and marjoram, wild mignonette, common spotted-orchid, squinancywort, yellow-wort and kidney vetch.

Tiny close-pruned sprays of dogwood, privet and hawthorn point to the efforts of scrub to invade the grassland, and a block of less closely grazed downland does indeed show more vigorous invasion. Where the nature trail climbs towards the woodland on Beacon Hill, a further step in the change from grassland may be seen. Rabbit-grazed clearings still show the typical small herbs but most of the slope is filled with a mix of scrub ash, beech, elder, hawthorn, wild privet, wild rose, wayfaring-tree, common whitebeam and yew. Approaching the woodland proper, woodland plants begin to appear and under the scrub, to which hazel, oak, rowan and willow are added, spreads of dog's mercury begin to show, together with deadly nightshade.

An even more important area of scrub contains a fine population of juniper which, with a mixed scrub of ash, beech, blackthorn, bramble and buckthorn, dogwood, hawthorn, wild privet and spindle, wayfaring-tree, common whitebeam and yew, forms the most northerly representative of such a community in Britain. As a whole the scrub forms an attractive habitat for birds and insects while the junipers have a notable range of insect specialities.

The woodland proper has developed on the cap of clay with flints, a superficial deposit on the hill top, but more spectacular deposits occur – one is in the car park – where sarsens, lumps of the sandstone which once lay above the chalk, have survived the erosion which removed the rest of the cover and remain poised on the top of the downland. Beech, typical of the Chiltern chalk, dominates the woodland and, casting a heavy shade, tends to deny a varied ground cover. Where light can penetrate, plants such as yellow archangel, bluebell, enchanter's-nightshade, wood melick, sanicle and woodruff may be seen or tangles of bramble grow under the trees and spread across the clearings. In clearings, too, guelder-rose may occur and, although the understorey tends to be thin, young beech, hawthorn, holly, rowan and sycamore may survive the shade.

Two plants of the deep beech woodland seem to delight in the lack of sun – both white and violet helleborine often occur on the bare forest floor. Two unusual grasses also grow at Aston Rowant, wood barley in the woodland and the rare mat-grass fescue in the pastureland, while downy oat-grass, generally a plant of damp lime-rich sites, may be found unexpectedly on a north-facing slope. Other uncommon plants include Chiltern gentian and candytuft, together with the better known but rather local pale toadflax. Chiltern gentian is limited to this area and to a part of the North Downs while candytuft is slightly more widespread but still restricted to central southern England.

The reserve contains a further range of habitat in pathways and sunken tracks, in the bare chalk faces of the motorway cutting which now bisects the escarpment, and in the open stands of juniper which grow in a grazed dry valley. The whole reserve is enormously varied, from the grassland slopes to the woodland, and holds a great diversity of animals.

The outstanding butterfly is probably silver-spotted skipper, a species which occurs only locally on southern chalk, but there are also good populations of dingy and grizzled skipper. Numbers of chalkhill blue are not as great as at Pewsey Down, which has larger colonies of horseshoe vetch, but the abundance of common rock-rose here encourages good numbers of brown argus while the chalk heath attracts green hairstreak which does not occur at Pewsey. Two other notables species are dark green fritillary, a large and beautiful insect, and Duke of Burgundy, like silver-spotted skipper mainly restricted to the south of England. The butterfly populations also include a wide range of commoner species and on a sunny summer day the slopes are filled with their colour and movement.

The scrub is the richest area for bird life, where the low shelter and abundance of insects provide nesting sites and plentiful food for many song-birds, but the woods also have their complement of birds and provide a habitat for great spotted woodpecker and nuthatch, for kestrel and sparrowhawk which hunt across the reserve, and for the rather uncommon hawfinch which, feeding on the woodland floor, can be easily recognised by its distinctive vertical take-off – where most birds fly to the side of a clearing, the hawfinch seems to rise straight upwards if alarmed.

Fox and badger are fairly common, fallow and muntjac deer may be present and the small mammals include harvest mouse. The main impression on the visitor, however, will probably be of the chalkland flowers and scrub, the butterflies and birds, and the cool shade of the woodland.

An excellent interpretative centre stands below the car park. It enjoys a quite spectacular view of the farmland spread below and gives a dramatic record of the national loss of chalk grassland of which Aston Rowant protects such a splendid example.

Blenheim Park

SP 442168; 897ha; Duke of Marlborough
Parkland, woodland and lake
Self-guided nature trail
Spring, early summer

A good variety of birds may be seen around the park or on the lake but the special interest of the site lies in its parkland oak trees, several centuries old.

Chinnor Hill

SP 766002; 26ha; BBONT reserve
Chiefly chalk scrub and woodland with some grassland
Spring, summer

There is a fine range of lime-loving trees such as whitebeam, wayfaring-tree and yew with a scrub that includes juniper and grassland species such as autumn gentian. The varied cover provides nest sites and territories for breeding songbirds while the berry-bearing species attract winter migrants.

Juniper scrub and woodland vary the chalk grassland of Aston Rowant.

The woodland rides of Bernwood Forest, on the borders of Buckinghamshire and Oxfordshire, are famous for their butterflies.

Cothill

Permit only; 2ha; NCC reserve
Pond, fen and woodland
Leaflet from NCC
Spring, summer

Once known as the Ruskin reserve, the fragile rich wetland contains several uncommon species such as fen pondweed. Together with adjacent PARSONAGE MOOR it forms an outstanding area for the richness and variety of its plants and animals.

Dry Sandford Pit

SU 467995; 8ha; BBONT reserve
Old sand digging
Spring, early summer

A lime-rich wetland, rich in plants such as fen pondweed, marsh helleborine and several orchid species, has developed in the old working. The range of flora provides a habitat which is enjoyed by numerous insect species.

Foxholes

SP 254206; 72ha; BBONT reserve
Woodland and riverside meadow
Spring, early summer

Protected from disturbance by its position at the heart of a private estate, Foxholes contains a very wide variety of habitats. The reserve slopes gradually from a fairly level plateau down to the wet meadowland beside the Evenlode, showing a range from rather acid woodland above to limestone-influenced woodland and grassland below.

The meadow has been unimproved for over a century; it has been neither ploughed nor dressed with chemical fertiliser throughout that period. This lack of human interference has protected the meadow plants which are generally lost when grassland is improved and species such as great burnet, marsh valerian and marsh speedwell may still be found here. The old ditch system which drained the lower wood has collapsed upon itself and parts of the meadow are very wet and marshy.

The lower wood lies immediately above the meadow, initially a narrow hedgelike strip, then widening, slopes up away from the river. The narrow belt contains mainly oak and ash over hawthorn, blackthorn and hazel with a variable ground cover according to the shade: dense bramble grows where the light is good but many woodland flowers survive among the bramble and along the pathway. Where the wood deepens more varied conditions occur; the structure of the woodland is improved by past coppicing of the hazel to give a good shrub layer or understorey, ideal for warbler species and full of song in early summer. The path is damp enough for meadowsweet to show in clearings, accompanied by a good display of common spotted-orchid. Above, the wood becomes more open, with oak and birch over dense bramble or deep bracken between coppiced hazel draped with honeysuckle, an ideal site for badger.

The rough grassland above the wood is thick with ragged-Robin and meadow crane's-bill while higher again, in a separate block, the upper woodland climbs to the plateau. The wealth of woodland types provides suitable sites for small mammals. These are hunting grounds for fox, stoat, weasel, tawny owl and sparrowhawk as well as safe retreats for fallow deer. The plateau woodland, like the slope, has much birch and oak and contains areas of planted conifers, damper areas of oak and ash, scrub grassland, rich in vetches and meadow flowers such as cowslip and common spotted orchid, and open parklike glades deep in bracken.

Henry Stephen

SP 560065; 2.8ha; BBONT reserve
Pond and woodland
Spring, early summer

An educational reserve formed by flooding old claypits, the pond and giant horsetail marsh is rich in wetland life while the woodland attracts many songbirds.

Hook Norton Railway Cutting

SP 360320; 7.6ha; BBONT reserve
Disused railway line
Spring, summer

Developing woodland, grassland and artificial rock faces, the old retaining walls afford a wide range of habitat utilised by lime-loving plants, insects and a good range of birds.

Lewknor Copse

SU 724976; 1ha; BBONT reserve
Small beech woodland
Spring, summer

The reserve protects a population of spurge-laurel and of white and narrow-lipped helleborine, uncommon and beautiful plants characteristic of undisturbed lime-rich woodland.

Oakley Hill

SU 755995; 4.5ha; BBONT reserve
Chalk downland
Spring, summer

The downland has been mainly colonised by scrub but there are still open areas with plants, including rock-rose, thyme, Chiltern gentian, clustered bellflower, spotted-orchid, yellow-wort, salad burnet and cowslips. There is a fringe of beechwood along the top of the slope.

Parsonage Moor

SU 461998; 5.2ha; BBONT reserve
Lime-rich fen
Spring, summer

The largest and most important section of an area which includes COTHILL Fen, Parsonage Moor is outstanding for the richness and variety it contains. Areas of tussocked purple moor-grass give way to small mires or to tall beds of common reed or seas of meadowsweet while reed-filled sedge-beds, wet underfoot, lift up to shoulders of drier ground thick with scrub. The whole is sheltered, full of aromatic wetland plants and filled with insects and the sound of songbirds.

The tussocks of purple moor-grass are spangled with yellow tormentil and patterned with the rounded heads of devil's-bit scabious, the food plant of the marsh fritillary caterpillar. In the mires the purple moor-grass gives way to *Sphagnum* mosses, sedges and rushes. Both common butter-wort and round-leaved sundew grow on the *Sphagnum*, representatives of two of our three families of insect-catching plants; common cottongrass and meadow thistle nod above lousewort or spikes of early and southern marsh-orchid and the beautiful marsh helleborine.

The taller herb communities, dominated by common reed, include common comfrey, food plant of scarlet tiger moth, hemp-agrimony, marsh valerian, meadowsweet and a great variety of sedges, including brown and tawny sedge, glaucous sedge and long-stalked yellow-sedge, together with black bog-rush, a distinctive plant of rich calcareous fens. Invading scrub is species-rich, with lime-loving shrubs such as privet and spindle growing among hawthorn, hazel and willow, with ash and guelder-rose, birch, oak and alder. Drier scrub-covered banks have a typical woodland ground cover and include cowslip and quaking-grass. One of the particular interests of the reserve is the population of scarlet tiger moth which, with its variety *bimacula*, has been studied here for many years.

Ridgeway Path

SU 259833–SP 770013; 58km (in two sections); CC
Long-distance way
Leaflet from CC or booklet from HMSO bookshops
Spring, summer

Generally following the line of chalk hills, past the White Horse of Uffington and the colourful slopes of ASTON ROWANT, the path gives a good idea of the richness of Oxfordshire wildlife.

Scarlet tiger moth, a subject of special study at Parsonage Moor.

Shotover Country Park

SP 561063; 1.2–4km (trails); Oxford City Council
Woodland, scrub, heath and grassland
Leaflet from site or from OCC
Spring, early summer

Five trails have been laid out to show the interest
of the area, once part of a royal hunting forest,
which contains a good range of habitat including
ancient woodland still managed as coppice with
standards, bird-rich scrub, heath containing
heather, a species uncommon in Oxfordshire, and
grassland where plants such as star-of-Bethlehem
and musk mallow may be found. Mammals include
both fallow and muntjac deer, while purple emperor and white admiral butterflies occur, together
with a good variety of other insects.

Vale Wood

SP 237040; 0.2ha; WdT
Small plantation
Spring, early summer

In an area devastated by Dutch elm disease, a small
plantation has been established to produce a future
woodland.

Vicarage Pit

Permit only; 8.8ha; BBONT reserve
Flooded gravelpit
Can be overlooked from SP 400056
Winter

The reserve, easily overlooked from the road, is a
favourite resting place for winter wildfowl such as
mallard, tufted duck and pochard.

Warburg

SU 720880; 102ha; BBONT reserve
Chalk woodland, scrub and grassland
Visitors must keep to marked pathways
Information centre open periodically
Spring, early summer

The largest and one of the most varied of the BBONT
reserves, Warburg lies in the chalk valley of Bix
Bottom, sheltered, sunny and particularly rich in
plant and animal life. Most of the reserve is wooded,
much of it with beech, but there are wide grassy
rides, old meadows, open banks and woodland clearings providing a very wide variety of habitat.

The open areas show the typical chalk grassland
range of plants such as salad burnet, wild mignonette and cowslip, with more unusual plants
including meadow clary, a tall spikelet of deep
blue-violet flowers, and orchids such as bee and fly
orchid.

The woodlands themselves are very varied with
beech, standing over shaded deep leaf-litter,
contrasting with areas of coppiced hazel or mixed
varieties such as dogwood, privet, spindle, field
maple, wayfaring-tree, ash, birch, hawthorn,
sweet chestnut and sycamore or the dense shade of

yew. Conifer plantations are being replaced with
species more natural to the chalk.

Beneath the trees, light is the great moderator.
Some plants thrive in the darkest sites but generally the more open woods, or places where the leaf
canopy is thin, will show the best variety of plant
life. Commoner rich-wood plants are plentiful
throughout the reserve – plants such as dog's mercury, varieties of violet, wood spurge, looping
ropes of traveller's-joy, path-edge plants such as
bugle and delicate wood melick, deep green splays
of ferns or tangles of bramble – but more unusual
plants abound and include such species as yellow
archangel, columbine, green hellebore, herb-Paris
and Solomon's-seal.

Breeding birds here include kestrel and
sparrowhawk, woodcock, willow tit and wood
warbler; the larger mammals include fallow and
muntjac deer, with fox, badger, stoat and weasel;
adder, grass snake, slow-worm and common lizard
may be found. The insects are equally varied and
a good range of butterflies is complemented by a
variety of moths which include maple prominent,
scarce footman, clay triple-lines, large twin-spot
carpet and map-winged swift.

Wychwood Forest

Permit only; 647ha; NCC reserve
Mixed woodland
Spring, early summer

Formerly a Royal Forest and at one time managed
by coppicing, the wood is very varied, containing
oak and ash together with large areas of hawthorn
and Midland hawthorn, of blackthorn, elder, field
maple and willow. Four small lime-rich ponds add
a wetland interest and the site is important for a
number of old-woodland lichens.

Ponds add wetland interest in Wychwood Forest.

Shropshire

It has been said that the only element required to render Shropshire the perfect county is a coastline although, ironically, such a feature would probably destroy its most precious asset, tranquillity. Although thousands rush lemming-like towards the Welsh cliffs every summer, few spare more than a glance at Shropshire on the way. For those who stop and explore, the county reveals itself as a place of extraordinary variety. In every sense it is a zone of transition between the cold, bleak English lowlands and the solid, reassuring mass of Wales. The dividing line between many of its contrasting features is the River Severn, once an important trade route. This ponderous waterway once flowed northwards to the Dee, but when blocked in the last ice age turned southwards and cut the impressive Ironbridge gorge. Within an almost complete meander of the river, in the centre of the county, lies the ancient county town, Shrewsbury.

The Severn divides the county into two. To the north and east, a low-lying landscape forms the beginning of the Midland plain. This is a very dry region and the predominantly arable farming needs extensive irrigation in order to grow its barley, wheat, potatoes and sugar beet.

To the south and west lie a great variety of hard rocks, including some of the oldest in Britain. Much of this area, wetter and warmer under the influence of the Welsh massif, lies over 130m and rises to 600m. Farming in this hill country is characterised by beef and sheep rearing. The local sheep breed, the Clun, is now internationally recognised.

Shropshire is a Mecca for geologists who come to see the classical exposures of 10 out of 12 recognised geological ages. Pre-Cambrian rocks, 600 million years old, can be seen in the same valley where there is evidence of a glacier 20,000 years ago.

It is assumed that the inhabitants of the many Iron Age ring forts were the first to change the Shropshire landscape. Most large hills were laid bare of trees at this time, and many remain so. The rich alluvial forests of the Severn plain too were cleared at an early date and this continued with Roman occupation. Clearance of the valley woods by Saxon settlers and those who followed them reduced the great Shropshire forests still more. Many vast areas remaining as oak coppice were cleared early this century and replaced with conifers, the oak bark no longer being needed for tanning.

Despite the industrial significance of Coalbrookdale, and recently Telford New Town, Shropshire has been little scarred by industry. Locally, the extraction of lead from the Stiperstones area, and limestone from Wenlock Edge and the north west, has had an impact on the countryside, but time has converted these original scars into important wildlife areas, notably disused lime quarries.

The complex interaction of different physical features and land use creates a naturalists' paradise, again characterised by contrasts. Many northern and western species mix with their southerly cousins: dormouse, nightingale and mistletoe go little farther north west, and dipper, bird cherry and globeflower little farther south east. Some plants like rock stonecrop have their English strongholds here, and least water-lily has its only English site.

Agricultural development has so fragmented natural habitats in the fertile north and east that only isolated sites remain. Early extensive heathlands have almost vanished and the area is now notable only for the meres and mosses. These large lakes, such as THE MERE, Ellesmere and COLEMERE, and the accompanying peat bogs like WEM MOSS, have developed in depressions left after the

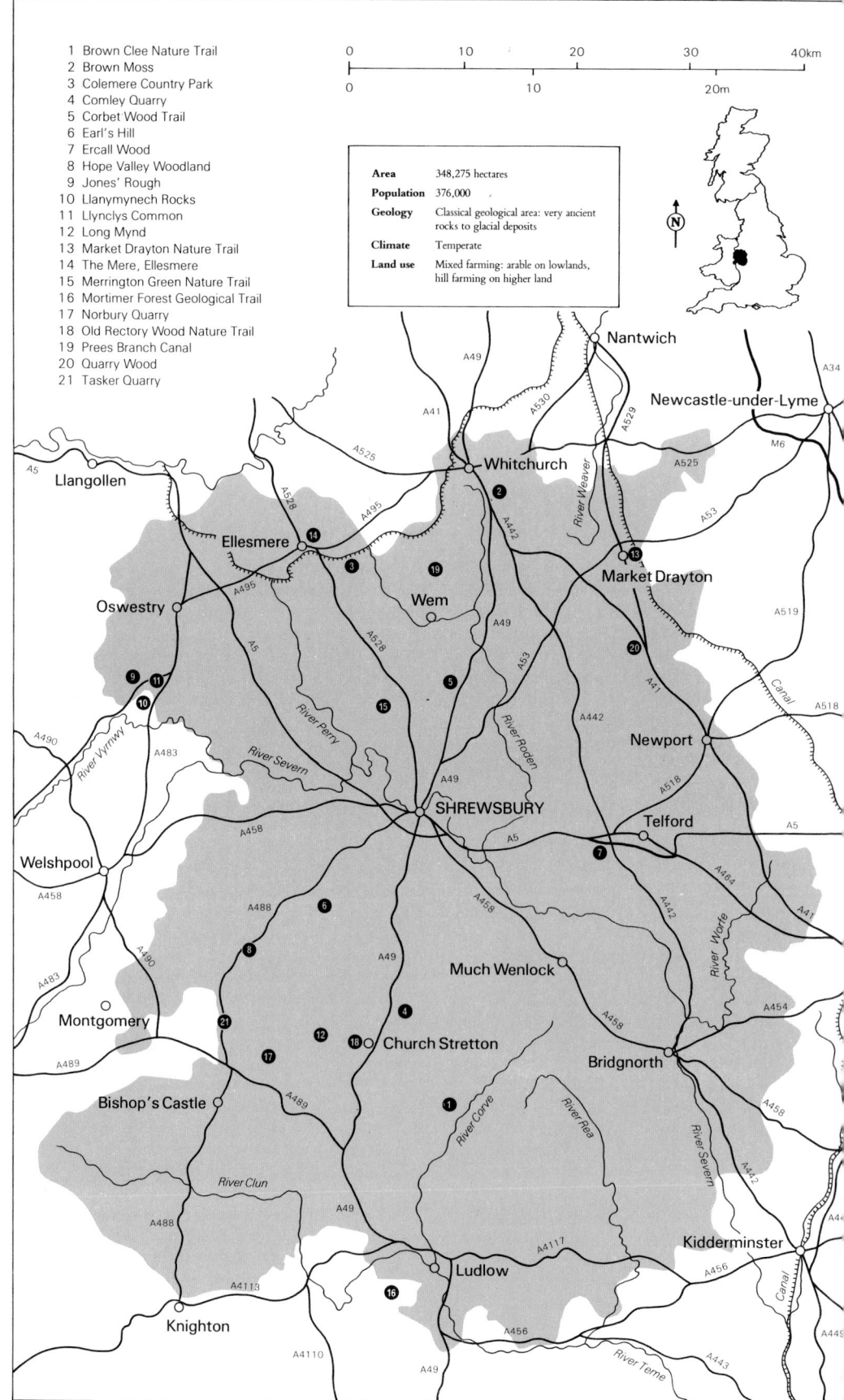

1 Brown Clee Nature Trail
2 Brown Moss
3 Colemere Country Park
4 Comley Quarry
5 Corbet Wood Trail
6 Earl's Hill
7 Ercall Wood
8 Hope Valley Woodland
9 Jones' Rough
10 Llanymynech Rocks
11 Llynclys Common
12 Long Mynd
13 Market Drayton Nature Trail
14 The Mere, Ellesmere
15 Merrington Green Nature Trail
16 Mortimer Forest Geological Trail
17 Norbury Quarry
18 Old Rectory Wood Nature Trail
19 Prees Branch Canal
20 Quarry Wood
21 Tasker Quarry

Area	348,275 hectares
Population	376,000
Geology	Classical geological area: very ancient rocks to glacial deposits
Climate	Temperate
Land use	Mixed farming: arable on lowlands, hill farming on higher land

0   10   20   30   40km
0   10   20m

N

Nantwich
Newcastle-under-Lyme
A34
A49
A530
A41
A529
M6
A525
Whitchurch
A525
A53
A885
Llangollen
A5
A528
A495
River Weaver
A442
Ellesmere
Oswestry
A495
Wem
A49
Market Drayton
A519
A5
A528
A53
A41
Newport
A490
River Vyrnwy
A483
River Perry
River Severn
River Roden
A442
A518
A518
A518
Welshpool
A458
SHREWSBURY
Telford
A5
A458
A464
A41
Montgomery
A488
A49
Much Wenlock
River Worfe
A454
A483
A490
A458
A442
Bishop's Castle
A489
Church Stretton
Bridgnorth
A458
A489
River Corve
River Rea
River Severn
A458
River Clun
A488
A49
A4117
Kidderminster
Ludlow
A456
A443
Knighton
A4113
A4110
A49
A456
River Teme

retreating ice. The fascinating meres, some under pressure from recreation, support rich freshwater life and harbour large numbers of wildfowl.

There are several 'groups' of Shropshire hills, each with its own geological history, and characteristic landscape and wildlife. The earliest Shropshire rocks, the Pre-Cambrian, form a long series of hog-back hills from the Wrekin to the Stretton Hills with vast stretches of acid grassland and some oak woodland. The remote and desolate LONG MYND provides a haunt for red grouse, merlin and hen harrier, while its valleys conceal many interesting plants. Similar plants and birds, with rarer species such as cowberry and crowberry, can be seen on the nearby gaunt and jagged Stiperstones. This ridge is set in wild country, dotted with small farms, lead miners' cottages and abandoned fields, now being rapidly changed by land reclamation schemes.

In the Clee Hills the distinctive peaks of BROWN CLEE and Titterstone Clee are surrounded by upland grassland and moorland, boggy flushes and scree. On the lower slopes are many tiny hay meadows, some traditionally managed and supporting yellow rattle and spotted-orchid. The fertile border country towards Hereford contains orchards and large, ancient woods. The rolling Clun Forest Hills hold several remaining coppiced oakwoods on the steeper valley sides, providing a habitat for pied flycatcher and redstart. The area's rivers, the Unk, Clun and Onny, are important arteries for wildlife in this otherwise well-farmed area.

Away from these windswept and rugged hills, the naturalist can find peace and quiet in the mellow Silurian limestone country of Wenlock Edge and the carboniferous limestone of the north west, near Oswestry. The 35km wooded scarp of Wenlock Edge is a rich storehouse of delights for the botanist, as are the limestone cliffs, screes and tiny meadows of the north west. Both for the ardent naturalist and the passing visitor, Shropshire is well worth a closer look.

WILL PRESTWOOD

Betton Dingle

Permit only; 2.4ha; STNC reserve
Steep valley woodland and scrub
Spring, early summer

Ash and wych elm, with small-leaved lime and wild cherry, provide dense tree cover to contrast with the slope of bracken and bramble beyond the stream. The ground cover includes species such as toothwort and alternate-leaved golden-saxifrage, while the bird interest is typical of scrub and woodland sites.

Jagged rocks cap the ridge of Stiperstones.

Brown Clee Nature Trail

SO 607872; 2km; STNC
Mixed woodland trail
Booklet from STNC
Spring, early summer

The trail is mainly through planted conifers, with some native hardwoods and open grassland on the lower slopes of Brown Clee Hill.

Brown Moss

SJ 564394; 32ha; SCC
Woodland, heath and wetland
Leaflet from SCC
Spring, summer

Drainage and cutting has changed the old peat bog to an area of dry acid heath surrounding a series of pools. Rare and locally uncommon wetland plants include orange foxtail, floating water-plantain, floating club-rush and water-violet which, with the bird life, including some 30 breeding species with visitors such as water rail and black tern, give considerable importance to the site.

Bushmoor Coppice

Permit only; 4ha; STNC–Shropshire Ornith. Soc. reserve
Mixed woodland
Spring, early summer

Tucked into a tiny valley, no more than a fold in the land between two of Shropshire's huge ridges, the reserve is a sheltered lowland wood, set in a pattern of farmland. The approach is a half-hour's stroll along an ancient lane, thickly hedged or sunken and tree-lined, filled with shade-loving ferns and grasses such as the delicate wood melick.

In the wood itself tall stands of coppiced trees lift above a tilted woodland floor; hazel with wild

The low-lying Shropshire meres contrast with the ancient rocks of the uplands.

cherry, with hawthorn and elder here and there, stands in a springtime show of bluebell, on the higher drier ground, with a rich-wood spread of dog's mercury and plants such as yellow pimpernel where the ground is damper and more clayey near the stream. The coppice has not been cropped for many years and generally the poles have become over-tall.

Beyond the stream, however, the structure is more varied. Alder grows along the valley bottom and passes upwards into more acid woodland where oak, holly and birch stand above glades of bracken, bramble and rosebay willowherb. The streamside area is damp enough for meadowsweet, marsh bedstraw and common valerian; and in places it is dry enough for field maple to stand over drifts of enchanter's-nightshade and woodruff, violets and wood-sorrel, or perhaps a flower-spike of broad-leaved helleborine.

One of the great attractions of the wood is its range of habitat within so small an area. The stream and marsh area attract large numbers of insects which in turn provide food for breeding and visiting birds. Native trees, too, are rich in insects — a long-growing tree such as the oak has some 300 insects associated with it. The wood may possess no national rarities but, as a sheltered retreat for plants and animals and a small but vital stronghold of native woodland, it is a place of interest and beauty.

Colemere Country Park

SJ 434328; 50ha; SCC
Lake, woodland and grassland
All year

By the end of the last ice age great spreads of sands, gravels and clays had been laid across these lowlands with, here and there, a sizeable hollow which filled with glacial melt-waters and formed a standing pool. These pools gave rise to the well-known meres and mosses – remaining, like Colemere and THE MERE, ELLESMERE, as open water, they form meres; grown over with vegetation based on peat, like WEM MOSS, they become mosses.

Colemere shows much of the magic of the open ice-born lakes. Meadows lie to the west and south east of the mere, while woodland stands around the rest, framing the dark, still waters. Some disturbance occurs from fishing and sailing but generally the site is calm and peaceful.

The meadows are fringed with plants such as water forget-me-not, with bulrush, great willowherb and hemlock at the woodland edge. The woods are very varied. To the north is high-forest woodland, curving round the mere and separating it from the Shropshire Union Canal which runs close by. Holly, birch and rowan grow over a tangle of bramble, raspberry and honeysuckle, beneath a mix of tall alder, ash and oak, birch, Scots pine and sycamore at the corner of the mere. Where the wood narrows between the mere and the canal, a strong spread of rhododendron shades out all other undergrowth. Occasional yew trees grow in this northern belt and it is interesting to see that even the smothering rhododendron is smothered by the yew. The southern bank and the slope above are chiefly planted with conifers and sycamore but also contain native species such as rowan, oak and birch.

A good variety of birds may be seen in the park, with woodland and meadow birds as well as water-birds. As with the Mere at Ellesmere, a few kilometres away, migration times bring terns and waders, while winter brings waterfowl and flocks of gulls.

Comley Quarry

SO 483964; 0.8ha; STNC reserve
Geological site
All year

The quarry shows an exposure of the type-section of the Cambrian Lower Comley limestones.

Corbet Wood Trail

SJ 525238; 1.6km; STNC
Mixed woodland trail
Booklet from STNC
Spring, early summer

An attractive variety of trees such as wild cherry and rowan are mixed with birch, beech, oak and conifers above a ground cover which may contain bramble and bilberry or plants such as alkanet, bluebell and common spotted-orchid. The bird life is typical of gladed woodland: blackcap and long-tailed tit, for instance. Jackdaw breed in the quarry face which shows a fine exposure from upper mottled sandstone to keuper marl.

Earl's Hill

SJ 409048; 40ha; STNC reserve
Hill grassland to valley woodland
Leaflet from STNC or visitor centre
Spring, summer

Above the level north Shropshire plain, Earl's Hill lifts to some 315m as a steep-sided bluff, skirted with woodland, once a high hill fort and now a sanctuary for wildlife. From the summit, where Iron Age lookouts must have stood, the view is quite stupendous: to the north the great spread of the plain, to the east the Wrekin; swinging southerly, Wenlock and Hoar Edges, Lawley, BROWN CLEE Hill and Caer Caradoc, the LONG MYND and the Stiperstones; to the west, Long Mountain and into Wales where the Berwyn Mountains rise behind the Breiddens.

Place your hand on the bare rock of Earl's Hill and you are touching something unimaginably old. These are not the oldest rocks in Britain – the MALVERN HILLS (Hereford and Worcester) and parts of Anglesey are older – but the hard grey stone of Earl's Hill was probably made more than 1200 million years ago, at a time when life was evolving

in the waters and nothing moved on land except the violent forces of volcanoes, rivers, rain and wind. Now the hill stands surrounded by farming land and is covered by grass, scrub and woodland but in those millions of years it has seen many changes. It has been repeatedly drowned by the sea and buried under younger rocks, only to be raised again and bared by erosion; ice has smoothed it and frost shattered it; time may eventually wear it down but this slow decay is important to its wildlife.

The hill has been modified by grazing, which once kept the slopes quite open, but scrub is now returning to the pasture and the reserve has become a mosaic of habitats. The summit and slopes are mainly grassed, where the soil is thin on the slow-decaying rock and where sheep could comfortably graze, preventing the rapid invasion of scrub. In the crags, where ledges and crevices can catch a deeper soil and sheep could not graze easily, an attractive scatter of woodland clings and climbs almost up to the summit. The bare rock faces provide a habitat for lichens and mosses while the screes, below, provide a site for one of the reserve's specialities. Rock stonecrop is native only in the west, where it grows on damp rocks and cliffs. This suggests that it may not be able to stand competition, that it needs clear light to survive, and the scree obviously offers it just what it needs. Few plants can survive on open scree, since deep roots are required to reach the moisture shaded below, and the slow erosion of the rocks above does not encourage the covering of soil which would be colonised by competitors – in midsummer the shattered rocks blaze with this beautiful plant.

Another western plant, navelwort, grows with wood sage on these screes, while a scrub of ash saplings is developing, but the major scrub invasion is on the old grassland. Here areas of bracken are widespread, together with bramble and woodland plants such as bluebell, lesser celandine and primrose; the scrub species include ash, elder, hawthorn, sycamore and wych elm. Another interesting plant occurs here in the scrub, meadow saffron, an autumn-flowering species with a very restricted distribution in Britain.

The woodland, on the deeper soils of the stream-cut valley below, is mainly of ash and wych elm with oak above a ground cover thick with dog's mercury. By the stream, alder grows with plants of rich damp woods, such as bugle, alternate-leaved golden-saxifrage and ramsons, and among the commoner trees in the wood are more uncommon species: large-leaved lime and wild service-tree. The stream itself is a breeding site for stonefly and mayfly and draws waterbirds, pied wagtail and dipper, to feed on the rich insect life. Other woodland birds include pied flycatcher, redstart and wood warbler with a fine variety of other warblers, six species of tit, both treecreeper and nuthatch and all three native woodpeckers. Sparrowhawk and kestrel have been recorded on the reserve and the high hill is a site from which buzzard, merlin and raven may be seen.

The wide range of habitat attracts good numbers of butterflies and some 29 species have been recorded, including dingy, grizzled, large and small skipper, green and white-letter hairstreak, grayling and holly blue, together with pearl-bordered and small pearl-bordered, silver-washed and dark green fritillary. Mammal interest includes a large badger sett while smaller mammals include dormouse, long-eared bat and pipistrelle.

A nature trail has been laid out which winds from the screes below the crags, through the scrub and woodland on the shales of the valley, to climb the thin rocky slopes up to the summit. These shallow soils, high above the farmland, contain attractive small plants, such as mouse-ear hawkweed, sheep's bit and carline thistle, together with taller hoary mullein and bushes of gorse and broom. It is difficult to say that any one part of this varied reserve is more fascinating than the rest, but these slopes, and the summit with its truly spectacular views, are quite superb on a sunlit summer day.

Perhaps, more than any other reserve, Earl's Hill captures the richness of the county; other sites may have more special features – the limestone of LLANYMYNECH, the raised bog of WEM MOSS – but here is a variation, from streamside woodland to high grazing, which embraces sites rich enough for sanicle and yellow archangel or for wall lettuce and bloody crane's-bill, together with places where hard fern and bilberry grow. In the short distance from valley bottom to hilltop, a range of birds might be seen which includes heron and moorhen, tawny owl and tree sparrow, yellowhammer, linnet and skylark. While the huge

Earl's Hill looms above the land around, seen here from Granhams Moor.

ridge of the Long Mynd may be more spectacular, Earl's Hill holds the fascination of even more ancient rocks. The reserve is also enhanced by the presence of an excellent visitor centre.

Edge Wood

Permit only; 10ha; STNC reserve
Mixed woodland
Spring, early summer

A spectacular long low wooded wall of hill, the famous Wenlock Edge runs for some 35km above the valley of Ape Dale. Before fast-growing conifers were planted for greater income, Edge Wood was mainly ash, with oak – for timber – and a mix of other species. Now, much of the wood is dark with conifers or planted with trees such as beech, native only further south and, like the conifers, casting deep shadow and dropping slow-rotting leaves, creating an environment in which few other plants can survive.

Areas still remain, however, of native ash and oak. These, with rides and clearings, and the more recent woodland invasion of old fields, allow a variety of smaller plants to grow, providing a range of habitat for many woodland animals. Hazel coppice with birch, wild cherry, guelder-rose, holly, rowan, spindle and willow grows above spreads of bramble, wild rose, wood anemone, bluebell, enchanter's-nightshade and dog's mercury.

Lime-rich damp clay soils encourage herb-Paris, yellow archangel, sanicle and woodruff, with marsh plants such as wild angelica, meadowsweet and ragged-Robin in the rides. Dry soils are suitable for wood-sorrel and wood spurge. Woodland plants such as primrose or common and early dog-violet may be contrasted with grassland species such as cowslip, lady's-mantle and pignut. Management practices affect the structure: some areas have been re-coppiced, some spot-planted to give a mixed-age wood; one area cleared for planting was then left derelict and has now become a stand of pure birch.

Woodcock probe the damp rides for worms and insect larvae; green, great spotted and lesser spotted woodpecker search bark and rotten timber for grubs; spotted flycatcher dart and swerve in the clearings taking insects on the wing. Six species of tit and six warblers may commonly be seen in early summer, while predators such as tawny and little owl, buzzard, kestrel and sparrowhawk may visit at any time. Yellow-necked mouse and badger are among the mammals; insects include moths such as oak beauty, peppered and winter moth.

Ercall Wood

SJ 646103; 15.2ha; SCC
Mixed woodland
Spring, early summer

Set on a ridge, part of the famous Wrekin Hills, the wood contains a good variety of plant species, birds and other animals and has considerable geological interest.

Llanymynech Rocks: quarried limestone has now become an important nature reserve.

Hope Valley Woodland

SJ 350018; 12.8ha; STNC reserve
Mixed woodland
Spring, early summer

The long narrow valley is to be returned to oak-wood by removal of planted conifers. Woodland birds include pied flycatcher and redstart while the stream attracts dipper and kingfisher and also exhibits unique geological exposures.

Jones' Rough

SJ 247247; 3.1ha; STNC reserve
Limestone woodland, cliff and scree
Spring, summer

The wood, part of which is thought to be ancient, contains many yew trees and some wild cherry. The ground cover includes spurge-laurel and stinking hellebore, while the cliff and scree above the wood is rich in hairy rock-cress, common rock-rose and wild thyme.

Knowle Wood

Permit only; 2.2ha; STNC reserve
Mixed woodland
Spring, early summer

Mainly the result of the natural colonisation of abandoned limestone workings, the wood contains more than 20 tree species including ash, wych elm, oak and grey willow. Mammals found in the reserve include badger and yellow-necked mouse and there is a very varied population of scrub and woodland birds.

Llanymynech Rocks

SJ 266218; 2.4ha; STNC–MTNC reserve
Disused limestone quarry
Spring, summer

Llanymynech Hill stands above farmland where the Afon Vyrnwy flows across the plain to join the River Severn – the reserve straddles the border between Wales and England. The carboniferous limestone of the hill has been quarried to leave a towering cliff above a spread of grassland, scree and scrub. Beyond the quarry floor and the scrub-covered spoil heaps, a sloping belt of woodland falls to the edge of the fields below.

The old spoil heaps, mounded away from the working floor, have been colonised by grasses and small bright flowers and carry a deep enough soil for woodland to develop. In places they have been planted with conifers or invaded by sycamore scrub but the attractive range of native species such as dogwood, ash and hawthorn implies an eventual mixed wood. The scrub, at present, stands above a show of grassland plants which will disappear as the woodland cover grows. Species such as dog's mercury will spread up from the established tree line below and, eventually, the brighter plants will only survive in the narrow grassland edging the paths.

The thin-turfed quarry floor acts as a storehouse of these grassland plants. In spring and summer, it is beautiful with species such as oxeye daisy and common bird's-foot-trefoil, tangling vetches and clovers, tiny blue milkwort, marjoram and wild thyme, spreads of common rock-rose and vivid star-like yellow-wort. Bright small butterflies

353

dance from flower to flower and the sheer rock-face echoes the sound of birdsong.

The grassland is varied by areas of scree, an open rough shingle of limestone on which little can grow except plants such as herb-Robert, a specialist in rocky places often seen on walls. When soil has accumulated, grassland species will populate the scree and it will be, in turn, a flower garden.

Llynclys Common

SJ 273237; 36ha; STNC reserve
Grassland, scrub and woodland
Spring, summer

Scrub and birch woodland is invading a splendid area of limestone grassland – a site which contains some eight species of orchid and attracts a good range of insects, including brown Argus butterfly.

Long Mynd

SO 425945; 1812ha; NT
Plateau moorland
Leaflets from Shropshire Hills Information Centre
Spring, summer

Bilberry, bracken and heather spread across a great plateau rising out of the level land below. At the highest point, 517m, it is possible to see far over the Cheshire plain, across to Wenlock Edge, the BRECON BEACONS (Powys), or CADER IDRIS (Gwynedd). This whale-backed huge plateau is a tilted mass of rocks formed under the sea hundreds of millions of years ago. It has weathered many eras, from the hot desert winds of the Devonian to the bitter cold and the weight of the Pleistocene ice.

The trees that returned after the ice have long been cleared and for centuries sheep have grazed here, preventing any return to woodland cover. The Mynd is now managed as a grouse moor, with a regular mowing programme to encourage the growth of young heather without allowing bracken to spread.

The plateau slopes, particularly on the east, are cut by deep winding valleys where ice and melt-waters have carved away the hill. The present streams rise from springs where bog plants such as *Sphagnum* mosses, bog pimpernel, common butter-wort and round-leaved sundew grow with less acidic plants such as marsh lousewort and marsh pennywort. The sheltered grassland slopes are scattered with hawthorn and rowan scrub.

The streams are ideal sites for stonefly larvae, which can only survive in such pure waters, for several of the more particular caddis flies, mayflies and dragonflies, and also for a bird which feeds on these insects. The dipper can walk upstream under-water, head-down, leaning forward, held to the bot-tom by the water flow. Yellowhammer sing from the hawthorn bushes while wheatear and ring ouzel flit from rock to rock. Buzzard or raven may also be seen.

Although the Long Mynd may seem bare and featureless, to the naturalist it is full of fascination. Tiny acid-loving plants such as tormentil and heath

bedstraw shine among the grasses, while navelwort grows on the rocks; northern eggar, moth and cater-pillar, may be seen among the heather and small brown trout swim in the lower valley streams.

Market Drayton Nature Trail

SJ 684343; 6.4km; STNC
Habitat trail, circulating through lanes near the town
Booklet from STNC
Spring, early summer

The trail includes a range of interest from river and canal to woodland, hedge and farmland.

The Mere, Ellesmere

SJ 403348; 46.4ha; SCC
Large glacial lake
Booklet from Meres Centre at site
Winter

Summer disturbance, pleasure-boating for in-stance, reduces the potential of the mere but in winter the water is a notable gull roost and draws numbers of wildfowl such as goldeneye, pochard, smew and wigeon. A heronry adds to the year-round interest and tern species are among migrant visitors.

Merrington Green Nature Trail

SJ 465209; 2km; STNC
Scrubland trail
Booklet from STNC
Spring, early summer

The trail has been established on the old Mer-rington Green Common which, now that grazing has ceased, is in the process of changing, through scrub, to secondary woodland. A number of pools add wetland interest.

Long Mynd: a magnificent sweep of moorland.

Mortimer Forest Geological Trail

SO 470730; 4.8km; NCC
Trail examining Silurian sediments
Booklet from NCC
All year

The trail, passing through progressively younger rocks in its passage eastwards, covers some 10 million years. From Easter to September the Ludlow Museum, near the end of the trail, is open to visitors daily.

Norbury Quarry

SO 358928; 0.8ha; STNC reserve
Geological site
All year

The quarry shows an exposure of fossiliferous Silurian pentamerous limestone.

Old Rectory Wood Nature Trail

SO 448959; 2.4km; SCC
Trail through mixed woodland
Spring, early summer

The trail circles through an attractive woodland of beech, varied with other tree species, beneath the slopes of the LONG MYND.

Prees Branch Canal

SJ 497332; 0.8km; STNC reserve
Disused canal
Spring, summer

The canal has been invaded by alder, reedswamp and yellow water-lily. Spring brings a waterside show of cowslip and marsh-marigold, while summer plants found in the reserve include frogbit and flowering-rush.

Preston Montford Nature Trail

Permit only; 275m; FSC
Short riverside trail
Booklet and permit from site at SJ 432143, also permit for hide
Spring, early summer

A variety of habitats, particularly the range associated with glacial materials overlying clay, is found on the trail, together with opportunities to study the bird life of the river from the bankside hide.

Quarry Wood

SJ 686273; 0.8ha; STNC reserve
Mixed woodland
Spring, early summer

Winter migrants, such as fieldfare and redwing, roost in the dense rhododendron cover which shades out much of the woodland floor. Some 20 other tree species add colour and variety to the reserve and encourage an interesting range of summer breeding birds.

Sallow Coppice

Permit only; 12ha; STNC reserve
Mixed woodland
Spring, early summer

At least 30 tree and shrub species may be found, in an area of ancient woodland on lime-rich soils which contains a rich ground flora. Varied management techniques increase the woodland diversity.

Tasker Quarry

SO 326957; 0.8ha; STNC reserve
Geological site
All year

The quarry shows an exposure of Ordovician Stapeley volcanic ashes interbedded with shales.

Wem Moss

Permit only; 20.8ha; STNC reserve
Lowland raised bog
Spring, summer

Contrary to the views of many people, most bogs are neither dangerous nor ugly. Undoubtedly some are dangerous – a schwingmoor or floating bog, for instance, may be a flimsy raft of peat above several metres of mud or water – but most bogs are wonderful places of subtle-patterned colour.

Wem Moss is a small raised bog, a post-glacial mere where mosses and wetland plants have built up peat into a low dome, like a giant sponge. The surface is dipped and hummocked, allowing plants to grow in either damp or wet conditions. The edges of the sponge are drier, a suitable habitat for a different range of plants.

The reserve, surrounded by woodland and fields, appears as a plain of heather-purple divided by a strip of wetter ground where alder and birch grow with tussocks of purple moor-grass and sprays of bog myrtle, with marsh-marigold, lesser spearwort and early marsh-orchid, lesser butterfly-orchid, meadow thistle and royal fern. Bog asphodel, cross-leaved heath and heather show the change to more acid conditions which marks the bog, where a spread of purple moor-grass and heathers is varied by tormentil and by the special plant life of the wet, small hollows.

These hollows are rich in sedges, such as white beak-sedge and common cottongrass, and are cushioned with *Sphagnum* mosses, decorated with round-leaved sundew and cranberry. Both the other British sundews occur, oblong-leaved and great sundew, together with bog-rosemary.

Adders are abundant on the moss; wetland and woodland birds may visit, hunting the plentiful insects; some notable dragonflies occur and the reserve protects a population of large heath butterfly. The large heath is limited to bogs and wet heathland where its food plants, white beak-sedge and cottongrass, survive, and it occurs in three distinct varieties. Wem Moss holds the one known only in Cumbria, Lancashire and north Shropshire.

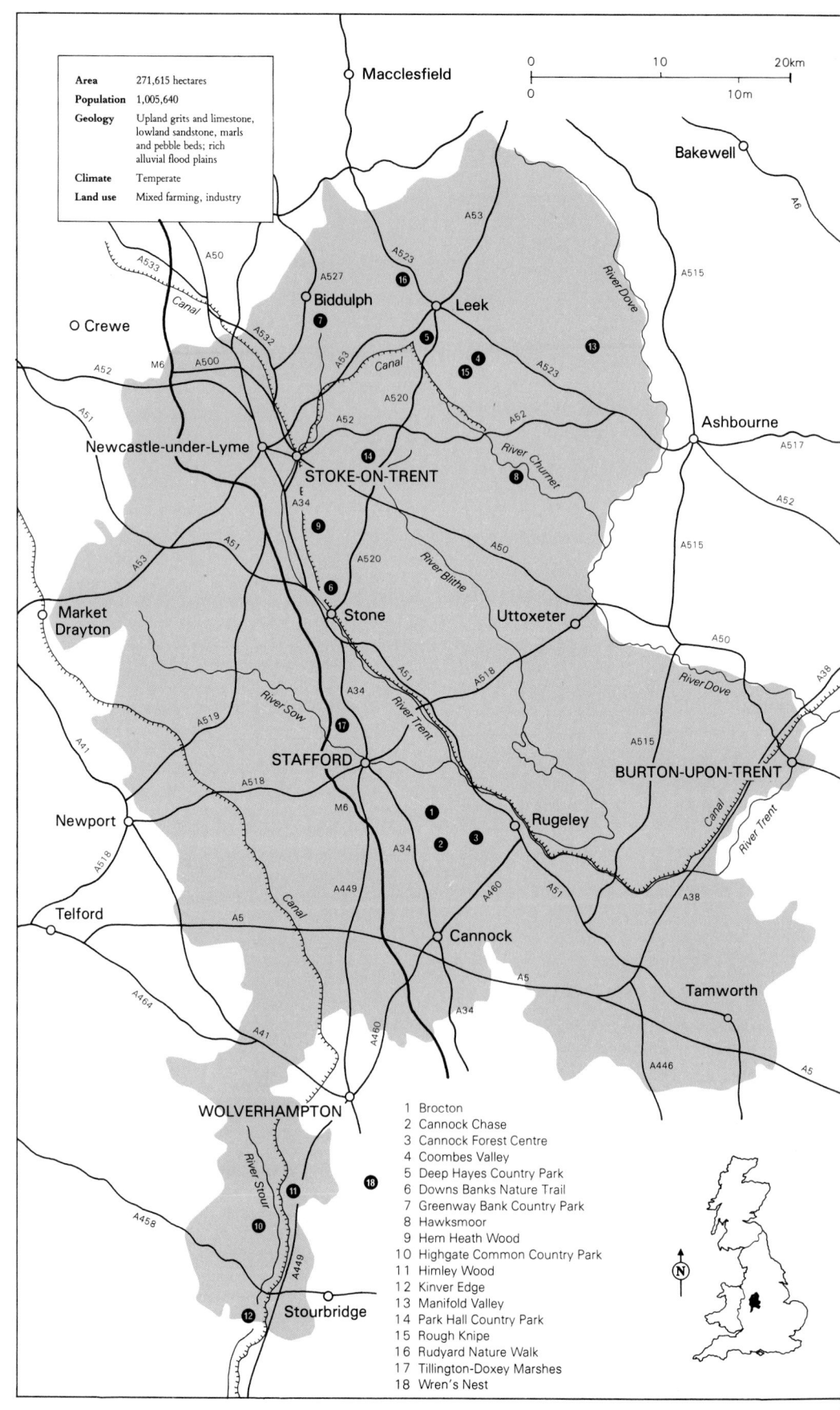

Area	271,615 hectares
Population	1,005,640
Geology	Upland grits and limestone, lowland sandstone, marls and pebble beds; rich alluvial flood plains
Climate	Temperate
Land use	Mixed farming, industry

0   10   20km
0   10m

Macclesfield

Bakewell

A6

A53

A533

A50

A527

Biddulph

A523

River Dove

A515

Crewe

A532

Leek

Canal

A53

A53

A500

M6

A52

Canal

A520

A523

Newcastle-under-Lyme

A52

A52

Ashbourne

STOKE-ON-TRENT

River Churnet

A517

A34

A51

A520

River Blithe

A50

A515

Stone

A520

A515

Market Drayton

Uttoxeter

A519

River Sow

A34

A51

A518

River Trent

River Dove

A50

STAFFORD

A515

BURTON-UPON-TRENT

Newport

A518

M6

Rugeley

Canal

River Trent

Telford

A41

Canal

Brocton

A34

A449

A460

A51

A38

A5

Cannock

A38

A464

Tamworth

A41

A460

A34

A5

A446

A5

WOLVERHAMPTON

River Stour

1 Brocton
2 Cannock Chase
3 Cannock Forest Centre
4 Coombes Valley
5 Deep Hayes Country Park
6 Downs Banks Nature Trail
7 Greenway Bank Country Park
8 Hawksmoor
9 Hem Heath Wood
10 Highgate Common Country Park
11 Himley Wood
12 Kinver Edge
13 Manifold Valley
14 Park Hall Country Park
15 Rough Knipe
16 Rudyard Nature Walk
17 Tillington-Doxey Marshes
18 Wren's Nest

A458

A449

Stourbridge

N

Staffordshire

Staffordshire is a county of exceptional variety. The wild moorlands in the north of the county have grouse and mountain hares, harriers and dipper-haunted streams. At the other extreme, in the south of the county, fossils from the limestone caves at WREN'S NEST (described under Warwickshire and West Midlands) indicate that the industrial sprawl of the Black Country was once on the bed of a semi-tropical sea.

Between the industrialised sprawl of the Potteries in the north and the heavy industries in the south is open, unspoilt countryside that strangers hardly ever discover. Its very anonymity rescues it from the fate of the Dukeries in Nottinghamshire, or parts of THE PEAK NATIONAL PARK (Derbyshire), both of which are being ruined by too much pressure from the people who love them well, but not wisely enough.

CANNOCK CHASE, to the west of this central area, consists of conifer plantations, oak and birch woods and open moorland. This acts as a major lung for the industrial areas to the north and south and the planners have done all that they can to supply 'honeypot' areas, to concentrate visitors and minimise damage through over-pressure. To the north east of the Chase a number of contiguous large estates stretch across to Needwood Forest and Marchington Woodlands, almost to the edge of Burton-on-Trent. Although these estates have recently been fragmented by taxation, the families who owned them for centuries shielded them from development, so that they now form a large area of beautiful, unspoiled, typical English countryside, still relatively undiscovered. As with other land composed of great estates, this area owes much to generations of hunting and shooting men who laid out their lands with strategically sited coverts for pheasant and fox, which supply ideal breeding and feeding habitat for insects, birds and animals not even remotely connected with sport!

On the edge of the Cannock Chase coalfield great crested newts and water-beetles, horse leeches and sticklebacks can be found in the subsidence pools or 'swags' created as land subsided, or sagged in, when coal was plundered way underground. The waste land around the swags and spoil banks has been for many decades rich with wild flowers that attract goldfinches, while skylarks sing in summer as over any windswept stretch of isolated downland. In recent years the value of such sites, especially for educational purposes, has been widely recognised and the Nature Conservancy Council and county conservation trusts have shown interest in preserving urban reserves.

Remnants of Needwood Forest and Cannock Chase still retain the last few ancient oaks that clothed the area before they were despoiled for charcoal for the iron and glass trades. Trees such as wild service-tree and plants and insects specific to ancient woodland still thrive there, and the light, sandy soil at Cannock is the perfect habitat for lizard and adder.

The rich dairying country round Uttoxeter grows more rugged and wooded to the north. The Rivers Dove, Churnet and Hamps provide superb scenery and a rich pattern of wildlife. Leaving the farmland of central Staffordshire behind, the clays and red marls give way to the millstone grit of the uplands. This is stone wall country, windswept in summer and desolate and forbidding in winter. Curlews sing the wildest song on earth and rabbits survive in crevices of rock, some man-made in walls and some in natural fissures, immune from dogs and spades and men with guns.

The Roaches, above Leek, support grouse and blue hare and also the remnants of a group of wallabies that started in the 1920s as a private collection, escaped during the war, and have survived ever since as a feral population. Besides dipper in the streams there are ring ouzel and stonechat in these wild hills, and red and fallow deer in the woods that clothe their slopes down to the farmland below.

The River Dove that divides Staffordshire from Derbyshire flows through some of the richest and most beautiful countryside in England, each county claiming that the best of all worlds is on their bank. The stretch flowing through Beresford Dale has been made immortal in Izaak Walton's *Compleat Angler*, and it still holds superb trout. Far more interesting from a naturalist's viewpoint is the fact that the whole valley is rich in wild flowers, and the insects that feed the fish are of no less delight to entomologists. The whole spectrum of bird life in the valley is a constant joy, ranging from curlew on the hills around to kingfisher and dipper along the river banks.

The choice of habitats to study and explore is almost limitless, ranging from the deer-haunted Needwood Forest and Cannock Chase to the wild beauty of the hills or the eerie atmosphere of CHARTLEY MOSS, a floating bog formed by vegetation creating a skin over a deep lake gouged out during the ice ages. In places the surface has formed peat on which large trees have grown. A single person jumping up and down can set the peat quaking until trees 6m high begin to rock and sway in rhythm. If they grow much higher, the weight causes a depression in the peat that makes the trees themselves sink until they die and collapse, to add to the thickness of the skin over the lake below. The next generation of trees will grow a little higher before they in turn sink and add their contribution of support for future generations.

Such curiosities give diversity to an already varied county. Whether your tastes are for woodland with its wide spectrum of birds and flowers, badger, deer and insects, or for the solitude of open hills, the countryside of great estates or wild moorland, you can satisfy them in Staffordshire.

PHIL DRABBLE

Allimore Green Common

Permit only; 2.5ha; SNCT reserve
Unimproved pasture
Spring, summer

The deep hedges containing oak, ash, hazel and holly spill into the meadow as a fringe of mixed scrub, bramble, hawthorn and wild rose, or alder, willow and alder buckthorn where the land lies wet. The grassland has not been ploughed or drained for many years and is filled with marshland plants while some areas, at least, show signs of lime enrichment.

The first impression is one of a deep herb meadow, with tall plants such as meadowsweet and hemp-agrimony standing above the grassland. In spring the meadow blazes with marsh-marigold and later the colours of ragged-Robin, greater bird's-foot-trefoil, marsh bedstraw, devil's-bit scabious and common knapweed lay a rich pattern across the spread of meadow grasses and of rushes and sedges which mark the wetter areas. Summer shows the beauty of marsh-orchids and common spotted-orchid, the blue flowers of water mint which are so attractive to butterflies and the fascinating plants of the damp rich spots where marsh pennywort and the white-flowered grass-of-Parnassus grow.

The fine hedges and clumps of scrub add an extra habitat and provide shelter and nest sites for birds as well as attracting insects, such as brimstone butterfly which lays on alder buckthorn.

The meadow is a small fraction of the pastures which were once a glory of the Staffordshire lowlands, the small hedged fields which, like the reserve, were filled with flowers and butterflies, with beautiful plants such as the decorative quaking-grass. This type of grassland is so vulnerable to the plough and to artificial fertilisers that very little remains in the country as a whole.

Alvecote Pools

Permit only; 225ha; WARNACT reserve
Pools and damp grassland
Nature trail booklet from WARNACT
All year

The reserve, mainly in Warwickshire, is described under Warwickshire and West Midlands.

Baldstones

Permit only; 25.2ha; SNCT reserve
Moorland and stream
Spring, early summer

Down the side of the Black Brook valley a small stream cascades to join the brook, cutting its way through the millstone grit to rush down rocky steps or curve through miniature valleys, draining the boggy moor above. The rocks are steeply tilted and the land above the stream is crowned with great steep slabs of stone which face towards the east. The view extends over long sweeps of moorland which are breeding sites for short-eared owl and ring ouzel, and over spreads of bracken and heather which fade into the distance.

The tilted rocks are bare, fissured and eroded on the east but rising steeply from the west in smooth slopes patched with lichens, heather, bilberry and moorland grasses. Below them the land falls back to the valley – moorland grazing with damper ground where hare's-tail cottongrass and *Sphagnum* mosses grow with purple moor-grass and rushes. These mires drain into the stream which, sheltered by its deep-cut banks, includes a great range of colour and interest. Rowan and willow lean across the water, where the shelter is sufficient for shrubs to grow, while the banks are topped with heather and bilberry, gorse, and sprays of rush and fern. Clumps of great woodrush grow in the damp deeper soils along the streamside, together with a particularly fine and interesting range of fern species.

Ground-nesting birds such as wheatear, whinchat and red grouse frequent the reserve. Red grouse is one of the few endemic British birds. It is regarded as an all-dark race of willow grouse, widespread in northern Europe. Grey mountain carpet and perhaps red carpet, both northern species of moth, may occur at Baldstones, together with beautiful yellow underwing.

Belvedere Observation Tower

Permit only; FC
Raised viewing hide
Open dawn–2 p.m. and 2 p.m.–dusk: apply during office hours to Chief Forester, tel. Rugeley 2035
Summer

Set in a sanctuary area of CANNOCK CHASE, the observation tower is open to deerwatchers in two sessions, as above.

Belvide Reservoir

Permit only; 122.4ha; West Midlands Bird Club reserve
Canal feeder reservoir
May be overlooked from public bridleway at SJ 856103
All year

The marshy vegetation of the margins is attractive to breeding birds in early summer and, in autumn, draw-down reveals muds to attract passage waders. The bays and shallows have floating spreads of amphibious bistort with clumps of rushes and stands of reed sweet-grass at the water's edge. Small well-vegetated or gravelled islands add further variety. The surrounding meadows are roosting and feeding grounds for waders and nest-sites for wetland birds, while the shallows are as attractive to dabblers and waders as the deeper waters are to diving birds.

In winter there may be large numbers of mallard, wigeon and teal with tufted duck and pochard, coot and mute swan. Goldeneye and goosander are usually present and, with BLITHFIELD, the reservoir may hold over 50 per cent of the national population of ruddy duck. Pintail and long-tailed duck, scaup, common scoter, shelduck and smew are often seen in bitter weather and, occasionally, true seabirds such as eider and red-breasted merganser may shelter here. Other visitors include geese, swans and rarities such as spoonbill, marsh sandpiper and black-winged stilt. Large numbers of gulls use the reservoir as a night-time roost and there are regular visits by glaucous and Iceland gull.

At times regular numbers of arctic, black and common tern fly through, with occasional visits from a range of other terns. Good numbers of migrant waders occur including spotted redshank and ruff, whimbrel, common, curlew, green and wood sandpiper.

Black Firs and Cranberry Bog

Permit only; 5.2ha; SNCT reserve
Wet woodland, fen and bog
Spring, summer

Swampy woodland covers an area of drained fen while the small floating acid bog is outstanding in that it lies surrounded by rich-fen plants. The bog contains cranberry, cross-leaved heath and common cottongrass, with species such as cowbane, water-violet and royal fern in the surrounding fen.

Blithfield Reservoir

Permit only; 760ha; South Staffs Waterworks Co.
Very large reservoir
May be overlooked from SK 058238 and lanes around
Autumn, winter

Most important for its winter wildfowl, with good numbers of mallard, teal and wigeon, pochard and tufted duck, the reservoir is also visited by passage migrants and provides a winter roost for gulls.

Brocton

SJ 967189; 48ha; SCC reserve
Deep-water gravelpit and woodland within Cannock Chase
Spring, summer

Gravel cliffs decorated with birch, broom, heather, rosebay willowherb, grasses and mosses stand above the waters of the pool which are overlooked by a small public hide. Canada geese, mallard, tufted duck and great crested grebe are among the waterfowl. The scrub woodland provides a habitat for smaller birds such as warblers.

Nightjar, the most important bird on Cannock Chase.

Staffordshire

Burnt Wood

Permit only; 12ha; SNCT reserve
Relict oak woodland
Spring, early summer

Much of the old oak woodland has been felled and turned over to conifers but areas of natural woodland remain, ensuring a continuity of oak which means that animals lost in other woods are able to survive here. For some moth species, Burnt Wood is the only remaining locality in the county.

The oaks stand above an understorey of birch, holly and rowan. The ground cover is mainly of bracken and bilberry with patches of bramble, honeysuckle and fine tussocked grasses. Mosses spread beneath the trees, often with plumes of broad buckler-fern. A characteristic of the wood is the amount of moss-covered fallen timber, while stumps, decorated with sprays of bilberry and moss, add to the dead wood so essential to many insects. Heather shows on the edges of the rides, where rosebay willowherb, raspberry and foxglove grow above tormentil, heath bedstraw, rushes and acid-loving grasses.

The birds include such characteristic woodland species as nuthatch and treecreeper, together with all three native woodpeckers, encouraged by the plentiful insect life. Tawny owl and sparrowhawk hunt the rides and woodland fringes which, in winter, may be busy with visitors such as redpoll and siskin. Damp places in the rides may show the probe marks of the long slightly flexible beak of the woodcock, unique among our native waders as a species almost completely adapted to woodland life.

Burnt Wood is important for small pearl-bordered fritillary and for a number of interesting species of spider, but is outstanding for its moths. It is the only known Staffordshire locality for least black arches, a site for the uncommon peacock moth and for three local species, beautiful snout, bilberry pug and silvery arches, which are limited to oak–birch woodlands over heather and bilberry. Other notable moths include oak beauty, grey birch, yellow-barred brindle and seraphim.

Cannock Chase

SJ 971842; 870ha; SCC
Heathland, bog and woodland
Leaflets from SCC or FC
Spring, summer

Late summer is perhaps the most spectacular time on Cannock Chase, when heather seems to blaze purple on the plateau, above spreads of bracken on long curves of the hillside. The plateau, made of coal measures capped with sandstones and gravels, has been cut by valleys and planed down by erosion, while boulder clays and rocks from as far as Scotland and Cumbria were left behind when the glaciers finally melted.

After the ice retreated and the climate began to improve the whole plateau was probably covered

by forest, but natural woodland is now very limited although much of the Chase is covered with conifers. The remarkably few prehistoric finds argue that pre-Roman man made little impact on the Chase, and certainly by Norman times it was protected as a Royal Forest, but gradually the woodland declined as charcoal-burning for iron works reduced the trees and grazing prevented natural regrowth.

By the end of the seventeenth century most of the Chase had become open heathland and extensive grazing kept it open. As with many other spreads of traditionally common land, once grazing is well established either pollarding or enclosure is necessary for woodland to survive – Cannock Chase, with its deer and sheep, was stripped of woodland cover. Grazing effects can be seen even now in the bushes on Brocton Field where young hawthorns are tightly pruned and taller shrubs show a browse-line as high as deer can reach.

The heathland, though, is beautiful, filled with plants such as bell heather and bilberry, with upland species such as crowberry and plants of the sandy lowland heaths, such as bird's-foot. Another upland species is cowberry, which not only underlines the link with the northern moors, but where it grows with bilberry forms a hybrid. The hybrid

360

shows attributes of both parents and grows here better than anywhere else in the country. Sometimes called the Cannock Chase berry, it is known only from two other sites in the county and, elsewhere, only from Derbyshire and Yorkshire.

Below the plateau the slopes curve down to a series of narrow valleys where old coppiced alders or willow shrubs mark the line of the streams. The valley bottoms have slowly filled to form narrow level flood plains through which the streams meander and which sometimes give way to valley mires where drainage is impeded. Here, as is so often the case in spreads of acid heath or moorland, some most attractive and interesting plants grow. In the more fertile valleys, bogbean and marsh cinquefoil, southern marsh-orchid, near the upper limit of its range, and marsh hawk's-beard, a northern plant close to its southern limit, may be found.

The valley bogs also contain species of both north and south but, except for plants such as grass-of-Parnassus, the accent is rather more southern: the bogs are said to be reminiscent of those in the NEW FOREST (Hampshire). Instead of the rich alluvium of the marshes, the bogs are based upon acid peats filled with *Sphagnum*, cross-leaved heath, purple moor-grass and greater tussock-sedge. Plants rare or uncommon in Staffordshire

Cannock Chase: bracken and heather, valley alders, scrub-covered slopes and forestry above.

include bog asphodel, common butterwort and cranberry, marsh pennywort and bog pimpernel, common spotted-orchid, great and round-leaved sundew, marsh valerian and marsh violet, together with narrow buckler-fern, marsh fern, dioecious and few-flowered sedge and wood horsetail.

Areas of broad-leaved woodland still remain on the Chase; pedunculate oak may be found at Sycamore Hill and Seven Springs, while sessile oak occurs in Brocton Coppice. These Brocton oaks, mainly around 150 to 200 years of age, support a number of beetle species which are thought to be indicators of ancient woodland, implying that oaks have survived here for many hundreds of years.

In fact, with the fall in grazing pressure, now that the sheep have gone, the Chase may be on its way to a return to woodland. Birch is spreading, pines are seeding themselves from the plantations, and sycamore has seeded from hedgerow trees. For the moment, the heath has the upper hand, with only a scatter of hawthorn, crab apple, elder, holly, rowan and willow to vary the birch and occasional oak. The woods have the typical springtime flowers of acid situations, wood anemone, bluebell,

361

lesser celandine and wood-sorrel, and also contain less widespread plants such as common cow-wheat and climbing corydalis. In late summer and autumn a wide variety of fungi may be found, with fly agaric and razor-strop fungus in the birchwood and blusher, funnel chanterelle, common earth-ball, shaggy ink-cap, sickener, edible ceps and other *Boletus* species in the mixed woodlands.

With its woods, heathlands, damp grasslands and bogs, the Chase is a vital reservoir for animals. Butterflies include green hairstreak and dingy skipper, with small pearl-bordered fritillary where its food plants, violets, grow in the small valley bogs. The spreads of purple moor-grass around the bogs support the eponymous moth while stream-side alders attract such moths as May highflyer, dingy shell and small yellow wave, and stands of willow may hold eyed hawk-moth. The heathlands are sites for typical heather feeders, such as emperor, oak eggar and beautiful yellow underwing, while areas rich in bilberry are sites for northern spinach, July highflyer and golden-red brindle. The woods hold species such as pale brindled beauty, scalloped hazel, September thorn and scorched-wing, with argent and sable, grey birch and pebble hook-tip flying among the birch trees. Brocton Coppice contains a population of angle-striped sallow, a moth that is typical of ancient woodlands.

Heathland, scrub and woodland birds include meadow pipit, linnet and great spotted woodpecker. Wetland birds may occur by the streams or, most often, in the flooded quarry at BROCTON, where sand martins breed in a dramatic exposure of the pebble beds of the Chase. The coniferous woodlands may be visited by wintering crossbill and hold, besides coal tit and goldcrest, occasional long-eared owl and sparrowhawk. The broad-leaved woods attract typical hole-nesting birds, treecreeper, nuthatch, redstart and tawny owl, with wood warbler, woodcock and hawfinch where hornbeam occurs and lesser spotted woodpecker where alder and willow grow in the valleys. The heathland and scrub provide a habitat for whinchat, tree pipit and grasshopper warbler, as well as for the most important bird of Cannock, nightjar, which seems to be losing ground throughout the country: two-thirds of the whole Midlands population breed here. The heaths are also important as a staging post for migrants such as ring ouzel, stonechat, wheatear, merlin and hen harrier and provide a regular wintering site for great grey shrike.

No discussion of the Chase is complete without mention of the deer. Small numbers of muntjac, red, roe and sika are present but fallow occur in good numbers and are the most likely to be seen. Few sights could come nearer to perfection than to see a group of these elegant animals moving through the dusk to drink at a valley stream. Even so close to great urban centres Cannock is wild and beautiful – a part of our national heritage that it is vital to protect.

Cannock Forest Centre

SK 017171; FC
Museum and information centre
Spring, summer

The deer museum and forest office provide a source of information about the forest and a starting point for waymarked walks.

Castern Wood

Permit only; 20.4ha; SNCT reserve
Mixed woodland, scrub and grassland
Spring, summer

The reserve is set on the steep slopes of the MANIFOLD VALLEY and ranges from open grassland, through mixed woodland, to scrub-invaded grassland beside the winter-born river. Limestone is exposed at the top of the reserve, where shallow turf carries wild thyme, harebell and many colourful plants and deeper grassland contains such species as musk mallow. The woodland contains a wide variety of trees above plants such as giant bellflower, although some parts are thick with bramble. The reserve as a whole is rich in animal life, particularly butterflies and woodland birds.

Chance Wood

Permit only; 2.8ha; WNCT reserve
Small woodland
Spring, early summer

The dry valley originally contained an ornamental woodland which now consists chiefly of oak and beech over a variety of other species. Snowdrop and bluebell make a fine show in spring. Typical woodland birds include nuthatch and tawny owl.

Chartley Moss

Permit only; 42ha; NCC
Large floating bog
Spring, summer

Woodland has formed on the edges of the bog and the thicker areas of floating peat, but generally the reserve consists of a spread of *Sphagnum* mosses, rich in bog plants such as cranberry, cross-leaved heath and bog-rosemary at the south eastern limit of its British distribution. There are important colonies of insects and large numbers of adder.

Coombes Valley

SK 005530; 104ha; RSPB reserve
Wooded valley, scrub and grassland
Visiting arrangements may be variable: contact RSPB
Leaflet from information centre
Spring, early summer

The woodland is chiefly oak with a range of species such as ash, birch, holly, rowan and wych elm over a shrub layer of blackthorn, bird cherry, hazel and guelder-rose. Bramble, gorse and wild rose appear where there is enough light and the stream, which was once large enough to carve out the whole valley, is lined with alder and clumps of fern. The woodland does not cover the whole reserve: meadowland lies above and beside the stream, filled with betony, common bird's-foot-trefoil, primrose, self-heal and tormentil, or wetland plants such as marsh-marigold. In heathland areas heather, bell heather and cross-leaved heath grow with bilberry and purple moor-grass. Early-purple orchid, common spotted-orchid and greater butterfly-orchid may be found in season.

Two observation hides have been built: one overlooking a streamside pool where dipper, kingfisher and grey wagtail may be seen, the other set in a tall oak to view birds such as goldcrest, nuthatch, redstart and treecreeper or the aerobatics of pied flycatchers. Woodland birds include woodcock, wood warbler, all three British woodpeckers, tawny and long-eared owl and sparrowhawk. Of a total of some 130 species, more than half breed on the reserve. Redpoll and siskin are a feature in winter while large flocks of fieldfare and redwing may make an occasional show.

Badger and fox are both present and there are many small mammals to feed the resident hunters. Adder, grass snake and common lizard are present and the pond provides a breeding ground for frog, toad and common and great crested newt.

The insect life of the reserve is particularly rich and interesting. There are more than 1200 species of beetle, 500 moths and some 24 butterflies, including high brown fritillary which has no other known breeding site within a 100km radius.

Deep Hayes Country Park

SJ 962535; 57.6ha; SCC
Pools, marshes, meadows and woodland
Spring, early summer

Adder's-tongue, dwarf elder, dyer's greenweed and greater butterfly-orchid are among the interesting plants. Adder and grass snake are plentiful and the birds include kingfisher.

Downs Bank

SJ 901365; 66.4ha; NT
Heathland, stream and woodland
Nature trail leaflet from SNCT
Spring, early summer

Bracken slopes dominate the Downs but there are still areas of bilberry and heather. The stream and marshy areas show pink purslane, ragged-Robin and marsh cinquefoil, marsh lousewort, round-leaved sundew and common spotted-orchid. Alder swamp in the wetland and drier oak–birch woodland with sycamore encourage a good range of birds including marsh tit and yellow wagtail, blackcap, whitethroat and garden warbler.

Doxey Marshes

Formerly known as TILLINGTON-DOXEY MARSHES.

Eccleshaw Castle Mere

Permit only; 8ha; SNCT reserve
Pool, meadow and woodland
Spring, summer

Typical birds of light woodland are abundant on the reserve. Waterbirds may visit the small mere, which is fringed by wet meadowland containing a wide variety of wetland plants.

George Hayes Wood

Permit only; 9.4ha; SNCT reserve
Mixed woodland
Spring, early summer

The mixed deciduous trees stand above an attractive diversity of woodland plants with a particularly fine display of wild daffodil in spring.

Greenway Bank Country Park

SJ 888552; 44ha; SCC
Woodland, old parkland and canal-feeder reservoir
Spring, early summer

Wetland areas are rich in species such as marsh-marigold, marsh violet and water avens, while the mixed woodlands and waters attract a good range of bird life including redstart, kingfisher and dipper. The Queen Elizabeth II Silver Jubilee Arboretum is an unusual collection of native or long-established British trees.

Meadowland and streamside trees increase the range of habitat at Coombes Valley.

The exposure of sandstone and pebbles, topped by heather, at Hawksmoor.

Hawksmoor

SK 033440; 122.8ha; NT reserve
Mixed woodland and heath
Spring, early summer

Birch, oak–birch and mixed woodlands stand on often steep slopes above bracken, heather and bilberry. The wood is set on the sides of a great ledge of sandstone and pebbles which looks out over the Churnet Valley. Opposite the entrance is a spectacular exposure of the underlying sandstone shelves and pebble beds.

Hem Heath Wood

SJ 885412; 8ha; SNCT reserve
Mixed woodland
Nature trail leaflet from SNCT
Spring, early summer

Some 34 trees and shrub species, including alder, ash, birch, beech, oak, wild cherry, wild privet and guelder-rose, grow in the wood, with an array of smaller plants including moschatel, yellow pimpernel, common twayblade and broad-leaved helleborine. A small pond shows wetland plants such as marsh-marigold and marsh cinquefoil. Woodland birds include nuthatch and treecreeper, wood warbler and sparrowhawk.

Highgate Common and Country Park

SO 844900; 111.2ha; SCC
Heath and woodland
Spring, early summer

The wide area of open heathland and spreads of birch woodland attract a bird life which ranges from skylark, yellowhammer and linnet to woodland species such as woodpeckers and warblers.

Himley Wood

SO 869916; 23.6ha; WdT
Mixed woodland
Spring, early summer

The wood is a fine stand of mature oak, ash, beech, sweet chestnut, lime and Scots pine.

Hodge Lane

Permit only; 1.4ha; Tamworth BC reserve
Derelict claypit
Leaflet from TBC
Spring, summer

Rough grassland, heathland, scrub and woodland have colonised the old working which also contains a small *Sphagnum* bog and a number of pools. Bulrush and water-plantain are among the wetland plants and a good range of birds is attracted to the gorse scrub and woodland.

Jackson's Coppice

Permit only; 6.4ha; SNCT reserve
Oak woodland and marsh
Spring, early summer

Jackson's Coppice lies in a narrow, shallow valley, a small steep wood above a spread of marsh. The road separates the wood from the marsh and each is full of interest. The wood is an acid oakwood with a splendid exposure of sandstone, a sudden wall where oak and beech stand above the rock. The wall of stone is rich in mosses, lichens, and ferns such as polypody, and faces out across the valley over the understorey of bramble, hazel and holly, rowan and sycamore. Broom, elder, sweet chestnut and wild cherry occur within or around the wood; the ground cover is varied, with dense bramble in well-lit areas or open acid grasses under the trees. Bluebell, foxglove, rosebay willowherb and wood sage, stands of bracken, broad buckler-fern and male-fern add to the show, together with honeysuckle and red campion.

The marsh is fed by a clear stream at its narrow upper end, a stream lined with great willowherb, banked with rosebay willowherb and decorated with the strange clusters of branched bur-reed. Below this point the marsh spreads, sheltered by a belt of willow and thick with reed sweet-grass, with deep stands of meadowsweet, with climbing marsh bedstraw and greater bird's-foot-trefoil. In early spring the brilliant yellow of marsh-marigold blazes from the reedswamp, contrasting with the delicacy of the attractive marsh fern, the subtle beauty of bogbean or the scented common valerian.

This varied plant life encourages a good range of animals including over 60 species of birds. Grasshopper warbler is among the smaller birds which breed here, a shy rarely-seen summer visitor with an unmistakable monotonous call. It is no shyer than another marsh-dweller, water rail. This bird, a little smaller than a moorhen, has an equally unmistakable call, sometimes likened to that of a fractious pig.

Kinver Edge

SO 838828; 123.2ha; NT–SCC
High heath and woodland
Spring, early summer

Despite the number of visitors, the oak–birch woodland over heather, gorse and wavy hair-grass or standing above sweeps of bracken is still attractive, particularly to scrub and woodland birds such as yellowhammer, nuthatch and a variety of tits.

Leomansley Pools

Permit only; 2ha; SNCT reserve
Pools and woodland
Spring, summer

Surrounded by wet woodland, the pools contain a good range of water plants and are fringed with wetland species, while the reserve forms a haven for many different birds.

Lime Tree Farm

Permit only; 1.2ha; SNCT reserve
Small wood
Spring, early summer

Hedgerows add to the habitat range of a small area of woodland, sloping down to a pool.

Loynton Moss

Permit only; 13.2ha; SNCT reserve
Wetland and bog
Leaflet from SNCT
Spring, early summer

Where CHARTLEY MOSS is a superb example of a floating bog, Loynton Moss derived from a similar depression in glacial clays but has been colonised by an immense reedbed. Until relatively recently the centre of the moss was an area of open water but common reed has now completely covered it. Surrounding the reedbed are wide areas of wet woodland and of the *Sphagnum* mosses which originally raised the peat bog to fill all the depression but the central pool of Blackmere. Less than half of the original basin remains undrained but there is still much of interest for the naturalist in the variety of habitat afforded by the site.

The reserve is approached by a bridge across the Shropshire Union Canal and is bounded by a bank thrown up when the canal was excavated. The bank is relatively rich in lime and is covered with a variety of tree and shrub species which contrast strikingly with the more acid conditions of the moss. Once off the bank, the footpath crosses an area of old grassland, now being invaded by the colonisers which will turn it, eventually, to woodland – plants such as bramble and bracken sheltering rowan saplings beneath birch and oak trees. Beyond the old field the path passes on to the moss.

The path marks an internal boundary within the reserve: towards the site of the mere the wetland is fenlike, rich in plants now uncommon in the Midlands, plants such as yellow loosestrife, yellow iris and greater spearwort, while the further side, lifted by the *Sphagnum* mosses above the richer water, is much more acid. Birch and rowan replace the stands of alder above a spread of broad buckler-fern growing on the *Sphagnum*. Bog myrtle is now limited to this one site in Staffordshire and the colony of alder buckthorn is probably the finest in the county.

Beyond the birch–rowan woodland, further away from the remaining wetter centre of the mere, oak and birch become the dominant trees, a further step in the eventual drying-out process – the whole reserve is a fascinating study in change.

Sweeps of bracken below birch woodland are one of the features of Kinver Edge.

Dipper, a characteristic bird of upland streams on both limestone and acid rocks.

Manifold Valley

SK 100543; 7km; NT–SCC
Limestone valley footpath
Booklet from SNCT
Spring, summer

Above Wetton Mill, water flows fast over the riverbed but, just below, it disappears into the stones, falling through swallet holes to reappear many kilometres south at the boil-holes of Illam. In winter the main flow carries over the swallets and the river runs throughout its course; by summer much of the bed is dry. Water, too, cut the valley itself and the high cave-mouths which gape on the cliffs mark an ancient level of the river.

Beside the present river, narrow meadows lie on the valley floor and give way to steep banks of limestone grassland, to slopes of woodland or to slabby cliffs which lift up to the crags. In some places small quarries have been cut out of the slopes. The whole area is rich in limestone plants. One small quarry, for instance, might show ash and sycamore over common bird's-foot-trefoil and salad burnet, eye-bright, harebell, lady's-mantle and marjoram, small scabious, saw-wort, wild rose and common rock-rose, quaking-grass, common spotted-orchid and greater butterfly-orchid, hart's-tongue and male-fern. Damper places in the valley bottom may show water avens, butterbur, great burnet, sweet cicely and comfrey, meadow crane's-bill, raspberry and common valerian, while the moist grottos below the woodland show woodruff and wood melick, giant bellflower and fleshy orpine. The sloping meadows are filled with herbs where devil's-bit scabious and oxeye daisy grow and green-winged orchid may be found in early summer. Mountain currant falls in curtains from the rocks above.

On the gorse and hawthorn of the higher slopes goldfinch, linnet and whinchat may be seen, while jackdaw haunt the high crags. Lower down, the more woodland-adapted birds occur: tree pipit and spotted flycatcher, garden and willow warbler, whitethroat and blackcap come to breed. The river is the site for two attractive and highly specialised birds, dipper and kingfisher.

Mottey Meadows

Permit only; 36ha; NCC reserve
Old-meadow grassland
Spring, early summer

As well as a range of grassland types, the meadows are chiefly notable as the most northerly native site for fritillary, an exotic-looking and very beautiful drooping flower which blooms in May and is limited to only a few areas outside the valley of the River Thames.

Old Macclesfield Forest Woods

Permit only; 92ha; SNCT reserves
Three separate woods
Spring, early summer

Close to the riverside, the woodlands are rich in typical plants and bird life, enhanced by the presence of species such as dipper, kingfisher and heron.

Park Hall Country Park

SJ 929447; 133.2ha; SCC
Heath, woodland, canyons and pools
Leaflet from visitor centre or SCC
Spring, early summer

The pools attract waders and wildfowl: golden and grey plover, mallard and tufted duck. Whinchat, stonechat and grasshopper warbler breed on the heaths; the area may be hunted by sparrowhawk, kestrel, short-eared and little owl, perhaps even merlin or great grey shrike.

Parrott's Drumble

Permit only; 12ha; SNCT reserve
Mixed woodland
Spring, early summer

A good diversity of woodland plants grows in the reserve which protects an area of mixed broad-leaved woodland.

Rough Knipe

SK 009534; 63ha; RSPB reserve
Valley woodland
Spring, early summer

A more mature woodland than nearby COOMBES VALLEY, the area is rich in plant and insect life and contains good populations of pied flycatcher, redstart, sparrowhawk and wood warbler. Dipper breed along the stream.

Rudyard Nature Walk

SJ 955579; 5km; SNCT
Disused railway line and canal-feeder stream
Leaflet from SNCT
Spring, early summer

The plant life is varied, with lime-loving species growing on the old railway gravels and more acid-loving plants such as tormentil on the sandy banks where gorse, broom and heather show. The wetter land is rich with marsh-marigold, cuckooflower and other wetland species, above which snipe and lapwing may be seen, together with large numbers of swallow, house and sand martin feeding on the summer insects.

St Margaret's Lakes

Permit only; 12ha; SNCT reserve
Lakes and woodland
Spring, summer

The spread of mixed deciduous woodland adds a range of typical plants to the wetland interest of the lakes and increases the variety and number of birds which may be seen.

School Lane Wood

Permit only; 6.4ha; SNCT reserve
Mixed woodland
Spring, summer

A pool, marsh and streams add variety to the mainly broad-leaved woodland which supports a good range of birds and insects among an interesting diversity of plants.

Spring Cottage

Permit only; 2.1ha; SNCT reserve
Moorland and grassland
Spring, summer

An interesting range of grasses and wild flowers may be seen in this small moorland and unimproved pasture reserve.

Stonehouse Drumble

Permit only; 1.2ha; SNCT reserve
Valley woodland
Spring, early summer

Oak, birch and holly stand on a steep valleyside above a stream attracting a good variety of birds to the reserve.

Swineholes Wood

Permit only; 24ha; SNCT reserve
Mixed woodland
Spring, summer

Areas of open moorland add to the interest of this acid upland reserve which contains a mix of oak, birch and pine woodland and has good populations of associated birds and insects.

Tillington-Doxey Marshes

SJ 915239; 36.8ha; SNCT reserve
Marshes and pools
All year

These riverside wetlands form a very important habitat for breeding and visiting waterbirds.

Ward's Quarry

Permit only; 0.3ha; SNCT reserve
Disused quarry
Spring, summer

The old limestone quarry has been colonised by a flora which includes five species of orchids among over 60 flowering plants.

Wren's Nest

SO 935923; 29.6ha; NCC reserve
Geological site
No access into fenced workings: many of them are exceedingly dangerous
Booklets from NCC
All year

The reserve is described under Warwickshire and West Midlands.

The rather uncommon greater butterfly-orchid may be found in the Manifold Valley.

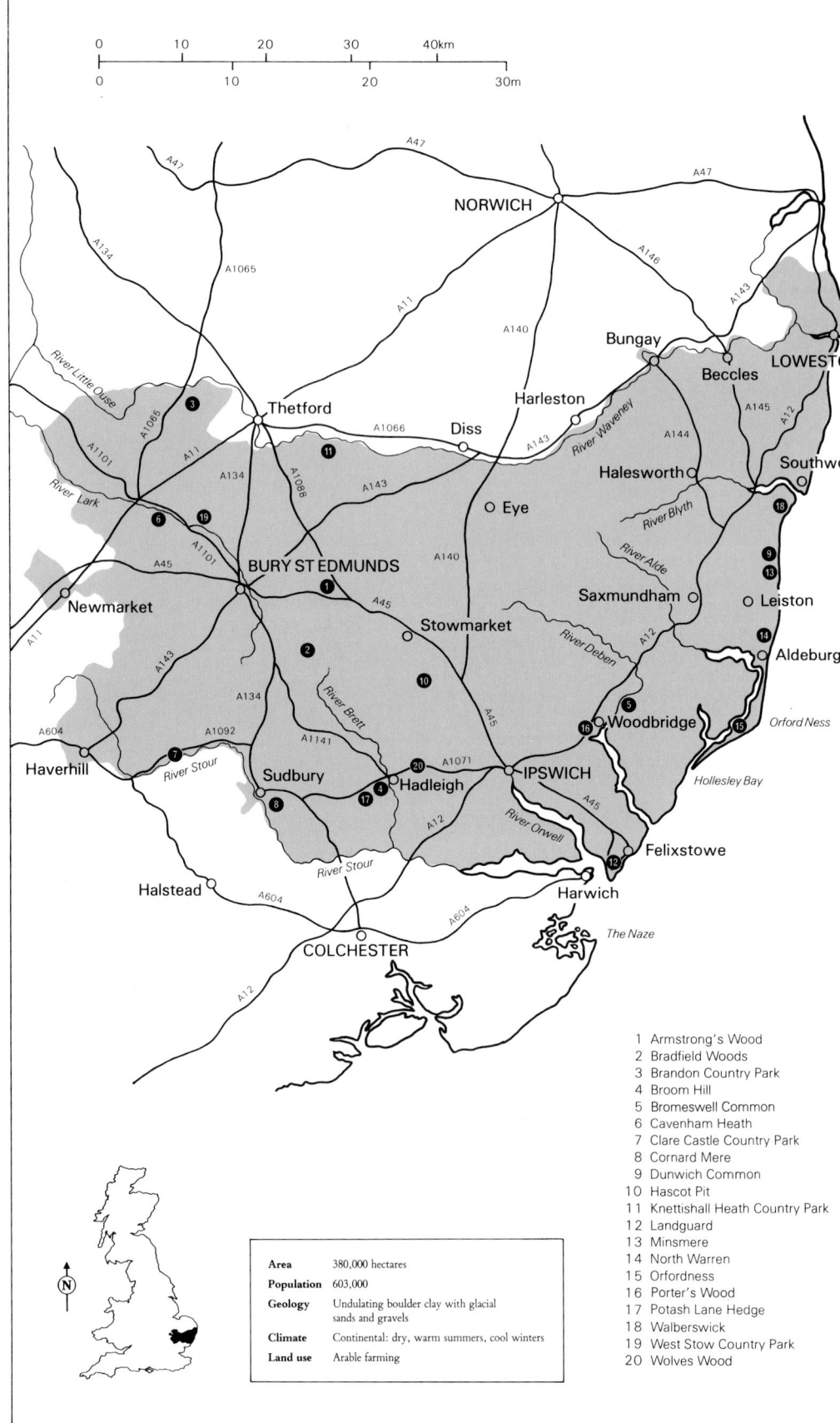

0 10 20 30 40km	
0 10 20 30m	

A47

NORWICH

A47

A47

A134

A1065

A11

A146

A140

River Little Ouse

A1065

A11

A1101

Bungay

Beccles

LOWESTO

A143

3

Thetford

A1066

Diss

Harleston

River Waveney

A145

A12

A134

A1088

A143

Eye

A143

A144

Halesworth

Southwol

River Lark

6

19

A1101

A45

BURY ST EDMUNDS

A140

River Blyth

18

River Alde

9

13

Newmarket

A11

A45

1

Stowmarket

Saxmundham

Leiston

A143

2

River Deben

A12

14

A134

10

River Brett

5

Aldeburgh

Haverhill

A604

7

A1092

River Stour

A1141

Sudbury

8

17

20

4

A1071

Hadleigh

16

Woodbridge

15

Orford Ness

IPSWICH

A45

Hollesley Bay

A12

River Orwell

Felixstowe

Halstead

A604

River Stour

A604

12

Harwich

The Naze

COLCHESTER

A12

N

1   Armstrong's Wood
2   Bradfield Woods
3   Brandon Country Park
4   Broom Hill
5   Bromeswell Common
6   Cavenham Heath
7   Clare Castle Country Park
8   Cornard Mere
9   Dunwich Common
10 Hascot Pit
11 Knettishall Heath Country Park
12 Landguard
13 Minsmere
14 North Warren
15 Orfordness
16 Porter's Wood
17 Potash Lane Hedge
18 Walberswick
19 West Stow Country Park
20 Wolves Wood

Area	380,000 hectares
Population	603,000
Geology	Undulating boulder clay with glacial sands and gravels
Climate	Continental: dry, warm summers, cool winters
Land use	Arable farming

Suffolk

Beloved of painters such as Constable and Gainsborough, Suffolk still retains much of its rural charm and is undeniably rich in all aspects of natural history. Many nationally rare species are protected in the various wildlife reserves, under the ever-varying and impressively open skies of this part of East Anglia.

Suffolk enjoys a dry climate, and severe weather is not usually prolonged, especially along the coast, where the sea has a warming effect in winter. The climate of the Breckland area in the north west is similar to a continental type, having higher summer and lower winter temperatures and lower rainfall than the rest of the country, with frosts even as late as July. Much of the county has a fertile boulder clay overlying chalk, but chalk comes to the surface in the north west, whereas the soil of the coastal belt is largely of poor-quality gravels and sands, but with rich alluvium and peats in the river valleys. Constantly eroding coastal cliffs of crag deposits are important for their rich fossil remains.

Agriculture is still the mainstay of the economy, with manufacturing industries in the towns and holiday facilities concentrated in the extreme north east. Elsewhere, people with leisure time are left alone to sail or enjoy the countryside and beaches. The landscape, rising to no more than 140m, has been greatly modified by man since agriculture and forestry have become intensive. Apart from the fringes, most of the county is an area of largely arable farming on clay soils, retaining very little deciduous woodland – what remains is mainly devoted to pheasant rearing. The protection and traditional management of a group of ancient woods surviving in the west of the county is a major objective of conservation policy. Commons, roadside verges and many churchyards preserve the natural and varied plant life of these habitats, so typical of rural Suffolk. The Suffolk Trust for Nature Conservation has been responsible for the conservation of several tiny meadows in mid-Suffolk which over the centuries have enjoyed traditional management for hay, with no chemical treatment. They now contain important colonies of the beautiful fritillary, meadow saffron and green-winged orchid. Large cornfields on the chalk exposure west of Bury St Edmunds have largely destroyed any natural downland, but small areas with typical populations of wildlife still occur on man-made earthworks and roadsides.

Undoubtedly the most interesting area in Suffolk for naturalists is the Breckland, which supports plant communities peculiar to the local climate and soil conditions. Many people think of Breckland as no more than an area of sand, but the landscape is more complicated than that. Variations in soil texture can be found within short distances; these give rise to differences in acidity, alkalinity and moisture retention, and in turn to different habitats and therefore also changes in the flora. Though many former habitats have been lost by land reclamation and some plants are now scarce, few species have been lost. Some species' existence depends on the – usually unwelcome – element of disturbance. Wind-blown sand, the scratching and burrowing of rabbits, and even soil compaction by wheeled traffic create the required habitat and thus contribute to the continued survival of certain rare annuals.

The Suffolk Breckland was originally a very open landscape but in the past 200 years large enclosures have been created by the planting of conifer shelter belts. The developments in farming methods in the past 40 years have caused a gradual loss of heathland, and over the same period an increasing area has been lost to conifer plantations. Breckland has been considerably broken up and the loss of large areas of heathland has disturbed the silence which attracted stone curlew and red-backed shrike; they remain, but in decreasing numbers. Unfortunately this rare shrike has completely disappeared from its former coastal haunt – the Sandlings, a narrow strip along most of the 55km of coast from Kessingland to Felixstowe. An area of acid heathland, dominated by gorse and heathers, it too is becoming ever smaller due to forestry and agricultural encroachment; it is also the site of two operational airfields.

Below the low, crumbling cliffs lies one of the most varied coastlines in Britain, with a rich range of animals and plants exploiting the sea and its adjacent shoreline of sand, shingle and saltmarsh. Rare species abound, and the tidal estuaries of the six main rivers are a birdwatcher's paradise, with the bonus of the nearby MINSMERE and WALBERSWICK reserves as well.

The Waveney and Little Ouse rivers rise at REDGRAVE and flow in opposite directions, forming the county boundary with Norfolk. Such fens as this are ecologically important, and several are now conserved, though maintenance for regulation of water levels is a major problem. One is the only site in Britain for great raft spider. A falling water table also presents problems in the nature reserves on the southern edge of broadland, where important areas of freshwater grazing marshes, dyke systems and natural reedswamp have been preserved from the ever-present threat of reclamation for arable crops. Such peatlands as exist in the county are in the extreme west round LAKENHEATH, and they are, of course, intensively farmed because of their high fertility. However even here several nature reserves exist, demonstrating diverse habitats, and interesting arable weeds can be found.

Considering that Suffolk is intensively farmed, it is still a county of enormous importance as far as all aspects of natural history are concerned. The work of the various conservation bodies in establishing more reserves must be encouraged and assisted to the maximum, as must close liaison with the farming community.

PETER LAWSON

Armstrong's Wood

TL 965638; 1.8ha; WdT
Mixed woodland
Spring, early summer

A long narrow woodland, Armstrong's Wood has lost a number of trees through Dutch elm disease, some of which have been left to provide a deadwood habitat for insects and birds and some of which have been replaced with saplings. A small pond adds wetland interest to the site.

Bradfield Woods

TL 935581; 64.4ha; STNC reserve
Ancient coppice woodland
Permit only off pathways
Leaflet from warden or STNC
Spring, early summer

Bradfield Woods are managed plots, fells where panels of woodland are cleared in regular rotation, where apart from the standard trees which grow above the underwood, each panel is filled with same-age coppice growth.

Coppicing in enclosed woods or pollarding in open forest is a very ancient skill: records of coppicing in Felsham Hall and Monk's Park woods, the Bradfield woods, date back to 1252. In either practice a tree is cut in such a way that a crop of poles may be taken. When woods are unfenced and stock can browse, eating the lower growth, trees are lopped some 3–4m above ground level and these pollard boles will sprout a crown of fresh shoots which grow above the reach of grazing animals. In woods which are enclosed, the stumps, or stools, are usually cut conveniently close to the ground and from these stools spring a crop of fresh poles, a replica of a pollard crown with the difference that it is far easier to harvest.

Compare the bulk of a forest tree with one which has been coppiced and you might think that the coppiced tree had been brought to an early death, a mere stump which sprouts a few stems from a gnarled low stool. The reality, though, is the opposite. The energy tied up in a giant tree may last for a long while but mature trees have their own death built in their bulk – windthrow, drought or disease will eventually tumble them. The same root-energy, though, can drive a coppice stool through many hundred years of regular growth – never the stress of tons of timber and a vast leaf canopy, just the strong springing of young poles which are allowed to leaf for perhaps a 10-year season and will then be harvested.

Maturing trees do stand in Bradfield Woods, for that has always been partner to coppicing. In competition, forest trees may grow spindly and unbalanced but, standing above the crop of coppice-wood, trees can grow sturdy and well-proportioned. The lot of the standard tree, however, has always been to be used for timber, so the fine tree is felled in its prime while the coppice-stools continue.

When management is abandoned, competition reduces the range, but here every shrub has an equal chance of success and, since the woods are a pattern of rich ground and acid, wet ground and dry, an amazing range of species may be found. The same applies to the ground cover, for every 10 years each panel passes from shadow into sunlight, lies bare for the first season of coppice clearance, then passes from woodland clearing to shade in the regrowth of the coppice. These woods have probably the finest range of plant life in East Anglia; they show a pattern of woodland which stretches back to medieval times and represents the way in which almost all English woods were maintained. The rides too have been unchanged for hundreds of years and are filled with flowers, butterflies and birdsong.

On the more acidic areas, the coppice is a mix of shrubs such as hazel, alder, holly and small-leaved lime, with birch seeding itself when the clearing is open; more lime-rich soils have such species as ash, elm, field maple, dogwood, spindle and guelder-rose while, throughout the woods, some 42 native trees and shrubs have been found, around two-thirds of the total for the whole of Britain. The smaller plants, like the shrubs, vary with soil conditions and, where honeysuckle tangles above the acid soils, spring brings a show of primrose, bluebell and wood anemone with a jungle of bramble in summer. On the richer clays, dog's mercury grows with a wonderful range of plants including oxlip, herb-Paris, water avens and early-purple orchid.

Over 350 flowering plants are known from the woods, where the pattern of change ensures there is always a niche available somewhere for plants of clearing, scrub or woodland, where sun-loving plants and shade plants can flower and lie dormant, turn and turn about. This richness, as described above, depends in part on the long tradition of woodland management but also results from the fact that most of the woods have never been cleared. Monk's Park contains a compartment of secondary woodland, a clearing in the ancient deer park kept open for grazing, and Felsham Hall holds a small block of old plantation, but generally the woodland cover seems to date back to the wild-wood. Both woods contain earth banks. Felsham Hall is surrounded by an immense wood bank, set with pollard trees; Monk's Park was divided by banks which were probably used to keep deer out of young coppice but were opened for grazing when the underwood had regrown.

Deer are no longer numerous enough to cause problems but fallow are resident and both roe and red deer occur, together with a typical range of woodland small mammals and of predators such as weasel, stoat and fox. Adder, grass snake, common lizard, common toad and frog occur, all of them extremely rare in the open farmland around.

Complementing the plant life, one of the notable features is birdsong. Willow and garden warbler, blackcap and nightingale sing within the woods. Other breeding species include woodcock, great spotted woodpecker and tawny owl, while winter brings brambling, redpoll and flocks of tits. Butterflies include brimstone, orange-tip, comma, wall brown and white admiral.

These are fascinating and complex woodlands where each close mosaic of plant life reflects a special habitat. In the wildwood of old, covering all but the highest hills in the country, the same sort of rich diversity must have existed; the variation here must represent most of the features found in East Anglia. While most of our managed woods are alien conifer plantations, Bradfield Woods are quite superb in their native richness and beauty.

Brandon Country Park

TL 788854; 12ha; SCC
Parkland in Thetford Forest
Information at site
Spring, summer, autumn

The fine parkland trees and ornamental lake provide interest within the park which is also a centre from which tracks through the conifer plantations of Thetford Forest may be explored on foot.

Broom Hill

TM 025422; 3.8ha; Babergh DC reserve
Scrub and heathland
Spring, early summer

The steep slopes of Broom Hill are scrubbed with gorse and broom, bramble, raspberry and plants such as rosebay willowherb, providing cover for heathland birds, while hawthorn, wild cherry and immense drifts of blackthorn provide singing sites for birds such as nightingale.

Bromeswell Common

TM 296503; 18ha; STNC reserve
Tidal riverside area
No access except to the 5ha common area
Spring, early summer

This is a most attractive small reserve, rich in bird life, which includes fringing common reed at the riverside with hawthorn, gorse and blackthorn scrub, overgrown hedges and a block of oak–birch woodland. Colour is provided by plants such as yellow iris and marsh-marigold while birds include those of both woodland and tidal wetland.

Wood warbler, an uncommon breeding bird in East Anglia, may be heard in Bradfield Woods.

Cavenham Heath: spreads of heather on the acid Breckland sands.

Bull's Wood

TL 925547; 11.6ha; STNC reserve
Mixed coppice and coppice-with-standards
woodland
Can be overlooked from footpath at TL 925547
Spring, early summer

Chiefly hazel and ash with some field maple and oak, the wood stands over a rich and varied ground cover containing plants such as oxlip, bluebell and early-purple orchid, herb-Paris, spurge-laurel and the exotic Oregon-grape.

Carlton Marshes

TM 508920; 45ha; STNC reserve
Species-rich wetland
Can be overlooked from footpath at TM 505918
Spring, summer

Close to the Norfolk border, Carlton Marshes contain many of the plants which make the broads so fascinating. Dyked grazing marsh, wet woodland, fen and old peat diggings contain species such as cowbane, frogbit and water-soldier, marsh pea and milk-parsley, attracting a great variety of insects and providing cover for many breeding birds.

Cavenham Heath

TL 757727; 140ha; NCC reserve
Breckland heath with woodland and fen
Permit only off nature trail and free access area
Spring, early summer

This is a superb area of great sweeps of heather, gorse and bracken varied with scrub and woodland, certainly among the finest of the acid Breckland heaths. The open sandy areas are colonised by small plants with little water demand, such as biting stonecrop, common centaury, common stork's-bill, thyme-leaved sandwort and sand spurrey, together with species such as common cudweed, hare's-foot clover, bird's-foot, mossy saxifrage and bearded fescue. The main area of heathland is spread with heather, deep-clumped over a ground cover of lichens and sheep's sorrel, with dazzling yellow bushes of gorse, with areas of wavy hair-grass, petty whin, wood small-reed, cross-leaved heath, narrow buckler-fern and the heather-parasite, dodder.

Birch – both silver and downy – is the chief tree of the heath. Damp ground beneath the trees may be filled with purple moor-grass, laced with honeysuckle and thick with broad and narrow buckler-fern or male-fern and lady-fern. The wettest areas may have common reed and meadowsweet, gipsywort, water mint, marsh horsetail and lesser pond-sedge. Ash Plantation, against the River Lark, has ash and alder among the birches and grades into rich fen towards the river with marsh fern and water dock, much reed sweet-grass, purple-loosestrife, yellow iris and yellow loosestrife, an amazing contrast with the dry heath.

The birds of the woods include magpie and jay, green, great spotted and lesser spotted woodpecker, woodcock and the heath-woodland lesser redpoll. On the open heath and scrubland the birds include linnet and yellowhammer, tree pipit, reed bunting, willow and grasshopper warbler, together with rarer species such as whinchat and nightjar.

A wide range of mammals is reinforced by the presence of a thriving population of roe deer. Grayling butterfly, unusually far inland, is present, together with a typical range of species such as small heath and beautiful yellow underwing and emperor moth.

Clare Castle Country Park

TL 768451; 10ha; SCC
Parkland set in grounds of a Norman castle
Information at site
Spring, summer, autumn

The wildlife interest of the park includes the old moats of the castle and a mill stream, enhanced by a butterfly garden and a wildfowl enclosure.

Cornard Mere

TL 887388; 5.2ha; STNC reserve
Small marshland
Spring, summer

Tufted-sedge and bogbean grow in the wettest part of the reserve which has a good range of marsh plants such as yellow iris and yellow loosestrife, purple-loosestrife and water mint.

Dunwich Common

TM 476685; 85.6ha; NT
Coastal heathland
Spring, summer

When the fortunes of Suffolk were built on wool the great coastal heathlands, the Sandlings, were an important grazing area for flocks of sheep which not only gave these areas economic value but, through consolidation brought about by the sheep treading and manuring them, contributed to the change to arable farming which now dominates the county. The Suffolk shepherds no longer lead their flocks out on to the heaths, but Dunwich Common remains as a fine example of the Sandlings, a wide stretch of heather and bracken standing above the sea.

All three commoner heathers are present here, but this heathland show of varied purples would not be complete without the yellow blaze of gorse and western gorse. Broom, too, grows on the heath and further colour is added by rosebay willowherb.

The damper areas are tussocked with purple moor-grass, a tall grass which dies back in winter to form a tangled mass of undergrowth ideal as cover for small mammals and many insects, while more open, drier areas are often filled with spreads of sand sedge, a characteristic duneland plant. Grassy areas often contain field wood-rush, an attractive tiny rush which flowers in spring and early summer, with grasses such as sheep's fescue, common bent and Yorkshire fog.

The heathland is gently rolling and is cut off at the beach by low cliffs of sands and gravels, readily eroding in winter storms, which show the materials which underlie the heath. The pebble beach, which stretches from WALBERSWICK to Sizewell, has typical shingle plants such as sea campion, sea-kale, sea pea and yellow horned-poppy.

The sandy cliffs provide nesting sites for colonies of sand martin which can be seen swooping and wheeling, taking insects above the beach, while the heathland itself is a suitable habitat for yellowhammer and linnet.

Flixton Holes

TM 517951; 1.2ha; STNC reserve
Ancient sand workings
Spring, early summer

The dominant feature of this reserve, pitted with old sand diggings, is a collection of yew trees estimated to be about a century old.

Fox Fritillary Meadow

Permit only; 2.4ha; STNC reserve
Finest East Anglian fritillary meadow
One open day a year, generally in early May, advertised in local press and national botanical journals

A most superb show of these elegant flowers, probably the second best in the country, can be found here. The small level meadow may have an overall density in excess of 250,000 plants per hectare.

Gromford Meadow

Permit only; 1.7ha; STNC reserve
Two small wet old meadows
Spring, early summer

The wet, peaty loam of the meadows supports an attractive marshland plant life including both common and marsh valerian, yellow rattle and adder's-tongue. Ditches contain plants such as bogbean, marsh-marigold and water-plantain while the pride of the reserve is grass-of-Parnassus.

Fritillary, now rare, is an elegant plant of water meadows.

Groton Wood

TL 977432; 20ha; STNC reserve
Remnant ancient woodland and more modern
coppice with standards
Spring, early summer

An outstanding woodland, in part made up of the
finest stand of small-leaved lime in Suffolk, Groton
Wood contains a fine variety of tree species over a
ground cover rich in woodland plants such as
bluebell and primrose, woodruff, wood spurge and
wood millet, herb-Paris, early-purple orchid and
violet helleborine. Mammals are well represented
and over 70 species of birds have been recorded.

Havergate Island

Permit only; 108ha; RSPB reserve
Lagooned island
Access seasonally restricted
April–August; November–February

A 3km boat ride down from Orford, the low-lying
island of Havergate divides the tidal estuary.
Originally the island was regularly flooded, a low,
wet world of saltmarsh and waterbirds, but later it
was largely embanked against the floods and cattle
were rafted to and from the island, to graze and
fatten there. Now the cattle are gone and the island
has returned again to the wildlife sanctuary it was
in earlier years.

The sea-wall conceals wide scrapes, islanded
spreads of water. The purpose of the embankment
is not to keep nature from flooding man's workings
but rather to keep man from disturbing nature. The
success of this strategy is self-evident: Havergate
Island now holds the largest breeding colony of
avocet in the British Isles. These beautiful and
elegant birds, the insignia of the RSPB, have been

Avocet breed at Havergate and Minsmere.

well publicised as an ecological success story. Since
they were lost as a British breeding species in the
early nineteenth century, the creation of suitable
habitats, in the form of islanded scrapes, encouraged a few pairs to nest in more recent years
and this has given rise to a spectacular increase in
the number of breeding pairs.

Other breeding species include short-eared owl,
a predator which is one of the few owls to hunt
regularly in daylight. Its main stronghold is in
Scotland and north eastern England but a breeding
population maintains itself along the East Anglian
coast as far south as the Thames Estuary. Short-
eared owl specialises in field vole as prey and is
closely bound to the availability of that animal.
Stoat and weasel also exploit the small mammals of
the island and certainly take the young of the large
hare population here.

Winter wildfowl include good numbers of teal,
pintail and shoveler, together with mallard,
shelduck and wigeon, and migration times bring
birds as varied as those which visit MINSMERE.

Hogmarsh

Permit only; 4.8ha; ENT reserve
Tidal saltmarsh
Spring, summer

A typical range of saltmarsh plants and animals
may be found on the reserve which lies within the
tidal estuary of the River Stour.

Knettishall Heath Country Park

TL 956806; 72ha; SCC
Breckland heath and woodland
Information at site
Spring, summer, autumn

A short frontage on the Little Ouse River adds to the
variety of the area which includes Breckland heath
with mixed woodland and is rich in plants and birds.

Lady's-mantle Meadow

Permit only; 3.6ha; STNC reserve
Ancient meadowland
Spring, early summer

The rich assembly of plants includes cowslip, restharrow and pepper-saxifrage together with common
twayblade, common spotted-orchid, early-purple
and green-winged orchid and lady's-mantle, known
from only one other site in East Anglia.

Lakenheath Poors Fen

TL 702827; 4.6ha; STNC reserve
Wet and dry sandy fen
Spring, summer

Great fen-sedge and purple small-reed grow with
copious creeping willow, sheltering marsh
valerian or early and southern marsh-orchid. Great
spearwort and water-violet show in the ditches
and the whole area is rich in insects and birds.

Landguard

TM 285319; 15.6ha; STNC–SCC reserve
Shingle, scrub and short turf
All year

Below the ridge where Landguard Fort was built to dominate the seaway into Harwich harbour, the tides have cast up a shingle bank. The oldest area of sand and shingle has become levelled and compacted, a fascinating narrow plain which lies behind the present pebble beach. Behind the plain is the scrub and woodland bank on which the fort was sited which, further north, becomes an old sea-wall. Situated as it is on the southernmost part of the Suffolk coast, Landguard is noted for its migrant species.

The shingle plants include sea campion, yellow horned-poppy, sea pea, sea-holly and sea-kale with sand or sand-and-shingle species such as marram, sea bindweed and sea sandwort. Curled dock occurs on the reserve, together with rue-leaved saxifrage, teasel, sheep's sorrel and the weirdly beautiful alien milk thistle. Areas of disturbed sand may be invaded by unusual grasses, such as sand cat's-tail and sea fern-grass, rush-leaved squirreltail and dune fescue or by taller plants such as prickly lettuce, narrow-leaved pepperwort and cotton thistle. Related to the narrow-leaved pepperwort, and a rarer plant, is dittander, a plant which grows here in abundance. One of the fascinations of Landguard is the way in which the vegetation changes from place to place; although effectively a level plain, the older beach is dipped and hummocked and each hollowed-out area or raised-up mound tends to have its own particular community of plants.

Offshore there is a continual movement of seabirds, while the shingle, plain, banked scrub and woodland are busy with nesting birds or massed with migrants. In some years little tern nest on the open shingle. Another shingle species, and one which is supremely camouflaged, is ringed plover, one of the most characteristic and attractive of our shore birds. Together with our smallest tern, our largest native duck, the strikingly handsome shelduck, may also be seen on the reserve. More typical land birds are also present: the heathland linnet, wheatear, red-legged partridge and skylark, with species such as garden warbler and black redstart in the bramble, tamarisk, elder and ilex scrub beneath the fort.

The reserve is also important for migrant insects such as butterflies – red admiral, painted lady and occasionally landfalls of clouded yellow.

Martins' Meadows

Permit only; 3.7ha; STNC reserve
Ancient meadowland
Spring, early summer, autumn

An exceptional variety of grassland species from cowslip, fritillary, early-purple and green-winged orchid to the autumn-flowering meadow saffron distinguishes the three small meadows which make up the reserve. Yellow rattle, pepper-saxifrage and adder's-tongue add to the range of colour and interest.

Mickfield Meadow

Permit only; 1.8ha; STNC reserve
Old meadow
Spring, early summer

Notable as a fritillary meadow, Mickfield became much overgrown and many of the plants were lost, but sympathetic management has reversed the trend. Other wetland plants include ragged-Robin and wild angelica.

Minsmere

TM 473672; 588ha; RSPB reserve
Lagoons, reedbeds, dunes and foreshore, woodland and heath
Public hide open at TM 477465 at all times; permit only to reserve proper
All year

Minsmere is probably the most famous of the RSPB holdings, chiefly for the area of freshwater marsh which attracts an exceptional number and variety of both typical and less common wetland birds. One of the important features of the reserve is the Scrape, where wide shallow lagoons have been bulldozed in an area of derelict marsh.

The marshland around the open water area contains fine stands of common reed, important for birds such as bittern and bearded tit, with very good numbers of the rare marsh sow-thistle, a spectacular yellow-flowered plant which may grow well over 2m tall. Hemp-agrimony and yellow iris add colour to the wetland edges where the reedbeds are varied with plants such as water dock and bulrush, while drier grassed ditch margins have colonies of common spotted-orchid, southern marsh-orchid and marsh-mallow.

The two other main types of habitat are heathland and woodland. The heathland, similar to DUNWICH COMMON, is chiefly heather and bell heather, with areas invaded by gorse and by birch and pine saplings. Birds such as linnet and yellowhammer breed here freely and the heaths remain a stronghold for nightjar. The woods are mixed and rich in woodland species with all the native tits except for the crested tit, with all three British woodpeckers, with tawny and occasional long-eared owl, with summer nightingale and most of the common warblers.

The birds, of course, and chiefly the birds of the wetlands, are really the basis of the special magic of Minsmere. In spring and summer the exotic-looking spoonbill often occurs and one or more purple heron may often be seen. Passage birds include black tern, osprey, sandpipers, godwits, a host of waders and waterfowl; over 280 species have been recorded on the reserve and some 200 occur here annually.

Stone curlew, a rare breeding bird of the Breckland heaths.

Moat Farm

Permit only; 3.2ha; STNC reserve
Ancient meadowland
Spring, early summer, autumn

Cowslip, primrose and plants such as ragged-Robin show in the meadow before the hay-cut – meadow saffron lifts from the aftermath in autumn.

Norman Gwatkin

TM 463767; 8.3ha; STNC reserve
Osier bed and marshland
Spring, early summer

Marsh plants such as yellow iris, purple-loosestrife and common valerian with branched bur-reed, wild angelica and water dock, and with varied sedges and rushes, make up an attractive wetland reserve with the extra interest of the crack, grey and white willows in the osier bed.

North Warren

TM 455587; 96ha; RSPB reserve
Grass heath, woodland and fen
Nature trail guide from RSPB
Spring, early summer

The woodland is mainly oak and birch with willow in the wetter areas, encouraging a typical range of woodland birds including willow warbler and red-poll. The stands of common reed, varied with plants such as marsh-marigold, meadowsweet and yellow iris, provide a habitat for reed and sedge warbler, bittern and, in autumn, occasional marsh harrier and bearded tit. The grass heath, a sandy heath modified by sheep-grazing, is scrubbed with gorse and broom, a suitable site for birds such as linnet and stonechat, for grayling and small heath butterflies.

Orfordness

TM 430480; 205.6ha; NCC reserve
Shingle spit and saltmarsh
Access impossible except by boat and landings should not be made near gull colonies in season
All year

Glasswort, thrift, sea aster, common saltmarsh-grass and small cord-grass typify the areas of salt-marsh while the shingle bank contains plants such as sea-kale, sea pea, yellow-vetch and yellow horned-poppy. Waders and wildfowl are seasonally plentiful, and the shingle to the north of the reserve provides a site for the largest colony of lesser black-backed and herring gull in East Anglia.

Pashford Poors Fen

TL 733835; 10ha; STNC reserve
Grassland, fen and woodland
Spring, summer

The heath grassland, fen, scrub and mixed woodland are rich in wetland birds such as snipe and mallard and songbirds such as nightingale and grasshopper warbler. Dragonflies are attracted by the wetland areas and there is a good variety of crickets, grasshoppers, butterflies and moths.

Porter's Wood

TM 263493; 3.6ha; WdT
Mixed woodland
Spring, early summer

A small stream drains the wet areas of the oak–beech woodland where opposite-leaved golden-saxifrage contrasts with sheets of ramsons on the drier woodland floor. The mature trees provide an ideal habitat for birds such as green woodpecker.

Potash Lane Hedge

TL 994404; 275m; STNC reserve
Ancient hedge
Spring, early summer

This unusual reserve dates back to around the time of the Norman Conquest. It contains standard trees and old pollards and includes some 20 tree and shrub species in a superb mix of plants such as Mildand hawthorn, wild cherry and dogwood, gorse, broom and crab apple.

Redgrave and Lopham Fens

TM 046797; 124ha; STNC reserves
Rich fen, river and pools
Spring, summer

The ancient river valleys which divide the counties of Suffolk and Norfolk, once peat-filled fens, have become a marvellous wetland mosaic of pools and ditches, wet heath and bog, marsh and fen, of areas of scrub and wet woodland, an oasis of wildlife between the two great agricultural counties. Peat digging destroyed or altered much of the original fenland and, with agricultural reclamation and drainage, has resulted in the loss of large areas, but the STNC has succeeded in protecting a nucleus at Redgrave, Lopham and two other small fens.

Wetter areas contain black bog-rush, purple small-reed and lesser tussock-sedge with wild angelica, fen bedstraw, bulrush, water mint, meadow-rue and marsh valerian. Other fen plants such as water dock, purple-loosestrife, tubular water-dropwort and great fen-sedge occur while

damp ground is massed with common reed, with purple moor-grass, with meadowsweet, hemp-agrimony and common valerian.

In some places ridges of sand provide wet-heath conditions where heather and cross-leaved heath stand above mosses; in others low hummocks carry tormentil, heath wood-rush, petty whin and flea sedge above a wetter spread of common cotton-grass. Common butterwort also occurs, as does the beautiful grass-of-Parnassus, a treasure on any reserve.

As would be expected, with this low, tall, tussocked, tangled reedbed, scrub and woodland variation, there is a very wide range of habitat for animals to exploit. Small mammals are plentiful, particularly water shrew and water vole, and the bird life includes mallard, shoveler and teal, together with eight warbler species, and regular winter visits from bearded tit and hen and marsh harrier.

Of outstanding interest here was the discovery in 1956 of Britain's biggest spider, great raft spider, still known nowhere else in the country.

Thetford Heath

Permit only; 100ha; NCC–NNT reserve
Typical Breckland heath
No access April–July inclusive
Spring, early summer

Grass-covered ridges of flint and chalk alternate with sand-filled trenches thick with heather, an effect associated with the ice ages. A fine range of heathland birds is attracted by varied vegetation.

Invading birch woodland is a feature of the acid heaths of the Brecklands.

Walberswick

TM 493742; 514ha; NCC reserve
Reedbeds, mudflats, woodland and heath
Permit only off rights of way
Spring, early summer

The reserve spans the heathland shoulder and includes the southern edge of the inland estuary at Blythburgh, a low-tide stretch of mudflats fringed with saltmarsh where shelduck, dunlin and redshank feed beside drifts of sea-lavender, sea aster and sea-purslane. In spring there may be parties of black-tailed godwit, in summer visiting avocet, in winter spotted redshank.

The heathland, a spread of heather, bell heather, occasional cross-leaved heath, clumped with gorse and scrub, is an important habitat for adder, slow-worm and common lizard, for birds such as nightjar, stonechat, red-backed shrike and winter predators such as great grey shrike. Like DUNWICH COMMON and the heathland part of MINSMERE, this is a relict of the Suffolk Sandlings, a face of the old county almost completely vanished.

The reedbeds are managed by cutting. This rotational harvest for thatching ensures areas of strong young reed for the future while keeping mature stands to provide nesting sites for bearded tit, bittern, reed warbler and water rail, sites in which marsh harrier can build its raft of reed, and areas of cover around the open pools where gadwall,

mallard, shoveler, teal and, occasionally, garganey can hatch their ducklings.

The tall stands of reed are varied by plants such as marsh pennywort and bogbean, wild celery and marsh sow-thistle, while summer-breeding duck are reinforced in winter by numbers of goldeneye, pochard, tufted duck and wigeon. In winter too more predators arrive: hen harrier, merlin and short-eared owl; occasionally buzzard or rough-legged buzzard may be observed hunting across the reserve.

The insect life, as would be expected with such a habitat range, is rich and varied, with less common butterflies including species such as comma, holly blue, green hairstreak and Essex skipper. The reserve is outstanding for rare and local moths which include Kent black arches together with the reed-feeding wainscots: Fenn's, powdered and the very rare white-necked wainscot.

Wangford Glebe

Permit only; 16ha; STNC reserve
Exceptional Breckland reserve
No access in breeding season
Spring, late summer

One of the few remnants of the Brecklands, which in the seventeenth century might bury a traveller in wind-blown sand, the reserve contains a most fascinating range of plants and animals.

Wangford Glebe: open sands were once widespread, but few remnants now remain.

Westleton Heath

Permit only; 46.8ha; NCC reserve
Sandy heathland
Access open to picnic area and rights of way
Spring, early summer

Close to DUNWICH COMMON, the reserve is a fine example of the sandy heaths, the Sandlings, which ran parallel with the sea and of which so little now remains. Woodland adds interest to the spreads of heather and bracken while the bird life includes species such as stone curlew, nightjar, red-backed shrike and woodlark.

West Stow Country Park

TL 801715; 50ha; St Edmundsbury BC
Grassland, lake and woodland
Spring, early summer

The park lies on the edge of the Breckland between King's Forest and the River Lark. Woodland, grassland and flooded old gravel workings provide a wide range of interest and there is added archaeological attraction in the reconstruction of the excavated fifth-century village.

Wolves Wood

TM 054436; 37ha; RSPB reserve
Mixed woodland
Nature trail open at all times
Leaflet from RSPB or site in summer
Spring, early summer

The general type of woodland here is coppice-with-standards, oak over hazel, with ash in the

Wolves Wood, on the wet Suffolk clays.

wetter places and field maple in the more chalky pockets. Hornbeam coppice is a feature, a shading, dense form of woodland, attractive to birds such as hawfinch. Aspen and grey willow appear where the watertable is high and newly coppiced blocks are rich in shrubs such as dogwood and guelder-rose.

The high watertable, held by impervious clays, makes this a wet wood, well supplied with ponds. Broad rides encourage the woodland plants which include some excellent shows of yellow archangel, with carpets of moss, with springtime flowers such as primrose, violet and bluebell. Ferns include broad buckler-fern with both male-fern and lady-fern and the woodland contains both early-purple orchid and common spotted-orchid, together with bird's-nest orchid and violet helleborine.

An excellent variety of woodland birds contains some six species of tit and ten of warbler, including the secretive garden warbler. Both great and lesser spotted woodpecker are present, with green woodpecker a frequent visitor. Kestrel and tawny owl are among the predators of the reserve which is made glorious in spring and early summer by the singing of a dozen or more nightingales.

The policy of coppice-with-standards management, together with the widening of glades and woodland rides, not only encourages bird life but also increases the insect life by ensuring greater variation in the woodland structure. Comma, orange-tip, red admiral and small tortoiseshell are among the numerous butterflies.

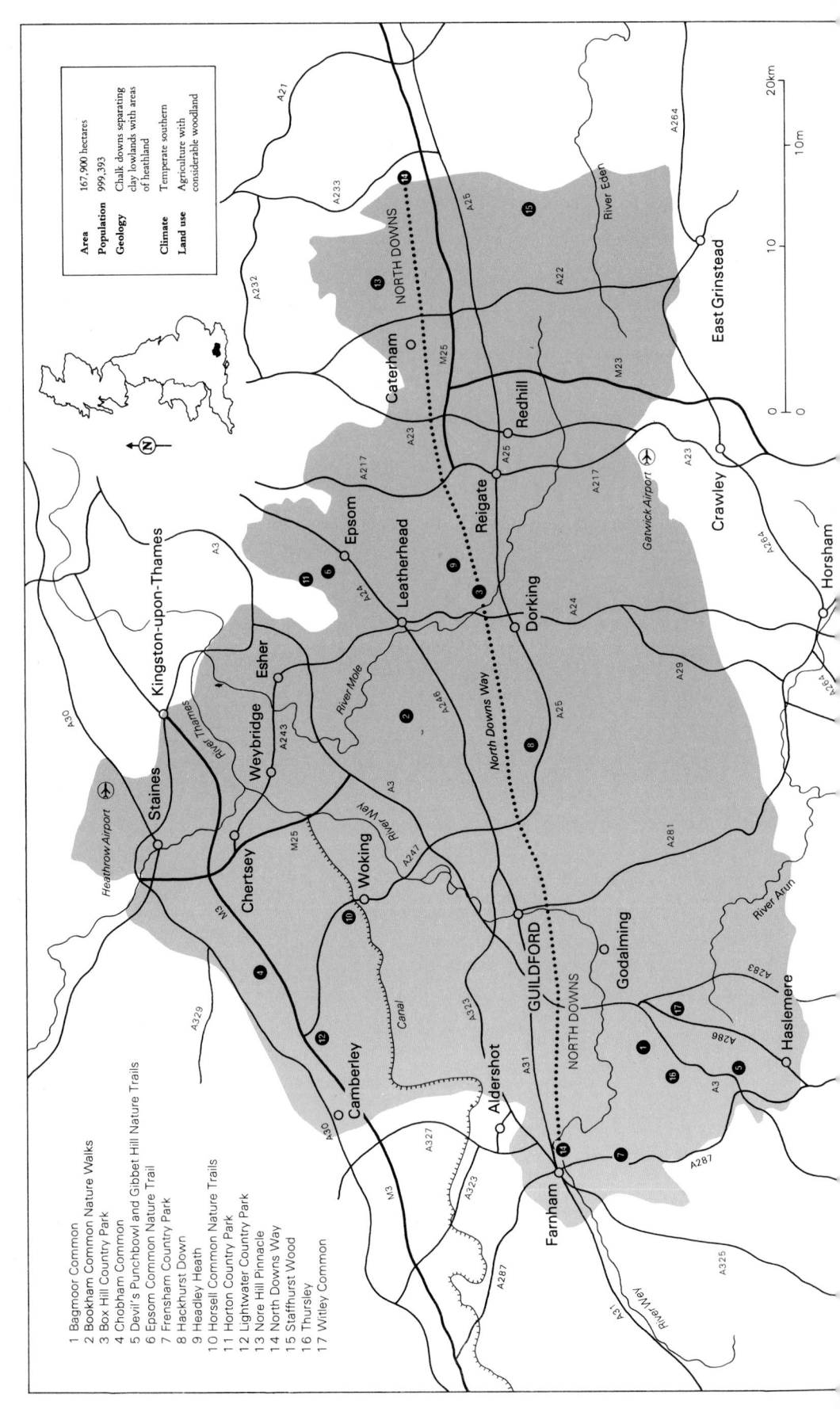

1 Bagmoor Common
2 Bookham Common Nature Walks
3 Box Hill Country Park
4 Chobham Common
5 Devil's Punchbowl and Gibbet Hill Nature Trails
6 Epsom Common Nature Trail
7 Frensham Country Park
8 Hackhurst Down
9 Headley Heath
10 Horsell Common Nature Trails
11 Horton Country Park
12 Lightwater Country Park
13 Nore Hill Pinnacle
14 North Downs Way
15 Staffhurst Wood
16 Thursley
17 Witley Common

Area	167,900 hectares
Population	999,393
Geology	Chalk downs separating clay lowlands with areas of heathland
Climate	Temperate southern
Land use	Agriculture with considerable woodland

Surrey

Surrey is not what it seems. It looks like a predominantly woodland county, just as it was for centuries past; but the abundance of trees hides the facts that about half Surrey's total area is urbanised, and that it has a higher density of population than almost any other county save the Metropolitan areas. However, this does not mean that wildlife has been squeezed out. On the contrary, much of the urbanisation includes relatively low-density, residential properties, in which wildlife is often encouraged. Moreover, many areas of industrial land include exhausted mineral workings which are often of very considerable wildlife value. For example, there are over 1000 ha of flooded gravel-pits in north Surrey alone. Together with some large and shallow reservoirs, these constitute a major wetland component, rich in wildlife and important at the national level for breeding and migrating birds. The urban areas of north Surrey have extensive parks and open spaces, and are penetrated by the radially arranged railway routes into London. These allow wildlife access well into the heavily built-up outskirts of the metropolis. The county is also traversed north–south and east–west by new motorways, the margins of which may, in the future, also prove to be important habitats and dispersal routes for plants and animals.

The more rural parts of Surrey, the south and west, are characterised by small farms and villages, abundant hedgerows and copses, small streams and ponds. There are no really extensive or unbroken areas of any single habitat; even the forestry plantations are relatively small. Thus, what characterises the landscape and wildlife of Surrey is not so much the apparent domination by trees and woods, but the extraordinary variety of small and diverse fragments, dominated by direct human influence.

These two factors, diversity and development, are interlinked. The development has been continuous for thousands of years: grazing, coppicing, digging, clearing and cultivation, and building. All have left their mark and contribute to the diversity. This in turn owes a lot to the varied geology of Surrey. The chalk hills of the North Downs form a transverse ridge right across the county. To the north are the clays and aggregates of the Thames Basin; to the south lie more sands and clays of different types, forming the Weald. In places the greensand ridge is higher than the Downs – as at Leith Hill, which (at 295m) is the highest point in south-east England. Some of the sandstones are hard enough to have been used for building purposes, and the old sandstone mines are the nearest thing in the south-east to natural caves – important sites for hibernating bats and other subterranean

life. The chalk has been quarried, mainly for making cement, leaving interesting sites for plants and insects. Removal of sand has left pits suitable for colonisation by sand martins and the little ringed plover. Digging clay for a great variety of bricks and tiles, so typical of Surrey's houses, has resulted in wet, overgrown claypits ideal for amphibians, including the great crested newt. The Weald's ironstone was at one time the basis of a major smelting industry which left a legacy of 'hammer ponds', constructed to provide a head of water to drive machinery. These tree-fringed waters, now often heavily silted up, are rich habitats for insects and the birds that feed upon them. Iron smelting was supported by extensive exploitation of coppiced woodland for charcoal, which was also needed for domestic fuel and for making gunpowder. Today large areas of woodland remain in the Weald, including much old coppice with a high content of dead wood. These are excellent sites for forest insects and mammals, the latter including deer and dormice.

The different geological deposits that underlie the Surrey landscape have given rise to very varied soils. These include clays and fertile sands, which are heavily cultivated, but also nutrient-deficient soils, ranging from very acid to very alkaline. These are of little economic value and have therefore often escaped extensive interference, leading to a rich and varied flora and fauna. This is especially true of the dry, thin and highly calcareous soils that cover the chalk. The downland turf that has developed here has its botanical specialities, including many beautiful orchid species, but it needs constant grazing to suppress the growth of taller vegetation and ultimately the spread of scrub and woodland. This process of succession shades out the smaller plants and also prevents the sun warming the soil – an important factor for the insects in this habitat, many of which are completely dependent on certain species of chalk grassland plants. In the past the grazing was by sheep and rabbits, but the latter were decimated by myxomatosis in the 1950s and 1960s and sheep farming is no longer an economic way of using the land. Consequently the maintenance of this important open downland habitat has become the responsibility of conservationists, but not before large areas have been lost to encroaching woodland.

In the west of the county, forest clearance several thousand years ago, followed by leaching of the sandy soils by rain, has created the heathlands that are perhaps Surrey's most important habitat type. The sun-warmed, well-aerated and nutrient-poor sands offer a set of environmental conditions found only here and in a few other areas of southern England. The associated flora and fauna are of particular interest and include national rarities such as the sand lizard and Dartford warbler. The heaths also have wet areas with acidic peat bogs, dominated by *Sphagnum* moss and supporting interesting plants such as the insectivorous sundews and butterwort. Shallow heathland pools are inhabited by many plants and insects (especially dragonflies) that are rare elsewhere. Like the downlands, these heaths suffer change and serious threats. There is little or no grazing now to stop the advance of birch and Scots pine scrub, and in places this process has been accelerated by conifer planting. As open spaces near to centres of population, the fragile heathlands are subject to heavy recreational use, which leads to erosion of the soft sandy soils. Fires are frequent, killing many animals and causing the development of a degraded habitat dominated by gorse or bracken. These can cope with being burnt but are less interesting than the ericaceous community that they replace. Frequent fires also mean that heather is burnt before it is old enough to form old woody clumps – the preferred habitat of sand lizards and an important source of insect food. Active conservation efforts include scrub clearance, relocation of threatened sand-lizard colonies and an attempt to re-establish the natterjack toad in suitable heathland pools.

There is only one National Nature Reserve in Surrey – THURSLEY heath and bog – but there are many small local reserves, including those managed by the Surrey Trust for Nature Conservation.

P. MORRIS

Alders

Permit only; 2ha; STNC reserve
Wet woodland
Spring, early summer

The small area of wet woodland lies within old quarry workings with the added wildlife interest of a number of pools including a sizeable colony of water-violet.

Bagmoor Common

SU 926423; 13.6ha; STNC reserve
Mixed woodland
Spring, summer

An acid woodland of birch and pine with mature oak and scrub areas, the reserve is notable for butterflies with over 23 species recorded, including white admiral and purple emperor.

Box Hill: the southern slopes of grassland and woodland, seen from Ranmore Common.

Bay Pond

No access; 6.8ha; STNC reserve
Lake and alder swamp
Can be overlooked from footpath at TQ 353516
All year

The lake is fringed with attractive wetland plants, such as marsh-marigold, yellow iris and purple-loosestrife, beneath tall stands of bulrush, together with more uncommon species such as skullcap, lesser water-parsnip and golden dock. Over 100 bird species have been recorded here, with breeding birds including little and, occasionally, great crested grebe and visiting birds such as heron, kingfisher, grey wagtail and several duck species.

Bookham Commons Nature Walks

TQ 121567; various lengths; NT
Woodland, scrub and grassland
Leaflets from the Warden, Merrit's Cottage,
Bookham Common, Leatherhead or NT
Spring, summer

The walks are set in 180ha of oakwood and scrub-invaded grassland which, with the added interest of old fishponds, holds a wealth of animal life and a range of plants in which well over 500 species have been recorded.

Box Hill Country Park

TQ 179513; 253ha; NT
Chalk downland and woodland
Spring, summer

Although it is not strictly a nature reserve, and although parts of it suffer enormous public recreational pressures, the Box Hill area of chalkland remains a dramatic and fascinating place.

The steep sweep of woodland on the slope above the River Mole gives the great shoulder of chalk its name, for it is filled with box – box and yew over young box. Among the sturdier yews, the box trees are slender trunks with long, stretching branches, adapted to trap the slightest glimmer of life-giving light. At the upper and lower woodland levels, where light strikes in most easily, smaller plants are able to survive; woodland species such as common twayblade or lime-loving plants such as deadly nightshade show beneath the trees.

The slopes beside the woodland are scrub and grassland – a scrub community of ash and birch, gorse, hawthorn and oak, wayfaring-tree, whitebeam and yew. There is open scrub over wild rose and lime-loving flowers such as marjoram, milkwort and salad burnet, horseshoe and kidney vetch and the vivid pink-rose pyramids of sainfoin. In some areas the scrub shelters species such as stinking hellebore, ploughman's-spikenard and the strange, small man orchid, while orchids of the grassland include autumn lady's-tresses with bee, musk, pyramidal and fragrant orchid.

On the plateau above, where a capping to the chalk begins to develop, woodland shows again. Beech, with oak, ash and wild cherry, stands above an understorey of holly, yew and box with a variety of other species which include large-leaved lime, over a varied ground cover of typical woodland plants. A further woodland type, ash over yew, box and elder laced with traveller's-joy, spreads above a rich-wood ground cover below the slopes of box. This complex of woodland and grassland, sometimes level, sometimes very steep, contributes much to the interest of the site.

The animals of the area include edible snail, a very large land snail imported by the Romans. Apart from any climatic consideration, it is limited to chalk or limestone areas by the need for calcium to build its shell. Butterfly species are numerous and include chalkhill blue and silver-spotted skipper.

Chobham Common

SU 965648; 198ha; SCC reserve
Wet and dry heathland
Spring, early summer

The dry heath is characterised by heather, purple moor-grass and the generally more western bristle bent, together with a considerable invasion of birch and pine. Wet areas have bog plants such as hare's-tail cottongrass and round-leaved sundew. The common is of outstanding interest for its spiders and insects, one species of ant being found nowhere else but the ISLES OF SCILLY (Cornwall), and one species of spider nowhere else in the British Isles.

Cucknells Wood

Permit only; 10ha; STNC reserve
Mixed woodland
Spring, early summer

Set on the spring-line where sandstone meets clay, the wood shows the variation from dry to damp, from more acid to enriched ground conditions which this circumstance implies. Woodland birds include marsh and willow tit with all three native woodpecker species.

Devil's Punchbowl and Gibbet Hill Nature Trails

SU 890357; 3 and 4km; NT
Two circular walks
Leaflets from site or Hon. Sec., Hindhead Committee, Littleshaw, Hindhead
Spring, summer

Superb views from the Chilterns to the South Downs together with the wildlife interest of heathland or woodland characterise these trails.

Epsom Common Nature Trail

TQ 196609; 3.5km; Epsom and Ewell BC
Circular walk in ancient common land
Leaflet from E and EBC Parks Dept
Spring, early summer

The trail passes through woodland and scrub with heathland and meadow grassland and the wetland interest of a stream-fed pond.

Frensham Country Park

SU 849406; 311ha; Waverley DC
Heath, woodland and ponds
Leaflets from interpretative centre or WDC
Spring, early summer

An example of the Surrey heaths, the country park has a range from dry heath with heather, bell heather, bracken, gorse, western gorse, birch and Scots pine to wet heath characterised by purple moor-grass, *Sphagnum* mosses and plants such as bog asphodel, white beak-sedge and round-leaved sundew. The Great and Little Ponds contain reed-beds of bulrush, yellow iris, common reed and sweet-flag which attract a variety of birds including a good population of reed warbler. A conservation trail has been laid out near the interpretative centre, and an area of land established as a nature reserve.

Godstone Reservoirs

Permit only; 18ha; STNC reserve
Two small reservoirs
Can be overlooked from footpath at TQ 362511
All year

A good variety of waterbirds may be seen on the reservoirs, with wintering duck, occasional passage migrants and breeding water and waterside birds such as great crested grebe, little ringed plover and a colony of sand martin.

Gracious Pond

Permit only; 12ha; STNC reserve
Mixed woodland
Spring, early summer

Formerly a monastic fishpond, Gracious Pond now consists mainly of dry and wet woodland above heather and its associate heathland species. A good range of dragonflies and water-associated spiders occurs.

Graeme Hendrey

Permit only; 10ha; STNC reserve
Mixed woodland
Spring, early summer

The mixed deciduous wood set within an old sand quarry makes an interesting contrast with CUCK-NELLS WOOD, which shows the transition from sandstone to damper clay. Here flowering plants include large numbers of bird's-nest orchid with a colony of common wintergreen while ferns include hart's-tongue and hard fern.

Hackhurst Down

TQ 096486; 32ha; SCC–NT reserve
Chalk downland
Spring, summer

A good chalkland plant life, including round-headed rampion and autumn lady's-tresses with more common species such as cowslip and horseshoe vetch, encourages an interesting variety of butterflies including a thriving colony of chalkhill blue.

Headley Heath

TQ 204538; 112.8ha; NT
Heathland, woodland and chalk grassland
Leaflet from NT
Spring, early summer

Slender birch scrub, with occasional rather small oak trees, banks of gorse and vivid sprays of broom, opens on long sweeps of heather and bracken heathland. Rides and pathways cut through the heath, showing the sandy soil, while a few natural hollows show a scatter of pools.

Birch scrub and gorse above great sweeps of heather typify the colourful Surrey heathlands.

Until at least the early 1930s, the site was an open spread of sheep-grazed heathland, with only a·scattering of birch. During World War II the area was used for tank-training exercises and the torn-up heath was churned into a perfect seed-bed for the tiny airborne seeds of birch. In the absence of sheep grazing, rabbits were not enough to control the spread of the trees and, in 1954, myxomatosis practically removed even that slight control on their growth. Sweeping fires were also encouraging bracken invasion and the heath looked set for complete destruction.

Fire is now used to assist the return of the heathers, for the charred birch stumps are removed from the ground and gorse and bracken mown above the height of regrowing heather until the latter is strong enough to shade out its competitors. Belts and spinneys of birch and oak are retained as windbreaks and as a habitat for heath-edge animals.

Below the heath, where the soil thins and gives way to the underlying chalkland, the scene changes dramatically. The wide horizon beyond the heath gives way to a smaller country where the curving sides of old dry valleys are thick with scrub or woodland. Blackthorn and hawthorn, dogwood, ash and yew, crab apple, holly and sycamore are tangled with wild rose and laced with swathes of traveller's-joy. With wild thyme and common rock-rose, tall mulleins, tiny milkworts, the delicate musk mallow, marjoram, eyebright, common bird's-foot-trefoil and viper's-bugloss, the grassland slopes are gardens of wild flowers.

Although the warblers and songbirds of the chalky scrub and woodland may be more obvious, many warblers breed on the heath above. Linnet, redpoll and meadow and tree pipit may be seen, together with more uncommon birds such as woodcock and nightjar. Winter flocks of goldfinch and siskin visit as well as occasional passage migrants or predators such as owls and shrikes.

A good range of butterflies includes chalkhill blue, green hairstreak and dark green fritillary with several skipper species, while there is a great variety of moths including orange underwing. This is also a noted site for Duke of Burgundy.

Headley Warren

Permit only; 31.2ha; STNC reserve
Chalk grassland and woodland
Spring, summer

The reserve lies on the slopes of a dry valley where a shallow soil has developed over the curves of chalk. Much of the woodland is coniferous plantation but areas of native woods contain yew, juniper and box with ash, buckthorn, dogwood, field maple, privet, spindle, wayfaring-tree and whitebeam. Other species include wild cherry and guelder-rose with tangles of traveller's-joy, bramble and wild rose. This variety gives a wide range of habitat from deep shade beneath the yews to well-lit grassland around the scrub. Woodland plants include yellow archangel, nettled-leaved bellflower, white and broad-leaved helleborine, woodruff and moschatel, but the greatest glory of Headley Warren lies in its herb-rich grassland.

Treecreeper, a common though often unnoticed small bird of British woods.

Here there is a pattern of colour which shows the full beauty of chalkland. Mounded anthills vary the slopes, each a cushion of small herbs such as wild thyme, sweet and hairy violet, eyebright and common bird's-foot-trefoil. The grassland itself is a mosaic of species – cowslip, common rock-rose, horseshoe and kidney vetch, yellow rattle and yellow-wort, milkwort and chalk milkwort, small scabious, clustered bellflower, marjoram, squinancywort and restharrow, wild basil and basil thyme – alive with butterflies and bees.

Here are strange small plants such as adder's-tongue and uncommon species such as wild candytuft, wild liquorice and grass vetchling. The reserve contains a splendid range of unusual plants such as the rare green hound's-tongue, while a good variety of orchids includes bee, fragrant, man and pyramidal orchid.

This profusion of plant life in a warm and sheltered site is obviously rich in insects and a butterfly list of some 35 species includes dark green and pearl-bordered fritillary, brown, green and white-letter hairstreak with Adonis blue, Duke of Burgundy and the migrant clouded yellow.

Horsell Common Nature Walks

TQ 989605, SU 002605, 007593 and 015611; each 2.4km; Horsell Common Preservation Soc.
Four varied walks
Booklet from HCPS or STNC
Spring, summer

The walks are set in 280ha of mainly sandy heathland invaded by birch and Scots pine. Wetter areas contain cross-leaved heath, cottongrasses and round-leaved sundew while the heather, bell heather, dwarf gorse and scrub attract a good range of heathland birds.

Horton Country Park

TQ 191618; 99ha; Epsom and Ewell BC
Meadowland and woodland
Leaflet from E and EBC
Spring, early summer

Since no herbicides are used, the hay meadows are rich in spring and summer flowers while the woodlands and hedges attract birds such as treecreeper, blackcap and chiffchaff.

Lightwater Country Park

SU 921622; 48ha; Surrey Heath BC
Woodland, heathland and wetland
Leaflet from SHBC
Spring, early summer

A nature trail has been laid out in the park which shows the habitat range from Scots pine and mixed woodland, through gorse and heather heathland, wet acid heath and bog, with *Sphagnum*, bog asphodel, cross-leaved heath, round-leaved sundew and purple moor-grass, to open pools fringed with bog myrtle where mallard, coot and moorhen feed.

Moor Park

No access; 6.8ha; STNC reserve
Wet alder woodland
Can be overlooked from footpath at SU 867459
Spring, early summer

The deep alder swamp lies in a curve of the River Wey. Rich in characteristic plant species, such as sedges, in spring it is filled with the sound of small songbirds. Breeding species include water rail.

Nore Hill Pinnacle

TQ 378576; 0.2ha; SCC reserve
Geological site
All year

The chalk pinnacle is of great geological interest as an example of a form of weathering unique in the British Isles.

North Downs Way

SU 844467–TQ 429561; 72km; CC
Long-distance way
Booklet from CC or HMSO bookshops
Spring, summer

Starting from Farnham and ending at Dover in Kent, the way mainly follows the crests of the downland in Surrey, with spectacular views across the lower farmland and with all the colour and beauty of chalk turf and wood-land.

Seale Chalk Pit: plants recolonise the quarry.

Nower Wood

Permit only; 43.3ha; STNC reserve
Mixed woodland
Spring, early summer

Nower Wood has long been noted for its show of spring flowers, particularly for its spread of bluebell. The wood has been much altered from its natural state, with planted species such as sweet chestnut and rhododendron, Scots pine, larch and Norway spruce, but it still contains a fine range of native trees and shrubs which, with its different soils and varying wetness, make it so fascinating.

The hill on which the wood is set is an outlier of acid sands and gravels mounded on chalk and capped by clay with flints. Five ponds provide open water and marshy areas.

The lower areas, on or near the chalk, are characterised by trees, such as ash, beech, field maple, wild cherry and yew, and show typical rich-wood plants including enchanter's-nightshade, bugle, woodruff and yellow archangel.

Hornbeam and wood-sorrel indicate the change through birch, sweet chestnut, holly over bramble, bracken and bluebell to the birch, oak, holly, honeysuckle and bracken which characterise the higher acid woodland. Rowan, a typical acid-loving tree, is also present. Where the clay with flints is damp, small bright plants such as yellow pimpernel flourish and the wetter areas may contain spreads of willow swamp with wetland plants such as soft rush and lesser spearwort. Ash, too, enjoys the wetland edge and the pools form an unexpected feature this high up the hill.

Pools where dragonflies breed add to the habitat range at Thursley.

The largest, topmost, pond is overlooked by a hide, which also overlooks the swamp below, an ideal spot for woodland clearing birds such as spotted flycatcher. The evening visitor might see a roe deer or a mallard at the willow-fringed water-side, watch the day-flying insects slow and the songbirds settle to rest as moths appear, and hear a nightingale's song across the pool.

Badger live in the wood and some 35 species of breeding birds have been recorded. There are interesting populations of dragonfly and a good range of moths and butterflies.

Ripszam's Wood

Permit only; 13.2ha; STNC reserve
Woodland and grassland
Spring, early summer

Oak and ash stand above hazel coppice, now being restored by active management, which together with a block of hornbeam contains a wide range of woodland plants including species such as common centaury and broad-leaved helleborine, unusual in Wealden clay woodlands but present here due to seams of palludina limestone. A good range of scrub and woodland bird life may be seen, together with butterflies such as white admiral, purple emperor and dark green, silver-washed and small pearl-bordered fritillary.

Seale Chalk Pit

Permit only; 1.2ha; STNC reserve
Disused chalk quarry
Spring, summer

The small quarry is being recolonised by chalkland plants including both bee and fly orchid, and its sunny position on the southern flank of the Hog's Back encourages a good variety of butterflies.

Staffhurst Wood

TQ 412483; 38ha; SCC reserve
Mixed woodland
Spring, early summer

Old oak pollards, hornbeam coppice and some fine wild service-trees indicate that this is probably an ancient woodland relict, a remnant of the old Weald clay forests. Oak and beech are the main standards above a varied ground cover, with the continuity of woodland here ensuring a habitat for an excellent variety of insects.

Thundry Meadows

Permit only; 15.2ha; STNC reserve
Damp and wet meadowland, some woodland
Bog areas are dangerous
Spring, summer

A variety of wetland habitats contains a fine range of plants including bogbean and fen bedstraw, common marsh-bedstraw and marsh cinquefoil, with petty whin and dyer's greenweed, with heath spotted-orchid and early marsh-orchid. Butterflies include woodland species such as purple emperor and pearl-bordered fritillary.

Thursley

SU 900399; 250ha; NCC reserve
Bog, heath and woodland
Leaflet from NCC
Spring, early summer

Like Thomas Hardy's Egdon Heath, this is a wild and mysterious place when mists and darkness spread across the bog. Broad-leaved forest once covered the Surrey heathlands, forest which early man burned and felled for arable land and grazing

387

– eventually the sandy soil became exhausted and heathland took over the farmland. Sheep, of course, still grazed, cropping seedlings as they grew, but when the grazing ceased in the early twentieth century birch and Scots pine invaded the open heath.

The dry heath is coloured with heather, bell heather, gorse and dwarf gorse, with areas of sand and stands of birch. Wetter heath is characterised by purple moor-grass grading into bog where *Sphagnum* mosses spread beneath cross-leaved heath and common cottongrass, where southern marsh-orchid shows in early summer and fascinating bog plants grow. The wet heath and the bog afford habitat for bog asphodel, white and brown beak-sedge, cranberry and both oblong-leaved and round-leaved sundew, while the open pools within the bog are rich in species such as bogbean, lesser bladderwort, bottle sedge and marsh St John's-wort.

The range of woodland, heath and bog is rich in bird life with over 140 species recorded. Some 65 breed on the reserve, with good numbers of redstart, with locally uncommon species such as curlew and with national rarities such as Dartford warbler. The heath is noted as a raptor site with records of 10 different species of falcon or hawk, including breeding sparrowhawk and kestrel, regular visiting hen harrier and occasional Montagu's harrier, merlin, osprey and peregrine. Great grey shrike are regular winter visitors.

Somewhere between 5000 and 10,000 insect species are present, including both silver-studded blue and grayling butterflies and the heather-feeding emperor moth. Of outstanding interest to entomologists, the reserve contains no fewer than 26 dragonfly species, probably more than any other single site in southern Britain.

Vann Lake

Permit only; 11.2ha; STNC reserve
Lake and woodland
All year

The old hammer pond is surrounded by mixed mainly deciduous woodland including wild service-tree, with a good ground cover of plants such as bluebell, primrose, common cow-wheat, early-purple orchid and common spotted-orchid. There is an exceptional variety of fungi, including over 560 species, one unknown to science before its discovery in 1973. Over 100 bird species have been recorded including waterbirds on the lake and songbirds such as nightingale in the woodland.

Witley Common

SU 936409; 150ha; NT
Large area of typical Surrey heathland
Nature trail leaflets from information centre
Spring, early summer

Great spreads of woodland and heather heathland demonstrate the plants and animals characteristic of the area, including heather, bell heather and gorse, whinchat and stonechat, together with adder and heathland insects.

Sand lizard, one of the rarest of our native reptiles.

Sussex

A great horseshoe-shaped rim of chalk hills encompasses an area in south east England called the Weald. Some 55km long by 23km broad, it comprises a large part of Kent and Surrey and almost the whole of Sussex (now administratively divided into East and West). Its long axis runs approximately WNW–ESE; the south east corner, isolated some 8000 years ago by the formation of the English Channel, now forms the Bas Boulonnais in the country around Calais. The Wealden geology conspires to make Sussex a region of strong contrasts, covering downland, sandstone hills, clay vales and alluvial plains.

The chalk hills of the South Downs rise from the sea to form an impressive line of cliffs, the SEVEN SISTERS, some 11km long between BEACHY HEAD in the east and SEAFORD HEAD in the west. West of Brighton the Downs swing inland until at the Hampshire border their southern edge lies about 10km from the sea. In a letter dated 1773 and written during one of his frequent visits to Sussex, the famous naturalist Gilbert White describes the South Downs as 'that chain of majestic mountains'. Impressive though they are, the Downs can hardly be dignified as mountains since at only three points do they exceed 260m! The range extends for over 90km from Beachy Head to the county boundary, and is broken up into five blocks by four rivers that breach the escarpment: from east to west the Cuckmere, the Ouse, the Adur and the Arun. East of the Arun the Downs are largely unwooded, while to the west lie large areas of fine beechwoods as well as more recent conifer plantations.

In 1761 a farmer from Hartfield near the Kent border moved to Glynde where he set about improving the polled, black-faced, speckled-legged sheep of the eastern Downs to produce what was to become the most famous of all breeds of sheep, the Southdown. The close-cropped turf of the southern chalk must be among the richest botanical habitats in Europe – it is possible to find more than 20 different species of flowering plant in a piece of ground 30cm square. Many of these, such as round-headed rampion and early spider-orchid, are confined to the southern chalk in Britain. The insects are no less exciting and include the now rare and threatened Adonis blue butterfly, whose caterpillar feeds on another chalk plant, horseshoe vetch.

Sheep farming has progressively declined on the Downs since World War I and much old downland pasture has been converted to arable land, much of it used for intensive barley production. Other areas of abandoned sheep walk are rapidly becoming invaded by coarse grasses and scrub. A survey by the Nature Conservancy Council has revealed that between 20 and 25 per cent of the area of old chalk grassland in the two counties has been lost in recent years.

North of the South Downs the Weald comprises a complicated series of alternating clays and sandstones. They culminate in the forest ridges of the High Weald, dominated by the large expanse of ASHDOWN FOREST, the biggest single tract of undeveloped countryside in southern England east of the New Forest. Lowland heath is one of the most rapidly disappearing of all habitats in western Europe, and the 25 sq. km of heath, bog and valley woodlands which represent the remains of John of Gaunt's medieval royal park are protected by their own Act of Parliament.

The Weald has traditionally produced the finest oaks in the kingdom, and East and West Sussex still form the most wooded area of almost the least wooded country in Europe. The wooded, deep, steep-sided rocky ravines of the High Weald, known locally as ghylls, are more reminiscent of Welsh oakwoods or parts of Exmoor than the

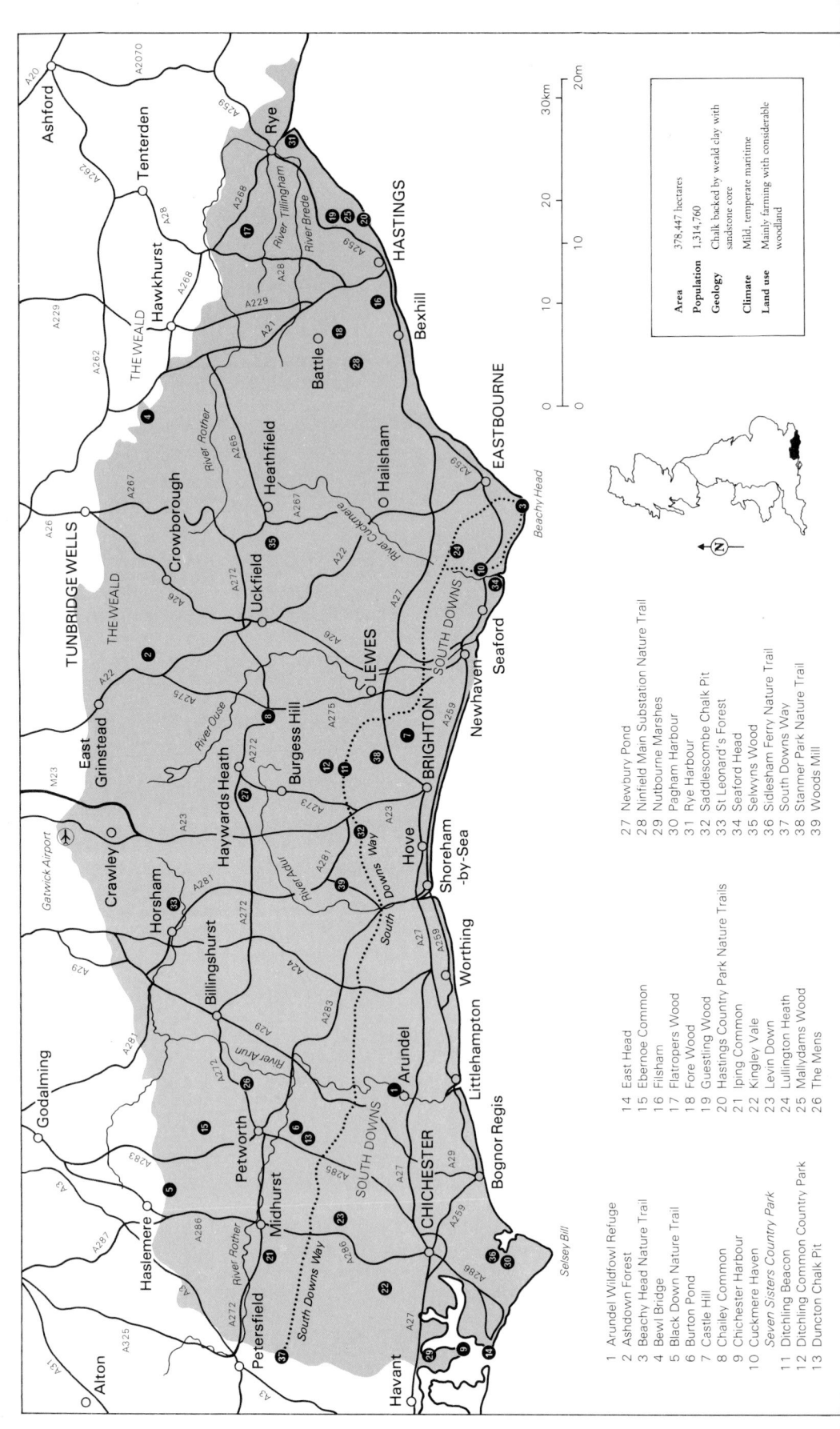

Area	378,447 hectares
Population	1,314,760
Geology	Chalk backed by weald clay with sandstone core
Climate	Mild, temperate maritime
Land use	Mainly farming with considerable woodland

20km

30km

20m

Ashford
A2070
A20
A262
Tenterden
A28
A28
Hawkhurst
A268
A268
A229
A262
THE WEALD
A26
TUNBRIDGE WELLS
Rye
A259
A268
River Tillingham
River Brede
17
19
25
20
HASTINGS
A28
A229
A21
16
Bexhill
A259
18
Battle
28
River Rother
Heathfield
A267
A265
A267
A272
River Cuckmere
Hailsham
EASTBOURNE
A259
Beachy Head
3
Crowborough
THE WEALD
A26
Uckfield
35
A22
A272
24
10
34
Seaford
SOUTH DOWNS
Newhaven
LEWES
A26
A259
East Grinstead
2
A22
A275
River Ouse
A272
Burgess Hill
8
7
BRIGHTON
12
11
38
Hove
Shoreham-by-Sea
Haywards Heath
A272
27
A273
32
South Downs Way
A23
Worthing
M23
Gatwick Airport
Crawley
A23
33
Horsham
A281
River Adur
39
A281
A27
A269
Littlehampton
Billingshurst
A24
A272
A29
Bognor Regis
River Arun
A283
Arundel
1
SOUTH DOWNS
Godalming
A3
A283
A286
15
Petworth
26
6
13
A285
CHICHESTER
A27
A29
A259
Haslemere
A287
5
A286
Midhurst
23
A286
A259
Selsey Bill
Alton
A31
A325
Petersfield
21
37
River Rother
A272
22
South Downs Way
29
30
39
9
14
A27
A3
Havant

1 Arundel Wildfowl Refuge
2 Ashdown Forest
3 Beachy Head Nature Trail
4 Bewl Bridge
5 Black Down Nature Trail
6 Burton Pond
7 Castle Hill
8 Chailey Common
9 Chichester Harbour
10 Cuckmere Haven
  Seven Sisters Country Park
11 Ditchling Beacon
12 Ditchling Common Country Park
13 Duncton Chalk Pit

14 East Head
15 Ebernoe Common
16 Filsham
17 Flatropers Wood
18 Fore Wood
19 Guestling Wood
20 Hastings Country Park Nature Trails
21 Iping Common
22 Kingley Vale
23 Levin Down
24 Lullington Heath
25 Mallydams Wood
26 The Mens

27 Newbury Pond
28 Ninfield Main Substation Nature Trail
29 Nutbourne Marshes
30 Pagham Harbour
31 Rye Harbour
32 St Leonard's Forest
33 Saddlescombe Chalk Pit
34 Seaford Head
35 Selwyns Wood
36 Sidlesham Ferry Nature Trail
37 South Downs Way
38 Stanmer Park Nature Trail
39 Woods Mill

populous south east. The similarity does not end there as they contain an extraordinary assemblage of both animals and plants, such as hay-scented buckler-fern and Tunbridge filmy-fern, that are far more characteristic of the oceanic west and are probably persisting in the south east as relics of the Atlantic forest period of 5000–6000 years ago.

The Weald clay country of West Sussex still has hundreds of hectares of mature oak forest including several well-known woodland nature reserves such as THE MENS and EBERNOE COMMON. These are the stronghold of many of Britain's rarest woodland butterflies, and the beautiful wild service-tree is a characteristic feature.

In common with other parts of the British coastline, the Sussex coast has experienced major changes in sea level over the last thousand years or so. In the extreme east the county boundary ends in that most extraordinary of British coastal features, the vast shingle expanse of the Dungeness foreland. As one travels eastwards the coastline is punctuated by a series of alluvial flats, each dissec-

ted by extensive systems of drainage dykes. Starting with the western edge of Romney Marsh and the area around Camber Castle south of Rye, this is followed by the Pevensey Levels to the east of Eastbourne and then the flood plains of the Sussex rivers: the Lewes Brooks, Adur Levels and AMBERLEY WILD BROOKS. With the reclamation and deterioration of areas such as the Somerset Levels and the Norfolk Broads these areas are now among the last remaining strongholds of our wetland flora and fauna.

Sussex is a county of paradoxes. In the north the tentacles of Gatwick Airport, with its attendant sprawl of industries, reach out into the countryside of the Sussex–Surrey borders. Sussex's 150km of coastline, with its holiday beaches and marinas, are the most developed in the British Isles. Yet the Weald itself, notwithstanding its proximity to London, can be counted among some of the last unspoiled landscapes in England.

DAVID STREETER

Amberley Wild Brooks

Permit only; 5ha; STNC reserve
Rich flood meadows
All year

The reserve and surrounding areas are of most interest to birdwatchers in winter, with good numbers of Bewick's swan, pintail, shoveler, teal and wigeon. However in spring and summer the ditches are filled with arrowhead, bladderwort and frogbit.

Arundel Wildfowl Refuge

TQ 020081; 24ha; WT
Open water, wet grassland and reedbed
Information from entrance building or WT
All year

Many birds are attracted to the wild area where a lake, wader scrape, reedbed and two marshy fields may be viewed from the observation hides. Lapwing, redshank and teal breed, and passage birds include regular common and green sandpiper and greenshank. Winter duck may include many pochard, teal and tufted duck, shoveler and wigeon, together with bittern, bearded tit and Cetti's warbler.

Ashdown Forest

TQ 432324; 2560ha; Conservators of Ashdown Forest
Heathland and woodland
Spring, summer

This wide area of High Weald heathland, once a royal hunting forest, is a splendid mosaic of dry, damp and wet heathland with valley mires, streams, scrub and woodland. Reduced grazing has accelerated the spread of woodland and accidental fires may help the invasion of bracken, but fine heather moorland still remains, typically with

bell heather in the drier areas and cross-leaved heath marking the damper sites. Gorse and dwarf gorse add colour to the open moorland stretches where purple moor-grass varies the stands of heather and, here and there, creeping willow, sawwort, petty whin and dodder may be found.

The wetter sites, where *Sphagnum* mosses grow, are also defined by common cottongrass, bog asphodel and round-leaved sundew, while some iron-rich mires contain fen bedstraw and marsh fern, and stream-cut gullies may hold not only sheltered narrow woodlands but also lemonscented fern and hay-scented buckler-fern. The woodlands themselves are considerably varied and

White admiral butterfly, the Sussex Trust emblem.

From Black Down, the view towards Telegraph Hill.

include invasive birch, oak, willow and Scots pine with alder and alder buckthorn by some of the streams and areas where woodland, often beech, was enclosed against grazing pressure in earlier years.

Animals include an important population of fallow deer with badger, fox, stoat, weasel and typical small mammals together with a wide range of birds. Woodland birds – blackcap, willow warbler and nightingale, for instance – sing in the scrub, while woodcock may be seen at dawn or dusk, when nightjar may hawk after insects. Predators include kestrel, sparrowhawk and an occasional pair of hobbies.

The wet heaths provide breeding sites for a fine range of dragonflies, and the forest as a whole is rich in such insects as silver-studded blue, grayling, dark green, pearl-bordered, small pearl-bordered and silver-washed fritillary butterflies and the emperor moth, a feature of the heathlands.

The forest is a splendid refuge for a wealth of wildlife and makes a magnificent contrast with the heavy clays of the Lower Weald and the dry chalk of the Downs.

Beachy Head Nature Trail

TV 586956; 2km; Eastbourne BC
Coastal chalk downland
Leaflet from natural history centre at site or EBC
Spring, early summer

The circular trail demonstrates the fascination of this spectacular chalk headland with its range of plants from kidney vetch to wayfaring-tree, and chalkland butterflies including five species of blue.

Bewl Bridge

No access; 51.4ha; SWA reserve
Part of Bewl Bridge Reservoir
Reserve may be overlooked from TQ 678318
and other rights of way
Leaflets from visitor centre at TQ 676337
Autumn, winter

Passage waders may be seen on the mud when the water level falls in autumn, while winter waterfowl include mallard, pochard, teal, tufted duck and wigeon with shoveler and great crested grebe.

Black Down Nature Trail

SU 921309; 2.4km; NT
Woodland and grassland walk
Leaflet from Haslemere Educational Museum
and bookshops
Spring, summer

The trail, on the highest point in West Sussex, leads through woods of Scots pine and oak where fallow and roe deer are resident. Meadow pipit, linnet and yellowhammer may be seen outside the woods, where there are magnificent views of the South Downs.

Burton Pond

SU 979180; 31.2ha; WSCC–STNC reserve
Lake, wood, heath and bog
Leaflet from WSCC
All year

Extensive reedbeds, containing lesser bulrush, branched bur-reed and cowbane at its only Sussex locality, stand around a lake bright with yellow water-lily. To the west, birchwoods slope down to a wet alder wood and the lake margins. On the other side Black Hole, an alder carr, has been bridged by a viewing causeway. The higher ground is mostly covered by birch heath. Teal, tufted duck, great crested and little grebe, water rail and reed and sedge warbler all breed. Many pochard are present in winter.

Castle Hill

TQ 367074; 45ha; NCC reserve
Fine chalk grassland
Permit only off public footpath
Leaflet from NCC
Spring, summer

Superb chalkland flowers include dropwort, yellow-wort and small scabious with field fleawort, chalk milkwort and round-headed rampion. Corn bunting, meadow pipit and skylark breed on the slopes, while scrub contains linnet, whitethroat and yellowhammer. Many chalkland butterflies are attracted to this warm, sheltered spot.

Chailey Common

TQ 386210; 173ha; ESCC reserve
Wet and dry heath
Spring, early summer

Despite invading bracken, heathland plants still include all three common heathers, tormentil, heath milkwort and petty whin. Scrub birch and woodland encourage a variety of birds.

Chailey Warren

Permit only; 2.5ha; STNC reserve
Damp and dry heath
Early September

The reserve protects a population of marsh gentian which flowers in early autumn.

Chichester Harbour

SU 775005; 1200ha; Chichester Harbour
Conservancy
Huge area of deeps, tidal mudflats and islands
All year

Twenty thousand dunlin can't be wrong: Chichester Harbour is fascinating in winter. At high tide the rising waters drive the birds off the mudflats to huddle, thousands strong, on roosts such as Thorney Island where they stand, head to wind, waiting until their feeding grounds are uncovered again.

The tide fills and drains through the channel east of Hayling Island where EAST HEAD lies like an opened door, a narrow spit of sand dunes. It is, indeed, a door which has been opened by tide and storm. In the late 1780s the land lay almost out to Hayling Island but, slowly, since that time, it has been worn back north and eastwards: the spur of East Head has swung back as if it were on a hinge.

East Head and NUTBOURNE MARSHES between them hold examples of much of the habitat of the harbour. The main habitat is the huge area of estuary muds, the lime-rich silts which hold the wealth of marine worms, molluscs and crustaceans that feed the winter waders. The mudflats also form low-tide grazing meadows where dark-bellied Brent geese feed on the eel-grass and *Enteromorpha* spreads. The geese fly in from their frozen breeding grounds in Arctic Russia and Siberia – some 8000 birds may be seen within the harbour. Large numbers of redshank, curlew, bar-tailed and black-tailed godwit, grey plover and sanderling may be present, with several thousand shelduck, with wigeon, mallard, pintail and teal, and with goldeneye and red-breasted merganser diving in the channels. Severe weather may see pochard and tufted duck fly in from the frozen gravelpits inland or, perhaps, a flock of white-fronted geese, spiralling down on to the mudflats.

The plant life of the Nutbourne Marshes mud is mainly restricted to eel-grass, the green alga *Enteromorpha* and common cord-grass, but East Head contains a number of interesting and typical plants. The saltmarsh is characterised by glasswort, sea-lavender, thrift and sea aster which grade into duneland sea bindweed and evening-primrose. Sea couch, marram, lyme-grass and sea rocket show in the open dunes, while specialities such as golden samphire and sea-heath also occur.

Breeding birds include common and Sandwich tern, and the only Sussex breeding colony of black-headed gull, together with ringed plover, redshank and shelduck. Smaller birds include a good population of reed bunting, and two woodlands nearby contain heronries.

The interest of the harbour is increased by its continuity with LANGSTONE HARBOUR (Hampshire). Together they form the largest area of estuarine mudflats on the south coast of Britain, of exceptional importance to wintering waders and wildfowl.

Black-tailed godwit on the tidal mud.

Cuckmere Haven

TV 519995; 392ha; ESCC–Lewes DC
Chalkland estuary, cliffs and downland
Leaflets from visitor centre, ESCC or LDC
Spring, summer

If you look towards Beachy Head from the western side of the Haven, some of the finest chalk coastland in the country lies before you. Rank upon rank of smoothly curving hillsides have been guillotined to form sheer white cliffs, the Seven Sisters, topped by a close green turf; below, the Haven itself is a wide meadow valley where the old river meanders form winding pools beside the now straightened course of the River Cuckmere. The SEVEN SISTERS COUNTRY PARK and the SEAFORD HEAD reserve make up the area called Cuckmere Haven.

After the last ice age the hills lay inland, higher above the deep-cut valley than now. They formed a barrier, between the thawing land and the sea, which was sculpted by the driving rush of water. Whereas rain now sinks fast through the porous chalk, at that time the chalk itself was frozen solid, so that rivers must have run on the surface to cut the hanging valleys. The sea was further south, and some 30m lower, so that the cutting effect was considerable and, in the case of the main valley, sliced deep into the hills to form the basis of the shape of the present Haven. As the sea rose towards its modern level, the deep channel became silted up. On evidence from similar estuaries, the valley is floored by bare chalk beneath a layer of flinty pebbles washed down from inland; above is a bed of peat which developed when the meltwater torrent slowed to leave a wide valley of swampland, and above the peat are the rich alluvial silts of the present meadows, the freshwater marshes and the spread of saltmarsh.

The rising sea level also brought the tides against the hills of the Seven Sisters and began to cut back the chalk. From the cliff top, when the tide and light are right, a wide spread of milky shallows indicates the wave-cut platform, the planed-off chalk of earlier hills beneath the present cliffs; the valleys which sloped towards the sea have been undercut, left hanging above a spectacular wall of chalk, and form one of the finest examples in the country of dry valleys cut back by marine erosion.

A shingle bank has been thrown up in the mouth of the Haven, formed mainly from flints which have washed out of the chalk; the bank provides a habitat for sea beet, yellow horned-poppy and sea-kale, and behind it an islanded lagoon provides nesting sites for ringed plover and common tern. The lagoon and the marshland beyond are a feeding point for migrant waders and winter wildfowl, while the marsh holds glasswort, sea aster, sea-purslane and sea wormwood, and the alluvial grassland adder's-tongue and marsh-mallow.

Chalk grassland curves up from the valley floor and caps the cliffs, a pattern of short and tall, species-rich swards, varied by shallow scrub, which stretches to Beachy Head. Early-purple and pyramidal orchid, common spotted-orchid and autumn gentian occur among typical chalkland salad burnet, common centaury, carline and dwarf thistle, squinancywort and wild thyme, while deeper grassland holds wild carrot, wild mignonette, viper's-bugloss, weld, yellow rattle and red bartsia.

Smooth curves of chalkland: the Cuckmere Valley below Firle Beacon.

Autumn gentian is one of the treasures of the chalk grassland of Cuckmere Haven.

heron, mute swan and shelduck are commonly to be seen, and winter brings further waterbirds such as little grebe, mallard, teal, tufted duck and wigeon.

Throughout the year this is a richly fascinating site, a haven for winter wildfowl, a landfall for migrants and a place of summer flowers. It is a place of contrasts, too, acid enough above Seaford Head for such insects as emperor and oak eggar moths, rich enough on the downland for chalkhill blue butterflies; the dry chalk slopes contrast with the water meadows below, and there is a further range of contrast between the saltmarsh and shingle ridge. The Haven provides a superb complex of habitats and is further adorned by an information centre in the Country Park, which publishes an excellent Park Trail guide and is possibly unique in possessing an informal reference library.

Ditchling Beacon

TQ 329133; 19.6ha; STNC reserve
Steep chalk grass and scrub
Spring, summer

A very steep north-facing scarp of the South Downs: from the top of the reserve there are enormous views clear across the Weald to the far North Downs. An excellent range of plants covers the slope, from rougher grassland above to lime-loving species on the thinnest soils, while scrub provides cover for bird life and grades into young ash woodland. Butterflies include chalkhill blue and brown Argus.

Ditchling Common Country Park

TQ 336181; 76ha; ESCC
Wealden common
Leaflet from site or ESCC
Spring, early summer

Oak woodland, scrub, spreads of gorse and bracken-filled grassland are supplemented by a sizeable lake. Spring brings a fine show of bluebell and wood anemone to contrast with tall bulrush round the lake. Birds include blackcap, chiffchaff, stonechat and linnet while butterflies include small pearl-bordered fritillary and green hairstreak.

Only three of the Seven Sisters lie wholly within the Country Park, but the coastal footpath runs on to Beachy Head and within this length of the highest chalk cliffs in Britain are several unusual plants. Field fleawort, burnt orchid and round-headed rampion bring splashes of colour to the grassland while coastal plants such as rock sea-lavender and sea radish may be found. Moon carrot, least lettuce and small hare's-ear occur, the last found elsewhere in mainland Britain only on the limestone cliffs of Devon.

Jackdaw, herring gull and fulmar nest on the cliffs, meadow pipit and skylark on the grassland, while the scrub, particularly on Seaford Head, is rich in small birds. This western side of the Haven is capped with glacial deposits of sand and mud which are deep enough to allow dense scrub to develop, important shelter for many migrants. Resident species include stonechat while spring brings redstart, blackcap, chiffchaff, common and lesser white-throat, grasshopper and willow warbler and a host of passage birds. Ring ouzel and pied flycatcher pass through, en route for the moors and western woodlands, while more uncommon visitors might include bluethroat and ortolan bunting, red-breasted flycatcher, hoopoe and wryneck.

In autumn the migrants rest on their return passage. Waders using the river as a migration route may pause to feed on the marshes or visit the lagoon and river meanders, where cormorant,

Duncton Chalk Pit

SU 961162; 2.4ha; STNC reserve
Disused chalk quarry
Spring, summer

Chalk woodland and scrub contain such interesting species as narrow-leaved everlasting-pea and wild liquorice.

East Head

SZ 765985; 30.4ha; NT
Dunes, saltmarsh and sandy foreshore
Leaflet from NT
All year

Part of CHICHESTER HARBOUR.

Ebernoe Common

SU 976278; 71.6ha; STNC reserve
Ancient beech–oak woodland
Spring, early summer

A fine example of high-forest woodland, the common contains many huge old beech trees with younger oak woodland, an area of scrub and old ponds. This variation encourages a good range of birds including nightingale and woodcock, and of insects including white admiral, purple emperor and silver-washed fritillary.

Filsham

No access; 17.1ha; Hastings BC–STNC reserve
Wetland
Reserve may be overlooked from right of way at
TQ 775098
All year

The area of reedbed, water meadows and drainage ditches is rich in spring and summer with arrowhead, yellow iris, marsh-marigold, water mint and water-soldier. Passage and winter waterbirds, including mallard, shoveler, teal, wigeon, snipe and jack snipe, ensure the year-round interest of the site.

Flatropers Wood

TQ 862229; 34.8ha; STNC reserve
Mixed woodland
Spring, early summer

Mainly oak, with birch and coppiced sweet chestnut over bluebell, bramble and honeysuckle, the reserve contains many characteristic woodland birds and has good populations of pearl-bordered and small pearl-bordered fritillary.

The fine spread of heathland at Iping Common.

Fore Wood

TQ 756128; 55ha; RSPB reserve
Mixed woodland
Spring, early summer

Where NAP WOOD is an acid central Wealden woodland and THE MENS a fine high forest on Wealden clays, Fore Wood is an interesting mix on clay and sands, like neither reserve but with echoes of both. Sweet chestnut flourishes on the sandstone areas, while richer clays carry a more varied plant life under hornbeam.

From a study of the plants it seems likely that Fore Wood is a primary woodland site, that woodland cover has been maintained, although much altered by management, for very many years. Later management, until shortly after World War II, consisted of coppice with standards, where hornbeam and sweet chestnut were coppiced beneath a spread of standard oaks. When this was discontinued the coppiced stools crowded the wood to produce a dense block of trees which depressed the growth of the woodland floor. Management now is concentrated on opening up the wood, recoppicing and letting in the light.

Roughly half the reserve is sweet chestnut coppice, a fast-growing tree probably imported by the Romans for its crop of edible nuts. Oak and birch occur rather sparsely throughout the area, while the dense shade and slow decomposing leaf litter limit the ground cover to spring bluebell and wood anemone with a later spread of bracken, bramble and ivy. By contrast the hornbeam coppice is much more varied. The spring show of flowers is chiefly wood anemone and the ground cover is later mainly honeysuckle, bramble and ivy, but oak standards are more plentiful and the hornbeam coppice is varied with ash, aspen, birch, field maple and grey willow. Other smaller areas include blocks of scrub, of alder, of oakwood, with standard and coppiced oak, of mixed woodland with an understorey of blackthorn, hawthorn, hazel and holly, elder, wild rose and guelder-rose over dog's mercury, yellow archangel and pendulous sedge.

An attractive facet of the reserve is its steep-cut ghylls, tree-lined along the stream bed and rich in ferns and mosses. An artificial pond, too, adds to the interest and, although much of the woodland floor is shaded and poor in species, small numbers of primrose, woodruff, wood spurge, wood-sorrel, moschatel and early dog-violet add to the springtime show. Orchids include early-purple, common spotted-orchid, common twayblade and broad-leaved helleborine, while among other interesting plants are tutsan and butcher's-broom.

The birds are chiefly those of woodland, woodland edge and scrub; they include some six species of tit, all three native woodpeckers, nuthatch, treecreeper and tawny owl. Hawfinch have probably bred in some years and sparrowhawk have certainly done so. Many other species should breed in or visit the reserve as the habitat range is further increased by sympathetic management.

Guestling Wood

TQ 863144; 12.4ha; WdT
Mixed woodland
Spring, early summer

The varied woodland includes areas which are to be allowed to develop to high forest to contrast with the sweet chestnut coppicing which has been the traditional management.

Hastings Country Park Nature Trails

TQ 860118; various lengths; Hastings BC
Sandstone sea cliffs, valleys and heathland
Leaflets from interpretative centre or HBC
Spring, early summer

The trails are laid out variously to demonstrate the interest of the cliffs where seabirds nest, the gorse and heather heathland, and the cool, damp, fern-rich glens or valleys.

Hooe Common

Permit only; 1.7ha; STNC reserve
Small area of marsh
Spring, summer

The marshland includes a variety of typical and attractive plants together with an interesting range of wetland insects.

Iping Common

SU 853220; 77ha; WSCC
Dry and wet heathland
Spring, summer

The common is a heathland, developed on acid sands. The thin cover of peaty soil supports spreads of heather and bell heather, mosses and lichens, with bracken on the drier banks – a splendid rolling pattern of colour which grades into woodland on its southern edge.

Lying beside the busy A272, Iping Common is highly susceptible to fire. Woodland, of course, would be the natural climax here, and seedling birches demonstrate how readily the change might come. Heather and bracken can both survive burning, due to their deep-buried roots, and bare ground is quickly recolonised by mosses and plants such as sheep's sorrel, forming a bright mosaic of colour until the taller plants grow up again. Large-scale fires can, however, deplete the populations of ground insects, amphibians and reptiles unable to move quickly to unburnt areas. Burning of the vegetation also reduces the habitat available for nesting birds in the first few years of recovery.

Small pockets of bog have developed in the dips and hollows of the common, marked by the white plumes of hair's-tail cottongrass, by the paler purple where cross-leaved heath takes over from bell heather and by clumps of sedges and rushes and tussocks of purple moor-grass. The wettest places are vivid with *Sphagnum* mosses and plumed with common cottongrass. The bogs and pools provide a fascinating contrast with the drier parts of the common, where fine grasses and small plants such as tormentil and heath bedstraw line the edges of the paths and where the sands show a hard bright sparkle – a clue to the problems of surviving in such an arid environment.

The plant life, however, modifies the dryness, giving shade and shelter to a wide variety of animals. Over 100 species of spider have been recorded, including a number of rarities, and other heathland animals, such as common lizard, find suitable habitats here. Breeding birds include reed bunting, meadow pipit, skylark and yellow-hammer while the woodland fringe adds its own range of characteristic species.

Kingley Vale

SU 824088; 146ha; NCC reserve
Yew woodland, chalk scrub and grassland
Leaflets from reserve centre or NCC
Spring, summer

Above the great horseshoe curve of Kingley Vale a memorial stone to Sir Arthur Tansley, first chairman of the Nature Conservancy, overlooks the view which he is said to have considered the finest in Britain: the view across land and water, across woodland, farmland, coastal lagoons and sea, past the landmark of Chichester Cathedral, clear across to the Isle of Wight.

Sir Arthur's personal preference may have many rivals but the naturalist's eye is unlikely to disagree with the claim of the yew wood below to be one of the finest in Europe. Great yews, gnarled and twisted, slopes of straight young yews, yew varied with ash and whitebeam, yew woodland mixed with oak – from the deeper soils on the valley bottom the trees have spread to cover the steep chalk slopes in a strange and wonderful, dark and mysterious forest.

Besides the woodland proper, spreads of scrub, of hawthorn, blackthorn, buckthorn, dogwood, juniper, spindle, wayfaring-tree, of a fascinating mix of varied species, laced with traveller's-joy, bramble, white bryony and thorned with wild rose, cluster the woodland edges and pattern the slopes. Chalk heath, too, where heather and bell heather, acid plants, grow mixed with lime-loving species, adds to the variation of the site.

Nothing grows on the chalk beneath the yews; these are the climax trees, the end of the succession, the trees that can weave and weld themselves together into multiple trunks with boughs so heavy that they break and sag to the ground but still grow on – slow powerful trees that make their own cathedral-cool climate on even the hottest day. But if the succession ends with bare chalk under the shade of the yews, it starts with the open downland, bright with sunlight: small herbs and grassland colonise the chalk, filling it with colourful plants before the scrub moves in to begin the change to woodland.

Kingley Vale: the chalk valley holds one of the finest yew woodlands in Europe.

Kingley Vale has just that herb-rich grassland, maintained by grazing to hold it at that stage, and this, with the scrub and woodland, affords a marvellous range of habitat. Within the grassland plants such as common bird's-foot-trefoil and horseshoe and kidney vetch are food plants for butterflies and add to the richness of colour. Common rock-rose, hawkbit and hawkweed contrast with chalk and common milkwort, harebell, clustered bellflower and round-headed rampion. Eleven orchid species have been recorded, including fly, bee and frog orchid, fragrant and pyramidal orchid, and autumn lady's-tresses.

The reserve is as rich in animals as in plants, with fallow and roe deer, a great variety of birds, with adder and common lizard, with spiders, beetles such as glow-worm and many species of moth. The butterflies include four blues, five fritillaries and five skippers, together with species such as white admiral and a record of purple emperor.

Levin Down

SU 886134; 10ha; STNC reserve
Chalk grassland and scrub
Spring, summer

The speciality of the reserve is a fine colony of juniper, but it also contains a most attractive range of chalkland flowers such as kidney vetch and common rock-rose, together with a rich and varied scrub which has developed around tiny secret lawns of herb-rich grassland. Scrubland birds are plentiful and the warm southern aspect is excellent for characteristic chalkland butterflies.

Lullington Heath

TQ 545018; 62ha; NCC reserve
Chalk heathland
Permit only off rights of way
Leaflet from NCC
Spring, early summer

Chalk heath occurs where shallow acid soils occur on the chalk, producing neither acid heath nor chalk downland but a mix of many species from both habitats. Heather and salad burnet, for instance, might grow side by side. In spite of the fact that gorse has invaded a considerable part of the reserve it still remains an area of great interest to botanists.

Mallydams Wood

TQ 857122; 24ha; RSPCA reserve
Mixed woodland and heath
Booklet from field centre or RSPCA
Spring, early summer

A very wide range of habitat characterises this mainly educational reserve where heather heath and small areas of *Sphagnum* mosses contrast with the woodland rides rich in gorse, broom and spreads of common spotted-orchid, the birch woodland over bluebell and bracken or the old pollards of oak and sweet chestnut. The underlying sandstone is shown in a stream-cut ghyll, typical of High Weald woodlands, and, even though much modified by earlier management, the reserve demonstrates much that is characteristic of East Sussex woods.

The Mens

TQ 024236; 155ha; STNC reserve
Mixed woodland
Leaflet from STNC
Spring, early summer

Where most of the Sussex woods have been managed as coppice, The Mens (extending its title to cover the seven continuous woods which combine to form the reserve) has generally been common land where grazing rights prevented coppicing because the animals would have cropped the growing shoots. Pollarding is often practised in such circumstances, but here the woodland was largely left to develop into high forest. From time to time trees must have been felled for timber, for few of the present trees are more than 100 years old, but the woodland has not been intensively managed since the nineteenth century and now all stages, from seedling to forest tree, may be seen growing naturally here.

Where the Wealden clays are lighter, huge beech trees tower above a tangle of holly and young beech, a dense understorey beneath which little can survive. Here and there a tall tree has fallen and the open glade allows more plants to grow, but generally the pure beech stands are cathedral-tall and dim.

Heavier clays are more varied, with oak and beech, a more open canopy, with an understorey of holly, yew and hazel, of Midland hawthorn and crab apple, with ash and spindle and an equally rich ground cover. Wood anemone, bluebell and bugle may be found, with wild rose, sanicle, violets and wood spurge. Other interesting plants occur, such as butcher's-broom, wood melick and pendulous sedge, and the woodland structure is varied with more open areas of birch and bracken or richer spots where ash stands over spiny tangles of blackthorn.

The Mens: bluebells beneath high-forest beech.

With tall high-forest trees forming the main part of the wood it is hardly surprising that there is a good population of true woodland birds, exemplified by all three woodpeckers, nor that woodland butterflies abound. The white admiral, the insignia of the STNC, occurs here but pride of place must go to the purple emperor, a rare and beautiful butterfly which flies in the sunlight round the upper branches of the taller oak trees.

Roe deer are abundant and their tracks may be found on the paths, while fallow and muntjac deer may be seen from time to time. Parts of the reserve are among the finest in the country for their fungal flora with more than 40 *Russula* species recorded, including three known from no other site.

Nap Wood

Permit only; 44.5ha; STNC reserve
Mainly oak woodland
Access on Sundays April–October only
Leaflets from STNC
Spring, early summer

By contrast with the heavier clays of THE MENS, Nap Wood lies mainly on the acid sandstone of the Tunbridge Wells sands; instead of the close high-forest woods of The Mens, much of Nap Wood consists of almost park-like oak trees over sloping bracken. Coppicing has been practised in Nap Wood, of the oak itself on the poorer ground, of hazel below oak standards, and of sweet chestnut and beech; alder, in the valley, also shows signs of coppicing.

The slopes of the reserve include a range from higher sandstone land to lower clays where the streams have cut down through the native rocks. The structure of the woods, and the pattern of their management, reflect this variation. Above, the oak trees could never reach a tall maturity because of the poorness of the soil, hence they were coppiced, particularly for bark for the tanning trade; here birch and rowan have invaded above a ground cover of bracken and bluebell. Lower down, where the soils are deep, oak was grown as standards, the trees for timber and naval needs, for houses and for ships. A richer understorey could develop: hazel for coppicing, crab apple, hawthorn, yew perhaps and holly, occasional wild cherry above a tangle of bramble and honeysuckle with further spreads of bluebell. Lower still the wet clays of the valleys encourage a growth of alder, hard, ideal for clog-making, and a range of heavy-soil plants such as ramsons, yellow archangel and pendulous sedge with damp shade-loving plants such as mosses and ferns. Sweet chestnut was planted for its timber and is not native to these sandstone woodlands but, with Scots pine, also planted, adds a further range of habitat to the reserve.

The mammals of Nap Wood include fox and badger. The birds include most of those typical of lowland oakwoods, with species such as redstart and wood warbler, both British breeding species which winter in Africa.

A fascinating aspect of the wood is that the damp valley bottoms, less variable in humidity and temperature than the rest of the Weald, hold certain Atlantic plants which have probably survived here for thousands of years. Plants such as hay-scented buckler-fern are generally limited to the west, and would not normally be expected in the modern climate here.

Newbury Pond

TQ 306243; 0.5ha; STNC reserve
Small pond
Spring, summer

Consisting of a small pond together with a marsh, the reserve contains an interesting variety of water plants, marsh plants, and insects associated with this kind of habitat.

Ninfield Main Substation Nature Trail

TQ 725117; 2km; CEGB
Circular trail around boundary of substation
Restricted to educational visits
Booklet from CEGB
Spring, early summer

The grazing meadows, water meadows, streamsides, pools and woodlands through which the trail passes demonstrate some of the interest of the East Sussex countryside.

Nutbourne Marshes

SU 766051; 360ha; Chichester Harbour
Conservancy reserve
Salting, creeks and tidal mudflats
Access along sea wall rights of way only
Autumn, winter

Part of CHICHESTER HARBOUR.

Pagham Harbour

SZ 857965; 440ha; WSCC reserve
Tidal saltmarsh and surrounding land
Leaflets from information centre
All year

With a great range of sand, shingle, saltmarsh and coastal plant life, including one national rarity, the reserve has attracted over 200 bird species and is rich in insects such as butterflies and moths. The larger area of CHICHESTER HARBOUR may be better known as a winter bird site but the mudflats and the sheltered Ferry Pool often contain a wealth of birds difficult to rival.

Powdermill Wood

Permit only; 1.9ha; STNC reserve
Wet woodland
Spring, early summer

The small reserve protects an interesting area of wet coppiced alder woodland and sedges, and is noted for its bird life.

Rye Harbour

TQ 942187; 356ha; ESCC reserve
Foreshore, shingle, saltmarsh, meadows and lagoon
Leaflets from warden
Visitors should keep to footpaths
All year

Looking inland from the shingle at the mouth of the River Rother, a low line of hills can be seen some 5km away. Between 3000 and 4000 years ago this was the coastline of Britain and the raised land represents the old sea cliffs of the time. From then until now, changes in sea level and drifts of shingle have moderated the bay until a whole new spread of land has been developed below the cliffs. Gravel extraction has given rise to a widespread series of pits, one of which lies within the reserve while the others may all be overlooked. It is these pits, together with the shingle ridges and foreshore, that form the most interesting and important features of the site.

Most visitors will probably come to see the spectacular bird life, the winter wildfowl, the passage birds and the colonies of terns, but the plant life of Rye Harbour is equally varied. The small saltmarsh shows all five native species of glasswort together with sea aster, sea-purslane and sea-heath, while the shingle carries a wide range of plants from yellow horned-poppy to biting stonecrop, from viper's-bugloss to sea pea, sea-kale and sea wormwood. The diversity of plants found on the reserve includes lesser bulrush, lesser centaury, henbane, blue fleabane, green-winged orchid, musk mallow, rock samphire, bladderwort and least lettuce.

In winter large numbers of waders – dunlin, lapwing, oystercatcher, golden plover, with curlew, ringed plover, redshank, sanderling and snipe – may be seen together with a congregation of coot, mallard, pochard, shoveler, tufted duck, wigeon, eider, goldeneye, gadwall, shelduck and teal. Spring brings many birds of passage including bar-tailed godwit, grey plover, turnstone and whimbrel, and sees the arrival of summer breeders such as common and little tern. Other breeding species include ringed plover, oystercatcher, redshank, black-headed and herring gull, little grebe, pochard, shelduck, tufted duck, yellow wagtail and wheatear, while heron which nest in a nearby wood may often be seen stalking their prey at the gravelpits.

Among the other animals of note are the introduced marsh frog, released on Romney Marsh in 1935, and the brown-tailed moth, a characteristic south eastern species which defoliates bramble and hawthorn.

Saddlescombe Chalk Pit

TQ 267122; 0.6ha; STNC reserve
Disused chalk quarry
Spring, summer

The reserve was established chiefly to protect a population of juniper.

St Leonard's Forest

TQ 208299, 216303 and 212308; 5.2ha; STNC
reserve
Three small woodland areas
Spring, early summer

Representatives of three specialities of the old
central Wealden forest are contained within these
sites. One is an area of old beech woodland with a
block of standard oak and coppiced birch, one is a
protected area of lily-of-the-valley, while the last
is a narrow sandstone valley containing unusual
bryophytes forming a link between this and the
wetter areas of western Britain.

Seaford Head

TV 505980; 112ha; Lewes DC reserve
Chalk cliffs, grassland and scrub
Spring, summer

Part of CUCKMERE HAVEN.

Selwyns Wood

TQ 552205; 11.2ha; STNC reserve
Mixed woodland
Spring, early summer

The mixed deciduous wood consists mainly of coppiced sweet chestnut on the acid Ashdown sands.
Active coppicing is intended to ensure and demonstrate the continuance of this form of management.

Seven Sisters Country Park

TV 519995; 280ha; ESCC
Chalk cliffs, downland, shingle and estuary
Leaflets from information centre
Spring, summer

Part of CUCKMERE HAVEN.

Sidlesham Ferry Nature Trail

SZ 857965; 2.5km; WSCC
Nature trail at Pagham Harbour
Leaflet from information centre
All year

The trail follows part of the western edge of the
harbour and illustrates much of the wildlife
interest of the reserve. Among winter wildfowl are
pochard, shoveler, teal and tufted duck, while
migrant waders include regular curlew, green and
wood sandpiper and little stint.

South Downs Way

SU 762193–TV 600972; 129km; CC
Long-distance way
Leaflet from CC or booklet from HMSO bookshops
Spring, summer

The route of the long-distance way follows the
South Downs clear across the county from the
Hampshire border to the coast at Beachy Head. The
wide range of wildlife includes that of the superb
chalk cliffs and of open herb-rich downland.

Stanmer Park Nature Trail

TQ 337097; 1.6km; Brighton BC
Woodland and parkland
Leaflet from BBC
Spring, early summer

The circular trail shows an attractive range of
spring flowers in an area rich in wildlife: mature
trees attract birds such as great spotted woodpecker
and there is a resident population of badger.

*Looking across the mouth of Cuckmere Haven:
Seaford Head to the Seven Sisters cliffs.*

Lime-rich waters drain from the Downs to fill the lake at Woods Mill.

Vert Wood

Permit only; 3.2ha; STNC reserve
Mixed woodland
Spring, early summer

Areas of scrub and a glade, together with a small pond, add to the variety of the woodland reserve which contains a good range of birds and insects.

Waltham Brooks

Permit only; 42.4ha; STNC reserve
Flood meadows
Winter

The winter floods encourage a good variety of wetland birds including Bewick's swan, shoveler, teal, wigeon and snipe. In spring the reserve is colourful with marsh-marigold, followed by a bright show of yellow iris. Redshank, lapwing, gadwall and shelduck may be seen.

West Dean Woods

Permit only; 15.4ha; STNC reserve
Old oak woodland on chalk
Spring, early summer

A fascinating relict woodland with areas of high forest and of hazel coppice under oak standards, the reserve is rich in species such as wild daffodil and bluebell growing on the non-calcareous mantle which covers the chalk. Early-purple orchid and toothwort are among the varied plants of the woodland floor, while bird and insect life includes woodcock and silver-washed fritillary. Fallow and roe deer may be present.

Woods Mill

TQ 218137; 6ha; STNC reserve
Woodland, grassland, marsh and lake
Leaflets from information centre
Spring, summer

The reserve buildings house not only the headquarters of the STNC but also an excellent information centre complete with an audio-visual room where slides and tapes are made use of to demonstrate many facets of the wildlife interest of Sussex. The reserve itself contains a small example of a damp wealden clay wood, but is most notable as a fine wetland area where lime-rich waters draining from the South Downs encourage a fine variety of plants and, therefore, a good range of interesting animal life.

Small though it is, the wood contains much of interest. It was managed as coppice with standards, oak and hazel, although only a few of the standards still remain and, except for a demonstration area, coppicing is no longer practised. Birch has invaded the wood but there is still a good mixed range of trees, with ash, beech, field maple, hawthorn, holly and wild service-tree above a rich ground cover of wood anemone, bluebell, lesser celandine and primrose, of early dog violet and moschatel, saw-wort, wood spurge, wood millet and wood sedge, with wood-edge banks of dogwood, stands of common spotted-orchid and sprays of male-fern and hart's-tongue.

The wetland areas are various – streams and ditches, an old water tank, the lake, marsh and reedbed. The water tank, a rectangular pool, is dipped into for invertebrates during educational demonstrations, and is also a water garden of species such as bogbean, bulrush and water dock, marsh-marigold, water mint and water-plantain. The marsh and lake edge are rich in plants such as meadowsweet and great willowherb, with wild angelica, bulrush, branched bur-reed, cuckooflower, hemp-agrimony, yellow iris and yellow loosestrife. Alder and willow stand upon the banks with brown and grey sedge, while yellow waterlily shows on the lake itself. Near the lake a small reedbed, edged with banks of bramble, adds to the variety of the wetland.

Kingfisher and heron visit the lake and the alders draw winter flocks of goldfinch, redpoll and siskin. In winter, too, redwing and fieldfare, thrushes from northern Europe, may be seen feeding on the hedges and fields around the reserve. Reed bunting and sedge warbler breed in the reedbed area, while the woodland affords nest sites for many species including several tits, nuthatch and treecreeper.

As with most wetlands, the area is particularly rich in insect life, in attractive dragonflies, including the broad-bodied libellula with its blue-bodied male and orange-bodied female, and damselflies such as common ischnura, azure and large red. Butterflies include peacock, small tortoiseshell, red admiral and comma.

Warwickshire and West Midlands

Situated at the very heart of England, Warwickshire and the West Midlands are counties of contrasts. Both have been moulded and shaped by the hands of man, but in very different ways. The most obvious effects are in the urbanisation of Birmingham, the Black Country and Coventry, which together have a population of nearly three million. Possibly less obvious but equally affected by man is the agricultural land of Warwickshire, now intensively farmed to maximise food production. Mixed in amongst this background of industry, housing and agriculture are areas rich in wildlife. Some are recent, having developed on derelict land, but others are more ancient, remnants of the countryside of long ago.

Although the entire region is lowland with few hills reaching 250m, Birmingham and the Black Country lie on a slightly raised plateau drained to the east and north by the River Tame. At the time of the second ice age a great lake covered most of Warwickshire, trapped between this plateau and the higher ground of Edge Hill to the south east by giant glaciers. When the ice eventually melted the lake poured out to the south west, creating the basin of the River Avon. Today the Avon flows more gently, crossing the county from Rugby through Warwick and Stratford and then on to the Severn.

The underlying geology of much of the region is keuper marl or 'Mercia mudstone', giving rise to red clay soils, although these are covered in many places by sands and gravels left after the ice ages. In the south east a scarp slope marks the grey calcareous clays of the lower lias, which have associated limestones and overlying ironstones. Coal measures and older, harder rocks are found in both north Warwickshire and the Black Country, the latter rocks outcropping in unique sites at HARTSHILL HAYES near Nuneaton and WREN'S NEST, Dudley.

Over 4000 years ago the region was almost entirely blanketed by a deciduous forest of oak, ash, alder and birch, but most of this had already been cleared before the Romans came. During the next thousand years agriculture developed in the fertile valleys of the Avon and Tame, with many small towns becoming established. Between these two rivers lay the Forest of Arden, once a continuous tract of woodland from Stratford to Nuneaton but considerably broken up even before the Domesday survey of 1086. By the seventeenth century most of the Birmingham plateau was farmland or heath. These habitats suffered considerably during the Industrial Revolution when large areas of land became covered by thriving factories. Industries, based initially on iron smelting and a multitude of manufactured goods, attracted more people to the towns and demanded more raw materials, more efficient transport and more intensive food production. Although these activities in turn destroyed more of the natural vegetation, by a strange paradox many of the old industrial sites now provide excellent habitats for a wide range of wildlife.

Today rural Warwickshire presents a picture of gently rolling farmland, a patchwork of arable crops and pasture. The destruction of hedgerows to create large, prairie-like fields has happened in only a few areas, so that most fields are still surrounded by living boundaries. Since the ravages of Dutch elm disease 'leafy Warwickshire' is no longer quite so leafy, but subsequent tree-planting schemes may go some way to restore the county's character over the next few decades. Despite the fact that Warwickshire contains large areas of grassland, most are short-term ryegrass leys. Thanks to fertilisers, herbicides and field drains, these are very productive for the farmer but have little value for wildlife and the naturalist. One of the few remaining traditional hay meadows,

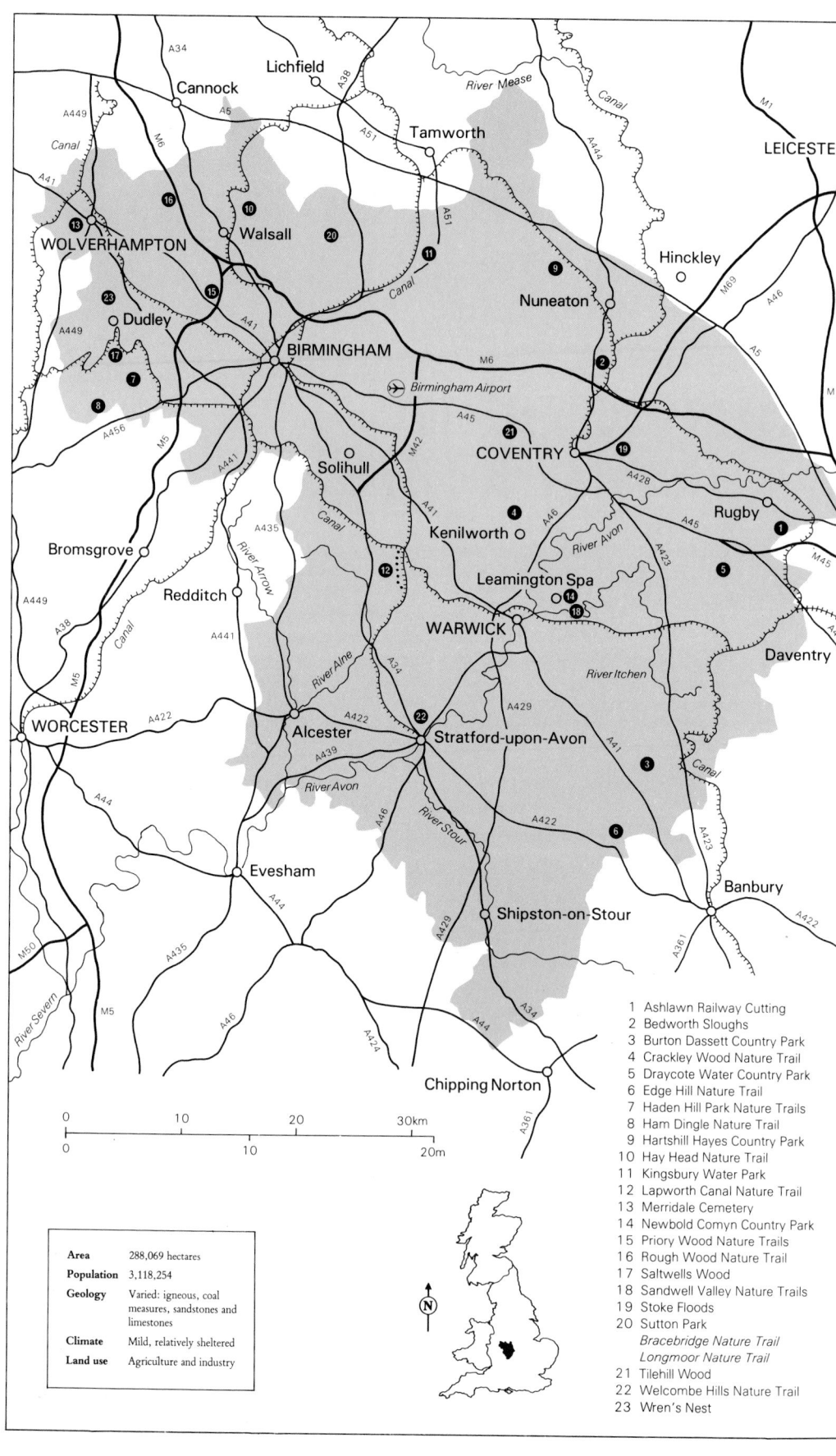

A34		

Lichfield

Cannock

River Mease

Canal

LEICESTER

A449

Canal

Tamworth

A38

A51

M6

16

WOLVERHAMPTON

13

10

Walsall

20

A5

11

Canal

Nuneaton

Hinckley

M69

A46

23

Dudley

15

A449

17

7

BIRMINGHAM

A41

M6

2

M1

A5

8

A456

M5

A441

Birmingham Airport

A45

21

COVENTRY

19

A428

Rugby

1

Solihull

M42

A41

A45

M45

Bromsgrove

A435

4

River Avon

A46

A423

5

Redditch

Canal

Kenilworth

12

Leamington Spa

14

18

Daventry

A422

River Arrow

River Alne

A34

WARWICK

River Itchen

A441

A449

Canal

A429

A41

WORCESTER

A422

22

3

Alcester

River Avon

A439

Stratford-upon-Avon

6

A422

A423

A44

Evesham

A46

River Stour

A44

Banbury

A422

M50

A44

A429

Shipston-on-Stour

A361

M5

River Severn

A44

A34

A361

Chipping Norton

0	10	20	30km
0	10		20m

N

1 Ashlawn Railway Cutting
2 Bedworth Sloughs
3 Burton Dassett Country Park
4 Crackley Wood Nature Trail
5 Draycote Water Country Park
6 Edge Hill Nature Trail
7 Haden Hill Park Nature Trails
8 Ham Dingle Nature Trail
9 Hartshill Hayes Country Park
10 Hay Head Nature Trail
11 Kingsbury Water Park
12 Lapworth Canal Nature Trail
13 Merridale Cemetery
14 Newbold Comyn Country Park
15 Priory Wood Nature Trails
16 Rough Wood Nature Trail
17 Saltwells Wood
18 Sandwell Valley Nature Trails
19 Stoke Floods
20 Sutton Park
    Bracebridge Nature Trail
    Longmoor Nature Trail
21 Tilehill Wood
22 Welcombe Hills Nature Trail
23 Wren's Nest

Area	288,069 hectares
Population	3,118,254
Geology	Varied: igneous, coal measures, sandstones and limestones
Climate	Mild, relatively sheltered
Land use	Agriculture and industry

DRAYCOTE MEADOWS near Rugby, is now owned by WARNACT. Every year in late May it becomes transformed into a carpet of purple and yellow by green-winged orchid, yellow rattle and cowslips.

Heathland, once so widespread throughout the Black Country and Birmingham, and reflected in so many district names, has now largely disappeared. The most important surviving relict is SUTTON PARK, a unique semi-natural area within the city of Birmingham where woodland, bog, heath and grassland give some indication of the landscape of 300 years ago.

As a whole the region is poorly wooded, although small copses are dotted throughout the landscape. Some of these woods may be remnants of the Forest of Arden, but nearly all are later plantings of broad-leaved trees or conifers. Privately owned Ufton Wood, one of the largest deciduous woodlands still managed by coppice rotation, has an excellent record of ground flora and wildlife. CLOWES WOOD near Birmingham, owned by WARNACT, is a more acid wood containing a small area of remnant heath.

Throughout the region the legacy of industrial dereliction has resulted in a wide range of valuable wildlife habitats, from calcareous grassland in old limestone quarries to marshes in worked-out clay-pits. More recent sand and gravel extraction in both the Tame and Avon valleys has created wetland sites such as KINGSBURY WATER PARK near Coleshill and BRANDON MARSH near Coventry. Together with mining subsidence pools and reservoirs, these now form vital links in bird migration routes as well as habitats for more permanent residents.

In a short account of the area, one might be forgiven for omitting the towns and cities entirely. However, recent surveys have shown that towns are not seas of lifeless concrete as is sometimes thought, but contain many oases of wildlife. These may be small fragments of wood, marsh or rough grassland, or larger areas with a diversity of habitats. Whatever their size or relative value, they all have what some may think a disadvantage, but in reality is an advantage – they are surrounded by people and so can bring home the message of conservation and the value of wildlife. Man's activities have moulded agricultural landscapes and shaped urban skylines – with the right guidance they can ensure a future for wildlife, too.

A. TASKER

Alvecote Pools

Permit only; 225ha; WARNACT reserve
Pools and damp grassland
Can be overlooked from road at SK 254047
Nature trail booklet from WARNACT
All year

The nature trail demonstrates both ecologically rich and polluted pools south of the railway line, but the wildfowl interest of the reserve is centred on the pools to the north, where in winter flocks of duck, including pochard, shoveler, teal and wigeon, may be seen. Breeding species include great crested grebe, redshank and snipe – the shallow pools and water meadows are particularly suitable for migrant waders.

Ashlawn Railway Cutting

SP 516732; 5.25ha; WARNACT reserve
Disused railway
Spring, summer

A rare urban example of lime-rich grassland, it contains many attractive orchids and butterflies.

Bedworth Sloughs

SP 350871; 5ha; Nuneaton and Bedworth BC
Small wetland
All year

The shallow pool, formed by mining subsidence, is surrounded by a deep bulrush reedmarsh and by small areas of herb-rich grassland. Over 70 species of birds have been recorded including wildfowl, waders and commoner woodland birds, but the major significance of the site is that it provides one of the largest and most regular roosts of autumn passage swallows in the Midlands, with up to 25,000 birds recorded in one night.

Bracebridge Nature Trail

SP 102980; 2.4km; City of Birmingham DC
Trail past woodland and lake
Leaflet from CBDC
Spring, summer

Set in SUTTON PARK, the trail runs through mainly Scots pine woodland with heather in well-lit glades and passes a large pond where great crested grebe may be seen.

Alvecote Pools attract a good range of birds.

Brandon Marsh

Permit only; 53.6ha; WARNACT reserve
Pools, marsh and scrub
All year

Former gravelpits offer a variety of wetland habitat at Brandon Marsh, well known for its bird life.

A superb wetland reserve has been developed on an area of worked-out gravelpits which now lie among a rich tangle of marsh plants and scrub. The pools are varied in size and depth, some steep-banked and lined with reedbeds or tall stands of bulrush, others edged with scrub or grading into rough meadowland, with beaches and spits on which waterbirds can preen. Willow and hawthorn scrub, providing shelter and nesting sites, merges into spreads of rosebay willowherb, meadowsweet and common nettle or drier slopes of bramble, clearings bright with ragwort, prickled with thistles and teasel. Damper parts contain rushes, sedges and marshland plants such as gipsywort, while damp grassland supports marsh-orchids.

The deep rich vegetation attracts a good range of insects, with butterflies such as comma, red admiral and an occasional clouded yellow, and moths with wonderful names such as pink-barred sallow, scalloped hazel, burnished brass and copper underwing. The main attraction of Brandon Marsh, however, must be its birds.

Probably the most common breeding species is reed bunting, the male with a bright white distinctive collar in contrast to the drab brown female, camouflaged to match her low, hidden nest. Other small birds include reed, sedge and willow warbler, all of them summer visitors, as are yellow wagtail and sand martin, which has a thriving colony here. Snipe and water rail are among the breeding species, together with dabbling duck such as gadwall and divers such as ruddy duck, little and great crested grebe.

The range of wildfowl recorded, particularly in winter, is excellent and includes gadwall, garganey, mallard, pintail, pochard, ruddy duck, shoveler, teal, tufted duck and wigeon. Goldeneye, ring-necked duck, scaup, shelduck and ruddy shelduck occur and the reserve may be visited by Bewick's swan or by wintering white-fronted geese. Migrants such as black-tailed godwit, greenshank, ruff and green sandpiper use the marsh as a feeding ground or roost, while predators such as hobby and merlin may visit, short-eared owl may hunt across the reserve and, occasionally, the great wings of a harrier may sweep the tips of the reeds.

Golden eagle and osprey have been sighted overflying Brandon Marsh, while the River Pool, an area of muddy shallows connected to the Avon, can boast a visit by a little egret, only the third recorded in Warwickshire this century. The birds are well studied here due to the work of an active bird-ringing group whose captures and releases include spotted crake, bearded tit, wryneck and barred and great reed warbler.

Burton Dassett Country Park

SP 397519; 38.8ha; WCC
Hilly grassland
Nature trail booklet from Warwickshire
Museum or WCC
Spring, early summer

Disused quarries, now richly overgrown, add interest to the large area of unimproved grassland with its fine views across the farmland plain below.

Clowes Wood

Permit only; 32.5ha; WARNACT reserve
Mixed woodland
Spring, early summer

Divided by a working railway line, Clowes is composed of two woodlands, both different, which provide a good variety of habitat. Big Clowes is mainly even-aged oak over a thin understorey of birch, holly, rowan and alder buckthorn. The oak trees are not tall, with an almost continuous canopy which shades the low ground cover of bilberry, bramble and grasses. At the bottom of the gentle slope variation is provided by blocks of beech and sweet chestnut, where bluebells stand thick beneath the trees and the clearings are filled with bracken. Alder appears where the ground is damp and wood-sorrel shows beneath spreads of broad buckler-fern.

Little Clowes is more varied, with mature oak and beech, more tilted and gullied, drained by a stream and containing pools where wetland plants contrast with the woodland around them. The pools are small but attractive, set in clearings and edged with alder, rushes, drooping clumps of cyperus sedge, and plants such as lesser spearwort and branched bur-reed. The woodland floor beneath the beeches is deeply shaded and bare, but where the canopy is mainly oak the understorey resembles that of Big Clowes with alder buckthorn, birch, holly, rowan, bilberry, bramble, honeysuckle, bracken and the occasional yellow flowers of common cow-wheat.

The soils throughout the reserve are considerably varied: in Big Clowes a change occurs from

bilberry–bramble to a richer mix, and in Little Clowes the western boundary is marked by the presence of ash, dog's mercury, enchanter's-nightshade, woodruff, wood melick and sprays of wild rose. Hazel and hawthorn appear in the understorey and coppicing has been practised, giving a more varied structure to the wood. Both woodlands are noted for mosses and fungi and contain some fine spreads of lily-of-the-valley.

The variation of the reserve makes it attractive to typical woodland birds. The coppiced areas, clearings and woodland edge provide a suitable habitat for warblers such as chiffchaff, willow and wood warbler, and for blue, great, coal and marsh tit. The bigger timber, the trees rich in bark-living insects, provide feeding grounds for great spotted woodpecker or for nuthatch.

Just as the birds are those characteristic of mixed woodland, so too are the mammals, which include grey squirrel, wood mouse and bank vole, all competitors for the annual harvest of hazelnuts. A splendid variety of moths includes over 50 scarce or local species amongst which are ear moth, dark spectacle and the very local grey shoulderknot.

Crackley Wood Nature Trail

SP 287737; 1.2km; Warwick DC
Woodland trail
Leaflet from WARNACT or Warwickshire Museum
Spring, early summer

An acid woodland, mainly oak and birch, Crackley Wood contains a fine show of spring flowers such as wood anemone and bluebell. Woodland and wood-edge birds are plentiful and the site is visited by badger.

Draycote Meadows

Permit only; 5.2ha; WARNACT reserve
Old-meadow grassland
Spring, early summer

No one who has seen a field of corn flushed over with common poppy can forget it; no one who has seen the vivid heads of hayfield cowslips can prefer a plain of grassland. Draycote Meadows are two small fields beside a stream which have escaped the march of progress. In spring and early summer they are rich in cowslips; rich in varied grasses too and filled with the delicate hooded flowers of green-winged orchid, the strange small adder's-tongue and the delicate feathery pignut. Any one of these plants might have survived an attempt at improving the meadow, but the presence of all four, together with a spread of yellow rattle, is a clear pointer to the probability that the meadows have been unploughed for a very long time. As well as adder's-tongue, one meadow contains another unusual fern, moonwort.

That the site was ploughed in earlier years can be seen in the curve and dip of ancient ridge-and-furrow patterns, but these now harbour plants not seen in modern fields. Common bird's-foot-trefoil,

Sand martins are burrow-nesters living in colonies.

selfheal, agrimony and pink-flowered spiny rest-harrow grow here, with a small invasion of gorse and hawthorn to demonstrate how scrub would begin the succession to woodland if the meadows were not maintained. A tree-lined disused claypit contains the same range of plants, and further variety is added by small areas of marshy ground where horsetails, rushes, meadowsweet and lady's-mantle contrast with the hay-meadow plants.

A most attractive hedge lines the stream which borders the reserve, where water mint and watercress are shaded by a mix of species which include alder, ash, bittersweet, elm, elder, guelder-rose, hawthorn, hazel, honeysuckle, ivy, oak, field maple, privet, willow and wild rose. From here birds fly out over the meadow, or butterflies such as red admiral may catch the sun; here small animals come to drink and the cattle to enjoy the shade when they graze the aftermath of summer haytime.

Draycote Water Country Park

SP 467692; 8.7ha; WCC
Hilly grassland
Leaflet from site or WCC
Spring, summer

Overlooking the reservoir, the grassland has the added interest of a ridge-and-furrow ploughing pattern which shows the remains of a medieval open-field system.

Earlswood Moathouse

Permit only; 3.6ha; WARNACT reserve
Mature and planted woodland
Spring, early summer

A variety of tree species have been planted in abandoned meadowland which, with a strip of mature woodland, is managed to provide a sanctuary for birds.

Eathorpe Marsh

Permit only; 1.4ha; WARNACT reserve
Small marshland
Spring, summer

Wild angelica, water mint and yellow iris add colour to a spread of reed sweet-grass and bulrush. Pools attract breeding birds such as reed bunting and snipe, which are joined by winter flocks of finches, corn bunting, linnet and redpoll. Insects include white ermine, small square-spot and Hebrew character moths.

Edge Hill Nature Trail

SP 370470; 3.2km; WARNACT
Trail through wide range of habitat with spectacular views
Leaflet from WARNACT or Warwickshire Museum
Spring, early summer

Grassland, wetland and woodland rich in plants, insects and birds provide considerable wildlife interest to which are added the spectacular views, said to extend to 12 counties, from this northern extension of the Cotswolds.

Haden Hill Park Nature Trails

SO 960856; 1.6–3.2km; Sandwell MBC
Trails through suburban park
Spring, summer

Small wild areas have been established to create pockets of natural vegetation and to encourage a varied range of wildlife.

Ham Dingle Nature Trail

SO 913828; 1.6km; Dudley MBC
Trail through oak woodland
Spring, early summer

The oak woodland contains a good range of typical mosses and attracts woodland birds such as nuthatch, treecreeper and great spotted woodpecker.

Harbury Spoil Bank

Permit only; 2.4ha; WARNACT reserve
Lime-rich grassland
Spring, summer

Formed by the colonisation of spoil from the railway cutting, the reserve is rich in plants, such as carline thistle, yellow-wort and quaking-grass, as well as many butterflies including green and white-letter hairstreak, little blue and marbled white. Hawthorn scrub provides winter roosts and feeding for migrants such as fieldfare and redwing.

Clowes Wood: beeches are the first trees to change colour in autumn.

Hartshill Hayes Country Park

SP 315945; 8.8ha; WCC
Hill grassland and woodland
Leaflet from site or WCC
Spring, early summer

The wildlife interest of the country park, set high up on a ridge overlooking the Anker Valley, is increased by the availability to the public of footpaths in the 45.6ha woodland of Hartshill Hayes which adjoins the park.

Hay Head Nature Trail

SP 041989; 1.2km; Walsall MBC
Old lime workings and canal basin
Spring, early summer

The old lime workings, now colonised by alder and hawthorn shrubs above a ground cover of plants such as ramsons, attract a range of woodland birds. The canal basin may be bright with marshmarigold in spring and is visited by wetland birds such as kingfisher.

Kingsbury Water Park

SP 204958; 213.8ha; WCC reserve
Flooded gravelpits
Leaflets from visitor centre or WCC
All year

A part of the much larger complex of flooded pits, grassland and scrub which make up the water park as a whole, the reserve lies at the most northerly, least disturbed end of the park. The water park is, effectively, man-made: gravel extraction has left wide pits, some of them open flooded waters, others filled with fly ash from the power station to form deep reedbeds or spreads of willow swamp. These stands of bulrush and willow form an integral part of the wildlife interest of the site because, though most of them lie outside the reserve, they create nest sites for many species, particularly warblers, and provide food and shelter for many important insects.

Warblers are a feature of the park, with blackcap, chiffchaff, whitethroat and lesser whitethroat, garden, grasshopper, reed, sedge and willow warbler breeding here. Kingfisher, kestrel and tawny owl all breed within the park, but the greatest interest probably lies in the shallow lagoons of the reserve. Two hides have been built overlooking the pools, and there is always something of interest to be seen.

In migration times arctic, black and common tern pause to rest and feed on the reserve; waders such as curlew, greenshank, spotted redshank and common sandpiper search the mud and, occasionally, a marsh harrier hunts low across the flood plain. Merlin and hobby, too, will visit in season, the latter following the autumn flocks of swallow and martin as they move south for the winter.

In winter the water and the meadows are roosts and feeding grounds for many species. As many as 5000 lapwing may be seen, with thousands of gulls – black-headed, lesser black-blacked and herring gull – flying in at evening time to roost on the darkening pools. Gadwall, goldeneye, pintail, pochard and wigeon increase the numbers of duck already here, while greylag and white-fronted geese or Bewick's swan add to the variety of waterfowl. Cormorant, water rail and waders such as dunlin and golden plover also winter here, while short-eared owl regularly hunt the meadows. Breeding birds include mallard, shoveler, teal and tufted duck, with little and great crested grebe, little ringed plover, lapwing and snipe, and common tern on the gravel islands.

Knowle

Permit only; 0.3ha; Knowle Soc. reserve
Educational reserve
Spring, early summer

The tiny reserve includes a spinney, grassland and wetland consisting of a pond and a stream.

Lapworth Canal Nature Trail

SP 186708–188678; 3.2km; NT
Waterside nature trail
Booklet from Warwickshire Museum
Spring, summer

The Stratford-on-Avon Canal falls through 15 locks as it passes down the trail. A fine variety of wetland plants and birds may be seen, together with hedgerow and farmland wildlife.

Longmoor Nature Trail

SP 091955; 3.2km; City of Birmingham DC
Heathland and mixed woodland
Leaflet from CBDC
Spring, summer

A SUTTON PARK trail, it circles through the typical heathland where gorse and heath bedstraw show among the heather, and through an area of sweet chestnut where woodland birds add their songs to that of the heathland yellowhammer.

Merridale Cemetery

SO 899979; 2ha; Walsall MBC
Old, well-wooded cemetery
Spring, early summer

The cemetery contains a fine range of mixed tree species both native and exotic, which attracts woodland birds such as nuthatch and spotted flycatcher and forms a wildlife oasis on the western outskirts of Wolverhampton.

Newbold Comyn Country Park

SP 329659; 128ha; Warwick DC
Riverside habitats
Leaflets from Tourist Information Centre, Jephson Gardens, Leamington Spa
Spring, early summer

Woodland, grassland, marsh and the river combine to form the basis for a varied and interesting nature trail.

Oxhouse Farm

Permit only; 7.2ha; WARNACT reserve
Lime-rich grassland and disused railway line
Spring, summer

If an insignia for Oxhouse had to be chosen one might suggest traveller's-joy. The rich limestone ridge on which the reserve proper lies is looped and laced with the plant; the open ballast of the old line is a tracery of tendrils which also climb and twist in the shrubs and trees; in autumn the banks are foamed with the creamy white feathery fruits. A lime-loving plant with vigorous sun-seeking growth, traveller's-joy epitomises the magic of the farm.

The old railway line runs down the spine of the ridge, here leaping the river on a bridge, there cut deep into the limestone to give steep banks of herb-rich grass and scrub. Trees and shrubs form a shelter for the line where ash, blackthorn, buckthorn, dogwood, elder, hawthorn, oak, privet, wayfaring-tree and willows are tangled with bittersweet, bramble, traveller's-joy and wild rose. Grassland banks and the ballast of the line are filled with lime-loving wild basil, salad burnet, cowslip, dyer's greenweed, carline thistle, yellow-wort and quaking-grass.

A pair of nuthatches at their nest hole.

Oaks in Saltwells Wood.

The meadow below the line is deeply grassed, humped with colonies of anthills and sheltered by spreading hedges. Pink musk mallow contrasts with vibrant yellow lady's bedstraw and agrimony or the subtler colours of small scabious and greater knapweed, while the spectacular woolly thistle dominates the grassland. A damp corner is thick with meadowsweet which hints at the riches of the river meadows. Although not strictly part of the reserve, these carry a most attractive range from banks of meadow crane's-bill to a vast spread of butterbur and the tall alder, grey poplar and willow trees shading the river.

The insect life is equally diverse and almost 30 species of butterfly have been identified including brimstone and little blue, small copper, dark green fritillary and marbled white, together with both green and white-letter hairstreak. Birds include all three woodpeckers, abundant willow warbler, a fluctuating count of nightingale and occasional redstart. Wide-ranging visitors include great grey shrike, hoopoe, peregrine and snow bunting.

Among the unusual plants of the reserve are continental fine-leaved vetch and, among some 45 grasses, spreading meadow-grass at one of its five known Warwickshire stations, an unusual variant of tall fescue, and a hybrid between marsh and meadow foxtail not known in the county since 1899.

Priory Wood Nature Trails

SP 020913; 1.2 and 2.4km; Sandwell MBC
Wet woodland
Spring, early summer

Oak and hawthorn above spring plants such as wood anemone provide a contrast with wetland areas rich in marsh horsetail and damp-loving species. The woods and scrub attract a good range of songbirds and provide a habitat for great spotted woodpecker.

Rough Hill Wood Nature Trail

Permit only; 1.4km; Redditch Dev. Corpn
Woodland trail
Leaflet from Landscape Section, Architect's Dept, RDC
Spring, early summer

The trail demonstrates a good range of woodland habitat with its associated animal species in a site on the county border south of Redditch.

Rough Wood Nature Trail

SJ 094010; 2.4km; WMCC
Trail through scrub woodland
Spring, early summer

The spread of scrub woodland includes oak, hazel and acid-loving alder buckthorn, and is particularly rich in birds such as redstart and whitethroat.

Saltwells Wood

SO 934874; 35ha; Dudley MBC
Woodland, pond and disused claypit
Spring, summer

Oak, with aspen, beech and white poplar, stands above a ground cover of bluebell and wood-sorrel and attracts such birds as spotted flycatcher, willow warbler and green woodpecker, while the marshy pool is a good site for dragonflies. The disused claypit is of particular geological importance.

Sandwell Valley Nature Trails

SP 017914; 1.2 and 2.4km; Sandwell MBC
Woodland and lakeside trails
Booklet from Recreation and Amenities Dept, SMBC
Winter, early summer

The trails are laid out in a valley, once parkland, which contains mixed woodland around a number of pools. Trees include oak, alder, ash, field maple, whitebeam and yew above a varied ground cover and hold woodland birds such as spotted flycatcher, willow warbler and kestrel. Wetland birds include passage waders and winter flocks of duck.

Stockton Railway Cutting

Permit only; 5.5ha; WARNACT reserve
Disused railway line
Spring, summer

Celebrated primarily for its 28 species of butterfly, the reserve supports limestone plants and a range of birds and mammals in mixed scrub and grassland.

Stoke Floods

SP 374791; 7.6ha; WARNACT reserve
Urban wetland area
All year

Summer brings a show of marshland plants to the wet grassland and reedbeds which, in winter, provide an important feeding site for wildfowl.

Sutton Park

SP 103963; 859ha; City of Birmingham DC
Lowland heath and woodland
Nature trail leaflets from CBDC
Spring, early summer

Roughly 10km from the heart of Birmingham's
bustle, Sutton Park has been preserved as a spread
of heath and woodland safe from development, an
urban rural escape. Enormous public pressures
occur around the fringes, and the popular sites are
popular indeed, but the park has woodlands where
people rarely venture and boggy valleys which
people tend to avoid. The land dips and rises, the
houses around are generally screened by trees,
wide spreads of heathland stretch to the horizon,
and one might easily imagine that the city had
disappeared.

The woods are mixed with areas of conifers but
include large stands of deciduous trees of varying
composition. In places the woods are of oak, with
birch and rowan over holly, often dense and impenetrable. The holly casts so much shade that
virtually nothing grows beneath, but clearings
show a mix of acid grasses, bramble, rosebay
willowherb, bracken and heath bedstraw, with
seedling birch and rowan and occasional oak saplings. Other areas have interplanted larch, with
beech and with tall rowan lifting sprays of berries
into the high tree canopy. Sweet chestnut and pine
trees also occur over a ground cover of bracken and
young holly. Parts of the heath have been invaded
by birch which stands over grassland, bracken,
bilberry and heather with a scrub of gorse and
grades into older oak–conifer woodland, again
with a holly understorey. Here and there blocks of
pure birch stand over spreads of grasses, a slender
well-lit woodland contrasting with the holly. A
further contrast appears where a small valley mire
is filled with an alder swamp standing in cushions
of *Polytrichum* mosses, with broad buckler-fern,
tussock-sedge and horsetail species.

As with so many acid areas, the wetter parts are
often most rich in species and there are several
attractive bogs where streams cut through the open
heath. The heath itself is mainly of acid grassland
with wide banks of gorse and spreads of purple
heather, with small copses varying the skyline and
with willow and birch marking the lines of the
streams. The bogs are marked by a change to
purple moor-grass, by cross-leaved heath appearing with the heather, by the soft white plumes of
common cottongrass. *Sphagnum* mosses spread in
the wettest places surrounded by rushes and
sedges. The plants are, perhaps, more marshland
than acid bog species and include such attractive
species as ragged-Robin, greater bird's-foot-trefoil,
devil's-bit scabious, marsh cinquefoil, marsh horsetail and marsh-marigold, with fine stands of
marsh-orchids.

Typical birds of heath and woodland include
yellowhammer, skylark, great tit and great spotted
woodpecker. Foxes hunt the woodland and the

heath, while insects include dragonflies at the
rather disturbed ponds, with moths such as fox
and emperor.

Although one would not recommend a Bank
Holiday visit, the sheer size of Sutton Park ensures
that despite the public pressures there is always
much of natural history interest.

Temple Balsall

Permit only; 4ha; WARNACT reserve
Woodland and wetland
Spring, summer

Reedswamp, wet and dry woodland attract a good
range of birds which include blackcap, coal tit and
great spotted woodpecker. Butterbur and yellow
iris may be found in the wetland, with species such
as ramsons and yellow archangel in the woods.

Tilehill Wood

SP 279790; 29.5ha; Coventry City Council
Mixed woodland
Spring, early summer

In spite of heavy urbanisation, the oak–hazel
woodland contains an attractive flora including
wood anemone, bluebell and wood-sorrel, together
with a good range of insects and birds.

Tocil Wood

Permit only; 4.4ha; WARNACT reserve
Urban oak woodland
Spring, early summer

The wood has been managed as a coppice with oak
standards over hazel and provides a show of spring
flowers such as bluebell and primrose together
with a characteristic range of woodland birds.

Ufton Fields

Permit only; 31ha; WARNACT reserve
Disused limestone workings
Spring, summer

Ufton Fields includes a tremendous range of
habitats in a relatively small area. Open-cast limestone mining has left a ridge-and-dip pattern
which has resulted in long narrow pools separated
by wooded hills and grassy slopes. Other areas are
open grasslands, invading scrub or spreads of level
marshland. Obviously the natural colonisers are
mainly lime-loving plants and, although a considerable part of the reserve has been planted with
conifers during early 'reclamation', there is a
splendid variety of plants to match the variation in
habitat.

The pools are fringed with alder and willow,
with sedges, rushes, bulrush and water-plantain –
sheltered areas where warblers sing from the
wooded slopes and hawking dragonflies flash as
they fly from shade into full sunlight. The slopes
– the ridges between the pools – may be covered
with conifers or scrubbed with hawthorn, ash,

guelder-rose, privet, wild rose and bramble above knee-deep grasses with clovers and vetches, ragwort and knapweeds. Where the ground has been most disturbed primary colonisers such as colt's-foot grow. Where the dips are damp, rather than deeply ponded, narrow marshes develop, thick with bulrush, great willowherb and horsetail species, with plants such as yellow melilot and rosebay willowherb at the drier edges. This marshland may open out on to drier grassland or change again to shallow pools which are surrounded by widespread sedgebeds.

The drier grassland varies according to the depth of the soil. Where a deeper soil has developed, the grasses are coarse, choking out many smaller plants and varied only by stronger species such as ragwort or a scrub of hawthorn, ash and wild rose. Shallow soils, however, give a wealth of lime-loving plants such as wild basil, eyebright, small scabious, yellow-wort and quaking-grass, with very good numbers of common spotted-orchid together with bee and man orchid.

Breeding birds include reed, sedge, willow and grasshopper warbler, with chiffchaff and white-throat, reed bunting, greenfinch and tree pipit, while winter may bring goldfinch, lesser redpoll and, occasionally, siskin to feed on the waterside alder. Insect life is varied and interesting, with a colony of marbled white among the butterflies and with a great variety of moths such as five-spot burnet, burnet companion, chalk carpet, Mother Shipton and northern eggar.

Wappenbury Wood

Permit only; 103.2ha; WARNACT reserve
Oak woodland
Spring, early summer

Mainly oak over old coppice, this Forestry Commission woodland also contains ash, birch, holly,

hawthorn, buckthorn, aspen and willow. The broad rides are attractive to deer, woodland butterflies – of which 37 species have been recorded – and moths, as well as woodlark, tree pipit and nightingale.

Welcombe Hills Nature Trail

SP 205564; 2km; Stratford DC
Grassland hills and woodland
Leaflet from WARNACT or Warwickshire Museum
Spring, early summer

A mixed spinney, beech woodland, parkland oak trees and conifers provide a good variety of interest and encourage such woodland birds as nuthatch and treecreeper, green and great spotted woodpecker.

Wren's Nest

SO 935923; 29.6ha; NCC reserve
Geological site
No access to fenced workings: many of them
are exceedingly dangerous
Booklets from NCC
All year

The colonising vegetation is fascinating for its lime-loving species, but the great importance of Wren's Nest lies in its exposures of Wenlock limestone. These are extremely rich in fossils and the site has long been a Mecca for geologists and palaeobiologists.

Wyken Slough

Permit only; 1.2ha; WARNACT reserve
Small urban reedbed
Spring, summer

In late summer the reedbed is an important night-time roost for migrant swallows, while throughout the flying season a good variety of dragonflies and damselflies may be seen.

A superb variety of habitats is contained in the old lime workings of Ufton Fields.

Wiltshire

Better known for its archaeological treasures than for its wildlife, Wiltshire nonetheless possesses a surprising variety of habitats and species of great interest to the naturalist. The county is well worth inspection by those who might otherwise pause only briefly to look at Stonehenge, Avebury or Salisbury Cathedral on their way to the holiday beaches and harbours of the West Country.

Since the earliest continental settlers left their traces at Windmill Hill, the history of Wiltshire has been one of forest clearance, with settlements put on the high ground, and then later at the major river crossings and confluences along the springs of the greensand. The county's chief industry has always been agriculture, and traditionally Wiltshire was known as the 'land of chalk and cheese' because of the two main types of grassland: the fine grasses of the chalk downland supported flocks of sheep, while the lusher meadows of the clay vales provided grazing for the cows whose surplus milk was converted into cheese.

Geologically, two-thirds of Wiltshire consists of chalk, either directly exposed or overlain by superficial deposits of varying thickness. Salisbury Plain and Marlborough Downs are the two distinct areas that make up the chalk downs. Limestone of another type, Jurassic, forms a border along the county's north west boundary. This part of the Cotswolds is separated from the chalk by the clay vale, which includes Oxford and Kimmeridge clays. In the south west of the county an eroded anticline exposes more Jurassic rocks in the Vale of Wardour. The Portland stone quarried from here was used in the construction of most of the important buildings in the south of the county, including Fonthill Abbey, Longford Castle and Salisbury Cathedral. Finally, in the south east of the county, a layer of tertiary deposits overlies the chalk and allows the development of some oak-with-hazel-coppice woodlands.

Wiltshire's most notable and fiercely protected habitat is undoubtedly the chalk downland, which comprises almost three-quarters of what remains of this habitat in Britain. Developed over hundreds of years, first by forest clearance and then by intensive grazing by rabbits and sheep, this habitat is now under threat from demands for increased agricultural productivity. When ploughed, chalk downland is very good for growing cereal crops, and when 'improved' with fertilisers the number of grazing cattle that a piece of land will support can be greatly increased. Agricultural improvement, however, involves the encouragement of coarse grasses and the elimination of the dozens of finer herbs and grasses that give the downland its distinctive character.

Typical good downland can contain up to 40 plant species per square metre, and these may include up to a dozen species of orchid, ranging from the rare lizard orchid through the uncommon musk orchid and marsh helleborine to the abundant early-purple orchid and common spotted-orchid. Other attractive flowers include milkworts, scabious, rampion (found only on the Marlborough Downs), gentian, stemless and tuberous thistle (the latter is one of Wiltshire's specialities), and numerous trefoils, including bird's-foot trefoil and horseshoe vetch.

Horseshoe vetch is the link to the downland's other attractive feature, the butterfly population, because it is the chief food plant for several species of blues. The powder-blue chalkhill blue, the increasingly rare Adonis blue, and the common and little blues may be found flying freely on sunny days alongside the commoner browns and marbled white and the day-flying burnet moth, whose pupal cases form such a distinctive feature on the larger flowering grass stalks.

In many parts of the county the downland is also under threat from the development of scrub, following the permanent reduction in the rabbit population after myxomatosis and the great decrease in the number of sheep kept. Although this scrub is being actively managed in many parts of Wiltshire, there are one or two sites where a sequence of progression through juniper and hawthorn scrub to ash wood can be clearly demonstrated. Mention must also be made of the role of the Ministry of Defence in the preservation of Wiltshire's downland, for a significant proportion of it comes within the boundaries of the army ranges, and hobby, stone curlew and the herds of deer on Salisbury Plain, as well as the much more plentiful skylark and lapwing, benefit greatly from this protection.

Woodland is comparatively uncommon in Wiltshire. Virtually no woods grow directly on chalk, although some fine old woodlands flourish on the clay-with-flints deposits on top of the chalk ridge between the valleys of the Wylye and the Nadder, and the largest ancient wood in the county, SAVERNAKE FOREST near Marlborough, is established on a similar deposit. On the Jurassic limestone of the north west, woods flourish which contain Bath asparagus and yellow star-of-Bethlehem, whereas the woods on the tertiary deposits south of Salisbury support many butterflies, including silver-washed fritillary, white admiral and the increasingly rare purple emperor.

Wiltshire offers three major river systems, a canal and several artificial lakes. The Salisbury Avon drains Salisbury Plain; the Bristol Avon drains the clay vale; and the Kennet drains Marlborough Downs and flows eventually into the Thames. The Salisbury Avon and the Kennet are typical chalk streams, supporting a rich fish, insect and plant life. Associated with these two rivers, especially the Avon, are the functioning remains of several old water-meadow systems, which originally operated by being periodically flooded in winter to encourage the growth of grass. The Kennet and Avon Canal crosses the county, and though still in the process of being restored it offers many undisturbed stretches where wildlife may be observed quietly. The main lakes in Wiltshire belong to the large estates, such as those at Fonthill, Bowood, Longleat and Stourhead. In the extreme north of the county the headstream of the Thames runs through some meadows growing over gravel deposits. Here, in some carefully managed reserves, grow the last Wiltshire remnants of fritillary, once so much more widespread.

The archaeological interest in Wiltshire has already been referred to, but to the all-round naturalist these historical sites often have a biological interest too. The tumuli, Iron Age forts and even the huge mound of Silbury Hill are clothed with good chalk turf. The standing sarsens of Avebury and Stonehenge bear a rich lichen flora, and the old droveways on the downs and the chalk ridges offer an abundance of plant and animal interest to the walker.

JOHN PRICE

Barbury Castle Country Park

SU 157761; 52ha; WCC
Chalk downland
Spring, summer

An Iron Age encampment set high on a north-facing scarp of the Marlborough Downs, Barbury Castle is an example of grazed downland and has superb views across the landscape round Swindon.

Woolly thistle, a spectacular plant of the chalk.

Blackmoor Copse

Permit only; 31.2ha; WTNC reserve
Old coppiced woodland
Spring, summer

Blackmoor Copse stands on a spread of clay with flints, a damp heavy soil contrasting with the thin chalk soils of the neighbouring downs. It is a splendid example of mixed woodland – both primary and secondary. Its ecology indicates that the northern part represents original forest while, in the southern part, woodland has recolonised ancient fields.

Most of the fine oak standards were felled in the 1940s and the wood was then left derelict. Thickets of birch invaded the wood, altering its traditional structure, but some fine oaks still remain. The hazel understorey is varied with shrubs such as dogwood and hawthorn, while chalk must be close to the surface in one small corner where wild privet, field maple, spindle and wayfaring-tree grow together with sanicle, wood melick and lime-loving traveller's-joy. Damp wide rides and clearings are filled with plants such as greater bird's-foot-trefoil and bugle, meadowsweet, yellow pimpernel and ragged-Robin, are edged with woodland species, with violets, primrose, woodruff and wood spurge, are bright with the movement of butterflies.

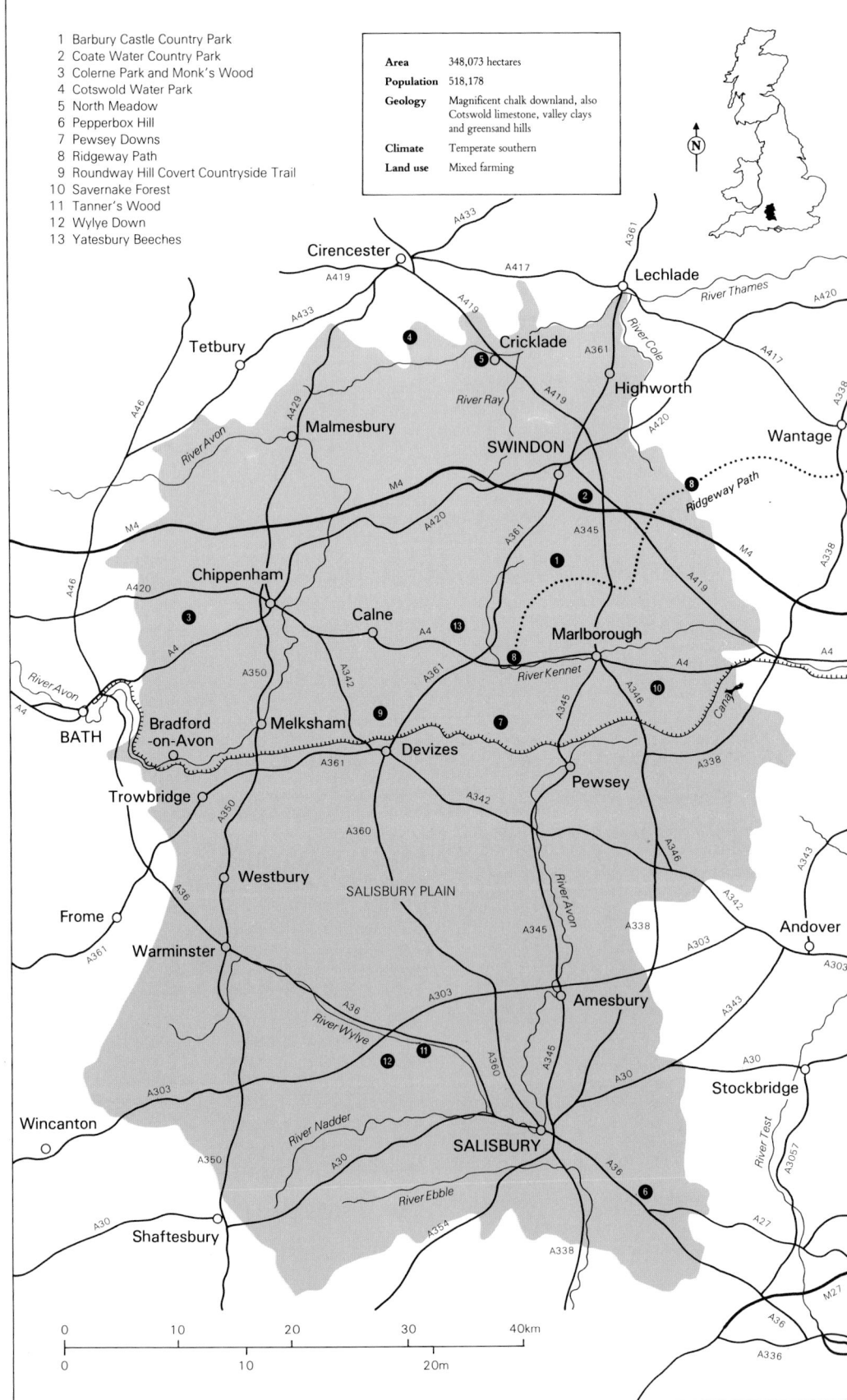

1 Barbury Castle Country Park
2 Coate Water Country Park
3 Colerne Park and Monk's Wood
4 Cotswold Water Park
5 North Meadow
6 Pepperbox Hill
7 Pewsey Downs
8 Ridgeway Path
9 Roundway Hill Covert Countryside Trail
10 Savernake Forest
11 Tanner's Wood
12 Wylye Down
13 Yatesbury Beeches

Area	348,073 hectares
Population	518,178
Geology	Magnificent chalk downland, also Cotswold limestone, valley clays and greensand hills
Climate	Temperate southern
Land use	Mixed farming

Chalkhill blue butterfly is found only in the south, usually near its food plant, horseshoe vetch.

The woodland is rich in animal life, from dormouse to roe deer, from warbler to woodcock, but its particular interest, and the reason for which it was originally acquired, is its wealth of woodland butterflies. Pride of place belongs to the purple emperor, but other attractive species occur, including white admiral, purple hair-streak and silver-washed fritillary. On a fine July day all four should be on the wing, although both purple emperor and purple hairstreak tend to fly around the topmost branches of the oaks. The damp rich clays are well suited to purple emperor since they also encourage the growth of willows, essential as its larval food plant. Like the white admiral, a related species which feeds on honeysuckle, it hibernates as a caterpillar, stitching a hammock from a leaf of its chosen food plant.

Coate Water Country Park

SU 178820; 45.8ha; Thamesdown BC
Wetland bird sanctuary
Permit only to hides
Leaflet from site
All year

An interesting variety of birds has been recorded here, including red-throated diver, woodlark, little stint and hobby.

Colerne Park and Monk's Wood

ST 835725; 44.4ha; WdT
Mixed woodland
Spring, early summer

In this fine example of old coppiced oak and ash woodland on limestone, the ground flora is notable for plants such as Solomon's-seal, angular Solomon's-seal and lily-of-the-valley.

Cotswold Water Park

SU 027955; 5666ha; WCC–Gloucestershire CC
Flooded gravel workings
Leaflets from WCC or GCC
All year

Most of the park lies in Gloucestershire, under which county it is described.

Hen Down

Permit only; 10ha; WTNC reserve
Chalk downland, scrub and woodland
Spring, summer

A small beechwood and scrubland provide cover and nest sites for birds, while the close-cropped grass is rich in small herbs such as chalk milkwort and includes both bee orchid and its variant *Ophrys apifera* var. *trollii.*

Hetley Hill

Permit only; 6ha; WTNC reserve
Chalk downland
Spring, summer

A superb variety of chalkland flowers includes restharrow, frog orchid and horseshoe vetch, the food plant for a thriving colony of chalkhill blue butterfly. Essex skipper, a grass-feeding species, has also been recorded.

Lavington Hill

Permit only; 9.2ha; WTNC reserve
Chalk grassland
Spring, summer

The downland turf of Lavington Hill is a reminder of what the chalk downlands must have been like when they were grazed by sheep, not ploughed for arable crops.

The reserve is particularly rich in plant species because the soil is shallow on the slope, but even the deep-grassed plateau is full of yellow rattle, greater knapweed and clusters of colourful vetches; with closer grazing far more species would show. The bank itself is a colourful tapestry shaped to the slope of the hill. White is picked out by oxeye daisy or the tiny eyebrights which often cushion the ant-hills. Vivid yellow is everywhere: tall spikes of agrimony show small yellow stars, common bird's-foot-trefoil clear yellow and orange, lady's bedstraw a fizzing brightness; earlier, cowslips gave a dancing show, telling of the summer yet to come. Dazzling sprays of ragwort attract bright butterflies and stand above the paler yellow of common rock-rose or horseshoe and kidney vetch, important food plants for some of the butterfly larvae. Yellow-wort is strikingly plentiful on the thinner, barer soils. Shades of pink, blue-purple, purple-red, a subtle show of colours can be seen in common centaury, restharrow, squinancywort, in clustered bellflower and harebell, in small scabious, selfheal, dwarf thistle and scented cushions of wild thyme.

A wonderful mosaic of meadow plants may be seen at North Meadow, famous for its fritillaries.

Bee and pyramidal orchid add their special beauty to the slope and, in early summer, there is the clear white of star-of-Bethlehem. One of the most spectactular plants at Lavington Hill is woolly thistle, while among several species of note bastard-toadflax, burnt orchid and lesser butterfly-orchid occur. The reserve also supports a good variety of butterflies, including chalkhill blue, green hairstreak and the beautifully marked marsh fritillary.

Nadder Island

Permit only; 0.4ha; WTNC reserve
Wooded island
Spring, early summer

The island, which is within the city of Salisbury itself, was formed artificially when a new channel was dug to drain a development area. It is now thick with willow species, banks of common nettle and stands of common reed.

North Meadow

SU 099944; 39ha; NCC reserve
Old-meadow grassland
No access off public rights of way
Leaflet from NCC
May, mid-June

An exceptionally fine ancient meadow, the reserve contains a rich mix of meadow plants: adder's-tongue, great burnet, cowslip, oxeye daisy, southern marsh-orchid and common meadow-rue. It is, however, most famous for fritillary, with per-haps 80 per cent of the total British population.

Oysters Coppice

Permit only; 5.6ha; WTNC reserve
Mixed woodland
Spring, summer

Oysters Coppice lies on upper greensand although standard ash trees among the oak-over-hazel sug-gest slightly less acid conditions, except where holly and rowan grow. The ground cover, with wild daffodil and bluebell, is more characteristic of western woodlands. A variety of mammals frequent the reserve and birds include a summer breeding population of wood warbler.

Pepperbox Hill

SU 212248; 34ha; NT
Rough chalk grassland and scrub, woodland
Spring, summer

The grasslands of PEWSEY DOWNS and LAVINGTON HILL are a richness of short-grazed herbs. Pepper-box Hill, in contrast, marks the progression towards woodland which, uncontained by man, would eventually cover these hills. This invasion of scrub is marked by clumps and banks of varied shrubs. The tiny scented herbs have faded away, drowned by the deep rank grassland, but in ex-change are thickets of colour with sheltered sun-traps where butterflies bask and yellowhammers sing. Dogwood, hawthorn, wild privet, wayfaring-tree and whitebeam are clustered together, barbed with wild rose, set among and around the dark contrast of yew and juniper. The hill is interesting as a juniper site, a plant which seems to be dying out; it is also very beautiful in its mix of berry-bearing shrubs, both for the individual change from blossom to fruit and for the mix of individual species, never the same in any two clumps of scrub.

Beneath the scrub, although small plants such as squinancywort and wild thyme only occur on ant-hills or in the paths, taller plants rise above the grasses. Pyramidal orchids occur, as do a host of other plants: agrimony, wild basil, lady's bedstraw, harebell, greater knapweed, wild mignonette, wild parsnip, ragwort, small scabious and dwarf thistle, plants which attract marbled white and gatekeeper butterflies or vivid burnet moths.

Beech has not yet spread from the woodland nearby, but it is interesting to note that the sunlit edges of the wood contain the same lime-loving shrubs as the grassland scrub contains, with the addition of elder and guelder-rose as well as more typical woodland species such as ash and holly, but without juniper. The ground cover is essentially that of woodland and varies from virtually nothing in the more densely shaded areas to spreads of ivy, dog's mercury and enchanter's-nightshade, with wood melick, sanicle, violets and woodruff.

Peppercombe Wood

Permit only; 0.8ha; WTNC reserve
Mixed woodland
Spring, early summer

Coppiced hazel under standards of oak, ash and wych elm grows above a ground cover of species such as bluebell, moschatel and snowdrop. The elms are diseased and have been replaced with a wider variety of trees.

Pewsey Downs

SU 115635; 166ha; NCC
Open chalk downland
Leaflets from NCC
Spring, summer

No one who travels in southern England can fail to be impressed by the sweep of chalkland which dominates so much of the area. Earth movements and the wear and tear of time have hollowed and rounded the landscape to a magnificent rolling stretch of country which is raised above the lower vales and edged with dramatic fluted slopes. For many centuries this was the land of sheep, of huge flocks which spread across the downland, crop-ping the fine short turf and preventing the return of the woodland which once had covered the hills. Today most of the sheep have gone or graze on reseeded pastures and the woods are kept at bay by the work of widespread arable farms. In a few areas, however, the herb-rich turf of unimproved grassland remains and Pewsey Downs is a splendid example of this very special downland.

The main slopes curve above the Vale of Pewsey like the flanks of some gigantic sleeping beast and look southwards to the great downland spread of Salisbury Plain. Despite its level sheltered farm-lands, the Vale was once a fold of chalk pushed up by the same forces that raised the Alps millions of years ago. The fold ran across southern England, from the Mendip Hills to the Hog's Back in Surrey,

and here erosion has worked a complete reversal. Whereas YR WYDDFA (Gwynedd), the summit of Snowdon, stands as a high peak because it was once compressed in the base of a giant down-fold, the top of the fold at Pewsey was stretched and loosened, so that the chalk became more easily eroded and was cut down to the clays and corn-brash which lay below. Pewsey Downs represents the steeper northern part of the fold and lies on the western edge of the chalk which runs north east-wards to include ASTON ROWANT (Oxfordshire).

Compared with Aston Rowant, Pewsey is far more exposed and has had a longer continuous record of grazing, with only a small plantation on a patch of superficial drift in contrast to the rich beechwoods of the Chilterns reserve, but it stands as a quite superb demonstration of the magic of open chalk grassland and contains a number of features which are special to the south western Downs.

The reserve is, typically, a sward of red and sheep's fescue with plentiful glaucous sedge, salad burnet and dwarf thistle, with upright brome but rather little tor-grass, and contains a particular range of plants which indicates its importance. Just as some woodland plants find it difficult to recolonise secondary woodland, so certain grass-land species are unable to return if they have been driven out. Ploughing, for instance, may totally destroy a community of plants which require a

Burnt orchid is rare in Britain.

very long time to become established; similarly, improvement by use of chemical fertilisers may eliminate plants either by making the habitat unsuitable or by encouraging other plants at their expense. Although one or two of the critical species might survive or recolonise, the presence of a group of these plants is thought to be clear evidence that the turf has been largely unaltered for many centuries. The plants indicating this ancient turf at Pewsey include bastard-toadflax, field fleawort, chalk milkwort, burnt orchid and horseshoe vetch, while the south western element is shown by the presence of betony, saw-wort and devil's-bit scabious which are rare on any chalk outside Wiltshire and Dorset.

These key species are part of a superb pattern of colourful plants which is spread across the downland and includes clustered bellflower, cowslip, hoary plantain, quaking-grass, yellow rattle and spiny restharrow, sainfoin, squinancywort, small scabious, kidney vetch and musk thistle. The slopes are often mounded with ant-hills which provide one of the special pleasures of chalklands, for each ant-heap becomes a tiny garden thick with small flowers such as lady's bedstraw, common bird's-foot-trefoil and eyebright, harebell, mouse-ear hawkweed, common rock-rose and wild thyme.

Besides burnt orchid, the reserve protects a range of other orchid species, including common spotted-orchid and bee, frog, fragrant, green-winged and pyramidal orchid. The strange-looking knapweed broomrape, which grows as a parasite on greater knapweed and is plentiful on the downlands of Salisbury Plain, is also found in the reserve. Here, too, are a number of uncommon plants – round-headed rampion near its western limit, early gentian and the rare hybrid between dwarf and tuberous thistle. Early gentian is mainly found on the southern central chalk and, unique among British gentians, does not occur in northern Europe, while the tuberous thistle is even more restricted in its British range and, apart from this area, grows in only two other districts in the country.

The wealth of plants supports a wide range of insects including large populations of downland butterflies. By early July the down may be enlivened by brown Argus, chalkhill and little blue and the fast-flying marsh fritillary which occurs here because of its food plant, devil's-bit scabious. Similarly, the others require common rock-rose, horseshoe vetch and a range of small trefoils and clovers respectively and it is this close relationship between food plant and range which provides much of the fascination of these beautiful butterflies. At Aston Rowant, for instance, marsh fritillary does not occur because devil's-bit scabious is absent, and the smaller colonies of horseshoe vetch support fewer chalkhill blues. An interesting part of the research conducted at Pewsey, where economics have forced a change from sheep to cattle grazing, is an enclosed area which is not grazed so that the effects on butterflies of the unchecked growth within may be studied – it also makes a striking contrast with the close-cropped turf around it.

While the farmed downs of Salisbury Plain make a wide and beautiful landscape, no one who visits Pewsey Down can fail to regret the loss of the far more beautiful earlier grasslands. Summer sun and a cool breeze on the hills make this a truly unforgettable place.

The grazed chalk grassland of Pewsey Downs, an example of ancient pasture.

Prescombe Down

Permit only; 47ha; NCC reserve
Chalk downland and scrub
Spring, summer

The reserve contains uncommon species, such as meadow saxifrage, saw-wort and early gentian, as well as commoner plants of chalk grassland and distinctive plants of the Wiltshire and Dorset Downs, such as dwarf sedge. The mixed scrub attracts breeding birds such as corn bunting, willow warbler and whitethroat.

Red Lodge Wood

Permit only; 4.4ha; WTNC reserve
Mixed woodland
Spring, early summer

Like SOMERFORD COMMON a relic of Braydon Forest, the reserve is a mixed-age woodland of oak over hazel, birch and hornbeam. In spring the ground cover includes wood anemone, bluebell and primrose, followed by plants such as broad-leaved helleborine. A characteristic range of birds occurs, while woodland butterflies include white admiral and purple hairstreak.

Ridgeway Path

SU 118681–259833; 30km; CC
Long-distance way
Booklet from HMSO bookshops
Spring, summer

The footpath, starting near Avebury, occasionally deflects from the ancient Ridgeway but follows the same line along the crest of the Downs to IVINGHOE BEACON (Buckinghamshire).

Roundway Hill Covert Countryside Trail

SU 005647; 2km; FC
Mixed woodland trail
Leaflet from FC
Spring, early summer

The trail circles through mixed woodland with an understorey of box above a high steep slope replanted with beech trees. Small clearings full of chalkland plants form platforms from which there are wide views across the countryside.

Savernake Forest

SU 225667; 1000ha; FC
Mixed woodland
Spring, early summer

A spread of ancient woodland on the clay-with-flints soil south east of Marlborough, Savernake Forest was held from Norman times until the sixteenth century as a royal hunting forest. Much of it has now been planted with conifers but some huge old trees remain: considerable areas are retained as broad-leaved woodland and some have been planted with young broad-leaved species including oak.

A small area of downland turf may hold an incredible number of colourful plants.

Some parts of the forest are dominated by beech, with a thin understorey of young beech and little ground cover but fallen leaves, although well-lit clearings may be carpeted with close grassland, mosses, rosebay willowherb and bracken. Other woodland blocks are far richer, with oak, ash, rowan and sycamore above a more varied herb layer, a contrast with the planted stands of beech, oak or conifers.

In common with many ancient parkland woods, the ground flora is often rather limited and the greatest variation of plants may be found in the rides and ride-edges. Here, where the shade is not as deep as it is within the trees, grassland plants such as agrimony, lady's bedstraw and meadowsweet, ragwort and hairy St John's-wort, selfheal and tormentil grow with species such as wood avens, enchanter's-nightshade, dog's mercury, wood spurge and wood-sorrel. As the dampness and type of top-soil change so do the woodland plants and, in autumn, meadow saffron may show in some of the richer areas, an uncommon beautiful flower with a rather limited range in England.

Grassland fields within the forest add to the habitat range which encourages a diversity of insects and other animals. Woodland birds include kestrel and sparrowhawk, while among the forest mammals are fallow and lesser numbers of red, roe and muntjac deer.

The woodlands are privately owned and leased to the Forestry Commission; rights of way are scarce but access is permitted on rides and paths.

Somerford Common

Permit only; 2.4ha; WTNC reserve
Mixed woodland
Spring, early summer

Like RED LODGE WOOD, Somerford is a remnant of the medieval Braydon Forest. The wood was clear-felled in the late 1950s and is now managed to provide the greatest range of variation. The ground cover includes primrose, cowslip and their hybrid, with a number of orchids, under a mixed shrub-layer with standard oak and ash. Birds are varied, and butterflies include speckled wood and white admiral.

Tanner's Wood

SU 033373; 1ha; WdT
Derelict woodland
Spring, early summer

The wood has been devastated by Dutch elm disease and is being replanted with a mix of tree species.

Upper Waterhay

Permit only; 2.7ha; WTNC reserve
Old-meadow grassland
Visitors must be accompanied by warden
May

The reserve was established to protect a fine display of fritillary, which is unusual because most of the plants have white flowers.

Vera Jeans

Permit only; 12ha; WTNC reserve
Small valley fen
Spring, summer

A shallow damp valley with a waterlogged peaty soil in a basin of clay, the reserve lies on ground once farmed as a water-cress bed. It is now managed in two halves, one a head-high fen, the other a marshy meadow astride a stream; the meadow may be grazed by cattle; the fen is fenced, sheltered and surrounded by trees.

The marshy meadow is rich in waterside plants such as water forget-me-not, water figwort and water mint, with water-cress in the clear fast-running stream. Marsh-marigold in the spring is followed later by comfrey and spiny-leaved marsh thistle. The meadow is often thick with rushes and plants such as square-stalked St John's-wort, a foretaste of the richness of the fen.

The fen is thick with tall plants such as bulrush, great horsetail, great willowherb and meadow-sweet or spread with a lower cover of sedges where more acid areas occur. The stream, in fact the Salisbury River Avon, meanders through the fen, encouraging the show of wetland plants. Among and around the taller plants, such as yellow iris, ragged-Robin, common valerian and hemp-agrimony, greater bird's-foot-trefoil and marsh bedstraw climb.

Bastard-toadflax, a tiny parasitic plant found mainly on the southern chalk.

Common spotted-orchid and southern marsh-orchid make a superb display among the sedges, but it is the acid-loving plants which are of greatest interest in this county of widespread chalk. Among the sedges is flea sedge, more commonly found on wet moors, bog pimpernel, a plant of wet peaty heaths, and bogbean, a typical plant of watery bogs. Many of the plants of the reserve are uncommon within the county and a number, such as marsh arrowgrass, have a somewhat local distribution in the country as a whole.

Breeding birds include insect-feeders which exploit the hatches so characteristic of wetland. Several species of warbler breed here and the fen and marshy meadow provide suitable habitats for water rail and snipe or hunting grounds for sparrowhawk and kestrel. Among the varied insects, the butterflies include marsh fritillary.

Whitesheet Hill

Permit only; 2.8ha; WTNC reserve
Disused chalk quarry
Spring, summer

The Hardway and Long Lane are remnants of the ancient drove-road which led from Castle Cary to Salisbury, and ran close by the chalk quarry at the foot of the Whitesheet Downs. Now long-abandoned, the quarry has largely returned to grassland and, with a range of habitat from open chalk scree to the short-cropped grassland above, has become a valuable nature reserve, a study in recolonisation.

The small chalk scree slope is largely populated by colt's-foot, a well-known primary coloniser, growing on bare ground anywhere, provided the soil is not too acid. The spring-time yellows of colt's-foot, cowslip and primrose make a beautiful display on the slopes around the entrance to the quarry, followed later by many of the characteristic chalkland plants such as lady's bedstraw, common bird's-foot-trefoil, salad burnet, harebell, yellow rattle and wild thyme.

The spread of many of the plants is clearly related to habitat, with plants such as carline thistle and quaking-grass more plentiful in the shallow turf near the open chalk and with taller plants such as meadow crane's-bill growing where the soil is deeper. Deeper soils, too, carry a developing scrub, where ash, blackthorn, hawthorn, wild privet and willow provide singing posts and nesting sites for birds. The shallow slopes beside the drove-way are brilliant with common rock-rose in summer, while the reserve as a whole holds good numbers of common spotted-orchid, together with bee and pyramidal orchid, common twayblade and, later, autumn gentian.

There are signs that fox and badger visit the reserve and it is frequently hunted by kestrel, while smaller birds include skylark, meadow pipit, willow warbler, corn bunting and yellowhammer.

The sheltered slopes full of colourful flowers attract many butterflies, including both marsh and dark green fritillary, with a colony of the chalk-loving marbled white.

Wylye Down

SU 002363; 34ha; NCC reserve
Chalk downland
Permit only off right of way
Leaflets from NCC
Spring, summer

The rich grassland contains much dwarf sedge, a species characteristic of south Wiltshire and Dorset but rare elsewhere, together with more common chalkland plants. Less common species include bastard-toadflax, field fleawort, dyer's greenweed, meadow saxifrage, saw-wort and a range of orchid species.

Yatesbury Beeches

SU 060714; 0.4ha; WdT
Roadside beeches
Spring, summer

The trees provide both shelter to the roadway and a sanctuary for birds and insects.

Wylye Down: slopes too steep to plough still hold the riches of chalk grassland.

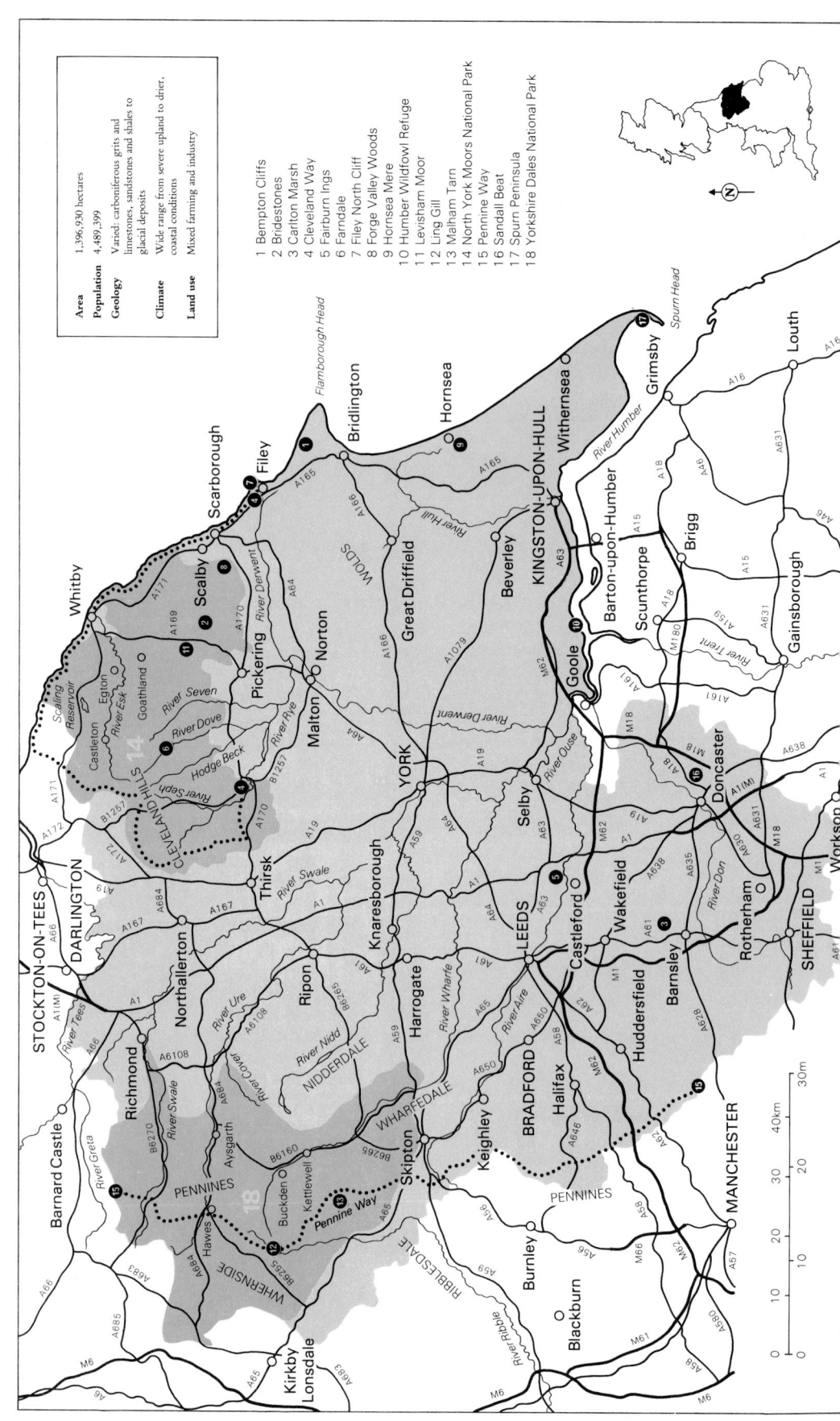

Area	1,396,930 hectares
Population	4,489,399
Geology	Varied: carboniferous grits and limestones, sandstones and shales to glacial deposits
Climate	Wide range from severe upland to drier, coastal conditions
Land use	Mixed farming and industry

1 Bempton Cliffs
2 Bridestones
3 Carlton Marsh
4 Cleveland Way
5 Fairburn Ings
6 Farndale
7 Filey North Cliff
8 Forge Valley Woods
9 Hornsea Mere
10 Humber Wildfowl Refuge
11 Levisham Moor
12 Ling Gill
13 Malham Tarn
14 North York Moors National Park
15 Pennine Way
16 Sandall Beat
17 Spurn Peninsula
18 Yorkshire Dales National Park

Yorkshire and North Humberside

Yorkshire, the largest county in England, comprises the administrative counties of North, West and South Yorkshire and, since boundary changes in the 1970s, North Humberside and parts of Cleveland, Durham, Cumbria and Lancashire. It probably boasts a greater variety of scenery, habitat and wildlife than any other part of the country.

Man's influence on the Yorkshire landscape began in very ancient times and in the eighteenth and nineteenth centuries in certain areas it was carried almost to the point of destruction, as in the industrial areas of South and West Yorkshire. Places such as Leeds and Sheffield were among the first to be affected by the Industrial Revolution, and to many people the name of Yorkshire still evokes a picture of 'dark satanic mills', coal mines and belching factory chimneys. In fact the vast proportion of its surface is covered with moorland, up to 800m high in places, and mixed lowland farming. It is to such areas that those interested in natural history will turn for enjoyment and interest.

The industrial belt, dense in places, is centred on the old West Riding conurbations. These densely populated towns arose wherever both water and coal were readily available on the eastern flank of the Pennines. By contrast North Yorkshire, which stretches westwards to within a few kilometres of the Lancashire coastline and over to Scarborough on the east coast, can claim to be one of the few counties with two national parks – part of the YORKSHIRE DALES NATIONAL PARK and the NORTH YORK MOORS NATIONAL PARK. Apart from York, Scarborough and Harrogate there are no really large centres of population in North Yorkshire.

Geologically Yorkshire can be divided into four main regions, each of which, because of its underlying rock structures, has distinctive features characteristic of the county. To the west is the Pennine range, which consists mainly of carboniferous rocks. In the centre is the Vale of York,

a continuation of the Vale of Mowbray. Here the softer Permian limestone (the stone used to build York Minster) and the Triassic rocks are sometimes extensively covered with glacial deposits. In the east, the third region and the most northerly part of lowland Britain, are the hills of the North York Moors and the Wolds, consisting of Jurassic and cretaceous rocks respectively. South and east of these hills is the Plain of Holderness, which stretches from the Wolds to the North Sea and consists of glacial boulder clay overlying chalk. Since the ice retreated at the end of the ice ages the North Sea has continued to erode this coastline, depositing material further south to form the sand spit called the SPURN PENINSULA which juts out into the Humber, and is now one of the Yorkshire Wildlife Trust's most valued reserves.

Rain is carried in on the prevailing south westerly winds and over the Pennines it is sometimes heavy and prolonged, while in the east drier conditions prevail. Northerly winter winds sometimes bring heavy snowfalls to the east coast. Where rain falls on to millstone grit, it is often retained as standing water. This leads to areas of dense peat or peat bog moors, with high acidity and little botanical interest apart from cottongrass, which is sometimes present in profusion. To the north of the millstone grit is the Askrigg carboniferous block, where the water filters through the limestone, often making extensive cave systems, to re-emerge as the streams and rivers that drain eastwards towards the Yorkshire Ouse.

Over the centuries the northern Pennine upland, predominantly heather moorland, has been almost completely denuded of trees. It is surrounded by limestone outcrops and stone-walled fields on the lower slopes, and has become for the most part man-made wetland desert, now partially grazed by sheep and used as grouse moors. Raven, buzzard, peregrine and merlin still survive in the remoter parts in spite of changing habitats, man's continuing persecution and persistent use of organochlorine pesticides. Associated with the areas are such waders as curlew, golden plover and redshank with, on the streams, grey wagtail and dipper. Little afforestation has taken place in the Dales.

Except for those rivers flowing through industrial areas, such as the Calder and Aire, most Yorkshire rivers that drain eastward from the Pennines or the southward flowing Derwent from the North York Moors are relatively unpolluted. The Derwent, described as the most unpolluted river in lowland England, has a great variety of wildlife, including a few otter in its upper reaches. In the lower Derwent valley the Yorkshire Wildlife Trust has established an internationally important wetland reserve at WHELDRAKE INGS. Here in the winter months thousands of wildfowl gather on the flood waters, including Bewick's and whooper swan.

Like other northern counties, Yorkshire lies at the northern and southern limits of some of Britain's flora and fauna, which adds considerably to its natural history potential. Such interesting plants as mountain pansy, bog asphodel and spring sandwort are found in the Dales, and deep in afforested areas around Pickering grow oak fern and the saprophytic yellow bird's-nest. Mammals include harvest mouse, Leisler's bat, roe deer and pine marten. Eight of Britain's amphibians and reptiles live in the county, with palmate newt in the upland districts and grass snake in wetland carrs around the River Don. Insect and spider species are both numerous and varied.

Nature reserves in Yorkshire are managed by the Yorkshire Wildlife Trust and other interested bodies, and include a variety of habitats and associated species. There are boglands such as ASKHAM BOG near York, and various heathlands in the Vale of York where long-eared owl, little ringed plover and nightjar regularly breed. In an area of intensive agriculture in North Humberside, remnants of the chalk flora of the Wolds are to be found at WHARRAM QUARRY. In South Yorkshire wetland flashes, often created by mining subsidence, have been established as reserves; the most important of them is POTTERIC CARR. Limestone pavement, sea cliffs and staging posts for migratory birds are among other important areas preserved for study and enjoyment by those who care about the preservation of Yorkshire's wildlife heritage.

MICHAEL J. THOMPSON

Adel Dam

Permit only; 8ha; YWT reserve
Artificial lake surrounded by woodland
All year

Two observation hides overlook the lake, which is fringed with birch, oak, sycamore and Scots pine above thickets of hawthorn, willow and bramble. The woodland encourages typical birds such as warblers, great spotted woodpecker, kestrel and tawny owl. Teal, mallard and heron may visit the lake.

Allerthorpe Common

Permit only; 6.1ha; YWT reserve
Wet heath with pools
Spring, summer

The reserve is a damp heathland invaded by oak woodland. The wetter areas hold *Sphagnum* mosses, round-leaved sundew, marsh cinquefoil and marsh gentian. Curlew, nightjar and whinchat represent the heathland birds and snipe and woodcock may occur in winter.

Ashberry

Permit only; 5.3ha; YWT reserve
Valley grassland and woods
Spring, summer

A deep, quiet valley fed by springs, it has a good range of limestone plants, including three species of quite exceptional beauty: bird's-eye primrose, globeflower and grass-of-Parnassus. The woodland areas are rich in bird and mammal life.

Askham Bog

Permit only; 42.5ha; YWT reserve
Good range of open fen to fen woodland
Spring, summer

Oak and birch woodland, with alder where the ground becomes damper, includes areas of willow swamp, alder buckthorn and bog myrtle. The numerous plant species include some rare sedges, royal fern and water-violet. The reserve has many species, particularly insects, in common with the East Anglian fens.

Bempton Cliffs

TA 197738; 4.8km; RSPB reserve
Chalk cliffs
The cliffs are extremely high and dangerous; visitors must keep to paths
Leaflet from RSPB
Spring, summer

If one never saw another big seabird colony Bempton Cliffs would amply explain the excitement and sense of awe that such places inspire. The reserve consists of a narrow strip of clifftop grassland, rich in lime-loving plants, and the magnificent cliffs themselves. These are the highest chalk cliffs in the country and drop sheer more than 120m to the North Sea below. In the breeding season even the smallest ledge or crevice seems to hold a nesting bird. Bempton Cliffs are the most southerly seabird cliffs on the east coast of Britain and the only mainland colony of gannets is to be found here: there may be over 350 pairs nesting on the broader ledges.

There are literally thousands of auks – guillemot, razorbill and puffin. The guillemots line the long narrow ledges, puffins peer from the deeper cracks and the razorbills huddle in the narrow, shallow crevices. The auks seem to throw themselves off the cliffs and then drop, arrowing out to sea. The return is equally swift and sudden: they drive themselves through the air, not sailing like the gulls but beating a fast straight path to a halt, feet out and wings back-pedalling, to drop into an impenetrable tangle of their peers.

The most successful breeding birds, however, are the kittiwakes; more than 65,000 pairs nest here. Of 160 bird species known from the reserve some 33 are regular breeders – the cliffs also afford nest sites for land birds such as jackdaw, rock pipit, rock dove and feral pigeon.

At other seasons the cliffs are a vantage point from which to watch migrant birds, waders in summer and large flocks of Sandwich and common tern, which may be harried by arctic skua; autumn birds may include Manx shearwater and common scoter, perhaps even sooty shearwater or great skua; winter brings flocks of redwing and fieldfare, shorelark and snow bunting and the occasional short-eared owl.

The 15 butterfly species identified include small copper and common blue with migrants such as red admiral and painted lady. The moths include the day-flying narrow-bordered five-spot burnet and chimney-sweeper. The rare great yellow bee is one of 12 bee species recorded.

Bretton Lakes

Permit only; 60ha; YWT–Bretton Hall College
Two ornamental lakes in wooded parkland
Spring, summer

The lakes' 20ha of open water support a resident population of Canada geese, coot, great crested grebe, mallard and tufted duck. In winter goldeneye, pintail, pochard, teal and wigeon may be seen. Plants such as bulrush, great willowherb, meadowsweet and yellow iris fringe the lakes, while alder grows on the northern edge of the Lower Lake and there are some fine standard oak, beech, ash, yew, sycamore and chestnut trees. In the north west of the reserve fine mature deciduous woodland is carpeted in spring with snowdrop and daffodil.

Bridestones

SE 880904; 140ha; YWT–NT reserve
Fine dry moorland with rock outcrops
Spring, summer, autumn

The moorland is chiefly heather, bilberry and occasional cowberry. Bracken grows on the slopes and birch, rowan and oak are invading the central portion. Small wet areas are shown by common cottongrass and cross-leaved heath. Roe deer, fox and badger may be seen and kestrel and sparrowhawk are resident.

The superb chalk cliffs of Bempton, over 120m high and Britain's only mainland gannetry.

Brockadale

Permit only; 6.4ha; YWT reserve
Mixed woodland and grassland
Spring, summer

False brome and dog's mercury carpet much of the ash–sycamore woodland. The dry grassland holds quaking-grass, common twayblade and early-purple orchid, with spring cinquefoil, carline thistle and common rock-rose, while yellow iris and hound's-tongue grow in the river meadows. There is a good variety of birds and mammals and both slow-worm and common lizard occur.

Carlton Marsh

SE 378104; 14ha; Barnsley MBC
Embankment, marshland and pools
All year

The plant life, ranging from dog rose, hawthorn and acid grasses to willow scrub, reed canary-grass, bulrush and southern marsh-orchid, attracts a variety of insects and other small animals. Mallard, whinchat and several warblers breed here, while the pools and marsh draw passage and wintering waterfowl.

427

The view from the Cleveland Way on Sutton Bank, across to the Vale of York.

Cleveland Way

SE 607837–TA 121808; 144km; CC
Long-distance way
Booklet from HMSO bookshops
Spring, summer

The walk curves around the mass of the NORTH YORK MOORS NATIONAL PARK, dips briefly into Cleveland, and shows a magnificent variety of upland and coastal scenery and wildlife.

Colt Park Wood

Permit only; 8.5ha; NCC reserve
Limestone woodland
Spring, early summer

A mainly open ungrazed ash woodland, set on an area of limestone pavement, the reserve contains a wealth of plants such as baneberry, alpine cinquefoil and melancholy thistle.

Denaby Ings

Permit only; 20ha; YWT reserve
Riverside flood marshes and subsidence ponds
All year

An observation hide overlooks Cadeby Flash, now a permanent pool as a result of mining subsidence. Reed and sedge warbler, great crested grebe, mallard, pochard, shoveler and tufted duck breed and the winter-flooded marshes attract many seasonal visitors and passage migrants.

Fairburn Ings

SE 460278; 247.2ha; RSPB reserve
Large subsidence ponds and marshland
No access away from footpaths
Leaflet from RSPB
All year

The results of mining have changed the area from one of extensive flood meadows to one of low hills and permanent lakes. Its attractiveness to birds, however, remains, for it forms part of a long-established migration route.

Of the 240 species recorded 170–180 are seen annually and up to 70 breed or have bred. There is a resident population of mute swan and Canada goose and breeding duck include gadwall, mallard, pochard, shoveler, teal and tufted duck, together with both great crested and little grebe. Waders include lapwing, redshank and snipe, with little ringed plover and, occasionally, ringed plover and oystercatcher. In winter whooper swan arrive from northern Europe and Russia, together with flocks of wigeon and goldeneye, with goosander and small numbers of scaup and smew, while vast numbers of gulls come in to roost, joining the resident breeding population of black-headed gull. Ruff, spotted redshank, greenshank, dunlin and green, wood and common sandpiper fly in on their spring and autumn migrations and, particularly in spring, numbers of black tern and little gull pass through. Very many smaller birds may be seen at these migration times and one of the most exciting sights is the autumn movement of the swallows, when around 20,000 birds may pass southwards, often harried by predators – a hobby, for instance, can fly down even a swift.

The spoil heaps are massed with colonisers of waste ground – rosebay willowherb, foxglove, tansy, weld and wild mignonette. The muddy edges of the open waters are lined with bulrush, yellow iris and celery-leaved buttercup. Both marsh dock, generally limited to south east England, and the slightly commoner golden dock, also occur. Buttonweed is one of the alien plants here, otherwise known only in the Deeside–Merseyside area.

Farndale

SE 666974; 1050ha; NYMNPC reserve
Valley daffodil fields
Spring

The headwaters of the Dove drain this narrow dale, which is most important for its spectacular spring show of wild daffodil.

Filey North Cliff

TA 115813; 46ha; Scarborough BC
Clifftop parkland and shoreline
Guidebook from information office, Filey Country Park
All year

A nature trail and bird hide have been established along the shoreline and cliffs of Filey Brigg.

Forge Valley Woods

SE 985860; 63ha; NCC reserve
Semi-natural woodland
Leaflet from NCC
Spring, summer

Oak on the upper slopes changes to ash and elm in the lower, more sheltered parts with alder and willow in the damp valley bottom. There is a good understorey of hazel, holly, hawthorn, elder and rowan, and the ground cover includes primrose, bluebell, wood anemone, wood-sorrel and early-purple orchid in spring, giving way to strong-smelling ramsons and then to summer green ferns and mosses. Common woodland birds are plentiful and include nuthatch and great spotted wood-pecker with chiffchaff, willow and wood warbler.

Garbutt Wood

Permit only; 24ha; YWT reserve
Rough grassland, woodland, scree and cliff
Spring, summer

The reserve drops from sheer cliffs, through a litter of scree and boulders, bracken-clad slopes and damp woodland, to the shores of Gormire Lake. There is a wide range of habitat, sometimes lime-rich, showing such plants as bloody crane's-bill, heath bedstraw, ragged-Robin and northern marsh-orchid. Red, roe and fallow deer visit and both badger and fox are resident.

Below Grass Wood, the River Wharfe runs beside banks of dazzling shingle.

Grass Wood

Permit only; 79.3ha; YWT reserve
Rich ash woodland on limestone
Spring, summer

When the ice melted away from Wharfedale the steep site of Grass Wood must have stood over a raging torrent driving through a bare white ravine. Now one can look out from a wonderful richness of limestone plants to a clear, curving, pebbled river set in a long green valley. The reserve is a place of crags and flagstoned pathways climbing through well-lit ash woodland. The grey of the ash trunks reflects the grey of the weathered limestone and both are grown around with flowers. Lily-of-the-valley follows the spring primrose and bluebell. These, in turn, are followed by ferns and white-flowered privet while honeysuckle climbs from the pavement areas and fills the air with scent. The grassland above the crags is yellow with common rock-rose, cushioned with mats of wild thyme and blazing with the crimson of bloody crane's-bill.

The scree slopes are pink with herb-Robert, thick with carpets of woodruff and dog's mercury. Above, the crags are clustered with burnet rose and here and there the white-flowered rock whitebeam. Small plateaus of limestone grassland cap the crags with tiny milkwort, salad burnet and the rare limestone bedstraw while, behind the grassland, the woods stand in a jumble of limestone pavement. Climbing upwards the slope lessens and damper, deeper soils give a fine high-forest of ash. The range, from crags through scrub to woodland, encourages a good variety of birds.

Hayburn Wyke

NZ 010970; 13.6ha; NT–YWT reserve
Wooded coastal valley
Spring, summer

Over many years, the Hayburn Beck has carved out a valley which curves to the sea and drops in a sudden small waterfall to the boulder-strewn beach below. The valley slopes are thickly wooded and the only grassland is on the open shoulders of the sea cliffs in the small cove; generally the coast here is high, sheer and wooded to the edge.

The woods are almost impenetrable, except along the paths, sometimes dry and shading great moss-covered boulders, in other places damp, tussocked with great wood-rush and sometimes hiding shallow wet mires, almost invisible in the gloom of the trees. Generally it is oak woodland, but ash, hazel, hawthorn and holly also grow here with sycamore and rhododendron. Wood millet grows where there is enough light and there are thick carpets of woodruff and enchanter's-nightshade; where the ground is damp yellow pimpernel and opposite-leaved golden-saxifrage may be found. More open parts of the reserve show fine clumps of elecampane, and there are small patches of grass-of-Parnassus.

Along the beach on to which the valley opens there is a most unusual mix of rocky beach and shingle where large boulders have been rounded by the power of the driving sea. Above the sea's normal reach the slopes are rich in a range of species from kidney vetch and common bird's-foot-trefoil to common spotted-orchid, ragged-Robin and common butterwort.

The Hayburn Beck falls to meet the sea.

Pied flycatcher and redstart nest while willow warbler, chiffchaff and blackcap represent the warblers here. Treecreeper and great spotted woodpecker are also resident and woodcock and goldcrest may be seen in autumn.

Hetchell Wood

Permit only; 11.6ha; YWT reserve
Mixed woodland with clearings
Spring, summer

Alder swamp by the stream contains wetland plants such as greater tussock-sedge, ragged-Robin and common spotted-orchid beneath slopes of acid grassland and hawthorn scrub. Higher slopes carry limestone woodland of ash, elm and hawthorn with a ground cover of dog's mercury, ramsons and sanicle, and areas of limestone grassland contain common spotted-orchid, crosswort and dyer's greenweed.

Hornsea Mere

TA 198473; 235ha; RSPB reserve
Lake, fields and woodland
Permit only off rights of way and to hide
Leaflet from RSPB or visitor centre; escorted tours
as advertised
All year

The largest natural freshwater lake in Yorkshire and less than 1km from the sea, the reserve contains a variety of interesting plants and small animal life but is most renowned for its bird life. Formed as a result of glaciation, the lake is fringed by reedbeds and fen, which include common reed, lesser bulrush, yellow iris, branched bur-reed, mare's-tail, water-plantain and flowering-rush. The mere has a large breeding population of reed warbler, close to its north eastern limit, and attracts impressive numbers of winter wildfowl.

The only general access to the reserve is on the footpath which runs through sloping fields from TA 198466. From here, in winter, thousands of mallard, very many pochard, wigeon, teal, tufted duck and goldeneye may be seen, with lesser numbers of gadwall, goosander and shoveler. Occasional bittern and bearded tit may visit the spreads of reedmarsh, or Bewick's and whooper swan pause on the mere.

Besides the reed warblers and some of the duck, reed bunting and sedge warbler breed, with a typical range of woodland birds, giving an average of 60 breeding species. In most years around 170 species are seen and these include many passage birds – curlew sandpiper, little stint and ruff are regular, while other migrants include wryneck, red-backed and the occasional great grey shrike, with continental birds such as blue-headed wagtail. Other regular passage birds include marsh harrier, hunting the reedbeds, snipe and jack snipe on the autumn muds, little gull and black tern.

The mere is rich in water animals and, although the range of hatching insects is relatively

Hornsea Mere: a rich glacial lake which attracts a great variety of birds.

small, their numbers are huge, feeding vast flocks of swallows and martins which rest in the reed-beds on passage. Other insects include butterflies such as common blue and small copper, with a range of over 200 moths, including bulrush wainscot, clouded border and least yellow underwing.

Humber Wildfowl Refuge

No access; 1280ha; Humber Wildfowl Refuge Committee
Saltmarsh, mudflats and sand banks
Can be overlooked from SE 864242 and 936263
Autumn, winter

The sanctuary harbours good numbers of wintering pink-footed geese, together with mallard, shelduck, teal, wigeon and large gatherings of waders.

Kiplingcotes Chalk Pit

Permit only; 4.4ha; YWT reserve
Chalk grassland and scrub
Spring, summer

Although small, this reserve is an exceptional demonstration of the richness of chalkland. There are four main habitats: open chalk on the old quarry face, recently colonised plant communities on the quarry floor, rich old grassland above the face, and scrub woodland.

Much of the quarry face is unvegetated chalk but the level floor is a mosaic of flowers: among them red, white and bladder campion, wild thyme, germander speedwell, wild pansy and lady's bed-straw. Cowslips flower in spring followed later by harebells. Among the grasses is quaking-grass, a lime-loving plant of great delicacy, while common spotted-orchid and pyramidal orchid are two of the orchids most commonly found.

On the grassland above the face oxeye daisy, kidney vetch, meadow vetchling, tufted vetch and hop trefoil grow. Orchids are again plentiful, while broom and dogwood provide both colour and shel-ter. The reserve holds two plants of particular interest: adder's-tongue, in a highly uncharacteris-tic habitat, and English stonecrop, which has a generally western distribution in Britain and is most uncommon in this part of the country.

This wealth of plant life encourages a similar wealth of animal life and butterflies and moths are abundant. The butterflies include large skipper, grayling, ringlet, meadow brown and small heath, together with small copper, dingy skipper and common blue. Moths include yellow underwing, cinnabar, elephant hawk-moth and burnet moth.

Bird species are increasing, with plantings that are designed to attract them, and include greenfinch, long-tailed tit, willow warbler and whitethroat.

Levisham Moor

SE 853937; 840ha; NYMNPC
Upland moorland, valleys and woodland
Spring, summer

The variety of habitats and wildlife make this area an important site for conservation. Heather moorland surrounds the enormous curving valley of the Hole of Horcum, a wide, level valley ending in slopes as steep as sea cliffs. The valley holds two arctic–alpine plants, chickweed wintergreen and dwarf cornel, at or near the southern limit of their British distribution.

There are large areas of bracken in the moorland, but there are also fine stands of heather with bilberry and crowberry. Large blue-green cushions are the acid-loving moss *Leucobryum glaucum* and, in open areas of mat-grass, tormentil, heath bedstraw and sheep's sorrel may be found.

From the moorland edge the ground drops away again, not in a valley like the Hole of Horcum, but into a wide rolling space of farmland and forestry with the North York Moors rising behind. Moorland birds include red grouse, meadow pipit, curlew, snipe and golden plover.

The woodlands have a rich mixture of trees and, although mainly oakwoods, include alder and willow along the streams with birch and rowan at the moorland edge and aspen, small-leaved lime, Scots pine and elm among the oak, together with beech, field maple and guelder-rose. Crab apple, hawthorn, blackthorn, gorse and broom occur. The water's edge in the lower valleys may be thick with meadowsweet and water mint and the small open streamlets with water-cress and brooklime while, on the woodland floor, primrose and bluebell grow. Further up the valleys, where the soil is thinner and more acid, common cow-wheat and foxglove show among the ferns and mosses. There is great diversity in the woodlands, from lowland valley woods and streamside alder fringes to thin oak scrubland on steep banks or by torrential moorland streams; the woods generally run

The lime-rich waters of Malham Tarn form the core of a most important reserve.

north to south but the valleys twist and merge and there are woodland slopes of every aspect, every angle and all combinations from open broken woodland to close-canopied dense woods.

The pastures add yet another range of habitat, with richer grasses, dog rose scrub, marsh and spear thistle, small wetland clusters of cuckooflower and ragged-Robin with globeflower in some ditches. On drier banks harebell, dog violet and fragrant orchid may occur.

Roe deer slip quietly out of the woodlands to graze the pastures and brown hare is not uncommon. Woodland birds are plentiful and dipper breed along the streams.

Ling Gill

SD 803778; 5ha; NCC reserve
Limestone gorge woodland
No dogs allowed
Leaflet from NCC
Late spring, summer

An area of dangerously steep woodland, preserved from grazing by its inaccessible position, the gorge represents a rich limestone habitat which once must have been far more common. Ash and wych elm grow where it is more sheltered, with birch, bird cherry, rowan and aspen on more exposed areas. Bracken, purple moor-grass and deergrass grow on the upper slopes while wood melick flourishes where shade is dense, and ferns cover parts of the damp valley bottom.

Little Beck Wood

Permit only; 12.6ha; YWT reserve
Steep oak woodland
Spring, summer

The woods, chiefly of oak with ash, alder along the streams and a hazel understorey, include holly, rowan, wych elm and a few conifers. Spring brings primrose, bluebell, wood anemone and early-purple orchid and wetter parts have moschatel and both opposite-leaved and alternate-leaved golden-saxifrage. Birds include great spotted and green woodpecker, marsh tit, woodcock and dipper; mammals include roe deer, fox and badger.

Malham Tarn

SD 890672; 73.6ha; FSC–NT reserve
Tarn, bog, fen, woodland and limestone grassland
Permit only off rights of way or nature trail
Booklets from field studies centre
Spring, summer

This exceptional reserve is one of the best documented in the country. Its mixture of lowland and upland and of northern and southern plant and animal species make it an important site for scientific research.

Maltby Low Common

Permit only; 6ha; YWT reserve
Mixed grassland, scrub and marsh, small woodland
Spring, summer

The marsh is rich in sedges, shaded by aspen, and has typical marsh plants including lousewort, sneezewort and pepper-saxifrage. Acid grassland, bracken and heath dog-violet contrast with a bank rich in orchid species and plants such as restharrow, small scabious, grass-of-Parnassus and columbine. There are many insect species and the scrub and small woodland attract birds such as redstart, whinchat and stonechat.

Moorlands

Permit only; 6.8ha; YWT reserve
Mixed woodland
Spring, summer

An old estate woodland planted with a great range of exotics, both conifers and broad-leaved trees, the reserve contains ginko, tulip tree and tree-of-heaven. The show of daffodil, narcissus, azalea and rhododendron in spring and early summer is especially fine.

North York Moors National Park

See map; 138,050ha; NYMNPC
Moorland, valleys and coast
Leaflets from NYMNPC
Spring, summer, autumn

FARNDALE, Bransdale, Rosedale and Westerdale are among the valleys carved in the North York Moors, valleys which a stranger might think should belong to the YORKSHIRE DALES NATIONAL PARK, draining the hills of the Pennines. Visit them, though, and no confusion is possible for these are cut into England's largest expanses of heather moorland, instead of the grass heath and limestone scars of valleys such as Wharfedale. Limestone occurs within the park and contributes much to its beauty but the high plateau of central moorland is mainly acid sandstone. The rocks, as a whole, are extremely varied and, terminating in some of the highest sea cliffs in England, provide evidence of the Jurassic which parallels parts of the Dorset coast in interest.

The valleys of the North York Moors are cut in England's largest heather moorlands.

Heather and wind-blown grasses on Danby High Moor above Westerdale.

The heather moorland is varied with bilberry, with bell heather and bracken on some slopes, with wetter areas where cross-leaved heath, mat-grass and heath rush grow and with spreads of deergrass where sandstones give way to wet shales. Crowberry and cowberry occur here and there while the park also contains a population of cloudberry. Where drainage is poor, in valley bottoms or occasionally in the heart of the upland peats, bogs develop which may hold a fine range of plants such as *Sphagnum*, common and hare's-tail cottongrass, cranberry, bog myrtle, bog rosemary and several species of sedge. Uncommon plants, such as bog-sedge, and northern species, including lesser twayblade and common wintergreen, occur on these upland moors, while the richer valleys have a splendid variety of species.

Farndale is noted chiefly for its spring display of wild daffodil but other areas of woods and grassland, enriched by limestone or varied minerals, hold a wide range of rare or uncommon plants. Greater butterfly-orchid and bird's-nest, burnt, frog, green-winged and small-white orchid may be found, together with yellow bird's-nest and marsh helleborine. Damp areas may show globeflower, grass-of-Parnassus and bird's-eye primrose. Plants of dry chalk or limestone also occur, and woodland species include baneberry and herb-Paris.

Ponds, lakes and rivers add further variation and this wide range is demonstrated by the park's wealth of bird life. Around 150 species are recorded as resident while the fine stretch of coastline encourages passage birds. The moors are managed for red grouse and support populations of predators such as kestrel, merlin and peregrine, while the areas of blanket bog provide breeding sites for curlew, dunlin and golden plover. Wetland reedbeds and streamside sites attract their characteristic birds and the open waters, such as SCALING DAM WILDFOWL SANCTUARY (Durham, Cleveland, and Tyne and Wear), draw winter wildfowl including good numbers of mallard, pochard, teal, tufted duck and wigeon, with goldeneye and a range of less common species. The coastal cliffs have breeding colonies of seabirds and form an excellent vantage point for sea-watching.

Mammals are well represented, with dormouse and harvest mouse occurring at the limit of their northern range. There are particularly good numbers of badger, fox and stoat. Fallow, roe and possibly red deer are present within the park, together with a small population of red squirrel, occasional otter and mink. A number of bat species have been recorded and the coast attracts non-breeding grey and common seal.

This whole highly varied area has a character all of its own. Unlike the Yorkshire Dales, which are part of the Pennines, it is bounded by the Cleveland Hills, the Hambletons and the Tabular Hills, with the North Sea on its eastern flank, to form an upland which stands on its own above the surrounding lowlands. Its western flanks look across to the Pennines, its northern heights to the distant Cheviot Hills, and southwards the Vale of York spreads beside the Yorkshire Wolds.

The legacy of the ice ages is marked on the North York Moors: boulders were carried from the Cheviots, from the Lake District and the Pennines, even from as far as Scandinavia, to be dropped in the region of Eskdale. Eskdale itself was probably once a huge lake, when the melting glacial waters were held back by the North Sea ice and the overflow of this violent flood cut the ravine of Newton Dale in escaping to the south. Many of the deep-cut valleys were probably formed in this way and their narrow winding courses are a feature of the park.

Water, too, has had its effect on the coastline, in valleys such as HAYBURN WYKE where the overlying boulder clay has been cut down to the rocks beneath, in the dramatic landslip of Beast Cliff and the splendid wave-cut platform to be seen in Robin Hood's Bay. The landslip, as in the jumbled parts of the Dorset coast, has provided a wilderness difficult to reach. A huge section of cliff has slumped seaward, forming a bench-like plateau, wooded with oak and ash. A scrub of birch, hawthorn, rowan, sycamore, broom, gorse and wild rose gives cover for many birds and other animals, while the smaller plants are also richly varied. Acid areas may show heather and devil's-bit scabious; rich damper sites contain marsh arrowgrass, fairy flax and grass-of-Parnassus; small pools contrast with sweeps of rosebay willowherb and bracken. The wave-cut platform is considered to be one of the finest in Britain and contains a wide range of marine plants and animals.

Its list of rare plants may nowhere approach that of the Yorkshire Dales, its peaks may be lower and its size considerably smaller, but the wealth of variation makes the park an area of exceptional wildlife value.

Pennine Way

SE 078047–NZ 897067; 160km; CC
Long-distance way
Booklet from HMSO bookshops
Spring, summer

The first and most famous long-distance footpath in the British Isles, the Pennine Way runs mainly along the mountain chain which forms the backbone of England.

Potteric Carr

Permit only; 104ha; YWT reserve
Wetland, small area of grassland and woods
British Rail Walking Permit required
All year

A complex of subsidence ponds, artificial pools, drainage dykes and areas of wetland together with wet and dry woods and grassland gives Potteric Carr a very wide range of habitat. The pools are fringed with common reed, bulrush and soft rush, with scrub and woodland providing shelter for a great variety of birds.

The many breeding waterfowl include shoveler, pochard, tufted duck and water rail with garganey, which outside the south east of England nests regularly only in Somerset and Yorkshire. Reed and sedge warbler breed in the fringing vegetation, there is a noisy black-headed gull colony, and the woodlands have their own range of breeding species.

Non-breeding birds visiting the reserve include goldeneye, pintail, wigeon, great crested grebe and bittern. Occasionally marsh harrier may be seen, or perhaps a great grey shrike, either wintering or pausing in its passage south. Wood sandpiper and black tern pass through on their autumn journey to Africa, and wryneck, once plentiful in Britain but now reduced to a very few breeding pairs, has been recorded.

The pools and marsh areas are rich in bright flowers: marsh-marigold in spring, yellow iris, yellow water-lily, water forget-me-not and water mint in summer. The woods are mixed – alder wetlands full of meadowsweet, marsh woundwort and plants of damp woodland contrast with areas of scrub and a tall, dry, open woodland. Ballast imported for the railway lines provides areas of lime-enrichment and the lines are fringed with unexpected plants such as hedgerow and meadow crane's-bill and evening primrose.

The water and wealth of plants encourage a great range of insects, including china mark moth which, as a caterpillar, makes itself a raft – it sandwiches itself between two leaves of duckweed and floats in this camouflage on the pond.

Saltmarshe Delph

Permit only; 3.6ha; YWT reserve
Small wetland and reedbeds
Spring, summer

This small wetland is of considerable scientific interest for the many tiny animals of its rich waters. The wealth of bird life is encouraged by beds of common reed, bulrush and lesser bulrush.

Golden plover: its plaintive whistling call and dramatic plumage distinguish this moorland bird.

Sandall Beat

SE 610044; 76.8ha; Doncaster BC
Mixed woodland
Booklet from Doncaster Museum
Spring, early summer

This secondary woodland, planted with a great mix of tree species in the early nineteenth century, includes an area of fen containing common reed, purple small-reed, bulrush and lesser bulrush. Breeding birds include woodcock, grasshopper warbler and nightingale.

Scar Close

Permit only; 93ha; NCC reserve
Limestone pavement
Spring, summer

The ungrazed pavement contains a splendid development of clint-and-grike flora including blue moor-grass, bloody crane's-bill and lily-of-the-valley on the slabs, with hart's-tongue, hard shield-fern and green spleenwort in the fissures.

Skipwith Common

Permit only; 240ha; YWT reserve
Wet and dry heath, marsh and woodland
Spring, summer

A nature trail laid out on a loop road to the old airfield demonstrates much of the range of habitat in this fine mixed heathland, and it has the additional advantage that it is sufficiently level to be negotiated by people in wheelchairs.

The woods are generally clumped, with scrub birch on the heaths and willow in the wetter areas, although there is considerable overlap and both birch and oak occur in the wetter areas. Bracken and heather with bell heather characterise the dry heaths, with heather, cross-leaved heath and clumped tussocks of purple moor-grass where the ground becomes wetter. The wet heaths grade into marshland and open water and a system of deep drainage dykes divides part of the area.

Broad-leaved helleborine follows common twayblade in the late summer woods, while common spotted-orchid occurs in the dyke-edge grasses. In the wetlands marsh pennywort, marsh bedstraw and skullcap may be found and the small pools of the heathland hold *Sphagnum* mosses, bog pimpernel and round-leaved sundew.

The common, with its level heathland broken by scrub and woodland, with open pools and wet marshes, with dense areas of bracken and with grassland and arable fields around, is most attractive to birds. One of the more uncommon species found here is nightjar, one of the most evident black-headed gull which has established a successful breeding colony.

South House Pavement

Permit only; 4ha; YWT reserve
Limestone pavement
Spring, summer

The reserve consists of several pavement areas of exposed rock, often deeply fissured and pock-marked with solution holes. Generally the pavements are grazed, which reduces vegetation to rough grassland, but the deeper cavities often contain a good range of characteristic species, particularly ferns such as green spleenwort, limestone fern, brittle bladder-fern and rigid buckler-fern.

Limestone pavement at Scar Close: protection from grazing conserves its special plant life.

Sprotbrough Flash

Permit only; 14.3ha; YWT reserve
Subsidence lake
All year

The long, open lake, formed by mining subsidence, has a good marshland vegetation including sedges and stands of common reed attractive to many waterside birds. With the lakeside willow and hawthorn scrub they also provide resting places for seasonal migrants. Great crested grebe and kingfisher breed.

Spurn Peninsula

TA 417151; 112ha; YWT
Narrow dune and shingle promontory, tidal mudflats
Vehicular access is controlled
Leaflets from information centre
Migration times

This narrow spine of shingle and sand protected by sea defences forms one of the finest sites in Europe for seeing migrant birds. The sea defences are necessary since the peninsula has had a history of growth and destruction dating back at least to the seventeenth century – affected by erosion of the coast of Holderness, the spit has been bodily moved inshore in a 250-year cycle.

At low tide the reserve increases in size by around 190 hectares: the area of mudflats and saltmarsh beyond the ridge. Wildfowl such as mallard and shelduck may shelter here in winter, while in passage times curlew, dunlin, knot, oystercatcher, redshank and turnstone may be seen. Terns, also, pass through – often harried by arctic skua – while smaller birds include pied and spotted flycatcher, redstart, whinchat and wheatear and large winter numbers of fieldfare and redwing which feed on the sea-buckthorn berries. Not only do many species use Spurn as a staging post but the sheer number of birds is often amazing – a fall of around 6000 blackbirds has occurred on a single day.

The dunes have a typical east coast cover of marram and sea-buckthorn, with sea bindweed, sea-holly and springbeauty. Perhaps influenced by chalk imported to strengthen the ridge, a variety of lime-loving plants such as yellow-wort, ploughman's-spikenard, restharrow and pyramidal orchid may be found.

Stocksmoor Common

Permit only; 11.6ha; YWT reserve
Damp grassland and mixed woodland
Spring, summer

Damp rough pasture, with newly planted trees, occupies over half the reserve. The woodland is chiefly of birch with oak and hawthorn. Grey willow grows along the stream and in the wetter areas where typical plants such as ragged-Robin, marsh bedstraw and bulrush occur. Over 40 bird species have been recorded and mammals include badger, fox and red squirrel.

Marsh gentian, an uncommon plant of wet heaths such as Skipwith and Strensall Commons.

Stoneycliffe Wood

Permit only; 40ha; YWT reserve
Oak–birch woodland
Spring, summer

The strong growth of young oak and birch trees forms an understorey to the mature trees, widening the range of habitat for woodland birds. Wet places show opposite-leaved golden-saxifrage and great wood-rush and in the drier parts bracken, bramble and bluebell grow.

Strensall Common

Permit only; 21.6ha; YWT reserve
Damp lowland heath
Spring, summer

Like SKIPWITH COMMON, one of the few lowland heaths remaining in the Vale of York, the reserve includes dry heath, with silver birch, bracken and heather, and wet heath with purple moor-grass and cross-leaved heath. Cottongrass and common reed grow in the wetter places and heath dog-violet and marsh gentian also occur. The common is a breeding site for nightjar and other heathland birds.

Thorpe Marsh

Permit only; 20ha; YWT–CEGB reserve
Open water, pasture and scrub
Leaflet from YWT
Spring, summer

Varied habitats include a new lake, an older pond, a disused railway track with a dry scrub area of hawthorn and oak, and pasture grassland. Curlew, lapwing, redshank and snipe breed in the pastures with hedgerow and woodland birds in the scrub. The reserve is regularly hunted by short-eared and barn owl, kestrel and sparrowhawk.

The Derwent Valley contains important wetlands such as Wheldrake Ings.

Wharram Quarry

Permit only; 4ha; YWT reserve
Open chalk, grassland and scrub
Spring, summer

Winter-cress grows on the chalk of the cliff face but a richer plant life has developed on the quarry floor. Here restharrow and common bird's-foot-trefoil grow among grasses such as crested dog's-tail and quaking-grass, and in some years there is a fine show of bee orchid. Ash, crab apple and gooseberry growing in hollows in the cliff face provide nest sites for birds such as linnet and yellowhammer.

Wheldrake Ings

Permit only; 160ha; YWT reserve
Flood meadows
Spring, summer

An old meadow flood plain, the Ings have a range of marsh and meadow plants. These include meadowsweet, great burnet and narrow-leaved water-dropwort, a rare wetland plant near its northern limit. Bewick's swan, duck and other waterfowl come to the great shallow lake which stretches across the reserve in winter. Breeding species include mallard, shoveler, curlew, lapwing, redshank and snipe; small birds may be hunted by kestrel or short-eared owl.

Willow Garth

Permit only; 5.4ha; YWT reserve
Subsidence pond and grassland
Spring, summer

Willow Garth is a wetland formed by mining subsidence. Reed canary-grass, meadowsweet and great willowherb surround the pool and Indian balsam has invaded the area. Harvest mice have bred and breeding birds include several warblers and tits.

Yorkshire Dales National Park

See map; 176,113ha; YDNPC
Uplands and valleys
Leaflets from YDNPC
Spring, summer

The third largest of Britain's ten national parks, the Yorkshire Dales contain some of the most spectacular scenery in the country. The park lies mainly on carboniferous rocks, with huge masses of hard pale limestone, gently tilted and overlain to the north and east by softer layers of shales, sandstones and limestones. These, the Yoredale beds, are in turn covered by hard acid millstone grit as they, too, slope gently north and east. This is not to say that the countryside is gentle: great hills rear up from terraced shoulders which stand above long sloping grasslands or sudden steep cliffs of rock or the winding valleys of the dales themselves. The huge hills, such as Ingleborough, are capped with millstone grit and rise as pyramids of Yoredale beds set on platforms of Great Scar limestone – the finest examples of such limestone scenery in Britain. The cliffs, too, such as Gordale Scar and Malham Cove, are spectacular sheer faces of pale, almost bone-white, limestone.

The Great Scar limestone plateaus are highly permeable: rainwater washes them into broken pavements of clints, dissected by deep-cut grikes, and sinks through pot-holes to drain down into fantastic cave systems, deep below the surface. Not only does the park hold almost half of the total exposure of limestone pavement in Britain, it also contains more cave systems than the whole of the rest of the country – over 320km of passages with more than 50 caves of national importance.

These rock and grassland plateaus, hills and pavements also carry a wonderful range of plants. Much of the uplands are over-grazed but the very broken terrain may allow many special plants to survive and, where the pressures are lower, it is possible to see an example of how the land must have looked before woodland clearance and grazing bared the uplands. The higher grits in the south may have been free of woodland but the lower north eastern millstone grit would probably have been forested with birch. The Yoredale beds might have carried woods more varied, according to the soil, but the Great Scar limestone was almost certainly dressed with woods of ash.

Where ungrazed pavements or steep ravine slopes support the clues to the original woodland, the pavement grikes and the slopes are wooded with ash, here and there with birch and wych elm, perhaps with alder along the lines of the streams. The ash trees may be rather sparse and stunted, giving a well-lit wood which has an understorey of bird cherry, hawthorn, hazel and rowan. The ground cover contains many lime-loving plants including those, like bird cherry, more typical of northern England. Plants such as water avens, herb-Paris, angular Solomon's-seal and yellow star-of-Bethlehem may occur with baneberry, giant bellflower, wood crane's-bill, globeflower, marsh and northern hawk's-beard and melancholy thistle. On the deeper soils of the Yoredale series giant bellflower and herb-Paris may be found, but most plants are generally those of more common lime-rich woods, such as dog's mercury, primrose and ramsons, while the more acid soils might have oak, birch and rowan with small-leaved lime above a typical flora.

The return to these characteristic woodlands might be seen in an ungrazed pavement where a mixed scrub is able to survive. Here, ash is probably the climax but, with the scrub, has a mix of grassland and relict woodland species which is really quite superb. The open scrub would probably consist of ash, bird cherry, blackthorn, hawthorn, hazel, oak, rowan, and willow. Patches of glacial drift might give rather acid areas, where plants such as heather, tormentil, wood sage and

Malham Cove is a spectacular cliff, a sheer face of Great Scar limestone.

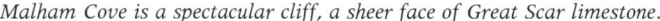

devil's-bit scabious could grow, but the main accent would be on the lime-loving species. On the pavement an ungrazed grassland can develop filled with a wonderful range of plants, including blue moor-grass and quaking-grass. The clints might carry bloody crane's-bill, zigzag clover, globe-flower, wall lettuce, lily-of-the-valley, hairy rock-cress, saw-wort and melancholy thistle while the grikes contain baneberry, rigid buckler-fern, limestone and holly fern, hart's-tongue and hard shield-fern.

The pavements of the park form an informal garden where plants of the north, of limestone, of mountains, woods and grasslands are able to meet. Here are mountain avens, alpine bartsia, northern bedstraw, brittle bladder-fern and dark-red helleborine, with alpine bistort, alpine cinquefoil, mountain everlasting, hutchinsia, dwarf milkwort, green spleenwort, grass-of-Parnassus, bird's-eye primrose and plants associated with lead mines: spring sandwort and mountain pansy. The higher crags have species such as roseroot and mossy, purple and yellow saxifrage, while on the acid hilltop plateaus and gritstone moors typical plants include heather, bilberry and crowberry and hare's-tail cottongrass heaths are patterned with *Sphagnum* bogs.

To match the richness of the pavements and caves, MALHAM TARN provides an unparalleled wetland site. Nowhere in Britain is there a compar-able area with such a wealth of mire vegetation. From acid *Sphagnum* to plants such as broad-leaved cottongrass, common reed, marsh-marigold and marsh valerian, together with a fine variety of sedges, the mires contain a remarkable range of plants. The neighbourhood streams include the Gordale Beck, which, plunging over a 60m scar in a series of spectacular falls through natural arches, forms one of the finest limestone waterfalls in the country. Semer Water, held back by an ice age moraine, is another natural feature, but its attractiveness for wildlife is diminished by watersports.

Just as the rocks, and their wildlife, are reflected in the ascent of Ingleborough, so are they seen in moving north east from Malham through the park. Malham and the Craven district show the Great Scar limestone, Wharfedale and Wensleydale display the gentler Yoredale beds, where lower scars alternate with rich green pastures, and the valley of Swaledale registers millstone grit. The park contains other, older rocks, where the Howgill Fells show the ancient rounded grassy slopes of their shales. The gritstone moors hold heathers to please red grouse; dunlin, lapwing, golden plover, snipe, ring ouzel and black-headed gull are among the birds of the uplands; and the valley woods are full of their own typical birds. But the special interest of this magnificent area must surely lie in its wonderful limestone richness.

Swaledale, cut in the millstone grit in the north of the Yorkshire Dales National Park.

Wales

Clwyd

Tucked in the north east corner of Wales between rugged Snowdonia and the fertile lowlands of the Cheshire and Shropshire plain, Clwyd offers a remarkable range of wildlife habitat. It is a county of contrasts, a modern amalgam of the former Welsh border counties of Flintshire and Denbighshire with part of old Merioneth, and named after the river which sweeps northwards to the Irish Sea in the Vale of Clwyd.

Apart from the industrial belt along the old coalfield, and recreational and tourist development on the coast, Clwyd is predominantly rural and mostly upland. Traditional sheep rearing on the Berwyn Mountains, Mynydd Hiraethog and elsewhere has perpetuated vast heather and grass moorlands, although afforestation has covered much of Mynydd Hiraethog and the Clwydian range. In the lowlands stock rearing and dairy farming predominate and a close-knit landscape of fields and hedgerows remains.

Land use reflects geological contrasts, with a general east–west succession from newer to older rocks and from lowland to upland. The climate also changes: rainfall ranges from less than 889mm in the lower Dee Valley to 1778mm on the Berwyn Mountains. To the east the east Denbighshire plain is an extension of the Cheshire plain beyond the Dee which, leaving its spectacular wooded valley between Chirk and Erbistock, meanders north to its estuary and Liverpool Bay. The underlying rocks are Triassic sandstones overlain extensively with clays and, in the Wrexham area, sand and gravels from the last ice age, when a glacier pushed up the DEE ESTUARY from the Irish Sea.

To the west the carboniferous shales and sandstone of the coal measures run north in an arc from the former north Shropshire coalfield to the western shore above the Dee Estuary, and to the west

again Ruabon Mountain, rising to 502m, and Hope Mountain are formed on gritstones of the same series. This gives way to a limestone outcrop reaching spectacular proportions in Eglwyseg Mountain in the south above the major fault line of the Vale of Llangollen, thrusting west deep into the uplands. The limestone broadens out to the north on Halkyn Mountain and ends above Prestatyn, separated from the sea by a narrow coastal plain. West again is the eastern flank of the great north–south rift valley of the Vale of Clwyd, the Clwydian range, dominated by MOEL FAMAU at 554m and formed of older Silurian rocks. These also underlie the great dome of Mynydd Hiraethog west of the Vale, separated by a narrow limestone outcrop which runs north to the coast and swings westwards into Gwynedd, terminating in the Great Orme above Llandudno. In the south are the Berwyn Mountains, rising to 827m on Moel Sych on a prominent ridge overlooking a bisected plateau which continues into Powys, and from which the Rivers Ceiriog and Tanat drain into the lowlands of north Shropshire.

In the eastern lowlands of the lower Dee and beyond into the Maelor, agricultural improvement has left little of the former woodland cover. Much of the wildlife interest is related to glacial activity: former small lake basins are now important peatland sites dominated by the extensive Fenns and Whixall Moss.

The industrial belt now only supports two deep coal mines, and much dereliction remains from past extraction of coal, limestone, sand and gravel. There is, however, plenty to interest the naturalist, for many such sites are rich refuges for wildlife.

Beyond Chester the Dee flows past land that was formerly part of the estuary, until it broadens into an estuary of international importance for wintering waders and wildfowl, that has so far survived the pressures of modern development. From the estuary mouth at the POINT OF AYR westwards to the county boundary at Rhos-on-Sea, holiday caravans and chalets between the resorts have left little of the coast undeveloped. However an extensive, if narrow, dune system runs eastwards from Prestatyn to the estuary mouth and supports a rich variety of dune plants and insects.

The limestone outcrops running south from the coast provide many contrasts: the upper slopes are still unploughed and grazed by sheep while, on the coast, they support a number of limestone plants rare in Wales. Elsewhere limestone ash woodland remains and COED CILYGROESLWYD is partly developed on limestone pavement. Lower down the landscape is dominated by small walled fields and, although most are now ploughed, a few flower-rich meadows remain and the roadside verges are awash with spring and summer colour. Limestone quarrying is a major industry in Clwyd, but some of the smaller disused quarries are rich in flowers and insects.

The most extensive uplands lie to the west of the Vale of Clwyd on Mynydd Hiraethog and the Berwyn Mountains south of the Vale of Llangollen, but extensive areas of heather moor survive on the Clwydian range, Ruabon Mountain and Llantysilio Mountain. Much of Mynydd Hiraethog is now clothed in conifers but the grass and heather moorlands to the west, dotted with reservoirs, and the heather moors on the Berwyn Mountains in southern Clwyd, provide important breeding sites for Welsh upland birds. The high ridges of the Berwyns support some of the most extensive and southerly blanket bog in Britain. Although agricultural improvement and commercial forestry have eliminated most of the original valley oakwoods, a few remnants survive on the lower slopes in the valleys which drain from the upland blocks.

From the vast mudflats and saltings of the Dee Estuary to the gentle uplands of Mynydd Hiraethog and the Berwyn Mountains, and from the spectacular limestone outcrops of MYNYDD EGLWYSEG in the beautiful Vale of Llangollen to the sombre peatlands of Fenns Moss, the county of Clwyd reveals all the contrast in landscape and wildlife between highland and lowland Britain.

A. J. DEADMAN

Bishopswood Nature Trail

SJ 068813; 2km; Rhuddlan BC
Woodland walk with limestone grassland and quarry
Booklet from RBC, Town Hall, Rhyl, and Prestatyn
Information Centre, Nant Hall Road, Prestatyn
Spring, summer

The trail climbs to high grassland where common rock-rose attracts brown Argus butterfly, and the woodlands below hold birds such as blackcap and wood warbler.

Bryn Euryn Nature Trail

SH 834802; 1.2km; Colwyn BC
Hill woodland, scrub and grassland trail
Booklet from CBC
Spring, summer

The woods include yew, spindle, spurge-laurel and wild privet while the rocky grasslands contain such plants as bloody crane's-bill, dropwort and hoary rock-rose.

Coed Cilygroeslwyd

Permit only; 4ha; NWNT reserve
Limestone woodland
Spring, early summer

Oak and ash form the tree canopy of this woodland, with an understorey of hazel, hawthorn, holly, sycamore and yew. This variety affects the amount of light reaching the ground and has a profound effect on the biology of the wood. Because of the darkness under the yews there is little ground cover but in more open areas there are broad carpets of woodruff while the edges of the clearings are tangled with traveller's joy. Old field walls within the wood are grown over with ivy, mosses and ferns. Three interesting and unusual plants are stinking hellebore, flowering in February and March, followed by greater butterfly-orchid and bird's-nest orchid in early summer. Of special interest is the presence of giant bellflower, generally typical of northern England, and nettle-leaved bellflower, more usually limited to the south.

The range of habitat provided by the different trees is exploited by many insects and birds. Green and great spotted woodpecker take insect food deep within the bark; coal, blue, great and long-

Stinking hellebore grows in Coed Cilygroeslwyd.

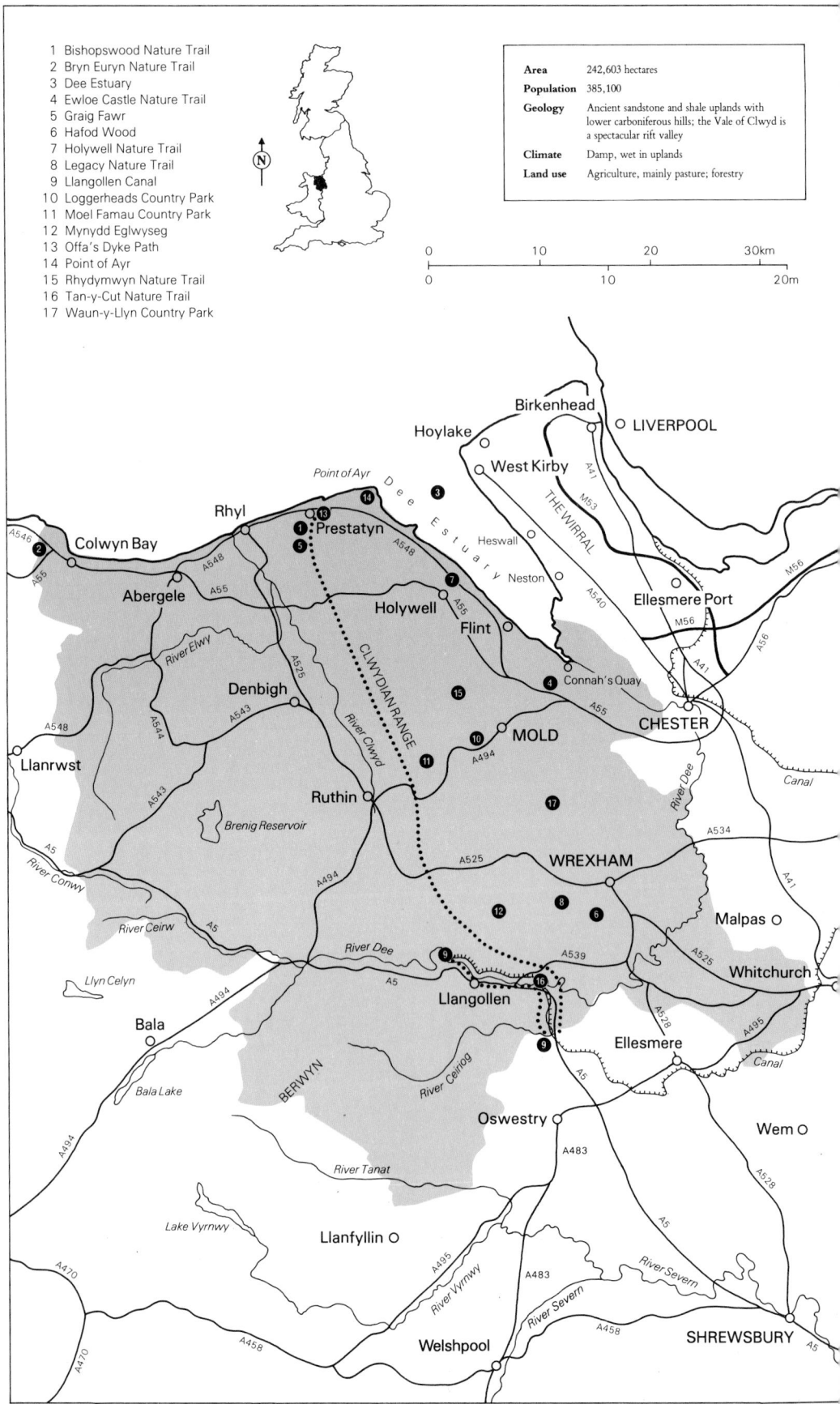

1 Bishopswood Nature Trail
2 Bryn Euryn Nature Trail
3 Dee Estuary
4 Ewloe Castle Nature Trail
5 Graig Fawr
6 Hafod Wood
7 Holywell Nature Trail
8 Legacy Nature Trail
9 Llangollen Canal
10 Loggerheads Country Park
11 Moel Famau Country Park
12 Mynydd Eglwyseg
13 Offa's Dyke Path
14 Point of Ayr
15 Rhydymwyn Nature Trail
16 Tan-y-Cut Nature Trail
17 Waun-y-Llyn Country Park

Area	242,603 hectares
Population	385,100
Geology	Ancient sandstone and shale uplands with lower carboniferous hills; the Vale of Clwyd is a spectacular rift valley
Climate	Damp, wet in uplands
Land use	Agriculture, mainly pasture; forestry

0   10   20   30km

0   10   20m

Connah's Quay: saltmarsh, mudflats and sandbanks stretch across to the Wirral Peninsula.

tailed tit may be seen in the high tree canopy. These, too, are chiefly insect-eaters, but feed in different parts of the tree from the specialist bark-feeding birds. Yet another strategy is used by yet another insect-eater: the pied flycatcher feeds in the air. It perches at the edge of a clearing and performs fast aerobatics to take its prey on the wing.

Wood mouse, a resident of the wood, moves mainly at night to avoid day-flying hawks, but is hunted by tawny owl instead. As well as wood mouse, voles and shrews find cover in the tangled tree roots, banks and old walls of the wood. These small mammals attract other predators – fox, stoat and weasel hunt through the wood and, very occasionally, polecat may be seen.

Connah's Quay

Permit only; 90ha; CEGB–DNS reserve
Estuarine saltings and mudflats, large pool, scrub area
Reserve report every two years by DNS
Spring, autumn, winter

Behind the huge towers of the Connah's Quay Power Station the tidal waters of the DEE ESTUARY rise and fall across wide expanses of sand, mud and saltmarsh. About 90 ha of foreshore, marsh and reclaimed land have been established as a reserve by the CEGB and are managed by the Deeside Naturalists' Society.

The reserve has three main areas. The flats and marsh represent the main features of the estuary and form about half of the site. Here, characteristic plants are common scurvygrass, lesser sea-spurrey and glasswort. Mallard and shelduck are present at all times, to be joined in autumn and winter by good numbers of pintail, wigeon and teal. Both bar-tailed and black-tailed godwit, together with commoner waders, may be seen on the saltmarsh, but it is most important for the autumn migration of spotted redshank.

The pool, flushed with fresh water from a nearby stream and flooded with salt water only at high spring tides, provides a different range of habitat and, although visited by saltmarsh birds, draws a different range of species. Both great-crested and little grebe may be seen on the pool and heron stalk the shallow waters; common and curlew sandpiper seem to prefer the area. Kingfisher often fish from the willows which grow on the islands and fringe the pool.

The third main area is the scrub on the reclaimed land to the east of the reserve. Here the profusion of clovers, vetches, tares and other flowering plants provides a special attraction for butterflies. Fourteen species were recorded during 1977 and 1978 including comma, around its northern breeding limit, grayling, essentially a coastal butterfly in Britain, and painted lady. This, too, is an ideal site for smaller birds such as blue tit, stonechat and whitethroat.

Grazed fields and a small wood add further interest, and, of course, there is always the chance of some unusual sighting. Oceanic birds such as Manx shearwater or storm petrel may be blown in by autumn gales; hen harrier or merlin are occasional winter visitors; green and wood sandpiper, little and Temminck's stint, arctic skua and Iceland gull have all been recorded here.

There is a field studies centre, complete with display room, to improve facilities for school groups and organised visits.

Ddôl Uchaf

Permit only; 4ha; NWNT reserve
Old marl workings and stream
Spring, summer

Although small, the reserve shows a great variety of habitats. In the woodland the ground cover is not spectacular because of the lack of light, although the commoner plants of rich woodland, such as dog's mercury, ground-ivy and wood avens, thrive, but the grassland area has a very rich variety of lime-loving plants. Here the plants have colonised bare marl workings with no competition

445

Oystercatchers and black-tailed godwits: winter brings thousands of waders to the Dee Estuary.

from the trees and there is a range of conditions from dry sunlit banks to damp meadow and small open pools.

On the dry banks cowslip, kidney vetch, perforate St John's-wort, wild strawberry and ploughman's-spikenard may be found. The damper grassland, from July to September, is graced by grass-of-Parnassus, meadowsweet and hempagrimony, while the pools are lanced with bulrush.

As well as the plants, the clearing is filled in spring with birdsong, in summer with butterflies, bees, dragonflies and damselflies.

The woodland, although less varied than the grassy clearing, still provides a good range of habitat with areas of sycamore wood, a mature wet willow wood, a young dry willow wood and an area of blackthorn scrub. This provides cover for a wide range of birds and over 40 species have been recorded here including all the more common woodland species such as tits, finches and warblers.

Some of the old farm buildings have been converted into an interpretative centre.

Dee Estuary

See map; 12,600ha; various bodies
Sand, mudflats and saltmarsh
All year

Walking out on to the sands of Dee, with the wide estuary spreading all around, it is hard to realise that this was once a huge river of sea ice, a groaning flow turned aside by the hills and glaciers of Wales to drive deep into the Cheshire plain. Imagine, too, how the meltwaters must have roared through here when the ice eventually melted. Since then the sea level has risen, relative to the land, and the estuary, now deeply silted, is formed from the drowned river mouth.

The silts and sands are the key to the wildlife value of the Dee. Upward of 140,000 waders – over 10 per cent of the British population – may be present here in winter, feeding on the rich food supplies of the estuary, together with large flocks of waterfowl and gatherings of finches and other small birds.

Sand and mud form a clogging, difficult environment, while the changing mix of fresh and salt water which occurs in an estuary adds further problems. For animals which can cope with the difficulties, however, the rewards are great and, although not many species can survive, those that can are present in amazing numbers. Common estuary shellfish, such as Baltic tellin, peppery furrow shell and laver spire shell, provide rich pickings for many birds, together with common cockle – a staple for oystercatcher. *Corophium volutator*, a small crustacean, is present in vast numbers, with ragworm at a density as high as 2500 per square metre and another worm, *Pygospio elegans*, reaching the staggering figure of almost half a million per square metre.

The plants, too, resemble the animals both in the problems they have to face and in the way in which relatively few species achieve success. Those that do are, however, again plentiful. The bare muds contain Townsend's cord-grass and glasswort; common saltmarsh-grass, sea aster and scurvygrass species abound where the mudflats are higher, while the creeks which drain the marshes are fringed with sea-purslane. Sea-milkwort and sea arrowgrass show on higher parts of the marsh and the fringes of the estuary may be marked by stands of common reed and sea club-rush. These marshes are feeding grounds for winter finches, when plant seeds are available to provide a ready supply of food.

The West Hoyle Bank in the estuary mouth is a notable site for grey seal – summer peaks of over 200 have been recorded. It is unusual for a haul-out to be so far away from any large breeding site and it is surprisingly close to a great industrial sprawl. Other sea mammals occur occasionally: bottlenosed and Risso's dolphin, common porpoise and killer whale may visit while, rarely, large whales have been stranded here.

Other summer animals include breeding duck such as mallard, shelduck, occasional shoveler and teal, waders such as lapwing, redshank, snipe and a few oystercatchers, and smaller birds: sedge and reed warbler, reed bunting, skylark, meadow pipit and yellow wagtail. Common tern nest on the rafts in the SHOTTON STEELWORKS and little tern may find undisturbed stretches of beach. Stonechat and grasshopper warbler occur in scattered pairs and the summer marshes are hunting grounds for kestrel and sparrowhawk.

Dunlin and sanderling breed in the tundra regions of Greenland, birds such as knot travel up to the Arctic, bar-tailed godwit to Russia – thousands of birds of many species make long migrations to breed and here, on the estuary flats and marshes, they pause to feed on passage or to spend the winter months. Of some 30 wader species normally noted in this country, 26 have been recorded here – in winter the most numerous are knot. These may occur in such numbers as to seem like a living carpet on the flats or, all flying together, like a billowing smoke-cloud whirling at the edge of the tide; over 40,000 dunlin may be present, with thousands of bar-tailed godwit, ringed plover and sanderling – for these five waders, the Dee is one of the six most important estuaries in Britain. Oystercatcher, black-tailed godwit, curlew, grey plover, redshank and purple sandpiper also winter here and, at high tide, the shores and rocky islets may be tightly packed with birds.

The estuary is just as important to wildfowl – 22 out of the 27 British species may occur here. Duck such as pintail and wigeon, from as far away as northern Russia, come to winter on the marshes. The estuary is a prime site for pintail, with flocks of over 5000 – among the largest in Europe; shelduck, too, may exceed 4000. With mallard, teal and other dabblers, these duck are generally gathered in the shallows or on the marshes, but deeper waters also attract diving duck. Smaller numbers of seaduck such as scaup, goldeneye, common scoter and red-breasted merganser may be seen, together with great crested grebe, redthroated diver, guillemot and razorbill.

The largest winter roosts of gulls are in the neighbouring Mersey Estuary but the West Hoyle Bank attracts a considerable roost and, with the commoner gulls, species such as glaucous, Iceland, little and Mediterranean gull occur. Winter is the time for gatherings of finches, for foraging groups of greenfinch and chaffinch, for other small birds such as reed bunting, rock and meadow pipit, brambling and twite, for water pipit working the edge of the tide. Hard weather may bring in Lapland and snow bunting, and times of high winter tides force out secretive birds such as spotted crake and water rail. The vast numbers of birds may draw such predators as hen harrier, merlin, peregrine and short-eared owl.

The estuary is a treasure-house of wildlife, a broad sweep of beautiful, rich wilderness. Millions of people live and work nearby but this great spread of water and silt retains its natural freedom.

Erddig Ponds

Permit only; 0.4ha; NWNT–NT reserve
Two small ponds
All year

In summer wetland plants include greater spearwort, fine-leaved water-dropwort and bulrush, together with lesser bulrush which is rare in Wales. Willow and hawthorn scrub and oak shelter small birds while the marsh areas attract winter duck, and waders during migration.

Ewloe Castle Nature Trail

SJ 292670; 2.4km; CCC
Trail through open farmland and wooded valley
Booklet from CCC
Spring, early summer

In spring the floor of the valley is filled with primrose and bluebell. The trail also passes a small pond where yellow iris grows and moorhen nests in summer. A good variety of birds may be seen, both those of open farmland and those of the woodland.

Graig Fawr

SJ 064802; 24.6ha; NT
Limestone crags, grassland and scrub woodland
Leaflet from NT, Llandudno
Spring, summer

Graig Fawr is a great limestone hill looking out over the Vale of Clwyd, near Prestatyn. The western and northern faces are steep, falling sharply to the valley floor, while the eastern and southern parts slope more gently into the land behind.

The shallow turf is rich with small herbs and lime-loving plants such as wild thyme, small scabious, lady's bedstraw, common bird's-foot-trefoil, harebell and common rock-rose. The presence of hoary rock-rose is of particular interest as it is limited to carboniferous limestone and is found in only a very few sites in Wales and northern England. Here, it grows in thick mats on the steep rocks of the western face. This whole area of rock and shallow turf is a treasure-house of lime-loving plants – others include biting stonecrop, carline thistle and salad burnet.

Where trees such as blackthorn, hawthorn and yew have become established they are generally small and stunted, but on the shallower slopes and at the foot of the steep faces there are areas of better developed woodland. In the south western part of the site there is a block of woodland scrub which has grown up over some old quarry workings, a typical hills-and-holes system. Here the banks of blackthorn scrub, bramble, gorse and wild rose alternate with clearings and grassy banks, rich with the limestone plants of the plateau above. This grades into semi-mature woodland and there is a similar block of woodland at the foot of the north eastern slope.

The birds of Graig Fawr are chiefly those of woodland, chaffinch and blue tit, for instance, and of scrub, including stonechat, linnet and whitethroat, which may be seen on the gorse clumps. The colourful limestone plants attract many butterflies, including meadow brown, small tortoiseshell and the beautiful common blue.

Hafod Wood

SJ 324477; 8ha; NWNT–NT reserve
Mixed woodland and wetland
Spring, summer

Most of the woodland is open alder wetland, with great horsetail, hemlock water-dropwort, bird cherry, red currant and guelder-rose. The drier woodland, at either end of the reserve, contains wild daffodil and wood spurge beneath a good range of native trees. Breeding birds include spotted flycatcher, lesser spotted woodpecker, tawny owl and kestrel, with mallard and moorhen on the open marsh and pools.

Common blue, a beautiful small summer butterfly.

Holywell Nature Trail

SJ 195764; 1.8km; CCC
Trail through wooded valleys and past old industrial ponds
Booklet from CCC
Spring, summer

The valleys have a good variety of trees including oak, ash, rowan and crab apple with characteristic plants such as wood anemone, wood-sorrel and woodruff. Several ponds provide shelter and food for waterbirds, where willow and alder, branched bur-reed, bulrush and yellow iris grow.

Legacy Nature Trail

SJ 295483; 1km; CEGB
Trail demonstrating the colonisation of man-made habitats
Dogs must be kept on leash; no smoking allowed
Leaflet from CEGB
Spring, summer

Mounds thrown up around the substation to preserve the area's rural appearance have been planted with trees and shrubs; the old railway embankment has been colonised by ash. A drainage ditch has been widened to establish a marshy wetland area and open turf provides a further habitat type. The area is populated by hedgerow and woodland birds and hunted by tawny and barn owl.

Llangollen Canal

SJ 198433–284378; 17km; CCC
Canal and towpath
Booklet from CCC
All year

The water of the canal may appear turbid and lifeless but it is filled with all manner of animals and plants, and even a short walk along the towpath will show a wide variety of hedgerow trees and plants, of marsh plants, birds and insects and further variation in the bankside meadows.

In spring, marsh-marigold is followed by cuckooflower and water forget-me-not. By midsummer the banks are full of colour, thick with meadowsweet, hemp-agrimony, great and rosebay willowherb, hedge and marsh woundwort and water mint. At the water's edge monkeyflower, a garden escape which has spread along waterways and now grows wild over most of the country, grows in a blaze of yellow. The hedgerow trees, oak, ash and sycamore, tower over hawthorn, hazel, field maple and dogwood.

Heron often visit while coot and moorhen busy themselves at the reedy edges of the canal; mallard dabble. Quick activity among the wagtails and flycatchers signals an insect hatch. Swallow and house martin dip and twist, as do the bats of an evening. Evening, too, is the time for other mammals. Water voles may be seen nibbling at plant material held in their forepaws or heard, especially in spring, chattering and squealing in their territorial squabbles.

Moel Famau: a fine spread of heather moorland above the Vale of Clwyd.

Beneath the surface of the water there is always much activity. Water snails graze the algae and are food for leeches. Dragonfly larvae, and the larvae of the great diving beetle, probably the most voracious of the underwater insects, stalk the canal bed, seizing anything that might be edible. Bream, carp, eel, perch, pike, roach, rudd and tench swim in the slow, dark water.

Although the whole stretch of the canal is an informal nature trail, there is a formal one, TAN-Y-CUT NATURE TRAIL, at SH 282411.

Loggerheads Country Park

SJ 198626; 27ha; CCC
Limestone crags, woodland and river
Nature trail booklet from CCC
Spring, summer

The summer sun strikes the 60m crags with an almost dazzling whiteness relieved only by the darker masses of the trees and the brilliant mosaic of the limestone flowers which cluster the terraces of the cliff. The river below is cold, fast-flowing and clear, a trout stream spangled with the flowers of common water-crowfoot.

Downstream the land falls in a series of steep banks and semi-dry valleys. Here the tree cover is thick with ash, beech, hazel and sycamore and the resulting lack of light restricts smaller plants to those adapted to this habitat. The limestone ensures a good supply of calcium-rich dampness, so there are dense masses of dog's mercury and enchanter's-nightshade. The parasitic toothwort may also be found – a plant which grows on tree roots, taking its food directly from the tree.

Above this high-forest area, on the slopes of the limestone hill, the ground becomes drier and a special fascination of such ground becomes apparent. Because water drains very freely through limestone the soil above is often much less rich than that below – the 'goodness' is washed downwards; acid-loving plants can therefore be found growing among the lime-loving plants one would expect to find. For this reason these slopes carry birch, rowan and gorse as well as shrubs such as dogwood.

The grassland plateau is filled with lime-loving plants – common rock-rose, bloody crane's-bill and wild thyme. Harebell, small scabious, common milkwort and eyebright grow on the banks and terraces while, lower down, the steep narrow cliff path is edged with the exotic rose-of-Sharon.

Moorhen, dipper, pied and grey wagtail and an occasional kingfisher may be seen at the river. The woodland shelters chiffchaff, treecreeper and pied flycatcher. The woodland edge is the home of tits and finches and the grassland holds skylark and meadow pipit.

Moel Famau Country Park

SJ 171611; 861ha; CCC
High rolling heather moor
Spring, summer, autumn

Moel Famau is a long escarpment, its wide slopes and steep valleys clothed with heather, bilberry and bracken. Gorse and bell heather add bright colour, particularly in sheltered dry stream gullies where rowan and hawthorn grow. A few wet areas show ferns, rushes and plants such as cross-leaved heath and marsh pennywort. A typical grouse moor, the slopes are often hunted by kestrel and buzzard.

Point of Ayr: saltmarsh backed by the dunes.

Mynydd Eglwyseg

SJ 233485; 490ha; Wynnstay Estates
Limestone crags and acid moorland
No access off rights of way
Spring, summer

The limestone cliffs of Mynydd Eglwyseg wind above the valley like crumbling battlements. The cliffs themselves are not high but stand above long, steep scree slopes, open and brittle, an apparently arid contrast to the purple moorland above and the green farmland below. The screes have been subjected to heavy sheep grazing, well illustrated by the squat hawthorns heavily pruned by their teeth. Where the scree is tumbled to provide sheltering crannies into which the sheep cannot reach, maidenhair spleenwort and herb-Robert flourish. On the cliffs themselves, less accessible to the sheep, are small scabious and wild thyme, with special plants of the limestone – rigid buckler-fern, limestone fern and uncommon species of whitebeam.

Keeping to the rights of way, one can leave the Eglwyseg scarp and cross over Ruabon Mountain, returning by another path to join OFFA'S DYKE PATH. This circuit shows the contrast between the limestone of Eglwyseg and the acid millstone grit of Ruabon.

The moorland is managed as a grouse-shoot, with regular burns to ensure a constant new growth of young heather. Bell heather shows where the peat is dry while cross-leaved heath generally indicates wetter places. Small heathland plants such as tormentil also occur, and where the peat thins over the underlying limestone wild thyme reappears. The dark, almost metallic, sheen of the millstone grit announces the change to Ruabon Mountain. The millstone grit does not drain as easily as Eglwyseg's carboniferous limestone, so that small areas of *Sphagnum* bog, marked by plants such as round-leaved sundew, become more frequent. The main feature of the moorland, though, is the rolling sweep of heather and bilberry.

Offa's Dyke Path

SJ 073822–267206; 85km; CC
Long-distance way
Booklet from HMSO bookshops
Spring, summer

Based upon the defensive dyke built to protect England from the Welsh, Offa's Dyke Path passes through farmland and moorland, upland and lowland, close to GRAIG FAWR and MYNYDD EGLWYSEG and through the great moorland slopes of MOEL FAMAU COUNTRY PARK.

Point of Ayr

SH 125847; 542ha; RSPB–Welsh Water Authority
Dunes, sands and saltmarsh
Spring, autumn, winter

Point of Ayr, the western corner of the DEE ESTU-
ARY, is an area of immense sands, shingle banks and
mudflats with a small dune system on its western
edge. It holds important bird populations, either
over-wintering or resting and feeding before continuing their migration, and from here birds may
be watched on the estuary or out at sea.

At high tide Point of Ayr may be a roosting place
for thousands of birds, waiting to return to feed on
the mudflats when the tide falls. Bar-tailed and
black-tailed godwit, dunlin, grey plover, knot,
redshank, sanderling and turnstone – rank upon
rank, they face into the wind and wait.

As well as a roost for waders, the marsh is a
feeding place for wildfowl and attracts good numbers of mallard, pintail, shelduck and shoveler.
Inland, the smaller birds shelter and feed – snow
bunting, shore lark and water pipit with the
commoner winter birds. These small birds, and the
plentiful small mammals, attract predators and the
marsh and its fringes are hunted by visiting hen
harrier, peregrine, merlin, kestrel, sparrowhawk,
barn owl, little owl and wintering short-eared
owl.

Short-eared owls may visit Point of Ayr in winter.

Summer brings holidaymakers to the wide sands
and the visible wildlife is reduced, but as the
autumn gales begin to threaten, the estuary
resumes its wildness. Winter storms bring in many
interesting vagrants and Leach's petrel, grey
phalarope and Sabine's gull have been recorded.

Rhydymyn Nature Trail

SJ 207668; 6.4km; CCC
Trail following River Alyn and returning on
higher ground above
Excellent booklet from CCC
Spring, early summer

At times of low rainfall the River Alyn disappears
– a swallow-hole takes the river on an underground course when there is insufficient water to
drive across the hole. The trail passes woods, small
meadows, banks and hedges bright with flowers,
especially in spring, and full of commoner birds of
woodland, waterside and open country. Twite, siskin and crossbill may be seen in winter.

Shotton Steelworks

Permit only; 22ha; British Steel Corpn reserve
Wetland and pools
Permit from BSC (Personnel Services), Shotton
Works, Deeside
All year

A reserve has been established in the marshes,
reedbeds and lagoons around the steelworks. Over
200 bird species have been recorded, ranging from
terns breeding on nesting rafts to passage waders
and winter wildfowl.

Tan-y-Cut Nature Trail

SH 282411; 0.5km; Wrexham Maelor BC
Woodland trail
Leaflet from WMBC, Guildhall, Wrexham
Spring, early summer

Lying between the Shropshire Union Canal and the
River Dee, Tan-y-Cut Wood is a damp mixed
woodland with areas of marsh. The wetland plants
here include great horsetail, pendulous sedge and
butterbur.

Waun-y-Llyn Country Park

SJ 284577; 29ha; CCC
Upland moorland
Spring, summer

The park is an example of heather moorland with
a small lake and areas of peat bog. There are good
views across the Cheshire plain and the Wirral
Peninsula.

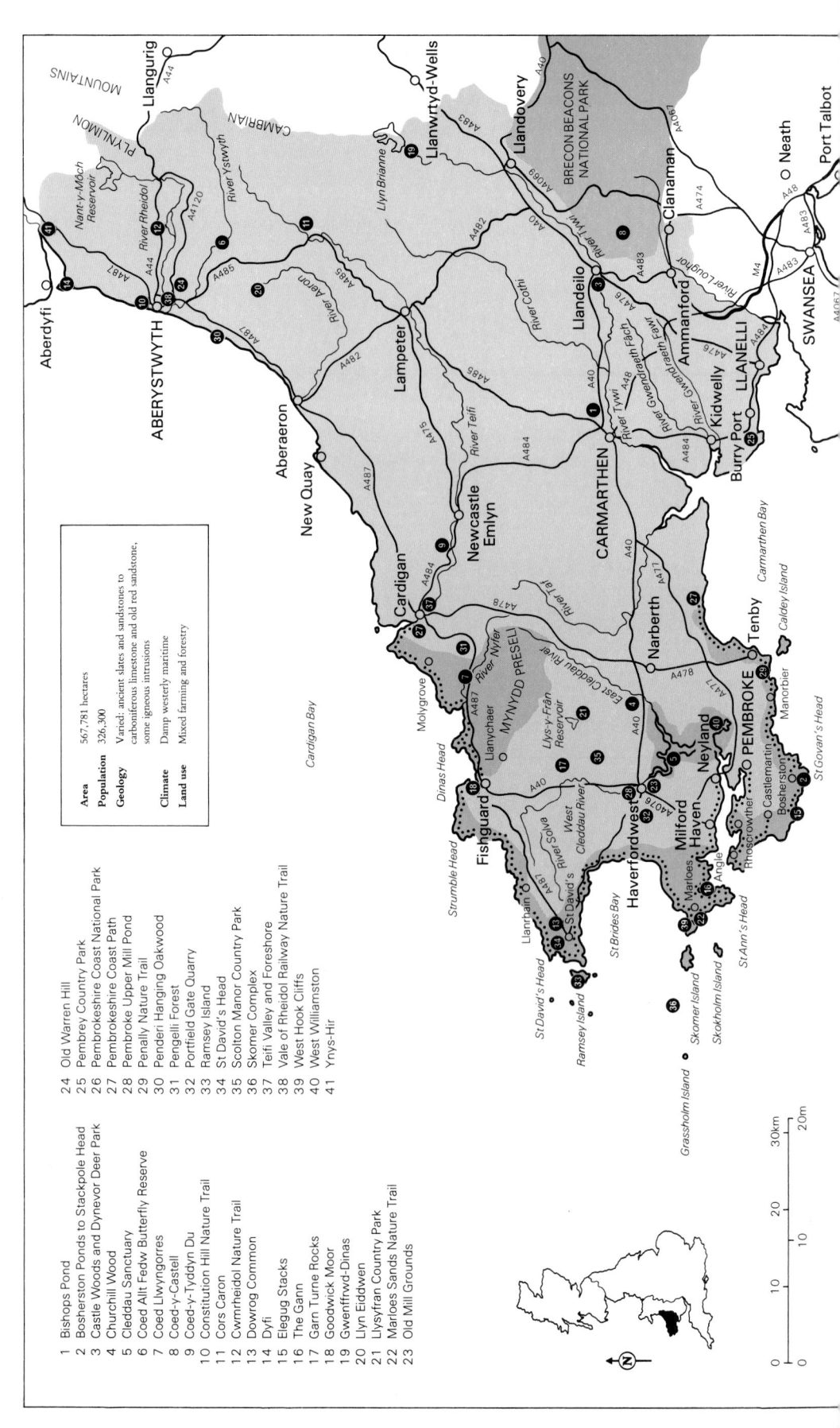

1 Bishops Pond
2 Bosherston Ponds to Stackpole Head
3 Castle Woods and Dynevor Deer Park
4 Churchill Wood
5 Cleddau Sanctuary
6 Coed Allt Fedw Butterfly Reserve
7 Coed Llwyngorres
8 Coed-y-Castell
9 Coed-y-Tyddyn Du
10 Constitution Hill Nature Trail
11 Cors Caron
12 Cwmrheidol Nature Trail
13 Dowrog Common
14 Dyfi
15 Elegug Stacks
16 The Gann
17 Garn Turne Rocks
18 Goodwick Moor
19 Gwenffrwd-Dinas
20 Llyn Eiddwen
21 Llysyfran Country Park
22 Marloes Sands Nature Trail
23 Old Mill Grounds

24 Old Warren Hill
25 Pembrey Country Park
26 Pembrokeshire Coast National Park
27 Pembrokeshire Coast Path
28 Pembroke Upper Mill Pond
29 Penally Nature Trail
30 Penderi Hanging Oakwood
31 Pengelli Forest
32 Portfield Gate Quarry
33 Ramsey Island
34 St David's Head
35 Scolton Manor Country Park
36 Skomer Complex
37 Teifi Valley and Foreshore
38 Vale of Rheidol Railway Nature Trail
39 West Hook Cliffs
40 West Williamston
41 Ynys-Hir

Area   567,781 hectares
Population 326,300
Geology   Varied: ancient slates and sandstones to
            carboniferous limestone and old red sandstone,
            some igneous intrusions
Climate   Damp westerly maritime
Land use   Mixed farming and forestry

Dyfed

The old counties of Carmarthen, Ceredigion and Pembroke together form the present-day county of Dyfed in south west Wales, which has an ancient landscape of great interest to geologists. The oldest rocks in South Wales, of the Pre-Cambrian and Cambrian, occur only in Pembrokeshire where in places they form picturesque outcrops, none more spectacular than Maiden Castle above the Treffgarne gorge. Elsewhere in the county, except for a small pocket of tertiary material, there are no rocks younger than the upper carboniferous period. Subsequently the landscape was shaped by glacial action as a great ice sheet gouged its way from north and central Wales, and by the incessant torrents of meltwater as the ice retreated.

The sea coast, of which Dyfed enjoys a superb variety, has always been a major factor in the development of the county. Most of the main towns are situated on or close to the coast or at the heads of estuaries. According to Nelson one of the finest harbours in the world, Milford Haven, once home port to a thriving fishing industry, now provides a major oil facility with several refineries and terminals together with an oil-fired power station. The only other major industrial zone in Dyfed is around Llanelli and inland along the Amman Valley; otherwise the county is essentially rural.

Iron Age man once lived on SKOMER island and most probably caught and ate seabirds. Nowadays large numbers of seabirds still thrive on the Pembrokeshire islands, of which GRASSHOLM, SKOKHOLM, Skomer and ST MARGARET'S are all nature reserves. Together they form the stronghold for seabirds in south west Britain and the fine colonies are now a major attraction for naturalists. For those unable to make a boat journey as the result of rough weather there are a number of mainland seabird colonies; the one at STACKPOLE HEAD forms part of a National Nature Reserve. Although the estuaries of Dyfed do not support the numbers of wildfowl and waders that occur at some English sites, they are of enough importance for those of the DYFI and CLEDDAU to be designated wildfowl refuges.

The sand dune areas, many of which contain rare plants such as dune gentian and fen orchid, have been much altered as the result of sand quarrying, agricultural reclamation and summer visitors. Four sites of considerable conservation interest do, however, remain – at Ynyslas in the north, and within the boundaries of three Ministry of Defence ranges in the south.

The heathlands of Pembrokeshire, especially those of the north west coastal zone, are especially important. At one time they provided extensive grazing areas, particularly for horses. Such activity would have maintained a more open habitat and allowed smaller plants to thrive, including scarce species such as yellow centaury, wavy St John's-wort and pale butterwort, which still occur. The first of these particularly likes the disturbed ground of animal tracks, a situation where, as the winter floods recede, dainty three-lobed crowfoot can be found.

The upland heather moors have largely vanished as the result of reclamation and afforestation, or are now dominated by purple moor-grass and mat-grass. A few pairs of merlin still nest at suitable sites while the sheep walk areas, which at times provide an abundant supply of carrion, attract that Welsh speciality, red kite. Concerted efforts by naturalists have enabled this superb bird to survive, and in 1983 no fewer than 46 pairs were present here.

There is a scarcity of open freshwater habitats in Dyfed, and extremely few at low altitude. The most important exception is Bosherston Ponds in Pembrokeshire, a major site for aquatic plants and winter wildfowl. Some of the upland lakes are of equal interest, especially those in areas where few changes have taken place in the surrounding catchments.

The two main rivers of Dyfed, the Tywi and the Teifi, both flow through broad valleys. It is to the former that virtually the only wild geese to winter regularly in Wales, a flock of Siberian white-fronted geese, come. The Teifi and its tributaries, and further south west the smaller rivers of Pembrokeshire, form one of the remaining strongholds of otter in England and Wales. Often associated with these rivers are areas of as yet unreclaimed marshland and carr which provide a feeding and resting area for this scarce animal.

Unimproved pastures are rapidly disappearing, and examples have been established in the nature reserves of RHOS GLYN-YR-HELYG and RHOS-Y-FFOREST. However, a number of other sites will have to be acquired if a representative series of pasture habitats with their wide botanical interest is to be maintained. With flowers such as spotted-orchid and marsh-orchid, slender whorled caraway, lousewort and devil's-bit scabious, they contrast strikingly with intensively cultivated farmland nearby.

Much of the semi-natural woodland of Dyfed is now retained only on steep valley slopes where the main species is sessile oak. Several interesting species indicating very ancient sites also occur, including small-leaved lime and wild service-tree. In much of Ceredigion and east Carmarthen the bird of the valley woodlands is pied flycatcher which nested in Pembrokeshire for the first time in 1983. By contrast to the valley woodlands a few remnants of lowland woodland remain, the most important being the pasture woodlands of DYNEVOR DEER PARK (see CASTLE WOODS), a treasure-store of lichens, invertebrates, birds and mammals.

DAVID SAUNDERS

Allt Crug Garn

Permit only; 0.3ha; WWNT reserve
Small block of heather
Spring, summer

The reserve contains the oldest lowland stand of unburnt heather in Ceredigion, a habitat that is now becoming rare.

Allt Rhyd-y-Groes

Permit only; 62ha; NCC reserve
Hanging oak woodland
Spring, summer

The wood, on a steep valley side, has some fine mature oaks and includes birch and rowan with ash and alder in the damper areas. Woodland grasses, bilberry and bluebell cover much of the ground, with wood sorrel, meadowsweet and opposite-leaved golden-saxifrage in wetter places. Ferns include oak fern and Wilson's filmy-fern.

Bishop's Pond

SN 446212; 4ha; WWNT reserve
Oxbow lake
No access beyond bridge
All year

The River Tywi once meandered here but bank erosion cut away the land inside the curve and eventually the river took a different course, straightening out the bend and leaving this pool like a footprint in the valley floor. Reed sweet-grass gives cover and nesting sites for small birds and there are some uncommon plants such as branched bur-reed and adder's-tongue. The wooded banks give further habitats for birds and an island provides a nest site for waterbirds; the pond is a wintering site for several species including Bewick's swan.

Bosherston Ponds to Stackpole Head

SR 966948; 797ha; NT–NCC
Freshwater lakes, dunes, calcareous grassland and sea cliffs
All year

Bosherston Ponds are part of a sea-drowned valley system. The wooded limestone slopes above the valleys and the sand dunes which cut the ponds off from the sea provide a variety of habitats.

The spurs between the ponds are scrub-covered with oak and ash standing among blackthorn, hawthorn and wild privet with a tangle of bramble, ivy and traveller's-joy. Rocky outcrops are thick with ivy-leaved toadflax, maidenhair spleenwort and hart's-tongue. The woodland spread of dog's mercury gives way to bracken and bramble in more open places, while beside the path are betony, slender St John's-wort and marjoram. On the open limestone heath above the woods gorse, bracken and rosebay willowherb grow. The grassland between, where the soil is shallow, is filled with ploughman's-spikenard, kidney vetch, salad burnet, wild thyme, carline thistle, wild privet and wild madder.

At the lake edge are stands of common reed, yellow iris, fleabane, purple-loosestrife and water mint. Nearer the sea typical duneland plants appear – dewberry, lady's bedstraw, common centaury and Portland and sea spurge. The grassland here is rather open and there is obviously much sand blown up from the beach below, but nearer the sea cliffs the plants change again.

The cliffs vary: sometimes a grassed slope with rocky outcrops, sometimes a jumbled series of shelves, sometimes a sheer drop to the sea's edge; caves, stacks and natural arches have been carved out by the waves and there are vertical shafts

Bosherston Ponds: a drowned valley system cut off from the sea by a sand-bar.

where blow-holes have collapsed. Here are clumps of rock sea-lavender, thrift, rock sea-spurrey and golden samphire.

Inland, however, the cliff-top plateau is still strongly affected by the dunes behind it and viper's-bugloss and common centaury show among the white flowers of sea campion. The dunes themselves, thrown up over limestone crags, do not have the damp slacks of normal sea-level systems such as KENFIG (Glamorgan), but there is a characteristic cover of mosses and lichens with yellow-wort, common bird's-foot-trefoil and mats of wild thyme.

The cliffs provide nest sites for an important colony of seabirds and the sheltered lakes attract waterfowl in winter.

Cardigan Island

Permit only; 16ha; WWNT reserve
Small island
Spring, summer, autumn

A herring gull colony of around 900 breeding pairs dominates this exposed island; other nesting species include great and lesser black-backed gull, fulmar, shag, oystercatcher, raven, jackdaw and rock pipit. Non-breeding kittiwake roost and other

visitors include chough. Since 1980 the WWNT has been endeavouring to establish a colony of Manx shearwater by transporting fledgelings from SKOMER.

Castle Woods and Dynevor Deer Park

SN 627220; 28ha; WWNT reserve
Fine mixed woodland
Occasional guided visits to Dynevor Deer Park: contact WWNT
All year

Castle Woods is one of the finest woodlands in this part of Wales. It overlooks Dynevor Deer Park and a wide area of the valley flood meadows which attract good numbers of wintering wetland birds. The woods lie on a limestone bluff above the River Tywi and, although there are now plantations within the reserve, the ash and wych elm may represent elements of the ancient primary woodland of Wales. Other tree species include some fine oaks, beech, wild cherry and holly with box and privet. The rich ground flora includes lime-loving spindle and early dog-violet. Parasitic toothwort, known only from two other areas in the old county of Carmarthenshire, also grows here.

455

Silver-washed fritillary butterfly.

Dynevor Deer Park is a rare example of fine old parkland, untouched by modern practices and containing a herd of fallow deer and a small group of red deer. The parkland is chiefly open woodland with copses, clumps of trees and some huge old single trees among rough grassland. It also contains ponds and is bordered by an oxbow lake. The trees are mainly oak with beech, sweet chestnut, elm, lime and a number of conifers.

Badger from the six active setts frequent the reserve. Foxes are not uncommon in the area and there are signs of otter on the river. The reserve holds a very good range of woodland birds, including all three British woodpeckers and all the characteristic woodland tit species, together with both nuthatch and treecreeper. Sparrowhawk, buzzard and raven are also present. In winter a wide variety of waterbirds may be seen on the ponds and the flood meadows, with commoner species including mallard, teal, wigeon, moorhen and coot.

The site contains some extremely fine lichen communities. Tree lungwort, a western lichen particularly sensitive to air pollution, is to be found in Castle Woods while the deer park supports a wide range of old parkland lichens now rarely seen in Wales.

Cleddau Sanctuary

SM 977116; 350ha; WWNT reserve
Inland estuary
No access beyond foreshore
Autumn, winter

A large part of the upper estuary has been designated a sanctuary to protect good numbers of migrant and wintering waders and wildfowl; some remain to breed.

Clettwr Valley

Permit only; 20.4ha; WWNT reserve
Lowland valley oak woodland
Spring, summer

The woodland has been coppiced and contains a rich ground cover. The wide range of habitat throughout, from marsh to dry cliff face, ensures great variety. Ferns are plentiful and the 16 species recorded include rustyback, oak and beech fern, and both filmy-ferns.

Coed Allt Fedw Butterfly Reserve

SN 667729; 3ha; FC–WWNT reserve
Small hilltop area
Leaflet from FC
Spring, summer

Rotational Christmas tree growing encourages butterflies, including silver-washed and small pearl-bordered fritillary, small skipper, small copper, speckled wood and grayling.

Coed Llwyngorres

SN 100390; 24.8ha; WWNT reserve
Woodland and river bank
Permit only off bridleway
Spring, summer

The steep woodland contains oak, holly and rowan at one end and sycamore, oak, ash, hazel and beech at the other. Fox and badger live in the wood where many typical birds may be seen. Willow and alder line the river – a spawning ground for salmon – where heron, kingfisher and dipper may occur.

Coed Penglanowen

Permit only; 6.5ha; WWNT reserve
Mixed woodland with stream
Spring, summer

Alder, grey, goat and crack willow grow by the stream, while the main woodland contains beech, oak, ash, sycamore and wych elm together with some tall conifers. Rhododendron in the shrub layer shades out other plants but, where there is sufficient light, the smaller plants are very varied. Birds include all three British woodpeckers with woodcock, pied and spotted flycatcher and sparrowhawk.

Coed Rheidol

Permit only; 75ha; NCC reserve
Steep oak woodland
Spring, summer

The woodland, cut by river gorges, is generally acidic – birch and rowan among the oaks with a ground cover of bilberry, common cow-wheat, purple moor-grass and wavy hair-grass. Richer areas contain sanicle, globeflower and Welsh poppy. There is a good range of ferns, mosses, liverworts and lichens.

Coed-y-Castell

SN 667193; 15.7ha; BBNPC
Ash and oak woodland
Leaflet from BBNPC
Spring, summer

Below limestone crags the scree slopes carry thick ash and hazel woodland which gives way to open acid slopes of bracken and oak woodland where the limestone gives way to old red sandstone. This diversity of habitat encourages a wide variety of birds, including wood warbler, pied flycatcher, raven and buzzard.

Coed-y-Tyddyn Du

SN 272426; 18.8ha; WdT
Mixed woodland
Spring, early summer

Mainly old farmland returning to forest, the ash–birch–oak woodland contains areas of herb-rich old pasture. Over 100 species of fungi and many insects have been recorded.

Constitution Hill Nature Trail

SN 583826; 5km; WWNT–Ceredigion DC
Circular trail on coastal hill above Aberystwyth
Leaflet from WWNT
Spring, summer

The trail demonstrates a variety of habitat. Coastal grassland gives way to inland woods and hedge bank habitats, each with their own plants and animals. Birds of the open fields, woodland, hedgerow, sea cliff and shoreline may all be seen.

Cors Caron

SN 696632; 800ha; NCC reserve
Raised peat bog and river
No access off right of way
Permit and booklet from NCC, Aberystwyth
All year

Cors Caron (formerly known as Cors Tregaron) is one of the classic peat bogs of Britain, demonstrating the development from aquatic conditions (the original shallow moraine lake) through flood-plain mire (still fed primarily by river water) to an ombrogenous (rain-fed) mire, the true raised bog. The River Teifi cuts the bog in two, from north east to south west, while the eastern bog is divided again into two. The west bog is the best preserved.

The sloping edge of the bog is tussocked with purple moor-grass which gives way to a belt of heather, cottongrass and deergrass with occasional small birches. The highest part of the bog is rich with *Sphagnum* mosses. Surface pools are filled with these mosses and with deergrass and white beak-sedge and above these are heather and the wet-loving cross-leaved heath. Other plants include crowberry, bog-rosemary, cranberry and bog asphodel, together with all three sundews. In places the tall fronds of royal fern rise from the covering heathers.

In winter the river floods widely and even in summer the general wetness makes the reserve unsuitable for many mammals, although water voles are plentiful and otter occur. The raised bogs are dry enough for adder, common lizard and slow-worm and may, occasionally, be hunted by polecat.

The great spread of Cors Caron, filling the Teifi Valley.

The wide variety of habitat, river terrace and reed canary-grass bed, raised bog and willow scrub, provides suitable feeding or nest sites for many kinds of bird. Water rail, moorhen, coot, mallard, teal, curlew, redshank and snipe are among the wetland species. Redpoll, willow tit and willow warbler may be found in the trees, with grasshopper warbler, sedge warbler and reed bunting by the river and small numbers of red grouse on the bog itself. In winter there are good numbers of whooper swan together with mallard, teal and wigeon, and hen harrier and merlin may be seen. One of the most exciting sights might be a red kite, wheeling effortlessly above the bog.

Cwm Felin-y-Gigfran

Permit only; 6ha; WWNT reserve
Steep valley side
Spring, early summer

Wood anemone, bluebell and primrose carpet the slope in spring, followed by bracken, while the riverside scrub of ash, oak and sycamore is fringed with alder. Buzzard, raven, dipper and grey wagtail may be seen.

Cwmrheidol Nature Trail

SN 697797; 4km; CEGB
Trail circling the reservoir at Rheidol Power Station
Leaflet from information centre or CEGB
Spring, summer

The trail overlooks the reservoir, a wintering site for Bewick's swan, goosander and tufted duck, and shows much of the plant and animal life of the acid rocky parts of Wales. Salmon and trout pass through the reservoir on their way to breed and a wide range of field, hedgerow, woodland and water birds may be seen.

Dowrog Common

SM 769268; 81.2ha; NT–WWNT reserve
Lowland heath and wetland
Spring, early summer

The reserve's habitat range is from damp heath to open pools, but with a wide range of variation; the common is a mosaic of plants, all reflecting the changes in wetness or in soil.

There is the gorse and heather typical of heathland with bell heather in the drier areas and cross-leaved heath in the wet. Purple-loosestrife, fleabane and sneezewort grow with saw-wort and bog asphodel. Small pools are ringed or hidden with wet cushions of *Sphagnum* mosses, and fringed with water mint, yellow iris, ragged-Robin, common cottongrass and bogbean. Nearly 300 plant species have been recorded, including a number of restricted distribution in Britain.

Clumps of grey willow and meadowsweet mark the streams and pools with their stands of bulrush and great willowherb above smaller marsh plants such as square-stalked St John's-wort, marsh lousewort and marsh cinquefoil. Here birds of the open water areas nest – coot, moorhen, water rail, sedge warbler and duck such as mallard. In winter other duck may visit, pintail, pochard, teal, tufted duck and wigeon, and both whooper and Bewick's swan are regularly observed. The birds also include short-eared owl and grasshopper warbler. Hen harrier and merlin are present throughout the winter, while buzzard, kestrel and sparrowhawk are seen regularly.

The wealth of water and flowering plants means that insects are plentiful and varied, with an abundance of dragonflies, including small red damselfly. The butterflies include green hairstreak and the much rarer marsh fritillary – localised in south and south west England, Cumbria and west Wales and using devil's-bit scabious as its food plant.

A change in sea level drowned an ancient forest at Ynyslas; low tide shows the petrified remains.

Dyfi

SN 609942; 1590ha; NCC reserve
Estuary, dune system and raised bog
Permit required, except to Ynyslas Dunes,
from NCC, Aberystwyth
Leaflets from information centre, Ynyslas
All year

Ynyslas Dunes, rising from a shingle beach, show typical dune development: at low tide sand is blown up to settle around the stems of plants, such as sea rocket and prickly saltwort, which are adapted to grow in the sandy shingle. As sand builds up around these plants marram begins to grow, sending out new shoots as fast as fresh sand covers it – it can tie together a dune as high as 7m. On the sheltered, landward side of the dune, sea spurge can grow and provide shelter in which restharrow, red fescue and duneland mosses begin to consolidate a surface.

When the surface has become more stable, smaller more delicate plants appear, for example Portland spurge, common centaury, biting stonecrop, hare's-foot clover and common bird's-foot-trefoil. In the meantime another dune may have been forming in front of this one and the whole cycle will repeat itself.

Between the ranks of dunes are damp hollows with their own special plants and, because these sands are rich in calcium, they are particularly suitable for many orchids. Among those found at Ynyslas are a subspecies (*coccinea*) of early marsh-orchid, northern marsh-orchid, marsh helleborine and bee and pyramidal orchid.

The reserve is a haven for rabbits, making the dunes a good hunting ground for fox, weasel, stoat and polecat. Small mammals generally are not plentiful, although hedgehogs find plenty of snails, particularly the characteristic duneland banded snail.

Birds, too, are neither plentiful nor widely varied, since the dunes offer little cover; many species, however, may be seen from the reserve – on the foreshore such birds as ringed plover, which nests there, and dunlin, sanderling and oystercatcher – the greatest variety, however, will be seen in the estuary. Summer sightings may include cormorant, shelduck and red-breasted merganser, while waders include bar-tailed godwit, curlew, whimbrel, greenshank, redshank and common sandpiper. During spring and autumn migrations the wader population increases dramatically, while the winter population of wildfowl may include about 2000 wigeon, together with mallard, pintail and teal. This is the only regular winter roost, south of the Solway, for Greenland white-fronted geese.

The bog, Cors Fochno, is open only to permit holders. The largest area of unmodified raised mire in the country, it has a magnificent range of wetland plants and insects, many of them of great interest for their range and distribution. It also has probably the lowest-altitude flock of black grouse in the country.

Razorbill are among the seabirds of Elegug Stacks.

Elegug Stacks

SR 926945; 1ha; MOD–PCNPA
Limestone pillars
Spring, summer

The coastal cliffs here are spectacular, carrying a striking range of plants, and the stacks just offshore provide breeding sites for guillemot and razorbill.

The Gann

SM 808066; 100ha; PCNPA
Coastal shingle, saltmarsh and freshwater pools
Spring, summer, autumn

Near the mouth of the Milford Haven Estuary the coastline bends back on itself, forming the sheltered bay of Dale Roads. The PEMBROKESHIRE COAST PATH crosses the head of the bay, at low water, by an embankment and a tidal ford. From here the Gann, a very wide range of habitat, can be seen.

The foreshore is of shingly sand with rock outcrops. The embankment has led to the development of a saltmarsh behind it and gravel extraction has left a number of pools, some flooded at high tide, some brackish and some freshwater, although these may be washed over at very high spring tides. This gives, in a very small area, an unusual amount of variation.

The bank is faced with shingle and supports typical shingle plants, such as sea beet and orache, but also some rather unexpected plants, woody nightshade, for instance, indicating that the tides rarely reach here. It is topped with gorse, ragwort, chamomile and mugwort, while common bird's-foot-trefoil and common vetch tangle the undergrowth.

At the eastern end the embankment breaks into a number of tidal islands, thick with sea-purslane, common scurvygrass and greater sea-spurrey. The largest, above normal tide levels, is covered with scrub. Where the shingle and sand-and-shingle become mud glasswort grows. It is at this point that the tidal ford allows crossing of the stream, while upstream of the ford the level ground opens on to the saltmarsh. The saltmarsh, rich in creeks and pools, is full of thrift, sea aster and lax-flowered sea-lavender. Curlew and redshank probe the mud of the marsh, which is also a hunting ground for heron.

The larger gravelpits lie behind the embankment and at the edge of the marsh and there is a good progression of saltwater to freshwater plants with, at the low hill which overlooks the estuary, stands of common reed, hemp-agrimony, fleabane, silverweed and water mint. A dense mass of thorn and bramble near the west end of the bank gives cover to such birds as stonechat and linnet and the position of the Gann, almost at the mouth of the estuary, means that in spring and autumn a good selection of passage birds should be seen.

Garn Turne Rocks

SM 979273; 3ha; WWNT reserve
Archaeological site
All year

The main interest of the site lies in the collapsed cromlech which was once a burial chamber.

Goodwick Moor

SM 946377; 15.2ha; WWNT reserve
Reedbed and marsh
Permit only away from footpath
All year

A superb mix of wetland – open water, extensive reedbed, marsh and bog – provides habitats for breeding sedge, reed and grasshopper warbler, while snipe and teal are regular winter visitors. Characteristic plants include *Sphagnum* mosses, marsh cinquefoil, bogbean and bog myrtle with bulrush, bur-reeds, reeds and sedges.

Y Goyalt

Permit only; 5.8ha; WWNT reserve
Oak woodland
Spring, summer

The reserve, in the upper valley of the Tywi, holds a good range of woodland birds. As in many of the drier Welsh oak woodlands, bracken is thick around the upper edges. There is an active badger sett.

Grassholm

Permit only; 30ha; RSPB reserve
Rocky offshore island
No visits before 15 June
Summer

Part of the SKOMER GROUP: an important gannetry.

The wheeling elegance of a red kite in flight.

Gwenffrwd–Dinas

SN 787470; 480ha; RSPB reserve
Upland hill and valley oakwoods and pasture
Permit only to the Gwenffrwd, April–August, Saturday, Monday and Wednesday
Leaflet from RSPB or Dinas information centre in summer
Spring, summer

This large tract of typical mid-Wales upland is in two blocks, the Gwenffrwd being the larger and more varied. The smaller is a steeply wooded knoll at the junction of the Towy and Doethie rivers. There are wide stretches of heather moorland, home of red grouse, snipe and meadow pipit, rich in wet mires with marsh St John's-wort, bog asphodel, bogbean and bog pimpernel. These heather moors provide breeding sites for skylark, whinchat and wheatear and, in spring, may be visited by merlin.

Dropping down from the moors the valley sides begin to show woodland, thin at first and then thickening into the typical woodland, oak and birch, of the wet acid valleys of much of Wales. This is pied flycatcher country, with redstart, wood warbler and woodcock: damp woodland with little ground cover but a tumble of rocks thick with mosses and ferns, with hard, oak and lemon-scented fern, lady-fern, polypody and Wilson's filmy-fern.

Dinas has a nature trail which shows a representative range of the steep valley habitats. The tumbled rocks and the mosses and ferns are here, the oaks climbing the tilted rocks, and, where more light penetrates, heather, bilberry, harebell and navelwort. Damp, thin grassland shows ivy-leaved bellflower and lousewort; in spring there are bluebells under the trees.

The rivers provide yet another type of habitat, a feeding ground for dipper, heron and kingfisher, a breeding ground for dipper, grey wagtail and common sandpiper. The Towy riverbank is the site for a colony of sand martin, and the rivers themselves hold resident brown trout and are spawning grounds for salmon and sea trout.

Buzzard, kestrel, sparrowhawk, tawny owl and red kite nest on the reserve and peregrine may visit. There are numerous foxes and a number of active badger setts, occasional polecat and a population of both red and grey squirrel.

Llanerch Alder Carr

Permit only; 2.6ha; WWNT reserve
Wet alder and grey willow woodland
Spring, summer

This is probably the best example in Pembrokeshire of a mature wet alder woodland with an abundance of rotten stumps, fallen trees and open marshy glades. Apart from the glades the tree canopy is dense and the ground cover is thick with bramble, reed canary-grass and greater tussock-sedge.

Llyn Eiddwen

SN 606674; 48ha; WWNT reserve
Upland lake and grassland
All year

A small water-catchment area of unimproved land has allowed the lake to remain unaltered and encouraged a community of water plants unique in Britain. Here awlwort grows, at its most southerly limit, with quillwort, least bur-reed, shoreweed, water lobelia and lesser and floating water-plantain. The growing basin mire is dominated by bottle sedge and water horsetail. Small numbers of whooper swan winter on the lake.

Llyn Nant-y-Bai

Permit only; 0.9ha; WWNT reserve
Pond and scrub-covered bank
Spring, summer

The shallow pond is covered by water horsetail in summer and is edged by soft rush, mosses and purple moor-grass, ideal cover for nesting reed warbler and mallard. The bank is thick with gorse, heather and characteristic heathland plants such as bilberry, heath bedstraw and tormentil. The pond is a breeding area for frog and a favourite site for heron.

Llys-y-Fran Country Park

SN 040244; 124.5ha; DCC
Reservoir and surrounds
All year

A nature trail demonstrates the interests of the park where moorland birds and waterbirds breed. In winter, wildfowl may shelter on the reservoir.

Marloes Mere

Permit only; 11.2ha; WWNT reserve
Species-rich wetland
All year

Soft rush covers much of the reserve and common cottongrass most of the rest. Reed bunting, curlew, snipe and mallard breed; winter duck include shoveler, for which it is one of the best sites in south Wales, and teal. Marsh fritillary butterfly has been recorded.

The narrow river valley where Dinas, steeply wooded, faces typical open grazed slopes.

Marloes Sands Nature Trail

SM 780082; 3.2km; WWNT–NT
Trail on coast overlooking Gateholm and
Skokholm, returning inland
Leaflet from WWNT
Spring, summer

The trail includes streamside interest, an old roadway overlooking MARLOES MERE, and a sunken
lane. The cliffs are rich with heather, thrift and
wild thyme. Sea and shore birds can be seen, with
raven and, occasionally, chough.

Nant Melin

Permit only; 2.8ha; WWNT reserve
Mixed woodland and damp grassland
Spring, summer

The slope above the river carries birch, oak,
sycamore and rowan, with alder and several
willow species in the wetter parts. Wet grasslands
on the wood's fringes have plants such as wood
horsetail, royal fern and globeflower. Birds characteristic of woodland and river can be seen.

Old Mill Grounds

SM 953161; 3.2ha; WWNT reserve
Marsh and woodland
Spring, summer

Mixed woodland slopes down steeply to the western CLEDDAU river, bordering a marsh which lies
between it and the water. The marsh has meadowsweet, purple-loosestrife, lesser pond-sedge and
wood club-rush. Grasshopper warbler breeds in
the marsh, with mute swan on the river islands and
birds such as nuthatch, treecreeper, blackcap and
goldfinch in the woods.

Old Warren Hill

SN 615787; 8.1ha; WWNT reserve
Mixed woodland
Spring, summer

Varied woodland species form the ground cover
under oak, ash, beech and birch and trees such as
sycamore and Scots pine. There is an open, bracken-
covered hillside, a wooded dingle and a deep valley
with a stream. This is a breeding site for many
species of birds and contains active badger setts.

Steeply tilted rock strata are a feature of the very varied cliffs of the Pembrokeshire coast.

Pant Da

Permit only; 4ha; WWNT reserve
Mixed woodland
Spring, early summer

The woodland, composed of a mix of planted larch
and regenerating oak, contains typical birds.

Pembrey Country Park

SN 415007; 210ha; Llanelli BC
Duneland and plantations
Booklet from visitor centre or LBC
All year

The country park is situated on an area of blown
sand at the mouth of the Burry Inlet. Four waymarked nature trails demonstrate some of the interest
of the pinewoods, scrub, grassland and sands.

Pembrokeshire Coast
National Park

See map; 58,275ha; PCNPA
270km of coastline and inlying land
Leaflets from PCNPA
Spring, summer

The park embraces most of the coast from Cardigan
to Amroth, swinging inland to include the heather
moors of the Mynydd Preseli and the estuary of the
CLEDDAU. A wide range of scenery is contained
within its area, including such diverse habitats as
islands and estuaries, sea cliffs and saltmarsh, freshwater lakes, heathlands and varied woodlands.

The coastal waters are extremely rich, encouraging an important wintering flock of common scoter
in Cardigan Bay and providing food for the grey seals
which breed on the inshore islands. These, such as
the SKOMER COMPLEX, hold colonies of seabirds while
the coastal cliffs and heathlands contain a superb
range of colourful plants. The long winding estuaries
– deep-cut drowned river valleys – provide shelter
and feeding grounds for wildfowl and waders and,
set in the south west corner of Wales, are important
migration routes for birds and insects. The woods
have been largely altered by man but form a habitat
for typically western as well as more widespread
species; the largest area of freshwater lakes, at
BOSHERSTON PONDS, has also been modified but is
both beautiful and rich in water plants and animals.

DOWROG COMMON, THE GANN and ST DAVID'S
HEAD are among a great number of fascinating areas
included in the park – the PEMBROKESHIRE COAST
PATH runs along its length. Although this is the
smallest national park in England and Wales, its
range of variety is quite superb: duneland, with
uncommon plants such as dune gentian and perennial centaury, give way to cliffs of hard rock above
the sea; when the sun is hot on the coast, narrow
valleys inland may be cool in the shade of steeply
sloping woodlands while the heather moors may be
high enough for a breeze. Its geology is as rich and
varied as its wildlife and its coastal scenery is
among the finest in Britain.

Teal may visit Pembroke Upper Mill Pond in winter.

Pembrokeshire Coast Path

SN 164468–174073; 270km; PCNPA–CC
Long-distance way
Booklet from CC or HMSO bookshops
Spring, summer

The waymarked footpath follows the coastline
through the length of the PEMBROKESHIRE COAST
NATIONAL PARK.

Pembroke Upper Mill Pond

SM 953161; 5.3ha; WWNT reserve
Good waterbird pond
Visitors must keep to right of way
Winter

The pond is the only Pembrokeshire site for horned
pondweed but its chief interest is probably its
waterbirds. Little grebe has nested here and late
summer visitors include green sandpiper. Winter
is the time for wildfowl – mallard, pochard, tufted
duck and teal are among the regular visitors.

Penally Nature Trail

SS 117991; 5.6km; Friends of Penally
Countryside trail
Leaflets from Penally post office, stores or pottery,
or PCNPA information centres
Spring, early summer

In an area of farmland set on old red sandstone and
limestone, the trail includes hedges, woods, grassland and marsh, together with an old cave system.

Penderi Hanging Oakwood

SN 550732; 12ha; WWNT reserve
Oak woodland and sea cliffs
Permit only away from coastal footpath
Spring, summer

Hanging oakwoods above the sea cliffs have been
stunted by exposure to the gales, yet still hold a good
variety of woodland plants and birds. Cormorant,
shag and herring gull nest on the cliffs and raven and
chough may be seen. Grey seal gather in autumn and
occasionally breed in inaccessible bays.

Pengelli Forest

SN 124395; 64.8ha; WWNT reserve
Oak woodland
Visitors must keep to marked paths
Spring, summer

Even on the hottest day it is cool and quiet under the oak trees of Pengelli. The woodland canopy is fairly high but dense and even, because the forest was clear-felled for charcoal around the time of World War I and so the effect is same-aged coppiced woodland throughout. It represents the largest block of primary oak woodland left in Pembrokeshire and is, in fact, two woods: one steep and dry on shallow soil and similar to many steep oakwoods in Dyfed, the other, separated from it by a deep ravine, damper and holding a different range of plants.

The drier wood is chiefly oak with birch and rowan while the wetter wood is more mixed, again with oak but with more birch, with ash and abundant alder. The understorey of the former is rather thin but contains a good range of species including hazel, holly, guelder-rose and gorse, some crab apple, red currant and gooseberry. The ground cover is mainly wavy hair-grass, common cow-wheat, heather and bilberry, the characteristic plants of dry acid Welsh oakwoods. In the damper wood heather is replaced by tufted hair-grass, woodruff, opposite-leaved golden-saxifrage and marsh violet.

Fox, polecat, badger and rabbit are among the mammals; frogs breed in the wetter places and both common lizard and slow-worm may be found. The range of birds is typical of such woodland and includes pied flycatcher, redstart, wood warbler and buzzard.

Light filters through the branches of the oaks in Pengelli Forest.

Portfield Gate Quarry

SM 923154; 0.7ha; WWNT reserve
Two small pools
Spring, summer

The two small pools in this tiny reserve are sheltered by willow and blackthorn scrub, and provide an attractive habitat for hedgerow and waterside birds and for dragonflies and damselflies.

Ramsey Island

SM 700235; 200ha
Inshore island
Daily boats from St Justinian's, June–September; otherwise by arrangement, tel. 0437 720648
Summer

The island's complex geology supports an unusual range of plants; its rugged coastline provides sheltered coves and beaches for the most important breeding colony of grey seal in Wales and its cliffs nest sites for the best population of chough.

Rhos Glyn-yr-Helyg

Permit only; 15.2ha; WWNT reserve
Wet pasture, bog and riverside
Spring, summer

The most important habitat here is an area of unimproved wet heathy pasture, herb-rich and increasingly rare as agricultural practice drains more and more marginal land.

464

Rhos-y-Fforest

Permit only; 1ha; WWNT reserve
Species-rich bog
Spring, summer

The reserve contains an exceptional assembly of
bog plants, including a wide range of sedges and
wavy St John's-wort, which has a very limited
range near western coasts in Britain.

Rosemoor

Permit only; 7.6ha; WWNT reserve
Lake, marsh, rough pasture, scrub and woodland
Spring, summer

Oak and ash, with an understorey of hazel and
elder, contrast with dry blackthorn scrub and a wet
area of willow scrub. The marsh adds further variation and the grassland contains a fine range of plants
including adder's-tongue, cowslip, heath spotted-
orchid and both northern and southern marsh-
orchid. The lake attracts a range of waterbirds.

St David's Head

SM 734272; 208ha; NT
Rocky headland, sea cliffs and
coastal moorland
Spring, summer, autumn

The tilted rocks and the open heathland topped by
the 180m peak with its battlemented tors make St
David's Head a popular beauty spot. The views are
certainly spectacular but, for the naturalist, are
only a part of the area's fascination.

The path rises steeply from the sandy beach of
Traeth-Mawr to the edge of the headland. Here
kidney vetch competes in brightness with goldenrod. Heather and bell heather, gorse and tormentil
clump the edges of the grassland, which runs to the
cliff edge and is backed by gorse and heather
heathland, broken by boulders and huge slabs of
rock before it finally gives way to bracken on the
steep slopes up to the tors.

East of St David's Head itself the coastline
stretches in a great arc to Strumble Head, a sweep
of sheer cliffs and steep gorse and bracken slopes
which fall into a sea sharp with rocks or washing
tiny unattainable beaches. The cliffs are topped
with heathland which rises and falls with the rock
beneath. Near the headland the rocks are slanted
and form steep, narrow gullies dropping towards
the sea. There are mats of rock sea-spurrey, of
biting stonecrop and English stonecrop. A near
relative, orpine, grows in the shelter of the rocks
or in the steep, damp gullies between them. On the
heathland above, harebell and saw-wort sway in
the strong sea winds which hardly stir the tiny,
close-growing heath pearlwort. Uncommon plants
of this coastline include *Limonium paradoxum*, a
species of sea-lavender, chives, hairy greenweed,
and the dwarf coastal form of oxeye daisy.

The hidden beaches and narrow coves beneath
the cliffs are hauling-out sites and breeding places
for the colonies of grey seal which live along these
coasts. The cliffs above the seal haul-outs provide
nest sites for buzzard, raven and small numbers of
chough and form an ideal site for seabird watching.

St Margaret's Island

Permit only; 5.6ha; WWNT reserve
Island with good bird populations
Landing is by permit only and often dangerous
Spring, summer

In summer there are frequent boat trips around the
island to see the bird colonies. The cormorant
population is huge and there are good numbers of
kittiwake, razorbill, guillemot and great black-
backed and herring gull. Manx shearwater are
seen regularly and storm petrel occasionally, as
well as many other species typical of open sea or
rocky shores.

Scolton Manor Country Park

SM 991218; 16ha; DCC
Leaflet from DCC or countryside centre
Spring, early summer

The park has a nature trail which circles through
the surrounding woodland, including a section in
Forestry Commission plantations.

Skokholm

Permit only; 96ha; WWNT reserve
Inshore island
Accommodation available: contact WWNT
Summer

Part of the SKOMER COMPLEX.

*Skomer's cliff-top turf may be a carpet of flowers
in summer.*

Skomer Complex

See map; 415ha; WWNT–RSPB reserves
Rocky islands
Leaflets from WWNT
April–September

Skomer, SKOKHOLM and the smaller Midland Island, or Middleholm, form a group at the base of the curve of St Bride's Bay. Skokholm differs from the others in being made of old red sandstone, repeated in St Anne's Head and the Angle Peninsula, while Skomer and Midland Island are mainly the old volcanic rocks of part of the Marloes Peninsula, a reef of rock which surfaces again as the small steep island of GRASSHOLM some 10km further out to sea.

Grassholm, managed by the RSPB, is little more than a cone of rock. Where vegetation exists it is mainly a spread of red fescue over the hummocked peat – the earlier deeper peats were tunnelled and eroded by puffins to such an extent that they ruined their own habitat: the tunnels collapsed and the puffins were forced to move on. A few may still nest here, together with other species of seabird, but the chief importance of Grassholm is as a gannetry. In 1860 very few gannets nested here; in 1893 numbers had risen to around 250. Now, although still the only western colony in southern Britain, the gannetry has grown to become the third largest in the North Atlantic and around 22,000 pairs may breed on the island.

The much larger island of Skokholm was the site of Britain's first bird observatory. Its coastline is carved into bays and islets ideal for nesting seabirds and, lying just off the mainland, it attracts large numbers of migrants. The cliff tops are lined with a mixture of coastal and common mainland plants, spring squill, Danish scurvygrass and thrift with bluebell, lesser celandine and primrose, while dry inner grasslands are closely cropped by rabbits and damper sites may carry a marsh of purple moor-grass. Unlike Skomer, only 3km away, neither common lizard nor toad is present and an effort to introduce them was a failure. Also a failure was an attempt to infect the rabbits with myxomatosis. Rabbits were introduced, as a food source, by the Normans in the twelfth century and do not carry the fleas which are the normal transmitters of the disease – nor, apparently, were infected fleas attracted to the Skokholm rabbits. Large numbers of seabirds breed here including Manx shearwater, storm petrel, puffin, guillemot and razorbill, together with land birds such as lapwing and raven.

Skomer is the largest of the islands and, like Skokholm, is spectacularly eroded. Much of it is heathland, a pre-glacial wave-cut platform around 60m high. Irish Sea ice must have covered Skomer, since boulders carried down from northern Britain are found on it, and at that time it would have been a flat-topped hill on the Marloes Peninsula. Rising sea levels later flooded the lower-lying land and cut Jack Sound to sever the hill from the mainland. Midland Island was then part of Skomer and the

narrow Little Sound was only eroded in relatively recent times. Erosion is a continuing factor and the narrow ridge of soft sedimentary rock between the main part of the island and the Neck will clearly be broken in the not too distant future.

The island contains a fine range of moorland and cliff habitats, together with those of old farmland, small marshes and pools. Bracken shelters woodland plants such as bluebell, lesser celandine, primrose and ground-ivy while grasslands are starred with heath pearlwort, rock sea-spurrey and English stonecrop. The heathland of heather, bell heather, tormentil and wild thyme contains cross-leaved heath and lesser skullcap in wetter

Grassholm: an island citadel of gannets; around 22,000 pairs may be present in summer.

sites and the streamside and damp valley bottoms may be filled with marshland skullcap, yellow iris and meadowsweet. Sea beet, rock samphire and sea spleenwort grow on the rugged cliffs and grade into clifftop turfs, bright with thrift, sea campion and sea squill. Around 200 flowering plants have been recognised on the island, including adder's-tongue, lanceolate spleenwort, wild madder, red goosefoot, lesser marshwort, shoreweed and yellow-eyed grass, the last an American plant possibly introduced by some migrant bird.

Large falls of migrants may occur in spring and autumn while breeding species are varied and numerous. Here is the largest kittiwake colony in Wales, with fulmar, lesser and great black-backed and herring gull. Guillemot and razorbill breed on the cliffs while puffin, storm petrel and Manx shearwater nest in burrows beneath the turf. The range of breeding birds is wide and includes waders, curlew, lapwing and oystercatcher, small birds such as wheatear and sedge warbler, and birds of the crags such as chough, raven and peregrine. Among other birds of prey seen on or above the island are buzzard, kestrel and short-eared owl.

467

Manx shearwaters nest in burrows under cushions of thrift and sea campion on Skokholm.

Predatory mammals are absent, allowing large numbers of rabbit, common and pigmy shrew, wood mouse and Skomer vole to survive on the island. Skomer vole is a race of bank vole, larger than the mainland variety, lighter in colour and different in skull and teeth. Another speciality of the reserve is the breeding population of grey seal – Skomer is one of the most important sites in south west Britain, second only to RAMSEY ISLAND, some 14km north.

Skomer may be visited from April until late September, on any day except Monday, Bank Holidays excepted. Sailings may be cancelled in times of severe weather and no more than 100 visitors are permitted on any one day. Details of visits to Skokholm and Grassholm are given under their respective headings.

This quite magnificent and fascinating group of island reserves is complemented by a marine reserve which embraces the inland waters around Skomer and the Marloes Peninsula. Some 1000ha are protected to conserve their underwater interest.

Teifi Valley and Foreshore

SN 185458; 60ha; WWNT reserve
Tidal muds and riverside
All year

An interesting range of plants is complemented by resident birds and a wealth of migrant and winter waterfowl which shelter in the reedbeds. Regular wintering species include snipe, woodcock, bartailed and black-tailed godwit, mallard, teal, goldeneye and pintail.

Vale of Rheidol Railway Nature Trail

SN 585816; 19.3km; BR
Britain's first railway nature trail
Leaflet, both English and Welsh editions, from WWNT and Aberystwyth bookshops
Spring, summer

The narrow-gauge line runs from Aberystwyth to Devil's Bridge, through the broad flood plain of the lower Rheidol Valley and up the side of the narrowing wooded slopes. The journey takes in a very wide range of man-made and natural habitat.

West Hook Cliffs

SM 762092; 8.8ha; WWNT reserve
Coastal cliffs and heathland
Visitors must keep to the coast path right of way
Spring, summer

Above the cliffs rich coastal heathland, thick with bramble, bracken and gorse, contains plants such as autumn squill, heath spotted-orchid and a prostrate variety of broom. Butterflies include small pearl-bordered and dark green fritillary, ringlet and green hairstreak. Buzzard and crow breed, together with heathland stonechat and linnet.

West Williamston

SN 028060; 22.4ha; NT–WWNT reserve
Mixed coastal and limestone habitats
Permit only away from foreshore
Spring, summer

A limestone outcrop against a saltmarsh deeply cut with tidal creeks provides an interesting reserve.

The typical limestone plants include yellow-wort, blue fleabane and bee orchid, while the saltmarsh contains sea couch and marsh-mallow. Woodland areas support characteristic bird species to complement those of the saltmarsh.

Ynys-Hir

SN 683963; 255ha; RSPB reserve
Woodland, moorland, estuary and saltmarsh
Access restricted: contact RSPB
Leaflet from RSPB or site
All year

Sixty-seven bird species nest at Ynys-Hir, mostly in the oak woodland. Eight breeding warblers include wood warbler while blackcap, garden and willow warbler are plentiful and there are usually several chiffchaff. Pied flycatcher, very characteristic of Welsh woods, nests here with more general woodland birds such as blue, coal, great and willow tit, redstart, nuthatch, treecreeper and all three British woodpeckers.

Outside the oak woodland there are conifers, nesting places for goldcrest and coal tit, and the moorland of Foel Fawr, a rocky bracken-covered hill with damp patches holding cross-leaved heath, bog pimpernel and common butterwort. Lesser skullcap and ivy-leaved bellflower also grow here and the drier areas are coloured with heather, bell heather, wild thyme and trailing St John's-wort. Foel Fawr provides nesting sites for wren, for tree and meadow pipit, for stonechat, whinchat, wheatear and yellowhammer, for nightjar and woodcock.

There is a small peat bog, rich with characteristic plants – all three British sundews, bog myrtle, bog-rosemary, bog asphodel, heath spotted-orchid and white beak-sedge. The saltmarsh has typical plants such as sea aster, common scurvygrass, sea-milkwort and thrift. Here are nest sites for grasshopper and sedge warbler, reed bunting, snipe, redshank and lapwing. Here and on the estuary wigeon, mallard, teal, goldeneye, red-breasted merganser, tufted duck and shoveler flock in winter. The Greenland white-fronted geese may move up from their more usual roost in DYFI. Mallard and red-breasted merganser are present all year and breed, as do shelduck, grey wagtail, common sandpiper and, sometimes, kingfisher and dipper. Buzzard, kestrel, sparrowhawk, tawny and barn owl are among the nesting predators and there is also a small heronry.

The range of habitat supports a wide variety of mammals – small mammals are prey to fox, stoat, weasel and polecat and to aerial predators which, in autumn and winter, may include hen harrier, merlin and peregrine.

Butterflies and moths are also encouraged by the diversity, and 31 species of butterfly have been identified, including pearl-bordered, dark green and marsh fritillary. The more uncommon moths include scarlet tiger, narrow-bordered bee hawk-moth, fox and northern eggar.

Ynys-Hir: a fine dissected saltmarsh spreads from the wooded slopes to the estuary.

Glamorgan

Most people think of Glamorgan as industrialised; few realise how much open country remains. Climb to the brink of a mining valley and houses, mines and factories disappear: a great expanse of mountain moorland stretches east and west, putting the ribbon development along the valley bottoms in perspective. To the north the coalfield hills ascend to 660m and beyond them the Brecon Beacons to almost 1000m. To the south they descend to 330m before dropping abruptly to the coastal plain and the Bristol Channel.

The region, now administratively divided into West, Mid and South Glamorgan, falls naturally into upland similar to the rest of Wales, and the sunnier, more fertile Vale of Glamorgan along the southern seaboard. In the west the grey cliffs of the Gower Peninsula stand four-square to the south westerlies.

On the roof of the coalfield, where dipper and ring ouzel nest, rainfall is high and the climate bleak. The southern shores receive less rain and plants and insects known in southern Europe thrive. The extremes of climate are governed largely by altitude, but it is the wide range of rock types that determines plant and animal life.

Devonian old red sandstones dip below the south Wales coalfield to surface north and south of it. Mid Glamorgan extends across the northern outcrop into the BRECON BEACONS NATIONAL PARK (Powys), where reservoirs harbour brown and rainbow trout and amphibians.

Carboniferous limestones over the old red marls, brownstones and quartz conglomerates offer the chance to see white trout, white cave spiders and other subterranean rarities. Crevice plants escaping the inexorable munching of sheep include saxifrages and meadow-rue, with endemic whitebeams in river gorges.

The alternation of hard grits and soft shales gives some splendid waterfalls. Mountain tops are of rain-soaked acid moorland, with deergrass, bilberry, cottongrass and bog asphodel. Corrie lakes lie under the north scarp of the coalfield and upper valleys. Quillwort, water lobelia and narrow bur-reed occupy the water, with cowberry, stone bramble and roseroot on the crags. Buzzard, raven, merlin and heron are typical; foxes roam the hills and there are polecat and badger.

Much of the coalfield is blanketed by 'Molinia desert' and mat-grass moor. Heathery slopes are sprinkled with cranberry and crowberry, inaccessible cliffs with club-mosses and filmy-ferns, quagmires with bog pimpernel and ivy-leaved bellflower, streams with monkeyflower and rare red algae.

Wooded tributary valleys are the home of redstart, pied flycatcher, wood warbler and woodpeckers. Sessile oakwood formerly clothed far more, but much fell to the charcoal burners who supplied the early iron foundries; mercifully coal took over as the source of power. Soil once forested is now usually bracken- or larch-clad.

To the south the mountain limestone surfaces as a ridge which is dolomitised in the east, the red, iron-stained magnesian limestone supporting a different flora from the purer limestones of the west. Much is beech-covered, with early-purple and bird's-nest orchid, broad-leaved helleborine and columbine, spindle and dogwood among the beech leaves, centaury and yellow-wort on the paths, green spleenwort and golden-saxifrage near ancient lead mines. In the west there is more rock-rose, horseshoe vetch and squinancywort and there are some fine limestone heaths.

The Triassic rocks near Cardiff and the flaky black Rhaetic strata are characterised by narrow-leaved everlasting-pea, dyer's greenweed and flax. Warm soils of the younger Jurassic limestones support woolly thistle and wild cabbage, with clustered bellflower and marjoram, tuberous thistle and pepper-saxifrage. Stinking hellebore, stinking iris and spurge-laurel defy the hungry sheep.

Bee orchid abounds locally and the insects are reminiscent of warmer climates. Herring gull, jackdaw and house martin nest on the vertical cliffs of the Vale and a remarkable platform has been carved from the soft strata by marine erosion. The northern part of the Vale lies under boulder clay; less suited to agriculture, it has some interesting heath and bogland and peaty pools, with riverside monk's-hood and orange balsam.

FLAT HOLM, 5km offshore, is of carboniferous limestone, its spray-washed slopes bringing thrift, sea campion and rock sea-lavender well up-channel. Herring, lesser black-backed and a few greater black-backed gull nest, with the inevitable impact on other wildlife, but there are still great sweeps of scurvygrass, cowslips are surviving the rain of guano, wallflowers clothe more sheltered cliffs and the rare wild leek is thriving.

Mainland Glamorgan is blessed with vast sand dunes, each with national rarities. Plants and insects encroach on the intrusions along with the advancing sand. Dunes started to build up in the Middle Ages, and at present sand is accreting at a phenomenal rate east of Swansea. Slacks are colourful with marsh-orchid and fragrant orchid, marsh helleborine and round-leaved wintergreen, dunes with viper's-bugloss and restharrow, spinneys with yellow bird's-nest and valerian. Burnet rose and dewberry cover more stable areas, creeping willow the older slacks.

KENFIG POOL adds an extra dimension with wintering waterfowl, the occasional bittern and bearded tit, harvest mouse and water shrew. CRYMLYN BOG and associated fenland are rich in plant and bird life, dragonflies and other insects, and have been classified as Grade I conservation areas.

Alluvial flats seaward of the old sea cliffs were once visited by thousands of white-fronted geese, but have suffered lamentably at the hands of the developers. Flowering-rush, arrowhead and frogbit persist, and yellow wagtail, reed bunting and water rail still nest, but the black-headed gull colony succumbed in 1977. Gulls, kestrel, crows, starling and pied wagtail now nest in and on the industrial sites.

Saltmarshes range from the vast sandy expanses at the mouth of the River Neath to the muddier saltings alongside the Bristol Channel at Rumney Mouth, just upstream from Cardiff. Both are wriggling with invertebrate life which attracts a wealth of shorebirds to feed. A fascinating complex of salt, brackish and freshwater marsh exists within a series of old and new storm beaches at ABERTHAW and there are fine ungrazed marshes around the Taff–Ely Basin.

Gower is a Glamorgan in miniature, having all these habitats from coalfield to saltmarsh. It is famous for its limestone cliffs backing sandy bays and pockets of sand dunes. Southerners like yellow whitlow-grass and spiked speedwell, clary and golden samphire, hoary rock-rose and spring cinquefoil find sanctuary on south-facing rocks. Old red sandstone pops up as moorland ridges, and the sandy saltings of the Burry Inlet are favoured by Brent geese and summering eider, well south of their breeding latitudes. Thousands of oystercatcher feed on the cockles of Penclawdd.

Gower nurtures rare fen orchid and dune gentian, strand beetle and money spiders and an awe-inspiring number of marine creatures. Kittiwake, fulmar, guillemot and razorbill breed and puffin have recently returned to a traditional site. The future for the conservation of this part of Glamorgan at least, now enjoying considerable official protection, is optimistic.

MARY E. GILLHAM

Aberdare Canal

SO 013024; 3ha; Cynon Valley BC reserve
Disused canal and woodland
Spring, summer

Part of the canal has been cleared to provide an open pool with a good stand of bulrush. Moorhen and heron may be seen at the pool while the rest of the reserve, grown over with large willow trees, provides a good habitat for warblers and other songbirds.

Abergelli Wood

Permit only; 1.1ha; GTNC reserve
Woodland with small pool
Spring, summer

Rowan, alder, alder buckthorn and downy birch grow above plants such as bluebell, opposite-leaved golden-saxifrage, yellow pimpernel and marsh violet. Buzzard nest in the woodland and heron visit the pool. There is a badger sett.

Hoary rock-rose, a rare limestone species.

471

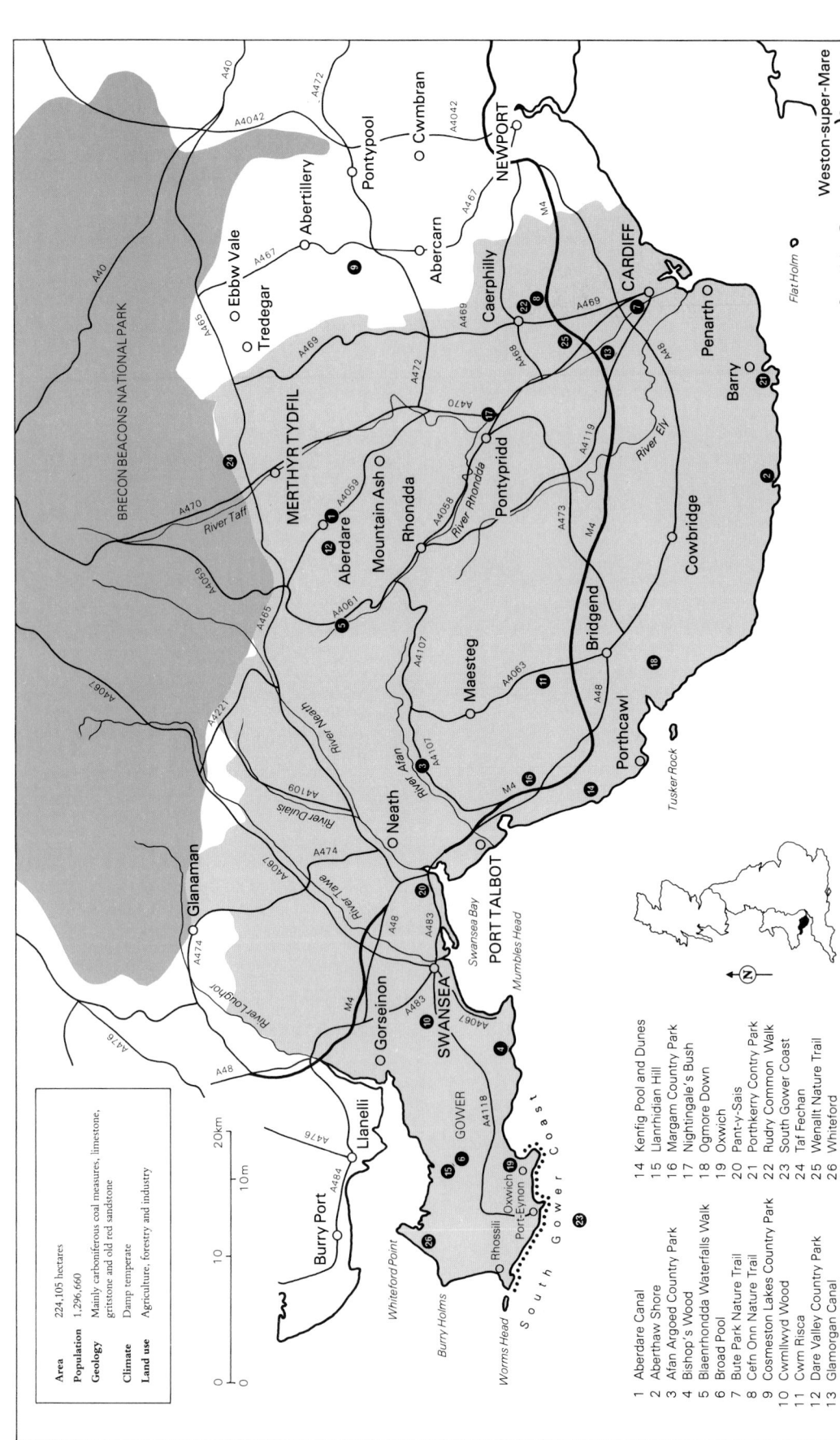

Area 224,105 hectares

Population 1,296,660

Geology Mainly carboniferous coal measures, limestone, gritstone and old red sandstone

Climate Damp temperate

Land use Agriculture, forestry and industry

BRECON BEACONS NATIONAL PARK

1 Aberdare Canal
2 Aberthaw Shore
3 Afan Argoed Country Park
4 Bishop's Wood
5 Blaenrhondda Waterfalls Walk
6 Broad Pool
7 Bute Park Nature Trail
8 Cefn Onn Nature Trail
9 Cosmeston Lakes Country Park
10 Cwmllwyd Wood
11 Cwm Risca
12 Dare Valley Country Park
13 Glamorgan Canal

14 Kenfig Pool and Dunes
15 Llanrhidian Hill
16 Margam Country Park
17 Nightingale's Bush
18 Ogmore Down
19 Oxwich
20 Pant-y-Sais
21 Porthkerry Country Park
22 Rudry Common Walk
23 South Gower Coast
24 Taf Fechan
25 Wenallt Nature Trail
26 Whiteford

0 10km 20km

10m

0

Aberthaw Shore

ST 043659; 36.3ha; GTNC reserve
Foreshore, saltmarsh and limestone cliffs
Spring, summer, autumn

The seaward edge of the reserve is bounded by a pebble storm beach where yellow horned-poppy and sea radish flower. In the lee of the storm beach is an extensive saltmarsh, dominated by sea purslane, sea aster and rock sea-lavender, and which supports several rare invertebrate species. Relict sand dunes at the eastern end of the marsh are decorated by sea-holly. Patches of the rare purple gromwell and maidenhair fern are present on the tall scrubby cliffs, where crevices and ledges provide nest sites for raven and shelter for a large population of adder. A variety of seabirds can be observed along the shoreline.

Afan Argoed Country Park

SS 821951; 56ha; West Glamorgan CC
Afforested steep valley
Leaflet from countryside centre or WGCC
All year

The fir forest rises above the twisting Afon Afan, a typical valley river. The area was once mined for coal but the tips are now grassed. Pockets of natural woodland occur among the conifers – oak, birch, ash and rowan, with alder and grey willow in the wetter places. Ivy-leaved bellflower and mountain fern may occur and the old tips have developed an interesting plant life. Woodland and waterside birds are plentiful.

Berry Wood

SS 436585; 6.8ha; GTNC reserve
Coastal oak woodland
Spring, summer

Although chiefly an oak woodland, there is a good mixture of other trees, including crab apple and aspen. As in many coastal woods the trees are pruned by salt-laden sea breezes. Lichens, mosses and ferns flourish in this unpolluted environment. Narrow buckler-fern grows here, as does wood millet. There is a good range of birds, from the tiny goldcrest to the broad-winged wheeling buzzard.

Bishop's Wood

SS 594878; 19.2ha; Swansea City Council
Dry limestone valley
Leaflet from SCC
Spring, summer

Above Caswell Bay, the reserve includes habitats ranging from cliff top, through slopes wooded with ash, oak, beech and sycamore, to open grassland in the valley bottom. A good variety of birds and mammals breed within the reserve.

At the head of the Rhondda Valley – Blaenrhondda Falls in winter.

Blaenrhondda Waterfalls Walk

SN 922021; 4km; Mid Glamorgan CC–FC
Moorland walk
Leaflet from MGCC
Spring, summer

A walk in the uplands at the head of the Rhondda Valley, it contains characteristic moorland vegetation such as heather, bilberry and tormentil, and birds such as buzzard, raven and wheatear. Grey wagtail and dipper may be seen at the streams below the waterfalls.

Broad Pool

SS 510910; 11ha; GTNC reserve
Freshwater pool and bog
Spring, summer, autumn

The pool contains white and fringed water-lily, the latter rare in west Wales. The bog is rich with bog asphodel and cross-leaved heath – a level mosaic of colour which lies in a shallow basin rising to dry heath on the slopes around.

Bunkers Hill

SS 428881; 0.4ha; GTNC reserve
Scrub and grassland
Spring, summer

This tiny hillside reserve is an area of bracken-covered grassland with open scrub, the haunt of linnet and stonechat.

Bute Park Nature Trail

ST 182767; 3.5km; Cardiff City Council
Parkland nature trail beside River Taff
Booklet from Leisure and Amenities Dept, CCC
Spring, summer

The variety of both native and exotic broad-leaved and coniferous trees and the range of natural and planted flowers make this an attractive trail. Other habitats include riverside, a feeder stream, and the castle moat. The native plants include woodland species such as dog's mercury and toothwort and wetland species such as water-plantain and meadowsweet. The many birds are characteristic of these habitats.

Castle Wood Field

SS 472931; 0.3ha; GTNC reserve
Saltmarsh
Spring, summer, autumn

This small area of saltmarsh within the extensive north Gower marshes supports typical plants of this habitat, such as thrift and sea plantain.

Cefn Onn Nature Trail

ST 184843; 2.5km; Cardiff City Council
Trail through limestone and sandstone woodlands
Booklet from Leisure and Amenities Dept, CCC
Spring, summer

The trail climbs out of the limestone ridges north of Cardiff to sandstone areas. Ash and birch, oak and hazel, oak and birch, beechwoods – all show their characteristics along the course of the trail.

Coed Garn-Llwyd

Permit only; 13ha; GTNC reserve
Limestone woodland
Spring, summer

Mixed deciduous woodland with tufa springs on a hillside shelters lime-loving shrubs such as spindle and wayfaring-tree; herb-Paris, goldilocks buttercup and butterfly-orchid thrive in the base-rich soils.

Coed Gawdir

SN 783007; 0.1ha; GTNC reserve
Small pool
Spring, summer

Sweet-grass, around the tiny artificial pool, forms an attractive habitat for small birds such as buntings and for waterbirds such as moorhen. There is a bird hide from which the pool may be observed.

Coed-y-Bedw

ST 117829; 16.6ha; GNT reserve
Rich valley woodland
Spring, early summer

In early spring, when the sunlight falls almost unfiltered to the valley floor, the dark trunks of the streamside alders stand out against the yellow of marsh-marigold. The main stream drains from west to east and the woodland grades with it from drier beech in the west to wet oak and birch woodland in the east. Alder, ash and hazel are found throughout. As these trees progressively leaf over, the shade within the wood deepens and the spring show of bluebell and ramsons becomes a variation of greens, broken by shrubs which can reach upwards for light – spindle, alder buckthorn and guelder-rose.

Another plant which can reach up from the shade is the climbing wild clematis, traveller's-joy; in autumn whole trees are cloaked with its fruit clusters. While the traveller's-joy flowers on the richer soils, the more acid eastern area has lousewort and heath bedstraw.

Among the trees there is a rich profusion of lichens, mosses and ferns and the spectacular great horsetail, which may grow as tall as a man. Trees do not cover the whole of the reserve and there are more open areas. Where spoil from the old coal workings was tipped there are two grassy clearings. Here brimstone and speckled wood may be seen, two of the 17 butterfly species recorded.

The reserve is frequented by many birds, including green and great spotted woodpecker, grey wagtail, pied flycatcher and woodcock. Above the calcium-enriched stream (the reserve lies on the junction between acid coal measures and carboniferous limestone, and receives water from both), Britain's largest lacewing, *Osmylus fulvicephalus*, may be seen.

Coed-y-Bwl

SS 909749; 2.4ha; GTNC reserve
Elm woodland
Spring, early summer

Elm, over ash and field maple, stands above a spring show of lesser celandine, wild daffodil, wood anemone and bluebell. Woodland birds include great spotted and green woodpecker, nuthatch, tawny owl and sparrowhawk.

Ring ouzel breed in sites such as Craig-y-Llyn.

Crymlyn Bog, constantly under threat, is the largest area of lowland fen in Wales.

Cosmeston Lakes Country Park

ST 180693; 84ha; Vale of Glamorgan BC–South
Glamorgan CC
Two large lakes, limestone grassland,
woods and scrub
Leaflet from VGBC or SGCC
Spring, summer

A large 'natural' area, within the park, includes one of the lakes. There is a good range of limestone plants, including some spectacular orchids, and, with water, wood and grassland, there is a great variety of bird and insect life.

Craig-y-Llyn

SN 905038; 16.2ha; GTNC reserve
Corrie lake and crags
Spring, summer, autumn

Llyn Fach lies in the curve of the Craig-y-Llyn crags, a double horseshoe of sandstone cliffs above steep fans of scree which spill down as far as the lake. A Forestry Commission plantation fringes the lake on its northern and eastern sides and there is a boggy wetland where water flows in at the western end. This type of lake was hollowed out by the action of ice, many thousands of years ago, and Llyn Fach is one of the most southerly examples of this geological process.

The lake and wetland contain many interesting plants, including spring quillwort, floating bur-reed and water lobelia, which grows here at its most southerly station in Britain. These plants are typical of northern and western high-level lakes and testify to the coldness and acidity of the waters of Llyn Fach.

The screes and higher slopes on the south of the lake vary in steepness and wetness and have a typical moorland cover of heather and bilberry, with cross-leaved heath in wet places. Their chief interest, however, lies in the presence of some high-altitude and arctic–alpine species such as roseroot and lesser meadow-rue. Three unusual ferns are found here – parsley fern, Wilson's filmy-fern and a dwarf variety of male-fern. Fir clubmoss, not really a moss at all, may also be found.

The birds of Craig-y-Llyn are as characteristic of Britain's high mountain areas as the plants. The crags, cold, wet and exposed, offer little to the more delicate species; raven, nesting in February and March, followed by ring ouzel in May, are the main species of the rocks. Peregrine used to nest here, but plantations and coalmining have now destroyed much of their territory and they will probably never return. Buzzard, kestrel and sparrowhawk, however, hunt the reserve and short-eared owl has been seen.

Crymlyn Bog

No access; 234ha; various bodies
Large wetland
Can be overlooked from lanes around,
e.g. at SS 700963
All year

A site of national conservation importance, this is the largest area of lowland fen in Wales. With a range from *Sphagnum* mosses through bulrush, common reed and great fen-sedge swamps, the bog contains many uncommon plants and provides a haven for bird life and a rich variety of insects.

Cwm George

ST 148721; 4.9ha; GTNC–FC reserve
Limestone woodland and scrub
Spring, summer

The reserve lies on the side of a deep gorge thick with oak, ash, beech, elm, birch and sycamore. The richness of limestone soils is indicated by plants such as herb-Paris, spurge-laurel and Italian lords-and-ladies, the latter normally only found in the south of England. The range of habitat encourages a good range of insects and woodland birds, including lesser whitethroat and lesser spotted woodpecker.

Cwm Ivy Wood

SS 443938; 5.5ha; GTNC reserve
Mixed wood and small quarry
Spring, summer

The mixed ash wood has a shrub layer which includes holly and dogwood and the quarry is thick with traveller's-joy. Spring flowers include primrose, cowslip and early-purple orchid, and in summer dog's mercury and hart's-tongue appear. Woodland birds are plentiful and there is a badger sett.

Cwm Leyshon

ST 213869; 1.2ha; GTNC reserve
Beech–yew woodland
Spring, summer

Some magnificent trees grow in the reserve, which is thought to be an example of the completed natural development of woodland on limestone in south Wales. Hazel and ash form the understorey with dogwood, spindle and field maple.

Cwmllwyd Wood

SS 610946; 6.4ha; West Glamorgan CC reserve
Woodland, grassland and marsh
Leaflet from WGCC
Spring, summer

Cwmllwyd has mixed oak woodland and bracken-covered grassland above marshland, each habitat showing characteristic plants. A tiny bog contains bog asphodel, heath spotted-orchid and cross-leaved heath. Typical woodland birds are present and in winter snipe and woodcock visit the marsh. There are two birdwatchers' hides.

Cwm Risca

SS 881843; 1.6ha; GTNC reserve
Woodland and pond
Spring, summer

The woods are chiefly oak, with ash, elm and some very fine small-leaved limes. The pond is bordered by marsh and wet grassland, fringed with willows and wetland flowers. Snipe visit the marsh and meadow and the willow scrub shelters tits and finches. Moorhen breed around the pool, which lies adjacent to the Glamorgan Nature Centre and Trust headquarters.

Puss moth caterpillar, found in wet woodlands.

Dare Valley Country Park

SN 962027; 320ha; Cynon Valley BC
Reclaimed mining valley
Leaflets from warden or CVBC
Spring, summer

The country park has been landscaped in a valley once mined for coal. Three nature trails have been established in the upper reaches of the valley to show examples of plants and animals typical of the coalfield.

Eglwys Nunydd

SS 794850; 101ha; GTNC reserve
Large reservoir
All year

Eglwys Nunydd is partly fringed by common reed where coot and great crested and little grebe breed. The reservoir often holds good numbers of dabblers such as mallard and shoveler and large flocks of diving ducks. Because it is close to the sea divers, scaup, smew and goosander may occur, and occasionally rare vagrants may shelter in hard weather.

Flat Holm

Permit only; 28.8ha; South Glamorgan CC reserve
Small island in Bristol Channel
Permit required for landing: from Project Manager, Flat Holm Project, Harbour Road, Barry
Leaflets from SGCC and Project Manager
Spring, summer

The island slopes from west to east, exposing much of the plateau to the prevailing off-sea winds. Dense clumps of nettles and thistles indicate the gull colonies' past domination, but the numbers of both lesser black-backed gull and herring gull have now declined. Because of the general lack of cover and the gull numbers, which are still high, other breeding species are few, although shelduck, oystercatcher and some smaller birds do nest. The island is one of the few British sites for wild leek.

Gelli Hir Wood

SS 563925; 28.7ha; GTNC reserve
Mixed lowland woodland
Spring, early summer

The open heathlands of East Gower were once covered with deciduous woodland like Gelli Hir but most were cleared for grazing. Much of the reserve is wet and acid, like the modern heaths, but is thick with oak and birch, with alder and willow by the pools and stream, and hawthorn and rowan in the drier places. Other parts of the wood are less acid and drier, and trees such as ash and wych elm with beech, hazel, sweet chestnut and small-leaved lime predominate. Boggy rides open on to narrow paths and sudden sunlit clearings. The whole wood is a complex of contrasting and interlocking habitats.

The smaller pools along the main ride are bright with lesser spearwort but the chief wetland interest is the main pool, perfectly circled by trees, sheltered and undisturbed. Bulrush grows at the water's edge with water-plantain, wild angelica, blinks, branched bur-reed, greater tussock-sedge and purple-loosestrife.

Mallard and teal nest here while, deeper in the wood, sparrowhawk, tawny owl and buzzard may breed. Of the many different moths and butterflies there are several which are uncommon in the area. These include comma, silver-washed fritillary and holly blue. The colony of silver-washed fritillary is of interest because it has changed from its normal food plant, heath dog-violet, to marsh violet.

Deep shade ensures a stretch of open water on the Glamorgan Canal.

Glamorgan Canal

ST 143803; 23ha; Cardiff City Council
Canal, old railway cutting, grassland,
marsh and woodland
Permit only to marsh
Spring, summer

The canal and marsh contain plants such as arrowhead, yellow loosestrife, branched and unbranched bur-reed, cyperus sedge and purple-loosestrife. The alder carr and mixed woodland support many spring flowers. Birds recorded include all three woodpeckers, kingfisher, siskin and redpoll.

Hambury Wood

SS 472929; 4.8ha; GTNC reserve
Oak woodland
Spring, summer

A small mixed, chiefly oak woodland with an understorey of coppiced hazel, Hambury Wood is a haven for a good range of woodland birds including breeding buzzard. There is an active badger sett.

Ilston Quarry

SS 555905; 7.6ha; GTNC reserve
Mixed woodland and pool
Spring, summer

The quarry is dominated by a steep limestone cliff, bare rock and scree slopes which are being colonised by plants. These, together with the plants of the woodland and pool, encourage many insect species and woodland insect-eating birds.

Scrub and reeds fringe the edge of the large freshwater pool at Kenfig.

Kenfig Pool and Dunes

SS 802815; 810ha; Mid Glamorgan CC
Dune system and pool
Leaflets from MGCC or reserve centre
All year

A superb spread of plant-rich dunes and a clear reed-fringed pool contrast with the heavy industry of Port Talbot not far to the north. The dune habitats range from open sand, through curving slopes of flowers, separated by damp slacks, to old dunes thick with vegetation developing into scrub woodland. The pool encourages marshland plants and a wet woodland of birch and willow. The reserve is a haven for many animals, including a range of wildfowl which visit the pool in winter.

The primary colonisers of the dunes are typical species such as sea couch, sea rocket, sea sandwort and prickly saltwort, followed by marram, sea-holly and sea spurge – then the lime-richness of the dunes encourages an enormous range of species. Over 500 flowering plants have been recorded: those of the dunes include restharrow, wild pansy, evening primrose and burnet rose with viper's-bugloss, carline thistle, wild thyme, kidney vetch and autumn lady's-tresses. In the damp slacks yellow rattle fringes round-leaved wintergreen and marsh-orchids set among creeping willow.

The pool is mainly fringed with a reedswamp of sea club-rush and common reed, with water horse-tail and bulrush and with an area rich in plants such as yellow loosestrife, tubular water-dropwort and purple-loosestrife. It lies among the older dunes which are now well grown with grasses, bramble and dewberry, tending to a scrub of hawthorn, birch and other trees.

Sedge and grasshopper warbler breed around the pool, where waterbirds may include mallard, tufted duck and great crested grebe, while winter brings goldeneye, pochard and teal, with Bewick's and whooper swan. Passage birds often visit the reserve and curlew, greenshank, redshank, sanderling and whimbrel may be seen. Kestrel and short-eared owl come here to hunt.

The pool and the dunes are rich in insects and other small animal life, with a good range of mammals including fox and hare.

Lavernock Point

ST 182680; 5.8ha; GTNC reserve
Limestone grassland and scrub
Spring, summer, autumn

Lavernock is a coastal reserve with areas of dense hawthorn scrub on rich limestone grassland. The grassland contains adder's-tongue and several orchids, including lesser butterfly-orchid, green-winged and bee orchid. Greenfinch and linnet are typical of the small birds of the hawthorn scrub which, during migration times, may shelter less common species.

Llanrhidian Hill

SS 497922; 3.1ha; GTNC reserve
Grassland, scrub and rock
Spring, summer

Two old quarry sites, together with elder, hawthorn and ash scrub and limestone grassland, provide a good habitat range rich in plant and insect life. Linnet and stonechat flick from shrub to shrub and kestrel hunt the steep slopes.

Margam Country Park

SS 813849; 240ha; West Glamorgan CC
Parkland and woodland
Permit only to Furzemill Heron Reserve
Leaflets from park or WGCC
All year

The park has several pools and some fine parkland trees. Several waymarked walks demonstrate the variation within the area. The ponds and streams have plants related to the acidity of the water, with water horsetail and shoreweed in the richest lake and water-plantain and marsh St John's-wort fringing the most acid. This is Furzemill Pond, established as a reserve to protect the heronry. A herd of over 300 fallow deer grazes the park.

Nightingale's Bush

ST 082898; 1.1ha; GTNC reserve
Disused canal
Spring, summer

Some 200m of the canal have been excavated, giving an area of slow-moving open water, rich in wetland plants. On one bank is a towpath, on the other a scrub of grey willow, osier, alder, sycamore and guelder-rose, harbouring a variety of woodland birds. Kingfisher visit the canal.

Ogmore Down

SS 897762; 26.5ha; GTNC reserve
Limestone grassland and heath
Spring, early summer

Sandwiched between quarries which have torn the heart out of the hillside, Ogmore Down is a reminder of the rich vegetation which once must have clothed the whole area. There is a superb early summer show of colour which varies with the depth of the soil. Where there are pockets of deeper soil on the hillside, the plants are often typical of lime-poor areas because much of the goodness of the limestone has been washed downwards; where the soil is shallow there is a rich mix of lime-loving plants because grazing pressures hold back the grasses and the soil is too thin for lime-haters such as gorse and heather.

The hilltop, like the pockets of deeper soil, is lime-poor for the same reasons – here is one of the fascinations of what is called limestone heath: acid-lovers such as gorse, heather and bell heather grow alongside limestone plants in a dense and colourful confusion. The soil is rich enough for common rock-rose, but acid enough for cross-leaved heath and tormentil.

On the thin soil of the steep grassland a wide variety of lime-loving plants may be seen – lady's bedstraw, common bird's-foot-trefoil, common centaury and eyebright, wild thyme, small scabious, salad burnet, harebell and autumn lady's-tresses, together with a rare subspecies of hairy violet, a diploid population of horseshoe vetch and mountain everlasting, a northern heath and mountain species.

This generally dry mosaic of open, short grassland and thick, tussocked heath with its scattered patches of gorse scrub is an ideal nesting area for such typical heathland birds as skylark, stonechat and yellowhammer.

One of the more unusual insects of the reserve is glow-worm, a nationally decreasing species. The larvae are very active predators, feeding mainly on snails, which are most plentiful in chalk and limestone grassland where there is a good supply of calcium for shell building. The decrease of these beetles is due, at least in part, to the destruction of such grasslands.

Oxwich

SS501865; 258ha; NCC reserve
Dunes, saltmarsh and freshwater marsh between wooded limestone headlands
Permit required except on dunes and on footpaths through woodlands
Booklets from NCC information centre in car park
Spring, summer, autumn

Two nature trails give the flavour of the reserve. The sand dune trail begins with the first land plants of the sandy beach. These, such as sea-holly and prickly saltwort, trap some of the blown sand to form foredunes. Marram continues the consolidation of the sand and as the dunes build up other plants begin to stabilise the surface. Dewberry and sea bindweed form a lattice of runners through which ragwort and common evening-primrose grow. The sand here is rich in calcium and in the damp hollows between the dunes lime-loving plants such as yellow-wort, common centaury and dune gentian grow among creeping willow and downy birch. In June both early and southern marsh-orchid and marsh helleborine may grow in these damp slacks.

Adder, Britain's only venomous native snake.

Behind the seaward dunes more stable slopes develop and more general plants such as bracken and wood sage grow where rain has washed most of the calcium out of the top layers of the soil. Wild privet and carline thistle, two characteristic lime-loving species, are plentiful. At the back of the dunes clovers and grasses form a more meadow-like sward and damp places are filled with meadowsweet and rushes.

The woodland trail passes through tall woods and scrub and out on to the clifftop grassland. The whole of this area is on limestone and has the expected richness and variety. The main woodland is of high-forest oak and ash with an understorey of hazel and holly. In spring there are bluebell, ramsons, wood anemone, common dog-violet and lesser celandine. Dog's mercury, enchanter's-nightshade and many ferns follow later in the year. The commoner woodland birds fill the woods with song and there is also a rookery.

The drier slopes are thick with bracken and the path crosses a scrub area of blackthorn, hawthorn and gorse, perfect cover for heathland birds such as stonechat and for badger, fox and weasel. Adder, slow-worm and grass snake may occur. From the clifftop grassland, rich in lime-loving plants such as common rock-rose, oystercatcher and redshank may be seen on the strandline.

The areas open only to permit holders are extensive freshwater marshes with fen, carr and open pools, and Crawley Wood, another limestone wood, with an interesting flora including the rare whitebeam *Sorbus rupicola*.

Pant-y-Sais

SS 713939; 17.8ha; Neath BC
Narrow strip of rich fen
Spring, summer, autumn

Tall stands of common reed, a belt of fenland unexpectedly surviving between the Skewen road and the Tennant Canal, crossed by a railway line, close to huge oil refineries, Pant-y-Sais is a rare and exciting treasure. The plants are very rich and varied: among the reeds are rosebay willowherb, greater bird's-foot-trefoil, bulrush and royal fern. In the canal, white water-lily lifts above the water.

A towpath separates the fen from the canal and has its own contrasting plants, such as common toadflax and the more unusual pale toadflax. Heather and gorse make a rather unexpected show here: with the railway clinker of the towpath, a number of plants not usual in this sort of habitat have been imported. Creeping willow, too, grows on the towpath and other trees in the area are the alders lining the east side of the canal and a scattering of birch and hawthorn in the fen itself. These obviously grow in the drier parts, a supposition reinforced by areas of bracken around some of them – bracken does not like wet conditions. Yellow iris and fleabane show where conditions are wet and here, and at the canal edge, skullcap, hemp-agrimony and marsh cinquefoil may be seen.

With its wealth of wetland plants and with the open water of the canal, Pant-y-Sais is a most important area, rich in insects and their predators, and a vital area for conservation.

Peel Wood

SS 607883; 1.2ha; GTNC reserve
Wooded old quarry
Spring, summer

Sycamore and elm, with oak and ash, form the main tree cover over a shrub layer which includes rhododendron and snowberry. The quarry is rich in ferns, including hart's-tongue and soft shield-fern, and there is a good range of woodland birds including breeding tawny owl.

Penmoelallt Forest

SS 995093; 7ha; NCC–FC reserve
Mixed woodland
Leaflet from NCC
Spring, summer

The tree cover varies from ash, with wych elm and rowan, on the limestone screes to oak with ash, elm, rowan and silver birch where the soil is deeper. Small-leaved lime and hazel are also present and there are many spring flowers. This diversity means a good range of woodland birds, but the reserve's chief interest is the presence of some rare whitebeams, one of which is known only in this valley.

Porthkerry Country Park

ST 092672; 91ha; Vale of Glamorgan BC
Woodland, grassland, cliff and shingle
Booklet from car park
Spring, summer

Only Cliff Wood, the coastal woodland, is actually scheduled as a reserve, but the whole park is a rich mix of varied habitats.

Purple gromwell, a rare plant of lime-rich woods.

Mewslade Bay shows some of the splendid sea cliffs that distinguish the South Gower Coast.

The long curve of the shingle beach which closes the mouth of the valley has typical plants such as sea beet, bulbous foxtail and yarrow. Above the beach is a spectacular limestone cliff on which maidenhair fern grows – this rare and delicate fern is found only on a few limestone sea cliffs in the west of Britain.

The cliff is topped by a typical limestone woodland, Cliff Wood, which was scheduled as a reserve to protect another rare plant, purple gromwell, a trailing, creeping plant with dark blue-purple flowers which show in early summer. The trees are chiefly oak and ash and have been managed in a coppice-with-standards system which, with the hawthorn, hazel, field maple and yew that also grow in the wood, has resulted in a very good woodland structure.

Beneath the tall standards the coppiced trees form an interlaced canopy over the smaller plants. This obviously poses problems for plants which depend on light, and most of them flower in spring when the shade is less dense. Some, such as wild madder on the sea edge of the wood, and traveller's-joy, can climb to reach the light, but much of the wood in summer is a rich pattern of green.

The park contains other spreads of woodland and areas of damp and close-cut grassland and this variety of habitat encourages a good range of mammals and commoner birds.

Redley Cliff

SS 589875; 3.6ha; GTNC reserve
Coastal grassland and scrub
Spring, summer

The north-facing slope is covered with scrub woodland – ash, hazel, hawthorn and blackthorn – with a dense ground cover of dog's mercury and ramsons. The south-facing slope is a more open coastal heathland. From the headland, seabirds such as oystercatcher may be seen.

Rudry Common Walk

ST 183865; 3.2km; Mid Glamorgan CC
Moorland and valley walk
Spring, early summer

A climb to the peak of Mynydd Rudry near Caerphilly which includes dry heathland with damp valleyland and small areas of *Sphagnum* bog. Typical grassland birds such as skylark and meadow pipit may be seen, with woodland birds in the lower scrub and in the nearby oakwood.

South Gower Coast

See map; 30km; GTNC–NCC–NT
Foreshore, cliffs, dunes and marshes
Leaflets from NCC
Spring, summer

The Gower Peninsula, with its amazing wealth of wildlife, is also subject to heavy pressure from visitors – on a summer bank holiday the roads may become completely clogged with traffic. Outside such popular times, and off the roads, the peninsula is rich in natural beauty and the south coast, in particular, is fascinating.

Hard, pale carboniferous limestone has been tilted, folded and faulted, planed off to form a coastal plateau and eroded into bays and coves, faced with sand or carved into pinnacles and caves. The cliffs are dramatic and beautiful, varied with sweeps of grassland, scrub and woodland, giving way to a bay of duneland and marsh where the sea has found a fold of softer rock. The mild climate and lack of pollution, together with the lime-rich rocks, encourage a wonderful range of wildlife.

The cliffs and shallow limestone grasslands contain coastal species such as thrift, spring squill, rock sea-lavender and rock and golden samphire, together with lime-loving common rock-rose, carline thistle and squinancywort. Horseshoe vetch, uncommon in Wales, occurs with other less common plants including bloody crane's-bill, wild cabbage, spring cinquefoil, hoary rock-rose and hutchinsia. Yellow whitlowgrass grows on this coast and nowhere else in Britain – its nearest European site is far inland in Belgium – while small restharrow and goldilocks aster are almost as restricted, occurring only in a few western coastal sites. These last two plants are of very special interest because they seem incapable of spreading. The sites where they do occur are often far-flung – BERRY HEAD (Devon) is one – but intermediate, apparently suitable areas have not been colonised; whereas most of our plants spread back across Britain at the end of the ice ages, these species seem unable to have done so. This suggests that the cliffs on which they grow may have escaped the worst of the ice and acted as reservoirs of plant life – one reason for their present richness and beauty.

Contrasting with the hard rocks are the dunes and marshes of OXWICH. Soft shales, folded into the limestone, have been eroded to form a bay, then altered to a lagoon by a bay-head barrier of sand. The lagoon now forms an expanse of freshwater marsh and saltmarsh, while a low dune system has developed behind the beach. Drainage from the millstone grit flushes the freshwater marsh – open pools lie among spreads of common reed and rich mixed fen filled with plants such as bogbean and flowering-rush, both bulrush and lesser bulrush, with yellow iris, marsh lousewort, greater bird's-foot-trefoil, lesser twayblade, marsh arrowgrass and a fine variety of sedges. The fen gives way through an area rich in marsh-mallow to a salt-marsh, draining into the bay, overlooked by the dunes which cut off the old lagoon.

The dunes show a good example of progression from open sand, with marram, sand sedge, sea spurge and sea-holly, to fixed dunes with an excellent lichen flora, bracken-clad where the sands are leached, coloured with common centaury, rest-harrow and dewberry. The slacks, in particular, may be filled with colour – low straggles of creeping willow patterned with early and southern marsh-orchid or marsh helleborine; other plant species include fen, green-winged and pyramidal orchid, autumn lady's-tresses and autumn and dune gentian.

On either side the bay is fringed with woodland, and areas of scrub also occur, a feature of this coastline where fine examples of wind-pruning may be seen, together with splendid spreads of limestone heath. The heaths may be as spectacular as the short-turfed coastal grasslands, curving above the sheer limestone in a sweep of bell heather, western gorse and heath bedstraw, common rock-rose, wild thyme and salad burnet. Gorse and western gorse appear in the scrub, together with blackthorn, wild privet and juniper, while, in the woodlands, dogwood, hawthorn, hazel, guelder-rose, spindle, wild privet and black-thorn predominate. The woods themselves vary from alder carr by the marshland to high-forest ash

Sparrowhawk, typical of valley woodlands.

and oak, occasionally with small-leaved lime and the rare whitebeam *Sorbus rupicola*. A thick ground cover of dog's mercury, enchanter's-nightshade, sanicle, woodruff and wood spurge may be plumed with hart's-tongue and broad buckler-fern or show ramsons and meadowsweet in damper places, while more open woods on thin rocky soils stand above lime-loving yellow-wort, bloody crane's-bill, common rock-rose and marjoram, with rustyback growing on the outcrops of rock.

This great diversity of habitat attracts an equal range of animals. Its south westerly position makes the Gower a staging post for migrant birds and the offshore waters shelter thousands of wintering common scoter. The marsh provides a breeding site for large colonies of reed and sedge warbler and has become a regular nesting site for bearded tit. Occasional visitors have included rarities such as little bittern and aquatic warbler. Worm's Head, a high tide island, holds the most westerly notable seabird colonies this side of the Bristol Channel, including numbers of guillemot, razorbill, fulmar, kittiwake, shag and cormorant. Some of the caves along the cliffs contain roosts of greater horseshoe bat and the remains of animals such as Irish elk, mammoth and woolly rhinoceros.

This is a coastline both beautiful and fascinating – rich in seashore and land animals, in butterflies and birds; but, however exciting these may be, for its plants and its geology the Gower is unique.

Taf Fechan

SO 045097; 41 ha; Merthyr BC–Merthyr
Naturalists' Soc.–GTNC
Steep river valley
Booklet from MBC
Spring, summer

The Taf Fechan flows through and by a fascinating range of habitat. The steep valley sides are wooded with oak, ash and sycamore, with areas of mature trees. Oak again, with Turkey oak, small-leaved lime, beech and bird cherry and an understorey of dogwood, field maple and guelder-rose, declares the limestone richness of the upper reaches. The valley floor varies from wide grassy swards to wet alder swamps, while the open slopes of the wider parts of the valley are covered with great spreads of bracken.

This wide variation is due to changes in the underlying rock, from acid millstone grit to rich limestone, to changes in the dampness, from dry slope to torrential river with a range of wetland areas in between, and to the effect of man. The limestone has been quarried here and has left a hummocked grassland thick with hawthorn and fairy flax, wild thyme, common bird's-foot-trefoil and quaking grass. Parts of the old woodland have been cleared for fuel and for grazing.

The greatest influence has been the river, either as ice or running water, cutting deep into the bedrock. Where the rocks are hard and wet there are rich clusters of liverworts, mosses and ferns; where the water shallows the yellow of mon-keyflower recalls the earlier brilliance of marsh-marigold. At the river edges greater tussock-sedge, water avens, common and water figwort and hem-lock water-dropwort grow.

The river is rich in animal life, busy with insects and their larvae, with snails and small shrimp-like gammarids. Brown trout lie up among the weeds or hang in a mid-water eddy. Dipper and kingfisher pillage the stream while pied and grey wagtail flick and bob at the water's edge, taking, at low level, insects similar to those that pied flycatcher and redstart capture in the air above. Other birds typical of north and mid-Wales woodlands include raven, buzzard and sparrowhawk, and among the smaller birds nuthatch, treecreeper, green and great spotted woodpecker, willow and wood warbler may be seen.

Wenallt Nature Trails

ST 153831; 1 and 1.6km; Cardiff City Council
Two trails in woodland and heath above Cardiff
Booklet from Leisure and Amenities Dept, CCC
Spring, summer

These trails show plants typical of the soils on which they grow. The open slopes are thick with bracken, gorse and broom. The woods are birch–oak, or plantations of beech or young conifers, with elder, hawthorn, rowan and holly in scrubland or as understorey to the trees, sheltering the many flowers on the woodland floor. The birds, too, are typical of the habitats through which the trails pass.

Whiteford

SS 438938; 800ha; NCC reserve
Sand dunes, saltmarsh and foreshore
Permit only off marked paths
Leaflet from information kiosk
All year

The dunes are separated from the saltmarsh by a well defined damp transition zone in which both dune and saltmarsh plants occur together with wetland plants. A bird hide overlooks the salt-marsh and the waters of Burry Inlet – the estuary of the Loughor (see PEMBREY COUNTRY PARK (Dyfed)) – which are renowned for winter waders and wild-fowl. Oystercatcher frequently exceed 10,000, with almost as many dunlin and knot, and large numbers of golden plover, turnstone and redshank. Other waders include bar-tailed and black-tailed godwit, purple sandpiper and spotted redshank.

The richness of a damp dune slack contrasts with a ridge at Whiteford.

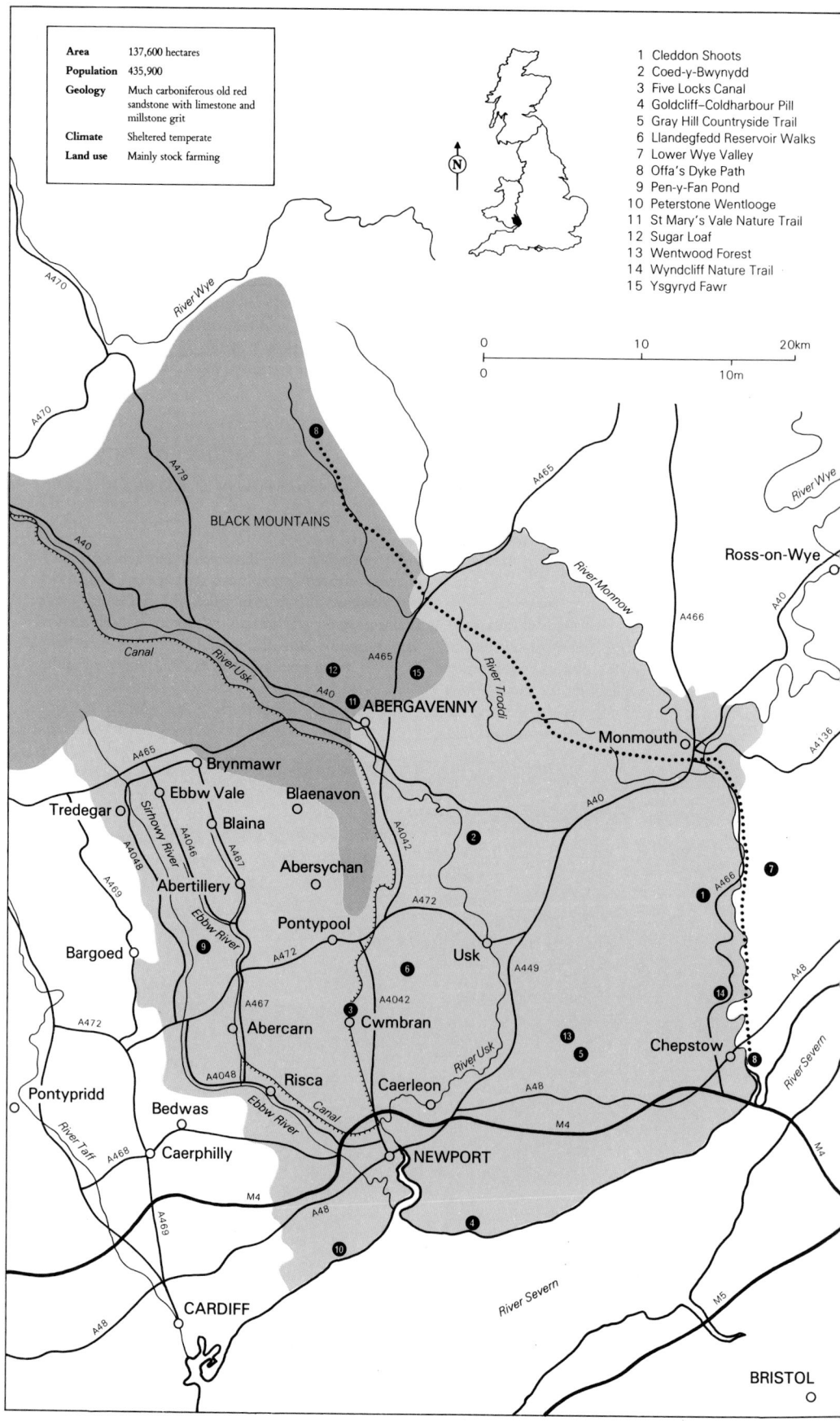

Area	137,600 hectares
Population	435,900
Geology	Much carboniferous old red sandstone with limestone and millstone grit
Climate	Sheltered temperate
Land use	Mainly stock farming

N

1 Cleddon Shoots
2 Coed-y-Bwynydd
3 Five Locks Canal
4 Goldcliff–Coldharbour Pill
5 Gray Hill Countryside Trail
6 Llandegfedd Reservoir Walks
7 Lower Wye Valley
8 Offa's Dyke Path
9 Pen-y-Fan Pond
10 Peterstone Wentlooge
11 St Mary's Vale Nature Trail
12 Sugar Loaf
13 Wentwood Forest
14 Wyndcliff Nature Trail
15 Ysgyryd Fawr

0   10   20km
0   10m

River Wye

A470

A470

A479

BLACK MOUNTAINS

A40

Canal

River Usk

River Wye

River Monnow

Ross-on-Wye

A40

A465

A466

A40

River Troddi

12   A465   15

11   ABERGAVENNY

Monmouth

A4136

A465   Brynmawr

Ebbw Vale   Blaenavon

Tredegar   Blaina

A4046   A467

Abersychan

A4042

2

A466   7

Abertillery

A472

Pontypool

A472

1

Bargoed

9   Ebbw River

6   Usk

A449

A48

Abercarn   A467

3   Cwmbran

A4042

13

14   Chepstow

A472

Risca   Caerleon

River Usk

5

8   River Severn

Pontypridd

A4048

Bedwas

A48

A48

M4

River Taff

A468   Caerphilly

NEWPORT

M4

A469

A48

4

10

River Severn

M5

CARDIFF

A48

BRISTOL

Gwent

The most southerly of the Welsh border counties, Gwent is probably still better known by its ancient name of Monmouthshire. A small county, it can nevertheless boast most habitats except the classic marine ones of dune, cliff and sandy beaches.

The northern third of Gwent is contiguous with mountainous Breconshire (now part of Powys) and contains much land over 330m, including the SUGAR LOAF and Skirrid Mountains, the Blorenge near Abergavenny and the Black Mountains, all within the BRECON BEACONS NATIONAL PARK (Powys). This area is rich in mountain wildlife and offers ample scope for walking, camping and pony trekking.

Between the mountains and the sea lies the agricultural heart of the county. This is largely a landscape of small farms and very little of the traditional patchwork pattern has been disturbed. There are a number of comparatively small deciduous woodlands and many more tiny ones. Although some corn and maize is grown, it is predominantly a stock-rearing district, beef, milk and lamb being the primary products. In the west, the farmland is bounded by the industrial valleys and former coalmining areas which once gave south Wales a bad name for dirt and dereliction; valleys run down to Newport at the mouth of the Usk where the river joins the Bristol Channel. Eastern Gwent is bordered by the Wye, one of the great salmon rivers of Britain, which carves a spectacular valley for itself, cutting down through the limestone between the FOREST OF DEAN (Gloucestershire) and the adjacent Tintern Forest in Gwent towards its confluence with the Severn at Chepstow.

A narrow strip of land, known locally as the Monmouthshire Moors, runs along the coast, defended against the ferocious tides of the Severn by a sea wall said to have been erected originally by the Romans. This area has a great reputation for grazing cattle, though at one time it supplied the vast quantities of hay needed for the horses working in the local industrial areas. On the other side of the wall lie the banks of silt and sand which, when exposed at low tide, form feeding grounds for countless waders and ducks which use the estuary as a refuelling station on their long migrations north and south.

Geologically the county consists of the eastern and western ridges of carboniferous limestone, those in the west overlying the coal measures which gave rise to the great mining industry of the nineteenth and early twentieth century. Some millstone grit is also present in the north west and forms a durable cap to the aptly named Sugar Loaf Mountain. Most of the rest of Gwent lies on the old red sandstone which gives a characteristically red colour to the soil, though not as red as in neighbouring Herefordshire. In the Llanthony Valley in the Black Mountains evidence of glaciation is very evident. In the coastal belt, for about a kilometre inland from the sea wall the reclaimed silt land lies on a deep layer of sedge peat, evidence of a former fenland type of habitat now only represented by the MAGOR marshland reserve. The climate is comparatively mild at least as far north as Usk, but in the mountainous areas of the north west the rainfall is about 1500mm annually, falling to about 1000mm in the central districts near Raglan and Usk.

The two main rivers, the Usk and the Wye, both rise in central Wales and are swift, clear and excellent for salmon and trout, being almost unpolluted except at their mouths. The Monnow, which joins the Wye at Monmouth, is a little-known and delightful river running for much of its course along the Herefordshire border. There are a number of smaller rivers and streams; some of the ones in the west of the county, such as the Ebbw and Affon Llwyd, have been more or less restored to normality after more than a century's gross industrial pollution. All the Gwent rivers are good for such species as dipper, kingfisher, grey wagtail and siskin, the last-named being common in the many alders that line the banks.

LLANDEGFEDD RESERVOIR, near Pontypool, carries large flocks of mallard, wigeon and coot in the winter, with smaller numbers of other species such as pochard, tufted duck and great crested grebe. Migrating terns are often recorded in late summer.

The mountains of the north and west support a typical plant life of moorland grasses with much bracken and patches of heather, bilberry and crowberry. The Blorenge and its neighbouring ranges still have a population of grouse, though much reduced from its heyday in the nineteenth century. Other birds to be seen are buzzard, wheatear, whinchat and ring ouzel as well as great numbers of meadow pipit and skylark. Raven, although nesting in many places in the county, are most commonly spotted in the mountains, giving voice to their ominous croak as they soar and dive in the wind.

A number of small mountain ponds support a remarkably large population of amphibians in the summer, including palmate newt in one or two places. A number of rare dragonflies and Lepidoptera have been recorded breeding in these districts too. Adder is the commonest reptile on the mountains and in the forestry rides, grass snake being mostly restricted to damper lowland habitats. Slow-worm and common lizard can also be found by those who know where to look for them.

In the east the principal habitat is that created by the Wye Valley, bounded by the great deciduous mass of the Forest of Dean and the lesser but still magnificent Tintern Forest. The whole area between Chepstow and Monmouth is a paradise for the botanist and lepidopterist and many species of rare plants, ferns, moths and butterflies can be discovered by the enthusiast. With the noble ruins of Tintern Abbey at its heart, the beauty of the Wye Valley, especially in the autumn, is internationally famous, and even in the spring and summer, with different but subtler shades lighting the woodlands, the region is full of interest.

The coast of Gwent is probably of no great attraction except to the ornithologist, the walker or the wildfowler. To others the great estuary of the Severn seems bleak and grey most of the time and is rarely very warm even in the summer; but there is a good path along the top of the sea wall and one can walk for hours and meet only the occasional farmer or birdwatcher. The ever-changing colours of the rushing water, sometimes lapping the sea wall but more often far away beyond the silt banks, together with the constantly shifting flocks of gulls and waders and the reflected patterns of the clouds, create a unique atmosphere, heightened by the constant music of curlew, dunlin, redshank, oystercatcher and lapwing and the strange discordant notes of shelduck as they continually search for food.

P. N. HUMPHREYS

Blackcliff–Wyndcliff Forest

Permit only; 81 ha; FC reserve
Mixed woodland
Spring, early summer

Part of the reserve, a mix of high-forest and old coppiced woodland on steep limestone slopes, may be seen from the WYNDCLIFF NATURE TRAIL.

Cleddon Bog

Permit only; 15 ha; GCC reserve
Lowland wet heath
Spring, summer

The finest small basin mire in Gwent, the bog is a spread of purple moor-grass sheltering typical wet heath species – heather, cross-leaved heath, hare's-tail cottongrass, *Sphagnum* mosses, bog asphodel and white beak-sedge. An area of willow carr and an open scrub of birch and conifers add further interest.

Cleddon Shoots

SO 520040; 8 ha; GTNC reserve
Steep mixed woodland with streams
Spring, summer

Cleddon Brook keeps the air damp and suitable for ferns and mosses. Wild cherry, oak and beech,

with holly and yew, show the richness of the underlying rock but throw a dense shade with little light for late-flowering plants, although providing nest sites for birds.

Wheatear, a characteristic upland bird.

Cwm Clydach clings to a steep valleyside, a fine spread of woodland sloping down to the river.

Coed-y-Bwynydd

SO 365068; 10ha; NT
Mixed woodland
Spring, summer

Bracken and rosebay willowherb give way to grassland under magnificent oak and beech trees at the top of this wooded hill. Ash and beech grow on the slopes where ivy-covered oaks make ideal nest sites for small birds. Holly and yew occur occasionally in the understorey together with field maple, hazel and elder.

Cwm Clydach

Permit only; 23.3ha; NCC reserve
Very steep valley and beech wood
Spring, summer

Beech, here at its western limit, shows a dense shade under which few plants can thrive, but the limestone of much of the reserve encourages a rich ground cover where there are gaps in the canopy, and in other open areas. Slender, delicate grasses and the rare soft-leaved sedge grow in the valley, together with early and common dog-violet, wild thyme and the rarer large thyme. Oak, wych elm, downy birch, holly, with yew and an uncommon whitebeam, *Sorbus porrigentiformis*, break the monopoly of the beech with which yellow bird's-nest and bird's-nest orchid grow. Another section of the wood, although still dominated by beech, is more acid in character with hard fern, scaly male-fern and wiry clumps of bilberry. There is a good variety of woodland birds and the river supplies another habitat range, where both grey wagtail and dipper breed. Common blue and small copper are among the butterflies recorded.

Cwm Coed-y-Cerrig

Permit only; 4.5ha; BBNPC
Wet alder woodland and marsh
Spring, summer

Cwm Coed-y-Cerrig is a narrow alder swamp where early marsh-orchid is followed by yellow loosestrife and alternate-leaved golden-saxifrage. Plentiful insects attract a good range of woodland birds.

Five Locks Canal

ST 287968–292978; 1km; GTNC reserve
Disused canal
Spring, summer

Slow-moving waters are uncommon in Gwent and the canal provides an opportunity to see plants and animals otherwise scarce in the county. The canal is bordered by fields, unfenced and lined with large alders on one side, hedged against the towpath on the other, so that a considerable range of habitat can be seen from the towpath itself.

Around 120 plants have been recorded from the water and the banks, and the reserve provides a breeding site for newts, frog and common toad. In the canal are water plants such as rigid hornwort, whorled water-milfoil and several species of duckweed, pondweed and water-starwort. Attractive plants such as arrowhead, yellow water-lily and water-plantain lift above the surface or float on the water while the margin and banks may be filled with colourful plants. Monkeyflower, a bright yellow alien which has spread through many of our waterways, complements yellow iris, contrasting with marsh woundwort and gipsywort. Stands of reed canary-grass and branched bur-reed provide cover for breeding moorhen.

The alders provide a winter feeding ground for redpoll, siskin and twite and, in summer, their over-hanging branches are often used as perches by king-fisher. The canal holds dace, more typical of faster streams, together with the chub, roach and tench characteristic of such sluggish waters. Good numbers of dragonflies and damselflies may be seen, with a range of water beetles, leeches and water snails which could not survive the surge of a rapid stream.

The reserve is managed mainly as an educational site but also includes an attractive walk by the old Monmouthshire–Brecon Canal.

Goldcliff–Magor Pill

ST 375820–ST 438848; 7km; GTNC reserve
Estuarine foreshore
No access off rights of way
Spring, autumn

The GTNC has acquired the shooting rights over the estuary foreshore, thus protecting an area of tidal flats important for many waders and migrant birds which use the River Severn as a flight path.

Gray Hill Countryside Trail

ST 429396; 5km; GCC
Moorland and woodland trail
Leaflet from GCC
Spring, early summer

From Gray Hill, above Wentwood Reservoir, the trail circles through WENTWOOD FOREST. A fine range of moorland and forest habitats may be seen.

Henllys Bog

Permit only; 0.6ha; GTNC reserve
Damp grassland
Spring, summer

The good diversity of plants here includes some which are rare or uncommon in the county.

Lady Park Wood

Permit only; 46ha; NCC reserve
Mixed woodland
Spring, early summer

An exceptionally rich mixed woodland, the reserve contains several rare tree species and, although in the past it was considerably modified by felling, it is to be left unmanaged so that natural return to the wildwood can be studied.

Llandegfedd Reservoir Walks

ST 329985–323978; 6.5–10km; GCC
Varied walks
Leaflet from GCC
All year

The walks circle in the hills, woods and steep valley around Llandegfedd Reservoir, itself of ornithological interest. Winter wildfowl include mallard, wigeon and coot, with great crested grebe, pochard and tufted duck. At migration times more unusual birds, including terns, may be seen.

The Lower Wye Valley: the pinnacles of the Seven Sisters look across to Lady Park Wood.

Llwyn-y-Celyn Bog

Permit only; 0.4ha; GTNC reserve
Lowland bog
Spring, summer

This very fine small marsh holds a great number of species, including water avens, bogbean, marsh lousewort, marsh-mallow, monk's-hood and lesser skullcap among a wealth of colourful wetland plants.

Lower Wye Valley

See map; 35km; various bodies
Spectacular river gorge
Spring, summer

Rising close to the source of the River Severn on the eastern slopes of Plynlimon, the River Wye cuts a more direct course to their confluence below Chepstow. This, one of the finest rivers in the country, has been scheduled as a Grade I site by the NCC: in its lower reaches it has cut a spectacular winding gorge which shelters one of the four most important woodland areas in Britain.

Having curved out of Powys to wind through the rich farmlands of Hereford, the Wye swings back into Wales as it leaves the limestone gorge below the DOWARD GROUP (Hereford and Worcester). For the rest of its course to the sea it either lies wholly in Wales or forms its border with Gloucestershire. Compared with the lower reaches of most of our major rivers, those of the Wye have been little altered by man and the geological interest and range of wildlife is possibly unequalled in the country.

The gorges, below the Doward and from Wyesham down to Chepstow, were caused by the imposition of river meanders on the rocks below. When sea levels were higher the Wye found its wandering course across a level plateau – falling sea levels caused the river to flow with greater speed and the wide meanders of the earlier slow-flowing river were carved downwards by its new-found urgency. Within the gorges the river is now deep and slow-flowing, tidal in the lower sections where it gradually changes to estuarine conditions. It holds a gradation of freshwater to brackish and marine animals and provides the route by which the uncommon Allis shad migrates to spawn in higher waters. It also provides a site where a number of uncommon insects breed.

The strata through which the river has cut its way are tilted layers of carboniferous rock laid upon Devonian Tintern sandstone. The carboniferous limestone forms spectacular cliffs in the gorges and is largely responsible for the magnificent range of unusual plants. The sandstones, though, increase the habitat range by providing more acidic areas and the woodlands here hold over 60 species – most of our native trees and shrubs – in essentially natural groupings.

The woods have been modified by man but mainly by coppicing, a practice which does not destroy the natural communities, and, except where alien species have been planted, these steeply sloping woods are considered to be ancient woodland.

Oak–beech woods occur on the sandstones, with a characteristic acid-loving ground flora, but many of the sites contain a mix of soils – light or heavy loams depending on their origin, areas of glacial drift and dry stony limestone soils. A typical sloping woodland might contain a mix of ash, beech, wych elm, small-leaved lime and yew at the rather acid summit falling through ash, wych elm and hazel to riverside alder on the damp rich valley flood plain. Species such as wild cherry might occur throughout and the ground cover would

Greater horseshoe bat in a Lower Wye Valley cave.

vary with the richness. Some of the finest lime-stone woods contain ash, wych elm and field maple with yew, wild service-tree, large-leaved lime and common whitebeam, with several rare whitebeam species including Cheddar whitebeam, *Sorbus rupicola*, *Sorbus porrigentiformis* and even the rare hybrid between common whitebeam and wild service-tree.

The ground cover of such woods is also extreme-ly rich. Dog's mercury often forms a dense green carpet but is varied with yellow archangel, bluebell, ramsons and woodruff, with hart's-tongue and soft shield-fern, with herb-Paris and spurge-laurel. Clearings and woodland edges might show lime-loving species such as marjoram and ploughman's-spikenard while less common plants of the woodlands include yellow bird's-nest, wood crane's-bill, wood fescue, mountain melick, fingered sedge, thin-spiked wood-sedge and com-mon wintergreen. The gorge, too, is a site for upright spurge, a small plant of clearings and open ground which occurs nowhere else in Britain.

This rich variety is underlined by the occurrence of almost half the British butterflies, including com-mon and holly blue, silver-washed fritillary and speckled wood. Both holly blue and speckled wood are interesting in being multiple-brooded: holly blue switches from holly to ivy, to provide its second brood with a seasonal food plant, while speckled wood, which sticks to grass as a food source, manages at least three broods by overwin-tering either as pupae or larvae – the pupae hatch in spring and produce a second, autumn, brood, while the larvae pupate in spring and hatch in summer. This device spreads the hatching period over the whole growing season of grass.

Mammals are those expected of a large and varied woodland area and include yellow-necked mouse with greater horseshoe bat which roost in limestone caves by the riverside cliffs. Typical woodland birds are complemented by those of river and estuary sites, such as heron and cor-morant, while the cliffs provide ideal nesting places for crag-loving birds such as jackdaw.

This is a truly spectacular area, from the deep ravine below LADY PARK WOOD to the dramatic curve of cliff at LANCAUT (Gloucestershire). Few views can be more impressive than that from the Eagle's Nest, on the WYNDCLIFF NATURE TRAIL, over 200m above a great curve of the river. Steep wooded slopes fall to the waterside, backed by limestone cliffs, by the gleam of water where the Wye runs into the Severn, and, across the Vale of the Severn, by the Cotswold and Mendip Hills.

Magor

Permit only; 24ha; GTNC reserve
Relict fen
Spring, summer

The reserve contains a remnant of the once exten-sive Monmouthshire fens and is a mosaic of damp old pasture fields, ditches (or reens) and pools. The old fields are, in places, reverting to scrub and woodland, adding to the wide range of habitat. The whole area is extremely wet and is filled with a wonderful variety of fen and marshland wildlife.

Grazing is continued in some of the drier fields but even these are wet enough for plants such as ragged-Robin, for lesser and greater spearwort, marsh-marigold and meadowsweet. Ungrazed fields are waist-high stands of wild angelica, purple-loosestrife, great willowherb and yellow iris, laced with marsh bedstraw, scented with water mint and filled with a fine variety of sedges. Reed canary-grass and common reed grow in these damper meadows while wetter areas hold stands of reed sweet-grass.

These densely overgrown fields form magnifi-cent jungles of marsh plants and grade into scrub willow or woodlands of alder and willow. Old willow pollards often stand by the reens and these ditches, paralleled by the rhynes of the Somerset Levels, contain some of the special plants of Magor. Arrowhead occurs, as at FIVE LOCKS CANAL, but here too are flowering-rush and frogbit – all three rare in Wales. Mare's-tail, scarce in Gwent, grows in one of the pools and the poolside stands of bulrush provide excellent cover for birds.

A hide overlooks the main pool and provides opportunities for seeing some of the many birds of Magor. This is a site, near the flight path of the Severn, where many rarities have been recorded, where garganey have bred and where one of the most important Gwent colonies of reed warbler breed. Other breeding species include reed bunt-ing, sedge and grasshopper warbler, mallard and water rail, yellow wagtail, redshank and snipe. The rich wetland encourages a good range of in-sects and small water-animals, including a number of nationally rare dragonflies.

Offa's Dyke Path

SO 267323–ST 553928; 70km; CC
Long-distance way
Booklet from HMSO bookshops
Spring, summer

The old defensive wall of the English against the Welsh, the path runs from Prestatyn (Clwyd) to Chepstow and passes through some of the most spectacular and richly interesting country in east Wales.

Old Church Wood

Permit only; 4ha; GTNC reserve
Valley woodland
Spring, early summer

The sloping oakwood lies on old red sandstone in the LOWER WYE VALLEY. A typical range of woodland birds adds to the beautiful spring display of wild daffodil.

Pen-y-Fan Pond

SO 197006; 13.5ha; GCC
Pond and heathland
Spring, summer

Although disturbed by rowing, model boat sailing and fishing, the park contains an interesting area of dry heath, with bracken, gorse and heather, which grades into acid bog beside the pool.

Peterstone Wentlooge

ST 278807; 4km; GTNC reserve
Extensive mudflats and saltmarsh
All year

The mudflats and saltmarsh are probably the most important habitat types here, but there is a further range to increase the variety and interest. The land behind the sea wall has been reclaimed and ditched. The influences here are more typical of farmland than of sea coast but there are a number of interesting plants including bristly oxtongue and spiny restharrow – both uncommon and usually found only near the coast in Wales.

Across the sea wall, stepped so that a small plateau is covered in places by high tides, annual sea-blite edges areas of open mud on which glasswort grows. The grassland is thick with sea plantain and sea aster around the small salt pans and greater sea-spurrey grows in the rock jumble of the lower wall. To the west is a common cord-grass saltmarsh, very open and muddy, clumped with common scurvygrass and sea aster on the landward side.

The drainage ditches behind the sea wall provide yet another habitat range. The land side of the sea wall is clumped with bramble and scrub and the dykes are often fenced with hawthorn hedges. In the dykes themselves are stands of common reed and bulrush, with branched bur-reed and water-plantain. The water is often covered with duckweed which shows the tracks of swimming moorhen or water vole.

The saltmarsh and mudflats are favourite sites for waders and wildfowl. On one day in 1977 a mixed flock of dunlin and knot was estimated at 11,000 strong. A number of duck uncommon in Gwent may occur here, including long-tailed duck, a winter visitor unusual anywhere in the west of England and Wales, with shoveler and common scoter. Other rarities in Wales, avocet, ruff, wood sandpiper and little stint, have been seen. In winter merlin, peregrine and short-eared owl may patrol the area. Redshank and yellow wagtail breed in summer, while autumn brings flocks of finches and other small birds, with swallows gathering before their long migration. Thousands of fieldfare and redwing feed on the hawthorn hedges in cold weather.

Beside the muds and saltmarsh of Peterstone Wentlooge, the levels add a further habitat.

St Mary's Vale Nature Trail

SO 283162; 3.2km; BBNPC–NT
Steep-sided valley walk in foothills of Sugar Loaf
Booklet from BBNPC
Spring, summer

The trail rises through woodland – alder and ash beside the stream with beech, probably planted, on one side and native oakwood on the other. The oaks grade into open moorland as the valley side climbs towards the SUGAR LOAF, with stands of heather, bilberry and bracken.

Strawberry Cottage Wood

Permit only; 6ha; GTNC reserve
Steep oak woodland
Spring, summer

This hanging oak woodland with some birch clings to the side of a steep old red sandstone slope. Buzzard, wood warbler and great spotted and green woodpecker frequent the wood.

Sugar Loaf

SO 268168; 852ha; NT
Fine upland
Spring, summer

The Sugar Loaf is one of the last of the old red sandstone hills which make up the greater part of the Brecon Beacons. The summit, capped with millstone grit, is bare and open but grades down through bilberry and bracken to sheltered woodlands on the lower slopes where buzzard and kestrel breed.

Wentwood Forest

ST 436936; 1005ha; FC
Mixed woodland
Spring, early summer

Wentwood is mainly larch forest, set on a ridge of old red sandstone above the lower meanders of the River Usk. Its southern slopes have been cut into valleys by the streams which fed the Monmouthshire fens – of which nearby MAGOR is a relic – while unwooded hills close to the forest are heather –bracken moors. Despite its mainly coniferous nature, areas of mature beech–oak woodland still remain and the varying richness of the soils encourages an interesting flora. Trails and bridleways provide ample scope for exploring the woodland and the GRAY HILL COUNTRYSIDE TRAIL, starting from the reservoir on the edge of Wentwood, includes both moorland and a part of the forest.

Its large size and the mosaic of conifers at various stages of growth, with blocks of broad-leaved trees, wide rides and clearings, offer a range of habitat which varies from areas of acid bog, where ivy-leaved bellflower occurs, to richer sites on lime-rich cornstone conglomerate where ash stands over woodruff. Broad-leaved helleborine may be found in the woodland, with adder's-tongue in remnants of old pasture, and, in unpicked areas, spring may bring a magnificent display of wild daffodil.

The mature native trees provide holes and crevices for long-eared, noctule and whiskered bat and larger mammals include fallow deer, badger and fox. Both dormouse and harvest mouse have

Sugar Loar and Ysgyryd Fawr, backed by the Black Mountains.

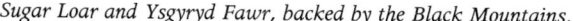

been recorded. The breeding birds are very varied and may range from shelduck on the reservoir to redstart and wood warbler in the native trees, nightjar in the clearings and occasional crossbill in the conifers. Other breeding species include raven, buzzard and sparrowhawk, tree pipit, grasshopper warbler and woodcock.

Pools provide breeding sites for all three British newts and for common toad and frog, while adder and common lizard are plentiful in the heathland. Heather attracts emperor moth, and other insects include peach blossom, Chinese character and wood tiger moths, with many butterflies in the forest rides as well as eyed ladybird, a species associated with conifers.

Wyndcliff Nature Trail

ST 525973; 1km; FC
Woodland walk
Leaflet from Welsh Tourist Board, Tintern or GTNC
Spring, early summer

The trail, in the BLACKCLIFF–WYNDCLIFF FOREST, includes the viewpoint of the Eagle's Nest with its spectacular outlook across the LOWER WYE VALLEY.

Yew trees grow on the sheer rocks of Wyndcliff.

Ysgyryd Fawr

SO 330180; 83ha; NT
Steep knoll, grassland and woods
Spring, summer, autumn

Ysgyryd Fawr, rendered into English as Skirrid Fawr, is a sudden shoulder of hill, rising from the farmland around, looking westward to the better-known SUGAR LOAF and inland, across the Vale of Usk, to the MALVERN HILLS (Hereford and Worcester). An outlier of the old red sandstone Black Mountains, the hill is flanked by woodlands to the west and south and has areas of open scrub around its lower slopes. There are high stands of bracken with gorse and foxglove and the scrub is chiefly hawthorn with a mixture of ash, birch, crab apple, elder and oak. The bracken opens where flushes and wet areas drain through the scrub and sheep-grazing keeps the turf short.

Above the scrub the hill rises steeply to reach the summit at 486m. Here there are extensive spreads of bilberry and rough grassland which run on the western side to the vertical crags of a rocky scarp. Below the crags long slopes of tumbled scree are broken by grassy plateaus and massive rock

outcrops with harebell, wild thyme and bilberry. Mosses and lichens cover the long-fallen rocks and among the screes herb-Robert and hart's-tongue can be found.

The woodlands grade from open scrub to more mature woods with attractive ash woodland in the damper, richer areas. Here there is a profusion of ferns with raspberry and in spring wood-sorrel and common dog-violet. The hill is long-backed, running from south to north, and scrub and woodland climb high up the sheltered southern slopes. This is a superb site for hill woodland birds such as redstart and the open scrub is a perfect hunting ground for both kestrel and sparrowhawk. Buzzard circle above the slopes or the farmland below.

Sheep grazing here is not over-hard and there is a good balance between close-grazed areas, the sweeter grasses around the streams and wet places, and the rough grassland on the slopes and summit. There is good variation in the range from open scrub, suitable for linnet and stonechat, rabbit and fox, to thicker woodland where bank vole and wood mouse may be prey to stoat, weasel or tawny owl.

Gwynedd

Nature has bestowed a magnificent mantle on Gwynedd – from its mountainous shoulders down to the vast and superbly varied coastline. The region's bold and breathtaking contrasts are mirrored by an abundance of nature reserves and conservation sites. Anglesey, Caernarvonshire and Merioneth have been administratively recombined to form Gwynedd, once the county of Welsh princes and now the stronghold of Welsh culture.

Half the county lies in the SNOWDONIA NATIONAL PARK, a land of hill farms that enjoys the true alpine scenery of Snowdonia and its neighbours. The coastal plateaus of Anglesey and the Lleyn Peninsula display a mosaic of ever more productive grassland mixed farms. Most of the few towns are strung along the coast. Upland climate, poorly developed soils and marshes have prevented man from greatly changing the vegetation of many parts of the county; in this lies much of its outstanding interest for nature conservation.

Gwynedd's diverse habitats owe much to its complex rock formations and the scouring of ice and water. This complexity, unusual even in Britain, ranges from some of the oldest to some of the youngest rocks; many of them are acid, with mineral-deficient soils. Other, more basic, soils are found on limestone, sand dunes and some of the volcanic rocks. Snowdonia's rugged land shows all the signs of the forces which squeezed and folded its rocks. Gwynant and Padarn are just two of the valley lakes bequeathed by ice age glaciers.

In contrast to Snowdonia the island of Anglesey is a succession of broad, flat-topped ridges and straight valleys, more or less parallel with the Menai Strait, itself deepened by moving and melted ice. Further south, on the Meirionnydd coast, are the broad triangular forelands, originally of shingle, of MORFA HARLECH and MORFA DYFFRYN.

Strong, warm, moist winds from the Irish Sea play their part in shaping the vegetation. Windy, sunny Anglesey is less often in cloud and rain than the mainland mountains where a varied landscape produces a range of local climates. The treeless natural vegetation on the thin soil of Snowdonia's harsh mountain slopes was mainly heather moor and grass fell. Deciduous forest covered the coastal lowlands and most valleys below the tree line, with marshes and fens on the extensive areas of poor drainage.

An interesting arctic–alpine flora survives on the higher mountains, on YR WYDDFA (Snowdon) and CADER IDRIS, for example. Here fescue dominates, reindeer-moss is found, and the cliffs are the habitat for some plants found also on the coast – sea-plantain, thrift and creeping willow. Man's main impact on the mountain vegetation has been through sheep, which favour grass rather than heath on the rough grazings; the Rhinogydd, inland of the Meirionnydd Ardudwy coast, are an exception. Elsewhere on the cold, wet, southern uplands purple moor-grass and mat-grass abound. East of Blaenau Ffestiniog are hill peats, cottongrass moors and flush bogs.

In Snowdonia, as elsewhere in Britain's uplands, there has been an ebb and flow of the upper limit of grassland management. Above the lowland winter grazing is a band of *ffriddoedd*. Rushes, heather and bracken have invaded parts of the less intensively managed hill farms. Overhead, kite, buzzard and kestrel hunt their prey.

Modified remnants of the once natural western oak woodlands can be found on many steep valley sides. Though mainly of sessile oak, a range of hybrids with pedunculate oak is common. Several woods are nature reserves notable for their abundant mosses and liverworts, and management of

494

these woods for conservation, beauty and timber is gaining attention. Under-planted conifers have altered many of the woods in recent years.

Coniferous afforestation, not only of deciduous woodland, has rapidly been changing wildlife habitats. Most of Gwynedd's lowland woodland has long been replaced by a patchwork of grass and arable fields interlaced with other vegetation less easily used for farming. The decline in rabbit numbers on farmland has reduced the supply of small flowering herbs, food plants for butterfly larvae.

Anglesey's valleys abound in small lakes, sluggish rivers and marshes, but it is the non-acidic fens, rich in nutrients and with high, fluctuating water levels, which are most prized, with their characteristic background of saw-sedge and black bog-rush. Columbine is an impressive early summer sight on CORS ERDDREINIOG, while orchids and pale dog-violet have been encouraged on CORS GOCH. One of the island's most attractive plants is the delicate blue marsh gentian, still found on some of the damp unimproved acid soils; another is spotted rock-rose, whose petals drop within hours of opening.

Over half the county's long boundary is coast, mostly very beautiful and much of outstanding conservation interest. From the Little Orme round to the southern DYFI (Dyfed), cliff-fronted head-lands of infinitely subtle variety separate sand and shingle beaches, estuaries and saltings. The Lleyn cliffs, including BARDSEY Island, are some of the least disturbed and, along with those around Anglesey, support populations of breeding seabirds. Puffin Island, beyond Beaumaris, supports more of the tougher guillemots, with their 'anti-roll'-shaped eggs. This island also possesses one of the largest herring gull colonies in Britain. The oil-spitting fulmar too has been competing successfully for cliff-nesting sites. Holyhead Mountain's SOUTH STACK CLIFFS are the finest place in Gwynedd for watching seabirds.

On the low-lying southern sector of the island's coast is the large NEWBOROUGH WARREN–YNYS LLANDDWYN reserve, the finest of its kind in Wales; it includes the Cefni Estuary, loved by Charles Tunnicliffe, the wildlife artist. The county's intertidal and marine habitats are almost as diverse as the British coast; the coast of Anglesey is an especially valued scientific resource. Along the dune-edged arc of Tremadog Bay, planning and conservation interests are working to protect the coast from excessive tourist pressures. This is the kind of co-operation that is essential to safeguard our wildlife and its natural environment for future generations.

D. M. EAGAR

Abercorris

Permit only; 1.1 ha; NWNT reserve
Mixed woodland
Spring, early summer

Ash, birch, oak and sycamore form a steep riverside woodland where nesting birds include pied flycatcher, wood warbler, dipper and grey wagtail.

Bardsey

Permit only; 175 ha; Bardsey Island Trust
Inshore island
Permit from observatory bookings secretary,
tel. Newton Abbot 68580
Spring, summer, autumn

The island is a landmark for migrant birds monitored by the observatory. Rabbits keep the coastal grassland short and the varied rocks encourage plants such as spring squill, gorse, bracken, sharp rush, Wilson's filmy-fern and lesser meadow-rue. There is a large population of Manx shearwater, with smaller numbers of kittiwake, guillemot, razorbill and shag. Grey seal are often plentiful.

Bron-y-Graig Nature Trail

SH 583311; 0.1 km; SNPC
Semi-natural woodland trail in old estate
Leaflet from SNPC
Spring, summer

The trail passes through mixed woodland, chiefly oak, with a small cliff overgrown with wood-sorrel and great wood-rush, and an area of tumbled boulders. Nest boxes attract the commoner woodland birds as well as pied and spotted flycatcher and tawny owl.

Bardsey Island seen from the Lleyn Peninsula.

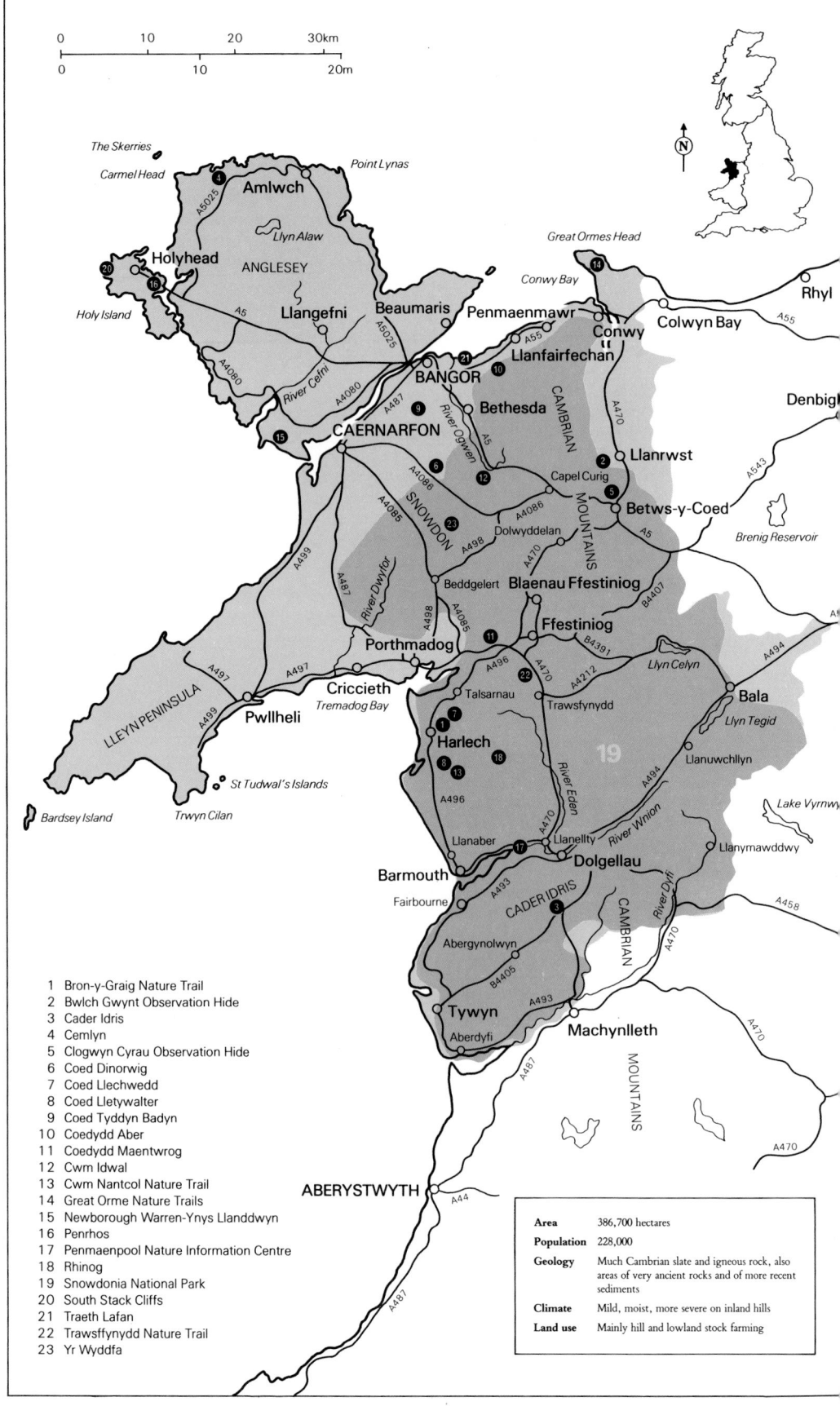

1   Bron-y-Graig Nature Trail
2   Bwlch Gwynt Observation Hide
3   Cader Idris
4   Cemlyn
5   Clogwyn Cyrau Observation Hide
6   Coed Dinorwig
7   Coed Llechwedd
8   Coed Lletywalter
9   Coed Tyddyn Badyn
10 Coedydd Aber
11 Coedydd Maentwrog
12 Cwm Idwal
13 Cwm Nantcol Nature Trail
14 Great Orme Nature Trails
15 Newborough Warren-Ynys Llanddwyn
16 Penrhos
17 Penmaenpool Nature Information Centre
18 Rhinog
19 Snowdonia National Park
20 South Stack Cliffs
21 Traeth Lafan
22 Trawsffynydd Nature Trail
23 Yr Wyddfa

Bryn Pydew

Permit only; 5ha; NWNT reserve
Limestone pavement, quarries and grassland
Spring, summer

The reserve is rich in such lime-loving plants as common rock-rose, bloody crane's-bill, lily-of-the-valley and dark-red helleborine, together with juniper, common whitebeam and yew. Insects include dingy skipper and brown Argus butterflies with reddish light arches, heath rustic and cistus forester moths. Glow-worm may also be seen.

Bwlch Gwynt Observation Hide

SH 774601; FC
Waterside bird hide
Spring, summer

The hide overlooks a small reservoir fringed with alder, birch and grey willow. Mallard, teal, moorhen and little grebe breed and a variety of other birds may be seen; buzzard, raven and sparrowhawk are not uncommon.

Cader Idris

SH 730114; 392ha; NT–NCC reserve
Mountain range, crags, lake and woodland
Permit only to enclosed woodland
Leaflet from NCC
Early summer

The path to Cader Idris rises steeply along the edge of the Afon Cau and through a mixed woodland of oak with alder, ash, hawthorn and rowan. The valley widens and then opens into the huge bowl which holds the lake of Llyn Cau. This bowl, with its 300m cliffs, is a superb example of an upland cwm. Climbing the valley towards the lake the impression is that of a traditional sheep walk: grazed mat-grass, heather and bilberry, but with richer grasses such as sheep's-fescue and common bent where the soil is better. Where poor drainage causes boggy areas, round-leaved sundew grows on the spongy masses of *Sphagnum* moss. Common butterwort may also be found here.

The crags are a mixture of hard, acid rocks and calcareous ashes and lavas. Their steepness protects the vegetation from sheep grazing and the north-facing aspect provides a suitable environment for plants of the last ice age. These plants, the arctic–alpines, are now found in only a very few places in Britain, their usual habitat being the high Alps and Arctic. A good example of these, flowering from June to July, is moss campion. Other attractive plants include globeflower, Welsh poppy, spring sandwort and purple and mossy saxifrage.

Of particular interest are a number of ferns: the rare alpine woodsia and both green and forked spleenwort. Green spleenwort is well known as a highly sensitive lime indicator and will only be found in the areas of calcareous rocks; forked spleenwort, on the other hand, grows only on the acid rocks. Their presence together underlines the highly varied nature of the reserve.

Globeflower grows in sites such as Cader Idris.

In February or March, raven nest in these crags, which in May become nest sites for ring ouzel. This is a summer visitor, staying from April to October, and with the raven is a typical bird of the high uplands. At about the same time wheatear nest among the lower rocks and meadow pipit in the open sheep walk.

The reserve rises to a maximum of 893m and, where the soil is deep enough, moles have been recorded 43m from the top.

Cemlyn

SH 336932; 16ha; NWNT reserve
Brackish pools and shingle bank; small enclosure
Permit only to enclosure at Ty'n Llan
Spring, winter

The shingle bar is a storm beach: once pebbles have been thrown above the normal tideline plants begin to move in. Nearest the waterline are strong, fleshy plants, sea kale, sea beet and orache, which can stand being battered by pebbles and drenched at spring tides. When out of reach of all but the heaviest gales the plants become more slender and include spring squill and, in some years, autumn lady's-tresses.

Behind the bank is the water of the pool, brackish and muddy, fringed by saltmarsh plants. These are not usually subjected to the battering that plants on the seaward side may suffer, but they are just as likely to be covered by a high tide, so have evolved similar protection. Glasswort grows at the water's edge, as fleshy as a smooth cactus; sea aster and thrift, both with fleshy leaves, can also stand occasional flooding.

In spring several hundred pairs of tern breed at Cemlyn. Three of Britain's native species, arctic, common and sometimes Sandwich tern, breed, together with a few pairs of black-headed gull.

Besides the terns and black-headed gulls, several other species nest on or near the reserve: oystercatcher on the shingle and shelduck in old rabbit burrows around the pool. Other breeding species include mallard, red-breasted merganser and redshank. In winter wigeon, mallard, shoveler and teal may be seen, together with diving duck such as goldeneye, red-breasted merganser and little grebe. Dunlin, turnstone, lapwing and golden and grey plover come into the reserve for shelter and food.

Tasselweed grows in the Ty'n Llan pool: it is a local plant generally limited to slightly brackish ditches near the sea. The enclosure beside the pool has an area of dense blackthorn and gorse scrub and at the western end an area of rushes.

Clogwyn Cyrau Observation Hide

SH 789574; FC
Woodland bird hide
Spring, summer

The hide is on a terrace overlooking the Llugwy Valley. The woodland includes broad-leaved and coniferous trees; typical chaffinch, green and great spotted woodpecker, treecreeper, wren and several tit species may be seen.

Coed Camlyn

Permit only; 63.5ha; NCC reserve
Oak woodland
Spring, summer, autumn

One of the Vale of Ffestiniog oakwoods, Coed Camlyn is damp and acid with bilberry and purple moor-grass in the wetter areas and bracken where it is dry enough. The dampness encourages a good range of mosses.

Coed Cymerau

Permit only; 26ha; NCC reserve
Oak woodland
Spring, summer, autumn

Coed Cymerau is more sheltered and damper than nearby Coed Camlyn. Birch is more common among the oaks and bilberry less common on the forest floor. In addition there are several small wet mires and a grassland area. There is a wide range of ferns, mosses, liverworts and lichens.

Coed Dinorwig

SH 586603; 50ha; GCC reserve
Old oak woodland
Leaflet from Padarn Country Park information centre
Spring, early summer

Part of the Padarn Country Park, on the steep slopes above Llyn Padarn, the reserve is unusual among similar Welsh hill oakwoods in having been ungrazed for many years. The wood was fenced, presumably to keep sheep from the Dinorwig quarries, and this has protected what must have been the typical ground cover of many other woods.

Cemlyn's birds include nesting Sandwich terns.

Under the often rather small oaks, heather, bilberry and bramble form a rich tangle while, in damper areas, the ground is thick with spreads of great wood-rush. Hazel and holly form a thin understorey, best in the deeper soils where bands of slate have eroded unevenly to give a ridge-and-channel effect which runs across the slope. The sheltered dampness encourages a good range of ferns and mosses and the oaks, often thick with ivy, carry attractive sprays of polypody. Lady-fern, hard and parsley fern occur on the woodland floor and wet rocky outcrops provide a habitat for Wilson's filmy-fern; drier rocks and jumbles of block scree provide a suitable site for maidenhair spleenwort. In places where the oakwood has been cleared, the Vivian quarry for instance, birch is invading – a first step towards new woodland cover.

Insects such as mottled umber moth will sometimes completely strip the leaves from many of the oaks, an attack balanced by a second spring of fresh leaves in July – but an attack which is most important for breeding birds: it implies enormous numbers of accessible caterpillars. Pied flycatcher specialise in oakwoods such as this, with a full canopy, sparse understorey and a richness of insects for food. Buzzard, kestrel and sparrowhawk are among the other birds and, while more common mammals include fox, stoat and weasel, the reserve is sometimes hunted by the far more uncommon polecat.

Coed Dolgarrog

Permit only; 69ha; NCC reserve
Mixed deciduous woodland
Spring, summer

Coed Dolgarrog's trees include oak, wych elm, ash, small-leaved lime and crab apple. On the woodland floor dog's mercury and enchanter's-nightshade grow with sanicle, ramsons, wild strawberry and common dog-violet. The bird and mammal life is similarly rich and the wood has a large badger population.

Coed Dol-y-Bebin

Permit only; 29ha; NWNT reserve
Woodland and rough hillside
Spring, summer

Oak woodland, with ash, birch, holly and rowan, stands on the steep rocky hillside, thick with bracken in the clearings. Two streams give wet areas which are rich in ferns. Buzzard hunt the hillside and stands of heather on the drier slopes support occasional red grouse.

Coed Ganllwyd

Permit only; 24ha; NCC reserve
Oak woodland
Spring, summer, autumn

Coed Ganllwyd is chiefly oak woodland but contains other tree species; the considerable variation in the soil gives a good range of ground cover. A waterfall makes part of the wood extremely damp, encouraging a rich variety of unusual ferns, mosses and liverworts.

Coed Gorswen

Permit only; 13.5ha; NCC reserve
Mixed deciduous woodland
Spring, summer

Coed Gorswen, like COED DOLGARROG nearby, is much richer than most other woods in Gwynedd and has a similar wide range of trees and smaller plants, including moonwort and broad-leaved helleborine.

Coed Llechwedd

SH 592318; 24.4ha; WdT
Steep sloping woodland
Spring, early summer

On the old sea cliff above MORFA HARLECH, the wood is mainly oak with a variety of other species including wild cherry. Since the wood has been fenced the ground flora has become more varied and interesting.

Coed Lletywalter

SH 602275; 37.6ha; WdT
Woodland and lake
Spring, summer

The area includes a large lake with boggy wetlands and a stream through the woodland. Rocky outcrops add to the habitat range and, although not a scheduled reserve, the whole complex is of great interest.

Coed Tyddyn Badyn

SH 565668; 3ha; WdT
Mixed woodland
Spring, summer

Although largely replanted with conifers, the wood still contains a mix of alder, birch and willow and is to be allowed to return to a broad-leaved woodland.

Rushing water encourages damp-loving plants in the woodlands of Coed Ganllwyd.

Polecat, a rare relative of stoat and weasel.

Coedydd Aber

SH 662720; 147ha; NCC reserve
Mixed valley woodland
Permit only off rights of way, from NCC, Bangor
Nature trail leaflet from NCC
Spring, summer

To walk to the spectacular Aber Falls at the head of the valley is to walk through an immense variety of woodland and valley habitat. The dry acid oak woodland on the higher slopes is typical of many Welsh oakwoods, but the lower slopes are richer and damper and there are also wet areas of alder woodland and a fine example of cliff woodland in the spray of the Falls themselves. On the lower slopes of the valley the woods are varied, with oak, ash, wych elm, birch and hazel, with primrose, bluebell, wood anemone and wood-sorrel in spring. Here, in wet boggy areas, are alder and grey willow with creeping buttercup and opposite-leaved golden-saxifrage. On the steep ravine slopes soft shield-fern is common and, where sheep cannot graze, tutsan grows on rock ledges and wood fescue, a rare grass, may also occur.

Towards the head of the valley the woodland becomes more open, wide glades and marshy areas give more openings in the leaf canopy, and the woodland eventually grades into hawthorn and crab apple scrub, open and standing in close-grazed grassland. A litter of boulders and low hummocks sparsely grown with hawthorn signals the head of the valley and the Aber Falls. On either side of the washed slabs the cliffs are terraced and broken, soaked with spray and rich with stunted oak, birch, rowan, gorse and heather and thickly clumped with great wood-rush. The reserve also

has a good lichen epiphyte flora, with a number of important rarities, and some very local Atlantic bryophytes on these cliffs situated near the Aber Falls.

This diversity of habitat encourages a wide variety of bird life. There are particularly good breeding populations of pied flycatcher, redstart and wood warbler. Willow warbler and chiffchaff may be heard throughout the woods and the stream attracts both dipper and grey wagtail. Wheatear and ring ouzel nest in the rocky areas around the head of the valley where merlin and buzzard hunt.

Coedydd Maentwrog

SH 652414–600410; 68.5ha; NCC reserve
Oak woodland in three blocks
Leaflet from NCC
Spring, early summer

Coed Llyn Mair, high above the Vale of Ffestiniog, is the smallest of the three woodland blocks; the NCC has laid out a nature trail to show the various facets of woodland life.

The trees are mostly oak with a scattering of birch, alder, rowan and sycamore, but the reserve also has small meadow-like clearings, a marshy wetland at the top of the wood, a good deal of woodland edge and a small area of rocky heathland. This heathland shows the sort of habitat over which the woods have grown, a thick springing stand of heather and bell heather, with bilberry, tormentil, heath bedstraw, harebell and goldenrod.

Under the trees the smaller plants change, the ferns, mosses and lichens come into their own and hard fern and polypody are common. There are also flowering plants, such as common cow-wheat, adapted to grow in shade. Primrose, lesser celandine and common dog-violet grow in the clearings.

Above and outside the present woodland is an open area of bracken with young hawthorn beginning to mark the change to scrub which precedes the change to woodland – when the hawthorns will shelter young oaks and then give way to them. The bracken is tangled with bramble and raspberry. Above this is a small area of wetland with grey willow standing above tussocks of purple moor-grass and meadowsweet, a warm scented corner loud with insects, very different from the shaded quiet of the woods and the stream which drops down through them into Llyn Mair below.

Although Llyn Mair is outside the reserve it adds another range of habitat to the area, with marshland becoming lakeside bog. The lake itself is fringed with willow, small birch and thick beds of rushes. This open water attracts mallard, coot, moorhen, heron and insect-taking birds such as swallow, contrasting with the reserve's typical woodland birds, pied flycatcher, wood warbler, nuthatch, treecreeper, green and great spotted woodpecker, jay and buzzard.

Two further blocks of woodland, to which access is restricted, complete the spread of the reserve.

Coed-y-Rhygen

Permit only; 27.5ha; NCC reserve
Oak woodland
Spring, summer

The underlying rocks cause alternating belts of dry woodland and wet boggy slopes. The moss *Leucobryum glaucum* forms green-grey cushions on the forest floor while purple moor-grass and bog myrtle grow in the wet mires. In more open areas are heather and cross-leaved heath. Buzzard, pied flycatcher and great spotted woodpecker frequent the woodland and mallard and common sandpiper breed on the lake. Polecat has been recorded.

Cors Bodgynydd

Permit only; 4ha; NWNT reserve
Small area of bog and heath
Spring, autumn

Bog myrtle, cross-leaved heath and purple moor-grass cover much of this reserve, important for the rare marsh clubmoss. The rich dampness encourages insects and green hairstreak butterfly and oak eggar, emperor and beautiful snout moths have been recorded, together with two national rarities: Ashworth's rustic and Weaver's wave moths.

Cors Erddreiniog

Permit only; 66ha; NCC reserve
Fen, birch woodland and heath
Spring, summer

Wetland and limestone combine to provide an exceptional range of habitat and species. There is a wide variety of fenland plants, including black bog-rush and great fen-sedge, together with orchid species such as northern marsh-orchid, fen orchid, narrow-leaved marsh-orchid and marsh helleborine.

Cors Goch

Permit only; 46ha; NWNT reserve
Rich fen, limestone grassland and acid heath
Spring, summer

Cors Goch is a reserve of splendid variety where rushes, sedges and great stands of common reed, scented with bog myrtle and water mint, combine with marsh fern and royal fern in one of the finest fen communities in Britain. The richness is due to drainage from the limestone higher ground. On the thickly grassed bank above the fen common rock-rose and fairy flax show among mats of salad burnet and quaking-grass. Here one of the reserve's many orchid species grows – never more than locally common, and rare in north Wales, green-winged orchid occurs in the limestone grassland. Lower down, where the grassland merges into fen, fragrant orchid and lesser butterfly-orchid grow. Rich areas of damp marshland occur around the fen and these are glorious with grass-of-Parnassus and early and northern marsh-orchid, common spotted-orchid and marsh helleborine, another orchid uncommon in north Wales.

To describe a reserve only in terms of its rarities is not really to give a true description, and the richness and colour of Cors Goch owe much to the commoner plants. The area of acid heath where a belt of sandstone shows above the fen is bright

The flanks of the Vale of Ffestiniog are clothed with splendid mixed oakwoods.

One of the artificial lakes which complement the heathland at Cors Tyddyn Du.

with gorse, heather and bell heather and, in April and May, it is starred with spring squill, more typical of coastal grasslands. In the more acid marshy places common butterwort grows, with lesser water-plantain, uncommon throughout the country and rare in north Wales. Another rarity is greater bladderwort which grows with lesser bladderwort in the more acid fenland pools. Lesser bulrush grows together with bulrush and common reed in the largest of the pools.

The great variety of chiefly wetland habitat encourages a wide range of animal life. Over 600 species of insect have been identified, including some 250 moth and butterfly species. Birds include grasshopper warbler, reed bunting, curlew, lapwing, redshank, snipe and nightjar.

Cors Tyddyn Du

Permit only; 5.5ha; NWNT reserve
Wet heath, scrub and two artificial lakes
Spring, summer

The drier parts of the heath are dominated by purple moor-grass with brown bent and sharp-flowered rush, dotted with devil's-bit scabious. Cranberry, marsh cinquefoil and marsh St John's-wort grow in the wetter parts and willow scrub fringes the stream. Branched bur-reed and typical water plants such as the three-petalled water-plaintain have colonised the stream and lakes. Reed bunting, grasshopper and willow warbler and whitethroat breed, and both corncrake and water rail have been recorded.

Cors-y-Sarnau

Permit only; 13ha; NWNT reserve
Marsh and alder carr
Spring, summer

The marsh formed where an old valley lake gradually silted up. Varied acid wetland plants include

bog asphodel, cranberry, cross-leaved heath and round-leaved sundew while purple moor-grass grows on parts of the swamp with marsh cinquefoil, bogbean and ragged-Robin. The wet alder woodland has greater tussock-sedge, meadowsweet and marsh-marigold.

Craig Wen

Permit only; 6ha; NWNT reserve
Damp acid heath
Spring, summer

Acid-loving plants such as bog pimpernel and bog asphodel, mountain everlasting and pale dog-violet contrast with lime-rich areas where black bog-rush may be found.

Cwm Glas Crafnant

Permit only; 15.5ha; NCC reserve
Partly wooded rocky hillside
Spring, summer

The slopes are mainly of a rich volcanic ash and the ledges carry a range of arctic–alpine plants which are unusual at such low altitude. The woodland is chiefly ash with hawthorn and hazel.

Cwm Idwal

SH 640590; 398ha; NCC reserve
High upland cwm, corrie lake and crags
Leaflet from NCC
Late spring, summer

Cwm Idwal, containing the hanging gardens of Twll Du, the Devil's Kitchen, lies at the head of the Nant Ffrancon, cupping Llyn Idwal, a small glacial lake, in the long curve of its tremendous crags. Like much of Wales it is heavily sheep-grazed but, like only a very few upland areas now, it shows how the hills must have been a glory of colour before sheep became so widespread.

Where the mat-grass cover of much of the reserve is fenced against sheep, purple moor-grass, heather and bell heather show; where the damp sward of common bent and sheep's fescue below the lime-rich cliffs is fenced, tufted hair-grass, Yorkshire-fog, bog asphodel, common cottongrass, heather, cross-leaved heath, milkwort and yarrow grow.

The cliffs above, where sheep cannot reach, are a treasure-house of flowers and ferns. Some are rarities, arctic–alpine plants which have survived here since plants first recolonised the cliffs after the last ice age; others are commoner plants enjoying the damp richness of the cliff ledges. April shows primrose, moschatel, early-purple orchid and purple saxifrage – the first of the arctic–alpines. By July the ledges are filled with flowers: alpine meadow-rue, moss campion, mossy and starry saxifrage and globeflower, with red campion, foxglove, thrift, goldenrod, sea campion, great wood-rush, brittle bladder-fern, oak fern, parsley fern and green spleenwort. These, of course, are only some of the plants of the rich rocks – the acid crags, too, have their characteristic flora. The lake has plants peculiar to its high altitude – awlwort, floating bur-reed, water lobelia, pillwort, quillwort, shoreweed, alternate water-milfoil and autumnal water-starwort.

There are trout and minnows in Llyn Idwal and it is fished by cormorant and heron. In winter goldeneye, pochard and whooper swan may be seen. Other birds of the reserve are those to be expected in high crags, such as raven and ring ouzel.

Cwm Nantcol Nature Trail

SH 605270; 1km; GCC–SNPC
Short trail in Nantcol Valley
Leaflet from car park or SNPC
Spring, summer

The trail passes through oak and birch woodland, by the rushing Nantcol stream, to the open sheep walk above. The small peat bog has common cottongrass and bogbean. The land formation and litter of great boulders shows the effects of the ice ages on the landscape.

Gogarth

Permit only; 2ha; NWNT reserve
Limestone grassland and scree
Spring, summer

Although heather and bell heather occur, this is an outcrop of carboniferous limestone with many limestone plants, including white horehound, wild madder and hoary rock-rose. Juniper shrubs and dense scrub shelter heathland birds and seabirds may be seen along the coast. The insects include the dwarf forms of grayling and silver-studded blue butterflies and the rare horehound plume moth, otherwise found only in southern England. Glow-worm may occasionally be seen.

Great Orme Nature Trails

SH 780832; 2.8–5.1km; Aberconwy BC
Trails on limestone grassland and sea cliffs
Booklet from tourist information centre, Llandudno
Spring, summer, autumn

The trails take in grassland with characteristic limestone flowers, and fine sea cliffs holding breeding colonies of birds such as fulmar, kittiwake, guillemot, razorbill, cormorant, shag, chough, jackdaw and raven. Some 85 bird species may commonly be seen around the Orme.

Morfa Bychan

Permit only; 11ha; NWNT reserve
Coastal dune system
Spring, summer

Morfa Bychan shows the range of duneland habitat from open seaward dune edge through stable dunes, overgrown with plants, to dune grassland and freshwater marsh. Partridge nest on the reserve and the bishop's mitre shield-bug, unusual in north Wales, has been found.

Morfa Dyffryn

Permit only; 202ha; NCC reserve
Coastal dune system
Spring, summer

These dunes have typical sand plants such as sand couch and prickly saltwort, and the sand stabiliser, marram. The stabilised dunes are rich with lichens, mosses and plants such as lady's bedstraw and thyme-leaved sandwort. In the damp slacks between the dunes sharp rush and glaucous sedge grow with sprawls of creeping willow. Seaside centaury and green-flowered helleborine are among the reserve's rarer plants.

Cwm Glas Crafnant: sloping woodland and crags.

Morfa Harlech

Permit only; 491ha; NCC reserve
Dune system and saltmarsh
Spring, summer

The saltmarsh, which is now being invaded by common cord-grass, grades into sandy grassland and then into a rich and complex system of dunes and damp dune slacks where plants such as moonwort, Portland spurge and sharp rush may be found. A freshwater marsh holds a black-headed gull colony in summer and a winter population of wildfowl, including shoveler, teal and whooper swan. Reed bunting, curlew, lapwing, oystercatcher, ringed plover, redshank and shelduck breed on the reserve.

Nantporth

Permit only; 7ha; NWNT reserve
Small limestone quarry, woodland and foreshore
Spring, summer

In the quarry the limestone plants include common rock-rose, burnet rose, yellow-wort and salad burnet. The woodland has common twayblade, columbine, early dog-violet and woodruff. The area between high and low water demonstrates muddy shore ecology, with animals ranging from the tiny shrimp-like *Corophium* to the giant king rag bristleworm.

Dune grassland and scrub at Newborough Warren, backed by Snowdonia's mountains.

Newborough Warren–
Ynys Llanddwyn

SH 406636; 633.5ha; NCC reserve
Dunes, saltmarsh, pool and rocky headland
Permit only off rights of way
Leaflet from NCC
All year

Newborough Warren is one of the finest dune systems in the country. The sand includes a high proportion of powdered shells which makes it rich in calcium and contributes much to the wealth of plants found here. Some 560 plant species have been identified in the open duneland and in Newborough Forest. Characteristic plants of the first, seaward, dunes are marram, sea spurge, sand cat's-tail and wild pansy, the food plant for the caterpillars of dark green fritillary. The more stable dunes have lady's bedstraw, common bird's-foot-trefoil, cuckooflower, meadow saxifrage and wild thyme. In the dune slacks creeping willow grows and the wide range of orchids includes dune helleborine.

The dunes are rich in insects but bird species are limited by lack of cover, and the characteristic birds are curlew, lapwing, oystercatcher, meadow pipit and skylark.

A large area of the duneland has been planted with trees and although most of them are conifers, generally Corsican pine, there are some broad-leaved trees and many characteristic duneland plants, as well as more typical and some more unusual woodland ones. Although it is outside the

Spotted rock-rose grows only on Anglesey.

reserve the NCC has scheduled Newborough Forest a Site of Special Scientific Interest.

Beyond the Forestry Commission plantations is the Cefni Estuary and an area of saltmarsh. This contains one of the country's largest continuous stands of sea rush. Other typical plants are sea aster, sea arrowgrass, annual sea-blite and thrift. In winter flocks of around 2000 duck, including 200 pintail, come to the estuary and several hundred Canada and greylag geese feed on the saltmarsh. Further up the estuary is Malltraeth Pool, another haven for waders and wildfowl. Most commonly seen are curlew, lapwing, redshank, cormorant and shelduck, but goldeneye, pintail, greenshank, bar-tailed and black-tailed godwit and Bewick's, mute and whooper swan have been recorded.

A narrow ridge of Pre-Cambrian rock, which runs through the middle of Newborough Forest, ends in the tidal island and rocky islets of Ynys Llanddwyn. Cormorant and shag nest on the islets, little more than ledged spikes sticking up out of the sea. The island is larger and, due to the acid rocks topped by glacial clays and lime-rich wind-blown sands, has a good range of plants reflecting this variety.

Penmaenpool Wildlife Information Centre

SH 695185; RSPB–NWNT
Bird observatory
Opening times: 11.30 a.m.–5.30 p.m.
June–September

From the observatory species such as cormorant, red-breasted merganser, curlew, lapwing, oyster-catcher and heron may be seen along the tidal riverway. From here an old railway line follows the estuary and overlooks a range of habitats: grazed saltmarsh with ditches and pools, freshwater marshes, oak woodland and patches of acid scrub.

Penhros

SH 276804; 140ha; Penhros Nature Reserve–
Anglesey Aluminium Ltd reserve
Coast, woodlands, scrub and marsh
Permit only to Specialist Sector: from Hon.
Director, Penhros Nature Reserve, Holyhead
Booklet from site
All year

The main part of the reserve consists of woodland, coastal grassland and rocky foreshore on the north east corner of Holyhead Island.

The mixed woods contain many typical wood-land birds while the foreshore may have breeding red-breasted merganser, shelduck, oystercatcher, ringed plover and redshank. Greenshank, spotted redshank, Slavonian grebe, black-tailed godwit and whimbrel may visit and artificial pools attract many other wild birds. The Specialist Sector, open only to bona fide ornithologists, consists of scrub and marsh and overlooks an important tern colony.

Porth Diana

Permit only; 2ha; NWNT reserve
Coastal heathland
Spring, summer

In this tiny reserve spring squill, bird's-foot and English stonecrop show beneath gorse, heather and cross-leaved heath. The real treasure, how-ever, is spotted rock-rose, which only grows in certain parts of north Wales.

Rhinog

SH 657290; 598ha; NCC reserve
Acid upland and crags
Leaflet from NCC
Late spring, summer, autumn

This highly inaccessible area (the map reference marks the peak of the reserve since the nearest road access is several kilometres away from any part of it) has a wonderful sweep of heather moor with bil-berry, cowberry and crowberry. Areas of blanket bog have *Sphagnum* mosses and purple moor-grass, with bog myrtle edging the wetter places. The crags provide nest sites for raven, ring ouzel and wren, while red grouse, meadow pipit and wheatear breed on the lower slopes.

Snowdonia National Park

See map; 218,455ha; SNPC
Mountains, moorland, valleys and coast
Leaflets from National Park centres
Spring, summer

The heights of Snowdon seen across the waters of Llynau Mymbyr.

Of the three main routes into Snowdonia, many visitors will enter by the A5 from Llangollen. Perhaps they might arrive on a day when the mountain ranges show as a clear sharp line of peaks above the broken plateau of the uplands; perhaps they might see little but driving rain. One of the most spectacular introductions to the mountains is to see the huge lift of the land ahead rising into cloud – a clear view of the slopes below but the peaks lost in mists which roll across the plateau to stream downward from the tops, a dreamlike waterfall which vanishes in the warmer air below.

Water is an essential part of the uplands, feeding the bogs and rivulets, streams and rivers which fill the lakes and cut through the rocks to the sea. While earth movements have raised the great massif, water and ice have refined the final form.

The sculpted plateau forms the core of the National Park which, excluding the Lleyn Peninsula and much of the coastal strip, covers most of the land between the River Conwy, Bala Lake and River Dyfi. It includes the ranges of Snowdon and the Carneddau, Arennig, Aran, CADER IDRIS and RHINOG in an area second only in size to the LAKE DISTRICT NATIONAL PARK (Cumbria). Among the mountains, valleys wind between long rocky slopes of sheep-grazed grass moorland or steeply tilted woodlands, between huge splays of shat-tered scree or dark cliffs of stone while, everywhere, the silver threads of streams or the cold ripples of upland lakes add their beauty to the scene. Below the uplands, rich agricultural valleys drain to the dunes and marshes of the coast.

Snowdon – YR WYDDFA, the highest mountain in Wales and England – is the remains of a worndown dip in the rocks. At one time this peak was buried in the fold of an ancient valley. In Devonian times, over three hundred million years ago, the layered rocks of earlier times were buckled by a driving force which thrust them up against the even older rocks of Anglesey and Padarn and heaved them into heights and valleys which were later attacked by time. As later earth movements lifted them out of the sea, wind and weather worked at the hills and slowly wore them away. By the time of the ice ages only the stumps of the buckled layers remained, with Snowdon standing as a peak since its rocks were harder than those around it. Being in the bottom of a fold, the layers of rock at the centre were compressed – they now form the rocks of the summit. The ice moved in glaciers which thrust slowly through the valleys, smoothing and scraping the slopes into long U-shaped curves, plucking the rock from the valley heads to form spectacular cwms, sculpting the rock into the shapes visible today.

When the ice withdrew, plants began to recolonise: first, those which could live in arctic conditions and then, as the climate warmed, those which preferred more temperate ones. Birch and pine woodland, similar to the relict Caledonian forests of Scotland, spread throughout the hills and then, with a further warming, sessile oak took over. Of course, the spread of plants varied: the folding and eroding, the volcanic intrusions and changes led to a widely varying range of rocks being exposed and each rock weathered to give a different soil. In a similar way the shape of the land affected exposure and wetness.

Some sites, high in the mountains, north-facing and cold in summer, retained their arctic plants – these are some of the specialities of Snowdonia which attract botanists to the region. With a change in climate, other areas became spreads of bog, trapping remains of the earlier woods in their peat. Yet other sites, the sheltered valleys, preserved their splendid oakwoods and provided cover for many mammals and woodland birds.

The heather moorland and all but the steepest valley woods have largely gone from the mountains; birds and mammals have been hunted for many generations and the rarer, less resilient ones are gone or only survive in hidden places. A few inland-breeding chough and peregrine remain and rare and beautiful plants still show on the higher rocky ledges. The arctic–alpines, the ice age relict plants, include Snowdon lily, at its only site in Britain – a plant that grows here on lime-rich ledges but which, elsewhere in the world, normally grows in mountain ranges close to perpetual snows. The splendid range of species includes mountain avens, alpine bistort, moss campion and alpine cinquefoil, mountain crowberry, alpine meadow-rue, arctic and alpine mouse-ear, alpine saw-wort, alpine saxifrage, mountain sorrel, holly fern and alpine woodsia. Together with these are more commonly lowland species and water avens, meadowsweet, early-purple orchid, primrose and great wood-rush may be found on the upland crags.

Below, the mat-grass moors have little variation but, where heather survives on the peat mires, plants such as lesser twayblade may occur. The woods, lower still, have a wide range from acid oakwoods to sheltered valley woodlands where clays have washed down to give suitable soils for a much wider range of trees. Modern coniferous woodlands add slight variety.

The lakes are as varied as the woods, ranging from shallow upland pools to deep-scoured narrow waters in the valleys. Many are of glacial origin, formed when mountain rubble dropped from the melt-face of the glacier to form a moraine which dammed the waters above it. These lakes have native populations of minnow and small brown trout and a few contain char. Char, like the arctic–alpines, is thought to be a glacial relict species; related to trout, it is a coldwater fish limited to its deep narrow lakes

and unable to survive elsewhere. Bala Lake holds gwyniad, another relict fish, which is found nowhere else in Wales.

To travel through the National Park, from the mountain tops to the sea, would encompass a marvellous range of country and a rich variety of wildlife. The mammals, of course, are seldom seen but a great diversity of birds might be observed. In the high hills buzzard and raven, wheatear and ring ouzel, meadow pipit and skylark may be seen. On the moors red grouse breed in the heather, there are curlew, lapwing, redshank, snipe, and perhaps golden plover or dunlin in the bogs, while merlin, sparrowhawk, short-eared owl, hen harrier and kite may occur. The kite nests in valley oakwoods outside the National Park but in the woods of Snowdonia a typical range of Welsh woodland birds may be seen. Here are pied flycatcher, wood warbler and redstart, with all three native woodpeckers and with buzzard, sparrowhawk and tawny owl. Where a rapid stream runs, dipper and grey wagtail come to breed and, where the valley broadens to give agricultural land, kingfisher nest in the clay banks and a whole variety of lowland birds occur. Follow the river down to the sea and there may be a wide drowned estuary, sheltered tidal waters fringed with salt-marsh, where wildfowl and waders feed. Onwards to the coastal dunes and yet another rich habitat unfolds, with waders feeding at the water's edge or probing the marshy slacks.

This great diversity is reflected in the many reserves of the park – underlining the national importance of the richness of its wildlife and conserving some of the beauty of its mountains, moors and valleys.

Merlin prey on the small birds of the uplands.

South Stack Cliffs

SH 205823; 316ha; RSPB reserve
Coastal cliffs and heathland
Leaflet from RSPB
Spring, summer

In spring and early summer the northern part of the reserve is probably the most exciting, for at least nine seabird species breed there. The 120m cliffs hold a breeding population which includes around 2000 guillemot, 500 puffin and 600 razorbill pairs. Stock dove and rock pipit are among the cliff-nesting birds which are not specifically coastal, as are four members of the crow family: carrion crow, raven, jackdaw and chough.

Plants of the sea cliffs characteristic of western coasts are golden samphire, rock sea-spurrey, spring squill and English stonecrop. Sea campion, common scurvygrass, kidney vetch and restharrow also cluster the hard white twisted rock. Gogarth Bay, between South and North Stack, is a regular hauling-out place for grey seal.

The other important habitats are heathland, the hill moorland of Holyhead Mountain and the coastal heath of Penrhos Feilw Common. Holyhead Mountain has typical acid plants such as bilberry and wavy hair-grass, with heather, bell heather, gorse and tormentil. Penrhos Feilw is more unusual, since good coastal heathland is not common in Britain. Dense masses of intermingled gorse and heather turn the heath into a deep-pile carpet of gold and green and purple, for exposure and salt-laden winds prune the heath so that it rolls smooth and even until, as it approaches the sea, the exposure becomes too great and it fades into coastal grassland. There are wet areas within the heathland, where bog pimpernel and cross-leaved heath appear. Two rarities grow here, field fleawort and spotted rock-rose.

There are small breeding populations of waders on the heathland in spring and dotterel are passage migrants in May and September. Adder and common lizard are plentiful here. Among the butterflies are marsh fritillary and silver-studded blue – the latter at its most northerly site in western Britain.

Traeth Lafan

SH 614724; 2000ha; GCC reserve
Inter-tidal flats
Autumn, winter

Over 1000 waders of 10 different species, together with large numbers of duck, add to the importance of the sands and mudflats where red-breasted merganser and great crested grebe gather to moult.

Trawsfynydd Nature Trail

SH 695383; 3km; CEGB
Nature trail along edge of Trawsfynydd Reservoir
Booklet from CEGB
Spring, summer

Herring gull, greater and lesser black-backed and black-headed gull and a few common tern nest on the islands, and common sandpiper on the stony shores, of this man-made lake. The planted woodlands hold spotted flycatcher, green woodpecker, buzzard and sparrowhawk, while natural woods below the Maentwrog Dam are rich in mosses, liverworts and ferns, with birds such as pied flycatcher, redstart, grey wagtail, dipper and barn owl.

Choughs nest on cliffs such as these at South Stack, or in upland crags, quarries and old mines.

Yr Wyddfa

SH 630530; 1677ha; NCC reserve
High upland crags, cwms and corrie lakes
Leaflets from NCC
Spring, summer

The Miner's Track runs on from Llyn Llydaw, by Crib Goch, below Yr Wyddfa.

The Miner's Track nature trail rises from Pen-y-Pas to Llyn Llydaw and gives a very good idea of the sort of influences – altitude, exposure, underlying rock and the effects of man – which have brought about the present face of Snowdon, Yr Wyddfa. Much of the way is through wide slopes of rocky grassland where grazing sheep reduce the plant cover to little more than a lawn of mat-grass. Higher up, though, where rich volcanic lavas break through and the soil is better, the grasses are more varied, softer, and more small herbs appear. But again sheep keep most of the more exciting plants from growing and only a few, heath bedstraw, tormentil and wild thyme, for instance, survive the continual grazing.

Higher again, the acid rocks reappear and there are small areas of bog, bright green with *Sphagnum* mosses and vivid with bog asphodel, while common cottongrass dances in the wind. Common butterwort and round-leaved sundew lay sticky traps for small insects, a special adaptation to secure extra nutrition in this difficult habitat. Many years ago trees grew where the bogs are now, and their remains can still be found preserved in the peat, but changing climate and the hand of man have banished them from almost all the hills and grazing sheep make sure that none will grow now, although a few rowans, brilliant with reddish-orange berries in autumn, survive on rock ledges too steep for sheep to reach.

Llyn Llydaw, at the end of the nature trail, looks calm and beautiful on a still summer day but the ripple of rising trout no longer stirs its surface: copper pollution from the mills where ore was crushed in the early part of the century has poisoned its waters.

Apart from predators, particularly peregrine, and the birds of the long-gone oakwoods, birds have not been greatly affected by man's interference here; indeed the high crags are still a haven for chough, once common on the western sea coasts and now very rare indeed. The important factor affecting mountain birds is the bleakness, and the characteristic birds are fairly few. With the chough on the crags are carrion crow, raven, ring ouzel and wren. Wheatear on the screes and meadow pipit on the grassland are the characteristic birds of the lower slopes.

Powys

Powys, the upland heart of Wales, comprises former Montgomery, Radnor and Brecon. Its western border follows the crest of the Cambrian Mountains, the spine of Wales, touching the sea only at the DYFI Estuary (DYFED). On the east the border with England follows ancient OFFA'S DYKE, now a long-distance footpath. The southern boundary follows the edge of the carboniferous limestone and millstone grit escarpment where it meets the coal measures of the south Wales valleys. This border is shared by the southern limit of the BRECON BEACONS NATIONAL PARK, which lies mainly in Powys and is the largest area of old red sandstone upland in Wales. These sandstones do not reach further than Builth Wells, for the rest of the county is largely of acidic shales of Silurian age.

The highest points in Powys, reaching just over 800m, are the Berwyns in the north and the Brecon Beacons in the south. Powys is essentially a county of rounded hills. On reaching the Severn, Wye and Usk, the streams which issue from these hills create superb farmland and beautiful countryside. The Wye is of sufficient environmental interest to be scheduled a Grade 1 site by the NCC, one of the few rivers in Britain to receive this premier grading.

Few of the major reservoirs are noted for wildfowl, but an exception is TALYBONT RESERVOIR. Its attractiveness to birds is partly due to the mineral-rich waters which act as a stimulus to the whole food chain. Some 6km north is the largest natural nutrient-rich lake in Wales, LLANGORSE LAKE, now somewhat over-exploited for recreation, but still worth visiting if only for the opportunity of glimpsing a migrating osprey.

Powys is the most sparsely populated county in England and Wales, and with less than 20 per cent of it below 180m sheep greatly outnumber people. In the north these quiet uplands are the territory of hen harrier, further south scavenging grounds for red kite. The relatively few craggy areas echo to the piercing cry of peregrine. In the heather above the crags the merlin rears its brood on a diet of meadow pipits.

Most of the uplands are blanketed with peat, some actively growing and supporting *Sphagnum* mosses, some eroding to leave remnants of the original surface as hags in a sea of treacherous peaty ooze. Here dunlin nests, along with scattered golden plover and redshank. Some of the plants of the uplands are distinguished more for being on the southern edge of their range than for their rarity.

In southern Powys the limestone shows itself in a maze of caverns, part of which, at OGOF FFYNON DDU, is Britain's first underground National Nature Reserve. Elsewhere limestone only outcrops at Dolyhir, midway along the eastern border, and at LLANYMYNECH HILL (Shropshire), which supports a wide range of lime-loving species, at its northern end.

Away from rocks and hills there is still much to interest the naturalist. Walk along the Montgomery Canal near Welshpool, or the Monmouthshire and Brecon Canal, both rich in plants. Look for otter along any river in this, one of its last strongholds in England and Wales. Look out for yellow rattle, saw-wort, meadow thistle, dyer's greenweed and wood bitter-vetch, which together indicate a field with an undisturbed history.

Well over 10 per cent of Powys is covered by softwood forests but some of the original sessile oakwoods still cling to hillsides. In spring these woods, some of which are the home of red kite, come alive with small migrant birds. Pied flycatcher is very common in oakwoods.

The county possesses certain plant rarities and specialities. The Wye Valley and some of the limestone crags in the south support rare species of whitebeam including three endemic to the county. At scattered volcanic outcrops spiked speedwell, sticky catchfly, perennial knawel and rock cinquefoil are found. On a few rocky ledges late winter is brightened by a small yellow crocus-like flower, *Gagea bohemica*; although native, it was only discovered a few years ago, the first distinct native flowering plant found in England and Wales for decades.

Powys has relatively few formal nature reserves, although if transposed into other regions much of the county would merit such status. So come and enjoy the freedom of its hills, the summer melody of its oak woodlands and the Wordsworthian splendour of the 'sylvan Wye' without, in general, recourse to a pocketful of permits.

F. M. SLATER

Aberithon Turbary

Permit only; 5.8ha; H and RNT reserve
Old peat cutting
Spring, summer

Common reed, bulrush and willow carr stand above a wetland flora which includes lesser bladderwort, meadow thistle and floating club-rush and provides a varied habitat for many birds and insects. The reserve is important for the lichen *Cetraria sepincola*, which is probably a glacial relict species.

Brecon Beacons National Park

See map; 134,421ha; BBNPC
Huge tracts of uplands and valley
Literature from BBNPC and several
information centres
All year

From the high ridge above CRAIG-Y-LLYN (Glamorgan), the view across the Brecon Beacons is breathtaking. The huge escarpments stand out in tiered ranks, cupping the shadowed valleys, showing a splendid range of dark reds, deep purples, greens and yellows. The reds are due to the old red sandstone which makes up most of the park, but there are also areas of limestone, at CRAIG-Y-CILAU, for instance, where the Agen Allwedd caves run for 25km, at OGOF FFYNON DDU, another cave system, and at Castell Cerrig where both limestone and acid old red sandstone show in COED-Y-CASTELL (Dyfed).

Sheep grazing has converted the great moors of heather and bilberry into long slopes of bents and fescues, great plains of mat-grass and wet places where hare's-tail cottongrass can be found among tussocks of purple moor-grass. Only the tiered ledges of the cliff faces show what the Beacons must have been like in earlier years. Here, where sheep cannot graze, globeflower grows, purple and mossy saxifrage curtain the damp rocks in early summer, and dense clumps of great wood-rush show dark green on the lower ledges.

The valleys, Cwm Sere below Pen-y-Fan, for example, open smoothly down to the lowlands from steep heads ending in the high terraced scarps of the peaks. Rain on the high land drains down through these valleys in streams that have cut into the valley bed. They start as bubbling streamlets, rising from small rushy bogs or falling clear down the hillside, but soon the streamlets join and the waters race and tumble, cutting steps where the rock is harder, often forming a series of small waterfalls. Rowans stand over the falls and the shelter and dampness there encourage a rich growth of ferns, mosses and lichens and a colourful show of flowering plants.

The park as a whole naturally contains a greater range of habitat than merely the Beacons themselves; there are the limestone areas already mentioned, there are woodlands such as those in NANT SERE WOOD, and there are wetlands such as CWM COED-Y-CERRIG (Gwent) and TRAETH MAWR.

Cefn Cenarth

Permit only; 4ha; H and RNT reserve
Hillside woodland
Spring, early summer

Mainly a steep oak woodland, the reserve also includes rowan and planted larch and rises to some 420m. Tree pipit, redstart, pied flycatcher and wood warbler breed.

The grass moorland of the Brecon Beacons, sculpted by deep curving cwms, rises to Pen-y-Fan.

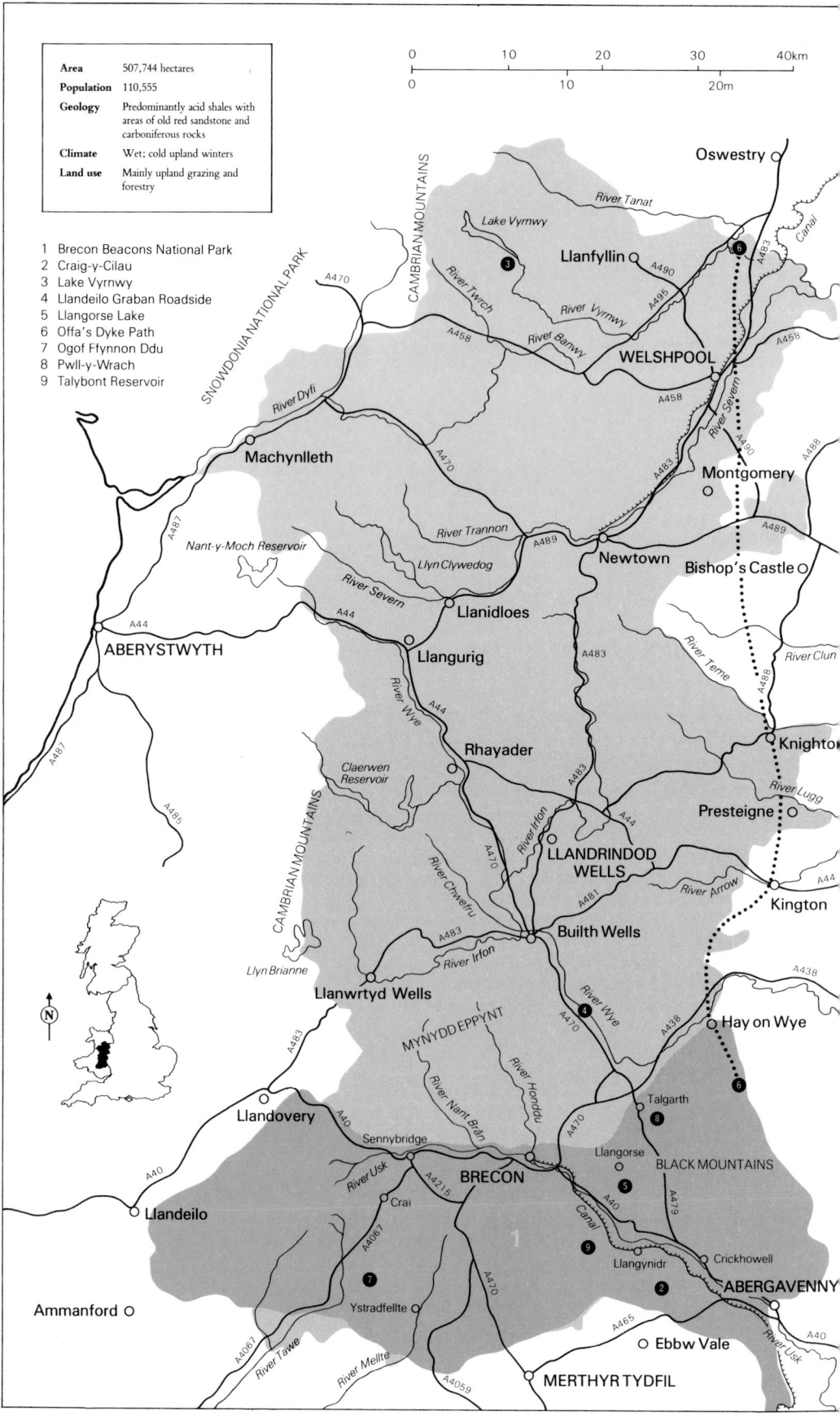

Area	507,744 hectares
Population	110,555
Geology	Predominantly acid shales with areas of old red sandstone and carboniferous rocks
Climate	Wet; cold upland winters
Land use	Mainly upland grazing and forestry

1 Brecon Beacons National Park
2 Craig-y-Cilau
3 Lake Vyrnwy
4 Llandeilo Graban Roadside
5 Llangorse Lake
6 Offa's Dyke Path
7 Ogof Ffynnon Ddu
8 Pwll-y-Wrach
9 Talybont Reservoir

0   10   20   30   40km
0   10   20m

Oswestry

River Tanat

CAMBRIAN MOUNTAINS

Lake Vyrnwy

Llanfyllin

A490

A495

6

Canal

A483

River Twrch

River Vyrnwy

WELSHPOOL

River Banwy

A458

A458

A470

SNOWDONIA NATIONAL PARK

River Dyfi

Machynlleth

A470

A483

A490

A483

River Severn

Montgomery

A488

A470

Nant-y-Moch Reservoir

River Trannon

A489

Newtown

A489

Bishop's Castle

Llyn Clywedog

River Severn

A44

Llanidloes

A483

River Teme

River Clun

ABERYSTWYTH

A44

Llangurig

A488

Knighton

A487

River Wye

A44

Rhayader

A483

A44

River Lugg

A495

Claerwen Reservoir

River Irfon

A470

Presteigne

LLANDRINDOD WELLS

A481

River Arrow

Kington

A44

CAMBRIAN MOUNTAINS

River Chwefru

Builth Wells

A483

River Irfon

Llyn Brianne

A438

N

Llanwrtyd Wells

River Wye

4

Hay on Wye

A483

MYNYDD EPPYNT

River Nant Bran

River Honddu

A470

6

Talgarth

8

BLACK MOUNTAINS

Llandovery

A40

Sennybridge

Llangorse

5

A479

River Usk

A4215

BRECON

A40

Crai

Canal

9

Llandeilo

A4067

1

Llangynidr

Crickhowell

2

ABERGAVENNY

Ammanford

7

Ystradfellte

A470

A465

River Usk

A4067

River Tawe

River Mellte

Ebbw Vale

A40

A4059

MERTHYR TYDFIL

Coed Pendugwm

Permit only; 3ha; MTNC reserve
Mixed woodland
Spring, summer

A good example of mature woodland, the trees are mainly oak and include beech, elm and ash above a typical woodland ground cover. The good range of insects reflects the wood's maturity. Both red and grey squirrel are present and the bird life includes the classic Welsh trio of wood warbler, pied flycatcher and redstart, with dipper on the boundary streams.

Craig Irfon

Permit only; 8.3ha; BNT reserve
Upland valley side
Spring, summer

In contrast with the rounded slopes of the BRECON BEACONS, the valley at Craig Irfon has been cut from harder rock and twists, craggy and narrow, through looming cliffs of rugged shales. Like so much of Wales the uplands here are grazed by sheep, so the sloping valley sides below the crags have lost their heather–bilberry cover and generally are blanketed with fescues, bents and mat-grass although the lower slopes have areas of scrub, hawthorn and rowan, lifting above thick stands of bracken.

The crags, where the sheep cannot graze, have a richer range of plants and stunted oak trees manage to survive. Fine clumps of heather, with bell heather and bilberry, decorate the crags.

The limestone cliffs of Craig-y-Cilau dominate wooded slopes above the bog.

Other acid moorland plants include heath bedstraw, tormentil and sheep's sorrel. The rocks also support a range of more widespread plants including wood sage, navelwort and ivy. Ferns, among them polypody, hard fern, lady-fern and the generally northern oak fern, grow on the ledges and in the crevices which also provide nesting sites for cliff-breeding birds.

An area of bog above the crags drains downwards through the long grass slopes, the course of the seepage marked by tussocks of purple moor-grass and *Sphagnum* moss. Below the slopes small mires hold *Sphagnum* with a good variety of rushes, sedges and acid wet-bog plants including cross-leaved heath, marsh lousewort, and bog asphodel.

The bird life is somewhat restricted by the open ruggedness of the valley but representative species occupy the broad habitat types available. At the lowest level, the stream is exploited by dipper; stonechat and whinchat occupy the scrubby areas; wheatear breeds on the open slopes below the rocks. The crags themselves provide nest sites for wren, ring ouzel and raven.

Craig-y-Cilau

SO 188159; 63ha; NCC reserve
Limestone crags, acid heath and bog
Permit only off right of way
Leaflet from NCC
Spring, early summer

The great white sweep of the limestone cliffs hides some well-known cave systems including the Agen Allwedd, which extends for some 25km. Limestone is the champagne rock of Britain and often the most forbidding cliffs effervesce with bright, unusual and fascinating plants.

Five rare whitebeams grow here together with beech, yew, wych elm, oak and silver birch, with hawthorn scrub on the slopes below. Harebell grows in the cliff crevices with brittle bladder-fern while mountain melick, angular Solomon's-seal and several uncommon subspecies of hawkweed grow on the cliff ledges. Limestone polypody and mossy saxifrage grow on the screes together with commoner plants such as herb-Robert.

The lower slopes are a jumble of moss-shrouded limestone blocks and steep slopes thickly grown with hawthorn scrub. At the base of the scarp, a small raised mire has formed in a glacial depression, with two streams at its edge, fringed with round-leaved sundew.

The caves shelter hibernating lesser horseshoe bat while fox and badger may occur on the slopes. Some 40 species of birds breed, including upland wheatear, ring ouzel and raven, with woodland species such as willow warbler and redstart.

Part of the gritstone plateau above the limestone crags lies within the reserve. This is acid moorland and heather is rather patchy, but there are good stands of bilberry and crowberry grading into common cottongrass mires and areas of mat-grass and heath rush.

Lake Vyrnwy lies below moorland slopes fringed with coniferous forests and small native woods.

Cwm-y-Wydden

Permit only; 4ha; MTNC reserve
Small steep woodland
Spring, summer

The wood is a mixture of generally acid areas and pockets of richer soils where rain washes minerals down. In the latter dog's mercury, herb-Paris and soft shield-fern grow beneath a canopy of wych elm, ash and willow. The acid parts have oak above a mossy ground cover with wavy hair-grass. Mosses and liverworts are particularly good along the stream and many lichens grow on the trees. Butterflies include speckled wood and purple hairstreak and there is a good range of typical woodland birds.

Glaslyn

Permit only; 160ha; MTNC reserve
Heather moorland
Spring, summer

The reserve protects a fine spread of heather, with bell heather, cross-leaved heath, bilberry, crowberry and areas of *Sphagnum* bog. The moorland and a steep rocky gorge provide a hunting ground for red kite, merlin and peregrine.

Lake Vyrnwy

SH 985215; 6500ha; RSPB
Flooded valley, grassland, moor and woodland
Leaflets and trail guide from visitor centre
All year

At the south western end of the Berwyn Mountains a deep steep-sided valley has been flooded to form the reservoir of Vyrnwy. Around and above the reservoir are some 2000ha of conifers, pockets of broad-leaved trees and great spreads of moorland,

part of the most extensive area of heather moor in Wales. Grass moor and old-meadow pastures increase the habitat range, together with crags and upland streams, scrubland and valley bogs. The reservoir is largely screened by a shelter belt of trees but the road which circles it offers several vantage points and a public hide provides views across the northern shallows to the towering crags beyond.

Its depth and the steepness of its banks are not ideal for waterbirds but mallard, teal and occasional great crested grebe nest here while goosander breeds at one of its very few Welsh sites. The stony edges of the lake provide nest sites for common sandpiper and grey wagtail which, with dipper and kingfisher, also breed on the feeder streams. In winter the reservoir may be bleak, at 250m above sea level, but mallard and teal may be joined by goldeneye, pochard and tufted duck, wigeon and whooper swan.

Over 120 species have been recorded on the reserve and the wide diversity of habitat attracts many breeding species. Few are resident because of the hardness of the winters – the moorland rises to 600m – but the valley provides an important flight-path for migrants and spring brings an influx of breeding birds to Vyrnwy. Crossbill, in the plantations, and raven, in the taller conifers or the crags, are the earliest to nest – usually sitting while snow is on the ground. Siskin and redpoll also breed in the conifers; black and red grouse, ring ouzel and wheatear nest in the moorland, together with curlew, lapwing, golden plover and snipe; the mixed woods and scrub provide habitats for pied and spotted flycatcher, redstart, wood warbler, tree pipit and whinchat. Breeding numbers may not always be large but the diversity is impressive, underlined by nesting predators: buzzard, kestrel, sparrowhawk and tawny owl.

Butterflies, too, respond to the habitat diversity and some 24 species have been recorded, including a fine range of fritillaries and hairstreaks with the now uncommon large heath on the moors. Among the mammals, pride of place must go to polecat, present but rarely seen, but there is also a good population of badger and thriving colonies of red squirrel, which may be seen feeding quite amicably with the much more widespread grey squirrel.

Ultimately, of course, these breeding species rely upon the plants of the reserve – either as a direct food source or as the crop on which their own food source feeds. The woods and the moors are the most important broad habitats and these are managed to increase diversity. In the native woodland, so much of which has been lost to conifers, new oaks are planted and natural growth protected by sheep-proof fencing. Grazing keeps the grass moors open for birds such as skylark and meadow pipit, while the heather is managed by rotational burning to encourage a mosaic of regrowth.

Over 200 flowering plants and 13 ferns have been recorded, together with a wide range of fungi, lichens, liverworts and mosses. The lakeside and roadside verges contribute such plants as betony, Welsh poppy and goldenrod, the grasslands harebell, sheep's-bit and heath bedstraw; the rocky crags have English stonecrop and navelwort while the woods contain species such as wood anemone, enchanter's-nightshade and climbing corydalis. The unimproved pastures hold an attractive range of hay-meadow plants including yellow rattle and field scabious with petty whin, pignut and heath spotted-orchid. Scattered here and there are uncommon ferns such as beech, oak and parsley fern and, as is so often the case in moorland areas, a wealth of beautiful plants occurs in and around the bogs.

The moorland and stream-fed valley bogs contain typical species such as common butterwort and round-leaved sundew with occasional bog asphodel and bog pimpernel. Ivy-leaved bellflower, globeflower, marsh lousewort and starry saxifrage are infrequent here but lesser twayblade, very rare in Wales, is fairly well represented.

This magnificent upland reserve of water, woodland and moor is almost entirely man-made. The reservoir was completed at the end of the nineteenth century, the conifers have been planted long enough to achieve commercial size and the grass moors and heather moorland are strongly influenced by man, but the site is nevertheless very important to natural wildlife. Not only is the valley a route for migrants – thousands of birds such as tree pipit, redstart and willow warbler, with ring ouzel and wheatear, pass through the reserve in the spring – but the lake itself has become a pre-breeding roost for up to 6000 black-headed gulls, which congregate before flying on to their nest sites. In autumn, too, a good passage occurs and, although they may not pause unless the year is a good one for rowan and hawthorn berries, large numbers of fieldfare and redwing may be seen.

The reserve was established mainly for the interest of its bird life and a measure of its potential was seen in August 1981. In a two-hour watching period, one hen harrier, one merlin, two buzzards and two sparrowhawks, four peregrines and five kestrels were observed: few birdwatchers could ask for a more exciting experience.

Llanbwchllyn Lake

Permit only; 12ha; H and RTNC–WWA reserve
Lake and marshland
All year

Greater spearwort, skullcap and lesser bulrush provide a breeding site for waterbirds. Passage migrants may occur in spring and autumn; winter wildfowl include mallard, pochard and tufted duck.

Llandeilo–Graban Roadside

SO 090438–112419; 3km; H and RTNC reserve
Old railway line
Spring, summer

Overlooking the River Wye, the reserve includes a range from meadowland to marsh and woodland plants. Slow-worm and common lizard occur on the slopes, with a good variety of butterflies and other insects, while the river and the wayside woods are rich in bird life.

Llangorse Lake

SO 133262; 22ha; WWA
Large shallow lake
All year

This shallow lake attracts a wide variety of wetland migrant and breeding birds. The lake is fringed with many plant species including common reed and bulrush; there are several species of pondweed and fringed, white and yellow water-lily occur. Roach, perch, pike and eel are among the fish in the lake, which would be an outstanding refuge for wildlife, were it subjected to fewer public pressures.

Goosander often nest in old trees.

Llyn Mawr

Permit only; 12ha; NWNT reserve
Lake and marsh area
All year

The margins of the lake are rich in plants typical of lower-level waters, such as marsh cinquefoil, marsh lousewort and early and northern marsh-orchid, as well as more characteristic species such as round-leaved sundew, butterwort and bog asphodel. The reserve is noted for its wetland birds including breeding black-headed gull, mallard and teal, with tufted duck, great crested grebe, snipe and curlew. Stonechat and whinchat nest in the scrubland. Pochard, wigeon, goldeneye, goosander and whooper swan may visit the lake in winter.

Mynydd Ffoesidoes

Permit only; 26.8ha; H and RTNC reserve
Upland moor
Spring, summer

This fine heather moorland, with bilberry, cowberry and crowberry, provides a breeding site for red grouse and a hunting ground for buzzard and merlin. Damper areas are marked by plants such as purple moor-grass, hare's-tail and common cottongrass with pockets of *Sphagnum* moss.

The Irfon Valley holds two reserves, Craig Irfon and Nant Irfon.

Nant Irfon

Permit only; 136ha; NCC reserve
Upland grassland and valley woods
Spring, summer

The grazed grassland contains the typical association of fescue, bent and mat-grass found in these hills, with extensive areas of purple moor-grass. High altitude hanging oak woodlands have generally uncoppiced oak, rowan, hazel and ash. There is a good range of woodland and upland birds including redstart, pied flycatcher, ring ouzel and winchat.

Nant Sere Wood

Permit only; 17.5ha; BNT reserve
Valley woodland
Spring, summer

Sheltered in the bottom of a spectacular BRECON BEACONS valley, the wood is a fascinating mosaic of wet and damp woodland with a varied range of habitat: grassland, scrub and woodland, sloping steeply down to a torrential stream.

Open grazing gives way to the woodland through old walled fields, thick with bracken where they are driest but otherwise grassed, with typical plants of the sheep walk such as heath bedstraw and tormentil. An open scrub of hawthorn spreads across these fields. The fairly dry grassland then grades into a wet meadow, full of rushes and sedges, showing a good range of marsh plants including meadowsweet, devil's-bit scabious, marsh

bedstraw, greater bird's-foot-trefoil, water mint and bog asphodel. Old walls within the fields show a contrasting, drier variation, supporting ash trees and clumps of heather. Alder and downy birch colonise the wet meadow area.

The woodland proper contains much alder – even the drier parts have pockets of waterlogged ground; other trees include oak, holly and field maple. An area of ash has a coppice-with-standards structure.

On drier slopes within the wood foxglove, common dog-violet, wood-sorrel and herb-Robert grow, with bluebell and the occasional rowan tree, while the damper areas have yellow pimpernel, wood horsetail and lesser spearwort. Most of the wood is damp and boggy, encouraging a strong and varied growth of ferns and mosses with a good range of liverworts and a rich autumn crop of fungi. The river and river edge provide a further range of habitat.

The birds are those characteristic of gladed lowland woods in Wales and include wood warbler, pied flycatcher, great spotted and green woodpecker, nuthatch, treecreeper, willow warbler, tree pipit and several species of tit.

Offa's Dyke Path

SJ 267206–SO 267323; 115km; CC
Long-distance way
Booklet from HMSO bookshops
Spring, summer

Generally following the line of the Welsh border, the footpath passes through spectacular countryside as rich in wildlife as it is beautiful.

Ogof Ffynon Ddu

SN 867155; 413ha; NCC reserve
Cave system, limestone pavement, grassland and heather moorland
Permit only off rights of way and to caves
Leaflet from NCC
Spring, summer

Above the extensive cave system, one of the largest and deepest in Britain, the reserve demonstrates the difference between rich limestone and acid millstone grit. Mountain everlasting, mossy saxifrage, mountain melick and lily-of-the-valley contrast with heather and bilberry. Ring ouzel and wheatear breed, and merlin and kestrel often hunt the area.

Pentwyn Reservoir

Permit only; 76ha; BNT reserve
Small reservoir
Autumn, winter, spring

Occasional migrant waders such as redshank and common sandpiper feed in the shallows and on exposed muds when the reservoir is low; duck include mallard, teal and wigeon. Scrub and woodland around the reservoir ensure a range of other birds and winter brings a good variety of wildfowl.

The mixed woodland of Pwll-y-Wrach falls to a swift clear stream.

Pwll-y-Wrach

SO 163327; 8.3ha; BNT reserve
Steep valley woodland
Visitors must keep to pathways
Spring, summer

The structure of Pwll-y-Wrach is good: tall oak trees stand above an understorey varied with ash, birch, hawthorn, hazel, holly, field maple and spindle. This richness, particularly the presence of lime-loving species such as spindle, is due to richer bands within the predominant old red sandstone. Along the river bed a shelf of cornstone, the lime-rich rock, is harder than the old red sandstone and forms a sculpted waterfall, where the rocks are thick with liverworts, mosses and ferns and ash takes over from oak as the main tree species.

The ground cover in this riverside ashwood has been virtually destroyed by grazing, but within the main body of the wood there is much variety, with an abundance of spring-flowering plants such as bluebell, wood-sorrel, woodruff, dog's mercury, enchanter's-nightshade, wild strawberry and common dog-violet. The edges of the paths in summer contain plants which cannot grow beneath the trees, such as devil's-bit scabious, betony and St John's-wort species. The range of habitat includes a boundary bank with heathland plants such as heather, gorse and broom growing together with lime-loving dogwood – perhaps the bank was mounded on a wall of cornstone.

The river itself and the river edge provide another range of habitat, from the pool below the waterfall to the rock and gravel stream bed. Dipper and grey and pied wagtail may be seen while other birds include a range of woodland species such as treecreeper and nuthatch.

Talybont Reservoir

SO 098190; 146ha; WWA–BBNPC reserve
Flooded valley reservoir
No access to the reservoir area
Autumn, winter, spring

The reservoir is a long, narrow body of water in a steep, forested valley. Generally deep, it is ideal for diving birds, and the southern end shallows into meadowland suitable for dabblers and waders. The shores are variable, sometimes gently sloping, sometimes with shallow muddy cliffs, so the range of 'edge' habitat is considerable.

Mallard, teal and wigeon are the commonest of the dabbling ducks seen here and may be joined at the water's edge by occasional waders such as curlew, redshank, common and green sandpiper and greenshank. The waders are wonderfully adapted to their environment. Their long legs hold them above the icy waters while their long beaks probe down deep into the mud. Of course, this similarity might lead to too many species feeding on the same prey, but a range of different styles of beak ensures that each species takes a different type of food, reducing competition to a minimum.

Three of the largest birds seen at the reservoir are the swans, resident mute swan and the two winter visitors, Bewick's and whooper swan, which fly in from Russia and northern Europe.

Traeth Mawr

Permit only; 5ha; BNT reserve
Wetland and bog
This site may be dangerous
Spring, summer

The heart of the bog is an area of mire and swamp, a dangerous place where sheep and ponies drown

Traeth Mawr: a level wetland set below the slopes of the Brecon Beacons.

each year, and this grades into a damp grassland filled with pools and then a grazing common with clumps of gorse and bracken. The whole area is grazed, so the drier parts are rather poor in species, a short-cropped turf where little can survive except the grasses, although the gorse and bracken provide good cover for heathland birds such as whinchat.

The pools contain more interesting plants with sweet-grass species standing above smaller water plants such as common water-crowfoot and shoreweed.

The bog–swamp central area is more diverse, not least because it is more difficult to graze, although invading downy birch shows that the progression to drier scrub and then to woodland is already under way. There is a good range of wetland species, with rich *Sphagnum* mires and typical wet-bog plants including bog pimpernel and cross-leaved heath, with common and hare's-tail cottongrass. Flea and bottle sedge occur with star sedge and with great fen-sedge in the more marsh-like areas while pockets of open water hold the unusual lesser marshwort.

The pools, marsh, bog and developing scrub provide a superb range of feeding and nesting sites for many bird species, a circumstance which is made even more attractive by the inaccessible nature of the wet heart of the area. Duck include mallard and teal. Black-headed gull nest and the wader population includes curlew and lapwing, together with snipe which make their wonderful drumming flights of courtship and territorial display over the reserve in spring and early summer. Other birds include heron, buzzard and raven.

Scotland

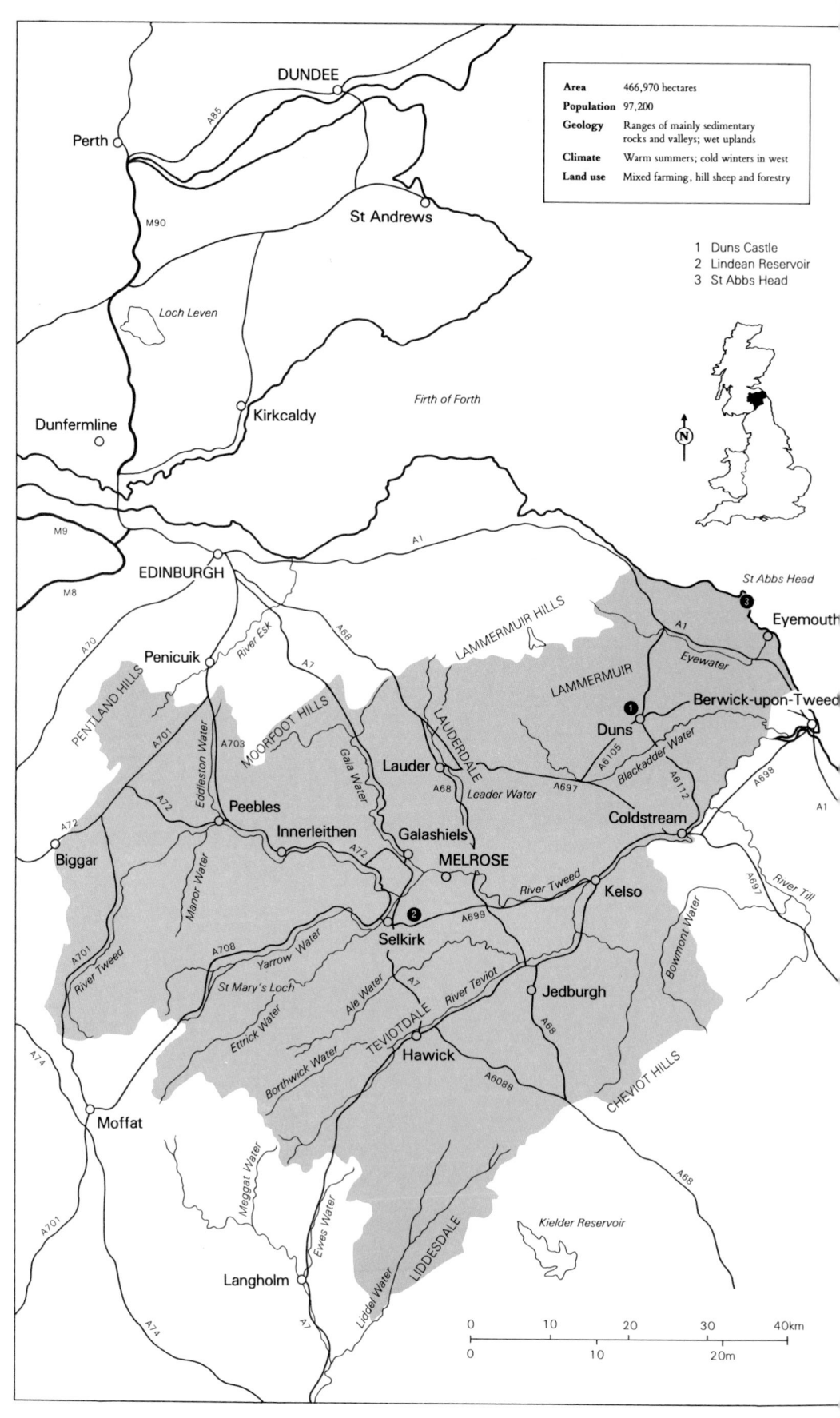

DUNDEE

Perth

St Andrews

Loch Leven

Dunfermline

Kirkcaldy

Firth of Forth

Area	466,970 hectares
Population	97,200
Geology	Ranges of mainly sedimentary rocks and valleys; wet uplands
Climate	Warm summers; cold winters in west
Land use	Mixed farming, hill sheep and forestry

1 Duns Castle
2 Lindean Reservoir
3 St Abbs Head

N

A85

M90

M9

M8

A70

EDINBURGH

Penicuik

River Esk

A68

A7

A701

PENTLAND HILLS

Eddleston Water

MOORFOOT HILLS

A703

A72

Peebles

Innerleithen

A72

Biggar

A72

A701

Manor Water

River Tweed

Gala Water

Lauder

A68

Leader Water

LAUDERDALE

LAMMERMUIR HILLS

LAMMERMUIR

St Abbs Head

A1

3

Eyemouth

Eyewater

A697

A6105

Blackadder Water

1

Duns

Berwick-upon-Tweed

A6112

A698

A1

Galashiels

MELROSE

River Tweed

Kelso

Coldstream

River Till

A697

Bowmont Water

2

Selkirk

A699

A708

Yarrow Water

St Mary's Loch

Ettrick Water

Ale Water

A7

River Teviot

Jedburgh

A68

TEVIOTDALE

Hawick

A6088

CHEVIOT HILLS

Moffat

A74

Meggat Water

Borthwick Water

Ewes Water

Liddel Water

LIDDESDALE

Kielder Reservoir

A68

Langholm

A74

A7

0	10	20	30	40km
0		10		20m

Borders

The Cheviot Hills are the natural frontier between England and Scotland, and visitors who come to the border at Carter Bar feel instinctively that they are entering a different land. To the east the ridge of the Cheviots points to the igneous massif of Cheviot itself, and to the west stretch successive ranges of hills, while to the north, across some odd, hummocky foothills, lies a clear view of the great expanse of the Tweed Valley. Far to the north again, the line of the Southern Uplands forms another natural frontier. The Borders Region can be seen as an independent unit built round the great river system of the Tweed, with its many tributaries pointing into hidden valleys in the hills.

The Border towns with their woollen industry stand at river crossings, their ruined abbeys testament to the riches of the valley. Not far away lie the historic houses of the great landed estates of the Borders, many now open to the public; they offer not just art and landscape, but wildlife in their parks and woodlands among prosperous agriculture. The Borders are famous for their green, sheep-grazed hills, but today Borderers are learning to accept afforestation as a competing use for this hill land.

The Silurian rocks of much of the Tweed Valley have been subject to extreme folding, which explains the rolling landscape with many a hollow to hold the mosses or mires so prized by naturalists. There is also a broad band of Devonian old red sandstone, easily recognisable in the architecture and red soils from Jedburgh to the Berwickshire coast. Evidence of volcanic activity is conspicuous in the triple peaks of the Eildon Hills and other isolated 'laws', and in spectacular coastal cliffs at St Abbs. The rainfall varies from over 1000mm on the western moors to 600mm in the Merse of Berwickshire. Severe frosts are a feature of the inland valleys, and a cold east wind with sea haar (mist) is prevalent on the Berwickshire coast in spring. The region is relatively sheltered, however, and the encircling hills often break a layer of cloud to dapple the landscape with sunshine.

The short coastline is rocky, with the highest cliffs in eastern Scotland. On the cliff ledges between St Abbs and Fastcastle seabirds nest in such numbers that they are of international importance. Offshore the exceptionally clear coastal waters support a marine life that is unusually rich for the generally murky North Sea; this interest is already acknowledged by the expanding scope of marine reserves around Eyemouth and St Abbs. The passage of bird migrants is very evident in spring and autumn, and the mixed habitats of the ST ABBS HEAD reserve are a happy hunting ground for birdwatchers. Steep grassy slopes among the coastal cliffs provide some of the richest grasslands remaining in the Borders, and here cowslip, early-purple orchid and wood vetch occur in abundance, as well as more maritime flowers.

The importance of the Tweed river system has received formal recognition by the Nature Conservancy Council. It contains many fish in addition to its famous salmon, but the otter which was widespread until a decade ago has now almost disappeared and mink have become common. Kingfisher are scarce, but the winter wildfowl are impressive with a large population of whooper swan. The vegetation of the lower reaches is somewhat marred by aliens, including forests of giant hogweed and the gaudy Indian balsam. In the upper reaches there are many fine river valleys including the Tweed itself at Tweedsmuir, Yarrow with St Mary's Loch, Ettrick, Teviotdale and the Jed Water. All these valleys have a varied wildlife interest and dipper are frequent everywhere, while ring ouzel breed by the higher burns. However, the wet meadows full of globeflower that

521

were a feature of such areas as Teviothead a century ago have been lost to agriculture.

Large lochs are scarce, consisting of St Mary's Loch in the west, and HOSELAW and YETHOLM Lochs together beneath the Cheviots. These last two are reserves and hold large wintering wildfowl populations including geese and wigeon. Elsewhere the wildfowl move between smaller lochs and the rivers in response to the availability of food supplies and to disturbance.

The mosses of the Borders are nationally important but relatively unknown: six of them are included in the Scottish Wildlife Trust reserves. Raised bogs, valley bogs, basin mires and fen are all well represented and occur at a variety of altitudes and in different water regimes. Unlike the long-lost ancient fens of the Berwickshire Merse, none of these mosses with their associated carr of willow and birch is large enough for its bird life to be exceptional, but they support a wide range of specialised plants and insects including some rare water beetles. Characteristic plants include greater spearwort, coralroot orchid and holy-grass. Most of the mosses have been disturbed by drainage and peat digging in the past, but perhaps the greatest threat today is the run-off, from adjacent arable land, of fertiliser and sprays.

Throughout the Borders one may still find rocky hillsides that have escaped the plough, where superb banks of rock-rose are mixed with fragrant thyme and locally with maiden pink. Mountain pansy is also abundant in these grasslands and butterflies such as common blue may be plentiful; the number of species is limited, but sometimes includes Scotch argus. These grasslands now need more protection.

Ancient deciduous woodland is rare in the Borders and is generally limited to fragments on steep river banks and up the hill burns; centuries of border warfare and intensive sheep farming have contributed to this. Way-marked countryside walks developed by the initiative of the Borders Regional Council lead through several of the remaining woodland areas, as by the Whiteadder at Abbey St Bathans, the Tweed at St Boswells and again at Neidpath Castle by Peebles. Red squirrel are still common in these areas.

There are nationally important moorlands including the superb landscape of the Tweedsmuir Hills, the wild wastes of the Langholm to Newcastleton Hills, the grouse moors of the Moorfoot Hills, Kielderhead Moor high on the Cheviots and the lowland Greenlaw Moor. Wild goat and mountain hare inhabit the high tops and, on a few crags, raven and peregrine still nest. These hills appear well rounded, but they conceal many a steep-sided cleuch with hidden botanical riches.

Some of the new conifer forests have been planted with sympathy to the wildlife interest by leaving a proportion of open ground, especially along the burns. Here the inevitable roe deer have prospered together with, more locally, the even more damaging sika deer; among birds that have found a place here are black grouse, long-eared owl, crossbill and siskin. Such gains to wildlife do something to balance the continuing losses of many habitats to agriculture.

MICHAEL E. BRAITHWAITE

Bemersyde Moss

Permit only; 27ha; SWT reserve
Marsh
April–August

Willow carr and continuous reed canary-grass and sedge marshland surround a central mosaic of open pools and marsh vegetation on this rather wet moss. Nodding bur-marigold and celery-leaved buttercup are among the less common plants present. About 2000 pairs of black-headed gull breed on the moss and grasshopper warbler is a typical species of the willow carr. Many wildfowl visit in winter, when the outflow is adjusted so that the open water area is more extensive.

Dunhog Moss and Hare Moss

Permit only; 4ha; SWT reserve
Peat bog and fen; loch with reedbeds
July–September

Both these small mosses are noteworthy for their water beetles; 23 species have been recorded, some of them relics of the ice ages. *Hydroporus glabriusculus* is known in Britain only from this site and a few other localities in the Borders Region. *Hydroporus elongatus* is similarly restricted but with one outlying site in Ayrshire. The complex of willow carr and marshland at Dunhog includes an interesting sequence from acid bog to base-rich fen with sedge–bryophyte communities and three species of tussock-sedge, all of local distribution in southern Scotland. Grass-of-Parnassus is plentiful at Dunhog and there are colonies of ringlet and Scotch argus butterflies there. Little grebe and tufted duck breed on Hare Moss, which was dammed in the 1960s to create a lochan, and now has extensive reedbeds.

Duns Castle

NT 778550; 77ha; SWT reserve
Loch, mixed woodland and grassland
Leaflet from SWT
April–July

In late spring this mixed woodland reserve is a riot of colour, with great drifts of early-blooming wild flowers. In some areas ramsons carpets the ground, elsewhere there is a sea of bluebells, or vivid red campion or purple wood crane's-bill; meadowsweet, foxglove and water avens continue the succession. Even the conifer plantations here have a green ferny floor. Beech dominates much of the woodland but there are also fine mature oak and

ash and occasional stands of slender poplars, their silvery grey leaves rustling gently in the breeze. In addition to the many well-known woodland plants the reserve contains some less familiar species, including toothwort, common twayblade and the waxy-flowered common wintergreen.

A good variety of birds inhabits the woodlands. Five species of tit have been recorded, including the very local marsh tit. Pied flycatcher breed regularly in the nest boxes provided and chiffchaff are among the warblers present.

The Hen Poo, an artificial loch of 7ha, provides additional habitat diversity. Yellow iris, bulrush and bogbean grow on the marshy margins and the plate-like leaves of yellow water-lily float on the surface. There are water shrew and tench in the loch and otter occasionally visit, while badger, roe deer and red squirrel occur in the woodland.

A network of rides and grassy glades crisscrosses the whole area and these sheltered spots, together with the variety of food plants present, ensure that the reserve is rich in butterflies and moths. The delicately marked green-veined white and more vividly coloured orange tip are among the butterflies recorded.

Yellow water-lily covers much of the Hen Poo at Duns Castle.

Gordon Moss

Permit only; 41ha; SWT reserve
Peat bog with scrub woodland
May–August

The superficially uniform lichen-covered jungle over much of this moss conceals a considerable diversity of habitat which is due to the effect of old peat workings and to the presence of strong springs of mineral-rich water. The woodland includes birch, willow (six species), alder and aspen and shelters roe deer and a varied bird population. Six species of orchid, including coralroot orchid and lesser butterfly-orchid, occur; lesser wintergreen, moonwort and greater spearwort are also present. The site is a good one not only for its plants but also for its entomological interest. It is a locality for a number of moths which are of limited distribution in Scotland; these include small chocolate tip, miller, northern drab, powdered Quaker and beautiful carpet. Gordon Moss also supports a colony of small pearl-bordered fritillary butterflies.

Hoselaw Loch and Din Moss

Permit only; 25ha; SWT reserve
Open water and raised bog
October–March: wildfowl; July: flowers

Situated at 200m and surrounded by farmland, the
12ha Hoselaw Loch is an important refuge for wintering wildfowl. Flocks of pink-footed and greylag
geese, mallard and wigeon use the open water for
roosting, and diving duck such as goldeneye,
pochard, tufted duck and goosander feed there
regularly. Curlew, lapwing and snipe frequent the
muddy shores in summer. The domed peat of Din
Moss is up to 10m deep and carries heather, crowberry, bilberry and cranberry. Along the edge a
strip of alder, birch and willow, with a few pines,
provides cover for roe deer and woodland birds.
Where bog and loch meet there is a rich fen vegetation with cowbane and greater pond-sedge.

Lindean Reservoir

NT 5128; 7.5ha; Borders RC
Reservoir with island and woodland
Hide; leaflet from BRC; further information from
BRC ranger, tel. St Boswells 2330
April–August

The western end of this reservoir, also used for
angling, is managed as a nature reserve. The
mineral-rich water supports a good variety of
aquatic life. Some 200 flowering plants have been
recorded in the area, among them grass-of-
Parnassus, skullcap and early marsh-orchid. The
reservoir is locally important for breeding and
wintering duck; whinchat, sedge warbler and linnet breed in the area.

St Abbs Head

NT 9168; 77ha; NTS–SWT reserve
Sea cliffs and grassland
Leaflet from NTS, SWT reserve ranger, or at car park
May–July: breeding birds; October: migration

Spectacular cliff scenery, a vast seabird colony,
rich marine life and a varied flora make this a site
of unusually diverse interest. For many visitors the
birds nesting on the precipitous lava cliffs provide
the main attraction. Some 10,000 guillemot breed
here, packed in serried ranks on steeply sloping
ledges and the tops of stacks. Several thousand
kittiwake cling to the smaller peaks and pinnacles;
brooding razorbill, wings adroop, tuck themselves
into the larger niches; and fulmar cackle from
ledges surrounded by hanging gardens of common
scurvygrass, thrift and sea campion.

Deep gaps or inlets give good cliff viewing in
many places, while the headlands afford extensive
views out to sea. In summer flights of gannet pass
to and from their BASS ROCK breeding ground, but
it is during migration periods, especially in
autumn, that the greatest variety of bird species
occurs. Sooty and Manx shearwater regularly pass
offshore, as do arctic and great skua. The Mire
Loch is visited by waders pausing there on their
travels. The small passerines recorded include such
uncommon visitors as red-breasted flycatcher,
greenish warbler and yellow-browed warbler,
wind-drifted across the North Sea to this
prominent stretch of coast.

Behind the cliffs short-turfed grassland rolls in
a series of humps and hollows down to the narrow
ribbon of the Mire Loch in the valley bottom. Some
of the humps are of mineral-rich rock; others give

St Abbs Head is notable for its spectacular scenery, seabirds, plants and rich marine life.

The Eildon Hills, rising above the rolling Border countryside.

rise to acid soil. The vegetation is correspondingly varied. Above Pettico Wick the natural rock garden is bright with yellow common rock-rose and bird's-foot-trefoil, dark purple mats of thyme, pink thrift and the dainty white stars of spring sandwort. Tormentil and milkwort flourish in the more acid areas; wood sage and foxglove grow near the wind-bowed hawthorns and sycamores by the loch; and tiny plants of purple milk-vetch abound along the cliff top.

The reserve's insect life is varied. Migrant species include Camberwell beauty butterfly and the large and spectacular death's head hawkmoth. More regularly seen are small copper, common blue and grayling butterflies and some of the larger day-flying moths, such as yellow shell, silver Y and colourful six-spot burnet.

Strong tides sweep along this exposed stretch of coast and help to ensure that the sea remains unpolluted. Skin divers and marine biologists take advantage of the good conditions to study the life of the submarine kelp forests which can be no more than glimpsed from land, and even then only at very low tide.

Yetholm Loch

Permit only; 26ha; SWT reserve
Loch and marshland
No access to marsh during breeding season
July: flowers; October–March: wildfowl

The marshland at the inflow end of the loch provides the principal interest of this site, which is enriched by drainage from the surrounding farmland. The vegetation types represented include willow carr and greater spearwort–bottle sedge fen. Great crested grebe, shoveler, teal and pochard breed regularly; winter visitors include whooper swan, pink-footed goose and large numbers of duck.

Central

The majestic peaks and shapely ridges of the southern Grampians, from Ben Lomond in the west to Ben Vorlich in the east, occupy almost half of Central Region and beckon the northbound visitor. However, the charm of these distant hills is only one of several attractions in a small area of Scotland in which scenic variety is the key to diversity of wildlife.

The changes in landscape from north to south are quite dramatic. North of the Highland Boundary Fault are windswept, towering bens and steep-sided, often loch-filled glens. These have been moulded by moving ice from a base of ancient sediments which were altered and contorted beyond imagination to form massive folds of schist, slate and grit, of which only the foundations now remain.

South of the bisecting fault are the abrupt humps of the Menteith Hills and the gentler terrain of the Braes of Doune, which are formed of sloping sandstone beds, liberally speckled with quartzite pebbles to form 'plum-pudding' rock. Continuing southward, these uplands suddenly give way to the flat Carse of Stirling, only a few metres above sea level, even at Aberfoyle. Its clay bottom is patched with peat mosses and incised by the meandering channel of the Forth, which snakes around the dolerite crags of the Stirling Gap. The Forth Estuary expands between levées which protect the eastern carselands of Falkirk and Clackmannan from the salt-laden tides.

Volcanic activity and faulting produced the precipitous south-facing scarp of the Ochil Hills east of Stirling, while later eruptions of lava created the cliff-edged massifs of the Gargunnock Hills and the Campsie Fells to the west. The Campsies terminate above Killearn in the sugar loaf of Dumgoyne, an old volcano. The smooth undulations in Falkirk and Clackmannan, here and there punctuated by heaps of colliery waste, are of glacial drift which covers the coal measures beneath. In the far south the relatively barren peatlands on the rolling Slamannan plateau yield a more accessible fuel source.

Such contrasts in land form and surface water assure the naturalist of a remarkably compact package of plant communities and wildlife habitats, perhaps unrivalled in the rest of Scotland. This is further enhanced by climatic variation; southern-based plants and insects find their northern outpost here, overlooked by hills which contain the southernmost limits of the arctic–alpine communities. Humid Atlantic air, which in a year drops over 2500mm of rain to the east of LOCH LOMOND, soon gives way to more continental influences east of Stirling, where 1000mm of rain in a year is the norm and where plentiful sunshine during the summer months ripens the farmers' hay and cereal crops two weeks earlier than in moist Strathendrick further west.

The hand of man, as elsewhere, has modified most of the native habitats, nowhere more than in the woodlands. In the Highlands especially, forests of oak, and in the far north Scots pine, were relentlessly felled over the centuries until only a few coppiced remnants of the oak were left to regenerate in the Trossachs and by Loch Lomond; mere vestiges of the Caledonian pine forest now exist near Crianlarich. The open hillsides of grass and heather which replaced the woodland support sizeable herds of red deer as well as the hill sheep and cattle, and spring fires indicate management of heather for red grouse on many estates. However, trees are once again growing in expanding conifer plantations, particularly in Strathyre and in the QUEEN ELIZABETH FOREST PARK, where red squirrel are regaining lost ground and capercaillie lek on forest roads.

The high tops above 800m are perhaps least affected by man and his livestock. Here, alpine turf and dripping rock ledges provide a paradise for botanists, notably on the northern hills of Breadalbane (see BEN LAWERS, Tayside), the Braes o' Balquhidder and on BEN LUI, where saxifrages, speedwells and a host of other plants nestle on the least accessible spots. Here too, the birdwatcher may be lucky enough to glimpse a soaring golden eagle or watch ptarmigan play hide-and-seek among lichen-covered rocks. Further south, the warmer southern slopes of the Ochils have a distinctive flora, while the wooded gorges on the fringes of these uplands, such as DOLLAR GLEN and BALLAGAN GLEN in the Campsies, have much of interest for all kinds of naturalists.

The freshwater lochs in the Highland zone, like Loch Katrine, utilised for its pure water, tend to be deep and cold. But where rivers flow in, valuable wetlands develop on the alluvial soils; the Laggan Fen area where the River Balvaig joins Loch Lubnaig contains several rare plants within its sedge-beds. In addition to the ubiquitous brown trout, char haunt Lubnaig's depths, and in the northern basin of Loch Lomond, the unique powan thrives. The small hill lochans, often set amid treacherous *Sphagnum* bogs, have breeding ducks and gulls; here and there rarer species like greenshank can occur. Of the lowland lochs, the best known is the Lake of Menteith whose reed-bordered bays are a summer home to great crested grebe. The Endrick mouth on the Loch Lomond reserve has attracted many rare birds, but its large wintering wildfowl population and wetland plant communities are more important; so too are the large flocks of duck which assemble on the man-made GARTMORN DAM.

FLANDERS MOSS on the carse west of Stirling is the largest raised valley bog in Britain; here a feeling of wilderness is sensed despite the surrounding arable fields. The peat vegetation supports rare insects and a huge gull colony covers the northern part, outside the reserve area. Nearby, otter inhabit the banks of the Forth as they do most major streams; the Region's rivers with their wooded banks and flood-plain meadows add an important element to the lowland wildlife scene.

It is the Forth Estuary, teeming with invertebrate fodder for the nationally important numbers of wintering wildfowl and waders on its mudflats, which deserves the final words. The out-of-season visitor should pay a visit to SKINFLATS when the incoming tide sneaks towards the salt-marsh edge on a February evening, sharpening the brilliant orange reflections of the refinery flares over Grangemouth. The sight of several thousand waders in massed flight against this backdrop brings into focus the urgent need to protect this most precious and vulnerable of the Region's natural assets.

W. R. BRACKENRIDGE

Ballagan Glen

Permit only; 5ha; SWT reserve
Wooded gorge with rock exposures
Part of the reserve is dangerous
April–June

More than 200 species of flowering plants and ferns have been recorded in this steep and well-wooded glen, which is of geological importance for its exposed Ballagan Beds, a series of narrow bands of variously coloured sandstones. These, forming part of the 45m high west wall of the glen, are very unstable and consequently dangerous.

About 150 species of mosses and liverworts occur. Where the sandstone boulders in the stream bed are kept constantly damp by spray from the falls the liverworts *Scapania aspera* and *Cololejeunea* and the moss *Eucalypta ciliata* are present.

Ben Lui

NN 2626; 798ha; NCC reserve
Mountainous area
Intending visitors should notify warden at NCC, Balloch
June–July

The northern cliffs of 1200m high Ben Lui are well known for their rich mountain flora. On and below the outcropping mica schists and limestone the vegetation is particularly luxuriant and interesting. On the cliff ledges are large patches of mossy, purple and yellow saxifrage, and round-leaved wintergreen occurs alongside roseroot, globe-flower and alpine saw-wort. Mountain avens, mountain bladder-fern and alpine bartsia are particularly abundant.

Mosses and liverworts flourish around Ballagan Falls.

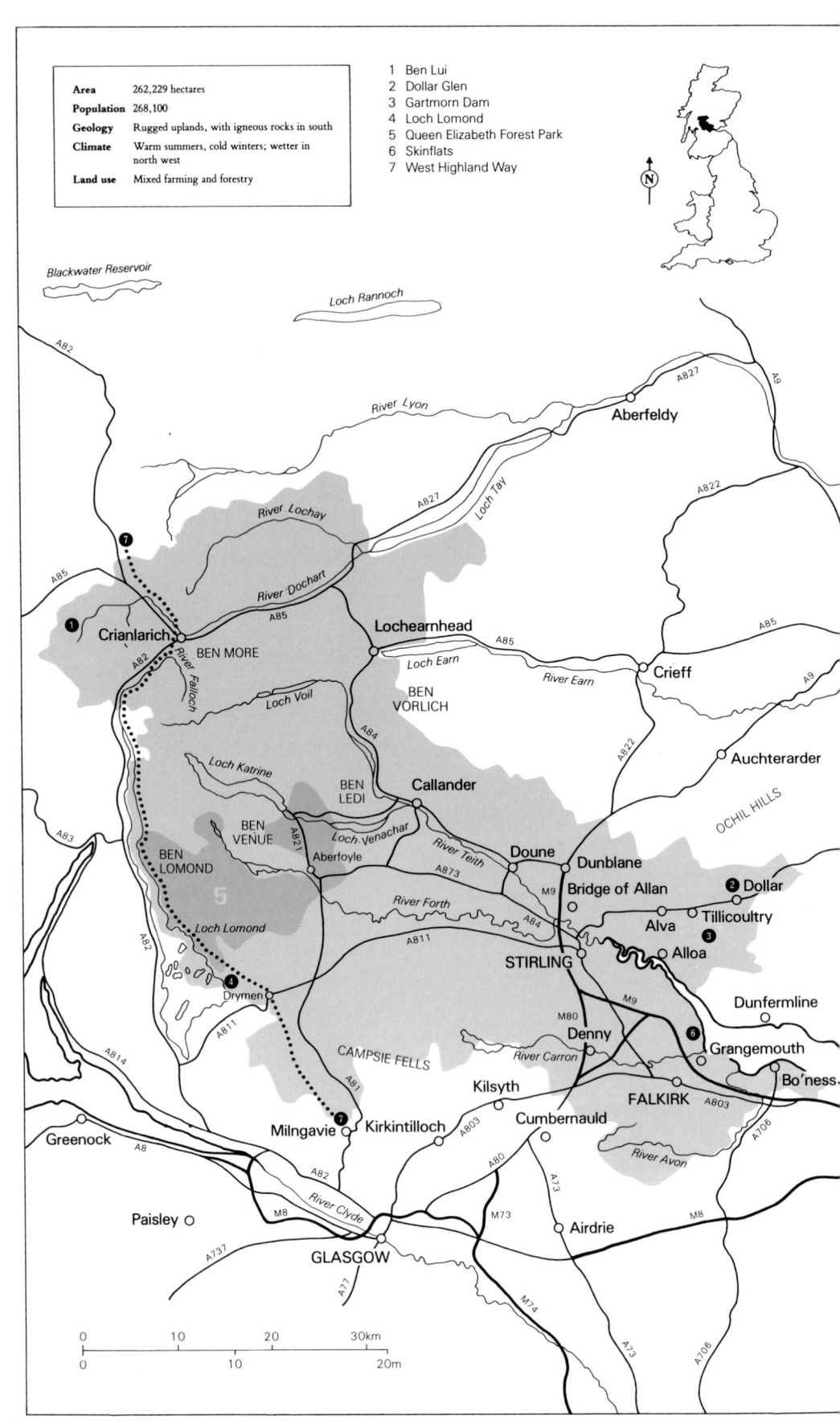

Area	262,229 hectares
Population	268,100
Geology	Rugged uplands, with igneous rocks in south
Climate	Warm summers, cold winters; wetter in north west
Land use	Mixed farming and forestry

1 Ben Lui
2 Dollar Glen
3 Gartmorn Dam
4 Loch Lomond
5 Queen Elizabeth Forest Park
6 Skinflats
7 West Highland Way

N

Blackwater Reservoir

Loch Rannoch

River Lyon

Aberfeldy

A82

A827

A9

A827

A822

River Lochay

Loch Tay

A85

River Dochart

A85

A827

7

1 Crianlarich

BEN MORE

River Falloch

Lochearnhead

Loch Earn

River Earn

Crieff

A85

A85

A9

BEN VORLICH

Loch Voil

A84

Auchterarder

Loch Katrine

BEN LEDI

Callander

A822

OCHIL HILLS

BEN VENUE

Loch Venachar

River Teith

Doune

A821

Aberfoyle

A873

Dunblane

M9

Bridge of Allan

2 Dollar

BEN LOMOND

5

River Forth

Alva

Tillicoultry

3

A84

STIRLING

Alloa

Loch Lomond

A82

A811

Dunfermline

4 Drymen

M80

M9

A814

CAMPSIE FELLS

A811

Denny

6

Grangemouth

River Carron

FALKIRK

A803

Bo'ness

Kilsyth

Cumbernauld

A706

Greenock

A8

7 Milngavie

Kirkintilloch

A803

River Avon

A80

A73

A706

Paisley

M8

River Clyde

M73

Airdrie

M8

A737

GLASGOW

A77

M74

A73

A706

0	10	20	30km

0	10	20m

Loch Lomond, seen from Inchcailloch. The two islands lie along the Highland Boundary Fault.

Dollar Glen

NS 9699; 24ha; NTS
Wooded glen
Paths can be dangerous after rain
April–June

Oak is predominant in the woodland clothing the steep slopes but there is also some ash, wych elm and sycamore. In spring ramsons, celandine, wood sorrel and dog's mercury carpet the ground, with mosses and golden-saxifrage in the steepest and dampest parts of the gorge. The summer woodland birds include wood warbler and spotted flycatcher.

Flanders Moss

Permit only; 45ha; SWT reserve
Raised peat bog
April–June

This is one of the least disturbed sections of the very extensive bog which once filled the upper Forth Valley. Much of the bog is wet, with *Sphagnum* actively growing in open pools and abundant cottongrass. Heather dominates the drier areas and there is a fringe of birch woodland, giving way to purple moor-grass and bog myrtle along the outer edge of the moss. Cranberry is quite widespread and bog-rosemary, a very local species, is present.

Gartmorn Dam

NS 9294; 67.6ha; Clackmannan DC
Reservoir with wooded island and shoreline scrub
Hide; visitor centre; leaflet from countryside ranger, Gartmorn Dam House, Sauchie, Alloa, tel. Alloa 214319
All year

This locally important site for wintering wildfowl holds up to 1500 mallard in midwinter, over 100 tufted duck, and smaller numbers of teal, wigeon, pochard and goldeneye. Greylag geese and whooper swan occasionally visit and a few great crested grebe attempt to breed. Three species of orchid and a wide range of aquatic plants are found.

Loch Lomond

NS 3598; 416ha; NCC reserve
Islands and marshy shoreline
Access to mainland section restricted; contact reserve warden, 22 Muirpark Way, Drymen, for advice; organised groups intending to visit Inchcailloch should contact NCC, Balloch Reserve leaflet from NCC, Balloch; Inchcailloch Nature Trail (4km) leaflet from village shop or boatyard, Balmaha
May–July: breeding birds and flowers; October–December: wildfowl

This, the largest freshwater lake in Britain, is famous for the beauty of its wooded shores and islands, its unusual variety of fish, and the winter concentrations of wildfowl near its south east corner. All are represented within the reserve which includes the five islands of Inchcailloch, Torrinch, Creinch, Clairinsh and Aber Isle, the marshy hinterland around the mouth of the River Endrick and part of the mainland shore.

Inchcailloch, the largest island, carries a fine example of the woodlands typical of this southern end of the loch and found also in the nearby QUEEN ELIZABETH FOREST PARK. Sessile oak is the dominant species, with alder and ash in the damper areas, Scots pine crowning the rocky summits, and guelder-rose, willow and bog myrtle along the shore. The island lies astride the Highland Boundary Fault and so has a variety of soil types with their associated ground flora. Conglomerate sandstone underlies about two-thirds of the island and forms the main ridge; beneath the oaks great woodrush flourishes. A band of serpentine separates this area from the old red sandstone to the north and provides conditions suitable for lime-loving plants such as maidenhair spleenwort, woodruff, dog's mercury and sanicle. Wavy hair-grass, honeysuckle, heather and bilberry dominate the ground cover on the more acid soils. These oakwoods support a large insect population and there are abundant caterpillars for the woodland birds. The

529

Wildfowl frequent the sheltered and marshy south east corner of Loch Lomond.

density of wood, willow and garden warblers is particularly high; redstart, tree pipit, great spotted woodpecker and jay also breed.

The most notable fish is the powan, popularly known as the freshwater herring, which is of very limited distribution in Britain. Salmon, sea trout and brown trout are widespread, whereas roach and perch are confined to the richer waters of the southern end. The aquatic invertebrate fauna includes a number of species known from very few other Scottish sites.

A patchwork of swamp, lagoons, fen and willow carr lies to the south of the slow-flowing, meandering River Endrick. Reed canary-grass lines the drainage channels, mats of bogbean, nodding bur-marigold and cowbane float on some of the pools and others are overgrown with mare's-tail, water horsetail and tufted loosestrife. The swamp is colourful in summer with yellow iris, yellow loosestrife, purple-loosestrife, skullcap, marsh willowherb and marsh forget-me-not. Angelica, meadowsweet, bittersweet and cuckooflower flourish where the ground is slightly drier.

The wildfowl breeding population is not large but several thousand ducks and geese spend at least part of the winter in this area. Greylag geese and whooper swan occur regularly and up to 100 Greenland white-fronted geese are sometimes present. Tufted duck, pochard, goldeneye and a few shoveler use the area, with very much larger numbers of mallard, teal and wigeon. If low water levels, exposing the invertebrate-rich mud, happen to coincide with migration periods waders, too, are attracted to the Endrick mouth: over the years no fewer than thirty-two species have been recorded there.

Queen Elizabeth Forest Park

See map; includes six sites
Guide, maps and leaflet on forest walks from David Marshall Lodge, open daily 9.30a.m.–6p.m. *April–October*

To many people the Trossachs, on the eastern edge of this area, are the epitome of Highland scenery. In the words of Sir Walter Scott, this is a

> Land of brown heath and shaggy wood,
> Land of the mountain and the flood.

The heather and bracken-covered moorland rises above the tree line and many of the 'shaggy' oak-woods remain. Ben Lomond and Ben Venue tower above the surrounding hills and the numerous streams and rivers are regularly swollen by flood water. The Queen Elizabeth Forest Park is a Mecca for tourists and also for day visitors from central Scotland.

Much of the western section remains unplanted. Along the eastern shore of LOCH LOMOND are semi-natural oakwoods, in early May alive with birdsong. Particularly noticeable are the shivering trill and plaintive 'teu-teu-teu' of wood warbler, high in the canopy, and the more varied song of tree pipit, floating downwards in their 'parachute' display flight. The ground cover varies. In some parts primroses nestle among the roots, and as the trees come into leaf the woodland is carpeted with lesser celandine, bluebell, dog's mercury and wood-sorrel. Elsewhere there is a jumble of mossy mounds and bilberry humps, with occasional clumps of heather and many small rowan saplings.

Above the band of conifers that backs the shoreline oakwood, the lower slopes of Ben

Lomond carry heather, cross-leaved heath and bracken, dotted with birch regeneration and straggling, shoulder-high bog myrtle. Redpoll and willow warbler are common and green tiger beetles sun themselves on the path. On this western side of the Ben patches of slender rush occur, mats of yellow saxifrage go right down to the loch side, and the delicate silvery-leaved alpine lady's-mantle grows as low as 300m. The flora is richest where streams come tumbling down the slopes, for example around the Bealach Buidhe burn. There globeflower, starry and mossy saxifrages and lesser clubmoss flourish, as do the tiny moss-like Wilson's and Tunbridge filmy-ferns.

Higher still on Ben Lomond, on both the upper grasslands and the crags and corries, the variety of arctic–alpines is impressive. Graceful fairy flax dances in the short turf with alpine meadow-rue, sibbaldia, cloudberry and spiky cushions of cyphel. On the crags purple saxifrage, moss campion, wood crane's-bill, mountain pansy, wild thyme and red campion contribute a variety of hues. Less colourful, but of equal interest, are holly fern, net-leaved willow, hoary whitlowgrass, mountain bladder-fern and interrupted clubmoss.

A few ptarmigan frequent the highest summits, and there are raven around the crags and ring ouzel in the corries. The lower moorland holds breeding curlew, skylark and meadow pipit, with occasional pairs of hen harrier and merlin. Northern eggar moths, a large day-flying species associated with heather moors, are one source of food for merlin chicks; their wings may be found scattered around the cock bird's plucking post, among the half-grown wing feathers of fledgling meadow pipits. Red deer and mountain hare are present in moderate numbers on the hills.

The woodlands are perhaps at their most diverse around Aberfoyle and Loch Ard, a mosaic of natural woodland and plantations that vary in age and species. Juniper among birch, spruce beside larch – such contrasts of form and colour belie the myth that afforested areas are monotonous. Species typical of coniferous woodland are found here: the thin, wavering song of goldcrest comes from every stand of well-grown spruce, and red squirrel shred the cones of Scots pine. Here too are species associated with deciduous woodland: oak and birch harbour tree pipit and great spotted and green woodpecker. Roe deer and wren take advantage of both worlds, feeding in the more open areas and finding cover in the denser plantations.

The oakwoods in the park and around the east end of Loch Katrine include examples on both acid and mineral-rich soils. Some, long protected from grazing, have a very natural ground flora, while others, among them the Fairy Knowe wood near Aberfoyle, have been woodland sites for at least 200 years.

The lochs, large and small, add to the charm of the area as well as to its natural history interest. Where Loch Lomond's shore is of sand and shingle, miniature storm beaches are formed by the wind-blown waves and are soon colonised by skullcap and gipsywort. Pied wagtail feed on insects along the 'tide line' and common gull occupy the rocky islands near Rowardennan Pier. Reed-fringed Dubh Loch, sheltered in contrast, holds little grebe and sometimes goosander. Mallard, teal and tufted duck occur regularly on the larger lochs within the park, and small numbers of wigeon, goldeneye and

A panorama of woods, moorland and hills north of Aberfoyle.

pochard are often on Loch Ard, Loch Chon and Loch Achray. Common sandpiper, dipper and grey wagtail are frequent along the streams and rivers, heron fish in shallows, and both water vole and otter are known to be present. Some of the lochs are of botanical interest, having marsh and fen communities of types that are scarce in this part of Scotland.

For many visitors the David Marshall Lodge (NN 520015) on a rocky knoll above Aberfoyle is the first stopping place. Its windows offer panoramic views of the hills and forests, and it contains an exhibition on the history and wildlife of the area. From here a short woodland trail leads through the forest to a waterfall. Heading northwards from the Lodge the Duke's Road climbs to a viewpoint above Loch Achray, passing abandoned slate quarries where a tunnel used by hibernating bats has been protected from disturbance by a metal grille. Stonechat can often be seen perched on the gorse bushes along this route.

Not far from the viewpoint at NN 515033 a forest drive branches off right and winds for 11km past Lochan Reoidhte, with its white water-lilies, along the shores of Loch Drunkie, and down to Loch Achray. Dragonflies hawk around these lochs and along the forest tracks, and butterflies flit across the sunny clearings. Many of the steep trackside banks are carpeted with mosses. At numerous stopping places it is possible to leave one's car and explore on foot, or sit by the loch shores watching birds and insects.

The park as a whole offers a wide selection of walking routes, ranging from short circular trails to the five-hour climb to the summit of Ben Lomond and back. Many of these routes, totalling over 110km in length, have been waymarked. An attractive section of the WEST HIGHLAND WAY runs through Rowardennan Forest on Loch Lomondside and among other cross-country routes are the paths from Aberfoyle to Callander along the Menteith Hills, and from Brig o' Turk through the hills to Balquhidder. Be properly equipped, and carry a map and compass, when tackling any of the hill routes. There is also a wayfaring course in Achray Forest, and three centres organising pony treks along the forest tracks, as well as the Achray Forest Drive for motor vehicles.

Skinflats

NN 9385; 410ha; RSPB reserve
Inter-tidal mudflats and foreshore
Access restricted; contact RSPB, Edinburgh for advice
September–March

This stretch of the upper Forth is of major importance for passage and wintering waders and wildfowl in an area increasingly subject to industrial development and disturbance. In winter it holds virtually the entire Forth population of pintail, an exceedingly local species in Scotland, and a very large concentration of shelduck. Significant gatherings of knot, redshank, dunlin, curlew and golden plover are a feature of the area, and a wide variety of species, including terns and arctic skua, has been recorded during autumn migration.

West Highland Way

NS 896744 – NN 113743; 152km; Central, Highland and Strathclyde RCs
Long-distance way through woodland, moor and mountain
Official guide and map from bookshops
All year

The first officially designated long-distance footpath in Scotland offers a superb walk of varied character through fine scenery. The path goes through woodland on the shores of LOCH LOMOND, over high moorland and through the wild and rugged mountainous country around GLENCOE (Highland South), and on via Glen Nevis to Fort William; the wildlife interest is correspondingly varied. Since much of the route is exposed and sparsely inhabited, adequate planning and equipment are essential pre-requisites for anyone intending to walk the full length of the Way.

The Loch Lomond dock grows on the fringes of wet land, and occurs only in the Loch Lomond area.

Dumfries and Galloway

A striking diversity of habitats is found here over a short distance: coastal mudflats, extensive salt-marshes, coastal and river valley oak woodlands, lowland grassland, lochs and south-flowing rivers, and heather moorland leading to uplands with arctic plant communities. The Region's south-facing aspect and geographical position have brought together a unique assemblage of plant and animal species at both their northern and southern limits. Its climate makes Dumfries and Galloway the Devon and Cornwall of Scotland; the coastal strip is mild and dry, but the hilly areas experience higher rainfall, days of snow cover and a quick decrease in temperature.

The Region consists of a line of uplands extending from eastern Wigtownshire to the Moffat Hills in Dumfriesshire. The lower Palaeozoic sediments are intensely folded, with major granite intrusions. Adjacent to the granite is a ring of outcrops of metamorphosed rock. The ridges of the Merrick (843m), the Rhinns of Kells (813m) and Lamachan (716m) all arise above the inner granite basin of the Loch Doon pluton.

The landscape of Galloway has been shaped by the long-continued effect of the rivers and the short-lived influence of the ice ages, and their melt-waters, on the foundation rocks. In the upland areas the forces of erosion are much more apparent than are those of deposition. Classic glaciation features are present at White Coomb in the Moffat Hills, with south-facing corries and a morainic dammed lake, and in the GREY MARE'S TAIL which is the best example of a hanging valley in the Southern Uplands. Galloway is the site of an ancient icecap, and glacial troughs occur at Loch Doon and Loch Trool.

Below 303m are the lowlands where glacial deposition has been the chief landscape-forming influence. Extensive drumlin fields occur between Kirkcowan and Burrow Head, Wigtownshire, and persist eastwards towards Dumfriesshire where at Locharbriggs there are impressive kame deposits.

The upland areas were formerly devoted to sheep farming, but its pre-war decline enabled the Forestry Commission to buy very large land holdings. By 1980, 187,500ha was under conifer afforestation, 30 per cent of the region's land area. Throughout the region dairy farming is important; some areas now rear beef, and there is subsidiary arable farming especially on the low ground. Sheep and stock rearing tend to dominate the unplanted moorland areas.

Much of coastal Galloway, parts of the Stewartry, and Dumfriesshire consist of raised beaches. In early spring the coastal cliffs of the south west are covered with the blue shimmer of spring squill. The south-facing aspect of the coast-line, shell-rich soils, and the occasional iron-rich podzols contribute to the unusual plant associations. Scots lovage is at its southern limit here and golden samphire at its northern one. Locally along the shingle are patches of oysterplant, a relic of former arctic plant communities.

The sand dune complex of Torrs Warren is of outstanding interest and importance. Solitary bees find the warm sandy soil ideal for egg laying, and butterflies such as pearl-bordered fritillary, dingy skipper and common blue are found here too. The coastal areas are the haunt of peregrine and raven; the latter was once common in upland areas, but afforestation and the removal of sheep have reduced its range and numbers.

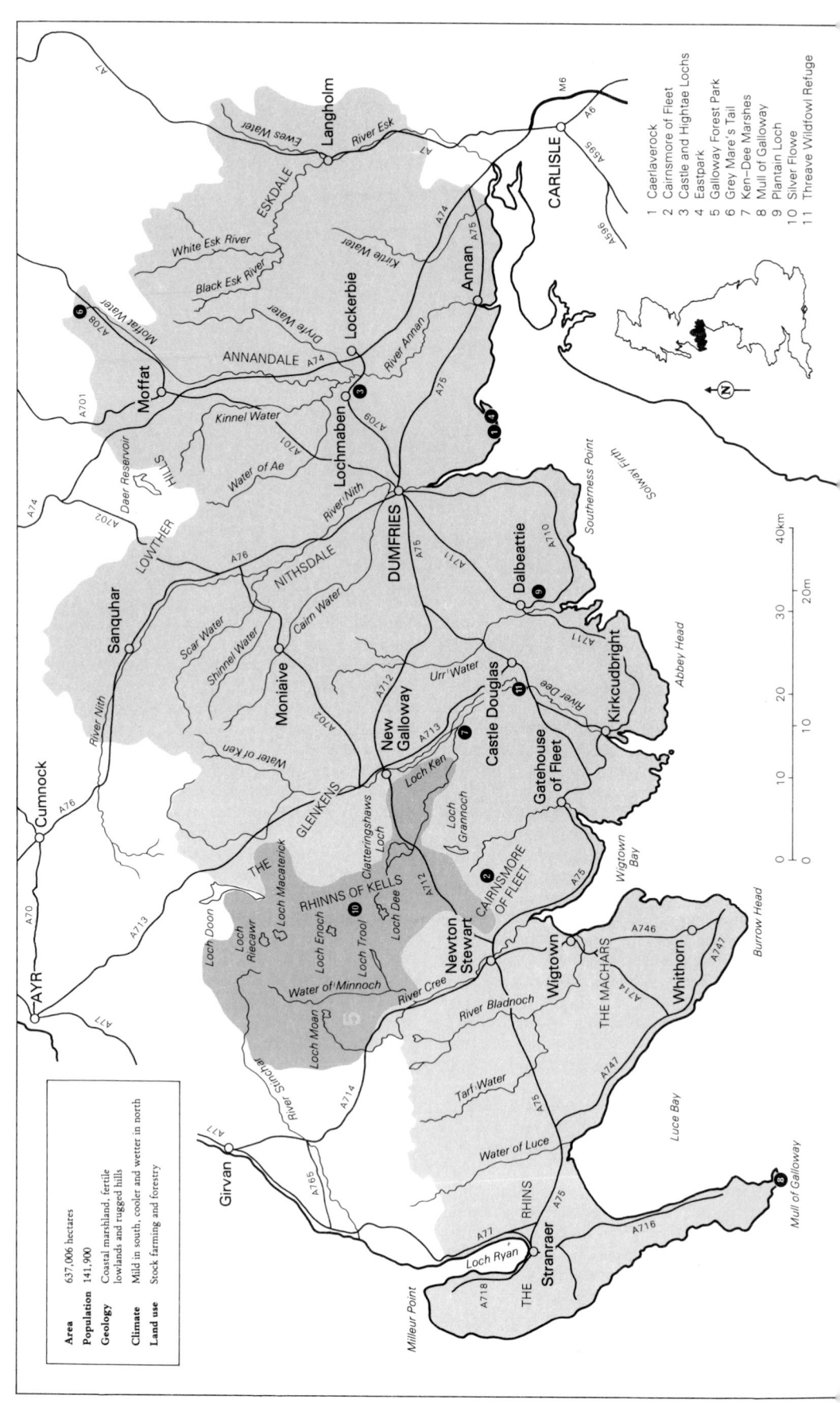

Area 637,006 hectares

Population 141,900

Geology Coastal marshland, fertile lowlands and rugged hills

Climate Mild in south, cooler and wetter in north

Land use Stock farming and forestry

1 Caerlaverock
2 Cairnsmore of Fleet
3 Castle and Hightae Lochs
4 Eastpark
5 Galloway Forest Park
6 Grey Mare's Tail
7 Ken–Dee Marshes
8 Mull of Galloway
9 Plantain Loch
10 Silver Flowe
11 Threave Wildfowl Refuge

The saltmarshes and mudflats of Wigtown Bay, Southwick Merse and the CAERLAVEROCK reserve are the feeding and roosting grounds of pink-footed, greylag and barnacle geese, wigeon, pintail, shelduck and thousands of waders. Up to 10,000 golden plover may career in the clear of a January day, or an elusive cloud of dunlin dance away from a peregrine or merlin. Banks of oystercatcher and trails of curlew occur throughout the Inner and Outer Solway, but it is only at Carse Bay that large gatherings of knot and pintail occur.

At Glencaple and DRUMMAINS the tall reedbeds are bordered by the short sward of sea aster and sea arrowgrass, food plants of the wintering wildfowl. Southerness Merse is the most westerly point in the range of the coastal-breeding natterjack toad, but its stronghold is at Caerlaverock where it breeds in shallow pools and hibernates in sandy banks. The coastal pebble beaches of Galloway at Port William, the saltmarshes and the shingle all provide breeding habitat for waders.

The hinterland contains the agricultural landscape of the Rhinns of Galloway, the home of corn bunting, summering corncrake and in winter hen harrier, which roosts nearby in the largest established roost in Britain. Farming threatens the lowland grassland, and DOWALTON is a sensitive jewel in a busy agricultural landscape. Field gentian, dyer's greenweed, bog pimpernel and dense communities of orchids flower on the floor of a drained loch amid the summer hum of hoverflies.

The dales and low hills occupy an extensive area which was once well wooded, but now the woodland is limited to remnants on inaccessible valley sides. On Shinnel Water, the woods are rich in bird cherry; Scaur Water has ash woodland and at Dryfe Water there is hazel. The size, composition and history of the relict oak woodlands of Castramon, Cree, Caldons, Buchan and Glenhead enable them to make a unique contribution to nature conservation. Cree and Castramon, considered as a unit, are the best example of this ecosystem and contain rich bryophyte communities. Dog's mercury and bluebell grow in profusion. The woodlands also contain pied flycatcher, redstart, green woodpecker, wood warbler and tree pipit, together with purple hairstreak, the localised and declining butterfly which flights in July.

In the lowlands, the glacial deposits and climate have encouraged blanket peat which at Raeburn Flowe still bears typical bog plant communities. Afforestation and peat extraction put the future of such rich ecosystems at risk.

At Lochmaben, Dumfriesshire, the Mill Loch is the habitat of vendace, a relict fish species, and the wetlands of CASTLE AND HIGHTAE LOCHS contain the localised narrow-leaved bulrush. The most extensive wetland within the region is the KEN–DEE complex, noted for its wintering wildfowl. In summer the site contains breeding shoveler and great crested grebe; its shores are surrounded by varied and rich wetland plant communities with numerous dragonflies. The nearby oak woodlands echo on summer evenings to the sound of reeling grasshopper warbler, the yaffle of green woodpecker, and the soft croaks of roding woodcock. The wetlands host that gem of the flood plains, the globeflower. Once again plants at their southern limits, such as spignel, and northern limits, for instance saw-wort, occur. The wetlands of the Upper Cree are dominated by bristle sedge and the river is the haunt of kingfisher, goosander and otter. Carlingwark contains winter gatherings of shoveler, tufted duck and goldeneye, and even the occasional American pied-billed grebe.

The undulating moorland of Grobdale–Laughenghie–Laghead represents probably the best golden plover, curlew and snipe breeding area in the mid-altitude parts of the region. Surrounded by afforestation, this habitat, which also contains ring ouzel, whinchat, kestrel, merlin, hen harrier, short-eared owl, peregrine and golden eagle, characterises the true open hill spirit of Galloway – but for how long?

In the western part of the region the recent increase in acid precipitation, on an acid geology where the main land use is conifer afforestation, gives cause for concern about the lochs and rivers. Afforestation near the edges of water catchment feeder streams exacerbates a water-quality problem at such places as Loch Dee. The increased acidification of waters threatens the successful breeding of trout, salmon and amphibians, together with a range of aquatic invertebrates which form links in the complex food chains. The proposed afforestation of a further 60,000ha by the year 2000 would have serious implications for the overall ecology of the area, in which agriculture, recreation and nature conservation all compete with forestry.

PETER G. HOPKINS

A bluebell glade in Castramon oakwood.

Spitsbergen's entire population of barnacle geese winters on the merse and farmlands of the Solway, especially around Caerlaverock.

Caerlaverock

NY 0365; 5501ha; NCC reserve
Saltmarsh, foreshore and freshwater marsh
The mudflats are dangerous
No access to sanctuary area; recommended access
points at NY 018653 and at Eastpark, NY 052656
Leaflet from watchtower or warden, Tadorna,
Hollands Farm Road, Caerlaverock
October–March

This great saltmarsh or merse is important as one of the largest unreclaimed saltmarshes in Britain, as the most northerly breeding site of the natterjack toad, and as a winter feeding ground for the entire Spitsbergen population of barnacle geese. It is a dangerous area as the flats are intricately laced with deep, muddy creeks which fill with alarming speed as the tide comes in. The wildfowl can be observed most conveniently and safely at EAST-PARK wildfowl refuge, where special facilities are available. Visitors wanting to go out on to the mudflats should first seek advice from the warden.

Since the reserve was established in 1957, and wildfowling controlled by introducing a permit system and a large sanctuary area, the Solway barnacle goose population has increased from about 1000 to over 8000. Up to 5000 pink-footed geese sometimes roost on the merse in the first three months of the year, with small numbers of greylag geese. Also important for pintail, this is one of the few Scottish locations where flocks of 1000 or more are recorded. Several hundred mallard, wigeon and teal spend much of the winter in the area. Large numbers of waders also pass through, with as many as 24 species being recorded in one season. Oystercatcher are by far the most numerous, with the peak roosting numbers, in October, estimated at around 15,000.

Red fescue dominates the vegetation on the merse, which is dotted with sea asters and has unusually extensive populations of saltmarsh flat-sedge and saltmarsh rush. These plant communities provide valuable grazing for cattle in summer as well as for geese in winter. On the western side of the merse the force of wind and tide is resulting in erosion, with great hunks of muddy turf being torn off and deposited on the flats below. At the eastern side, corresponding accretion is taking place.

The thriving colony of natterjack toad, a specially protected species, is based on the pools fringing the saltmarsh. These very vocal creatures find there the warm, shallow, unshaded water necessary for successful breeding.

Cairnsmore of Fleet

NX 5266; 1900ha; NCC reserve
Granite uplands
Access restricted: contact warden, Falbae
Cottage, Falbae, Creetown for advice
Leaflet from warden or NCC, Balloch
June–September

The great granite hump of Cairnsmore, domed on its western flank, falls away to the east in sheer cliffs and steep slab-strewn slopes around a basin of undulating moorland. On much of the lower ground the vegetation is dominated by purple moor-grass, heather and bog myrtle, with bog mosses in the wetter areas. Bare white granite is exposed in many place higher up, but on the long spur below the Knee of Cairnsmore heather-covered peat banks stand proud of the general ground level. No paths or tracks penetrate the interior of the reserve.

The lower ground was formerly grouse moor; more recently it has carried sheep and a flock is still maintained. Past management has included drainage, and stumps buried deep in the peat demonstrate the previous existence of tree cover on the site; present management is aimed at encouraging a more widespread growth of heather.

The Cairnsmore of Fleet is now the only site in the district including unafforested ground through an altitude range from 167m up to the summit at 710m. The reserve is important for upland red deer, feral goat, golden plover and raven. It is also valuable for ecological research, since much of the adjoining ground has been afforested and so permits comparative studies of animal populations in contrasting conditions yet close proximity.

Castle and Hightae Lochs

NY 0881 and 0880; 137ha; Annandale and Eskdale DC reserve
Lochs, reedbeds and woodland fringe
January–March

These lochs are of most interest after the shooting season, when considerable numbers of greylag geese, and sometimes also pink-footed geese, come in to roost on Castle Loch. Smallish numbers of mallard, wigeon and tufted duck are present for much of the winter. Hightae Loch is rich in invertebrates and there is a good variety of warblers, tits and other small birds in the woodlands around the lochs.

Dowalton

Permit only; 61.5ha; SWT reserve
Willow carr and grassland on site of drained lake
Access to some areas restricted March–June
April–June: flowers; November–March: wildfowl

Both dry and wet meadow, as well as willow carr, are represented on this reserve and the correspondingly varied flora includes some 180 flowering plants. Among the more interesting species present are brooklime, lesser water-plantain, marsh pennywort, quaking-grass, dyer's greenweed and several orchids. The drier patches of woodland contain birch, elder, hawthorn and wild roses; five species of warbler are among the birds breeding there. In winter much of the carr and the reed canary-grass is flooded and attracts a variety of duck and also whooper swan. The reserve is rich in dragonflies, hoverflies and butterflies, although surrounded by intensively cultivated farmland.

Drummains Reedbed

Permit only; 5.5ha; SWT reserve
Reedbed and saltings
Hide
April–June: flowers; October–March: wildfowl and waders

Part of the Solway tideflats, this reserve includes farmland, reedbed, saltings and mudflat, and part of the tidal channel of the River Nith. Reed bunting and sedge warbler breed in the reedbeds, which serve as a winter roost for a variety of species. The merse, with its sea plantain, sea aster and common saltmarsh-grass, is grazed in winter by wigeon and barnacle geese. The mudflats support breeding shelduck and a wintering population of pintail, mallard, curlew, oystercatcher and dunlin.

Eastpark

NY 052656; 524ha; WT–NCC reserve
Farmland and tidal merse
Open daily 16 September–30 April (except 24 and 25 December) at 11 a.m. and 2 p.m., no access to merse; all visitors escorted by warden; groups limited to 50, and those of 20 + should book, tel. Glencaple 200.
Observation buildings and hides; educational display; binoculars for hire; leaflet from Eastpark or Slimbridge (Gloucestershire)
Early October–end March

This extensive wildfowl refuge often holds the entire Solway population of barnacle geese and a good variety of other wildfowl, waders and birds of prey. The birds can be observed at close range thanks to comprehensive viewing facilities and the fact that the birds receive minimal disturbance. Most of the farmland around Eastpark was purchased by the Wildfowl Trust to ensure undisturbed feeding grounds, while the merse section lies within the Sanctuary Area of CAERLAVEROCK. A large pond in front of the observation building draws many birds – on occasion 17 wildfowl species – to within 10m or less of the observers.

The flock of up to 8500 barnacle geese provides the most spectacular sight. Hides and towers help to ensure good views of these immaculately patterned birds, on all parts of the refuge. The barnacle geese start arriving from Spitsbergen early in October, reach peak numbers in November, and leave in mid-April. Pink-footed geese arrive later and only reach their maximum of around 3000 in late January or early February. Very much smaller numbers of greylag geese are also fairly regular in winter.

Among the most important and impressive visitors are whooper and Bewick's swan. Whooper numbers are highest in November–December, Bewick's slightly later. Construction of a large decoy-type trap has recently enabled a research programme on the whoopers to be undertaken. The flock of Bewick's swan has been gradually building up since the refuge was established; now over 70, it is by far the largest regular gathering of this species in Scotland.

Over 2000 wigeon and teal winter on the grassland and small numbers of pintail, gadwall, shoveler, pochard and tufted duck are regularly recorded; in recent years blue-winged teal and scaup have been observed. The waders most often seen are curlew, golden plover and lapwing, but many others visit occasionally including long-billed dowitcher, black-tailed godwit and green and wood sandpiper.

At high tide large numbers of waders are sometimes visible on the merse. These, and the duck feeding out on the saltings, attract peregrine, merlin, hen harrier and sparrowhawk, all frequently seen in winter.

Fountainbleau and Ladypark

Permit only; 5.5ha; SWT reserve
Wet woodland
Visitors should keep to the marked path
Nature trail (1km); leaflet from SWT
April–June

Deep drainage ditches criss-cross this woodland, which has a high watertable and frequently floods. As a result abundant rotten birches support prolific fungi and mosses. The decaying stumps are also important as nesting sites for the resident willow tits. Alder grows along the ditches, willows are widespread and a few oak, rowan and hawthorn grow in the driest areas. Marsh cinquefoil, marsh pennywort, marsh thistle, woody nightshade and water-pepper are characteristic plants of the wetter ground, with climbing corydalis and common St John's-wort on drier soil. In summer willow warbler, sedge warbler, reed bunting and redpoll are numerous; long-tailed tit, spotted flycatcher and tree pipit are also known to nest. Water vole and water shrew frequent the ditches and roe deer breed in the wood.

Boggy peatland pools lie below the rugged hills in the heart of the Galloway Forest Park.

Galloway Forest Park

See map; includes eight sites
Guide from HMSO bookshops and forest centres; trail guides at Caldons and Talnotry caravan sites; further information from Clatteringshaws Deer Museum, open April–October, 10a.m.–5p.m., or recreation forester, Glentrool Forest, Bargrennan, Newton Stewart
All year

Rugged granite mountains, rushing hill streams with sparkling falls, and trackless wastes of bog combine to create an atmosphere akin to 'wilderness' in much of the unplanted section of the park. Such treeless hill country accounts for nearly 40 per cent of its 66,000ha and offers a great variety of walking routes. Forest trails lead through the woodlands around Loch Trool and elsewhere, red deer and wild goats can be watched in large roadside enclosures, there is a deer museum at Clatteringshaws, and along the Raiders' Road Forest Drive reed-fringed Stroan Loch is alive with dragonflies in late summer.

The Merrick, at 843m the highest of the ten hills exceeding 600m, lies at the core of the Range of the Awful Hand, a five-fingered cluster of summits and glens. Crags and corries scar the northern and eastern faces of the Merrick, home of arctic–alpines such as dwarf juniper and starry saxifrage; dwarf willow and stiff sedge grow on the exposed ridges and parsley fern among the loose boulders below. From the summit the view eastwards takes in the much indented Lochs Enoch and Neldricken, lying in the basin of bogs and peat mosses which also

Colourful feral goats can be seen close to the road from Clatteringshaws to Newton Stewart.

holds the SILVER FLOWE reserve. Silvery granite sand lines many of the bays and gives the water an iridescent quality. Beyond lies the remote granite bastion of Mullwarchar.

Trees dominate the view westward too, crowding in around Loch Moan, with its big black-headed gullery, and along either side of the road leading from Bargrennan to Straiton. Here afforestation has had the greatest impact visually and on animal life. Much of the planting was carried out in the 1950s and early 1960s, on rolling moorland once the haunt of curlew, golden plover, red grouse, skylark, wheatear and merlin. In those days all available ground was planted up – here with Sitka spruce and Japanese larch – so that trees now blanket the landscape. The moorland birds were forced out, to be replaced first by short-eared owl, whinchat and willow and grasshopper warbler, which find suitable food and nest sites among the rank growth associated with young plantations. As the trees closed up, creating a dark jungle of leafless twigs, these species left too. Today few birds are seen away from the forest edge, the rides and the few small unplanted enclaves. There tits, willow warbler, goldcrest, chaffinch and siskin can be expected, along with the odd blackbird and thrush, an occasional jay and perhaps a sparrowhawk.

In more recent plantings the ranks of conifers have been broken up, creating vistas, introducing a greater diversity of species, retaining areas of natural woodland, and leaving land unplanted around lochs and streams. Around Glen Trool substantial remnants of the original oak and birch woodlands survive at either end of the loch, at Buchan, Glenhead and Caldons. They hold a good variety of flowering plants and ferns and in summer are alive with birds such as wood warbler, redstart, tree pipit and pied flycatcher, the last often choosing nest boxes in preference to natural holes. The ground to the north is largely unplanted, comprising open rocky moorland of heather, purple moorgrass, rushes and bracken. The plantations stretch irregular fingers up the hillside.

There are other noteworthy stretches of semi-natural woodland in the area. The Wood of Cree, an oakwood once coppiced, then managed jointly by the FC and the NCC, and now an RSPB reserve (see Stop Press), lies just outside the south western boundary of the park. It contains much hazel and some rowan and birch; the ground vegetation includes bilberry, cow-wheat, ramsons and woodruff, and abundant mosses and ferns. On the eastern boundary, in Bennan Forest, the woodland strip along the shore of Loch Ken is predominantly alder, with birch and willow. Bog asphodel, bog myrtle, hemlock water-dropwort, sneezewort, angelica and greater bird's-foot-trefoil grow in this wet woodland, also the habitat of willow tit.

The Bennan Forest includes the oldest plantations in the park, dating from 1922, of Scots pine, European larch, Douglas fir, and Norway and Sitka spruce. Many are now mature and felling has started. The forest currently holds a fair population of crossbill, and siskin are common. Nightjar 'churr' in summer in the clearings and flit silently along the rides at dusk; green woodpecker breed here and little owl have been seen.

Red and roe deer are present in large numbers. Red deer can be seen both in their wild state and in the big enclosure on Brockloch Hill, beside the A712 and not far from the Clatteringshaws Deer Museum. Between the deer park and Murray's monument another enclosure holds a flock of the multi-coloured feral goats seen on the remoter hills.

Other animals include red squirrel, fox, rabbit and mountain hare. Wild cat are absent but there are a few badger and otter have been increasing since otter-hunting ceased in the area. Mink are regrettably widespread but grey squirrel have not yet arrived. Fallow deer, originally from a deer park, occur only in Kirroughtree Forest. In recent years attempts have been made to re-introduce pine marten, once native. Groups have been released in the Caldons, Glen Trool and also in Clatteringshaws Forest. They have been seen on several occasions since and it is hoped that they may soon successfully establish themselves.

Dragonflies frequent many of the park lochs in late summer and early autumn. One of the easiest places to see them is beside Stroan Loch, near the southern end of the Raiders' Road Forest Drive. Rushes and sedges provide suitable stances for the emerging insects and white granite boulders along the shore attract adults to rest in the sun. Perhaps the most numerous is a darter dragonfly, the Scottish sympetrum. Other species include small blue damselfly and the very much larger common aeshna.

Those who stay by the roads can only taste what the Galloway Forest Park has to offer. This is really a place for the walker, for a network of paths and forest tracks invites exploration and frequently also offers a challenge, as many of the long routes lead through uninhabited country. Although most of the recreational facilities are along the southern fringe of the forest and around Loch Trool, opportunities for exploration and discovery are just as great in Carrick Forest to the north, with its scattered lochs of varying size and type, and in Clatteringshaws Forest to the east. Those who can spend several days on the hills and moors may sight hen harrier – there is a communal winter roost of around 30 birds in one boggy area; merlin – still present although decreased in numbers; or one of Galloway's golden eagles – sadly unsuccessful breeders in recent years. Short-eared owl, black grouse, buzzard and possibly raven may be seen, although the last has become scarcer with the absence of sheep carrion from the hills. Even short trips may reveal the unexpected – golden pheasant in Kirroughtree Forest, grass-of-Parnassus and fairy flax near Murray's monument, or even (as in 1976) a nuthatch in Glen Trool.

Grey Mare's Tail

NT 182150; 1016ha; NTS
Grass heath, cliffs, loch and waterfall
Paths and slopes slippery: take great care
Further information from NTS, Edinburgh,
or ranger on site in summer
April–August

Falling some 60m from the lip of a hanging valley, this is one of the highest waterfalls in Britain. Lush vegetation flourishes on the wet and inaccessible sides of the gorge; heather, roseroot, harebell, wood-rush, scabious, goldenrod, dog's mercury and wood sage are among the more obvious species. Where the cliffs give way to scree, however, all accessible plants are hard grazed by the multi-coloured feral goats, which scrabble their way across astonishingly steep slopes, starting a series of stone slides as they go.

Above the fall Loch Skeen lies in an upland basin, with lime-rich cliffs breaking the rolling grassland to west and south; these cliffs have an unusually rich flora for the southern uplands. Common gull nesting by Loch Skeen and raven playing above the cliffs are among the breeding birds of the area.

Ken–Dee Marshes

NX 6376 and 6869; 158ha; RSPB reserve
Marsh and deciduous woodland
Access restricted; visiting by arrangement only
but viewing possible from roadside
*October–March: wildfowl; May–June:
breeding birds*

Loch Ken and the River Dee wind for 16km along the valley floor, fringed variously with marsh, woodland and fields. Peninsulas and bays scallop the shores and extensive mudflats are exposed at the northern end when hydroelectric activities lower the water level. This diversity of habitats supports a varied population of breeding and wintering birds, and the woodlands and marshes are of botanical interest. The two areas comprising this reserve include a large canary-grass marsh, dotted with willows and seamed by open channels; wet meadows with birch, hazel and willow scrub; and fine open oak woodlands.

This is the wintering ground of the largest mainland flock of Greenland white-fronted geese, currently about 200 strong. Much larger numbers of greylag geese regularly roost on the river, while pink-footed, barnacle and bean geese and whooper swan all occur occasionally. Pintail and shoveler regularly nest and are often present in autumn among the dabbling ducks gathered near the north-end marshes. The muddy shallows there also attract waders passing along the natural migration route through the valley.

In summer the patches of wet meadow and adjoining marsh are alive with sedge and grasshopper warbler. In these rough grasslands, once cut for hay, meadowsweet, valerian and marsh cinquefoil are abundant and there are good stands of such local species as spignel, saw-wort and wood bittervetch. On slightly higher ground gnarled old hawthorns and crab apples, and the occasional guelder-rose, are scattered through a jungle of bracken, birch, hazel and willow. This dense cover is favoured by the resident willow tits whose distinctive calls can be heard throughout the year.

Although limited in area the mature oakwoods contain many fine trees and show signs of regeneration. Pied flycatcher and wood warbler breed in these woodlands and green and great spotted woodpecker occur in the vicinity.

Kirkconnell Flow

Permit only; 155ha; NCC reserve
Raised bog
Permit from warden, Tadorna, Hollands Farm
Road, Caerlaverock
May–July

The most important feature of this remnant peat moss is its extensive colonisation by Scots pine; birchwood is also present on some parts. Heather, cross-leaved heath and *Sphagnum* mosses dominate the vegetation and such typical mire species as bog-rosemary and cranberry are widespread. The reserve has a rich and varied insect population.

Knowetop Lochs

Permit only; 27.5ha; SWT reserve
Moorland with two small lochs
Nature trail (4km); leaflets, details with permit
April–July

Birch woodland separates the two small lochs, which are fringed with reedswamp, bog and willow carr. The surrounding moorland ranges from wet peat moss to grassy heath, and a belt of conifer plantation gives shelter to the north. There are four species of willow in the marshy thickets; whorled caraway, bogbean and intermediate bladderwort in the bog; petty whin among the heather of the drier moorland, and grass-of-Parnassus on the heath.

Four species of owl hunt over the reserve and many small woodland birds breed among the birches and willows. In spring blackcock display at a lek nearby, snipe drum over the bog and woodcock 'beat the bounds' of their territory. Whooper swan are regular winter visitors, as are several species of duck. Buzzard, kestrel, sparrowhawk and hen harrier are not uncommon.

Mull of Galloway

NX 157305; 16ha; RSPB reserve
Sea cliffs
May–July

Rising to a maximum height of 87m, this rugged cliff supports a moderate-sized colony of seabirds, including cormorant, shag, kittiwake, guillemot, razorbill and fulmar. Spring squill and purple milk-vetch are abundant on the cliff top; roseroot

Shags nest on the rocks of the Mull of Galloway.

and Scots lovage are also present. Rock sea-spurrey, golden samphire, rock samphire and rock sea-lavender are at their northern limit here.

Plantain Loch

NX 841602; 4ha; FC
Shallow loch
July–September

This small loch is notable for the extensive colony of oblong-leaved sundew on its northern shore and for its dragonflies, many of which, trapped among the sundews, can be examined at close range. Species positively identified include common aeshna, four-spotted libellula, large red damselfly, common ischnura, green lestes, common blue damselfly and Scottish sympetrum; others probably also occur.

Silver Flowe

NX 4782; 191ha; NCC reserve
Blanket bog
Access restricted: contact warden, Falbae Cottage, Falbae, Creetown
May–August

Within this reserve, situated on the floor of a glacial valley in one of the remoter parts of the GALLOWAY FOREST PARK, lies the most varied and least disturbed area of acid peatland in southern Scotland. The seven distinct bog areas together represent a unique series of mire types.

Threave Wildfowl Refuge

NX 7462; 348ha; NTS
River, islands and marshes
Hide; further information from visitor centre at NX 753605, leaflet from NTS
Open 1 November–end March

The marshes along this section of the River Dee provide good feeding grounds for wildfowl, especially when they are flooded. Greylag geese, wigeon, mallard and teal are all regular autumn and winter visitors. A hide on the old railway at NX 745613 offers a good viewpoint; the river itself is best seen from NX 740619 or NX 744625 (access from Kelton Mains Farm).

Tynron Juniper Wood

Permit only; 4ha; NCC reserve
Shrub woodland
Permit from warden, Tadorna, Hollands Farm Road, Caerlaverock
April–July

A dense growth of columnar and prostrate juniper is the main feature of this reserve, on which the regeneration of this species is being studied. A few ash and wild cherry are present among the juniper and the ground flora is quite varied but does not include any unusual species. Several local insect species, such as juniper carpet and juniper pug moth, have been recorded.

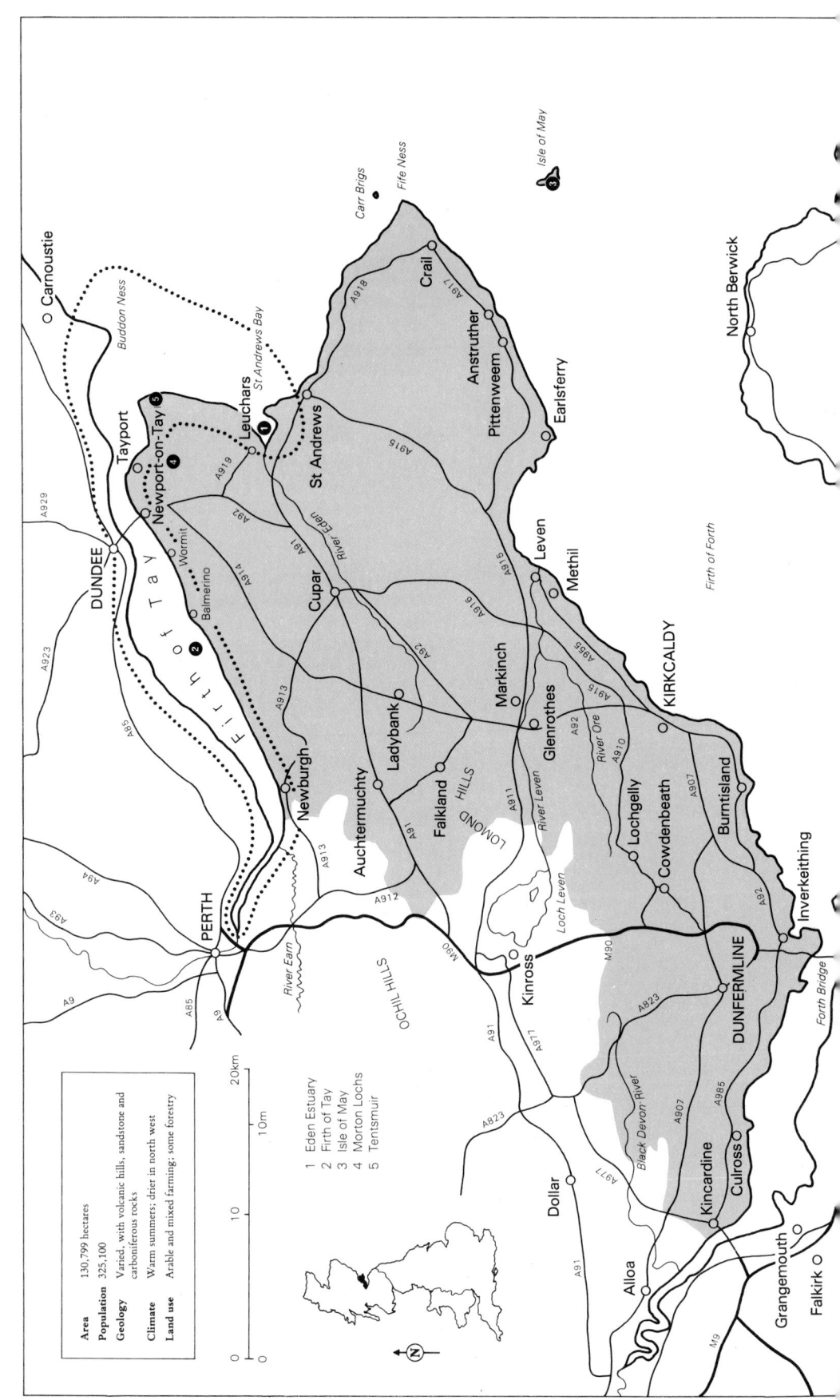

Fife

In effect Fife is a large promontory dominated on three sides by salt water, and cut off physically from the rest of Scotland by these waters and the mass of the Ochil Hills to the west. This created an isolation that disappeared only with the building of the Forth and Tay road bridges during the 1960s, and made for a particular identity reflected in the past in its proud title, the Kingdom of Fife.

The county's southern shores are lapped by the tides of the Firth of Forth, which exhibits a wide range of habitat as it gradually widens from the infant Firth above Kincardine and flows east under the rail and road bridges. Here the estuary suddenly opens out, with Edinburgh in the distance to the south. On the Fife side are the regular series of villages and towns running east which prompted James VI of Scotland and I of England to describe Fife 400 years ago as 'a beggar's mantle fringed with gold', owing to the importance of these harbours and ports.

The islands of the Forth, in particular the ISLE OF MAY, have long fascinated both locals and visitors. Ranking with FAIR ISLE (Shetland) as one of the two most important east coast migratory points in Britain, since the 1930s this island's reputation as a place where a great variety of birds may be seen has spread far and wide, and the reserve is well worth a visit. The FIRTH OF TAY, forming Fife's northern coastline, differs from the Forth. It is much more gentle and estuary-like, and the tide goes out a long way to reveal large sand- and mud-banks while trees reach down to the water's edge and reedbeds fringe the shores, the haunt of geese and shelduck.

The eastern littoral – exposed directly to the North Sea – presents a further contrast. The east coast of Scotland possesses few major sand dune systems and Fife is fortunate to have the unique TENTSMUIR at its extreme north eastern corner. At one time this was a wind-blown tract of wilder-

ness, but though its character has been greatly altered by afforestation much of it remains full of interest, especially the eastern coastal strip at Kinshaldy just south of the reserve. This area's maritime plants, birds and insects are markedly dissimilar from those of MORTON LOCHS a few kilometres inland, with its pools, marshes and reeds favoured by wildfowl.

Just to the south is the EDEN ESTUARY, echoing to the cry of rare migrant waders, not far from St Andrews and its famous golf links. From here the coast is rock-girt around most of the East Neuk, and the shore walk brings such strange rock formations as the Rock and Spindle, and compact salt-marshes full of uncommon plants. Rounding Fife Ness and continuing up the Forth the cliffs and braes of Kincraig present a fine spectacle in scenic, wildlife and geological terms; the columnar basalt outcrops and the classic sequence of raised beaches are particularly remarkable. Further west the influence of man is much more pronounced and industrialisation looms large, but this has unexpected wildlife benefits in the large numbers of wintering duck that frequent the offshore waters.

Inland, man's effect on the landscape is even more marked. Until recently much of it was scarred by ugly pit bings and spoil heaps, products of an intensive coalmining industry; but these have now very largely gone, thanks to an imaginative land reclamation policy, to be replaced by such attractive open areas as Lochore Meadows Country Park, which includes a small nature area. The reclamation of other derelict land and its conversion to agriculture emphasises that Fife is predominantly a farming region. While there is still a fair amount of woodland much of it is now coniferous, and arable fields and pasture land dominate. There are no rivers to speak of – the Eden flowing through north east Fife is no more than a wide burn – but several lochs and reservoirs provide the freshwater environment necessary for a diversity of wildlife. Of the few raised bogs remaining, that at BANK-HEAD MOSS has been made into a reserve. Moor and heath are now but fragments except in the Lomond Hills, which overlook much of Fife.

The twin peaks of the Lomonds are low by mountain standards, reaching a mere 519m, but they are of considerable interest. Though much affected by grazing and planting they still retain good areas of moorland and rough ground, with rocky outcrops here and there. The Lomonds district forms a natural country park and already there is a ranger service to look after this inland lung of Fife and Kinross.

To anyone standing on either peak, the broad effect of glaciation on much of the landscape is clear. During the ice ages the glaciers moved west to east, and these flows created an undulating topography pleasing to the eye. To the north east lie the eastern outposts of the Ochils, falling to the Tay on one side and sheltering the fertile Howe of Fife to the south. Both hills and strath are composed of old red sandstone, whereas the inland hump of the East Neuk is capped by dolerite sills and old volcanoes such as Largo Law (as are the Lomonds themselves). These volcanic features also occur in the south and west of the region, but here the underlying rocks belong to the carboniferous, its large coal measures now mostly exhausted. Scarps appear here and there, notably in the Cleish Hills which form part of the boundary between Kinross and Fife.

Owing to its comparative geographical isolation Fife tends to have a microclimate of its own – the fact that the weather in Edinburgh can be quite different from that in Dundee has played no small part in moulding both Fife and Fifers. This is particularly true of the coast, where a low shivering haar or sea fog at times blots out visibility all day while inland the sun is blazing down! Fife can also be subject to biting easterly gales, but its sheltered position does mean that rainfall is low and it shares with East Lothian some of the driest and sunniest spots in Scotland.

The old Kingdom of Fife thus provides a varied range of landscape, scenery and habitat for the lover of both coast and country, especially those with an interest in natural history and wildlife. Although there are as yet comparatively few declared reserves, there are many areas worthy of that status and all have much to offer.

G. H. BALLANTYNE

Bankhead Moss

Permit only; 4ha; SWT reserve
Raised bog
May–September

One of the few surviving in Fife, this peat bog is encircled by farmland. The peat is 7m deep at the centre and, although raised above the surrounding land, carries open pools with at least six different species of actively growing *Sphagnum* mosses. There is a rich growth of lichens among the heather-dominated ground cover. Scattered Scots pine and birch regeneration is taking place towards the centre of the moss and birch woodland is well grown around the fringe.

Eden Estuary

NO 4819; 891ha; NE Fife DC reserve
Estuary with sandbanks and mudflats
Access points at West Sands (NO 497195) and along shore from Kinshaldy car park (NO 498243)
April–June: breeding birds; August–May: waders and duck

Sandbars and low dunes protect the mouth of this small estuary and make it very sheltered in comparison with St Andrews Bay. Much of the estuary itself is also sandy, but the flats become muddier towards Guardbridge. The reserve is fringed by a number of small but botanically interesting salt-marshes, brackish reedswamps and sand dunes.

The estuary supports large numbers of waders, especially bar-tailed godwit, redshank, dunlin, oystercatcher and knot. It is one of the very few Scottish sites regularly holding more than 100 grey plover and black-tailed godwit, and is visited briefly by many wader species on migration, particularly in autumn. At high tide the waders roost either on Shelly Point, on the north side of the estuary, or on the saltmarsh near Guardbridge. Over 1000 eider sometimes gather off the Eden mouth and many of the birds nesting on TENTSMUIR bring their ducklings down to the estuary. Rafts of common scoter can often be seen in St Andrews Bay and several hundred mallard, teal and wigeon use the area in winter. Shelduck, which breed around the estuary, are at their peak in March, when the numbers present are of international importance. Common seal regularly visit the Eden and haul out on the sandbanks between Shelly Point and the river mouth.

Eden Estuary: grey plovers occur regularly here.

Firth of Tay (Tay–Eden Estuary)

See map; includes eight sites
Estuary with sandbanks and mudflats
April–June: breeding birds; August–May: waders and duck

Vast flocks of pink-footed geese arrive on the Tay Estuary in autumn.

The Firth of Tay, with its off-lying Abertay Sands, has long been important for wildfowl and waders but recently it has been recognised as the only site in Britain to hold an internationally significant gathering of eider; the flocks of 15,000 or more on the outer Firth in winter represent 1.3 per cent of the north west European population and 20 per cent of the British stock. In addition the estuary itself attracts nationally important numbers of grey geese and of several wader species, while the contiguous St Andrews Bay and EDEN ESTUARY also hold significant populations of duck and waders.

From Perth to just above its confluence with the Earn the Tay is narrowly confined between steep slopes and fringed with scrub and marsh; this stretch of the river holds comparatively few waterbirds. From Earnmouth to Kingoodie the estuary gradually widens, revealing at low tide a vast expanse of muddy sand, divided into discrete banks in a number of places by deep channels.

Many waders feed over the mudflats, especially in autumn and particularly around Invergowrie Bay. Large numbers of redshank, dunlin and oystercatcher are often present, with smaller numbers of bar-tailed godwit, curlew, lapwing, golden plover and knot. Some less common waders, such as black-tailed godwit, ruff, curlew sandpiper and spotted redshank, are also recorded quite regularly. This can be a difficult area to observe but reasonably good views can be obtained around Kingoodie and Port Allen. The extent of the mudflats makes it pointless to visit at low tide, when the birds at the water's edge are far beyond comfortable viewing range.

Many thousands of geese also use this section of the estuary, but only for roosting. The pink-footed geese generally roost over the Dog Bank and Carthagena Bank, while the greylag geese are concentrated around Mugdrum Island, off Newburgh. Most of the pink-footed geese flight off at dawn to north or west, to feed over the rich farmlands of the Carse of Gowrie, Strathmore and Strathearn. The greylags generally fly less far and often feed on the steep grass fields on the south bank of the Tay. There are several points along the minor road from Newburgh to Balmerino from which good views of the flighting geese can be obtained.

Although there are several responsible local wildfowling clubs, many 'cowboy' wildfowlers also visit this area, resulting in a high level of disturbance to the geese. At the same time complaints about the damage caused by the geese are quite often and sometimes justifiably made by local farmers particularly in April. Migrating geese pass through in successive waves that may total 20,000 or more, each batch pausing for a day or two to feed ravenously on the young spring grass before setting off again.

At Dundee the Tay narrows again and for about 5km is little wider than it was at Newburgh, more than 25km upstream. Common seal are regular visitors to this stretch and can often be seen off Riverside Drive or hauled out on the sandbanks between the road and rail bridges. In winter the sewage outfalls at the Stannergate and near Monifieth are popular with goldeneye, tufted duck and mute swan. In summer this stretch of the river is heavily used for recreation.

East of Tayport both shores are stony with mussel beds for a short distance before giving way to the sands of Barry on the north and of TENTSMUIR on the south. Here again the shores attract waders, including sanderling and knot. The extensive dunes and dune slacks of the Barry Links, lying behind Buddon Ness Point, are of considerable botanical interest and the area also holds an important breeding bird population. Barry–Buddon is an army firing range and so has been protected from the recreation pressures experienced by other dunes and beaches nearby. The restrictions on access are frustrating to naturalists but so far as the wildlife is concerned occasional disturbance by army activities is much less harmful than would be the major industrial developments recently proposed for the site.

The Tay's famous gathering of eider is found right at the mouth of the Firth, around the outer Abertay Sands. Because the birds sit well offshore for much of the time and the nearest land is very low-lying, shore-based observers have found it impossible to make realistic counts of these great rafts of duck; over the years estimates ranged from 2000 to 'uncountable masses'. Subsequent aerial counting showed that eider numbers here were at least as high as had been guessed, with over 15,000 birds present in the autumn of 1979.

Two incidents of oil pollution in the Firth of Tay have demonstrated just how vulnerable a great concentration of seaduck can be. In February 1968 a tanker discharging her cargo at Dundee leaked around 87 tons of oil into the river. The oil contaminated the beaches at Broughty Ferry and Tayport and spread out over the Abertay Sands and southwards to foul the salmon nets on Kinshaldy beach and the common scoter in St Andrews Bay. An estimated 2000 eider died as a result of this incident. Only two years later waste fuel oil dumped by a ship somewhere well off the east coast was carried inshore by wind and tide. Over 2100 dead eider were found on the coasts of Fife and Angus, together with over 300 scoter and 130 divers. As the Tay wintering eider flock includes a substantial part of the very important Ythan Estuary breeding flock (see SANDS OF FORVIE AND YTHAN ESTUARY, Grampian), as well as birds that nest in the immediate area, it is vital that the east coast population is protected from pollution of any kind.

Most of the eider breeding around the Firth of Tay do so between TENTSMUIR POINT and the Eden mouth, though small numbers also nest on Barry – Buddon. The Eden Estuary is the most intensively used 'nursery' area, but there are also smaller creche areas at St Andrews, beneath Score Cliff and at the north end of Kinkell Braes.

Further offshore, the bay is an important area for scoter; both common and a few velvet occur regularly. Red-throated diver are also regular in autumn and winter and can often be seen close inshore near the Eden mouth.

From the mouth of the Eden fine beaches stretch to north and south for a total of over 10 km. Those to the south, St Andrews' popular West Sands, are crowded with holiday-makers in fine weather, while those of Tentsmuir Point, at the north, are accessible only after a long walk or, in the case of organised groups, by vehicle through prior arrangement with the warden. The beach at Kinshaldy, which can easily be reached from the Forestry Commission car park at NO 498243, offers good opportunities for both seawatching and exploring the dune fringe.

Morton Lochs: management has increased both habitat and species diversity.

Isle of May

NT 6599; 57ha; NCC reserve
Cliff-girt island
Access by boat from Crail, Anstruther or
Pittenweem; summer day trips dependent on
tides and weather
Permission required to carry out research on
island: contact NCC, Edinburgh
Bird observatory, with limited residential
accommodation: contact Isle of May Bookings
Sec., c/o 21 Regent Terrace, Edinburgh EH7 5BT
May–July: breeding birds; April–May and
August–October: migrants

This small island on the seaward edge of the Firth
of Forth has been a site of ornithological importance for over 50 years. Since a bird observatory
was set up in 1934 many thousands of birds have
been ringed, the hundreds of species involved including many 'first records' for Scotland. More
recently the island's seabirds have been the main
focus of attention. During the last 30 years some
very striking changes have occurred in the breeding populations and also in the island's vegetation.
These have been the subject of detailed studies,
whose findings are now being used in managing
the island's flora and fauna.

Forty years ago much of the Isle of May was carpeted with thrift and sea campion; then, 8000 pairs
of four species of tern nested and there were only
800 pairs of gulls. By 1972 the terns, thrift and sea
campion had largely gone, unable to survive alongside the 34,000 herring gull and 5000 lesser black-
backed gull occupying the island, their nests set on
bare ground or among a tangle of chickweed, sorrel,
orache and scurvygrass. A gull control programme
reduced numbers to around 2500 herring and 250
lesser black-backed gull, and in 1979 common tern
laid on the island for the first time since 1957.

Some of the other changes have been equally
spectacular and even more difficult to explain.
Puffin numbered only seven pairs in 1955; now
they are by far the most numerous species, with the
estimated 8500 occupied burrows stretching to the
centre of the island and young birds en route to the
sea occasionally wandering into the various buildings. Shag too have shown a vast increase; over
1000 pairs now build their untidy nests on the low
cliffs where only six pairs were present in 1934.
Several thousand pairs of kittiwake and guillemot
also breed, with a few hundred razorbill and a
steadily expanding population of fulmar.

The excitement of the migration period is an
important attraction: when strong east winds combine with poor visibility at peak migration times
dawn often reveals an astonishing number and
variety of tired birds. There could be a big fall of
a relatively common species, such as brambling –
over 1000 appeared on one occasion; an assortment
of waders; or something really rare – perhaps a
Sabine's gull, scarlet rosefinch or gyr falcon.

Rona, the northern tip, is the breeding ground
for a growing colony of grey seal; over 300 pups
were counted there in November 1980. Interesting

Seabird numbers on the Isle of May have been
increasing rapidly.

insects occasionally turn up, dragonflies for example,
or a large influx of painted lady butterflies, or the
rare humming-bird hawkmoth – recorded in 1980
for only the second time this century. The vegetation, both land-based and marine, is still yielding new records after many years of study. One
of the most recent additions has been common
lungwort.

Morton Lochs

NO 4626; 24ha; NCC reserve
Man-made lochs with surrounding marsh and
woodland
Three hides, one open to the public (suitable for
the disabled) and two accessible to permit holders
only: apply NCC, Edinburgh; booklet on
rehabilitation management from NCC
April–June: breeding birds: August–January:
waders and wildfowl

Originally created for fish-rearing, these lochs at
one time attracted large numbers of waders and
wildfowl and had a high conservation interest.
During the 1960s, however, their interest
progressively declined as deposition of silt and
blowing sand gradually led to them drying out
completely. The smaller south loch, now a marsh
with virtually no open water, demonstrates the
sequence of plant colonisation, from rushes and
reeds to alder and willow carr.

In 1976 a major programme was carried out to restore the north and west lochs, which involved complete drainage and mechanical excavation of large quantities of silt. Islands and promontories, designed to increase the areas available for nesting, roosting and feeding, were created from the excavated material and were sown with grass and planted with rushes, sedges, willow, birch and hawthorn. The flourishing growth already provides adequate nesting cover and food for a variety of birds.

Migrant waders, such as redshank, greenshank and lapwing, visit this loch to feed and rest on the exposed mud of the sloping shores. Mallard, teal and mute swan breed, and several other duck species, including gadwall, are fairly regularly recorded in autumn and winter. Willow, sedge and grasshopper warbler are among the small birds breeding in the scrub woodland and reedbeds, and heron are often seen on both north and south lochs. Nine distinct species of willow and a variety of hybrids are represented on the reserve.

Tentsmuir Point

NO 5072; 505ha; NCC reserve
Foreshore, dunes and scrub woodland
No access to Abertay Sands
*May–August: flowers and butterflies;
September–March: waders and wildfowl*

The foreshore and the offshore Abertay Sands, which account for more than 80 per cent of the reserve area, are of major importance as roosting and feeding grounds for large numbers of waders and wildfowl. At times the wader population totals around 9000 and includes significant numbers of grey plover, sanderling and little stint as well as dunlin and oystercatcher. In late summer the offshore sandbanks are white with roosting gulls and terns, and during the winter both pink-footed and greylag geese roost there, the former in the largest numbers. The sands are also used regularly by common and grey seals, which haul out on to the banks and lie there like fat slugs.

Many of the duck wintering in the Tay—EDEN ESTUARY area gather at times off Tentsmuir. Autumn eider flocks there may exceed 15,000 and there are sometimes sizeable gatherings of common scoter, red-breasted merganser, scaup, mallard and wigeon.

The dune section of the reserve has been expanding in area as a result of lateral accretion; much of the ground is less than 50 years old. All stages of plant colonisation, from pioneering lyme-grass on the fore-dunes, through lichen-rich heath, to alder, birch and willow scrub, are represented and the flora is rich and varied. Over 400 flowering plants have been recorded. Grazing by rabbits keeps much of the herbage short and in summer the lawn-like turf carries an astonishing abundance of grass-of-Parnassus, the delicately-veined white flowers set off to advantage by the sharply contrasting pinks of common and seaside centaury. Purple milk-vetch and coralroot orchid are also plentiful.

A variety of butterflies and moths frequent the dune area. Grayling are particularly abundant at times and there are good numbers of small copper, dark green fritillary and ringlet. Six-spot burnet moths are frequently seen and the striking orange and black caterpillars of cinnabar moth can often be found on ragwort growing near the woodland edge of the reserve.

Tentsmuir Point: as the dunes creep seawards, a succession of plant communities is established behind them.

Grampian

Contrast and space are Grampian's features. It is a broad land of sweeping mountains and beaches and wide skies, where the view often includes the distant hills and grey sea together. The Cairngorms (partly in Grampian and partly in Highland South, where they are described) are not sharp, small peaks but a great range of rounded hills and boulder-strewn plateaus, at all seasons providing Britain's only truly arctic–alpine experience. Here you walk in awe, realising that you are in a place where great climatic forces are dominant, and where only a handful of hardy plants and animals can snatch their living in the short summer. These impressive hills are approached by attractive valleys and skirted by an agricultural plain running to Aberdeen, Peterhead, Elgin and the sea. The valleys are Deeside, with its Caledonian pine forests; Donside, wider, more fertile and equally beautiful; and the smaller vales to the north, where the clean springs allow production of the finest whisky anywhere.

Agriculture dominates the lowlands and the great Buchan plain stretches from BENNACHIE to the sea. This treeless, unrelieved area has its own sad charm, and the breadth of view means that its skies are dramatic and immense. A winter storm can be a thrilling event when you can watch it building up from a great distance, but there is no relief from the fierce wind which is so much a part of Buchan life. To the north the Moray coastal strip is relatively dry and warm, and so is pleasant and fertile even though it has light, sandy soil, with many small woods and valleys to make it a varied and interesting place.

Grampian's coast is also impressive. The dramatic cliffs hold huge seabird colonies, as at FOWLS-HEUGH, or are natural rock gardens, as at Muchalls; and in other places great dunes and beaches are backed by colourful maritime heaths. There is always space in Grampian and the visitor is often alone with the hills or the sea.

The scenery and wildlife are overwhelmingly influenced by the climate and the presence of the Cairngorms. Most of the rocks are acid and the summers are cool, so man's activities do not reach far up into the hills. The lowland agricultural zone is dominated by barley, beef, turnips and potatoes, but this soon merges into upland farming where cattle and sheep graze hard for their living. On these fairly dry, eastern hills heather grows well and so grouse moors are a feature of the landscape: their pattern of burnt stripes and the purple blossom in August are characteristic, especially on Donside, where the more fertile rocks allow profitable shooting estates to flourish. Finally, above the grouse moor, comes the dwarf shrub vegetation and the sedges and lichens. The Cairngorm tops are the largest remnant of reasonably undisturbed natural vegetation in Britain and are of international importance. In contrast little of the natural lowland vegetation remains in Grampian, except at the coast. Some lowland mosses survive in damp hollows; a few valley woods exist, as at Gight; and there are the birch, juniper and Scots pine woodlands in the middle valleys. Many of these areas are now reserves.

The climate on the high tops is truly arctic with frost and snow likely in any month, and some snow patches are almost permanent. The plants and animals surviving here have a fascination for the naturalist which is increased by the real achievement of climbing to find them in the corries and boulder fields. A snow bunting by the coast in winter is not the same prize as one seen nesting in the hills.

It is not only the hills, however, which have a continental climate. The upper valleys, which can be fiercely cold, as at Braemar where a British record low of −27°C has twice been recorded, can also be very hot in summer. These valleys escape the coastal breeze which keeps lowland Grampian cool, and it can be a revelation to experience

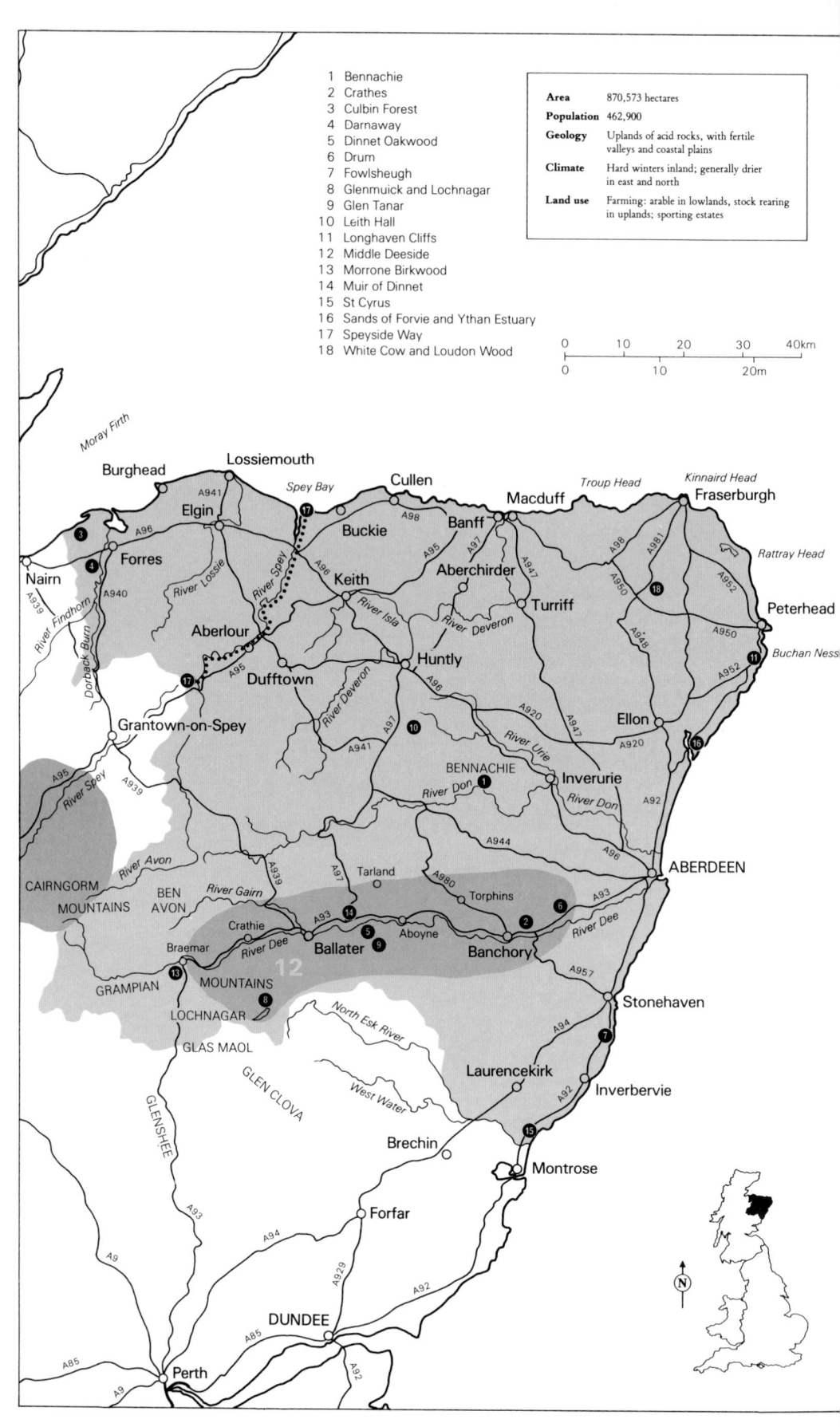

1 Bennachie
2 Crathes
3 Culbin Forest
4 Darnaway
5 Dinnet Oakwood
6 Drum
7 Fowlsheugh
8 Glenmuick and Lochnagar
9 Glen Tanar
10 Leith Hall
11 Longhaven Cliffs
12 Middle Deeside
13 Morrone Birkwood
14 Muir of Dinnet
15 St Cyrus
16 Sands of Forvie and Ythan Estuary
17 Speyside Way
18 White Cow and Loudon Wood

Area	870,573 hectares
Population	462,900
Geology	Uplands of acid rocks, with fertile valleys and coastal plains
Climate	Hard winters inland; generally drier in east and north
Land use	Farming: arable in lowlands, stock rearing in uplands; sporting estates

0   10   20   30   40km

0   10   20m

stifling days in the hills. The red deer range high in the summer to avoid the heat and flies of the valleys. Generally Grampian is cool but dry and there are many brilliant, cloudless days, though usually accompanied by a breeze or a sea mist.

The acidity of much of the rock is relieved in places. Serpentine rocks, and limestone in a narrow belt from Blair Atholl to the Banff coast at Cullen, allow a richer flora to develop. An energetic and observant botanist can find exciting and unusual plant communities on these rocks, and the extra searching needed for these in the Cairngorms is rewarded by a rarer satisfaction.

A naturalist in Grampian will find the coastline very worthwhile. The seabird colonies at Fowlsheugh, LONGHAVEN and Troup are dramatic, with vast numbers of kittiwake and guillemot and other common species, and, at SANDS OF FORVIE especially, terns and eider duck abound on the sand dunes. Winter brings grey geese to coastal lochs in their thousands, as at LOCH OF STRATHBEG, and waders and ducks to the estuaries. The coastal plants are also exceptional, ranging from the luxuriant dunes at ST CYRUS with many species at their northern limit, to the maritime heaths of crowberry and ling, and the cliffs with their banks of roseroot and Scots lovage as at Bullers of Buchan. The varied rock types and microclimate on the coast make it a mosaic of interest at all seasons, and the base-rich sands near Cullen and Portsoy, with their banks of kidney vetch, contrast attractively with the pines at CULBIN or spring squill at Troup.

Deeside is described elsewhere and deserves its fame, but all Grampian's river valleys are of interest and the clear streams are rightly famous for trout and salmon. The lowlands need a more selective itinerary, but many areas remain of interest and in the spring the bird cherry and blackthorn are especially attractive. Even Buchan has its wooded river valleys and mosses and is worth visiting, but naturalists in Grampian will be inevitably and rewardingly drawn to the varied coastline or to the Cairngorms, one of Britain's last few wildernesses.

MARK YOUNG

Bennachie

NJ 6821; 2344ha; FC
Plantations and open moorland
Information centre; forest walks; guide booklet
All year

A good variety of tree species is represented around the fringes of this forest; many of them are labelled near the Don View Centre at NJ 672190. Ferns, mosses, lichens and fungi are abundant along the edges of the tracks. The open heather moorland above the plantation includes the summits of Millstone Hill, the Mither Tap and Craigshannoch, displaying characteristic tor weathering of the granite.

Crathes

NO 7396; 241ha; NTS
Woodlands
Trails leaflet on site; guided walks programme; ranger-naturalist
All year

The grounds of Crathes Castle include a variety of habitats, among them mature deciduous woodland, conifer plantations, ponds and an old sand quarry. Many tree species are represented: introduced exotics; birch, rowan and wild cherry colonising the quarry; and Scots pine crowning a rocky outcrop. The ground vegetation is equally varied, with marsh thistle and herb-Robert in the damper areas; heather, tormentil and wood-sorrel along the forest tracks; and mullein, red campion and wild pansy in the quarry. Roe deer are numerous in the woodland and red squirrel quite common. A good range of woodland birds is also present.

Culbin Forest

NH 9861; 2400ha; FC
Afforested sand dunes and adjoining saltmarsh
Access, on foot only, from Wellhill (NH 997614) and Cloddymoss (NH 983599); organised groups wanting guided tours should contact chief forester, Newton Nursery, by Elgin, tel. Elgin 2832
Forest may be closed in periods of acute fire danger
April–August

A large tract of planted forest today clothes and anchors the sands of Culbin, once notorious for their mobility and their tendency to bury both farmland and dwellings. The history of the area is fascinating, and equally interesting to the naturalist is the way in which the relatively recent forest has been colonised by native species.

The planted forest area is largely Scots pine but includes some Corsican pine and lodgepole pine. Birch is widespread and there are willows in the damper hollows. Creeping lady's-tresses, coralroot orchid, chickweed wintergreen and one-flowered wintergreen occur among the heather and sand sedge ground flora.

Culbin Forest is notable for its crested tits; first recorded in 1948, this species has steadily increased to a current population of 150–200 pairs. There are also good numbers of capercaillie and goldcrest. Other breeding species include buzzard, sparrowhawk, short-eared and long-eared owl, water rail and great spotted woodpecker, and there is a variety of small passerines associated with the birches and the forest edge.

About 200 roe deer inhabit the forest and there is a resident population of around 50 badgers. Red squirrel are fairly common and both pine marten and wild cat have been recorded.

The saltmarsh along the western shore of Findhorn Bay and fringing the unplanted Culbin Sands

Dinnet Oakwood: one of the few remaining oakwoods in this area, it has a varied plant and bird life.

is dominated by sea aster, thrift and sea milkwort; other plants of interest include long-bracted sedge and Baltic rush. Due to the very mild climate of the Moray Firth some 48 plants occur here at their northern limit in Britain, making the area one of considerable botanical interest.

Darnaway

NH 9951; 2857ha; Moray Estates
Woodland and river gorge
Access restricted to waymarked paths unless accompanied by countryside ranger
Visitor centre at Tearie Farm (NH 989569) open May–September; guided walks in summer; leaflets from Moray Estate Office, Forres
Summer

This large estate includes extensive areas of both deciduous woodland and conifer plantation which support a very varied flora and fauna. Waymarked paths through the woodland start from car parks at NJ 013525 and NH 996514 and both offer views of the spectacular gorge of the River Findhorn.

Dinnet Oakwood

NO 464980; 13ha; NCC reserve
Semi-natural oakwood
May–June

Both sessile and pedunculate oak, as well as many hybrids, are present in this small wood, one of the few remaining oakwoods in north east Scotland. Although probably planted, the woodland has much of the character of a natural upland oakwood. The ground flora is varied and includes such northern species as chickweed wintergreen, common wintergreen and stone bramble. A variety of woodland birds is present, among them wood warbler, spotted flycatcher, jay and great spotted woodpecker. Several locally uncommon insects occur in the wood.

Drum

NJ 7900; 166ha; NTS
Woodland
Leaflet from NTS, Crathes and Drum Castle; guided walks in summer; ranger-naturalist
April–July

The old Forest of Drum has been a woodland site for several centuries. Today it carries magnificent mature beech, oak and Scots pine, well spaced and consequently natural in form. Wych elm, juniper, venerable yews and ancient twisted wild cherries are also present. Much of this open woodland has a lush carpet of grasses, ferns and wood anemone. Great clumps of rhododendron add colour and cover and here blackcap and garden warbler sing. Redpoll trill above the more open birch areas, woodcock 'rode' overhead and great spotted woodpecker drum on the dying limbs of ancient oaks. Rooks nest in a group of Scots pine and the woodland holds an important winter roost serving most of lower Deeside. Roe deer, hare and rabbit are common and the old forest holds several species of moths, snails and fungi that are very local in their distribution.

Fowlsheugh

NO 880798; 11ha; RSPB reserve
Coastal cliff
Access by path from Crawton
May–mid-July

Fowlsheugh can aptly be described as a seabird city; a total of around 80,000 pairs of six species breed on this magnificent cliff, which is 1.6km long and up to 65m high. In May and June the place is alive with the noise and movement – not to mention smell – of its inhabitants. There is a ceaseless crying of kittiwake, especially from the non-breeding birds which alternately sit about in groups and then fly off in sudden 'panics', to alight out at sea for a brief spell before returning. Where trickles of water muddy a gully in the cliff the nesting kittiwakes busy themselves gathering mud, and where a stream topples over the edge they bathe in and drink the fresh water.

Unlike many major seabird sites Fowlsheugh is a city of detached apartments rather than crowded tenements. Many of the guillemot and kittiwake nests, as well as those of razorbill, are sited in individual niches formed where a large stone has worked loose and fallen from the surrounding conglomerate. Only in a few places are there long ledges where the guillemots can pack tightly together. The off-duty guillemots dot the surface of the sea below the cliff, showing now brown, now white as they turn and twist to preen in the water. A substantial proportion have the white eye-ring of the bridled form.

Herring gull occupy many of the sites near the clifftop and their nest-building activities leave the coarse grass nearby looking as though it has been raked. Nesting fulmar are scattered fairly thinly among the gulls, and a few puffin are present, though Fowlsheugh is not well provided with terrain suitable for burrow-nesters. Nor is it well suited to shag; those that do nest mostly occupy ledges in caves.

This is one of the largest seabird colonies on the eastern mainland of Scotland; it probably holds over 30,000 pairs each of kittiwake and guillemot together with several thousand razorbill and smaller numbers of fulmar, shag, herring gull and puffin. Deep indentations in the cliffs make it easy to observe the colony without disturbance to the birds or danger to the observer, although care must, of course, be taken to keep well back from the cliff edge.

Red deer can be seen all year round in Glenmuick.

Glenmuick and Lochnagar

NO 2585; 2572ha; Balmoral Estates–SWT reserve
Mountainous area with lochs
Visitor centre; reserve booklet; ranger service; further information from Balmoral Estates Office or ranger
May–September: birds and flowers; November: deer

Upper Glenmuick is an impressive place at any season. The boulder-strewn slopes of 'dark Lochnagar' rise abruptly from the shore of Loch Muick and conceal much of the higher ground, allowing just a glimpse of the knobbly tor of Cac Carn Beag from the visitor centre at the Spittal (NO 307851). This is wild country – especially in winter: the haunt of peregrine, golden eagle and red deer.

Crowberry, bilberry, bearberry and cowberry are scattered among the heather by the shore of Loch Muick. Sundew, butterwort, petty whin and alpine lady's-mantle also occur, and there are a few aspens, rowans and birches near the Black Burn. Adder and lizard bask by the path on sunny days, snipe and redshank frequent the boggy areas in the valley bottom, and common sandpiper bob at the waterside. In early summer large northern eggar and emperor moth are on the wing, while in July and August butterflies and several species of dragonfly are likely to be seen.

Trailing azalea makes vivid splashes of colour among the wind-dwarfed heather around the 700m level, while above 1000m patches of bare granite gravel are interspersed with clumps of stiff sedge, mounds of woolly fringe-moss and prostrate mats of least willow. Three-leaved rush grows in the most exposed situations of all and lichens are unusually abundant for a Scottish summit. Ptarmigan and dunlin breed high up on Lochnagar, red grouse and golden plover at a somewhat lower level. Mountain hare are not uncommon on the moorland and the red deer move freely from high ground to valley bottom, according to the season and weather conditions.

The greatest scientific interest of the reserve undoubtedly lies in the plant life of the corries. Ledges and gullies on the cliffs, continuously dampened and enriched by trickles of water and inaccessible even to deer, carry a luxuriant growth of flowers, such as red campion, globeflower, roseroot and melancholy thistle, and big tufts of great wood-rush. Saxifrages flourish in the wettest spots, among them starry saxifrage and yellow saxifrage. Alpine speedwell, alpine willowherb and Norwegian cudweed are also present. At the foot of the cliffs alpine lady-fern and parsley fern grow among the scree of granite blocks that litters the ground. Where the snow lies longest on the floor of this north-facing corrie the growth of bilberry is particularly lush and there are scattered plants of dwarf cornel, chickweed wintergreen and bog bilberry.

From the visitor centre, paths offer a variety of routes. The low-level track to Loch Muick is easy going but the route up Lochnagar is steep, rough and very exposed; adequate footwear and equipment are essential. The old drove road over the Capel Mount to Glen Clova provides an interesting alternative high-level path with a good viewpoint less than 1.5km from the visitor centre. Visitors are asked to keep to the tracks and to avoid disturbing the deer, both during the stalking season and in winter, when they normally conserve energy by moving as little as possible. Stag stalking lasts from 1 July to 21 October and hinds are stalked between 20 October and 16 February.

Glen Tanar

NO 4891; 4185ha; Glen Tanar Estate–NCC reserve
Caledonian forest
Permit only, from Glen Tanar Estate Office,
off waymarked paths
Visitor centre open April–September;
countryside ranger service in summer
May–September

This is one of the finest, and the driest and most easterly, remnants of the old Caledonian forest. It contains large areas of fine mature native Scots pine, mainly on the banks of the River Tanar and around the Water of Allachy, and natural regeneration is taking place on an unusually extensive scale, in some places on open moorland adjoining the forest. Juniper is scattered through the forest and there are occasional rowan, aspen and birch.

Many of the plants and animals characteristic of pinewoods occur here. Heather, bilberry, cowberry, hair-grass and mosses dominate much of the ground cover; creeping lady's-tresses and chickweed wintergreen are widespread; and lesser twayblade, twinflower, common wintergreen and intermediate wintergreen are present. Crossbill,

siskin and capercaillie, all birds associated with pinewoods, are present in good numbers, while the more varied woodland along the River Tanar and around the policies attracts a wide range of species. The site is good for birds of prey. Fencing has kept red deer to the higher hill ground but there are roe deer in the valley woodlands. Red squirrel are occasionally seen and wild cat, otter, fox and mink are known to be present.

The small visitor centre at Braeloine, run by Glen Tanar Estate, contains an exhibition on the wildlife and land use of the area. Walks of various lengths have been waymarked for visitors and two ancient high-level drove roads, the Mounth road and the Firmounth road, lead southwards through the Estate to Glen Esk.

Leith Hall

NJ 5429; 116ha; NTS
Woodland, moor and farmland
Hide; trail leaflet on site;
ranger-naturalist
May–August

Two trails, each 2.5–3km long, lead through this small estate. One climbs through mixed plantation, where the herb layer includes wood-sorrel, leopard's-bane and pink purslane, to a viewpoint on open moorland. Roe deer occur in the woodland and in one grassy glade Scotch argus and ringlet butterflies can be seen in August.

The second trail passes a wide variety of native trees; a side track leads off to the ponds with their observation hide. Mallard, tufted duck, teal and heron are among the birds that visit these pools, which are an important breeding site for common toad.

Natural regeneration of Scots pine is a feature of the old Caledonian forest in Glen Tanar.

Loch of Strathbeg

Permit only; 942ha; RSPB reserve
Loch, marshes, dunes and woodland
Open all year, Wednesday and Sunday, by advance
arrangement only; apply RSPB warden, The Lythe,
Crimonmogate, Lonmay, Fraserburgh AB4 4UB
Access limited to reception area and hides;
approach is across MOD land and visitors must
obtain permit in advance
Reception hut with display; two hides; leaflet from
warden or RSPB, Edinburgh
October–March; wildfowl; April–July;
breeding birds

This very large, shallow loch, lying only a few
hundred metres from the east coast, acts as a magnet to migrating wildfowl. Many thousands of
duck, geese and swans rest and feed there, some
staying only a few hours or days and others spending the winter on the reserve. At times the number
of wildfowl on the loch exceeds 20,000 and the
sight and sound of their flights to and from the
farmland on which many of them feed is an ex-
hilarating experience.

Mallard are the most abundant of the wintering
duck, with tufted duck coming a close second.
Several hundred goldeneye are sometimes present
and pochard, red-breasted merganser and goosander are all regular visitors. So too are barnacle geese,
which often appear at Strathbeg in early October,
en route from Spitsbergen to their winter grounds
at CAERLAVEROCK on the Solway. However the
majority of wintering geese are pink-footed and
greylag.

Mallard, tufted duck, eider and shelduck breed
on the reserve and water rail nest in the dense
vegetation of the marshes. The reedbeds at the
north west end of the loch and the willow and
alder scrub there hold populations of reed bunting,
sedge and willow warbler, and wren.

Both marshes and scrub attract a variety of
migrants. Sparrowhawk, merlin and short-eared
owl can often be seen as they hunt over the reserve,
and the cover available draws small birds that have
made a landfall on the coast nearby. The 185 or so
species recorded since 1973 have included such
exciting rarities as pied-billed grebe, little egret,
crane, Caspian tern and red-footed falcon.

Roe deer can often be watched as they browse in
the surrounding scrub and badger are occasionally
seen. Otter are also present but seldom observed
and mink have unfortunately become established
in the area, presenting a threat to breeding wildfowl.

With habitats ranging from freshwater marsh to
lime-rich dunes the reserve has a diverse flora and
a good variety of insects. Grass-of-Parnassus, field
gentian and Scots lovage occur on the dunes and
angelica, early marsh-orchid and greater butterfly-
orchid in the marsh. Migrant butterflies such as red
admiral, peacock and painted lady occur quite
often; resident species include dark green and
small pearl-bordered fritillary, common blue and
small copper.

Longhaven Cliffs: flowers flourish in sheltered
areas.

Longhaven Cliffs

NK 1239; 2.5km; SWT reserve
Coastal cliffs
Access from NK 116393
May–July

The coastline in this part of Buchan is really
spectacular; its pinky red granite cliffs are deeply
indented and carved into impressive stacks and
holes, the best known of which, the Bullers of
Buchan, lie just south of the reserve boundary.
Nine seabird species breed on these cliffs, the total
population numbering somewhere around 23,000
pairs. The distribution of most species is uneven,
governed by the form of the weathered rock and
the availability of suitable ledges and niches, but
every stack and headland has its quota of wailing
herring gull. Perhaps 2000 pairs nest in the area,
along with a few pairs each of greater black-backed
and lesser black-backed gulls. Kittiwake too are
numerous but their nests here are widely scattered.
Huddles of guillemot pack the lower ledges and
crannies, those with eggs or small chicks recognisable by their half-squatting posture with drooping
wings. Shag favour the lowest sites of all,
sometimes building their untidy seaweed nests
only just clear of the high-tide mark. As the sun
catches their iridescent plumage it turns them from
black to green snakelike creatures whose 'back
hair' is blown about by the breeze. There are numbers of puffin to be seen here too, standing outside
their burrows or hurtling by on whirring wings,
orange feet thrust out astern and multi-coloured
bills ahead.

The sparkling river, varied woods and hills give Deeside great scenic and wildlife interest.

Not all the Buchan cliffs area is sheer and bird-strewn. Here and there steep slopes lead down to bays and inlets bright with flowers: sheets of red campion tossing in the wind, rounded cushions of thrift, primroses and violets tucked into sheltered nooks, and marsh-marigold and celandine where water seeps down. There are bluebells too, in both blue and white forms. Along the clifftop much of the vegetation is low and stunted by the wind. Patches of heath occur here, with bell heather, heather, crowberry and bearberry. Scots lovage and burnet rose are among the more interesting species present, with abundant roseroot.

Middle Deeside

See map; includes 17 sites
Information from tourist offices in Ballater or Banchory
All year

Middle Deeside, with its imposing string of castles – Balmoral, Braemar, CRATHES and DRUM are simply the better-known few among many – has been a tourist haunt since Queen Victoria's day. The two main features of this central section of Deeside are rather neatly summed up by a local jingle which runs:

> The River Dee for fish and tree,
> The River Don for horn and corn.

The Dee is one of Scotland's most famous salmon rivers, while its banks and hillsides carry woodlands of great attraction and variety; but as farmland Deeside is poor and unproductive in comparison to neighbouring Strathdon.

One of the few large Scottish rivers unaffected by hydroelectric schemes, the Dee is also free of industrial pollution except in its lowermost reaches. It has the additional advantages of a large-ly granite bed and the greatest altitudinal range of any river in Britain. Pure, well-oxygenated water such as this is ideal for salmon; for the angler there can be few more scenic places in which to pit his wits and strength against those of the king of fish.

Other fishers on the Dee include mink and otter, both of which have been studied from the Institute of Terrestrial Ecology's research station at nearby Hill of Brathens. It was found that mink in this area fed largely on rabbits in summer and duck in winter, while otter took mainly eels in summer and small salmon and trout in winter. Quiet waters with plenty of cover, such as Loch Davan on the MUIR OF DINNET reserve, proved important as 'nursery' areas where the otter cubs could be reared to independence in peace, and thickly wooded stretches of river bank were also valuable in ensuring the necessary seclusion.

A colourful early summer feature is the great swatches of brilliant blue nootka lupin that adorn the riverside shingle banks downstream from Ballater. At this time of year the cascading white blossom of bird cherry is also very evident along the roadsides and in some of the mixed woodlands, while thickets of gorse and broom glow vivid yellow in odd corners. The contrasting forms of silver and downy birch, the one pendulous and the other erect and angular, are both represented. Rowan and wild cherry are also common and aspen occurs more locally. There are oaks on Deeside too, notably at DINNET OAKWOOD, Aboyne and Craigendarroch, on the north side of Ballater, with a few real old worthies still surviving in the ancient forest of Drum. The Craigendarroch oaks have been there at least since the early nineteenth century and were once coppiced; the Dinnet wood, although planted, has much of the character of a semi-natural oakwood. There are also many fine mixed policy woodlands, such as those at Crathes.

Birch and pine are, however, the trees most typical of middle Deeside. Although often forming separate woods they sometimes grow intermixed, as happens near Crathie in a wood where juniper is also present, and both readily regenerate in this area when conditions are right. Young birches are rapidly colonising, and changing the appearance of, the Muir of Dinnet, and in GLEN TANAR pines are becoming established in open moorland. Even in the ancient forest of the Ballochbuie, where little regeneration has taken place for many years due to pressure of deer grazing, a recent fencing programme has already resulted in the appearance of thriving young trees. Deer pressure is heavy in GLENMUICK too, where there are virtually no young trees outside the fenced plantations.

With its good diversity of woodland types, interspersed with scrub, moorland, rough pasture and wetlands, middle Deeside supports a rich variety of bird species. Interesting changes in bird populations have taken place in recent years. Green woodpecker are now well established in the mixed woodland and have even been recorded from pinewoods. Jay have spread widely, breeding in plantations as well as deciduous woods. Buzzard too have increased greatly: scarce on Deeside until about 1945, they have become a regular sight. While Scottish crossbill remain firmly associated with the native pinewoods, the smaller-billed common crossbill appears to be colonising some of the conifer plantations. Perhaps more surprising was an influx of crested tits during the 1970s. Other recent exciting records include wryneck and goshawk; the latter, once widespread in Scotland, now shows signs of re-establishing itself in several areas with extensive plantations.

There have also been changes in mammal populations. Since grey squirrel were first reported on Deeside, in Glen Tanar in 1971, they have spread through many of the valley's hardwoods, despite endeavours to exterminate them. A more welcome expansion of range has been that of pine marten, with sightings now being reported well down the valley.

Changes in the distribution of birds and mammals cannot always be explained by changes in habitat availability, however. Lochs Davan and Kinord have not undergone any significant change in recent years, but goldeneye are summering there increasingly. Soon, perhaps, the pairs displaying there will breed, as they have done on Speyside since 1970. The recent breeding of red-throated diver on a hill loch in Deeside, after an absence from the area of over 95 years, is not easy to explain; nor is the upsurge in breeding redwing and fieldfare in the Highlands from the late 1960s.

To enjoy middle Deeside's wildlife to the full leave the main tourist route up the A93. Explore the minor roads south of the river and up into the Forest of Birse, and to the north around Tarland, Lumphanan and Torphins. Follow the 'high roads' on to the moorlands, from Banchory up to the Cairn o' Mount and from Ballater up the notorious Cock-

bridge to Tomintoul route. Take to the hills at the head of Glenmuick and Glen Tanar.

This is not to suggest, of course, that you should avoid such popular places as the Burn O' Vat on the Muir of Dinnet, or the woodlands of Crathes and Drum. But go there in the early morning or the evening, and avoid the weekends, if you want to see anything of the wildlife. The same applies to the various forest walks and the walkways along the former railway line.

Morrone Birkwood

NO 1390; 225ha; NCC reserve
Birch–juniper woodland
Access restricted to waymarked paths, starting from car park at NO 143911
May–July

With many features typical of similar woods in Norway, this is the best example in Britain of a subalpine birchwood on basic soils. The wood is pure downy birch, with a few stands of aspen and an understorey of low, heavily grazed juniper. The combination of lime-rich soils, the protection from grazing provided by the juniper bushes, and many flushes and wet hollows, has resulted in a rich and varied flora; some 280 species of flowering plants and ferns have been recorded.

This is one of the few places in Britain where mountain plants such as alpine cinquefoil, Scottish asphodel, alpine rush, three-flowered rush and hair sedge grow in a woodland setting, and the flora has changed comparatively little since postglacial times. The limestone schist crags and the scrub above the wood hold an interesting plant life which includes serrated wintergreen, twinflower, small-white orchid and holly fern. The wood is also notably rich in bryophytes and lichens.

Morrone Birkwood is subalpine in character.

Muir of Dinnet

NO 4399; 1408ha; NCC reserve
Moorland, woodland, bog, open water and
striking landform features
Landform trail; leaflet at tearoom, NO 429997, or
from NCC, Aberdeen; comprehensive reserve
report from NCC
*May–July: birds and flowers; October–December;
wildfowl*

Spring, when the birches are just coming into leaf, and late summer, when the heather is in full bloom, are when the Muir of Dinnet is perhaps most visually attractive. But it has something to offer at all seasons. The famous rock cauldron of the Vat, a gigantic pothole, is even more spectacular in wet or frosty weather than on a sunny summer day; and the twin lochs of Davan and Kinord hold many more birds in autumn and winter than in summer.

The landscape setting of the reserve is well known for its wealth of features formed by ice and water towards the end of the ice ages. Mounds and ridges of material deposited as the ice melted are widespread, deep channels cut by streams running under the ice score the hillsides, and the two lochs lie in basins formed where massive hunks of ice slowly thawed while deposition continued around them. The Burn O'Vat occupies one of the deepest meltwater channels. With this variety of landforms goes a corresponding diversity of vegetation, the dominant species in any area being largely dependent upon the wetness and the quality of the soil.

On the lower granite hills and gravel moraines of the western part of the reserve, heather and heather–bearberry heathland cover much of the ground. Rapid colonisation of Scots pine and birch has taken place in the last 20 years since muir-burning ceased. This moorland carries a species-rich heath in which mosses and lichens are abundant and intermediate wintergreen and petty whin quite common. The wet granite walls of the Vat support a rich bryophyte flora and a variety of ferns. Lemon-scented fern, brittle bladder-fern and beech fern are present along the Burn O'Vat.

Silver birch dominates the woodland which clothes some 243ha of the reserve. Much of the ground cover is grassy but in the older wood at New Kinord, where aspen, ash, hazel and blackthorn are present, there is a more varied plant life with abundant primrose, dog's mercury and wood anemone. Fungi grow profusely in the birchwoods in late summer and species represented include fly agaric, chanterelle and woolly milk-cap.

Lochs Davan and Kinord are shallow and have a moderately rich aquatic flora; the display of white and yellow water-lily in places sheltered from wind and waves is particularly impressive. Other plants include 11 species of pondweed, water lobelia, shoreweed, stonewort, greater bladderwort and six-stamened waterwort. Several different types of reedbed are represented, and the local downy-fruited sedge dominates large areas. Extensive stands of bog myrtle are also present.

The lochs are an important feeding ground for otter; family parties are regularly seen although there is no evidence of breeding on the reserve. Visitors hoping to see otter should watch from the A97 beside Loch Davan or the north shore of Loch Kinord near the Celtic Cross, but should not enter the surrounding vegetation as this disturbs them. Mink are known to breed here, fox and wild cat visit occasionally, as do red deer, and there is a large resident population of roe deer.

Loch Kinord is regularly visited by otters, which find good fishing and cover in the marshes.

St Cyrus: the cliffs and dunes support a remarkable variety of flowering plants.

Some 140 bird species have been recorded, 76 of them breeding regularly. Populations of willow warbler, redpoll, great tit and woodcock are notably high. Numbers of breeding wildfowl are not large but the autumn and early winter flocks of duck, geese and whooper swan are often substantial. Peak counts of greylag goose have been nearly 8000 and of pink-footed goose on passage 2000. Pintail, gadwall, shoveler and pochard are recorded annually in small numbers and goldeneye occasionally summer on the lochs. Moorland birds include wintering merlin and hen harrier and breeding black grouse.

More than 380 species of moth have been noted in the reserve, among them several uncommon and local species such as Kentish glory, scarce prominent, cousin german, and large red-belted clearwing. This site is important for dragonflies; rare beetles and bugs have also been recorded.

St Cyrus

NO 7464; 92ha; NCC reserve
Foreshore, dunes and cliff
Access restricted in tern breeding area,
May–August
Leaflet from NCC, Aberdeen; comprehensive
report also available
*April–July; flowers and breeding birds; July:
butterflies; September–November: migrants*

A 4km sweep of golden sand, backed by narrow dunes, and a relict cliff, makes St Cyrus an attractive beach to the casual visitor. To the naturalist this reserve, although nowhere more than 400m wide, offers a surprising diversity of habitats and a remarkable range of wildlife. Foreshore, sand dunes, saltmarsh, dune pasture, aprons of scree and blown sand below the cliff, and the cliffs themselves – of mineral-rich volcanic rocks – are all represented, and each has it own special interest. A bonus is the active salmon fishery, with its traditional netting methods, which also influences the wildlife of the area.

The reserve musters an impressive 350 flowering plants and ferns, including several species at the northern limit of their distribution here. Most of the latter occur on the inland cliffs, which are dry, sheltered and of south eastern aspect. The night-scented Nottingham catchfly grows on the drier ledges, as do the small annual soft clover, with pale pink flowers, and rough clover, with tiny white flowers; all three are very local. Tall yellow spikes of great mullein and vivid blue viper's-bugloss make splashes of colour where there is a slippage of unstable slopes. Marjoram, carline thistle and wild liquorice are among the less common plants of the cliff grassland, and henbane occurs at the northern end of the sea cliffs.

Despite the increasingly rank growth on the dune pastures since myxomatosis decimated the rabbit population, this area is still rich in wild flowers. Cowslip, purple milk-vetch, hairy violet, clustered bellflower and maiden pink are among the most interesting and colourful. Where tracks and rabbit scrapes have disturbed the ground winter annuals such as spring vetch and common corn-salad are found. Since a major sand blow in 1967 the saltmarsh has almost disappeared and many of the typical saltmarsh species have been replaced by 'weed' and pasture plants.

The Sands of Forvie dunes hold large numbers of breeding eiders and terns.

St Cyrus is important for insects, with 13 species of butterfly and over 200 moths recorded; several of the latter have not been found anywhere else in Scotland. Among the butterflies present are the brightly coloured small copper, small blue and grayling. Moths recorded include the day-flying cinnabar, near its northern limit in Britain, Mother Shipton, six-spot burnet and bordered grey, of particular interest as its only known food plant is heather, which is very scarce here.

Although the land area of the reserve is so limited, 47 bird species have bred there. The little tern colony on the sand and shingle at the south end of the reserve has had varying success, on occasion suffering serious predation from crows, rats, stoats and kestrels. The colony is fenced and wardened during the breeding season. A small population of grasshopper warbler breeds and stonechat, whitethroat and yellowhammer frequent the gorse scrub. Fulmar and herring gull nest on the cliffs and eider throughout the reserve. This area is also good for migrants, with regular autumn passage of skuas and shearwaters, winter records of all three divers, and a total of 29 wader species listed.

Otter tracks are occasionally found on the river bank and common porpoise are sometimes seen off-shore. Grey seal occur regularly, but common seal are rare locally.

Sands of Forvie and Ythan Estuary

NK 0227; 1018ha; NCC reserve
Estuary, saltmarsh, dunes, moorland, sea cliffs and sandy foreshore
Permit only away from footpaths and foreshore; apply NCC, Aberdeen
Hide overlooking ternery; leaflet and reserve handbook from NCC, Aberdeen
April–July: breeding birds; August–December: waders and wildfowl

The largest concentration of eider in Britain breeds here during the summer months, nesting among the dunes and moorland and leading the newly hatched ducklings down to the estuary and seashore to feed. By May many of the ducks are incubating; their finely speckled plumage and habit of freezing motionless make them difficult to spot. On the river parties of drakes still court any unattached ducks, oo-hooing as they bow and then lay back their heads to display their salmon-pink breasts to full advantage. In June ducklings are everywhere, dark fluffy balls diving in shallow water, bouncing on the waves, and gradually being gathered into large creches. Many eider leave the estuary in autumn to moult but some remain throughout the year, feeding on the mussels that throng the river bed.

Shelduck also breed in the dunes, generally in rabbit burrows where the eggs are safe from marauding crows and gulls. Each pair defends its feeding patch on the snail-rich inter-tidal mud and territorial disputes are common.

Other important summer visitors are terns. Four species nest in the dunes: Sandwich tern in a large, dense colony, common and arctic in smaller numbers and often within the limits of the black-headed gull colony, and little tern, at present making use of an 'inland beach' well away from the hazards of waves and wind-blown sand to which nests on the open beach are exposed. Terns are notoriously temperamental, frequently abandoning apparently suitable sites for no obvious reason, and at Sands of Forvie strict measures are taken to ensure that disturbance does not cause desertion.

The movements of the dunes themselves, however, can force the birds to change their nesting area. This is the least man-disturbed large dune system in Britain and winter gales regularly alter the shape and location of the Sahara-like mounds of loose sand. All stages in the development of a dune system can be seen here, from marram-covered ridges to dune-heath vegetation of heather, abundant crowberry and many different lichens. The habitats represented, which vary widely in soil moisture, support a great range of flowering plants.

In autumn and winter the Ythan Estuary attracts large numbers of waders: sanderling run along the seaward shore, the lower estuary with its mussel beds and pools holds turnstone, ringed plover, redshank, curlew and bar-tailed godwit, and the creeks and flats of the upper estuary are visited by spotted redshank, greenshank, little stint and green sandpiper.

The area is important too for passage and wintering wildfowl. The flocks of pink-footed geese which gather on the estuary and feed on nearby farmland sometimes number as many as 10,000. Wigeon, teal, red-breasted merganser and whooper swan all winter in fair numbers and in rough weather long-tailed duck and goldeneye quite often enter the river mouth. Large flocks of scoter, divers and merganser occur offshore from autumn to spring.

Speyside Way

NJ 349654–167367; 48km; Moray DC
Long-distance walk by River Spey
Leaflets from Moray DC; exhibition in Tugnet Ice House, Spey Bay; ranger service
All year

From Spey Bay, with its terns, waders and seals, the route follows first a footpath and later the line of the former Strathspey railway, passing through varied landscapes and habitats. Osprey sometimes fish in the Spey below Fochabers, butterflies are plentiful along the tree-sheltered stretches of track, and a wide variety of flowering plants grows by the path.

White Cow and Loudon Wood

NJ 9550; 270ha; FC
Plantations
Forest walk at NJ 957513
All year

In the largely tree-less Buchan countryside all size-able stands of trees are important to wildlife. These spruce woods are particularly notable for their badger setts and heronry.

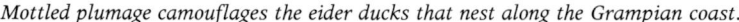

Mottled plumage camouflages the eider ducks that nest along the Grampian coast.

Highland North

The districts of Ross and Cromarty, Sutherland and Caithness together constitute one-sixth of the area of Scotland, yet their joint human population contributes only 1.3 per cent of the total and their burghs would be accorded village status south of the border. This is a land of violent contrasts, from the great Torridonian mountains of Wester Ross towering over 900m straight out of the sea, and the terrible barrens of west Sutherland, to the rich, fertile farmlands of Caithness and the Dornoch Firth. These, together with offshore islands, ancient woodlands, innumerable freshwater lochs, desolate moorland and many kilometres of the finest cliff coastline in Britain complement an equivalent diversity of wildlife with many reserves of national and international importance.

There are no averages, only extremes: rainfall may vary in Ross-shire from 2500mm or more in the Atlantic influence of the south west to a mere 500mm on the east coast of the Black Isle. The effect of wind is reflected in the vegetation: west of the Kyle of Durness trees cannot grow, but there is a 'forest' of juniper heath a few centimetres high. In the same district, in Migdale Wood on the Dornoch Firth, juniper grows as a columnar tree 3m high in the shelter of the old pines.

During the last ice age the thickest and heaviest part of the ice-cap lay over west Sutherland and Ross; it scoured the land bare, leaving a few pockets of soil on the coast only. This effect is seen most vividly on the hard, acid Lewisian gneiss of west Sutherland, where there is literally no soil and little glacial drift, only pockets of peat in the hollows and a magnificent array of 'perched rocks' and glacial erratic boulders unchanged for 10,000 years. Much of the west coast, however, including most of the mountains of Wester Ross, is Torridonian sandstone. This is a more recent, softer

and less acid rock which has weathered into spectacular cliffs and stacks like Rudha Reidh, Point of Stoer (with the Old Man) and, notably, the famous bird colonies of HANDA and the Clo Mor where the bedding of the Torridonian forms such admirable ledges for auks and kittiwakes.

The Durness limestone shows its influence in a narrow strip from Kishorn to Faraid Head, in the limestone pavement of RASSAL ASHWOOD, the botanically rich area of INCHNADAMPH, and finally in Durness itself, an oasis of calcareous grassland and lime-rich lochs in a sour and barren landscape. To the east, large tracts of Ross and Sutherland are of Moine schist, much overlain by peat and blanket bog but elsewhere with a rich flora – Ben Dearg and Seana Bhraigh are considered to have the finest montane flora in the north Highlands, surpassed in Scotland only by the CAIRNGORMS (Highland South) and BEN LAWERS (Tayside).

Finally there is the old red sandstone of the east, well known for its spectacular cliff scenery and fossil fish beds. It underlies the high-quality arable farmland covering most of Caithness, east Sutherland and the whole of Easter Ross and the Black Isle, so different from the narrow strip of glacial drift forming the croft lands of the north and west. It is no coincidence that the fertility of these lands is reflected in the rich feeding in the bays, firths and shallow seas of the east for the incredible numbers of wildfowl and waders which frequent these coasts, and are protected there in several reserves of international importance.

Geology apart, however, the north Highlands today are a product of the activities of man. Pastoral people inhabited these lands in pre-Roman times and 2000 years of grazing, burning and felling have reduced the natural woodlands to a few pitiful relics. Sutherland suffered most in this respect, and at an early date lost all the original pine and most of the oak. Ross-shire suffered rather less, and fortunately has retained several fine examples of the old pine forest such as those at BEINN EIGHE, LOCH MAREE and TORRIDON.

Man's influence has not been entirely on the debit side; reafforestation by estates began in the eighteenth century, notably in Sutherland. At LOCH FLEET occurs what is probably the only example in Britain of natural regeneration of pine on sand dunes, seeded from one of the original estate plantations, and on the adjacent reserve are the magnificent MOUND ALDERWOODS, a spontaneous growth on land reclaimed from the sea by the erection of the Mound barrier in 1816.

More recently the Forestry Commission has transformed much of Sutherland's 'wet desert' into coniferous forest. This is a source of much criticism, although welcomed by many, and certainly provides new habitats for birds and mammals. The older plantations are gradually acquiring some of the characteristic plant and animal life of primary forest, for example one-flowered wintergreen at Loch Fleet; and crested tit and Scottish crossbill are now breeding in the Shin Forest.

The diversity of landscape and habitat, mountain, moorland, sea coast and woodland in the northern Highlands is unsurpassed elsewhere in the kingdom. Fortunately the nature reserves carry a fair representation of all these. A few, such as STRATHY BOG and ACHANARRAS QUARRY, are of such specialised interest that they have little to offer the casual visitor. Handa is an island gem even without its famous seabird cliffs, although ornithologists on holiday will probably find much more on the east coast firths. The vast wilderness areas, however, such as Torridon with Beinn Eighe or INVERPOLLY with BEN MORE COIGACH, may be enjoyed by everyone from bryologists or ecological historians to lovers of fine scenery.

I.D. PENNIE

Achanarras Quarry

Permit only; 44ha; NCC reserve
Disused quarry
Collection restricted and by permit only, from
NCC, Golspie
All year

This site is of international importance for the very rich fossil vertebrate fauna preserved in a 5m exposure of Caithness flagstone.

Allt nan Carnan

NG 8940; 7ha; NCC reserve
Wooded gorge
April–June

Carved through calcareous schists, this 1.6km long gorge is up to 30m deep, with dangerously slippery, sheer sides. Oak and birch dominate the woodland, with some bird cherry, ash, rowan, holly, aspen and hazel, and a good range of bryophytes on both trees and exposed rocks. The rich and varied ground flora includes stone bramble, yellow saxifrage, opposite-leaved golden-saxifrage and alpine lady's-mantle.

Beinn Eighe

NG 9862; 4800ha; NCC reserve
Mountainous area with remnant Caledonian pine forest
Access restricted 1 September–21 November; contact wardens (Kinlochewe 254 or 244) or Aultroy Visitor Centre (Kinlochewe 257) for advice
Nature trail and reserve leaflets from Aultroy Visitor Centre (open weekdays May–September) or from NCC, Inverness
May–August

The jagged ridge of Beinn Eighe, with its long snow-white skirt of quartzite scree, gives the southern aspect of this reserve a somewhat forbid-ding look. In contrast, the north east slopes present a more welcoming appearance, with native pine-woods extending from the shores of Loch Maree up to about 400m above sea level. This fragment of Scots pine forest, with its scattering of birch, rowan and holly, carpets of heather, bilberry and cowberry, and colourful mounds of bog mosses, is full of interest for both general and specialist visitors. So too are the slopes above the tree line, where dwarf shrub heath is interspersed with patches of lusher vegetation and outcropping bands of fossil-bearing lime-rich rock. Beinn Eighe has been internationally recognised and designated a Biosphere Reserve under UNESCO's Man and Biosphere Programme.

Alpine lady's-mantle is found at Allt nan Carnan.

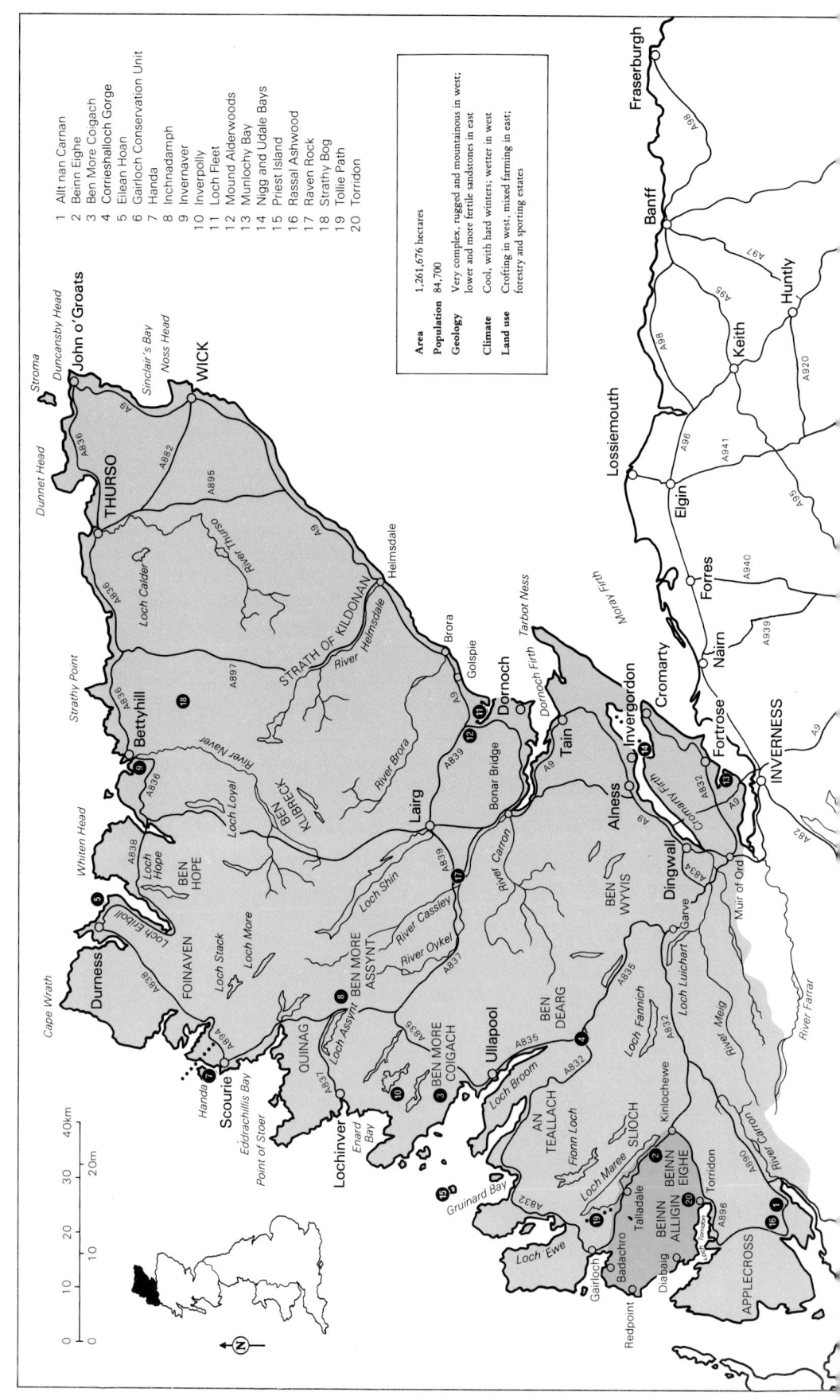

Area	1,261,676 hectares
Population	84,700
Geology	Very complex, rugged and mountainous in west; lower and more fertile sandstones in east
Climate	Cool, with hard winters; wetter in west
Land use	Crofting in west, mixed farming in east; forestry and sporting estates

1 Allt nan Carnan
2 Beinn Eighe
3 Ben More Coigach
4 Corrieshalloch Gorge
5 Eilean Hoan
6 Gairloch Conservation Unit
7 Handa
8 Inchnadamph
9 Invernaver
10 Inverpolly
11 Loch Fleet
12 Mound Alderwoods
13 Munlochy Bay
14 Nigg and Udale Bays
15 Priest Island
16 Rassal Ashwood
17 Raven Rock
18 Strathy Bog
19 Tollie Path
20 Torridon

Beinn an Eoin rises steeply from the moorlands of Ben Mór Coigach; the distant hill is Stac Pollaidh.

The shorter (1.5km) of the reserve's two trails, both of which start from the car park at NH 000650, winds through a representative section of the pinewood, including a few open clearings where mineral-rich water seeps through the soil and species such as water avens, globeflower and melancholy thistle can be found. Roe deer are fairly common in the woodland, and in winter many red deer come down from the hills to find shelter and food. Pine marten and wild cat, although present, are rarely seen. The bird population is rather limited in both variety and numbers, with only 15 woodland species breeding and 27 recorded: willow warbler and coal tit are among the commonest; goldcrest, siskin, redpoll and crossbill are resident throughout the year; redstart and tree pipit are present in fair numbers in summer. A number of rare invertebrate species, not recorded elsewhere in the area, are found in the woodland.

The second trail (6.5km) climbs to an altitude of 540m and passes through a variety of montane habitats. Immediately above the tree line, dwarf juniper, heather and bearberry sprawl through a dense carpet of mosses and liverworts; slightly higher up, the vegetation is more varied and includes creeping willow, crowberry, trailing azalea, dwarf cornel and moonwort. This is ptarmigan, red deer and mountain hare country, though they are not abundant; their predators are correspondingly scarce, but golden eagle, buzzard, merlin and fox all hunt here occasionally.

A pony path which leaves the road at NH 022628 provides the best approach route to the highest ground. Up on the exposed ridges and summit plateau woolly fringe-moss–mat-grass heath is the most widespread form of vegetation. Where weathering of mineral-rich rocks has produced a more fertile soil, arctic–alpine species such as moss campion, mossy saxifrage, alpine saw-wort, alpine meadow-rue, sibbaldia and northern rock-cress are present while the larger cliff ledges carry mountain sorrel, globeflower, purple saxifrage and the more local Highland saxifrage and pyramidal bugle. Hill walking equipment is essential in these areas.

The bryophyte and lichen flora of Beinn Eighe is of special interest. Some northern Atlantic liverworts, usually found on treeless hills, occur within the upper limit of the woodland, including *Herberta hutchinsiae*, *Bazzania pearsonii* and *Jamesoniella carringtonii*, and the conspicuous leafy liverwort *Herberta borealis*, known elsewhere only in Norway, is present in quantity amongst the dwarf juniper–heather–bearberry heath. The woodland is also rich in lichens and in Atlantic mosses, among them *Daltonia splachnoides* and *Hylocomium umbratum*. Lungwort grows abundantly on the pines.

Ben Mór Coigach

NC 0807; 6075ha; SWT–RSNC reserve
Mountain and moorland, coastline and islets
No access to islets
May–July

Shapely Ben Mór Coigach (743m) and the twin peaks of Beinn an Eoin dominate all views of this vast area of rock and wet heath. To the north the steep sandstone slopes of Beinn an Eoin give way to heather–grass moorland streaked with brighter green, mineral-rich flushes. Scrub birch lines the gullies running down to the lowland around the shores of Loch Lurgainn, whose barrenness is relieved by scattered small birchwoods containing some aspen, rowan and holly. Deergrass and cottongrass blanket bog with sundews and bog asphodel covers the undulating western moorland, while the smoother slopes above Achiltibuie are largely heather-clad. Much of the croftland included in the reserve is no longer actively cultivated, but is still used for grazing stock and should not be entered without permission from the crofters. Barnacle geese graze this ground in winter and eider can frequently be observed on the shoreline and islets.

The botanical interest of the reserve centres largely on the woodland, and on the crags and summits of the hills. Brittle bladder-fern, northern buckler-fern, alpine scurvygrass, three-leaved rush, trailing azalea and dwarf juniper are among the species present.

Breeding birds on the reserve include ptarmigan, raven, ring ouzel, golden plover, greenshank and twite. Large numbers of red deer roam the hills and pine marten, otter, badger and wild cat may be seen. Although the insect life has not yet been studied in detail five species of dragonfly and at least five of butterfly have been recorded.

Corrieshalloch Gorge

NH 204777; 14ha; NTS–NCC reserve
Wooded gorge
April–September

This spectacular gorge, a fine example of a box canyon, is 1.6km long and reaches a maximum depth of 60m at the Falls of Measach. A narrow strip of woodland, mainly of mixed native species, fringes the ravine, and a rich variety of mosses and liverworts grows on the sheer walls of the gorge and on the boulders in the stream bed. The bridge offers good views of the falls and of the inaccessible depths of the River Droma below.

Drummondreach Oakwood

Permit only; 7.5ha; SWT reserve
Deciduous woodland
April–July

The richness of the ground flora under these near-mature oaks suggests that they were planted on an old natural oakwood site. Regeneration of oak, ash, rowan and birch is taking place in the wood, which also contains beech, wild cherry, bird cherry, blackthorn and juniper, over herb-Paris, moschatel, enchanter's-nightshade, meadow cow-wheat and hard shield-fern.

Eilean Hoan

NC 4567; 40ha; RSPB reserve
Uninhabited island
Access very difficult
All year

Although this low grassy island is not far from the mainland, the sea between is rough enough to ensure that the bird population is little disturbed. In winter the most northerly regular flock of barnacle geese grazes here and in summer eider, oystercatcher, ringed plover, lapwing and terns nest among the thrift, sea campion and bird's-foot-trefoil. Great northern diver in breeding plumage gather off Eilean Hoan in spring before migrating to Iceland, and are visible with a telescope from the coast road.

Gairloch Conservation Unit

See TORRIDON AND LOCH MAREE.

Gualin

Permit only; 2522ha; NCC reserve
Mountain, moorland, lochs, bogs and river
Permit from NCC, Inverness
April–July

This vast wilderness includes the quartzite ridges of Foinaven (908m), extensive areas of undulating and rugged gneiss plateau, and the intricately patterned peat bogs of Strath Dionard. It supports an interesting variety of northern montane and bog plant communities.

Handa

NC 1348; 310ha; RSPB reserve
High inshore island
Day visits (not Sundays) April–August
Leaflet from RSPB, Edinburgh; access by small boat, weather permitting, from Tarbet, NC 1648
May–July

In summer many thousands of seabirds throng the near-vertical cliffs which bound Handa on three sides. Some 140m high on the north side, the cliffs gradually decrease in height southwards, finally giving way to sandy bays. The horizontally layered rock weathers unevenly, forming ideal breeding ledges which attract guillemot, the most numerous species. They are seen most dramatically on the sides of the famous Great Stack of Handa. Numbers of razorbill are also high, around 9000 pairs, with large populations of kittiwake and fulmar, and a few hundred pairs each of puffin and shag.

Handa's Great Stack is a multi-storey for seabirds.

Black-throated divers nest by many Highland lochs.

Six lochans enliven the moorland interior of the island and provide freshwater bathing sites for the birds. A plantation of lodgepole pine and alder near the bothy gives cover for small migrants and for breeding robin, song thrush and dunnock. Deergrass and heather dominate the moorland, with heath spotted-orchid, northern marsh-orchid, bog asphodel and pale butterwort giving colour in the damper areas. Other plants of interest include royal fern, few-flowered spike-rush and Scots lovage. Details of a comprehensive survey of the flora are available from the Summer Warden.

Wheatear, skylark and meadow pipit are the commonest birds on the moorland, which has been colonised since 1964 by both great and arctic skua. Several pairs of each now breed along with shelduck, eider, ringed plover, stonechat and occasionally golden plover and red grouse. Visitors are asked to keep to the marked paths to avoid disturbance to the birds. Divers are often seen offshore, and in winter a small flock of barnacle geese grazes on the island.

Inchnadamph

NC 2719; 1300ha; NCC reserve
Moorland with limestone outcrops
Access restricted: contact warden, tel. Assynt 208
Leaflet from NCC, Inverness, or Knockan Visitor
Centre, Inverpolly
May–June

This reserve is best known for the great range of erosive features contained in the limestone plateau, including caves, swallow-holes and underground streams. The Allt nan Uamh caves have yielded relics of human occupation dating back to the late Stone Age and bones of animals now extinct in Scotland. The reserve's rich plant life includes mountain avens, holly fern and serrated wintergreen, and several uncommon willow species.

Invernaver

NC 6961; 552ha; NCC reserve
Seashore, dunes, raised beach, and rocky
moorland with lochans
Access easiest from Borgie, at NC 681612
May–July

A strange combination of physical features and climatic conditions makes this a site of particular ecological interest. Exposure to frequent northerly gales inhibits tree growth in all but the most sheltered spots, and carries sand from the beach and dunes far up on to the hinterland of acid moorland. This shell-sand enriches the otherwise poor soils and supports an unusual mixture of plants. Montane and oceanic species appear in close proximity with lime-loving plants and those typical of acid moorland.

Dwarf juniper grows at all levels, from the moorland plateau almost down to the shore, and there are great mats of dwarf shrubs like mountain avens, crowberry, bearberry and creeping willow, and abundant thrift, sea campion, moss campion, yellow and purple saxifrage and alpine bistort. Scottish primrose is among the less common species present and the rich bryophyte flora includes one moss not yet recorded from any other British site.

A strip of birchwood along the lower slopes by the Naver adds habitat diversity and attracts bird species like sparrowhawk and woodcock which would not otherwise be found on the reserve; kestrel and buzzard hunt along the hillside and snipe and greenshank breed on the moorland lochans and bogs. Fox, badger, otter and wild cat have all been recorded.

Inverpolly

NC 1312; 10,856ha; NCC reserve
Moorland, mountain, woodland, lochs, bogs,
seashore and islands
Access restricted 1 September–21 October:
contact wardens, tel. Lochinver 204 or Elphin 234
Reserve and trail leaflets available at Knockan
Visitor Centre (NC 187094) or from NCC,
Inverness
April–May

Suilven forms a fine backdrop to Inverpolly's undulating moorland.

This vast area of rock hummocks, interspersed with numerous lochs and boggy hollows and dominated by the spectacular peaks of Stac Pollaidh, Cul Mor and Cul Beag, is in many senses a wilderness: no roads penetrate it and there are few tracks. Away from the approach routes to the peaks it is possible to lose sight of 'civilisation' within a few minutes of leaving the road and to wander all day without encountering another human being. The roughness of the terrain, the apparently endless undulating platform of gneiss, and the unreliability of the weather make a venture into the interior of Inverpolly quite an undertaking. But fortunately it is possible to get an impression of the reserve by walking the peripheral roads and the trails of Knockan Cliff on the eastern boundary. Those who do decide to tackle Stac Pollaidh (613m) should note that the summit ridge is crumbling and thus potentially dangerous.

The wide range of habitats at Inverpolly supports a corresponding variety of plant and animal life typical of the north west Highlands. One hundred and four bird species have been recorded, including golden plover, wheatear, ring ouzel, greenshank and stonechat on the moorland; wood warbler, treecreeper, long-tailed tit, spotted flycatcher and long-eared owl in the woodland; divers, mallard, wigeon, red-breasted merganser and goosander on the lochs; and shag, fulmar and black guillemot on the coast. Barnacle geese visit the islands in winter, ptarmigan and raven breed on the hills, and several birds of prey frequent the reserve.

Around 500 red deer roam freely over Inverpolly, generally moving up the corries and away from the road during the summer months and feeding on the flats near Elphin in winter. Otter fish along the shoreline and in the lochs, which contain char and eels as well as trout and salmon. Wild cat and pine marten are occasionally seen, as are badger, which often live in holes among the rocks rather than in setts.

The many small woods represent all that remains of what were once extensive birch–hazel woodlands. Birch is now the dominant species with some hazel, and rowan, holly, oak and bird cherry are also present. Some of the woodland soils are moderately fertile and support a varied ground cover including such species as selfheal, primrose, common dog-violet, melancholy thistle, meadowsweet, hay-scented buckler-fern, and a variety of mosses, liverworts and lichens. Lemon-scented fern and Wilson's filmy-fern are abundant in some areas.

Much of the undulating gneiss plateau is covered with wet heath dominated by heather, cottongrass, deergrass and purple moor-grass. Bog myrtle flourishes in the wetter areas, with the pools supporting bogbean and intermediate bladderwort, and great sundew and common butterwort around the margins. Lesser bladderwort and pale butterwort are more localised in their distribution. Altogether some 360 plant species have been recorded.

Although the Inverpolly reserve is of great natural history interest it is probably best known for its geological importance. Knockan Cliff played a major part in the history of geological discovery: from studying this cliff geologists first realised that forces arising deep within the earth can cause great masses of rock to slide up a gently inclined fault line and eventually come to rest on top of much younger rock. The basis for this discovery is clearly demonstrated along the Knockan Cliff Geological Trail.

Loch A' Mhuilinn

Permit only; 67ha; NCC reserve
Woodland, heath, fresh water and coast
Permit from NCC, Inverness
April–July

Set in a characteristically undulating Lewisian gneiss landscape, this reserve is a mosaic of different habitats. Small patches of lichen-rich birch woodland are of special scientific interest as they include oak, near its northern limit in Britain. The heathy areas, marshes and coastline support a variety of flora and fauna typical of the area.

Loch Fleet

NH 7796; 709ha; SWT reserve
Tidal basin, dunes and pine woodland
Access to woodland restricted to path
*May–July: flowers and breeding birds;
October–March: wildfowl*

Only a narrow channel between shingle bars separates Loch Fleet from the sea, and when the tide is out mudflats are exposed over most of the basin.

In summer shelduck, redshank and oystercatcher feed on the rich invertebrate life in the mud, and eider on the mussel beds along the course of the river. In autumn many different species of wader appear, some on passage and some to winter in the area. Curlew, golden plover and knot are often present in large numbers. This is also an important resort for wintering duck: mallard, teal and wigeon in and around the basin, goldeneye, red-breasted merganser, common scoter, eider and long-tailed duck commuting between sheltered water and open sea according to weather and tidal conditions. Common seal can often be seen on the sandbanks – the minor road along the south shore provides good viewpoints – and fishing arctic and common tern hover over the shallows in summer.

Although the woodlands are largely planted, natural regeneration of the Scots pine is occurring and the ground flora, typical of old-established pinewood sites, includes one-flowered wintergreen, creeping lady's-tresses, twinflower and lesser twayblade. Capercaillie, siskin and crossbill all breed here, and in one part of the woodland herring gull have established a small colony.

Loch Maree Islands

Permit only; 220ha; NCC reserve
Island group
Permit from NCC, Inverness
April–June

The reserve consists of about 40 small islands and three large ones which are interesting principally for their native Scots pine and well-grown juniper cover. Most of the species present are also found on BEINN EIGHE.

Mound Alderwoods

Permit only; 267ha; NCC reserve
Wet woodland, fen and open water
Viewing possible from public road at NH 775983
April–June

This unusual alderwood developed on the estuary of the River Fleet after the construction of the Mound embankment stopped tidal flow into the area. Sluices hold back the waters of LOCH FLEET on the seaward side of the bank at high tide and at the same time prevent adult salmon and their fry from moving upstream and downstream respectively. As the tide drops, there are often fine views from the bridge of the fish waiting for the sluice gates to open. Many of the wildfowl frequenting Loch Fleet visit the marshes on the downstream edge of the alderwood and terns fish in the open water.

The alderwood itself is of specialist, as distinct from special, interest. It contains no plant rarities but its fascination lies in the way in which the communities vary with changes in the watertable and level of salinity. Drainage cuts and the unevenness of the woodland floor make access very difficult in wet weather.

Nigg Bay: the rich mudflats attract vast flocks of wildfowl in autumn and many wintering waders.

Munlochy Bay

NH 6753; 443ha; Highland RC reserve
Tidal mudflats and saltmarsh
Open days, advertised locally; otherwise viewing from car park on A832 at NH 657537
September–March

This very sheltered inlet on the northern shore of the Moray Firth attracts up to 1000 wigeon in midwinter and around 200 shelduck in the first three months of the year. Several hundred teal and smaller numbers of mallard also frequent the bay, and greylag and pink-footed geese roost there fairly regularly in late winter.

Nigg and Udale Bays

NH 7873 and 7367; NCC reserve
Inter-tidal flats
Access difficult but much of the area can be viewed from the road
August–December

This reserve lies within the larger area of the Cromarty Firth, which is by far the most important site for wintering and passage wildfowl and waders in north east Scotland. Despite nearby industrial developments, the sheltered bays and great stretches of sand and mud are still internationally important for migratory wildfowl.

A good growth of eelgrass is largely responsible for attracting the thousands of wigeon and hundreds of whooper and mute swans that feed on the two sections of the reserve and elsewhere in the

Firth, while an abundant invertebrate population provides food for the several thousand waders generally present in autumn. Oystercatcher, redshank, curlew, knot and dunlin are the most numerous. Fair numbers of goldeneye winter on the Firth, and teal, pintail, shelduck, scaup and pink-footed geese are also regularly recorded. The autumn greylag goose population in Easter Ross often exceeds 10,000; many of these birds roost on the estuary.

Priest Island

NC 9303; 121ha; RSPB reserve
Uninhabited island
Landing is extremely difficult
All year

This grassy sandstone island is notable for its colony of storm petrel, estimated at over 10,000 pairs and the largest known in the United Kingdom. Other breeding species include greylag geese, which nest beside the small freshwater lochs, otter, and a few seabirds.

Rassal Ashwood

NG 8443; 85ha; NCC reserve
Ashwood on limestone
April–June

The ashwood, which occupies only 13ha of the reserve, is a prominent feature in a landscape of heath and rough grassland and the most northerly true ashwood in Britain. Some of the trees are large and the woodland is open in character with a curious hummocky floor produced by limestone ridges. Although subject to heavy grazing the

Thousands of wigeon visit Nigg Bay in autumn.

wood contains abundant hazel and some rowan, blackthorn and hawthorn. Woodland flowers are common only within the fenced enclosures or on the steep sides of the Allt Mor Gorge, part of which lies in the reserve.

On the lime-rich wet ground outside the wood, field gentian is present, broad-leaved cottongrass and black bog-rush flourish and there are drifts of yellow saxifrage around the many small rivulets. Further away from the limestone outcrop the ground cover is of bracken-dominated grassland and heather moor.

The lichens of Rassal Ashwood are of particular interest, with a number of relatively uncommon species growing on either the trees themselves or the rocks on the woodland floor.

Raven Rock

NC 5001; 2km; FC
Plantation and gorge
Leaflet, *Kyle of Sutherland Forest Walks*, from Lairg tourist office
All year

The steep-sided, damp gorge which lies at the heart of this plantation is particularly rich in mosses and ferns.

Strathy Bog

NC 7955; 49ha; NCC reserve
Blanket bog
Access by foot only; no road suitable for vehicles
April–June

This reserve represents one of the best remaining examples of low-lying blanket bog in Britain. Its physical features suggest the pattern of its past development and indicate how it may change in the future. Among a large variety of species of bog plant present are dwarf birch, sundews and bearberry.

Talich

Permit only; 13.5ha; SWT reserve
Alderwood and grassland
May–June

Talich includes both dry pasture, believed never to have been ploughed, and wet grassland with boggy flushes where a wide range of orchids can be found, among them fragrant and early-purple orchid, and lesser butterfly-orchid. The alder wood, in which cattle graze in winter, shows signs of previous coppicing.

Tollie Path

NG 889723–859790; 8km; FC
Conifer plantation and open hill
All year

This rough track gives fine views of the LOCH MAREE ISLANDS as it climbs from the loch shores up through rugged open hill country to join the A832 above Poolewe.

Torridon

NG 9059; 6518ha; NTS
Mountainous country
Visitor centre at NG 905557, open 1 June–30
September; display and audio-visual programme; deer
museum; booklet, from centre or NTS, Edinburgh;
guided walk programme;
contact ranger-naturalist
May–September

This vast wilderness area is one of the most scenically splendid in Scotland. Viewed from the
southern side of Loch Torridon, the fine peaks of
Liathach (1054m), Beinn Alligin (985m) and Beinn
Dearg (914m) cannot fail to impress with their steep
crags and soaring ridges. At closer range it is the
great corries and the towering shelves of sandstone, skirted with loose grey scree and riven by
stone chutes, that take the eye. Rock and water
dominate the scene, the latter not only as streams
and rivers rushing down the hillsides but also as
mist veiling the summits and swirling in the corries. These mountains are not for the inexperien-
ced, but fortunately they can still be appreciated,
and much of their natural history interest enjoyed,
from the safety of well-marked tracks.

That Scots pine once covered the lower slopes of
the hills is evident from the many twisted stumps
preserved in the peat. Today, apart from plantations and the woodland by Loch Torridon, only
scattered pine, birch, rowan and, surprisingly, the
occasional oak tree, struggle for survival in this
barren country. Heather, cross-leaved heath, deer-

*Under the humid conditions of Torridon, woolly
fringe-moss is wrinkled by its own wet weight.*

grass, cottongrass and purple moor-grass dominate
the vegetation on the lower ground, with bog
myrtle, in some places shoulder-high, in the wetter
areas, and crowberry, bearberry and dwarf juniper
where it is drier. Woolly fringe-moss and bog
mosses are plentiful, the former sometimes growing so luxuriantly on rock surfaces that it sags into
wrinkles under its own wet weight. Spotted-
orchids, bog asphodel, sundew and butterwort are
widespread, and water lobelia and bogbean grow
in the peaty lochans.

Higher on the hillsides, where bands of lime-rich
rock and absence of grazing animals encourage a
more varied and lush vegetation, many of the sandstone ledges are veritable rock gardens. Roseroot
and alpine scurvygrass are particularly abundant,
often accompanied by lowland meadow species
such as water avens, globeflower and marsh-
marigold. Starry and mossy saxifrage, alpine bistort and alpine willowherb grow around streams
and gullies, while on the drier slopes dwarf cornel,
parsley fern, alpine lady-fern and bog bilberry
occur. The most local plants of these mountains,
found at the highest levels among screes and on the
exposed ridges, include northern rock-cress, arctic
mouse-ear, least willow and curved wood-rush.

Birds and animals are comparatively scarce on
these bare hills; only the wooded shores of Loch
Torridon hold any variety of species. Torridon's

red deer population, like that of neighbouring BEINN EIGHE, forms part of the huge GAIRLOCH CONSERVATION UNIT and is carefully controlled. No access restrictions are imposed, however, within the NTS property. Small numbers of roe deer and mountain hare live here and fox is fairly common.

On the lower slopes of the hills the birds most likely to be seen or heard are golden plover, wheatear, ring ouzel and meadow pipit. Red-throated diver nest by some of the hill lochans and a few greenshank in the remoter bogs; there is a chance, too, of seeing golden eagle and peregrine over the high corries.

Torridon and Loch Maree (Gairloch Conservation Unit)

See map; includes two sites
Seasonal access restrictions: see below
All year

Extending over some 40,500ha of mountainous country, the land between Lochs Torridon and Maree can truly be described as one of Scotland's last great wildernesses. No roads penetrate its interior, nor do any encircle it. In some respects the beauty and grandeur of the area can best be appreciated from a distance: looking across the calm waters of Upper Loch Torridon towards the soaring peaks of Liathach, or down Glen Docherty to Loch Maree, stretching away between its guardian mountains, BEINN EIGHE and Slioch. But such spectacular views normally arouse a desire for closer acquaintance and it is fortunately quite easy to see much of interest in the area without expending vast amounts of time and energy. Those who wish to explore and enjoy its wild beauty to the full must, however, be prepared to do so on foot, adequately shod and equipped to cope with rough terrain, long distances and often unreliable weather.

Before embarking upon any such expedition the visitor should take note of the fact that virtually the whole of this area lies within the Gairloch Conservation Unit, in which the large herds of red deer are managed on a co-operative basis by the various landowners involved. Deer do not recognise estate boundaries – unless marked by a 2m fence – so the herds move at will between the large privately-owned deer forests of Grudie and Gairloch, the Beinn Eighe reserve, the TORRIDON estate, and the Forestry Commission's Slattadale property. The deer may represent, according to one's own particular viewpoint, a tourist attraction, a threat to young trees, potential competition with sheep and cattle, or a valuable source of income from stalking rents and sales of venison. Perhaps most importantly, deer are the creatures best able to thrive in an area of such poor grazing, and so are a natural resource of considerable economic importance.

Management of the deer involves cropping the natural population increase, to keep the herd size within the carrying capacity of the ground, and also upgrading the environment for them by drain-ing and burning to improve the grazing and by providing more sheltering woodland. Accurate counting of the stock and selective culling of the surplus stags and hinds both depend on freedom from disturbance; walkers are asked to co-operate by checking with local agents before entering the core of the Gairloch Conservation Unit, where this work is carried out. There is freedom of access at all times to the fringes of the Unit and to the Torridon estate; elsewhere restrictions are most likely to be in force during September, October and November.

Many walkers and climbers use the routes leading into the hills from the car parks on the Torridon estate and Beinn Eighe, but several long paths head southwards from the A832. One of these, up Glen Grudie, offers an 8km walk culminating in a magnificent vista of Coire Mhic Fhearchair, the most north westerly of Beinn Eighe's many corries. Justly regarded as among the finest in the Scottish Highlands, this ice-carved amphitheatre with 400m vertical walls of red sandstone topped with white quartzite rises as a horseshoe around its cold corrie loch. Three huge buttresses crown its southern rim and offer quite a challenge to the rock climber.

There is abundant evidence of the action of ice elsewhere in the area at low levels as well as high among the corries and ridges. Just south of Lochan an Iasgair, in Glen Torridon, the mounds of glacial deposit are so thick on the ground that the place is called the 'Corrie of a Hundred Hills'. When this

The remnant of old Caledonian forest by Loch Maree is an attractive feature of Beinn Eighe.

Greenshanks generally nest in remote wet moorlands.

mass of hummocks is lit at just the right angle it looks for all the world like a cardboard egg tray!

Ice-deposited boulders are scattered liberally almost everywhere, some large and apparently awaiting only a gentle push to start them moving again, while others litter the more level ground. The great lumps of exposed bedrock often bear the scars left by moving glaciers with their burden of sharp stones.

The road along the northern shore of Loch Torridon is well worth exploring – but should not be attempted by those in a hurry. Single-tracked, with steep gradients and hairpin bends, it first skirts the lochside and then climbs above the scattered crofting townships of Inveralligin and Alligin Shuas and on over the Beallach na Gaoithe, or Pass of the Winds, to a fine viewpoint overlooking Loch a Mhullaich. Here clubmosses and lichens grow by the roadside among heather, cottongrass and bog asphodel. At Diabaig the road drops again, with staggering suddenness, to sea level and ends by the pier in a rocky bay where cormorant fish and heron nest on the cliffs.

The road starts again at Redpoint, some 13km up the coast. The youth hostel at Craig, about 5km from Diabaig, is the only habitation along this lonely stretch of coastline. For the energetic the walk from Torridon hostel to Craig and on to Gairloch is not unduly arduous, and Craig certainly offers a fine chance to get away from it all. Most visitors, however, will approach Redpoint from the north, via the narrow road which leaves the A832 near Kerrysdale and winds through knobbly low hills to the attractive little village of Badachro. From there to Redpoint the hinterland consists of undulating and rather monotonous moorland, dotted with lochs large and small, but the coastline is enlivened by several sandy bays.

Although these bays are not under anything like the recreational pressures experienced by beaches on the Sutherland coast, for example at Achmelvich, they nevertheless illustrate clearly just how fragile an environment these 'soft' coastlines are. Wherever the thin *machair* turf of grasses and wild flowers is broken through by wheeled traffic, human trampling or over-grazing, wind-blow soon starts, creating breaches in the vegetated dunes and spreading sand far inland. Once started, such erosion is difficult to stop and it is not long before the appearance of the area is radically altered. Sometimes the level of almost the entire *machair* grassland is lowered, leaving only a few resistant tufts to show how things once were, and sometimes the blown sand causes problems by drifting on to the roads and penetrating buildings and caravans.

This coastline does not attract many seabirds, although a few shag, cormorant and black guillemot may be seen. Eider and red-breasted merganser breed in small numbers, and heron often stand out on the rocks, patiently waiting for an unwary fish to come along. Near the coast, and especially in the woodlands around Loch Shieldaig and Badachro and along Loch Torridon, there is a good variety of small birds; both whinchat and stonechat are fairly common. But this is really a land of moorland and mountain birds. Out in the trackless hinterland you might expect to hear the haunting cry of golden plover and the anxious yelping of a greenshank disturbed on its breeding ground. Both black-throated and red-throated diver find lochs here to suit their respective, and very different, requirements; the red-throats regularly make their presence known as they fly to and from their fishing trips at sea, calling gutturally as they go. There are insignificant-looking brown twite here too, with ring ouzel, raven, ptarmigan, peregrine and golden eagle in the hills. Many of these species are sensitive to disturbance, either abandoning their nests altogether or leaving them unattended until the intruder is well away, by which time a marauding crow or gull has probably helped itself to the eggs. Such birds are under ever greater pressures in the more accessible parts of their breeding range, so trackless areas like this, where they can nest in peace, are increasingly important refuges.

Fortunately many visitors to the area come primarily to enjoy the superb scenery – and preferably to do so from the roadside. Wester Ross sunsets are often truly spectacular and fine views of Skye and the Western Isles can be obtained from several places, among them Redpoint. The Torridon mountains and Slioch, viewed across Loch Maree, are renowned for their magnificent scenery and also act as magnets for hill-walking and rock-climbing enthusiasts. To see something of the area's wildlife the best starting points are undoubtedly the visitor centres at Torridon and Beinn Eighe. These provide both a general introduction and also more detailed information on specific aspects of natural history for those who want it.

Highland South

Spanning the breadth of the Highlands from the Moray Firth to the sea of the Hebrides is the massif of the central Grampians and west Highlands. It is a landscape of superlatives and comprises a highly dissected 914m plateau rising to some 1340m at the summit of Ben Nevis, and to nearly 1300m on the Braeriach summit of the CAIRNGORMS, encompassing no fewer than 36 peaks over 914m. This plateau is deeply cleft by the Great Glen fault, plunging over 300m below sea level in a north east to south west gash from Inverness to Fort William.

Glaciers, their meltwaters and the fast, spating rivers have further incised the mountains: the River Spey, for example, separating the Cairngorms from the Monadhliath; and Glen Spean, isolating the southern Nevis and GLENCOE ranges. The water-filled glacial troughs of Loch Ness, Loch Morar and Loch Shiel are the deepest and among the largest freshwater bodies in Britain. Drowned by rising sea levels in the past, other glaciated valleys form a fretted coastline of deepwater sounds and fiord-like sea lochs, penetrating inland 30km or more.

The climate is also one of contrasts. It ranges from the wet and mild Atlantic west coast, through the arctic–alpine summits of the Grampians, to the more continental dry east coast with above-average sunshine.

The ring faults of Ardnamurchan and the cauldron subsidence of Glencoe help to make these places world-famous to volcanic geologists. A hard-rock structure produces a rocky, cliffed coastline with maritime heaths and oak or hazel scrub on promontories and sheltered inlets, with stony or sandy beaches in a few small bays in Ardnamurchan and Morar. In such a geologically young landscape, soils are immature or rudimentary and natural fertility is usually low. In contrast, the soft coast of the north-facing Moray Firth has sandbanks and dunes forming unstable bars and forelands from the CULBIN SANDS to Whiteness Head at the entrance to the shallow, silted Beauly Firth. These softer shores provide nesting sites for terns and ringed plover, wide feeding grounds for knot and bar-tailed godwit in winter, and for pintail, scoter, goldeneye and long-tailed duck offshore. Inland here is the only arable land where grain and root crops can be grown successfully.

The land is chiefly used for hill sheep farms, conifer forestry and sporting estates, the last varying from grouse moors in the heather-clad eastern Highlands to deer forests on the wetter moor-grass- and deergrass-covered western hills, with salmon and trout fisheries throughout. This east–west climatic gradient is quite apparent: the heather moors towards the east become richer in dry heath flowers – bell heather, cowberry, petty whin and wintergreen – while the western moors become upland grasslands with bracken or blanket bogs containing sparse heather, cross-leaved heath, bog asphodel, bog myrtle, sundews, moor-grass and *Sphagnum* moss. There are similar contrasts in woodlands, with juniper and the pendulous silver birch in the eastern woods, and grey and eared sallow and hairy birch in the west, where the tree line is much lower.

The summits of the mountains with their barren crags, stony 'fell-field' and thin cover of lichen, moss and sedge heath are the habitat of arctic birds such as dotterel, ptarmigan and snow bunting, and of mountain hare. Colourful cushion alpines soon come into bloom when the winter snow cover melts. This montane environment covers large areas of country both north and south of the Great Glen. Cliff ledges out of reach of grazing animals support tall herbs including angelica, roseroot, stone bramble, mountain sorrel and holly fern. Golden eagle, peregrine falcon, merlin and raven

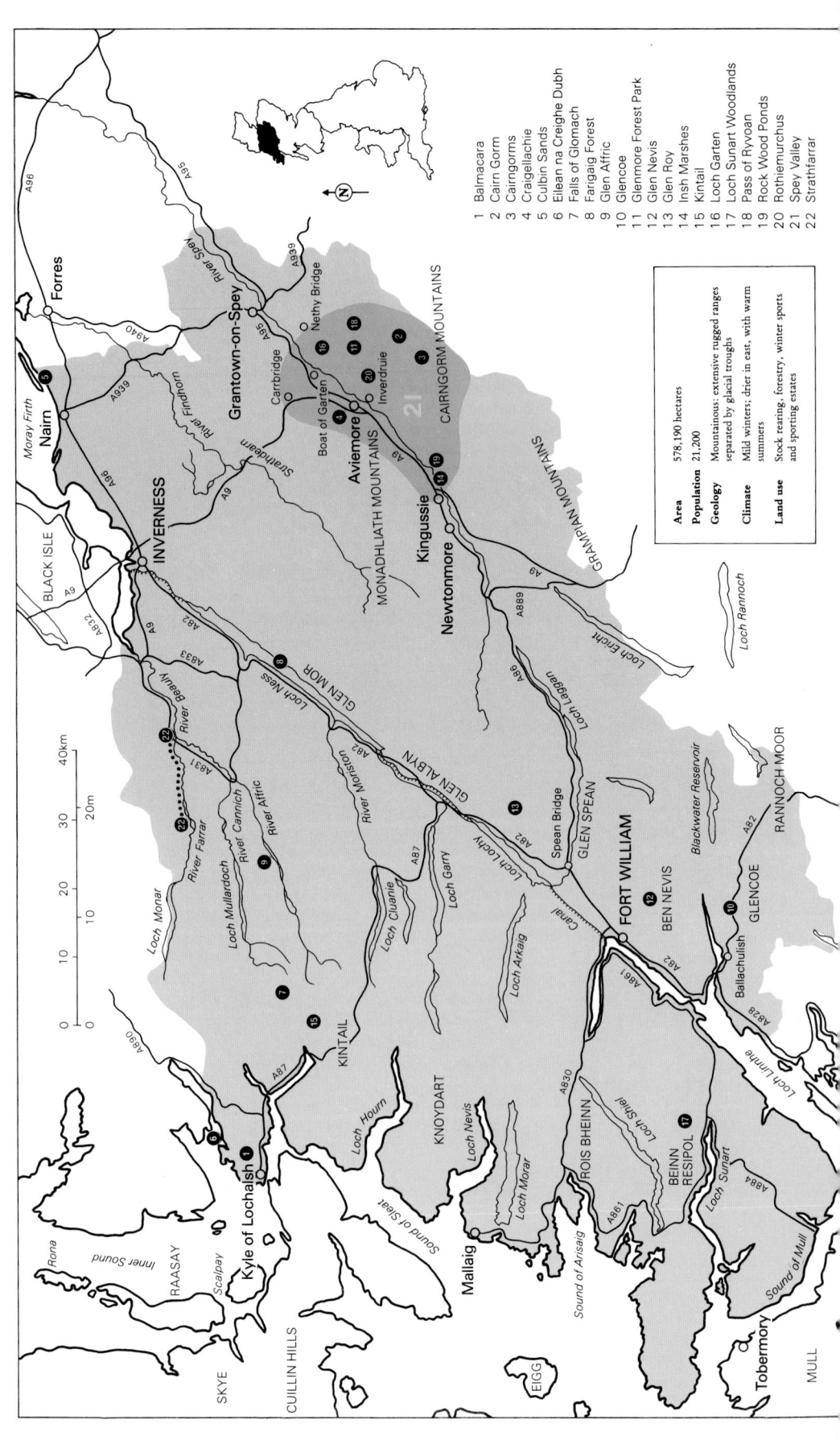

Area	578,190 hectares
Population	21,200
Geology	Mountainous: extensive rugged ranges separated by glacial troughs
Climate	Mild winters; drier in east, with warm summers
Land use	Stock rearing, forestry, winter sports and sporting estates

1 Balmacara
2 Cairn Gorm
3 Cairngorms
4 Craigellachie
5 Culbin Sands
6 Eilean na Creighe Dubh
7 Falls of Glomach
8 Farigaig Forest
9 Glen Affric
10 Glencoe
11 Glenmore Forest Park
12 Glen Nevis
13 Glen Roy
14 Insh Marshes
15 Kintail
16 Loch Garten
17 Loch Sunart Woodlands
18 Pass of Ryvoan
19 Rock Wood Ponds
20 Rothiemurchus
21 Spey Valley
22 Strathfarrar

hunt over wide areas, and red deer also range over large expanses of hill and glen according to weather and season.

Summit areas are far less extensive in the west Highlands; for example, from Kintail through Knoydart, Morar and Moidart to Glencoe the dominant features are generally steep, rugged crags, cliffs and acute ridges and peaks offering sparse roothold to mountain vegetation. Characteristic alpines here are starry saxifrage, parsley fern, Scottish asphodel and alpine lady's-mantle.

Where the foothills flatten out near the west coast, valley bogs and raised bogs form extensive peat mosses, as at the outflow of Loch Shiel and by the River Shiel. Too wet ever to have developed woodland cover, the layers of undecomposed sedge and moss with their preserved pollen grains tell the story of vegetation succession since the last glaciation. These mosses are the habitat and nesting place of greenshank and the wintering ground of white-fronted geese, which feed on the nuts of sedges and on other bog plants.

All the glens which dissect the Highlands were once clothed by the old Caledonian forest, of Scots pine and birch in inland areas, and oak, ash, elm and hazel lower down near the coast, especially on the warmer, south-facing aspects. The flat riversides of the lower straths were once covered with impenetrable alder and willow thickets.

The bulk of the remaining native Scots pinewoods are found in this central Highland area, and most are now protected within reserves. In these forests survive the predatory pine marten, wild cat and golden eagle, the growing population of osprey, with crossbill and crested tit. Northern pinewood plants of the forest floor include orchids – creeping lady's-tresses, lesser twayblade and coralroot orchid.

The broad-leaved woods are equally rich, containing butterflies such as speckled wood, chequered skipper, pearl-bordered fritillary and Scotch argus, mammals such as wild cat, badger and roe deer, and a good variety of woodland birds. Oakwoods with birch, hazel, holly and ash cover the steep slopes beside Loch Ness and many of the west coast sea lochs and freshwater lochs. The oak gives place to ash and sometimes wych elm over more calcareous rocks. Of particular interest to botanists are the hundreds of species of epiphytic lichens, mosses and leafy liverworts which luxuriantly clothe all twigs, branches and trunks. They survive here only because of an unbroken history of forest cover, a pristine atmosphere and high humidity. The woodland flora, as well as the ubiquitous bluebells, primroses, wood-sorrel and anemones, has a field layer rich in ferns including mountain fern, hay-scented buckler-fern and the diminutive filmy-fern.

The mixed woodland, farmland and moorland country where Loch Ness opens into the Moray Firth is particularly rich in relatively small, shallow lochs which are a haven for waterfowl such as tufted duck and mallard, and the rare Slavonian grebe which nests in the fringing sedgebeds. The Beauly Firth attracts large numbers of wintering waders and wildfowl including greylag and pink-footed geese, wigeon, tufted duck, mallard and goldeneye, but particularly the sawbills, goosander and merganser, which feed on the herring and sprat shoals. The food resource is also exploited by common seal, dolphin and porpoise which are regular visitors. In summer the firth also holds a flock of moulting Canada geese, and a substantial population of breeding shelduck.

M. E. BALL

Balmacara

NG 7930; 2274ha; NTS
Rocky shores and islands, hilly ground, woodland, lochs and croft ground
Booklet from NTS, Edinburgh and local centre; visitor centre, open Easter–October, at Lochalsh House; guided walks programme
All year

This extensive property covers most of the rugged promontory lying between Loch Alsh and Loch Carron. Small rocky islets are scattered thickly along the coastline and the hinterland displays the mosaic of heathery hillocks, bare knobs of rock and small lochans so characteristic of Wester Ross. Much of the land is crofted and visitors are asked to respect this traditional form of land use and not to enter croft land without permission. The policy woodlands of Lochalsh House are open all year.

Wild cats, though seldom seen, are by no means rare animals.

Cairn Gorm

NJ 0005; 2422ha; HIDB
Mountainous country
All year

Stretching from the limits of afforestation up to the summit of Cairn Gorm, this is the area on which facilities for skiing are concentrated; the roads into Coire Cas and Coire na Ciste provide easy access to the middle slopes, where many species typical of the CAIRNGORMS can be found. Even when low cloud blankets the summits there is much to see, for example on the shoulder of An t-Aonach, between the two car parks. The striking variation in the growth of heather, stunted and low on the exposed faces and luxuriant where a hollow gives shelter from wind, is well demonstrated here, while even a short search should soon reveal most of the berry-bearing shrubs, including dwarf cornel and cloudberry. Clubmosses are widespread, several species of fern are tucked away in crannies among the rocks, and there is an abundant growth of lichens. The last are among the food plants of reindeer, once native to Scotland and reintroduced here some years ago. Ptarmigan and red deer can sometimes be seen quite near the roads but a greater variety of birds will be found away from the populous areas, in the eastern corries.

Cairngorms

NJ 0101; 25,949ha; NCC reserve
Mountain, moorland and forest
Access unrestricted, but visitors are asked to avoid certain areas during deer cull, August–October
Visitor centre, open May–September, nature trail, publications; further information from Aviemore tourist office or NCC, Achantoul, Aviemore
April–August

This vast reserve, the largest in Britain, stretches both north and south from the high tops of the Cairngorms down to the pinewoods of the low ground. Only the toughest plants can survive among the pink granite gravel and boulders of the exposed summit plateaus, but the great corries hold a more varied flora and the native pinewoods of the lower slopes have their own special plants and animals. This is a land of red deer and wild cat, of golden eagle and crested tit, and of mountain avens and twinflower. It impresses from afar by the scale and grandeur of its landscape features, it arouses feelings of isolation and awe in those who penetrate to its remoter areas, and it offers a wealth of interest to visitors who take time to study it at close range.

The reserve lies astride the Lairig Ghru, the rugged and steep-sided pass which links Speyside with Deeside and separates CAIRN GORM and Ben Macdhui – at 1310m the highest point in the range – from Braeriach, Cairn Toul and Carn Ban Mor. Corries large and small, many of them with spectacular cliffs and some of them notable for their late-lying snow beds, bite into these western plateaus and provide shelter and suitable con-

ditions for many species unable to stand extremes of exposure. On the windswept summits moss campion, spiked wood-rush, curved wood-rush and three-leaved rush are among the few flowering plants present with the mosses and lichens. In the corries the flora, which is predominantly one of acid rocks, includes many widespread montane species, such as roseroot, mountain sorrel, purple saxifrage and alpine saw-wort, and a number of rare or very local ones, including mountain hawkweeds, starwort mouse-ear, hare's-foot sedge, arctic mouse-ear and alpine hair-grass. Least willow and sibbaldia flourish where snow regularly lies late, as do parsley fern and alpine lady-fern.

Heather and deergrass dominate the vegetation lower down the mountain slopes, with bell heather in relatively dry areas and cross-leaved heath where the ground is wetter. Bog bilberry, mountain crowberry, bearberry and trailing azalea are widespread, the latter most often on very exposed sites between 750 and 1000m. Dwarf cornel, cloudberry, interrupted clubmoss and chickweed wintergreen are also abundant, and dwarf birch occurs locally.

The most extensive of the pinewood areas lie on the northern and north western edges of the reserve, in ROTHIEMURCHUS Forest and on the slopes above Loch an Eilein, where the trees growing sparsely at 625m above sea level are probably near the upper limit for native Scots pine in Britain. Some of the oldest and finest specimens, around Loch an Eilein, are at least 250 years old; good natural regeneration is now taking place on open moorland nearby. The visual attraction of these woodlands lies largely in their diversity: in some

Peregrines may nest among vegetation, like this one, or on much barer ledges.

Conditions on the Cairngorm plateau can be arctic, even in mid-summer.

places the trees are densely packed above a mossy carpet, and in others widely spaced among heather, bilberry, cowberry and juniper. The two small and unobtrusive pinewood orchids, creeping lady's-tresses and lesser twayblade, are widespread; both lesser and intermediate wintergreen are fairly common but serrated wintergreen is less abundant; one-flowered wintergreen and twinflower are very local in their distribution.

A feature of these native pinewoods is their high population of wood ants. Their big mounded pine needle nests are scattered through the forest and there is constant traffic of ants across the gravelly tracks. Many very local insects – beetles, plant bugs, caddis flies, moths and also spiders – are known only from Rothiemurchus and from the Cairngorms.

Crested tit and crossbill are typical birds of these pinewoods, but though widespread neither species is numerous. Siskin and redstart are quite common, wren and chaffinch abundant, and tree pipit and willow warbler present where birch, rowan and aspen grow in clearings and along the water's edge. Capercaillie and black grouse also breed in moderate numbers, the former deep in the forest and the latter often along its moorland edge. Above the tree line peregrine and ring ouzel haunt the cliffs and screes. On the summits, among the scattered boulders and sparse vegetation, dotterel and ptarmigan rear their young in a situation so exposed that disturbance can all too easily lead to chilling of eggs or chicks. Several pairs of golden eagle nest on the reserve and these magnificent birds can often be seen soaring high above the tops

or riding the up-currents along a corrie rim. Their breeding success has, however, fallen in recent years, largely due to disturbance. Other breeding birds of the reserve include greenshank, merlin, buzzard and sparrowhawk.

Large herds of red deer roam the hills, descending into the valleys in winter, and there are fair numbers of roe deer in the woodlands. Pine marten is scarce on Speyside but red squirrel is quite common, though more often found near mixed plantations than in pure pine forest. Badgers have been increasing in recent years and otter tracks are occasionally seen by lochs and streams.

The visitor centre at Loch an Eilein provides a good introduction to the reserve and its wildlife, while the 5km nature trail round the loch leads through a variety of typical habitats. Many of the species found on the reserve are also present on Rothiemurchus Estate, in GLENMORE FOREST PARK or on Cairn Gorm itself, where high-level roads and a chairlift provide easy access.

Claish Moss

Permit only; 563ha; NCC reserve
Raised peat mire
Permit from NCC, Inverness
May–August

This large, unevenly domed mire area is patterned by a linear series of ridges, pools and streams. Several species of *Sphagnum* moss are present and the ridges carry woolly fringe-moss. A major interest of the site is the fact that its vegetational history since postglacial times has been traced in the peat.

Craigellachie: the open birchwood is alive with birdsong in early summer.

Craigellachie

NH 8812; 260ha; NCC reserve
Birchwood, cliff and moorland
May–August

Open birchwood clothes the lower slopes of this reserve, which lies on the western edge of Aviemore. Above are sheer cliffs of schistose rock and open heather moorland rising to around 600m. On the upper slopes the jumble of fallen trees and mossy boulders harbours a good range of ferns, lichens and fungi and there is a rich ground flora.

Both silver and downy birch are present in the wood, which is one of the largest birchwoods in Speyside. Rowan, aspen, hazel, wych elm, oak, bird cherry and juniper are scattered thinly among the birch and there is a wet area with bog myrtle and *Sphagnum*. Grasses and mosses dominate the ground vegetation, with common rock-rose and alpine bistort in a few localities and local species such as shining crane's-bill, alternate-leaved golden-saxifrage and serrated wintergreen growing on the rocks.

In summer the wood is alive with birdsong; typical birchwood species such as tree pipit, willow warbler, spotted flycatcher, blue tit and long-tailed tit are particularly abundant. Great spotted woodpecker, woodcock, treecreeper and mistle thrush are also among the breeding species. Red grouse nest on the moorland and black grouse at the woodland edge, while kestrel and jackdaw favour the cliffs for their nest sites. But the most notable breeding bird of the reserve is undoubtedly peregrine; for many years, and generally successfully, a pair of these dashing and handsome predators has nested on the sheer cliff overlooking the busy Aviemore Centre.

On a warm day in summer multitudes of moths, many of them tiny, dance in the sunlit glades among the birches. Craigellachie is well known for its insects, which include several very local moths such as Rannoch sprawler, the delicately-patterned Kentish glory and angle-striped sallow. All these moth species are associated with birch trees.

Culbin Sands

NJ 9362; 862ha; RSPB reserve
Sandflats, saltmarsh and shingle bars
Access, on foot only, along the shore from
Kingsteps (NJ 905575) or through Culbin Forest
from Cloddymoss (NH 983599)
September–March: duck and waders;
May–August: flowers and breeding birds

This remote stretch of coastline, backed by CULBIN FOREST (Grampian), is a very important wintering area for wildfowl, especially sea duck, and waders. Two shingle bars lie 1.5km out from the high-water mark; stretching for nearly 8km along the coast, they are constantly changing in size and shape under the action of wind and waves. Greylag geese roost on the bars in winter and several thousand common scoter, long-tailed duck and velvet scoter regularly gather on the seaward side. Ringed plover, oystercatcher, redshank, gulls and a few pairs of common tern breed on the shingle of the reserve's Nairn Bar; in late summer several species of tern rest there in large numbers as they pass through the area on migration.

Between bar and beach lie the flats and saltmarsh, a rich feeding ground for waders and duck such as wigeon, mallard and shelduck. As many as 1000 bar-tailed godwit and 2000 oystercatcher use these flats in winter, and many knot, dunlin, ringed plover and curlew are generally present. These gatherings of waders draw predators into the area and peregrine, merlin and hen harrier are frequently seen.

Nairn Old Bar, towards the western end of the reserve, is also of physiographical and botanical interest. Its pattern of raised shingle ridges is particularly well marked and it carries an interesting plant succession, from pioneering lichens and stonecrop through to heathland dominated by heather, crowberry and gorse.

Doire Donn

Permit only; 28ha; SWT reserve
Woodland
April–July

By Highland standards this deciduous woodland is unusually rich, with a well-developed shrub layer and varied ground flora. Sessile oak, ash, birch, alder and wych elm all contribute to the canopy and there is an understorey of hazel, rowan, holly, willows and a few guelder-rose and bird cherry, together with seedlings of most of them. The ground vegetation includes both acid-loving plants, such as heather and bilberry, and those typical of richer soils, for example woodruff and sanicle. Many species of woodland birds are present.

Eilean na Creige Duibhe

NG 824335; 1ha; SWT reserve
Wooded island
Access restricted March–June
July–August

The Scots pinewood on this small rocky island holds a flourishing heronry. Eider nest in the dense ground cover of heather, bilberry and bracken and otter frequently visit the island. Drifts of sand-like material along the southern shore are in fact the remains of a lime-covered red seaweed which grows nearby in deep water.

Falls of Glomach

NH 017258; 1134ha; NTS
Waterfall and surrounding valley
Access, on foot only, from Killilan (NG 946302) or Dorusduae (NG 983227)
All year

This spectacular fall is one of the highest in Britain. Confined within a narrow ravine some 180m deep, the mountain torrent drops 100m in a single wild plunge, then jets off a projecting rock to fall a further 20m to the pools below. The falls lie in a remote mountain area and both routes mentioned above are steep and rugged; the wet ground around the falls can be dangerously slippery and visitors should take great care.

Farigaig

Permit only; 5ha; SWT reserve
Scrub woodland
April–July

Situated on steeply sloping ground above the Farigaig River, near Loch Ness, this small area of scrub woodland contains a good variety of species. The wood is open and dominated by birch, with a few relict oak on the drier ground and alder, aspen and willow in the wetter hollows. Juniper, hazel and rose species occur in the shrub layer and common wintergreen is found in the predominantly heather and bilberry ground cover.

Farigaig Forest

NH 523237; 2.5km; FC
Woodland
Leaflet at centre or from Inverness tourist office; forest centre with display; trail
All year

The trail climbs steeply, through a mixture of native deciduous woodland and planted conifers, to a mountain viewpoint. An exhibition on the wildlife of the forest is included in the display.

Glen Affric

NH 2424; 1265ha; FC reserve
Native pinewood
Trail leaflet from Inverness tourist office or forest office
April–October

Glen Affric is widely acknowledged to be one of the most attractive places in Scotland; hills, lochs, islands, river, waterfalls and woodlands combine to create a remarkable variety of scenery, much of it visible from the road that winds up the glen. The pine forest, lying along the southern side of Lochs Affric and Benevean (Beinn á Mheadhoin), which contributes so much to the beauty of the area, is managed as a Native Pinewood Reserve. Strict measures have been taken to control deer, in order to allow natural regeneration to take place, and a programme of planting with stock raised from seed gathered in the reserve has been carried out.

Scottish crossbill, typical of the native pinewoods, breeds very early in the year.

The most natural areas of pinewood are those near Dog Fall (NH 2928), and at Pollan Buidhe, between Lochs Affric and Benevean. At both points there are many fine old trees and a good sprinkling of younger ones, with abundant birch and rowan giving spectacular colour contrasts in spring and autumn. The hummocky ground is thickly carpeted with heather, bilberry and a good variety of mosses. Purple moor-grass, cottongrass and *Sphagnum* flourish in the damper hollows, and in autumn many different fungi appear along the edges of the sandy forest tracks.

Scottish crossbill, capercaillie and black grouse breed in the pinewoods and there is a varied population of small birds in summer. Goosander and mallard occur regularly on the lochs and dipper and grey wagtail by the river; the chances of seeing one of the larger birds of prey over the glen are quite high. Because deer control is strict there are only a few roe deer in the forest, but red squirrel are fairly common and red deer may be seen on the open hills to the north.

Glencoe

NN 1556; 5749ha; NTS
Mountainous country
Visitor centre (NN 127565) open Easter–
mid-October; guided walks programme;
ranger-naturalist
All year

The spectacular mountains of Glencoe, where walls of rock rise steeply on either side and great corries

Glen Nevis offers good opportunities for eagle-spotting.

are carved from the peaks above, has long made this place famous for its scenery as well as its notorious massacre. This is climbers' country, demanding a high degree of fitness and skill from those who would venture to the tops. The traveller through the glen is unlikely to see anything of particular natural history interest, although both golden eagle and peregrine sometimes pass overhead. Golden plover and ptarmigan breed in small numbers and red deer are present but generally stay well away from the busy floor of the glen. The mountain flora is richest where calcareous rocks outcrop – usually on the most inaccessible cliffs.

Glenmore Forest Park

NH 9810; 2644ha; FC
Coniferous woodland, loch and heather moor
Map-guide and booklet from Glenmore forest
office (NH 977097) or Aviemore tourist office
April–September

Remnants of the old native pinewoods still survive here in a few places, for example the PASS OF RYVOAN, but most of the plantable land in the Forest Park now carries commercial woodlands. These are predominantly of Scots pine, Sitka spruce and Norway spruce; natural birch, rowan and willow are widespread along streams and in clearings. Many of the pinewood birds and animals have colonised the plantations and are as likely to be seen along the forest tracks as among the old pine trees. Above the economic planting limit of around 500m the heather-dominated moorland supports a good range of plants typical of the lower slopes of the CAIRNGORMS reserve. The hills on the north side of the park rise to around 800m; the higher ground to the south, on which the skiing facilities are located, and the summit ridge itself, are described under CAIRN GORM. Scenic Loch Morlich, set against a backdrop of the high peaks and corries, lies almost entirely within the park.

Wherever the tree canopy is open enough, heather dominates the ground flora, with bilberry, cowberry, cow-wheat and hairy wood-rush often abundant. Juniper is frequent along the forest edge and lesser twayblade, chickweed wintergreen, creeping lady's-tresses and lemon-scented fern are not uncommon. Intermediate wintergreen, mountain everlasting and bearberry are among the plants of the more open moorland.

Scottish crossbill, crested tit, capercaillie, siskin and goldcrest all breed in the afforested areas, while moorland birds include red grouse and curlew, with black grouse common along the forest fringe. Dipper, grey wagtail, teal, goosander and common sandpiper frequent the streams and loch shore, and the famous Speyside osprey sometimes fish in Loch Morlich.

There are many roe deer and red squirrels in the plantations and both can often be seen along the forest trails. Red deer are discouraged from entering the forest but they roam the moorland and hills, where mountain hares are also found.

Despite persecution, Scotland's golden eagles are holding their own.

Glen Nevis

NN 1669; 873ha; Highland RC
Mountainous country
All year

The chance of seeing golden eagle from the roadside is as good here as anywhere in Scotland. These majestic birds can often be seen soaring above the crags which rise steeply on either side of the glen. There are also spectacular views around the upper car park (at NN 167692) and along the right-of-way path to Steall and beyond. A countryside ranger is based in the area.

Glen Roy

NN 3090; 1168ha; NCC reserve
Series of ice-age geological features
Booklet from NCC, Inverness; viewpoint
All year

The best-known of the ice-age features visible in Glen Roy are the spectacular 'parallel roads', three distinct horizontal terraces on the hillside, which can be clearly seen from the viewpoint at NN 297854. Scientific investigation has demonstrated that these terraces mark successive shorelines of a large lake formed when ice blocked the entrance to the glen. The processes involved, and the many other glacial features visible in the area, are fully described in the booklet, *The Parallel Roads of Glen Roy.*

Insh Marshes

NH 7799; 509ha; RSPB reserve
Marsh, wet pasture and woodland
Open April–August, Wednesday, Friday and Sunday, 10a.m.–5p.m.; access limited to area around car park on B970 (NH 775998)
Leaflet from RSPB, Edinburgh or RSPB warden, Ivy Cottage, Insh, Kingussie; reception hut; hides
April–July

This vast tract of wetland along the flood plain of the River Spey is important for breeding and wintering wildfowl and also for breeding waders. Although few birds of prey nest on the reserve, many hunt over the marshes and along the woodland fringe; hen harrier and osprey are regular visitors. A good variety of small birds inhabits the birchwoods and the marshland shrub layer of willow carr and bog myrtle. The area is also rich in insects.

In the past numerous attempts have been made to drain these marshes for agriculture. Flood banks were constructed along the riverside and an elaborate network of ditches dug, but the Spey is not an easy river to tame. Severe floods continued to occur, the ditches gradually silted up and eventually all attempts at reclamation were abandoned. Today the reserve is largely fen – marsh, which covers great stretches of the valley floor and is interspersed with willow carr, drainage ditches and areas of open water, and fringed with birch and juniper on the higher ground. In midwinter a metre or more of water or ice often covers the area, but in summer many of the smaller pools dry out. New, deeper pools are being created, and summer grazing by cattle has been reintroduced to improve conditions for breeding birds.

Good numbers of mallard, wigeon, teal and tufted duck nest on the reserve; shoveler, goosander and red-breasted merganser occasionally breed and pochard did so for the first time in 1978. All the common wetland waders, such as curlew, snipe, redshank, lapwing, oystercatcher and common sandpiper, breed in these wetlands, and the much rarer wood sandpiper regularly feeds there. The dense beds of water sedge, a local northern species, and other marsh plants provide ideal cover for water rail and sometimes also for spotted crake – both more likely to be heard than seen.

The reserve boasts an impressive list of birds of prey observed from the hides. Buzzard, sparrowhawk and hen harrier are the most frequently recorded, while osprey fish the river and pools regularly between April and August. Peregrine, kestrel and merlin occasionally hunt over the marshes and there have been sightings of golden eagle, goshawk and marsh harrier. A sudden panic in the big black-headed gull colony often gives the first hint that a raptor is around.

Seventeen species of butterfly and over 200 moths, including the very local Kentish glory and Rannoch sprawler, have been recorded on the reserve. Both elephant hawk-moth and poplar hawk-moth are seen every year. Other insects of interest include the very locally distributed bee beetle, which looks like a bumble bee, and several species of dragonfly.

A number of roe deer spend most of their time in the marsh, where the tall vegetation gives good cover for the young kids. Fox and badger are also present and are sometimes seen from the hides.

Many wetland birds visit the Insh Marshes, now being managed to increase habitat diversity.

Kintail

NH 0019; 5182ha; NTS
Mountainous country
Possible seasonal restrictions: see below
Booklet; visitor centre at Morvich (NG 961211)
open June–September; guided walks;
ranger-naturalist
All year

The clustered peaks of the Five Sisters of Kintail form the core of this site. Rising steeply from near sea level at the head of Loch Duich, several of the Sisters just top the 1000m mark. Crowned with a spectacular array of corries, crags and precipices, these are among the sheerest grassy mountains in Scotland. Advice on the best routes into these hills, and on any restrictions because of deer stalking on adjoining properties, can be obtained from the National Trust for Scotland representative at Morvich Visitor Centre.

Although not carrying the wealth of plants found on BEN LAWERS (Tayside), these mountains support a varied and interesting flora. Among the more notable species on the grassy slopes are pale butterwort, fragrant orchid, greater and lesser butterfly-orchid, dwarf cudweed and mountain azalea, while the corries support alpine rue, dwarf willow, three-flowered rush and starry, purple and mossy saxifrage. There are herds of red deer and wild goats in the area and a good variety of moorland birds.

Loch Garten

NH 9718; 895ha; RSPB reserve
Pine forest, lochs and wet moorland
Access within statutory bird sanctuary strictly
confined to marked path leading to osprey
observation post; elsewhere on reserve along
pinewood paths
Leaflet from hide or RSPB, Edinburgh; observation
hide, open 10a.m.–8.30p.m. end April–end August
Mid-April–August

Famous as the site which initiated the osprey's successful recolonisation of the Scottish Highlands, Loch Garten is the only nature reserve in Scotland that can justifiably claim to attract over 50,000 visitors a year. Most visit the observation hide, which is open at the times stated above provided the ospreys are nesting, but comparatively few see anything more of the reserve. Yet with its old-established pinewoods and variety of other habitats Loch Garten contains a wealth of interest for the botanist and entomologist as well as the ornithologist.

The reserve forms part of Abernethy Forest, a remnant of the ancient Forest of Caledon and now the largest surviving area of semi-natural wood-land in Britain. Around Lochs Garten and Mal-lachie the pines are well grown and mature; elsewhere on the reserve are scattered trees more than 200 years old, and areas of active regenera-tion. In the wetter stretches of peat bog the stunted growth of the moribund trees belies their age, and a 6m stem may represent a 100-year-long struggle to survive. An important feature of the pine forest is the many dead and decaying stumps, for it is here that the crested tit makes its nest. A thriving po-pulation of 40–50 pairs of these delightful little birds breeds on the reserve. Other breeding birds particularly associated with the pinewoods include Scottish crossbill, capercaillie and siskin. Redstart, spotted flycatcher and willow warbler are regular summer visitors and among the residents are wren, goldcrest and the four commoner tit species.

Many of the typical northern pinewood plants are represented on the reserve. Heather, bilberry and cowberry are abundant and juniper is the dominant shrub. Cow-wheat, wood-sorrel and chickweed wintergreen are widely distributed, and less common species such as creeping lady's-tresses, lesser twayblade, serrated, common and intermediate wintergreen and moonwort also occur. In the peat bogs yellow bog asphodel and the insectivorous sundew and butterwort flourish, while field gentian, rock-rose and goldenrod are found on the drier gravelly ridges. In July white water-lily adorns the rather acid lochs, which also support water lobelia and greater bladderwort.

The lochs hold only small populations of breed-ing wildfowl, such as mallard, teal, tufted duck and sometimes wigeon, but they are important roosting sites, for black-headed gull in spring and for duck, greylag geese and whooper swan in win-ter. Buzzard, kestrel and sparrowhawk breed on the reserve and other birds of prey, such as hen harrier, merlin and peregrine, are often observed.

Roe deer and red squirrel are common on the reserve and frequently seen; badger, fox and wild cat occasionally visit but are often identified only by tracks left in the snow. Otter too visit regularly and at one time bred on an island in the middle of Loch Mallachie.

Both the long history of Scots pine on the site and the presence of many small pools among the waterlogged peat contribute to the richness of the reserve's insect life. About 350 beetle species, some of them rare and very closely associated with old pinewoods, have been identified. The 11 dragonfly species recorded include white-faced dragonfly, here close to its northern limit in Britain. Over 260 moths and 18 butterflies are known to occur, among the latter the very local dingy skipper.

With all this variety of interest in addition to the 144 bird species recorded, 73 of which have bred, Loch Garten is indeed a place worth exploring. The track leading into the forest a short distance to the west of Loch Garten itself offers a 2km route through a variety of habitats, to Loch Mallachie and back.

Loch Sunart Woodlands

NM 8464 and 6558; 163ha; NCC–FC reserve
Natural woodland
Access to Glencripesdale (NM 6558) by permit
only: apply NCC, Inverness
Booklet from Strontian information centre or FC,
Inverness; forest trail (11km) in Ariundle Wood
April–August

This reserve comprises two contrasting woodlands on opposite sides of Loch Sunart. Ariundle Wood (70ha), in Strontian Glen on the north side of the

The striking elephant hawk-moth is regularly recorded on the Insh Marshes.

loch, is predominantly oak, with scattered birch, hazel and rowan. Much of the oak has been coppiced in the past. The Strontian Glen trail starts at the road junction below the old manse and passes through the wood to disused lead mines beyond. Glencripesdale Wood (93ha), situated on steep north-facing slopes and on more fertile soil than Ariundle, is an ashwood, with some alder and hazel and a lot of birch.

The scientific interest of these woodlands lies largely in the luxuriant growth of mosses, leafy liverworts and lichens resulting from the high humidity of the area and the long history of woodland on these sites. Many local and some rare species flourish on the woodland floor, especially on the rock surfaces, and on the trees themselves.

Pass of Ryvoan

NJ 9910; 122ha; SWT reserve
Natural pinewood and scree slopes
April–July

Between the steep sides of this narrow pass, which links GLENMORE and Strathnethy, lies the intriguing Green Loch – in Gaelic Lochan Uaine. Not algal growth but a quirk of reflected light is responsible for its strange olive green colour. The muted shade of the loch contrasts with the vivid greens of bilberry and birch, which in turn stand out against the background of dark Scots pine, heather and grey scree. On the southern wall of the pass a cascade of loose stones falls right to the loch shore. On the northern, more stable, slope the rock is richer in minerals, giving rise to unusually varied plant life for natural woodland of this type.

Dense stands of juniper, some upright and some sprawling, are scattered through the open pinewood and there are clumps of silvery-grey willows among the birches. Primroses, violets, woodruff and moschatel grow on the reserve, as do petty whin and common wintergreen. The marshy floor of the pass holds butterwort and a variety of mosses and sedges.

Crossbill, goldcrest and crested tit are among the resident bird species, while summer visitors include tree pipit, redstart and grey wagtail. Red deer and red squirrel occur regularly on the reserve, through which the public path to Abernethy passes.

Rahoy Hills

Permit only; 1766ha; RSNC–SWT reserve
Mountainous country
Permit from SWT
Botanical list available with permit
May–July

The basalt-capped peaks of Beinn Iadain and Beinn na h'Uamha, with their arctic–alpine plants, are the focal points of this large reserve. On their unstable crags and screes the mineral-rich soil supports a luxuriant flora including four species of saxifrage, alpine meadow-rue, roseroot, globeflower, moss campion, northern rock-cress, Norwegian sandwort and holly fern.

The northern shore of Loch Arienas carries the largest area of woodland on the reserve. Oak, coppiced in the past, is dominant, with much birch and a shrub layer of hazel, alder, holly, rowan and aspen. Blanket bog and acid grassland covers most of the moorland, with marshy ground fringing the several small lochans. Red-throated diver and greenshank breed on this ground and golden eagle and peregrine are regularly recorded.

The Loch Sunart Woodlands are notably rich in mosses, liverworts and lichens.

Rock Wood Ponds

NH 8302; 17.5ha; FC
Lochans, bog and plantation
Signed trails (1.6 and 2.1km) from NH 8302; hide
All year

Red squirrel, roe deer, goldcrest and crossbill frequent this forest area and a variety of duck visit the lochans. Many typical bog and moorland plants grow in the open areas and insects include red damselflies.

Rothiemurchus

NH 9110; 8800ha; Rothiemurchus Estate
Native pinewood, lochs and hill ground
Access restricted to waymarked paths through forest, to specified hill routes and by arrangement
Visitor centre at Inverdruie (NH 903109), with exhibition, open all year 9a.m.–dusk; visitor guide leaflet; guided walks programme in summer; for further information tel. Aviemore 810647
All year

The Rothiemurchus Estate includes 800ha of pine forest and 5000ha of hills, plateau and moorland, all lying within the boundary of the CAIRNGORMS reserve, and 3000ha outside it. Most of the finest stands of native pine in the area are found on the estate and many of the typical pinewood species, such as creeping lady's-tresses and chickweed wintergreen, can be seen along the forest paths. Crested tit, redstart, crossbill and tree pipit are quite numerous and there are many red deer and roe deer on the hills and in the woods.

Spey Valley

See map; includes nine sites
Visitor centre at Carrbridge with display and audio-visual programme; tree-top trail and bookshop; exhibition at Aviemore tourist office; further information and guided walks programme from Rothiemurchus Estate ranger service, Inverdruie, and Highland Guides
All year

There can be few visitors to the Scottish Highlands who do not at least pass through the Spey Valley, the most visited stretch of countryside in Scotland. Pressures on LOCH LOMOND-side (Central) are heavy in summer, especially at weekends, and Deeside is a busy tourist corridor, but it is only on Speyside that so many people spread over such a wide area during so much of the year. Some come to ski, others participate in canoeing, rock climbing, sailing or pony trekking. Some come to pursue a particular natural history interest – and this is one of the richest areas in Scotland for wildlife. But the majority, especially in summer, want to enjoy the magnificent scenery, the pure air, and the freedom to walk, to laze around or to explore.

Between the mighty rampart of the CAIRNGORMS, scalloped by corries and cleft by the deep V of the Lairig Ghru, and the comparatively featureless rolling plateaus of the Monadhliath to the north,

In recent years crested tits have spread north from Speyside to the Moray Firth.

the Spey winds its leisurely way along the valley floor. From Kingussie to Kincraig its pace is so slow, and the valley floor so flat, that much of the adjoining land forms one of the largest fens remaining in Britain. Part of this great swamp, INSH MARSHES, is now actively managed to make it even more attractive to wetland birds.

At Loch Insh the pattern changes. Scattered across the valley floor between Kincraig and Boat of Garten lies a jumble of humps and hollows, relics of the last ice age. Most of the hummocks are wooded, with graceful birches or sombre pines above a carpet of heather and bilberry, and many of the hollows hold lochs, some large and windswept like Loch Alvie and some little more than pools. It is this mosaic of different landforms and woodland textures, of contrasting colours and of light and shade, that makes this section of the valley so attractive.

Among the best known and most popular of the lochs in the Spey Valley are LOCH GARTEN, with its famous ospreys, and Loch an Eilein, at the edge of the vast Cairngorms reserve. Few people penetrate beyond the well-beaten tourist track, yet at each of these sites a comparatively short walk will take you away from the coach parties and picnickers into the quiet of the old pine forests, where on a still day you may hear the cracking of crossbills extracting the seeds from cones, the scratching of a squirrel's claws as it scampers along a branch, or the purring calls of a family of dainty little crested tits. The pines themselves have richly coloured bark and massive limbs; there are many fine specimens on ROTHIEMURCHUS Estate and in the PASS OF RYVOAN.

Scots pine, juniper and birch, typical species of the Caledonian forest, frame a view of Cairn Gorm.

It is to the mountains, however, that the eye inevitably keeps straying. The massive rolling plateaus of the Cairngorms form the most extensive area of land above 1000m anywhere in Britain. Impressive from any angle, they are at their magnificent best when viewed across Loch Morlich, with snow capping the summits and highlighting the great northern corries. Small wonder that, since the advent of the chairlift, tourists flock to experience the view from on high as well as that from below. Many who visit in summer must find the contrast in climate between valley and mountaintop a shock; the Cairngorms can be arctic even in July and visitors are often ill-prepared for the chill winds. But if conditions are right the view from the summit can be truly superb. Below lies Loch Morlich, tree-fringed and with a beach of golden sand at its eastern end, and virtually as far as the eye can see, in every direction, are mountains. To the south and west the summits of Ben Macdhui, Cairn Toul and Braeriach all rise above CAIRN GORM itself, while Beinn a Bhuird to the east is only slightly lower. Beyond Aviemore stretches the barrier of the Monadhliath and far away to the north stands Ben Wyvis.

Mountains may seem permanent and indestructible features of the landscape, but changes are taking place, both through natural processes such as weathering and also as a result of man's impact. In the early 1950s Aviemore was a quiet Highland village, the dirt road to Glenmore was little better than a forest track, and only a few hundred came regularly to climb and walk and ski in the Cairngorms. Today a continuous stream of cars and buses pours along the tarred road leading to high-level car parks in Coire Cas and Coire na Ciste, and many thousands of skiers in winter and tourists in summer pound the upper slopes of Cairn Gorm each year.

Many of the changes resulting from these developments are obvious – new roads and buildings, a clutter of pylons and snow fences on the ski slopes, construction scars on the hillsides and the alien green swards where such scars have been reseeded. But there have been other, more insidious, changes too. High on Cairn Gorm, where plant life has a constant struggle to survive and regeneration may take many years, trampling feet have bared the thin gritty soil over an ever-widening area. Around the ski slopes the easy pickings provided by discarded picnics have attracted gulls and crows to scavenge in areas where they were formerly seldom seen – and both are potential predators of the eggs of scarce mountain birds. Conservationists are understandably concerned about the long-term effects of such changes in an area of unique and fragile habitats and animal communities.

The Cairngorms and Spey Valley represent an enormously valuable resource in terms of habitat and species diversity, of scenery and 'wilderness' qualities, and of recreational opportunities. The last is the only aspect measurable in economic terms, but must not any significant losses of wildlife and amenity also affect the recreational value of the area? The task of reconciling the often conflicting needs and demands of conservation and recreation is never easy; here, in one of Scotland's most important scenic and wildlife heritage areas, it is an increasingly pressing problem.

From the ruins of Ruthven Barracks dominating the marshy flood plain of the Spey below Kingussie, to the picturesque old arch across the River Dulnain at Carrbridge, and from the crags of CRAIGELLACHIE to the summit of Cairn Gorm, the Spey Valley offers an impressive variety of opportunities to those who wish to discover something of the area's wildlife. Two good starting points are the Aviemore tourist office and Landmark visitor centre, Carrbridge (see above for facilities). Once armed with a map and a little basic information you can go where and when you like – though this may well be influenced by the weather. Highland Guides hire out boots and protective clothing – essential for anyone planning to leave the well-marked lowland paths and venture on to high ground or off the beaten track. For the less adventurous there is the Highland Wildlife Park at Kincraig, where deer, snowy owl, pine marten, wild cat and many other Scottish species can be admired at close quarters. And at GLENMORE visits can be made to the famous herd of reindeer, reintroduced into the area after being extinct in Scotland for many hundreds of years and now well established.

As to the best season for visiting the Spey Valley, each has something to commend it. There is a special enchantment about a bright winter's day with snow on the mountains and hoar frost shimmering on every twig and stem in the valley. In spring the soft green of unfolding birch leaves forms a delicate tracery against the dark background of heather and pine. Summer sun brings out the resiny scent of the forest and encourages even the less energetic to head for the high tops. And in autumn there is a veritable feast of colour – golden birch, russet rowan, pink and red bilberry leaves and vivid scarlet and white toadstools. Whatever the season, those who have eyes to see will find plenty to look at here.

Strathfarrar

NH 2737; 2189ha; NCC reserve
Native Scots pinewood
Vehicular access is restricted; apply gatekeeper's house, NH 395406, for permit; organised groups should contact warden, Eilean Aigas, Hughton, Beauly, tel. Kiltarlity 310
Leaflet from NCC, Inverness
March–July

The pinewoods of Glen Strathfarrar represent the largest surviving remnant, in this part of Scotland, of the ancient Forest of Caledon. Obstacles such as alder marshes and deep gorges, which presented major problems for early timber extractors, resulted in these woods being left unscathed when more accessible forests were cleared. Little regeneration has taken place here for many years but the Strathfarrar woods still display the mosaic of fine mature pines, clumps of birch, and hummocks of heather and bilberry so characteristic of native pinewoods.

The finest stands of pine are on the south side of the River Farrar at Coille Garbh, the Rough Wood,

where the trees, many at least 200 years old, grow on rocky knolls and morainic terraces. Aspen, rowan and holly, as well as birch, are scattered among the pines and old stands of juniper grow on the flatter ground by the river. Some of the massive pines in this area are especially magnificent and may be up to 300 years old. Crossbill and crested tit, both breeding locally, frequent these pinewoods and red squirrel and roe deer are plentiful. Pine marten are also present, but less likely to be seen.

Beneath the pines the uneven ground is thickly carpeted with bilberry, cowberry and mosses, among which are many of the wild flowers particularly associated with pinewoods, for example chickweed wintergreen, intermediate wintergreen, lesser twayblade and creeping lady's-tresses.

The woodland on the south-facing slopes of the reserve contains a much higher proportion of birch – mainly the graceful pendulous variety. Aspen, rowan, alder, holly and willow are more abundant here and there are a few sessile oaks. A more varied ground flora is present on the richer soils of the birchwood floor. Woodland flowers such as wood sorrel, wood anemone and lesser celandine are widespread and the wetter hollows hold sundew, heath spotted-orchid and bog asphodel.

To ensure the continued existence of this important pinewood a long-term programme to encourage regeneration is under way. This involves fencing to exclude both deer and domestic animals, so that natural seedlings stand a better chance of survival. Since the youngest trees currently on the site are at least 100 years old, this programme will have to be carried on for a full century.

Colourful fly agaric is among the fungi that appear in autumn in the Spey Valley.

Lothian

In many ways a microcosm of Scotland, Lothian Region ranges in its landscapes from the wide sand dunes of the EAST LOTHIAN COAST to the rounded tops of the Pentland Hills, which reach 579m at Scald Law. Despite the high population density centred on Edinburgh, Scotland's capital and second largest city, the region is not highly industrialised. Although man's influence is always evident, some remarkably wild corners remain, their unexpectedness adding to their charm. Watching sea duck dive in the Forth on a crisp winter's day, or a skein of pink-footed geese fly in to a reservoir in the Pentlands while a grouse scolds on the hill behind, one can feel miles away from civilisation.

Each of the four administrative districts has its own character. East Lothian is a fertile coastal plain shaped by increasingly intensive agriculture. West Lothian is predominantly upland acid moor, sweeping up to the Pentlands themselves, although there has been extensive afforestation in recent years. Midlothian is an area of mixed farming and some industry based around several coal mines. Much woodland remains, as ribbons along the various dissecting rivers, as shelter belts, and as policy plantations from the last century. Even Edinburgh has a number of wild areas, centred on its open hills.

The climate is relatively temperate, although winter temperatures as low as −18°C have been recorded, and temperatures on the hottest summer days can be reduced by the coastal fog known as east coast haar. Strong winds are not uncommon, but rainfall is typical for eastern Britain.

The Pentlands, Robert Louis Stevenson's 'old huddle of grey hills', dominate the landscape of the Lothians. Essentially they are an eroded mass of volcanic lavas and old red sandstone, on a base of more ancient rock. The surrounding plains are considerably younger, dating from a time, 340 million years ago, when Scotland lay close to the Equator and the plains were lush tropical forests of fernlike plants interspersed with freshwater swamps. The vestiges of this plant life remain today as the extensive Midlothian coalfield, mined for at least 750 years, while the hard shells of the animals of the swamp and encroaching sea form the fossil-rich limestones found north west of Edinburgh.

The active vulcanism of this period has also left a dramatic impression on the region. The 251m high Arthur's Seat in the centre of Edinburgh is the remnants of a complex volcano, while Edinburgh's Castle Rock, North Berwick Law in East Lothian, and the gannet-populated BASS ROCK in the Forth Estuary are all old volcanic plugs. Later, glaciation scooped away all but the hardest rock, isolating the rounded tops of the Pentlands and sculpting the volcanic cores into distinctive crag-and-tail features, most clearly seen at the Castle Rock, where the tail forms Edinburgh's Royal Mile. This whole intricate landform can be seen impressively displayed from Soutra Hill on the A68 road south of Edinburgh.

The glacial plains left in East Lothian and Midlothian were probably once covered largely in oak woodland, but only remnants remain at ROSLIN GLEN and near Dalkeith. The rest were cleared to make way for agriculture, but in the late eighteenth and nineteenth centuries the local lairds planted new policy woodlands to provide cover for game and shelter for their houses, and as an investment. Many of these remain, together with a well-established alien flora including leopard's-bane, white butterbur, pink purslane, and even, in places, patches of the giant *Gunnera*. These woods provide refuge for a large roe deer population and small numbers of red squirrel. Tits and other woodland species abound, and woodcock can still be seen roding in the spring twilight.

West Lothian, too, must have been partially wooded, recorded in the name of towns like East Calder ('calder' being an oak wood). In much of the area, however, the soils were so poor and water-logged that large boggy mosses developed, with their characteristic plants and insects and only scattered trees of birch or alder. Extensive draining and fertilisation have largely converted these to upland sheep pastures, but to this day farmers have to battle against the invasion of these pastures by rushes and other poor acid vegetation. Remnants of the mosses can still be found at TAILEND MOSS and the RED MOSS OF BALERNO, while small bogs in the Pentlands are still the home for rare plants like hairy stonecrop and the yellow marsh saxifrage.

The natural vegetation of the high Pentlands was the more typically northern forest of birch and Scots pine, and fragments of juniper scrub remain. Today, however, this has largely been converted to sheep run and grouse moors which are still burnt to maintain the heather. Red grouse are common, along with mountain hare which were introduced to the area from 1834. Peregrine are occasional visitors.

Several reservoirs in the Pentlands, including Cobbinshaw and Threipmuir, as well as GLADHOUSE in the Moorfoot Hills, provide winter roosts for large numbers of greylag and pink-footed geese, whooper swan, wigeon, teal and other duck. The only large natural bodies of water in the area are DUDDINGSTON and Linlithgow Lochs, where duck winter in large numbers and great crested grebe nest in summer. Several medium-sized rivers flow through the area, providing fishing for dipper and heron, but some are polluted and, partly as a result, the otter is close to extinction in the region. Ponds are scarce.

Edinburgh's volcanic hills provide refuge for much wildlife. Among the rough grassland and gorse of Holyrood Park, dominated by Arthur's Seat, snow bunting can be seen in winter, while short-eared owl and, occasionally, sparrowhawk hunt in summer. Rare plants like maiden pink and forked spleenwort grow amongst the crags, and fulmar have recently begun nesting. Craiglockhart and Corstorphine Hill have badger and fox, and grey squirrel abound in the city parks, successors of a group that escaped from Edinburgh Zoo in 1913.

The Forth shoreline of Edinburgh is famous for its wintering sea duck. In the past up to 30,000 scaup could be seen near the sewage outfalls. Improved sewage treatment has drastically reduced these numbers, but quantities of long-tailed duck, scoter, eider, great crested grebe and merganser can still be seen from Seafield or by the ash lagoons at Musselburgh.

Certainly the most important and impressive natural feature of the region is the long coastline of cliffs, dunes and saltmarsh, together with the FORTH ISLANDS, including the Bass Rock with its gannetry and kittiwakes, Fidra and Inchmickery with terns, and Craigleith with puffins and guillemots. The increasing use of the Forth by oil tankers is an ever-present threat to these birds.

MICHAEL M. SCOTT

Aberlady Bay

NT 4681; 582ha; East Lothian DC reserve
Open bay with sand and mudflats, saltings, dunes and grassland
Access points at NT 472806 (car parking for permit holders only) and Gullane Dunes (NT 465831)
Access restricted from time to time; organised groups should contact warden, Dairy Cottage, Craigielaw, Longniddry, tel. Aberlady 588, in advance
April–July: breeding birds and flowers;
September–March: wildfowl and waders

Aberlady Bay is best known for its birds. The area also has considerable botanical interest, since its communities represent the full plant successsion from mudflat through saltmarsh and dune to dune scrub and grassland. Most of the reserve lies below the high-water mark.

The list of some 228 bird species recorded reflects the importance of the site for migrants as well as regular visitors, and the thoroughness with which it has been observed for many years. Fifty-five species breed, among them ringed plover, over 100 pairs of eider and a good number of shelduck.

Many shelduck nest at Aberlady Bay, and some now moult on the Inner Forth.

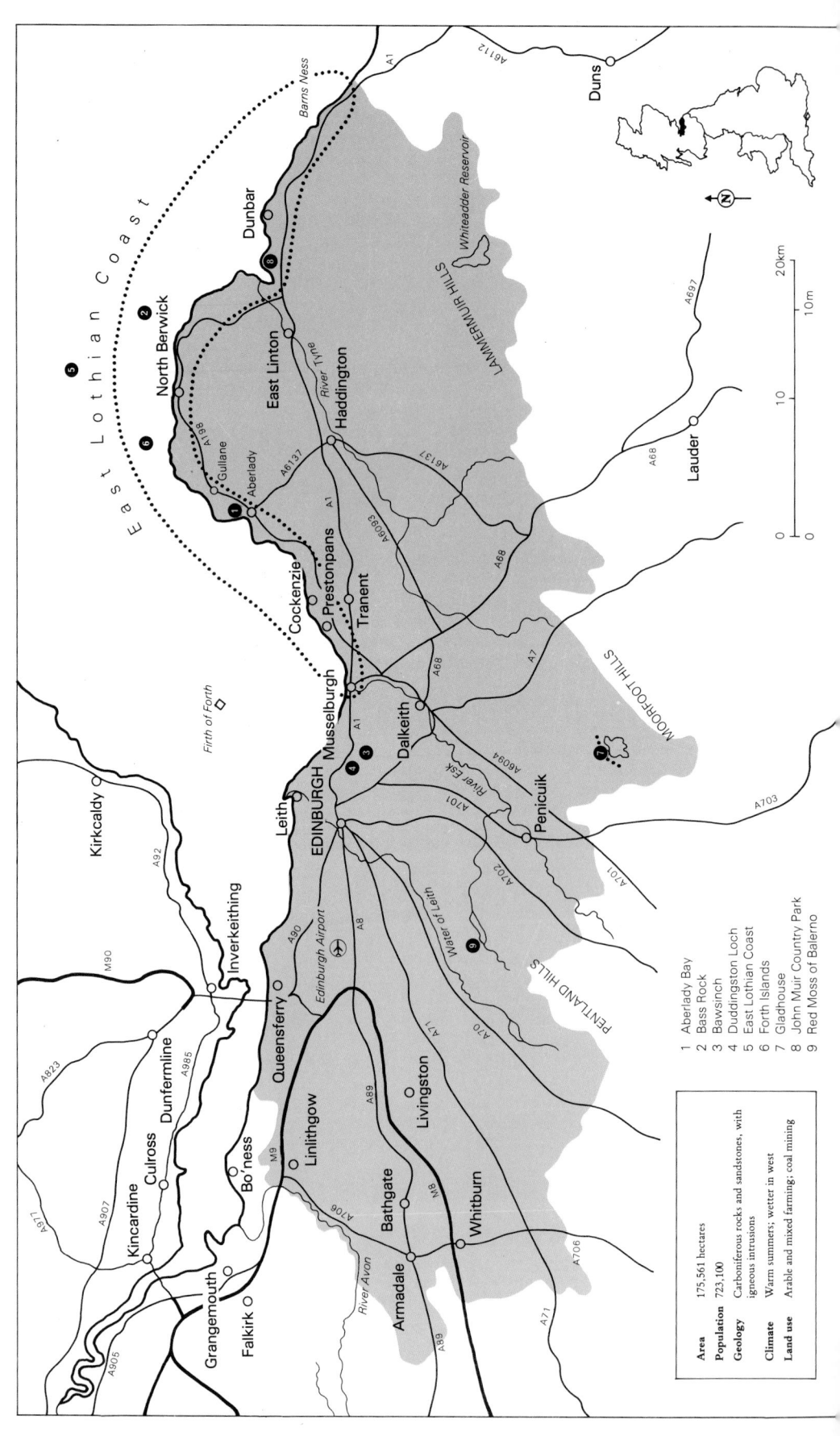

Area	175,561 hectares
Population	723,100
Geology	Carboniferous rocks and sandstones, with igneous intrusions
Climate	Warm summers; wetter in west
Land use	Arable and mixed farming; coal mining

1 Aberlady Bay
2 Bass Rock
3 Bawsinch
4 Duddingston Loch
5 East Lothian Coast
6 Forth Islands
7 Gladhouse
8 John Muir Country Park
9 Red Moss of Balerno

In winter several thousand scoter gather in the open Firth off Gullane Bay, and grebes and divers are regularly seen there. Several hundred mallard and wigeon feed on the mudflats, the latter generally concentrated where glasswort is most abundant. The bay is used as a roost by up to 3000 pink-footed geese which flight to and from the rich East Lothian farmland to feed. Waders are present in large numbers in autumn and winter, especially bar-tailed godwit, knot and grey plover; dunlin are also numerous.

All three species of eelgrass grow in the bay and some unusual saltmarsh mosses are present. The grey-hummocky fixed dunes carry abundant mosses and lichens and in some areas autumn gentian, grass-of-Parnassus, burnet rose and moonwort. Bog pimpernel, early marsh-orchid, northern marsh-orchid and 15 species of sedge occur in the dune slacks, and the Marl Loch holds bogbean, amphibious bistort and intermediate bladderwort.

Both grey and common seal are frequently seen off Hummel Rocks, near the eastern boundary of the reserve in Gullane Bay. This area is also of geological interest.

Northern marsh-orchid favours lime-rich soil.

Bass Rock

NT 602873; 10ha; privately owned
Cliff-girt island
Permission to land obtainable through local boatman
Regular daily sailings, weather permitting, in summer: contact Fred Marr, 24 Victoria Road, North Berwick, tel. 2838
May–July

This volcanic neck, rising to over 90m, is famous for its gannets, an association recognised in the bird's scientific name, *Sula bassana*. Some 9000 pairs nest on the island; the colony has outgrown the cliff sites and spread on to the sloping summit. Other breeding seabirds include kittiwake, puffin, guillemot, razorbill, shag and fulmar. A stand of tree mallow is of botanical interest.

Bawsinch

NT 284725; 7ha; SWT reserve
Variety of habitats on former waste ground
Open Wednesday and Saturday by appointment with SWT
Some restrictions on access 1 March–30 June
Hide, with bird and plant list
April–June: flowers and insects;
September–December: wildfowl

This small reserve is a fine example of habitat creation to benefit wildlife. Acquired to form a buffer zone along the southern edge of DUDDINGSTON LOCH, the once derelict ground now supports thriving trees and shrubs. Nearly all the native Scottish and British species are represented and most specimens are of known origin. Among the trees grow various flowering plants: some garden escapes, presumably dumped in the past, some

self-seeded, and some introduced. The last include teasel to attract goldfinches – which it has done; buddleia for butterflies; and species such as cowslip, increasingly rare in natural habitats.

Five small ponds of varying size and depth have been excavated; each now holds its own distinctive flora and fauna. Water-starwort, broad-leaved pondweed and common duckweed arrived by natural means; water-milfoil, water-crowfoot and white water-lily were introduced. The pond snails too were 'imported' but water fleas, pond skaters and whirligig beetles just appeared.

About 66 bird species have been recorded on the reserve, and many more seen from the hide which overlooks Duddingston Loch. The resident Duddingston greylag geese regularly move across to graze on the 'goose green' established for them. Foxes occasionally visit and grey squirrel, water vole and pipistrelle have all been seen.

Blawhorn Moss

Permit only; 69ha; NCC reserve
Peat moss
Permit from NCC (SE Region), Edinburgh
April–July

This peatland is one of the few in central Scotland still relatively unaffected by peat-cutting, drainage or afforestation. Both raised and blanket mire are represented and the predominant vegetation is heather, hare's-tail cottongrass and cross-leaved heath on the hummocks, with crowberry, common cottongrass and *Sphagnum* moss in the damper hollows.

Duddingston Loch

Aerial view of Bass Rock.

NT 2872; 8ha; Scottish Dev. Dept (Ancient
Monuments)–SWT
Loch with reedbeds
Access restricted to north shore near car park
October–March

Duddingston is best known for its wintering
pochard. Numbering up to 8000 at its peak in the
late 1970s, the flock spends the day bathing and
resting on the loch, and flights at dusk to feed on
the Firth of Forth. Recent years have seen a drop in
numbers, probably associated with the reduction
in sewage pollution of the Forth. Pochard and feral
greylag geese breed near the loch and the geese also
visit other lochs in Holyrood Park. In winter the
reedbeds are an important roosting area for small
birds such as pied wagtail and yellowhammer.
Heron are frequent visitors and water rail are
occasionally heard calling in the reeds. The
BAWSINCH hide gives good views over the loch.

East Lothian Coast

See map; includes 11 sites
Information and nature trail booklets from tourist
offices in North Berwick and Dunbar, or from East
Lothian DC; countryside ranger service
All year

A quite remarkable range of land uses and habitats
is displayed along the East Lothian coast. There are
power stations at Cockenzie and Torness, at either
end of the district, the former coal-fired and the
latter a much-debated nuclear plant, the first in
eastern Scotland. Between them, the land immediately behind the foreshore supports industry,
a nature reserve, world-famous golf courses, public
open space, private woodlands, holiday resorts,
intensive farming and a large cement works. The
foreshore itself includes mudflats, fine sandy
beaches, low rocky coastline and steep cliffs, with
a scatter of small islands offshore. Much of this
coast is heavily used for recreation; industrial
pollution is widespread around Musselburgh; and
the heavy shipping on the Firth of Forth, which
includes large oil tankers, presents a constant
threat to bird life. Yet despite these pressures the
coast is rich in natural history interest, by no
means confined to the reserve at ABERLADY BAY.

In the built-up section of the coast the Musselburgh lagoons are one of the local birdwatchers'
most popular haunts and a good illustration of how
industrial development may sometimes benefit
wildlife. These lagoons are used for the disposal of
waste ash from the Cockenzie power station;
originally flooded, they now offer an extensive flat
area with a mud-like surface. Almost concurrently
with the construction of the lagoons reclamation
was taking place on the shore nearby, where
waders roosted at high tide. As the birds were
driven from their traditional sites they started to
roost on the lagoons, choosing areas where the ash

had not dried out and become compacted. Secure from human disturbance, this roost rapidly increased until the former Musselburgh population of around 800 birds had reached a winter average of about 7000. Knot (sometimes numbering 10,000), oystercatcher and curlew particularly favour this site, which is also used by many golden plover, turnstone, redshank, bar-tailed godwit and ringed plover.

Some 10km further east lies Gosford Bay, so exposed to westerly winds that the woodlands of Gosford House are trimmed to an even slope above the level of the boundary wall. With a largely stony shore and scattered scrub on the strip of ground between the A198 and the high-tide line, Gosford Bay looks unprepossessing, but it is probably the best place in Scotland for wintering grebes. Over 100 Slavonian grebe are regularly present in midwinter, often with 20–30 red-necked grebe and a few great crested; the bulk of the 500 or so great crested grebe that winter on the Firth of Forth tend, like some of the diving ducks, to be found further west, between Musselburgh and Leith.

Gullane Point is good for observing the large flocks of sea duck on this section of the Firth. Common scoter are present for much of the year: counts of 1500 in August and 1000 in May are not uncommon; autumn counts of velvet scoter are usually in the region of 300, and over 200 long-tailed duck are often in the area in February–March.

Gullane Bay is the finest and most popular beach within easy reach of Edinburgh. Not many years ago erosion was a serious problem: the fore-dune was virtually destroyed and major blow-outs of sand took place. Fortunately a restoration programme was initiated by the local authority, using brushwood and fencing to stabilise the sand, planting marram and lyme-grass to anchor it, and using sea-buckthorn and board-walks to channel pedestrian traffic.

At Yellowcraig the shore is rockier again, though still backed by dunes. A nature trail has been laid out along the shore, where rock pools and shells provide varied interest. There are good views from here of the FORTH ISLANDS.

North Berwick, a popular holiday resort, has both sandy and rocky shores and a small harbour busy in summer with sailing craft and boat trips to the BASS ROCK. Gannets from the Bass often dive quite close inshore; the rocks beyond the swimming pool provide a good vantage point. Tantallon Castle, another good viewpoint, is notable for nesting fulmar.

The next stretch of coast is much less frequented, being backed by farmland and accessible on foot only over considerable distances. At JOHN MUIR COUNTRY PARK however, better known as the Tyninghame Estuary, there is much of interest to botanists and ornithologists, as well as a magnificent beach.

Dunbar's rich red cliffs and busy little harbour add to its attractions. Kittiwake nest on the old castle ruin and on many of the harbour buildings, while the cliffs have considerable botanical interest. They also provide good viewpoints for sea-watching and the passage migrants seen along this north east facing stretch of coast are many and varied. In August arctic and great skua sometimes pass at up to 20 and 50 an hour respectively, and both long-tailed and pomarine skua are occasionally recorded. Little gulls are also regularly seen, while in winter large numbers of red-throated diver gather offshore.

Slightly further down the coast, at Barnsness, a lighthouse, patches of scrub and freshwater pools attract small migrants off the sea. Many species have been recorded, their arrival often coinciding with similar arrivals on the ISLE OF MAY (Fife), which is usually visible from Barnsness. Among the less common ones are woodchat shrike, lesser whitethroat, red-breasted flycatcher, wryneck and hoopoe.

The stretch of coastline from just north of Barnsness south to Torness displays a succession of lower carboniferous limestones and calciferous sandstones along the foreshore. At low tide these rocks, many of them fossil-bearing, can be clearly seen. One of the most spectacular sections, not far from an old lime kiln, is a creamy white wave-cut platform of nodular limestone, the surface dimpled

The Bass gannetry now extends on to the slopes above the cliff.

The fossil-rich rocks at Barnsness are pitted with shallow pools.

with basin-shaped hollows. This rock is extremely rich in fossils, the colonial reef coral (*Lithostrotion*) being abundant enough to justify the description 'spaghetti and macaroni rock'. The lime-rich grassland here carries purple milk-vetch and bird's-foot-trefoil; autumn gentian grows on some of the limestone outcrops.

Here, at the outermost end of the East Lothian coast, industrial pressures are again in evidence. The limestones provide raw material for locally produced cement, and on the headland at Torness stands the new nuclear power station.

Forth Islands

Fidra NO 513867; Eyebroughty NO 495863; The Lamb NO 535866; 2ha; RSPB reserve
Small inshore islands
No landing on The Lamb; access to Fidra by boat from North Berwick: several boat hirers run round trips; Eyebroughty can be reached by foot at low tide
May–July

Although small, these islands are important seabird breeding sites. Eyebroughty is also a moulting ground for large numbers of eider.

Rapid colonisation by several species has occurred in recent years. Cormorant bred first on The Lamb in 1967, built up rapidly to 250 pairs, and then spread to Eyebroughty and the nearby small island of Craigleith. Razorbill and guillemot colonised The Lamb in the 1960s and Fidra about ten years later; over 1000 pairs of guillemot now breed on the reserve. Kittiwake first bred in the 1960s and have increased steadily: over 450 pairs now nest on Fidra. Until 1967 the only regularly used puffin colony was on Craigleith but a small group has recently settled on Fidra.

Other regular breeders include shag, eider, lesser black-backed and herring gull. Small numbers of common and arctic tern have bred occasionally.

Gladhouse

NT 3054; 162ha; Lothian RC reserve
Reservoir with islands and woodland fringe
No access at present but good views obtainable from public road
All year

Up to 13,000 pink-footed geese roost here in autumn. Other wildfowl include up to 700 mallard, several hundred teal, wigeon and tufted duck, and smaller numbers of goldeneye and goosander. Mallard, teal and a few shoveler breed. A recent decrease in duck is possibly attributable to feral mink, but numbers should rise now that the mink are actively controlled. The exposed mud around the shores has attracted more than 20 species of migrant waders.

John Muir Country Park

NT 6480; 675ha; East Lothian DC
Estuary, dunes, beach and cliffs
Leaflets from Dunbar tourist office or ELDC; guided walks programme in summer
May–June: flowers and breeding birds;
September–March: waders and duck

The park is named after the naturalist and explorer John Muir, born in nearby Dunbar; as a boy he emigrated to America, where he became much involved in conservation and the national parks movement.

Better known to many naturalists as Tyninghame, this estuary, with its prominent headland to the north, surrounding woodland, and sheer cliffs to the south east, attracts a wide variety of migrant birds. Two long sand spits, Sandy Hirst and Spike Island, shelter the inner part of the Tyne Estuary and provide nesting sites for ringed plover; an extensive growth of sea-buckthorn on the spits gives good cover for small migrants. The invertebrate-rich mud of the estuary attracts shelduck and wintering waders, while Whitberry Point and the Dunbar cliffs offer good vantage points for watching offshore bird movements.

Eelgrass and glasswort on the mudflats are succeeded first by sea-blite, sea plantain and common saltmarsh-grass and then, on ground that is seldom inundated, by saltmarsh rush, sea-milkwort and red fescue. Around the volcanic rocks of Whitberry Point wild thyme, bloody crane's-bill and buck's-horn plantain occur and there is a patch of heather and cross-leaved heath, with green-ribbed sedge and sneezewort. The near-vertical cliffs at Dunbar, also largely volcanic, carry meadow saxifrage, cowslip, primrose and oxlip.

More than 30 wader species have been recorded on the estuary, most of them during peak migration periods. Numbers are largest in winter, with big populations of oystercatcher, dunlin, knot, ringed plover and redshank; grey plover, bar-tailed godwit and turnstone are also generally present. Several hundred mallard, teal and wigeon use the area in winter and small groups of greylag and pink-footed geese occasionally roost on the estuary. There is a wintering mute and whooper swan flock of up to 80 birds. Divers are frequently seen offshore in winter, and great, arctic and pomarine skua are recorded regularly in autumn.

A good variety of lichens, including several locally uncommon species, is present on the dune areas. The marine invertebrate fauna includes seven species of crab, soft coral and several sponges, with shells of many different molluscs on the beach.

Milkhall Pond

Permit only; 2ha; SWT reserve
Disused reservoir and associated marsh
April–June

A variety of aquatic invertebrates inhabits this shallow pond 350m above sea level. Frog, toad and newt all breed and sedge warbler and reed bunting nest in the surrounding rosebay willow-herb, bramble and meadowsweet.

Pepper Wood

Permit only; 1ha; SWT reserve
Semi-natural woodland
April–August

This tiny wood holds most common native woodland plants and a large number of other species introduced over 150 years ago. It is now notable for lily-of-the-valley, leopard's-bane, butterbur and heart-leaved valerian.

Red Moss of Balerno

NT 165638; 23ha; SWT reserve
Peat moss
Public access only on advertised open days
or by permit from SWT
June–September

Formerly a peat 'common' regularly cut for fuel, the Red Moss is one of the finest peatlands left in the Edinburgh area. Reaching a maximum depth of around 6m, the heather-covered peat rises to a perceptible dome in the centre. Wet woodland, predominantly birch, willow and rowan, fringes the moss, and scattered birch and Scots pine dot its surface.

The boggy areas hold the most varied vegetation. At least six species of *Sphagnum* moss are known to be present, as are bog asphodel and round-leaved sundew, both uncommon in the Lothians. In summer the marshy margins of the reserve are colourful with ragged-Robin, marsh ragwort, lesser spearwort, cuckooflower and heath spotted-orchid.

Red Moss is rich in insects. Swarms of small moths flit over the heather and marsh; these and the water beetles have been the subject of special study. Frog and toad frequent the area and common lizard sun themselves on the drier hummocks. A good variety of moorland and scrub woodland birds use the reserve; among the more interesting are redpoll, tree pipit, short-eared owl and, occasionally, hen harrier.

Red Moss of Balerno is of interest for its mosses, marsh vegetation and varied insect life.

Roslin Glen

Permit only; 19.2ha; SWT reserve
Mixed woodland in steep-sided valley
April–June

Steep slopes and luxuriant ground cover give this woodland an air of impenetrability that will help safeguard its wildlife interest. Oak, ash and wych elm are dominant, with 14 other broad-leaved species and a few Scots pine and yew. Honeysuckle is everywhere – sprawling over the ground, twining up tree trunks and hanging in great festoons from branches – and provides admirable nesting cover for woodland birds. The more open areas, where oak predominates, hold a good population of wood warbler; redstart and pied flycatcher have been recorded and no fewer than 60 bird species are known to breed.

Much of the wood is carpeted with a typical oak –ash flora including dog's mercury, wood anemone, woodruff and ramsons. Hairy wood-rush abounds and there are clumps of pendulous sedge where the slope steepens and falls away abruptly to the River North Esk below. Beech fern and hard fern are among the six or more fern species, and the woodland is rich in bryophytes. Garden escapes are not infrequent and include several patches of leopard's-bane.

Both red and grey squirrel are found on the reserve, the latter having appeared first in 1968. Roe deer, badger and fox also visit, probably sometimes spending long periods in the wood and at other times passing through it on their way to or from the Roslin Glen Country Park further upstream.

Tailend Moss

Permit only; 29ha; SWT reserve
Peat bog with open pools
Leaflet from SWT
April–July: flowers and insects;
November–February: wildfowl

Cranberry, sundew and bog asphodel grow on the wetter sections of this heather-dominated moss. Mallard, teal, snipe, curlew and redshank breed and wintering wildfowl include whooper swan, wigeon, shoveler, tufted duck, pochard and goldeneye. Six of the seven species of dragonfly and damselfly found in the Lothians have been recorded, as have oak eggar and emperor moths.

Thornton Glen

Permit only; 6ha; SWT reserve
Natural woodland in steep glen
April–June

Apparently virtually untouched for several hundred years, this woodland is predominantly ash, elm, holly and hazel. Various escapes, such as privet and gooseberry, have become naturalised and field maple is present, here at the northern end of its range in Britain. The glen is cut through calciferous sandstone and the resultant soil fertility is reflected in very varied ground cover. Seven species of fern, including hart's-tongue, are present, with abundant bryophytes.

Despite its proximity to built-up areas, Roslin Glen is still a refuge for roe deer.

Orkney

Orkney is a crossroads where north and south, Atlantic and North Sea, sea and land, man and wildlife meet. Its landscape is a mosaic of sea and softly curved landforms. Especially when viewed from the air, the well-stocked, dyke-crossed farms and the moorlands form a smooth patchwork with nothing harsh or angular. Even where sea and land meet the transition is mostly gentle; only when some angle of view profiles the higher cliffs does the skeleton of old red sandstone give any indication of the forces of wind and wave which have exposed it there.

Nearer to the Arctic Circle than to London, the islands are in the track of the Atlantic depressions, making them vulnerable to wind and cloud; gales are frequent, yet the annual rainfall is well under 1000mm. The Gulf Stream brings warmth, and winter temperatures compare well with those of English south coast resorts. Snow rarely lies long, and severe frosts are virtually unknown. Summers are mild and fairly dry, although the coasts and higher land may experience cool onshore winds; this is the season when the sun seems reluctant to set at night and eager to rise again in the early dawn.

Land that has bent under the ice sheets of the Pleistocene and bowed to wind and sea has also proved amazingly docile under the hand of man, who has cultivated its fertile soil for more than 4000 years. As elsewhere, wildlife is under pressure; compared with the islands of the Hebrides, Orkney carries a higher density of human population, which, after a long decline to the early 1970s, is now rising. Luckily the impact of North Sea oil is hardly discernible to the visitor, but farming is expanding.

Although modern Orkney appears predominantly agricultural, so cunningly are the fields spaced out by lochs and moorland, and so surrounded are they by vast areas of coastal features, that abundant wildlife still manages to exist cheek-by-jowl with the human presence. Even though drainage proceeds at an alarming rate, there are still many small fens dominated by shrubby willows and bright with orchids. There are dune slacks where great clumps of grass-of-Parnassus open 50 or more green-veined white cups at a time, and there are beds of reeds beloved by waterfowl. A glorious jumble of meadow, bog and alpine plants grows together in roadside flushes, and the great eutrophic lochs of the west mainland, with their unique range of water from fresh to salt, are still important for wintering duck and for trout.

The prehistoric mixed birch, hazel and rowan scrub, with its understorey of ferns and flowers, manages to maintain itself in tiny remnants on the cliffs of Scapa Flow and in the gullies of Hoy, and a place name including 'dale' indicates a moorland valley rich with plants of a woodland character. On the higher, exposed hills of Westray, Rousay, and especially Hoy, dwarf shrubs lie flattened among slabby pavement and lime-loving alpines cling to the crumbling outcrops and wet screes.

On the coast, several rare northern plants are relatively abundant. Dunes and sunny, grassy sea banks are good for insects, including butterflies. Most of Orkney's land mammals are probably introductions, but Orkney vole is found elsewhere in the British Isles only on Guernsey; it forms a prey species for several raptors. The absence of ground-based animal predators, apart from the

Area	97,591 hectares
Population	18,400
Geology	Mainly sandstones yielding fertile soils
Climate	Windy; winters less harsh than on mainland
Land use	Agriculture, largely pastoral

1 Copinsay
2 Dale of Cottasgarth
3 Hobbister
4 Marwick Head
5 North Hill, Papa Westray
6 Noup Cliffs, Westray

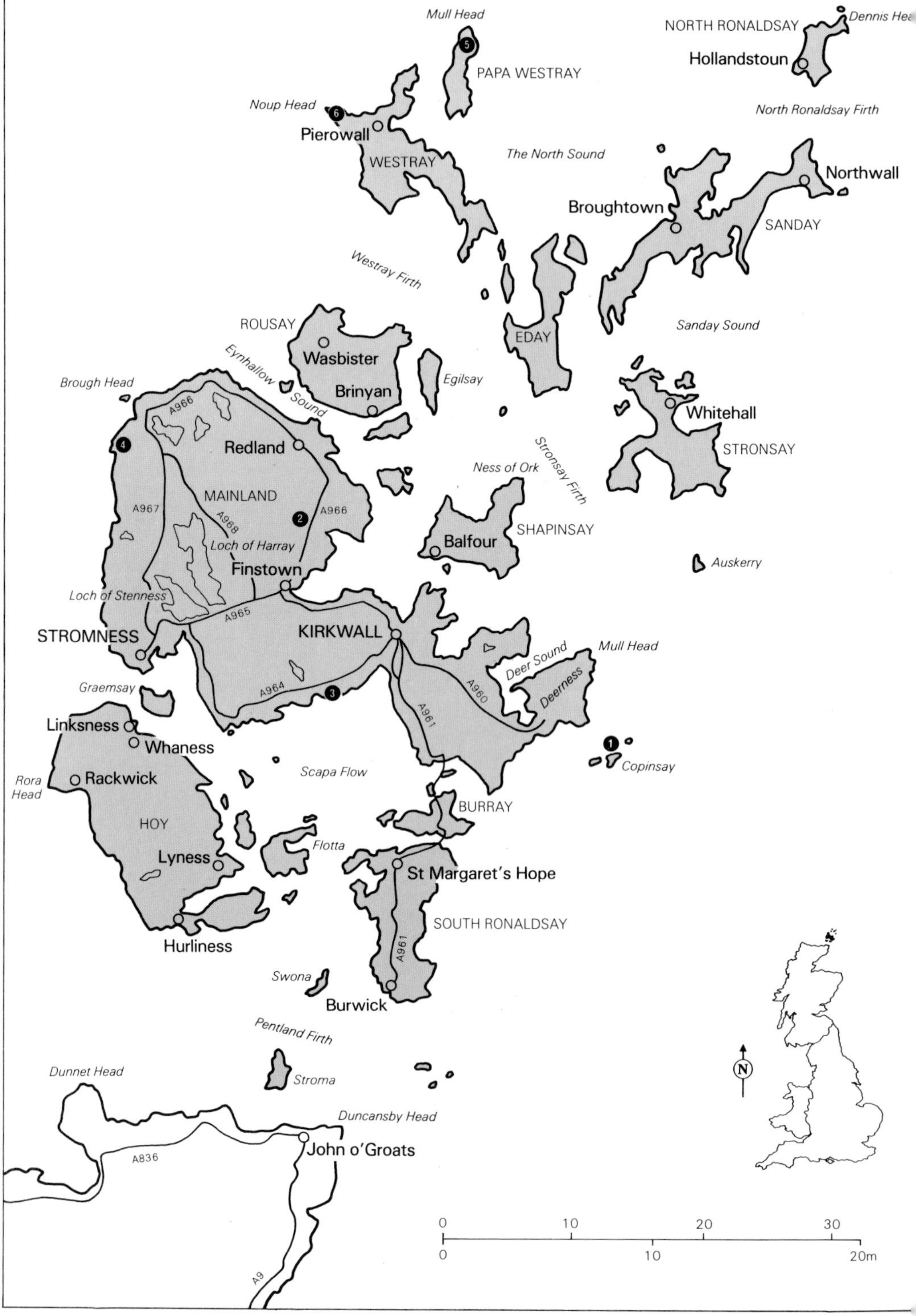

Mull Head

NORTH RONALDSAY   Dennis Hea

Hollandstoun

PAPA WESTRAY

North Ronaldsay Firth

Noup Head   6

Pierowall

WESTRAY

The North Sound

Broughtown

Northwall

SANDAY

Westray Firth

ROUSAY

Wasbister

Brinyan

Eynhallow Sound

Egilsay

EDAY

Sanday Sound

Brough Head

A966

Redland

MAINLAND

A967

A966

2

A968

Loch of Harray

Finstown

Loch of Stenness

STROMNESS

A965

Graemsay

Linksness

Whaness

Rora Head

Rackwick

HOY

Lyness

Scapa Flow

Flotta

KIRKWALL

A964

3

A961

A960

Deer Sound

Deerness

Mull Head

1

Copinsay

BURRAY

St Margaret's Hope

SOUTH RONALDSAY

A961

Hurliness

Swona

Burwick

Ness of Ork

SHAPINSAY

Balfour

Stronsay Firth

Whitehall

STRONSAY

Auskerry

Pentland Firth

Stroma

Dunnet Head

A836

Duncansby Head

John o'Groats

A9

0   10   20   30
0   10   20m

N

domestic cat, makes low-nesting birds comparatively safe, even though woodland is so scarce.

What Orkney lacks in land mammals is more than balanced by its breeding colonies of grey seals and by the fewer but less timid common seals, which often haul out on reefs quite close to public roads. Out to sea the observant watcher may spot schools of whales and occasionally other cetaceans, while at the opposite end of the scale a moist climate and the Gulf Stream combine to ensure a rich and varied shore life.

If the open Orkney landscape is now almost treeless, the towns and gardens are overshadowed by more big sycamores than many a southern centre. The rooks cawing among Kirkwall trees could be those of any English cathedral close.

ELAINE R. BULLARD

Copinsay

HY 6001; 152ha; RSPB reserve
Island and nearby holms
Access by boat (30 mins) from Newark Bay lighthouse pier (HY 568042) or Skaill; booking necessary; tel. Deerness 245 or
S. Foubister, Deerness 252; landing only possible in calm weather
Visitors should go first to information room in farmhouse
May–July

Sheer cliffs, rising to 60m along the south east coast of the grassy island of Copinsay, hold breeding populations of some 30,000 pairs of guillemot and 10,000 pairs of kittiwake. Several hundred pairs of fulmar, razorbill and great black-backed gull also nest on the island, along with smaller numbers of puffin, black guillemot, shag, and lesser black-backed, herring and common gulls. The little island of Corn Holm, which is connected to Copinsay by a storm beach exposed at low water, usually has a small colony of arctic tern, and cormorant nest on the Horse of Copinsay, 1 km off the main island.

Along the north coast of Copinsay, where the old red sandstone has been eroded to form a medley of stacks, geos and promontories, the cliff vegetation is luxuriant. Sea aster is particularly abundant, sea pearlwort and sea-spurrey are plentiful, and sea spleenwort and northern saltmarsh-grass are also present. Oysterplant grows abundantly on Corn Holm.

Dale of Cottasgarth and Birsay Moors

HY 3719; 2000ha; RSPB reserve
Moorland
Access from Lower Cottasgarth (HY 370194), where cars can be parked, along track to the Dale
May–August

This large area of rough moorland is typical of the habitats that are progressively disappearing in Orkney as heather and deergrass are replaced with cultivated grasses and clovers. The gently rolling moorland, with its mosaic of shortish heather, worked-out peat banks, small lochans and sheltered dales, is the home of those Orkney specialities, hen harrier and short-eared owl. Both need large territories for hunting, ground cover to nest in, and freedom from disturbance for successful breeding.

Other species breeding on the reserve include curlew, snipe, redshank, meadow pipit, skylark and wheatear. Kestrel and merlin occasionally nest – on the ground among the heather – and both great and arctic skua are sometimes present too. Most of the breeding species can usually be seen from the ruined farm buildings at Dale or the small hide nearby.

Inland, fields are taking over Orkney's moors.

Guillemots pack together on the larger ledges.

Hobbister

HY 3806; 759ha; RSPB reserve
Moorland with loch
Access restricted to area between A964 and sea;
approached via minor road on east side of
Waulkmill Bay (HY 381067) with car park; the
houses there and surrounding ground are private
property
May–August

Bounded to the south by Scapa Flow and to the
west by tidal flats in Waulkmill Bay, this reserve
has a greater diversity of habitat than the purely
moorland DALE OF COTTASGARTH AND BIRSAY
MOORS, and consequently a greater variety of
breeding birds. As Scapa Flow is encircled by
islands its shoreline cliffs are not occupied by
seabirds, but its sheltered waters attract large
numbers of wintering duck including long-tailed
duck and velvet scoter. On the more sheltered
stretches of cliff the luxuriant vegetation includes
shrubby species which provide cover for small
migrants. Raven, jackdaw and rock dove breed on
the cliffs, generally choosing sites tucked in below
an overhang. Eider and shelduck also nest on the
reserve, often quite far inland, later leading their
newly hatched broods over the cliff edge to the
safety of the sea below.

The moorland area, still actively worked for
peat, is largely heather-covered, with cottongrass,
deergrass and sedges in the wetter areas. Four
predators, hen harrier, kestrel, merlin and short-
eared owl, breed regularly on the moor which also
supports a few pairs of red grouse. Curlew, snipe

and redshank are among the breeding waders,
while the freshwater loch holds teal, tufted duck
and red-throated diver. A small area of saltmarsh
behind the shingle bar across Waulkmill Bay
provides additional feeding ground for waders,
but the tidal flats of the bay itself, though visually
attractive, are not rich enough in invertebrate life
to attract many birds.

Marwick Head

HY 2224; 19ha; RSPB reserve
Sea cliffs
For car parking and viewpoints see below
May–July

This is the most accessible and easily viewed of the
large seabird colonies in Orkney.

Like NOUP CLIFFS, WESTRAY, those around Marwick Head have abundant flat nesting ledges
which are packed with seabirds during the summer
months. Kittiwake and guillemot are the most
numerous species, with more than 10,000 pairs of
each in the colony; smaller numbers of razorbill
and fulmar and a few puffin are also present. Great
and arctic skua often fly past offshore, ready to
give chase whenever they spot a fish-laden
kittiwake coming in from the sea. Other birds likely
to be seen along this stretch of cliff include raven,
jackdaw and the unobtrusive little twite.

Part of the bay of Mar Wick is included in the
reserve. Eider, oystercatcher, ringed plover and
redshank can be seen there and occasionally seals
come well inshore. Sloping slabs of rock form the
shoreline at the north end, where the cliff starts to
rise. It is at this point (HY 228243) that visitors
should park their cars; a path leads along the cliff
top to the grey stone memorial to Lord Kitchener
which stands on the summit of Marwick Head. A
substantial part of this seabird colony is not visible
from the land and in some places the cliffs are
dangerous. Visitors can obtain a close view of the
birds from a point roughly halfway up the path, just
below a rock face bearing the painted number 129.

North Hill, Papa Westray

HY 4953; 206ha; RSPB reserve
Maritime heathland
All visitors must contact RSPB warden, Gowrie,
Papa Westray, preferably in advance by letter,
before entering the reserve
Mid-May–July

In the breeding season this rather barren-looking
stretch of heath is literally seething with birds. The
5000–6000 pairs of arctic tern breeding in one vast
colony, the largest in the UK, are constantly in
motion; successive 'panics' send waves of screaming birds up into the air to circle for a few minutes
before returning to their nests. On the fringes of
this throng 100 pairs of arctic skua harry the terns
coming in from the sea with fish, streaking after
them, twisting and turning until the luckless terns
eventually drop their catch. Great skua nest in
the area too, as well as a sizeable population of

great black-backed, lesser black-backed, herring and common gull. Breeding on the heathland are eider, ringed plover and dunlin, and there are notably high numbers of oystercatcher.

The North Hill is of botanical as well as ornithological interest and importance. It represents the best example of maritime sedge heath in northern Scotland; exposure, salt spray and grazing have combined to produce a ground cover which gradually changes from a sward dominated by thrift, spring squill and sea plantain near the cliff top, to heather, crowberry and creeping willow further inland. Sizeable patches of tiny Scottish primrose add to the attractions of the site.

Although small in comparison with such sites as NOUP CLIFFS and MARWICK HEAD, the colony of cliff-nesting seabirds on Papa Westray is particularly easy to observe. Situated on Fowl Craig, at the south east corner of reserve, the colony holds several thousand pairs of kittiwake and guillemot and small numbers of razorbill, puffin and black guillemot.

Noup Cliffs, Westray

HY 3950; 14ha; RSPB reserve
Sea cliffs
Access from road to Noup Head lighthouse
(HY 391503)
No dogs allowed
May–July

This 2km stretch of cliffs running south from Noup Head (HY 391503) is arguably the most densely populated seabird city in Britain. Indeed, so closely are the 40,000 pairs of guillemot packed that slum conditions might be said to prevail, with chicks being roughly jostled, dead birds trampled underfoot, and many of the inhabitants liberally bespattered with guano from the floors above. The scene is one of perpetual motion as continuous streams of

birds leave for the fishing grounds and return with sand eels for their young. Below, rafts of guillemot are scattered far out over the sea, many of the birds bathing with such energy and enthusiasm that the pattering of their wings on the water is audible even through the background chorus of raucous 'aaarghs'. The smell is equally impressive.

It is the combination of rich, readily accessible feeding grounds and the generous supply of suitable nesting ledges that has made Noup Cliffs and several others in Orkney, for example MARWICK HEAD, such important seabird colonies. Wherever flagstone rocks of varying hardness lie horizontally, the sea erodes the softer layers faster than the hard ones, and creates a series of level shelves of varying depth and length. Fulmar, razorbill and shag occupy the smallest, detached, residences; kittiwake, of which there are 40,000 pairs on the reserve, favour the longer and shallower shelves, spacing their nests along them at regular intervals or, in the case of the non-breeding groups, just staking their claim and returning quickly after their frequent 'panic' flights along the cliff face. Puffin are present in small numbers.

On the heathland behind the cliffs arctic skua nest and perform their mock-pathetic wing-trailing distraction display when their chicks are too closely approached. Both they and the great skuas that gather to bathe at the small lochans and to stand around on prominent – and well-fertilised – green knolls, can have little difficulty in obtaining food with a kittiwake colony as big as this one so close at hand. Arctic tern and several wader species also breed in the area.

Although the moorland is not part of the reserve visitors are allowed to walk across the unenclosed land, but are asked to be careful to close all gates.

Copinsay: the James Fisher Memorial Seabird Reserve.

Area	289,798 hectares
Population	30,700
Geology	Peatland over hard, acid rock; beaches and *machair* on Atlantic coast
Climate	Wet and windy; mild winters, cool summers
Land use	Crofting

1 Balranald
2 Loch Druidibeg
3 Monach Isles
4 North Rona and Sula Sgeir
5 St Kilda

0   10   20   30   40km

0   10   20   30m

Sula Sgeir   ④ *North Rona*

Butt of Lewis
Port of Ness
Cellar Head
A857
Carloway   **Barvas**
Tolsta Head
Great Bernera   A858
Gallan Head   A857
STORNOWAY   *Tiumpan Head*
Broad Bay   *Eye Peninsula*
Aird Brenish   **Callanish**   A866
Loch Roag
Mealasta Isle
Loch Langavat
Scarp   A859   *Loch Erisort*
Kebock Head
LEWIS
Flannan Isles
West Loch Tarbert   *Loch Seaforth*
Taransay   **Tarbert**
Toe Head   A859   *Scalpay*   *Shiant Islands*
HARRIS
Pabbay   *East Loch Tarbert*
Berneray   **Rodel**
⑤ *St Kilda*   *Boreray*
Haskeir Island   *Renish Point*
Sound of Harris   *The Little Minch*
①   **Sollas**   A865
A867   **Lochmaddy**
③   **NORTH UIST**
Monach Islands   **Carinish**
Baleshare
Creagorry   **BENBECULA**
Wiay
②   **SKYE**
Howmore
A865   **SOUTH UIST**
Lochboisdale
Sound of Barra   *Eriskay*
Scurrival Point   *Canna*
Barra   A888
Vatersay   **Castlebay**   *Rhum*
Pabbay
Mingulay
Berneray

N

Outer Hebrides

From North Rona and Sula Sgeir to Barra Head, and from the Shiant Isles to Rockall, the Outer Hebrides embrace some 120 named islands used for agriculture, of which only 14 are now permanently inhabited: Lewis, Harris, Great Bernera, Scalpay, Berneray, North Uist, Grimsay, Baleshare, Benbecula, South Uist, Eriskay, Barra, Vatersay and ST KILDA. Breached only by the shallow, reef-strewn sounds of Harris and Barra, the Long Island itself (Butt of Lewis to Barra Head) stretches 210km across the prevailing westerly winds and Atlantic surges, and has long been the home of a proud and hardy race with a distinctive culture and ethos, derived from an ancient language, strongly held religious beliefs and an age-long struggle with elemental forces.

The origins of Hebridean man are obscure. It has been suggested that the post-neolithic colonisers were Iberian, but were sparsely distributed when the Viking occupation took place in the ninth century. This may account for the predominance of Norse place names, especially in Lewis, where the Scandinavian element in the population is also more evident than in Harris and the Southern Isles.

The land itself is all that remains of an ancient eroded platform of Lewisian gneiss, 3000 million years old, and mostly under 90m above sea level. Raised and convoluted by subsequent earth movements, its hills have been shaped by glacial action and its surface overlain by glacial deposits, and by peat to a depth of 4.5m in some places.

Along the low-lying western seaboard, lime-rich shell sand has been blown inland by the prevailing westerlies and has transformed the peat into fertile grassland or *machair*, which plays a vital part in the economy and landscape of the islands and which is studded with shallow lochs rich in vegetation, invertebrates and fish. The east coast, on the other hand, is fragmented and intersected by deep, labyrinthine sea lochs, rendering communi-cations difficult and modern roads tortuous. The freshwater lochs here and inland are acidic and, with a few exceptions, support little life.

Blessed with an equable, oceanic climate, yet one which to visitors may seem excessively wet and windy, the islands never suffer the climatic extremes which affect less fortunate parts of the British Isles. Certainly gales occur, on average, on 50 days of the year, but in this respect familiarity breeds tolerance and self-preservation; tolerance, too, of the 1270mm of annual rainfall which ensures that gardens can always be watered, cars washed and salmon, sea trout and brown trout fished for in most of the 6000 lochs.

Wind and rain, often salt-laden, have played a great part in the vegetation of the Outer Hebrides, restricting the number of species and often their shape and structure too. The impervious, underlying gneiss has weathered to produce a topsoil of peaty podsol overlain by blanket bog on which sedges and heather flourish. In accessible areas, beside main roads and unsurfaced side roads, this peat is cut for fuel in spring and carted home after drying to form conspicuous and familiar stacks at each homestead. Within the last 30 years convenient parts of the moor have been reclaimed, by fencing, drainage and liming, to provide pasture for stock, and are now green oases among the heather. Away from the fertile *machair*, the thin soil has been cultivated and gathered into lazybeds to supply subsistence crops of oats and potatoes, and ancient corrugations may still be made out near the sites of former dwellings, abandoned for an easier life in the townships.

The moorland flora of acid-tolerant plants comprises, for example, heathers, butterwort, milkwort, tormentil, bird's-foot-trefoil, sundews, royal fern, lesser spearwort, bogbean, water-lily and water lobelia. The post-glacial scanty cover of trees and shrubs was mostly destroyed by fire, sheep and the growth of peat, but some vestiges may still be found on freshwater islets and sheltered cliffs. Lately, shelter belts of conifers have been planted near townships, and the Forestry Commission and the North of Scotland College of Agriculture have established woodlands in Lewis and the Uists which are already contributing to a diversity of landscape and fauna. However the most substantial wood in the Outer Hebrides is that surrounding Lews Castle at Stornoway. Planted by Sir James Matheson in the mid-nineteenth century, it is now a mature and diverse mixture of exotic and native coniferous and deciduous trees and shrubs which has attracted some bird and insect species elsewhere absent from the islands; it includes the Outer Hebrides' only rookery.

Some 296 species of birds have occurred in these islands: corncrake, wintering waders and the native mute swan and greylag goose populations are of national significance. The importance of the off-lying island populations of gannet, Leach's petrel, puffin and grey seal are mentioned under the relevant reserves.

Grey seals are a common sight offshore of the main islands, and a few have become almost tame in Stornoway harbour where they scavenge on the waste products of the fishing fleet. In the Sound of Harris and off the Southern Isles common seal is a feature of the shallow western littoral and reefs. Otters are more common than is generally supposed, but are more marine than their mainland counterparts. Mink, the descendants of escapees from Lewis farms, and feral ferrets have over-run Lewis and Harris, and the former may soon gain a foothold in the Uists. Red deer are to be found in Lewis, Harris, Pabbay and North and South Uist. Mountain hares have survived in very small numbers on Lewis and Harris but the rabbit, introduced in the nineteenth century, infests all the main islands. A more recent introduction to Lewis is the hedgehog, which has become established since 1970 around Stornoway. The only bat is pipistrelle, confined to Stornoway. Apart from a recent discovery of palmate newts in South Uist and intermittent introductions of frogs and toads there are no amphibians and only one reptile, slow-worm. Pygmy shrew, long-tailed fieldmouse, house mouse and brown rat are widespread, but short-tailed vole is confined to the Uists and Benbecula.

Perhaps the main attractions of the Outer Hebrides to the birdwatcher are the seabirds and the possibility of encountering Arctic migrants and transatlantic vagrants; to the botanist, the treasures of the *machair* and the vestigial woodlands; to the angler, the wealth of sequestered trout lochs; to the entomologist, a world as yet largely undocumented; and to the visitor wide, unpolluted spaces where time seems to stand still.

PETER CUNNINGHAM

Balranald, North Uist

NF 7070; 658ha; RSPB reserve
Machair, marshes and coastline
Visitors are requested to call at reception cottage on arrival
Display and reserve leaflet at cottage, Goular, Hougharry
April–September

The core of this varied reserve is the shallow Loch nam Feithean and its extensive surrounding marshland. A rich invertebrate fauna, together with the cover provided by great sweeps of emergent fen vegetation – sedges, amphibious bistort, bogbean, marsh-marigold, mare's-tail, yellow iris and grey club-rush – make this an important breeding site for duck and waders. Gadwall, wigeon, shoveler, tufted duck, snipe and redshank are among the regular breeders, while red-breasted merganser and red-necked phalarope nest occasionally. Crofting land surrounds the marshes and in summer the rasping calls of corncrake sound on all sides.

Machair ground lies between the loch and the coastal dunes. Strip-cultivated to varying degrees of intensity, the summer *machair* is a patchwork of contrasting colours: here the dominant rusty-red of sorrel, there the red and orange of poppy and corn marigold, the vivid blue and strong purple of green alkanet and tufted vetch, or the bright pink of stork's-bill. This rich flora and associated insect life supports many pairs of twite, skylark and corn bunting, the latter often singing from clumps of umbels in the absence of more substantial songposts. Most spectacular of all are the nesting waders: an astonishing density of lapwing, oystercatcher, redshank, ringed plover and dunlin, all thriving on the cultivated *machair* and wet grassland. Arctic tern and little tern breed on the silver-grey sandy beaches and dunes, with shag and black guillemot on the rocky headlands. Some 50 species nest annually on the reserve.

Arctic terns nest on many of the islands.

Loch Druidibeg holds an important colony of native greylag geese.

Balranald is also important for migrant and wintering birds. The marshes and the tidal strand of Loch Paible between them attract a wide variety of waders: grey plover, whimbrel, black-tailed godwit, little stint and ruff are among the regular visitors. Offshore all three species of diver occur regularly, as do sooty shearwater, and great, pomarine and arctic skua. The passage and wintering wildfowl include pintail, scaup, common scoter, five species of goose and whooper swan. Hen harrier, merlin and peregrine are among the recorded visiting predators, sometimes visible at close range hunting over the marshes.

Like other western isles North Uist has a flourishing population of otter and these delightful animals are frequently seen on Balranald's shores and lochs. A colony of grey seal breeds on the small rocky island of Causamul and porpoises, dolphins and whales have been observed during seawatches.

Although the northerly latitude limits the likely range of butterflies, eight species have been recorded to date, together with 56 kinds of moth. Green-veined white, common blue and meadow brown – an especially bright Hebridean form, are the most frequent butterflies; moth species include garden tiger, yellow underwing, dark arches and the much less common Portland moth and brindled beauty.

Loch Druidibeg, South Uist

NF 7937; 1677ha; NCC reserve
Lochs, moorland, croftland, *machair* and seashore
Permit only during bird breeding season; apply
NCC, Inverness
May–July

The two widely contrasting sections of this large reserve are neatly separated by the road that bisects it. To the east lies Loch Druidibeg, home of the largest surviving British colony of native greylag geese. Its shallow waters are dotted with islands large and small, many of them fringed with tawny royal fern and crowned with scrub woodland of Scots pine, rowan, willow and juniper, often draped with honeysuckle. Undulating peat moorland backs most of the loch's convoluted stony shoreline. Grazing, peat cutting and heather burning have helped to create a wide variety of micro-habitats within this superficially monotonous looking area. Floating club-rush and delicate water lobelia grow in the pools; clumps of vivid yellow bog asphodel and silvery tufts of cottongrass stand out against the dark peaty background; and wind-pruned willows, only a quarter of a metre high but with stems several centimetres thick, sprawl over the exposed rocks at the loch's edge.

In addition to the geese the breeding birds of this eastern part of the reserve include a varied assortment of species such as buzzard, red-breasted merganser, mute swan, heron, red grouse, common

In early summer the Hebridean machair *lands are carpeted with colourful flowers.*

gull and wren; golden eagle, hen harrier, merlin and short-eared owl are also regularly seen.

In comparison with the moorland section, the western part of the reserve is both more obviously influenced by human activity and much richer in species. Within it lie two crofting townships, a series of shallow lochs, lagoons and marshes, and a stretch of dunes with their associated *machair*. The shell–sand *machair* is carpeted with flowers in summer, the predominant colours and species varying from one place to the next according to the way the land is managed. Lesser meadow-rue, wild thyme, daisy, and selfheal are among the constants: red and white clovers dominate the more intensively farmed areas, and yellow seaside pansies and bright pink stork's-bill star the barer sandy patches. Orchids abound, in every shade from nearly white to wine red; many of them are hybrids between heath spotted-orchid and northern marsh-orchid.

Loch Druidibeg is rich in bird life, with important breeding populations of waders such as snipe, redshank, dunlin and lapwing. Corncrake, corn bunting and twite frequent the fields of meadow hay and barley—the latter colourful with poppies, small bugloss and corn marigold. Arctic tern and ringed plover nest where the sand is bare of vegetation, and several species of duck breed in the wetland areas.

Monach Isles

NF 6462; 577ha; NCC reserve
Island group with associated reefs
Access restricted; landing permit from North Uist Estate, Lochmaddy or NCC warden, Loch Druidibeg, South Uist

Shillay, Ceann Iar and Ceann Ear, the three main islands of the group, are low-lying and largely *machair*-covered, with a few marshy areas and pools. Arctic tern breed here, and small numbers of seabirds live on the rockier outlying islets. The islands support an important grey seal colony and are a wintering ground for barnacle and white-fronted geese.

North Rona and Sula Sgeir

HW 8132 and 6230; 130ha; NCC reserve
Isolated islands
Landing permit from Barvas Estates Ltd; NCC, Inverness must be informed of proposed visits

Both these remote islands are well known for their contrasting, but equally important, wildlife interest. In summer the great barren rock of Sula Sgeir, a few hectares in area and rising to 100m, is white with gannets. This is the only place in Britain where fat young gannets can legally be harvested for food, and the men of Ness in Lewis still take their traditional crop of *gugas* despite the danger and privation involved.

North Rona, 20km away and also 100m high, is a much larger green island which still shows the pattern of the lazybed cultivation of the past; it is now grazed by sheep. The island's importance is as a breeding place for grey seal; several thousand gather from September to December and each year about 2000 pups are born. By the peak of the breeding season the peninsula of Fianuis, the seals' nursery-ground, has become a sea of mud, churned up by their comings and goings.

There are also important colonies of Leach's and storm petrel on the island and large numbers of guillemot, razorbill, kittiwake, puffin and fulmar nesting on the cliffs.

St Kilda

NA 1000; 846ha; NTS–NCC reserve
Isolated island group
Permission to stay on the island must be
obtained from NTS
May–July

Everything about St Kilda, the premier seabird breeding station in Britain, demands superlatives. Hirta, the principal island, is the remotest inhabited island in British waters and has the highest sea cliff, almost 430m of precipice on the north face of Conachair. The walls of the smaller islands of Boreray and Soay rise absolutely sheer to over 360m. Stac an Armin, where Britain's last great auk was killed in 1840, and Stac Lee, at 191m and 165m respectively, are the two highest rock stacks in the country. St Kilda holds the oldest, and by far the largest, colony of fulmar in Britain. The gannetry, on Boreray and the adjacent stacks, is the largest in the world, with over 50,000 pairs. This combination of spectacular scenery and vast seabird populations ensures that every visit to these islands is a truly memorable experience.

Approaching St Kilda by sea, as most visitors must, the first impressions are of the scale and ruggedness of the islands and of the great throngs of seabirds: a snowstorm of gannets, circling and plunging off Boreray; a continuous procession of puffins, whirring to and from the steep grassy slopes of Dun; crowds of guillemot, scattered over the surface of the water as far as the eye can see. These are immediately obvious even when low cloud screens the summit of Conachair and the stacks. The important populations of Leach's and storm petrel and of Manx shearwater are much less readily appreciated, since these species are active only at night and tend to favour rather inaccessible spots for their nesting burrows. Few of today's visitors to these islands would care to tackle the cliffs that the old St Kildans climbed as a matter of course when gathering the birds and eggs that provided them with both food and fuel.

The St Kilda wren, a distinct sub-species which is larger and greyer than the mainland version, lives mostly around the old village street and among the dry stone *cleitean*, little turf-roofed chambers in which the islanders stored their crops, fuel and dried birds for winter food. The St Kilda field mouse, here often occupying the house mouse niche left vacant when that species failed to survive the island's uninhabited period, 1930–57, is another local speciality. Flocks of the primitive Soay sheep, left behind when the island was evacuated, run wild on Soay and Hirta, and there are feral blackface sheep on Boreray. More recent arrivals are grey seal, now breeding in considerable numbers on Hirta and Dun, and great skua that have colonised the grassy moorland.

Despite the fact that drenching with salty spray is a frequent occurrence, the cliff vegetation is strikingly rich. Roseroot, primrose, honeysuckle, moss campion and purple saxifrage are among the flowers blooming on the ledges and in the gullies. Over 130 species of flowering plants have been recorded from the island group, while the bryophyte population includes at least one liverwort with Mediterranean affinities – though wet, St Kilda's climate is also relatively mild.

For long notorious as the most inaccessible island group in British waters, St Kilda is now easier to get to than it ever has been in the past. Since 1957, when the island was bequeathed to the National Trust for Scotland (and the army established a base there for tracking rockets), a programme of rehabilitation has been carried out in the village. The Trust now runs regular working holidays to Hirta during the summer months, accommodating the participants in some of the houses which have been restored. Several independent charter companies also run shorter trips which generally involve sleeping on board the vessel.

The isolated islands and stacks of St Kilda are home to vast numbers of seabirds.

Shetland

People are always attracted to extremes: the highest mountains, the widest plains, the furthest corners of the Arctic, the Antarctic and the tropics have been visited by intrepid explorers. But most people have neither the means nor the opportunity to follow in their footsteps, and must be satisfied with exploring the more remote parts of their own country. A map of Britain may or may not show that the most northerly point of the United Kingdom is Shetland. Lying some 160km north of John o' Groats, it does not fit comfortably into the format of such maps; as often as not the islands are fitted into a box frame in some convenient corner of the page.

The true situation of Shetland is about 320km north of Aberdeen and 290km west of Bergen, the largest town in western Norway. Physically it comprises a group of about 100 islands totalling 142,450ha in area. Only 15 of the islands are now populated; the rest are made up of stacks, skerries and holms inhabited by sheep, seals, otters, rabbits and seabirds. Shetland gives the impression of rolling, heather-clad, treeless hills, spangled with peaty lochs and pools, its coastline bitten into by arms of sea, locally called 'voes', some steep-sided like a tiny Norwegian fiord.

On the largest island, Mainland, lies the only town, Lerwick, which boasts a fine natural harbour visited by ships of all nations and summer yachtsmen. Farther north is the gigantic oil terminal at Sullom Voe. Although physically the huge industrial complex has been absorbed remarkably well into the landscape, the social and economic effects reach into every corner of the islands.

Outside these two centres the rest of the 22,000-odd population lives in small villages in the larger of the islands. These are usually near the shores of some sheltered voe, witness to former dependence on the sea for a livelihood, and dwellings tend to be scattered because originally each family's house or croft was built on its own patch of land which provided basic food.

Ever since the first naturalists visited and wrote about Shetland over 200 years ago, the islands have been acknowledged to contain flora and fauna unique in Britain. The reasons lie in Shetland's geological and physical development, as well as in its geographical situation.

It would seem that, as the climate became warmer, Shetland emerged from the last great ice age as a set of barren mountain tops, cut off by the rising waters and so barred from natural colonisation by any land-based animals. Today Shetland has no deer, foxes, badgers, voles or shrews, nor any evidence that they have ever existed in the islands. However hares, rabbits, stoats, hedgehogs, house and field mice are there in plenty, but have been introduced by man since his colonisation 5000 or 6000 years ago. The field mice are interesting in that, although recognisably different forms occur on different islands, all show genetic affinities to the mice of western Norway, suggesting that Viking colonisation took many forms.

Species that swim, of course, had no problems, and there are considerable numbers of both grey and common seal, but Shetland's large and healthy population of otters gives rise to doubts about whether they arrived spontaneously or were escapes from captivity. Wherever otters came from originally, the absence of rivers in Shetland has forced them to adapt to a lifestyle which, like that of seals, is almost wholly dependent on the sea.

There is little doubt that man and his domestic animals have had a profound effect on the landscape. Abundant evidence exists in the peat deposits that Shetland was once extensively covered in scrub woodland, and in the few places inaccessible to sheep there still remain examples of native birch, rowan and aspen. The attentions of grazing animals are the main factor inhibiting the regeneration of any trees or bushes. However there is plenty of herb vegetation, with currently some 600 varieties of flowering plant.

Spring comes late at this latitude, and it is May before splashes of yellow marsh-marigold and primrose herald an explosion of colour as successive waves of wild flowers make recompense for the drabness of winter. Along the cliff edge swards, the purple haze of spring squill is replaced by pink carpets of thrift, while many of the grassy cliff slopes are a blaze of scarlet as Shetland red campion takes over.

The heather hills change only slowly to subtle shades of purple in late summer, but crofting areas and 'improved' pasture share in the rush of summer colour. In places some of the several species of orchids are abundant enough to provide the dominant colour. On higher hills and screes alpines can be found, and azaleas, saxifrages, mountain rock-cress and arctic sandwort all occur, while a variety of arctic chickweed found nowhere else in the world can be seen on the island of Unst.

Shetland is particularly rich in bird life, which can be placed in three overlapping categories, all tied in with climate and geography. First, Shetland lies in a sea full of fish, for the relatively shallow North Sea basin is constantly enriched by nutrients carried by the warm Gulf Stream. The food attracts huge numbers of seabirds, and since the long coastline, over 1500km, contains a variety of nesting habitats, Shetland has a seabird population of international importance.

Second, the northerly situation of Shetland encourages a number of species whose main distribution is towards the sub-Arctic: breeding seabirds like black guillemot, great and arctic skua and red-throated diver, waders such as whimbrel and red-necked phalarope, and other occasionals like snowy owl and glaucous gull. In the winter Shetland is regularly visited by other birds from the Arctic: long-tailed duck and whooper swan, great northern diver and little auk can all be seen, and rarer species like ivory and Ross's gull, king and Steller's eider turn up from time to time.

Third, there is the excitement of the great seasonal bird migrations. Regular passage birds such as vast flocks of fieldfare, redwing and song thrush pass through in spring and autumn on their way to and from northern breeding grounds. With them appear a bewildering variety of small birds – warblers, chats, flycatchers, shrikes, finches, buntings and many others. The more remote an island – providing it is on or near a bird migration route – the better chance it has of 'collecting' migrants in suitable weather, and FAIR ISLE is justly famous among birdwatchers on this account.

BOBBY TULLOCH

Fair Isle

HZ 2172; 830ha; NTS
Cliff-girt inhabited island
Bird observatory with hostel, open March–October
(FIBOT)
Booklet on birds and brochure from FIBOT or NTS
May, September–October: migration;
May–July: breeding birds

Long famous as a migration station, Fair Isle boasts an impressive list of rare bird visitors. First records – for Scotland, Britain and even Europe – are a regular occurrence, with birds arriving from as far afield as Siberia and North America.

Red sandstone cliffs edge most of the shoreline, rising to 200m on the west coast and on Sheep Craig. The rock is soft, weathering readily into caves, arches and stacks, and demands extreme caution. Grey seal breed in the caves and lie out on the rocks singing their sad songs, and colonies of around 25,000 pairs of fulmar, 20,000 pairs of guillemot, 12,000 pairs of kittiwake and 2500 pairs of razorbill occupy the cliff ledges. Gannet first bred successfully in 1975 and this new colony has now grown to over 150 pairs. Some 30,000 puffin and 100 pairs of storm petrel nest in burrows among loose stones and earth where the cliffs and gullies are steep rather than sheer, and Leach's petrel have been caught on the island though not yet proved to breed there.

Puffins find abundant supplies of sand-eels in Shetland waters.

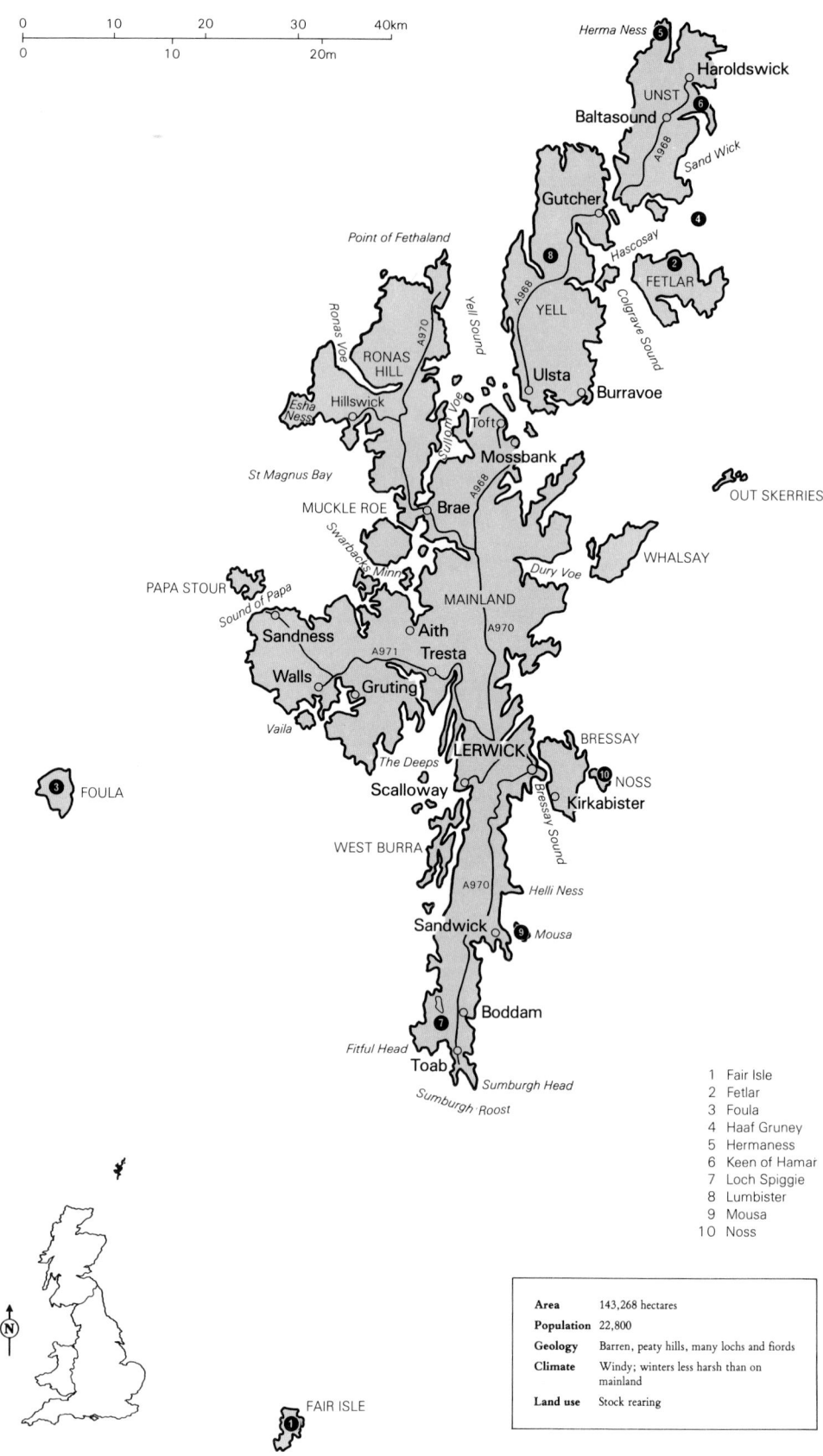

0	10	20	30	40km
0	10	20m		

Herma Ness
UNST
Haroldswick
Baltasound
Sand Wick
Gutcher
Hascosay
FETLAR
Point of Fethaland
Ronas Voe
YELL
Colgrave Sound
RONAS HILL
Yell Sound
A968
A970
Esha Ness
Hillswick
Ulsta
Burravoe
Toft
St Magnus Bay
Mossbank
OUT SKERRIES
MUCKLE ROE
Brae
A968
Dury Voe
WHALSAY
Swarbacks Minn
PAPA STOUR
Sound of Papa
MAINLAND
A970
Sandness
Aith
A971
Tresta
Walls
Gruting
Vaila
BRESSAY
LERWICK
The Deeps
NOSS
FOULA
Scalloway
Kirkabister
Bressay Sound
WEST BURRA
A970
Helli Ness
Sandwick
Mousa
Fitful Head
Boddam
Toab
Sumburgh Head
Sumburgh Roost

1 Fair Isle
2 Fetlar
3 Foula
4 Haaf Gruney
5 Hermaness
6 Keen of Hamar
7 Loch Spiggie
8 Lumbister
9 Mousa
10 Noss

Area	143,268 hectares
Population	22,800
Geology	Barren, peaty hills, many lochs and fiords
Climate	Windy; winters less harsh than on mainland
Land use	Stock rearing

N

FAIR ISLE

Much of the rough hill ground is skua territory; the colony, now numbering about 120 pairs of arctic skua and 40 of great skua, has been studied intensively over many years. During the summer months visitors need walk only a few hundred metres from the observatory hostel to experience the realistic injury-feigning distraction display and the aggressive dive-bombing of skuas safeguarding their nests and young.

The Fair Isle Bird Observatory is best known for its work in recording and ringing migrants. Well over 300 species have been recorded, more than at any other British locality. Over 150,000 birds, representing around 250 species, have been ringed, and reports of recoveries have come from places as distant as Greece, Siberia and Brazil. Visitors are encouraged to participate in the daily recording of birds and to observe the work of the licensed ringers.

Fair Isle's flora is varied, with well over 200 recorded species, many associated with the cultivated croft ground. Spring squill is widespread along the cliff tops and field gentian has been recorded at the south end of the island; both species occur in the white form as well as the usual blue one. Lesser twayblade and frog orchid are among the five orchids present, and ferns include Wilson's filmy-fern, moonwort and adder's-tongue. With so much rough grassland and heath with boggy areas, the list of sedges, rushes and grasses is a long one. A full list of plant species is given in *Fair Isle Bird Observatory Report*, 1971.

The tidal rock pools, regularly flushed with the unpolluted waters of the North Sea and Atlantic, hold a rich variety of seaweeds and other marine life. Lobsters provide a source of income, saithe and mackerel are caught for home consumption, and large shoals of sand eels supply food for the breeding seabirds. Porpoises, sharks and whales are frequently sighted offshore.

For many visitors it is the island as a whole, rather than any one facet, that arouses enthusiasm, since it is rare these days to find a thriving community on an island as isolated as Fair Isle, separated from the nearest land by 40km of sea.

Fetlar

HU 6091; 699ha; RSPB reserve
Island moorland with lochans and marshes
Island accessible April–August
Access restricted mid-May–end July; contact warden on arrival
Information sheet from RSPB warden, Bealance, Fetlar
May–July: breeding birds; September: migrants

Although Fetlar, one of Shetland's greenest islands, is probably best known for the snowy owls which bred there between 1967 and 1975 and are still often present, it also has a regular breeding bird community of national importance. None of the species nests solely on the reserve and all may be seen elsewhere on the island when access to the bird sanctuary is restricted.

Fetlar is the only site in Britain where snowy owls have bred.

Much of northern Fetlar, in which the reserve lies, is bare grassy moorland over serpentine rock. Here golden plover, dunlin, curlew and many whimbrel breed, filling the air with plaintive and wilderness-evoking courtship songs. In the wetter areas snipe and redshank nest, and there are many lapwing, oystercatcher and ringed plover. Red-throated diver occur on many of the lochs and red-necked phalarope are best seen at one of their feeding areas, such as Loch Funzie, rather than risking disturbance of the breeding marshes. A large, though fluctuating, population of arctic tern is scattered over 20 or more colonies, while the main concentration of arctic and great skua is on the heather moorland of Lambhoga, outside the reserve.

Fetlar supports populations of both storm petrel and Manx shearwater; a night out along the cliffs of Lambhoga, listening for the purring calls of the incubating petrels and the wild shrieks of shearwaters flighting in from Tresta Bay, can be an exciting and rewarding experience. Compared to other Shetland islands Fetlar's cliff-nesting seabird population is small. Puffin are the most numerous with around 2500 pairs; black guillemot are widely distributed around the island, as are the 300 or so pairs of shag.

Both common and grey seal breed, the population of the latter among the largest on any one Shetland island. Otter also occur, and the marine life is rich. Among the more interesting plants are northern rock-cress, northern marsh-orchid, field gentian and creeping willow.

Foula is the British stronghold of the aggressive great skua.

Foula

HT 9639; 1380ha
Isolated inhabited island with high cliffs
Access by boat from Walls (HU 243495):
details from Lerwick tourist office
May–July

Spectacular scenery and vast colonies of seabirds make this one of the most impressive islands in Shetland. To the west precipitous cliffs of old red sandstone rise sheer from the Atlantic, reaching 370m at the Kame, the second highest cliff in the British Isles. From the Sneug, the high point of the central ridge, the ground slopes steeply down to low-lying croft ground on the east coast. Much of the island is, or once was, peat-covered and carries a range of heath and bog vegetation. The high humidity is reflected in widespread Wilson's filmy-fern and varied mosses and liverworts.

The seabird colonies are the outstanding wildlife feature; Foula holds one of the largest and most varied breeding populations in the North Atlantic. At 3000 pairs Foula's great skua colony accounts for half of Shetland's total and nearly 30 per cent of those breeding in the northern hemisphere. Numbers have increased threefold in the last 20 years but now show signs of levelling off. The arctic skua population of about 270 pairs is small in comparison and has grown only slowly since the turn of the century.

It was on Foula that the first Shetland breeding of fulmar occurred in 1878; the cliffs now hold some 40,000 pairs. Auk numbers are also the highest, in total, in Shetland, with around 35,000 pairs of puffin, 30,000 of guillemot, 5000 of razorbill and 60 of black guillemot. Important colonies of shag (3000 pairs), kittiwake (6000 pairs) and arctic tern (3000 pairs) are present and the storm petrel population of over 1000 pairs is by far the largest in Shetland. Foula is as yet the only proven breeding site for Leach's petrel in Shetland and is one of the two known locations for Manx shearwater (the other is FETLAR). With 16 species of nesting seabirds and a total population of over 125,000 pairs, Foula is an internationally important seabird station.

Haaf Gruney

HU 6398; 18ha; NCC reserve
Low uninhabited offshore island
May–July

This small island, accessible only in calm weather, is low and fertile with a plant life reflecting the underlying serpentine rock and the influence of salt spray. Spring squill and the very local northern saltmarsh-grass are present. The boulder beach holds breeding storm petrel and black guillemot and the island is a favourite resting place for common and grey seal.

Hermaness

HP 6016; 964ha; NCC reserve
Cliff-girt moorland peninsula
and associated skerries
Visitors are asked to keep to marked path and cliff
top during breeding season, to minimise disturbance
May–July

Hermaness is at the northernmost tip of Britain. With several miles of bird-thronged cliffs, gannet colonies that can be viewed from above, and an expanse of rough moorland alive with skuas, it is one of Europe's major seabird stations. Fourteen species of seabird breed within the reserve.

The skuas on Hermaness have been protected for nearly 100 years, in which time great skua have increased from only a few pairs to over 800, but arctic skua have declined. Walking across the skua grounds in June means constant dodging of dive-bombing territory defenders! Gannet too have shown a spectacular increase; nesting first around 1920, they now number well over 5000 pairs. Those nesting on some of the stacks can be watched in comfort from the 200m high cliff as they come and go, often harried by great skuas. Since 1972 a black-browed albatross, a wanderer from south of the Equator, has returned annually.

Puffin are the most numerous species present, breeding in tens of thousands on the steep grassy and scree slopes. Some 16,000 pairs of guillemot jostle in tightly packed scrums on the lower ledges of the cliffs; 2000 pairs each of razorbill and shag and a few black guillemot occupy the boulder-strewn shore; 5000 pairs of kittiwake and 10,000 pairs of fulmar ceaselessly call and patrol.

A few red-throated diver nest beside the small lochans scattered over the moorland area. Whimbrel, golden plover and dunlin also breed on the heather-, grass- and *Sphagnum*-dominated moor, and there are twite and Shetland wren around the cliffs. The plant life of the rather acid cliffs is quite varied and includes such northern species as Scots lovage and roseroot. Moss campion occurs right down to sea level and the Shetland race of red campion is present. Otter and common seal frequent the rocky shores and the grey seals that breed in the caves often haul out on the rocks.

Dark local forms of certain moths occur in Shetland, and many have been recorded on Hermaness, including northern rustic, autumnal rustic, square-spot rustic and the less common arctic northern arches.

Keen of Hamar

HP 6409; 30ha; NCC reserve
Stony hillside
May–June

Montane and maritime plants grow side by side on this Icelandic-type fellfield. As low as 50m above sea level the frost-shattered debris lying around on the serpentine bedrock displays the characteristic striped patterning more frequently encountered at higher altitudes. An imbalance in the essential soil minerals, combined with unusually high concentrations of toxic metals, has resulted in distinct races of thrift and mouse-ear chickweed. Norwegian sandwort, northern rock-cress, moss campion and stone bramble are among the arctic–alpine species present.

Loch Spiggie

HU 3716; 115ha; RSPB reserve
Loch and associated marshland
October–November: swans and ducks;
March–April: long-tailed duck

Sheltered from the west by the headlands of Foraness and Fitful and from the north by a narrow ridge of sand dunes, shallow Loch Spiggie and its neighbouring Loch Brow are the most important freshwater site for wintering wildfowl in Shetland. This is a regular stopping-off place for migrant duck and geese and early-winter home for a sizeable herd of whooper swan. Tufted duck, pochard and goldeneye are present for much of the winter and in spring as many as 50 long-tailed duck come in off the sea to undergo their pre-migration moult on the sheltered loch.

The two lochs are separated by a floating marsh with varied vegetation. This and the boggy areas around the loch shores hold breeding waders in summer, and the surrounding farmland is often alive with birds during the peak migration periods in spring and autumn.

Until facilities are provided on the reserve the loch is best viewed from the public road along its north and west sides.

Whimbrel breed locally in Shetland.

Lumbister

HU 4995; 1720ha; RSPB reserve
Peat moorland with lochans and cliff
May–mid-July

The peat-blanketed island of Yell, on which this reserve is situated, is not visually attractive but its moorlands and lochs hold important breeding populations of several birds that are of limited distribution. Whimbrel occasionally nest on the higher heather moorland, which reaches no more than 150m, and red-throated diver by many of the 20 or so lochs and smaller pools. The guttural calls of divers on their way to or from a fishing trip at sea and the weird wailing of their courtship 'song' are familiar sounds here.

Great and arctic skua also breed on the moor, dive-bombing intruders and threatening the survival of the eggs and young of divers and other birds. The wader population is large and varied: golden plover, curlew, oystercatcher, ringed plover, lapwing, snipe and dunlin breed. One or two pairs of merlin prey on twite, meadow pipit and wheatear, while cliff-nesting raven and hooded crow are efficient scavengers. Few seabirds nest on Yell, surrounded as it is by other islands, but there are arctic and common tern by the Lumbister lochs and a colony of great black-backed gull on the moorland.

Although there is little variety in the vegetation, in the Daal of Lumbister, a steep gorge cut by the stream that drains Lumbister Loch with its sandy bays of sparkling mica crystals, juniper, honey-suckle and roseroot grow, protected from wind and grazing animals. And along the cliff tops, where the peat gives way to grassland, there are wild thyme, moss campion and sundew.

As elsewhere in Shetland, otter are not uncommon, and the reserve supports a flourishing population of them.

Mousa

HU 4624; 180ha
Low uninhabited inshore island
Access by small boat from Sand Lodge, Sandwick (HU 438248): details from Lerwick tourist office
May–July

Famous for its extraordinarily well-preserved Pictish broch, this is one of the most interesting, attractive and accessible of the smaller Shetland islands, with a range of animals and plants typical of the lower grassy islands around the coast. Great and arctic skua nest on the rough grassland and there is a colony of several hundred arctic tern. Other breeding birds include fulmar, black guillemot, shag and eider, while the purring of incubating storm petrels enlivens the dry stone walls of the broch in summer. A large rock-bound tidal pool forms a narrow neck linking the wider ends of the island and is a regular hauling-out place for the large local population of common seal. Grey seal also frequent the island's shores.

Long inlets cut deeply into Shetland's north mainland.

Haaf Gruney: common seals haul out to rest.

Noss

HU 5540; 313ha; NCC reserve
Uninhabited island
Access is from Lerwick via the island of Bressay;
summer ferry service across Noss Sound operated
by NCC: details from Lerwick tourist office
Visitors are asked to stay on the clifftop path while
on the reserve
Small visitor centre open in summer
Leaflet from tourist office, Lerwick and NCC,
Lerwick or Aberdeen
May–July

One of Europe's most spectacular seabird colonies
occupies this easily accessible island, a site of
international importance. Cliffs nearly 200m high
fringe the eastern and southern shores, their sandstone layers weathered and eroded to form shelves
ideal as nesting sites. Birds throng every shelf, with
over 5000 pairs of gannet dominating the headland
of the Noup and the area around Rumble Wick.
Some 63,000 guillemot shoulder one another on the
lower ledges, while many of the 10,000 pairs of
kittiwake nest below overhangs and in cave
mouths where their cries are drowned by the
booming sea.

Gannet and kittiwake are relentlessly pursued
by the skuas that nest on Noss's moorland interior.
With over 200 pairs of great skua and around 40 of
arctic skua present in summer there is always some
luckless victim being forced to disgorge its freshly
caught fish for a skua to catch in mid-air. The great
skuas also threaten eider ducklings hatched on the
skua grounds, and indeed any unprotected eggs
and young. The great black-backed gull colony on
the flat summit of Cradle Holm is one of the largest
in Shetland, with over 200 pairs.

Noss is a 'green' island with sedges and grasses
dominant among the moorland vegetation. Chickweed wintergreen occurs on the moor and in early
summer the cliff tops are bright with spring squill
and thrift. Sea and red campion, roseroot and
scurvygrass flourish on the cliffs around the nesting fulmars; in contrast the concentrated guano on
Cradle Holm has resulted in a lush growth of sorrels.

Yell Sound Islands

Permit only; 162ha; RSPB reserve
Uninhabited islands
May–July

These six small islands represent a wide variety of
habitats and the seas around them are an important
wintering area for eider, long-tailed duck and
divers. The activities at nearby Sullom Voe have
already caused some wildlife losses through oil
pollution of sea and beaches.

The steep cliffs of Ramna Stacks and Gruney hold
big seabird populations: guillemot and kittiwake on
both, with puffin as well on Gruney. Barnacle geese
sometimes visit in winter. Unyarey and Fish Holm
are flatter and grassier; shag, eider, puffin and black
guillemot breed here. On Muckle Holm the cliffs are
high enough to attract fulmar and gulls, though not
other cliff-nesting seabirds, and small colonies of
arctic tern and puffin breed. The largest island,
Samphrey, has great and arctic skua, dunlin, snipe
and skylark on the hill ground; a large colony of arctic
tern on the once-cultivated fields; and storm petrel,
black guillemot and starling in the ruined crofts.

A colony of grey seal breeds on Gruney, hauling
out well above sea level, the only place they do so in
Shetland. Common seal breed on Muckle Holm and
Samphrey, while otter, which are seen regularly,
breed on Samphrey and may do so on other islands
also.

Skye and the Small Isles

The late Seton Gordon, a notable naturalist of the Inner Hebrides, called Skye 'The Winged Isle' because of its shape, with its great peninsulas and deep inlets of sea lochs. The 'wings' are overlooked by the ragged ridge of the Cuillins, towering up to almost 1000m, and surrounding hill ranges such as the Red Hills and Lord Macdonald's Forest. The Small Isles – RHUM, EIGG, Canna and Muck in descending order of size – lie south of Skye. The contrasts between them are striking: Rhum is almost entirely mountainous, reaching over 800m on Askival; Eigg's An Sgurr rises to nearly 400m; Canna and Muck are low-lying by comparison.

Some of the complex and diverse geological features have special significance for the vegetation: for instance the tertiary basalt and Jurassic limestone of north Skye, the ultrabasic rocks of central Rhum and the Cambrian limestone in south Skye. Plant communities dominated by mountain avens occur in Raasay and Rhum, but are best seen on the Durness limestone pavement near Ben Suardal in Skye, where herb-Paris, dark-red helleborine and mountain melick are also present.

The climate is oceanic, dominated by westerly winds from the Atlantic. Weather conditions are varied locally by the higher hills, which give rise to higher rainfall and frequent low cloud. Though the winds are less severe than in the Outer Hebrides, they still contribute to lower summer daytime temperatures than those on the mainland. On the other hand, the winds ensure that winter snow does not normally lie long, and the islands escape the severe winters of central Scotland.

About 1 per cent of the islands' surface is standing water, much less than in the Outer Hebrides; most lochs are small, with relatively little plant and bird life. Rivers and streams are short and weather-sensitive, being often either torrential floods or a mere trickle. The moist climate has given rise to widespread and extensive peatland and blanket bog. On the highest hills, the development of plant communities like those on the mainland has been restricted by the limited ground area.

Crofting is a major activity, along with hill and upland farming; though good land for cultivation is scarce, the climate is well suited to pasture and stock rearing. Most native woods have been felled or burned in the last few hundred years; only fragments survive. Little moorland has not been burnt to its detriment, and 'muirburn' is still a major threat to the surviving natural vegetation.

The influence of the sea is felt throughout the islands. Rocky shores make up the entire coastline, with coastal cliffs, stacks and islets providing a major habitat for plant and bird life; the whole range of maritime habitats may be seen in the Rhum reserve. *Machair* is virtually absent from Skye and the Small Isles, but there are a few sand dunes in scattered places such as Glen Brittle in Skye, Kilmory in Rhum and Laig in Eigg. The best saltmarshes are at the heads of Skye's many sea lochs. As a result of the strong winds, coastal influences can extend well inland, giving rise to maritime heaths and grasslands and accounting for sea plantain on moorland. In contrast some mountain flowers grow near sea level, including purple and mossy saxifrage, roseroot, hoary whitlowgrass and moss campion.

Despite the sea cliffs seabird colonies are small; guillemot, razorbill, kittiwake and fulmar are the main species. A few puffin occur at isolated sites such as the Ascrib Islands, and terns nest on a few islets, but it is the huge Manx shearwater colonies of the hills of Rhum which are outstanding, while storm petrel also nest in north Skye and Canna. A few wildfowl and waders winter along the coasts, with large numbers of eider in the Inner Sound of Raasay, and small groups of wigeon round the Skye coast at Broadford, Portree and Dunvegan. Divers and auks winter in the Inner Sound. Mallard, merganser, eider, shelduck, oystercatcher and ringed plover are among the summer nesting birds.

Freshwater lochs, such as Loch Suardal near Dunvegan, in Skye, hold limited numbers of wintering birds including whooper swan, goldeneye, tufted duck and pochard. In summer, common sandpiper nest by lochs and streams, while here and there may be found pied and grey wagtail and dipper. Red-breasted merganser nest in this habitat, and on Skye there are a few pairs of little grebe. Many of the lochs carry fine clumps of white water-lily, bogbean or bottle sedge, and a few near Sligachan in Skye have the rare pipewort. Royal fern grows on islands in some lochs, and here trees and scrub survive in the absence of grazing and burning. Salmon, brown trout and arctic char are among the freshwater fish present.

The native woodland which survives is mainly birch, seen in Raasay, Skye and Eigg, but there are also good examples of oak, ash, hazel and alder. The best ashwood is at TOKAVAIG WOOD, where ash grows on Durness limestone with birch and rowan, in contrast to oak which chooses the adjacent Torridonian sandstone. Mixed deciduous woodland occurs in Skye in the shelter of narrow ravines such as the Geary Ravine and Allt Grillan, and fine coastal woodlands may be seen in Strathaird. Hazel scrub clothes some of the slopes below the sea cliffs of Skye and Eigg, and where muirburning has not been too severe willow carr grows strongly, especially on the reserve at Blàr Dubh, in Eigg. Rich moss and lichen communities are associated with the older woods, and include a fine range of oceanic bryophytes. Birds are at their best in the mixed woodlands, and include woodcock, tawny owl, great, blue and coal tit, redstart, willow and wood warbler, treecreeper and tree pipit.

Peatland and bog are represented in oceanic type, with distinctive plants which include great sundew, pale butterwort, lesser skullcap and white beak-sedge. Moorland provides nesting habitats for small birds like meadow pipit, skylark and wheatear, and for waders including curlew, greenshank and golden plover, while the moorland lochs may have breeding red-throated and occasionally black-throated diver. Moorland and hillside provide territories for birds of prey, especially buzzard which also frequent woodland. Golden eagle may be seen soaring high on wind currents, particularly on Skye, and peregrine falcon still occupies a few eyries. Kestrel are present on Skye, Eigg and Rhum, as are sparrowhawk and merlin, and on occasion short-eared owl can be seen quartering the ground.

It is the high hills that are the finest attribute of these isles, often obscured by impenetrable cloud, but at other times sparkling in bright sunshine. On Rhum alpine plants such as Scottish asphodel and two-flowered rush can be found. The famous Cuillins of Skye support a range of alpines on their limited surfaces, and Blaven has richly vegetated limestone cliffs with tall-herb communities. The best place to see mountain vegetation in Skye is on the basalt escarpment of Trotternish Ridge, with its banks of yellow saxifrage and lawns of alpine lady's-mantle, as well as the recently discovered Iceland purslane. Birds of the hills include ring ouzel, ptarmigan and raven, while over all may soar the golden eagle.

ANDREW CURRIE

Clan Donald Centre, Skye

NG 6105; Clan Donald Lands Trust
Woodlands, hill and lochs
Access restricted to waymarked walks unless accompanied by countryside ranger
Visitor centre at Armadale Castle, Sleat, open April–October; leaflets
All year

The planted woodlands around the castle include an extensive and long-established arboretum with some fine specimen trees. From their seaward edge otters and seals can sometimes be seen in the Sound of Sleat. The main interest of the area, however, lies in the natural woodlands, which are predominantly birch and hazel with a scattering of rowan, willow, ash and oak. They occur on mineral-rich soils which support a varied ground flora, including herb-Robert, lesser twayblade, stone bramble and melancholy thistle. These woods also hold roe deer and a wide variety of woodland birds.

Mountain avens carpets lime-rich soil on Skye and Rhum.

	0		10		20		30km
	0		10				20m

Rubha Hunish

Loch Gairloch

Kilmaluag

A855

Waternish Point

Staffin

Loch Torridon

Uig

RONA

Loch Snizort

A856

A855

Dunvegan Head

Sound of Raasay

APPLECROSS

Loch Dunvegan

A850

Dunvegan

MACLEOD'S TABLES

Portree

SKYE

Inner Sound

RAASAY

Loch Bracadale

A863

A850

Loch Kishorn

Idrigill Point

SCALPAY

Kyle of Lochalsh

A850

Kyleakin

CUILLIN HILLS

A850

❷

Broadford

Kylerhea

A881

Loch Scavaig

Loch Eishort

SOAY

Elgol

❺

A851

Loch Hourn

CANNA

Sound of Sleat

Sound of Canna

Point of Sleat

❶

Armadale

Loch Nevis

❹

RHUM

Mallaig

Sound of Rhum

Loch Morar

❸

EIGG

Sound of Eigg

A830

MUCK

Sound of Arisaig

N

1 Clan Donald Centre
2 Corry Walk
3 Eigg
4 Rhum
5 Tokavaig Wood

Area	142,696 hectares
Population	7,800
Geology	Mainly igneous rocks, locally ultrabasic
Climate	Cool and wet
Land use	Stock rearing

Natural woodland, predominantly hazel, is wind-pressed against this basalt cliff on Eigg.

Corry Walk, Skye

NG 625255; 1.9km; FC
Coast and young conifer plantation
All year

This walks follows the shore for much of its route, providing opportunities to watch seabirds, for instance gannet fishing in Scalpay Sound, and sometimes waders in the muddy bays, as well as woodland species such as siskin and redpoll. Many typical moorland plants can still be seen along the edge of the plantation.

Eigg

Permit only; 608ha; SWT reserve
Lime-rich upland area, mixed woodland and small lochans
May–July

Visually most striking of the three separate sections comprising this reserve is that including the Sgurr, a narrow pitchstone lava ridge rising steeply above a hinterland of heather moor and dominating the island landscape. On the bare slopes surrounding the base of the hexagonally columned pitchstone least willow – with its tiny round leaves – sprawls close to the ground, and the moisture-loving Wilson's filmy-fern flourishes among the grass in the damp conditions created by the high rainfall and frequent low cloud. A lime-rich dyke provides one area of markedly more varied vegetation than elsewhere in the section. Here, cushions of pink moss campion, clumps of white-flowered mountain avens and the woolly yellow heads of kidney vetch brighten the scene; moonwort is also found.

At the opposite end of the island the Beinn Bhuide plateau falls away in steep craggy cliffs to both east and west. Those overlooking Cleadale are much fissured, with spectacular pillars and perched boulders along the rim. Here, buzzard and raven ride the up-currents, and golden eagle are not infrequently seen. Below the plateau rim moss campion and the uncommon Norwegian sandwort occur, with roseroot on the cliff ledges beneath. Steep scree slopes, some unstable and bare and others grassed over, form a 'skirt' below the cliffs, and it is here that Eigg's Manx shearwater colony is now located, the former site below the Sgurr having apparently been deserted.

Scrub woodland clothes the lower slopes, its canopy wind-smoothed to give a bank-like effect. Hazel predominates in the woodland but willow, rowan, hawthorn and blackthorn are also present. Ferns flourish among the jumble of mossy boulders concealed by the trees; those found include lemon-scented fern, broad and narrow buckler-fern, and scaly male-fern. Typical woodland flowers such as wood-sorrel, wood anemone, ramsons, wood sage and wild strawberry grow here, along with yellow pimpernel and great patches of bluebell which extend beyond the woodland to the surrounding bracken-covered slopes. Burnet rose is abundant, too, its thickly spined stems often crowded together in dense clumps.

The third section of the reserve lies above Laig Farm, where two wooded ravines cut through a low stepped basalt escarpment. Hart's-tongue and Wilson's filmy-fern are among the plants growing in the damp shade of the ravines; on the acid moorland above, several species of stunted willow are scattered among the heather, sometimes as isolated

621

Manx shearwaters from Rhum's vast colony gather offshore before flighting to their nests at night.

specimens and sometimes forming miniature woods in the shallow valleys. At the foot of the escarpment a deceptively deep pool, known as the Giant's Footprint, exhibits a classic pattern of colonisation, with quantities of horsetail, bogbean and cottongrass, as well as floating *Sphagnum* islands, on the largest of which grow heather and two or three small willows.

There is also much to interest the naturalist on Eigg beyond the reserve areas. Towards the eastern end of Laig Bay a band of lime-rich rock forms outcrops on the shore, and just beyond lie the 'Singing Sands' – an area of rounded quartz grains. The croft land is dotted with orchids, while primrose and speedwell are massed on the Laig dunes and the areas of low marshy ground are bright with yellow iris. There are snipe in the marshes, corncrake in the meadows, eider and shelduck along the tideline, and porpoises and sharks offshore. The 68 bird species known to breed on the island include red-throated diver, long-eared owl, short-eared owl and golden eagle.

Rhum

NM 3798; 10,684ha; NCC reserve
Large and mountainous island
Access from Mallaig and Arisaig: day trips, but accommodation also available (see below)
Permit required to visit parts of the island away from the Loch Scresort area: apply NCC, Inverness
Nature trail and reserve leaflets at Kinloch Castle and Rhum post office, or from NCC, Inverness
May–September

When seen from afar, whether from EIGG, Skye or the mainland, Rhum is dominated by the cluster of spectacular peaks and ridges towards its southern end – all relics of volcanic activity in the distant

past. A great variety of rock types, some of them unique to Rhum, are represented in these uplands; they range from the acid granites of Sgurr nan Gillean to the magnesium-rich rock of which pyramid-shaped Askival (812m) and Hallival are formed. Only at closer quarters, however, can the full natural diversity of the island be appreciated; it includes limestone cliffs and lava flows, flourishing plantations of native tree species and relict natural woodland in isolated ravines, re-introduced sea eagle, an established population of golden eagle and an intensively studied herd of red deer. This wealth of interest, together with the fact that for more than 20 years the NCC has managed the reserve so as to minimise disturbance, explains the great value of Rhum for ecological research – a value recognised by the reserve's designation as a Biosphere Reserve in accordance with UNESCO's Man and Biosphere Programme.

The wide range of soil types represented on Rhum is reflected in the variety of the vegetation. Although the area of lime-rich rock is not extensive it has an interesting plant life including mountain avens, alpine saxifrage, alpine meadow-grass and alpine penny-cress. Scottish asphodel, stone bramble and mountain everlasting flourish on volcanic soils high in the hills, with arctic sandwort, purple saxifrage, cyphel and abundant northern rock-cress growing right up to summit level. Wood bitter-vetch and pyramidal bugle occur on the low-lying Torridonian sandstone soils, while the sandy bays of the north coast are made colourful by gentians, trefoils, pansies and a variety of orchids, including fragrant, frog and marsh-orchid.

Rhum's vast breeding colony of Manx shearwater is one of its ornithological specialities; over 130,000 pairs have their nesting burrows in the deep, loose soil high on the slopes of Askival and

Hallival. The heavy manuring of the soil outside the burrows produces lush grass which attracts the deer herds in summer. The other bird of particular interest is sea eagle. Once regular breeding birds on Rhum and elsewhere in Scotland, sea eagles were persecuted until they became extinct early this century. Now, in a project started in 1975, young sea eagles from Norway are being reintroduced and successfully released to the wild. Some are now sufficiently mature to breed, and in 1981 a pair occupied a nest site for the first time.

The bird life of the island has been significantly affected by the extensive afforestation with native species carried out during the last 15 years. Policy plantings around Kinloch Castle initially provided the only suitable habitat for woodland birds such as robin, blackbird, song thrush and dunnock, all relatively scarce in semi-natural woodlands in north west Scotland. These four species, together with chaffinch, willow warbler, wren and gold-crest, have now effectively colonised the new woodlands. Other breeding birds on Rhum include peregrine, merlin, raven, red-throated diver and corncrake, and there are modest seabird colonies along the southern cliffs.

Rhum is notably rich in insects, including the more vividly coloured Hebridean forms of species such as dark green fritillary butterfly. Small pearl-bordered fritillary, green hairstreak, common blue and large heath butterflies are all abundant. Among the larger and more obvious moths are emperor, fox, drinker and northern eggar, and three species strongly associated with aspens: puss moth, poplar hawkmoth and pebble prominent moth. Speckled wood butterfly and giant wood wasp are examples of insects which have colonised the island's new woodlands.

It is now possible to stay on the island, in Kinloch Castle, run for the NCC by Hebridean Holidays Ltd, to whom visitors should apply for hotel or hostel accommodation (tel. 0687 2026).

Tokavaig Wood (Coille Thocabhaig)

NG 6112; 81 ha; NCC reserve
Relict semi-natural woodland
May–June

The sheltered and very humid location of this mixed woodland, together with the variety of the underlying rocks, are responsible for its botanical richness. Ash is the dominant species on the limestone outcrops, with some hazel and bird cherry; the Torridonian sandstone areas support oak. The wood has a varied ground vegetation, and of notable interest are its bryophytes, lichens and ferns.

Contrasting rock types, shelter and high humidity account for Tokavaig Wood's botanical richness.

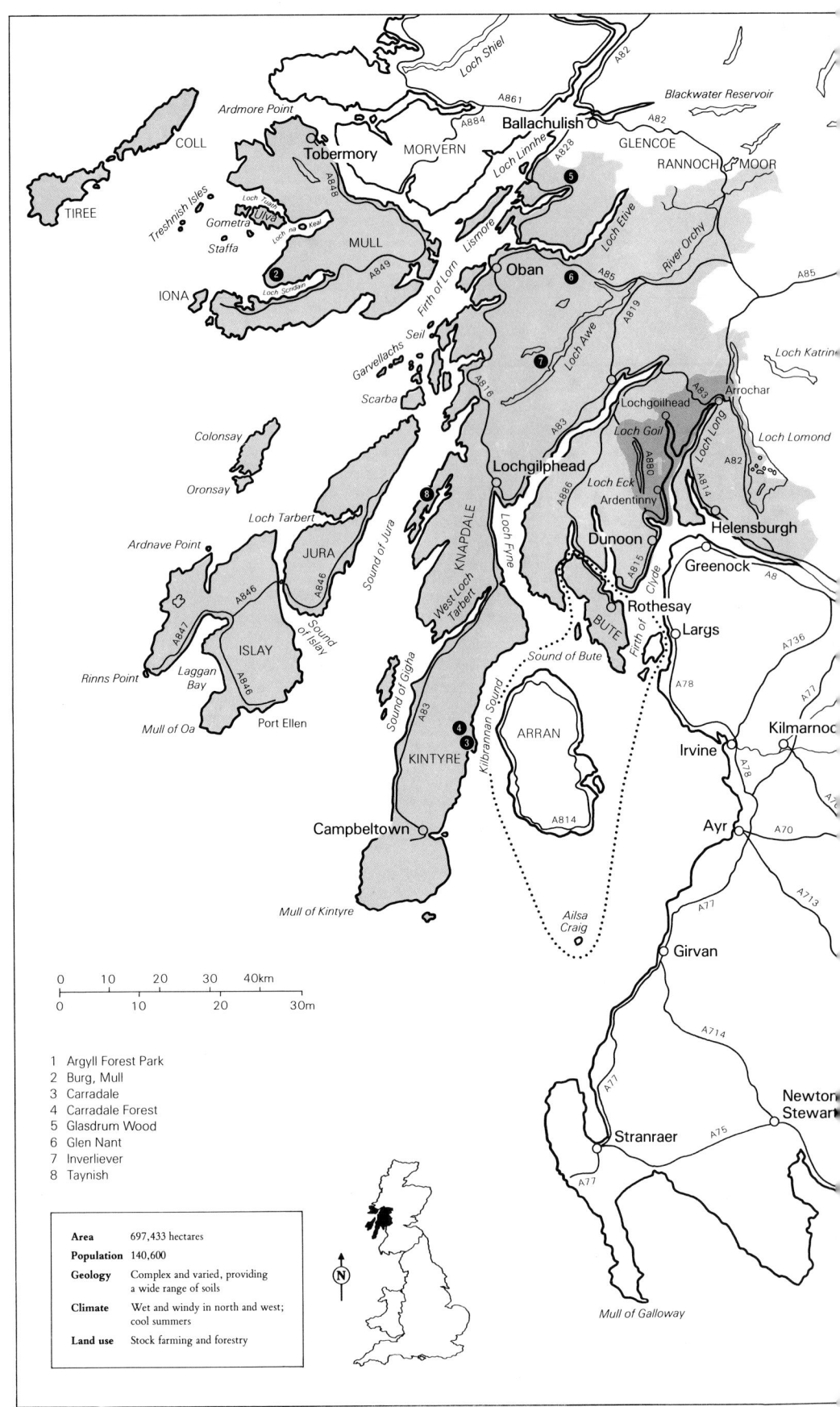

COLL

TIREE

Ardmore Point

Tobermory

MORVERN

Treshnish Isles

Gometra

ULVA

Staffa

MULL

A848

A849

IONA

Loch Shiel

A861

A884

Ballachulish

Blackwater Reservoir

A82

GLENCOE

Loch Linnhe

A828

RANNOCH MOOR

5

Lismore

Loch Etive

River Orchy

A82

A85

Oban

6

A85

A85

Loch Awe

A819

Loch Katrine

Firth of Lorn

Loch na Keal

Loch Tuath

Loch Scridain

2

Garvellachs

Seil

Scarba

7

A816

Arrochar

A83

Lochgoilhead

Loch Goil

Loch Long

Loch Lomond

A82

Colonsay

Oronsay

Loch Tarbert

JURA

A846

Sound of Jura

KNAPDALE

A83

Loch Eck

A880

A814

A886

Ardentinny

Loch Fyne

Dunoon

Helensburgh

Ardnave Point

A846

Sound of Islay

West Loch Tarbert

A815

Greenock

A8

Lochgilphead

Rinns Point

A847

ISLAY

A846

Laggan Bay

Sound of Gigha

A83

Rothesay

BUTE

Firth of

Clyde

Largs

A78

A736

A77

Mull of Oa

Port Ellen

Sound of Bute

4

3

Kilbrannan Sound

ARRAN

Kilmarnoc

KINTYRE

A814

Irvine

A78

Campbeltown

Ayr

A70

A713

Mull of Kintyre

Ailsa Craig

Girvan

A77

A714

0   10   20   30   40km

0   10   20   30m

Newton
Stewar

1 Argyll Forest Park
2 Burg, Mull
3 Carradale
4 Carradale Forest
5 Glasdrum Wood
6 Glen Nant
7 Inverliever
8 Taynish

Stranraer

A77

A75

Area	697,433 hectares
Population	140,600
Geology	Complex and varied, providing a wide range of soils
Climate	Wet and windy in north and west; cool summers
Land use	Stock farming and forestry

N

Mull of Galloway

Strathclyde North

From the Clyde Estuary north into the mountains and islands of Argyll lies a countryside of ceaseless change in mood and endless variety in landform. Peninsulas reach out into the island-studded sea of the Hebrides. From the vast peatlands of Rannoch Moor to the unspoiled beaches of Tiree, and from the Mull of Kintyre to Loch Linnhe, Argyll probably contains a greater variety of natural formations and richer assemblages of plants and animals than any other part of Scotland. There are mountains supporting tundra and alpine flowers; raised bog and valley peatlands; open waters ranging from small peat pools to lime-rich lochs fringed with reed and fen communities; rolling dunes; steep, herb-rich coastline; and native deciduous woodlands. It all starts some 30km from the centre of Glasgow by LOCH LOMOND (described under Central), studded with tree-covered islands and fringed with fine, mixed woodlands.

Sea lochs cut deep into the hinterland, providing shelter from the Atlantic rollers. Unpolluted lagoons contain myriads of inshore marine organisms. Clear rivers run down to the head of these long fiords, and in some the great volume of fresh water affects the salinity of the loch, resulting in a gradation of animal and plant communities from near-freshwater to full salinity.

Wet days can be expected at any time of year, but rainfall is usually heaviest in late summer, autumn and winter. In early summer it is possible to experience the weather of all four seasons in one day. The climate varies within and between islands. Tiree and Coll enjoy longer periods of sunshine than most of Scotland, while the mountain mass of central Mull, only 32km east, is very wet. The islands usually escape heavy snow, but inland it can lie deep in the hills for long periods. The influence of the Gulf Stream is felt along Argyll's deeply indented coastline and around the offshore islands, which usually escape extreme frosts.

The action of weather on complex geological formations has led to a wide range of soil conditions. Granite hills produce generally infertile soils around upper Loch Etive, while black, base-rich schists to the east of Dalmally support some of the richest upland plant communities in the Highlands. Nearer the coast, a north east to south west configuration of the terrain is created by the bedding of metamorphic Dalradian rocks; and there are limestone bands within these formations. Around Oban, the underlying rock is mostly igneous andesite and the vegetation is influenced by intrusions of basalts.

The geology of the Inner Hebrides is even more complex. Lismore is entirely limestone and the landscape is verdant; three lime-rich lochs support aquatic and fen communities very rare in Scotland. Jura is mainly quartzite, whereas Islay has the full range of Dalradian rocks. The underlying rock of Tiree and Coll is Lewisian gneiss, but Coll has rocky hillocks, and low-lying Tiree is largely raised beach. Both contain dune and *machair* formations, but blown shell sands influence the soil all over Tiree. On Colonsay and Oronsay the underlying rocks are Torridonian sandstones, phyllites, grits, mudstones and flags. Some of the finest raised beaches in Britain are found on Jura, Islay and Colonsay.

The Isle of Mull with its smaller satellites is geologically outstanding. Mull was the centre of violent volcanic activity in the tertiary period. There are granite exposures on the Ross of Mull, but over the rest of the island layers of lava flow have resulted in a terraced landscape with columnar formations along the coast, the most spectacular forming the pillars of Fingal's Cave on Staffa. The great plateau lavas of the central Mull complex contain an almost perfect ring dyke. Formations such as this, the coastal exposures where the plateau lavas cover sedimentary rocks, and sites such as the Ardtun leafbeds, where fossilised ancient forest debris is sandwiched between lava flows, make Mull a petrologist's paradise.

Some islands in the Inner Hebrides support plant communities dependent on sands derived from seashells. The air is seldom still here and the fine, calcium- and phosphate-rich sand is taken up by the wind and deposited over the islands, which bear a *machair* turf studded with wild flowers. This in turn supports distinctive insect and bird communities. *Machair* is most extensive on Tiree, probably the biggest blown sand formation in Britain unaffected by rabbit grazing: although brown hare are present, rabbits were never introduced to Tiree.

Argyll contains more relict native woodlands than other parts of Scotland. Fragments of fine old native pinewoods survive by Loch Tulla, near Bridge of Orchy and along Glen Orchy. Nearer the coast and on many islands the original forest cover consisted mainly of deciduous species – oak, ash, wych elm, wild cherry, birch, alder, rowan, hazel, with sallows, holly, bird cherry and guelder-rose sometimes present in the shrub layer. It is not surprising that three of Argyll's National Nature Reserves, GLASDRUM, TAYNISH and GLEN NANT, were designated primarily as examples of native deciduous forest. These woods have been exploited by man over the centuries, first for fuel, tools and building timber, and later also to supply charcoal for the iron smelting industry centred on Loch Fyne and Loch Etive, and oak bark for tanning. Had it not been for the management of woods by coppicing, for a sustained yield, all these ancient forests would perhaps have long since been destroyed.

An interesting feature of the oceanic deciduous woodlands of western Scotland is the profusion of lichens, mosses and liverworts, which cover tree trunks as well as the forest floor. Over 200 species of lichens may occur in a single wood, with a similar number of mosses and liverworts, while some of the oceanic species existing here are found nowhere else in Europe. Many of the oceanic lichens are sensitive even to low levels of atmospheric pollution, and their survival here is evidence of clean air.

Man's past use of the land has been mainly pastoral. Until the nineteenth century cattle were herded in the hills in summer and brought down to the glens in winter. Later sheep were introduced in enormous numbers and muirburning became a regular practice, aimed at encouraging young growth of the moorland vegetation in early spring. At the same time deer stalking developed as a popular sport on the large estates. The coppicing system came to an end and the woods were exposed to browsing by sheep and deer and the effects of fire. For over 100 years natural regeneration has only been possible where grazing has been relaxed for periods.

Today dramatic changes are taking place. In the past 40 years extensive areas have been commercially afforested, and conifers now grow on hillsides where native woodlands have long since vanished. Dense, dark spruce woods blanket the hills, suppressing the natural vegetation, but the potential threats to wildlife have been recognised. Streamsides and river courses are left unplanted or planted with alder and willow, and native woodland relics are protected as wildlife refuges within areas of afforestation. In the ARGYLL FOREST PARK care is being taken to achieve a greater diversity of species in second-generation forests, and woodlands developing by Loch Goil and Loch Eck have an uneven canopy structure and contain a wide range of conifers as well as substantial areas of native deciduous species.

The larger animals and birds are all well represented in this corner of Scotland. Golden eagles soar around coastal cliffs as well as the high corries. Peregrine, merlin, hen harrier, sparrowhawk, kestrel and buzzard are abundant. Fox and badger are widespread on the mainland and otter occur around the coastline and on most of the islands. Red and roe deer play an increasingly important part in current land use.

PETER WORMELL

Fingal's Cave, Staffa, is formed of columnar basalt.

Ardmore Point

NS 319786; 194ha; SWT reserve
Rocky foreshore, mudflats and wet moorland
Nature trail leaflets from SWT
*April–July: flowers, breeding birds; September–
March: wildfowl and waders*

The promontory of Ardmore juts out from the
northern shore of the Clyde and is joined to it by
a narrow neck of land, flanked by muddy bays.
Rocky shore, saltwater and freshwater marsh, wet
meadows, boggy moorland, gorse thickets, alder
scrub and planted woodlands are all represented
within the reserve, providing a very diverse range
of habitats. The promontory enjoys a slightly
milder climate than the adjoining mainland and
this, too, influences the species found here – particularly the insects. The reserve also has geological
interest, firstly in the unconformity between the
beds of upper and lower old red sandstone exposed
on the shore and secondly because of its landforms.

Marine life is rich and varied in the rock pools
and inter-tidal zone, with abundant shellfish, crustaceans and seaweeds. Among the fish are butterfish and three-spined stickleback, with viviparous
blennies inhabiting pools around the south bay. In
the bays, many waders and duck feed on the
plentiful lugworms and other invertebrates, and a
small patch of eelgrass. Whimbrel, greenshank,
bar-tailed godwit and golden plover are recorded
regularly, along with the more common waders.
Duck wintering in the bays include wigeon and
teal, while eider, goldeneye, scaup and red-
breasted merganser occur offshore.

The vegetation on the raised beach below the
wooded Ardmore Hill includes moorland plants
such as bog asphodel, marsh-orchid, yellow rattle
and sundew. Small copper butterflies occur in this
area, and the gorse and bramble scrub attracts
linnet, whinchat and yellowhammer. Wetter areas
at the foot of the relict sea cliffs support yellow iris,
marsh cinquefoil and sedges, and attract dragonflies and other insects. The small areas of saltmarsh
and alder scrub represent further plant communities with their own characteristic species. Although no individual species on the reserve can be
described as rare, the presence of so many plants
and animals typical of such a variety of habitats
makes this a site of great interest.

Argyll Forest Park

See map; c.240sq.km; FC and others
Information from forest offices at Ardgartan
(NN 272034), Glenbranter (NS 112977) or Kilmun
(NS 160825); guide from FC, or HMSO bookshops
All year

This forest park is unique in that roughly half its
perimeter is bounded by sea water. The narrow,
fiord-like fingers of Loch Long and Loch Goil
thrust far into the forested hills, the former reaching, at Arrochar, to within 2.5km of LOCH LOMOND,
and the latter almost bisecting the park. This was

*Hen harriers breed on open moorland, above the
tree-line, in several of Scotland's forest parks.*

the first forest park to be set up in Great Britain, in
1935, and it has demonstrated with ever-increasing
success how commercial forestry can be combined
with a wide variety of recreational facilities and
still maintain great natural history interest. Today
the park, within easy weekend visiting distance of
the most densely populated area of Scotland, caters
for holiday-makers, outdoor activity enthusiasts,
and those who seek solitude and a chance to study
wildlife. From seashore to mountain top the range
of habitats is wide, and there is an abundance of
natural history to be discovered.

Much less than half of the land within the park
has been afforested, the upper limit of planting
being around 350–400m, depending on exposure. Above this fringing band of conifers lies
open hill ground, rising to a maximum height of just
over 1000m in the 'Arrochar Alps' near the northern
boundary, and around 700m in the rest of the park.
Much of this ground is grassy moorland, with heath
rush, cottongrasses, bog mosses and sedges on the
peaty wetter areas, and bracken, heather and bilberry where the drainage is freer. Arctic–alpines
such as alpine lady's-mantle, mountain everlasting,
alpine meadow-rue and moss campion are not uncommon from 700m, with dwarf willow and three-
leaved rush on the summits, and holly fern, alpine
lady-fern and alpine saw-wort also occurring.
Where glacial action has carved out corries, or water
has worn through the rock to form gorges, one can
often find good displays of globeflower, goldenrod,
purple saxifrage and roseroot.

Argyll Forest Park: the semi-natural woodlands support a more varied bird life than do the plantations.

This high ground is used for sheep grazing, and also supports several hundred red deer; in autumn the hills ring with the roars of rutting stags. A few ptarmigan are present on the summits, and the birds of the lower moorlands include red grouse, curlew, skylark, twite and stonechat. Hen harrier breed in some areas, buzzard and raven are fairly common, and one may see a golden eagle soaring overhead or flying low in pursuit of a mountain hare. There are many good walking routes over the high ground, one of the most spectacular being that along the ridge in the Ardgoil peninsula, taking in the peaks of the Saddle, Beinn Reithe, Cnoc Coinnich and the Brack.

The hills of the 'Arrochar Alps' are higher and steeper and therefore more challenging. Ben Arthur (881m), better known as the Cobbler, attracts hill walkers and rock climbers; its crags and corries look wild and forbidding in misty weather but there is a comparatively easy route, by grassy and scree slopes, to the Centre Peak, the highest point. The striking South Peak, crag-bound on all sides, is best left to experienced rock climbers. However modest the objective remember that the weather is singularly unreliable, and mist and low cloud can blot out landmarks with dismaying speed; a map and compass should always be carried.

The forests offer a maze of tracks, some way-marked as circular routes and others simply working forestry roads. Crossbill, capercaillie, sparrowhawk, goldcrest and siskin breed in the plantations, with black grouse along the forest fringe, where trees give way to moorland. Both red and grey squirrel live in these woods, but neither is very numerous.

Semi-natural woodlands still survive in many parts of the park. Oak dominates the woods along the shore of Loch Lomond, north of Tarbet, and in Glen Loin there is a virtually untouched stand of mixed ash, hazel, birch, alder and oak. In Glen Branter natural woodland lines the hillside gullies, and along the east shore of Loch Eck are mixed woods with much beech and oak. Many of these woods produce masses of primroses, bluebells, wood anemones and violets in spring. The fact that no part of the park is more than 6.5km from sea water means that the climate is relatively mild and this, together with the high rainfall, results in an exceptionally rich growth of ferns, mosses, liverworts and lichens. Beech and oak fern are widespread, and the tiny Wilson's filmy-fern – easily overlooked – often grows among the mosses on wet rocks and in damp shaded gorges.

These areas of mixed woodland support a more varied bird population than do the plantations. Long-tailed tit occur in them, as well as blue, great and coal tit; willow warbler are numerous in summer and jay are most abundant where there are oak trees. Magpie are very local – often the case in Scotland – and are most likely to be seen around Strachur. The best prospect of hearing the delightful shivering trill of wood warbler is in the predominantly oak woodland, while blackcap, garden warbler and chiffchaff are most likely to be found in the exotic surroundings of the Younger Botanic Gardens at Benmore, or in the Kilmun Arboretum.

Although in no way resembling natural woodland, these two sites are well worth a visit. Both owe their success to the temperate climate which enables many non-hardy exotics to be grown. At

Kilmun there is an interesting and varied collection of trees from all over the world; trails have been set out and a guide book is available. In the Younger Botanic Gardens the unrivalled collection of rhododendrons takes pride of place, but there are also many magnificent specimen trees of such species as noble fir and redwood. In the soft west-coast climate rhododendron naturalises readily and spreads rapidly; along the eastern shore of Loch Goil young plants are plentiful. A more unexpected exotic, also abundant in this area, is flowering nutmeg, rampant on some of the rocky slopes beside the forest track.

The park's extensive shoreline offers many opportunities for exploring the natural life between the tidal zones. Sandy areas are few and far between, occurring only at the heads of Loch Goil and the Holy Loch, and near Ardentinny. Elsewhere the shores are mostly composed of stones set in sand and gravel, but there are interesting and easily accessible rock pools around Strone Point on the southern tip of Kilmun. Because the narrowness of the sea-lochs restricts tidal scour, dense beds of seaweeds flourish in the inter-tidal zone; a great variety of species may be found, representing a wide range of colours and sizes. Among the seaweeds and stones beadlet sea-anemones and the grey sea-slugs that feed on them, sea-lemons and starfish, sea-urchins and well-camouflaged, armadillo-like chitons all flourish. Mussels – both the common variety and the larger horse-mussel – are abundant on the gravelly shores, providing food for the eider that frequent the coasts, and there are many other 'shellfish' such as periwinkles, limpets and whelks. In the rock pools shore crabs, shrimps, sea-scorpions and the almost transparent aesop prawns hide among the fronds of seaweed, while bread-crumb and purse sponges, star sea-squirts and jellyfish occur in the deeper water. Grey seal frequently visit the sea-lochs and basking shark have been seen both in Loch Goil and as far up Loch Long as Arrochar.

There is much more that is equally worthy of mention in the Argyll Forest Park – otter in the rivers and sea-lochs, for example, golden-ringed dragonflies hawking over the track-side ditches, hart's-tongue fern on a shady wall, or powan and char in Loch Eck. There is scope, too, for those less devoted naturalists who wish to vary their wildlife watching with other activities. Within the park are four outdoor education centres, offering many facilities to the general visitor. Hill walking and climbing, fishing – both freshwater and sea – orienteering, sailing, canoeing and pony trekking can all be enjoyed, while subaqua enthusiasts can explore the underwater caves in Loch Long. There are endless subjects for the photographer too, but a permit should first be obtained from the FC.

Burg, Mull

NM 426266; 617ha; NTS
Cliff, grassland and shoreline
Access by foot only, from Tiroran (NM 478278)
Further information at Burg Farm (NM 427266)
All year

Situated at the western end of the Ardmeanach peninsula, this site is famous for its fossil tree, believed to be 50 million years old. Known as McCulloch's tree, it is embedded in columnar basalt and can be seen only at low tide. The area is notable for its rich and varied plant life, and also for its Lepidoptera.

Spikes of mare's-tail in a moorland pool on Jura.

Carradale

NR 8137; 70ha; SWT reserve
Coastal grassland, low cliffs and island
April–June

There is rich coastal and marine life around this grassy peninsula, which affords good views over Kilbrannan Sound. Otter frequent the shoreline and porpoise, white-beaked dolphin, bottle-nosed dolphin and killer whale are regularly seen offshore. A variety of seabirds can be seen in summer, and there is a small though long-established herd of white feral goats.

Carradale Forest

NR 8038; 700ha; FC
Conifer plantations and moorland
All year

This is probably the only area in Scotland with both sika and fallow deer, as well as roe deer. The sika deer originated from an enclosure at CAR-RADALE, and have colonised the Kintyre peninsula. Fallow deer occur only in the Deerhill section of the forest (NR 8039).

Glasdrum Wood

NN 0545; 169ha; NCC reserve
Hanging woodland
Access restricted: contact NCC, Cairnbaan,
by Lochgilphead, Argyll
Leaflet from NCC, Balloch
May–August

This trackless, closed-canopy woodland rises steeply from just above sea level to an altitude of 530m; above it lies open hill. A band of alder occupies the damp lower slopes; ash and hazel dominate the middle section, in which lime-rich rocky outcrops occur; and above the main escarpment sessile oak and birch gradually give way to moorland. The herb-rich ground flora includes a variety of ferns, and such typical woodland flowers as dog's mercury, wood anemone and enchanter's-nightshade. Many maritime bryophyte and lichen species are present and the reserve has an interesting insect population.

Ferns, mosses and lichens flourish in steeply sloping Glasdrum Wood.

Glen Nant

NN 0128; 200ha; NCC–FC reserve
Native deciduous woodland
Access restricted: contact NCC, Cairnbaan,
by Lochgilphead, Argyll
Nature trail (4km) on forest nature reserve
April–July

The mark of man's past activities is still apparent in these woods, once the source of charcoal for the iron furnace at nearby Bonawe. Stumps of coppiced oaks, some around 400 years old, and the levelled circles of charcoal hearths, are widely scattered through the mixed woodland that clothes the slopes of Glen Nant today. A variety of tree species is now present, including oak with abundant ash, hazel and birch. Bird cherry, rowan and holly are well represented, with the occasional wych elm and wild cherry, and alder and willow in the wetter areas.

The shrub layer is minimal – only a few blackthorn, hawthorn and guelder-rose. In some places ferns dominate the ground vegetation: oak fern, lemon-scented fern, hay-scented buckler-fern, scaly male-fern and Wilson's filmy-fern are among the species present. Elsewhere feathery clumps of tufted hair-grass tower above a carpet of ramsons, primrose and wild strawberry. Both living and fallen tree trunks carry a luxuriant growth of mosses, and there are many lichens.

Wood warbler, redstart and great spotted woodpecker are among the breeding birds in the wood. Roe deer are common – the ground cover is networked by their tracks – and voles, fieldmice and hedgehogs are plentiful. Insect life is also varied. Scotch Argus, dark green fritillary and green-veined white butterflies dance in the clearings and the more open boggy areas, and golden-ringed dragonflies zip to and fro along the tracks. Beneath the trees wood ants work around their mounded nests, some of which have been there sufficiently long for bilberry to colonise their summits.

The Forest Nature Reserve accounts for considerably more than half of the total woodland area. It lies on the west side of the valley, and is separated by the River Nant from the NNR, which is in private ownership and not open to the public.

Inverliever

NM 9410; 13,383ha; FC
Conifer plantations, oakwood and open hill
ground
Forest walks; further information from forest office,
Dalavich, Taynuilt (NN 970126)
All year

This vast scenic area includes hill grazings, unplanted hill tops, lochs and broad-leaved woods, as well as coniferous forest. The large stretches of untouched heathery hill ground support red deer and such typical moorland plants as purple moorgrass, deergrass, bog asphodel and bog myrtle. Hen harrier nest on the moorland, and golden eagle and peregrine can sometimes be seen flying over. The forest itself holds breeding buzzard, sparrowhawk, jay and crossbill, and there are red, roe and sika deer and badger in the area. Several remnants of the old oakwoods remain along the shores of Loch Awe and a variety of other native species, such as alder, ash, wych elm and hazel, are present. The woods and wet gullies are rich in ferns, mosses and lichens and hold many smaller birds and mammals.

Loch Lomond

Described under Central.

Taynish

NR 7384; 320ha; NCC reserve
Woodland, heath, bog and foreshore
Permission required to visit areas away from
road: apply to NCC, Cairnbaan,
by Lochgilphead, Argyll
Leaflet from NCC, Balloch
April–July

The oakwoods clothing the schist ridges of this reserve represent one of the largest remnants of this type of woodland surviving in Scotland. Ash, hazel, rowan, honeysuckle and holly occur among the even-aged oaks, and there is a luxuriant growth of mosses on the boulders littering the woodland floor. Between the ridges open areas of boggy ground, heath and wet meadow fringed with mixed woodland increase the habitat diversity. Heath spotted-orchid and northern marsh-orchid grow in these areas, which attract a wide variety of butterflies. Scotch argus are abundant in late summer, when their warm brown colouring stands out against the grasses and rushes as they flit low over the ground.

Taynish is rich in lichens as well as mosses; many of the tree trunks are completely swathed in luxuriant growths – which often represent several species. Lungwort is common and other species confined to the Atlantic coast also occur.

There is unusually little tidal variation in the sheltered waters around the Taynish peninsula, and the warm shallows hold a variety of marine species normally found over a much wider range of depth. Herons stalk over the tangles of golden-tawny seaweeds, and sea-urchins, starfish and various species of sponge flourish in the unpolluted water. Common seal and otter frequent the nearby islets, and wigeon visit Linne Mhuirich in winter to feed on the eelgrass.

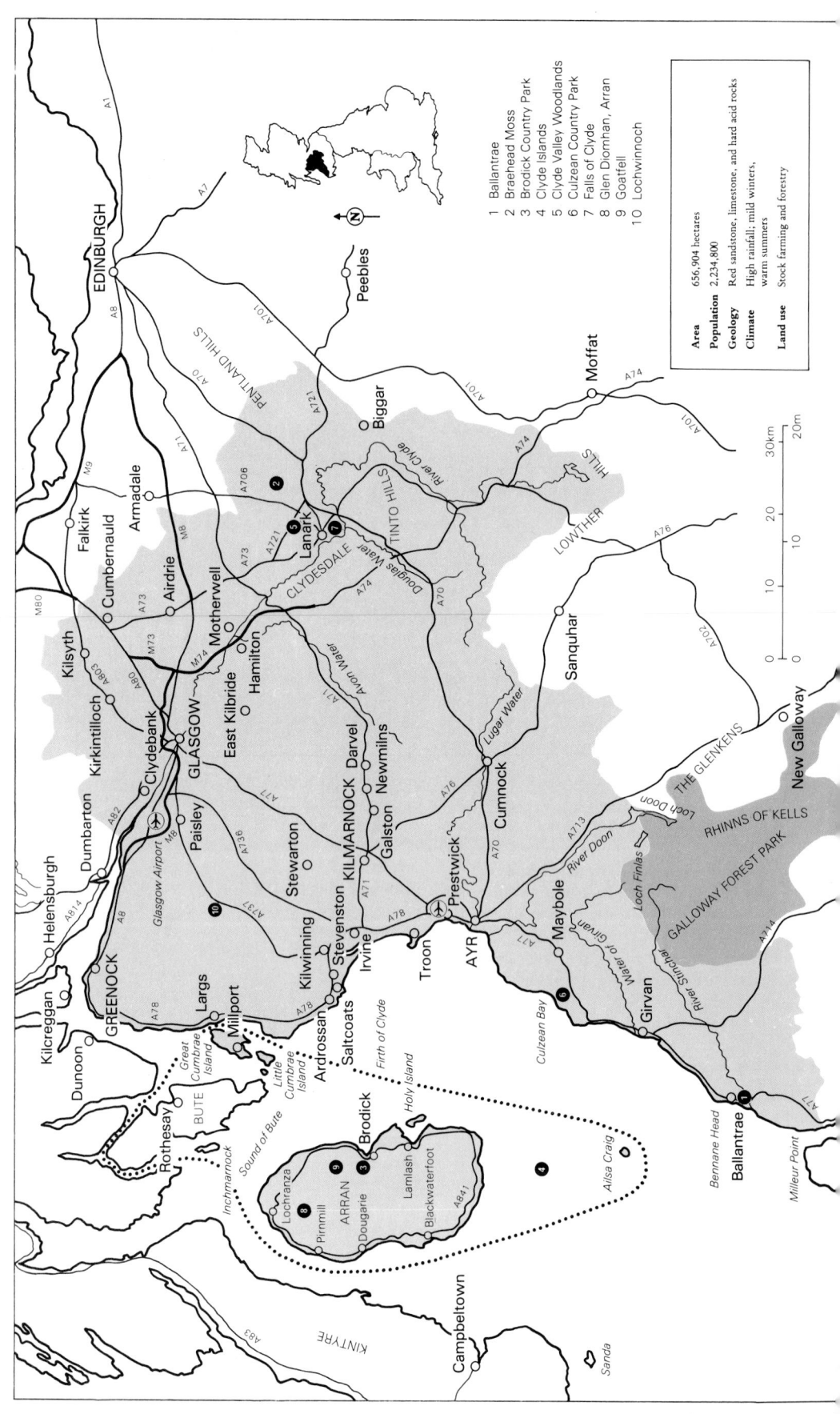

1 Ballantrae
2 Braehead Moss
3 Brodick Country Park
4 Clyde Islands
5 Clyde Valley Woodlands
6 Culzean Country Park
7 Falls of Clyde
8 Glen Diomhan, Arran
9 Goatfell
10 Lochwinnoch

Area	656,904 hectares
Population	2,234,800
Geology	Red sandstone, limestone, and hard acid rocks
Climate	High rainfall; mild winters, warm summers
Land use	Stock farming and forestry

EDINBURGH

Peebles

Moffat

Biggar

Armadale

Falkirk

Cumbernauld

Airdrie

Kilsyth

Motherwell

LANARK

CLYDESDALE

TINTO HILLS

LOWTHER HILLS

Sanquhar

Kirkintilloch

Clydebank

GLASGOW

Hamilton

East Kilbride

Darvel

KILMARNOCK

Newmilns

Galston

Cumnock

Paisley

Stewarton

Dumbarton

Helensburgh

Kilcreggan

Dunoon

GREENOCK

Largs

Millport

Kilwinning

Stevenston

Irvine

Saltcoats

Ardrossan

Troon

Prestwick

AYR

Maybole

Girvan

Glasgow Airport

Rothesay

BUTE

Great Cumbrae Island

Little Cumbrae Island

Firth of Clyde

Inchmarnock

Sound of Bute

Lochranza

Pirnmill

Dougarie

ARRAN

Brodick

Lamlash

Blackwaterfoot

Holy Island

Alisa Craig

Bennane Head

Ballantrae

Milleur Point

Sanda

KINTYRE

Campbeltown

New Galloway

THE GLENKENS

Loch Doon

RHINNS OF KELLS

GALLOWAY FOREST PARK

Loch Finlas

River Stinchar

Water of Girvan

River Doon

Lugar Water

Avon Water

Douglas Water

River Clyde

PENTLAND HILLS

Culzean Bay

0   10   20   30km

0   10   20m

Strathclyde South

Southern Strathclyde extends from the inland hills and valleys of Lanark north to the shores of the Clyde Estuary and west to the coast of the Firth of Clyde. In the lowlands of Lanark, Renfrew and Ayrshire, once deciduous woodland, the important dairy industry developed to meet the expanding demands of nineteenth-century Glasgow. Farming today is less intensive than in eastern Scotland, and the abundant wildlife reflects the sheltered habitats created by the hedgerows, copses and rough pastures of the less fertile areas.

The uplands are largely rolling hills and moorlands, mountains being found only in the south. Rough grass and bracken clothe the well-drained steeper slopes, while heaths dominate the rocky outcrops and great peat bogs cover the flat, poorly drained areas. This is sheep country, though conifer plantations are becoming more evident. Rural depopulation has made its mark, and isolated ruined cottages bear witness to a more dynamic past.

The Clyde coast provides habitats ranging from rocky shore, raised beaches and cliffs to sand dunes. Despite increased pressures from man these habitats remain generally unspoilt, and even the shore of the inner Clyde Estuary between Port Glasgow and Erskine is still nationally important for waders.

The climate is temperate throughout the year. Prevailing south to south westerly winds maintain a warm, damp airstream and relatively high rainfall in the uplands; areas around Ayr and Troon, however, have the lowest rainfall (around 890mm per annum) on the west coast of Scotland. The Gulf Stream is responsible for the relatively mild winters; snow rarely lies long, particularly along the coast.

Southern Strathclyde's geology is reflected in its scenery and vegetation. The uplands of the south and Galloway comprise hard, relatively acidic rocks of the Ordovician and Silurian periods, exemplified by the granites of the Loch Doon area. To the north of Loch Doon, across the Southern Upland Fault, the old red sandstone of Ayrshire and Lanark has been more readily eroded to produce a rolling landscape, while the sandstones, shales and limestones of the central basin of Ayrshire form low-lying, gently undulating ground.

During the later ice ages the Merrick region in Galloway was an area from which glaciers moved north and west, creating U-shaped valleys such as the upper Nith Valley and features such as drumlins and moraines. Glasgow's steep streets are the result of its being built on drumlins while the rushy upland grassland to the south may reflect moraine and boulder clay deposition resulting in poorly drained soils. Post-glacial raised beaches formed by wave action during glaciation are prominent along the Clyde coast, particularly at BALLANTRAE, Dunure, Portencross and the CLYDE ISLANDS.

Deciduous woodland is now largely confined to copses and river banks. The trees are generally beech, sycamore, wych elm, ash or oak; shrubs and herbs are more diverse under the last two, since they come into leaf last and have an open leaf canopy. In spring the drier woodlands are coloured by wood anemone, wood-sorrel, lesser celandine and bluebell, followed by avens, herb-Robert and other shade-loving species. Wetter soils are dominated by alder and willow, with which are associated marsh-marigold, golden-saxifrage, ramsons, meadowsweet and marsh valerian. The woodlands shelter roe deer, foxes, badgers, shrews, field mice and voles, and occasionally heronries.

Notable deciduous woodlands include the FALLS OF CLYDE reserve near Lanark, and further to the west ENTERKINE WOOD; both are rich in woodland birds and have a spring carpet of bluebells. The country parks of CULZEAN and BRODICK also include woodlands: at Brodick, the grounds contain mature oak and beech, which provide a shady habitat for mosses, liverworts, lichens and ferns, while Culzean has extensive policy woodlands and formal ponds. The cliffs at Culzean support heathland and maritime species, and the pebble or sandy beaches are rich in marine life and shore birds.

The Culzean seashore is typical of the Clyde coast: sand dunes or shingle beaches are often flanked by rocky headlands and cliffs. The dunes contain sea lyme-grass and marram, red fescue, sand sedge, silverweed and bird's-foot-trefoil. The shingle beaches are often colonised by salt-loving plants such as sea sandwort, grass-leaved orache or silverweed, among which may be found the nests of oystercatcher, ringed plover or terns. At Ballantrae, about 24km south of Culzean, a reserve has been established on a shingle spit at the mouth of the River Stinchar. Little, common and arctic tern nest on the shingle, while shelduck, red-breasted merganser, common sandpiper and gulls frequent the lagoons. Plant life includes the salt-loving sea campion, sea sandwort and oysterplant.

Rocky shores form a micro-habitat for seaweeds, shellfish, crabs, sea anemones and fish. The shoreline south of Girvan is particularly unspoilt, while Turnberry, Dunure and Portencross have a raised beach and cliffs with interesting flora and fauna. In mid-May the cliffs of south Ayrshire are tinged by brilliant blue spring squill, occasional patches of rock-rose, bitter vetch and spotted-orchids which complement the bird's-foot-trefoil, sea campion and sea pink.

Inland again is a birdwatchers' reserve at LOCH-WINNOCH. Beds of reed canary-grass and sedges, with scattered willow scrub, provide good cover for breeding black-headed gull, great crested grebe, mallard, tufted duck, coot, moorhen and the occasional teal and shoveler. Marsh plants include common spotted-orchid and lesser butterfly-orchid, marsh valerian, meadowsweet and purple-loosestrife. Among winter wildfowl are wigeon, pochard, goldeneye, greylag goose and whooper swan. A similar habitat is found at LOCH LIBO where the plant life includes sedges, pondweeds, and white and yellow water-lilies. POSSIL MARSH, similar in character to these two wetland reserves, is remarkable since it lies within the boundary of the city of Glasgow.

Base-rich meadowland is scarce in the west of Scotland, and two meadow reserves have recently been established south of Ayr – AUCHALTON MEADOW and FEOCH MEADOWS. Both support greater and lesser butterfly-orchid, fragrant and frog orchid and field gentian; a wide variety of butterflies has been recorded at Feoch Meadows, including large skipper.

In the moors and hills of the Clyde coast the most interesting areas are often the gullies and glens, colonised by ferns and other shade-loving species. The fringes of Shielhill Glen above Inverkip are typical moorland, while the birch, oak and alder within shelter brown and mountain hare, fox, stoat, weasel and roe deer, as well as a variety of small mammals. Wood pigeon, willow warbler, tawny owl, chiffchaff, wood warbler, spotted flycatcher, carrion crow and buzzard are among the breeding birds.

Southern Strathclyde contains a wealth of wild-life interest, reflecting the climate, geology and traditional farming practice. While the development of Glasgow and the associated urban and industrial complexes have had a marked effect locally, the greater part of the area is relatively unspoilt and has suffered less from man's interference than has much of lowland Britain.

RALPH KIRKWOOD

Auchalton Meadow

Permit only; 4ha; SWT reserve
Lime-rich grassland
Mid-June–July

At one time three lime kilns were in operation on this site, which supports a wide variety of herbs and grasses. Adder's-tongue, common twayblade, greater and lesser butterfly-orchid, frog orchid, field gentian and quaking-grass are among the more interesting of the 98 plant species present.

Ballantrae

NX 0882; 22ha; SWT reserve
Shingle spit and lagoons
Access restricted mid-May–mid-August, when terns are breeding
Leaflet from warden on site May–August
April–September

Sea campion, mats of fleshy sea sandwort and blue-grey oysterplant crown this shingle spit, composed largely of grey stones worn flat by the waves. The ridge of the spit lies parallel to the tideline; behind it the waters of the River Stinchar mingle at high tide with the sea in a series of brackish lagoons.

A colony of little tern, small in number but still the largest in the Clyde Estuary, breeds on the spit, where common and arctic tern, ringed plover and oystercatcher also nest. Shelduck, red-breasted merganser and common sandpiper frequent the lagoons, and common gull roost at the river mouth. Around the landward fringe of the reserve bird's-foot-trefoil, meadow crane's-bill and naturalised *Rosa rugosa* provide patches of bright colour to contrast with the background greys and greens, and in early summer the area between the river and the lagoons is covered with the frothy white flowers of wild carrot.

Braehead Moss

NS 9551; 87ha; NCC reserve
Raised and blanket bog
Information from warden, 22 Muirpark Way,
Drymen
All year

This reserve represents the best example of its type in southern Strathclyde, having remained largely free from agricultural operations, severe burning or forestry in the recent past. Its major interests are typical peat bog plants and less common species of *Sphagnum*. There are no tracks or paths and most parts are very wet underfoot.

Brodick Country Park

NS 0138; 72ha; NTS–Cunninghame DC
Mature policy woodlands
Nature trail; guided walks; access path to Goatfell;
visitor centre: ranger-naturalist
April–August

The wide variety of trees includes some particularly fine mature specimens of oak and beech. Mosses, liverworts, lichens and ferns flourish in the damp shade of the woodland paths. The combination of tall trees and rhododendrons provides a habitat for birds such as chiffchaff, garden warbler and blackcap; nightjar breed in the more open woodland nearby.

Clyde Islands

See map; includes 16 sites
All year

From the rugged grandeur of Arran to the almost featureless plateau of Great Cumbrae, and from the bird-dominated rock of Ailsa Craig to the fertile farmland of Bute, the Clyde Islands offer a remarkable variety of scenery and natural history. Each of these islands, and many of the smaller ones, too, has its own distinctive character and wildlife specialities.

Arran, at 427sq.km by far the largest in the group, exhibits a greater geological complexity than any other British island of comparable size. The discovery, in 1975, of the fossil trail of a giant centipede preserved in the rock of one of the island's quarries added yet another aspect to Arran's geological interest.

Lying astride the Highland Boundary Fault, the island is part highland and part lowland, and is sometimes described as a microcosm of Scotland. GOATFELL and its attendant granite peaks, with their ice-carved corries and jagged ridges reaching to nearly 900m, give the northern half an impressively wild character. Here eagle and raven fly, arctic–alpines flourish, and rock climbers respond to the challenge of the summits. South of 'The String,' the road which bisects the island, lies a gently undulating plateau seldom exceeding 400m in height. Much of this area has been afforested in the last 20 to 30 years, providing exten-

sive stretches of new habitat for woodland birds. Crossbill first bred in these plantations in 1980, goldcrest and siskin are well established, and sparrowhawk and buzzard are on the increase. Hen harrier hunt over the adjoining moorlands, and several pairs of peregrine breed on the island. Both red-throated and black-throated diver occur, and there is a regular breeding population of nightjar near BRODICK.

Red deer are present in large numbers on the Arran hills, but are absent from all the other Clyde Islands. Badgers also occur on Arran, having been introduced at the end of the last century, but there are neither mountain hares nor foxes on any of the islands. Red squirrels were introduced to Arran in the 1920s and are still present, but grey squirrels have not yet reached the islands. The Arran Nature Centre at Brodick contains a wealth of detailed information on the island's natural history specialities, among them the rare trees that grow in remote GLEN DIOMHAN.

Although seabirds are a regular feature of the Arran scene, comparatively few nest on the island due to a lack of suitable sites. The cliffs at Drumadoon have held breeding fulmar since 1948 and this species now nests at several places on the west coast. One or two pairs of black guillemot breed among the boulders at Dippen Head, but there are no breeding records of guillemot, razorbill or kittiwake, and the small colonies of common and arctic tern can perhaps most appropriately be described as 'of no fixed abode'. Pladda, the smaller of Arran's two off-lying islands, once held large numbers of breeding terns, including a few pairs of

Ailsa Craig, premier seabird site of the Clyde.

The mild, damp climate encourages lush wild flower growth on the scree slopes below Ailsa's cliffs.

roseate tern. However, its close proximity (only 1.5km offshore), and popularity for picnickers, have resulted in such disturbance that the tern colonies are now much reduced. Large numbers of duck breed on the island, however; eider, shelduck, mallard and red-breasted merganser are all plentiful.

Holy Island, Arran's other offlier, is much larger, steeper and rougher than Pladda, and rises to over 300m. Buzzard and raven nest on the cliffs, while there is a sizeable mixed colony of gulls and a large population of stonechat, whinchat and wheatear. A herd of white wild goats and a few Soay sheep roam the rocky hills, a few grey seal have bred, and the island shares with Arran the distinction of supporting adder, a species absent from all the other islands in the group.

The isolated rocky hump of Ailsa Craig is the Clyde's premier seabird station. With 150m vertical cliffs, crowned with a grassy dome rising to 350m and fringed by a narrow, boulder-strewn foreshore, Ailsa holds a population of around 35,000 pairs of seabirds, nearly half of them gannets. The Ailsa gannetry has existed since at least 1526, and was for long a locally important source of human food. A 2.5km stretch of the west cliffs is densely packed with nests, and the constant circling and plunging of the birds provides a dramatic spectacle. Other seabirds breeding on Ailsa Craig include several thousand kittiwake, guillemot, razorbill and gulls, with smaller numbers of fulmar, puffin and black guillemot.

Bute, unlike Arran which has granite mountains, has hummocky acid moorland, rising no higher than 278m and covered with bracken, heather and grass. Sycamore dominates much of the woodland on the steep inland cliffs, but there is ash and elder too. These woods, and the tangled scrub on the uncultivated sections of Bute's raised beaches, hold good populations of tits and other small birds as well as buzzard and sparrowhawk.

The island is well endowed with freshwater lochs, several of them large, secluded and with adjacent marshy ground which provides nesting cover for waterbirds. Tufted duck breed regularly in some numbers and shoveler do so occasionally. The larger lochs are important roosts for the substantial winter population of greylag geese, which reaches a maximum of around 4000. On Greenan Loch there is an attractive summer show of waterlilies.

Much of Bute's shoreline is rocky, and carved by the sea into a series of ridges and contorted pinnacles. Eider, red-breasted merganser, oystercatcher and ringed plover are frequent around the coast but the biggest gatherings of both duck and waders occur in the beautiful sandy bays of Kilchattan, Scalpsie, St Ninian's and Ettrick. Many curlew, oystercatcher, wigeon and mallard use the mudflats here, and a wide variety of waders is recorded in migration periods. There are also significant numbers of turnstone on the nearby rocky shores in winter.

The small island of Inchmarnock is farmed, but subject to much less disturbance than the popular holiday resort of Bute. Several species of bird breed there in impressively large numbers, notably eider (at least 50 pairs) and gull (around 300 pairs of herring and lesser black-backed, 100 common and a dozen or so great black-backed). Fulmar and black guillemot also nest on Inchmarnock, as do peregrine, buzzard and raven. Access to the island is from Straad on Bute, by private arrangement.

Perhaps not surprisingly, in view of its extensive farmland, Bute has a large population of moles, absent from both Arran and Great Cumbrae. Hedgehogs are also abundant on Bute and were introduced to Inchmarnock in 1972, resulting in a population explosion about five years later. Numbers have since declined, but hedgehogs are still occasionally seen on the shore at dusk, where they have been observed eating winkles. A small herd of multi-coloured wild goats lives at the northern end of Bute and there are substantial numbers of roe deer in the woodlands. The displays and trail guide available at the Buteshire Natural History Society's Museum in Rothesay provide a useful introduction to the island's natural history.

The last of the larger Clyde Islands, Great Cumbrae, is capped with heather moor and girdled by an inland cliff of red sandstone conglomerate. Below the cliff the flat rim of the island is marshy, with spears of yellow iris alternating with newly unfurled bracken in early summer. A jungle of gorse, bramble, rowan, hawthorn and elder straggles up the cliff face, often neatly shaped by the wind, and clumps of sycamore give additional shelter. This scrubland is busy with stonechat and whitethroat, common gull nest in the bog, and all around curlew and redshank engage in their display flights.

It is the roadsides and the shore that most catch the eye, however. In June the verges are colourful with yellow rattle, marsh lousewort, heath spotted-orchid and a few northern marsh-orchids. The rocky shoreline is equally colourful, with patches of grey-green lichen adorning the red rocks, and clumps of pink thrift, yellow bird's-foot-trefoil and pinky-white English stonecrop brightening the surrounding ground.

Few seabirds breed on Great Cumbrae, but neighbouring Little Cumbrae has a small tern colony, nesting black guillemot, and a miniature sea cliff on which shag and cormorant nest. Eider and red-breasted merganser are common around both islands, and there is a surprising variety of birds of prey.

It is, however, for marine life that Great Cumbrae is best known. The Marine Biological Station at Keppel, near Millport, runs a museum and aquarium which is open to the public; there the visitor is given some idea of the complexity of marine communities and also of the varied, and surprisingly exotic, forms of life found in the waters around the Clyde Islands.

Clyde Valley Woodlands

NS 9045; 24ha; NCC reserve
Deciduous woodland
Information from warden, 21 Ardmore Gardens, Drymen
April–July

Cleghorn Glen, part of the Clyde Valley Woodlands, is a nationally important site whose main conservation feature is its diverse and varied woodland cover. The woods, largely of elm, ash, oak and alder, support a range of interesting plants. Uncommon species such as rough horsetail, wood fescue, herb-Paris and stone bramble add to the reserve's importance.

Culzean Country Park

NS 2310; 229ha; NTS
Woodland, ponds and coastline
Visitor centre open April–October; exhibition and audio-visual programme; guided walks programme covering specialist and children's interests; publications; ranger-naturalist
May–September

The extensive policy woodlands and formal ponds within this country park support a very varied population of plants and animals, offering excellent opportunities to study many aspects of natural history. It is along the 5.5km of coastline, however, that the richest natural communities are found.

The familiar kestrel, equally at home in town or country, often hunts along roadside verges.

Low cliffs back the beach. For 2km southwards from the castle they are composed of lava, and rise from a rock platform pitted with a multitude of pools. To the north, the cliffs are of old red sandstone, heavily vegetated, and support relics of the pre-improvement heathland flora, such as heather and tormentil, as well as the typical maritime species sea campion and thrift. Caves in the lava cliff, now well above the high-tideline, house hibernating herald moths in winter.

The pebble beach is rich in agates and the rock pools are well populated with seaweeds, as well as with animals such as beadlet sea-anemone, sea-slug, brittle star, sea-urchin, butterfish and chiton. At Port Carrick the shore is sandy, and several pairs of shelduck take up territory in spring before nesting in rabbit burrows on the cliffs. Most of the more usual shorebirds can be seen in summer; winter visitors include occasional less common species such as great northern diver and long-tailed duck.

Enterkine Wood

Permit only; 5ha; SWT reserve
Mixed woodland
Nature trail (1km): leaflet from SWT
April–October.

This attractive and varied mature woodland contains 16 broad-leaved tree species, including lime, and three species of conifer. Many of the trees were probably planted, but natural regeneration of several species is now occurring. Bramble, hazel,

Long-tailed tits suffer badly in severe winters.

hawthorn, honeysuckle and sapling trees give good nesting cover for a large population of woodland birds. Thirty-four species breed, among them blackcap, chiffchaff, goldfinch and woodcock. Bluebells carpet parts of the wood in spring; wood anemone, enchanter's-nightshade, dog's mercury, comfrey, woodruff and great wood-rush all cover considerable areas; and in one place the feathery wood horsetail is common.

A stream runs through the wood, forming a pond where it is checked in its progress by a dam. The strap-like leaves of hart's-tongue adorn a second dam, now in disrepair, and marsh-marigold, yellow iris and golden-saxifrage flourish nearby. The tiny moschatel is less obvious and needs to be searched for.

Above the south bank of the stream, where the ground slopes steeply, is a badger sett. Two tree hides enable visitors to watch these fascinating animals as they go about their nocturnal business.

Falls of Clyde

NS 8841; 55ha; SWT reserve
River gorge and surrounding woodland
Access restricted in Corehouse section of reserve
Visitor centre in New Lanark, tel. Lanark 65262;
ranger service; reserve leaflet
April–July

The spectacularly stepped gorge of the River Clyde separates the two distinct sections of this reserve: Bonnington on the north east bank and Corehouse to the south west. Viewpoints on both banks offer vistas of the river and its falls, framed in mixed woodland. Above the uppermost fall, Bonnington Linn, the river flows deep and still, edged by overhanging banks and small sandy beaches which attract mink and otter. Much of the flow is diverted for hydroelectric purposes at Bonnington and returned to the river below Cora Linn. This middle fall drops 30m in two steps and when the Clyde is in spate, or the water is deliberately released – as happens several times a year by arrangement with the electricity board – spray drenches the basin below and rises mist-like above the level of the gorge. The force of the water in the past has smoothed and pot-holed the rocky floor of the gorge, now exposed and dry for much of the year.

Dundaff Linn, the lowest of the three falls, lies just above New Lanark, once famous for its cotton mills powered by the Clyde, and now being refurbished. Dipper haunt the old mill stream as well as the river; grey wagtail flick their immaculate yellow tails as they flutter from rock to rock; and occasionally a kingfisher streaks over the dark water. The Clyde, here clean and healthy, is well stocked with minnow, trout, grayling and pike, while lamprey have been seen in the mill stream.

Inaccessible ledges on the precipitous gorge sides afford secure nesting sites for kestrel and safe lodging for such interesting plants as purple saxifrage, butterwort and meadow saxifrage. Ferns and mosses abound on the wetter sections of the cliffs and in parts of the woodland.

Falls of Clyde, a famous beauty spot.

Although much of the Bonnington reserve is under conifer plantation there are many deciduous species, and the ground vegetation reflects the fact that this is an area of long-established woodland. Near New Lanark the spring flowers are typical of oakwood – lesser celandine, dog's mercury, bluebell and red campion, with wood avens and marsh-marigold in the damper areas. Further up-river, where the soil is more acid, bilberry, great wood-rush, heather and wood anemone carpet the woodland fringe. Northern marsh-orchid, with its wine-purple flowers, wood vetch and the slender and graceful grass wood millet are among the less common plants on the Bonnington bank.

The Corehouse reserve, originally formal policy woodlands, contains introduced species such as *Sequoia* and rhododendron, as well as native species including oak, alder and yew. Several hundred flowering plants have been recorded here and the variety of the vegetation is increased by marsh-land and an artificial lake. Bogbean, bulrush, water-plantain and an unusual hybrid yellow water-lily grow in or beside the water, while marsh thistle, marsh woundwort and marsh cinquefoil flourish in the surrounding boggy ground.

Garden warbler, chiffchaff and spotted flycatcher are among summer visitors to the woodlands, both green and great spotted woodpecker occur and five species of tit, including long-tailed and the very local willow tit, are present. The woods are rich in fungi and insects – the latter also well represented in the gorge. Badger, roe deer, red squirrel, pipistrelle and Natterer's bat are among the mammals recorded.

Feoch Meadows

Permit only; 10ha; SWT reserve
Meadow on lime-rich rock
Mid-June–July

An unusually rich vegetation – some 140 species of herbs and grasses have been noted – reflects the fact that this site is ancient meadowland. Orchids include fragrant, frog and small-white, and greater and lesser butterfly-orchid. The area attracts a variety of butterflies: 14 species have been recorded, among them the very local large skipper.

Glen Diomhan, Arran

NR 9246; 10ha; NCC reserve
Woodland
No access to fenced part of reserve
Information from NCC, Cairnbaan,
by Lochgilphead, Argyll
May–September

This remote woodland remnant, situated in a steep-sided gorge at over 300m, contains two rare native species of whitebeam, *Sorbus arranensis* and *Sorbus pseudofennica*; both are restricted to north Arran. The scrub includes rowan, birch, juniper, willow, holly and aspen, together with a few specimens of burnet rose.

Goatfell

NR 9941; 2673ha; NTS
Mountainous country, woodland on lower slopes
Guided walks programme: access path from
Brodick Country Park; ranger-naturalist
All year

Goatfell (874m) and its attendant peaks have long been famous among climbers. Sheer slabs, huge hunks of rock and jagged, knife-edge ridges are features of these peaks, many crowned with blocks of granite intricately fissured in all directions. Extensive stretches of the south east slopes have been afforested, but a remnant of older mixed woodland remains near Merkland.

Raven haunt the high corries, and golden eagle are quite often seen over the glens. On the moorland slopes of Beinn a Chliabhain a few golden plover breed, and redpoll nest in the woodlands of lower Glen Rosa. Moorland plants such as heath milkwort and heath spotted-orchid grow on the lower ground and in the glens, where dwarf juniper also occurs. High on the peaks starry saxifrage, mountain sorrel, goldenrod and alpine buckler-fern are among the plants of the granite pavement.

Merkland Wood (NS 023385), with its mature birch, pine, beech and oak, attracts many different woodland birds. Breeding warblers include blackcap, chiffchaff, garden warbler, and wood warbler, and there have been sightings of pied flycatcher.

Lady Isle

Permit only; 11ha; SWT reserve
Small inshore island
May–July

This little island formerly held a very large tern colony which included roseate and Sandwich as well as common and arctic tern. In recent years numbers have decreased greatly, while the population of the larger gulls has shown a marked increase. Eider, mallard, red-breasted merganser and a few shelduck breed, and grey and common seal are present.

Loch Libo

Permit only; 18ha; SWT reserve
Loch, wetland and woodland
April–June: flowers; October–December: wildfowl

White and yellow water-lilies grow in the mineral-rich water of the loch; mare's-tail and several species of pondweed also occur. The surrounding marshland vegetation includes nine species of sedge – among them the very local lesser pond-sedge – bogbean, marsh cinquefoil and cowbane. Moorhen, coot, mallard and mute swan breed on the reserve, the woodland attracts a variety of small birds, and wintering wildfowl include species such as tufted duck, pochard, wigeon, goldeneye and whooper swan.

Lochwinnoch

NS 3558; 230ha; RSPB reserve
Open water, marsh and woodland
Open all year, Thursday, Friday, Saturday and
Sunday, 10a.m.–5.15p.m.; school parties welcome:
contact warden, Largs Road, Lochwinnoch; access
limited to marked paths
Nature centre with displays etc.; two hides; leaflet
from centre or RSPB, Edinburgh
*April–June: breeding birds; October – March:
wildfowl*

The panoramic windows of a tower at the Nature Centre offer commanding views of this reserve and the surrounding countryside. To the north lies Aird Meadow, a stretch of shallow open water surrounded by varied marshland, and edged with trees through which a path leads to the observation hides. Barr Loch, larger, deeper and more open, lies to the south west, on the far side of the A760; access is not allowed. The two stretches of water hold sizeable populations of breeding and wintering birds and support a variety of wetland plants.

Dense beds of reed canary-grass and sedges, with scattered willow scrub, give good cover around Aird Meadow, and additional nesting sites have been provided in the form of small, floating raft-islands. Located within easy viewing distance of the hides, these help visitors to observe breeding species such as black-headed gull and great crested

Secluded pools, like this at Aird Meadows, attract the more secretive ducks such as teal and shoveler.

grebe. With a population of around 11 pairs, the chances of seeing the grebes performing their elaborate courtship display are unusually good for a Scottish site. Mallard, tufted duck, coot and moorhen can often be watched at close range as they lead their broods through the patches of bog-bean in front of the hides. A few teal and shoveler also breed, but they tend to be more secretive and spend much of their time in thick cover.

The strip of mixed woodland along the eastern side of Aird Meadow contains oak, birch, beech and lime with an understorey of rhododendron, hawthorn and dog rose. Many common woodland birds can be seen here, and typical plants such as wood-sorrel, red campion and ramsons are present. Common spotted-orchid and lesser butterfly-orchid occur, and meadowsweet, valerian and purple-loosestrife flourish along the edge of the marsh. Where the water level is higher yellow iris, marsh-marigold and marsh cinquefoil add colour among the sedges and rushes.

In winter Aird Meadow and Barr Loch attract substantial numbers of wildfowl. Wigeon, pochard and goldeneye are usually present as well as mallard, teal and tufted duck, and Barr Loch is used as a roost by greylag geese and whooper swans. As long as the marshes remain unfrozen snipe and heron feed in the shallows; cormorants are also among the regular visitors. Over 154 bird species have been recorded on the reserve in recent years, and 65 species are known to have nested.

The displays in the nature centre describe various aspects of the reserve and its management, and there are facilities for talks and films. Educational use of the reserve is particularly encouraged; school parties are welcome on Monday, Tuesday and Wednesday by arrangement.

Impressive ridges and corries crown Goatfell.

Possil Marsh

Permit only; 28ha; SWT reserve
Open water, marsh and scrub
All year

On the northern edge of Glasgow an exciting and well-known wetland area can be found. This loch with its surrounding marshland and scrub of willow and birch has long been recognised for its variety of plants and animals. The marshland has reedmace beds, marsh cinquefoil meadows and bottle sedge swamp in which greater spearwort, mare's tail and tufted loosestrife all occur. Sedge warbler, reed bunting, and whitethroat breed and the reserve attracts many wintering and migrant birds. Eight species of Tardigrade have been recorded here.

Tayside

Like much of Scotland, Tayside is a region of contrasts, with the imposing Grampians to the north and the green lowland straths and coastal strip to the south and east. This diversity of scenery and habitat is reflected in the variety of wildlife in the region, which includes species characteristic of the mountains, glens and coast. The hills are the home of rare alpine plants and the lowlands are memorable for the vast numbers of grey geese and wildfowl which winter on the many lochs. The hand of man has largely fashioned the lowlands of Tayside, but his impact has been much less in the uplands. A small area around Dundee is industrial, but agriculture predominates in the lowland south, and sporting interests such as deer stalking, game shooting and salmon fishing are catered for farther north.

The scenery and habitats of Tayside relate to its geological skeleton which is dominated by the Highland Boundary Fault, running south west to north east. To its north lie the uplands, mainly metamorphic in origin and composed largely of schists which are locally lime-rich. A band of limestone crosses this area. To the south of the faultline are Devonian sandstones and conglomerates forming the straths, and upwellings of volcanic lavas which have produced the Sidlaw and Ochil hill ranges. Superimposed on the geological skeleton is the reshaping produced by the last glaciation. After the ice sheets melted colonisation by tundra vegetation took place, followed by vast forests of oak, elm and hazel in the lowlands, pine and birch in the highlands. Above these forests grew montane scrub of dwarf birch, dwarf willow and juniper.

Man's impact began with clearance of this forest and scrub, and has continued ever since; now the remaining areas of wildlife habitat are very fragmented, and in the lowlands virtually islands in a sea of intensively farmed land. The other main influence on Tayside is its climate, which has an exceptional range, from the wet, relatively mild, semi-oceanic west to the drier, more continental east. The weather on the mountains can be truly arctic while the sheltered straths are basking in balmy sunshine.

Visitors to the highland area of Tayside find high mountains alternating with sheltered glens. The mountains in the west, the part known as Breadalbane, consist of very lime-rich rock on which grow many rare alpine plants. Queen of these mountains is BEN LAWERS, renowned for its flora, and in the east CAENLOCHAN is of equal interest, although supporting different species partly because of its more continental climate. Other hills have limestone outcrops and Schiehallion even boasts limestone pavements, the quarrying of the best of which has now been made illegal throughout Great Britain. In the north the hills are less lime-rich and so more heathery; here breed peregrine falcon, golden eagle, and the rare but trusting dotterel. Red deer can be seen on most of these hills and are important to the economy of local estates, such as ATHOLL. However this traditional use of the hills is increasingly being replaced by afforestation, skiing, and even mining, with consequent threat to wildlife. In the far west lies the desolate, boggy RANNOCH MOOR, from which the last ice sheet is thought to have radiated.

The highland glens are largely pasture, enhanced by many large lochs – most are harnessed for hydroelectric power, and many enlarged or even created specially for this purpose. In these glens most of the remnants of primeval forest and scrub are to be found, their survival reflecting the attitude of large estate owners who have retained them for their amenity and sporting value. There are Caledonian pinewoods at the BLACK WOOD OF

RANNOCH, mixed gorge woodlands at the PASS OF KILLIECRANKIE, LINN OF TUMMEL and KELTNEYBURN, oakwoods such as at Queen's View and juniper scrub at BALNAGUARD GLEN. These woods, where not in nature reserves, are gradually being either felled or converted to faster-growing conifers as in parts of the HERMITAGE. The pastureland in between has largely been fertilised or reseeded, but here and there untouched areas retain a rich flora with many orchids, as at Keltneyburn, or an old hayfield mixture, as at BRERACHAN MEADOWS.

In the lowland area are many small lochs formed in hollows after the ice sheets retreated. These lochs are spectacular for the thousands of grey geese which roost there on winter evenings after feeding on nearby farmland during the day. Many species of duck also winter on these lochs, the largest of which, LOCH LEVEN, is of international importance and has the VANE FARM Nature Centre alongside. Other places worth a winter visit are BALGAVIES LOCH, LOCH OF KINNORDY, LOCH OF LINTRATHEN, LOCH CRAIGLUSH and the LOCH OF THE LOWES. Many are important for breeding ducks and grebes, but their best-known breeding bird is osprey which has nested at the Loch of the Lowes since the early 1970s. Their plant life is also of interest: in the case of a few lochs high up the stream system it is still relatively unaffected by pollution. Increasingly the sands and gravels surrounding the lochs are being exploited, but afterwards flooded pits can become wildlife habitats in their own right.

The lowlands are bounded to south and east by the sea. Estuaries, sea cliffs and extensive sand dunes are all represented, together with the largest reedbeds in Britain. MONTROSE BASIN is an almost unique landlocked tidal basin whose mudflats are home to large flocks of waders at low tide, and also to ducks and geese. Almost as fine is the TAY ESTUARY (Fife), whose vast reedbeds are now being harvested for thatch. Also worth seeing, especially in summer, are the red sandstone cliffs north of Arbroath, where seabirds nest and many northern and southern plants meet in a blaze of colour. Part of these cliffs is included in the reserve at SEATON CLIFFS. North Sea oil and gas put much of this coastline, particularly the dunes and estuaries, under threat from industrial development and pollution. Recreation too has a considerable impact: many dune systems have been flattened for golf courses and caravan sites.

ROSALIND A.H. SMITH

Atholl

See map; includes 12 sites
All year

For the naturalist Atholl is an area of great interest, as much for its contrasts as for its individual sites or species. For those with little time, a varied collection of reserves, with visitor centres and guided walk programmes, offers a speedy introduction. For those with time to explore at leisure, there are marked right-of-way paths across the lower hill ground, and long-distance routes leading through the mountains to the north. In addition there are many tracks across Forestry Commission land, both among the plantations and out on to the unplanted hill ground above.

As one drives north through central Scotland, approaching Dunkeld a very different type of landscape begins to unfold. A range of low but rugged hills, broken only by occasional passes, stretches away on either side. These hills mark the line of the Highland Boundary Fault, the junction between the rolling landscape of the lowlands and the mountainous country of the north.

Beyond Dunkeld the valley widens to a broad U shape, its steeply sloping sides levelling off above to heathery plateaus, and now runs straight as far as Pitlochry. There the hills again change in character, becoming higher and wilder, topped with peaks instead of plateaus, and at KILLIECRANKIE they close in to form a narrow, gorge-like pass. At Blair Atholl the landscape opens up once more as the road turns slightly westward and heads for exposed Drumochter Summit, at 500m the lowest of the major passes to the north.

This stretch of country provides a wealth of natural history interest. Varied rock types, glacial deposits and river conditions have resulted in a diversity of plant communities. Woodlands of contrasting types clothe the lower hill slopes and fringe the lochs and rivers, and physical difficulties limit cultivation.

The turkey-sized capercaillie, widely distributed in Tayside.

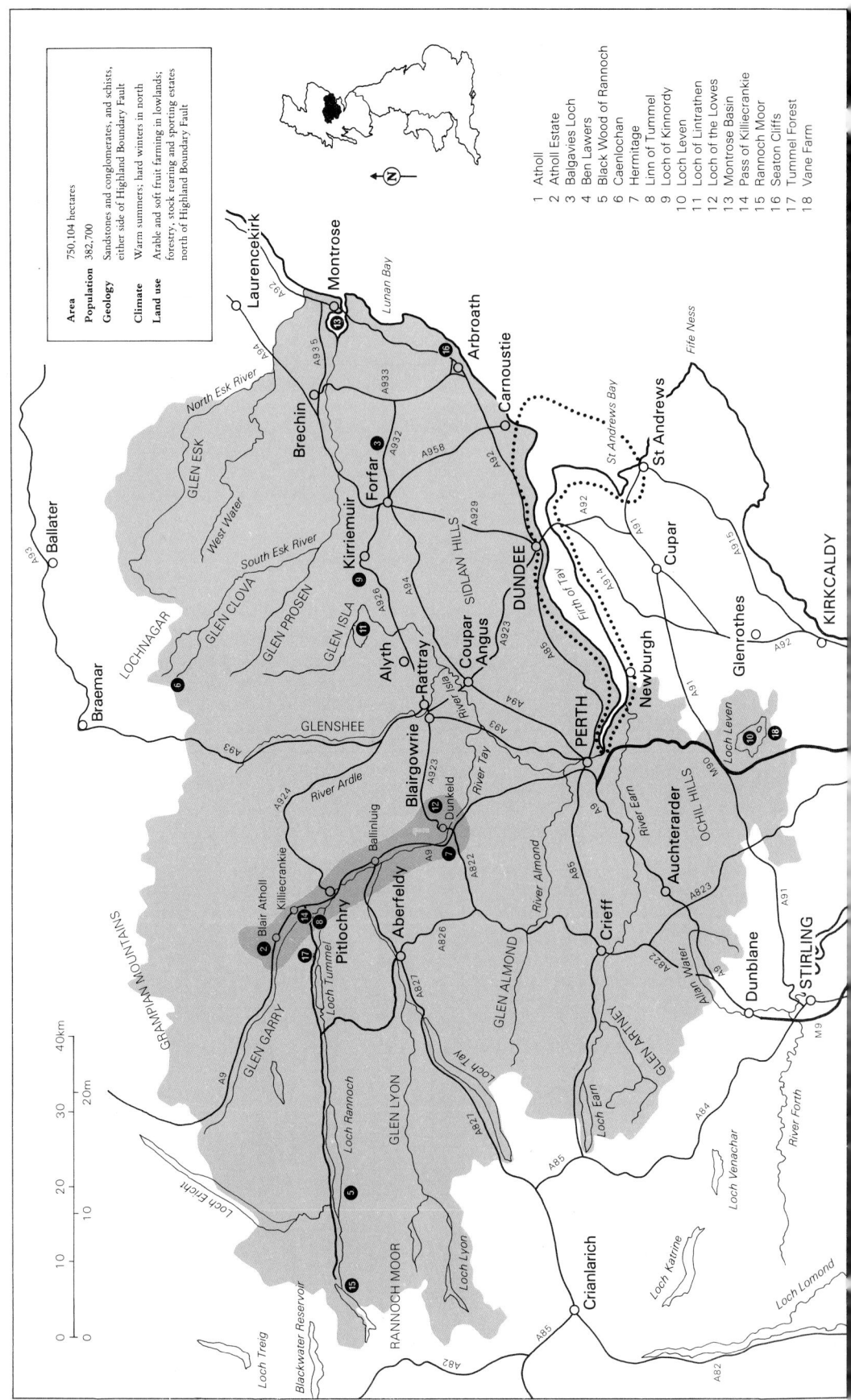

Area	750,104 hectares
Population	382,700
Geology	Sandstones and conglomerates, and schists, either side of Highland Boundary Fault
Climate	Warm summers; hard winters in north
Land use	Arable and soft fruit farming in lowlands; forestry, stock rearing and sporting estates north of Highland Boundary Fault

N

1 Atholl
2 Atholl Estate
3 Balgavies Loch
4 Ben Lawers
5 Black Wood of Rannoch
6 Caenlochan
7 Hermitage
8 Linn of Tummel
9 Loch of Kinnordy
10 Loch Leven
11 Loch of Lintrathen
12 Loch of the Lowes
13 Montrose Basin
14 Pass of Killiecrankie
15 Rannoch Moor
16 Seaton Cliffs
17 Tummel Forest
18 Vane Farm

Although it looks like a single entity the valley has, in fact, three rivers running through it. The Garry, rising high in the hills, is joined by the Tummel above Pitlochry, and at Ballinluig the Tay flows in from the west. The two northernmost, the Garry and the Tummel, have been greatly affected by hydroelectric developments. Beyond Blair Atholl the Garry is reduced to a trickle of water in summer, and can no longer support brown trout. By the time it reaches Killiecrankie tributaries have added greatly to the river's volume, but the flow through the pass, although impressive in spate, is still small in comparison with its former scale. Similarly, the construction of the Clunie Dam has reduced the flow in the Tummel. However, the Faskally Dam at Pitlochry, fed by both the Tummel and the Garry, created a new, large and very beautiful loch. Provision of a fish ladder ensured that the dam did not prevent the movement of salmon upstream to their spawning grounds, while the loch itself attracts a variety of wildfowl.

Below Pitlochry the Tummel spreads itself over a shingly bed and meanders from one side of the valley floor to the other. The same pattern is maintained after it has joined the Tay at Ballinluig, with a variety of oxbow lakes, backwaters and marshy hollows marking the river's earlier routes. Although the River Tay is free of dams and generating stations it has been affected by the reduced flow in its tributaries and by the periodic artificial spates when surplus water is released by the power stations, giving sudden fluctuations in level, even in summer.

A notable feature of the Pitlochry to Dunkeld stretch is the shingle islands. Continuously influenced by erosion and deposition, these islands represent habitats in a constant state of flux. They vary greatly in size and degree of permanency, and carry widely differing plant communities. Many have well-established cover of willow and alder scrub; on some, Scots pine is regenerating nat-urally, with seedlings and young trees of various ages; yet others support colourful stands of blue nootka lupin, yellow broom, red campion, comfrey, stone bramble and melancholy thistle.

Road realignment has threatened some of the surviving remnants of meadowland along the valley. Most of the riverside meadows have long been under cultivation, and it is only on steep banks and in odd pockets that the attractive, varied meadow vegetation remains. Where such pockets survive they are often rich in orchids, and sometimes support such locally uncommon species as maiden pink, giant bellflower, cowslip, kidney vetch and purple milk-vetch. The meadow flora is especially rich where limestone occurs, as it does near Blair Atholl.

In contrast to the situation in many other parts of Scotland, planted conifers have been a familiar sight in this area for well over 100 years. Some 15 million conifers, mostly larches, were planted around Dunkeld by successive dukes of Atholl between 1738 and 1830; trees were even established on the rocky slopes of Craig a Barns, using a cannon to sow the seed! The dukes also carried out extensive amenity planting of hardwoods at Dunkeld and Blair Atholl. Horse-chestnut, beech, walnut and maple were chosen for their form and colour as much as for their timber value; those planted in the grounds of Dunkeld House are still glorious in autumn.

The largest oakwood in the area, Craig Wood, on the ridge between Dunkeld and the LOCH OF THE LOWES, was probably also planted and was at one time coppiced. Invading sycamore, rhododendron and beech are now making it less like an oakwood but offer more cover for birds and animals in the shrub layer. Roe and fallow deer regularly visit this wood, the latter – like the larches – introduced to the area many years ago by a duke of Atholl, and wood warbler, jay and great spotted woodpecker breed here.

Autumn's gold and rust tint the mixed woodlands in the Pass of Killiecrankie.

Some quite large areas of semi-natural birch-wood also still exist, and at BALNAGUARD birch and juniper grow together on the hillside. These woodlands of little or no commercial value are gradually dwindling, their place being taken by conifers. Even the once heather-covered plateaus are beginning to be encroached upon.

The inaccessibility of some of the steeper slopes, together with a series of woodland reserves, should help to ensure that some sizeable areas of semi-natural tree cover survive, however. Such areas are important not only for breeding and wintering birds, but also for migrants. In spring many small, insectivorous migrants, such as warblers and flycatchers, work their way northwards through these sheltered valley woodlands well in the vanguard of the main arrival. The almost continuous tree cover has also allowed green woodpecker, a resident woodland species currently expanding its range, to colonise as far as Blair Atholl without encountering treeless areas.

It is not only woodland species that use this valley as a migration route. Swallow, martin and wagtail follow the river itself, and wheatear and whinchat move along the hillsides above. Geese, both greylag and pink-footed, regularly use this route through the high hills in autumn and in spring. And osprey – including, perhaps, some of those reared at the Lock of the Lowes – follow the rivers, fishing as they go northwards to Speyside.

Ospreys have been regular summer visitors to Tayside since they first nested at the Loch of the Lowes in 1970.

Atholl Estate

NN 8666; 54,000ha; Atholl Estates
Woodland and mountainous countryside
Access restricted to waymarked routes unless accompanied by countryside ranger
Nature trails leaflet from Blair Castle or caravan site

This very large estate includes policy woodlands, extensive conifer plantations and a vast area of open hill ground. Particularly notable is the arboretum at Blair Castle, known as Diana's Grove, which contains an exceptional collection of large conifers. Red deer are plentiful on the hills and the estate as a whole supports a varied collection of plants and animals. Nature trails follow the banks of the River Tilt; the middle section of Glen Tilt is a classic geological site. Right-of-way footpaths lead through Glen Tilt to White Bridge and Deeside, and through Glen Bruar to Glen Feshie and Speyside; both are long, rugged routes requiring adequate equipment and preparation.

Balgavies Loch

NO 528508; 40.5ha; SWT reserve
Loch, fen, carr and woodland
Hide open to public on first Sunday of month, 1–4p.m. groups welcome: apply SWT; access to areas other than hide restricted: apply SWT
April–July: flowers and breeding birds; October–March: wildfowl

Woodland and marsh fringe this sheltered loch, which is important for plants and winter wildfowl. Mixed woodland, willow carr and reedbeds add to the habitat diversity, and a stretch of abandoned railway track demonstrates the rapidity with which the succession towards woodland proceeds. The hide (for which members may obtain a key) overlooks open water, an island and part of the marsh and woodland near the shoreline.

Yellow water-lily and amphibious bistort cover substantial areas of the water surface, bogbean and bulrush also occur, and the fringing vegetation includes yellow iris and cowbane. Osier and crack willow are among the several willow species represented. Tufted loosestrife and coralroot orchid grow in the sedge-dominated fen and fen carr.

Greylag geese coming in at dusk to roost on the loch provide one of the reserve's most spectacular sights and sounds. Other wintering wildfowl include wigeon, shoveler, pochard, goldeneye and goosander. Heron and cormorant often roost in the larger trees near the water, and water rail, woodcock and snipe are regular in winter. Many of the duck species breed in small numbers and great crested grebe are usually present in summer. Kingfisher, whooper swan and ruddy duck visit, the latter probably arriving from LOCH OF KINNORDY.

Otter have been seen on the reserve, and there is a resident population of roe deer. The loch's very rich population of aquatic invertebrate animals has been the subject of intensive study; at least 10 species of pond snail are known to occur.

Ben Lawers: its cliffs and corries are well known for their botanical interest.

Balnaguard Glen

Permit only; 67ha; SWT reserve
Birch–juniper woodland and wooded gorge
Information sheet with permit
April–July

The birch and juniper woodland on the higher ground represents one of the finest examples of this habitat in Tayside. Prostrate and upright forms of juniper are scattered through the open birchwood. Grazing pressure in the past has discouraged regeneration, but some young plants are present, especially on the steep eroding slopes of glacial drift on the northern side of the gorge. Heather and bilberry dominate the ground cover, and there is abundant harebell and bird's-foot-trefoil. Common blue and Scotch argus butterflies are plentiful.

The gorge itself is thickly wooded, with dense thickets of blackthorn, hawthorn and tall bracken on the steeper north west facing slopes. Tree species include alder, ash, oak, elm, hazel, rowan and wild cherry, with occasional whitebeam, aspen, field maple and guelder-rose. The ground flora is richest near the stream, especially around the waterfall. Stone bramble, burnet-saxifrage, alpine bistort, cowslip, rock-rose, fragrant orchid and both mountain and wood melick are among the species present. The site is rich in fungi, and many species of bryophyte are also found.

Birds known to breed include green woodpecker, sparrowhawk, redstart and grey wagtail. Short-eared owl and black grouse frequent the adjoining moorland, and wood warbler and pied flycatcher have been recorded in the woodland. Roe deer are resident in the area, red deer occasionally visit, and both brown and mountain hare have been seen.

Ben Lawers

NN 6138; 3104ha; NTS–NCC reserve
Mountain and moorland
Access to area north of Beinn Ghlas–Ben Lawers–Meall Garbh ridge, and to Meall nan Tarmachan area, restricted 12 August–15 February
Visitor centre open Easter–end September, with display; nature trail; guided walks programme; publications
May–August

Ben Lawers has long been renowned for its arctic–alpine flora. The schists of which this mountain and its neighbours Beinn Ghlas and Meall Garbh are largely composed are rich in lime and other minerals, and very friable. One result is an extensive area of steep, constantly eroding cliff face which supports a varied plant life. The altitude (Ben Lawers summit is 1214m) and exposure of these hills, on which snow often lies late, particularly favour montane species, represented here in great variety. Scree slopes, mountain springs and the grassy sides of corries also hold plant communities of great interest, including several species of very local distribution.

The most luxuriant vegetation is found on the cliff ledges, inaccessible to sheep and deer. Roseroot, angelica, wood crane's-bill and red campion flourish in such places, alongside less common species such as alpine forget-me-not, alpine cinquefoil and alpine saw-wort. Shady crevices among block scree hold woodland plants such as oak fern, wood anemone and moschatel, while yellow saxifrage, hairy stonecrop, alpine scurvygrass and various sedges favour wet gravel springs with a high proportion of bare ground. Even on the lower slopes many of the commoner mountain species, such as alpine lady's-mantle, tormentil and heath bedstraw, are widespread among both the mat-grass-dominated grassland of the glacial drift soils and the bilberry- and lichen-rich vegetation at the lower edge of the schists. Some of the arctic–alpine plants can be seen along the nature trail.

Bird life is comparatively sparse on these rather bare hills, but golden eagle and peregrine are seen occasionally, and buzzard and kestrel more often. Ring ouzel frequent the gullies, and raven sometimes play over the high ridges. A few red grouse and ptarmigan are present, but the species most certain to be visible are carrion and hooded crow, meadow pipit, skylark and wheatear.

Red deer, which move freely between the reserve and the adjacent hill ground, are occasionally seen on the south-facing slopes. Mountain hare are found on high ground, but brown hare are to be seen on the lower slopes only. Common shrew and mole can both penetrate to surprisingly high altitudes.

The insect fauna is rich; northern eggar, fox moth, emperor moth and yellow underwing are among the larger moths likely to be seen. One of the most interesting insects is small mountain ringlet butterfly, for which the Breadalbane hills represent its Scottish headquarters.

Black Wood of Rannoch

NN 5755; 2350ha; FC reserve
Pine forest
Access restricted to forest tracks, starting at
NN 589561 and 536540; there is no vehicular
access to these points
April–August

This important remnant of the Caledonian pine and birch forest is managed as a Forest Nature Reserve, with the aim of conserving, and where necessary restoring, the natural pinewood ecosystem. In parts of the reserve the woodland is open, with fine mature pines from 160 to 250 years old, and a good sprinkling of birch and rowan. Some natural regeneration is occurring, and the trees are of mixed ages. Exotic species planted prior to declaration of the reserve will gradually be removed. Much of the ground cover is bilberry and long heather, with abundant mosses in the damper hollows. Chickweed wintergreen, common wintergreen and lesser twayblade are among the more interesting plant species.

Substantial populations of capercaillie and black grouse inhabit the forest, siskin are common, and Scottish crossbill are known to breed. Summer visitors include redstart, spotted flycatcher and tree pipit. Roe deer are plentiful, and in winter a few red deer are sometimes present.

The Black Wood and the birchwoods on its western fringe are internationally important for their insects; many rare and local species are recorded. The Camghouran birchwoods are particularly noted for their moths.

The Black Wood of Rannoch represents a habitat that once covered much of the Highlands.

Many of the species in the Black Wood can also be seen along the forest trails starting from Carie (NN 617573), where there is ample car parking. From there it is also possible to join the right-of-way path leading from Loch Rannoch over the hills to Innerwick in Glen Lyon.

Brerachan Meadows

Permit only; 0.5ha; SWT reserve
Uncultivated meadow
May–July

Globeflower, spignel, melancholy thistle and quaking-grass are among the 119 plant species recorded in this remnant of former hay meadow, part of which is subject to periodic flooding.

Caenlochan

NO 2070; 3639ha; NCC reserve
Mountains and steep glens
Access restricted 1 June – 20 October; contact NCC
(SE Region), Edinburgh for advice
April–May

Stretching from the Devil's Elbow road to Glen Isla
and Glen Clova, this large reserve includes high
level plateaus and several steep corries with exposures of lime-rich rocks. The cliff ledges in these
corries support a very varied flora including many
arctic–alpine species; among them are montane
willows, purple saxifrage, alpine bistort, alpine
meadow-rue and northern bedstraw. *Cladonia*
lichens, stiff sedge and woolly fringe-moss are
widespread on the summit plateaus, each dominating the plant community where it occurs. Carnation sedge and broad-leaved cottongrass are
found on the Glen Shee side, with yellow saxifrage
around open lime-rich flushes.

Large numbers of red deer frequent the corries
and summits, and fox and blue hare are not uncommon. There is a large population of ptarmigan
on the reserve, golden plover and dunlin breed on
the plateaus, ring ouzel haunt the corries, and
golden eagle are quite often seen over the glens.

Hermitage

NO 0142; 15ha; NTS
Woodland, gorge and falls
Booklet from Pass of Killiecrankie Visitor Centre,
The Ellshop, Dunkeld or NTS, Edinburgh; guided
walks; nature trail; ranger-naturalist
April–October

There is a long history of conifer planting around
Dunkeld and the trees close to the River Braan
include many particularly fine specimens of Douglas and silver fir, Norway spruce and larch. Along
the river bank alder, birch and wild cherry
contrast with the conifers, and attract birds such as
long-tailed tit and willow warbler. Dipper and
grey wagtail nest near the falls and can often be
watched from the bridge over the gorge, as can
salmon making vain attempts to leap up the falls.

649

Keltneyburn

Permit only; 31 ha; SWT reserve
Meadow and wooded gorge
Parties by arrangement with SWT
Reserve booklet
Mid-May–mid-July

In the meadow section of this reserve – part of which is marshy – comparatively lime-rich soil and minimal management for agricultural purposes have resulted in a very varied flora. Greater butterfly-orchid, frog, small-white and fragrant orchid are among the abundant orchids recorded. Other species of interest include field gentian, globeflower, spignel, burnet-saxifrage, mountain everlasting and the curious little fern, moonwort. Encroaching bracken and birch scrub are a potential threat to this attractive meadow, and active management is needed to keep them in check.

The gorge section of the reserve, the Den of Keltney, is precipitous and difficult of access, with much loose material on the steep upper slopes. Broad-leaved woodland – predominantly ash, hazel, wych elm and oak at the lower end, and birch above – clothes the sides of the den. Typical woodland herbs such as dog's mercury and ramsons occur, and lily-of-the-valley is also present. The humid conditions deep within the gorge are reflected in a rich growth of ferns, mosses and liverworts.

Killiecrankie

Permit only; 380 ha; RSPB reserve
Deciduous woodland, cliffs and moorland
May–July

Stretching from the rock-strewn bed of the River Garry to the heather moorland over 300m above, this reserve encompasses a wide variety of habitats. Perhaps the most important is the oak-dominated woodland which clothes the lower slopes: here wood warbler, redstart, green woodpecker and great spotted woodpecker breed. The birch-clad hillside and rugged cliffs above hold redpoll, tree pipit, buzzard, kestrel and raven, while on the moorland curlew nest and blackcock gather to display at the lek.

The reserve is of considerable botanical interest. A variety of ferns grows among the jumble of rocks and moss-covered tree trunks in the gorge, and other plants include wood vetch, yellow saxifrage and shining crane's-bill. Many of the species on this reserve can also be seen in the PASS OF KILLIECRANKIE, to which there is unrestricted access.

Linn of Tummel

NN 9160; 20 ha; NTS
Wooded river banks
Nature trail (3.5km); booklet from Pass of Killiecrankie Visitor Centre and The Ellshop, Dunkeld; car park at NN 913610; ranger-naturalist
April–October

Varied woodland, largely deciduous, covers much of this area, which lies at the confluence of the Rivers Garry and Tummel. Oak and beech are dominant in some places, a mixture of birch, hazel and alder predominates in others, and there is a stand of Scots pine on the north bank of the Tummel. Many exotic conifers are also present. The ground vegetation varies with the tree cover, being quite rich in the most natural areas of the woodland. Here mountain and wood melick, stone bramble, primrose, common wintergreen, goldilocks buttercup, lily-of-the-valley and common dog-violet occur. Elsewhere heather is dominant, and there is abundant bilberry and bracken.

Red-breasted merganser, goosander, dipper and grey wagtail are among the birds regularly seen along the rivers, while greylag geese from the feral flock on Loch Faskally often graze on the fields beside the path. Breeding woodland birds include siskin, redpoll, long-tailed tit and treecreeper; capercaillie visit the heathery glades, and great spotted and green woodpecker frequent the area. Roe deer and red squirrel are also quite common.

Loch of Craiglush

Permit only; 35.5 ha; SWT reserve
Loch with fringing marsh and woodland
All year

Similar in many ways to the neighbouring LOCH OF THE LOWES, and linked to it by a wide canal, this loch can be viewed from the A923. The area around the loch is kept as free from disturbance as possible, and permits are granted only to bona fide research workers.

Loch of Kinnordy

NO 3653; 81 ha; RSPB reserve
Loch with surrounding marsh and woodland fringe
Reserve visiting April–August, Wednesday, Saturday, Sunday; September–November, Sunday only, 10a.m.–5p.m.
Two hides with information display
April–June: breeding birds; October–November: wildfowl

Birds dominate the scene virtually all year round. In summer there is the constant noise and movement of the several thousand-strong colony of black-headed gulls and in winter up to 5000 greylag geese flight in at dusk to roost on the loch. But these are only the most obvious of the great variety of waterbirds that breed on, or visit, the loch.

Vast mats of the tangled rhizomes of bogbean and cowbane form floating islands on which the gulls nest. There is constant bickering between adjacent birds for the available space. Amidst all this activity the presence of other waterbirds can easily be overlooked, but patient scanning of the open water between islands is likely to reveal at least six duck species as well as coot, moorhen, dabchick and great crested grebe. Of the ducks, the shoveler drakes, resplendent in chestnut, green and white, are the most noticeable. The waters of

Kinnordy, enriched by drainage from adjoining farmland, and also by the droppings of the huge bird population, are ideal for this species. Mallard, teal, gadwall, pochard and tufted duck are also regularly present in summer. A much more surprising record is that of breeding ruddy duck. This dumpy, stiff-tailed duck is a North American species which now breeds wild in England; to date Kinnordy is its only Scottish nesting site.

Reeds and willow scrub, with a windbreak of spruce and an isolated group of pines, fringe the loch and provide habitat for woodland birds. Sedge warbler and reed bunting nest in the willow scrub, while waders such as snipe, curlew and redshank breed in the drier areas of the marsh. The mud exposed by the low water levels of summer is an ideal feeding ground for waders: soft enough for easy probing, yet firm enough to support the weight of a bird. Waders on passage are attracted to the mud, too: ruff, greenshank and spotted redshank have all been recorded here in autumn. It was in spring, however, that another Kinnordy 'special' appeared – a cattle egret, one of only a very few seen in Scotland in recent years.

Much of the summer marshland vanishes under a sheet of water in winter. Many more duck are on the loch at this season, including sizeable flocks of wigeon. From October onwards the greylag geese appear at dusk: clamorous flocks flight in from their feeding grounds on the surrounding farmland and whiffle down on to the tree-fringed loch, to

bathe and rest until dawn. Only when ice covers the water do wildfowl numbers drop right away, leaving only a few mallard, with coot and moorhen sheltering in the willow scrub. It is in this kind of weather that birds of prey such as hen harrier and short-eared owl are most likely to be seen, hunting over the tall marsh vegetation for mice and voles.

Loch Leven

NO 1501; 1597ha; NCC reserve
Large freshwater loch
Access restricted to Kirkgate Park, Findatie, Burleigh Sands and Loch Leven Castle; permit required to visit other parts of reserve and granted only to bona fide research workers: apply NCC (SE Region), Edinburgh
Late September–March: wintering wildfowl; April–August: breeding duck

Loch Leven is one of the most important wildfowl sites in Europe and holds the greatest concentration of breeding duck in Britain. Its shallow waters and the surrounding fertile farmland provide rich winter feeding grounds for a wide variety of wildfowl species, and its islands offer a relatively safe nesting place for large numbers of duck.

The loch is one of a small number of major arrival points for pink-footed geese in autumn, and in years when they arrive in daylight a continuous stream of skeins can be seen coming in from the north and dropping on to the water. Once down, the geese rest on and around St Serf's Island before

Many duck nest on Loch Leven's islands and lead their broods to the sheltered eastern shore.

Man-made lagoons attract waterbirds near Vane Farm.

dispersing to feed on nearby fields or moving on to their wintering grounds elsewhere. Greylag geese arrive later and in smaller numbers, but a much larger proportion of the birds remain in the area all winter. Barnacle, brent, Canada, white-fronted and snow geese appear as stragglers in most seasons, and whooper swan are present throughout the winter.

Most of the 1000 or so pairs of breeding duck nest on the 42ha St Serf's Island, the majority among tussocks of tufted hair-grass or reed canary-grass, and often surprisingly close together. Many of the 500–600 pairs of tufted duck choose sites within the several thousand-strong colony of black-headed gull. Mallard, gadwall, wigeon, shoveler and shelduck also nest on the island.

Although the once-extensive areas of marsh were greatly diminished when the water level was lowered 150 years ago, the wetter fields around the loch still hold quite large numbers of breeding waders, such as lapwing, oystercatcher, snipe, curlew and redshank. A few common sandpiper and ringed plover also nest near the shore. In late summer large areas of mud are exposed along the north side of St Serf's Island, attracting a variety of passage waders. Dunlin, jack snipe, greenshank and ruff occur regularly in small numbers, and golden plover are found in flocks of up to 500. Other species, such as green sandpiper, black-tailed godwit and spotted redshank, are occasionally recorded.

Many changes in Loch Leven's animal and plant populations have been noted in recent years, largely resulting from enrichment of the loch by run-off from the surrounding farmland. Only small patches of common reed and reed canary-grass

now remain where there used to be extensive reed-beds. Once-dense beds of Canadian pondweed and stonewort have virtually disappeared, pondweed species of value as waterfowl food plants have much decreased, and thick algal blooms have become a frequent occurrence. There have also been associated changes in invertebrate life; dragonflies and mayflies are no longer seen, and freshwater shrimps are less abundant, but there are still vast numbers of the non-biting chironomid midge, upon whose larvae many of the duck feed. These large midges are so numerous that on a still summer's day they look like clouds of smoke as they rise and fall in columns above the trees.

Loch Leven is also famous for its fish, especially brown trout. Perch, pike and stickleback are also present, and there are roach and brook lamprey in the inflow streams. Both fishing and wildfowling on the loch are carried out on a commercial basis and under strict control, as they have been for many years. In addition to these traditional uses and its well-established importance for wildfowl research, Loch Leven now also serves, through the RSPB's activities at Loch Leven Nature Centre, VANE FARM, as a valuable resource for conservation education. This site is listed under the Ramsar Convention for the conservation of wetlands.

Loch of Lintrathen

NO 2755; 162ha; SWT reserve
Reservoir
Access to hide restricted to members except on advertised open days; no access elsewhere on reserve
October–April

Very large numbers of wildfowl visit this deep loch during the winter. In late October and November the numbers of greylag geese coming in from neighbouring farmland to roost may be as high as 5000, and their arrival and descent on to the water at dusk looks and sounds impressive. The number of mallard occasionally exceeds 3000; like the geese they leave the loch to feed elsewhere. Diving ducks, dependent on the loch for their food supply, are less numerous, although several hundred tufted duck are sometimes present along with smaller numbers of goldeneye. Shoveler generally appear for a short time in October and teal, wigeon and whooper swan all occur regularly. There is a heronry near the loch, and at times as many as 30 of these handsome birds gather in the vicinity of the hide.

Loch of the Lowes

NO 0544; 98ha; SWT reserve
Loch with fringing woodland and marsh
Access limited to centre, hide and unfenced section of south shore
Visitor centre open April–September (see below); hide open at all times; handbook and leaflets; parties and educational groups should book, tel. Dunkeld 337; ranger service
April–June: breeding birds; July: young ospreys, if present; late October–March: geese

Although the view from the hide is always attractive, with a backdrop of rugged hillside setting off the reed- and tree-fringed loch, the most rewarding times for a visit to this reserve are early morning and late evening in midsummer. Then mallard ducklings may feed almost under the hide, diving terns may make an audible splash as they hit the water, and water rails may be screaming in the reedbeds. By mid-July the fat buds of white water-

lilies are opening, and if the ospreys have nested successfully the young birds are likely to be indulging in energetic bouts of wing flapping. It is even possible that the observer will share the hide with a treecreeper busily feeding its brood.

The reserve's chief interest lies in the diversity of habitats and species it contains. Here, at the very edge of the Highlands, plants and animals typical of both upland and lowland Scotland occur. Most of the reserve is water, much of it shallow, but the narrow fringe of woodland and marsh are significant in contributing towards species diversity. In the loch aquatic plants typical of nutrient-poor Highland lochs – quillwort, shoreweed, water lobelia and bogbean – grow near species characteristic of silts rich in nutrients, such as yellow water-lily and amphibious bistort. Common reed, reed canary-grass and sedges border the western bay, and provide cover for nesting grebes and for resident roe deer as they come down to drink.

The loch's wealth of invertebrate life supplies food for brown trout, perch, pike and eels, as well as diving ducks. Tufted duck, mallard and teal breed on the reserve, and goldeneye, goosander, red-breasted merganser, wigeon and pochard occur regularly. Over 1000 greylag geese usually roost on the loch in late autumn.

The Loch of the Lowes has been noted for its great crested grebes since the first Scottish breeding was recorded there in 1870. The normal population is now four or five pairs, and their display dance is a fascinating sight. Little grebe also breed on the reserve, and in 1973 the very decorative Slavonian grebe nested here, the first recorded breeding south of the Grampians.

Containing both highland and lowland species, the Loch of the Lowes is of particular interest.

The bird most people hope to see from the hide is the handsome osprey. These birds have not nested successfully every season, however, since they first appeared in 1969 shortly after the reserve was established. One year there was an 'eternal triangle' with two females incubating side-by-side, amicably but unproductively, and in other seasons they have sometimes failed to lay. But they have reappeared at the loch and spent some time there every year.

Scots pine, the species most favoured by nesting osprey, is just one of the wide range of native trees in the reserve's fringing woodland. Oak, ash, hazel, holly, alder and five species of willow are present, and juniper, wild cherry and bird cherry are frequent. Because the woodland strip between loch and road is so narrow, the ground flora includes not only the expected species, such as wood anemone, wood-sorrel and primrose, but also plants much more commonly associated with disturbed ground, for example pineappleweed and colt's-foot.

The mixed woodland attracts a varied bird population. Both green and great spotted woodpecker occur; common redstart, spotted flycatcher, grasshopper and wood warbler are among the summer visitors and siskin and redpoll are common in winter. Capercaillie occasionally visit the reserve; black grouse can be heard at their lek on a nearby hillside; and goldcrest and long-tailed tit frequent the birch and juniper near the Centre.

Few of the reserve's mammals are likely to be seen during the day, but badger, otter, wild cat, fox and red squirrel are known to occur. Roe deer appear quite often at dawn and dusk, and fallow deer, from a long-established herd on the hills to the north, sometimes forage in the woodland.

The visitor centre contains a display and tape-slide programme on the reserve and its wildlife; full lists of all species recorded to date are available for reference. High-powered binoculars are provided in the hide during the summer.

Montrose Basin

NO 6957; 1125ha; SWT–Angus DC reserve
Large estuarine inlet
Permit only to hides.
Leaflet and ranger
October–March

At low tide this almost circular basin is a vast expanse of mud, with the deep trough of the River South Esk winding near the southern shore, and minor channels patterning the main flats. Emerald-green sea lettuce provides splashes of colour on the mud, and the mussel beds along the course of the Esk give a strong contrast in textures. Many thousands of wildfowl and waders come to this estuary in autumn and winter, some soon moving on while others remain throughout the winter.

The Basin is particularly noted for its populations of redshank, knot, oystercatcher, curlew and dunlin. Each species reaches peak numbers at a different time: curlew in August and March; redshank in September and March; oystercatcher in October and November; knot in January; and dunlin in February. Although birds are widely scattered over the mud at low tide, the feeding area most favoured is near the river channel. Most birds roost at the north west corner of the Basin, with curlew, redshank and dunlin moving on to the

Viewed from above, the network of channels in the Montrose Basin mud is clearly visible.

A cormorant 'hangs out to dry'.

fields behind the seabank during very high tides, although oystercatcher tend to gather in the south east corner, where there is a shingle ridge. Many other wader species are recorded on migration, often being found in the pools and marshy mud channels around the Lurgies. Small numbers of oystercatcher, redshank and snipe breed in the area.

It is the rich feeding provided by invertebrates, and especially the abundant *Hydrobia* snail, in the mud that attracts these large numbers of waders. The presence of glasswort and three species of eelgrass helps to draw large flocks of duck to the area. Several thousand wigeon are often present, with smaller numbers of mallard, teal and pintail; this is one of the few Scottish east coast sites where pintail appear regularly. There is a sizeable winter population of shelduck, which also breed on the reserve. Eider, too, are year-round residents, nesting on the seabanks and around the edges of the fields, and feeding on the mussels. A group of non-breeding mute swans is also present throughout the year, the numbers peaking in July and August when the area is an important moulting ground. Both greylag and pink-footed geese use the estuary for roosting; the site is of national importance for the latter. Numbers are smaller than in the past, but it is hoped that the flocks will build up again as disturbance decreases.

Other birds of the Basin include cormorant – often seen 'hanging out to dry' on sandbanks – and both common and arctic tern, fishing 'in the shallows. Sedge warbler breed in the area and both they and swallow use the reedbeds at the west side as a migration roost; water rail have also been recorded here. Salmon and sea trout pass up the

South Esk – there is an old-established salmon-netting station near the mouth of the estuary – and seals occasionally follow them into the Basin. Eels are trapped as they make their way down to the sea, and local fishermen farm the mussels and dig in the mud for bait. To reconcile these traditional activities with wildfowling and the more recently introduced recreational sailing and wind-surfing presents a great challenge to those responsible for managing and conserving this relatively new reserve.

Pass of Killiecrankie

NN 917627; 22ha; NTS
Wooded gorge
Visitor centre, open Easter–September (see below); guided walks; ranger-naturalist
April–October

Oak dominates this woodland on the steep banks of the River Garry, but many other tree species, including bird cherry, are also present. The ground flora includes very local flowering plants such as wood vetch, bird's-nest orchid, stone bramble, melancholy thistle and giant bellflower, as well as many more widespread species.

Wood warbler, redstart and spotted flycatcher are among the small birds breeding in the oakwood; dipper and grey wagtail frequent the rocky gorge; and woodcock and great spotted woodpecker are also regularly recorded. The gorge itself is of considerable geological interest.

The visitor centre contains a display on the wildlife of the area, and serves as base for ranger-guided walks. Paths from the pass link up with the LINN OF TUMMEL trail.

Looking east from Loch Ba, Argyll, the wet wilderness of Rannoch Moor stretches away into Perthshire.

Rannoch Moor

NN 4053; 1499ha; NCC reserve
Peaty moorland, lochs and bogs
April–July

This is an area of trackless, hummocky terrain with an intricate mosaic of bogs, peat hags, lochans and small pools occupying the hollows. The reserve, which includes part of Loch Laidon, lies at an altitude of about 360m and is notoriously bleak in bad weather. The diversity of mire types provides the main scientific interest of the area. Plants associated with the mires and of particular interest include Rannoch-rush, for which Rannoch Moor is now the only British site. All three species of bladderwort are present, and dwarf birch also occurs. Red and roe deer graze the reserve, and a variety of moorland birds and waterbirds breed there.

Seaton Cliffs

NO 667416; 10.5ha; SWT reserve
Coastal cliffs
Nature trail (5km); booklet from information centre, 105 High Street, Arbroath
May–August

There is colour here whatever the weather or season, with the sandstone cliffs glowing richly red against grey sea and green grass. In early summer sweet-smelling white scurvygrass cascades down the slopes, and clumps of thrift and bird's-foot-trefoil provide splashes of pink and yellow. Primroses and violets bloom in the most sheltered corners, and where springs create marshy conditions there is a lush growth of meadowsweet and meadow crane's-bill. In a few places scattered spikes of marsh-orchid, early-purple orchid and heath spotted-orchid occur. The vetches growing along the cliff top represent an interesting mixture of maritime and non-maritime species; tufted vetch and wood vetch grow alongside the more truly maritime purple milk-vetch.

The cliff vegetation attracts a variety of butterflies and moths. Green-veined white butterflies are among the earliest to appear, visiting the scurvygrass; common blue and meadow brown are abundant in summer. The vividly coloured six-spot burnet moth flaunts its metallic green and red body in leisurely flight, and in the sandy bank alongside the path solitary bees excavate their burrows. Several species of snail occur among the vegetation of these lime-rich cliffs, many of them attractively banded or mottled.

Seaton Cliffs harbour few seabirds since the alternating layers of coarse sandstone and pebbly conglomerate, which slope to seaward, do not provide suitable nest sites. They do, however, weather to form spectacular arches, blow-holes and caves, some of which are occupied by breeding house martin. Fulmar, kittiwake and guillemot can be seen offshore in summer, while eider and seals are regular visitors to the bays. Many migrant birds have been recorded in the area in autumn and winter. The flat shelves of seaweed-strewn rock exposed at low tide attract waders, as well as being of interest for the marine life contained within the pools.

Tummel Forest

NN 865597; 6800ha; FC
Woodland and lochs
Visitor centre open April–September; guided walks
programme; audio-visual programme; leaflet
All year

Below the famous Queen's View overlooking Loch
Tummel a walk leads through the mixed deciduous
woodland which still clothes the steep slopes. Oak,
ash, hazel, alder and birch are the most abundant
trees in this area, over dog's mercury, wood
anemone, wood-sorrel, marsh hawk's-beard, herb-
Robert, climbing corydalis and broad buckler-fern.
Redstart, wood warbler, spotted flycatcher, jay
and great spotted woodpecker breed.

Limestone ridges are exposed around Lochan na
Leathain at 400m on the hills above Queen's View,
where the vegetation includes thyme, quaking-
grass, fairy flax, bearberry and common reed. The
more acid lochs nearby support water horsetail,
water lobelia and common spike-rush. Mallard,
teal, wigeon and Canada geese breed near these
lochs, and there is a colony of black-headed gulls
on Lochan na Leathain. There are capercaillie and
goldcrest in the conifer forest, with black grouse
along the fringes.

Vane Farm

NT1699; 185ha; RSPB reserve
Loch shore, woodland, moor and farmland
April–December: open daily except Friday,
10a.m.–5p.m.: January–March: open weekends
only 10a.m.–4p.m.; parties should book, tel.
Kinross 62355; access limited to nature trail and
picnic area
Nature centre; trail; hide; educational facilities (see
below); leaflet from centre or RSPB, Edinburgh
October–March

From the upper floor of the reserve's nature centre,
using the high-powered binoculars provided, the
late autumn spectacular of LOCH LEVEN's vast flocks
of geese can be enjoyed in comfort whatever the
weather. The windows have a panoramic view of the
southern part of the loch and the farmland around,
and it is possible to observe both the movement of
the geese and the many duck that frequent the area
between Vane Farm and St Serf's Island.

Much of the farmland included in the reserve is
managed at least partly for the benefit of birds, and
the two main arable crops, barley and potatoes,
provide good autumn gleanings for the geese and
attract them close to the centre. Another feature
that brings a variety of species within easy viewing
distance is a lagoon, complete with islands, created
some years ago in a low-lying marshy field. This
offers shelter, feeding grounds and nesting sites for
both ducks and waders in an area where the loch
shore is rather bare and exposed.

In addition to the autumn invasion of pink-
footed geese and the wintering flock of greylag,
there are occasional sightings of barnacle, Canada,
brent and white-fronted geese. Tufted duck, mallard and pochard are regularly seen from the
centre, and quite often other species such as teal,
wigeon, gadwall and goldeneye are also present.
Waders either breeding in the area or likely to be
recorded on migration include curlew, redshank,
greenshank and ringed plover.

The lower slopes of Vane Hill behind the Centre
carry rather sparse birch woodland, which gives
way to heather moor above. It is through this area
that the nature trail is routed. A programme of
fencing and planting is under way with the aim of
increasing the woodland cover. Many of the commoner small woodland birds breed either among
the birches or in the nearby conifer plantation.
Insects include digger bees and wasps which
burrow in the trailside sandy banks; and several
species of aquatic invertebrates inhabit the small
streams. From the viewpoint high on the moorland
the view of Loch Leven and its surrounding hills
is spectacular.

Although the range of habitats is limited, and
the bird life not particularly rich, there is much
here of value for educational purposes – and education is a primary aim on this reserve. In addition
to the observation windows, the nature centre contains a display on the history and ecology of Loch
Leven, and a variety of identification games and
other items designed to interest children. Special
facilities are available for primary school groups:
these include preparatory and follow-up materials,
and the services of a teacher-naturalist during the
visit.

Supplement

England

Avon and Somerset

Axbridge Hill

Permit only; 11.5ha; STNC reserve
Limestone grassland and scrub
Spring, summer

The south-facing steep grassland slopes above Ax-bridge support the rare Somerset hair-grass. The scrub area is important for breeding birds, and there is a cave (which is not open to the public) containing greater horseshoe bats.

Beer Wood

ST 413316; 13ha; STNC reserve
Ancient woodland
Spring

The reserve of oak, ash, small-leaved lime and maple has a rich understorey and ground flora. There are superb views over the Somerset Levels.

Bickenhall Old Churchyard

ST286197; 0.2ha; WdT reserve
Trees, grassland
Spring, summer

Old churchyards can be important for wildlife and this one, which has now been deconsecrated, is no exception. It contains areas of unimproved grassland with many meadow flowers. There is a massive ancient yew tree, in the tradition of churchyards.

Bishops Knoll

ST 553754; 2.4ha; WdT reserve
Mixed woodland
Spring, summer

An attractive wood at the western end of the Avon Gorge. Mature trees and new planting enhance the scenery leading to the Clifton Suspension Bridge.

Boon's Copse

Permit only; 3.6ha; STNC reserve
Ancient woodland
Spring

The copse, a remnant of the medieval Neroche Royal Forest, is mainly ash and oak, with an abundance of wild service-tree and aspen. Nightingales can often be heard singing, and the good selection of woodland butterflies includes the white admiral.

Cheddar Wood Fields

Permit only; 2.5ha; STNC reserve
Limestone grassland and scrub
Summer

The south-facing grasslands adjoin CHEDDAR WOODS and are important for blue gromwell, a British *Red Data Book* plant. Invertebrates are also of interest.

Chilton Moor

Permit only; 2.8ha; STNC reserve
Grazing marsh
Summer

A key area of the Somerset Levels, snipe and redshank breed here, and there is a good wetland flora.

Chivers Knoll

ST657569; 0.2ha; WdT reserve
Mixed woodland
Spring, summer

This small but prominent wood is an important landmark in the area. It originated as the spoil heap of a small coal-mine that operated for a short time in the eighteenth century.

Holford

Permit only; 5.3ha; STNC reserve
Ancient woodland
Spring

Also known as the Kelting reserve, this oak–ash woodland with alder, willow and thorn scrub lies at the downstream end of Holford Glen.

Littleton Wood

Lies only in Gloucestershire (see p. 183), not in Avon.

Mounsey

Permit only; 57ha; STNC reserve
Ancient woodland and marshes
All year

Many rare lichens and bryophytes are associated with this very important western oak and ash wood in the Barle Valley. Redstarts, pied flycatchers and wood warblers all breed in high numbers. The valley meadows support interesting plant and butterfly populations.

North Lodge Copse

ST 397123; 0.5ha; WdT reserve
Mixed woodland
Spring, summer

A small roadside wood with a good variety of tree species.

Otterhead Lakes

ST 224141; 8ha; STNC reserve
Woodland, marsh and lakeside
Nature trail leaflet from STNC or on site
All year

The reserve surrounds two lakes managed by Wessex Water Authority as a fishery and water-supply source. The marsh and woodland are of interest for breeding birds, dragonflies and bog plants.

Perry Mead

Permit only; 2.5ha; STNC reserve
Meadowland
Summer

A small area of meadows which adjoins the River Cary and has a good wetland flora.

Searts Copse

ST 671302; 0.3ha; WdT reserve
Deciduous wood
Spring, summer

Despite its small size, the copse – with large oaks and a hazel understorey – is rich in plants and insects. Its variety is enhanced by an interesting wet area.

Swell Wood

ST 361238; 30ha; RSPB reserve
Deciduous woodland
Spring, summer

On the south side of WEST SEDGEMOOR wetland reserve lies this strip of woodland. A deciduous wood with a good variety of trees and shrubs, the site is most important for its heronry. Over 60 pairs of herons have been counted, making it one of the largest colonies in southern England. Jackdaws, marsh tits, nuthatches and woodpeckers also nest in the mature oaks, while nightingales, blackcaps and garden warblers are found in the open areas with a dense shrub layer.

Upton Cheyney

ST 699704; 2.8ha; WdT reserve
Mixed woodland
Spring, summer

Three fields have been planted up with mixed broadleaf trees to create a small woodland characteristic of the rolling countryside of the area.

Wellington Hill

ST 139175; 10ha; STNC reserve
Ancient woodland and meadowland
Spring, early summer

A very attractive reserve below the Wellington Monument which overlooks the Vale of Taunton Deane. The meadows are full of interesting plants and butterflies, and lie within a scattering of oak–hazel coppice.

Wells Conservation Centre

ST 564458; 1ha; STNC reserve
Wildlife education centre
Group visits by arrangement
All year

An old cemetery and chapel restored as a wildlife garden, display centre and educational facility.

Westhay Heath

Permit only; 6ha; STNC reserve
Peat workings, reedbed and scrub
Dangerous site, permit must be obtained from STNC
Summer

The area of worked-out peat excavations has been flooded to create open water pools, reedbeds and fringing marsh vegetation. The reserve supports important populations of water-rail.

Withial Combe

ST 576375; 7ha; STNC reserve
Ancient woodland
Spring

The steeply incised gully and waterfall has fringing woodland of oak, ash and small-leaved lime, but unfortunately parts of the area have been decimated by Dutch elm disease. There is a rich ground flora.

Wyndham Woods

Permit only; 16.6ha; STNC reserve
Ancient woodland
Spring, summer

Two wet, low-lying woods near Williton which support a rich ground flora with several typical ancient woodland indicator plants.

Bedfordshire and Huntingdonshire

Barton Hills

TL 089297; 44ha; NCC reserve
Chalk grassland, scrub, deciduous woodland
Leaflet available from NCC, East Midlands Region
Spring, summer

The reserve lies in a chalk coombe with steep slopes covered by grassy downland grading into scrub and woodland. A spring rises at the head of the coombe and feeds a chalk stream which runs along the valley. An old quarry has recolonised with a rich variety of downland flowers. In spring the cowslips and pasqueflower can be seen, and these are followed by field fleawort, fragrant and spotted orchids, the clustered bellflower, carline thistle and knapweed. The flowers attract a number of butterflies, including brown argus and chalkhill blue, as well as many species of beetle. At the top of the east-facing valley lies Leete Wood, an ancient beech woodland, which also contains wayfaring tree, spindle and yew.

Dropshort Marsh

Permit only; 2ha; B and HWT reserve
Grassland and marsh
Spring, summer

A large number of both marsh and meadow species occur. In May several large blocks of marsh-marigold are in flower with bugle and cuckoo-flower. The summer flowers include marsh valerian, lesser spearwort, marsh arrowgrass, ragged robin, common spotted-orchid, marsh pennywort and fen bedstraw in the wet areas and devil's-bit scabious, lady's-mantle, betony, harebell, tormentil, yellow rattle and quaking grass in the grassland. Blackcaps and willow warblers, reed buntings and yellowhammers are some of the birds likely to be seen.

Millbrook Pillinge

Permit only; 14ha; B and HWT reserve
Water-filled brick pit with islands
All year

Ducks, geese and gulls, with great crested grebe, dabchick and the occasional cormorant can be seen from the hide. Goldfinches often feed on the teazels near the water's edge.

Mowsbury Hill

Permit only; 2.8ha; North Bedfordshire BC
Woodland and grassland
All year

The reserve is on calcareous boulder clay and consists of a medieval moated site within an Iron Age hill-fort. Bee orchid, hound's-tongue, wild liquor-ice and adder's-tongue fern grow on the ramparts on the western side. Woodland species include moschatel and stinking iris. All three species of woodpecker and six species of warbler can be seen on the reserve in summer; in winter there is a large starling roost. Grass snakes and slow-worms have been sighted and a fox earth is also present.

Sandy Banks

Permit only; 1ha; B and HWT
Greensand grassland
Late summer, autumn

These three small areas of greensand are linked by a circular walk. Goldenrod, hawkweeds and the bright blue sheep's-bit flower. The bare sandstone is a favourite basking place for slow-worms and lizards, and the area abounds with butterflies.

Sewell Cutting

SP 995227–TL 004227; 3.2ha; B and HWT–South Bedfordshire DC reserve
Old railway cutting
Leaflet from B and HWT
Summer

The cutting is a first-class site for chalk grassland butterflies, with marbled white, chalkhill blues, brown argus and small blues. The reserve has a rich flora, including cowslips, bird's-foot-trefoil, greater knapweed, yellow-wort and bladder campion.

Berkshire

Bowdown Woods

SU 504657; 20ha; BBONT reserve
Mixed woodland
Open to public along path only
Spring, summer

The wooded scarp which drops down to the floor of the Kennet Valley is deeply incised with numerous valleys carrying small, spring-fed, nutrient-poor streams. They are clothed mainly with alder, which grows from large old coppice stools. The higher ground supports oak, birch, hazel, rowan and cherry. The ground flora is rich and includes an unusual number of woodland plant species indicative of its ancient woodland status.

Buckinghamshire

Rushbeds Wood

SP 668157; 45ha; BBONT reserve
Ancient woodland
Spring, summer

Nearly 100 species of flowering plants have been recorded, reflecting the reserve's ancient status.

The wood is excellent for butterflies, with purple emperor, black hairstreak and white admiral. Fallow deer are occasionally seen and there are large, thriving populations of both fox and muntjac.

Tenterden Spinney

SU 967995; 2ha; WdT reserve
Mixed woodland
Spring, summer

A mixed woodland now surrounded by houses. A footpath running through the wood provides good access.

Whitecross Green Wood

See Oxfordshire, p.686.

Cambridgeshire

Arthur's Meadow

Permit only; 0.7ha; B and HWT reserve
Grassland
Spring, early summer

Four species of orchid, as well as a wide range of other meadow flowers, can be found in this small, damp 'ridge and furrow' meadow.

Aversley Wood

TL 158815; 62ha; WdT reserve
Mixed woodland
Closed for shooting 4 days in winter; check dates with WdT office
Spring, summer

One of the largest woods in the county, it is traditionally managed as coppice with standards. The main trees are oak, ash, field maple and hazel, but this ancient woodland is noted for its wild service-trees. In spring the wood is carpeted with bluebells, and black hairstreak butterfly has been recorded. There are three ponds in the wood, one of which is a fine example of an armed pond – one of the few remaining in the East Midlands.

Far Close

TL 293717; 1.7ha; B and HWT reserve
Grassland
Spring, early summer

This unimproved 'ridge and furrow' meadow, a relict of medieval cultivation, supports plants such as crosswort, green-winged orchids, yellow rattle and salad burnet. Cowslip are plentiful on the dry ridges, while cuckooflower prefers the damp furrows.

Gransden Wood

Permit only; 15ha; B and HWT reserve
Ancient woodland
Leaflet available from Trust
Spring, early summer

Adjoins WARESLEY WOOD and is a similar habitat.

Nene Washes

TL 277992; 225ha; RSPB reserve
Flood meadows
Access by arrangement with Warden, 59 Headlands Way, Whittlesey, Cambs
All year

Like the OUSE WASHES, the area was created in the seventeenth century as a storage area for floodwater as part of the scheme to drain the fens. While flooding in winter continued, the area was immensely important for wildfowl. However, improved flood control in the 1960s restricted the overflow of water, resulting in a decline in wintering species and also in the loss of traditional hay meadows rich in flowers, as these areas were ploughed. Acquired as a reserve just in time, the remaining meadows will be managed traditionally and other areas restored, while control of the water levels will enable flooding once more to provide a safe winter haven for large flocks of Bewick's swans as well as wigeon, pintail and gadwall. Short-eared owls hunt the area for voles.

In spring the exposed meadows are a rich feeding area for passage waders like black-tailed godwits. The reserve also supports a large population of breeding ducks of several species, including shoveler, gadwall, pintail and garganey. Lapwing, redshank, snipe and yellow wagtail also nest.

Riddy Wood

Permit only; 8.5ha; B and HWT
Deciduous woodland
Spring, summer

One of the few ancient woodlands remaining in the north Huntingdon area, Riddy Wood still contains mature oak and ash trees with an understorey of field maple, hazel, blackthorn and Midland hawthorn. Bluebells carpet the woodland floor in spring with patches of primrose and yellow archangel, and meadowsweet, ragged robin and lesser spearwort in the damper rides and glades. Typical woodland birds occur and Chinese water deer visit the reserve from nearby WOODWALTON FEN.

Sapley Spinneys

Permit only; 3ha; B and HWT reserve
Deciduous woodland
Spring

The area is a remnant of the sixteenth-century Royal Forest of Sapley, which was subsequently cleared and the two spinneys have developed from old hedges. Small-leaved elm now dominates the reserve, with some oak, ash, sycamore and hornbeam. A number of ancient woodland indicator plants occur, such as dog's mercury, bluebell, wood anemone and goldilocks buttercup. Thirty species of birds have been recorded.

Sutton Wash

Permit only; 3.5ha; B and HNT reserve
Winter-flooded fen meadows
Can be viewed from parking place on B1381 at TL 416777
All year

Part of the OUSE WASHES

Cheshire

Heswall Dales

8.9ha; Wirral BC reserve
Dry heath
Contact WBC for further information
Spring, summer, autumn

Cornwall and the Isles of Scilly

Anne's Wood

SW 547372; 0.6ha; WdT reserve
Mixed woodland
Spring, summer

A small wood on the banks of the HAYLE ESTUARY.

Breney Common

SX 055610; 55ha; CTNC reserve
Heathland, ponds, scrub and grassland
Nature-trail guide available from CTNC
Spring, summer

There is a remarkable array of habitats of biological importance on this reserve. The wet heath area supports fine stands of royal fern, marsh cinquefoil and various sedges, with heath spotted-orchid in the drier areas. Nightjar and tree pipit are two of the 97 bird species recorded breeding, and there are good butterfly and moth populations. The emperor dragonfly frequents the ponds along with a number of other uncommon dragonflies and damselflies.

Carn Moor

SW 795538; 1ha; CTNC reserve
Wet heathland, bog and carr
Late spring, summer

A mosaic of black bog-rush, purple moor-grass, bog myrtle and ericaceous shrubs cover this small reserve, while the hollows support bog asphodel, sundews and the spectacular royal fern. Fringing scrub and willow carr encourage a variety of birds and mammals, including snipe and curlew which use the area in winter.

Kennall Vale

SW 747370; 8ha; CTNC reserve
Broadleaved woodland, river, quarry and lake
All year

This fascinating reserve, which ranges from majestic limes planted along a track to small pockets of semi-natural oakwood, surrounds the remains of a nineteenth-century gunpowder works. Among the wood-sorrel and bluebells less common plants such as sweet woodruff and wood spurge may be seen. The lake formed from a disused quarry is reputed to contain carp, and dippers feed along the river. The area is also a favourite feeding ground for bats.

Lavethan Wood

SX 104730; 10ha; WdT reserve
Valley woodland
Spring, summer

The wood lies in a valley of a tributary of the River Camel on the slopes of Bodmin Moor. It consists of oak, beech and other broadleaved trees with attractive riverside walks.

Loveny

SX 183744; 160ha; CTNC–Cornwall Bird Watching and Preservation Soc. reserve
Open water, heathland and grassland
Western margin of reserve only
All year

Loveny reserve covers the northern limb of Collingford Reservoir, which lies in the St Neot river valley on Bodmin Moor. The reservoir is likely to become an important ornithological site and already mallard, wigeon, teal and tufted duck use the water. Lapwing, curlew, green sandpiper, redshank and dunlin feed at the edge, while golden plover, short-eared owls and hen harriers are occasionally seen in winter. Marsh fritillary is just one of the interesting range of butterflies recorded.

Milltown and Lantyan Woods

SX 110570 and SX 108578; 33ha; WdT reserve
Deciduous woodland
Spring, summer

These two woodlands, linked by a narrow belt of trees, lie on the western shore of the Upper Fowey Estuary. Clothing the side of the valley right down to the edge of the river, these oaks form an essential feature of this beautiful Cornish river.

Penhale Training Camp, Perran Sands

SW 764585; 8km; MOD–NT
Coastal walk through large sand dunes with lime-loving plants
Visitors should read all notice boards carefully and keep to marked coastal footpath, as this is an MOD training area (although there is no live firing)
All year

Phillips' Point Cliffs

SS 200044; 0.5km; CTNC–North Cornwall DC reserve
Coastal clifftop grassland and heath
All year

In spring thrift, bladder campion and wild carrot add colour to the grassland, while the area of western maritime heath supports bell heather and western gorse with dodder. Wheatear, stonechat, and meadow and rock pipit breed along the clifftops, and gulls, raven and fulmars can often be seen. Seals also frequent the area.

Southern Red Moor

SX 076607; 50ha; CTNC reserve
Heathland, bogs, ponds, grassland and scrub
Summer

This is a recently acquired extension to RED MOOR. The wetlands are of special interest, supporting royal fern, marsh cinquefoil and several uncommon sedges. In drier areas hare's-tail and heath spotted-orchid carpet the heath, whilst the delicate ivy-leaved bellflower may be found in the more open grassland. The many silted-up ditches crossing the site are particularly good for dragonflies and damselflies.

Stithians Reservoir

SW 715372 and SW 709373; 40ha;
SWWA–Cornwall Bird Watching and Preservation Soc. reserve
Reservoir
Permit from Cornwall Bird Watching and Preservation Soc., but can be viewed from the road
Summer, autumn, winter

There are two nature reserves on Stithians Reservoir – at Polighey Moor and at the 'cut off' opposite the Golden Lion Inn. The area is particularly important for its rare migrant wader and waterfowl, which are attracted from the Arctic, North America and the Mediterranean. In recent years solitary sandpiper, lesser yellowlegs, pectoral and semi-palmated sandpipers, blue-winged teal and white-winged black tern have all been recorded. There is also an annual passage of the more common waders, wildfowl and terns.

Cumbria

Abbotswood

SD 220716; 7.7ha; Barrow-in-Furness BC reserve
Mixed woodland
Leaflet from CTNC
Spring, summer

The older areas of woodland can be distinguished by their ground covering of wood anemones, wood-sorrel, primroses and bluebells, but there are also many exotic trees as part of the reserve was once formal gardens. The area is rich in birdlife, including treecreepers, long-tailed tits and spotted flycatchers.

Argill Woods

Permit only; 6.8ha; CTNC reserve
Steep valley woodland
Spring, summer

Set on the steep north side of Argill Beck, the woodland is dominated by oak, ash and birch, with elm, rowan, hazel and hawthorn, and a ground cover of melancholy thistle, globeflower, wood sanicle, bluebells, betony, wood crane's-bill and great burnet. Birds include dippers, warblers and tawny owls, and red squirrels and roe deer are present.

Ash Landing

SD 386951; 2.5ha; CTNC reserve
Young woodland, grassland and ponds
Information centre; apply to CTNC for entry
Spring, summer

This reserve is on the west shore of Lake Windermere and consists of a small heather and rhododendron garden with three ponds and a stream which are very good for invertebrates, particularly dragonflies. Woodland, wetland and grassland habitats are in the process of being created. There is also a small wildlife garden and some newly planted hedges.

Clints Quarry

Permit only; 17.5ha; CTNC reserve
Limestone quarry
Summer

The base of the quarry is colonised with a wide variety of limestone-loving plants, including several species of orchids – bee, common spotted and northern marsh orchids, common twayblades and several hybrids. The top of the cliffs are wooded with ash, willows and hawthorn, and two pools provide additional interest.

Cumbria Coastal Way

NX 966180–NX 960119; 13km; various bodies
Coastal nature trail
Leaflet from CTNC
Spring, summer

A fine walk along the cliffs from Whitehaven to St Bees, passing ST BEES HEAD, which is particularly interesting geologically as a wide variety of rocks can be seen, especially in the old coal-workings south of Whitehaven. Plants on the cliffs include rock samphire and rock sea-lavender, while on the grassy tops there is scurvygrass, bloody crane's-bill, orpine and yarrow. Excellent views of sea-birds. This is first section of way to be opened.

Gowk Bank

NY 679739; 4ha; NCC reserve
Hay meadows
Permit only from NCC
Spring, early summer

This reserve is one of the finest examples of traditionally managed meadow systems in northern Britain. Typical meadow flowers are found in the areas cut for hay; the uncut sections contain globeflower, melancholy thistle and a good range of orchids.

Knipefold Coppice

NY 342002; 1.6ha; WdT reserve
Mixed woodland
Spring, summer

This wood lies on a steep, exposed hillside with wonderful views over the LAKE DISTRICT NATIONAL PARK. Dominated at present by a belt of mature larch, the coppice has in fact a variety of trees, though much of the land is sparsely wooded. However, planting of mixed native trees and shrubs will enhance the scenery and wildlife of the wood.

North Walney

SD 170725; 136ha; NCC–CTNC reserve
Sand-dunes, heath, saltmarsh and open water
Spring, summer and winter

A large sand-dune system at the north end of Walney Island. The reserve is a long, narrow peninsula with extensive saltmarsh on the east side and a shingle beach leading to open water on the west side. The dunes are full of colour in the spring, with northern and early marsh-orchid and the 'Walney geranium' (a local form of bloody crane's-bill). The dune heath has acid-loving plants, such as sundew, and the saltmarsh has extensive areas of thrift and sea aster. Over 300 flowering plants have been recorded on the reserve. Disused gravelpits and dune slacks provide breeding sites for common and natterjack toad and palmate and smooth newts. In winter wigeon graze the salt-marsh and many species of wildfowl can be seen, including eider and red-breasted merganser.

Ravenglass and Eskdale Railway Nature Trail

SD 095978–NY 173007; 11km; CTNC
Railway nature trail
Leaflet from CTNC
Late spring, summer, autumn

A nature trail for the lazy viewed from the windows of the Ravenglass and Eskdale Railway trains. The 'Ratty' passes between the Irish Sea and Eskdale Fell; the rich variety of habitats include saltmarsh, moorland, crags, wet meadows, fresh and salt water, and old woods.

The Ridge Wood

NY 540618; 10ha; WdT reserve
Mixed woodland
Spring, summer

As its name suggests, this wood is situated on a prominent ridge with fine views across the surrounding countryside. The reserve has a fine back-drop of mature beech trees, and although parts of the wood have been felled and replanted with conifers, it is still predominantly broadleaved in character, with areas of oak as well as beech.

Sandscale Haws

SD 185750; 264ha; NT reserve
Sand-dunes
Summer

Extensive dune system with marram grass, also supporting sea holly and sea spurge in the base-rich areas. In the more acid areas there are plants of dune heath such as bell heather and burnet rose. The wetter slacks have a richer plant community, including marsh helleborine, grass of Parnassus and common wintergreen. Natterjack toads breed in the pools.

Scroggs Wood

SD 512906; 1.2ha; WdT reserve
Mixed woodland
Spring, summer

An amenity woodland on the south side of Kendal with access to the banks of the River Kent.

Serpentine Woods Nature Trail

SD 510928; 1km; CTNC
Woodland and open fell nature trail
Leaflet from CTNC
All year

The trail passes through mixed woodland and up on to open fell with splendid views across the Kent valley. The wood is one of the best areas near Kendal for woodland birds, and curlew, wheatear and little owl can often be seen in the more open country.

Shank Wood

NY 468706; 8ha; WdT reserve
Deciduous woodland
Spring, summer

The reserve is a tranquil lowland wood in a steep gorge of the tributary of the River Lyne. The main tree species are oak, ash, elm and hazel. There is a rich ground flora and the site is noted for its bryophytes.

Talkin Tarn

NY 545588; 74ha; CCC reserve
Grassland, lake and woodland
Leaflet available on site
All year

A mountain tarn with woodland on its north side, supporting fox, badger and red squirrels, typical deciduous woodland plants and an interesting range of fungi. Swifts, swallows and martins feed over the tarn in summer, and in winter goosander, tufted duck and coot can be seen.

Ullswater Nature Trail

NY 943197–NY 394161; 12km; CTNC
Lakeland nature trail
Leaflet from CTNC
Spring, summer

Along the south-east shores of Ullswater, the trail passes between Howtown and Patterdale and, in summer, the return journey can be made by steamer. The walk follows the lakeside through meadows and woodland with beautiful views of the fells.

Derbyshire

Burrs Wood

SK 305755; 12ha; WdT reserve
Mixed woodland
Spring, summer

A wood in a steep valley on the edge of the PEAK NATIONAL PARK. It has a variety of trees and shrubs but is dominated by very old coppice oak, ash and sycamore. There is an area of elm as yet unaffected by Dutch elm disease, as well as rowan, silver birch, yew, sallow and hazel.

A stream runs through the wood and several rocky ridges and steep gullies give the wood an unusual character.

Elvaston Castle Country Park

Permit only; 12ha; DCC
Wetland
A phased development; contact DCC for latest information
All year

Devon

Bailey Wood

SS 521275; 0.4ha; WdT reserve
Oak woodland
Spring, summer

A small area planted up to create an oak woodland.

Bere Alston and Bere Ferrers Copses

SX 456670 and SX 452639; 0.4ha; WdT reserve
Mixed woodland
Spring, summer

These two small copses are conspicuous features of the very open landscape at the southern end of the high ridge between the Rivers Tamar and Tavy.

Buck's and Keivell's Woods

SS 357234; 13ha; WdT reserve
Coastal woodland
Spring, summer

The woodland lies along three cliffs and in a valley running down to the sea. The trees are mainly oak, which is suited to the exposed site. The North Devon Coast Path runs along the clifftops and through Buck's Wood.

Capton Wood

SX 835539; 4.4ha; WdT reserve
Deciduous woodland
Spring, summer

The reserve is part of a larger area of woodland lying on the steep sides of a secluded tributary valley on the River Dart. It contains oak, ash, cherry, beech, birch and sweet chestnut, with shrubs such as hazel, hawthorn and elder. In spring the ground is covered with a carpet of bluebells.

Clayton Wood

SY 068929; 1ha; WdT reserve
Mixed woodland
Spring, summer

A new woodland planted in 1980, which, as it matures, will provide a valuable haven for wildlife and fit in well in a landscape of scattered small woods.

Cleaveland Wood

SX 437651; 1.8ha; WdT reserve
Mixed woodland
Spring, summer

A mixed woodland in the Tamar Valley. An ivy-covered chimney near the edge of the wood is a reminder of the former mining industry for which the area is renowned.

Crowndale Wood

SX 474733; 1ha; WdT reserve
Mixed woodland
Spring, summer

A narrow wood of mature trees following the foot-path of the Tavistock Canal.

Dishcombe Wood

SX 660933; 1.8ha; WdT reserve
Mixed woodland
Spring, summer

A small field bounded by a line of fine hedgerow beech trees which has been planted up to create a mixed broadleaved woodland for the future.

Exe Reedbeds

SX 955885; 25ha; DTNC reserve
Reedbeds
Can be viewed from the banks of Exeter Canal
All year

These extensive reedbeds within the tidal reaches of the River Exe are important for birds. In winter jack snipe, black-tailed and bar-tailed godwits, and common and green sandpiper all frequent the area, while mute swan, reed and sedge warbler and reed bunting find the area ideal for nesting.

Fernworthy Reservoir

SX 665840; 30.8ha; SWWA
Reservoir
All year

Unlike most of the other Dartmoor reservoirs, Fern-worthy has shallow, reedy banks which give ex-cellent cover for water-birds. The nature reserve area is situated at the inlet of the reservoir and is surrounded by scrub and mature deciduous trees. Summer migrants include swift, redstart, siskin, redpoll and crossbill, while in winter goldeneye, teal, great crested grebe, goosander and heron fre-quent the reserve.

Fordy Park Wood

SS 818058; 0.7ha; WdT reserve
Woodland
Spring, summer

A small woodland that is a vital feature of the landscape.

The Grange

SX 895500; 11ha; DTNC reserve
Coastal woods and cliffs
All year

Good views of the sea and the Dart Estuary can be obtained from the South Devon Coastal Footpath, which passes through pinewoods on this reserve.

Halsdon

SS 554131; 57ha; DTNC reserve
Woodland, grassland and river
Spring, summer

The large block of ancient woodland supports a wide range of birds and mammals, and slopes down the side of the Torridge Valley to marshes along-side the river, where kingfishers and sand martins may be seen.

Hardwick Wood

SX 530555; 21ha; NT–WdT reserve
Mixed woodland
All year

High on a hill on the eastern edge of Plymouth, the wood is an important feature of the city's land-scape. There are many rides and paths through the wood, giving excellent views over Saltram House and Plymouth to the south, and over the lower slopes of DARTMOOR to the north.

Hemborough Beeches

SX 828522; 0.7ha; WdT reserve
Beech wood
Spring, summer

These beeches on the Totnes to Dartmouth road are a well-known landmark.

Hollacombe Woods and Quarry

SX 527506; 6.6ha; WdT reserve
Deciduous woodland
Spring, summer

A varied broadleaf woodland that contains a worked-out quarry and a profusion of wildlife.

Littlewood

SX 539684; 0.4ha; WdT reserve
Mixed woodland
Spring, summer

The wood is an important feature in the village of Dousland.

Liverton Copse

SY 025823; 2.8ha; WdT reserve
Mixed woodland
Spring, summer

A copse in the centre of Exmouth which was once planted with conifers. These have now been felled, except for a shelter belt on the seaward side, and the wood replanted with oak, ash and lime trees.

Longlands Brake

SX 502492; 0.7ha; WdT reserve
Broadleaf wood
Spring, summer

The reserve on a steep slope with the village of Heybrook Bay is a haven for birdlife.

Longstone Wood

SX 467753; 1ha; WdT reserve
Mixed woodland
No public access

This clump of mature beech and ash trees is a well-known landmark between Tavistock and Launceston.

Martyn's Wood

SS 336031; 0.8ha; WdT reserve
Scrub and hedgerow
Spring, summer

A field of bracken and brambles adjacent to a hedge with tall trees forms a valuable wildlife habitat.

New Cross Pond

Permit only; 11ha; DTNC reserve
Clay pond, scrub and woodland
Winter

The disused clay pond is an important refuge for wintering wildfowl. It is surrounded by a mixture of other habitat types.

Northdown Wood

SS 923062; 9ha; WdT reserve
Mixed woodland
Spring, summer

This wood has a great variety of tree species and a rich flora. It has a long tradition of management as a nature reserve, for the Fursdon family who owned it for over 150 years also looked after it with conservation in mind.

Otter Estuary

SY 075825; 18ha; DTNC reserve
Saltmarsh
Winter

The saltmarsh, a rare habitat in the south-west, shows characteristic zonation from glasswort and sea-blight through sea club-rush to patches of common reed. In winter several hundred snipe are often present, along with little grebe, heron, brent goose and shelduck. Meadow and rock pipits and stonechats breed on the adjacent fields.

Page Wood

SY 137879; 0.4ha; WdT reserve
Mixed woodland
Spring, summer

A prominent small wood on the west side of Salcombe Hill.

The Plantation

SX 734385; 0.8ha; WdT reserve
Mixed woodland
Spring, summer

This small area of mature mixed broadleaved trees forms part of the background to the town of Salcombe when seen from the estuary.

Point and Whitehall Woods

SX 483879; 9.4ha; WdT reserve
Mixed woodland
No public access
Spring, summer

An important wildlife and amenity woodland just outside the DARTMOOR NATIONAL PARK.

Rectory Field

SX 842696; 2.2ha; WdT reserve
Meadow and scattered trees
Spring, summer

A field with several groups of young trees, and mature trees in the hedgerow, is being managed by grazing to create an area of pasture woodland.

Scanniclift Copse

Permit only; 11ha; DTNC reserve
Broadleaved woodland
Spring

A block of ancient woodland in the Teign Valley which exhibits a range of different woodland types and has a rich ground flora.

Shears Copse

SS 614097; 1.2ha; WdT reserve
Scrub woodland
Spring, summer

A coppice of naturally regenerated scrub woodland on the edge of the old Winkleigh aerodrome. It has an especially plentiful and varied bird population.

Snakey Copse

SX 874675; 0.4ha; WdT reserve
Mixed woodland
Spring, summer

A small woodland of mainly local interest.

South Plantation

ST 114094; 12ha; WdT reserve
Mixed woodland
Spring, early summer

A mixed wood of conifers and broadleaves which will gradually be converted to a pure deciduous wood by felling the conifers as they reach maturity and replanting with native broadleaved trees.

Devon

Uplyme Pinetum

SY 316936; 28ha; WdT reserve
Woodland and arboretum
Spring, summer

The pinetum is partly a deciduous wood of fine
oaks and beeches and partly an arboretum of
specimen conifers. It contains the country's tallest
Prince Albert's yew and Japanese red cedar. There
are also fine specimens of Caucasian fir and
Wellingtonia.

Warleigh Point

SX 446610; 31ha; DTNC reserve
Woodland and mudflats
Spring, summer

Wild service-tree, an ancient woodland indicator
species, grows alongside the estuarine fringe.
Much of the wood was clear-felled in the early
1960s and is now being re-coppiced in rotation.
The reserve also includes mudflats and part of the
fundus of the River Tavy.

Wedd's Copse and Tanglewood

SX 484745; 1.2ha; WdT reserve
Mixed woodland
No public access
Spring, summer

An area of disused railway line and associated
woodland.

Westcott Wood

SX 785873; 5.6ha; WdT reserve
Coniferous woodland
Spring, summer

A conifer wood in the valley of a small tributary of
the River Teign within the DARTMOOR NATIONAL
PARK. The conifers will eventually be replaced by
broadleaved trees.

Weston Mouth

SY 163879; 1ha; DTNC reserve
Coastal scrub and grassland
Spring, summer

From the footpath through the reserve can be seen
its speciality – purple gromwell – growing amongst
the scrub.

Whitleigh Wood

SX 482599; 15.3ha; WdT reserve
Deciduous woodland
Spring, summer

A mixed broadleaved woodland with a series of
attractive walks. The opening up of a glade and
ride has increased the variety of habitats much
enjoyed by the people of Plymouth. The wood lies
on a hillside in the centre of Tamerton Foliot and
is an important landscape feature.

Woodcot Wood

SX 734384; 2.8ha; WdT reserve
Woodland
Spring, summer

A prominent woodland on the west side of the
Salcombe Estuary.

Yeo Copse

SS 801151; 5.6ha; WdT reserve
Oak woodland, river
Spring, summer

An attractive area of oak woodland lying on the
south side of the valley of the River Sturcombe. An
old mill leat is situated by the public footpath at the
bottom of the wood.

Dorset

Duncliffe Wood

ST 825225; 88ha; WdT reserve
Mixed woodland
Spring, summer

The reserve forms one of the largest areas of woodland in north Dorset, set like a saddle on top of two
hills overlooking the Blackmoor Vale. This ancient
wood was once all oak and hazel coppice but has
now been substantially replanted. The woodbank
is surmounted by huge pollards, one of which is
thought to be the oldest living thing in Dorset.

Higher Hyde Heath

Permit only; 40ha; DTNC reserve
Heathland, acid bog and carr woodland
Summer, early autumn

The dry heath is home for both the smooth snake and
the sand lizard, while the attractive marsh gentian
occurs locally in the wetter areas. The acid bog is
scattered with small pools, which, together with
nearby streams, have given rise to a particularly rich
and interesting dragonfly and damselfly fauna.

Holt Heath

SZ 060040; 450ha; NCC reserve
Heath and oak woodland
Spring, early summer

Dry, damp and wet heath occur widely on the
reserve, together with valley bogs that merge into
a flat mire at the southern end. To the north the
land rises to its highest point at Bulbarrow and
from here, looking south, it is possible to obtain an
impression of wild Dorset as it must have appeared
for many years. The heath's large size and diversity
allow a rich fauna with good populations of characteristic heathland birds and insects.

In Holt Forest the massive pollarded oaks, standing over a dense understorey of holly, support
many lichens and invertebrates.

Kingsettle Wood

ST 865255; 21ha; WdT reserve
Mixed woodland
Spring, summer

The reserve sits on top of a ridge overlooking Blackmoor Vale, straddling the Dorset–Wiltshire county boundary. In the last 35 years much of the wood has been felled and replanted, mainly with conifers and some beech. The Trust plans to restore the site to native broadleaves but in the meantime it provides a wonderful place to enjoy the views over the River Stour.

Lodmoor

SY 686807; 61ha; RSPB reserve
Damp pasture, reedbeds, dykes and scrub
All year

Behind Weymouth's seafront lies a wetland area with an outstanding variety of birds. By following the footpath from the Sea Life Centre, the reserve can be viewed from three different hides. In the breeding season bearded tits, water-rails and sedge warblers can be heard, and sometimes seen, in the reedbeds, and Cetti's warblers lurk in the scrubby areas. On the wet pasture yellow wagtails and redshank nest, while stonechats, linnets and whitethroats are found in the drier grassland with scrub. In autumn passage waders use the reserve and there is always the chance of seeing North American rarities, such as grey phalaropes and pectoral sandpipers. Winter visitors to the reserve are large flocks of lapwing and snipe, with smaller numbers of jack snipe and water pipits, while floods bring shoveler, wigeon, teal, pintail, gadwall and Brent geese.

Luscombe Valley

SZ 045891; 4.5ha; Poole BC reserve
Grassland, heathland and scrub
All year

The valley supports a wide variety of flowering plants and grasses indigenous to this low-lying land. The area is interspersed with trees, predominantly pine and silver birch, with heather and other heathland flora. There is a good variety of wildlife, particularly birds.

Upton Country Park

SY 995930; 22.3ha; Poole BC
Formal gardens, farmland, woodland, saltmarsh and mudflats
9 a.m. until dusk. Nature trail leaflet available from Upton House
All year

A traditional English country estate, but the hide overlooking Poole Harbour allows good views of the waders and wildfowl. There is also an interesting selection of woodland birds.

Durham, Cleveland and Tyne and Wear

Coatham Marsh

Permit only; 54ha; NCT reserve
Brackish marsh
All year

Coatham Marsh is of particular interest to birdwatchers in the autumn and winter, when 31 species of wader have been recorded. Rarities include white-winged black tern, little egret, red-throated pipit, ring-billed gull and bluethroat. Thirty-four species of birds have bred on the reserve in recent years.

Cow Close Wood

NZ 700138; 11ha; WdT reserve
Deciduous woodland
Spring, summer

A horseshoe of woodland running up two stream valleys on the northern edge of the NORTH YORK MOORS NATIONAL PARK. The trees are mainly oak, ash, alder and beech, with hazel dominant in the understorey. There is a wide variety of plants of old woodland.

Mount Pleasant Marsh

NZ 341609; 2.4ha; DCCT reserve
Marsh, open water and rough grassland
Permit only from DCCT
Summer

The large stand of false fox-sedge is probably the largest in the county. Elsewhere the plants around the edge of the water include hard rush, common spike-rush and bulrush. Celery-leaved water crowfoot, lady's smock and pepper saxifrage are also present. Orange-tip butterflies are numerous in the spring, and throughout the summer the whole area is alive with freshwater invertebrates. Moorhen, reed bunting, sedge warbler and whitethroat all breed, with wintering water-rail and jack snipe.

Pontburn Woods

NZ 147562; 24ha; WdT reserve
Deciduous woodland
Spring, summer

This is one of the largest and most important broad-leaved woods remaining in the Derwent Valley west of Newcastle. This part of the valley is of considerable beauty. The huge Hamsterley Viaduct, which carries the Derwent Valley Walkway, is a focus of the valley and provides a unique view of the woods from above.

Saltburn Gill

NZ 675210; 16.9ha; CNCT reserve
Broadleaved woodland and heath
Spring, summer

This valley woodland reaches the coast at Saltburn-by-Sea. It includes open gorse and bracken-covered slopes.

Thorpe Wood

NZ 404247; 16.8ha; Cleveland CC reserve
Deciduous woodland and ponds
Leaflet from field centre at Thorpe Thewles Station
Spring

The woodland is carpeted with wood anemones in the spring, and populations of giant bellflower are particularly good in the summer. Many woodland birds are present and there are several notable species of spiders, molluscs and butterflies. The pond contains a good variety of wildlife, including great-crested newts.

Timber Beach

NZ 369584; 1.8ha; DCCT reserve
Saltmarsh
Summer

This small saltmarsh is the most northerly example of its type on the east coast. There is a zonation of plant communities from sea-blite and glasswort through a low turf of common saltmarsh-grass and red fescue with sea aster and thrift to an upper saltmarsh of sea couch with spear-leaved orache. Timber Beach is a good site for watching gulls, cormorants and the more common waders. During spring and autumn passage more uncommon birds may be seen.

Essex

Copperas Bay

TM 190320; 225ha; RSPB reserve
Saltings, mudflats
All year

This bay lies on the south side of the Stour estuary, partly flanked by the woodland reserves of STOUR WOOD and COPPERAS WOOD, which come right down to the tideline. The three reserves form a fine complex of different habitats, all being managed for conservation. The saltings and mudflats of the bay provide a wintering area for Brent geese, shelduck, wigeon, oystercatcher, redshank and dunlin. The site is also important for passage waders, especially for a large flock of black-tailed godwits that feed here regularly each autumn.

Cudmore Grove Country Park

TM 064147; 14.4ha; ECC
Open grassland, oak copse and beach, overlooking mudflats of Colne Estuary
All year

Danbury Country Park

TL 769048; 16.5ha; ECC
Mixed woodland and lakes
All year

Hanningfield Reservoir

Permit only; 354ha; Essex Water Co.
Large reservoir, important for birds
Can be overlooked from public roads around, e.g.
TQ 732980
All year

Harrison Sayer

Permit only; 1ha; ENT reserve
Boulder-clay grassland
Spring, early summer

Bee orchid, wild liquorice, fairy flax and blue fleabane all flower on this small reserve, which is one of the few of its type remaining in north-west Essex.

Hawksmere Springs

Permit only; 1.7ha; ENT reserve
Unimproved grassland, woodland and stream
Spring, summer

The meadow flora is extremely rich, with cowslip, yellow rattle, betony, ragged robin, sulphur clover and sneezewort. There is also a remnant of ancient damp woodland.

Iron Latch Meadow

Permit only; 2.4ha; ENT reserve
Meadow and scrub
Spring, early summer

Clearance work undertaken on this scrub-infested meadow has already shown good results with a healthy increase in the number of green-winged orchids. With careful management the area should be returned to its flower-rich glory.

Loshes Meadow

TL 873371; 7ha; CEGB–ENT reserve
Grassland, marsh, woodland and brook
Permit only from ENT
Spring, summer

The reserve is rich in wildlife, with birds such as nightingale, willow tit, and grasshopper warbler among the nesting species. Plants including ransoms, yellow archangel, opposite-leaved saxifrage and tree orchid species. Ringlet and white-letter hairstreak butterflies are also found here.

Old Hall Marshes

TQ 958122; 459ha; RSPB reserve
Grazing marsh, saltmarsh, reedbeds and meres
Permit only off public footpaths
All year

The reserve is mainly unimproved grazing marsh, a habitat which over the last 30 years has largely been reclaimed and turned into arable land. At Old Hall the marshes are still grazed by sheep and cattle much as they have been for hundreds of years and they provide breeding sites for shelduck, redshank and yellow wagtail. Botanically the banks of the sea walls are most interesting with spring rest-harrow, grass-leaved vetchling and sea clover. The meres and ditches are also good for aquatic plants, as well as supporting large populations of dragon-flies. Duck, such as pochard breed on these open-water areas.

The saltmarsh and mudflats are most important for the huge flocks of waders they support in autumn, winter and spring, the main species being dunlin, knot, grey plover and curlew, and for Brent geese which feed on the eelgrass on the mudflats of the reserve, as well as the improved grassland. The glasswort on the saltmarsh attracts large flocks of passerines, especially twite.

Waterhall Meadows

TL 759073; 2.3ha; ENT reserve
Grassland and scrub
Access along public footpath only
Spring, summer

Situated on the west bank of Sandon Brook, the reserve consists of unimproved flood meadows that support an interesting flora with a variable bird and insect fauna. There is also a small spinney and an area of blackthorn thicket.

Gloucestershire

Bigsweir Wood

SO 544056; 44ha; WdT reserve
Deciduous woodland
Spring, summer

The wood is a part of the LOWER WYE VALLEY woodlands, which are some of the richest in the country. The wood is an excellent example of the acid woodlands of this complex. Lying on sandstone, the wood is dominated by sessile oak and beech high forest; ash occurs in areas of slightly less acid soils. There are areas of coppice, including both beech and small-leaved lime. The ground flora includes great woodrush, cow-wheat, hard fern and honey-suckle.

Offa's Dyke, marking the old Welsh border, runs through the wood, as does the long distance footpath OFFA'S DYKE PATH.

Causeway Grove

SO 089536; 5ha; WdT reserve
Deciduous woodland
Access from road difficult due to steep bank
Spring, summer

The woodland lies on a steep valley side overlooking the River Wye and is an excellent example of the ancient woodland of this area. It is dominated by ash, small-leaved lime and wild cherry. The flowers are varied, with drifts of the strongly scented ransoms.

Coombe Hill Canal

SO 887273; 4.8km; GTNC reserve
Canal and grassland
All year

The aquatic and bankside vegetation is the main botanical interest of the reserve. There are fine stands of grey club-rush, and purple and yellow loosestrife provide attractive splashes of colour. Fine-leaved water-dropwort and flowering-rush are two of the rarer species found in the area. In winter, when the surrounding meadows are flooded, the canal provides a superb viewing point to observe the flocks of wildfowl, which include white-fronted goose, teal and pintail.

Parish and Oldhills Woods

SO 906027; 14ha; WdT reserve
Deciduous woodland
Spring, summer

These woods lie on the banks of the River Frome in an area called the Golden Valley. In autumn this is a very apt name, as the woods are dominated by beech trees. Oldhills Wood has a large proportion of elm, most of which has died and is being replaced by other mature trees.

Ridley Bottom

ST 564985; 1ha; GTNC reserve
Grassland and coppice
Spring, summer

The coppice contains small-leaved lime with maple, gean and yew, and the groundcover includes herb-Paris and hard and hart's-tongue ferns. There is a rich birdlife, and brimstone butterflies are common.

Siccaridge Wood

Permit only; 27ha; GTNC reserve
Mixed woodland
Spring, summer

Lily-of-the-valley and angular Solomon's seal occur in this interesting woodland.

Stanley Wood

SO 895015–SO 817022; 38ha; WdT reserve
Mixed woodland
Spring, summer

The wood stretches for 1½ miles along the scarp slope of the Cotswolds above the villages of Kings Stanley and Leonard Stanley. It forms part of the wooded edge of the Cotswolds that can be seen from much of the Severn Valley. From the wood itself there are superb views across the valley to the FOREST OF DEAN and the MALVERN HILLS. Much of the wood was felled in the 1950s and parts were replanted with conifers. However, there was considerable natural regeneration of beech and ash and the Woodland Trust's management involves a programme of thinning to promote the broadleaved trees. This will not only improve the wood from a landscape point of view but will help to conserve the rich ground flora so characteristic of ancient woodland on limestone in this area. The Cotswold Way long-distance footpath runs through the wood and the Coaley Park Picnic Site is next to the wood making a good starting place for those who wish to explore the network of footpaths through the wood.

Three Groves Wood

SO 911030; 2.8ha; GTNC reserve
Mixed woodland
Spring, summer

Beech woodland that was planted up some 50 years ago with larch and beech; oak, ash, wych elm and whitebeam have regenerated naturally. Badgers occur.

Wimberry Quarries

SO 594121; 2ha; GTNC reserve
Disused quarries
Spring, summer

The reserve consists of a complex of four disused quarries which have been colonised by a rich flora of ferns and mosses, including oak fern. There is an area of mixed woodland with beech, ash, oak and sweet chestnut. Above the quarries there is a small area of heathland with ling and bilberry.

Woorgreens Lake and Marsh

SO 630129; 9ha; GTNC reserve
Lake and marsh
All year

In winter the lake supports dabbling ducks, including teal, while the marsh attracts large numbers of snipe; other waders that can be seen on passage are spotted redshank, greenshank and green sandpiper. In drier areas among recent plantations there are good breeding populations of whinchats and tree pipits. Seventeen species of dragonfly and damselfly have been recorded. The reserve is the best site in the FOREST OF DEAN for brown argus and grayling butterflies.

Greater London

Battersea Park

Queenstown Road, SW8; 75ha; GLC–LWT reserve
Grassland, shrub and woodland
All year

Mist's Pitch just inside the Chelsea Bridge entrance, established in 1985, is the first reserve inside the GLC inner-city parks since the setting up of the Hampstead Heath Conservation Unit in 1968 to manage wildlife areas within HAMPSTEAD HEATH. There is a leaf dump covered by cinders from the nearby power station and former miniature railway; its variety of habitats attracts 65 bird species and 18 types of butterfly. The informally maintained fringe of trees and understorey along the eastern edge of the park also provides a complementary contrast to the attractions of the rest of the park.

Bayhurst Wood Country Park

TQ 068889; 39.5ha; LB Hillingdon
Woodland and lake
Nature trail leaflet available on site
All year

A woodland, linked by paths to RUISLIP, which once formed part of the ancient Middlesex Forest, it contains interesting standard and coppiced hornbeam, as well as fine standards of oak and beech. There is a good diversity of woodland plants and animals.

Bramley Bank

Riesco Drive, Croydon; 10ha; LWT reserve
Woodland, acid grassland and ponds
All year

Oak, ash, hazel and sycamore are the main constituents of this woodland left to the people of Croydon by the Riesco bequest. A good understorey of hawthorn and rowan, together with the bramble-dominated ground layer provide a good habitat for birds such as treecreeper, nuthatch, great spotted woodpecker and tits. Bluebells, dog's mercury, sanicle and wood-sedge are found. A large pond supports all three species of newt.

Coppetts Wood

Colney Hatch Lane, North Finchley, N12; 8ha; LWT reserve
Ancient woodland
All year

Oak-dominated woodland with an understorey of derelict hazel. hornbeam and sweet chestnut coppice which is a remnant of the former Finchley Common. A variety of scrub and trees is colonising the grassland, where plants such as harebell, and perforate and imperforate St John's-wort are found. The adjacent glebeland has unrestricted access.

Crane Island

Carlton Avenue, off Hounslow Road, Feltham;
1.8ha; LWT reserve
River island
Permit only from warden, tel. 01-892 0035
All year

The island's habitats include ash, horse chestnut,
elder and hawthorn woodland, where 45 of the
larger fungi have been recorded. The backwater is
dominated by crowfoot, while arrowhead has a
footing in the main stream. The central third is
occupied by the former millpond, which now
forms a marsh favoured by butterflies and grass
snakes.

Devonshire Road

Devonshire Road, Forest Hill, SE23; 2.8ha; LB
Lewisham—local management committee reserve
Railway cutting
Saturday afternoons, educational access at other
times; contact warden, tel. 01-650 6695
All year

An interpretation centre and nature trail are
features of this woodland, scrub and grassland area
created along a railway cutting.

Fryent Country Park

Fryent Way, NW9; 20ha; LB Brent reserve
Woodland and farmland
Nature trail leaflet available from council's leisure
department, tel. 01-903 1400 ext. 529
All year

Not far from BRENT RESERVOIR is Fryent Park, an
area bought by the local council in 1927 and
managed for its wildlife interest. The nature trail
that guides you round the woodland also covers
the 82ha of hay meadows and hedgerows across
Fryent Way.

Gunnersbury Triangle

Bollo Lane, Chiswick, W3; 2.4ha; LWT reserve
Damp woodland and scrub
All year

Bounded by railways, this triangle of wet birch and
sallow woodland is to be served by a field studies
centre. The damper zones give rise to lush vegetation, including ferns, horsetails and sedges as well
as hemp-agrimony, celery-leaved buttercups and
nettles. Thickets of bramble, elder and holly
provide nesting places for blackcaps, chiffchaffs,
willow warblers and sedge warblers, while the
more open grassy areas attract butterflies such as
orange-tip, small copper and holly blue.

Ham Lands

Riverside Drive, Ham, Richmond; 80ha; LB
Richmond—local management committee reserve
Grassland and scrub
All year

An extensive area of grassland with patches of
scrub has colonised infilled diggings next to the
Thames and supports a large population of bee
orchids plus some pyramidal and common spotted
orchids. Other uncommon plants recorded here
include moth mullien, bloody crane's-bill, hairy
vetchling, dittander and salad burnet. Woodpeckers, spotted flycatcher and various warblers
are among the 100 birds recorded here. An area of
relict flood meadow survives near the Thames
bank.

Hither Green

Green Chain Walk, Baring Road, Lewisham, SE12;
2.4ha; LB Lewisham—local management
committee reserve
Woodland, scrub, grassland and pond
Nature trail leaflet from warden, tel. 01-650 6695
All year

The mixture of habitats on a former railway siding
now form an educational reserve with a nature trail
and an interpretation centre in prospect.

Lonsdale Road Reservoir

Lonsdale Road, Barnes, SW13; 9ha; LB
Richmond—local management association reserve
Shallow lake
Permit only from council
All year

A former reservoir, this is also known as the Barnes
Wildlife Sanctuary and, because of its shape, the
Leg 'o Mutton reservoir. The margins of the lake
show the stages of plant succession. Pochard, tufted duck, goosander and goldeneye are among the
diving ducks that feed on the reserve in winter,
and raft-type islands have been provided for
breeding purposes. A classroom is planned.

Rotherhithe Ecological Park

Salter Road, Rotherhithe, SE1; 3ha; Ecological
Parks Trust reserve
Recreated habitats
All year

A new reserve replacing the former William Curtis
Ecological Park is being established next to the
local council's ambitious new Russia Dock Wood.
The part next to the wood has open access while
the remainder will become an educational site with
a planned interpretation centre.

Rowley Green

TQ 217961 Rowley Lane, Barnet; 12ha; H and
MTNC—LWT reserve
Grassland and scrub
All year

Common land designated an SSSI, its acid grassland
species have become overgrown with trees—
predominantly oak and birch, and, in the damper
zones, willow alder and downy birch. Appropriate

management is planned to retain the grassland areas with their mat-grass, tufted hair-grass and purple moor-grass. Heath bedstraw, tormentil, devil's-bit scabious and patches of heather and petty whin have also been recorded. Small areas of *Sphagnum* bog contain jointed rush, lesser spearwort, sweet-grass and various sedges, while a small pond is used by a variety of woodland birds.

St Philomena's Lake

Shorts Road, Carshalton; 1ha; LWT reserve
Open water
Permit only, except on open days
All year

This large spring-fed pond within the grounds of Carshalton House, now a convent school, has been desilted and its weir reconstructed. The original vegetation – mostly small reed-grass, water mint and watercress – is being replaced along with more plantings of water dock, water celery, large bittercress and the nationally rare water sedge. Newts, toads and frogs are also found, as well as a rare aquatic snail *Limnea palustris* and good numbers of dragonflies.

Scadbury Park

Perry Street, Sidcup; 60ha; LB Bromley reserve
Woodland, meadows, pools, streams and hedges
All year

Opened by the council in 1985, the park includes oaks from Elizabethan times when the estate was a hunting park, 58 acres of woodland managed by Bromley's forestry department, and farmland including old hedgerows. The wide range of habitats supports a diversity of plant and animal life and is particularly rich in bird species.

Stratford Butterfly Garden

Great Eastern Road, Stratford, E15; 0.5ha;
Newham Wasteland and Allotments Association reserve
Wildflower meadow, scrubland and pond
All year

A recently created nature garden that already attracts over 14 species of butterfly.

Tump 53

Carlyle Road, Thamesmead, SE28; 1.4ha;
GLC–LWT
Small island
By arrangement with LWT
All year

The Tump, an island surrounded by a moat, is a survival from the munitions industry on the Woolwich marshes – along with several dozen other tumps, it was once used to store explosives. Retained amid the new housing development at the centre of Thamesmead for its amenity and nature conservation interest, it is being managed by an LWT warden who also has responsibility for keeping an eye on other sites of ecological value in the area.

The Warren

Sheepcote Lane, St Mary Cray, Orpington; 35ha;
LWT reserve
Acid grassland, woodland and lake
Permit only
All year

Part privately owned and part belonging to LB Bromley, the Warren is gradually being restored. The woodland is a haven for the three woodpecker species and the lake for amphibians, including the endangered great crested newt.

Hampshire and the Isle of Wight

Bramley Frith Wood

SU 513920; 27ha; CEGB reserve
Deciduous woodland
Educational or youth groups only
Nature-trail leaflet from nature centre
Spring, summer

An electricity substation has been sited in the centre of the ancient wood of mainly coppice with oak and a few ash standards. In spring there are many bluebells, primroses, Solomon's-seal and common spotted-orchids. Speckled wood and white admiral butterflies may be seen along the sunny rides, and mammals include dormouse and roe and fallow deer.

Dodnor Creek and Dickson's Copse

SZ 505915; 11ha; IWCC reserve
Freshwater ponds and woodland
Spring, summer

A former mill pond associated with cement mills on the bank of the Medina River has reverted to freshwater marshes and now provides a habitat for breeding wetland birds, including mute swan and reed and sedge warbler. Dickson's Copse provides a wooded fringe of pedunculate oak noted for mosses, liverworts and ferns.

Flexford

SU 424220; 9.3ha; H and IOWNT reserve
Alder carr woodland and grassland
Spring, summer

Carpets of ransoms, opposite-leaved golden saxifrage and wood anemones cover the woodland floor in summer, with scarce wood-rush and Solomon's seal also present. The peaty grassland is equally rich in wood horsetail, water avens and marsh-orchids. Butterflies such as the ringlet, brimstone and white admiral have all been recorded.

Pamber Forest

SU 616605; 115ha; Englefield Estate–Pamber
Forest Management Committee
Mixed woodland
Spring, summer

The reserve is an extensive acid oakwood, with a few plantations of Douglas fir, larch and sweet chestnut. It is probably primary woodland as it was recorded in Roman times and is a remnant of the much larger thirteenth-century royal hunting forest of Pamber. More recently it has been managed as hazel coppice with oak standards, some of which are very large. There is a great variety of trees and shrubs, including aspen, wild service, whitebeam, butcher's broom and alder buckthorn. In addition to the usual flowers of ancient woodland there are lily-of-the-valley, early-purple orchid, nettle-leaved bellflower and orpine. Wide rides and glades are ideal areas for butterflies, and white admiral and silver-washed fritillary can be plentiful; purple emperor and purple hairstreak also occur.

Rew Down

SZ 552775; 4.6ha; IWCC reserve
Chalk grassland
Spring, summer

The nature reserve is situated on the steep south-facing chalk slope above Ventnor and gives commanding views over the English Channel. A wide range of basic alkaline and acid soils supports a rich variety of chalk grassland flora and fauna. Large populations of early gentian and horseshoe vetch provide seasonal colour, the latter supporting a colony of Adonis blue butterflies.

Shide Chalk Pit

SZ 506882; 5ha; IWCC reserve
Abandoned chalk quarry
Spring, summer

The deep man-made pit sunk into an escarpment of the Upper Chalk exhibits all stages of succession from bare chalk, important for geological research, through a chalk grassland plan community to tall scrub. Over 160 flowering plant species have been recorded, including, at the pit floor, some unusual flora associated with spring.

Solent Way Walk

SZ 569994; MOD
Coastal walk which passes through Browndown
Ranges at high-water mark
All year

No live firing, but when training is taking place and flags are flying follow public highway (Browndown Road and Privett Road) between Stokes Bay and Lee-on-Solent. The coastal walk is not dedicated as a public highway.

Winnall Moors (southern area)

SU 486300; 16.2ha; H and IOWNT reserve
River and water meadows
Summer

The land here differs from that in WINNAL MOORS (the northern area) in that it is not grazed and supports a rich, tall fen vegetation. Reeds and sedges are plentiful and provide a rich bird and insect habitat with many of the taller-growing marsh plants adding their burst of colour. The River Itchen flows beside this section and the birds noted in WINNAL MOORS occur here as well. However, great densities of reed, sedge and grasshopper warblers are to be seen and heard in the taller vegetation.

Hereford and Worcester

Betts

Permit only; 2ha; WNCT reserve
Mixed woodland
Summer

Typical sessile oak woodland of the Wyre Forest dominates this steeply sloping reserve above the Lem Brook. Dipper, pied wagtail and redstart breed in the reserve. The steep acid slopes with bilberry and hard fern contrast with the valley floor, where wild daffodil, wood anemone and primroses grow under hazel coppice.

Cleeve Prior

SP 079496; 11.3ha; WNCT reserve
Limestone scrub and grassland
Summer

Stretching for about 1.6km along the edge of the Avon Valley, the Rhaetic limestone grassland supports species such as bee and pyramidal orchids. Under the hawthorn scrub is a dense growth of deadly nightshade in its only site in the county.

Lion Wood

Permit only; 3.2ha; WNCT–WARNACT reserve
Acid oak woodland
Summer

Oak dominates this woodland established on acid gravelly ground. The dense shrub layer is of hazel, birch, holly, rowan and alder buckthorn, the latter supporting a large brimstone butterfly population. The ground flora is not rich but has abundant bilberry.

Mousecastle Wood

SO 245427; 21ha; WdT reserve
Mixed woodland
Spring, summer

This beautiful oak woodland overlooks Hay-on-Wye, giving magnificent views of the valley. Within the reserve there is a motte-and-bailey castle that is a scheduled ancient monument.

Redstone

SO 810703; 7ha; Wyre Forest DC reserve
Marsh, wet woodland and damp meadows
Access restricted in accordance with bye-laws
Spring, summer

Hemlock water-dropwort, fine-leaved water-dropwort and slender tufted sedge are amongst the more unusual plants found on this small but valuable Local Nature Reserve. Thirty species of birds were recorded breeding in 1984.

Symonds Yat Wood West

SO 557158; 5.6ha; WdT reserve
Deciduous woodland
Visitors are advised to keep to footpaths due to several derelict mineshafts
Spring, summer

This broadleaved wood is part of the geologically important LOWER WYE VALLEY woodlands. It is noted for the wide variety of tree and shrub species found here and for its rich ground flora. It is an important part of the famous view from Symonds Yat Rock.

Tiddesley Wood

SO 930458; 75.2ha; WNCT reserve
Mixed woodland
Avoid access to south end when red flag is flying
Spring, summer

In the 1950s and '60s, this wood was planted with conifers by the Forestry Commission; since then much has reverted to native broadleaved coppice dominated by oak, ash, field maple, birch and hazel. Over 300 plant species have been recorded, including herb-Paris, violet helleborine, meadow saffron, bird's nest orchid and wild pea. Nightingale and sparrowhawk breed, and amongst the 30 species of butterfly found are white-letter hairstreak and white admiral.

Wassell Wood

SO 795775; 22ha; WdT reserve
Deciduous woodland
Spring, summer

This wood is an important landscape feature, standing as it does on a prominent hill overlooking the Severn Valley. Much of the mature oak woodland was felled before the site became a reserve. A planting programme is now in progress to restore the tree cover.

Hertfordshire

Digswell Lake

Permit only; 7.2ha; H and MTNC reserve
Lake, marsh and woodland
All year

On one side the spring-fed lake lies in a formal setting, but there is an interesting alder wood with a ground flora that includes greater pond-sedge, meadowsweet and hemp-agrimony. The woodland birds are diverse with all three species of woodpeckers and various warblers, while the lake attracts birds of open water; in winter this includes pochard and teal.

Frogmore Meadow

Permit only; 3ha; H and MTNC reserve
Grassland
Spring, summer

Frogmore is an alluvial meadow lying adjacent to the River Chess and is particularly interesting for its large number of ant hills and variety of sedges. The flowers are typical of a flood meadow and the ancient hedgerows that surround the reserve add to its interest.

Hoddesdonpark Wood

TL 348088; 60ha; WdT
Deciduous woodland
Spring, summer

This wood is part of a large woodland complex including WORMLEY WOOD. The reserve consists of oak forest with areas of hornbeam coppice. There is an abundance of oak regeneration. There is rich ground flora and a good variety of bryophytes. Ermine Street, the Roman road, runs along the western boundary and is bordered by a number of fine pollarded hornbeams.

Maple Lodge

TQ 040975; 16ha; TWA
Gravel-pits, woodland and grassland
Permit from TWA
Leaflet available from information centre
All year

The reserve is mainly a man-made wetland area of old gravel-pits and a sludge lagoon. The open water is a haven for ducks, little grebe, kingfisher heron and water-rail, and for a variety of waders on passage. Sweet violet and yellow archangel occur in the woods, while meadowsweet and common spotted orchids grow in the wet grassland. The 130 species of moths recorded include elephant hawk moth, large emerald and Hebrew character. Butterflies such as comma, speckled wood and brimstone are present.

Northaw Great Wood Country Park

TL 284042; 100ha; Welwyn–Hatfield DC
Broadleaved woodland
Groups and organisations by arrangement only
Leaflet available on site
All year

A mixture of oak-and-birch and oak-and-hornbeam woodland with considerable areas of coppice. Birds include nightingales, wood warbler, tree pipit, woodcock and redpoll, as well as all three species of woodpecker. Muntjac deer, badgers and foxes are also resident in the wood.

Telegraph Hill

TL 117298; 3ha; H and MTNC reserve
Grassland, scrub and plantation
Access by walking from TL 109283
Spring, summer

As part of the Icknield Way along the Chiltern ridge, the reserve widens into a series of parallel hollow ways with steep banks that have allowed the development of a rich chalk flora, which includes field fleawort, purple milk-vetch, squinancywort, several species of orchid and horseshoe vetch. Variety is added to the site by a plantation and two dew ponds.

Kent

Berengrave Lane

TQ 820670; 10ha; Gillingham BC reserve
Former chalkpit with small pond and trees
All year

In the 30 years since the quarry closed a great variety of habitats has developed. The ponds contain breeding populations of frogs, toads and newts, and a number of species of dragonflies. A reedbed has grown up around where reed warblers and reed buntings nest. Much of the rest of the area has reverted to woodland of birch, ash and sycamore with shrubs such as dog rose, clematis and dogwood.

Canterbury

TR 159596; 12ha; CEGB reserve
Freshwater lakes, grassland, recent woodland and River Stour
Restricted site for use by Kent Education Authority and KTNC
Nature-trail guide from CEGB and study centre
All year

The site is noteworthy for freshwater life, resulting from recolonised abandoned gravel workings, but the recent woodland and open grassland add diversity. Over 200 plants have been recorded and 90 species of birds, including kingfisher, water-rail and Cetti's warbler.

Church Wood

TR 123593; 142ha; RSPB reserve
Deciduous woodland
Spring, summer

The reserve is part of one of the most extensive ancient oakwoods in southern England; BLEAN WOODS is also a piece of this complex. The structure of the wood is mixed, including areas of oak high forest, with scattered wild service-trees, oak standards over coppice of hazel, chestnut and hornbeam; there are also blocks of pure chestnut coppice, and scrub spindle and dogwood has developed in areas of recent felling. Small stands of beech occur on gravelly soils, while alder and sallow grow along the streams. There is a good breeding population of nightingales and a variety of warblers, including wood warbler, which, like the redstart, is scarce in this area. In the clearings nightjars can be heard and long-eared owls have nested in a small conifer plantation. Among the woodland flowers there are large colonies of lily-of-the-valley and lesser periwinkle. Cow-wheat is common and supports the threatened heath fritillary butterfly.

Gazen Salts

TR 327587; 4.8ha; KTNC–Dover DC
Wet meadow with ponds and ditches
Spring, summer

The reserve is noted for its birdlife, and over 150 species have been seen, including such rarities as osprey, spoonbill, bittern and great grey shrike. In summer reed and sedge warbler, whitethroat, willow warbler, yellow wagtail and swallow frequent the area, and redwings and fieldfare, water-rail, short-eared owl and snipe are winter visitors. Wildfowl on the lake include pochard, shoveler, shelduck, and barnacle and greylag geese. There is a good selection of butterflies, including Essex skipper, holly blue and wall.

Hurst Wood

TQ 568405; 17ha; WdT reserve
Mixed woodland
Spring, summer

The woodland lies in a small valley with a stream running through it. Over the last 40 years most of the mature trees have been felled, but the Trust has replanted with oak, sweet chestnut and hazel. A small area of land was planted in 1963. There are some open glades in the woodland which are covered by a sea of bluebells in spring.

Marden Meadow

Permit only; 1.5ha; KTNC reserve
Unimproved meadow with hedgerows and ponds
Spring, early summer

Green-winged orchids, dyer's greenweed and adder's-tongue are all found on this rich meadow.

Oare Marshes

TR 011645; 65ha; KTNC reserve
Unimproved coastal marshes
Access along public footpath on sea wall
Spring, early summer

The reserve is chiefly noted for its good selection of wildfowl. The pasture has an interesting selection of native grasses and herbs, including some rare clover species.

Westerham Mines

Permit only; 2000m; KTNC reserve
Old mine tunnels
Winter

These old tunnels are an important site for hibernating bats.

Lancashire, Greater Manchester and Merseyside

Cabin Hill

SD 284052; 28ha; NCC reserve
Sand-dunes
Spring, summer

Part of the extensive sand-dune system stretching from Liverpool to Southport, the reserve shows a range from embryo dunes on the shore to stabilised ones inland. The flora is especially interesting as the reserve is grazed and provides a contrast with the unmanaged areas. Natterjack toads breed in the large pool.

Ravenmeols

SD 274064; 70ha; Sefton MBC reserve
Rich coastal dune system
Leaflet available from SMBC
Spring, summer

The best example of the early stages of dune formation on the Sefton coast is protected here, along with examples of most other dune habitats. There are many notable plants, including dune helleborine, intermediate wintergreen and bee and pyramidal orchids. A good variety of butterflies and moths occurs.

Walton Park Cemetery

SJ 358958; 10ha; Walton Parish Church—Rice Lane Community Association reserve
Scrub and heathy grassland
Leaflet available from RLCA and LTNC
Spring, summer

This ancient burial ground provides a quiet haven for wildlife within a crowded urban setting. There is an attractive mixture of heathy grassland and mature scrub, the latter supporting many breeding birds, including willow warbler, chiffchaff and whitethroat, for which there are few other sites in the city. A remarkable total of 70 species of spiders has been recorded, reflecting the relatively undisturbed nature of the area.

Warton Crag

SD 497724; 19ha; Lancaster City Council reserve
Limestone cliffs, grassland, scrub and scree
Leaflet available from LTNC or LCC
All year

The very varied habitats on the terraced south face of the Crag support a wealth of plants, birds and insects. Horseshoe vetch, bird's-foot-trefoil, spring cinquefoil, thyme, red valerian and spring sandwort are among the many colourful plants that adorn the cliffs and short turf in the spring and early summer. The geological interest, coupled with fine views over MORECAMBE BAY, the Bowland Fells and the Craven Pennines, make the reserve attractive and of interest at any time of the year.

Leicestershire and Rutland

Knighton Spinney

Permit only; 2.6ha; L and RTNC reserve
Oak—ash spinney
All year

Situated along the northern edge of Knighton Park in south Leicester, the wood provides a useful educational resource for local schools. Originally planted as a fox covert in the 1840s, the wood has a shrub layer of hawthorn, hazel, field maple and holly, and a ground flora which includes wood anemone, goldilocks buttercup and yellow archangel. Great and lesser spotted woodpecker, treecreeper and nuthatch all breed in the spinney.

Loughborough Big Meadows

Permit only; 2.9ha; L and RTNC reserve
Unimproved flood meadow
Spring, autumn

Periodic flooding by the River Soar has produced a very rich flora, such as great burnet, pepper saxifrage and the rare sulphurous water-dropwort. The proximity of the river adds interest, and breeding birds include sedge warbler, whitethroat, reed bunting and possibly whinchat. Redshank breed on adjacent areas and are usually present during the spring and autumn migration.

Lucas's Marsh

Permit only; 1.5ha; L and RTNC reserve
Marshland
Spring, summer

The marsh developed as a result of excavation for building materials at the turn of the century, taking drainage from the surrounding farmland. It is now dominated by stands of great willowherb, together with rushes (including the uncommon straw-coloured rush) and sedges. Drier areas support uncommon grassland species such as adder's-tongue. Stands of common reed, sallow and willow provide cover and food for a variety of insect- and birdlife. Willow warbler, lesser whitethroat and reed warbler breed on the site and, during the summer, house martins attract regular visits by a hobby. The rich hedgerow provides food and autumn roosts for blackbirds and thrushes, and redwing numbers have exceeded 1000. Common snipe, with occasional jack snipe and woodcock, are winter visitors.

Piper Way

SK 562053; 1ha; Leicester City Council reserve
Urban nature area
All year

This small area provides a wildlife oasis in a built-up area of Leicester and is being developed by the L and RTNC's City Wildlife Project. Habitats include new plantations, scrub, rough grassland and a pond.

Rally Nature Garden

SK 579041; 0.5ha; Leicester City Council
Urban nature area
All year

The mixed habitats of this small area – scrub, meadow, tall herbs, a rockery and a small pond – form part of a larger community park. Butterflies are a dramatic feature of the site, especially in late July and August, when many hundreds can be seen feeding on the buddleia. Redpolls, siskins and goldfinches are commonly seen feeding in the area.

Tilton Railway Cutting

Permit only; 7.1ha; L and RTNC reserve
Geological site
All year

Tilton Cutting was excavated in the 1870s for the railway from Melton Mowbray to Market Harborough, and was closed in 1965. The cutting is the type locality for a number of species of fossil brachiopods, gastropods and ammonites, and for the so-called Tilton faunal province. The rocks exposed are maring sandstones, ironstones and clays of Liassic (Lower Jurassic) age (about 190 million years old). The floor of the cutting supports a fairly rich flora, including cowslips, square-stalked St John's-wort and a variety of grasses, sedges and rushes. The scrub attracts a wide range of the commoner small birds, including great, coal and blue tits, willow warbler and robin.

Watermead Ecological Park

SK 598079; 1ha; L and RTNC reserve
Flood meadow
All year

This educational reserve provides a variety of habitats for use by local residents and schools. The site experienced regular flooding until 1976, when a flood bank was constructed along the River Soar. The meadow grassland is now dominated by couch grass and cock's-foot, but with sizable areas of meadowsweet, great willowherb and stinging nettles. Great burnet, meadow vetchling and other meadow species can also be found. Extensive tree planting has included alder, willow and guelder rose, and a new pond is being stocked with a range of aquatic plants from nearby gravel-pits.

Lincolnshire and South Humberside

Ancaster Valley

SK 988430; 9.7ha; L and SHTNC reserve
Limestone grassland
Spring, summer

On the eastern slope of this steep-sided valley is a hanger of beech and ash with box, yew and barberry, whilst the western slope carries herb-rich limestone grassland with pyramidal orchid, pasqueflower and dyer's greenweed.

Ashing Meadow

Permit only; 2.8ha; L and SHTNC reserve
Meadow
Spring, summer

A wealth of wildflowers grows on this old meadow, including garlic mustard, great burnet, fleabane, tufted vetch and cowslip. The large hedgerow contains ash and hawthorn, purging buckthorn, blackthorn, black bryony, field maple and dogwood.

Far Ings

TA 015234; 36ha; L and SHNTC reserve
Open water, reedbed and saltmarsh
All year

The reserve includes over 2km of saltmarsh and the Humber bank on which the Viking Way long-distance footpath runs from its start at the nearby Humber Bridge. However, the chief interests of this major reserve are the reedbeds and lakes with adjoining grazing marsh and scrub. Reed warbler, bearded tit, water-rail, shoveler and pochard breed, whilst in winter snipe, jack snipe and goosander, together with a wide variety of duck, are to be seen. Bittern sometimes occur, as do hen and marsh harriers.

Freshney Bog

TA 242090; 14ha; L and SHTNC reserve
Grassland and marsh
Summer

Lying beside the River Freshney on the outskirts of Grimsby, this is the site of a major urban conservation project involving the local community, where trees are being planted, meadows created and ponds excavated. Local schools are involved and it is hoped that a rich and varied wildlife area will be created. Already there is a good range of wildflowers and birds. There is a reedbed and wet flushes with ragged robin, lady's smock and forget-me-not. Frogs and newts are abundant.

Horbling Line

TF 112362–115347; 2.5ha; L and SHTNC reserve
Grassland and scrub
All year

The hawthorn and blackthorn scrub of this disused railway line supports many birds, including flocks of finches and thrushes in winter, while nesting birds include whitethroat, lesser whitethroat, spotted flycatcher and nightingale. Tufted vetch, rough hawkbit, yellow toadflax and restharrow all occur on the reserve, and there is a good selection of butterflies such as ringlet, meadow brown, and small and large skippers.

Messingham Sand Quarry

SE 908032; 36ha; L and SHTNC reserve
Lakes, marsh and heathland
All year

The varied water depth in the lakes provides conditions suitable for wading birds as well as wildfowl. Migrant waders commonly seen include dunlin, redshank, curlew sandpiper and common sandpiper, while little ringed plover, redshank, yellow wagtail, shelduck and shoveler all breed. Marsh-orchids, pillwort, sneezewort and bog pimpernel are among the many wildflowers.

Moulton Marsh

TF 330330; 25ha; South Lincs Nature Reserves Ltd–AWA
Lagoons and islands
All year

When the sea defences along the River Welland were improved, a series of lagoons, scrapes and islands was created with a connection to the tidal river. The site provides an ideal environment for waders and waterfowl to feed at high tide. Oystercatcher, dunlin, snipe, ruff, curlew and redshank are all common on the reserve.

Muckton Wood

Permit only; 16.7ha; L and SHTNC reserve
Ancient deciduous woodland
Summer

Ash and oak standards grow over ash and hazel coppice, with a rich ground flora which includes early-purple and butterfly orchids, moschatel, herb-Paris, wood anemone and primrose. Both hard and soft shield-fern occur. Green and great spotted woodpecker, spotted flycatcher, blackcap and garden warbler all nest on the reserve and there is a large heronry.

Nettleton Wood

TF 098994; 10ha; WdT reserve
Deciduous woodland
Spring, summer

The reserve lies just below the edge of the Lincolnshire Wolds. It is partly covered by woodland, while the rest of the area is an abandoned field which has been planted up with ash, hazel, small-leaved lime and field maple to create a coppice woodland. Growth rates and productivity of trees, and changes in flora and fauna associated with a new coppice are being monitored.

The Pine Woods

TR 193633; 7ha; WdT reserve
Mixed woodland
Spring, summer

This attractive square of woodland lies right in the centre of the town of Woodhall Spa, and yet it is an important site for a great many insects, birds and flowers.

Robert's Field

Permit only; 0.7ha; L and SHTNC reserve
Limestone grassland
Spring, summer

A fragment of surviving Kesteven limestone grassland with a rich flora which includes pyramidal orchid, clustered bellflower, dwarf thistle, wild basil, autumn gentian, rockrose and wild thyme.

Whisby Pits

Permit only; 20.8ha; L and SHTNC reserve
Lakes, woodland and scrub
All year

A great variety of wildflowers are to be seen in this disused sand quarry, including harebell, knapweed, blue fleabane, trailing St John's-wort, gypsywort and marsh-orchid. Great crested and little grebes, kingfisher, shoveler and sand martins all breed on the reserve, while in winter there are large flocks of ducks such as teal, wigeon, shoveler, pochard, goldeneye and pintail. Seventeen species of butterfly have been recorded.

Yalta Woods

TF 320910; 2.4ha; WdT reserve
Young woodland
Spring, summer

The reserve has been planted up with a variety of trees. These are already beginning to make a contribution to the landscape of north Lincolnshire, where there are few small woods.

Norfolk

Dick Buck's Burrows

TG 212406; 3ha; WdT reserve
Deciduous woodland
Spring, summer

The reserve contains some fine mature trees, mainly oak, beech and chestnut. The wood lies alongside the Weaver's Way long-distance footpath.

Litcham Common

TF 888173; 24ha; Norfolk CC reserve
Heathland, scrub, woodland and ponds
Summer

An area of heathland, a habitat once widespread in Norfolk. A good variety of woodland birds occurs and there is an interesting heathland flora.

Surlingham and Rockland Marshes

TG 305605; 87ha; RSPB reserve
Grazing marsh, fen and reedbeds
Surlingham Marsh may be viewed from public footpath from church, Rockland Marsh from footpath starting opposite New Inn, Rockland St Mary
All year

The riverside marsh below Surlingham church has been grazed and sometimes cut for hay for at least 250 years. Throughout this period it has been subjected to intermittent flooding. Through neglect it has become partly overgrown by sweetgrass and sedges; however, there are areas of fen meadow where marsh-orchids and water avens flower, while in wetter patches bogbean can be found. There are small reedbeds and three pools, as well as a network of dykes. Gadwell, pochard and mute swans can be seen with their young on these areas of open water, while redshank, snipe and yellow wagtails nest among the sedgy tussocks and waterrails lurk in the reedbeds. It is the distinctive songs of the reed, sedge, grasshopper and Cetti's warblers and brief views of the bearded tits that reveal that these birds all nest in the reserve. Marsh harriers hunt over it regularly. A number of waders, including spotted redshank and wood sandpiper, visit the marshes in passage. The winter brings parties of shoveler, teal and wigeon, and occasionally short-eared owls and hen harriers.

The land has been combined with Rockland Marshes, which lie downriver, to form one reserve. Across the River Yare lies another RSPB reserve, STRUMPSHAW FEN.

Northamptonshire and the Soke of Peterborough

Byfield Pool

SP 500527; 4.4ha; NTNC reserve
Reservoir, reedbeds and willow carr
All year

The reserve is an old feeder pool for the Grand Union Canal now made obsolete by the adjacent, more extensive reservoir. The open water of the pool attracts a range of wildfowl, great crested and little grebe and kingfishers, whilst the extensive surrounding fringe of common reed forms an attractive nesting site for visiting sedge and reed warblers and for the elusive water-rail. Mature willow carr lines the stream entering the pool, which holds good communities of marsh plants, marsh-marigold and figwort. Areas of open grassland and mature hedges on the boundary of the reserve add diversity and are frequented by gatekeeper, meadow brown and large skipper butterflies.

Farthinghoe Railway

SP 516403; 2ha; NTNC reserve
Grassland scrub
Spring, summer

The sheltered clearings of this disused railway encourage a range of insect life, including 10 species of butterfly. Birdlife is well represented: sparrowhawk and kestrel hunt over the reserve; little and tawny owl are also present. The common finches, linnet and yellowhammer are seen throughout the year with redwing and fieldfare visiting in winter, and whitethroat and spotted flycatcher in the summer months. A restored landfill site has been extensively planted with native trees and scrubs.

High Wood and Meadow

SP 589548; 16.5ha; NTNC reserve
Oak–ash woodland, acid grassland
Spring, summer

Unlike many other ancient woodlands in Northamptonshire, High Wood has been unaffected by recent replanting. Parts of the wood contain a well-preserved structure of mainly oak standards with hazel coppice, while other areas show a high degree of naturalness with unusually abundant aspen and wild cherry. Characteristic woodland plants such as bluebell, primroses, wood sorrel, wood anemone and yellow archangel are abundant. A small stream flows through the wood, the banks of which and other wet flushes hold the less common moschatel, opposite-leaved golden saxifrage, yellow pimpernel and hairy wood-rush.

The adjacent cattle-grazed meadow is an excellent example of an acid grassland community which is now confined to a few sites in the west of the county. The yellow flowers of cat's-ear and tormentil stand out among other herbs such as heath bedstraw and sheep sorrel. Adjacent to the wood is an area of more neutral grassland and base-rich marsh with scattered willows. It holds interesting marshland plants, including spotted orchid. The meadow holds good populations of the more common grassland butterflies, and the large and prolific anthills of the yellow meadow ant are a particular feature. Areas of open sandy ground support colonies of solitary bees and wasps as well as forming sites for several badger setts. Large patches of scrub, scattered gorse and thick adjoining hedgerows extend the range of habitats for wildlife, especially birds.

Northfield Avenue

SP 861799; 1ha; NTNC reserve
Rough grassland and scrub
Spring, summer

A disused railway on the northern fringe of Kettering provides an important urban reserve. Some of the grassland supports attractive displays of bird's-foot-trefoil, ox-eye daisy and yellow stonecrop, whilst gorse and larger numbers of dog rose add interest to the scrub. Small heath, common blue and small copper butterflies breed in the grassland and a good range of birds frequents the site, including finches, yellowhammer, linnet and visiting cuckoo, willow warbler and lesser whitethroat.

Stoke Wood

SP 802864; 10.4ha; WdT
Deciduous woodland
Spring, summer

The wood is a remnant of the ancient Rockingham Forest, which is still managed traditionally as a coppice. Most of the wood consists of an oak and ash cover with an understorey of hazel coppice. A rich ground flora has survived and includes a number of species that are rare locally.

Stoke Wood End Quarter

SP 799855; 1ha; NTNC reserve
Oak woodland
Spring, summer

This small reserve is part of the more extensive STOKE WOOD. It is a fine example of a coppice woodland with some large oaks and ash and a hazel understorey. A good range of ancient woodland plants includes wood anemone, bluebell, primrose, yellow archangel, sanicle and widespread herb-Paris. In addition, honeysuckle and dog rose can be found and there are some fine specimens of crab apple

along the small stream that forms the north-eastern edge of the reserve. The commoner woodland birds are present, as well as tawny owls which breed.

Yelvertoft Fieldside Covert

SP 616760; 6.4ha; WdT reserve
Woodland and scrub
Spring, summer

The wood lies on either side of the Grand Union Canal in a rich agricultural area with little other woodland. Although devastated by Dutch elm disease and felling, the trees are regenerating and the reserve provides a valuable place for birds and insects.

Northumberland

Annitsford Pond

NZ 267743; 0.5ha; NWT–North Tyneside DC reserve
Subsidence pond
Spring, summer

This small urban subsidence pond between arable land and allotments has a good amphibian and invertebrate fauna. Breeding birds include coot, moorhen and mute swan. The flora is diverse with a well-developed area of marginal vegetation and scrub.

Borough and Scotch Gill Woods

NZ 183857; 23ha; Castle Morpeth BC reserve
Semi-natural woodland
Spring, summer

Both woods are fine examples of Northumberland woodland and are being managed to restore their ancient character. The ground flora includes toothwort, woodruff, Dutch rush, great horsetail and 'ne, while roe deer, badger and red squirrel are known to be present.

Hartburn Glebe Woods

NZ 088864; 3ha; WdT reserve
Mixed woodland
Spring, summer

The reserve is a strip of woodland lying on a steep slope above the Hart Burn. The woodland consists of oak, beech and cherry, though two large areas have recently been felled and replanted with conifers. However, present management is designed to re-establish broadleaved trees by natural regeneration. Historically, the wood is full of interest. The Devil's Causeway, an old Roman road, runs through the reserve, while a system of walks and architectural features laid out by a local vicar in the eighteenth century still survives. The most interesting of them is 'The Grotto', which is now a listed building.

Hauxley

NT 285021; 20ha; NWT reserve
Coastal lake and islands
All year

The whole reserve has been created from open-cast coal workings, and many trees have been planted and water plants introduced. The five islands are already used by breeding terns, which can be viewed from one of the three hides. The area is good for passage waders, and for wintering wildfowl and gulls.

Nottinghamshire

Ashton's Meadow

SK 787801; 3.6ha; NTNC reserve
Unimproved meadow
Spring, summer

The ancient ridge-and-furrow pattern is clearly visible in this meadow, which becomes a carpet of flowers in late spring. Species include cowslip, yellow rattle, green-winged orchid, adder's-tongue and quaking grass.

Brickyard Plantation

SK 493419; 1ha; WdT reserve
Scrub woodland and wetland
Spring, summer

The wood suffered badly from Dutch elm disease and many of the trees have now become waterlogged owing to altered drainage caused by the surrounding mining activities. The area provides an attractive wetland for insects and birds and is beginning to regenerate with alder and willows. As such, it provides a valuable addition to OLDMOOR WOOD, which lies close by.

Bunny Old Wood

SK 585284; 15.4ha; NTNC reserve
Deciduous woodland
All year

The reserve was originally an unusual coppice wych elm wood, with ash, oak, field maple and cherry. Much of the elm has died as a result of Dutch elm disease, and other native species are being planted to replace it. The wood has a flora typical of the heavy lias clay, and many insects and birds.

Daneshill

SK 666867; 50ha; NTNC–Notts CC reserve
Gravel-pits
All year

The varied mixture of birch woodland, willow scrub, marsh and open water attracts a variety of bird species, including wintering wildfowl. In summer little ringed plovers can be seen on the reserve, and dragonflies, damselflies and butterflies are abundant.

Dukes Wood

Permit only; 8ha; British Petroleum–NTNC reserve
Woodland
Spring, summer

The reserve is an ancient woodland, and the site of Britain's first on-shore oil field, which has now been restored.

Eaton Wood

SK 726775; 24.3ha; NTNC reserve
Ancient coppice woodland
All year

This mixed deciduous woodland contains oak, ash and field maple. It was formerly managed as coppice and produces an excellent show of spring flowers, including primroses, bluebells, wood anemones and herb-Paris. The reserve contains a wide variety of woodland birds.

Gamston Wood

SK 727767; 41ha; NTNC reserve
Ancient coppiced woodland
Permit only from NTNC
All year

Together with EATON WOOD, which it adjoins, this reserve forms one of the largest remaining blocks of ancient deciduous woodland in the county. Despite being clear-felled and replanted in the 1960s, the conifer replanting has been overwhelmed by coppice regrowth of native species.
   The roadside verges next to the wood have an exceptionally diverse grassland flora.

Holly Copse

SK 501424; 0.6ha; WdT reserve
Deciduous woodland
Spring, summer

A small remnant of ancient woodland dominated by oak and beech with hazel and holly as an understorey and a rich ground flora.

Kirton Wood

SK 707687; 18.6ha; NTNC reserve
Deciduous woodland
Permit only from NTNC
Spring, summer

An old deciduous woodland with a rich ground flora and good bird populations, Kirton Wood is immediately adjacent to the ancient open-field system of the Laxton Estate.

Rainworth Heath

Permit only; 16ha; NTNC reserve
Heath
Summer

A remnant of heathland which lies within the old Sherwood Forest.

Skylarks

SK 621391; 9.7ha; NTNC–Winged Fellowship Trust
Flooded gravel-pit and willow scrub
Access by key from Skylarks Holiday Centre,
tel. Nottingham 820962
Spring, summer

The Skylarks Nature Reserve for the Disabled is part of the Holme Pierrepoint complex. The easily accessible hides and well-surfaced paths are specially designed for wheelchair users. Sedge and willow warblers breed, while great crested grebe, mallard and other ducks visit the area, as do waders on passage.

Spa Ponds

SK 572628; 6.5ha; NTNC reserve
Ponds
Spring, summer

The restored medieval ponds on Bunter sandstone lie on the Meden Valley scarp, and are surrounded by scrub oak. The reserve is good for dragonflies.

Teversal Pastures

SK 492617; 5.9ha; NTNC reserve
Calcareous grassland
Permit only from NTNC; can be viewed from
Ashfield District Embankment Trail
Spring, summer

These old damp pastures on magnesium limestone still retain ridge-and-furrow patterning and old dividing hedges. There is a good range of flowers and butterflies.

Oxfordshire

Bernwood Meadows

SP 606110; 7.3ha; BBONT reserve
Neutral grassland
Keep to footpaths from mid-May until hay is cut;
dogs not allowed when stock grazing
Spring, early summer

Over 100 species of plants have been recorded, including 23 grasses and there is a good display of green-winged orchids and adder's-tongue. Both fallow and muntjac deer frequent the reserve and rutting stands are clearly visible in the autumn.

Iffley Meadows

SP 324037; 33ha; BBONT reserve
Ancient wet meadow
Early spring

Fritillaries used once to be found in profusion over the whole area, but are now concentrated around the centre of the northern section, their numbers having been decimated mainly by picking but also by lack of appropriate management. Marsh thistle, marsh-marigold, great burnet, ragged robin and adder's-tongue flower here.

North Grove

SU 647832; 21ha; WdT reserve
Deciduous woodland
Spring, summer

This attractive Chiltern beech wood has been well managed along traditional lines. Selective felling has encouraged natural regeneration of beech and allowed the remaining trees to grow into fine specimens. There are also areas of ash and hazel coppice, which add variety to the reserve.

Sutton Courtenay

SU 643600; 14ha; CEGB reserve
Meadows, ponds and scrub
Educational or organised groups only; book with
the Head Teacher, Sutton Courtenay Primary
School, tel. (0235) 848333
Booklets from Sutton Courtenay Primary School
and the Public Relations Department, CEGB,
South-Western Region Headquarters, Bridgewater
Road, Bedminster Down, Bristol BS13 8AN
Spring, summer

Lying at the edge of Didcot Power Station, two ponds on the site provide feeding areas for mallard, teal, coot and little grebe, and both frogs and common newts breed. The stream, Moor Ditch, is known to be at least 900 years old and is a good place to see water voles and dragonflies. Cowslips, heath spotted orchids and meadow crane's-bill flower in the herb-rich grassland, while in the scrub willow warblers and chiffchaffs nest and thrushes feast on the hawthorn berries in winter.

Trigmoor Wood

SP 256229; 3.6ha; WdT reserve
Mixed woodland
Spring, summer

The reserve is a former area of railway sidings and track where planting of conifers and broadleaved trees has complemented natural regeneration.

Tuckhill Meadow

SU 240900; 5.3ha; BBONT reserve
Grassland, stream and spinney
Summer

The higher ground supports typical limestone grassland plants, while in the wetter areas there is southern marsh-orchid and marsh valerian; this section is excellent for dragonflies and damselflies. Kingfishers may breed on the reserve.

Uffington Gorse

SU 314900; 4ha; WdT reserve
Mixed woodland
Spring, summer

This reserve lies in the Vale of the White Horse, an area lacking much woodland cover. The wood at present consists of a ring of Scots pine and oaks, the central section having been felled. Plans to replant this area with a mixture of native trees and shrubs will enhance the wood for wildlife and ensure its survival as a landscape feature.

Whitecross Green Wood

SP 603145; 62ha; BBONT reserve
Mixed woodland and pond
Spring, summer

Straddling the county boundary between Oxfordshire and Buckinghamshire, a small portion of this reserve once formed part of the ancient Royal forest of Bernwood. Unfortunately some 60 per cent of the wood at the north-west end was planted with conifers between 1963 and 1965 by the Forestry Commission, but the reserve still boasts over 200 species of flowering plants. Wood white, purple emperor and black hairstreak butterflies have all been recorded. Birds are well represented, with most woodland warblers, nightingale and, in very recent years, the nightjar. Mammals include fallow and muntjac deer and a large population of foxes.

Shropshire

Craig Sychtyn

SJ 232256; 2ha; STNC reserve
Limestone cliff and ancient woodland
Leaflet available from STNC
Summer

The northern edge of this reserve is bordered by a disused quarry which has its own typical lime-loving species, including at least six species of orchid. The quarry is also of geological interest, as fossil specimens of various brachiopods, bivalves and sea lilies may be found. Beneath the cliff the woodland is composed of oak, ash, sycamore, hazel, aspen and wild service-tree, with a shrub layer of dogwood spindle and spurge laurel. The ground flora is dominated by dog's mercury but includes orchids, hart's-tongue fern, cowslip, false oxlip, slender St John's-wort and three species of violet.

Dolgoch Quarry

Permit only; 2.75ha; STNC reserve
Disused quarry
Summer

A thin limestone grassland has formed on the quarry floor with felwort and blue fleabane in late summer, whilst on the vertical walls viper's bugloss maintains a tenuous hold. Brown spikes of reedmace ring a small pond where great crested newts and frogs can be found, along with a multitude of damselflies and dragonflies. Following the richer grassy slopes up to the precarious narrow walk between the two quarry faces, the more intrepid will find bee and pyramidal orchids and golden rod.

Ruewood

Permit only; 2.6ha; STNC reserve
Wet unimproved meadow
Leaflet available from STNC
Early summer

The wet western field is a blaze of purple from marsh-orchids, with ragged robin, devil's-bit scabious and creeping-Jenny amongst them. The eastern field is drier and harbours yellow rattle, common knapweed, plantains and buttercups.

Stiperstones

SO 369976; 437ha; NCC reserve
Moorland with geological exposures
All year

The landscape of the reserve in characterised by steep slopes and deep valleys, and is renowned for its stone stripes and polygons. The block scree, which forms the stripes, split away from the summit by frost action to form the tors of more durable rock like the Devil's Chair, Manstone Rock and Cranberry Rock.

The moorland is dominated by heather and bilberry, and other plants such as cowberry, crowberry and western gorse also occur.

At Resting Hill there is an area of oak coppice woodland which used to provide the charcoal for smelting. There are several wet flushes and bogs where cottongrass, bog asphodel and bog violet can be found. There is a small area of unimproved grassland among the abandoned smallholdings on the reserve, where a large population of the yellow mountain pansy grows. Redstarts and tree pipits live among the old hedges and walls.

Sweeny Fen

Permit only; 1ha; STNC reserve
Calcareous peat fen
Leaflet available from STNC
Late spring, summer

This rare Shropshire habitat results from the soil being a mixture of water-logged peat, boulder clay and alluvium fed by the base-rich run-off from the surrounding limestone rocks. From late spring onwards there is a continuously shifting patchwork of colour, from the delicate pinks of water avens and ragged robin to the rich creamy heads of meadowsweet. The rare marsh helleborine, fragrant orchid and bogbean can also be found. In the drier areas, globeflower, cowslip and false ox-lip grow.

Workhouse Coppice

SJ 667028; 5.4ha; WdT reserve
Deciduous woodland
Spring, summer

The wood overlooks the Severn Gorge above the historic Ironbridge where the Industrial Revolution had its roots. Once this coppice provided the wood that fuelled the new factories. Today the wood has a different function as an amenity area where residents and visitors alike can stroll among the mature oaks and enjoy the rich wildlife.

Staffordshire

Churnet Valley Woodlands

SK 000480; 74ha; RSPB reserve
Deciduous woodland, river
Spring, summer

The Churnet Valley has many reminders of north Staffordshire's industrial past. Chase Wood has an imposing set of disused limekilns, built from stone excavated from the large quarry within the wood. There is also a network of overgrown tracks of the old horse-drawn railways, known as plateways. The River Churnet, which adjoins part of the reserve, has been deepened to form part of the Cauldon Canal. Booth Wood, part of this reserve, and ROUGH KNIPE — as well as Chase Wood — provided the wood to power the local industries of coal- and iron-mining and charcoal-burning. Rotational cutting has created an uneven-aged woodland ideal for wildlife. There are areas of mature woodland containing oak, birch and ash trees, old coppice of varying ages, and a good shrub layer of birch, cherry, blackthorn, hazel and guelder-rose. In spring the woods are carpeted with wild flowers: bluebells, wood anemones, moschatel and great sweeps of white strong-smelling wild garlic. There are patches of giant bellflower and clumps of broad-leaved helleborine.

The woods are especially important for their large populations and varieties of migrant warbler, including wood warbler, whitethroat, garden warbler, blackcap and willow warbler; chiffchaff and lesser whitethroat occur in smaller numbers. The old trees are ideal for woodpeckers and all three species occur, together with treecreepers, nuthatches, redstarts and five species of tits. Smaller numbers of tree pipit and woodcock occur and sparrowhawks are the main predator. Despite Dutch elm disease, elm is still widespread on the reserve and supports the scarce white letter hairstreak butterfly.

Suffolk

Fen Alder Carr

TM 088568; 2ha; SCC reserve
Alder carr
Information at site
Spring, summer

High Lodge

TL 740755; 1ha; STNC reserve
Grassy pits in forest
All year

A selection of the more common breckland plants are found, such as viper's-bugloss, centuary and harebell. The area is a site of former archaeological excavations.

Iken Cliff

TM 398561; 1.5ha; SCC reserve
Rough grassland with viewpoint over estuary
Information at site
All year

Lavenham Walk

TL 916497; 2.4km; SCC reserve
Disused railway line with scrub and grassland
Spring, summer

Norah Hanbury Kelk Memorial Meadows

Permit only; 7.7ha; STNC reserve
Grazing marshes, dykes
Spring, summer

Lady's smock, ragged robin and greater bird's-foot-trefoil occur on the meadows, and a variety of plants borders the dykes. Ducks and waders breed.

Rodbridge

TL 859438; 8ha; SCC reserve
Freshwater lakes and riverbank
Information at site
Spring, summer

Valley Walk

TL 875409; 4km; SCC reserve
Disused railway line with scrub and grassland; views over water meadows
All year

Surrey

Chiphouse Wood

TQ 260570; 8ha; WdT reserve
Deciduous woodland
Spring, summer

The reserve consists of mature oak woodland and newly planted trees. The planting has been designed to link areas of existing woodland while leaving wide rides and glades for the benefit of wildlife and visitors.

Glover's Wood

TQ 230410; 25.5ha; WdT reserve
Deciduous woodland, bog
Spring, summer

The reserve is an excellent example of the Wealden woods. It lies across the valley of Welland Gill, which has created two distinct types of woodland. On the steep side of the gill there is extensive hornbeam coppice with a scattering of other species, such as ash, wych elm, maple, hazel, small-leaved lime and wild service-tree. Here the ground flora is dominated by bluebells, yellow archangel and dog's mercury. This part of the wood is possibly primary – that is, ancient woodland that has never been cleared – whereas the plateau area is woodland of oak, birch and hazel which has developed more recently on abandoned fields. There is also an area of *Sphagnum* bog.

Hammond's Copse

TQ 213442; 29ha; WdT reserve
Mixed woodland
Spring, summer

This ancient woodland consists partly of hazel coppice with oak standards and a rich, varied ground flora. The rest of the wood has been cleared and replanted with conifers. However, many of the planted trees have failed and natural regeneration of native species is taking over once again.

Sussex

Arlington Reservoir

TQ 533073; 100ha; Eastbourne Waterworks Company reserve
Open water
Access on footpath and bridleway only
Late summer, winter

Completed in 1971, the reservoir is particularly good for wildfowl. Canada geese, mallard, pochard, tufted duck and shoveler winter, while the migration brings in unusual waders such as spotted redshank.

Beechland Wood

TQ 414205; 0.8ha; WdT reserve
Deciduous wood
Spring, summer

A small valley oak woodland which has been augmented by the planting of a variety of native trees.

Brock Wood

TQ 644250; 4.8ha; WdT reserve
Deciduous woodland
Spring, summer

An attractive woodland reserve with many fine oak trees and hazel coppice.

Kiln Wood

TQ 527203; 3.6ha; WdT reserve
Deciduous woodland, grassland
Spring, summer

A fine oak wood with a number of other tree species, including birch, beech, holly and willow, and a shrub layer composed of coppiced hornbeam, chestnut and hazel. There is an adjacent area of rough grazing.

Malling Down

TQ 430108; 37.6ha; STNC reserve
Chalk grassland and scrub
Dogs must be kept on leads as reserve is grazed
Spring, summer

Part of the reserve is a series of chalk pits and spoil heaps renowned for their varied communities of chalkland flowers. The remainder is a deep and steep-sided dry valley with flourishing colonies of chalkland butterflies. The scrub provides a rich diversity of bird species.

Pevensey Levels

TQ 667056; 44ha; NCC reserve
Meadows and drainage ditches
Permit only, obtained from NCC SE office
Spring, summer, autumn

The reserve represents one of few remaining areas of undrained land on the marsh and consists of a series of undrained fields intersected by drainage dykes. The aquatic flora of the dykes is very rich, and species such as frogbit, bur-reed and reedmace are common, whilst rarer plants such as narrow-leaved water-plantain may also be found. Invertebrates, too, are an important aspect of the ditches. Dragonflies and water beetles are well represented, and the site is one of the best in Britain for freshwater molluscs. Breeding birds include reed and sedge warbler, reed bunting and yellow wagtail. In winter, high water levels attract a wide variety of waterfowl such as shoveler, teal and wigeon, as well as waders like snipe and golden plover. Short-eared owl and hen harrier are also common. The traditional management of grazing cattle and sheep, together with periodic dyke maintenance, ensures that the variety of habitats is conserved.

Steadham Common

SU 855219; 35ha; STNC reserve
Wet and dry heathland
All year

Parts of the reserve have reverted to their woodland origins but regular and accidental fires have kept this change in check in other areas, allowing heather and gorse to flourish. The reserve is predominantly dry heath, but some small areas of wet heath result in a wide range of plant species. Heathland bird species such as stonechats, tree pipits and nightjars are present but the most noteworthy group of animals is the invertebrates, with the rich spider fauna a particular feature.

Warwickshire and West Midlands

Bishops Bowl

SP 390590; 50ha; WARNACT reserve—commercial fishery
Lakes, wood and grassland
Summer

The lakes left by abandoned limestone quarrying now support a thriving commercial fishery, but the surrounding land has been allowed to develop naturally into a range of wildlife habitats. A carefully laid out nature trail gives excellent views over the main lake, with mute swan, tufted duck and occasionally kingfisher. The small pools, with dense stands of commmon reed and lesser reedmace, are the breeding grounds of moorhen, reed warbler and reed bunting. On the drier slopes, the calcareous grassland, rich in orchids, is a haven for meadow butterflies, including marbled white and common blue.

Decoy Spinney

Permit only; 1.6ha; WARNACT reserve
Small wood and pools
Spring, summer

A disused duck decoy, now surrounded by developing oak woodland and coniferous plantation, the reserve is situated in the centre of a thriving farm. The broadleaved wood has a hazel understorey with dog's mercury and bluebell, whilst the pools are surrounded by common reed and sedges, home for moorhen, coot and reed bunting.

Elmdon Manor

Permit only; 6ha; WARNACT reserve
Walled garden, wood and ponds
All year

The walled garden in the centre of the reserve is being converted into a wildflower nursery and tree bank, where threatened species can be grown on for later use on reserves or other wildlife areas. The remainder of the site contains a mixture of habitats, with some mixed woodland, a wet meadow and two shaded ponds.

Hampton Wood

Permit only; 11.1ha; WARNACT reserve
Broadleaved woodland with grass and scrub
Spring, early summer

An excellent wood for its springtime display of flowers, with carpets of primrose and bluebell mixed with red campion and yellow archangel. The hawthorn scrub provides good cover for woodland birds, including goldcrest, wren, spotted flycatcher and whitethroat. Two streams and a deep gulley provide moister areas where hard shield-fern and hart's-tongue thrive alongside mosses.

Ladywalk

SP 215920; 50ha; CEGB–West Midlands Bird Club reserve
Islands, lagoons and scrub
Permit only from West Midland Bird Club
Leaflet from CEGB or West Midland Bird Club
All year

The reserve, at Hams Hall Power Station, lies in a loop of the River Tame and attracts many wetland birds. There is an environmental studies centre at the site.

Lion Wood

Permit only; 3.4ha; WARNACT–WCNT reserve
Acid oak woodland
Spring, summer

This woodland is unusual for the county in being acidic, with bilberry, rowan, alder buckthorn and holly flourishing under a canopy of oak and birch. Despite the wood's small size, blue tit, great tit, wren and robin are all resident, and migratory fieldfare and redwing can reach large numbers.

Nether Whitacre

Permit only; 21.7ha; WARNACT reserve
Willow scrub, marsh and pools
Spring, summer

Bordered by the River Tame, this reserve was previously part of a sand and gravel quarry. It now supports a dense thicket of willow and alder scrub on the drier areas, with marsh grassland and pools in the centre. Although the scrub is generally poor for flowering plants, it provides shelter for the many reedbeds and their associated birds, such as reed warbler, sedge warbler and water-rail. The wetland is rich in invertebrate life, and in summer the emperor dragonfly and banded agrion damselfly flash their irridescent colours over the water. In the open grassier places are centuary and both common spotted and marsh-orchids.

Newton Gorse

Permit only; 3.4ha; WARNACT reserve
Mixed woodland
Early summer

Situated in a treeless part of north Warwickshire, this reserve provides a welcome haven for woodland birds such as blue tit, great tit and even woodcock. The predominance of coniferous trees has led to a poor ground flora, but has encouraged both goldcrest and siskin.

Old Nun Wood

Permit only; 2.1ha; WARNACT reserve
Broadleaved woodland
Spring, early summer

Although small, this reserve is close to the much larger WAPPENBURY WOOD, and so much of the rich animal life moves freely between the two. Predominantly oak and ash, there is a coppice of hazel with field maple, birch and willow also in the scrub layer. Its ancient woodland origins are hinted at by the spring displays of wood sorrel, wood anemone, bluebell and yellow archangel. A recent coloniser is the muntjac deer.

Priory Fields

SP 099789; 5.4ha; WARNACT reserve
Grassland
Summer

A damp meadow area on the Birmingham–Solihull boundary fed by a small spring and bounded by the Stratford Canal. The main interest of the site lies in its grassland, where all the common meadow grasses are intermixed with an assortment of colourful flowering plants, including yellow rattle, knapweed, vetches and trefoils.

Ryton Wood

Permit only; 68ha; WARNACT reserve
Oak woodland
Spring, summer

Probably one of the largest remaining fragments of the Forest of Arden, Ryton is of outstanding wildlife value in every respect. It is a pedunculate oak wood, with an understorey of hazel and patches of small-leaved lime and both birches. Also in the understorey are spindle, guelder-rose, dogwood and field maple, while the ground flora contains primrose, bluebell, wood sorrel, wood anemone and wood millet. The sunlit rides are home to white admiral, wood white, purple hairstreak, comma, ringlet and brimstone butterflies, while a small pool and damper areas add to the overall diversity.

A breeding population of nightingales adds a welcome melody to the six species of tits, six warblers, and tree pipits, while all three woodpeckers, nuthatch and treecreeper are also found.

Wiltshire

Clanger Wood

ST 873538; 52.5ha; WdT reserve
Mixed woodland
Spring, summer

This reserve was formerly broadleaved woodland, but has now been substantially replanted with mixed conifers. However, blocks of the original oak woodland remain among the areas of replanting. The wood is renowned for its wildlife and is an especially rich site for birds and butterflies. In spring and summer the ground is covered with a mass of woodland flowers.

Kingsettle Wood

See Dorset, p. 669.

Parsonage Down

SU 045412; 276ha; NCC reserve
Chalk downland
Permission required from warden
Spring, summer

This area of downland is unusual in that it is gently undulating and is normally grazed by cattle. The diversity of plants in relation to the topography is the most interesting feature of the reserve. There is a varied invertebrate fauna and the adonis blue butterfly occurs.

Yorkshire and North Humberside

Bilton Beck and Rudding Bottoms Woods

SE 315584; 18.7ha; WdT reserve
Mixed woodland
Spring, summer

The reserve lies in the Nidd Gorge north-west of Harrogate, with the impressive railway viaduct dominating the area. Once a deciduous woodland of oak with ash and alder in the wetter valley bottom and shrub species of predominantly hazel and holly, much of the area has now been cleared and replanted with beech and conifers. Some semi-natural areas still remain.

Church Plantation

NZ 580064; 1.6ha; WdT reserve
Deciduous woodland
Spring, summer

The wood was replanted in the 1950s with an unusual mixture of broadleaved trees, sycamore, poplar and hornbeam. It is, however, an important landscape feature within the NORTH YORK MOORS NATIONAL PARK. A stream runs through the wood, which has great potential for improvement with careful management.

Nabs Wood

SE 296039; 4.8ha; WdT reserve
Deciduous woodland
Spring, summer

The reserve is an attractive broadleaved wood of oak, ash and beech with a number of healthy mature elms. The ground flora is varied and interesting, and a stream which runs through the area adds to its appeal.

Oakwell Hall Country Park

SE 218270; 35ha; Kirklees MDC
Grassland, woodland and wildlife garden
Nature-trail booklet available on site
All year

There are fragments of sessile oak–birch woodland with rowan, holly and whitebeam. In an abandoned railway cutting linnets occur in the open areas and several species of tits are to be found in areas where scrub is developing into woodland. There are small streams with wetland plants, such as brooklime, and a pond where smooth newts breed.

Rother Valley Country Park

SK 469824; 300ha; South Yorkshire CC
Lakes, grassland, marsh, scrub and woodland
No public access to reserve area but ample viewing points
Leaflets available on site
Summer, winter

The country park is a former open-cast coal-mining site. Two of the five lakes have been set aside as a nature reserve, and at present they attract large numbers of gulls, as well as tufted duck, pochard, whooper and Bewick swans. It is hoped that future control of the water levels will attract waders on passage. A few small areas of hay meadow escaped mining and still support colonies of southern marsh-orchid and grass snakes, while common toads, frog and great crested and smooth newts breed in the old ditches.

Scar and Castlebeck Woods

SE 947970; 27ha; WdT reserve
Broadleaf woodland
Spring, summer

This important woodland in the NORTH YORK MOORS NATIONAL PARK lies on a steep scar overlooking the Jugger Howe Beck. It is predominantly an oak/birch wood with hazel understorey. In the wetter parts, ash and alder dominate. There is an area of hazel coppice in the southern part of the reserve where coppicing is being reinstated. This will help to promote the rich ground flora.

Thorne Moors

SE 721152; 78ha; NCC reserve
Peat bog
Strictly by permit only from NCC
Summer

Between the rivers Aire and Trent lies a lowland raised mire of 2000ha, the largest in England. Thorne Moors is just part of this complex. Peat has always been cut on the reserve and the original bog surface has been destroyed. It has now been colonised by peat-loving plants and is developing in parts into birch woodland. Interesting plants include bog-rosemary, cranberry, sundew and royal fern. The moors are also notable for insects and birds. Large heath butterflies are at their most southern locality, whilst nightingales reach their northern limit here.

Thrybergh Country Park

SE 476959; 28.3ha; Rotherham MBC
Lake and grassland
Leaflets available from visitor centre
All year

Based on an old water-supply reservoir, this country park has great ornithological interest. Wildfowl counts have shown that 900 ducks and 9000 gulls can be present on a single day in winter. As many as 170 plants species and over 225 species of invertebrate have been recorded.

Worsbrough Hill Country Park

SE 346033; 38.5ha; S Yorks MCC
Woodland, grassland, reservoir and willow carr
Leaflet available on site
All year

Birds are of particular note, with lesser spotted woodpecker, sparrowhawk, tawny and little owl being recorded around the woodland, and migrant waders, kingfisher and water-rail visit the reservoir area. All three species of newt occur, along with common toad, frog and grass snake.

Wales

Clwyd

Coed Tyddn halen

SJ 155725; 2.8ha; WdT reserve
Mixed valley woodland
Spring, summer

A secluded woodland in a quiet valley with a wide variety of trees and shrubs and a rich ground flora. A fast flowing stream and marshy area provide added interest.

Coed y Glyn

SJ 104732; 1.3ha; WdT reserve
Deciduous woodland
Spring, summer

The wood is on the steep side of a valley with several springs making it very wet in parts. Alder coppice dominates the area, with larger oak and ash over hazel coppice in drier parts. The ground flora is very rich, especially in the damp flushes.

Pwll-gwyn Wood

SJ 127723; 2.3ha; WdT reserve
Deciduous woodland
Spring, summer

Situated on a prominent hill above the River Wheeler, the coppiced woodland of oak, ash and sycamore was last cut during the Second World War. Older trees are found around the woodland edge and, although Dutch elm disease has had its effect, the gaps created by the loss of elms have now been filled by ash regeneration.

Sontley Moor

SJ 337476; 5ha; NWNT–NT reserve
Wet grassland, marsh and scrub
Permit only from NWNT
Spring, summer

The reserve comprises a complex mosaic of dry to wet grassland. The marsh area is dominated by giant horsetail, *Juncus* species and great willowherb, while in the wide range of sub-habitats species include bird cherry, wood and water avens, black bindweed and yellow rattle. Birds are not abundant, but willow tit, reed bunting, tawny owl and mallard all breed. Grass snake, frog and toad are common, and polecats have been recorded.

Dyfed

Allt Ddol Lan

SN 422402; 12.5ha; WWTNC reserve
Coppice woodland
All year

A woodland of high scenic value on the south bank of the Afon Teifi near Llandyssul comprised mainly of mature coppice with sessile oak and downy birch dominant in the canopy.

Allt Fedw Cutting

SN 665730; 1ha; WWTNC reserve
Disused railway cutting
Spring, summer

This section of cutting and embankment close to the village of Trawscoed was formerly known as Birchgrove Railway Line. The cutting is a shady, sheltered area with numerous mosses, liverworts and ferns, and several species of orchids. The embankment, an open, sunny area, is a particularly rich habitat for butterflies, with some 24 species recorded.

Brunt Hill

SM 816074; 3.4ha; WWTNC reserve
Coniferous plantation with some mixed woodland
All year

Numerous oak and birch trees have been planted so as to gradually convert this reserve from coniferous to broad-leaved woodland. There are active badger setts and raptors regularly roost in the quarry. Particularly fine views can be had of the adjoining saltmarsh from the top of the reserve.

Caeau Llety Cybi

SN 603535; 3.4ha; WWTNC reserve
Four small herb-rich pastures
Spring, summer

These dry fertile fields have fortunately escaped agricultural improvement and provide a sward rich in herbaceous plants. By far the most interesting species is the greater butterfly orchid, rarely seen elsewhere in Ceredigion. The reserve is surrounded by and divided by mixed hedges managed in the traditional manner.

Cemaes Head

SN 132500; 16ha; WWTNC reserve
Coastal cliffs
Permit only away from coastal footpath
All year

A spectacular section of the Pembrokeshire coastline with a range of cliff scenery – steep slopes, cliffs, gullies and small beaches. There is a small population of choughs and peregrines are regularly seen. The seabird population is small and includes cormorant, shag and fulmar, while other species are regularly seen offshore, as are grey seals.

Coed Allt Troed-y-rhiw Fawr

SN 413255; 15.8ha; WdT reserve
Deciduous woodland
Spring, summer

The wood stands at the entrance to the wooded gorge of the Afon Gwili and, rising almost vertically from the river to the top of the valley, dominates the view from the south. The reserve is dominated by oak and ash with smaller numbers of birch, cherry and sycamore.

Coed Cwm Ddu

SN 309429; 26ha; WWTNC reserve
Sessile oakwood
All year

The three blocks of woodland on the steep slopes of the Ceri Valley are mostly coppice regrowth from felling during the First World War. There is a well-developed ground flora. The woodland birds include redstart and pied flycatcher, while kingfisher, grey wagtail and dipper occur along the river.

Coed Perthneidr

SN 416584; 3.2ha; WdT reserve
Deciduous woodland and scrub
Spring, summer

The small hillside wood is a mixture of oak and ash with some sycamore and a good shrub layer dominated by hazel. At the top of the hill, which provides fine views, are some former fields now becoming overgrown with scrub.

Coed Simdde Lwyd

SN 720786; 29ha; WWTNC reserve
Sessile oakwood
All year

This superb section of the Rheidol Valley woodland on a south-facing slope includes the Rheidol Falls, a hanging valley of great geomorphological interest. The sheltered valley at the east end of the reserve has a great variety of tree species, with cherry, wych elm and small-leaved lime. Of special interest in west Wales are the large colonies of wood ant.

Commins Capel Betws

Permit only; 7ha; WWTNC reserve
Marsh, heath and unimproved neutral grassland
Spring, summer

Part of an area of former commonland in central Ceredigion, the reserve contains many interesting heath and marsh species, including lesser butterfly orchid, petty whin and whorled carraway. Curlew, snipe and mallard breed.

Cors Goch

Permit only; 11ha; WWTNC reserve
Raised mire
Spring, summer

Two sections of the raised mire on the south side of the Carmarthen to Haverfordwest railway line. The larger western section has had a number of drainage channels dug at some time in the past. This has resulted in an invasion by birch, and current management includes the blocking of the channels to raise the water table, and the removal of the birch. Interesting species include royal fern, cranberry, bog asphodel and bog myrtle. The marsh fritillary butterfly, bog bush cricket and black sympetrum dragonfly are just three of the invertebrates found.

Cors Gorsgoch

SN 482504; 17ha; WWTNC reserve
Soligenous valley mire
Spring, summer

The whole of the southern section of the mire which lies to the south of Gorsgoch village is a Trust reserve. The stream forming the headwaters of the Afon Grannell flows north-west through the site, which contains a number of glacial features known as pingoes in which mires have developed, with dominant bog mosses and species like white sedge, round-leaved sundew, cranberry and bog asphodel. The pond close to the eastern boundary attracts wildfowl in winter and is a good dragonfly habitat in summer.

Ffrwd Farm Mire

SN 420026; 25ha; WWTNC reserve
Fen
Spring, summer

The reserve, which is bounded by a road, disused canal and mineral railway, has a diversity of wetland habitats including species-rich fen, reedswamp, drier raised dune area, open water in ditches, and rough pasture. Several scarce species occur, including the marsh pea, frogbit, tubular water-dropwort and floating club-rush.

Fign Blaen Brefi

SN 717547; 45ha; WWTNC reserve
Blanket mire
Spring, summer

This blanket mire shows a good deal of erosion more usually associated with the peatlands of north-west Scotland. This has been caused by the Afon Brefi eating into the peat-covered watershed, resulting in large areas of peat wastage. The drier sections support heather, cross-leaved heath, bilberry and crowberry, while bog pondweed, bogbean, cottongrass, bog asphodel and star sedge occur in the wetter gullies.

Gelli Aur Country Park

SN 596198; 36ha; Dyfed CC
Estate parkland
Open spring and summer only, except to organised parties
Leaflets from DCC or warden on site
Spring, summer

The park has a series of natural trails through a variety of habitats. Fallow deer are also present.

Llyn Fanod

SN 604645; 0.25ha; WWTNC reserve
Upland lake
All year

The Trust owns only the northern section of this upland lake, which may aptly be described as a sister to LLYN EIDDWEN to the north. The range of aquatic plants is similar but with the addition of both white and yellow water-lilies.

Poor Man's Wood

SN 784356; 18ha; WWTNC reserve
Sessile oak woodland
All year

An ancient woodland gifted to the nearby town of Llandovery in the sixteenth century with the condition that any wood removed had to be carried away by the person. The area has been coppiced, though some large maiden trees remain. A small number of wild service-trees occur at one spot within the reserve.

Rhos Fullbrook

Permit only; 2ha; WWTNC reserve
Herb-rich, unimproved grassland
Spring, summer

The grassland contains a number of slightly base-rich flushes, alluvial marsh and some scrub. Over 100 high plants have been recorded, including devil's-bit scabious, lesser butterfly orchid, heath spotted-orchid, dyer's greenweed, petty whin, round-leaved sundew and butterwort.

Rhos Pil-Bach

Permit only; 10.4ha; WTNC reserve
Sedge-rich grassland
Spring, summer

One of the most species-rich and extensive areas of neutral–slightly base-rich, damp meadows in Ceredigion. Two of the five fields that form the reserve are superb examples of ancient ridge-and-furrow pastures. The grassland is particularly rich in orchids, with heath spotted, northern marsh and common spotted orchids. Three small ponds add diversity to the site.

Stackpole

SR 977950; 199ha; NT–NCC reserve
Sea cliffs, dunes, calcareous grassland and fresh-water lakes
Leaflets from NT, NCC or PCNPA
Spring, summer, winter
See also BOSHERSTON PONDS TO STACKPOLE HEAD, p. 454.

Tregeyb Wood

SN 641217; 28ha; WdT reserve
Mixed woodland
Spring, summer

The wood is of great landscape significance within the BRECON BEACONS NATIONAL PARK. While under commercial management, a large area was felled and replanted, but now that it has been acquired by the Trust no further large-scale felling will take place. A field within the wood is being allowed to regenerate naturally and a good system of rides throughout the wood provides a variety of attractive walks.

Wern ddu Wood

Permit only; 1.5ha; WWTNC reserve
Mixed woodland and rough pasture
All year

A section of woodland kindly gifted to the Trust. It contains a number of particularly fine oak and beech trees and a typical woodland ground flora. The bryophytes include several species rarely recorded elsewhere.

Western Cleddau Mire

Permit only; 13ha; WWTNC reserve
Flood-plain mire
Spring, summer

Part of the largest remaining flood-plain mire in Wales, through which flows the Western Cleddau. The range of wetland habitats includes superb high tussocks (up to 2m high) of greater tussock sedge. The water dock occurs frequently in the wettest parts of the fen, while there is a stand of the scarce northern bay willow. The Western Cleddau is of exceptional importance for otters and the reserve provides much cover for undisturbed feeding and resting areas.

Glamorgan

Clyne Valley Country Park

SS 610915; 294ha; Swansea City Council
Wet valley floor and wooded hillside
Leaflet from SCC
All year

The Clyne River is quite out of proportion to its valley, which was enlarged during the Ice Age when the soft coal-measures were easily eroded. The valley was exploited for its coal and also for clay, which was used at the nearby brickworks. The pathway occupies the track of the LMS route into Swansea. The wet valley floor is noted for its show of marsh-marigolds beneath the predominantly alder woodland. The oak woods of the valley sides are partly invaded by rhododendrons, and in places the three-cornered leek is found – both invaders from the private estates that formerly owned much of the area.

Dunraven Park

SS 890729; 22.7ha; Glamorgan Heritage Coast
Project – South Glamorgan CC
Parkland and restored gardens
Leaflets from Heritage Centre
Spring, summer

The parkland has magnificent views and historic walled gardens interpreted according to various themes, including a plant-explorers' garden. Nearby are limestone cliffs and Dunraven beach.

Llantwit Major Beach

SS 956675; 17.8ha; Glamorgan Heritage Coast
Project – South Glamorgan CC
Coastal cliffs and rocky shore
Five leaflets from Glamorgan Heritage Coast Project
Spring, summer

Col-huw Beach, Llantwit Major, is the starting point for walks, which take in the vertical sea cliffs and wide rocky platform exposed at low tide. The varied flora includes sea cabbage, wild carrot, rock sea-lavender and various algae on the rocky shore. Goldfinch, stonechat, yellowhammer and whitethroat may be seen on the cliffs and, on sunny days, there are many butterflies such as tortoiseshell, gate-keeper and common blue.

Summer House Point

SS 995665; 6.1ha; Glamorgan Heritage Coast
Project – South Glamorgan, by agreement with
South Wales Christian Outreach Trust
Cliffs with woodland
Leaflet from Glamorgan Heritage Coast Project
Spring, summer

An eighteenth-century summerhouse was built within a large Iron Age promontory fort and the undisturbed scrubland habitat of the ancient monument forms an oasis for wildlife. Woolly thistles, sea cabbage and hemlock are among the variety of plants found, and garden warblers, pigeons and yellowhammers take shelter in the copses. Just to the east is a fine example of a storm beach.

Swansea Canal

(Godre'rgraig to Ynysmeudw)

SN 743060; West Glamorgan CC reserve
Derelict canal with carr woodland; good for
dragonflies
Spring, summer

Gwent

Brockwells Meadows

ST 471896; 4.6ha; GTNC reserve
Limestone hay meadows
Permit from GTNC, otherwise 3 public open days
per year
Spring, summer

In spring the limestone flora is at its best, with green-winged orchids being the main attraction. Midsummer is the best time to see insects on the reserve, the highlight being the nationally rare great robber fly, while in late summer there is a fine display of autumn lady's-tresses.

Burness Castle Quarry

ST 461884; 2ha; GTNC reserve
Disused limstone quarry, grassland and woodland
Permit only from GTNC
Spring, summer

This shallow disused limestone quarry is an interesting mixture of grassland and secondary woodland. Many of the species present are scarce in Gwent, including star-of-Bethlehem and viper's-bugloss. There is also a good selection of mosses.

Caldicot Bee Orchid Site

ST 487877; 1.5ha; GTNC reserve
Limestone grassland
Permits required from GTNC
Spring, summer

The sites lie above the Severn tunnel between a rapidly expanding housing estate and the main South Wales railway line. There is a typical limestone flora, including bee orchid, kidney vetch and yellow-wort. It is also a good area for butterflies and the locally distributed marbled white can be seen.

Cwm Merddog

SO 185065; 20ha; GTNC reserve
Ancient woodland and wet flushes
Spring, summer

The reserve is a mixture of old beech woodland, wet flushes with alder and willow, regenerating spoil-tips and moorland. It is a good site for lichens, ferns and orchids, and there are fine views down the valley. The area of common land above the reserve is one of the most attractive heather moors in Gwent.

Dixton Embankment

SO 524147; 2ha; GTNC reserve
Limestone grassland
Spring, summer

The reserve lies between the A40 and the River Wye, and is very similar to the CALDICOT BEE ORCHID SITE, with a good range of lime-loving plants, including bee orchids. The area also supports a variety of butterflies.

Great Triley Wood

SO 310182; 6.4ha; WdT reserve
Deciduous woodland
Spring, summer

Lying on the marsh banks of the River Gavanny, the wood contains many fine oak and ash trees, while in the wetter areas there are large alders and willows. The ground flora is rich and varied, including herb-Paris.

Penhow Woodlands

ST 418901; 24ha; NCC reserve
Woodland
Access to south-western part of reserve only
Spring, summer

These woods contain a large variety of tree species and support a wealth of characteristic woodland plants and insects.

Priory Wood

SO 352057; 5ha; GTNC reserve
Mixed woodland
Spring, early summer

This small wood has a tremendous variety of woodland types within it, including oak, birch, cherry and beech above the old quarry. The birdlife is particularly rich, with pied flycatchers being a recent addition to the breeding list.

Sirhowy Valley Country Park

ST 200908; 325ha; Gwent CC
Woodland, grassland and riverside
Spring, summer, autumn

The Country Park is based on a disused railway line with regenerating birch, oak and alder, and adjoining woodland and meadowland next to the River Sirhowy. Buzzards, herons and foxes frequent the area and bluebells carpet the woodland in spring. There is a visitor centre at the former Babell Chapel, Cwmfelin Fach.

Gwynedd

Caeau Tan y Bwlch

SH 432489; 5ha; NWNT reserve
Unimproved grassland and mire
Summer

There is a very large colony of greater butterfly orchids on the meadows, along with heath and common spotted orchids, fairy flax, lady's-mantle, knapweed and yellow rattle. The soligenous mire is dominated by rushes with purple moor-grass tussocks. Bilberry and cranberry are common and sundew can easily be found. Grasshopper warblers breed and buzzard, raven, curlew and snipe are frequent visitors. Butterflies recorded include green-veined white, small heath, ringlet, peacock and small tortoiseshell.

Coed Allt

SH 620357; 3.2ha; WdT reserve
Deciduous woodland
Spring, summer

A young oak woodland which has been developed naturally on a steep slope after the area was fenced to exclude grazing sheep. Ravens nest in the older trees near the rocky crags.

Because of the steepness of the ground, access to the reserve is not recommended.

Coed Avens

SH 476923; 0.7ha; WdT reserve
Young broadleaf woodland
Spring, summer

A field overlooking the sea was planted up with mixed broadleaved trees. The site faces north-west so is protected from the prevailing south-west winds on Anglesey. A public footpath runs through the reserve, which as it matures will become an important broadleaved wood on the windswept island where even individual trees are uncommon.

Coed Bron Garth

SH 821793; 5.5ha; WdT reserve
Mixed woodland
Spring, summer

The wood supports a wide range of tree and shrub species, including small-leaved lime, hornbeam, yew and spindle — all species uncommon in the country except on this small area of limestone rocks around Llandudno and Colwyn Bay. Underplanted with some conifers before it became a reserve, these are now being removed to prevent the loss of the interesting ground flora of lime-loving plants.

Coed Crafnant

SH 618289; 20ha; NWNT reserve
Sessile oakwood
All year

For much of the year this woodland, which adjoins COED DOL-Y-BEBIN, is drenched by gales sweeping off the Atlantic and, being untouched by all but the evening and high summer sun, it has developed a special character of its own. The dimness and humidity offer 130 species of mosses and liverworts freedom from competition from other more robust plants and the woodland is therefore considered of international importance for its bryophytes. Species with extremely restricted national distribution occur here, such as the liverworts *Jamesoniella autumnalis* or *Cephaloziella pearsonii*. Other rare species include the moss *Dicranum scottianum*, the liverworts *Porella pinnata* and *Lepidozia pinnata*, and the lichen *Sphaerophorus melanocarpus*.

Coed Cymerau Isaf

SH 691425; 32ha; WdT reserve
Deciduous woodland, unimproved meadows and marsh
Spring, summer

The mixture of woodland, herb-rich grassland and marsh surrounds an old farmhouse dating back to the seventeenth century. The woodland of oak and birch with hazel in the more fertile areas has been heavily grazed in the past and this has impoverished the ground flora. The contrast between this reserve and the adjoining COED CYMERAU which is ungrazed, emphasises this effect. Several of the meadows are rich in flowers and the marshes are also interesting botanically, with both species of cottongrass. From the upper parts of the woods there are fine views of the Festiniog Valley.

Coed Garth Gell

SH 687191; 46ha; RSPB reserve
Deciduous woodland
Spring, summer

This sessile oak and birch wood lies on a hillside overlooking the Mawddach Estuary in the SNOWDONIA NATIONAL PARK. It supports a typical bird community, including pied flycatchers, redstarts, wood warblers and great spotted woodpeckers. Buzzards and ravens also nest here. The woodland is bounded by a dramatic river gorge where grey wagtails and dippers are found. The reserve is in part of the old Dolgellau goldfield and there are the remains of a number of worked out nineteenth-century mines.

Coed Porthamel

SH 508678; 2.4ha; NWNT reserve
Mixed woodland
Key for gate from warden at Porthamel Old Farm House or from Trust office
Spring

The reserve includes Coed Brain, a 0.5ha wood of sycamore. Green hellebore and golden-leaved saxifrage grow near the stream and ransoms cover much of the ground. The main part of the reserve is mixed deciduous woodland with good patches of brambles and nettles which attract many butterflies and provide food for birds later in the year. The most notable species of the 43 which have been recorded are merlin, stock dove, long-tailed tit and wood warbler. Records of *Catoptria falsellus* and *Teichobia filicivora* were both the first for these moths on Anglesey.

Coed Tremadoc

SH 569405; 20ha; NCC reserve
Deciduous woodland and cliffs
Strictly no access
Spring, summer

The woodland lies on the steep slope of the hill overlooking the village of Tremadoc. Much of the hillside is made up of scree of huge tumbled blocks of slate – here only a few scattered sessile oaks occur. But where there is soil – in pockets on the hill and at the base of the slope – a mixed woodland of sessile oak, ash and sycamore is found. The smaller plants are of the acid-loving type – wavy hairgrass, bilberry and wood sage, with the cliff ledges holding a richer selection, including orpine, marjoram and stonecrop.

Cors Bodeilio

SH 500775; 6ha; NCC reserve
Fen
Strictly no access
Spring, summer

The reserve lies in a shallow valley surrounded by limestone hills, which give the peat an interesting variety of lime-loving plants. Of particular note are the orchids, with fragrant, fly, frog, lesser butterfly, and a selection of marsh-orchids and marsh helleborines.

Great Orme Country Park and LNR

SH 767834; 291ha; Aberconwy BC
Coastal headland with grassland and heath
Booklet from visitor centre on site
Spring, summer, autumn

This fine carboniferous limestone headland has now become a country park and LNR, (see GREAT ORME NATURE TRAILS). The interesting calicole flora includes wild cabbage, spring squill, bloody crane's bill and common and hoary rockrose. Apart from the usual breeding seabirds, spring and autumn migrants such as golden plover, ring ouzels and whinchat often stop over on the reserve, and gannets, skuas and Manx shearwaters pass offshore. In winter snow buntings and black redstarts are seen, and divers and grebes often shelter in the bays.

Mariandyrys

SH 604809; 6ha; NWNT reserve
Limestone grassland
Spring, summer

The patchwork of vegetation on this reserve includes species-rich grassland with autumn gentian, rock-rose, ploughman's-spikenard, burnet saxifrage and spring squill; a sloping area dominated by Western gorse and bell heather, with grassy patches containing carline thistle, columbine and fragrant orchid; and a quarry, the floor of which supports pale flax and a small colony of bee orchids. Ten species of butterflies, including grayling, common blue, brown argus and large skipper have been recorded, and adders occur on the reserve.

Marle Hall Woods

SH 798791; 12ha; WdT reserve
Mixed woodland, limestone pavement and cliffs, species-rich grassland
Do not attempt to reach the top of the wood by going up the cliff face
Spring, summer

The reserve has a wide range of different habitats, including limestone pavement, cliffs, important grassland rich in limestone plants, and several different woodland types with a number of unusual plants.

Parc Mawr

SH 760740; 34ha; WdT reserve
Mixed woodland
Spring, summer

Situated on a hillside overlooking the beautiful Conway Valley on the edge of the SNOWDONIA NATIONAL PARK, part of the broadleaved woodland has been felled and replanted with conifers, but sympathetic management will eventually restore the whole reserve to broadleaves once again.

The Skerries

SH 270950; 17ha; RSPB reserve
Offshore islands
No access

A small group of rocky islets 2 miles off the north-west coast of Anglesey. The islands were once a major tern colony but were deserted by the terns during the 1960s. However, arctic terns returned in 1979 and have now built up to 150 pairs. There is also a large colony of herring and lesser black-backed gulls, as well as puffins and oystercatchers breeding. The reserve is an important site for autumn migrants.

Powys

Cwm Wood

SN 952633; 8ha; RSPB reserve
Deciduous woodland
Spring, summer

This mixed deciduous wood in the upper Wye Valley has typical breeding birds such as pied flycatchers, redstarts, wood warblers and tree pipits. The wood also has a good variety of mosses and liverworts.

Dolifor Wood

SN 960655; 11.6ha; WdT reserve
Mixed woodland
Spring, summer

A recently planted woodland in the Elan Valley, an area of dramatic landscape where the young trees are beginning to make impact, though the wood blends in well with the surrounding scenery.

Gaer Fawr Wood

SJ 223128; 30ha; WdT reserve
Mixed woodland, grassland
Spring, summer

The reserve is set on a steep, saddlebacked hill overlooking the Severn Valley close to the Welsh border. From the top of the hill it is possible to see for many miles. This natural look-out was once a hill fort and the banks and ditches of this important archaeological site can still be seen clearly today. The wood itself has a wide variety of trees and shrubs, including naturally regenerated birch, old coppice, oak and many other species of broadleaf trees. Small groups of conifers can be seen near the summit. There is an area of open ground on the south-western slope.

Graig Wood

SJ 175085; 3.2ha; WdT reserve
Deciduous woodland
Spring, summer

This lovely hillside wood consists largely of sessile oak standards over coppice with a few beech and ash trees on the boundaries.

Park Wood

SO 167338; 57ha; WdT reserve
Mixed woodland
Spring, summer

The reserve is sited on a prominent hillside above Talgarth on the lower slopes of the Black Mountains on the north-east edge of the BRECON BEACONS NATIONAL PARK. A former broadleaf woodland, which follows the hillside above the upper Wye Valley for about 3km, is an important feature of the landscape. About half has been converted to a mixture of conifers and hardwood, but fortunately the rest remains in a semi-natural state.

Roundton Hill

SO 294949; 35ha; MTNC reserve
Unimproved heath grassland
Spring, summer

Roundton Hill rises to 365m, giving fine views over both England and Wales. It is an important site for its unusual plant communities developed on thin volcanic-derived soils. Species include rock stonecrop, wild thyme and carline thistle, and over 100 species of lichen have been recorded. The area supports an interesting range of birds such as wheatear, redstart and woodpeckers.

Stanner Rocks

SO 262583; 5ha; NCC reserve
Deciduous woodland with rocky outcrops and grassland
Access to quarry floor only
Leaflet from Dyfed–Powys Office
Spring, summer

Sessile oak, with occasional ash and wych elm, and a hazel and elder shrub layer form the woodlands. The cliffs, facing south-east and some 230–300m in height, are subject to summer drought, thus maintaining open communities of plants of base-rich and base-poor soils. There are some interesting mosses and lichens.

Scotland

Borders

Cragbank Wood

Permit only; 9ha; NCC reserve
Deciduous woodland
Apply to South-East Scotland Office
Spring, summer, autumn

The wood is a mixture of ash, wych elm, alder and hazel with a wide diversity of associated flowering plants, ferns and lichens, which indicate the ancient, undisturbed nature of the site and include some species now extremely scarce in south-east Scotland. The dead and dying timber provides ideal habitat for many species of insect. Herb-rich grasslands at the edge of the wood add variety.

Whitlaw Wood

Permit only; 9ha; SWT reserve
Broadleaved valley woodland
Spring, summer

The underlying Silurian rocks of greywackes and shales are base-rich in parts and support elm–ash woodland with pockets of beech and oak; coppiced hazel is common, with bird cherry, rowan and blackthorn. The rich ground flora of primrose, early-purple orchid, woodruff, wood-sedge, goldilocks buttercup and sanicle is enhanced by wet flushes running down the steep slopes with angelica and meadowsweet. Great spotted woodpecker, woodcock and sparrowhawk all frequent the wood and an adjoining river enhances the reserve.

Central

Ben Lomond

NN 3602; 2173ha; NTS–FC reserve
Woodland and mountain heathland
Access by footpath from Rowardennan or Kinlochard
Late spring, summer

Ben Lomond, the most southerly of Scotland's mountains over 1000m, is also one of the most frequently climbed, being less than 50km from the centre of Glasgow. Lying within the QUEEN ELIZABETH FOREST PARK, the lower slopes of the Ben have been planted with conifers, but extensive areas of older oakwoods remain around the Rowardennan car park and to both north and south along the loch shore. These contain an attractive diversity of woodland birds, including treecreeper, wood warbler and redstart.

The upper slopes of the Ben belong to the NTS and are devoted to hill sheep-farming. On the ledges of the north-east cliffs, where sheep cannot graze, a luxuriant moss heath survives and in the wetter areas bog myrtle and willow scrub predominate. Birdlife is rather sparse but there are meadow pipits and grouse in the area. Both roe and red deer live in the woods and a herd of wild goats may occasionally be encountered.

Dumfries and Galloway

Southwick Coast

NX 9155; 16ha; SWT reserve
Coast, marsh and wood
Path down track to Needle's Eye
All year

Located at the western end of the Inner Solway complex of mudflats and saltmarshes, this area is of outstanding importance because of the vast flocks of geese (greylag, pink-footed and barnacle), duck and waders that overwinter. On the landward side a stranded cliffline supports a unique ancient oakwood. The presence of hazel and holly in the woodland bears testimony to its undisturbed character and the rich ground flora with early-purple orchid confirms this. Base-rich springs flush the lower slopes of the woodland and then flow into an area of brackish water fen, transitional to saltmarsh with sea lavender.

Wood of Cree

NX 382708; 212ha; RSPB reserve
Deciduous woodland, marsh, small burns and
lochs, moorland
Spring, summer

There are references to the Wood of Cree as early
as the thirteenth century and the reserve forms
part of the largest remaining ancient woodland in
the south of Scotland. Much of the area consists of
overgrown coppice of birch, ash, hazel, rowan and
willow, which were last cut in the 1920s. Most of
the oaks are of a similar age – about 100 years old,
as the woodland was all felled in 1875.

Despite the uniformity of age and lack of
management, the wood is rich in birdlife. There is
a large population of wood warblers, as well as
redstarts, tree pipits, garden warblers and spotted
flycatchers. A small number of pied flycatchers
and willow tits breed here, both unusual species in
Scotland. Tawny owls occur throughout the wood
and buzzards and sparrowhawks occasionally
nest. Dippers and grey wagtails can be seen along
the burns cascading through the wood. The
removal of the sitka spruce planted recently on the
adjoining moorland will allow the meadow pipits,
black grouse and snipe to stay here.

The reserve's woodland flowers include bluebells, primroses, ramsons, cow-wheat and woodruff, while in the marsh loosestrife, sneezewort and
meadowsweet occur.

Among the butterflies seen on the reserve are
Scotch argus and purple hairstreak.

Highland North

Ben Wyvis

NH 460680; 3334ha; NCC reserve
Mountain and moorland
Permit only from North-West office
Spring, summer

Ben Wyvis is the highest mountain in Easter Ross.
The broad summit plateau, coupled with a rainfall
that is considerably less than that of the hills in the
west, supports an almost continuous carpet of moss
heath and is the largest single area of this type of
vegetation in Britain. The mountain also contains
fine examples of lichen-rich blanket bog, rich in
northern species such as dwarf birch, alpine bearberry and mountain crowberry; on the ground
where the snow lies late bilberry covers the
ground. The two main corries expose pelitic greiss,
which supports relatively few arctic–alpine
flowers but a wide variety of vegetation characteristic of acid rocks. Parsley fern and Alpine lady-
fern are well represented. The block screes carry
snow late into the year and these patches also contain a number of rare mosses and liverworts.

Blar nam Faoileag

ND 144450; 2126ha; NCC reserve
Blanket bog
Permit only from NCC, Old Bank Road, Golspie,
tel. Golspie 3602
Spring, summer

One of the best examples of an undisturbed watershed mire in Britain. The vegetation is largely
heather, cottongrass and deer sedge growing
through a carpet of bog mosses. Other characteristic peat-bog plants are found – bog asphodel, the
insectivorous sundews and, in the pools, bogbean.
The area is important for breeding moorland birds
including several species of waders and wildfowl.

Dunnet Links

ND 2269; 536ha; NCC reserve
Rich dune and links grassland
Permit required for all area other than forest
Spring, summer, autumn

Shell sand blowing inland from Dunnet Bay has
caused a lime-rich, sand soil over a large area,
which, with the uneven nature of the ground and
high-water table, gives a great diversity of soil
types, from lime-rich fens to acid heath and the
natural transition between the two. The Scottish
primrose and the Baltic rush grow here in their
normal habitat, while others, such as hair sedge
and mountain everlasting, are montane species
growing at sea-level. The reserve is a good butterfly locality, especially in the forest where shelter is
provided by the trees.

Highland South

Balmacaan Woods

NH 500290; 39ha; WdT reserve
Mixed woodland
Spring, summer

Situated high on the hillside overlooking Urquhart
Bay and Loch Ness, the reserve is a mixture of oak
and birch woodland and pine plantations. There
are fine specimen conifers in and around the former gardens of the now demolished Balmacaan
House. The view point at Craig Mony is at the
north end of the wood and gives wonderful views
of Loch Ness and the surrounding hills.

Lothian

Erraid Wood

Permit only; 4ha; SWT reserve
Mixed woodland
Information booklet for primary school teachers
from SWT
Spring, early summer

A mixed woodland situated on the edge of Edinburgh and used for educational purposes. The land is steeply sloping and the woodland contains beech, oak, elm, ash and sycamore. There are good views of the Pentland Hills and regular sightings of roe deer and foxes.

Hermand Birchwood

Permit only; 9ha; SWT reserve
Birch wood
Spring, summer

A small birchwood on a remnant raised bog in West Lothian. Small areas of planted Scots pine and beech, together with marsh and rough grassland, bring diversity to this reserve on a remnant of raised bog. Great spotted woodpecker, redstart, treecreeper and tree pipit all breed. The rough meadow supports adder's-tongue and greater butterfly orchid.

Orkney

The Loons

HY 245242. 66ha; RSPB reserve
Marsh
Access to hide only from the road on the north side
Spring, summer

This reserve lies in a shallow basin surrounded on three sides by low hills and by the Loch of Isbister on the fourth. Peat cutting has resulted in many water-filled holes, and the variation in ground conditions has led to a rich flora with species such as bog pimpernel, knotted pearlwort, grass-of-Parnassus and small bladderwort. The marsh is most noteworthy for its high density of breeding ducks and waders. Of the ducks, wigeon and pintail are most interesting, while among the waders, lapwing, redshank, curlew, snipe, oystercatcher, ringed plover and dunlin all nest. In addition there is a gull colony with both common and black-headed gulls, and by the loch 250 pairs of arctic terns are found.

The bizarre name indicates the antiquity of this area: it derives from the Norse word *lon* which means a flat meadow beside water.

North Hoy

HY 220010; 3925ha; RSPB reserve
Moorland, sea cliffs and hill lochs
Daily boat service from Stromness to Moness Pier, or ferry from Houton to Lyness
Spring, summer

The island of Hoy differs from the rest of Orkney in that it consists almost entirely of Upper Old Red sandstone. The weathering by sea, wind and rain has produced the spectacular coastal scenery of this reserve. Jutting out from the cliffs is the famous Old Man of Hoy, 140m high, the highest sea stack in Great Britain. While the sheer cliffs of St John's Head over 300m high provide ideal nesting sites for a large colony of kittiwakes, guillemots and fulmars, puffins, razorbills, shags and Manx shearwaters nest along the coast in smaller numbers.

On the moors there are large colonies of great black-backed gulls and great skuas, and smaller numbers of arctic skuas. Red-throated divers breed on the hill lochans. Of the waders, golden plover, dunlin, curlew and snipe breed, as do smaller species such as wheatear, stonechat and twite. Merlin, peregrine, sparrowhawk and kestrel nest, while short-eared owls and hen harriers are less often seen. There is a large population of mountain hares and otters are occasionally seen.

The reserve has a rich flora of alpine plants such as alpine meadow-rue and purple and yellow mountain saxifrage. The small area of birch, aspen and rowan forms the most northern remnant of native woodland in Britain. Butterflies of 19 species have been recorded, including a good population of large heath. A Neolithic tomb called 'dwarfie stones', formed from a hollowed out boulder, can be seen on the reserve.

Skye and the Small Isles

Canna

NG 2705; 1515ha; NTS
Large island
Access by Caledonian MacBrayne ferry from Mallaig
Leaflet from NTS or Canna Post Office
Late spring, summer

Canna (the most westerly of the small isles of the Inner Hebrides) and the smaller island of Sanday are designated SSSIs for biological and geological reasons. The cliffs shelter breeding seabirds such as puffins, razorbills and Manx shearwaters, and several species of birds of prey may be seen, including the sea eagle, which has been reintroduced to Rhum. Snipe, curlew and other waders are abundant, and the number of woodland bird species has increased with the establishment and growth of the plantations. Raised beaches of coarse shingle occur at Tarbert and An Coroghon. It is possible to walk along the cliffs or the shore but access between is precipitous and dangerous. Visitors are reminded that the whole island is farmed and disturbance must be minimal.

Strathclyde North

Ballachuan Hazel Wood

Permit only; 49ha; SWT reserve
Hazel wood, marsh, rocky shore
Spring, summer

Ballachuan Wood lies in the south-west corner of Seil Island, south of Oban. From early spring the ground is carpeted with flowers and the narrow-leaved helleborine is worth looking out for. As with many hazel woods, Ballachuan was once coppiced but the 'trees' have now run wild and some are over 8m high. The hazel and bird cherry are draped in lichens, for which the wood is a site of international importance with over 250 species. The local heronry and nesting buzzards add ornithological interest, and marsh fritillary butterflies are abundant in the wet, marshy grassland.

Fairy Isles

NM 7688; 21ha; SWT reserve
Woodland and small islands
Spring, summer

The Faery Isles consist of 6 small islands at the head of Loch Sween in the small sea loch north of Rubh'an Oib and east of Caol Scotnish. All the islands except one are tidal but access to some is difficult, even at low tide, due to the very soft, muddy substrate. The reserve also consists of a narrow coastal strip of broadleaved woodland. All the islands are slightly different but generally have a cover of oak, birch and rowan together with a few 'exotic' trees. Woodrush, bilberry, heather and bluebell are some of the components of the ground layer, which also includes pennywort and Scots lovage. Treecreeper and willow warbler are found but more evident are the birds of the coast – eiders, herons, terns and red-breasted mergansers. Loch Sween itself is an area of exceptional marine biological interest.

Loch Gruinart, Islay

NR 280670; 1229ha; RSPB reserve
Farmland, estuary, saltmarsh and moorland
View from road on south and west side of Loch Gruinart
Autumn, winter and spring

The reserve consists of farmland and moorland on the south and west sides of Loch Gruinart and is one of the two most important wintering areas for barnacle geese in Britain. Islay is renowned for its wintering geese: the 18,000 barnacles form two-thirds of the Greenland race, while up to 4000 Greenland white-fronts represent one-third of the world population. A significant proportion of both these species can be seen on or around the reserve. Other birds include nesting lapwing, redshank, eider and shelduck on Gruinart flats and around the shore, while on the moorland black and red grouse and curlew breed. Peregrines, golden eagles, merlins and hen harriers all hunt over the reserve.

Strathclyde South

Ayr Gorge Woodland

NS 4524; 15ha; SWT reserve
River valley woodland
Path along west bank of river
Spring, summer

The sessile oak woodland lies on steep slopes where the river has cut through the soft beds of Permian sandstone, and there is also birch, rowan, holly and hazel. Woodland plants include hairy wood-rush, Yorkshire fog, wood-sorrel and bluebell; in acid areas heather, bilberry and the local cow-wheat grow in carpets of moss. Many interesting insects and spiders have been found on the warm, south-facing slopes, and there is a good variety of mammal and bird species.

Barons Haugh

NS 755552; 97ha; RSPB reserve
Woodland, parkland and marsh
All year

This reserve lies on the outskirts of Motherwell and consists of woodland, parkland and marshes running down to the River Clyde. The best area for birds is on the marshes and parks along the riverside. Here whooper swans winter, along with a variety of ducks, including teal, pochard and goldeneye. In summer mute swan, little grebe and water-rail breed, while kingfishers, grey wagtails and sand martins nest in the river banks. Whinchats and reed buntings are plentiful on the marshland. The woodlands support the common bird species, as well as willow tit at the northern edge of its range. Red squirrels and roe deer are present.

Dalmellington Moss

Permit only; 28ha; SWT reserve
Peat bog, fen and fen woodland
Spring, summer

Heather, *Sphagnum* mosses and cottongrass, together with great sundew and bog-rosemary, are of special interest on this reserve. The fen-carr of birch and willow is undisturbed and in many places impenetrable, being a tangle of fallen and half-fallen trees and dissected by numerous water-filled channels and pools. The Moss is also home for many unusual insects and is a safe refuge in winter for roosting birds of prey.

Nethan Gorge

NS 8246; 7ha; SWT reserve
Gorge woodland
Path through reserve to Tillietudlem Castle
Spring, summer

The Clyde Valley woodlands are of classic conservation interest as remnants of the mixed deciduous forest that once clothed much of the

Scottish Highlands. High above the river, a fringe of oak and birch trees marks the more acid soils along the top of the wood, but the major part of the reserve is on unstable slopes of lime-rich carboniferous rocks where the trees are predominantly ash and elm and the spring flowers are a lush carpet of wood anemone and bluebell, ransoms and dog's mercury.

Shewalton Sandpits

NS 326370; 17ha; SWT reserve
Scrub, grassland and lagoon
Spring, summer, autumn

The sandy grassland around this worked-out sand- and gravel pit forms a suntrap for numerous species of insects, many of which are at the northern extremity of their range. Grasshoppers, grayling butterflies, darter dragonflies, six-spot burnet, cinnabar moths and green tiger beetles are all found on the reserve. The pools and scrapes are important for wildfowl and waders, and attract migrants such as bar-tailed godwits, ruff and greenshank in the autumn.

Tayside

Ballinluig Shingle Islands

NN 9753; 23ha; SWT reserve
River islands
Path along river bank
Spring, summer

These shingle islands are found along the western bank of the River Tummel. They support a great array of different habitats, from bare open shingle through 'unimproved' herb-rich grassland to mixed woodland with alder, birch, Scots pine and some juniper. Over 350 species of plants have been recorded — goldilocks buttercup in the woods, thyme, meadow rue, globeflower, meadow saxifrage, cowslip and yellow rattle in the grassland, with sea campion and mountain sorrel also present. Common tern, ringed plover, common sandpiper, common gull, redshank, oystercatcher and lapwing are found on the reserve. Scotch argus and common blue butterflies fly in the meadows and there are a number of interesting species of cranefly.

Northern Ireland

Northern Ireland is a large, diverse province with much beautiful scenery and many geological features and wildlife habitats that deserve to be, and in some cases are, protected as Nature Reserves. These interesting places are set amidst a good deal of fairly commonplace rural landscape. A naturalist arriving from crowded Britain will at first notice with pleasure the low degree of urbanisation and industrialisation, and the abundant small fields and hedgerows. He will soon, however, become aware of the effects of modern subsidised agriculture and technological over-optimism. As in Britain, most of the better farmland and much of the marginal land has been 'improved' with almost total loss of its wildflowers. Bogs are being exploited, wetlands drained, watercourses scoured. Along many roadsides the hedges bear witness to mechanical cutting, and the masses of cow parsley on the verges to ill-advised and now abandoned spraying with herbicides. Magnificent, underused roads slash brutally through the countryside, carrying juggernaut lorries laden with fertilisers and feedstuffs, and contrasting painfully with the many miles of abandoned canals and railways.

These recent phenomena are superimposed upon the no less drastic effects of earlier human activity. Most notable of these, perhaps, was the almost complete removal of the province's natural forest cover, for which the recent tree plantings — comprising mostly exotics — do not adequately compensate. The overpopulation, then famine, of the last century, the cutting of bogs for fuel, the

frequent, unmethodical burning of moorland, and the rise and decline of industries have all left their mark. The conservationist's task is to do the best he can for wildlife in this complicated heritage, where human intervention has perhaps played a greater part than in most countries. This situation is increasingly reflected in the kinds of sites being chosen as Nature Reserves.

Geology forms a convenient basis for a review of the Northern Ireland scene. Very broadly speaking, there are five large geological regions. In the north-east is a great tertiary plateau of black basalt lying on white cretaceous chalk, which is interestingly exposed, showing dykes, on the coast and in quarries. The basalt carries base-rich grasslands, grading at high altitudes into blanket bog, which is well developed on the wild, lonely Garron Plateau. The largely calcicole flora of the remaining unimproved grasslands is beautiful and rich in species; one valley has 160 kinds of vascular plants, including eight orchids. The basalt plateau ends at the north coast with spectacular cliff scenery, such as the GIANT'S CAUSEWAY, and the RATHLIN ISLAND CLIFFS with their great breeding colonies of seabirds. Arctic-alpine relict plants, such as juniper and purple saxifrage, survive on some relatively inaccessible cliff ledges. The eastern edge of the plateau is intersected by the Glens of Antrim, containing remnants of oak and hazel woodland and interesting bryophytes. Its western side has sunk and become inundated, forming Lough Neagh, the largest sheet of fresh water in the

British Isles. Because of its flat setting and vast swarms of midges the Lough is not a great tourist draw, but it is interesting to naturalists for its bird life (large wintering populations of tufted duck, pochard and whooper swans, and breeding great crested grebes), its relict fish, the pollan (conspecific with one found in Siberia and Alaska) and the botanical riches of its shores, where the Irish lady's-tresses with American affinities grows. On the southern side of the Lough is the largest tract of lowland raised bog in the province; though greatly altered by cutting, burning and drainage, it is scenically beautiful and rich in wildlife, and much of it is now protected in the Birches Peatland Park.

The north-west of the province lies mainly on Dalradian schists, giving rise to species-poor acid grassland and, on the Sperrin Mountains, large tracts of blanket bog. A striking feature in the south of this region is the hilly glacial gravel deposits (kames), a sample of which, covered with dry-heath flora, is preserved in MURRINS FOREST.

Much of the carboniferous limestone in the province is in the south-west, mainly in Co. Fermanagh. With its lakes and hills, this beautiful region strongly attracts British and continental visitors and is biologically very rich. Here many road-verges are still bright with flowers. There is some karst scenery, with swallow holes, caves and small patches of limestone pavement. There are wide expanses of unimproved limestone grassland, the home of interesting lepidoptera. The purple hairstreak butterfly, found nowhere else in the province, frequents oakwoods of considerable age, while the region of Lough Erne is the breeding area of the brimstone butterfly and common scoter duck in Ulster. The impressive sandstone scarp of Cuilcagh Mountain can only be reached by a three-mile trek across the bog, worth making for the feeling of remoteness and isolation. The woods around Lough Erne show exceptional development of fruticose and foliose lichens in the clean, moist Atlantic air. Extensive reedbeds fringe parts of the Lough shores, while in other parts can be seen the blue-eyed grass (with American affinities) and the attractive grass-of-Parnassus. Upper and Lower Lough Erne are big enough for there to have been a substantial development of boating with, so far, no excessive congestion or noise.

Much of the south-eastern counties of Armagh and Down lies on Silurian shales, largely covered with drumlins – low, rounded hills of glacial drift. The drumlin landscape consists of rolling grass and arable farmland interspersed with hollows containing small, pretty lakes and fens. Strangford Lough, fed by the sea through The Narrows, is a drowned drumlin area in which some of the hill-tops form small islands. It is of international importance for its marine life and birds: grey seals are common; a quarter of all the terns in Ireland nest on its islands; while the rich feeding and mild winter climate bring in thousands of pale-bellied Brent geese, ducks and waders, especially knot.

Southern Co. Down is the site of the highest mountains in the province, the Mournes, which are mainly composed of a tertiary granite intrusion. Fortunately, pressures for insensitive development of this popular area have been successfully resisted, and the grandest and loneliest parts of the Mournes are still the reward of those prepared to walk quite a long way from the nearest road. The flora ranges from acid grassland, through heather heath on fairly thin, eroding peat, to *Rhacomitrium* heath on the summits. There are typical mountain birds, such as ring ouzel, whinchat and peregrine, and a few arctic-alpine plants, but the Mournes are not remarkable for their wildlife by, say, Scottish standards, and their appeal lies principally in their scenery and rugged glacial topography. Much of the fine coast nearby is under protection. It includes as Nature Reserves the Dundrum Dunes (probably the best example of dune zonation in Ireland) and KILLARD POINT, which has species-rich sandy grassland.

Like Ireland generally, Ulster has fewer species of animals and plants than Britain, but these include some notable Irish endemic forms, such as the Irish hare, regarded by some as a distinct species. Some species scarce in England are commoner in Ulster – for example the otter, red squirrel and wood white butterfly.

The conservation of wildlife habitats began late in Northern Ireland, which has had its own legislation since 1965. At the time of writing (1985) the powers of the Northern Ireland Office in conservation are much as in Britain, but the equivalent functions of the Nature Conservancy Council in Britain are performed in the province by the Conservation Branch of the Department of the Environment, advised by the (honorary) Committee for Nature Conservation. The Forest Service (Department of Agriculture) also accepts responsibility for conservation and has its own Nature Reserves. In the voluntary sector, the Ulster Trust for Nature Conservation, founded in 1978, is setting up reserves on a broad front, adding to the earlier and continuing work of the Royal Society for the Protection of Birds and the National Trust. Despite slow progress in some important directions (bogs and fens, and grasslands), the achievements of all these bodies are a matter of pride and augur well for the future, provided the present momentum is maintained by all concerned.

H.HEAL

Co. Antrim

Breen Forest

D 125338; 19ha; DOE(NI)–FS reserve
Deciduous woodland
Leaflet available from FS or warden at Portrush
Countryside Centre, 8 Bath Road, Portrush
Spring, summer

Northern Ireland is poorly endowed with native woodland and this small, mainly sessile oak, wood is therefore of importance. Birch is common along the wood margin and there are scattered rowans, hazel, holly and ash. Being on acid soils, the ground flora is fairly poor, with greater woodrush dominant; however, lemon-scented fern, hay-scented buckler-fern and Wilson's filmy-fern also occur.

Fair Head and Murlough Bay

D 185430–D 199418; 390ha; NT reserve
Cliff headland and wooded bay
Spring, summer

The top of the massive Tertiary dolerite sill of Fair Head is thinly covered with wet acid moorland vegetation and small lakes. Cliff-nesting birds, including chough, inhabit the cliff face of the head. Below lies an extensive block scree, on the gentler slopes of which, at the western end of Murlough Bay, are remnants of ancient hanging hazel–birch–rowan woods rich in lichens, bryophytes and ferns, including Wilson's filmy-fern. The eastern slopes of Murlough Bay have a rich assemblage of plants, as the vegetation types vary from chalk grassland to neutral grassland with wet flushes, and woodland. The buzzard is just one of the many woodland birds to be found.

Garry Bog

C 938298; 6.5ha; FS reserve
Raised bog
All year

Cranberry, round-leaved sundew and bog asphodel are common on this very wet acid habitat. The reserve is a small representative section of a much larger low-lying raised bog.

Giant's Causeway and North Antrim Cliff Path

C 952452; 16km; NT
Unique rock formation and coastal footpath
Leaflets from NT information centres
All year

This geological wonderland is the result of extensive volcanic activity in the Tertiary era, some 60 million years ago. Lava poured out from the fissures and vents in the earth's surface and flowed slowly over the white chalk, eventually solidifying into columnar basalt cliffs. A dry heath vegetation grows along the clifftop, but maritime grassland has developed on all but the steeper or more unstable scree slopes of the cliff face; it is here that the fulmar, rock dove and chough find suitable breeding ledges. Eider, oystercatcher and ringed plover nest along the rocky shoreline, and a good range of seabirds can be seen offshore throughout the year.

Glenariff Lakes

D 195188, D 189194; 12ha; FS reserve
Acid lakes
All year

The three small mountain lakes, Evish Lough, Loughnaweeland and Loughaniroona, support mallard, teal and redshank in the nesting season, and tufted duck and pochard in the winter. The rare, few-flowered sedge has been recorded along the shoreline.

Glenariff North

Permit only; 20ha; DOE(NI) reserve
Basalt cliffs, scrub and grassland
Permits available from warden
Spring, summer

The reserve is situated on the south-east facing wall of the classic U-shaped valley of Glenariff. The top of the reserve is fringed by basalt cliffs, which hold plants such as juniper, yew, spring sandwort and red broomrape. Tall hazel scrub with some ash clothes the lower slopes and there is a good range of associated woodland herbs. The unimproved pastures above the road contain fragrant orchid and lady's-mantle. Peregrine and buzzard regularly hunt the area.

Glenariff Waterfalls Forest

D 210205; 8ha; DOE(NI)–FS reserve
Gorge woodland
All year

In contrast to GLENARIFF NORTH, this is a humid gorge with a series of waterfalls and cascades situated within the Forest Park at the head of Glenariff. The site is mainly notable for its mosses and liverworts, although there is a good variety of woodland plants.

Kebble

D 095515; 123ha; DOE(NI) reserve
Cliffs, grassland, heath, fen and open water
Leaflet available on site
Spring, summer

Situated at the western end of RATHLIN ISLAND, the reserve consists of a range of the habitats and the major seabird colonies of the island. The thousands of birds which nest on the 120m cliffs and sea stacks include guillemot, black guillemot, razorbill, puffin, kittiwakes and fulmars. Tree-mallow, roseroot, thyme broomrape, spring squill and a number of orchids all flower in the area, and a lake and marsh add diversity with saw-sedge, mud sedge and bladderwort. Eleven species of butterfly have been recorded, including dark green fritillary and grayling, and as many as 52 species of spiders in the grassland.

Kinramer

D 101520; 59ha; FS reserve
Woodland
By boat from Ballycastle
Spring

The reserve includes the whole of the FS property on Rathlin Island. Experimental attempts 30 years ago to establish woodland on the island have resulted in the development of only patches of deciduous and coniferous scrub. However, the woodland, being the only area of trees on the island, does provide important shelter and nesting habitat for small passerines. Small colonies of seabirds occur at the northern end. The reserve adjoins KEEBLE to the west.

Larrybane/Carrick-a-Rede

D 062450; 36ha; NT reserve
Chalk sea cliffs
Rope bridge at Carrick-a-Rede open early May to mid-September
Leaflets at NT information centres
Spring, summer

Razorbills, guillemots, fulmars and kittiwakes nest on Carrick-a-Rede, which comes from the Celtic meaning 'rock on the road'. The road is the path of the salmon on their way to northern rivers and the rock is the small island itself. The sea cliffs and the old quarry, which is rich in fossils, are interesting geologically as they are chalk overlain by basalts; Carrick-a-Rede is a volcanic plug and ash cone. Those who brave the rope bridge to the island will have excellent views of swimming auks over the chalk seabed.

Muck Island

D 466024; 5.6ha; UTNC reserve
Offshore island
Boat by arrangement with UTNC, views from road to Portmuck
Early summer

The long, thin island has a full complement of cliff-nesting seabirds, with a few puffins and great black-backed gulls nesting on the plateau along with many herring gulls.

Portrush

C 856412; 1ha; DOE(NI) reserve
Geology
Leaflet available from adjoining Countryside Centre
All year

This tiny reserve was established for reasons connected with the history of geological thought. During the controversy that raged between the Neptunist and Vulcanist schools regarding how rocks were formed, this site was used in the discussions; the rock appeared to be volcanic in origin but included many fossil ammonites. In fact, the rock in question is a Liassic shale which was severely baked by subsequent dolerite intrusions to the consistency of porcellanite. Several seabird species, including eider duck and black guillemot, may be seen offshore.

Randalstown Forest

J 088872; 6ha; DOE(NI)–FS reserve
Mixed woodland on alluvium and lough shore
Permit only from FS
Leaflet from FS or Randalstown Forest Education Centre
All year

The water level of Lough Neagh has been lowered at intervals since the middle of the nineteenth century, most recently in 1959. In the parts of the shore which have been relatively undisturbed, each successive lowering can be identified by a break in slope, change in soil and different vegetation. One such unspoilt area is at Randalstown Forest, where the interest in the vegetation and insects is augmented by the water-birds that inhabit the lagoons just inside the shoreline. Breeding birds include great crested grebe, sedge warbler and blackcap; in winter wildfowl usually include teal, gadwall and goldeneye, and kingfishers are frequently observed. The offshorewaters form part of the extensive north-east Lough Neagh Wildfowl Refuge.

Rathlin Island Cliffs

D 120530; 50ha (4km); RSPB reserve
Cliffs
By boat from Ballycastle
Spring, summer

Peregrines, ravens, buzzards and choughs are the important breeding birds on this stretch of the basalt cliffs on the north coast of Rathlin Island. The main seabird colonies are at KEBBLE. Sea passage includes gannets, skuas and, in autumn, occasional sooty shearwaters and petrels. Manx shearwaters are present in summer and autumn.

Rea's Wood Forest

J 142855; 26ha; DOE(NI)–FS reserve
Woodland and fen
Leaflet from warden at Oxford Island
All year

Rarities such as summer snowflake, large bittercress and elongated sedge occur in this wet alder woodland and reedswamp along the shores of Lough Neagh. The site is particularly noted for its rich and diverse invertebrate life, and a wealth of insects can be seen feeding on the flowers along the extensive path system. The clear, rich song of the blackcap can be heard in spring and early summer; and in winter, pochard, goldeneye and tufted duck can be seen from the edge of the lough.

Shanes Castle

J 111880; 32ha; RSPB reserve
Mixed woodland, park, marsh and lough
All year

The hide along the nature trail gives good views of dabbling and diving ducks such as mallard, teal, pochard and goldeneye in winter. Heron, long-eared owl, sparrowhawk, buzzard, blackcap and magpie nest in the woodland. Red squirrel, badger and fallow deer occur, and plants include heath-spotted orchid, adder's-tongue and broad-leaved helleborine.

Slievenorra Forest

D 132865, D 135265, D 147174, D 155280; 57ha; DOE(NI)–FS reserve
Blanket bog
Summer

This reserve comprises four plots in an extensive area of blanket bog, much of which has been afforested. The sites were selected to show developing bog with fine hummock and sinuous pools on the lowest part, through mature peat on the shoulder of Orra Beg to two areas at the summit of Slievenorra. There are areas of deep peat which have been seriously eroded by wind and rain, providing a micro-landscape of unusual and striking quality.

Slievenorra Moor

D 140265; 225ha; FS reserve
Moor and coniferous forest
All year

The red grouse is a rapidly declining species in Ireland and the management of this reserve is aimed at increasing and perpetuating the population. The moor encompasses SLIEVENORRA FOREST.

Swan Island

D 424996; 1ha; DOE(NI)–RSPB reserve
Island ternery
No access
Summer

This diminutive island on Larne Lough holds an important mixed colony of terns – common, Sandwich and roseate. A few pairs of red-breasted merganser also breed.

Tardee

J 191948, 0.2ha; FS reserve
Geological
All year

This very small reserve consists of an old disused quarry, which exposes the acid igneous rock rhyolite, known locally as 'Tardee stone'. It is one of the few exposures of this rock in the country.

Upper Glenarm

D 304110; 100ha; Antrim Estates Company
Woodland and river gorge
Permit only from UTNC
Spring, summer

The Glenarm rivers cuts through steep forested slopes with plunging rapids and deep pools. Herons fish where the river is wide and pebbly at the entrance to the reserve.

Whitepark Bay

D 023440; 74ha; NT reserve
Sandy bay backed by chalk cliffs
Spring, summer

This beautiful beach of white sand is flanked on both the east and west by headlands of limestone and basalt, and fringed by grassy slopes on which there are masses of primroses and violets in the spring. At the back of the bay, small deep stream valleys are filled with willow and hazel scrub, and blackthorn is found on the drier ground.

Co. Armagh

Argory Mosses

H 879577; 17ha; UTNC–NT reserve
Bog, dry and wet heath, riverside vegetation
Permission from custodian, tel. Moy 84753
Spring, summer

The upper moss, being dominated by heather, is the most interesting and has a large variety of lichens and moorland moths. The lower moss is now mostly dry and wet heath surrounded by birch scrub and pine. The banks of the River Blackwater and adjacent ditches contain interesting aquatic and emergent vegetation and insects.

Brackagh Moss

J 019507; 110ha; DOE(NI) reserve
Cut-over bog, fen and pools
Access easiest through northern part of reserve via peat banks; rest of reserve completely surrounded by drainage ditch
Early summer

Extraction of peat has left a series of pools with only a tiny remnant of lowland raised bog remaining. The site is rich in plant species, and many fen and wetland varieties occur. The most outstanding discovery was in 1892 when the previously unknown Irish lady's-tresses was found by the great Irish naturalist R. Lloyd Praeger.

Carnagh

H 828295; 12ha; FS reserve
Old estate woodland and lakes
All year

A good variety of birdlife inhabits the mainly beech woodland and the willow and alder scrub around the edges of the three small lakes. An interesting selection of wildfowl visit the lake in winter and otters occasionally occur. The whole area is rich in bryophytes and fungi.

Coney Island, Lough Neagh

H 939642; 3.5ha; NT reserve
Wooded island
Access by boat through regional office or by local boatman at weekends during summer
Spring, summer

A wooded island in Lough Neagh with fringing reedswamp vegetation. Evidence of Neolithic and Bronze Age settlements exists.

Hawthorn Hill

J 038193; 29ha; FS reserve
Mixed woodland
All year

The reserve was created to conserve an area of semi-natural woodland with a wide variety of habitats and a rich diversity of flora. The tree cover varies from mainly oak through mixed deciduous woodland of beech and rowan to mixed conifers of Scots pine and larch and finally to an old pure Norway spruce stand. Red squirrels are common and a herd of wild goats from Slieve Gullion shelter in the area in winter.

Milford Cutting

H 859428; 1ha; UTNC reserve
Disused railway cutting
Summer

The wildflowers of the grassland bank attract many butterflies. The opposite slope is covered with native shrubs and the floor of the cutting is marshy.

Mullenakill and Annagarriff

H 893610 and H 905611; 22ha and 77ha; DOE(NI) reserve
Peat, both cut and uncut, and wooded drumlins
Late spring, summer

The tract of land south of Lough Neagh is low-lying and was formerly subject to periodic flooding. Peat covered most of the lower ground but this has been largely worked out for domestic purposes. However some commercial exploitation did take place and the largest such area, over 250ha, has been developed as the Birches Peatland Park. The two areas of NNR status fall inside this Park. Mullenakill is largely woodland and cut-over peat; Annagarriff is woodland and uncut bog and

occupies the floor of a lake drained in 1938. In each case the mixed woodland of largely oak and birch is on a drumlin, the only more fertile ground in the general peat area. Some of the plants found in the Park are very rare for Northern Ireland. These include marsh club-moss, bog-rosemary and alder buckthorn.

Oxford Island

J 305362, 113ha; Craigavon BC reserve
Lake shore, reedbeds, woodland and damp meadows
Nature trail leaflet from visitor centre
All year

Oxford Island is a peninsula on the south-east shore of Lough Neagh – the largest freshwater lake in the British Isles and of international importance for wintering diving ducks. The two hides afford excellent views of the wildfowl, and both great crested grebes and corncrakes breed on the reserve. The damp meadows are rich in wildflowers and much of the shoreline is covered with mixed woodland of predominantly alder planted in the 1960s when the lough was lowered.

Co. Down

Ballydyan Railway Cutting

J 418545; 3ha; UTNC reserve
Scrub and wet meadow
Permit only from UTNC, tel. (0232) 612235
Spring, summer

Half the 530m of disused cutting is covered with scrub and the other half is grazed by sheep in winter. Cuckooflower encourages orange-tip butterflies.

Ballymacormick Point, Cockle Island and Orlock Point

J 525837; 9.3ha; NT reserve
Low rocky shoreline and coastal walk
No access to island in May, June and July
All year

Rough maritime grassland with patches of marsh and scrub occur on these low rock headlands along the shore of Belfast Lough. There are also small areas of saltmarsh and mudflats. The wide expanse of rocky shore is good for birds at all seasons, especially waders in the autumn and winter, and seaduck can sometimes be spotted offshore. Cockle Island has nesting terns.

Belvoir Park

J 342698; 15.4ha; FS reserve
Mixed woodland and scrub
Leaflet and nature trail guide from FS Education Centre, Belvoir Park, Belfast BT8 4QT
Spring

The reserve forms part of Belvoir Park Forest, which lies within the Belfast City boundary and is heavily used by the public for recreation. The mixed woodland and scrub provides an oasis for many songbirds.

Bohill

J 396459; 2.8ha; FS reserve
Scrub woodland
April–June

Bohill provides optimum conditions for the holly-blue butterfly, which is scarce in Northern Ireland. The reserve consists of secondary re-growth with abundant holly, the result of clear-felling and coppicing many years ago.

Bohill Forest

J 396461; 1ha; DOE(NI)–FS reserve
Scrub woodland
Visitors should be accompanied by warden of
QUOILE PONDAGE
Spring, early summer

A tiny pocket of native scrub, largely of holly with oak standards, which lies within a planted coniferous forest. The steeply sloping, south-east facing, Silurian shale hill was, until the mid-1960s, an area of mixed scrub. Bracken and bilberry dominate the small clearings in which holly-blue butterflies are found in May. This is a key site for this species, which is rare in Northern Ireland. Several woodland bird species abound.

Cairn Wood

J 455774; 40ha; FS reserve
Old semi-natural woodland and scrub
All year

Rising to an altitude of 200m, the woodland was once an outlier of the Clandeboye estate and is important locally not only for its conservation value but also as a landscape feature in North Down. The tree cover of the reserve is mainly beech with some oak, alder and birch; a few conifers, mostly Scots pine, also occur. The open areas are predominantly grass–rush complex and at the highest elevations there is a bilberry–cranberry heath. A good variety of small songbirds may be seen and many of the more common raptors frequent the area.

Castle Ward Ponds

J 572492; 3.8ha; NT reserve
Freshwater ponds and marsh
Spring, summer

Interesting breeding birds and insects occur on this series of small ponds with surrounding marsh. There is a good range of aquatic and emergent vegetation developing to fen and fringing willow carr.

Cloghy Rocks

J 594478; 28ha; DOE(NI) reserve
Marine foreshore, rocks and mud
All year

This reserve comprises 2km of the foreshore on the western side of the Narrows – the constricted entrance to Stangford Lough. The complex pattern of rocks and inlets swept by the powerful tide supports a rich invertebrate fauna around the low-water mark. A large breeding colony of common seals uses the rocks just offshore as a low-water haul-out. In winter a good range of waders can be seen.

Dorn

J 595580; 800ha; DOE–NT reserve
Marine foreshore and seabed
Collecting by permit only
All year

This extensive reserve lies on the eastern side of Strangford Lough. It includes a complex inlet where three sheltered bays converge on a narrow channel or 'dorn'. A rock sill across this channel forms a tidal rapid where numerous filter-feeding and associated invertebrates, generally only found sub-tidally, encrust the boulders. Dense beds of seaweeds, especially of kelp, flourish. Large flocks of waders and wildfowl feed on the mudflats and common seals frequent the rocky 'pladdies' – low platforms of rock exposed at low tide. The reserve includes a portion of seabed.

Dundrum Coastal Path

J 420392; 3.2km; NT
Estuary edge and coastal path
All year

Part of the Ulster Way, this footpath runs along a disused railway line lying alongside and crossing the mudflats of Dundrum Inne Bay. Fringing areas of saltmarsh and strandline vegetation grade into grassland and scrub rich in plants, birds, butterflies and other insects. From late summer to spring the mudflats hold a good range of waders, wildfowl and gulls.

Edenderry Reserve

J 318680; 1ha; UTNC reserve
Mixed woodland with marsh
All year

The woodland, once part of an estate, has extensive banks of rhododendron and bamboo, as well as a good selection of deciduous trees. The flat marsh is bounded by beech and oak.

Glastry Clay Pits

J 633628; 17ha; NT reserve
Disused clay pits
Spring, summer

These flooded and abandoned clay pits contain a variety of aquatic and emergent vegetation, and invertebrate animal life.

Granagh Bay

J 604488; 24ha; DOE(NI) reserve
Marine foreshore and small inlets
Collecting by permit only
All year

This reserve consists of 1.5km of foreshore off the eastern side of the Narrows – the constricted entrance to Strangford Lough. Powerful tidal currents sweep among a complex of rocks and inlets, creating extremely diverse sediments and supporting a wide range of burrowing and encrusting invertebrates.

Green Island and Green Castle Point

J 241111; 1ha; RSPB–NT reserve
Small rocky islet and promontory
No access to islands but good views from coast road at Greencastle reached via Kilkeel
Spring, summer

Common, arctic, Sandwich and roseate terns all nest on this reserve, together with the occasional pair of gulls, oystercatchers and ringed plovers.

Hollymount

J 466399; 12.5ha; FS reserve
Alder carr and fen
Restricted access October to January
April–June

The wide stagnant ditches of this fine alder and willow carr reserve contain water-violet, which is very rare in Ireland. There is also a wide variety of sedges, perhaps the most spectacular being the extensive bed of greater tussock-sedge; greater pond-sedge is also common.

Hollymount Forest

J 466438; 5ha; DOE(NI)–FS reserve
Alder–willow carr and reedswamp
Visitors preferably accompanied by warden of
QUOILE PONDAGE
Summer

Prior to a major reclamation scheme of 1745, this site was a tidal pool. The subsequently formed Downpatrick Marshes were further drained by a major scheme in 1957, and the reserve is one of the remnants of a once extensive reedswamp and carr. The underlying deep fen peat is colonised by a sedge ground flora and mature carr woodland of alder and willow with fine epiphytic lichens. There is an adjoining reedbed. This is one of the very few Irish localities for water violet.

Inishargy Bog

J 615645; 8ha; UTNC reserve
Cutover bog
Permit only
Spring, summer

The lowland bog is surrounded by typical fen vegetation with heather on the higher ground. Royal fern, which is uncommon in the eastern part of the province, occurs.

Killard Point

J 610433; 68ha; DOE(NI) reserve
Maritime heath and grassland, foreshore and cliff
Midsummer

Killard Point forms the southern limit to Strangford Lough on the western side of its narrow entrance. The Point, of rugged vertically aligned Silurian slate with fine maritime lichen growth and pockets of saltmarsh, is backed by a lime-rich boulder-clay plateau flanked by grassland. Behind a fine sandy beach is a 20m-high cliff on which fulmars nest. The reserve is renowned for its colourful flora, especially orchids, several of which are very rare in Northern Ireland.

Lighthouse Island, Copeland Islands

J 596858; 2ha; NT–Copeland Bird Observatory
Bird observatory island
Visits by arrangement only with Observatory Boat Officer, tel. Belfast 655081
Spring, summer, autumn

A small island situated at the mouth of Belfast Lough and used as a bird observatory for recording and ringing migratory birds. Breeding birds include water-rail, Manx shearwater, eider and common gulls. A small Atlantic grey seal colony is associated with the island.

Mourne Coastal Path

J 389269; *c.*5.5km; NT
Rocky coastal footpath
All year

Fulmars, rock doves and black guillemots breed at the rocky northern end of the path. The wet flushes on the lower slopes of the boulder-clay cliffs support a rich fen vegetation with a high diversity of plant species, including sedges, rushes and other wetland plants. There are some interesting maritime and marsh insect species, and yellow-horned poppy and oysterplant can be found on the beach at the southern end.

Murlough National Nature Reserve

J 410350; 282ha; NT reserve
Sand-dunes, dune heath and woodland
Permit only off public footpaths from Warden,
Murlough NNR, Dundrum, Newcastle
Leaflets available from NT information centres
All year

This superb system of dunes was Ireland's first nature reserve and was given NNR status in 1977. The well-developed range of vegetation from dune grassland, through heather and lichen heaths to sycamore woodland at the northern end of the reserve, supports a wealth of interesting and rare plant and insect life. Large numbers of passerines feed on the dune scrub in the winter; waders and wildfowl can be seen on the mudflats of the Inner Bay, and seabirds are present offshore in Dundrum Bay.

Quoile Pondage

J 500478; 198ha; DOE(NI) reserve and Dept of Agriculture (NI) reserve
Impounded former river estuary, now a freshwater lake, marsh and scrub woodland
Access to southern part of right bank only
Leaflet and nature-trail guide from visitor centre at J 487471
All year

The first tidal barrage on the Quoile Estuary, 2km north of Downpatrick, was built in 1745. A new barrage was created 4km downriver as a flood-control measure in 1957. The intervening foreshore provides a pondage where floodwaters gather until the tide turns and the river can flow out through a sluice into the south-western corner of Strangford Lough. The former estuary has been colonised by freshwater marsh plants and willow scrub over the mud, and by ash, oak and thorn scrub on the upper stony shore. The luxuriant flora now supports a rich insect fauna with many woodland and wetland birds, especially breeding and over-wintering wildfowl.

Rainey Island

J 525630; 16ha; UTNC reserve
Partly wooded island in sea lough
By boat, but good views from Sketrick and Mahee Islands, both accessible by causeways
Spring, summer

The oakwood which dominates the north side of the island stretches right down to the shore – this is an uncommon occurrence around Strangford Lough. The variable vegetation and distinctive shoreline are also notable.

Rostrevor Forest

J 186170; 19ha; DOE(NI)–FS reserve
Sessile oakwood
No access off paths
Leaflet from FS or warden
All year

The mixed-aged oakwood is situated on a well-exposed west-facing slope overlooking Carlingford Lough, and ash, hazel, rowan, wych elm and wild cherry add variety. At the top of the wood great woodrush is the dominant ground cover, while on the lower slopes wild garlic is common. Local plants include bird's-nest orchid, wood millet and wood melick.

Co. Fermanagh

Aghagrefin

H 210657; 40ha; FS reserve
Varied vegetation on cut-over bog
May-July

The reserve consists of a low-lying bog which has been extensively used for turf cutting in the past; difficulties with drainage now prevents further cutting. Vegetationally the reserve is very varied. Wet areas support a wide variety of *Carex* and *Sphagnum* species, while small pools of permanent water have led to the development of colonies of reed-mace and water-horsetail. Birch woodland, with some hazel, rowan and holly has formed on the drier ridges, and further colonisation by trees is likely. Mallard, snipe and woodcock frequent the area in winter.

Aghatirourke

H 161315; 695ha; FS reserve
Upland limestone and bog
Spring, summer

The upper part of the area extending south-west to the summit of Cuilcagh (684m) is largely blanket bog with a typical western flora. In the sheltered gullies shrub woodland occurs with ash, hazel and rowan being predominant but also including some oak, yew and juniper. Dense rank heather covers most of the intervening land.

Bolusty Bog

H 050569; 6.8ha; FS reserve
Bog complex
All year

Both great and round-leaved sundew occur on this good example of pool and hummock bog. The hummocks are largely composed of *Rhacomitrium* and the pools are rich in *Sphagnum* species.

Carricknagower

H 012544; 86ha; FS reserve
Upland vegetation, lakes, marsh and cliff
All year

The reserve is in two sections. The smaller (8.5ha) to the west comprises Carricknagower Lake, associated marsh with a variety of sedge species and sundew, and cliff faces with wintergreens growing on them. The larger eastern section has a typical wet moorland vegetation with pale butter-wort present, and north-facing cliffs that support the rare Tunbridge filmy-fern. There is another small lake, Lough Naman, which provides good wildfowl habitat.

Castle Archdale Island Forest

H 144593, H 150604, H 158588; 74ha;
DOE(NI)–FS reserve
Wooded islands
Spring, summer

The reserve consists of a group of wooded islands – Inishmakill, Clennishgarve, Cleenishmeen, Gay and Strongbow – situated offshore from Castle Archdale Country Park. The main tree species are ash and oak with a fringe of willow and alder, and the islands have an interesting range of plants such as buckthorn, broad-leaved helleborine and bird's-nest orchid. Breeding birds include two of Lower Lough Erne's specialities – the common scoter and the garden warbler.

Castlecaldwell Forest

H 007603; 239ha; RSPB–DOE(NI)–FS reserve
Conifer forest, fen, lake shore and islands
All year

A major breeding area for common scoter, which nest on the islands together with mallard, tufted duck, red-breasted merganser, Sandwich tern and common and black-headed gull. Both great crested and little grebes breed on the lough, and water-rail can be found in the reedswamps along its margins. In the forest there are siskins, sparrowhawks and long-eared owls. In winter flocks of wigeon, goldeneye, teal, pochard, tufted duck and whooper swan gather on the reserve. In early summer, butterwort, grass-of-Parnassus and northern marsh-orchid can be found flowering in the loughside fens.

Castle Coole Loughs

H 260430; 30ha; NT reserve
Lake and small loughs
Spring, summer

Greylag goose and great-crested grebe nest around and on these three loughs in the Castle Coole Estate. There is an interesting succession of aquatic vegetation through reed swamp and sedge bed to wet meadow around Lough Coole, to willow carr at Breandrum Lough, and wet ash woodland around Lough Yoan. The area is ideal for dragonflies and damselflies.

Conagher

H 071538; 120ha; FS reserve
Varied upland vegetation
All year

Scrub of oak, hazel, birch and rowan occur on the cliff faces in this reserve, while the wet flushed areas on the slopes support typical bog communities. There is a small area of open water – Largalinny Lough – the bordering vegetation of which includes the great fen-sedge. The north-western edge of Conagher borders CORREL GLEN FOREST, and the long-distance footpath, the Ulster Way, bisects the area.

Cornagague Wood and Lough

H 474303; 3.1ha; FS reserve
Scrub woodland and lake
Spring

The lake is rich in aquatic insects, particularly dragonflies; great-crested grebes nest here and an interesting variety of wildfowl gather in the winter. The scrub woodland is mainly of willow and alder, with some birch and holly in a drier corner. In spring there is a good show of wildflowers.

Correl Glen Forest

H 080544; 85ha; DOE(NI)–FS reserve
Mixed deciduous woodland and heath
Spring, summer

This interesting mixture of woodland and heath has an excellent range of plants that are mainly found in north or west Britain. These include the serrated and lesser wintergreens, cowberry, both species of filmy-fern, hay-scented buckler-fern and pale butterwort.

Corry Point Wood

H 095378; 3.7ha; FS reserve
Mixed deciduous woodland
Spring

The reserve forms a promontory on the south shore of Lower Lough Macnean. The main characteristic of the area is the number of small but quite distinct plant communities present. There is a wide range of common deciduous trees and the ground vegetation includes many species typical of natural woodland. The area is particularly rich in mosses and the shoreline vegetation includes many species of sedge.

Crossmurrin

H 112348; 96ha; DOE(NI) reserve
Limestone grassland and hazel scrub
Spring, summer

The limestone grassland is rich in plant species, including blue moor-grass, early-purple orchid, mountain-everlasting and adder's-tongue. Where cracks in the limestone pavement preclude grazing, ferns such as soft shield-fern and brittle bladder-fern predominate. The hazel scrub contains a range of woodland plants, including stone bramble. In parts of the reserve blanket bog has developed and the vegetation of deer sedge and sundew contrasts strongly with the limestone area.

Dohatty Glebe

H 180310; 29ha; FS reserve
Limestone cliff vegetation
All year

The reserve rises almost to the summit of the prominent Benaughlin Mountain (375m). Fine limestone cliffs and scree slopes support a wide variety of plants on base-rich soils. Whinchats, uncommon in this area, frequent the slopes and upper boundaries of the plantation.

Glen Wood

H 172330; 4.7ha; FS reserve
Oak wood
April–June

The wood is not of natural origin but is old enough to have an established ground flora extremely similar to that of a natural oak wood. The interest of the site is increased by a small stream and associated wet shaded areas which have interesting bryophyte communities.

Hanging Rock and Rossaa Forest

Permit only; 15ha; DOE(NI)–FS reserve
Limestone cliffs and ash woodland
Spring, summer

Situated close to MARBLE ARCH FOREST and CROSS-MURRIN, the reserve is a north-facing limestone cliff with a well-developed moist ash wood at its base. Yew, juniper and Welsh poppy grow on the cliffs, while soft shield-fern, water avens, goldilocks buttercup and toothwort are found in the wood. In addition to the usual woodland birds, peregrines can be seen in the area.

Knockaginney

H 714453; 6.2ha; FS reserve
Semi-natural woodland and scrub
All year

This small, mainly oak, woodland has a shrub layer of spindle and guelder-rose which provides nesting sites for a good population of songbirds. Fallow deer are present in small numbers.

Lough Naman Bog

Permit only; 40ha; DOE(NI) reserve
Blanket bog
Permits available from warden at H 175586
Summer

An area of blanket bog which has a fine hummock development of *Racomitrium lanuginosum* and various species of *Sphagnum*. Dunlin and golden plover breed on the site.

Magho

H 080578; 74ha; FS reserve
Deciduous woodland
All year

The woodland scrub bordering the shore of Lower Lough Erne is used by nesting common scoters. The rest of the woodland extends over a considerable area of limestone cliff and scree slopes with numerous sheltered gullies. Mossy saxifrage, Tunbridge filmy-fern and several species of spleenwort are present on the dry rocky areas.

Marble Arch Forest

H 123350; 24ha; DOE(NI)–FS reserve
Mixed deciduous woodland in limestone gorge
Leaflet from interpretative centre at southern entrance
Spring, summer

The reserve is a moist, mixed deciduous woodland set in a narrow, steep-sided glen cut into the north-facing limestone escarpment, part of which forms HANGING ROCK. At its head the River Cladagh issues from an underground cavern beneath a limestone feature known as Marble Arch. The caves in this area have recently been opened to the public by Fermanagh DC. The reserve has been planted with a variety of trees in the past, although the main species is naturally regenerated ash. The ground flora includes both soft and hard shield-ferns, brittle bladder-fern, goldilocks buttercup, early-purple orchid, water avens and shady horsetail. There is a good selection of woodland birds, and dippers and grey wagtails can be seen along the river's edge.

Naan Island

H 296318; 4.6ha; FS reserve
Reedbeds, wooded islands and shoreline
Access only possible by boat
All year

The extensive areas of reedbed are comprised of common club-rush and common reed. The lagoon contains various species of pondweed together with water horsetail, needle spike-rush and bottle-sedge. The reserve includes Naan Island East and Naan Island West, both of which are covered with thick scrub of alder, birch and willow.

Reilly and Gole Woods

Permit only; 67ha; DOE(NI) reserve
Oak woodland, pasture, hay meadow and
reedswamp
Permits from warden at H 175586
Spring, summer

These two woods are situated on the shores of
Upper Lough Erne, where the flooded drumlin
landscape forms a confusing maze of interconnected loughs and channels. Reilly Wood is a
mature oakwood in contrast to Gole Wood, which
has a younger growth of birch, willow and alder.
The heavy clay soil has a characteristic wet-
woodland flora, which includes bird cherry,
aspen, water avens, early-purple orchid, wood
horsetail and thin-spiked sedge. Around most of
the two drumlins is open water. At Reilly Wood a
small lough has saw-sedge, and the reedswamp
along the shore of Upper Lough Erne contains
marsh pea, marsh stitchwort, tubular water-
dropwort, greater water-parsnip and cowbane.
Marsh-fern and blue-eyed-grass grow just outside
the reserve. A good variety of both woodland and
wetland birds breed in the area. Butterfly species
include the silver-washed fritillary and purple
hairstreak at one of its few Northern Ireland
localities.

Ross Lough Forest

H 143467; 9ha; DOE(NI) reserve
Ungrazed fen
Spring, summer

Ross Lough is set between drumlins in limestone
country: some years ago the water level was
lowered and, with the exception of the small area
that is now the reserve, the emergent shores are
used for cattle grazing. The luxuriance of this area
contrasts markedly with the remaining shore and
includes a wide range of typical fen plants, among
them several sedges. Whooper swans and wigeon
are present on the lough in winter.

Co. Londonderry

Ballymaclary

Permit only; 139ha; DOE(NI) reserve
Calcareous dune system
Permit from warden at C 857410; open at certain
times of year only as within military training area
Summer

The reserve consists of a number of parallel dune
ridges which grade from mobile dunes of marram
grass to fixed dunes with a development of blackthorn and burnet-rose scrub. Between these ridges
are well-developed dune slacks which hold a number of notable plants, including marsh helleborine,
variegated horsetail, grass-of-Parnassus and northern marsh-orchid.

Banagher Glen

Permit only; 30ha; DOE(NI) reserve
Mixed deciduous upland wood
Permits from warden at C 857410
Spring, summer

The rather open tree canopy in three deep river
valleys consists of a mixture of birch, oak and
hazel. The reserve contains a good range of woodland flora such as tutsan, lemon-scented fern, hay-
scented buckler-fern and Wilson's filmy-fern.
Buzzards are just one of the breeding woodland
birds, and butterflies include the silver-washed
fritillary.

Bar Mouth

C 792355; 17ha; NT reserve
Estuary
Access to hide by arrangement with warden
All year

This reserve has an interesting mixture of coastal
grassland, wet meadow and saltmarsh overlooking
mudflats at the mouth of the Bann Estuary. The
area is well known for sightings of rare passage
birds and vagrants.

Craig-na-Shoke

C 746005; 90ha; FS reserve
Peat erosion, landslips and montane grassland
Spring, summer

The reserve comprises three distinct areas. On the
highest, Mullaghmore (560m), erosion has led to
the development of peat 'mushrooms' and erosion
channels, and two interesting clubmosses, *Lycopodium selago* and the rarer *Lycopodium alpinum* are
present. An area of stepped terraces is an important
geomorphological feature, while on the drier slopes
a varied montane grassland flora has developed.

Creighton's Wood

H 928112; 32ha; UTNC reserve
Hazel—oak wood with lowland bog
Permit only from UTNC, tel. (0232) 612235
Spring, summer

Typical flora and fauna are found on these two oak-
and hazel-covered drumlins, with an intervening
area of lowland bog.

Loughan Island

C 878288; 1.6ha; FS reserve
Mixed deciduous woodland
Access only possible by boat
All year

The reserve is a small island in the River Bann,
probably enlarged during a major drainage scheme
in the early 1930s.

Lough Foyle

C 545236–630290; 1340ha; RSPB reserve
Mudflats
Good views at Longfield Point, Ballykelly and
Faughanvale
Spring, autumn, winter

Lough Foyle is at its most impressive in the winter
months when the beds of eelgrass are busy with over
20,000 wigeon, more than 1000 teal, nearly 1000
pale-bellied Brent geese and smaller numbers of
other ducks. The neighbouring agricultural land
also attracts over 1100 whooper swan, more than
200 Bewick's swans and smaller numbers of grey
geese. Equally impressive are the numbers of
waders – 8000 curlew, 3000 bar-tailed godwit and
2000 oystercatcher. Spring and autumn are much
less spectacular, but regular passage species include
curlew sandpiper, little stint and spotted redshank.

Magilligan Point

C 665387; 57ha; DOE(NI) reserve
Calcareous dune system
Permit required for part of reserve used for military
training from warden at C 857410
Leaflet from warden
All year

This reserve, together with BALLYMACLARY NNR
and the UTNC reserve at THE UMBRA, forms part of
one large calcareous dune system. Magilligan Point
is situated at the western extremity and is the most
dynamic part of the dune system; it is subject to
rapid change, with sand being added during
periods of calm weather or being removed by gales
and storms. A good range of typical dune plants
occur, although slacks are not well developed on
this site. The Point is a good place for observing
seabirds throughout the year, and little terns
occasionally breed at what is their only Northern
Ireland site. Of special interest is the variety of
seashells – some are quite rare and are normally
confined to warmer waters.

Portstewart Strand and Sand Dunes

C 720360; 43ha; NT reserve
Sand-dune peninsula
Spring, summer

Small areas of burnet rose brighten up the scrub
areas of the dunes, and a good range of typical
plants, insects and birds can be found. A narrow
margin of saltmarsh occurs on the edge of the Bann
estuary.

Roe Estuary

C 640295; 468ha; DOE(NI) reserve
Tidal estuary and mudflats
Autumn, winter

This reserve forms part of the extensive mudflats
and sand-dunes of Lough Foyle and supports large
autumn concentrations of wigeon. Other wildfowl
include mallard, teal, pintail and Brent goose, and
bar-tailed godwit, curlew, oystercatcher, redshank,
knot, dunlin and golden plover also feed on this
rich area.

The Umbra

C 724355; 44ha; UTNC reserve
Dunes
Permit only from UTNC
Spring, summer

This reserve forms part of the largest area of unspoilt duneland in Northern Ireland, and is rich in
typical duneland species and rare plants and insects. See also BALLYMACLARY NNR and MAGILLIGAN
POINT, which are part of the same dune system.

Co. Tyrone

Altadavan

H 596495; 1.9ha; FS reserve
Old semi-natural mixed woodland
All year

This old woodland is growing on a small rocky hill
enclosed by a stone wall. Oak predominates, with
birch, hazel, rowan, holly and hawthorn also present. The surrounding open land is dominated by
typical acid moorland plants. Altadavan is the only
example of this type of woodland in the locality.

Altamullan

H 160820; 8ha; FS reserve
Old woodland scrub and marsh
All year

The reserve consists of ash, oak, rowan, alder,
willow, hazel and holly scrub, as well as beech,
sycamore, lime, Scots pine and larch, which were
planted around the now demolished farmhouse
and sawmill, and are overmature and dying. The
whole reserve is a valuable habitat for many songbirds. The collapse of the old mill race has allowed
water to seep down through the area. This, combined with the shelter provided by the trees, has
led to the development of rich communities of
mosses and liverworts. The old mill dam provides
an interesting stretch of marsh.

Black Bog

H 642812; 48ha; FS reserve
Raised bog
All year

The area displays an excellent bog flora, including
pool and hummock complexes. The reserve is
bounded to the east by a minor stream, which adds
variety. Butterflies, in particular marsh fritillaries
and green hairstreaks, are plentiful.

Blessingbourne

H 449484; 10ha; UTNC reserve
Lake and woodland
All year

The lake attracts heron, coot, moorhen and water-rail. Warblers breed in the extensive reedbeds, and the mixed deciduous woodland adds a range of typical woodland plants, birds and small mammals.

Boorin

H 497846; 59ha; DOE(NI) reserve
Mixed woodland and heath
Summer

The glacial history of the Sperrin Mountains is complex, and this reserve is in an area of depositional features which also includes a series of kettle-hole lakes. On the drier morainic soils a heath has developed which grades into poor bog on the lower stretches. The very steep northern face of the reserve is woodland – predominantly oak but with a high proportion of birch. Though perhaps planted in association with charcoal-burning practices and grazed by sheep until its acquisition as a NNR, the wood does have many of the attributes of the native woodlands that once covered much of the Sperrin Valley sides.

Drumlish

H 353665; 1ha; FS reserve
Mixed woodland
September–November

Over 60 different fungi have been listed for this reserve, which is a strip of old broadleaved trees beside a commercial coniferous woodland. The majority of the trees are beech and the fungi are therefore of the type associated with this species.

Favour Royal

H 620532; 23ha; FS reserve
Mixed woodland
April and October

A high seat overlooking an open grass area gives excellent views of the resident fallow deer. The woodland is managed for deer as well as for timber production.

Killeter Forest

H 086821 and H 090808; 22ha; DOE(NI)–FS reserve
Blanket bog
Intending visitors should contact the warden at Castle Archdale Country Park, Lisnarick, Irvinestown, Co. Fermanagh (H 175586)
Summer

Most of the forest has been planted up with trees but the two small sections of wetter ground which form the reserve support several uncommon species of *Sphagnum* and a few unusual flowering plants such as white-beaked sedge, oblong-leaved sundew and intermediate bladderwort. Situated at the extreme west of Tyrone, this area records one of the highest annual rainfalls in Northern Ireland.

Killeter Forest Goose Lawns

H 093798 and H 078826; 15.8ha; FS reserve
Upland blanket bog
December–March

Greenland white-fronted geese, a declining species in Ireland, feed on the white beak-sedge which grows in these areas. The vegetation is typical of an acid upland bog, but it is interesting to note that great, oblong-leaved and round-leaved sundew all occur.

Knockmany

H 541550; 31ha; FS reserve
Lake and scrub
No access October–January
Spring

Ardunshin Lough and its associated reedbeds and shoreline scrub is an important breeding area and winter refuge for a variety of common wildfowl.

Meenadoan

Permit only; 20ha; DOE(NI) reserve
Upland raised bog
Permit from warden at Castle Archdale Country Park, Lisnarick, Irvinestown, Co. Fermanagh (H 175586), but reserve can be viewed from adjoining road
Summer

Great sundew, white-beaked sedge, cranberry and mud-sedge are found on this reserve which consists of a small raised bog within a general area of blanket bog on the surrounding sloping ground. Breeding birds include dunlin.

Moneygal Bog

H 241880; 47ha; FS reserve
Raised bog
All year

A wide variety of wildfowl and wader use the area including mallard, golden plover, redshank, snipe and jack snipe. The reserve is particularly rich in bog mosses, among which the rather rare *Sphagnum imbricatum* is found.

Mullyfamore

H 105797; 13.2ha; FS reserve
Pool and hummock bog complex
All year

A small number of Greenland white-fronted geese feed on this species-rich bog in the winter. A wide range of mosses and sundews occur.

Murrins Forest

H 565780; 54ha; DOE(NI)–FS reserve
Heath and bog developed on glacial outwash feature
Summer

In the complex landscape of Co. Tyrone there is one very fine example of a glacial outwash fan – the Murrins, whose name relates to a series of small prominent hills standing out over the adjoining moorland. The reserve encompasses only parts of the fan, and was designated because of the heath vegetation established on the dry, free-draining glacial soils. There are no unusual species on the heath, but on the bog part of the reserve tall bog-sedge – a rarity in Northern Ireland – occurs.

Pomeroy

H 712723; 21.4ha; FS reserve
Old estate woodland and scrub
Access restricted October–January, visitors report to Forestry School, 56 Tandragee Road, Pomeroy, Dungannon
Nature Trail guide from Forestry School
Spring, summer

The woodland consists of two basic types – mixed deciduous with Scots pine, and birch and willow scrub in the wetter area – and, being of considerable ecological interest, is used by the nearby Forestry School for conservation education.

Slaghtfreedan

H 728859 and H 735862; 18.6ha; FS reserve
Pool and hummock bog
All year

The Golan Water, a minor stream which borders the western part of the reserve, is used by wildfowl in winter, particularly mallard and teal. The rest of the reserve is comprised of two very low-lying areas of pools with a wide range of *Sphagnum* species and *Rhacomitrium* hummocks.

Strabane Glen

H 358990; 11ha; UTNC reserve
Woods and marsh in gorge
Permit only from UTNC
Spring, summer

The wooded gorge is 1.5km long with an area of marsh at its upper end. Ravens and birds of prey nest on the crags, while the woods support typical flowers, butterflies and birds.

Teal Lough

H 731880; 40ha; FS reserve
Bog complex
All year

Colonies of black-headed gulls nest on the reserve, as do teal. A wide range of wildfowl frequent the lough in winter. The area is particularly rich in cranberry and sundew.

Isle of Man

The Isle of Man – which, at 52km by 22km, is more than twice the size of the Isle of Wight – lies near the middle of the Irish Sea. Its central chain of hills runs in a north-east–south-west direction and the rocks are mainly Manx slate, save for the northern plain which is wholly the gift of the last Ice Age. The land bridge to England was cut some 8000 years ago. There may never have been one to the west, although Man has a race of Ireland's distinctive stoat and the two have several peculiar insects in common.

Early isolation produced a less diverse fauna and flora than that of England. Snakes, toads, moles and voles are absent. Common English plants such as cowslips, dog's mercury and white deadnettle occur only as very rare and quite recent introductions. Yet the island's wildlife had a similar history to that of its neighbours. In neolithic times there was oak–hazel woodland with red deer, wild cat and fox, but by the Middle Ages Man was almost entirely deforested. There was no suitable woodland left for the jay, bullfinch and woodpeckers, and the stoat was the only surviving carnivorous mammal until the now abundant feral polecat-ferret was introduced to hunt the rabbit population and escaped.

A little over 60 per cent of the island lies above the 76 contour, but the highest point, Snaefell (621m), is too low for most mountain plants, the exception being dwarf willow. The climate is cloudy and damp without extremes of temperature but with great variation in rainfall, from about 70cm at Port St Mary or the Point of Ayre to nearly twice that amount in the central hills. There is considerable diversity of unspoilt habitat, with only native woodland, true saltmarsh and inland limestone exposures being rare.

Man has its own very ancient parliament (Tynwald), government agencies and laws. The most important legislation in conservation terms is the Wild Bird Protection Acts of 1932 and 1975, and the Manx Museum and National Trust Acts of 1951 and 1959. The first, in addition to affording essentially similar protection to Manx birds as that given by the UK and Irish Acts, give the Lieutenant-Governor (the Queen's representative) power to create bird sanctuaries. This is customarily done at the request of the landowners.

The 1951 Act created the Manx National Trust as an insular government body responsible, amongst other duties, for 'the permanent preservation of properties ... and their natural aspects, features and animal and plant life.' Interpretation of law has increasingly led the Manx Museum and National Trust into a nature conservancy role. It has collected non-marine biological records since 1922 and has now been formally recognised as the Biological Records Centre for the Island. The Isle of Man Forestry, Mines and Lands Board manages the National Glens and much of the hill land, as well as its plantations. It is currently pursuing a policy of improved access, with car parking, combined with environmental enhancement for wildlife. There is an increased awareness of the need for conservation and, despite their small staff and budgets, Manx government agencies are attempting to protect their island for future generations.

LARCH S. GARRAD

The Ayres

NX 433033; 39ha; MMNT–10M Forestry, Mines and Lands Board reserve
Dunes and maritime heath.
All year

Although there are some 10km of unspoilt shoreline, only two sites – Ballakesh and Ballakeyl – are formal reserves. The area is of immense wildlife importance, with a unique lichen heath in which *Usnea articulata* grows on the ground and the only British colony of dense-flowered orchid outside Ireland. The heath also supports many locally uncommon plants and the most southerly major tern colony on the western side of Britain.

Ballamoar

SC 252812; 1.4ha; MNCT reserve
Open water and mixed woodland
Permit only from MNCT
Spring, summer

The stream which runs down the wooded – mainly ash and elm – valley was dammed in the nineteenth century to form a reservoir. Fifty-two species of birds have been recorded, of which 20 are probably breeders. Mammals include rabbits and bats.

Ballamodha

Permit only; 0.9ha; private reserve
Grassland and scrub
Permits from David Leesley, The Willows, Ballamodha, Castletown, Isle of Man
All year

At least 80 species of bird have been recorded, of which 24 breed on this sanctuary of damp unimproved grassland with some willow scrub and young trees.

Ballaugh Curraghs

SC 365950; 300ha; IOM Government Property Trustees–MMNT–private
Willow carr and wetlands
All year

A unique area of wetland showing complete succession from open water to willow carr within a larger protected area. This area has the longest continuous history of any site on the island, many species having being present for thousands of years. The MMNT owns 7.3ha of virtually inaccessible tussock grassland and a small private trust manages 1ha of damp hay meadow to preserve its abundant orchids.

Calf of Man

SC 160660; 250ha; NT–MMNT reserve
Bird sanctuary and observatory
By boat from Port Erin or Port St Mary. Limited hostel accommodation must be booked in advance with the Secretary, The Manx Museum, Douglas, Isle of Man, tel. Douglas 75522
Spring, summer, autumn

The islet, 600m off the south-west tip of the Isle of Man, was given to the National Trust, who in turn leased it to the Manx National Trust when it was founded in 1951. The Calf's shearwater colony was mentioned in a Norse saga as early as 1014, and the Manx shearwater was first described from specimens taken from the isle in 1678. An intensive anti-rat campaign has saved the much diminished colony.

The 8km shoreline is rocky, with cliffs for cormorants, shags, guillemots, razorbills, kittiwakes and fulmars. Choughs breed on the cliffs and in the walled-up towers of the two disused lighthouses. Part of the MMNT's flock of loghtan sheep (Man's native brown-fleeced breed, the rams of which often have four horns) grazes the heath. The Mill Glen, a mill pond and several boggy areas, adds variety to the habitats available for the very numerous passage migrants. The observatory ringing totals have passed 99,000 of over 130 species. About 200 species of flowering plants have been recorded.

Cooil Dharry

SC 314902; 7ha; MNCT reserve
Wooded glen
Spring, summer

The glen was at one time laid out for formal recreation and some paths and exotic species of trees still remain. In the wilder parts some 35 species of birds breed. The ground flora includes spring woodland flowers, giant hogweed and yellow iris.

Dhoon

SC 455865; 13ha; MMNT reserve
Coastal cliffs
All year

A buffer zone between the coastal agricultural land south of National Glen. Attractive wildflowers can be seen in the spring, as well as seabirds.

Early Cushlin and Creggan Mooar

SC 217750; 158ha; MMNT reserve
Rough grassland, maritime heath, stream and coastal cliffs
All year

Flocks of up to 40 choughs, as well as ravens and seabirds, frequent the area. The cliff-top vegetation is a good example of maritime heath and the caterpillars of the rather uncommon dew moth feed on the cliff lichens. Pigmy shrews are abundant in the grass and bracken areas.

Gob ny Rona and Maughold Head

SC 485925; 47ha; MMNT reserve
Coastal cliffs
All year

Spectacular cliff scenery, and the birds likely to be seen include chough, raven, peregrine, a good selection of seabirds and cliff-nesting house martins.

Kitterland Islet

SC 170667; 3.9ha; MMNT reserve
Small island
Virtually inaccessible because of strength of currents
All year

Good views of the gull colony on this small islet between the Calf and Isle of Man may be obtained from the Sound.

Langness and St Michael's Isle

SC 285665; 2km coastline and 25.5ha;
MMNT–private
Saltmarsh and maritime heath
All year

The intertidal area in Castletown Bay is the main Manx wintering ground for waders and wildfowl, and a superb place for viewing migrants, insects as well as birds. Locally rare plants include purple-milk vetch, dodder, field gentian, celery-leaved buttercup and cord-grass. The area is also the sole site in Britain for the grasshopper *Stenobothrus stigmaticus*.

Lough Cranstal

SC 444019; 1ha; MNCT reserve
Alder carr and open water
All year

Although small, Lough Cranstal benefits from being on the edge of a much larger area of wetland. The rich community of sedges, grasses and rushes includes mossy pearlwort and greater pond-sedge, two species very rare elsewhere on the island. The pools support a good selection of dragonflies, and wildfowl winter on the larger stretches of water beyond.

Silverdale

SC 277708; 1ha; MMNT reserve
Stream, millpond and woodland
All year

This reserve was originally a private garden and has naturally regenerating gulley woodland and planted hornbeam.

Spanish Head, The Chasms and The Sound

SC 180660; 153ha; MMNT
Coastal cliffs
All year

The cliffs rise to over 76m with abundant breeding birds, including chough, fulmar, kittiwake, razorbill and guillemot. Spring squill blooms in May.

The Channel Islands

Their geographical position and small-island status confer on the Channel Islands climatic characteristics unlike those found elsewhere in the British Isles, and provide conditions for the survival of many plant and animal species more typically found in southern European and Mediterranean regions. Thus a rich and varied flora and fauna exists in what is a comparatively small land area, giving credence to the claim that the Channel Islands are richer in wildlife than any other area of comparable size in the British Isles.

Certainly their botanical wealth is unquestioned. For example, with a total of almost 1000 species, Guernsey supports more than double the average number of plants marked for the standard 10km square in the *Atlas of British Flora* (about 400), although it is only two-thirds the area of such a square, while in Jersey that number is exceeded within a single and relatively small sand-dune system of only 90 hectares. Thus the naturalist is sure to find a visit to these islands a rewarding experience, especially if travelling in the spring and/ or autumn when, apart from reduced tourist pressure, numbers of migratory birds are likely to be at their highest. Probably spring offers the most visually exciting period for the botanist, although much of interest can be seen all year round. The inter-tidal and sublittoral areas of the seashore must not be forgotten, as the naturalist with marine inclinations is also extremely well catered for. The exceptional 12m rise and fall of the spring tides uncover enormous areas of those beaches which shelve gently and expose gullies and rock pools supporting a profusion of seaweeds and animal life. However, such tidal extremes can be hazardous and the enthusiastic explorer must always check local tidal conditions.

Although the islands have much in common, each has its own special characteristics related to its topography, geology and land-use patterns, and it is not unusual for a plant or animal species to exist only on one of the islands. This may reflect, specifically, geological differences. For example, Alderney possesses sandstone rocks not found in the other islands, and Sark's topography – in essence a plateau – is unique. The rate and timing of the islands' separation from the Continent in prehistoric times is considered also to have greatly influenced inter-island wildlife differences.

Interestingly, in view of their many rarities, the islands lack species common in the UK. This is true for some woodland species, for example. The islands are not well endowed with woodland even now and it seems likely that such plant deficiencies relate, in part, to the meagre tree cover of times past. Nevertheless, the islands are generally blessed with an extensive network of hedgerows (55km per 260ha in Jersey), which creates a unique landscape tapestry. These hedges often harbour plants of woodland character, and provide shelter and food for many of the small woodland birds. The visitor will also encounter many plants of a somewhat exotic origin. Over many years, flowers have been introduced to the islands' gardens from literally all over the world and, aided by a favourable climate, a significant number of such plants now thrive 'in the wild'. Some have become too successful; for example, the hottentot-fig hangs in masses on the sea cliffs of both Jersey and Guernsey, producing a vivid summer colour but unfortunately often blanketing out existing vegetation in a manner that is ecologically undesirable.

Jersey, the largest of the islands, has a rectangular shape with a pronounced tilt to the south along its longer east–west axis. Thus the north is marked by high cliffs that in places fall sheer to the sea, while the south, east and west coasts are characterised by broad sandy beaches set between rocky promontories. A series of steep-sided valleys with a predominantly north–south orientation run towards the lower-lying areas of the coastal plain,

and most of the island's woodlands exist along the sides of these. Jersey's most extensive, and ecologically most valuable, open areas are LES QUENNEVAIS sand-dunes that dominate the west coast, and the heathland of LES LANDES in the north-west. The sand-dunes support 400 vascular plants, 16 of which have British *Red Data Book* status. Wetland areas are much reduced compared with the past, but six sites of considerable ecological importance remain.

Guernsey, the second largest island, is roughly triangular in shape and, in contrast to Jersey, it slopes away from its south coast and experiences a slightly cooler climate. Its southern part is mostly high plateau with many small, sheltered coves nestling at the foot of sheer cliffs that still retain a wild magnificence and remoteness despite the good access afforded by a coastal footpath. The landscape in Guernsey is somewhat blighted by much ribbon development and by the numerous greenhouses servicing the local horticultural industry, but a noteworthy feature of its countryside is the water lane (simply a country lane with a running stream in the middle) where ferns grow in abundance. Generally wetland is scarce and duneland is much reduced compared to that of Jersey, but the island is certainly not without its wildlife attractions. For example, many rarities exist on L'ANCRESSE COMMON, a rolling expanse of dune turf much modified by use as a golf course.

Alderney, the most northerly island, is remote and its topography offers little shelter from strong winds. Its landscape, not surprisingly, is notable for its lack of trees. It is about 16 km² in area, with steep cliffs in the south and west bordering a high plateau that slopes gently towards sandy bays in the north and east. The sea cliffs are the major landscape and wildlife feature of Alderney. Supporting many of the coastal plants characteristic of these islands, they are an ornithologist's paradise. Amongst the many species, gannets have colonised the rocks of Les Etac for many years, and storm petrels and puffins nest on the nearby uninhabited island of BURHOU.

The remaining, much smaller, islands of Sark and Herm share the characteristic botanic richness of the other Channel Islands and their 'car-less' environments make them well worth a visit, even if only for a day trip. Sark, a plateau with few accessible bays, is blessed with one richly wooded valley, which perfectly complements the maritime flora of its cliffs. Herm, little more than 200 hectares, has an impressively varied flora, reflecting its wide range of habitats. Lime-loving plants thrive on the calcareous northern dunes that border Herm's famous shell beach. Marine specialists will also find much of interest on Herm, as the spring low tides uncover a wealth of inter-tidal areas almost doubling the island's surface area.

Several outlying rocky reefs are also noteworthy. Les Minquiers and Les Ecrehous, 24km southeast and 11km north-east of Jersey respectively, both fall under that island's administration. Enormous areas of rocky shore are exposed at low tide, but their ornithological value is also highly prized. A varied selection of shore birds nest on these isolated reefs, but the greatest interest occurs when they are densely populated by birds resting on their migration. These migrants are also very much the attraction of the Casquets, a small group of rocks about 11km west of Alderney, renowned for their lighthouse and their maritime history. Visits to these outlying reefs offer the naturalist a truly unique experience, but they do require special arrangement with local contacts.

DR MICHAEL ROMERIL

Alderney

1554ha; States of Alderney
Inhabited island with interesting coastal heathland and cliffs
Daily flights; standard accommodation; round-island boat trip see notices in capital, St Anne
Spring, summer, autumn

The most northerly and remote of the Channel Islands, Alderney is considered an ornithologist's paradise and is especially noteworthy for migrating birds of prey. The cliff scenery from Fort Nummery around the south coast to Fort Tourgis matches that of its sister islands, and the slopes are rich in characteristic flora. There are three locations on the island that should not be missed by the visiting naturalist.

At the island's south-west corner, Giffoine Point is a relatively short walk from the airport and appears as a massive, natural, wild garden with a plethora of flora, including many rarities. There are extensive areas of prostrate broom and gorse where Dartford warblers nest and a multitude of other birds feed and rest during migration. Numerous seabirds breed on the rocks and cliffs around the headland, and it makes an excellent point from which to view the 3000-strong gannet colony on the nearby Les Etacs rocks.

Also on the main island, Longy Common, to the north-east, is a particularly good area for migrating birds. Many species of marsh birds use the reedbeds surrounding Longy Ponds and waders can be observed in the bay.

Two-and-a-half kilometres off the west coast is the bird sanctuary of Burhou, which is visited on the round-island boat trip. Storm petrels and puffins are amongst the birds nesting on the islet, although the latter are now much reduced from the 100,000 nesting there in the early 1950s.

L'Ancresse Common, Guernsey

Perry's Guide, p.6, B4; 160ha; L'Ancresse Commons Council
Sand-dune
All year

This is one of the few places in Guernsey where lime-loving plants such as autumn squill can be found. The area is good for birdwatchers, with North American waders, dotterel and snow bunting often seen in winter. Adjacent Chouet headland and Jaonneuse Point provide excellent viewpoints for seabirds.

La Clare Mare, Guernsey

Perry's Guide, p.12, C4/5; 1.2ha; La Société Guernesiaise reserve
Visitors should contact La Société Guernesiaise
Marsh
All year

The emphasis is on birdwatching – especially waders – on this reserve and a hide is being provided. Pipits, stonechats and larks nest on the landward side.

Coastal Footpath, Guernsey

Perry's Guide, p.25, H3–p.32, B2; 26km; States of Guernsey
Mixed woodland, scrub and heathland
All year

From St Peter Point on the east coast to PLEINMONT POINT at the south-west corner, this path crosses a wide variety of habitats – the soft, pine-dotted slopes and steep cliffs draped in evergreen oak of the east coast, to the wild gorse and bramble scrub and heathland along the cliffs towards PLEINMONT POINT. There is a good coastal flora, and the green lizard may be seen along the south slopes. Amongst the many possible detours, the stream in the south-coast valley at Le Gouffre (Perry's Guide p.28, D5) attracts many finches and warblers in summer. The gorse-covered slopes contain Dartford warblers and stonechats, and the clifftops west of the valley support some of Guernsey's rarest birds and butterflies, including the Glanville fritillary.

Le Couperon, Jersey

OS 706540; 4ha; NTJ–private
Mixed woodland
'Fisherman's track' provides through path
Spring, summer

The ground flora here has a character very much reflecting the soil-enhancing influence of salt spray from the sea.

Grouville Marsh, Jersey

OS 699493; 8ha; NTJ–private
Grazed and ungrazed marsh
Access restricted – check with ornithological section of Société Jersiaise. Good view point from La Cache des Pres off A3.
Spring, autumn

Very wet in winter and largely uncultivated, the area attracts an exceptional variety of birds, especially during migration periods. It is thought to be one of the best ornithological areas on the island, which is perhaps due, in part, to the marsh's proximity to the Cherbourg peninsula.

Herm Island

200ha; Major P. Wood, tel. Herm 22377
Sand-dunes and sea cliffs
Daily boat trips from Guernsey; limited
accommodation
Spring, summer, autumn

The northern part of Herm is dominated by the mainly fixed sand-dunes that make up the Common. Although burnet rose is present in exceptional quantity, the sand is particularly rich in shell fragments and many lime-loving plants, as well as rarities such as dwarf pansy and autumn squill, can be found. Stonechats and whitethroats can also be seen here. Although they do not match the stature of Guernsey's cliffs, the south cliffs of Herm resemble them and offer good birdwatching. Puffins are resident until the end of July in Puffin Bay, and the gully at Barbara's Leap is an ancient nesting site for ravens. The whole island is good for spring and autumn migrations.

Les Landes, Jersey

OS 547554; 99ha; States of Jersey
Heathland, coastal cliffs and bog
All year

An exposed site in the north-west of Jersey, Les Landes is the largest continuous area of heathland on the island. On the seaward side it is bounded by 3km of west- and north-facing cliffs, which fall dramatically to the sea. Dwarf-scrub heath is the dominant vegetation, with scattered stands of bracken, gorse scrub, dry acidic grassland and maritime grassland. Several rare plant species can be found, as well as a number of less common animal species, including the Glanville fritillary butterfly. There is much of ornithological interest, and significant numbers of Dartford warblers nest here. The Gros Nez headland is an excellent viewpoint for passing birds in bad weather and from here fulmars may be seen.

Almost a 'site within a site', the wetland area of Le Canal du Squez (OS 546556) is a diverse flushed bog dominated by purple moor-grass and supporting many plants that are local or rare; these include St John's wort and bog pimpernel. It is also reputed to be a site for the protected agile frog, though its exact present-day status is uncertain.

La Mare au Seigneur, Jersey

OS 567520; 11ha; NTJ reserve
Open water
Contact ornithological or botanical section of the
Société Jersiaise
All year

The only large naturally occurring open stretch of water in Jersey, La Mare au Seigneur is surrounded by extensive reedbeds and is an important site for wintering and migrating birds. Inclement weather has sent Brent geese in from the sea, and Cetti's warbler may be seen in this area. The wet meadows bordering the reedbeds are rich in orchids, including the rare Jersey orchid.

Noirmont Headland, Jersey

OS 607470; 28ha; States of Jersey
Coastal headland with grassland and cliffs
No access across cultivated fields
All year

Much of the plateau of this south-facing headland is covered with tall gorse, bracken and bramble scrub, with some holm oak. The cliff grassland, however, contains several nationally rare plants, including autumn squill and spotted rockrose. Dartford warblers nest and there are some interesting insects. A small pond to the south-west supports that declining, unique Jersey rarity, the Jersey forget-me-not.

North Coast Footpath, Jersey

OS 691548–548549; *c.*25km; States of Jersey
Coastal cliffs
Visitors must keep to the path as parts of these
cliffs are very dangerous
Spring, summer

Mostly bracken and gorse scrub with some heather and maritime grassland, the cliff areas are not rich in rarities but do support a number of locally uncommon species and one *Red Data Book* species, balm-leaved figwort, which grows alongside the path. A wealth of bryophytes can be found on the peaty, wet banks of the cliffs. The wall lizard can be seen in reasonable numbers at Bouley Bay, and puffins nest on the cliffs east of Plemont. It supports a rich coastal flora.

Pleinmont Point, Guernsey

Perry's Guide, p.32, B2; 59ha; States of Guernsey
Coastal cliffs, scrub and grassland
Spring, summer, autumn

At the end of the COASTAL FOOTPATH, Pleinmont Point is an excellent birdwatching station, particularly during migration times. Many passerines can be seen, including Dartford warblers, which breed, and stonechats. Fulmars nest on the cliffs.

Port Soif and Fort Hommet, Guernsey

Perry's Guide, p.8, C1 and p.13, E2; 1.2ha; La
Société Guernesiaise reserve
Coastal headlands
Spring, summer, autumn

Both areas are very rich in sea-cliff flowers and
Port Soif is the only bee-orchid site in the Channel
Islands. Wheatears occasionally nest, and gannets,
skuas, shearwaters and terns can be seen out at sea.

Les Pres Dormants, Jersey

OS 675480; 11ha; JCNS reserve
Wet meadow and marsh
Permit only from Mike Stentiford, JCNS, tel.
Jersey 6114
Spring, autumn, winter

Particularly good for wintering birds, but also
migrants can be seen here; the quality and quantity
depends on the severity of the winter both on the
island and elsewhere in Europe. The reserve supports what is probably the largest population of the
Jersey orchid, as well as other local species.

Les Quennevais, Jersey

OS 573493; 100ha; States of Jersey
Sand-dunes
Pamphlets from interpretation centre
Spring, summer

Considered a naturalist's paradise, the Quennevais
sand-dunes have an extraordinary diversity of
plant life with well over 400 different species
recorded in their relatively small area. The
topography itself is unique, with a stable dune
plain separating the primary dunes from the secondary dunes that form a plateau inland. The alkaline
shellsand of this plateau supports many species
characteristic of calcareous grasslands. There is an
abundance of southern European or Mediterranean
species, which in part explains the presence of 16
plants listed in the British *Red Data Book*. The
dunes are home to many of the island's insect
fauna, and also the green lizard, which occurs
naturally in the British Isles in Jersey alone.

The sand-dunes are the ecological focus of Les
Mielles, a specially designated area along the west
coast of Jersey with similarities to a UK National
Park. Dune flora and fauna can be observed along
this whole coastal strip between the sea wall and
the coast road. Plants more typical of saltmarshes
will be found where the sea frequently washes
over the wall. The Interpretation Centre is at
Kempt Tower, a converted martello tower.

Rue des Vicheris, Guernsey

Perry's Guide, p.20, C3; 1ha; La Société
Guernesiaise reserve
Traditional water meadows
Permit required
May, June

The meadows contain the largest colony of loose-
flowered orchids in the British Isles. Other orchids
may also be seen.

St Catherine's Woods, Jersey

OS 700529; 29ha; private reserve
Deciduous woodland
Access restricted to footpath over common land
Spring, summer

Valley woods contain an interesting assemblage of
plants uncommon in Jersey, such as dog's mercury
and yellow archangel. The valley bottom is especially rich in bryophytes, and the area is good for
invertebrates and birds.

St Peter's Valley, Jersey

OS 610514; 8ha; NTJ reserve
Woodland
Spring, summer

An attractive woodland, which contains some fine
oaks and has a wealth of wildflowers in the spring.

Sark

520ha
Sea cliffs, grassland and valley woodland
Day trips from Guernsey, plus standard
accommodation
Spring, summer, autumn

Sark is formed of two peninsulas connected by a
very narrow bridge 77m high. The island does not
lend itself to subdivisions and can rightly be considered a nature reserve in its entirety. Sheer cliffs
climb from the sea around the whole coast to
produce its plateau topography and, not unexpectedly, Sark is rich in cliff flora. It is also very good
for small migrants in spring and autumn, when
large numbers often congregate in the fields. Eper-
querie Common in the north is a good site for
migrants, while a little further westwards along the
coast Les Autelets Rocks support 150 pairs of
guillemot. On the headland above, the sand crocus
– a Channel Island speciality – may be found. Dix-
cart Valley is richly wooded and highly rated for
its plant and insect life, especially its summer butterflies. The valley leading to La Greve de la Ville
on the east coast is good for birds.

Silbe, Guernsey

Perry's Guide, p.20, D5; 1ha; La Société Guernesiaise reserve
Mixed woodland, stream and open water
Unrestricted access, but check if bird-ringing activities in progress
All year

Excellent area for birdwatching, with influxes of migrants. Summer-breeding birds include the yellowhammer (rare in Guernsey) and long-tailed tit, while winter flocks of siskins and firecrests feed on the site. Among the flowers recorded are spotted-orchid and some interesting marsh and water plants.

Vale Pond, Guernsey

Perry's Guide, p.6, B5; 1ha; Bucktrouts' Ltd–La Société Guernsésiaise reserve
Brackish pond and saltmarsh
Public access to bird hide, but permission for detailed botanical exploration must be obtained from La Société Guernsésiaise
All year

The extensive reedbeds shelter many migrating birds, and waders are regular visitors to the pond. Grey mullet and bass can sometimes be seen in the water. The flora is interesting and includes the bulbous foxtail, a grass species absent from all the other islands.

Abbreviations Used in the Guide

Note: county councils are given in the following form, e.g. ACC for Avon County Council; the county is always the same as the section title unless otherwise stated, and these abbreviations do not appear in the list below. All county names beginning with the letter N are spelt out to avoid confusion with the NCC (Nature Conservancy Council); CC alone stands for the Countryside Commission. For convenience the managing body named in line 1 of each entry is sometimes given an obvious abbreviation in line 3, when indicating for instance the availability of a leaflet (e.g. KAMT for Kenneth Allsop Memorial Trust). Such abbreviations are not listed below.

AWA	Anglian Water Authority
AWT	Avon Wildlife Trust
B and HWT	Bedfordshire and Huntingdonshire Wildlife Trust
BBNPC	Brecon Beacons National Park Committee
BBONT	Berkshire, Buckinghamshire and Oxfordshire Naturalists' Trust
BC	After a place name: Borough Council
BNT	Brecknock Naturalists' Trust
BR	British Rail
BTCV	British Trust for Conservation Volunteers
BWB	British Waterways Board
Cambient	Cambridgeshire and Isle of Ely Naturalists' Trust
CC	Countryside Commission/ after a place name: County Council
CCT	Cheshire Conservation Trust
CEGB	Central Electricity Generating Board
CNCT	Cleveland Nature Conservation Trust
CPRE	Council for the Preservation of Rural England
CTNC	Cornwall Trust for Nature Conservation/Cumbria Trust for Nature Conservation (according to context)
DBWPS	Devon Bird Watching and Preservation Society
DC	After a place name: District Council
DCCT	Durham County Conservation Trust
DNPA	Dartmoor National Park Authority
DNS	Deeside Naturalists' Society
DNT	Derbyshire Naturalists' Trust/Dorset Trust for Nature Conservation (according to context)
DTNC	Devon Trust for Nature Conservation
ENPC	Exmoor National Park Committee
ENT	Essex Naturalists' Trust
ESCC	East Sussex County Council
FC	Forestry Commission
FSC	Field Studies Council
GTNC	Glamorgan Naturalists' Trust/Gloucestershire Trust for Nature Conservation/Gwent Trust for Nature Conservation (according to context)
H and IOWNT	Hampshire and Isle of Wight Naturalists' Trust
H and MTNC	Hertfordshire and Middlesex Trust for Nature Conservation
H and RNT	Herefordshire and Radnorshire Nature Trust
HIDB	Highlands and Islands Development Board
HMSO	Her Majesty's Stationery Office
IOW	Isle of Wight
IWCC	Isle of Wight County Council
JCNS	Jersey Conservation and Naturalists' Society

KTNC	Kent Trust for Nature Conservation
L and RTNC	Leicestershire and Rutland Trust for Nature Conservation
L and SHTNC	Lincolnshire and South Humberside Trust for Nature Conservation
LDSPB	Lake District Special Planning Board
LNR	Local Nature Reserve
LTNC	Lancashire Trust for Nature Conservation
LWT	London Wildlife Trust
MBC	After a place name: Metropolitan Borough Council
MOD	Ministry of Defence
MNCT	Manx Nature Conservation Trust
MTNC	Montgomery Trust for Nature Conservation
NCC	Nature Conservancy Council
NNR	National Nature Reserve
NNT	Norfolk Naturalists' Trust
NOA	Norfolk Ornithologists' Association
NT	National Trust
NTJ	National Trust for Jersey
NTNC	Northamptonshire Trust for Nature Conservation/Nottinghamshire Trust for Nature Conservation (according to context)
NTS	National Trust for Scotland
NWA	Northumbrian Water Authority
NWNT	North Wales Naturalists' Trust
NWT	Northumberland Wildlife Trust
NWWA	North Western Water Authority
NYMNPC	North York Moors National Park Committee
PC	After a place name: Parish Council
PCNPA	Pembrokeshire Coast National Park Authority
PPJPB	Peak Park Joint Planning Board
RC	After a place name: Regional Council
RSNC	Royal Society for Nature Conservation
RSPB	Royal Society for the Protection of Birds
RSPCA	Royal Society for the Prevention of Cruelty to Animals
SNCT	Staffordshire Nature Conservation Trust
SNPC	Snowdonia National Park Committee
SSSI	Site of Special Scientific Interest
STNC	Shropshire Trust for Nature Conservation/Suffolk Trust for Nature Conservation/ Surrey Trust for Nature Conservation/Sussex Trust for Nature Conservation (according to context)
SWT	Scottish Wildlife Trust
SWWA	South Western Water Authority
TC	After a place name: Town Council (now defunct – see Stop Press Sites)
TWA	Thames Water Authority
UTNC	Ulster Trust for Nature Conservation
WARNACT	Warwickshire Nature Conservation Trust
WdT	Woodland Trust
WNCT	Worcestershire Nature Conservation Trust
WSCC	West Sussex County Council
WT	Wildfowl Trust
WTNC	Wiltshire Trust for Nature Conservation
WWA	Welsh Water Authority/Wessex Water Authority (according to context)
WWNT	West Wales Naturalists' Trust
YDNPC	Yorkshire Dales National Park Committee
YWT	Yorkshire Wildlife Trust

Addresses

The following is a list of the major wildlife organisations in Britain, together with those owners and managing bodies from whom information and/or permits may be obtained, but whose addresses are not already given in the text. All requests should be accompanied by a stamped addressed envelope, and readers should understand that permits may be refused at the managing bodies' discretion.

The nature conservation trusts of England, Wales and Scotland

Avon Wildlife Trust
The Old Police Station
32 Jacob's Wells Road
Bristol BS8 1DR

Bedfordshire and Huntingdonshire Wildlife Trust
Priory Country Park
Barkers Lane
Bedford MK41 9SH

Berkshire, Buckinghamshire and Oxfordshire Naturalists' Trust (BBONT)
3 Church Cowley Road
Rose Hill
Oxford
OX4 3JR

Birmingham
See Urban Wildlife Trust

Brecknock Naturalists' Trust
Chapel House
Llechfaen
Brecon
Powys LD3 7SP

Cambridgeshire and Isle of Ely Naturalists' Trust (Cambient)
1 Brookside
Cambridge
CB2 1JF

Cheshire Conservation Trust
c/o Marbury Country Park
Northwich
Cheshire
CW9 6AT

Cleveland Nature Conservation Trust
The Old Town Hall
Mandale Road, Thornaby
Stockton on Tees
Cleveland TS17 6AW

Cornwall Trust for Nature Conservation
Trendrine
Zennor
St Ives
Cornwall
TR26 3BW

Cumbria Trust for Nature Conservation
Church Street
Ambleside
Cumbria
LA22 0BU

Derbyshire Naturalists' Trust
Elvaston Country Park,
Derby DE7 3EP

Devon Trust for Nature Conservation
35 New Bridge Street
Exeter
Devon
EX4 3AH

Dorset Trust for Nature Conservation
39 Christchurch Road
Bournemouth
BH1 3NS

Durham County Conservation Trust
52 Old Elvet
Durham
DH1 3HN

Essex Naturalists' Trust
Fingringhoe Wick Nature Reserve
Fingringhoe
Colchester
Essex
CO5 7DN

Glamorgan Trust for Nature Conservation
Glamorgan Nature Centre
Tondu
Bridgend
Mid Glamorgan
CF32 0EH

Gloucestershire Trust for Nature Conservation
Church House
Standish
Stonehouse
GL10 3EU

Gwent Trust for Nature Conservation
16 White Swan Court
Church Street
Monmouth
Gwent NP5 3BR

Hampshire and Isle of Wight Naturalists' Trust
8 Market Place
Romsey
Hampshire
SO5 8NB

Herefordshire and Radnorshire Nature Trust
25 Castle Street
Hereford
HR1 2NW

Hertfordshire and Middlesex Trust for Nature Conservation
Grebe House
St Michael's Street
St Albans
Hertfordshire
AL3 4SN

Kent Trust for Nature Conservation
The Annexe
1a Bower Mount Road
Maidstone
Kent ME16 8AX

Lancashire Trust for Nature Conservation
Cuerden Valley Park
Cuerden Pavilion
Bamber Bridge
Preston
Lancashire PR5 6AX

Leicestershire and Rutland Trust for Nature Conservation
1 West Street
Leicester
LE1 6UU

Lincolnshire and South Humberside Trust for Nature Conservation
The Manor House
Alford
Lincolnshire
LN13 9DL

London Wildlife Trust
80 York Way
London N1 9AG

LWT can provide information on all sites within the GLC area, regardless of management

Manx Nature Conservation Trust
Ballacross
Andreas
Isle of Man

Montgomery Trust for Nature Conservation
8 Severn Square
Newtown
Powys
SY16 2AG

Norfolk Naturalists' Trust
72 Cathedral Close
Norwich
Norfolk
NR1 4DF

Northamptonshire Trust for Nature Conservation
Lings House
Billing Lings
Northampton
NN3 4BE

Northumberland Wildlife Trust
c/o Hancock Museum
Barras Bridge
Newcastle upon Tyne
NE2 4PT

North Wales Naturalists' Trust
154 High Street
Bangor
Gwynedd
LL57 1NU

Nottinghamshire Trust for Nature Conservation
2-12 Warser Gate
Nottingham
NG1 1PA

Scottish Wildlife Trust

Headquarters
25 Johnston Terrace
Edinburgh
EH1 2NH

Ayrshire area
30 Woodend Road
Ayr

Glasgow area
1 Westbank Quadrant
Glasgow W2

Shropshire Trust for Nature Conservation
Agriculture House
Barker Street
Shrewsbury
SY1 1QP

Somerset Trust for Nature Conservation
Fyne Court
Broomfield
Bridgwater
TA5 2EQ

Staffordshire Nature Conservation Trust
Coutts House
Sandon
Staffordshire
ST18 0DN

Suffolk Trust for Nature Conservation
Park Cottage
Saxmundham
Suffolk
IP17 1DQ

Surrey Trust for Nature Conservation
Hatchlands
East Clandon
Guildford
GU4 7RP

Sussex Trust for Nature Conservation
Woods Mill
Henfield
West Sussex
BN5 9SD

Urban Wildlife Trust
11 Albert Street
Birmingham
B4 7UA

**Warwickshire Nature Conservation Trust
(WARNACT)**
1 Northgate Street
Warwick
CV34 4SP

West Wales Naturalists' Trust
7 Market Street
Haverfordwest
Dyfed

Wiltshire Trust for Nature Conservation
19 High Street
Devizes
Wiltshire

Worcestershire Nature Conservation Trust
Hanbury Road
Droitwich
Worcestershire
WR9 7DO

Yorkshire Wildlife Trust
3rd Floor
10 Toft Green
off Micklegate
York YO1 1JT

Other organisations

Allerdale District Council
Holmewood
Cockermouth
Cumbria
CA13 0DW

Anglian Water Authority
Ambury Road
Huntingdon
PE18 6NZ

Arnside Parish Council
c/o South Lakeland District Council
Ashleigh
Windermere
LA23 2AG

Barvas Estates Ltd
c/o Smiths Gore
The Square
Fochabers
Moray

Basildon Development Corporation
Gifford House
Basildon
Essex
SS13 2EX

Basildon District Council
Fodderwick
Basildon
Essex
SS14 1DR

Basildon Natural History Society
80 Sparrows House
Basildon
Essex
SS16 5EN

Batsford Estate Office
Moreton-in-Marsh
Gloucestershire
GL56 9QF

Bedfordshire County Council
Planning Dept
County Hall
Bedford
MK42 9AP

Borders Natural History Society
The Reenes
Bellingham
Hexham
Northumberland
NE48 2DU

Borders Regional Council
Planning Dept
Newton St Boswells
Roxburghshire
TD6 0SA

Bournemouth Borough Council
Town Hall
Bournemouth
BH2 6DY

Bracknell District Council
Easthampstead House
Town Square
Bracknell
RG12 1AQ

Brecon Beacons National Park Committee

Information centres
Monk Street
Abergavenny
Gwent
NP7 5NA

Glamorgan Street
Brecon
Powys
LD3 7DP

Broad Street
Llandovery
Dyfed
SA20 0AR

Brighton Borough Council
Town Hall
Bartholomews
Brighton
BN1 1JA

Bristol City Council
Council House
College Green
Bristol
BS1 5TR

Bristol Naturalists' Society
c/o Bristol City Museum
Queens Road
Bristol
BS1 5AQ

Bristol Waterworks Co.
Recreations Dept
Woodford Lodge
Chew Stoke
Bristol
BS18 8XH

British Waterways Board
Melbury House
Melbury Terrace
London NW1

Cardiff City Council
City Hall
Cardiff
CF1 3ND

Central Electricity Generating Board
The Surveyor
Sudbury House
15 Newgate Street
London EC1A 7AU

Cheshire County Council
County Hall
Chester
CH1 1SF

Chorley Borough Council
Town Hall
Chorley
Lancashire
PR7 1DP

City of Birmingham District Council
The Council House
Birmingham

Clwyd County Council
Shire Hall
Mold
CH7 6NB

Colwyn Borough Council
Civic Centre
Abergele Road
Colwyn Bay
Clwyd

Cornwall Bird-Watching and Preservation Society
Trendain
Perranwell Station
Truro
Cornwall

Cornwall County Council
County Hall
Truro
TR1 3AY

Countryside Commission
John Dower House
Crescent Place
Cheltenham
Gloucestershire
GL50 3RA

Cynon Valley Borough Council
Rock Grounds
High Street
Aberdare
CF44 7AE

Dartmoor National Park Authority
Parke
Haytor Road
Bovey Tracey
Newton Abbot
Devon
TQ13 9JQ

Daventry District Council
Church Walk
Daventry
NN11 4BJ

Deeside Naturalists' Society
Melrose
38 Kelsterton Road
Connah's Quay
Deeside
Clwyd

Derbyshire County Council
County Offices
Matlock
Derbyshire
DE4 3AG

Devon Bird Watching and Preservation Society
Wichmor
Dousland
Yelverton
Devon

Dorset County Council
County Hall
Dorchester
Dorset
DT1 1XJ

Durham County Council
County Hall
Durham
DH1 5UF

Eastbourne Borough Council
Town Hall
Eastbourne
BN21 4UG

East Lothian District Council
Recreation and Tourism Dept
Brunton Hall
Musselburgh
EH21 6AF

East Sussex County Council
Pelham House
St Andrew's Lane
Lewes
BN7 1UN

Ecological Parks Trust
c/o The Linnean Society
Burlington House
Piccadilly
London W1V 0LQ

Epsom and Ewell Borough Council
Parks Dept
Ewell Court House
Ewell Court Avenue
Ewell
Surrey

Essex Water Co.
342 South Street
Romford
Essex
RM1 2AL

Exmoor National Park Committee
Exmoor House
Dulverton
Somerset
TA22 9HL

Information centre
Minehead and West Somerset
Publicity Association
Market House
Minehead
Somerset

Fair Isle Bird Observatory Trust
21 Regent Terrace
Edinburgh
EH7 5BT

Warden
Bird Observatory
Fair Isle
Shetland

Forestry Commission

Headquarters for England, Wales and Scotland
231 Corstorphine Road
Edinburgh
EH12 7AT

England
North
1A Grosvenor Terrace
York
YO3 7DB

East
Great Eastern House
Tennison Road
Cambridge
CB1 2DU

West
Flowers Hill
Brislington
Bristol
BS4 5JY

Wales
Victoria House
Victoria Terrace
Aberystwyth
Dyfed
SY23 2DA

Scotland
South
Greystones Park
55/57 Moffat Road
Dumfries
DG1 1NP

Mid
Portcullis House
21 India Street
Glasgow
G2 4PL

North (North Sunart woodland, Highland)
21 Church Street
Inverness
IV1 1EL

Glen Tanar Estate Office
Aboyne
AB3 5EU

Gloucestershire County Council
Shire Hall
Gloucester
GL1 2TG

Gosport Borough Council
Town Hall
Gosport
Hampshire
PO12 1EB

Great Harwood Civic Society
2 Wimblefold Lane
Great Harwood
Blackburn
Lancashire
BB6 7PT

Gwent County Council
County Hall
Cwmbran
Gwent
NP4 2XH

L.G. Harris and Co. Ltd
Stoke Prior
Bromsgrove
B60 4AE

Hastings Borough Council
4 Robertson Terrace
Hastings
East Sussex
TN34 1JE

Hereford and Worcester County Council
New County Office
Farrier Street
Worcester
WR1 3BH

Her Majesty's Stationery Office

Government bookshops
258 Broad Street
Birmingham
B1 2HE

Southey House
Wine Street
Bristol
BS1 2BQ

41 The Hayes
Cardiff
CF1 1JW

13A Castle Street
Edinburgh

49 High Holborn
London
WC1V 6HB

Brazennose Street
Manchester
M60 8AS

Horsell Common Preservation Society
Fairbanks
Pembroke Road
Woking
Surrey
GU22 7DP

Isle of Wight County Council
County Hall
Newport
Isle of Wight
PO30 1UD

Isle of Wight Natural History and Archaeological Society
66 Carisbrooke Road
Newport
Isle of Wight
PO30 1BW

Isle of Wight Tourist Board
The Old Town Hall
Leigh Road
Eastleigh
Hampshire
SO5 4DE

Jeffery Harrison Memorial Trust
Sevenoaks Experimental Wildfowl Reserve
Tadorna
Bradbourne Vale Road
Sevenoaks
Kent
TN13 3DH

Kenneth Allsop Memorial Trust
Knock-na-Cre
Milborne Port
Sherborne
Dorset
DT9 5HJ

Knowle Society
1712 Warwick Road
Knowle
West Midlands

Lancashire County Council
County Hall
Preston
PR1 8XJ

Landmark Trust
21 Dean's Yard
Westminster
London SW1 3PA

Leicestershire County Council
County Hall
Glenfield
Leicester
LE3 8RA

Lewes District Council
Lewes House
Lewes
East Sussex
BN7 2LX

Llanelli Borough Council
Elwyn House
Llanelli
Dyfed
SA15 3AP

Manchester Ornithological Society
5 Church Cottages
Holmes Chapel Road
Chelford
Cheshire SK11

Mansfield District Council
Carr Bank
Mansfield
Nottinghamshire

Merseyside Metropolitan Borough Council
Metropolitan House
PO Box 95
Old Hall Street
Liverpool
L69 3EL

Merthyr Borough Council
Town Hall
Merthyr Tydfil
CF47 8AN

Mid Glamorgan County Council
County Hall
Cathays Park
Cardiff

Ministry of Defence
Lands Dept
Tolworth Tower
Ewell Road
Surbiton
Surrey
KT6 7DR

Moray District Council
Planning Dept
High Street
Elgin
Morayshire
W30 1BX

National Trust
42 Queen Anne's Gate
London SW1H 9AS

*There are also 15 regional offices in England and
Wales: their addresses are obtainable from the
address above*

National Trust for Scotland
Chief Ranger
Suntrap
43 Gogarbank
Edinburgh
EH12 9BY

104 West George Street
Glasgow
G2 1PS

Pitmedden House
Ellon
Aberdeenshire
AB4 0PD

109 Church Street
Inverness

Nature Conservancy Council

Headquarters
19–20 Belgrave Square
London SW1X 8PY

England
North East
Archbold House
Archbold Terrace
Newcastle upon Tyne
NE2 1EG

North West
Blackwell
Bowness-on-Windermere
Windermere
Cumbria
LA23 3JR

East Anglia
60 Bracondale
Norwich
NR1 2BE

West Midlands
Attingham Park
Shrewsbury
Shropshire
SY4 4TW

East Midlands
PO Box 6
Godwin House
George Street
Huntingdon
PE18 6BU

South East
Zealds
Church Street
Wye
Ashford
Kent
TN25 5BW

South
Foxhold House
Thornford Road
Crookham Common
Headley
Newbury
Berkshire
RG15 8EL

South West
Roughmoor
Bishops Hull
Taunton
Somerset
TA1 5AA

Wales
North
Penrhos Road
Bangor
LL57 2LQ

Dyfed–Powys
Plas Goggerddan
Aberystwyth
Dyfed
SY23 3EE

South
44 The Parade
Roath
Cardiff
CF2 3AB

Scotland
North East (Grampian, Orkney, Shetland and Speyside)
17 Rubislaw Terrace
Aberdeen
AB1 1XE

North West (Highland (except Speyside), Outer Hebrides, Skye and the Small Isles)
9 Culduthel Road
Inverness
IV2 4AG

South West (Dumfries and Galloway, Strathclyde)
The Castle
Loch Lomond Park
Balloch
Dunbartonshire
G83 8LX

South East (Borders, Central, Fife, Lothian, Tayside) and headquarters
12 Hope Terrace
Edinburgh
EH9 2AS

Newbury District Council
Cheap Street
Newbury
Berkshire
RG14 5BJ

Norfolk Ornithologists' Association
Aslack Way
Holme next Sea
Hunstanton
Norfolk
PE36 6LP

Northumberland County Council
County Hall
Newcastle upon Tyne

Northumbrian Water Authority
Northumbria House
Regent Centre
Gosforth
Newcastle upon Tyne
NE3 3PX

North York Moors National Park Committee
The Old Vicarage
Bondgate
Helmsley
York
YO6 5BP

Oxford City Council
Recreation Dept
Town Hall
Oxford
OX1 1BX

Peak Park Joint Planning Board
Aldern House
Baslow Road
Bakewell
Derbyshire
DE4 1AE

Pembrokeshire Coast National Park Authority
Dyfed County Council
County Offices
Haverfordwest
Dyfed

Peterborough Development Corporation
Touthill Close
City Road
Peterborough
PE1 1UJ

Peterlee Development Corporation
Lee House
Yoden Way
Peterlee
SR8 1BB

Redditch Development Corporation
Landscape Section
Architect's Dept
Holmwood
Plymouth Road
Redditch
B97 4PD

Rochdale Metropolitan Borough Council
Town Hall
Rochdale
OL16 1AB

Royal Society for Nature Conservation
The Green
Nettleham
Lincoln
LN2 2NR

Royal Society for the Protection of Birds

England and Wales
The Lodge
Sandy
Bedfordshire
SG19 2DL

Scotland
17 Regent Terrace
Edinburgh
EH7 5BN

Royal Society for the Prevention of Cruelty to Animals
Causeway
Horsham
West Sussex
RH12 1HG

Sandwell Metropolitan Borough Council
Town Hall
West Bromwich
Staffordshire

Selborne Society
7 Glebe Court
Church Road
Hanwell
London W7 3BY

Shropshire County Council
The Shirehall
Abbey Foregate
Shrewsbury
SY2 6ND

Shropshire Ornithological Society
13 North Hermitage
Shrewsbury

Snowdonia National Park Committee
Snowdonia National Park
Penrhyndeudraeth
Gwynedd
LL48 6LS

Somerset County Council
County Hall
Taunton
TA1 4DY

South Glamorgan County Council
Newport Road
Cardiff
CF2 1XA

South Staffordshire Waterworks Co.
50 Sheepcote St
Birmingham
B16 8AR

South West Water Authority
3–5 Barnfield Road
Exeter
EX1 1RE

South Wight Borough Council
41 Sea Street
Newport
Isle of Wight
PO30 5DN

Staffordshire County Council
County Buildings
Stafford
ST16 2LH

Stockport Metropolitan Borough Council
Town Hall
Stockport
SK1 3XE

Surrey Heath Borough Council
Bagshot Manor
Green Lane
Bagshot
Surrey
GU19 5NN

Swansea City Council
The Guildhall
Swansea
SA1 4PA

Tamworth Borough Council
Municipal Offices
Church Street
Tamworth
B79 7BZ

Thames Water Authority
Nugent House
Vastern Road
Reading
Berkshire
RG1 8DB

Torbay Borough Council
Town Hall
Torquay
TQ1 3DR

University Botanic Garden
1 Brookside
Cambridge

Vale of Glamorgan Borough Council
Town Hall
Barry
CF6 6EU

Wansbeck District Council
Council Offices
Newbiggin-by-the-Sea
NE64 6PL

Warwickshire County Council
Shire Hall
Warwick

Warwickshire County Museum
Market Hall
Market Place
Warwick

Waverley District Council
Council Offices
Bury Fields
Guildford
Surrey
GU2 5AY

Water Authority reservoirs
See British Waterways Board

Wells Natural History and Archaeological Society
c/o The Museum
Wells
Somerset

Welsh Water Authority
Cambrian Way
Brecon
Powys
LD3 7HP

Wessex Water Authority
Wessex House
Passage Street
Bristol
BS2 0JQ

West Glamorgan County Council
Guildhall
Swansea

West Midland Bird Club
1 Lansdowne Road
Studley
Warwickshire
B80 7JG

West Sussex County Council
County Hall
Chichester
PO19 1RQ

Wildfowl Trust

England and Wales
Slimbridge
Gloucester
GL2 7BT

Scotland
Eastpark
Caerlaverock
Dumfriesshire

Wiltshire County Council
County Hall
Trowbridge
Wiltshire
BA14 8JG

Wirral Borough Council
Town Hall
Brighton Street
Wallasey
Merseyside
L44 8ED

Wokingham District Council
Council Offices
Shute End
Wokingham
Berkshire
RG11 1BN

Woodland Trust
Westgate
Grantham
Lincolnshire
NG31 6LL

Woodspring District Council
Town Hall
Weston-super-Mare
BS23 1UJ

Yeovil District Council
Maltravers House
Petters Way
Yeovil
Somerset

Yorkshire Dales National Park Committee
Colvend
Hebden Road
Grassington
Skipton
North Yorkshire
BD23 5LB

The nature conservation trusts of the Channel Islands

L'Ancresse Commons Committee
c/o Mr H. Niles
Lucksall
L'Ancresse
Guernsey

Jersey Conservation and Naturalists' Society
c/o Mr M. Stentiford
Naparima
Victoria Village
Trinity
Jersey

National Trust for Jersey
The Elms
St Mary
Jersey

La Société Guernesiaise
Candie Museum
St Peter Port
Guernsey

La Société Jersiaise
Pier Road
St Helier
Jersey

States of Alderney
States Office
New Street
Alderney

States of Guernsey Board of Administration
St Julian's Emplacement
St Peter Port
Guernsey

States of Jersey
c/o The Conservation Officer
Planning Office
South Hill
St Helier
Jersey

Northern Ireland

Craigavon Borough Council
Town Hall
Edward Street
Portadown
Craigavon
BT62 3LZ

Department of the Environment (Northern Ireland)
Stormont
Belfast
BT4 3SS

Forest Service
Department of Agriculture
Dundonald House
Upper Newtonards Road
Belfast
BT4 3SB

National Trust for Northern Ireland
Rowallane House
Saintfield
Ballynamhinch
Co Down
BT24 7LH

Ulster Trust for Nature Conservation
Barnett's Cottage,
Barnett Demesne
Malone Road
Belfast BT9 5PB

Isle of Man

Ballamodha Bird Sanctuary and Nature Reserve
The Willows
Ballamodha
Castletown
Isle of Man

The Manx Museum and National Trust
Douglas
Isle of Man

Glossary of Naturalists' Terms

The following is a list of terms which may not be familiar to all readers of this Guide. It includes expressions such as Local Nature Reserve (LNR), National Nature Reserve (NNR) and Site of Special Scientific Interest (SSSI): these are used only rarely in the text because such sites are subject to frequent redesignation, which might prove confusing. However readers may well come across the terms in other literature.

Algae Seaweeds and related species, often microscopic.

Alien A non-native species breeding successfully in the wild: e.g. Indian balsam (Himalayan), mink (American).

Alluvial Describes sands and silts deposited by freshwater floods.

Ancient woodland *See* Primary woodland.

Andesite A fine-grained igneous rock.

Arboretum A collection of tree species.

Arctic–alpine Usually upland species, thought to have survived *in situ* since the last ice age, now normally found only in the Alps and the Arctic.

Area of Outstanding Natural Beauty (AONB) Area agreed between local authority and Countryside Commission as worthy of controls in planning and development.

Basin mire A bog, marsh or fen developed over a dip in the ground.

Belemnite Ancient group of animals related to modern cuttlefish. The bullet-like skeleton, equivalent to the cuttle-bone beloved of budgerigars, is frequently found in rocks such as the lias at Lyme Regis (Dorset).

Blanket bog Bog formed across upland plateaus, fed by rain direct – rather than spring-fed or drainage-fed as in a basin mire.

Boulder clay Glacial deposit of fine clay containing pebbles and boulders.

Box canyon Steep-sided, deep and narrow valley.

Brachiopods Group of two-shelled animals, more plentiful in prehistory than now, which superficially resemble bivalves such as cockles. They were often fixed to rocks by a stalk or pedicle.

Brae Slope.

Broad-leaved woodland A deciduous wood filled with trees which lose their leaves in autumn.

Bryophytes Liverworts and mosses.

Bunter sandstone Sandstones and conglomerates forming part of the new red sandstone, laid down in the Triassic.

Calcareous Highly alkaline: chalk, limestone, etc.

Carboniferous Geological period in which carboniferous limestone, millstone grit and coal measures were deposited on Devonian old red sandstone, *c.* 350–270 million years ago. A time of dense vegetation, shark-like fish, amphibians, the first reptiles, the first spiders and the first flying insects.

Carr A woodland, usually alder and/or willow, growing in very wet sites.

Carse Alluvial plain.

Cetaceans Marine mammals of the order including whales and porpoises.

Clay with flints A varying mixture of clay, sand and flints which caps much of the higher land in the south. It represents the insoluble parts of eroded chalk, mixed with later deposits, spread across the Downs by melting ice-age snow and ice.

Cleugh A steep wooded valley; in the south west, a cleave.

Clint The slabs of a limestone pavement.

Clitter The jumble of large rocks littering slopes below south western tors.

Coal measures Upper carboniferous deposits, typically alternating sandstones and shales with coal seams.

Colonisers Plants which can spread into new habitats. Primary colonisers, e.g., invade freshly cleared areas.

Combe/coomb/cwm Valley cut by ice-age action. Usually a dry valley in chalk or limestone in the south; a glacial scooped valley in Wales.

Conglomerates Rounded pebbles cemented by sand, silt, clay, etc.

Conservation Area Area recommended by NCC (in *A Nature Conservation Review*, 1977) as nationally important and meriting special safeguards, above those for an SSSI.

Coppicing Woodland management in which young trees are cut close to the ground to give a regrowth of shoots from the stumps (or stools). Provides a regular harvest for basketwork, fencing, firewood etc. Some standards are usually left to grow to maturity.

Corrie Cirque or cwm, an armchair-shaped hollow on a mountain formed by glacial erosion.

Crag-and-tail Roche moutonee, an asymmetrical rock outcrop owing its distinctive shape to glacial smoothing; the smooth slope or tail faces the direction of former ice advance and the steep slope or crag is on the lee side.

Cretaceous Geological period when Wealden sands and clays, lower greensand, gault, upper greensand and chalk were deposited on Jurassic Purbeck rocks, *c.* 135–70 million years ago. The second half of the age of dinosaurs, which ended with their extinction.

Crinoid Feather-stars and sea-lilies. Usually stalked, immobile starfish with long, branched, feathery arms.

Crustaceans Mainly aquatic animals such as crabs, lobsters, shrimps, sand-hoppers, etc. Also fixed forms such as barnacles.

Dabblers Duck which feed by grazing, dabbling or up-ending in shallow waters.

Devonian Geological period in which old red sandstone, including also marine deposits, was laid down on Silurian Ludlow beds, *c.* 400–350 million years ago. The age of fishes, the first bony fish and the first wingless insects; ended with the first amphibians.

Diploid Having pairs of similar chromosomes, one of each pair donated by either parent.

Diptera Two-winged insects: flies, mosquitoes, etc.

Dolerite A medium-grained igneous rock.

Drumlin A low ridge of glacial boulder clay.

Eocene First part of the tertiary era. Time of the first modern mammals, including early horses and elephants.

Epiphyte Plant which grows on another, for support rather than parasitic reasons.

Eutrophic Rich in nutrients.

Exotic Non-native species, usually planted for decorative reasons.

Feral Animal species which have escaped captivity and now breed in the wild: mink, Canada goose, etc.

Ffriddoedd Sheepwalks, upland grass moors, as opposed to the crags of the *mynydd*, or mountains.

Firth A wide estuary.

Flush Area flushed by drainage water, usually lime-enriched.

Gabbro A coarse-grained igneous rock.

Gammarid Small sand-hopper-like crustacean found in fresh and salt water.

Gault Cretaceous clay deposit between lower and upper greensand. Where the latter is absent it may directly underlie the chalk.

Ghyll A narrow, water-cut valley, usually with rock exposures.

Glacial drift The cover of clays, sands, pebbles and debris deposited by a melting ice sheet. Often used synonymously with boulder clay.

Gneiss A very hard and ancient metamorphic rock.

Great limestone Also great scar limestone. The standard limestone of the Pennine massifs, laid down in the carboniferous.

Green belt Undeveloped land around urban area, agreed by local authority to remain as such.

Greensand Sandstone containing glauconite, a green iron-bearing mineral, causing the rock to weather to an orange or yellow colour.

Grike A water-dissolved fissure in a limestone pavement.

Gritstone Typically, a coarse-grained sandstone, generally from the Carboniferous.

Guano Bird droppings.

Haar Sea mist, typical of east-coastal Scotland.

Hag The gully-and-hummock pattern of a blanket bog heavily eroded by rainwater run-off.

Hammer pond Pond formed by damming a stream to drive the mill wheels that in the eighteenth and nineteenth centuries powered giant hammers for iron workings.

Hanger, hanging woodland Wood growing on the side of a steep slope.

Hanging valley A tributary valley which terminates high above the floor of the main valley due to the deeper erosion of the latter.

Heritage Coast Length of coastline agreed between local authority and Countryside Commission as worthy of controls in planning and development.

High forest Wood allowed to grow unmanaged so that all the trees are tall.

Holm A small rocky island.

Igneous Rock solidified from molten or semi-molten material; magma.

'Improved' pasture Grassland sprayed, fertilised or reseeded to encourage a grass monoculture.

Invertebrate Any animal without a backbone.

Kame A steep-sided heap of stratified sands and gravels formed by glacial meltwaters.

Jurassic Geological period during which lias rocks were laid down on Triassic deposits, followed by limestones and clays, ending with the Purbeck beds, *c.* 180–135 million years ago. First half of the age of the dinosaurs, ending with the first birds.

Lamellibranch Bivalve. Two-shelled mollusc such as cockle, mussel, oyster, etc.

Law Scottish name for a small conical hill, usually of volcanic origin.

Lazybed Traditional method of cultivation practised in the Western Isles; seaweed and manure were mixed with the poor soil to form rectangular areas about 2 metres wide and about half a metre above the surrounding ground.

Leguminous Describes pod-bearing plants: peas, vetches, gorse, etc.

Lek A courting ground, especially for black grouse. Special area where males congregate to compete for watching females.

Lepidoptera Butterflies and moths.

Ley Traditionally, a hay-field.

Lias Beginning of the Jurassic: a period when clays, shales and clayey limestones were deposited on the Rhaetic rocks. Time of the first crocodiles and flying reptiles. Lias beds in Britain are particularly rich in fossils.

Lignite 'Brown coal'. The first stage in development from peat or partially decayed vegetable matter to coal. Found in late cretaceous and tertiary deposits.

Limestone pavement Slabby exposures of limestone divided by water-dissolved fissures, usually containing a characteristic plant life.

Littoral Of the shallows where light can reach. Includes the tidal seashore.

Local Nature Reserve (LNR) Nature reserve declared by a local authority.

Lochan Tarn, a small area of water.

Lusitanian Describes animals and plants found, in Britain, only on the western and south western coasts where the climate is warm and wet. Also found in western France, Spain and Portugal.

Machair Grass sward on calcareous ground behind beaches, typical of certain Hebridean islands.

Magma The molten rock which lies beneath the world's surface layer; the source of volcanic eruptions.

Magnesian limestone Limestone of the early Permian.

Maritime Of the sea.

Marl A mix of clay and lime-rich minerals, often with silts. The mix is variable: keuper marl, for instance, is a red mudstone only slightly calcareous.

Melanistic Dark colour form, genetically transmitted.

Mere Usually, a flooded glacial depression.

Metamorphic Altered. Heat, pressure and other factors may alter existing rocks – sediments to slates, for instance.

Micro-habitat Within the larger habitat of a wood, e.g., the sites beneath a damp stone and high on a sunlit branch are micro-habitats for small plants and animals.

Millstone grit Thick beds of sandstones and shales laid down on the carboniferous limestone. So called because the sandstones were often used for millstones.

Molluscs Mainly aquatic animals, usually with shells. Include shellfish, snails, squids and octopuses, etc.

Monocline Sudden increase in the dip of rock strata to a near-vertical, with a subsequent return to the original slope.

Montane Of mountains.

Moraine A ridge of rock particles dropped from the melt-face or sides of a glacier.

Moss Raised bog, usually formed on the site of a former mere.

Muir Moor, heath.

National Nature Reserve (NNR) Nature reserve declared by the NCC.

National Park Area administered by its own authority in concert with local and central government to protect its character and facilitate public access.

Old meadow Unimproved grassland. Pasture containing a rich variation of species slow to recolonise after improvement.

Oolite Sedimentary rock, usually limestone, built of small rounded grains. Inferior and great oolite are Jurassic deposits laid above the lias.

Ordovician Geological period between the Cambrian and Silurian, a mix of igneous and sedimentary rocks, c. 500–440 million years ago. An age of trilobites and brachiopods, of the first corals and primitive jawless fish.

Oxbow lake A curve cut off from the parent river by a straightening of the water-course.

Paleozoic The geological period from the Cambrian to the Permian.

Paludina limestone 'Purbeck marble'. A reddish or greenish limestone packed with freshwater fossils, laid down at the end of the Jurassic. A similar limestone occurs in the Wealden beds of the start of the Cretaceous.

Passerine A perching bird, e.g. sparrow or finch.

Pentamerus limestone Limestone containing the fossil *Pentamerus*, characteristic of the Silurian.

Permian Geological period following the carboniferous. Apart from the magnesian limestone of north eastern England, Permian rocks are inseparable from those of the Triassic in Britain, c. 270–225 million years ago.

Petrologist One who studies rocks.

Pinetum A collection of conifer species.

Podsol/podzol An acid soil type with pale upper layer from which the nutrients and minerals have been washed downwards, often forming a lower, impermeable pan, so may become waterlogged.

Pollarding Traditional management whereby grazed woodland could yield coppice-like growth. Trees are polled – cut off above grazing height – stimulating fresh shoots from the crown. Pollarded trees are often seen in hedges and by riverbanks.

Pre-Cambrian More than 600 million years old; the rocks laid down before the Cambrian are metamorphic. Life, both plant and animal, had evolved by the end of this period.

Primary woodland Woods which, even if clear-felled and allowed to regrow, have not been essentially altered by man since the last ice age.

Raised beach A platform above present high-tide mark, bearing sand or shingle and formed during a past period of relatively higher sea level.

Raised mire Bog domed by peat above an earlier wetland. In this way an acid bog can be raised above a lime-rich marsh.

Raptor A bird of prey.

Relict Species of habitat isolated from a previous environment. Char, for instance, are relict fish, trapped since the ice ages in deep glacial lakes.

Rhaetic Geological period transitional from Jurassic to Triassic.

Rhizome An underground stem (not a root) budding from small, scale-like underground leaves.

Rhyne A drainage ditch.

Rich wood Woodland, usually lowland, with a typical plant life including dog's mercury, primrose, violets, etc.

Ride Wide pathway in woodland.

Ridge and furrow Traditional ploughing technique, now long abandoned, which banks the land between the opening furrows, allowing dry strips for cultivation, with the furrows for drainage. Signs of ridge-and-furrow work in a grassland suggest considerable antiquity.

'Right to roam' Slogan and object of the protesters who asserted that access to the open moors of the Peak District should be allowed to all.

Ripple bedding Ripple patterns in sedimentary rocks due to water currents.

Roding Display flight of woodcock. Usually at dusk and dawn. solitary, with slow wing-beats but fast speed, accompanied by a strange, low, repetitive, grumbling call.

Scar An edge or cliff of exposed bedrock.

Schist A metamorphic rock altered to a finely layered mineral structure which will readily split into thin flakes.

Schwingmoor A floating bog, a raft of peat above a flooded depression.

Scrape A shallow pool excavated to attract waders.

Secondary woodland Woodland which has recolonised completely cleared land.

Sedimentary All rocks not igneous or metamorphic. Properly, rocks formed by the consolidation of sediments.

Serpentine/serpentinite A greenish or reddish mineral containing magnesium. Serpentinite is an igneous rock converted as a whole to serpentine. In Britain found only on the Lizard (Cornwall), on Anglesey (Gwynedd) and in the Scottish Isles.

Silurian Geological period following the Ordovician, preceding the old red sandstone of the Devonian, *c.* 440–400 million years ago. The beginning of the age of fishes and time of the first land plants.

Site of Special Scientific Interest (SSSI) Area recommended by the NCC as meriting special safeguards.

Skerry Isolated off-shore rock.

Spring line Springs often show where the junction between pervious and impervious rocks appears at or close to the surface.

Stack Rock pinnacle in the sea, often formed when the roof of a natural arch or cave collapses due to erosion.

Standard Tree allowed to grow to maturity for timber.

Strath A flat-bottomed highland valley (cf. glen, which is V-shaped rather than U-shaped).

Tertiary Geological period following the Cretaceous, *c.* 70–1 million years ago. Fossils show increasingly modern life forms; by the end of the tertiary, man is present.

Triassic Geological period when the new red sandstone was laid down (a process probably starting in the Permian), *c.* 225–180 million years ago. The first ichthyosaurs (fishlike reptiles) occurred.

Trilobite Extinct but once abundant marine animal superficially resembling a giant woodlouse.

Turbary The right to dig turf. Hence often incorporated in the names of old peat-digging areas.

Understorey The shrub layer. Young trees and shrubs below the taller tree layer in a woodland.

Voe Shetland term for a sea loch or fiord.

Waders Generally long-legged birds feeding at or in the water's edge. Include avocet, oystercatcher and woodcock.

Wealden beds Sands and clays, seen chiefly in the Weald area, marking the start of the Cretaceous.

Whip A slender branch or clump of new springs regrowing from a cut stump (*see* Coppicing).

Winter-borne/winter-bourne A river or section of a river which, drying out in the summer, runs only in the wet season.

Zonation Distribution of plants and animals in response to environment. The seashore, for instance, has a progression of different species from the splash zone, only wetted by high tide waves, to the lower shore, only exposed at lowest tides.

Index of Species

Avens, mountain, 99, 440, 507, 527, 567, 578, 618, 621, 622

Avens, water, 99, 107, 109, 114, 143, 149, 151, 153, 199, 204, 214, 261, 285, 290, 319, 363, 366, 371, 439, 483, 488, 507, 522, 565, 572

Avens, wood, 32, 149, 151, 153, 285, 421, 445, 633, 639

Avocet, 73, 89, 118, 125, 293, 294, 301, 374, 378, 491

Awlwort, 461, 503

Azalea, 433, 611

Azalea, mountain, 584

Azalea, trailing, 553, 565, 566, 578

Azure, 402

Badger, 17, 22, 24, 44, 78, 88, 96, 98, 103, 115, 118, 123, 124, 134, 138, 139, 143, 149, 151, 152, 154, 165, 176, 197, 199, 208, 215, 218, 221-223, 226, 227, 229, 234, 244, 251, 253, 281, 283, 286, 321, 325, 343, 344, 346, 352, 353, 358, 363, 387, 392, 399, 401, 407, 423, 427, 429, 433, 434, 437, 456, 460-462, 464, 470, 471, 476, 477, 480, 492, 498, 513, 515, 523, 539, 551, 555, 561, 566, 568, 577, 579, 584, 585, 591, 598, 610, 626, 631, 633, 635, 638, 639, 654

Balm, bastard, 90

Balsam, Indian, 186, 222, 257, 331, 438

Balsam, orange, 36, 186, 238, 471

Balsam, touch-me-not, 93, 97, 206

Baneberry, 96, 428, 434, 439, 440

Barley, 240

Barley, wood, 221, 342

Barnacles, 141

Bartsia, alpine, 440, 527

Bartsia, red, 394

Basil, wild, 109, 110, 385, 410, 413, 419

Bastard-toadflax, 137, 202, 211, 237, 418, 420, 423

Bat, 119, 181, 196, 229, 262, 434, 448, 532

Bazzania pearsonii, 565

Beadlet anemone, 83, 148, 629, 638

Beak-sedge, brown, 140, 206, 388

Beak-sedge, white, 95, 100, 118, 133, 206, 355, 383, 388, 457, 469, 486, 619

Bearberry, 99, 329, 553, 556, 558, 565, 567, 571, 572, 578, 582, 657

Beautiful golden Y, 261

Beauty, brindled, 607

Beauty, oak, 352, 360

Beauty, pale brindled, 362

Bechstein's bat, 139

Bedstraw, fen, 222, 237, 377, 387, 391

Bedstraw, heath, 23, 41, 49, 61, 96, 103, 104, 112, 121, 151, 234, 272, 277, 286, 296, 328, 337, 342, 354, 360, 397, 410, 412, 429, 432, 461, 474, 482, 500, 509, 513, 515, 516, 648

Bedstraw, lady's, 19, 29, 32, 43, 70, 100, 136, 137, 184, 199, 201, 208, 210, 211, 224, 229, 258, 271, 284, 301, 342, 411, 417, 419-421, 423, 431, 447, 454, 479, 503, 504

Bedstraw, limestone, 429

Bedstraw, marsh, 20, 237, 246, 274, 331, 350, 358, 364, 387, 422, 436, 437, 490

Bedstraw, northern, 259, 440, 649

Bee, 44, 288, 293, 385, 413, 420, 446

Bee, bumble, 263

Bee, digger, 657

Bee, great yellow, 427

Bee, mason, 44

Bee, solitary, 533, 656

Beech, 16, 19, 24, 26, 27, 40, 43, 44, 48, 51, 53-56, 59, 87, 88, 94-96, 106, 107, 109, 111, 112, 117, 123, 124, 127, 129, 131, 137, 148, 151, 153, 157, 163, 164, 173, 175-179, 181-184, 191, 194, 195, 198, 199, 201, 204, 205, 208-210, 213, 219, 231, 232, 234, 235, 240, 241, 244-246, 248-253, 256, 257, 259, 260, 265, 266, 277, 281, 286, 304, 313, 314, 322, 330, 337, 338, 341, 342, 345, 346, 351, 352, 362, 364, 381, 383, 386, 387, 389, 392, 396, 399, 401, 402, 407, 411-413, 417, 419, 421, 427, 432, 449, 455, 456, 462, 470, 473, 474, 476, 477, 482, 483, 486, 487, 489, 492, 513, 552, 566, 628, 633-635, 640, 641, 645, 650

Beet, sea, 84, 104, 161, 170, 204, 303, 394, 459, 467, 481, 497

Beetle, 42, 51, 126, 164, 398, 559, 579, 585

Beetle, bark, 47

Beetle, bee, 584

Beetle, musk, 186, 304

Beetle, strand, 471

Beetle, water, 30, 238, 304, 339, 357, 488, 522, 597

Beetle, whirligig, 593

Beetle, wood tiger, 144

Bell moth, lesser, 241

Belle, lesser, 248

Bellflower, clustered, 43, 59, 61, 131, 137, 179, 182, 183, 185, 199, 201, 208, 211, 237, 270, 385, 398, 417, 420, 470, 559

Bellflower, giant, 74, 103, 114, 149, 151, 186, 217, 218, 227, 272, 274, 338, 362, 366, 439, 443, 645, 655

Bellflower, ivy-leaved, 27, 122, 460, 469, 470, 473, 492, 515

Bellflower, nettle-leaved, 24, 30, 39, 107, 114, 182, 202, 210, 213, 223, 272, 310, 311, 316, 338, 385, 443

Bellflower, spreading, 227

Bent, 47, 334, 511, 513, 516

Bent, bristle, 25, 79, 86, 121, 206, 383

Bent, brown, 502

Bent, common, 23, 96, 373, 497, 503

Beta trigyna, 48

Betony, 23, 44, 74, 79, 80, 87, 141, 179, 210, 229, 270, 276, 277, 363, 420, 454, 515, 517

Bilberry, 22, 25, 27, 28, 30, 69, 74, 80, 88, 93, 99, 100, 106, 107, 110, 111, 113, 119, 121, 129, 151, 155, 181, 184, 218, 221, 224, 228, 229, 260, 269, 271, 277, 325, 329, 351, 352, 354, 358, 360, 362-364, 407, 412, 427, 432, 434, 440, 449, 450, 454, 456, 460, 461, 464, 470, 473, 475, 486, 487, 492, 493, 497, 498, 500, 505, 508, 511, 513, 514, 516, 517, 524, 529, 530, 539, 553, 554, 563, 579, 581, 582, 585-587, 589, 627, 631, 639, 647, 648, 650

Bilberry, bog, 553, 572, 578

Bindweed, sea, 84, 102, 104, 120, 143, 161, 249, 293, 375, 393, 437, 479

Binion, brown-spot, 261

Birch, 19, 20, 25, 27, 28, 33, 38, 39, 41, 45, 47-49, 55, 69, 71-73, 75, 80, 82, 87, 88, 90, 94-97, 100, 103, 104, 106, 107, 109-111, 114, 117, 119-121, 123, 126, 127, 130, 131, 133, 134, 137, 138, 142, 143, 153, 154, 160, 162, 164, 172, 175, 180-182, 185, 191, 195, 197, 199, 201-203, 205, 209, 213, 214, 218, 219, 221-224, 228, 232-237, 239, 245, 246, 248, 256, 257, 260-262, 271, 276, 277, 279, 281, 282, 285-287, 289, 294-296, 298, 303-305, 311, 313, 319, 321, 322, 324, 325, 329-331, 333, 337, 338, 344, 345, 346, 350-352, 355, 359-365, 367, 371, 372, 375, 376, 382-386, 388, 392, 393, 396-399, 401-403, 407, 412, 413, 415, 421, 426, 427, 432, 435-437, 439, 449, 454, 457, 460, 462, 464, 473, 474, 476-478, 480, 483, 492, 493, 495, 497-501, 503, 507, 517, 522-524, 529, 531, 537-541, 544, 548, 549, 551, 553, 554, 557, 558, 560, 563, 565-568, 572, 577, 579-583, 586, 587, 589, 591, 597, 599, 611, 619, 626, 628, 630, 631, 634, 639-642, 646-650, 654, 657

Birch, downy, 214, 282, 372, 471, 479, 487, 517, 518, 556, 557, 580

Birch, dwarf, 571, 578, 642, 656

Birch, grey, 360, 362

Birch, hairy, 575

Birch, pendulous, 589

Birch, silver, 16, 111, 151, 214, 259, 313, 316, 331, 339, 372, 437, 480, 513, 556, 558, 575, 580

Bird's-foot, 283, 287, 360, 372, 505

Bird's-foot, orange, 84

Bird's-foot-trefoil, common, 19, 23, 27, 29, 43, 56, 70, 71, 74, 78, 79, 84, 103, 107, 111, 118, 136, 137, 148, 149, 151, 184, 210, 213, 219, 223, 224, 229, 247, 248, 252, 267, 270, 271, 277, 284, 288, 335, 342, 353, 363, 366, 384, 385, 398, 407, 414, 417, 420, 423, 430, 438, 447, 455, 459, 479, 483, 504, 525, 566, 596, 605, 634, 637, 647, 656

Bird's-foot-trefoil, greater, 23, 33, 214, 246, 277, 358, 364, 412, 415, 422, 480, 482, 517, 539

Bird's-foot-trefoil, slender, 79

Bird's-nest, yellow, 178, 426, 434, 471, 489, 490

Bistort, alpine, 440, 507, 567, 572, 580, 647, 649

275, 281, 283, 285, 290, 303, 318, 326, 393, 400, 445, 447, 451, 459, 468, 483, 505, 544, 545, 561, 575, 580, 593, 595, 596, 627

Godwit, black-tailed, 18, 21, 33, 39, 61, 64, 71, 82, 125, 133, 186, 202, 203, 204, 207, 226, 239, 244, 250, 264, 275, 288, 378, 393, 406, 445, 447, 451, 468, 483, 505, 537, 544, 545, 607, 652

Gold, purple-bordered, 100

Gold tail, 164

Goldcrest, 16, 33, 50, 54, 85, 88, 100, 104, 118, 124, 128, 149, 151, 173, 181, 183, 191, 197, 219, 222, 226, 251, 266, 286, 301, 362, 363, 430, 469, 473, 531, 539, 551, 565, 582, 585-587, 623, 628, 635, 654, 657

Goldeneye, 21, 39, 55, 61, 64, 72, 82, 87, 99, 114, 125, 127, 136, 150, 154, 156, 159, 161, 195, 204, 226, 239, 258, 263, 264, 272, 276, 282, 285, 296, 298, 301, 314-316, 324, 325, 327, 331, 354, 359, 378, 393, 400, 406, 410, 427, 428, 430, 434, 435, 447, 468, 469, 478, 498, 503, 505, 514, 516, 524, 529-531, 535, 545, 555, 557, 559, 561, 569, 571, 575, 577, 596, 598, 615, 619, 627, 634, 640, 641, 646, 653, 657

Goldenrod, 27, 223, 465, 500, 503, 515, 540, 585, 627, 640

Golden-saxifrage, 470, 529, 633, 638

Golden-saxifrage, alternate-leaved, 222, 283, 290, 349, 351, 433, 487, 580

Golden-saxifrage, opposite-leaved, 74, 88, 114, 149, 151, 283, 290, 315, 327, 376, 430, 433, 437, 454, 464, 471, 500, 563

Goldfinch, 25, 37, 114, 156, 213, 214, 236, 275, 285, 301, 331, 357, 366, 385, 402, 413, 462, 593, 638

Goosander, 38, 55, 72, 82, 99, 127, 150, 159, 194, 204, 213, 244, 272, 276, 314, 316, 325, 331, 359, 428, 430, 458, 476, 514, 516, 524, 531, 535, 555, 568, 577, 582, 584, 596, 646, 650, 653

Goose, 18, 21, 69, 250, 301, 303, 329, 522, 536, 543, 545, 555, 559, 607, 615, 643, 653, 657

Goose, barnacle, 168, 186, 314, 535, 536, 537, 540, 555, 565-568, 608, 617, 652, 657

Goose, bean, 186, 294, 295, 324, 540

Goose, Brent, 136, 157, 166, 168, 169, 170, 186, 203, 204, 207, 212, 240, 244, 249, 290, 294, 301, 303, 314, 318, 471, 652, 657

Goose, Brent dark-bellied, 125, 160, 161, 165, 166, 168, 202, 204, 285, 393

Goose, Brent light-bellied, 168, 326

Goose, Canada, 38, 48, 125, 166, 168, 186, 190, 197, 202, 213, 226, 239, 275, 281, 282, 303, 317, 359, 427, 428, 505, 577, 652, 657

Goose, Egyptian, 303

Goose, greylag, 38, 156, 264, 275,

303, 324-326, 331, 410, 505, 524, 529, 530, 535-537, 540, 541, 545, 548, 551, 559, 570, 571, 577, 580, 585, 591, 593, 594, 596, 606, 607, 634, 636, 641-643, 646, 650-653, 655, 657

Goose, pink-footed, 186, 255, 263-265, 281, 285, 294, 301, 303, 314, 324, 524, 525, 535-537, 540, 545, 548, 559, 570, 571, 577, 590, 591, 593, 596, 646, 651, 655, 657

Goose, snow, 652

Goose, white-fronted, 81, 90, 186, 244, 245, 294, 301, 314, 393, 406, 410, 471, 577, 608, 652, 657

Goose, white-fronted Greenland, 459, 469, 530, 540

Goose, white-fronted lesser, 186

Goose, white-fronted Siberian, 454

Gooseberry, 438, 464, 598

Goosefoot, red, 467

Gorse, 16, 19, 21, 23, 25, 28, 30, 38, 42, 48, 49, 55, 56, 71, 74, 78, 80, 82, 84-86, 88, 90, 103, 104, 113, 121, 123, 127, 129, 133-137, 141, 143, 151, 156, 162, 165, 168, 172, 195, 197, 199, 201, 203, 204, 206, 208-211, 214, 218, 219, 221, 224, 227, 231, 244, 247, 262, 271, 272, 277, 283, 286, 287, 289, 290, 295, 303, 305, 313, 315, 319, 321, 324, 331, 337, 338, 352, 358, 362, 364-367, 371-373, 375-378, 383-385, 388, 391, 395, 397, 398, 408, 412, 432, 435, 448, 449, 454, 458, 459, 461, 464, 465, 468, 479, 480, 482, 483, 491, 493, 495, 498, 500, 502, 505, 508, 517, 518, 532, 556, 560, 580, 591, 627, 637

Gorse, dwarf, 47, 48, 133, 199, 205, 206, 214, 385, 388, 391

Gorse, western, 22, 25, 30, 79, 84, 86, 90, 118, 180, 184, 277, 383, 482

Goshawk, 262, 557, 584

Grass snake, 111, 139, 164, 197, 244, 246, 282, 285, 286, 296, 346, 363, 371, 426, 480, 486

Grasshopper, 39, 249, 335, 376, 409

Grasshopper, heath, 140

Grasshopper, large marsh, 140

Grass-of-Parnassus, 61, 96, 101, 109, 148, 256, 266, 302, 326, 329, 358, 361, 373, 377, 426, 430, 433-435, 440, 446, 501, 522, 524, 540, 541, 548, 555, 593, 599

Grayling (butterfly), 48, 80, 118, 138, 181, 263, 341, 352, 372, 376, 388, 392, 431, 445, 456, 503, 525, 548, 560

Grayling (fish), 638

Grebe, 161, 197, 282, 593, 641, 643, 653

Grebe, black-necked, 55, 99, 159, 194, 303, 314, 315

Grebe, great crested, 21, 39, 55, 61, 69, 71, 110, 114, 128, 147, 159, 187, 190, 192, 202, 212, 213, 220, 226, 233, 236, 239, 250, 266, 275, 276, 281, 286, 289, 294, 298, 299, 303, 304, 310, 312, 314, 315, 317,

337, 359, 382, 383, 392, 393, 405, 406, 427, 428, 435, 437, 445, 447, 476, 478, 486, 488, 508, 514, 516, 525, 527, 529, 535, 591, 595, 634, 640, 646, 650, 653

Grebe, little, 39, 50, 71, 73, 96, 104, 110, 135, 152, 154, 156, 161, 165, 199, 202, 212, 214, 218, 234, 239, 244, 245, 275, 276, 282, 285, 286, 289, 296, 303, 304, 331, 337, 382, 393, 395, 400, 406, 410, 428, 445, 463, 476, 497, 498, 522, 531, 619, 650, 653

Grebe, pied-billed, 535, 555

Grebe, red-necked, 159, 281, 314, 315, 317

Grebe, Slavonian, 55, 61, 82, 99, 110, 159, 204, 212, 289, 314, 315, 317, 505, 577, 595, 653

Green pea, cream-bordered, 63

Greenfinch, 50, 172, 236, 244, 275, 301, 413, 431, 447, 478

Greenshank, 21, 39, 41, 55, 61, 71, 82, 90, 125, 149, 156, 161, 165, 197, 203, 212, 226, 239, 244, 264, 275, 283, 288, 304, 337, 391, 406, 410, 428, 459, 478, 505, 518, 527, 548, 561, 566-568, 573, 574, 577, 579, 586, 619, 627, 651, 652, 657

Greenweed, dyer's, 44, 74, 80, 87, 103, 152, 171, 191, 193, 218, 219, 247, 285, 286, 296, 312, 319, 345, 363, 387, 410, 423, 430, 470, 510, 535, 537

Greenweed, hairy, 79, 87, 465

Gromwell, common, 167

Gromwell, purple, 20, 24, 30, 118, 473, 481

Grosbeak, pine, 326

Ground-ivy, 32, 74, 84, 167, 173, 445, 466

Grouse, 357, 486, 522, 537, 549, 575, 590, 591

Grouse, black, 96, 321, 325, 330, 459, 514, 522, 540, 559, 579, 580, 582, 628, 647, 648, 654, 657

Grouse, red, 95, 96, 99, 101, 110, 113, 123, 215, 321, 325, 349, 359, 432, 434, 440, 458, 460, 499, 505, 507, 514, 516, 526, 539, 553, 567, 580, 582, 591, 602, 607, 628, 648

Grouse, willow, 359

Guelder-rose, 20, 24, 32, 33, 41, 63, 66, 74, 82, 88, 103, 106, 107, 111, 113, 134, 153, 156, 171, 181, 186, 214, 226, 229, 237, 246, 251, 262, 270, 272-274, 285, 299, 311, 336, 338, 339, 342, 345, 352, 362, 364, 371, 379, 385, 396, 408, 413, 419, 432, 448, 464, 474, 479, 482, 483, 529, 540, 581, 626, 631, 647

Guillemot, 26, 79, 81, 85, 103, 119, 126, 133, 139, 211, 323, 427, 447, 459, 465-467, 471, 482, 495, 503, 508, 524, 541, 547, 551, 553, 555, 566, 591, 593, 596, 601-603, 608, 609, 611, 614, 615, 617, 618, 635, 636, 656

Guillemot, black, 103, 568, 574, 601, 603, 606, 611, 613-617, 635-637

Gull, 38, 39, 70, 72, 114, 179, 190,

Index of Sites

Picture Acknowledgements

Aerofilms Ltd: 594, 603, 654. Simon Andrew: 69. AQUILA PHOTOGRAPHICS/photo A.J. Bond 637; photo A.W. Cundall 218, 228; photo A.W. Cundall and Worcestershire Nature Conservation Trust 225; photo G.F. Date 366; photo N. Rodney Foster 497; photo Dennis Green 574; photo J.V. and G.R. Harrison 222, 227, 229, 365; photo E.A. Janes 181, 639; photo Neill King 221; photo S. Kill 591; photo J. Lawton Roberts 359; photo Michael Leach 353; photo M. and V. Lane 223, 405, 408–9; photo R.T. Mills 446, 498; photo W.S. Paton 578; photo D. Platt 583; photo J. Russell 371, 571, 611; photo Don Smith 646; photo E.K. Thompson 335, 595; photo P.D.V. Weaving 194; photo M.C. Wilkes 314, 385, 407, 655; photo M.B. Withers 486. ARDEA LONDON/jacket photo Yann Arthus-Bertrand; photo J.A. Bailey 167, 170, 276; photo Ian Beames 303, 500; photo R.J.C. Blewitt 159, 176, 226, 239, 258, 317; photo A. and E. Bomford 616; photo J.B. and S. Bottomley 125, 129, 133, 393, 435, 474, 479; photo Arthur Brook 123; photo K.J. Carlson 62, 179, 287, 515; photo M.D. England 410, 482, 567, 627; photo Bob Gibbons 190, 212, 252, 260, 524; photo C. Knights 285; photo J. Marchington 536; photo John Mason 22–3, 182, 213, 217, 271, 312, 373, 436, 553; photo P. Morris 461; photo S. Roberts 581; photo Robert T. Smith 20, 95, 210, 262; photo D. and K. Urry 249, 263, 465, 466–7, 545, 602; photo R. Vaughan 290, 507, 606; photo Wolfgang Wagner 460. Desmond J. Arnold 233, 237. I.P Bainbridge 325. BBONT: 48; photo Ian Buchanan 54. Bedfordshire County Council: 41, 44. Geoffrey Berry: 98–9. John S. Beswick: 80, 81, 90, 124, 128. BIOPHOTO ASSOCIATES/photo D.K. Mardon 560, 648–9; photo Chris Pellant 448. Roy Bowden: 74. Brecon Beacons National Park: 518. W. Brown/RSPB: 622. Graham Burton/RSPB: 652. Andrew Campbell: 639. Cardiff City Council: 477. J. Allan Cash: 163, 164. John Cleare/Mountain Camera: 110, 354, 401, 428, 434, 511. BRUCE COLEMAN LTD/photo Eric Crichton frontispiece, 141; photo Jennifer Fry 224; photo Gordon Langsbury 238; photo A.J. Mobbs 505; photo Hans Reinhard 118. Neil Cook: 643. R. Courtman: 406. Robin Crane Films: 396, 399, 402, 437. C.R. Cuthbert: 214: Deeside Naturalists' Society/photo Raymond A. Roberts: 445. Durham County Conservation Trust/photo Julie Gaman: 147. Exmoor National Park Authority: 26. Courtesy of D.H. Gantzel: 56. K.F. Giles: 30. Arthur Gilpin/RSPB: 438. Dennis Green/RSPB: 70. Frank Hamilton/RSPB: 584, 640. John Hines: 490. G. St J. Hollis/RSPB: 463. Eric Hosking: 614, 615. S.C. Hutchings: 82, 87. Jeremy Hywel-Davies: 93, 96, 100, 144, 151, 281, 364, 449, 464, 517. K. Jagger: 241. R. Jarman: 29, 32. D.J. Jeffray: 413. Kent Trust for Nature Conservation: 253. A.F. Kersting: 33, 49 below, 79, 142, 247, 322, 323, 382, 392, 462. Joy Ketchen: 94. Lancashire Trust for Nature Conservation/photo Peter Jepson: 267. Jorge Lewinski: 525. N.R. Lewis: 338, 339. Lincolnshire and South Humberside Trust for Nature Conservation/photo R.W. Dowlman 291; photo G. Trinder 266; photo R. B. Wilkinson 288, 289. London Wildlife Trust/photo Chris Rose: 191, 196, 197. Don MacCaskill: 577, 598. John Mason: 39, 42, 43, 66, 72, 171, 208, 246, 284, 456. Peter Merrin/RSPB: 40, 273, 363. Mid-Glamorgan County Council: 473, 476. The National Trust: 24, 88–9, 135, 209, 211, 506. NCC: 17, 18, 19, 28, 31, 51, 83, 85, 86, 107, 117, 119, 120, 138, 139, 143, 149, 160, 161, 168, 177, 178, 203, 204, 206, 251, 256, 259, 295, 299, 301, 307, 311, 236–7, 343, 346, 350, 352, 378, 388, 395, 398, 411, 417, 418, 419, 420, 421, 422, 423, 431, 450, 455, 457, 458, 471, 475, 478, 480, 481, 483, 487, 488–9, 491, 495, 499, 503, 513, 516, 529, 548, 552, 554, 556, 557, 559, 563, 570, 582, 586, 589, 607, 619, 623, 630, 647, 651. NATURE PHOTOGRAPHERS LTD/photo S.C. Bisserôt 36, 121, 122, 126; photo Frank V. Blackburn 207, 384, 386; photo B. Burbidge 49 above; photo N.A. Callow 349, 394; photo K.J. Carlson 302; photo A. Cleave 136, 250, 509; photo A. Davies 169; photo M.E. Gore 134; photo Dennis Green 541; photo J.V. and G.R. Harrison 84, 275, 277, 297, 336, 360–1; photo E. A. Janes 57, 165, 232, 286; photo M. Leach 337; photo R. Mearns 264–5; photo C.K. Mylne 527, 547; photo O. Newman 127; photo M.D.E. Oates 140; photo C. Palmer 530, 573; photo W. S. Paton 153, 635; photo D. Sewell 78; photo Don Smith 451; photo Robert T. Smith 156; photo E.K. Thompson 73; photo D. Washington 387; photo N. Wilmore 257. Northamptonshire Trust for Nature Conservation/photo James Frith 315; photo Angela Walker 316. Northumberland National Park Countryside Committee/photo Eric Dale 328; photo Karen Melvin 330. Northumberland Wildlife Trust: 324. W. H. Palmer: 65. W.S. Paton/RSPB: 152. Peak Park Joint Planning Board: 103, 113. F.B. Pearce: 25, 101. Peterlee Development Corporation/photo W.J. Monck: 150. R.K. Pilsbury: 201. Fritz Pölking/RSPB: 459. S.C. Porter/RSPB: 376, 544. Premaphotos Wildlife/photo K.G. Preston-Mafham: 180. Dr M.C.F. Proctor: 130. Dr D.A. Ratcliffe: 40, 97, 102, 104, 109, 154, 184–5, 192, 205, 220, 234, 296, 300, 305, 329, 344, 372, 377, 433, 501, 504, 535, 538, 558, 565, 568–9, 585, 593, 629, 636, 645, 656. Richard Revels: 27, 37, 61, 63, 129, 162, 166, 313, 345, 391, 468. Michael W. Richards/RSPB: 64, 235, 243, 245, 261, 304, 374, 508. Michael Rose: 193. RSPB: 469. Philippa Scott: 187, 306. Scottish Tourist Board: 626. Severn–Trent Water Authority/photo John Hemming: 514. Don Smith: 532. Robert T. Smith: 579, 587, 609. Gavin Stewart; 653. Alex Tewnion/RSPB: 566. Valerie M. Thom: 523, 531, 539, 546, 555, 561, 572, 580, 588, 596, 597, 601, 608, 621, 628. Brian Thomas: 21. T.J. Thomas: 38. Colin Titcombe: 492, 493. Bobby Tulloch: 613, 617. Peter Wakely: 367, 415, 443. Simon Warner/RSPB: 379. Tom Weir: 641. Derek G. Widdicombe: 429, 432, 439, 440. Derek G. Widdicombe/photo Simon Warner: 427. Peter Wild: 502. The Wildfowl Trust/photo Brian Gadsby: 155. Mike Williams: 112. Robin Williams: 195. Metropolitan Borough of Wirral Dept of Leisure Services and Tourism: 75. Yorkshire Wildlife Trust: 430.